The
INTERNATIONAL CRITICAL COMMENTARY
on the Holy Scriptures of the Old and New Testaments

GENERAL EDITORS:

J. A. EMERTON, F.B.A.

Fellow of St. John's College
Regius Professor of Hebrew in the University of Cambridge
Honorary Canon of St. George's Cathedral, Jerusalem

C. E. B. CRANFIELD, F.B.A.

Emeritus Professor of Theology in the University of Durham

AND

G. N. STANTON

Professor of New Testament Studies,
King's College, University of London

FORMERLY UNDER THE EDITORSHIP OF

S. R. DRIVER
A. PLUMMER
C. A. BRIGGS

THE GOSPEL ACCORDING TO SAINT MATTHEW

VOLUME I

A CRITICAL AND EXEGETICAL COMMENTARY

ON

THE GOSPEL ACCORDING TO SAINT MATTHEW

BY

W. D. DAVIES, F.B.A.

Fellow of the American Society of Arts and Sciences
Emeritus Professor of Christian Origins, Duke University

AND

DALE C. ALLISON, Jr., Ph.D.

Research Scholar, Saint Paul School of Theology

IN THREE VOLUMES

VOLUME I

Introduction and Commentary on Matthew I–VII

EDINBURGH
T. & T. CLARK LIMITED, 59 GEORGE STREET

Copyright © T. & T. CLARK LTD, 1988

TYPESET BY C. R. BARBER & PARTNERS (HIGHLANDS) LTD, FORT WILLIAM
PRINTED IN THE U.K. BY MARTIN'S OF BERWICK
BOUND BY HUNTER & FOULIS LTD, EDINBURGH

FOR

T. & T. CLARK LTD, EDINBURGH

First printed 1988

British Library Cataloguing in Publication Data
Davies, W. D.
A critical and exegetical commentary on the Gospel according to Saint
Matthew : in three volumes.—(The international critical commentary).
Vol. 1 : Introduction and commentary on Matthew I–VII
1. Bible, N.T. Matthew—Commentaries
I. Title   II. Allison, Dale C.   III. Series
226.207   BS2575.3
ISBN 0-567-09481-2

Dedicated
to
Eurwen and Kristine
οὐκ ἔχομεν ἀνταποδοῦναι ὑμῖν

PREFACE

Two main objections have been urged against the publishing of biblical commentaries at the present time. First, and most seriously, there has been an explosion of knowledge in the last half-century which has impinged upon the study of the Bible, and also developments in methodology in the study of documents which have led to new forms of biblical criticism demanding a radical rethinking of the genre of the commentary. Some have accordingly concluded that until the new information we now have has been more assessed and assimilated and the proposed new methodologies more tried, it is premature to write new commentaries. Any such, it is implied, will be out of date even before printed.

This conclusion is unacceptable. There certainly has been an explosion of information, perhaps particularly in areas which bear especially on the First Gospel: the Qumran documents, the Apocrypha and Pseudepigrapha, and Rabbinic and Gnostic sources. But many of the new, as well as the old, sources involved have been much scrutinized and to a considerable extent can already be exploited for the purposes of exegesis. The newer methodologies, which also are in the process of being tested, do not preclude the use of older more established methods: most of the former still presuppose the latter and demand their continuance. We cannot wait upon complete knowledge and fully adequate methodologies, even if such were ever attainable, before putting pen to paper. As it is important that each generation translate the Bible for itself, in its own idiom, so each generation should express its own interpretation of it. This will necessarily rest to a large degree on the work of previous generations. Any significant commentary will be an agent in the transmission of exegetical traditions: its wisdom accumulative. But each generation also brings its own peculiar insights to add to those of the past and helps to ensure that the Bible remains a living reality and not a static deposit.

The second objection urged is that there already exist many excellent commentaries: to add to their number is to bring coals to Newcastle. As far as the present commentary is concerned, this can hardly be maintained. In recent times the commentaries on the First Gospel in the English speaking world at least have not been as numerous as those on the other gospels. Willoughby C. Allen published his volume in this series in 1907, and A. H. McNeile's commentary in the Macmillan series appeared in 1915. These were on a large scale and based on a scrupulous scholarship. The recent work of Robert H. Gundry (1982) is massively learned and instructive but not a little idiosyncratic. There have also appeared, among others on a smaller scale, the commentaries by W. F. Albright and C. S. Mann, F. W. Beare, Floyd Filson and David Hill. The first of these was much criticized; and most of the others—admirable as they are, especially that of Professor Hill—were limited by the nature of the series in which they appeared, and the same applies to the English translation of Eduard Schweizer's influential commentary. On all these we have gratefully drawn as upon the countless, often excellent, monographs dedicated to the First Gospel. But in the conviction that the time is ripe for a fresh attempt at a large scale commentary on Matthew we accepted the invitation of the editors of this series.

The present volume is to be followed by two others, dealing with chapters 8 to 18 and 19 to 28 respectively. Considerations of cost and exigencies of printing have required restraint. We could have wished for more expansive treatments of many aspects of the text but have had to prefer leanness to fullness both in the introductory sections and in the body of the commentary.

Certain other considerations have led us to postpone the treatment of two overall themes to the end of the third volume: the theology of the gospel and its place and rôle in the development of early Christianity. What was the Matthean understanding of the gospel and how did it fit into or relate to the life of the Christian movement as a totality, for example, its history, theological cross-currents, liturgy, catechetical activity, etc.? These themes can be satisfactorily treated only after the whole of the gospel has been commented upon and assessed, and the discussion of them is rightly placed at the close of all the volumes. Such a postponement will have the advantage of allowing the authors to take more into consideration recent developments in biblical criticism to which reference is made below in the Introduction on pp. 1–5.

This is a collaborative work. Our joint engagement with the gospel began several years ago at Duke University: its authorities have been unfailingly supportive, as has more recently been Dean D. M. Campbell. Since then we have continued our concentration on the study of the gospel through the co-operation of Texas Christian University, which we here warmly acknowledge. We thank especially Duke Divinity School and the Department of Religion-Studies at T.C.U. for providing a congenial ambience for our work. Ms. Astrid Berger, a research assistant from Göttingen University, was particulary helpful in the preparation of the charts on pp. 34–57 and in many other ways, and Ms. Lu Bacus gave indispensable secretarial help. Professor David Hill of Sheffield University generously read through the whole typescript. The contribution of our wives, Eurwen Davies and Kristine Allison, is immeasurable. They both shared gladly in the demands made by the preparation of such a commentary as this. In addition, Mrs. Allison made herself responsible for the meticulous typing of a very difficult and always highly complex manuscript. Finally, we thank the publishers for their patience and encouragement, and particularly the New Testament editor of the series, Emeritus Professor Charles Cranfield, for a courtesy which combines efficiency with forbearance, as well as for very detailed criticisms.

Although we cannot be sufficient for this, our aim has been to be loyal to the tradition of disinterested and objective study in biblical criticism. We hope that this commentary will prove not unworthy of it.

W. D. Davies
D. C. Allison, Jr.

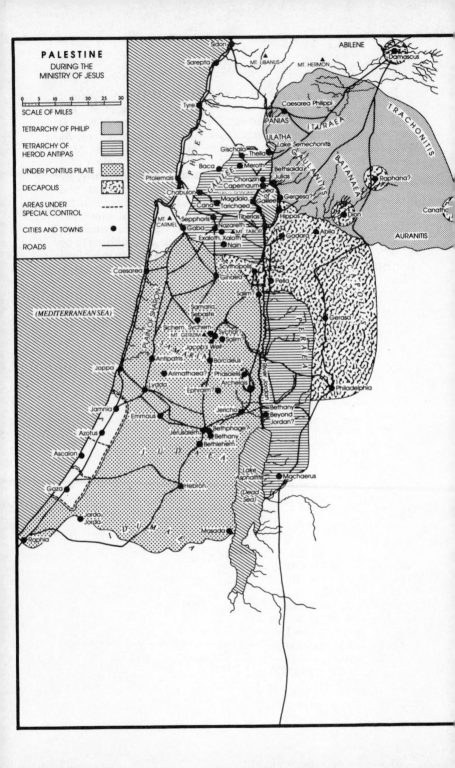

PALESTINE
DURING THE
MINISTRY OF JESUS

SCALE OF MILES
0 5 10 15 20 25 30

TETRARCHY OF PHILIP

TETRARCHY OF
HEROD ANTIPAS

UNDER PONTIUS PILATE

DECAPOLIS

AREAS UNDER
SPECIAL CONTROL

CITIES AND TOWNS

ROADS

ABILENE

Sidon

Sarepta

MT. LIBANUS

MT. HERMON

Damascus

Tyre

Caesarea Philippi

PHOENICIA

PANIAS

ITURAEA

TRACHONITIS

ULATHA

Lake Semechonitis

Gischala

Thella

Meroth

Baca

Chorazin

Capernaum

Bethsaida
Julias

BATANAEA

Raphana?

Ptolemais

Chabulon

GALILEE

Magdala

Tarichaea

Cana

Sea of
Galilee

Gergesa?

GAULANITIS

Canatha

Sepphoris

MT. CARMEL

Gaba

Nazareth

Tiberias

Hippos

Dion

AURANITIS

Exaloth

MT. TABOR

Xaloth

Nain

Gadara

Abila

Caesarea

Scythopolis

Ginaea

Pella

DECAPOLIS

(MEDITERRANEAN SEA)

PLAIN OF SHARON

Samaria,
Sebaste

Salim

Gerasa

Sichem, Sychem

MT. GERIZIM

Sychar

Salim?

SAMARIA

Jacob's Well

PERAEA

Antipatris

Borceus

Joppa

Arimathaea?

Lydda

Phasaelis

Jordan River

Ephraim?

Archelais

Philadelphia

Jamnia

Jericho

Emmaus

Bethany
Beyond
Jordan?

Azotus

Jerusalem

Bethphage?

Ascalon

JUDAEA

Bethlehem

Bethany

Gaza

Hebron

Lake
Asphaltitis

Machaerus

(Dead
Sea)

Jarda,
Jorda

IDUMAEA

Masada

Raphia

CONTENTS OF VOLUME 1

Preface ix

Abbreviations and Bibliography xv

INTRODUCTION

I	INTRODUCTORY MATTERS	1
II	THE AUTHORSHIP OF MATTHEW	7
III	THE STRUCTURE OF MATTHEW	58
IV	LITERARY CHARACTERISTICS	72
V	THE SOURCES OF MATTHEW	97
VI	THE DATE OF MATTHEW	127
VII	THE LOCAL ORIGIN OF MATTHEW	138
VIII	THE TEXT	147

COMMENTARY

I	TITLE (1.1)	149
II	FROM ABRAHAM TO JESUS (1.2–17)	161
	EXCURSUS I THE SOURCES OF MT 1.18–2.23	190
III	CONCEIVED OF THE HOLY SPIRIT (1.18–25)	196
IV	MAGI FROM THE EAST (2.1–12)	224
V	THE MESSIAH'S FLIGHT AND RETURN (2.13–23)	257
VI	JOHN THE BAPTIST AND JESUS (3.1–17)	285
VII	THE BEGINNING OF THE MINISTRY (4.1–22)	350
VIII	INTRODUCTION TO THE SERMON ON THE MOUNT (4.23–5.2)	410
IX	THE BEATITUDES (5.3–12)	429
	EXCURSUS II THE BEATITUDES (Mt 5.3–12 = Lk 6.20–23)	431
X	SUMMARY STATEMENT OF THE TASK OF GOD'S PEOPLE (5.13–16)	470
XI	JESUS FULFILS THE LAW (5.17–20)	481
XII	THE BETTER RIGHTEOUSNESS (5.21–48)	504
	EXCURSUS III THE INTERPRETATION OF MT 5.21–48	505
XIII	THE CHRISTIAN CULT (6.1–18)	572
	EXCURSUS IV THE LORD'S PRAYER (Mt 6.9–13 = Lk 11.2–4)	590
XIV	GOD AND MAMMON (6.19–34)	625
XV	THE TREATMENT OF ONE'S NEIGHBOUR (7.1–12)	667
XVI	THREE WARNINGS AND THE CONCLUSION (7.13–29)	693

ABBREVIATIONS AND BIBLIOGRAPHY

1. *Books of the Bible*

The abbreviations for the names of books of the OT and NT and of the Apocrypha, which are printed without full point, will be readily understood.

References to the Bible are generally cited according to the chapter and verse divisions of the RSV. References to the Septuagint are indicated either by the abbreviation, LXX, or by citing a book's title in Greek (e.g. 1 Βασ = 1 Sam, 3 Βασ = 1 Kgs). References to the Hebrew are signalled by the abbreviation, MT.

Biblical quotations, unless otherwise noted, are usually from the Revised Standard Version of the bible, copyright 1946, 1952, 1971, 1973, by the Division of Christian Education of the National Council of the Churches of Christ in the U.S.A., and are used by permission.

2. *Pseudepigrapha*

Apoc Abr, Dan, Elijah, Sed, Zeph = Apocalypse of Abraham, of Daniel, of Elijah, of Sedrach, of Zephaniah; As Mos = Assumption of Moses; Asc Isa = Ascension of Isaiah; 2, 3, 4 Bar = 2, 3, 4 Baruch; 1, 2, 3 En = 1, 2, 3 Enoch; Ep Arist = Epistle of Aristeas; 4 Ezra; Gk Apoc Ezra = Greek Apocalypse of Ezra; Hist Rech = History of the Rechabites; Jos Asen = Joseph and Aseneth; Jub = Jubilees; LAB = Liber Antiquitatum Biblicarum (Pseudo-Philo); LAE = Life of Adam and Eve; Liv Proph Isa, Jer, etc. = Life of the Prophet Isaiah, Jeremiah, etc.; 3, 4 Macc = 3, 4 Maccabees; Pry Jacob = Prayer of Jacob; Ps-Phoc = Pseudo-Phocylides; Ps Sol = Psalms of Solomon; Quest Ezra = Questions of Ezra; Rev Ezra = Revelation of Ezra; Sib Or = Sibylline Oracles; T Abr, Adam, Asher, Benj, Dan, Isaac, Iss, Jacob, Job, Jos, Judah, Levi, Naph, Reub, Sim, Sol, Zeb = Testament of Abraham, Adam, Asher, Benjamin, Dan, Isaac, Issachar, Jacob, Job, Joseph, Judah, Levi, Naphtali, Reuben, Simeon, Solomon, Zebulon; Vis Ezra = Vision of Ezra.

Quotations from the Pseudepigrapha are usually either from the collection edited by R. H. Charles or from that edited by J. H. Charlesworth (see bibliography), and are used by permission.

3. *The Dead Sea Scrolls*

The conventional sigla are used (see J. Fitzmyer, *The Dead Sea Scrolls: Major Publications and Tools for Study*, Missoula, 1977).

4. *Rabbinic Materials*

The conventional sigla are used (*m.* = *Mishnah*, *t.* = *Tosefta*, *b.* = *Babylonian Talmud*, *y.* = *Jerusalem Talmud*).

5. Classical Sources

The conventional sigla are used (see LSJ, pp. xvi–xxxviii, and Lewis and Short, pp. vii–xi). Quotations from classical sources are usually from the translations in The Loeb Classical Library and are used by permission.

6. Early Christian Literature

Apoc Pet = Apocalypse of Peter; Barn = Epistle of Barnabas; 1, 2 Clem = 1, 2 Clement; Did = Didache; Ep Diog = Epistle of Diognetus; Gos Eb, Heb, Naz, Pet, Phil = Gospel of the Ebionites, of the Hebrews, of the Nazaraeans, of Peter, of Philip; Herm v, m, s = Shepherd of Hermas, vision, mandate, similitude; Ignatius, *Eph, Magn*, etc, = Ignatius, *Epistle to the Ephesians, to the Magnesians*, etc; M Polyc = Martyrdom of Polycarp; Odes Sol = Odes of Solomon; Polycarp, *Ep* = Polycarp, *Epistle*; Prot Jas = Protevangelium of James; Ps-Clem Hom, Rec = Pseudo-Clementine Homilies, Recognitions.

7. Nag Hammadi Literature

Acts Pet 12 Apost = Acts of Peter and the Twelve Apostles; Ap Jas, Jn = Apocryphon of James, of John; Apoc Adam = Apocalypse of Adam; 1, 2 Apoc Jas = 1, 2 Apocalypse of James; Apoc Paul, Pet = Apocalypse of Paul, of Peter; Auth Teach = Authoritative Teaching; Dial Sav = Dialogue of the Saviour; Disc 8–9 = Discourse on the Eighth and Ninth; Ep Pet Phil = Letter of Peter to Philip; Gos Eg, Phil, Thom, Truth = Gospel of the Egyptians, of Philip, of Thomas, of Truth; Hyp Arch = Hypostatis of the Archons; Melch = Melchizedek; Orig World = On the Origin of the World; Pr Paul, Thanks = Prayer of Paul, of Thanksgiving; Soph Jes Chr = Sophia of Jesus Christ; Testim Truth = Testimony of Truth; Thom Cont = Book of Thomas the Contender; Thund = Thunder, Perfect Mind; Treat Res = Treatise on Resurrection.

8. Other Ancient Sources

CMC = Cologne Mani Codex; Mur. = Wadi Murabba' at texts; Sent. Syr. Men. = Sentences of Syriac Menander.

9. Journals and Series

AB: Anchor Bible.
AcOr: *Acta orientalia* (Copenhagen).
AfTJ: *African Theological Journal* (Arusha, Tanzania).
AGJU: Arbeiten zur Geschichte des antiken Judentums und des Urchristentums.
AJBI: *Annual of the Japanese Biblical Institute* (Tokyo).
ALGHJ: Arbeiten zur Literatur und Geschichte des hellenistischen Judentums.
AnBib: Analecta biblica.
ANF: The Ante-Nicene Fathers.
ASNU: Acta seminarii neotestamentici upsaliensis.
AsSeign: *Assemblées du Seigneur* (Paris).
ASTI: *Annual of the Swedish Theological Institute* (Leiden).
ATANT: Abhandlungen zur Theologie des Alten und Neuen Testaments.

ATR: *Anglican Theological Review* (Evanston, Illinois).
AusBR: *Australian Biblical Review* (Melbourne).
AzNTT: Arbeiten zur neutestamentlichen Textforschung.
BASOR: *Bulletin of the American Schools of Oriental Research* (Philadelphia).
BBB: Bonner biblische Beiträge.
BETL: Bibliotheca ephemeridum theologicarum lovaniensium.
BFTh: Beiträge zur Förderung christlicher Theologie.
BGBE: Beiträge zur Geschichte der biblischen Exegese.
BHT: Beiträge zur historischen Theologie.
Bib: *Biblica* (Rome).
BibB: Biblische Beiträge.
BJRL: *Bulletin of the John Rylands Library* (Manchester).
BK: *Bibel und Kirche* (Stuttgart).
BLit: *Bibel und Liturgie* (Klosterneuberg).
BR: *Biblical Research* (Chicago).
BS: Biblische Studien (Neukirchen).
BSac: *Bibliotheca Sacra* (Dallas).
BT: *The Bible Translator* (London).
BTB: *Biblical Theology Bulletin* (Jamaica, N.Y.).
BU: Biblische Untersuchungen.
BuL: *Bibel und Leben* (Düsseldorf).
BVC: *Bible et vie chrétienne* (Bruges).
BWANT: Beiträge zur Wissenschaft vom Alten und Neuen Testament.
BZ: *Biblische Zeitschrift* (Paderborn).
BZNW: Beihefte zur *ZNW*.
CB: Coniectanea biblica.
CBQ: *Catholic Biblical Quarterly* (Washington, D.C.).
CBQMS: *CBQ* Monograph Series.
CH: *Church History* (Chicago).
ConNT: *Coniectanea neotestamentica* (Uppsala).
CQR: *Church Quarterly Review* (London).
CTM: *Concordia Theological Monthly* (Fort Wayne, Indiana).
CV: *Communio Viatorum* (Prague).
DR: *Downside Review* (Bath, U.K.).
EB: Études bibliques.
EF: *Estudios Franciscanos* (Barcelona).
EKKNT: Evangelisch-katholischer Kommmentar zum Neuen Testament.
ER: *Ecumenical Review* (Geneva).
EstBib: *Estudios Bíblicos* (Madrid).
ETL: *Ephemerides theologicae lovanienses* (Louvain).
ETR: *Études théologiques et religieuses* (Montpellier).
EvQ: *Evangelical Quarterly* (Aberdeen).
EvT: *Evangelische Theologie* (Munich).
ExpT: *Expository Times* (Edinburgh).
FB: Forschung zur Bibel.
FBBS: Facet Books, Biblical Series.
FRLANT: Forschungen zur Religion und Literatur des Alten und Neuen Testaments.
FTS: Frankfurter theologische Studien.

FV: *Foi et Vie* (Paris).
GuL: *Geist und Leben* (Munich).
HDR: Harvard Dissertations in Religion.
HeyJ: *Heythrop Journal* (London).
HKNT: Handkommentar zum Neuen Testament.
HNT: Handbuch zum Neuen Testament.
HNTC: Harper's NT Commentaries (= Black's NT Commentaries).
HR: *History of Religions* (Chicago).
HTKNT: Herders theologischer Kommentar zum Neuen Testament.
HTR: *Harvard Theological Review* (Cambridge, Mass.).
HTS: Harvard Theological Studies.
HUCA: *Hebrew Union College Annual* (Cincinnati, Ohio).
IBS: *Irish Biblical Studies* (Belfast).
ICC: The International Critical Commentary.
IEJ: *Israel Exploration Journal* (Jerusalem).
IER: *Irish Ecclesiastical Record* (Belfast).
IKZ: *Internationale katholische Zeitschrift* (Cologne).
Int: *Interpretation* (Richmond, Virginia).
ITQ: *Irish Theological Quarterly* (Maynooth).
ITS: *Indian Theological Studies* (Bangalore).
JAAR: *Journal of the American Academy of Religion* (Atlanta, Georgia).
JBL: *Journal of Biblical Literature* (Atlanta, Georgia).
JBR: *Journal of Bible and Religion* (Boston, Philadelphia).
JDS: Judean Desert Studies.
JETS: *Journal of the Evangelical Theological Society* (Wheaton, Illinois).
JHS: *Journal of Hellenic Studies* (London).
JJS: *Journal of Jewish Studies* (Oxford).
JLA: *Jewish Law Annual* (Leiden).
JNES: *Journal of Near Eastern Studies* (Chicago).
JQR: *Jewish Quarterly Review* (Philadelphia).
JQRMS: *JQR* Monograph Series.
JR: *Journal of Religion* (Chicago).
JRelS: *Journal of Religious Studies* (Cleveland, Ohio).
JRS: *Journal of Roman Studies* (London).
JSJ: *Journal for the Study of Judaism in the Persian, Hellenistic and Roman periods* (Leiden).
JSNT: *Journal for the Study of the New Testament* (Sheffield).
JSNTSS: *JSNT* Supplement Series.
JSS: *Journal of Semitic Studies* (Manchester, U.K.).
JSSR: *Journal for the Scientific Study of Religion* (Storrs).
JTC: *Journal for Theology and Church* (New York).
JTS: *Journal of Theological Studies* (Oxford).
KD: *Kerygma und Dogma* (Göttingen).
LB: *Linguistica Biblica* (Bonn).
LCL: Loeb Classical Library.
LD: Lectio divina.
LumV: *Lumière et Vie* (Lyons).
MeyerK: H. A. W. Meyer, Kritisch-exegetischer Kommentar über das Neue Testament.
MNTC: Moffatt NT Commentary.
MTZ: *Münchener theologische Zeitschrift* (Munich).

NCB: New Century Bible.
Neot: *Neotestamentica* (Pretoria).
NESTTR: *Near Eastern School of Theology Theological Review* (Beirut).
NHS: Nag Hammadi Studies.
NICNT: New International Commentary on the New Testament.
NKZ: *Neue kirchliche Zeitschrift* (Erlangen).
NovT: *Novum Testamentum* (Leiden).
NovTSup: *Novum Testamentum* Supplements.
NPNF: Nicene and Post-Nicene Fathers.
NRT: *La nouvelle revue théologique* (Tournai).
NTAbh: Neutestamentliche Abhandlungen.
NTD: Das Neue Testament Deutsch.
NTF: Neutestamentliche Forschungen.
NTL: New Testament Library.
NTS: *New Testament Studies* (Cambridge).
NTTS: New Testament Tools and Studies.
NV: *Nova et Vetera* (Geneva).
OBO: Orbis biblicus et orientalis.
OCP: *Orientalia Christiana Periodica* (Rome).
OTL: Old Testament Library.
PEQ: *Palestine Exploration Quarterly* (London).
PAAJR: *Proceedings of the American Academy of Jewish Research* (Philadelphia).
PSTJ: *Perkins (School of Theology) Journal* (Dallas).
PTMS: Pittsburgh Theological Monograph Series.
QD: Quaestiones Disputatae.
RB: *Revue Biblique* (Jerusalem).
RBén: *Revue Bénédictine* (Maredsous).
RechB: Recherches bibliques.
RefTheoRev: *Reformed Theological Review* (Melbourne).
REJ: *Revue des Études Juives* (Paris).
RelS: *Religious Studies* (London).
RelSRev: *Religious Studies Review* (Macon, Georgia).
RestQ: *Restoration Quarterly* (Abilene, Texas).
RevB: *Revista biblica* (Buenos Aires).
RevExp: *Review and Expositor* (Louisville).
RevQ: *Revue de Qumran* (Paris).
RevScRel: *Revue des sciences religieuses* (Strasbourg).
RevThom: *Revue thomiste* (Toulouse).
RHPR: *Revue d'histoire et de philosophie religieuses* (Strasbourg).
RHR: *Revue de l'histoire des religions* (Paris).
RivB: *Rivista biblica* (Brescia).
RNT: Regensburger Neues Testament.
RSPT: *Revue des sciences philosophiques et théologiques* (Paris).
RSR: *Recherches de science religieuse* (Paris).
RTL: *Revue théologique de Louvain* (Louvain).
SANT: Studien zum Alten und Neuen Testament.
SBB: Stuttgarter biblische Beiträge.
SBFLA: *Studii biblici franciscani liber annuus* (Jerusalem).
SBLDS: Society of Biblical Literature Dissertation Series.
SBLSBS: Society of Biblical Literature Sources for Biblical Study.

SBLSCS: Society of Biblical Literature Septuagint and Cognate Studies.
SBLTT: Society of Biblical Literature Texts and Translations.
SBM: Stuttgarter biblische Monographien.
SBS: Stuttgarter Bibelstudien.
SBT: Studies in Biblical Theology.
SC: Sources chrétiennes.
ScEs: *Science et esprit* (Montreal).
SCHNT: Studia ad corpus hellenisticum novi testamenti.
Scr: *Scriptura* (Stellenbosch, S. Africa).
SD: Studies and Documents.
SEÅ: *Svensk exegetisk årsbok* (Uppsala).
Sem: *Semeia* (Atlanta, Georgia).
SJ: Studia Judaica.
SJLA: Studies in Judaism in Late Antiquity.
SJT: *Scottish Journal of Theology* (Edinburgh).
SNT: Studien zum Neuen Testament.
SNTU: Studien zum Neuen Testament und seiner Umwelt.
SNTSMS: Society for New Testament Studies Monograph Series.
SPAW: *Sitzungsberichte der preussischen Akademie der Wissenschaften* (Berlin).
SPB: Studia postbiblica.
SR: *Studies in Religion/Sciences religieuses* (Waterloo).
ST: *Studia theologica* (Oslo).
STDJ: Studies on the Texts of the Desert of Judah.
SUNT: Studien zur Umwelt des Neuen Testaments.
SyBU: Symbolae biblicae upsalienses.
TB: *Theologische Beiträge* (Wuppertal).
TD: *Theology Digest* (Duluth).
TextS: Texts and Studies.
TGl: *Theologie und Glaube* (Paderborn).
THKNT: Theologischer Handkommentar zum Neuen Testament.
TLS: *Times Literary Supplement* (London).
TLZ: *Theologische Literaturzeitung* (Leipzig).
TQ: *Theologische Quartalschrift* (Tübingen).
TRev: *Theologische Revue* (Münster).
TRu: *Theologische Rundschau* (Tübingen).
TS: *Theological Studies* (Washington, D.C.).
TSK: *Theologische Studien und Kritiken* (Berlin).
TTZ: *Trierer theologische Zeitschrift* (Trier).
TU: Texte und Untersuchungen.
TynBul.: *Tyndale Bulletin* (Cambridge).
TZ: *Theologische Zeitschrift* (Basel).
UNT: Untersuchungen zum Neuen Testament.
USQR: *Union Seminary Quarterly Review* (New York).
VC: *Vigiliae christianae* (Leiden).
VetChr: *Vetera Christianorum* (Bari).
VT: *Vetus Testamentum* (Leiden).
WD: *Wort und Dienst* (Bethel).
WMANT: Wissenschaftliche Monographien zum Alten und Neuen Testament.
WTJ: *Westminster Theological Journal* (Philadelphia).

WUNT: Wissenschaftliche Untersuchungen zum Neuen Testament.
ZAW: *Zeitschrift für die alttestamentliche Wissenschaft* (Berlin).
ZDPV: *Zeitschrift des deutschen Palästina-Vereins* (Wiesbaden).
ZKT: *Zeitschrift für katholische Theologie* (Innsbruck).
ZNW: *Zeitschrift für die neutestamentliche Wissenschaft* (Berlin).
ZST: *Zeitschrift für systematische Theologie* (Gütersloh, Berlin).
ZTK: *Zeitschrift für Theologie und Kirche* (Tübingen).
ZWT: *Zeitschrift für wissenschaftliche Theologie* (Jena, Leipzig).

10. *Commentaries and Other Literature*[1]

Abrahams: I. Abrahams, *Studies in Pharisaism and the Gospels*, 2 vols., reprint ed., New York, 1967.

**Albertus Magnus: Albertus Magnus, *In Evangelium secundum Matthaeum luculenta expositio*, in vols. 20 and 21 of A. Borgnet, *Opera omnia*, Paris, 1893–94.

Albertz: M. Albertz, *Die synoptischen Streitgespräche*, Berlin, 1921.

**Albright and Mann: W. F. Albright and C. S. Mann, *Matthew*, AB, Garden City, New York, 1971.

**Alford: H. Alford, *The Greek Testament, volume I: The Four Gospels*, reprint edition, Chicago, 1968.

**Allen: W. C. Allen, *A Critical and Exegetical Commentary on the Gospel According to St. Matthew*, ICC, 3rd ed., Edinburgh, 1912.

Allison: D. C. Allison, Jr., *The End of the Ages has Come: An Early Interpretation of the Passion and Resurrection of Jesus*, Philadelphia, 1985.

*Allison, 'Structure': D. C. Allison, Jr., 'The Structure of the Sermon on the Mount', *JBL* 106 (1987), pp. 423–45.

Ambrozic: A. M. Ambrozic: *The Hidden Kingdom: A Redaction-Critical Study of the References to the Kingdom of God in Mark's Gospel*, CBQMS 2, Washington, D.C., 1972.

Anderson: H. Anderson, *The Gospel of Mark*, NCB, London, 1976.

ANET: J. B. Pritchard, ed., *Ancient Near Eastern Texts*, Princeton, 1950; Supplement, 1960.

ANRW: *Aufstieg und Niedergang der römischen Welt*, ed. W. Haase and H. Temporini, Berlin and New York, 1979ff.

**Anselm: Pseudo-Anselm, *Enarrationes in Matthaeum*, in PL 162, cols. 1227–1500.

Arens: E. Arens, *The ΗΛΘΟΝ-Sayings in the Synoptic Tradition: A Historico-Critical Investigation*, OBO 10, Göttingen, 1976.

**Argyle: A. W. Argyle, *The Gospel According to Matthew*, Cambridge, 1963.

**Augustine, *De con. ev.*: Augustine, *De Consensu Evangelistarum libri 4*, CSEL 43, Vienna, 1904; English trans. in NPNF first series, vol. 6, pp. 77–236.

*Augustine, *De serm. mont.*: Augustine, *Commentary on the Lord's Sermon on the Mount* (trans. by D. J. Kavanagh of *De sermone domini in Monte*), Washington, D.C., 1951. See PL 34.1230–1308.

---

[1] A double asterisk (**) indicates a commentary on Matthew, a single asterisk (*) a work on the sermon on the mount. A dagger (†) indicates a survey of Matthean studies.

Aune: D. E. Aune, *Prophecy in Early Christianity and the Ancient Mediterranean World*, Grand Rapids, 1983.

AV: The Authorized King James Version of the Bible, 1611.

Avi-Yonah: M. Avi-Yonah, *The Holy Land*, rev. ed., Grand Rapids, 1977.

Bacon: B. W. Bacon, *Studies in Matthew*, London, 1930.

BAGD: W. Bauer, W. F. Arndt, F. W. Gingrich, F. Danker, *A Greek-English Dictionary of the New Testament*, Chicago, 1979.

Bailey: K. E. Bailey, *Poet and Peasant*, Grand Rapids, 1976.

Baly: D. Baly, *The Geography of the Bible*, rev. ed., New York, 1974.

Bammel, *Trial*: E. Bammel, ed., *The Trial of Jesus*, SBT, Second Series 13, London, 1970.

Bammel and Moule: E. Bammel and C. F. D. Moule, eds., *Jesus and the Politics of His Day*, Cambridge, 1984.

Banks: R. Banks, *Jesus and the Law in the Synoptic Tradition*, SNTSMS 28, London, 1975.

Barrett, *Jesus*: C. K. Barrett, *Jesus and the Gospel Tradition*, London, 1967.

Barrett, *John*: C. K. Barrett, *The Gospel According to St. John*, 2nd ed., London and Philadelphia, 1978.

Barrett, *Spirit*: C. K. Barrett, *The Holy Spirit and the Gospel Tradition*, London, 1947.

K. Barth: K. Barth, Church Dogmatics (trans. of *Die kirchliche Dogmatik*, 1932–67), Edinburgh, 1936–69.

*Bauman: C. Bauman, *The Sermon on the Mount: The Modern Quest for its Meaning*, Macon, 1985.

Baumbach: G. Baumbach, *Das Verständnis des Bösen in den synoptischen Evangelien*, Berlin, 1963.

BDB: F. Brown, S. R. Driver, C. A. Briggs, *Hebrew and English Lexicon of the Old Testament*, Oxford, 1907; reprinted 1953 (with corrections).

BDF: F. Blass, A. Debrunner, R. W. Funk, *A Greek Grammar of the New Testament*, Chicago, 1961.

**Beare: F. W. Beare, *The Gospel According to St. Matthew*, London, 1981.

Beasley-Murray: G. R. Beasley-Murray, *Jesus and the Kingdom of God*, Grand Rapids and Exeter, Devon, 1986.

**Bede: Pseudo-Bede, *In Matthaei Evangelium expositio*, in PL 92, cols. 9–132.

Beginnings: F. J. Foakes Jackson and K. Lake, eds., *The Beginnings of Christianity*, 5 vols., London, 1920–33.

**Bengel: J. A. Bengel, *Gnomon of the New Testament* (trans. of *Gnomon Novi Testamenti*, 1742), 2 vols., Philadelphia, 1864.

**Benoit, *Matthieu*: P. Benoit, *L'Évangile selon saint Matthieu*, Paris, 1961.

Benoit, *Passion*: P. Benoit, *The Passion and Resurrection of Jesus Christ* (trans. of *Passion et resurrection du Seigneur*, 1966), New York and London, 1969.

Berger, *Amen*: K. Berger, *Die Amen-Worte Jesu: Eine Untersuchung zum Problem der Legitimation in apokalyptischer Rede*, BZNW 39, Berlin, 1970.

Berger, *Gesetzesauslegung*: K. Berger, *Die Gesetzesauslegung Jesu: Ihr historischer Hintergrund im Judentum und im Alten Testament. Teil I: Markus und Parallelen*, WMANT 40, Neukirchen-Vluyn, 1972.

*Berner: U. Berner, *Die Bergpredigt: Rezeption und Auslegung im 20. Jahrhundert*, Göttingen, 1979.

Best, *Temptation*: E. Best, *The Temptation and the Passion: The Markan Soteriology*, SNTSMS 2, Cambridge, 1965.

Betz, *Essays*: H. D. Betz, *Essays on the Sermon on the Mount*, Philadelphia, 1985.

O. Betz, *Jesus*: O. Betz, *What Do We Know About Jesus?* (trans. of *Was wissen wir von Jesus?*, 1965), London, 1968.

Beyer: K. Beyer, *Semitische Syntax im Neuen Testament, Band I*, 2nd ed., Göttingen, 1968.

*Beyschlag, 'Bergpredigt': K. Beyschlag, 'Zur Geschichte der Bergpredigt in der Alten Kirche', *ZTK* 74 (1977), pp. 291–322.

Black: M. Black, *An Aramaic Approach to the Gospels and Acts*, 3rd ed., Oxford, 1967.

Blair: E. P. Blair, *Jesus in the Gospel of Matthew*, New York, 1960.

*Bligh: J. Bligh, *The Sermon on the Mount*, Slough, 1975.

*Böcher, *Bergpredigt*: O. Böcher et al., *Die Bergpredigt im Leben der Christenheit*, Göttingen, 1980.

Böcher: O. Böcher, *Christus Exorcista*, BWANT 96, Stuttgart, 1972.

**Bonnard: P. Bonnard, *L'Évangile selon saint Matthieu*, 2nd ed., Neuchâtel, 1970.

Borg: M. J. Borg, *Conflict, Holiness and Politics in the Teaching of Jesus*, New York, 1984.

Boring: M. E. Boring, *Sayings of the Risen Jesus: Christian Prophecy in the Synoptic Tradition*, SNTSMS 46, Cambridge, 1982.

*Bornhauser: K. Bornhauser, *Die Bergpredigt*, Gütersloh, 1927.

*Bornkamm, 'Bergpredigt': G. Bornkamm, 'Der Aufbau der Bergpredigt', *NTS* 24 (1978), pp. 419–32.

Borsch: F. H. Borsch, *The Son of Man in Myth and History*, NTL, London and Philadelphia, 1967.

Boucher: M. Boucher, *The Mysterious Parable*, CBQMS 6, Washington, D.C., 1977.

Bousset: W. Bousset, *Kyrios Christos* (trans. of *Kyrios Christos*, 1921), Nashville, 1970.

*Bowman and Trapp: J. W. Bowman and R. W. Trapp, *The Gospel from the Mount*, Philadelphia, 1957.

**Box: G. H. Box, *The Gospel of St. Matthew*, London, 1922.

Branscomb: B. H. Branscomb, *Jesus and the Law of Moses*, London, 1930.

Braun, *Jesus*: H. Braun, *Jesus of Nazareth* (trans. of *Jesus*, 1969), Philadelphia, 1979.

Braun, *Qumran*: H. Braun, *Qumran und das Neue Testament*, 2 vols., Tübingen, 1966.

Braun, *Radikalismus*: H. Braun, *Spätjüdisch-häretischer und frühchristlicher Radikalismus*, BHT 24, Tübingen, 1957.

Breech: J. Breech, *The Silence of Jesus*, Philadelphia, 1984.

Broer: I. Broer, *Freiheit vom Gesetz und Radikalisierung des Gesetzes:*

Ein Beitrag zur Theologie des Evangelisten Matthäus, SBS 98, Stuttgart, 1980.

Brown, *Essays*: R. E. Brown, *New Testament Essays*, Milwaukee, 1965.

Brown, *John*: R. E. Brown, *The Gospel According to John*, AB, 2 vols., Garden City, New York, 1966, 1970.

Brown, *Mary*: R. E. Brown et al., *Mary in the New Testament*, Philadelphia, 1978.

Brown, *Messiah*: R. E. Brown, *The Birth of the Messiah*, Garden City, New York, 1977.

Brown, *Peter*: R. E. Brown et al., *Peter in the New Testament*, Minneapolis and New York, 1973.

**Bruno: Bruno of Segni, *Commentaria in Matthaeum*, in PL 165, cols. 63–314.

Buchanan: G. W. Buchanan, *Jesus: The King and his Kingdom*, Macon, 1984.

Bultmann, *History*: R. Bultmann, *The History of the Synoptic Tradition* (trans. of *Die Geschichte der synoptischen Tradition*, 3rd ed., 1958), Oxford, 1963.

Bultmann, *Theology*: R. Bultmann, *Theology of the New Testament*, 2 vols. (trans. of *Theologie des Neuen Testaments*, 1948, 1953), Oxford, 1951, 1955.

*Burchard: C. Burchard, 'The Theme of the Sermon on the Mount' (trans. of 'Versuch, das Thema der Bergpredigt zu finden', in Strecker, *Jesus Christus*, pp. 409–32), in Fuller, *Love*, pp. 57–91.

Burger: C. Burger, *Jesus als Davidssohn*, FRLANT 98, Göttingen, 1970.

Burkitt: F. C. Burkitt, *Evangelion da-Mepharreshe II*, Cambridge, 1904.

Burnett: F. W. Burnett, *The Testament of Jesus-Sophia: A Redaction-Critical Study of the Eschatological Discourse in Matthew*, New York, 1981.

Burney: F. C. Burney, *The Poetry of Our Lord*, Oxford, 1925.

Burton: E. de Witt Burton, *Syntax of the Moods and Tenses in New Testament Greek*, Chicago, 1900.

Butler: B. C. Butler, *The Originality of St. Matthew*, Cambridge, 1951.

Cadoux: C. J. Cadoux, *The Historic Mission of Jesus*, New York and London, n.d.

Caird: G. B. Caird, *Saint Luke*, Pelican New Testament Commentaries, Harmondsworth, 1963.

**Calvin: J. Calvin, *Commentary on a Harmony of the Gospels* (trans. of *Joannis Calvini commentarius in harmoniam evangelicam*, 1555), reprint ed., 3 vols., Grand Rapids, 1956, 1957.

Carlston: C. E. Carlston, *The Parables of the Triple Tradition*, Philadelphia, 1975.

*Carson: D. A. Carson, *The Sermon on the Mount*, Grand Rapids, 1978.

Casey: M. Casey, *Son of Man: The Interpretation and Influence of Daniel 7*, London, 1979.

Charles: R. H. Charles, ed., *Apocrypha and Pseudepigrapha of the Old Testament*, 2 vols., Oxford, 1913.

Charlesworth: J. H. Charlesworth, ed., *The Old Testament Pseudepigrapha*, 2 vols., New York, 1983, 1985.

Chilton, *Rabbi*: B. D. Chilton, *A Galilean Rabbi and His Bible*, Wilmington, 1984.

Chilton, *Strength*: B. D. Chilton, *God in Strength: Jesus' Announcement of the Kingdom*, SNTU, Series B, Band I, Freistadt, 1979.

CHJ: *The Cambridge History of Judaism*, ed. W. D. Davies and L. Finkelstein, Cambridge, 1984–.

Christ: F. Christ, *Jesus Sophia: Die Sophia-Christologie bei den Synoptikern*, ATANT 57, Zürich, 1970.

**Christian of Stavelot: Christian of Stavelot, *Expositio in Matthaeum Evangelistam*, in PL 106, cols. 1261–1504.

**Chromatius of Aquileia: Chromatius of Aquileia, *Tractatus XVII in Evangelium S. Matthaei*, in PL 20, cols. 327–68; see also R. Étaix, ' "Tractatus in Mattheum", partiellement inédits, pouvant être attribués à Chromace d'Aquilée', *RBén* 70 (1960), pp. 469–503.

**Chrysostom, *Hom. on Mt.*: John Chrysostom, *Homilies on the Gospel according to St. Matthew* (trans. of *Commentarius in sanctum Matthaeum Evangelistam*, in PG 57 and 58), in NPNF 10.

CIG: *Corpus Inscriptionum Graecarum*, Berlin, 1828–77.

CIJ: J. B. Frey, *Corpus Inscriptionum Judaicarum*, Rome, 1936, 1955.

CIS: *Corpus Inscriptionum Semiticarum*, Paris, 1887–90.

**Clark, *Matthew*: K. S. L. Clark, *The Gospel according to Saint Matthew*, London, 1974.

Cohen: S. J. D. Cohen, *Josephus in Galilee and Rome*, Leiden, 1979.

Conzelmann: H. Conzelmann, *The Theology of St. Luke* (trans. of *Die Mitte der Zeit*, 1957), London and New York, 1960.

Cope: O. L. Cope, *Matthew: A Scribe trained for the Kingdom of Heaven*, CBQMS 5, Washington, D.C., 1976.

Cowley: A. Cowley, *Aramaic Papyri of the Fifth Century B.C.*, Oxford, 1923.

**Cox: G. E. P. Cox, *The Gospel of St. Matthew*, London, 1952.

CPJ: V. A. Tcherikover, A. Fuks, et al., *Corpus Papyrorum Judaicarum*, 3 vols., Cambridge, Mass., 1957–64.

Cramer: J. A. Cramer, ed., *Catenae Graecorum Patrum in Novum Testamentum. I Catenae in Ev. S. Matthaei et S. Marci*, reprint ed., Hildesheim, 1967.

Cranfield, *Bible*: C. E. B. Cranfield, *The Bible and Christian Life*, Edinburgh, 1985.

Cranfield, *Mark*: C. E. B. Cranfield, *St. Mark*, 2nd ed., Cambridge, 1963.

Cranfield, *Romans*: C. E. B. Cranfield, *A Critical and Exegetical Commentary on the Epistle to the Romans*, 2 vols., Edinburgh, 1975, 1979.

CRINT: *Compendia Rerum Iudaicarum ad Novum Testamentum*, Assen/Philadelphia, 1974ff.

Crossan, *Aphorisms*: J. D. Crossan, *In Fragments: The Aphorisms of Jesus*, New York, 1983.

Crossan, *Other Gospels*: J. D. Crossan, *Four Other Gospels*, New York, 1985.

CSCO: Corpus Scriptorum Christianorum Orientalium, Paris, 1913ff.

CSEL: Corpus Scriptorum Ecclesiasticorum Latinorum, Vienna, 1866ff.

'*CTA*: A. Herdner, *Corpus des tablettes en cunéiformes alphabétiques*, Paris, 1963.

Cullmann, *Christology*: O. Cullmann, *The Christology of the New Testament* (trans. of *Die Christologie des Neuen Testaments*, 1957), rev. ed., London and Philadelphia, 1959.

**Cyril of Alexandria, *Comm. on Mt.*: Cyril of Alexandria, *Commentariorum in Matthaeum quae supersunt*, in PG 72, cols. 365–474.

Dahl, *Jesus*: N. A. Dahl, *Jesus in the Memory of the Early Church*, Minneapolis, 1976.

Dautzenberg: G. Dautzenberg, *Sein Leben bewahren: Ψυχή in den Herrenworten der Evangelien*, SANT 14, Munich, 1966.

Dalman, *Jesus-Jeshua*: G. Dalman, *Jesus-Jeshua: Studies in the Gospels* (trans. of *Jesus-Jeschua*, 1922), London, 1929.

Dalman, *Words*: G. Dalman, *The Words of Jesus* (trans. of *Die Worte Jesu*, 1898), Edinburgh, 1902.

Danby: H. Danby, trans. and ed., *The Mishnah*, Oxford, 1933.

Daube: D. Daube, *The New Testament and Rabbinic Judaism*, London, 1956.

Davies, *COJ*: W. D. Davies, *Christian Origins and Judaism*, Philadelphia, 1962.

Davies, *JPS*: W. D. Davies, *Jewish and Pauline Studies*, Philadelphia, 1984.

Davies, *Land*: W. D. Davies, *The Gospel and the Land*, Berkeley, 1974.

Davies, *PRJ*: W. D. Davies, *Paul and Rabbinic Judaism*, rev. ed., Philadelphia, 1980.

*Davies, *SSM*: W. D. Davies, *The Setting of the Sermon on the Mount*, Cambridge, 1964.

Davies, *TDJ*: W. D.Davies, *The Territorial Dimension of Judaism*, California, 1982.

Davies, *Torah*: W. D. Davies, *Torah in the Messianic Age and/or the Age to Come*, JBLMS 8, Philadelphia, 1952.

DBSup: *Dictionnaire de la Bible, Supplément*, ed. L. Pirot, A. Robert, H. Cazelles, and A. Feuillet, Paris, 1928ff.

Deissmann, *Light*: A. Deissmann, *Light from the Ancient East* (trans. of *Licht vom Osten*, 1923), London, 1927.

Deissmann, *Studies*: A. Deissmann, *Bible Studies* (trans. of *Bibelstudien* and *Neue Bibelstudien*, 1895 and 1897), Edinburgh, 1901.

Delobel: J. Delobel, ed., *Logia: Les paroles de Jésus*, BETL 59, Louvain, 1982.

†Dermience: A. Dermience, 'Rédaction et théologie dans le premier évangile: Une perspective de l'exégèse matthéenne récente', *RTL* 16 (1985), pp. 47–64.

Derrett, *Law*: J. D. M. Derrett, *Law in the New Testament*, London, 1970.

Derrett, *Studies*: J. D. M. Derrett, *Studies in the New Testament*, 4 vols., Leiden, 1977, 1978, 1982, 1986.

Descamps: A. Descamps, *Les justes et la justice dans les évangiles et le christianisme primitif hormis la doctrine proprement paulinienne*, Gembloux, 1950.

*Descamps, 'Discours': A. Descamps, 'Le discours sur la montagne:

Esquisse de théologie biblique', *RTL* 12 (1981), pp. 5–39.

Descamps, *Mélanges*: A. Descamps and A. de Halleux, eds., *Mélanges bibliques*, Gembloux, 1970.

Dibelius, *James*: M. Dibelius, *James* (trans. of *Der Brief des Jakobus*, 1964), rev. by H. Greeven, Philadelphia, 1976.

*Dibelius, *Sermon*: M. Dibelius, *The Sermon on the Mount* (trans. of 'Die Bergpredigt', reprinted in *Botschaft und Geschichte*, vol. 1, 1953, pp. 80–174), New York, 1940.

Dibelius, *Tradition*: M. Dibelius, *From Tradition to Gospel* (trans. of *Die Formgeschichte des Evangeliums*, 1933), New York, 1935.

Didier: M. Didier, ed., *L'Évangile selon Matthieu: Rédaction et Théologie*, BETL 29, Gembloux, 1972.

DJD: Discoveries in the Judaean Desert (of Jordan), Oxford, 1955ff.

D.-K.: H. Diels and W. Kranz, *Die Fragmente der Vorsokratiker*, 3 vols., 11th ed., Zürich/Berlin, 1964.

Dodd, *Founder*: C. H. Dodd, *The Founder of Christianity*, London, 1971.

Dodd, *Interpretation*: C. H. Dodd, *The Interpretation of the Fourth Gospel*, Cambridge, 1953.

Dodd, *NTS*: C. H. Dodd, *New Testament Studies*, Manchester, 1953.

Dodd, *MNTS*: C. H. Dodd, *More New Testament Studies*, London, 1968.

Dodd, *Parables*: C. H. Dodd, *The Parables of the Kingdom*, rev. ed., New York, 1961.

Dodd, *Scriptures*: C. H. Dodd, *According to the Scriptures*, London, 1952.

Dodd, *Tradition*: C. H. Dodd, *Historical Tradition in the Fourth Gospel*, Cambridge, 1963.

Doeve: J. W. Doeve, *Jewish Hermeneutics in the Synoptic Gospels and Acts*, Assen, 1954.

Donaldson: T. L. Donaldson, *Jesus on the Mountain: A Study in Matthean Theology*, JSNTSS 8, Sheffield, 1985.

Donfried: K. P. Donfried, *The Setting of Second Clement in Early Christianity*, NovTSup 38, Leiden, 1974.

Doudna: J. C. Doudna, *The Greek of the Gospel of Mark*, SBLMS 12, Philadelphia, 1961.

Dox. Gr.: H. Diels, ed., *Doxographi Graeci*, Berlin, 1879.

Drury: J. Drury, *The Parables in the Gospels*, New York and London, 1985.

Dunn, *Christology*: J. D. G. Dunn, *Christology in the Making*, London and Philadelphia, 1980.

Dunn, *Spirit*: J. D. G. Dunn, *Jesus and the Spirit*, London, 1975.

*Dupont: J. Dupont, *Les Béatitudes*, 3 vols., Paris, 1958, 1969, 1973.

Dupont, *Jesus*: J. Dupont, ed., *Jésus aux origines de la christologie*, Gembloux, 1975.

**Durand: A. Durand, *Évangile selon Saint Matthieu*, Paris, 1929.

Edwards, *Q*: R. A. Edwards, *A Theology of Q*, Philadelphia, 1976.

Edwards, *Story*: R. A. Edwards, *Matthew's Story of Jesus*, Philadelphia, 1985.

*Eichholz: G. Eichholz, *Auslegung der Bergpredigt*, BS 46, 2nd ed., Neukirchen, 1970.

Ellis, *Jesus*: E. E. Ellis and E. Grässer, eds., *Jesus und Paulus*, Göttingen, 1975.

Ellis, *Luke*: E. E. Ellis, *The Gospel of Luke*, NCB, London, 1974.

Ellis, *Neotestamentica*: E. E. Ellis and M. Wilcox, eds., *Neotestamentica et Semitica*, Edinburgh, 1969.

Ellis, *Prophecy*: E. E. Ellis, *Prophecy and Hermeneutic in Early Christianity*, WUNT 18, Tübingen, 1978.

P. F. Ellis: P. F. Ellis, *Matthew: His Mind and Message*, Collegeville, 1974.

Eltester: W. Eltester, ed., *Judentum—Urchristentum—Kirche*, Berlin, 1964.

**Euthymius Zigabenus: Euthymius Zigabenus, *Commentarius in quatuor Evangelia*, in *PG* 129, cols. 107–766; also the edition of C. F. Matthaei, Leipzig, 1792.

EWNT: *Exegetisches Wörterbuch zum Neuen Testament*, ed. H. Balz and G. Schneider, Stuttgart, 1978ff.

Farmer, *Jesus*: W. R. Farmer, *Jesus and the Gospel*, Philadelphia, 1982.

Farmer, *Problem*: W. R. Farmer, *The Synoptic Problem*, New York, 1964.

Farmer, *Studies*: W. R. Farmer, ed., *New Synoptic Studies*, Macon, 1983.

Farrer: A. M. Farrer, *St. Matthew and St. Mark*, London, 1954.

**Fenton: J. C. Fenton, *The Gospel of St. Matthew*, rev. ed., London, 1977.

*Fiebig: P. Fiebig, *Jesu Bergpredigt*, FRLANT 20, Göttingen, 1924.

**Filson: F. V. Filson, *The Gospel according to St. Matthew*, London, 1960.

Finkelstein: L. Finkelstein, *The Pharisees*, 2 vols., 2nd ed., Philadelphia, 1940.

Fitzmyer, *Advance*: J. A. Fitzmyer, *To Advance the Gospel*, New York, 1981.

Fitzmyer, *Aramean*: J. A. Fitzmyer, *A Wandering Aramean*, Missoula, 1979.

Fitzmyer, *Background*: J. A. Fitzmyer, *Essays on the Semitic Background of the New Testament*, Missoula, 1974.

Fitzmyer, *Luke*: J. A. Fitzmyer, *The Gospel according to Luke*, 2 vols., AB 28, Garden City, 1981, 1985.

Flew: R. N. Flew, *Jesus and His Church*, New York, 1938.

France 1, 2, 3: R. T. France and D. Wenham, eds., *Gospel Perspectives*, vols. 1–3, Sheffield, 1980, 1981, 1983.

Frankemölle: H. Frankemölle, *Jahwebund und Kirche Christi*, NTAbh, n.F. 10, 2nd ed., Münster, 1984.

*Frankemölle, 'Bergpredigt': H. Frankemölle, 'Neue Literatur zur Bergpredigt', *TRev* 79 (1983), pp. 177–98.

Franzmann: M. H. Franzmann, *Follow Me: Discipleship according to St. Matthew*, St. Louis, 1961.

Freyne: S. Freyne, *Galilee from Alexander the Great to Hadrian*, Wilmington, 1980.

*Friedlander: G. Friedlander, *The Jewish Sources of the Sermon on the Mount*, London, 1911.

Fuller, *Christology*: R. H. Fuller, *The Foundations of New Testament Christology*, London, 1965.

Fuller, *Formation*: R. H. Fuller, *The Formation of the Resurrection Narratives*, New York, 1970.

Fuller, *Love*: R. H. Fuller and I. Fuller, eds., *Essays on the Love Commandment* (trans. of four essays originally appearing in G. Strecker, ed., *Jesus Christus in Historie und Theologie*, 1975), Philadelphia, 1978.

Fuller, *Mission*: R. H. Fuller, *The Mission and Achievement of Jesus*, SBT 12, London, 1954.

Furnish: V. P. Furnish, *The Love Command in the New Testament*, Nashville, 1972.

**Gaechter, *Kommentar*: P. Gaechter, *Das Matthäus-Evangelium: Ein Kommentar*, Innsbruck, 1963.

Gaechter, *Kunst*: P. Gaechter, *Die literarische Kunst im Matthäus-Evangelium*, Stuttgart, 1965.

Gärtner: B. Gärtner, *The Temple and the Community in Qumran and the New Testament*, SNTSMS 1, Cambridge, 1965.

Garland: D. E. Garland, *The Intention of Matthew 23*, NovSup 52, Leiden, 1979.

Gaston: L. Gaston, *No Stone on Another*, NovTSup 23, Leiden, 1970.

Gerhardsson, *Acts*: B. Gerhardsson, *The Mighty Acts of Jesus according to Matthew*, Lund, 1979.

Gerhardsson, *Memory*: B. Gerhardsson, *Memory and Manuscript: Oral Tradition and Written Transmission in Rabbinic Judaism and Early Christianity*, 2nd ed., Uppsala and Lund, 1964.

Giesen: H. Giesen, *Christliches Handeln: Eine redaktionskritische Untersuchung zum δικαιοσύνη-Begriff im Matthäus-Evangelium*, Frankfurt am Main, 1982.

Ginzberg: L. Ginzberg, *The Legends of the Jews*, 7 vols., Philadelphia, 1942.

GK: *Gesenius' Hebrew Grammer*, ed. and enlarged by E. Kautzsch, trans. by A. E. Cowley, 2nd ed., Oxford, 1910.

Glasson: T. F. Glasson, *The Second Advent*, 3rd ed., London, 1963.

**Glossa Ordinaria*: *Glossa Ordinaria*, in PL 114, cols. 63–178.

Gnilka, *Kirche*: J. Gnilka, ed., *Neues Testament und Kirche*, Freiburg, 1974.

Gnilka, *Markus*: J. Gnilka, *Das Evangelium nach Markus*, EKKNT II/1–2, 2 vols., Zürich, 1978, 1979.

Gnilka, *Verstockung*: J. Gnilka, *Die Verstockung Israels*, Munich, 1961.

Goguel: M. Goguel, *The Life of Jesus* (trans. of *La vie de Jésus*, 1932), London, 1933.

Goodenough: E. R. Goodenough, *Jewish Symbols in the Greco-Roman Period*, 11 vols., New York, 1953–64.

Goodspeed: E. J. Goodspeed, *Matthew, Apostle and Evangelist*, Philadelphia, 1959.

Goppelt, *Theology*: L. Goppelt, *Theology of the New Testament* (trans. of *Theologie des Neuen Testaments*, 1975, 1976), 2 vols., Grand Rapids, 1981, 1982.

Goppelt, *Typos*: L. Goppelt, *Typos* (trans. of *Typos*, 1939), Grand Rapids, 1978.

Goulder: M. D. Goulder, *Midrash and Lection in Matthew*, London, 1974.

Grässer: E. Grässer, *Das Problem der Parusieverzögerung in den synoptischen Evangelien und in der Apostelgeschichte*, BZNW 22, Berlin, 1957.

F. C. Grant: F. C. Grant, 'Matthew, Gospel of', in *IDB* 3, pp. 303–13.

*R. M. Grant: R. M. Grant, 'The Sermon on the Mount in Early Christianity', *Semeia* 12 (1978), pp. 215–31.

*Grayston: K. Grayston, 'Sermon on the Mount', *IDB* 4, pp. 279–89.

**Green: H. B. Green, *The Gospel according to Matthew*, Oxford, 1975.

**Gregory I, *Hom.*: Gregory I (the Great), *XL Homiliarum in Evangelia libri 2*, in PL 76, cols. 1075–1314.

Grimm: W. Grimm, *Weil ich dich liebe. Die Verkündigung Jesu und Deuterojesaja*, Frankfurt am Main, 1976.

**Grundmann: W. Grundmann, *Das Evangelium nach Matthäus*, THKNT, Berlin, 1968.

*Guelich: R. A. Guelich, *The Sermon on the Mount*, Waco, 1982.

Güttgemanns: E. Güttgemanns, *Candid Questions concerning Gospel Form Criticism* (trans. of *Offene Fragen zur Formgeschichte des Evangeliums*, 1971), Pittsburgh, 1979.

**Gundry, *Commentary*: R. H. Gundry, *Matthew: A Commentary on his Literary and Theological Art*, Grand Rapids, 1982.

Gundry, *OT*: R. H. Gundry, *The Use of the Old Testament in St. Matthew's Gospel*, NovTSup 18, Leiden, 1967.

**Guy: H. A. Guy, *The Gospel of Matthew*, London, 1971.

Haenchen: E. Haenchen, *Der Weg Jesu*, Berlin, 1966.

*Häring: B. Häring, 'The Normative Value of the Sermon on the Mount', *CBQ* 29 (1967), pp. 375–85.

Hagner, *Clement*: D. A. Hagner, *The Use of the Old and New Testaments in Clement of Rome*, NovTSup 34, Leiden, 1975.

Hahn, *Hoheitstitel*: F. Hahn, *Christologische Hoheitstitel*, FRLANT 83, 3rd ed., Göttingen, 1966.

Hahn, *Mission*: F. Hahn, *Mission in the New Testament* (trans. of *Das Verständnis der Mission im Neuen Testament*, 1963), SBT 47, London, 1965.

Hahn, *Titles*: F. Hahn, *The Titles of Jesus in Christology* (abridged trans. of *Christologische Hoheitstitel*, 1966), New York, 1969.

Hahn, *Worship*: F. Hahn, *The Worship of the Early Church* (trans. of *Der urchristliche Gottesdienst*, 1970), Philadelphia, 1973.

**Hamann: H. P. Hamann, *Chi Rho Commentary on the Gospel according to Matthew*, Adelaide, 1984.

Hamerton-Kelly, *Pre-Existence*: R. G. Hamerton-Kelly, *Pre-Existence, Wisdom and the Son of Man*, SNTSMS 21, Cambridge, 1973.

Hare: D. R. A. Hare, *The Theme of Jewish Persecution of Christians in the Gospel according to St. Matthew*, SNTSMS 6, Cambridge, 1967.

Harnack: A. Harnack, *The Sayings of Jesus* (trans. of *Sprüche und Reden Jesu*, 1907), New York and London, 1908.

†Harrington: D. J. Harrington, 'Matthean Studies since Joachim Rohde', *HeyJ* 16 (1975), pp. 375–88.

Harvey: A. E. Harvey, *Jesus and the Constraints of History*, London and Philadelphia, 1982.

Harvey, *Approaches*: A. E. Harvey, ed., *Alternative Approaches to the New Testament*, London, 1985.

Hasler: V. Hasler, *Amen*, Zürich, 1969.

Hawkins: J. C. Hawkins, *Horae Synopticae*, Oxford, 1909.

Hay: D. M. Hay, *Glory at the Right Hand: Psalm 110 in Early Christianity*, SBLMS 18, Nashville, 1973.

Heil: J. P. Heil, *Jesus Walking on the Sea*, AnBib 87, Rome, 1981.

*Heinrici: C. Heinrici, *Die Bergpredigt (Matth. 5–7; Luk. 6.20–49) begriffsgeschichtlich untersucht*, Leipzig, 1905.

Hendrickx, *Infancy Narratives*: H. Hendrickx, *The Infancy Narratives*, London, 1984.

Hendrickx, *Passion*: H. Hendrickx, *The Passion Narratives of the Synoptic Gospels*, London, 1984.

Hendrickx, *Resurrection*: H. Hendrickx, *The Resurrection Narratives of the Synoptic Gospels*, London, 1984.

*Hendrickx, *Sermon*: H. Hendrickx, *The Sermon on the Mount*, London, 1984.

*Hengel, 'Bergpredigt': M. Hengel, 'Die Bergpredigt im Widerstreit', *TB* 14 (1982), pp. 53–67.

Hengel, *Atonement*: M. Hengel, *The Atonement* (trans. of 'Der stellvertretende Sühnetod Jesu', *IKZ* 9 (1980), pp. 1–25, 135–47, with substantial additions by the author), London and Philadelphia, 1981.

Hengel, *Charismatic Leader*: M. Hengel, *The Charismatic Leader and His Followers* (trans. of *Nachfolge und Charisma*, 1968), Edinburgh, 1981.

Hengel, *Crucifixion*: M. Hengel, *Crucifixion* (trans. of '*Mors turpissima crucis*: Die Kreuzigung in der antiken Welt und die "Torheit" des "Wortes vom Kreuz" ', in J. Friedrich et al., eds., *Rechtfertigung*, 1976, with substantial later additions by the author), London and Philadelphia, 1977.

Hengel, *Jesus and Paul*: M. Hengel, *Between Jesus and Paul* (trans. of six articles originally appearing in German in various publications), London, 1983.

Hengel, *Judaism and Hellenism*: M. Hengel, *Judaism and Hellenism* (trans. of *Judentum und Hellenismus*, 1973), 2 vols., London and Philadelphia, 1974.

Hengel, *Mark*: M. Hengel, *Studies in the Gospel of Mark* (trans. of three articles originally appearing in German in various publications), London and Philadelphia, 1985.

Hengel, *Property*: M. Hengel, *Property and Riches in the Ancient Church* (trans. of *Eigentum und Reichtum in der frühen Kirche*, 1973), London and Philadelphia, 1974.

Hengel, *Zeloten*: M. Hengel, *Die Zeloten*, AGJU 1, Leiden, 1961.

HG: A. Huck, *Synopse der drei ersten Evangelien*, 13th ed., fundamentally revised by H. Greeven, Tübingen, 1981.

Hennecke: E. Hennecke, *New Testament Apocrypha*, edited by W. Schneemelcher and R. McL. Wilson (trans. of *Neutestamentliche Apokryphen*, 1959, 1964), 2 vols., London, 1963, 1965.

Hiers, *Historical Jesus*: R. Hiers, *The Historical Jesus and the Kingdom of God*, Gainesville, 1973.

Hiers, *Tradition*: R. Hiers, *The Kingdom of God in the Synoptic Tradition*, Gainesville, 1970.

Higgins, *JSM*: A. J. B. Higgins, *Jesus and the Son of Man*, London, 1964.

Higgins, *SMTJ*: A. J. B. Higgins, *The Son of Man in the Teaching of Jesus*, SNTSMS 39, Cambridge, 1980.

**Hilary: Hilary of Poitiers, *In Evangelium Matthaei Commentarius*, in PL 9, cols. 917–1078.

Hill, *Greek Words*: D. Hill, *Greek Words and Hebrew Meanings*, SNTSMS 5, Cambridge, 1967.

**Hill, *Matthew*: D. Hill, *The Gospel of Matthew*, NCB, London, 1972.

Hill, *Prophecy*: D. Hill, *New Testament Prophecy*, London and Atlanta, 1979.

*Hill, 'Sermon': D. Hill, 'The Meaning of the Sermon on the Mount in Matthew's Gospel', *IBS* 6 (1984), pp. 120–33.

†Hill, 'Trends': D. Hill, 'Some Recent Trends in Matthean Studies', *IBS* 1 (1979), pp. 139–49.

Hirsch: E. Hirsch, *Frühgeschichte des Evangeliums II: Die Vorlagen des Lukas und das Sondergut des Matthäus*, Tübingen, 1941.

Hoehner: H. Hoehner, *Herod Antipas*, SNTSMS 17, Cambridge, 1972.

*Hoffmann, 'Bergpredigt': P. Hoffmann, 'Auslegung der Bergpredigt', *BuL* 10 (1969), pp. 57–69, 111–22, 175–89, 264–75; 11 (1970), pp. 89–104.

Hoffmann, *Logienquelle*: P. Hoffmann, *Studien zur Theologie der Logienquelle*, Münster, 1972.

Hoffmann, *Orientierung*: P. Hoffmann, ed., *Orientierung an Jesus*, Freiburg, 1973.

**Holtzmann: H. J. Holtzmann, *Die Synoptiker*, 3rd ed., Tübingen, 1901.

Hooker, *Servant*: M. D. Hooker, *Jesus and the Servant*, London, 1959.

Hooker, *Son of Man*: M. D. Hooker, *The Son of Man in Mark*, London, 1967.

Horbury: W. Horbury and B. McNeil, eds., *Suffering and Martyrdom in the New Testament*, Cambridge, 1981.

Horsley: G. H. R. Horsley, *New Documents illustrating Early Christianity*, North Ryde, 1981ff.

Howard: V. Howard, *Das Ego Jesu in den synoptischen Evangelien*, Marburg, 1975.

*Huber: H. Huber, *Die Bergpredigt*, Göttingen, 1932.

Hübner: H. Hübner, *Das Gesetz in der synoptischen Tradition*, Witten, 1973.

**Hugh of St. Victor: Hugh of St. Victor, *Allegoriae in Novum Testamentum liber II: In Matthaeum*, in PL 175, cols. 763–802.

Hull: J. M. Hull, *Hellenistic Magic and the Synoptic Tradition*, SBT 28, London, 1974.

Hultgren: A. J. Hultgren, *Jesus and his Adversaries*, Minneapolis, 1979.

Hummel: R. Hummel, *Die Auseinandersetzung zwischen Kirche und Judentum im Matthäusevangelium*, 2nd ed., Munich, 1966.

*Hunter: A. M. Hunter, *Design for Life: An Exposition of the Sermon on the Mount*, London, 1953.

IB: *Interpreter's Bible*, ed. G. A. Buttrick, 12 vols., New York and Nashville, 1952–57.

IDB: *Interpreter's Dictionary of the Bible*, ed. G. A. Buttrick, 4 vols., Nashville, 1962.

IDBSup: *Interpreter's Dictionary of the Bible, Supplement*, ed. K. Crim, Nashville, 1976.

IG: *Inscriptiones Graecae*, Berlin, 1873ff.

IG²: *Inscriptiones Graecae*, editio minor, Berlin, 1913ff.

IGA: *Inscriptiones Graecae Aegypti*, Cairo, Leipzig, Nancy, 1901ff.

IGLS: *Inscriptiones Grecques et Latines de la Syrie*, Paris, 1929ff.

† Ingelaere: J. C. Ingelaere, 'Chronique Matthéenne', *RHPR* 61 (1981), pp. 67–79.

**Ishodad: Ishodad of Merv, *New Testament Commentaries*, vol. I, ed. and trans. by M. D. Gibson, Cambridge, 1911.

Jastrow: M. Jastrow, *A Dictionary of the Targumim, the Talmud Babli and Yerushalmi and the Midrashic Literature*, 2 vols., Brooklyn, n.d.

JBC: R. E. Brown et al., eds., *The Jerome Biblical Commentary*, Englewood Cliffs, 1968.

JE: *The Jewish Encyclopedia*, ed. I. Singer, 11 vols., New York and London, 1901–1907.

G. Jeremias, *Tradition*: G. Jeremias et al., eds., *Tradition und Glaube*, Göttingen, 1971.

Jeremias, *Abba*: J. Jeremias, *Abba*, Göttingen, 1966.

Jeremias, *Eucharistic Words*: J. Jeremias, *The Eucharistic Words of Jesus* (trans. of *Die Abendmahlsworte Jesu*, 1960), London, 1966.

Jeremias, *Heiligengräber*: J. Jeremias, *Heiligengräber in Jesu Umwelt*, Göttingen, 1958.

Jeremias, *Jerusalem*: J. Jeremias, *Jerusalem in the Time of Jesus* (trans. of *Jerusalem zur Zeit Jesu*, 1962), London, 1969.

Jeremias, *Lukasevangelium*: J. Jeremias, *Die Sprache des Lukasevangeliums*, MeyerK, Göttingen, 1980.

Jeremias, *Parables*: J. Jeremias, *The Parables of Jesus* (trans. of *Die Gleichnisse Jesu*, 1970), 2nd rev. ed., London, 1972.

Jeremias, *Prayers*: J. Jeremias, *The Prayers of Jesus* (trans. of four essays appearing in *Abba*, 1966), SBT, London, 1967.

Jeremias, *Promise*: J. Jeremias, *Jesus' Promise to the Nations* (trans. of *Jesu Verheissung für die Völker*, 1956), London, 1958.

*Jeremias, *Sermon*: J. Jeremias, *The Sermon on the Mount* (trans. of *Die Bergpredigt*, 1959), FBBS, Philadelphia, 1963.

Jeremias, *Theology*: J. Jeremias, *New Testament Theology* (trans. of *Neutestamentliche Theologie I. Teil*, 1971), London and New York, 1971.

Jeremias, *Unknown Sayings*: J. Jeremias, *The Unknown Sayings of Jesus* (trans. of *Unbekannte Jesusworte*, 1963), 2nd ed., London, 1964.

**Jerome, *Comm. on Mt.*: Jerome (Hieronymus), *Commentariorum in Matthaeum libri* IV, in vol. 7 of D. Vallarsi, *Opera omnia*, Verona, 1769, pp. 1–244 (also in PL 26).

Jervell: J. Jervell, *The Unknown Paul*, Minneapolis, 1985.

Juel: D. Juel, *Messiah and Temple*, SBLDS 31, Missoula, 1977.

Jülicher: A. Jülicher, *Die Gleichnisreden Jesu*, 2 vols., 2nd ed., Tübingen, 1910.

Käsemann, *Essays*: E. Käsemann, *Essays on New Testament Themes* (trans. of selections from *Exegetische Versuche und Besinnungen*, I, 1960), SBT 41, London, 1964.

Käsemann, *Questions*: E. Käsemann, *New Testament Questions of Today* (trans. of selections from *Exegetische Versuche und Besinnungen*, 2, 1965), London, 1969.

*Kantzenbach: F. W. Kantzenbach, *Die Bergpredigt*, Stuttgart, 1982.

Kennedy: G. Kennedy, *New Testament Interpretation through Rhetorical Criticism*, London, 1984.

Kertelge, *Mission*: K. Kertelge, ed., *Mission im Neuen Testament*, QD 93, Freiburg, 1982.

Kertelge, *Rückfrage*: K. Kertelge, ed., *Rückfrage nach Jesus*, QD 63, Freiburg, 1974.

Kertelge, *Tod*: K. Kertelge, ed., *Der Tod Jesus*, QD 74, Freiburg, 1976.

Kertelge, *Wunder*: K. Kertelge, *Die Wunder Jesu im Markusevangelium*, SANT 23, Munich, 1970.

Kilpatrick: G. D. Kilpatrick, *The Origins of the Gospel according to St. Matthew*, Oxford, 1946.

Kingsbury, *Matthew*: J. D. Kingsbury, *Matthew*, Proclamation Commentaries, Philadelphia, 1977.

Kingsbury, *Parables*: J. D. Kingsbury, *The Parables of Matthew 13*, Richmond, 1969.

Kingsbury, *Structure*: J. D. Kingsbury, *Matthew: Structure, Christology, Kingdom*, Philadelphia, 1975.

*Kissinger: W. S. Kissinger, *The Sermon on the Mount: A History of Interpretation and Bibliography*, Metuchen, 1975.

*Kittel, 'Bergpredigt': G. Kittel, 'Die Bergpredigt und die Ethik des Judentums', *ZST* 2 (1925), pp. 555–94.

KJV: see AV.

Klauck: H. J. Klauck, *Allegorie und Allegorese in synoptischen Gleichnistexten*, NTAbh 13, Münster, 1978.

Klausner, J. Klausner, *Jesus of Nazareth* (trans. of Hebrew original, 1922), New York and London, 1925.

**Klostermann: E. Klostermann, *Das Matthäusevangelium*, HNT 4, 2nd ed., Tübingen, 1927.

Knox: W. L. Knox, *The Sources of the Synoptic Gospels*, 2 vols., Cambridge, 1953, 1957.

Koester, *Überlieferung*: H. Koester, *Synoptische Überlieferung bei den apostolischen Vätern*, TU 65, Berlin, 1957.

Kopp: C. Kopp, *The Holy Places of the Gospels* (trans. of *Die heiligen Stätten der Evangelien*, 1959), Edinburgh, 1963.

Kratz: R. Kratz, *Auferweckung als Befreiung*, SBS 65, Stuttgart, 1973.

Kretzer: A. Kretzer, *Die Herrschaft der Himmel und die Söhne des Reiches*, Würzburg, 1971.

Kümmel, *Introduction*: W. G. Kümmel, *Introduction to the New Testament* (trans. of *Einleitung in das Neue Testament*, 1973), rev. ed., Nashville, 1975.

Kümmel, *Promise*: W. G. Kümmel, *Promise and Fulfilment* (trans. of *Verheissung und Erfüllung*, 1956), SBT 23, London, 1961.

Kümmel, *Theology*: W. G. Kummel, *The Theology of the New*

Testament (trans. of *Die Theologie des Neuen Testaments*, 1969), Nashville, 1973.

Künzel: G. Künzel, *Studien zum Gemeindeverständnis des Matthäus-Evangeliums*, Stuttgart, 1978.

*Kürzinger, 'Bergpredigt': J. Kürzinger, 'Zur Komposition der Bergpredigt nach Matthäus', *Bib* 40 (1959), pp. 569–89.

Kuhn: H.-W. Kuhn, *Ältere Sammlungen im Markusevangelium*, SUNT 8, Göttingen, 1971.

*Lachs, 'Sermon': S. T. Lachs, 'Some Textual Observations on the Sermon on the Mount', *JQR* 69 (1978), pp. 98–111.

**Lagrange: M. J. Lagrange, *Évangile selon saint Matthieu*, 7th ed., Paris, 1948.

Lambrecht, *Apocalypse*: J. Lambrecht, ed., *L'Apocalypse johannique et l'Apocalyptique dans le Nouveau Testament*, BETL 53, Gembloux, 1980.

Lambrecht, *Parables*: J. Lambrecht, *Once More Astonished: The Parables of Jesus* (trans. of *Terwijl Hij tot ons sprak*, 1976), New York, 1981.

*Lambrecht, *Sermon*: J. Lambrecht, *The Sermon on the Mount* (trans. of *Maar Ik zeg u: De programmatische rede van Jezus*, 1983), Wilmington, 1985.

Lampe: G. W. H. Lampe, *A Patristic Greek Lexicon*, Oxford, 1961.

Lane: W. L. Lane, *The Gospel according to Mark*, NICNT, London, 1974.

Lange, *Erscheinen*: J. Lange, *Das Erscheinen des Auferstandenen im Evangelium nach Matthäus*, FB 11, Würzburg, 1973.

Lange, *Matthäus*: J. Lange, ed., *Das Matthäus-Evangelium*, Darmstadt, 1980.

*Lapide, *Bergpredigt*: P. Lapide, *Die Bergpredigt*, Mainz, 1982.

*Lapide, *Feinde*: P. Lapide, *Wie liebt man seine Feinde?*, Mainz, 1984.

Laufen: R. Laufen, *Die Doppelüberlieferungen der Logienquelle und des Markusevangeliums*, BBB 54, Bonn, 1980.

K. Lehmann: K. Lehmann, *Auferweckt am dritten Tag nach der Schrift*, QD 38, Freiburg, 1968.

M. Lehmann: M. Lehmann, *Synoptische Quellenanalyse und die Frage nach dem historischen Jesus*, BZNW 38, Berlin, 1970.

Léon-Dufour: X. Léon-Dufour, *Études d'Évangile*, Paris, 1965.

Levine: A.-J. Levine, 'The Matthean Program of Salvation History', unpublished Ph.D. Dissertation, Duke University, 1984.

Lewis and Short: C. T. Lewis and C. Short, *A Latin Dictionary*, rev. ed., Oxford, 1958.

Lightfoot: J. Lightfoot, *A Commentary on the New Testament from the Talmud and Hebraica* (trans. of *Horae Hebraicae et Talmudicae*, 1658–74), 4 vols., Oxford, 1859; reprint ed., Grand Rapids, 1979.

Lindars, *Apologetic*: B. Lindars, *New Testament Apologetic*, London, 1961.

Lindars, *John*: B. Lindars, *The Gospel of John*, London, 1972.

Lindars, *Son of Man*: B. Lindars, *Jesus Son of Man*, London, 1983.

Lindenberger: J. M. Lindenberger, *The Aramaic Proverbs of Ahiqar*, London, 1983.

Linnemann, *Parables*: E. Linnemann, *Parables of Jesus* (trans. of *Gleichnisse Jesu*, 1964), London, 1966.

Linnemann, *Studien*: E. Linnemann, *Studien zur Passionsgeschichte*, FRLANT 102, Göttingen, 1970.

Livingstone: E. A. Livingstone, ed., *Studia Biblica 1978 II: Papers on the Gospels*, Sheffield, 1980.

Ljungman: H. Ljungman, *Das Gesetz erfüllen*, Lund, 1954.

Lövestam: E. Lövestam, *Spiritual Wakefulness in the New Testament*, Lund, 1963.

Lohmeyer, *Markus*: E. Lohmeyer, *Das Evangelium des Markus*, MeyerK, 17th ed., Göttingen, 1967.

**Lohmeyer, *Matthäus*: E. Lohmeyer, *Das Evangelium des Matthäus*, MeyerK, 4th ed., revised by W. Schmauch, Göttingen, 1967.

*Loisy, 'Discours': A. Loisy, 'La discours sur la montagne', *Revue d'histoire et de littérature religieuses* 8 (1903), pp. 97–132.

**Loisy, *Évangiles*: A. Loisy, *Les Évangiles Synoptiques*, vol. 1, Ceffonds, 1907.

LSJ: H. G. Liddell and R. Scott, *A Greek-English Lexicon*, new ed., ed. by H. Stuart Jones and R. McKenzie, Oxford, 1940.

LSJSup: Supplement to *LSJ*, ed. by E. A. Barber, Oxford, 1968.

Longenecker: R. N. Longenecker, *The Christology of Early Jewish Christianity*, SBT 2/17, London, 1970.

van der Loos: H. van der Loos, *The Miracles of Jesus*, NovTSup 8, Leiden, 1965.

*Luck: U. Luck, *Die Vollkommenheitsforderung der Bergpredigt*, Munich, 1968.

Lührmann: D. Lührmann, *Die Redaktion der Logienquelle*, Neukirchen, 1969.

*Luther: M. Luther, *Luther's Works, Volume 21: The Sermon on the Mount and the Magnificat*, ed. J. Pelikan, Saint Louis, 1956.

Lutteroth: H. Lutteroth, *Essai d'interprétation de quelques parties de l'évangile selon Saint Matthieu*, 3 parts, Paris, 1860, 1864, 1867.

Lutteroth, *Dernières parties*: H. Lutteroth, *Essai d'interprétations des dernières parties d l'évangile selon Saint Matthieu chapitres XIV–XXVIII*, Paris, 1876.

**Luz: U. Luz, *Das Evangelium nach Matthäus, 1. Teilband: Mt 1–7*, EKKNT I/1, Zürich, 1985.

*McArthur: H. A. McArthur, *Understanding the Sermon on the Mount*, London, 1960.

McConnell: R. S. McConnell, *Law and Prophecy in Matthew's Gospel*, Basel, 1969.

*McEleney, 'Sermon': N. J. McEleney, 'The Principles of the Sermon on the Mount', *CBQ* 41 (1979), pp. 552–70.

**McKenzie: J. L. McKenzie, 'The Gospel according to Matthew', *JBC*, vol. 2, pp. 62–114.

**McNeile: A. H. McNeile, *The Gospel according to St. Matthew*, London, 1915.

**Maier: G. Maier, *Matthäus-Evangelium*, 2 vols., Stuttgart, 1979–80.

Maloney: E. C. Maloney, *Semitic Interference in Markan Syntax*, SBLDS 51, Chico, 1981.

Manson, *Sayings*: T. W. Manson, *The Sayings of Jesus*, London, 1949.

Manson, *Servant-Messiah*: T. W. Manson, *The Servant-Messiah*, Cambridge, 1953.

Manson, *Teaching*: T. W. Manson, *The Teaching of Jesus*, Cambridge, 1935.

W. Manson: W. Manson, *Jesus the Messiah*, London, 1943.

Marguerat: D. Marguerat, *Le Jugement dans l'Évangile de Matthieu*, Geneva, 1981.

Marshall: I. H. Marshall, *Commentary on Luke*, London, 1978.

†Martin, 'Recent Study': R. P. Martin, 'St. Matthew's Gospel in Recent Study', *ExpT* 80 (1968–69), pp. 132–36.

Marxsen: W. Marxsen, *Mark the Evangelist* (trans. of *Der Evangelist Markus*, 1959), New York and Nashville, 1969.

Massaux: E. Massaux, *Influence de l'Évangile de saint Matthieu sur la littérature chrétienne avant saint Irénée*, Louvain, 1950.

Meier, *Antioch*: R. E. Brown and J. P. Meier, *Antioch and Rome*, New York, 1983.

Meier, *Law*: J. P. Meier, *Law and History in Matthew's Gospel*, AnBib 71, Rome, 1976.

**Meier, *Matthew*: J. P. Meier, *Matthew*, Wilmington, 1980.

Meier, *Vision*: J. P. Meier, *The Vision of Matthew*, New York, 1979.

Merklein: H. Merklein, *Jesu Botschaft von der Gottesherrschaft*, SBS 11, Stuttgart, 1983.

Metzger: B. M. Metzger, *A Textual Commentary on the Greek New Testament*, London, 1971.

**Meyer: H. A. W. Meyer, *Kritisch-exegetischer Handbuch über das Evangelium des Matthäus*, 2nd ed., Göttingen, 1844.

Meyer, *Aims*: B. F. Meyer, *The Aims of Jesus*, London, 1979.

MHT: J. H. Moulton, F. W. Howard, and N. Turner, *A Grammar of New Testament Greek*, 4 vols., Edinburgh, 1906, 1929, 1963, 1976.

**Michaelis: W. Michaelis, *Das Evangelium nach Matthäus 1–2*, Zürich, 1948–49.

Micklem: P. A. Micklem, *St. Matthew*, London, 1917.

*Miegge: G. Miegge, *Il sermone sul monte*, Turin, 1970.

MM: J. H. Moulton and G. Milligan, *The Vocabulary of the Greek Testament*, London, 1930.

Moffatt: J. Moffatt, *An Introduction to the Literature of the New Testament*, New York, 1911.

Mohrlang: R. Mohrlang, *Matthew and Paul*, SNTSMS 48, Cambridge, 1984.

Montefiore, *Rabbinic Literature*: C. G. Montefiore, *Rabbinic Literature and Gospel Teaching*, London, 1930.

**Montefiore, *Synoptic Gospels*: C. G. Montefiore, *The Synoptic Gospels*, 2 vols., 2nd ed., London, 1927.

Montefiore and Loewe: C. G. Montefiore and H. Loewe, *A Rabbinic Anthology*, London, 1938.

Moore: G. F. Moore, *Judaism in the First Centuries of the Christian Era*, 3 vols., Cambridge, Mass., 1927–30.

Moule, *Birth*: C. F. D. Moule, *The Birth of the New Testament*, 3rd ed., San Francisco and London, 1982.

Moule, *Christology*: C. F. D. Moule, *The Origin of Christology*, Cambridge, 1977.

Moule, *Essays*: C. F. D. Moule, *Essays in New Testament Interpretation*, London, 1982.

Moule, *Phenomenon*: C. F. D. Moule, *The Phenomenon of the New Testament*, SBT 2/1, London, 1967.

**Mounce: R. H. Mounce, *Matthew: A Good News Commentary*, New York, 1985.

Munck: J. Munck, *Paul and the Salvation of Mankind* (trans. of *Paulus und die Heilsgeschichte*, 1954), London, 1959.

NA²⁶: Nestle-Aland, *Novum Testamentum Graece*, 26th ed., Stuttgart, 1979.

NEB: The New English Bible.

Neirynck, *Evangelica*: F. Neirynck, *Evangelica*, ed. F. Van Segbroeck, BETL 60, Leuven, 1982.

Neirynck, *Minor Agreements*: F. Neirynck, *The Minor Agreements of Matthew and Luke against Mark*, BETL 37, Gembloux, 1974.

Nepper-Christensen: P. Nepper-Christensen, *Das Matthäusevangelium: Ein judenchristliches Evangelium?*, Aarhus, 1958.

Neusner: J. Neusner, *The Rabbinic Traditions about the Pharisees before 70*, 3 vols., Leiden, 1971.

Nineham: D. E. Nineham, *The Gospel of St. Mark*, rev. ed., London, 1977.

Nolan: B. M. Nolan, *The Royal Son of God*, OBO 23, Göttingen, 1979.

Norden: E. Norden, *Agnostos Theos*, Leipzig, 1913.

Ogawa: A. Ogawa, *L'histoire de Jésus chez Matthieu*, Frankfurt am Main, 1979.

Oppenheimer: A. Oppenheimer, *The 'Am Ha-Aretz*, Leiden, 1977.

Opus Imperfectum: Pseudo-Chrysostom, *Diatriba ad opus Imperfectum in Matthaeum*, in PL 56, cols. 601–946.

**Origen, *Comm. on Mt.*: Origen, *Commentary on St. Matthew*, in ANF 10, pp. 409–512; see also the critical edition of E. Klostermann for the series, Die griechischen christlichen Schriftsteller, 3 vols., Leipzig, 1933 (Latin translation), 1935 (Greek text), 1941 (Fragments and Indices); and H. J. Vogt, ed., Origenes, *Der Kommentar zum Evangelium nach Mattäus* 1, Stuttgart, 1983.

Otto: R. Otto, *The Kingdom of God and the Son of Man* (trans. of *Reich Gottes und Menschensohn*, 1934, with revisions by the author), new and rev. ed., London, 1943.

**Paschasius Radbertus: Paschasius Radbertus, *Expositio in Evangelium Matthaei*, in PL 120, cols. 31–994.

Patsch: H. Patsch, *Abendmahl und historischer Jesus*, Stuttgart, 1972.

Paul: A. Paul, *L'Évangile de l'enfance selon saint Matthieu*, Paris, 1968.

PCB: *Peake's Commentary on the Bible*, ed. M. Black and H. H. Rowley, Sunbury on Thames, 1962.

Percy: E. Percy, *Die Botschaft Jesu*, Lund, 1953.

Perrin, *Kingdom*: N. Perrin, *The Kingdom of God in the Teaching of Jesus*, NTL, London, 1963.

Perrin, *Language*: N. Perrin, *Jesus and the Language of the Kingdom*, Philadelphia, 1976.

Perrin, *Rediscovering*: N. Perrin, *Rediscovering the Teaching of Jesus*, New York and London, 1967.

Pesch 1, 2: R. Pesch, *Das Markusevangelium*, 2 vols., Freiburg, 1977.

Pesch, *Menschensohn*: R. Pesch and R. Schnackenburg, eds., *Jesus und der Menschensohn*, Freiburg, 1975.

Pesch, *Naherwartungen*: R. Pesch, *Naherwartungen*, Düsseldorf, 1968.

Pesch, *Taten*; R. Pesch, *Jesu ureigene Taten?*, QD 52, Freiburg, 1970.

W. Pesch: W. Pesch, *Matthäus der Seelsorger*, Stuttgart, 1966.

**Peter of Laodicea: Peter of Laodicea, *Erklärung des Matthäusevangeliums*, ed. C. F. G. Heinrici, Leipzig, 1908.

PG: Patrologia Graeca, ed. J. P. Migne, 162 vols., Paris, 1857–66.

PGM: *Papyri Graecae Magicae*, ed. K. Preisendanz, 2 vols., Leipzig and Berlin, 1928, 1931.

**Philoxenus: Philoxenus, *The 'Matthew-Luke Commentary' of Philoxenus*, ed., D. J. Fox, Missoula, 1979.

PL: Patrologia Latina, ed. J. P. Migne, 221 vols., Paris, 1844–64.

**Plummer: A. Plummer, *An Exegetical Commentary on the Gospel according to St. Matthew*, London, 1909.

*Pokorný, *Bergpredigt*: P. Pokorný, *Der Kern der Bergpredigt*, Hamburg, 1969.

Polag, *Christologie*: A. Polag, *Die Christologie der Logienquelle*, WMANT 45, Neukirchen-Vluyn, 1977.

Polag, *Fragmenta*: A. Polag, *Fragmenta Q*, Neukirchen-Vluyn, 1979.

de la Potterie: I. de la Potterie, ed., *De Jésus aux Évangiles*, Gembloux, 1967.

Potwin: L. S. Potwin, *Here and there in the Greek New Testament*, Chicago, 1898.

P. Oxy.: *The Oxyrhynchus Papyri*, ed. B. P. Grenfell and A. S. Hunt, London, 1898ff.

Preisgke: F. Preisgke and F. Bilabel, *Sammelbuch griechischer Urkunden aus Ägypten*, Strasbourg, 1915–1950.

Preiss: T. Preiss, *Life in Christ*, SBT 13, London, 1957.

Przybylski: B. Przybylski, *Righteousness in Matthew and his world of thought*, SNTSMS 41, Cambridge, 1980.

PW: *Paulys Realencyclopädie der classischen Altertumswissenschaft*, new ed. by G. Wissowa et al., Stuttgart, 1893ff., 1914ff.

PWSup: Supplements to *PW*.

**Rabanus Maurus: Rabanus Maurus, *Commentariorum in Matthaeum libri VIII*, in PL 107, cols. 727–1156.

RAC: *Reallexikon für Antike und Christentum*, ed. T. Klauser, Stuttgart, 1950ff.

**Radermakers: J. Radermakers, *Au fil de l'évangile selon saint Matthieu*, 2 vols., Heverlee-Louvain, 1972.

Rehkopf: F. Rehkopf, *Die lukanische Sonderquelle*, WUNT 5, Tübingen, 1959.

Reumann: J. Reumann, *Righteousness in the New Testament* Philadelphia, 1982.

**Reuss: J. Reuss, *Matthäus-Kommentare aus der griechischen Kirche*, Berlin, 1957.

RGG: *Die Religion in Geschichte und Gegenwart*, ed. K. Galling et al., 3rd ed., Tübingen, 1957–62.

Riches: J. Riches, *Jesus and the Transformation of Judaism*, London, 1980.

Ridderbos: H. Ridderbos, *Matthew's Witness to Jesus Christ*, New York, 1958.

**Rienecker: F. Rienecker, *Das Evangelium des Matthäus*, Wuppertal, 1953.

Riesenfeld: H. Riesenfeld, *The Gospel Tradition and its Beginnings*, London, 1957.

Riesner: R. Riesner, *Jesus als Lehrer*, WUNT 2/7 Tübingen, 1981.

Rigaux: B. Rigaux, *The Testimony of St. Matthew* (trans. of *Témoignage de l'Évangile de Matthieu*, 1967), Chicago, 1968.

Ristow: H. Ristow and K. Matthiae, eds., *Der historische Jesus und der kerygmatische Christus*, Berlin, 1963.

Robertson: A. T. Robertson, *A Grammar of the Greek New Testament in the Light of Historical Research*, 2nd ed., New York, 1914.

Robinson, *Coming*: J. A. T. Robinson, *Jesus and His Coming*, 2nd ed., London, 1978.

Robinson, *More Studies*: J. A. T. Robinson, *Twelve More New Testament Studies*, London, 1984.

Robinson, *Redating*: J. A. T. Robinson, *Redating the New Testament*, London, 1976.

Robinson, *Twelve Studies*: J. A. T. Robinson, *Twelve New Testament Studies*, SBT 34, London, 1962.

**T. H. Robinson: T. H. Robinson, *The Gospel of Matthew*, MNTC, London, 1928.

†Rohde: J. Rohde, *Rediscovering the Teaching of the Evangelists* (trans. of *Die redaktionsgeschichtliche Methode*, 1966), NTL, London, 1968.

Roloff, *Apostolat*: J. Roloff, *Apostolat-Verkündigung-Kirche*, Gütersloh, 1965.

Roloff, *Kerygma*: J. Roloff, *Das Kerygma und der irdische Jesus*, Göttingen, 1970.

Rothfuchs: W. Rothfuchs, *Die Erfüllungszitate des Matthäus-Evangeliums*, Stuttgart, 1969.

**Roux: H. Roux, *L'Évangile du royaume: commentaire sur l'Évangile de Matthieu*, Paris, 1947.

Rowland: C. Rowland, *The Open Heaven*, New York, 1982.

RSV: The Revised Standard Version of the Bible.

**Rupert of Deutz: Rupert of Deutz, *In Opus de gloria et honore Filii Hominis super Matthaeum*, in PL 168, cols. 1307–1634.

Ruppert: L. Ruppert, *Jesus als der leidende Gerechte?*, SBS 59, Stuttgart, 1972.

Sabbe: M. Sabbe, ed., *L'Évangile selon Marc*, BETL 34, Gembloux, 1974.

**Sabourin: L. Sabourin, *The Gospel according to St. Matthew*, 2 vols., Bombay, 1982.

Sand: A. Sand, *Das Gesetz und die Propheten*, BU 11, Regensburg, 1974.

Sanders, *Jesus*: E. P. Sanders, *Jesus and Judaism*, London and Philadelphia, 1985.

Sanders, *Paul*: E. P. Sanders, *Paul and Palestinian Judaism*, London and Philadelphia, 1977.

Sanders, *Tendencies*: E. P. Sanders, *The Tendencies of the Synoptic Tradition*, SNTSMS 9, Cambridge, 1969.

SB: H. L. Strack and P. Billerbeck, *Kommentar zum Neuen Testament aus Talmud und Midrasch*, 6 vols., Munich, 1921–1961.

Schaberg: J. Schaberg, *The Father, the Son and the Holy Spirit*, SBLDS 61, Chico, 1982.

Schenk: W. Schenk, *Der Passionsbericht nach Markus*, Gütersloh, 1974.

Schenke, *Studien*: L. Schenke, *Studien zur Passionsgeschichte des Markus*, Würzburg, 1971.

Schenke, *Wundererzählungen*: L. Schenke, *Die Wundererzählungen des Markusevangeliums*, Stuttgart, 1974.

Schille: G. Schille, *Die urchristliche Wundertradition*, Stuttgart, 1967.

**Schlatter: A. Schlatter, *Der Evangelist Matthäus*, 3rd ed., Stuttgart, 1948.

Schlatter, *Kirche*: A. Schlatter, *Die Kirche des Matthäus*, Gütersloh, 1930.

Schlosser: J. Schlosser, *Le Règne de Dieu dans les dits de Jésus*, EB, 2 vols., Paris, 1980.

**Schmid, *Matthäus*: J. Schmid, *Das Evangelium nach Matthäus*, RNT, 5th ed., Regensburg, 1965.

Schmid, *Studien*: J. Schmid et al., eds., *Synoptische Studien*, Munich,1953.

Schmid, *Verhältnisses*: J. Schmid, *Matthäus und Lukas: Eine Untersuchung des Verhältnisses ihrer Evangelien*, Freiburg, 1930.

Schmidt: K. L. Schmidt, *Der Rahmen der Geschichte Jesu*, 2nd ed., Berlin, 1919.

*Schnackenburg, *Bergpredigt*: R. Schnackenburg, *Die Bergpredigt*, Düsseldorf, 1982.

Schnackenburg, *John*: R. Schnackenburg, *The Gospel according to St. John* (trans. of *Das Johannesevangelium*, 1965, 1971, 1976), 3 vols., New York, 1968, 1980, 1982.

Schnackenburg, *Kirche*: R. Schnackenburg et al., eds., *Die Kirche des Anfangs*, Freiburg, 1978.

Schnackenburg, *Moral Teaching*: R. Schnackenburg, *The Moral Teaching of the New Testament* (trans. of *Die sittliche Botschaft des Neuen Testaments*, 1962), New York, 1965.

Schnackenburg, *Schriften*: R. Schnackenburg, *Schriften zum Neuen Testament*, Munich, 1971.

*Schneider: G. Schneider, *Botschaft der Bergpredigt*, Aschaffenberg, 1969.

Schnider: F. Schnider, *Jesus der Prophet*, Göttingen, 1973.

Schnider and Stenger: F. Schnider and W. Stenger, *Johannes und die Synoptiker*, Munich, 1971.

**Schniewind: J. Schniewind, *Das Evangelium nach Matthäus*, NTD, 12th ed., Göttingen, 1968.

Schoeps, *Paul*: H. J. Schoeps, *Paul* (trans. of *Paulus*, 1959), London, 1961.

Schoeps, *Theologie*: H. J. Schoeps, *Theologie und Geschichte des Judenchristentums*, Tübingen, 1949.

Schoeps, *Zeit*: H. J. Schoeps, *Aus früchristlicher Zeit*, Tübingen, 1950.

Scholem: G. Scholem, *Sabbatai Ṣevi* (trans. of *Shabbatai Ṣevi*, 1957), Princeton, 1973.

Schrage: W. Schrage, *Das Verhältnis des Thomas-Evangeliums zur synoptischen Tradition und zu den koptischen Evangelien-Übersetzungen*, BZNW 29, Berlin, 1964.

Schramm: T. Schramm, *Der Markus-Stoff bei Lukas*, SNTSMS 14, Cambridge, 1971.

*Schubert, 'Sermon': K. Schubert, 'The Sermon on the Mount and the Qumran Texts', in Stendahl, *Scrolls*, pp. 118–28.

Schulz, *Q*: S. Schulz, *Q. Die Spruchquelle der Evangelisten*, Zürich, 1972.

Schulz, *Stunde*: S. Schulz, *Die Stunde der Botschaft*, Hamburg, 1967.

Schürer: E. Schürer, *The History of the Jewish People in the Age of Jesus Christ* (trans. of *Geschichte des jüdischen Volkes im Zeitalter Jesu Christi*, 1901–1909), a new and rev. English version edited by G. Vermes and F. Millar, Edinburgh, 1973ff.

Schürmann, *Lukasevangelium*: H. Schürmann, *Das Lukasevangelium*, vol. 1, HTKNT III/1, Freiburg, 1969.

Schürmann, *Tod*: H. Schürmann, *Jesu ureigener Tod*, Freiburg, 1975.

Schürmann, *Untersuchungen*: H. Schürmann, *Traditionsgeschichtliche Untersuchungen zu den synoptischen Evangelien*, Düsseldorf, 1968.

Schürmann, *Ursprung*: H. Schürmann, *Ursprung und Gestalt*, Düsseldorf, 1970.

Schweitzer: A. Schweitzer, *The Quest of the Historical Jesus* (trans. of *Von Reimarus zu Wrede*, 1906), London, 1910.

*Schweizer, *Bergpredigt*: E. Schweizer, *Die Bergpredigt*, Göttingen, 1982.

Schweizer, *Gemeinde*: E. Schweizer, *Matthäus und seine Gemeinde*, Stuttgart, 1974.

Schweizer, *Lordship*: E. Schweizer, *Lordship and Discipleship* (trans. of *Erniedrigung und Erhöhung bei Jesus und seinen Nachfolgern*, 1955), SBT 28, London, 1968.

Schweizer, *Luke*: E. Schweizer, *The Good News according to Luke* (trans. of *Das Evangelium nach Lukas*, 1982), London and Atlanta, 1984.

Schweizer, *Mark*: E. Schweizer, *The Good News according to Mark* (trans. of *Das Evangelium nach Markus*, 1967), Atlanta, 1970.

**Schweizer, *Matthew*: E. Schweizer, *The Good News according to Matthew* (trans. of *Das Evangelium nach Matthäus*, 1973), Atlanta, 1975.

Schweizer, *Neotestamentica*: E. Schweizer, *Neotestamentica*, Zürich, 1963.

Scott: B. B. Scott, *Jesus: Symbol-Maker for the Kingdom*, Philadelphia, 1981.

Senior, *Invitation*: D. Senior, *Invitation to Matthew*, Garden City, 1977.

Senior, *Passion*: D. Senior, *The Passion Narrative according to Matthew*, Louvain, 1975.

†Senior, *What are they saying?*: D. Senior, *What are they saying about Matthew?*, New York, 1983.

Sherwin-White: A. N. Sherwin-White, *Roman Society and Roman Law in the New Testament*, Oxford, 1963.

Shuler: P. L. Shuler, *A Genre for the Gospels: The biographical character of Matthew*, Philadelphia, 1982.

SIG: *Sylloge Inscriptionum Graecarum*, ed. W. Dittenberger, 3rd ed., Leipzig, 1915–24.

Smallwood: E. M. Smallwood, *The Jews under Roman Rule*, SJLA 20, Leiden, 1976.

**B. T. D. Smith: B. T. D. Smith, *The Gospel according to St. Matthew*, Cambridge, 1950.

G. A. Smith: G. A. Smith, *The Historical Geography of the Holy Land*, 25th ed., London, 1931.

H. Smith: H. Smith, *Antenicene Exegesis of the Gospels*, 5 vols., London, 1925–28.

M. Smith, *Clement*: M. Smith, *Clement of Alexandria and a Secret Gospel of Mark*, Cambridge, 1973.

M. Smith, *Magician*: M. Smith, *Jesus the Magician*, New York, 1978.

M. Smith, *Parallels*: M. Smith, *Tannaitic Parallels to the Gospels*, SBLMS 6, Philadelphia, 1951.

Soares Prabhu: G. M. Soares Prabhu, *The Formula Quotations in the Infancy Narrative of Matthew*, AnBib 63, Rome, 1976.

*Soiron: T. Soiron, *Die Bergpredigt Jesu*, Freiburg, 1941.

Solages: *Composition*: M. de Solages, *La composition des Évangiles de Luc et de Matthieu et leur sources*, Leiden, 1973.

Sparks: H. F. D. Sparks, ed., *The Apocryphal Old Testament*, Oxford, 1984.

Spicq: C. Spicq, *Agape in the New Testament* (trans. of *Agape dans le Nouveau Testament*, Paris, 1958, 1959), 2 vols., London, 1963, 1965.

Spicq, *Notes*: C. Spicq, *Notes de lexicographie néo-testamentaire*, OBO 22.1–3, Göttingen, 1978, 1982.

**Staab: K. Staab, *Das Evangelium nach Matthäus*, Würzburg, 1963.

*Stalder, 'Bergpredigt': K. Stalder, 'Überlieferung zur Interpretation der Bergpredigt', in *Die Mitte des Neuen Testaments*, ed. U. Luz and H. Weder, Göttingen,1983, pp. 272–90.

*Stange, 'Bergpredigt': C. Stange, 'Zur Ethik der Bergpredigt', *ZST* 2 (1924), pp. 37–74.

Stanton: G. N. Stanton, ed., *The Interpretation of Matthew*, London, 1983.

Stanton, *Jesus*: G. N. Stanton, *Jesus of Nazareth in New Testament Preaching*, SNTSMS 27, Cambridge, 1974.

†Stanton, 'Origin and Purpose': G. N. Stanton, 'The Origin and Purpose of Matthew's Gospel: Matthean Scholarship from 1945 to 1980', *ANRW* II.25.3 (1983), pp. 1889–1951.

*Staudinger: J. Staudinger, *Die Bergpredigt*, Vienna, 1957.

Stauffer: E. Stauffer, *Jesus and his Story* (trans. of *Jesus: Gestalt und Geschichte*, 1957), London, 1960.

Steck: O. H. Steck, *Israel und das gewaltsame Geschick der Propheten*, WMANT 23, Neukirchen, 1967.

Steinhauser: M. G. Steinhauser, *Doppelbildworte in den synoptischen Evangelien*, FB 44, Würzburg, 1981.

**Stendahl, 'Matthew': K. Stendahl, 'Matthew', in *PCB*, pp. 769–98.

Stendahl, *Meanings*: K. Stendahl, *Meanings*, Philadelphia, 1984.

Stendahl, *School*: K. Stendahl, *The School of St. Matthew and its Use of the Old Testament*, rev. ed., Philadelphia, 1968.

Stendahl, *Scrolls*: K. Stendahl, ed., *The Scrolls and the New Testament*, New York, 1957.

*Stöger: A. Stöger, *Die Bergpredigt*, Klosterneuburg, 1982.

Stonehouse: N. B. Stonehouse, *The Witness of Matthew and Mark to Christ*, London, 1944.

Strauss: D. F. Strauss, *The Life of Jesus critically examined* (trans. of *Das Leben Jesu kritisch bearbeitet*, 1840), 2nd ed., New York and London, 1892.

*Strecker, *Bergpredigt*: G. Strecker, *Die Bergpredigt*, Göttingen, 1984.

Strecker, *Jesus*: G. Strecker, ed., *Jesus Christus in Historie und Theologie*, Tübingen, 1975.

Strecker, *Weg*: G. Strecker, *Der Weg der Gerechtigkeit*, FRLANT 82, Göttingen, 1962.

Streeter: B. H. Streeter, *The Four Gospels*, rev. ed., London, 1930.

*Strobel, 'Bergpredigt': A. Strobel, 'Die Bergpredigt als ethische Weisung heute', *TB* 15 (1984), pp. 3–16.

*Stuhlmacher, 'Bergpredigt': P. Stuhlmacher, 'Jesu vollkommenes Gesetz der Freiheit: Zum Verständnis der Bergpredigt', *ZTK* 79 (1982), pp. 283–322.

Stuhlmacher, *Evangelium*: P. Stuhlmacher, ed., *Das Evangelium und die Evangelien*, WUNT 28, Tübingen, 1983.

Suggs: M. J. Suggs, *Wisdom, Christology, and Law in Matthew's Gospel*, Cambridge, Mass., 1970.

Swanson: R. J. Swanson, *The Horizontal Line Synopsis of the Gospels, Greek Edition, Volume I: The Gospel of Matthew*, Dillsboro, 1982.

Swete: H. B. Swete, *The Gospel according to St. Mark*, London, 1927.

Talbert: C. H. Talbert, *Literary Patterns, Theological Themes and the Genre of Luke-Acts*, SBLMS 20, Missoula, 1974.

Tannehill: R. C. Tannehill, *The Sword of his Mouth*, Philadelphia, 1975.

**Tasker: R. V. G. Tasker, *The Gospel according to St. Matthew*, London, 1961.

Taylor, *Essays*: V. Taylor, *New Testament Essays*, London, 1970.

Taylor, *Formation*: V. Taylor, *The Formation of the Gospel Tradition*, 2nd ed., London, 1935.

Taylor, *Mark*: V. Taylor, *The Gospel according to St. Mark*, 2nd ed., London, 1966.

Taylor, *Passion*: V. Taylor, *The Passion Narrative of St. Luke*, SNTSMS 19, Cambridge, 1972.

TDOT: G. J. Botterweck and H. Ringgren, eds., *Theological Dictionary of the Old Testament* (trans. of *Theologisches Wörterbuch zum Alten Testament*, 1970ff.), Grand Rapids, 1974ff.

Theissen, *Sociology*: G. Theissen, *Sociology of early Palestinian Christianity* (trans. of *Soziologie der Jesusbewegung*, 1977), Philadelphia, 1978 (published in London, 1978, under the title, *The First Followers of Jesus*).

Theissen, *Stories*: G. Theissen, *The Miracle Stories of the Early Christian Tradition* (trans. of *Urchristliche Wundergeschichten*, 1974), Edinburgh, 1983.

**Thomas Aquinas, *Catena*: Thomas Aquinas, *Catena Aurea*, 3 vols., ed. I. Nicolai, Lyon, 1863.

**Thomas Aquinas, *Evangelium*: Thomas Aquinas, *Super Evangelium S. Matthaei Lectura*, Turin and Rome, 1951.

Thompson: W. G. Thompson, *Matthew's Advice to a divided Community: Mt. 17,22–18,35*, AnBib 44, Rome 1970.

Thrall: M. E. Thrall, *Greek Particles in the New Testament*, NTTS 3, Leiden, 1962.

*Thurneysen: E. Thurneysen, *The Sermon on the Mount* (trans. of *Die Bergpredigt*, 1963), Richmond, 1964.

Thysman: R. Thysman, *Communauté et directives éthiques: La catéchèse de Matthieu*, Gembloux, 1974.

van Tilborg: S. van Tilborg, *The Jewish Leaders in Matthew*, Leiden, 1972.

TIM: G. Bornkamm, G. Barth, and H. J. Held, *Tradition and Interpretation in Matthew* (trans. of *Überlieferung und Auslegung im Matthäusevangelium*, 1960), NTL, London, 1963.

Tödt: H. E. Tödt, *The Son of Man in the Synoptic Tradition* (trans. of *Der Menschensohn in der synoptischen Überlieferung*, 1963), NTL, London, 1965.

Torrey: C. C. Torrey, *The Four Gospels*, 2nd ed., London, 1947.

Trilling: W. Trilling, *Das wahre Israel*, 3rd ed., Munich, 1964.

**Trilling, *Matthew*: W. Trilling, *The Gospel according to St. Matthew* (trans. of *Das Evangelium nach Matthäus*, 1961, 1965), 2 vols., London, 1969.

Trocmé: E. Trocmé, *The Formation of the Gospel according to Mark* (trans. of *La formation de l'Évangile selon Marc*, 1963), London, 1975.

TTEC: J. M. Robinson and H. Koester, *Trajectories through Early Christianity*, Philadelphia, 1971.

Tuckett, *Revival*: C. M. Tuckett, *The Revival of the Griesbach Hypothesis*, SNTSMS 44, Cambridge, 1983.

Tuckett, *Studies*: C. M. Tuckett, ed., *Synoptic Studies*, JSNTSS 7, Sheffield, 1984.

TWNT: *Theologisches Wörterbuch zum Neuen Testament*, ed. G. Kittel and G. Friedrich, 10 vols., Stuttgart, 1933–79.

van Unnik: W. C. van Unnik, *Sparsa Collecta*, 2 vols., Leiden, 1973, 1980.

Urbach: E. E. Urbach, *The Sages* (trans. of the Hebrew 2nd ed., 1971), Jerusalem, 1975.

de Vaux: R. de Vaux, *Ancient Israel* (trans. of *Les Institutions de l'Ancien Testament*, 1958, 1960), 2 vols., London, 1961.

Vermes, *Jesus the Jew*: G. Vermes, *Jesus the Jew*, London, 1973.

Vermes, *Studies*: G. Vermes, *Post-biblical Jewish Studies*, Leiden, 1975.

Vermes, *Tradition*: G. Vermes, *Scripture and Tradition in Judaism*, Leiden, 1961.

Vermes, *World*: G. Vermes, *Jesus and the World of Judaism*, London, 1983.

Vielhauer: P. Vielhauer, *Aufsätze zum Neuen Testament*, Munich, 1965.

Vögtle, *Evangelium*: A. Vögtle, *Das Evangelium und die Evangelien*, Düsseldorf, 1971.

Vögtle, *Zukunft*: A. Vögtle, *Das Neue Testament und die Zukunft des Kosmos*, Düsseldorf, 1970.

Wacholder: B. Z. Wacholder, *The Dawn of Qumran*, Cincinnati, 1983.
Waetjen: H. C. Waetjen, *The Origin and Destiny of Humanness*, Coret Madera, 1976.
Walker: R. Walker, *Die Heilsgeschichte im ersten Evangelium*, FRLANT 91, Göttingen, 1967.
W. O. Walker: W. O. Walker, ed., *The Relationships among the Gospels*, San Antonio, 1978.
Wanke: J. Wanke, *'Bezugs- und Kommentarworte' in den synoptischen Evangelien*, Leipzig, 1981.
Weder: H. Weder, *Die Gleichnisse Jesu als Metaphern*, FRLANT 120, 3rd ed., Göttingen, 1984.
*Weder, 'Bergpredigt': H. Weder, 'Die "Rede der Reden": Beobachtungen zum Verständnis der Bergpredigt Jesu', *EvT* 45 (1985), pp. 45–60.
Weinrich: W. C. Weinrich, ed., *The New Testament Age*, 2 vols., Macon, 1984.
Weiser: A. Weiser, *Die Knechtsgleichnisse der synoptischen Evangelien*, SANT 10, Munich, 1971.
**B. Weiss: B. Weiss, *Das Matthäus-Evangelium*, 9th ed., Göttingen, 1898.
J. Weiss, *History*: J. Weiss, *Earliest Christianity* (trans. of *Das Urchristentum*, 1917), 2 vols., reprint ed., New York, 1959.
J. Weiss, *Kingdom*: J. Weiss, *Jesus' Proclamation of the Kingdom of God* (trans. of *Die Predigt Jesu vom Reiche Gottes*, 1892), Philadelphia, 1971.
Wellhausen, *Einleitung*: J. Wellhausen, *Einleitung in die drei ersten Evangelien*, 2nd ed., Berlin, 1911.
**Wellhausen, *Matthaei*: J. Wellhausen, *Das Evangelium Matthaei*, 2nd ed., Berlin, 1914.
Wenham, *Rediscovery*: D. Wenham, *The Rediscovery of Jesus' Eschatological Discourse*, Sheffield, 1985.
Wenham, *Tradition*: D. Wenham, *Gospel Perspectives, vol. 5: the Jesus Tradition outside the Gospels*, Sheffield, 1985.
Westerholm: S. Westerholm, *Jesus and Scribal Authority*, CB, New Testament Series 10, Lund, 1978.
**Wettstein: J. J. Wettstein, Ἡ Καινὴ Διαθήκη. *Novum Testamentum graecum* . . ., 2 vols., Amsterdam, 1751–52.
*Windisch: H. Windisch, *The Meaning of the Sermon on the Mount* (trans. of *Der Sinn der Bergpredigt*, 1937), Philadelphia, 1951.
Wink: W. Wink, *John the Baptist in the Gospel Tradition* SNTSMS 7, Cambridge, 1968.
Winter: P. Winter, *On the Trial of Jesus*, SJ 1, 2nd ed. revised and edited by T. A. Burkill and G. Vermes, Berlin and New York, 1974.
*Wrege; H.-T. Wrege, *Die Überlieferungsgeschichte der Bergpredigt*, WUNT 9, Tübingen, 1968.
**Zahn: T. Zahn, *Das Evangelium des Matthäus*, 4th ed., Leipzig, 1922.
Zeller, *Kommentar*: D. Zeller, *Kommentar zur Logienquelle*, Stuttgart, 1984.
Zeller, *Mahnsprüche*: D. Zeller, *Die weisheitlichen Mahnsprüche bei den Synoptikern*, FB 17, Würzburg, 1977.

Ziesler: J. A. Ziesler, *The Meaning of Righteousness in Paul*, SNTSMS 20, Cambridge, 1972.
Zumstein: J. Zumstein, *La condition du croyant dans l'Évangile selon Matthieu*, OBO 16, Göttingen, 1977.

Note on transliteration

In transliterating Hebrew and Aramaic, we have followed the system described in the Society of Biblical Literature Member's Handbook, 1980.

INTRODUCTION

I. INTRODUCTORY MATTERS

Recent studies on the nature of written documents have challenged the assumptions which have long governed commentators on the gospels,[1] and new questions are being raised about the dominance of traditional concerns. In the past, scholars have sought to 'excavate' the gospels in the hope of determining: (1) the sources they drew upon and the historicity of the events they purport to record (the historical concern); (2) the nature of the communities which helped to fashion their materials (the form-critical concern); and (3) (though perhaps to a lesser extent) the mind or intent of their final redactors or authors (the interpretative and hermeneutical concern). It is claimed that by focusing on these issues, usually subsumed under the umbrella terms 'historical criticism' or, more adequately, 'biblical criticism',[2] commentators have transformed the gospels into 'museum pieces', thereby placing a gulf between them and the reader and removing interest from the texts of the gospels themselves to factors extraneous to them—history, the early Christian communities, the evangelists. Whereas the actual texts of the gospels are tangible, present realities, these extraneous factors are intangible: they belong to a very distant, nebulous past and are necessarily uncertain. The text as an independent body, existing in its own right, has not been allowed to speak for itself. The search for what the gospels meant has replaced and hindered the understanding of what they mean. Moreover, it is further asserted that the text does not contain an original meaning or intention that can be recovered. Rather, it produces or evokes a meaning for the reader as he reads 'closely'. Those who wrote the gospels created their own literary world which becomes the primary world within which the gospels are to be understood. Hence the meaning which the gospels give is not to be reached by asking the traditional historical-critical questions. To answer these questions is not to interpret but only, at best, to

[1] The term 'gospel' means literally in English 'good story' or 'good news'. The term is used both of the message, 'the good news', proclaimed by early Christians, and the written documents called 'gospels'—a usage established in Mk 1.1 and used in the second century in the titles given to the NT's first four books—ΕΥΑΓΓΕΛΙΟΝ ΚΑΤΑ ΜΑΘΘΑΙΟΝ, etc. (see Hengel, *Mark*, pp. 65–7).

[2] See J. Barr, *Holy Scripture, Canon, Authority, Criticism*, Philadelphia, 1983, pp. 33–4, 105ff.

1

supply the preconditions for interpretation. It is urged that henceforth commentators should pay primary attention to the texts themselves as literary entities—their plots, the signals they offer, the references they make. The traditional themes—date, place, authorship, sources, form and redaction criticism—are more fitting in appendices than in introductions. In sum, historical criticism (interpreted rather one-sidedly and unfairly, because it was seldom merely historical in interest as now often alleged) is given only a preliminary rôle in interpretation.

Alongside this literary emphasis, there has arisen another. Literary critics have emphasized the importance of form, as well as content, as a component of the meaning of any text. Some biblical critics now point to the significance of the canonical form or shape of a gospel for the full understanding of it. Under their influence the study of the NT as a totality, that is, as 'canon', and the implications of this for exegesis, has burgeoned. The name 'canonical criticism' (although sometimes objected to and replaced by 'canon criticism')[3] has been given to this study, which in some of its forms at least also militates against the traditional concentration on historical-criticism.[4]

Because of this complex situation, it is necessary to state the approach adopted in this commentary. Exponents of 'The New Criticism',[5] so-called, insisted that all texts must be read in isolation, as they stand, in terms of their own inner dynamics. Considerations of their authorship and of the circumstances, the time and place of their origin are very secondary, if not irrelevant, to their interpretation. Accordingly the determination of their genre becomes important. We must agree with such critics, but only to a certain degree. It is essential to let the text of Matthew speak for itself in the sense indicated, in its nakedness as it were. But, in purely literary terms, this faces us at the very start with a conundrum. We cannot gather grapes from briars nor figs from thistles: our expectation of the fruit to be harvested depends on the nature of the plant. So with texts: what is the genre to which

[3] See J. A. Sanders, *Canon and Community*, Philadelphia, 1984, pp. 1–20 for a review of the discussion.

[4] For further discussion of 'canonical criticism'—which is still in a comparatively inchoate state—see Barr, as in n. 2; Sanders, as in n. 3; idem, *Torah and Canon*, Philadelphia, 1972; idem, review of Barr's *Holy Scripture*, in *JBL* 104 (1985), pp. 501–2; B. S. Childs, *The New Testament as Canon: An Introduction*, Philadelphia and London, 1984.

[5] See Cleanth Brooks, *The Well Wrought Urn*, New York, 1947; W. K. Wimsatt, *The Verbal Icon: Studies in the Meaning of Poetry*, Kentucky, 1954; R. Wellek and A. Warren, *Theory of Literature*, 3rd ed., London, 1966; Frank Lentricchia, *After the New Criticism*, Chicago, 1980; Nigel M. Watson, 'Authorial Intention: Suspect Concept for Biblical Scholars', forthcoming *Australian Biblical Review* (1987): the last item is a salutary corrective.

Matthew belongs? What can we expect it to yield? Is it a biography, or a myth, or a history set in a mythological framework, or simply disjointed memorabilia? Again, is it a manual of discipline designed for moral teaching, or an apocalypse to reveal mysteries, or an allegory to present riddles, or a lectionary for use in worship, or a catechism for initiates, or an apology directed to outsiders? A glance at the contents of Matthew reveals that there is much to suggest that each of these questions could, in part at least, be answered in the affirmative. But a close reading would indicate that not one of these categories taken in isolation does justice to the totality of the gospel, even though it includes examples and elements of them all: history, myth, moral instruction, apocalyptic teaching, liturgy, catechism, and apologetics. In a literary sense, as in others, the text is an omnibus of genres.

All this means that no one method should be exclusively employed: the multiplicity of genres in Matthew calls for flexibility in method and aim. No one approach or aim should have a monopoly: each needs the stimulus of the other. Many, if not most, literary and structuralist scholars, for example, assume the necessity and importance of the historical approach as well as of their own.[6] And biblical critics from the beginning have frequently employed historical-critical and literary methods simultaneously and have sometimes raised the question of the place of documents in the Canon. The choice of method or methods will, however, inevitably vary according to the competence of the commentators.[7]

In this commentary, although it is informed by what a colleague, R. P. Forrer, has taught us to call a 'principled eclecticism', the more traditional historical-critical approach will be dominant. This is not only because we have not been sufficiently involved in recent literary scholarship, from the New Criticism onwards, or in structuralist and canonical criticism. Our concentration on the historical-critical method is due to our understanding of the central demands which the text itself makes upon the reader. The text of Matthew has a history in the sense that it has taken up into itself pre-existing sources. Like a nation or a person, a text *is* its history. To a large degree it is conditioned, if not determined, by that history, knowledge of which is necessary for its full understanding. This calls for attention to source, form, and redaction criticism. This is not to deny that literary and

[6] E.g. D. Via, Jr., *The Ethics of Mark: In the Middle of Time*, Philadelphia, 1985, p. 3 *et passim*.
[7] See J. Barton, *Reading the Old Testament: Method in Biblical Studies*, Philadelphia, 1984.

canonical criticism have their subsequent place. But what we
cannot concede is that the text can be adequately dealt with in
isolation from its historical character in the sense indicated.

And there is a further, perhaps more fundamental, reason for
our concentration on the historical-critical method. Like all the
NT, the text of Matthew makes the indisputable assumption that
behind it and the community within which and to which its author
wrote, stands the life, death, and resurrection of an actual person,
Jesus of Nazareth. This implicit and explicit historical reference
demands historical investigation.[8] The text of Matthew provides
no direct access to Jesus. His words and deeds had already been
interpreted by the sources incorporated in it; and these sources
were in turn arranged and moulded afresh to offer further
interpretation. Still, that text always presupposes an historical
figure, Jesus, as its *raison d'être*. If it be legitimate to use the literary
term, 'genre', for our canonical gospels—an uncertain issue—, this
should not prevent us from recognizing that they are not 'art for
art's sake': their aims, even those of Luke, are not primarily
literary so that from a classical point of view 'gospel' is not a
literary genre;[9] rather do they intend to point to the manifold

[8] Literary critics further compelled the recognition of the difficulty of this task
very forcefully; it was already insisted on by historical criticism. If, as literary critics
urge, those who wrote the gospels created their own literary world, which becomes
the primary world within which the gospels are to be understood, their
understanding of history is not ours and its relation to historical reality as
customarily understood becomes problematic. The question becomes ever more
urgent at what point such a primary literary world becomes so distinct, and even
divorced from the historical, that it becomes an illusory world. Such issues are
beyond the intent of this commentary to deal with directly but necessarily haunt it.

[9] See G. Kennedy and W. A. Meeks in Walker, pp. 137 and 160 respectively.
Admittedly, there are those who disagree, or at least think our gospels should be
classified as instances of ancient biography. See C. H. Talbert, *What is a Gospel?*,
Philadelphia, 1977, and Shuler, *Genre*. Although the problem demands lengthy
investigation, we may here record our disagreement and refer to four helpful
studies: D. E. Aune, 'The Problem of the Genre of the Gospels', in France 2,
pp. 9–60; R. Guelich, 'The Gospel Genre', in Stuhlmacher, *Evangelium*,
pp. 183–219; R. H. Gundry, 'Recent Investigation into the Literary Genre
"Gospel" ', in *New Dimensions in New Testament Study*, ed. R. N. Longenecker
and M. C. Tenney, Grand Rapids, 1974, pp. 97–114; and F. G. Downing,
'Contemporary Analogies to the Gospels and Acts', in Tuckett, *Studies*, pp. 51–66.
Three observations are crucial. (1) The structural and thematic similarities between
the synoptics can be explained in terms of literary connexions: they do not of
themselves demand a common, recognized genre. (2) The gospels do share motifs
and themes which also play important rôles in hellenistic biography. But common
elements do not require a common genre. The same pieces can be put together to
make quite different wholes. (3) Matthew, like the other gospels and like all literary
texts, does not exist in isolation but is unconsciously and consciously related to
other documents. To use a technical term from literary criticism, we find an
intertextuality in Matthew, especially with regard to the OT, in both its Hebrew
and Greek forms. Consider the first chapter. Mt 1.1 reproduces a phrase from
Gen 2.4 and 5.1 and recalls the title of the OT's first book, Γένεσις (see on 1.1).

significance of Jesus of Nazareth for the communities within which they wrote and for humankind and his *mysterium tremendum*.[10]

Our task, then, is to examine the text of Matthew so as to understand what it says. To do this is not to abandon concerns and aims which have traditionally served commentators but to refuse to allow any of them to dictate our findings. We seek what has been called the 'plain sense' of the text. This is not its 'literal' sense and not its 'original' sense, which varies in different parts of it, but the sense which the sentences, the paragraphs, and longer units, the structure, shape and flow of the gospel as a totality present. To seek the 'plain sense' requires dealing with its original language; with its historical and cultural setting; with its history, and, therefore, with its sources; with the literary forms and the final literary and canonical shape with which it confronts us, so that the interpretation arrived at is not strained or against the grain of the text, but is governed by the criteria which the text itself supplies.

A few additional observations on the nature and structure of the present commentary are in order. First, each sub-section of the commentary proper has five different divisions, numbered i–v. The first (i) addresses questions of form or structure: how is a paragraph or passage put together or arranged? The second division (ii) deals with source criticism: how does the text bear on the different solutions to the synoptic problem? The third division (iii), which is the most substantial, contains exegesis. It includes philological notes, word statistics, synoptic parallels, NT parallels, extra-canonical parallels, history of religion parallels, and reflections on the historical worth of the material. In the fourth section (iv), the exegetical results are briefly summarized and then related to Matthean theology as a whole. Section v lists selected bibliography.

Secondly, as commentators we have thought it one of our chief

---

Next follows a genealogy, which, for the most part, reproduces information to hand in 1 Chronicles. Following 1.2–17 is the annunciation narrative, 1.18–25, in which Isa 7.14 is cited and certain OT narratives imitated (see p. 196). All this is characteristic. From first to last Matthew draws upon the OT: the Scriptures are explicitly cited and constantly alluded to. This moves us to suppose that the First Gospel should be explained in terms of Jewish literary precedent, if any. But biography, although found in Philo of Alexandria, is altogether absent from the OT, from the Apocrypha and Pseudepigrapha, and from rabbinic literature. It cannot be considered typical for Jewish literature. So one hesitates to label as 'biographies' documents as strongly rooted in Judaism as are the synoptics. (The Pentateuch, although it cannot by any stretch of the imagination be labelled 'biography', does more or less cover, and in a roughly chronological fashion, the life of Moses from beginning to end. Perhaps scholars need to make more of this fact in coming to terms with how the canonical gospels present the story of Jesus.)

[10] At the end of the commentary we shall return to the question of what exactly Matthew is. We also put off to the conclusion the problem of whether our gospel was composed for a liturgical or catechetical purpose.

duties to cite extra-biblical parallels to Matthean formulations and ideas. Three comments are in order.

(1) As indicated above, some scholars influenced by modern literary critics might protest that the great number of parallels adduced detracts from understanding the gospel as it lies before us. That is, instead of paying sufficient heed to the text as such, our attention has been distracted, and we have too frequently sought illumination in foreign lands. The protest would miss its mark, for it posits a false alternative. Matthew, we freely acknowledge, is the best interpreter of Matthew, and we trust that the commentary reflects this important fact. But the evangelist, like his first readers, lived in an extra-textual world, and, in so far as it is possible, his gospel should not be isolated from that world, lest we, the inhabitants of another place and a very different time, lose too much of Matthew's meaning. To illustrate: how can one really understand the meaning of 'Son of God' in Matthew without looking at other first-century texts, pagan, Jewish, and Christian? And how does one grasp the significance of the parallels drawn between Jesus and Moses or the exact connotations of δικαιοσύνη without going outside the First Gospel? Context defines meaning; and if our gospel text is the foreground, then it cannot be placed in perspective without its background. It is no more sensible to interpret Matthew as an isolated text than it is to define the meaning of a defunct Greek word by considering its use in only one ancient source. And as with the meaning of words, so is it with the narratives they combine to make: the task of compiling parallels is indispensable for interpretation. Comparison illuminates and instructs, and it often unearths treasures that would otherwise remain buried. For this reason, then, we have continued the historical-critical approach of citing parallels.

(2) While we recognize the interpenetration of Hellenism and Judaism, recently rightly emphasized, it is our conviction that the ancient Jewish sources (although not to be rigidly isolated from Hellenistic influences) put in the interpreter's hands the most important tool with which to fathom the First Gospel. The First Evangelist was a Jew whose mind was first of all steeped in the OT and Jewish tradition (see section II of the Introduction). So while we have, from time to time, taken notice of interesting and significant Graeco-Roman parallels, we have concentrated on Jewish texts.

(3) Some readers might be distressed at our frequent citation of rabbinic sources. Recent studies have made abundantly clear how difficult it is to date rabbinic traditions. The ascription of an utterance to Rabbi X is hardly a guarantee that Rabbi X actually

made the utterance. Contemporary scholars have in fact come so far from Strack-Billerbeck that some write as though it were a sign of naïveté when someone tries to elucidate the NT by citing material from the Talmud or Mishnah. In some instances it undoubtedly is. Nonetheless, if it is all but impossible to date many rabbinic texts, this unfortunate circumstance by no means implies that the NT specialist need no longer know rabbinic sources. The rabbinic mentality shows strong elements of conservatism, and the antiquity of at least some rabbinic traditions is accepted by all. In our judgement, then, while we must be very cautious in drawing inferences from rabbinic parallels, we would do wrong to ignore them altogether. This is why we have judged it expedient to cite texts from the Mishnah, the Mekilta, Sipre, the Talmuds, and so on. But it must be plainly said that our citation of these sources, when unaccompanied by comment, assumes only that they *might* be of historical-critical or interpretative significance. Nothing more is implied.

II. THE AUTHORSHIP OF MATTHEW[11]

In their search for the identities of the authors of ancient documents, biblical critics, like scholars of the Greek and Latin classics, have traditionally taken external evidence very seriously, often as their point of departure. And to judge from the external evidence (Papias and the title, ΕΥΑΓΓΕΛΙΟΝ ΚΑΤΑ

[11] Without prejudging the issue of authorship, we shall from here on, and throughout the commentary refer to the author of this First Gospel as 'Matthew'. Lit.: E. L. Abel, 'Who wrote Matthew?', *NTS* 17 (1970–71), pp. 138–52; Albright and Mann, pp. clx–clxxxvi; Bacon, pp. 3–49; K. W. Clark, 'The Gentile Bias in Matthew', *JBL* 66 (1947), pp. 165–72; M. J. Cook, 'Interpreting "Pro-Jewish" Passages in Matthew', *HUCA* 53 (1984), pp. 135–46; Cope, pp. 124–30; E. von Dobschütz, 'Matthäus als Rabbi und Katechet', *ZNW* 27 (1928), pp. 338–48, reprinted in Lange, *Matthäus*, pp. 52–64, and translated and reprinted in Stanton, pp. 19–29; Gundry, *Commentary*, pp. 609–22; D. Guthrie, *New Testament Introduction*, Downers Grove, 1970, pp. 33–44; D. A. Hagner, 'The *Sitz im Leben* of the Gospel of Matthew', in *Society of Biblical Literature 1985 Seminar Papers*, ed. K. H. Richards, Atlanta, 1985, pp. 244–70; Hill, *Matthew*, pp. 22–7; G. Kennedy, 'Classical and Christian Source Criticism', in W. O. Walker, pp. 125–55; J. Kürzinger, 'Das Papiaszeugnis und die Erstgestalt des Matthäusevangeliums', *BZ* 4 (1960), pp. 19–38; idem, 'Irenäus und sein Zeugnis zur Sprache des Matthäusevangeliums', *NTS* 10 (1963), pp. 108–15; Luz 1, pp. 62–5; W. A. Meeks, 'Hypomnēmata from an Untamed Sceptic', in Walker, pp. 157–72; A. Meredith, 'The Evidence of Papias for the Priority of Matthew', in Tuckett, *Studies*, pp. 187–96; J. Munck, 'Die Tradition über das Matthäusevangelium bei Papias', in *Neotestamentica et Patristica*, NovTSup 6, ed. B. Reicke and W. C. van Unnik, Leiden, 1962, pp. 249–60; P. Nepper-Christensen; C. S. Petrie, 'The Authorship of "The Gospel according to Matthew": A Reconsideration of the External Evidence', *NTS* 14 (1967), pp. 15–33; N. B. Stonehouse, *Origins of the Synoptic Gospels*, Grand Rapids, 1964, pp. 1–47; Strecker, *Weg*.

MAΘΘAION), already by about A.D. 125, which is less than fifty years after the gospel's genesis, the first of our canonical gospels was widely ascribed to Matthew, the apostle of Jesus (named in Mt 9.9; 10.3; Mk 3.18; Lk 6.15; Acts 1.13). The title of the gospel cannot, however, be taken as indisputable evidence. It was not in the autograph, and EYAΓΓEΛION KATA MAΘΘAION is not the only title to appear in the ms. tradition (see p. 129, n. 90). Moreover, in the case of Matthew, the witness of Papias and others is such that many have dismissed it as negligible (e.g. Kümmel, *Introduction*, pp. 120–21).

The main item of external evidence is a statement attributed by Eusebius, Bishop of Caesarea (ca. 260–340), to Papias, Bishop of Hierapolis in Asia Minor (for his dates see p. 128). This is usually given in isolation, as here—a fact not without significance, as we shall see below.

Ματθαῖος μὲν οὖν Ἑβραῖδι διαλέκτῳ τὰ λόγια συνετάξατο, ἡρμήνευσεν δ' αὐτὰ ὡς ἦν δυνατὸς ἕκαστος.

Now Matthew made an ordered arrangement of the oracles in the Hebrew (or: Aramaic) language, and each one translated (or: interpreted) it as he was able (*H.E.* 3.39).

The view of Papias is reiterated by Irenaeus (ca. 130–200), Bishop of Lyons:

ὁ μὲν δὴ Ματθαῖος ἐν τοῖς Ἑβραίοις τῇ ἰδίᾳ αὐτῶν διαλέκτῳ καὶ γραφὴν ἐξήνεγκεν εὐαγγελίου, τοῦ Πέτρου καὶ τοῦ Παύλου ἐν Ῥώμῃ εὐαγγελιζομένων καὶ θεμελιούντων τὴν ἐκκλησίαν.

Matthew also among the Hebrews published a written gospel in their own dialect, when Peter and Paul were preaching in Rome and founding the church there (Eusebius, *H.E.* 5.8.2, quoting Irenaeus, *Adv. haer.* 3.1.1).

Irenaeus wrote around A.D. 180.

The belief that the apostle Matthew wrote a gospel in Hebrew also appears in a story recounted in Eusebius, *H.E.* 5.10.3. Here we read that Pantaenus, the teacher of Clement of Alexandria (ca. 150–215), 'went to India, and the tradition is that he there found his own arrival anticipated by some who were acquainted with the gospel according to Matthew; for Bartholomew, one of the apostles, had preached to them and left them the writing of Matthew in Hebrew letters, and this writing was preserved until the time mentioned'.

Those church Fathers who, after Papias, connect the canonical Matthew, in a Semitic version, with the apostle[12] are usually

---

[12] In addition to Irenaeus, *Adv. haer.* 3.1.1 and Eusebius, *H.E.* 5.10.3 see Origen,

assumed to have relied upon his testimony, so their evidence is thought to be of no independent worth. Furthermore, it is claimed that the tradition, taken at face value, presents insurmountable difficulties. (1) Our canonical Matthew is in Greek, there is certainly no extant Semitic Matthew, and the gospel is not likely to be the work of a translator. (2) It is inconceivable that a Semitic document, such as Papias speaks of, would have incorporated a Greek document, the gospel of Mark, almost in its entirety. (3) It is even more inconceivable that, in writing his gospel, an apostle who had accompanied Jesus would have allowed the Greek gospel of Mark to determine the ordering of his material. These difficulties, along with Eusebius' assertion that Papias was a man of little intelligence (presumably because of his chiliastic views: see *H.E.* 3.39.12–13), have caused many to dismiss the testimony of the Bishop of Hierapolis as well as the subsequent evidence claimed to be based upon it.

Combining the external and internal evidence, then, the situation would appear to be this: the external evidence points to a Palestinian or Hellenistic-Jewish author who wrote in Hebrew or Aramaic, the internal to someone who wrote in Greek and used Greek sources. It is, accordingly, no surprise to learn that many modern scholars have come to reject the external evidence altogether, or even that some have come to ascribe the First Gospel to a Gentile. However, because the impact of the external evidence, taken, we repeat, at face value, and of certain obvious elements in the gospel seemed so strongly to point to a Jewish author, the view that the evangelist was a Gentile emerged surprisingly late. Indeed, the chart on the following pages, though not exhaustive, makes it clear that this view only appears in the twentieth century. It had no earlier proponents (although note Tertullian, *Adv. Marc.* 4.11, and Altercatio Simonis et Theophili 20). And, in fact, by far the greater number of scholars still favour some form of Jewish authorship. Yet the majority view has often been too easily espoused while the case in favour of the minority view has frequently been cavalierly dismissed. The matter is complex. In order, then, to give the issue the attention it deserves, we shall, in what follows, consider in detail both the arguments brought against the proposal of Jewish authorship and those favouring it.

(1) *The external evidence relating to authorship.*

The most powerful advocates of Gentile authorship dismiss the

---

in Eusebius, *H.E.* 6.25; Origen, *Comm. in Jn.* tom. 1.6; 6.32; Eusebius, *H.E.* 3.24.6; idem, *Ad Marin. quaest.* 2; Cyril of Jerusalem, *Cat.* 14; Epiphanius, *Haer.* 2.1.51; Jerome, *De vir. ill.* 3; *Prol. in Mt.*; *Praef in quat. ev.*; *Comm. in Oseam* 11.2; *Comm. in Jesai.* 6.9; Augustine, *De con. ev.* 1.2.4.

OPINIONS ON THE AUTHORSHIP OF MATTHEW

The apostle Matthew	Jewish Christian	Gentile Christian
	1886, H. J. Holtzmann (Hellenistic)	
	1898, B. Weiss (Hellenistic)	
1899, T. Zahn		
	1905, O. Pfleiderer (Hellenistic)	
	1914, J. Weiss (Hellenistic)	
	1915, A. Plummer	
	1918, J. Moffatt	
	1927, C. G. Montefiore (Hellenistic)	
	1928, E. von Dobschütz (converted rabbi), T. H. Robinson (Palestinian)	
	1930, B. W. Bacon	
	1933, F. C. Grant (Hellenistic)	
	1946, G. D. Kilpatrick (Hellenistic)	
	1947, M. Albertz (Palestinian)	1947, K. W. Clark
	1948, W. Michaelis (Palestinian)	
1953, A. Wikenhauser		
	1954, K. Stendahl (Hellenistic)	
		1958, P. Nepper-Christensen
		1959, W. Trilling
1959, E. J. Goodspeed	1960, F. V. Filson, E. P. Blair (Hellenist)	
		1962, G. Strecker

1963, N. B. Stonehouse

1963, P. Gaechter (translating and editing an apostolic Hebrew document), R. Hummel
1964, G. Bornkamm (Hellenistic)
1967, D. R. A. Hare (Hellenistic)
1968, W. Grundmann (Palestinian), B. Rigaux

1967, R. Walker

1971, W. F. Albright and C. S. Mann

1971, A. Kretzer (Hellenistic), H. A. Guy
1972, E. Lohse
1973, W. G. Kümmel
1974, P. F. Ellis, M. D. Goulder, H. Merkel
1975, H. B. Green (Hellenistic)
1976, L. Cope
1977, J. D. Kingsbury

1972, S. van Tilborg
1973, W. Pesch
1974, H. Frankemölle

1976, J. P. Meier

1980, S. Brown

1981, E. Schweizer, F. W. Beare

1983, M. J. Cook

1982, R. H. Gundry

1985, D. A. Hagner (Hellenistic)
1985, U. Luz

external evidence. Nepper-Christensen, who has examined the patristic testimony in great detail, is typical. He comes to the following conclusions. First, the traditions which mention a Matthew written in Hebrew for Hebrews all go back ultimately to Papias and therefore have no cumulative weight. Instead of many witnesses we have only one. Secondly, Hieronymus (Jerome) is not to be trusted. One may well doubt his claim to have seen and copied the Hebrew gospel to which he refers in a work written ca. 392, *De viris illustribus* (PL 23.643; cf. the conclusions of P. Vielhauer, in Hennecke 1, pp. 126–36). Thirdly, if Papias' statement preserved in Eusebius, *H.E.* 3.39 be taken in the usual sense, that is, as referring to a Hebrew or Semitic original behind our canonical Matthew, then it has to be rejected. The First Gospel, which depends upon the Greek Mark, is not a translation.

But there are nagging questions about the too confident dismissal of Papias (cf. Luz 1, p. 77). To begin with, it is not easy to determine whether an ancient text, especially one so clearly bearing, as does Matthew, the marks of two cultures, is or is not a translation. Eusebius, 'the father of church history', Origen (ca. 185–225), the prodigious exegete and editor of the Hexapla, Clement of Alexandria, the head of the catechetical school of Alexandria and the author of some very learned books, and Irenaeus, the great apologist—all no mean figures—, were Greeks. Presumably they knew the Greek language better than most, if not all, modern scholars; and they all, it would appear, took canonical Matthew to be the translation of a Semitic original. Is it, then, out of the question that our gospel is indeed a translation, perhaps of a Semitic original enlarged by the later addition of Greek Mark and other materials? Especially since the dependence upon Papias of all subsequent patristic testimony concerning Matthew is not proved but, in the last resort, simply assumed or asserted, should not the acceptance of Matthew as a translation by Greeks as eminent as Clement and Origen give pause? Some modern scholars, including T. Zahn, C. C. Torrey, B. C. Butler, and A. Debrunner have been of the same view as the Fathers mentioned.

Again, the objection that an apostle, Matthew, would not have included so much of Mark, can perhaps be met in terms of the usage of then contemporary historians, who used previously written works somewhat freely, imitating their style, grammar, phrases, and techniques of description.[13] Holding that an Aramaic Matthew was earlier than Greek Mark, George Kennedy has written:

If a gospel had been written in Greek at a fairly early date and was reasonably well-known, and if subsequently someone undertook to

---

[13] In addition to what follows see Gundry, *Commentary*, pp. 621–2.

translate an Aramaic gospel, rather fuller in content, into Greek, it would be·in accordance with Greek conventions for the translator to have taken the language of the existing Greek gospel as his model, even to the extent of borrowing some of that familiar language to translate passages of Aramaic that were not literally identical to his text. I understand that when Matthew cites passages of the Old Testament that are also cited by Mark or Luke, these citations are close to the Septuagint and highly consistent in language, whereas when Matthew cites passages of the Old Testament not found in the other gospels, his version is characteristically not that of the Septuagint (Kennedy here refers to Stendahl, *School*, p. 45). To me this suggests that the Greek text of an earlier gospel was a more potent influence on the translator than was the Septuagint itself.[14]

Although Kennedy's all-too-brief summary of and appeal to Stendahl does not do justice to the complicated issue of the OT textual traditions in the First Gospel, this does not invalidate his major point.

Once again, the claim that, in a church expanding vigorously into the Gentile world, at a time when (biblical) Hebrew was a dead language (so Nepper-Christensen), the author of a gospel would not have thought it worth his while to write in Hebrew, is no longer tenable. It is increasingly recognized on archaeological and other grounds that first-century Palestine was trilingual. Aramaic, Hebrew, and Greek were in use (cf. Fitzmyer, *Aramean*, pp. 29–56). To an extent that cannot be precisely assessed, Hebrew lived, not only in the worship of the Jews but in their daily transactions. Once this is granted, it is no longer acceptable to dismiss an originally Hebrew Matthew on the grounds that it would have found no readership.

A further minor point: scholars have made too much of Eusebius' castigation of Papias as a man of little intelligence. Eusebius' use of sources suggests that he himself did not always exercise the soundest of critical judgement, and his negative assessment of Papias was in all likelihood dictated simply by a distrust of chiliasm. But all this apart, in Judaism (and the same may have been true outside it) intelligence was not taken to be the mark of a reliable transmitter of tradition. Quite the opposite. The less intelligent the *tanna*' the more reliable he was deemed (see Gerhardsson, *Memory*, pp. 93–112). The intelligent tend to modify and alter what they pass on, unintentionally and otherwise. In a context of the transmission of tradition, Papias' *alleged* lack of intelligence (we have no proof of it) would not have been a disqualification. Beyond this, if the church Fathers, as is usually claimed, did all follow Papias' testimony, they could hardly have regarded him with great disdain. In any case, none

---

[14] 'Classical and Christian Source Criticism' (as in n. 11), p. 146.

seems to have disputed him. There was, as far as we know, no challenge in early Christian times to the Matthean authorship of the First Gospel.

Nor, finally, should the very early nature of Papias' evidence be overlooked. According to Irenaeus, Papias was 'a hearer of John' and 'a companion of Polycarp' (ca. A.D. 60–155; see *Adv. haer.* 3.3.4); and Polycarp could write of 'the apostles who preached to us' (*Ep.* 6.4) while Irenaeus could affirm that Polycarp 'had familiar intercourse with John and with others who had seen the Lord' (Eusebius, *H.E.* 5.20.6, quoting from a lost letter of Irenaeus to the Roman presbyter Florinus). Eusebius denied that Papias had been a listener or eyewitness of the apostles, but the passage Eusebius quotes hardly supports his denial (*H.E.* 3.39.3–4); and regardless of that problem, the connexion between Papias and the immediately post-apostolic Polycarp is not to be denied. Moreover, Papias himself wrote that he learnt from 'the elders' and from those who had heard 'the elders' (Eusebius, ibid.). Whoever those 'elders' were, they must have been the bearers of tradition, and that puts Papias' connexions well back into the first century. See further Petrie, as in n. 11.

The nagging considerations we have heretofore reviewed are, admittedly, of a general nature. But from two different quarters the evidence of Papias has been reassessed in minute detail, the result being two different reconstructions which yet resemble each other in taking Papias as an important witness to gospel origins. These we must now consider.

First, George Kennedy, who is sceptical of the scepticism of modern scholars and of every simplistic solution to the synoptic problem, has looked afresh at Papias' evidence and accused NT students of isolating the sentence quoted on p. 8 (above) from its immediate context and from other passages in Eusebius. The outcome of his provocative discussion is this: the gospels were written in the order, Aramaic Matthew (which was translated or paraphrased into several Greek versions), Mark's *hypomnēmata* (these, and not Mark's gospel, being the probable subject of Eusebius, *H.E.* 3.39.15–16), Mark's gospel, Luke (which may depend not only upon Mark but also on the notes of Matthew or Mark, the Aramaic Matthew, or a Greek translation of Matthew), Matthew in Greek, John. Although his reflections on the use of note-taking in the preparation of ancient historical works are very suggestive, the reasons Kennedy gives for his views are not in every instance persuasive. He has, however, fruitfully reopened the question of the meaning of Papias' evidence, and he has also, through an investigation of ancient methods of composition, made more plausible the possibility that Papias' tradition accurately reflects the way in which the synoptics were composed.

The second challenger, Kürzinger, begins with a minute analysis of Eusebius, *H.E.* 3.39.16. He refuses to deal with the reference to Matthew in isolation. He treats it instead as part of its context, *H.E.* 3.39.14–16, which he prints as follows:

... ἀναγκαίως νῦν προσθήσομεν ... παράδοσιν ἣν περὶ Μάρκου τοῦ
τὸ εὐαγγέλιον γεγραφότος ἐκτέθειται διὰ τούτων·
  καὶ τοῦθ' ὁ πρεσβύτερος ἔλεγεν·
  Μᾶρκος μὲν ἑρμηνευτὴς Πέτρου γενόμενος,
  ὅσα ἐμνημόνευσεν, ἀκριβῶς ἔγραψεν,
  οὐ μέντοι τάξει
  τὰ ὑπὸ τοῦ κυρίου ἢ λεχθέντα ἢ πραχθέντα.
  οὔτε γὰρ ἤκουσεν τοῦ κυρίου
  οὔτε παρηκολούθησεν αὐτῷ,
  ὕστερον δὲ, ὡς ἔφην, Πέτρῳ,
  ὃς πρὸς τὰς χρείας ἐποιεῖτο τὰς διδασκαλίας,
  ἀλλ' οὐχ ὥσπερ σύνταξιν τῶν κυριακῶν ποιούμενος λογίων,
  ὥστε οὐδὲν ἥμαρτεν Μᾶρκος
  οὕτως ἔνια γράψας ὡς ἀπεμνημόνευσεν.
  ἑνὸς γὰρ ἐποιήσατο πρόνοιαν,
  τοῦ μηδὲν ὧν ἤκουσεν παραλιπεῖν ἢ ψεύσασθαί τι ἐν αὐτοῖς.
Ταῦτα μὲν οὖν ἱστόρηται τῷ Παπίᾳ περὶ τοῦ Μάρκου·
περὶ δὲ τοῦ Ματθαίου ταῦτ' εἴρηται·
  Ματθαῖος μὲν οὖν Ἑβραῖδι διαλέκτῳ
  τὰ λόγια συνετάξατο,
  ἡρμήνευσεν δ' αὐτὰ ὡς ἦν δυνατὸς ἕκαστος.

Originally, according to Kürzinger, in Papias' lost work the statements about Matthew and Mark were combined. That about Matthew was an additional note to make the statement about Mark clearer, and it should therefore stand under the sentence, καὶ τοῦθ' ὁ πρεσβύτερος ἔλεγεν.

Papias was, in Kürzinger's view, concerned to justify the literary way in which Mark wrote his gospel with great accuracy (ἀκριβῶς ἔγραψεν) but without literary order or form (τάξις). The evangelist followed—he had no other choice—the way in which Peter presented the words and deeds of Jesus. Mark himself had never seen the Lord (οὔτε γὰρ ἤκουσεν τοῦ κυρίου οὔτε παρηκολούθησεν αὐτῷ). So he made no attempt to put together the dominical sayings in an orderly fashion. According to Kürzinger's understanding Peter used what was called in the terminology of the Greeks the χρεία (ὃς πρὸς τὰς χρείας ἐποιεῖτο τὰς διδασκαλίας). χρεία as a technical term was often used in rhetorical literature to describe a style in which short phrases, anecdotes, etc. in various forms were woven around a specific person or object. Mark followed Peter's use of χρεία. He did not aim at producing a work of literary art. His one goal was to be faithful to his source. But in the mind of Papias, in Hierapolis of Asia Minor, Mark could have been criticized for his lack of style. Papias lived in a world where there were many scholars devoted to grammar and rhetoric, and Papias himself, according to Kürzinger, must have had a rhetorical education. (Epictetus, he reminds us, was born in Hierapolis.) Thus, Kürzinger affirms, we can easily understand how Papias came to be concerned to defend Mark against the criticism of sophisticated contemporaries and why he stressed that despite its literary simplicity Mark's gospel remained an important document: it was faithful to Peter's recollections of the words and deeds of Jesus.

Kürzinger finds in the words of Papias several technical terms from Greek rhetoric, including these: (i) ἡρμήνευσεν. This word, whose basic meaning was not 'to translate' but 'to mediate thoughts and facts', was a technical term for the way in which thoughts and facts were presented (Kürzinger cites examples from Philostratus, V.S.). Mark as ἑρμηνευτὴς Πέτρου was therefore, it is claimed, not a translator but a mediator who transmitted Peter's teaching. (Note that when referring to 'translating' the NT generally prefers μεθερμηνεύειν.) (ii) συνετάξατο. This was also a technical term in Greek rhetoric (cf. (Ps.-) Aristotle, Rh. Al. 30–8). It referred to the structure and compositional organization of a literary work. Papias regarded Mark as having no structure of any kind in this sense, as being without orderly fashion. (iii) διαλέκτῳ. This is usually translated as 'dialect' or 'language'. But it too was a technical term in rhetoric and referred to a specific rhetorical technique (cf. Dionysius of Halicarnassus, Comp. 3.15–16, 20; 4.26; 11.58; 20.145). The word, according to Kürzinger, referred not to vocabulary or language but style and way of speaking (cf. Gundry, Commentary, pp. 619–20). Ἑβραῖδι διαλέκτῳ (which is, significantly, anarthrous) refers not to the Hebrew or Aramaic language but to the style and method of composition customary in Jewish writings, things Papias would have been familiar with from his reading of Jewish-Greek literature, especially the LXX. (Kürzinger refers in this connexion to the frequency of numerical patterns, symbolism, and parallelism.)

The outcome of all this is inevitable. By τὰ λόγια Papias, in Kürzinger's view, understood not a collection of sayings of the Lord but the gospel of Matthew. Papias regarded Mark's gospel as λόγια (τῶν κυριακῶν . . . λογίων) concerning the words and deeds of the Lord (τὰ ὑπὸ τοῦ κυρίου ἢ λεχθέντα ἢ πραχθέντα). τὰ λόγια in the note about Matthew was then a reference to the λόγια already mentioned in the comments on Mark. Matthew was not a translation. It was originally composed in Greek—but in the Jewish pattern or style. Kürzinger claims to find in Irenaeus support for this understanding of Papias' words. Irenaeus, so it is claimed, understood Papias as does Kürzinger. Confusion came only later, when Eusebius and other church Fathers misunderstood the Bishop of Hierapolis. They took him to refer to the Semitic language of the primitive Matthew and then added error on top of error by confusing this non-existent Semitic Matthew with the Gospel of the Hebrews (on which see esp. P. Vielhauer, in Hennecke 1, pp. 117–65).

As with Kennedy, Kürzinger has not convinced. Is his translation of πρὸς τὰς χρείας, on which his case rests so heavily, justified as over against the more customary one of 'towards the needs (of his audience)'? Can διαλέκτῳ bear the weight put upon it? And does Irenaeus really reproduce Kürzinger's reading of Papias? Whatever the answers, for our purpose, which is the search for authorship, one thing has become clear. In the light of the general considerations adduced and of the work of Kennedy and Kürzinger, the simplistic understanding of Papias which dismisses him out of hand must be questioned if not abandoned. We should also observe, given our concerns, that while Kennedy posits an original Matthew in Aramaic or Hebrew, Kürzinger posits an author familiar with the Hebrew or Semitic style of writing. In neither case are we likely to be dealing with a Gentile.

Two more observations need to be made before we turn to the next subject. First, although Papias and those after him identified the λόγια of Matthew with our First Gospel, one cannot be so certain that this was true for Papias' predecessors. That is, if indeed Papias did receive a tradition about the Matthean logia Ἑβραΐδι διαλέκτῳ, it is possible that the tradition was, somewhere along the line, attached to the First Gospel erroneously. If so, and as many others have remarked, the Q document might well account for the birth of the tradition.[15] An early form of Q could have been both apostolic and composed in Hebrew or Aramaic, and a later form of it taken up into Matthew. Certainly the conjecture—and that is all it is—gives us a reason for what is otherwise without explanation, namely, the association of the First Gospel with the relatively obscure apostle Matthew. To be sure, we are, as indicated, trading here in the realm of speculation. Nevertheless, the proposal has the great virtue of taking seriously the external evidence while at the same time being consistent with the conclusions of many modern scholars. It could very well be correct.

Secondly, let us suppose, despite Kennedy and Kürzinger and all that we have said, that Papias is to be rejected, his testimony dismissed. One is still left with a question. How do we explain the bishop's statement about Matthew? Surely he did not concoct it out of thin air. Surely he had some basis for his assertion. What might that have been? At the minimum, and if τὰ λόγια did not before Papias mean Q, it would seem that he knew of a tradition according to which the author of the First Gospel, the apostle Matthew, wrote for Jews who believed in Jesus (cf. Eusebius, *H.E.* 6.14.2).[16] In that case, however, one must concede that already before Papias' time our gospel was thought of as Jewish and as having been written by a Jew.

(2) *Linguistic usage and the issue of authorship.*

A. Matthew's use of φυλακτήριον, 'phylactery', in 23.5 is the only such reference in the NT. The Hebrew *ṭôṭāpôt* (Exod 13.16; Deut 6.8–9; 11.18) is translated in the LXX only by ἀσάλευτος (sing.). It is rendered by *tepillîn* in the Peshitta and in the targum. But in Mt 23.5 the *tepillîn* are evidently referred to as φυλακτήρια (although this has been disputed; see on 23.5). K. W. Clark, in his famous article on 'The Gentile Bias in Matthew' (see n. 11),

---

[15] This has been argued most forcefully by T. W. Manson, *Sayings*, pp. 15–20; idem, 'The Gospel of St. Matthew', in *Studies in the Gospels and Epistles*, ed. M. Black, Edinburgh, 1962, pp. 68–104. Cf. Streeter, p. 501, and those listed by Kümmel, *Introduction*, p. 120, n. 69.

[16] Cf. A. F. J. Klijn, 'Patristic Evidence for Jewish Christian and Aramaic Gospel tradition', in Best, *Text*, p. 170.

accepted G. G. Fox's explanation for this: the evangelist has attributed Gentile superstitition to the Pharisees; he has misrepresented the more reverent understanding of the *tepillîn* (which were designed to recall the Exodus) by calling them phylacteries, that is, amulets.[17] This misrepresentation or misunderstanding cannot go back to Jesus (whose criticism was of ostentatious use, not misuse) and hence is due to Matthew, a Gentile. So, at least, Clark.

This position fails for several good reasons. 1. Most commentators take 23.5a to be a redactional transition designed to combine 23.4 and 5bff. 23.5b belongs to the M material of Mt 23, which is generally—and rightly—taken to have had its origin in Jewish-Christian circles. It is probable, therefore, that it was a Jewish-Christian community, not an uninformed Gentile, who translated *tepillîn* by φυλακτήρια. The view of Clark breaks down on redactional grounds. 2. Both Jerome and Chrysostom, who were familiar with Jewish customs, state quite plainly that Jews called their *tepillîn* 'phylacteries' (PL 26.168 and *Hom. on Mt* 72.2 respectively; cf. Justin, *Dial.* 46.5). 3. That *tepillîn* could be employed in an ostentatious or hypocritical manner appears from Jewish texts (e.g. *Ruth. Rab.* on 4.1; see further J. H. Tigay, 'On the Term "Phylacteries" (Mt 23:5)', *HTR* 72 (1979), pp. 46–8); and the *tepillîn* found at Qumran vary considerably in size, which recalls Matthew's charge about 'making broad' (see Y. Yadin, *Tefillin from Qumran*, Jerusalem, 1969). 4. Sacred objects inevitably attract superstitious veneration, and one might have anticipated that the *tepillîn* would come to be thought of by some as amulets. It is no surprise that in several Jewish texts *tepillîn* are clearly thought of as a means of protection against demons, sin, or bad fortune (e.g. Tg. on Cant 8.3; *b. Menaḥ.* 43b; *y. Šabb.* 6.2.8b; *y. 'Erub* 10.11.26c). The development was wholly natural because the *tepillîn* contained Scriptures which promised God's protection (cf. Ep. Arist. 159; Josephus, *Ant.* 4.212–13; G. Vermes, 'Pre-Mishnaic Jewish Worship and the Phylacteries from the Dead Sea', *VT* 9 (1959), pp. 65–72). 5. Other Jewish texts mention *tepillîn* in close connection with the *qāmêa'* (= 'amulet'; see e.g. *m. Šabb.* 6.2; *m. Šeqal.* 3.2; *m. Kelim* 23.1). Moreover, in *Masseket Tefillin* 9 and 12, *qāmêa'* is actually used for *tepillâ* (first observed by Tigay, pp. 49–50). This should settle the issue. Even though the date of *Masseket Tefillin* is disputed (the earliest possible date being ca. 400), the saying in 9 is attributed to R. Judah b. Ilai, a *tanna'*; and already in *t. Dem.* 2.17 *tepillîn* are associated with the verb *qm'*

---

[17] 'Gentile Bias', p. 170, citing G. G. Fox, 'The Matthean Misrepresentation of Tephillin', *JNES* 1 (1942), pp. 373–7. Because of the importance of Clark's article for subsequent discussion, we shall, in what follows, take up all of his points one by one.

(= 'to tie'; cf. *b. Ber.* 30b). In view of this and the other considerations we have noted, one may reasonably surmise that, in Matthew's time, in Greek-speaking areas, Jewish-Christians who wore *tepillîn* may well have called them φυλακτήρια. And Mt 23.5 probably does not criticize the *tepillîn* themselves (equated with amulets) but only their ostentatious use.

B. Matthew uses Σατανᾶς, διάβολος, ὁ πονηρός and ὁ πειράζων for the devil, while two earlier Christians, Mark and Paul (both of whom Clark took to have been Jews), use the Semitic form Σατανᾶς without exception. Clark urges that this supports his thesis of a Gentile authorship. But most probably these terms were interchangeable among first-century Christians. Moreover, the temptation narrative from Q, which probably originated among skilled Jewish scribes, uses ὁ διάβολος instead of Σατανᾶς (see Lk 4.3). It should also be noted that Paul does not use only the term Σατανᾶς, as Clark implies. In 1 Th 3.5 we read of ὁ πειράζων, a title which also appears in the First Gospel: 4.3. As for Mark, many have taken him to be a Gentile. His ethnic character is at least open to doubt.

C. Matthew avoids words like Βοανηργές and ταλιθα κουμ found in Mark. He uses Greek words for κορβᾶν, Βαρτίμαιος, ῥαββουνεί, and Ἀββά. He hellenizes Mark's Ἰσκαριώθ to Ἰσκαριώτης (Mt 10.4 = Mk 3.19). He misunderstands (so it is claimed) ὡσαννά and Γολγοθᾶ and bothers to explain the meaning of the names 'Jesus' and 'Emmanuel'. For Clark these data indicate that Mark's gospel shows a better understanding of Aramaic than Matthew's gospel. Yet the avoidance of the majority of words and expressions just cited is probably due to Matthew's desire, often remarked upon, to improve the quality of Mark's Greek. Consider, for example, Βοανηργές (Mk 3.17 = Mt 10.2). The name is problematic. It is hard to explain the vowels in Βοα or to derive ργες from a Semitic word meaning 'thunder'. So Matthew's omission of Βοανηργές may have been due to his awareness of the difficulties of explaining it—in which case we should find here a sign of Matthew's knowledge, not his ignorance. Beyond this, the word is omitted by Luke also (Lk 6.14). Possibly the two evangelists follow traditions different from Mark about the sons of Zebedee. Or perhaps Matthew is simply trying to conform the first part of his list to the call of the disciples in 4.18–22.

Matthew's ἐλθόντες εἰς τόπον λεγόμενον Γολγοθᾶ (27.33) seems a stylish improvement over Mark's ἐπὶ τὸν Γολγοθᾶν τόπον (15.22); and the juxtaposition of the Semitic term and its Greek meaning was part of the tradition which our evangelist had received (see the Markan parallel). There is here no misunderstanding of the Aramaic by Matthew.

Concerning the Βαρτίμαιος of Mk 10.46, missing in Mt 20.30, is not this just part of the shortening of the whole pericope by Matthew (Mk 10.46–52: 123 words, Mt 20.29–34: 78–79)? Our evangelist also omits that the blind man (which he turns into two blind men) was a beggar. There is further the possibility that ὁ υἱὸς Τιμαίου Βαρτίμαιος would have been a good candidate for omission simply because of its awkwardness: the translation should come after, not before, the foreign word.

In 9.25 Matthew drops ταλιθα κουμ from Mk 5.41. Because, however, he has greatly abbreviated the whole pericope where it occurs (Mark has 383 words, Matthew only 187), his omission is not surprising. It has also been plausibly suggested that he avoided the phrase because it could have been interpreted as suggesting magical practices.

Why does Matthew omit the κορβᾶν of Mk 7.11 and use the Greek δῶρον? δῶρον became a loan word in rabbinic Hebrew and was used as a technical term for *qorban* (cf. Jastrow, s.v. *dôrôn*). It seems altogether probable that the equation was also known to Matthew's Jewish-Christian congregation. The redactor uses δῶρον nine times (Mk: 1; Lk: 2). Except in 2.11, the term always has the same meaning as *qorban* (5.23–4; 8.4; 23.18–19); so too in Hebrews 5.1; 8.3–4; 9.9; 11.4. Apparently Greek-speaking Jews understood δῶρον to mean 'offering' and equated the word with *qorban*. So Matthew's avoidance of *qorban* hardly implies his ignorance of the Hebrew term. In the same context, Mark (7.3–4) has to explain the Jewish custom of the washing of the hands whereas Matthew does not need to do so, presumably because his congregation was familiar with this as with the use of δῶρον for *qorban*.

Matthew's failure to reproduce ραββουνεί in 20.33 (from Mk 10.51) and his preference for κύριε are theologically motivated. He avoids 'rabbi' and 'teacher' and instead places 'Lord' in the mouths of disciples. Within the writer's circle the title 'teacher' was inadequate. Of the disciples, only Judas calls Jesus 'rabbi'. A Jew is more likely to have been sensitive on this point, especially after A.D. 70, when the term 'rabbi' became a title in Judaism. 'Lord' alone was to be used by Christians. And in 20.34 the two blind men become disciples ('and they followed him').

Similarly, nothing negative about Matthew's Jewishness can be deduced from his avoidance of Ἀββά in 26.39 where he gives πάτηρ for Mark's Ἀββὰ ὁ πάτηρ (14.36). The explanations offered for this are numerous: that Matthew's congregation did not use Ἀββά because of its opposition to its use in the Pauline congregations; or that in Greek-speaking churches the translation πάτηρ for 'Αββά had become fixed; or—and this is the best guess—that Matthew attempted to connect the scene in Gethsemane with the Lord's Prayer in 6.9.

Matthew's use of ὡσαννά as a shout of glory is no misunderstanding of the word's meaning. See on 21.9. As for the words 'Jesus' and 'Emmanuel' (1.21 = Ps 130.8; 1.23 = Isa 7.14; 8.18, 10), they are explained from the OT in order to emphasize the fulfilment of prophecy, not to enlighten readers who would not otherwise have known their meanings.

D. It is often asserted that Matthew was Jewish because of his avoidance of the divine name θεός in such typically rabbinic phrases as 'the kingdom of heaven' and 'your Father in heaven'. Clark has rejected this argument. He observes that Matthew did use the term 'the kingdom of God' in several cases (6.33; 12.28; 21.31, 43), and that two Jews—Mark (so Clark) and Paul—had no difficulty in using θεός, so why should we think the deliberate tendency to avoid this term necessarily Jewish? Against this, Mark, as previously noted, is not always taken to be a Jew, and Paul's epistles are addressed to Gentile churches. Had we letters by him to Jewish Christians we might see greater sensitivity to periphrastic usage. More significantly, the expression of an intimate relationship to God the Father was characteristic of earliest Christianity. This helps explain the uninhibited use of the divine name among the first Christians. And that Matthew—who uses the term 'Father' more than any other synoptic writer—has 'the kingdom of God' four or five times is, in view of this, not surprising. At the same time, it would be natural for a Jew who had no inclination to deny his roots to prefer 'the kingdom of heaven'.

All in all, Matthew's linguistic usage, while in itself not supporting the claim for his Jewishness, does not exclude this. The linguistic penetration of Judaism by Hellenism by the first century A.D. probably accounts for most of the data discussed above.

(3) *Doctrinal elements relating to authorship.*

A. The virgin birth. According to Clark, the story of the virgin birth betrays the Gentile bias of Matthew. This is because while there are no parallels in Judaism, there are in pagan literature, as in the tales about the miraculous births of Plato and Alexander (see on 1.23). A Gentile Matthew, it is implied, would have been much more likely to have adopted this kind of story than a Jewish Matthew. Certainly the Messiah was not expected to be of non-human origin.

But Clark has overlooked several things. To begin with, the details of the virgin birth of Jesus are rather different from the pagan parallels. There is, for example, no description of how the Holy Spirit came to Mary or of what form it took. In fact, Mt 1 differentiates itself by having to do with parthenogenesis in the strict sense: there is no male element. (The Hebrew *rûaḥ* is feminine, and 'Holy Spirit' is neuter in Greek.) Perhaps even more telling is the thoroughly Jewish character of Mt 1.18–25. The structure of the passage is common to certain OT annunciation narratives (see pp. 196–7). An OT text, Isa 7.14, is cited. Jewish law plays a central rôle (see on 1.19). Jesus is presented as a new Moses (see Excursus I). There is a Hebrew language wordplay (see on 1.21). These Jewish features put the burden on those who would affirm that Mt 1.18–25 arose in a Gentile environment.

B. Mt 22.41–6. In the words of Clark, Mt 22.41–6 clearly declares 'that the true Messiah need not, indeed cannot, be a descendant of David'. If true, this would surely be a strange thing for a Jewish Christian writer, especially when compared with the emphasis on Jesus as the son of David elsewhere in the Jesus tradition. Looked at more closely, however, Clark's analysis is not convincing. In fact, it makes no sense at all. Matthew cannot possibly have intended to deny the Davidic sonship of Jesus. The gospel opens with this redactional sentence: 'Jesus Christ, son of David, son of Abraham' (1.1); and throughout Matthew, often in redactional verses, Jesus is called by others the Son of David (e.g. 9.27; 12.23). So whatever interpretation be given to Mt 22.41–6 (see the commentary), one can scarcely view it as a refutation of Jesus' Davidic ancestry.

C. The rejection of Israel. The most famous argument put forward by Clark was this: the Jewish colouring in Matthew belongs only to the sources, not to the redactor. Matthew's own view is obvious (i) from the definite and final rejection of Israel—which can hardly have come from a Jewish Christian because 'at the time of the writing of Matthew a Jew did not feel the need to renounce Judaism'—, (ii) from the denunciation of the Pharisees and Sadducees, (iii) from the great commandment as the epitome of the law[18]; and (iv) from the great commission (28.16–20).

Clark refers to Paul, who 'illustrates a less vehement reaction of one who still insists that God had not repudiated His people'. We ourselves, however, have argued in the commentary that the question of the Jewish destiny is, in Matthew, still open (see e.g. on 2.6 and 23.39). Even if one thinks otherwise, it is perhaps not fair to compare Paul and Matthew on the issue at hand. For one thing, the former wrote two to four decades earlier than the latter, and prior to A.D. 70. Moreover, the opposition of the Jewish leaders to Christianity was probably more intense during the period of

---

[18] Why this should be a reason for Gentile authorship is not stated, and it is difficult to fathom, for there are very good Jewish parallels. See on 7.12.

Jamnian reconstruction, when Johannan ben Zakkai and others sought to consolidate Judaism in a period of trial and tribulation. One might expect *a priori*, then, that a document composed around Matthew's time might contain more polemic than one composed earlier.

We should also like to observe that one should not underestimate the hostility that could have existed between Jews and Jewish Christians. The covenanters at Qumran rejected the temple establishment in Jerusalem, damning it in the strongest possible terms. And Jesus himself presumably had very harsh things to say about the Pharisees and Sadducees. The apostle Paul, a Jew who may have had rabbinic training, and a man who had no doubt about the final salvation of 'all Israel' (Rom 11), could write that 'God's wrath has come upon them at last' (1 Th 2.16; on this see on 2.6). Passionate in-fighting and polemic within Jewish circles cannot be regarded as unlikely.[19] Indeed, debates within a religion are typically more vicious and passionate than debates between members of different religions. When Martin Luther began protesting against Roman Catholicism, he had no intention of founding a new church—but his attack was not the less vigorous for that. Clark's assertion that Jewish Christians in Matthew's time would have felt no need to 'renounce Judaism' is problematic on two counts. First, there is no 'renunciation' of Judaism in Matthew, only severe censuring of certain Jewish elements (esp. the leaders). Secondly, if in the Jamnian era there was increased Jewish opposition to Christianity, we might expect a polemical and apologetical response from Jewish Christians. And surely Matthew's gospel could in large measure be just such a response.

Clark writes of a total and final rejection of the Jews. This is an exaggeration. The Jews as such are no longer the stewards of God's kingdom (21.43). But the 'nation' to whom it has been entrusted is not an ethnic entity. It is rather the church, consisting of both Jew and Gentile. For Matthew the mission field is all the world: it includes Jew as well as non-Jew (see on 4.23 and 28.19). Admittedly, this is hardly the consensus of Matthean scholarship; but scholars, who tend to read the gospel through later ecclesiastical lenses, often approach Matthew with subtle biases. Only this explains why, whenever Jewish figures oppose Jesus, it is regularly assumed that their opposition foreshadows Israel's complete rejection of her Messiah and portends God's rejection of Israel; and why, conversely, whenever Gentiles (such as Pilate and the Roman guard) oppose Jesus, no such inference is made.

---

[19] Cf. H. Frankemölle, ' "Pharisäismus" in Judentum und Kirche', in *Gottesverächter und Menschenfeinde?*, ed. H. Goldstein, Düsseldorf, 1979, pp. 142–8.

Similarly, whenever Gentiles appear in Matthew in a positive light, commentators always see this as foreshadowing the great commission and the future influx of Gentiles; yet the significance of the ethnic identity of Jews such as Joseph, Mary, and Peter is passed over in silence. A more objective analysis would have to hold that, in the First Gospel, both Jew and Gentile are assumed to belong to the Christian church; and Matthew's animus is not directed against the Jewish people as an indivisible whole but against the Jewish leaders, Matthew's intellectual counterparts, who mislead others down the wrong path, away from the Christian church door (cf. T. Levi 10.2). The Pharisees and Sadducees do not simply stand for all Israel. They stand for its non-Christian leaders. Our gospel nowhere excludes faithful and fruit-bearing Jews from the ecclesia; and there is still hope for the nation as a whole (see on 2.6; 23.39).

What of 27.25, where 'all the people' are made to say, 'Let his blood be upon us and upon our children'? Is it not difficult to imagine one of Jewish birth inserting such a sentence into the Markan narrative (cf. Meier, *Vision*, p. 18)? And does the line not imply the rejection of all Israel? We think not. Too much emphasis should not be put upon '*all* the people', as though the Jews as a whole are rejecting Jesus as they stand before Pilate. Certainly no one would dream of taking the comparable πάντων τῶν ἐθνῶν of 24.9 as entailing that all the Gentiles will reject the gospel. And what of 3.5–6, where 'Jerusalem and all Judea' respond to John the Baptist's call for repentance? Room for overstatement must be allowed. More importantly, Matthew's harsh words against Israel and her leaders do not disallow the promise of ultimate salvation. There are Jewish and Christian documents from antiquity in which sentences of condemnation are passed only to be followed by prophecies of redemption. This is true, for instance, of some of the OT prophets, at least in their canonical forms (Hosea and Amos being examples). It is also true of the Dead Sea Scrolls (note esp. 1QS 1.1–2), Jubilees (see esp. 1.5–26), the Pauline corpus (cf. 1 Th 2.16; Rom 11.26), the Testaments of the Twelve Patriarchs, in their present form Christian (e.g. T. Levi 10 and 16), and even Justin Martyr (*Dial.* 108). It would be nothing extraordinary for Matthew to look forward to the eschatological redemption of Israel. As Hosea prophesied, God 'will say to Not my people, "You are my people" ' (Hos 2.23). For further discussion see G. N. Stanton, 'Aspects of Early Christian-Jewish Polemic and Apologetic', *NTS* 31 (1985), pp. 377–92. (Also helpful for the problem of Mt 27.25 is Cope, pp. 128–9, who argues that the verse is an explanation for the disaster of A.D. 70 and that it by no means imputes guilt to all Jews for all time.)

D. Jewish theology. We have looked at three theological themes that have been appealed to by proponents of a Gentile authorship. Our conclusions have been negative. The themes do not prove what they have been taken to prove. What, then, of the other side, the theological themes that have been thought to imply Jewish authorship? Perhaps the most impressive of these is the gospel's understanding of the Torah, especially as this is set forth in the programmatic 5.17–20. But there are also other seemingly Jewish theological tendencies in redactional material, such as the emphasis upon Davidic descent (see on 1.1) and on OT fulfilment (note esp. the formula quotations). On the surface, these appear to indicate a Jewish author. It is certainly telling that Clark's 'The Gentile Bias in Matthew' passes over entirely the subject of Torah. There is, nevertheless, room even here for doubt. One might argue that the Jewish theology in Matthew is to be explained in terms of its sources. Our author, a Gentile, was faithful to his tradition. This explains why his gospel contains, for instance, 5.17–20. It is an imperfectly digested piece of tradition that does not necessarily reflect the redactor's own Gentile viewpoint. In other words, Jewish theological elements come from the tradition: their significance can be too easily overemphasized (cf. Strecker, *Weg*, as in n. 11). There is also the real possibility that a Gentile could have made Jewish ways of thinking completely his own. A non-Jew, freshly converted to Christianity, full of zeal for his new found faith and wanting to lay aside his former pagan conversation, may well have been less radical than the Jewish 'Hellenists' of Acts or a Jew like Paul (cf. perhaps the situation of Paul's Gentile converts in Galatia). It follows, therefore, that while Matthew's conservative attitude towards the Law and his presentation of other themes are more than consistent with Jewish authorship, we cannot exclude the Gentile option. Can one really deny categorically that a Gentile could have approved of Mt 5.17–20?

(4) *Style and the issue of authorship.*

It has been argued that the stylistic corrections of Mark by Matthew and the finished Greek of the First Gospel (see pp. 72–4) are unlikely to have been achieved by a man whose first language was Aramaic or Hebrew. Such a one would not have set for himself the task of systematically improving, as has Matthew, the Greek of Mark. This is highly questionable. Apart from the fact that the Greek of the First Gospel hardly comes up to the level of Josephus (whose mother tongue was Aramaic), the recognition of the interpenetration of Hellenism and Judaism has become a commonplace among modern scholars: the ancient Jewish and Greek worlds cannot be neatly contained in separate compartments. In particular, the evidence for the use of the Greek language by even Palestinian Jews is now considerable. If our evangelist had been born in Palestine, he could very well have learned enough Greek to write the First Gospel, especially if he had had the aid of trained assistants. And if, on the other hand, Matthew lived in a Greek-speaking diaspora community, he could have learned to read the Hebrew OT in a Jewish school. In either case a bilingual or trilingual environment could have obtained. We further note that bilingual writers (for example, Welshmen—not the Anglo-Welsh—writing in English) often write in their second language with a more conscious effort at exactitude and elegance than those who write only in their native tongue. Perhaps, then, a bilingual Matthew, from long habit and stance, would have been prone to correct the poor language of Mark.

What of the Semitisms of Matthew? We have examined this issue elsewhere in the Introduction (in the chapter on style and literary characteristics). Our conclusion there is that Matthew's text is not really less Semitic in style than Mark; and in fact the first evangelist has on his own introduced a number of undoubted Semitisms (see pp. 80–5). This is some evidence for Jewish authorship.

(5) *Additional Jewish features and the issue of authorship.*

Matthew's special material contains much that has a distinctively Jewish flavour. To illustrate:

a. The structure of the genealogy seems to reflect gematria: the emphasis upon the number fourteen and its rôle in organizing the list of ancestors derives from the numerical value of David's name (see pp. 163–65).

b. Mt 1–2 presents Jesus as a new Moses (see Excursus I).

c. In 4.5 and 27.53 Jerusalem is 'the holy city'.

d. The παρεκτὸς λόγου πορνείας of 5.32 seems to reflect Shammaite teaching (see the commentary).

e. 5.33–7 is thoroughly Jewish in its discussion of oaths and the forms they might take.

f. The 'cult-didache' in 6.2–18 contrasts Christian behaviour with behaviour in the synagogue.

g. Matthew, more so than Mark or Luke, shows a special interest in the Pharisees, in the Sadducees, and in the scribes (see on 2.4 and 3.7).

h. 10.5 and 15.24 confine Jesus' ministry to 'the lost sheep of the house of Israel'.

i. 10.23 sets the preaching ministry of the disciples within the borders of Israel.

j. The terminology of 'binding' and 'loosing', used in 16.17–18 and 18.18, has a special Jewish background (see the commentary).

k. 23.3 enjoins obedience to those who sit on Moses' seat.

l. Proper piety is contrasted with the behaviour of the ἐθνικοί in 5.47 and 6.7 (cf. 18.17).

m. In 24.20 believers are to pray that their eschatological flight be not on a Sabbath.

These examples—all without parallel in the other synoptics—would seem very strongly to suggest a Jewish author. One might, of course, argue that this inference is not necessary. Given Matthew's penchant for preserving tradition the Jewish elements could be relics from the past, from an earlier stage in the history of Matthew's community, the Jewish-Christian stage. The problem with this position is two-fold. First, Matthew surely had the freedom to omit traditional materials if they did not fit his perspective and interests. And if he was given to inserting materials with a Jewish cast, that must tell us something not only about his community but about Matthew himself. Secondly, some of the relevant clauses or features or verses are almost certainly redactional (e.g. the gematria of 1.1–17, 'the holy city', παρεκτὸς λόγου πορνείας, 'nor on a Sabbath'). Strecker, who recognizes this, has recourse at this point to oral tradition (*Weg*, pp. 17–19). But when even redactional insertions show very strong Jewish features, is it not more natural to think of our author as having Jewish interests and a Jewish perspective, and as therefore being a Jew?

Let us consider 24.20. 'Pray that your flight be neither in winter nor on a sabbath'. Mk 13.18 has this: 'Pray that it be not in winter'. Because there is no evidence that the first part of Mt 24 draws upon any source other than Mk 13, 'nor on a sabbath' must be redactional. Why then was it added? If Matthew were a Gentile writing for a Gentile church, it is hard to answer this question. Recourse to oral tradition—which is in this case unproven and not obviously plausible—explains nothing. The question only becomes, Why did the redactor bother to record the oral tradition? 'Nor on a sabbath' was, assuming a Gentile readership, of no practical relevance for Matthew's audience. It is, admittedly, conceivable that the editor inserted the clause in order to lend to his narrative an archaic, authentic ring. But one hardly comes away from the First Gospel with the feeling that the Jewish features have been artificially sprinkled here and there for good effect: they are instead ubiquitous and seem to be an organic part of the whole. One thus inclines to the conclusion that Mt 24.20 was added because it was appropriate to the Matthean *Sitz im Leben*. Which is to say: the verse presupposes a Jewish-Christian audience.

(6) *Miscellaneous considerations relating to authorship.*

A. Mt 21.5. In 21.5 the evangelist quotes Zech 9.9 and construes it so that Jesus rides into Jerusalem 'on an ass and on a colt, the foal of an ass'. In the eyes of some the line reveals Matthew's Gentile character (see Meier, *Law*, pp. 16–18). He has misunderstood the Hebraic parallelism of Zechariah and, consequently, in the interests of the literal fulfilment of prophecy, has made one animal into two. Matthew cannot, therefore, have been a learned Jewish-Christian. But is this really a safe inference? One can hardly contend that the rabbis were always in agreement with the natural sense of the MT. It is not difficult to find in the Talmud examples of far-fetched exegesis which bends grammar and vocabulary in the interests of theology (see e.g. the interpretation of Deut 9.9 discussed in the commentary on 5.1). Next, one must observe that the formula quotation in 21.5 disagrees in several respects with the LXX while it agrees with the MT. Someone has apparently consulted the Hebrew (cf. Gundry, *OT*, pp. 197–9). But is it natural to think of a Gentile as knowing enough Hebrew to find and translate the Hebrew of Zech 9.9? Thirdly, E. von Dobschütz (as in n. 11, p. 7) actually took Mt 21.5 to be a point in favour of Matthew's Jewishness: 'A pupil of the rabbis and only a pupil of the rabbis would think of getting a literal fulfilment of Zech 9.9 . . .' (cf. Stendahl, *School*, p. 119). The assertion has force because some rabbinic sources agree with Matthew in finding two animals in Zech 9.9, and this in connexion with messianic expectation (see SB 1, pp. 842–4). Perhaps already in Matthew's time the interpretation preserved in *Gen. Rab.* on 32.6—or something like it—was already known. Lastly, perhaps the making of one animal into two should not be considered an isolated phenomenon. The demoniac of Mk 5.1–17 becomes two demoniacs in Mt 8.28–34; and while Mk 11.1–10 is about a certain Bartimaeus, Mt 21.1–9 is about two blind men. So there are other texts in which our evangelist has multiplied by two. Whatever be the explanation for this strange circumstance, it might also help account for the ass and the colt of 21.5. If so, Matthew could not be said to have misunderstood Zech 9.9 any more than he misunderstood Mk 5.1–17 or Mk 11.1–10.

B. Matthew's Gentile bias is, according to Clark, evident in the 'heightening of miracle'. Unfortunately, he does not elaborate on the point and only refers to M. S. Enslin, *Christian Beginnings*, New York, 1938, pp. 395–6. A look at this, however, shows that Clark was a bit too hasty. Enslin refers to Mt 9.22; 15.28; 17.18; and 21.19, in the first three of which Matthew uses a set phrase in connexion with healings—'and' + subject + verb of healing + 'from that hour'. This phrase is absent from Mark. But if we compare the Matthean stories with their Markan counterparts, there is no real heightening of the miraculous. Quite the opposite is the case. Matthew shortens and omits details given by Mark. Therefore the phrase cited seemingly does not have the function of heightening the miraculous but rather of shortening healing pericopae. Embellishment of the sort Clark implies just is not to be found. Matthew drops details from healing stories and makes the miracles instantaneous. Even if we were to speak of this as a heightening of the miraculous, the motive is Matthew's desire (1) to emphasize the sovereignty of the Messiah and (2) to discourage any hint of magical practices. He is not satisfying the appetite of a miracle-craving Gentile congregation. See further H. J. Held in *TIM*, pp. 165–299, and Hull, pp. 116–41.

C. The fulfilment of Scripture. To state the obvious, Christians had long before Matthew's time been intensely interested in scriptural proof texts and prophecies. Matthew's constant appeal to the OT is therefore nothing extraordinary. Clark, who makes this observation, backs it up by referring to Westcott and Hort, who list 123 quotations and allusions for Matthew—but also 109 for Luke and 133 for Acts; and Clark affirms that, in addition to the scriptural references drawn from Mark, Matthew uses about forty quotations, Luke about fifty. He then states: 'Unless we argue from these data that Luke also was a Jew, it is not logical to contend that this [frequent use of the OT] calls for a Jewish author for Matthew'.

Is it really the case that Matthew's treatment of and interest in the OT is no argument at all for his having been Jewish? The first Christians were Jews, and quoting and alluding to the Law and the prophets was their natural way of thinking, arguing, and interpreting. Certainly a Gentile Christian who did not from birth live and move and have his being in the Torah would not have caught and appreciated OT allusions as well as his Jewish-Christian brother. And a Gentile Christian author, it stands to reason, would have been less inclined than a Jew to add allusions to his text; he might even—often unwittingly—have omitted some from his sources. A Jewish writer, on the other hand, would, almost certainly, not only adopt the allusions and quotations of his sources but would also possibly if not probably expand them and even create some new ones. In view of this, the distinction between traditional and redactional material must be the starting point for the issue at hand. Clark has only counted verses. At first glance the result seems convincing. According to Westcott and Hort, there are as many quotations and allusions in Luke as in Matthew; and in the material not drawn from Mark or Q, Luke has more quotations and allusions than Matthew. There are, however, significant differences between the treatment of traditional allusions in Matthew and Luke. Matthew has a strong tendency to expand, Luke to shorten, omit, or make stylistic changes (cf. J. Dupont, 'L'utilisation apologétique de l'Ancien Testament dans les discours des Actes', *ETL* 29 (1953), pp. 298–327). Luke, for example, takes over many allusions from the Markan material but omits, shortens, or moves away from OT phraseology in four quotations and almost thirty allusions. For his part, Matthew brings several allusions closer to OT phraseology and expands others (see below). Scrutiny of the redactional treatments of OT references accordingly indicates that Matthew and Luke took different approaches. But the question remains, why does Luke have so many quotations and allusions peculiar to him?

While there are many quotations and allusions peculiar to Luke, most of these appear to have come from pre-Lukan sources (which explains why they often appear in a Semitic form). Thus many have plausibly argued that Luke found most of Lk 1–2 in a written source which had a marked Semitic character;[20] and when we examine the Lukan quotations and allusions as listed by Westcott and Hort, it becomes apparent that well over half of those unique to the Third Gospel belong to chapters 1–2. Even if Westcott and Hort's catalogue is incomplete, the direction in which it points seems highly significant. As if that were not enough, Jeremias (*Lukasevangelium*, pp. 77–89, 99–103) has argued that in Lk 1–2 Luke's creative hand is most evident in the Christmas narrative (2.1–20, especially at the beginning and the end) and in the story of the twelve-year old Jesus in the temple (2.41–52). For these sections Westcott and Hort list only one allusion.

Matters are completely different when we turn to the First Gospel. We find here not only editorial expansions of quotations (both in LXX and non-LXX text forms) but also several new quotations from the hand of the redactor. Even if one denies that the formula quotations are not his but derive from a pre-Matthean source (we think otherwise), many scriptural allusions remain which are very probably redactional (see e.g. on 5.39; 7.22; 25.31; 28.18). So in opposition to Luke, Matthew often uses the OT on his own, independently of his sources.

What, then, is the conclusion? The First and Third Gospels preserve distinctly different uses of the OT. The author of the latter often took over quotations and allusions from his sources.

---

[20] E.g. H. Schürmann, 'Aufbau, Eigenart und Geschichtswert der Vorgeschichte von Lukas 1–2', *BK* 21 (1966), pp. 106–11, and S. Farris, *The Hymns of Luke's Infancy Narratives*, JSNTSS 9, Sheffield, 1985. For an overview of the discussion see Brown, *Messiah*, pp. 244–7.

Sometimes he shortened or omitted them. He rarely if ever created quotations and allusions on his own. But Matthew rarely if ever shortened or omitted the OT references from his sources while he frequently expanded allusions and added quotations. Matthew, obviously, knew and treasured the OT in a way Luke apparently did not.

Clark claims that 'although "Matthew" is more deliberate in pointing to fulfilled prophecy, a similar significance is implicit in Luke, as it is also in other Gentile Christian writings. Such an application of the Jewish Scriptures to validate the Christian development was a common practice among contemporary Christian writers—Gentile as well as Jewish'.[21] Clark offers no evidence for this assertion. It may well be that in later Christian writings the Jewish Scriptures are commonly used. But to judge from the differences between Matthew and Luke, matters were probably different at an earlier time.

Two recent monographs deal with Luke's treatment of the OT—T. Holtz, *Untersuchungen über die alttestamentlichen Zitate bei Lukas*, Berlin, 1968 and M. Rese, *Alttestamentliche Motive in der Christologie des Lukas*, Gütersloh, 1969. Both authors emphasize that Luke quoted only the LXX. In opposition to Holtz, however, Rese contends that the OT text was not sacrosanct for Luke and that he therefore had no scruples about changing it in the interests of stylistic improvement. Both Holtz and Rese claim that Luke used the OT in a different way and for different reasons from Matthew's. Holtz even thinks that Luke was familiar only with an LXX copy of the twelve prophets, Deutero-Isaiah, and the Psalms. He makes a case that Luke did not know the Pentateuch, especially Deuteronomy. Needless to say, even if Holtz be thought incorrect, one cannot imagine somebody even beginning to make such a case for Matthew.[22]

Holtz argues for the redactional origin of a handful of quotations and allusions in Luke. But the number of these is not large, and in every instance it is the LXX that Luke is quoting. Again the difference from Matthew is undeniable.

D. The Sadducees. According to Meier (*Law*, pp. 18–19), Matthew's ignorance of the Sadducees—unthinkable for a Jew—appears in two places, 16.5–12 and 22.23. In the first Matthew (against Mark) writes of τῆς διδαχῆς τῶν Φαρισαίων καὶ

[21] 'Gentile Bias', p. 168.
[22] We reject Luz's conjecture (1, p. 135) that Matthew's community had no copy of either the twelve prophets or Jeremiah, and that it perhaps lacked other books as well. E.g. the προφητῶν of 2.23 does not show that Matthew was not able to find the author of the citation (see the commentary); and the introduction to 21.4 fails to name the minor prophet Zechariah simply because that would serve no redactional purpose (see on 2.15; 3.3; and 4.14; and cf. Gundry, *Commentary*, p. 408).

Σαδδουκαίων, a phrase which, it is asserted, shows ignorance of the doctrinal conflicts between Pharisee and Sadducee. (There is only one teaching—τῆς διδαχῆς—and only one article before 'Pharisees and Sadducees'.) Then in 22.23 Mark's 'the Sadducees, who say there is no resurrection' becomes 'Sadducees, saying there is no resurrection'. The Markan text attributes to the Sadducees a doctrinal position. The Matthean text simply tells us what certain Sadducees were saying as they once approached Jesus.

Should we conclude that Matthew knew nothing of the Sadducees? We have our doubts. If Matthew had no informed opinion, then surely he would have accepted the import of Mk 12.18: the Sadducees do not believe in the resurrection; in which case, Mt 22.23 cannot be taken to prove what Meier thinks it does. Furthermore, it is possible that οἱ should be restored in Matthew's text, giving us essentially what Mark has: 'the Sadducees, who say there is no resurrection' (so McNeile, p. 320; א² K L Θ 0107 565 pm bo arm eth and other witnesses have οἱ, and it is easy to see how it could have been omitted after Σαδδουκαῖοι). And if not, one could simply hold that Matthew altered Mark's prosaic statement of Sadducean doctrine in accordance with a fondness for direct discourse (contrast e.g. Mt 21.26 and 26.1–2 with the Markan parallels) and in order to gain a more vivid picture.

As for 16.5–12, a point just made is again relevant: if Matthew did, as most scholars suppose, work with the gospel of Mark, then he knew perfectly well that the Sadducees denied the resurrection (Mk 12.18). He therefore could not have been persuaded that the Pharisees and Sadducees had no significant doctrinal differences. How then do we explain the phrase, τῆς διδαχῆς τῶν Φαρισαίων καὶ Σαδδουκαίων? Mt 16.5–12 does not tell us precisely what the false teaching is. But to judge from the broader Matthean context, it must simply be all that leads away from Jesus. Certainly on that score there was, in Matthew's eyes, much agreement between the Sadducees and Pharisees. We propose that 'the teaching of the Pharisees and Sadducees' is no more than a convenient phrase indicating shared error, and to read into it ignorance of the Sadducees is to read too much into it. 'The teaching of the Pharisees and Sadducees' no more implies doctrinal consensus between the Pharisees and Sadducees than the comparable 'the righteousness of the scribes and Pharisees' (5.20) tells us exactly what Matthew thought to be the relationship between the scribes and Pharisees.

(7) *Non-LXX text forms and the issue of authorship.*

According to Bacon (p. 477), Clark ('Gentile Bias'), and Strecker (*Weg*, pp. 24–85), the redactor of the First Gospel knew only the LXX. In order to evaluate this judgement it is necessary to re-examine in detail the use of the OT in Matthew.[23] The following charts (=pp. 34–57) supply a synopsis of the pertinent data.[24]

The data given in the charts presented lead irresistibly to this conclusion: Matthew knew Hebrew. This follows from the following facts:

1. Matthew preferred a form of the *šĕma'* which stands close to the MT.
2. Several Matthean texts stand closer to Jewish tradition or interpretation than the Markan and Lukan parallels.
3. Matthew and Luke dealt in very different ways with the allusions in Mark and Q. Matthew generally preserved and expanded. Luke often omitted and shortened.
4. Several times Matthew brought his sources closer into line with the OT.
5. Matthew's redactional expansions or changes of allusions and his redactional allusions frequently depart from the LXX and often agree with the MT.
6. Matthew's unique quotations show the same mixed text form as the synoptic allusions.
7. Some of the allusions unique to Matthew but with a non-allusive parallel in Mark or Q show agreement with the MT or Jewish tradition.

Matthew, it would seem, lived in a bilingual or trilingual milieu, was familiar with Jewish traditions, had much more interest in and familiarity with the OT than Luke, and knew the OT both in Greek and Hebrew (cf. Goulder, pp. 123–7).

What follows for our purposes? Since Matthew knew Hebrew, he was almost certainly a Jew. The only alternative is to suppose that he was a man like Origen or Jerome, a Gentile who learned Hebrew. But surely this would be a desperate hypothesis.

In the light of all the discussion in the previous pages we can now present our conclusions on the issue of authorship. The external evidence makes our evangelist a Jew writing for Jews. Is it in this regard correct? Our discussion has shown that while, on the one hand, nothing in the First Gospel demands that its author was a Gentile, there are, on the other hand, several facts that are most easily explained by the supposition that our author was a Jew. Particularly weighty are these two considerations: first, much of Matthew's special material—including redactional material—contains a distinctively Jewish flavour (see section (5)); and

[23] On this subject Stendahl's *School*, Gundry's *OT*, and Soares Prabhu's *Formula Quotations* are indispensable. For what follows we are highly indebted to these three works.

[24] The authors wish to acknowledge the help of Ms. Astrid Berger in drawing up the following charts.

Chart I

QUOTATIONS COMMON TO MATTHEW AND MARK

OT text	Mt = Mk = LXX	Mt = Mk both against LXX	Mt against Mk both against LXX	Mt against Mk and LXX Mk = LXX
Isa 40.3	3.3			
Exod 23.20	11.10b (the ἐγώ is a stylistic improvement)			
Mal 3.1		11.10c		
Exod 20.12 Deut 5.16	15.4a (Mt has dropped possessive pronouns)			
Exod 21.16 Lev 20.9	15.4b (Mk and Mt have dropped possessive pronouns)			
Isa 29.13	15.8–9 (LXX A; cf. 1 Clem. 15.2; LXX B may here be hexaplaric; Mt slightly alters Mk's word order)			
Gen 1.27	19.4 (LXX = MT)			
Gen 2.24				19.5 (Mt is not closer to the MT despite his deviations)
Exod 20.13–16			19.18–19 (catechetical text; Mt has the word order of LXX A, MT, the targum, and Mk against LXX B)	
Isa 56.7	21.13a (Mt abbreviates)			
Jer 7.11	21.13b			

Chart I—*continued*

OT text	Mt = Mk = LXX	Mt = Mk both against LXX	Mt against Mk both against LXX	Mt against Mk and LXX Mk = LXX
Ps 118.22–3	21.42 (LXX = MT)			
Exod 3.6			22.32 (Mt is closest to LXX A)	
Deut 6.4–5				22.37 (Mk is essentially LXX; Mt is closer to the Hebrew)
Lev 19.18	22.39 (LXX = MT)			
Ps 110.1	22.44 (ὑποκάτω is from Ps 8.7)			
Zech 13.7			26.31 (Mt is close to LXX A; Mk is close to LXX Q; Mt's changes do not bring him nearer the MT)	

Comments:

Matthew and Mark share seventeen quotations. Eleven are Septuagintal. Two are closest to LXX A (22.32; 26.31), which may in these instances be original LXX. In three texts (19.18–19; 22.23; 26.31) Mark and Matthew both differ from the LXX but in different ways. In two places (19.5; 22.37) Mark follows the LXX while Matthew deviates from both Mark and the LXX. In one case this brings him closer to the MT: 22.37 (the *šĕmaʿ*, a text with an oral existence). On the whole, then, the Markan quotations are almost purely Septuagintal, the Matthean parallels a little less so. Allen was therefore mistaken when he asserted (p. lxii) that 'in the quotations borrowed by him from Mark the editor shows a tendency to assimilate the language more closely to the LXX'. See further Soares Prabhu, pp. 81–4. From Luke the following passages are missing: 15.4a, 4b, 8–9; 19.4, 5; 26.31. It is noteworthy that the only text in Matthew to show traces of Semitic influence is the *šĕmaʿ*. It stands to reason that, in catechetical texts, the evangelists would probably have reproduced the forms best known to themselves and to their readers; so Mt 22.37 is some evidence for supposing that the catechetical texts of the Matthean community had been influenced by speakers of a Semitic language.

Chart IIa

POSSIBLE ALLUSIONS COMMON TO MATTHEW AND MARK

OT text(s)	Mt = Mk = LXX	Mt = Mk both against LXX	Mt against Mk both against LXX	Mt against Mk Mt against LXX Mk = LXX	Mt = LXX Mk against LXX	Mt against Mk both LXX
2 Kgs 1.8	3.4					
Ezek 1.1 Isa 63.19					3.16	
Isa 42.1 Ps 2.7			3.17 (cf. 12.18)			
Lev 13.49	8.4 (LXX = MT)					
Num 27.17 1 Kgs 22.17 Ezek 34.5 2 Chr 18.16			9.36			
Mic 7.6	10.21 (contrast 10.35)					
1 Sam 21.6–7 12.3–4						
Isa 6.9			13.13			
Dan 4.9, 18 Ezek 17.23; 31.6			13.32 (Mt expands; there is some agreement with Theodotion, some with the LXX)			

Chart IIa—continued

OT text(s)	Mt = Mk = LXX	Mt = Mk both against LXX	Mt against Mk both against LXX	Mt against Mk Mt against LXX Mk = LXX	Mt against Mk Mt against LXX Mk against LXX	Mt = LXX Mk against LXX	Mt against Mk both LXX
Deut 18.15 Ps 2.7 Isa 42.1				17.5 (Mt adds ἐν ᾧ εὐδόκησα from Isa 42.1; cf. 3.17)			
Mal 3.23–4		17.11 (Mt changes Mk's ἀποκαθιστάνει to ἀποκαταστήσει which makes conformity to the LXX perfect)					
Deut 24.1			19.7 (Mt's word order is closer to the OT)				
Gen 18.14 Job 42.2 Zech 8.6			19.26 (Mt changes Mk's word order)				
Isa 53.10–12	20.28						
Ps 118.25–6			21.9 (partial agreement with the LXX in both gospels; Mt adds 'to the son of David')				
Isa 5.1–2						21.33 (Mt's ἐν αὐτῷ brings him a bit closer to the LXX)	
Gen 38.8 Deut 25.5			22.24 (Mt abbreviates and crosses over to Gen 38.8 one step before Mk and Lk; ἐπιγαμβρεύειν appears in Aquila's text of Deut 25.5 and in Lucian's version of Gen 38.8)				
Dan 2.28	24.6						

Chart IIa—*continued*

OT text(s)	Mt = Mk = LXX	Mt = Mk both against LXX	Mt against Mk both against LXX	Mt against Mk Mt against LXX Mk = LXX	Mt = LXX Mk against LXX	Mt against Mk both LXX
Isa 19.2 2 Chr 15.6			24.7 (LXX influence is unmistakable but there are also differences)			
Dan 12.12–13			24.13 (partial agreement with Theodotion)			
Dan 12.11 9.27; 11.31	24.15a					
Dan 12.10			24.15b (νοείτω may represent *yābînû*, for which LXX and Theodotion have other words; note Mt's addition, 'the word through the prophet Daniel'; this proves that our evangelist has noticed the allusions to Daniel in Mk 13; contrast Lk, who omits the Markan allusions in Mt 24.15a, 15b, 21, 24, 31 and moves away from OT phraseology in Lk 21.19, 21, 25–6)			
Dan 12.1				24.12 (Mt is perhaps closer to the MT than is Mk)		
Deut 13.1–3				24.24 (the 'false Christs' of Mt and Mk is closer to targumic renderings than to the LXX or MT)		
Isa 13.10; 34.4					24.29 (Mt has what could be an independent rendering of the MT)	
Zech 12.10, 12 Dan 7.13–14					24.30 (Mt expands the allusions)	

Chart IIa—*continued*

OT text(s)	Mt = Mk = LXX	Mt = Mk both against LXX	Mt against Mk both against LXX	Mt against Mk Mt against LXX Mk = LXX	Mt = LXX Mk against LXX	Mt against Mk both LXX
Isa 27.13 Zech 2.10 Deut 30.4			24.31 (see Gundry, *OT*, pp. 54–5, for connexions with the Peshitta and the targumim)			
Ps 31.14 Exod 21.14						26.3–4 (Mt alone has the possible allusion to Ps 31.13)
Deut 15.11		26.11				
Exod 24.8 Isa 53.12 Jer 31.31, 34 Zech 9.11				26.28 (Mt alone alludes to Jer 31.34, agreeing with the MT against the LXX; see Gundry, *OT*, pp. 58–9)		
Ps 42.6, 12; 43.5; Jon 4.9	26.38					
Ps 51.12	26.41 (Mt and Mk both agree with the MT)					
Zech 12.10 Ps 110.1 Dan 7.13					26.64	

Chart IIa—continued

OT text(s)	Mt = Mk = LXX	Mt = Mk both against LXX	Mt against Mk both against LXX	Mt against Mk Mt against LXX Mk = LXX	Mt = LXX Mk against LXX	Mt against Mk both LXX
Isa 50.6						26.67
Ps 22.19						27.35 (Mt's first verb agrees with the LXX perfectly, this against Mk)
Lam 2.15 Ps 22.8		27.39 (Gundry, OT, pp. 62–3, finds agreement with the OT Peshitta)				
Ps 22.2				27.46a (Mt has thought himself qualified to alter Mk's transliteration of a Semitic sentence)		
Ps 22.2					27.46b (Mt's ἰωτί agrees with the LXX; his Attic vocative θεέ does not)	
Ps 69.22	27.48 (LXX = MT)					

Chart IIb

LUKE'S TREATMENT OF THE ALLUSIONS COMMON TO MATTHEW AND MARK

No parallel in Luke	Luke follows Mark	Luke agrees with Matthew against Mark	Luke moves away from the OT	Luke is closer to the OT
Mt 3.4				
		Mt 3.16		
	Mt 3.17			
	Mt 8.4 (stylistic changes)			
Mt 9.36				
Mt 10.21				
	Mt 12.4			
	Mt 13.13			
		Mt 13.32		
				Mt 17.5 (one might detect influence from Isaiah in 'the chosen one'; but it should be kept in mind that ἐκλέγομαι is a favourite of Luke)

Chart IIb—continued

No parallel in Luke	Luke follows Mark	Luke agrees with Matthew against Mark	Luke moves away from the OT	Luke is closer to the OT
Mt 17.11				
Mt 19.7				
	Mt 19.26			
Mt 20.28				
			Mt 21.9	
			Mt 21.33	
	Mt 22.24			
	Mt 24.6			
	Mt 24.7			
			Mt 24.13	
Mt 24.15a				
Mt 24.15b				
Mt 24.21				
Mt 24.24				
			Mt 24.29	

Chart IIb—*continued*

No parallel in Luke	Luke follows Mark	Luke agrees with Matthew against Mark	Luke moves away from the OT	Luke is closer to the OT
	Mt 24.30			
Mt 24.31				
			Mt 26.3–4	
Mt 26.11				
				Mt 26.28 (Luke's 'new' is from Jer 31.31 but is scarcely a redactional creation; cf. 1 Cor 11.25)
Mt 26.38				
Mt 26.41			Mt 26.64	
Mt 26.67				
		Mt 27.35 (stylistic changes)		
				Mt 27.39 (although Lk lacks the allusions in Mk, he has another in LXX form from Ps 22)

Chart IIb—*continued*

No parallel in Luke	Luke follows Mark	Luke agrees with Matthew against Mark	Luke moves away from the OT	Luke is closer to the OT
Mt 27.46a				
Mt 27.46b				
Mt 27.48				

Comments on IIa and IIb:

Luke omits eighteen of the Markan allusions and in six instances moves away from the Markan (=OT) phraseology, sometimes so far that it is no longer possible to speak of an allusion. In only two or three instances does Luke add an allusion to the OT (the parallels to Mt 26.28; 27.39; and perhaps 17.5). For the rest Luke follows Mark. Note that it is especially in the allusions to Daniel and in his passion narrative that Luke exhibits a tendency to omit or to move away from Mark's OT phraseology.

Matthew presents a completely different picture. He always takes over the Markan allusions. He also adds a number of his own and brings some of Mark's even closer to the OT. Moreover, Matthew's editorial activity would seem to show a great deal of textual diversity. Thus in 3.16; 17.11; 26.3–4, 64; and 27.35 and 46b Matthew makes the Markan allusion closer to the LXX while in 24.21, 29, 31; and 26.28 there would appear to be closer approximation to the MT; and in 22.24 and 24.31 there are changes which stand near to targumic or other Jewish traditions. This supplies some evidence that the evangelist was familiar with different OT text forms in Greek and Hebrew. No less telling is the textual form of Matthew's expansions. Whereas Luke often omits, shortens, or changes the Markan allusions, Matthew sometimes expands (13.32; 17.5; 24.30; 24.31; 26.3; 26.28). And while in 26.3 the expansion clearly displays LXX form, in the remaining verses this is not the case. This too fits ill with the supposition that the LXX was Matthew's Bible. The objection that the changes and expansions could be pre-Matthean is hard to credit. It is very unlikely that the enlargements which are so closely connected with Markan allusions stem from M or some other source. All presumption is that they are Matthew's own work, created as he composed his gospel. Also deficient is the objection that we know too little about OT text forms in the first century to make any inferences about Matthew, and that therefore our evangelist might have used a non-LXX Greek text which has not survived. (1) If Matthew did in fact use a Greek OT which differed greatly from the LXX, all other traces of it have disappeared. There is, for example, no evidence for a Greek edition of Isaiah that would explain Matthew's readings for that prophet. (2) Neither the gospel of Mark nor that of Luke gives us any reason to suppose that their authors were familiar with anything but a Greek OT very similar to what we have in our hands today. The same is true of John. While Jn 19.37 could bear witness to a proto-Theodotionic recension, and while Jn 13.18 just might depend upon the Hebrew, all the other quotations in the Fourth Gospel either agree with the LXX or are too insubstantial to make their basis certain. See E. D. Freed, *Old Testament Quotations in the Gospel of John*, NovTSup 11, Leiden, 1965. (3) How do the Pauline epistles bear on the issue? (For what follows we depend largely upon E. E. Ellis, *Paul's Use of the Old Testament*, Edinburgh, 1957, pp. 150–85—although we have, in some particulars, disagreed with Ellis.) Paul cites the OT eighty-six times in Romans, 1 and 2 Corinthians, and Galatians (there are no quotations in Philippians, Colossians, 1 or 2 Thessalonians). Of these, thirty-one agree with the LXX and another twenty-two differ only slightly. Of the remaining texts, three seem to depend upon the MT (Rom 11.35; 1 Cor 3.19; 2 Cor 8.15), one upon the targum (Rom 12.19), and the vast majority of the others are probably to be explained in terms of Paul's redactional freedom: we are dealing with paraphrases or revisions for the sake of context (e.g. Rom 2.24; 3.10–12; 9.9, 17; 10.6–8, 15; 1 Cor 2.16; 15.55). (This explains why A. F. Kautzsch, *De Veteris Testamenti Locis A Paulo Apostolo Allegatis*, Lipsiae, 1869, could claim that out of eighty-four OT quotations in Paul (his count differing slightly from our own), approximately seventy agree with the LXX or do not vary considerably from it while twelve more, despite differences from the LXX, yet display signs of affinity.) Perhaps less than ten of the apostle's OT quotations present true variants from the LXX (Rom 9.25, 27–8, 33; 10.11; 11.3, 4; 1 Cor 15.54; Gal 3.10, 13); and even here one can find possible agreement with LXX tradition (e.g. Rom 9.25 could be a re-writing of Hos 2.25 LXX B V) and explain some of the texts as taking a form common to early Christian exegetical or testimony traditions (cf. Rom 9.33 and 10.11 with 1 Pet 2.6, 8 and Gal 3.13 with Acts 5.30; 13.28–30). So Paul, whose Bible was obviously the LXX or something quite close to it, confronts us with a different phenomenon from that which Matthew presents. In particular, while, according to Ellis, the apostle agrees with the MT against the LXX on a scant three occasions, the evangelist does so often, in most of his formula quotations and in many of his redactional allusions. This striking fact demands explanation and entails that the key to explaining Paul is not the key to explaining Matthew. (4) Hebrews is one more first-century witness which does not betray the existence of a non-LXX Greek OT in early Christian circles. In this book, LXX B or LXX A is usually followed, and where this is not the case the author's interpretative hand seems manifest (cf. F. F. Bruce, *The Epistle to the Hebrews*, NICNT, Grand Rapids, 1964, p. xlix). To sum up, then: because Matthew is the only NT writer frequently to agree with the MT against the LXX (see further below), and because we lack any corroboration for the hypothesis that our evangelist had a now defunct Greek OT, we must strongly suspect not that the author of the First Gospel alone among early Christians had a non-LXX OT that has altogether disappeared but rather that he could read the Scriptures in their original language.

Chart III

QUOTATIONS COMMON TO MATTHEW AND LUKE (FROM Q)

Mt = Lk = LXX	Mt against Lk both LXX	Mt = Lk both against LXX
	Mt 4.4 (Matthew expands)	
Mt 4.6 (Luke expands slightly)		
Mt 4.7		
		Mt 4.10

Chart IV

POSSIBLE ALLUSIONS COMMON TO MATTHEW AND LUKE (Q)

OT text(s)	Mt = Lk = LXX	Mt = Lk both against LXX	Mt against Lk Lk = LXX	Mt against Lk Mt = LXX	Mt against Lk both against LXX	Mt against Lk both LXX
Isa 61.1			5.3 (for the addition 'in spirit' cf. Isa 66.2 MT and 1QM 14.7)			
Isa 61.2				5.4 (LXX = MT; Lk has probably missed the allusion)		
Gen 15.1					5.1 (for targumic connexions see Gundry, *OT*, p. 72)	
Ps 6.9					7.23 (the texts are mixed: both Mt and Lk in turn agree and disagree with the LXX)	
Ps 107.3 Isa 49.12					8.11 (see the commentary)	
Ps 112.10		8.12 (cf. 13.42, 50; 22.13; 24.51; 25.30)				
Mic 7.6					10.35–6 (OT Peshitta has *waw*'s where Mt has καί's; and 10.36, which has no parallel in Luke and seems to be redactional, could be an independent translation of the Hebrew)	
Isa 35.5, 6; 61.1	11.5 (Mt adds καί's)					

Chart IV—*continued*

OT text(s)	Mt = Lk = LXX	Mt = Lk both against LXX	Mt against Lk Lk = LXX	Mt against Lk Mt = LXX	Mt against Lk both against LXX	Mt against Lk both LXX
Deut 21.20		11.19 (for targumic connexions see Gundry, *OT*, pp. 80–81)				
Isa 14.13, 15		11.23 (the form is mixed: καταβήσῃ is LXX, ὑψωθήσῃ is not)				
1 Kgs 10.4, 6, 8			12.42 (the OT has φρόνησις, the NT σοφία)			
Deut 32.5, 20			17.17 (cf. Phil 2.15, which agrees with the LXX)			
Dan 2.34–5, 44–5				21.44 (minor stylistic differences between Mt and Lk; HG omits the verse from Mt)		
Ezek 21.26	23.12 (the vocabulary is LXX, the word order slightly different)					
2 Chr 24.20–2 Lam 4.13						23.35–6 (Mt is closer to the OT and seemingly shows knowledge of the Hebrew; see Gundry, *OT*, p. 86–8)

Chart IV—continued

OT text(s)	Mt = Lk = LXX	Mt = Lk both against LXX	Mt against Lk Lk = LXX	Mt against Lk Mt = LXX	Mt = LXX	Mt against Lk both against LXX	Mt against Lk both LXX
Jer 12.7 22.5					23.38 (in their agreement Mt and Lk could be independent of the LXX; but Mt's addition—ἔρημος— seems to draw upon Jer 22.5 LXX)		
Ps 118.26	23.39 (cf. Mk 11.9)						
Job 39.30						24.28 (see Gundry, *OT*, pp. 88–9)	
Gen 7.7	24.38 (LXX = MT)						

Comments:

Of the nineteen common (Q) allusions we have listed, four clearly have a Septuagintal character in both gospels while twelve are seemingly non-Septuagintal in both gospels. It is probable that, in Q, Mt 5.3 and 4 alluded to the LXX. In perhaps six cases Matthew shows a closer linkage with the OT and Jewish tradition (5.3, 12; 10.35–6; 23.35–6, 38; 24.28). Whether Matthew has simply been more faithful to Q or whether he has instead increased the number of OT connexions does not admit of an easy answer. Probably both are true in turn. In any case Matthew's links to the OT are more numerous and more solid than those in Luke.

Chart V

QUOTATIONS PECULIAR TO MATTHEW

OT text(s)	Formula quotation	LXX	Against LXX	Mixture: LXX and against LXX
Isa 7.14	X	1.23 (with καλέσουσιν for καλέσει(ς))		
Mic 5.1, 3 2 Sam 5.2 1 Chr 11.2	?		2.6	
			2.15 (independent rendering of the Hebrew)	
Hos 11.1	X		2.18 (Mt is nearest to the MT)	
Jer 31.15	X		2.23 (there is a Hebrew word play; see the commentary)	
Judg 13.5 Isa 11.1	X			
Isa 8.23–9.1	X			4.15–16 (it seems impossible that just one OT textual tradition lies behind this; some type of targumic conflation has taken place; see Soares Prabhu, pp. 84–106)
Deut 5.17 Exod 20.13		5.21 (LXX = MT; see Soares Prabhu, pp. 79–80)		
Deut 5.18 Exod 20.14		5.27 (LXX = MT)		

Chart V—*continued*

OT text(s)	Formula quotation	LXX	Against LXX	Mixture: LXX and against LXX
Deut 21.1-4		5.31 (Mt abbreviates)		
Lev 19.12 Ps 50.14 Num 30.3			5.33 (ὅρκος is the only word shared with Lev and Num)	
Lev 24.20 Exod 21.24-5 Deut 19.21		5.38 (LXX = MT)		
Lev 19.18		5.43a (LXX = MT)		
Isa 53.4	X		8.17 (agreement with MT)	
Hos 6.6			9.13 (Mt has καὶ οὐ, LXX B ἥ; note the rabbinic introduction: 'going, learn what it is')	
Hos 6.6			12.7 (cf. 9.13; LXX B is probably original)	
Isa 42.1-4 cf. Hag 2.23; Isa 11.10; 41.8; 44.2; 1 Kgs 15.12; Hab 1.4	X			12.18-21 (there are several agreements with the targum; 12.21 is almost purely LXX; much of the passage seems to be an independent rendering of the Hebrew)
Isa 6.9-10	?	13.14-15 (cf. Acts 28.26-7; this is probably an interpolation)		

Chart V—continued

OT text(s)	Formula quotation	LXX	Against LXX	Mixture: LXX and against LXX
Ps 78.2	X			13.35 (the first clause is LXX; the second agrees with the MT)
Isa 62.11 Zech 9.9	X			21.5 (the Isaiah quotation is LXX; that from Zechariah shows knowledge of the Hebrew)
Ps 8.3		21.16 (in Markan material)		
Zech 11.13	X		27.9-10	

Comments:

There are twenty-one quotations peculiar to Matthew. Ten to twelve are formula quotations. Of the rest, six quotations appear in chapter 5, in the sermon on the mount. Five to six appear in the remaining material peculiar to Matthew.

The non-formula quotations are generally LXX in form or exhibit only minor variations from the LXX. Because, however, the non-formula quotations tend to be short and because the LXX always correctly renders the MT in the pertinent instances, dependence upon the MT cannot be altogether excluded.

The formula quotations are much more helpful. They display the same mixed text form as the allusions in the synoptic tradition. What is the explanation? There are two alternatives. Either (1) the formula quotations are redactional, in which case we must credit our evangelist with a knowledge of Hebrew, or (2) Matthew found the formula quotations in some source.

How does one make a decision on this matter? These are the most important facts. (1) Matthew's redactional expansions of Markan allusions and quotations show the same mixed text form as the formula quotations. (2) Some of the formula quotations are very closely connected with their Matthean context and it is very hard to imagine them as having had a pre-Matthean existence (e.g. 2.15, 18; 4.15–16; 8.17). (3) Those who argue for a source behind the formula quotations and deny Matthew's knowledge of Hebrew must explain why the evangelist has not assimilated these quotations to the LXX where possible. Matthew's high fidelity to his sources does not solve the problem, for the redactional expansions of allusions show the same mixed text form. (4) Some of the formula quotations contain seemingly redactional material (see e.g. Soares Prabhu, pp.101–4, on Mt 4.15–16). The conclusion seems inevitable: Matthew could read the OT in Hebrew.

Chart VI

POSSIBLE ALLUSIONS PECULIAR TO MATTHEW

OT text(s)	LXX	Against LXX	Mixture: LXX Against LXX
Gen 2.4; 5.1	1.1		
Gen 16.11; 17.19 Isa 7.14; 1 Kgs 13.2	1.21		
Ps 130.8		1.21 (possible dependence upon the MT)	
Num 23.7; 24.17	2.1–2		
Ps 72.10–11, 15 Isa 60.6	2.11		
Exod 2.15		2.13 (possible use of the MT)	
Exod 4.19	2.15		
Exod 4.19–20			2.20–1
Ps 37.11	5.5 (LXX = MT; τὴν γῆν agrees with the targum against the MT and LXX)		
Ps 24.3–4	5.8 (LXX = MT)		
Isa 51.7		5.11 (Gundry, OT, pp. 71–2, thinks the MT is presupposed)	

Chart VI—continued

OT text(s)	LXX	Against LXX	Mixture: LXX / Against LXX
Deut 24.1			5.32 (Jewish tradition is probably presupposed; see the commentary)
Isa 66.1		5.34 (the divergences from the LXX seem insignificant)	
Isa 66.1 Ps 48.3		5.35 (LXX = MT; the differences from the LXX are insignificant)	
Isa 50.6	5.39 (contrast Lk 6.29)		
Deut 18.13 Lev 19.2	5.48 (contrast Lk 6.36)		
Isa 26.20 2 Kgs 4.33		6.6 (the disagreement with the LXX may be of no consequence)	
Jer 14.14; 27.15	7.22		
Jer 50.6	10.6 (LXX = MT)		
Amos 3.5	10.29 (if this allusion stood in Q it was lost on Lk)		
Jer 31.25 Exod 33.14		11.28 (agreement with the MT)	
Jer 6.16			11.29
Jon 2.1	12.40 (LXX = MT)		

Chart VI—*continued*

OT text(s)	LXX	Against LXX	Mixture: LXX Against LXX
Zeph 1.3		13.41 (LXX omits; there may also be some influence from Ps 37.1 LXX)	
Dan 12.3			13.43 (cf. Theodotion)
Ps 62.13 Prov 24.12		16.27 (contrast Rom 2.6; 2 Tim 4.14; Rev 2.23; 20.12; 2 Clem. 11.6)	
Exod 34.29–30		17.2 (Ἔλαμψεν is nearer to the Hebrew than is the LXX's δεδόξασται)	
Lev 19.17	18.15 (contrast Lk 17.3)		
Deut 19.15; 17.6	18.16 (Gundry, *OT*, pp. 138–9, argues for dependence upon an Ur-Lucianic text)		
2 Sam 5.8	21.14		
Ps 1.3	21.41 (this is in Markan material; there are minor stylistic differences from the LXX)		
Ps 2.2	22.34 (there is no allusion in Mark)		
Exod 29.37		23.19 (Mt understands the indeterminate Hebrew to be a thing, the offering; the LXX, OT Peshitta, and targums (except the Old Palestinian) understand it to be a person, the priest)	
Dan 11.41		24.10 (agreement with the MT in σκανδαλισθήσονται, and with Theodotion in masculine πολλοί)	

Chart VI—*continued*

OT text(s)	LXX	Against LXX	Mixture: LXX Against LXX
Ps 104.27	24.45 (contrast Lk 12.42)		
Zech 14.5		25.31 (see Gundry, *OT*, p. 142; Mt may have worked with a Hebrew text different than our MT)	
Isa 58.7			25.35–6 (γυμνός and περιεβάλετε agree with the LXX; ἐδώκατέ μοι φαγεῖν does not)
Dan 12.2			25.46
Zech 11.12			26.15 (contrast Mk 14.11)
Isa 50.11		26.52 (agreement with the targum against MT and LXX)	
Deut 21.6-9 Sus 46	27.24		
Ps 69.22	27.34 (contrast Mk 15.23)		
Ps 22.9		27.43 (this is in Markan material; there are agreements with the OT Peshitta; dependence upon a Hebrew text seems probable)	

Chart VI—continued

OT text(s)	LXX	Against LXX	Mixture: LXX Against LXX
Zech 14.5 Ezek 37	27.51-3		
Isa 53.9		27.57 (contrast Mk 15.43; there is agreement with the MT)	
Dan 10.6; 7.9			28.3 (contrast Mk 16.5)
Ps 22.22		28.10 (cf. Heb 2.12)	
Dan 7.14; 4.14	28.18 (against Theodotion and MT)		
Dan 12.13	28.20		

Comments:

There are approximately fifty allusions peculiar to Matthew. They show the same mixed text form as the allusions in Mark and Luke and as the quotations unique to Matthew. Slightly over half depend upon the LXX. Seven show a mixture of agreement and disagreement with the LXX. The remainder are in non-LXX text forms and show contact with Theodotion (13.43; 24.10), with the targumim (5.5; 26.52), with the OT Peshitta (27.43), and with rabbinic tradition (5.32).

In several instances a Matthean verse with a parallel in Mark or Luke has an allusion while Mark and Luke do not: 22.34 = Mk 12.28; 26.15 = Mk 14.11; 27.34 = Mk 15.23; 27.43 = Mk 15.32; 27.57 = Mk 15.43; 28.3 = Mk 16.5; 5.11 = Lk 6.22; 5.32 = Lk 16.18; 5.39 = Lk 6.29; 10.29 = Lk 12.6; 18.15 = Lk 17.3; 24.45 = Lk 12.42. Of these twelve texts, precisely half have a pure LXX text form. Four could well show knowledge of a Hebrew text or Jewish tradition (5.11, 32; 27.43, 57). The same holds true for 1.21; 2.13; 11.28; 17.2; 23.19; 25.31; 26.52.

57

secondly, a close examination of our author's use of the OT strongly implies that he could read the OT in Hebrew (see section (7)). In our judgement, then, the signs point in one direction: the author of the First Gospel was a member of the Jewish people.

III. THE STRUCTURE OF MATTHEW[25]

The one incontestable fact about the structure of Matthew is this: the gospel's narrative portions follow a rough chronological

[25] Lit.: Allison, 'Structure'; Bacon; idem, 'The "Five Books" of Matthew against the Jews', *The Expositor* 15 (1918), pp. 56–66, translated and reprinted in Lange, *Matthäus*, pp. 41–51; D. Barr, 'The Drama of Matthew's Gospel', *TD* 24 (1976), pp. 349–59; D. R. Bauer, 'The Structure of Matthew's Gospel', unpublished Ph.D. Dissertation, Union Theological Seminary, Richmond, 1985; D. J. Clark and J. de Waard, 'Discourse Structure in Matthew's Gospel', *Scriptura* Special 1 (1982), pp. 1–97 (Matthew consists of three acts—1–9, 10–18, and 19–28); H. J. B. Combrink, 'The Structure of the Gospel of Matthew as Narrative', *TynBul* 34 (1983), pp. 61–90; Davies, *SSM*, pp. 14–25; M. S. Enslin, 'The Five Books of Matthew', *HTR* 24 (1931), pp. 67–97; Farrer; Cope (suggestions about the arrangement of portions of Matthew but not the whole); Fenton, pp. 14–17; idem, 'Inclusio and Chiasmus in Matthew', *Studia Evangelica* 1, TU 73, ed. F. L. Cross, Berlin, 1959, pp. 174–9; J. A. Findlay, 'The Book of Testimonies and the Structure of the First Gospel', *The Expositor* 20 (1920), pp. 388–400; Frankemölle, pp. 331–47; Gaechter, *Kunst*; D. W. Gooding, 'Structure littéraire de Matthieu XIII, 53 à XVIII, 35', *RB* 85 (1978), pp. 227–52; H. B. Green, 'The Structure of St. Matthew's Gospel', *Studia Evangelica* 4, TU 102, ed. F. L. Cross, Berlin, 1968, pp. 47–59; W. Hammer 'L'intention de la généalogie de Matthieu', *ETR* 55 (1980), pp. 305–6 (the genealogy is a table of contents); C. J. A. Hickling, 'Conflicting Motives in the Redaction of Matthew', *Studia Evangelica* 7, TU 126, ed. E. A. Livingstone, Berlin, 1982, pp. 247–60; J. C. Ingelaere, 'Structure de Matthieu et histoire du salut', *FV* 78 (1979), pp. 10–33; T. J. Keegan, 'Introductory Formulae for Matthean Discourses', *CBQ* 44 (1982), pp. 415–30; Kingsbury, *Structure*; idem, 'The Structure of Matthew's Gospel and his Concept of Salvation-History', *CBQ* 35 (1973), pp. 451–74; E. Krentz, 'The Extent of Matthew's Prologue', *JBL* 83 (1964), pp. 409–14, translated and reprinted in Lange, *Matthäus*, pp. 316–25; Kürzinger, 'Bergpredigt'; X. Léon-Dufour, 'Vers l' annonce de l' Église', in *Études*, pp. 231–54; C. H. Lohr, 'Oral Techniques in the Gospel of Matthew', *CBQ* 23 (1961), pp. 403–35; M. Meye Thompson, 'The Structure of Matthew', *Studia Biblica et Theologica* 12 (1982), pp. 195–238; J. Murphy-O'Connor, 'The Structure of Matthew XIV-XVII', *RB* 82 (1975), pp. 360–84; F. Neirynck, 'Le rédaction matthéenne et la structure du premier évangile', in de la Potterie, pp. 41–73; *Neotestamentica* 11, 16 (1977, 1982) (contributions from various authors on the structure of Matthew); Nolan, pp. 98–108; Ogawa, pp. 17–21; L. Ramaroson, 'La structure du premier évangile', *ScEs* 26 (1974), pp. 69–112; C. Rav, *Das Matthäus-Evangelium*, Stuttgart, 1976 (he divides Matthew into nine sections, corresponding to nine sections of the Lord's Prayer); R. Riesner, 'Der Aufbau der Reden im Matthäus-Evangelium', *TB* 9 (1978), pp. 172–82; A. Schieber, 'Konzentrik im Matthäusschluss', *Kairos* 19 (1977), pp. 286–307; Senior, *What are they saying?*, pp. 20–7; T. B. Slater, 'Notes on Matthew's Structure', *JBL* 99 (1980), p. 436; K. Smyth, 'The Structural Principle of Matthew's Gospel', *IBS* 4 (1982), pp. 207–20; D. O. Via, 'Structure, Christology and Ethics in Matthew', in *Orientation by Disorientation*, ed. R. A. Spencer, Pittsburgh, 1980, pp. 199–217; W. Wilkens, 'Die Komposition des Matthäus-evangeliums', *NTS* 31 (1985), pp. 24–38 (six major sections—1.1–4.22; 4.23–9.34; 9.35–11.24; 11.25–16.12; 16.13–21.46; 22.1–28.20).

sequence—birth, baptism, ministry in Galilee, journey to Jerusalem, passion, resurrection—, and into this sequence large sections of teaching material have regularly been inserted. Unfortunately, this single indubitable fact does not take us very far. It is consistent with a host of different structural analyses, including, most notably, these:

(1) B. W. Bacon's pentateuchal theory. The best-known and most influential modern hypothesis about Matthew's arrangement came from the Yale scholar, B. W. Bacon (*Studies*).[26] He divined in the First Gospel a counterpart to the Mosaic Torah. Just as the Torah consists of five books containing both narrative and discourse, so too does the gospel. The evangelist Matthew, a 'converted rabbi', a 'Christian legalist', ordered his sources so as to produce a new Pentateuch:

Preamble or Prologue:
1–2: The birth narrative

Book I: (a) 3.1–4.25: Narrative material
(b) 5.1–7.27: The sermon on the mount
   Formula: 7.28–9: '*And when Jesus finished these sayings*, the crowds were astonished at his teaching, for he taught them as one who had authority, and not as their scribes'.

Book II: (a) 8.1–9.35: Narrative material
(b) 9.36–10.42: Discourse on mission and martyrdom
   Formula: 11.1: '*And when Jesus had finished instructing his twelve disciples* . . .'.

Book III: (a) 11.2–12.50: Narrative and debate material
(b) 13.1–52: Teaching on the kingdom of Heaven
   Formula: 13.53: '*And when Jesus had finished these parables* . . .'.

Book IV: (a) 13.54–17.21: Narrative and debate material
(b) 17.22–18.35: Discourse on church administration
   Formula: 19.1: '*Now when Jesus had finished these sayings* . . .'.

Book V: (a) 19.2–22.46: Narrative and debate material
(b) 23.1–25.46: Discourse on eschatology: farewell address
   Formula: 26.1: '*When Jesus finished all these sayings*, he said to his disciples . . .'.

Epilogue: 26.3–28.20: From the last supper to the resurrection

[26] For scholars in general agreement with Bacon, see Kingsbury, *Structure*, p. 3, n. 13, to which add Meier, *Matthew*, pp. vii–viii. For critical discussion see Davies, *SSM*, pp. 14–25.

(2) C. H. Lohr's chiastic outline. The alternation between narrative and discourse—a feature emphasized by Bacon—can be set forth to generate a chiastic scheme. This is C. H. Lohr's analysis:[27]

1–4	Birth and beginnings	Narrative
5–7	Blessings, entering the kingdom	Discourse
8–9	Authority and invitation	Narrative
10	Mission discourse	Discourse
11–12	Rejection by this generation	Narrative
13	Parables of the kingdom	Discourse
14–17	Acknowledgement by disciples	Narrative
18	Community discourse	Discourse
19–22	Authority and invitation	Narrative
23–5	Woes, coming of kingdom	Discourse
26–8	Death and rebirth	Narrative

(3) J. D. Kingsbury's three-fold division. According to J. D. Kingsbury, the key to unlocking the structural plan of Matthew is the phrase repeated in 4.17 and 16.21: ἀπὸ τότε ἤρξατο ὁ Ἰησοῦς. This leads to a tripartite division—1.1–4.16: the person of Jesus Messiah; 4.17–16.20: the proclamation of Jesus Messiah; 16.21–28.20: the suffering, death, and resurrection of Jesus Messiah.[28]

(4) M. D. Goulder's lectionary hypothesis. Taking his cue from the divisions in Codex Alexandrinus, and boldly arguing that Matthew is a 'midrash' on Mark, M. D. Goulder avers that our gospel was composed in accordance with an annual weekly

---

[27] Lohr, 'Oral Techniques', p. 427. For other chiastic approaches see Combrink, 'Structure'; Fenton, 'Inclusio and Chiasmus'; Gaechter, *Kunst*; Green, 'Structure'; Schieber, 'Konzentrik'; Waetjen, pp. 33–4. Supportive of the chiastic approaches are the oft observed parallels between the beginning of Matthew and its conclusion. Frankemölle, pp. 321–25, for example, lists the following correlations between Mt 1–2 and 28:

1.23	the divine presence ('with')	28.20
1.2ff.; 2.1ff.	Gentiles	28.19
2.2, 8, 11	see + worship	28.17
1–2	kingship/authority	28.18
1.20, 24; 2.13, 19	angelic appearance	28.5
2.3	troubled	28.17
2.1, 9, 13, 19	and behold	28.20
1.2–17	genealogy/all the days	28.20
2	Father/Son/Holy Spirit	28.19

For a critical response to the chiastic analyses of Matthew see Meye Thompson, 'Structure', pp. 203–12.

[28] Cf. Lohmeyer, *Matthäus*, pp. 1, 64, 264; Stonehouse, *Witness*, pp. 129–31; Krentz, 'Prologue'; Slater, 'Structure'; Sabourin, 1–2. For Kingsbury's own work see n. 1. For critical discussion see on 3.1 and 4.17 and Meye Thompson, 'Structure', pp. 224–33.

lectionary cycle. More particularly, the Jewish festal year supplied the pattern by which the evangelist ordered his material. Matthew's structure is, therefore, liturgical in nature.[29]

(5) R. H. Gundry's indefinite plan. Robert Gundry is not alone in urging that 'we should avoid imposing an outline on Matthew'.[30] In his judgement, the first evangelist did not think in terms of any fixed arrangement, so no grand scheme is there to be unearthed.

Of the five options just introduced, we have the most sympathy for the first and the last. Matthew's gospel does feature five major discourses (so rightly Bacon).[31] At the same time, Matthew's architectonic grandeur does not appear to derive from a clear blue-print (so rightly Gundry). We, in any case, cannot claim to have found the blue-print, and we cannot credit anyone else with the discovery. The claimants just do not persuade. Thus, the chiastic analyses are too uncertain, Kingsbury's tripartite outline too precariously based, and Goulder's hypothesis too hypothetical (see ns. 27–9). But is that really the end of the matter?

Even if we cannot embrace Bacon's theory of five books comprising a new Torah, and even if we cannot accept any of the speculative chiastic constructions, the alternation in Matthew between narrative and discourse is firmly established, as is the number of major discourses, five (see n. 31). These two certainties constitute the foundation stone upon which all further discussion must build. But there is another foundation stone, one which has

[29] Goulder, passim. For discussion of Goulder's work see esp. L. Morris, 'The Gospels and the Jewish Lectionaries', in France 1, pp. 129–56. In addition to all the problems surrounding our ignorance of ancient Jewish liturgies (see Morris), Goulder's theory that Matthew is a midrash on Mark is problematic. Among other things, the claim that Matthew knew and used a collection of Paul's epistles (including Ephesians) is dubious. The birth date of the Pauline corpus is unknown and could easily be post-Matthean. Furthermore, when the synoptic tradition and the apostle's letters have material in common, Paul is usually closer to Luke than to Matthew; see D. C. Allison, 'The Pauline Epistles and the Synoptic Gospels: The Pattern of the Parallels', NTS 28 (1982), pp. 1–32; idem, 'Paul and the Missionary Discourse', ETL 61 (1985), pp. 369–75; W. O. Walker, Jr., 'Acts and the Pauline Corpus Reconsidered', JSNT 24 (1985), pp. 12–14. On Goulder's view of things this makes no sense, for he postulates that Matthew used Paul and that Luke in turn used Matthew. On the difficulty of using the textually marked 'divisions' in the gospels with any certainty, see Davies, COJ, pp. 67–95.

[30] Commentary, p. 10. Cf. Nolan, pp. 98–108.

[31] See esp. Keegan, 'Introductory Formulae'. Mt 23, which is clearly separate from the eschatological discourse in 24–5 (note the new beginning in 24.1), does not constitute a sixth discourse. It lacks the fixed formula found at the end of 5–7, 10, 13, 18, and 24–5. In addition, the chapter, which, despite 23.1, is less teaching material for the disciples than a complaint directly addressed to the Jewish leaders, is very like the debate material in certain narratives (cf. e.g. 12.25–37, 39–42). 23 is, accordingly, to be considered the extension and conclusion of the polemical narrative in 21–2.

been, if not rejected, then at the least ignored by students of Matthew. We refer to the pervasiveness of triads in the gospel.[32]

One of the authors of this commentary has elsewhere established that the sermon on the mount is, from first to last, constructed of triadic groupings (Allison, 'Structure'). His conclusions, which are upheld in this commentary, lead to the outline of Matthew's inaugural sermon shown on the following page. For discussion and defence of this analysis the reader is referred to Allison's article and to the appropriate sections of the present volume. What we wish to emphasize here is that, even if certain details of the proposal be doubted, the presence of triads cannot be gainsaid. 5.21–48 clearly divides itself into two groups, each with three members (see p. 504). 6.1–18 treats of three subjects: almsgiving, prayer, and fasting. And 6.19–7.12 contains two more triads, these in perfect parallelism (see pp. 625–7). Matthew, it is manifest, was thinking in triplicate as he composed his first discourse. (For a full list of the possible triads in Mt 5–7 see the chart, page 64.)

For our present purposes, the all-important observation is this: the sermon on the mount is not the only Matthean discourse to enshrine tripartite structures. Consider, for example, chapter 13. Up to 13.23 Matthew largely agrees with Mark. But from 13.24 on the First Evangelist goes his own way. And, as soon as he does, there are three consecutive parables of growth: 13.24–30, 31–2, 33. Each is introduced by this formula: ἄλλην παραβολήν + αὐτοῖς + ὡμοιώθη/ὁμοία ἐστὶν ἡ βασιλεία τῶν οὐρανῶν + dative. 13.24–33 is then followed by a small, interpretative discourse of Jesus (13.34–43), which is in turn succeeded by a second triadic grouping: 13.44, 45–6, 47–50. Once again there are three parables, and once again they all have similar introductions: (πάλιν) ὁμοία ἐστὶν ἡ βασιλεία τῶν οὐρανῶν + dative. The link between these three is all the closer as the formula in the second and third parables is prefaced by πάλιν. Matthew is counting as clearly as possible: ὁμοία ἐστίν, πάλιν ὁμοία ἐστίν, πάλιν ὁμοία ἐστίν: one, two, three.

Matters are very similar in Mt 24–5, the final discourse. Up to Mk 13.32 = Mt 24.36, a good measure of agreement obtains between the First and Second Gospels. But as soon as the two depart company, Matthew again starts manufacturing triads. There is first 24.37–42, the parable of who will be taken and who will be left on the day of the Son of man (cf. Lk 12.40; 17.26–7; 34–5; Mk 13.35). Secondly, there is 24.43–4, the parable of the

[32] The phenomenon was noted by Allen, p. lxv, but has yet to receive just treatment. Note also Moffatt, p. 257, and Luz 1, p. 20.

Introduction: the crowds on the mountain, 4.23–5.1
Nine(= 3 × 3) beatitudes for the people of God, 5.3–12
The task of the people of God in the world, 5.13–7.12
  (1) Summary statement: salt and light, 5.13–16
  (2) The three pillars, 5.17–7.12
    Introductory statement—the law and the prophets, 5.17
    A. Jesus and the Torah, 5.17–48
      1. General principles, 5.17–20
      2. Two triads of specific instruction, 5.21–48
        a. The first triad, 5.21–32
          i. On murder, 5.21–6
          ii. On adultery, 5.27–30
          iii. On divorce, 5.31–2
        b. The second triad, 5.33–48
          i. Do not swear, 5.33–7
          ii. Turn the other cheek, 5.38–42
          iii. Love your enemy, 5.43–8
    B. The Christian cult, 6.1–18
      1. General principle, 6.1
      2. A triad of specific instruction, 6.2–18
        a. Almsgiving, 6.2–4
        b. Prayer, 6.5–15
          i. How to pray: not as the 'hypocrites' in the synagogue, 6.5–6
          ii. How to pray, continued, 6.7–15
            (a) Not as the Gentiles, 6.7–8
            (b) The Lord's Prayer, 6.9–13
              (i) The address, 6.9b
              (ii) Three 'Thou' petitions, 6.9c–10
              (iii) Three 'we' petitions, 6.11–13
            (c) On forgiveness, 6.14–15
        c. Fasting, 6.16–18
    C. Social issues, 6.19–7.12
      1. God and mammon, 6.19–34
        a. A triad on true treasure, 6.19–24
          i. Exhortation: store up treasure in heaven, 6.19–21
          ii. Parable: the good eye, 6.22–3
          iii. Second parable: the two masters, 6.24
        b. Encouragement: 'Do not worry', 6.25–34
      2. On one's neighbour, 7.1–12
        a. A triad on attitude towards others, 7.1–6
          i. Exhortation: do not judge, 7.1–2
          ii. Parable: the log in the eye, 7.3–5
          iii. Second parable: pearls and swine, 7.6
        b. Encouragement: 'Ask', 7.7–11
    Concluding statement—the golden rule, the law and the prophets, 7.12
Three warnings, the prospect of eschatological judgement, 7.13–27
  The two ways, 7.13–14
    Beware of false prophets, 7.15–23
    The two builders, 7.24–7
Conclusion: the crowds and the mountain, 7.28–8.1

64

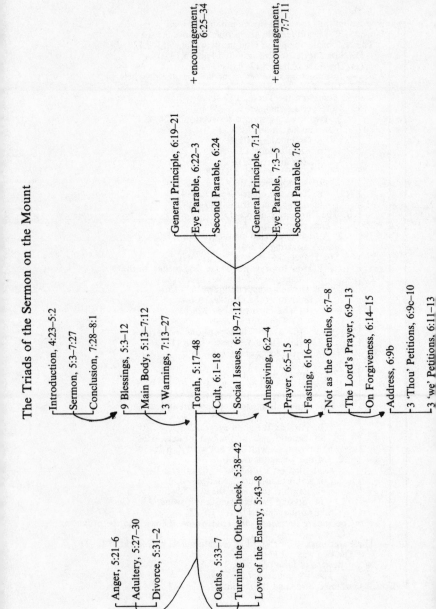

The Triads of the Sermon on the Mount

Introduction, 4:23–5:2
Sermon, 5:3–7:27
Conclusion, 7:28–8:1

9 Blessings, 5:3–12
Main Body, 5:13–7:12
3 Warnings, 7:13–27

Torah, 5:17–48
Cult, 6:1–18
Social Issues, 6:19–7:12

Anger, 5:21–6
Adultery, 5:27–30
Divorce, 5:31–2

Oaths, 5:33–7
Turning the Other Cheek, 5:38–42
Love of the Enemy, 5:43–8

Almsgiving, 6:2–4
Prayer, 6:5–15
Fasting, 6:16–8

Not as the Gentiles, 6:7–8
The Lord's Prayer, 6:9–13
On Forgiveness, 6:14–15

Address, 6:9b
3 'Thou' Petitions, 6:9c–10
3 'we' Petitions, 6:11–13

General Principle, 6:19–21
Eye Parable, 6:22–3
Second Parable, 6:24

General Principle, 7:1–2
Eye Parable, 7:3–5
Second Parable, 7:6

+ encouragement, 6:25–34

+ encouragement, 7:7–11

thief and householder (cf. Lk 12.39–40). Thirdly, there is 24.45–51, about the faithful and wise servant (cf. Lk 12.41–6). All three units are about being prepared for the Lord's return, and all three have closing sentences which speak of Jesus coming on a day or hour which is not expected or known. What then comes after 24.51? Chapter 25, which has *three* long eschatological parables— the parable of the ten virgins (25.1–13), the parable of the talents (25.14–30), and the parable of the sheep and goats (25.31–46).

When we turn to chapter 18, the discourse on community regulations, structural clues are harder to find. Nevertheless, the chapter naturally falls out into six paragraphs (cf. Huck-Greeven, pp. 141–7), the first three of which have to do with children or 'little ones', the second with the reconciliation of brothers:

On the 'little ones'

18.1–5	Who is the greatest?
18.6–9	On offences
18.10–14	The lost sheep

On the reconciliation of brothers

18.15–20	The sins of a brother
18.21–2	Forgiving seventy times seven
18.23–35	The parable of the unmerciful servant

Given the tripartite groupings in the other discourses so far examined, this result seems too striking to be dismissed as undesigned.

The remaining discourse to be considered is chapter ten. Does it too contain triads? The answer depends upon the position assigned to 10.26–31. This paragraph stands out in bold relief from the rest of the chapter. While all around are instructions, imperatives, and prophecies of hardship, 10.26–31 proffers encouragement. The key is the command, μὴ φοβεῖσθε. It really means, as the sequence shows, 'there is no need to fear'. The reason? The Father in heaven, who cares even for the sparrow, must care even more for the disciples of Jesus. Now in many ways 10.26–31 is very much like 6.25–34 and 7.7–11 (see on 10.26–31). The three paragraphs are intended to console and give heart. They break the rhythm of their respective contexts by intruding with good news: despite all apparent hardship, the heavenly Father will take care of his own. Further, our three paragraphs are centred around key words or phrases: do not be anxious (6.25, 31, 34), ask (7.7, 8, 9, 10, 11), do not fear (10.26, 28, 31). What is the significance of all this for the present discussion? 6.25–34 and 7.7–11 call attention to themselves not only by reason of their unique content: they also stand out because they break Matthew's

rule of three. In order to signal the different character and function
of 6.25–34 and 7.7–11, the evangelist has placed the two passages
outside his triadic framework. He has cleverly matched an
interruption in content with an interruption in structure. When
harsh imperatives give way momentarily to consolation, the triads
cease. We should like to propose that the same phenomenon exists
in chapter 10. That is, 10.26–31 is an interruption of both the
content and structure of chapter 10. The result is, as one might
have anticipated, the obvious creation of triads. 10.26–31 is
followed by three units and preceded by three units (cf. the RSV).

Setting/Introduction, 9.35–8
   The calling of the twelve, 10.1–4
      The commissioning—two triads, 10.5–42
         1. Missionary instructions, 10.5–15
         2. The messenger's fate, 10.16–23
         3. Disciples and teachers, 10.24–5
      Encouragement: do not fear, the Father cares, 10.26–31
         1. Confession and denial, 10.32–3
         2. Not peace but a sword, 10.34–9
         3. Receiving prophets and others, 10.40–2
Conclusion/Transition, 11.1

Our results so far may be succinctly summarized thus: the five
major Matthean discourses are largely made up of triads.[33] This
moves us to wonder how things stand with the narrative material.
Are threes to be found outside the discourses? Such would seem to
be the case. The gospel opens with a title containing three names
(1.1: Jesus, David, Abraham). This is followed by a genealogy
which the redactor has explicitly partitioned into three sections
(1.2–17). After the genealogy there are three infancy stories:
1.18–25 (the virginal conception), 2.1–12 (the visit of the magi),
2.13–23 (Herod and the infants).[34] Next comes chapter 3, which is
about John the Baptist and Jesus. It also has three parts. 3.1–6
introduces John. 3.7–12 gives us his words. And 3.13–17 recounts
the baptism of Jesus. Chapter 4 continues the story and the string

---

[33] This result seems to us to call into question H. D. Betz's theory that the sermon
on the mount is not from the final redactor of the First Gospel. The compositional
procedure that created the sermon on the mount is apparent in the other Matthean
discourses. While this does not prove that they were all conceived by the same
mind, it does make the supposition probable.

[34] We cannot follow those who would separate 1.18–25 from chapter 2 and join it
instead with 1.1–17, arguing that 1.1–25 answers the question of who Jesus is while
2.1–23 answers whence he is (so K. Stendahl, '*Quis et Unde*? An Analysis of
Mt 1–2', in Eltester, pp. 94–105). The theme of Jesus' identity remains prominent
in chapter 2—he is the true king (as opposed to Herod), he is the one like Moses (see
pp. 61–3), and he is God's 'son' (2.15). And the geographical orientation of chapter
2 continues through chapters 3 and 4. Cf. Luz 1, pp. 86–87.

of threes by telling us first about Jesus' temptation (4.1–11), secondly about Jesus' withdrawal to Galilee (4.12–17), and, thirdly, about the calling of four disciples (4.18–22). The sermon on the mount (4.23–7.29) follows.

What of 8.1–9.34, the narrative portion falling between the discourses in 5–7 and 10? It readily splits up into three separate sections: 8.1–22; 8.23–9.17; and 9.18–38. These three are near relatives in that each recounts first three miracle stories and then tacks on teaching material. Which is to say: 8.1–9.34 contains three sets of three:[35]

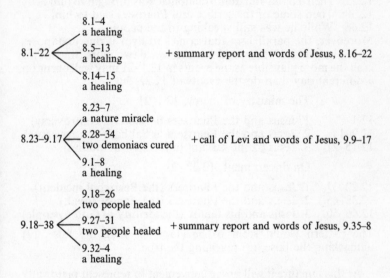

Note that the miracles in the central section, 8.23–9.17, take place either on the sea or on the sea shore. This further binds them together and serves to divide 8.1–9.38 into three parts.

Although the two chapters between 10 and 13 contain a diversity of material, certain thematic units seem obvious enough. Chapter 11, which apparently narrates the events of one day, opens with a tripartite unit about John the Baptist: 11.2–6 (John's question and Jesus' answer) + 11.7–15 (Jesus' estimate of John) + 11.16–19 ('this generation's' response to John and Jesus). After this there is 11.20–4, which records woes against three cities.

---

[35] There are, to be precise, ten *miracles* in Mt 8–9. But the two miracles in 9.18–26 are part of one indissoluble unit; hence there are only nine miracle *stories*; cf. Meier, *Matthew*, pp. 79–80.

Thirdly, there is 11.25–30, which consists of (1) a thanksgiving (11.25–6), (2) a christological declaration (11.27) and (3) an invitation to come to Jesus (11.28–30). Moving on to chapter 12, Matthew has done everything but give us a table of contents. The following six transitional phrases mark the six episodes of the chapter:

12.1: 'At that time Jesus went through the grainfields on the sabbath'.

12.9: 'And he went on from there, and entered their synagogue'.

12.15: 'Jesus, aware of this, withdrew from there'.

12.22: 'Then a blind and dumb demoniac was brought to him . . .'.

12.38: 'Then some of the scribes and Pharisees said to him . . .'.

12.46: 'While he was still speaking to the people . . .'.

Moreover, the parallelism that comes to light if one juxtaposes 12.1–21 with 12.22–50 would seem to reveal two more triads. This is all the more plausible as the events in 12.1–21 may well occur on a different day than do the events of 12.22–50.

> The ministry of mercy, 12.1–21

12.1–8	1. Jesus and the Pharisees (a Sabbath controversy)
12.9–14	2. Jesus and the Pharisees (a Sabbath controversy)
12.15–21	3. Jesus as the servant (a formula quotation)

> On discernment, 12.22–50

12.22–37	1. Jesus and the Pharisees (the Beelzebul incident)
12.38–45	2. Jesus and the Pharisees (the sign of Jonah)
12.46–50	3. Jesus and his family (the identity of God's people)

The pattern would seem to be (1) unmasking the false, (2) unmasking the false, (3) revealing the true.

At this juncture it will prove convenient to represent pictorially our conclusions on the structure of Mt 1–12. Leaving aside 1.1 (the book's title), 1.2–17 (the genealogy, which is not properly narrative material), and the discourses in 5–7, 10, and 13, the discussion leads to this outline:

I. Early history (1.18–4.22)
  1. The conception and infancy of Jesus (1.18–2.23)
    A. The virginal conception (1.18–25)
    B. The visit of the magi (2.1–12)
    C. The infants and Herod (2.13–23)
  2. John the Baptist and Jesus (3.1–17)
    A. John introduced and described (3.1–6)
    B. John's words (3.7–12)
    C. John baptizes Jesus (3.13–17)

3. The beginning of Jesus' ministry (4.1–22)
   A. The temptation (4.1–11)
   B. The return to Galilee (4.12–17)
   C. The calling of four disciples (4.18–22)
(The sermon on the mount, 4.23–7.29)

II. A cycle of nine miracle stories (8.1–9.34)
   1. Three miracles (8.1–15)
      A. The healing of a leper (8.1–4)
      B. The healing of a centurion's son (8.5–13)
      C. The healing of Peter's mother-in-law (8.14–15)
      Summary statement + teaching material (8.16–22)
   2. Three more miracles, on and around the sea (8.23–9.8)
      A. Jesus stills the storm (8.23–7)
      B. Jesus cures two demoniacs (8.28–34)
      C. Jesus heals a paralytic (9.1–8)
      The calling of Levi + teaching material (9.9–17)
   3. Three more miracles (9.18–31)
      A. The healing of two people (9.18–26)
      B. The healing of two blind men (9.27–31)
      C. The healing of a dumb demoniac (9.32–4)
      Summary statement + teaching material (9.35–8)
(Instructions to the twelve, 10.1–42)

III. Confrontation with 'this generation' (11.2–12.50)
   1. John, Jesus, and 'this generation' (11.2–30)
      A. The meaning of John and Jesus (11.2–19)
      B. The woes against three cities (11.20–4)
      C. The great invitation (11.25–30)
   2. The ministry of mercy (12.1–21)
      A. A sabbath controversy (12.1–8)
      B. A sabbath controversy (12.9–14)
      C. A formula quotation: Jesus as servant (12.15–21)
   3. On discernment (12.22–50)
      A. The Beelzebul controversy (12.22–37)
      B. The sign of Jonah (12.38–45)
      C. The family of Jesus (12.46–50)

The sight of such perfect symmetry ought, we freely confess, to cause some uneasiness. Is not our structural analysis too good to be true? Can the beautiful mathematical proportion really belong to the text? Is not the proposed scheme more likely to be an artificial construct imposed by an overactive imagination? We all know how to make out faces in the clouds, and it is possible to use the same talent to force an ancient text to fit a modern outline. It is, after all, a natural proclivity of the human mind to bring order out of chaos. Nonetheless, despite legitimate reservations we remain fairly confident that our structural analysis of Mt 1–12 is not a dubious and unjustified imposition. Two considerations in particular encourage us to think we are on the right track. To begin with, the Matthean proclivity for the triad just cannot be denied. The evangelist is explicit concerning his tripartite division of the genealogy, and the triadic arrangement of such units as 5.21–32, 33–48; 6.1–18; 13.24–33, 44–50; 24.37–51; and 25.1–46 is beyond all cavil. This cannot but spur one on to seek triads elsewhere. Secondly, try as we might, we have not been able to unearth significant triads in the narrative material after chapter 13. This is important because it indicates that triads cannot be pulled from the air at will or made to appear anywhere and everywhere. But this is not all. When one puts the entirety of Matthew beside the entirety of Mark, it becomes evident that, in their narrative portions, the two books travel the same road beginning with Mt 14.1 = Mk 6.14. This can best be appreciated by studying Allan Barr's *A Diagram of Synoptic Relationships*, Edinburgh, 1976. The Markan material in Mt 1–12 appears in different contexts in the first two gospels, and in Matthew that material is often combined with so-called Q passages. After Mt 14.1 this is no longer true. From here on a common order displays itself, and so-called Q material does not, with only a few insignificant exceptions, enter Matthew's narrative. The upshot is this: the point at which Matthew and Mark join up is precisely the point at which Matthew ceases to exhibit triadic groupings. The inference is inevitable. It being all but impossible to explain this circumstance on the Griesbach hypothesis (cf. pp. 102–3), this generalization commends itself: when Matthew composes on his own (as in 1–12 and the major discourses), he composes in triads; when he follows Mark (as he does from 14.1 on and in 13.1–23 and 24.1–36), the triads disappear.

Before we conclude, two questions pose themselves. The first is this: what is the significance of the fact that Matthew chose to arrange his material in threes? In our judgement, the correlation between the triadic structure of the sermon on the mount and a famous saying attributed to Simeon the Just (*m. 'Abot* 1.3) is highly significant. Matthew has fashioned his great sermon so that it corresponds with the three traditional pillars of Simeon (see pp. 134–5). For the rest, we have not been able to detect theological meaning in Matthew's compositional habit. That, however, is not the last word. We do have some idea why he arranged his material as he did. Jesus, it appears, liked threefold structures.[36] So did the

---

[36] See C. L. Mitton, 'Threefoldness in the Teaching of Jesus', *ExpT* 75 (1964), pp. 228–30.

author of the pre-Markan passion narrative,[37] and Mark himself.[38] The triad is also a conspicuous feature of *m.* '*Abot* 1, a chapter which purports to pass on in pithy summaries the wisdom of ancient teachers; see 1.1, 4, 5a, 6, 7, 9, 15, 16, 17, 18.[39] The data would seem to be sufficient to permit the conclusion that it was popular, in Matthew's environment, to group material in triads. Granted this, the practice probably had its origin in the oral world: thinking in threes aided the memory and maintained an ordered mind. But the convenient method of organizing oral matter could also be carried over into the writing process—as with Matthew, Mark, and the editor of *m.* '*Abot* 1.

The second question our results raise is: why does Matthew's gospel line up with Mark's only after 14.1? Why not follow Mark from the start? or restructure the Markan material all the way through? Gundry, who notices the relative lack of creativity in the last half of our gospel, speaks of 'editorial fatigue'.[40] Whether this conjecture about Matthew's lack of stamina is appropriate or not, how could one ever tell? Our evangelist's capacity for work and his compositional circumstances are hid from our eyes for ever. We should, however, call attention to a similar phenomenon in the enigmatic 11QTemple. Although the document as we have it is incomplete, there is a marked difference between the first fifty-one columns and those thereafter. The former are characterized by a good deal of rewriting: radical departures from the Pentateuch are frequent and sometimes extensive. The later columns, by contrast, largely reproduce the OT with only minor irregularities. Perhaps editorial fatigue accounts for this too. However that may be, we have a different explanation of the situation in Matthew. Granted the truth of the two-document hypothesis, Matthew has, by the time he arrives at 14.1, used up almost all of his Q material. And most of what is left he wishes to save for the discourses in 18 and 24–5. This means that, beginning with 14.1, the reservoir of tradition has been drained of much, and he can no longer draw from it as freely as before. It was relatively easy to be creative when all of Q and Mark were to hand. But when Q is almost exhausted, Matthew is forced to change his procedure. And up against the necessity occasioned by diminishing sources, he opts to get in line and follow his worthy predecessor, Mark.

To sum up, the most important conclusions about the structure

[37] See Pesch 2, pp. 19–20.

[38] See Neirynck, *Evangelica*, pp. 546–61; note also P. M. Beernaert, 'Structure littéraire et lecture théologique de Marc 14, 17–52', in Sabbe, pp. 241–67.

[39] For the triadic form of so much of '*Abot* see the translation of J. Neusner, *Torah from the Sages*, Chappaqua, 1984, pp. 23–4, 28–32, 39–44, 71–9, 99, 112–14, 136–41.

[40] *Commentary*, p. 10. Cf. Farrer, pp. 193–4.

of Matthew are these: there are five major discourses; the discourses and the narrative material are regularly alternated; from 14.1 on, Matthew's narrative faithfully follows Mark; the Matthean discourses and the narrative through chapter 12 feature triads. Unfortunately, these conclusions do not add up to any grand scheme. Leaving aside chronology, Matthew's arrangement has for its explanation no one structural principle. Sometimes our author has built triads, other times he has just been Mark's disciple. So despite its 'massive unity' (Moffatt, p. 244), Gundry is right: our gospel is 'structually mixed' (Gundry, *Commentary*, p. 11).

IV. LITERARY CHARACTERISTICS[41]

(1) *Introduction*. 'The Greek of the Gospel is not so full of Aramaisms and of harsh constructions due to translation from Aramaic as is the Greek of the Second Gospel. Nor, on the other hand, has it the Septuagintal and, so, Hebraic ring of the language of the Third Gospel. It has rather the lack of distinction which characterises any narrative compiled from previous sources by an editor who contents himself with dovetailing together rather than rewriting the sources before him.' These words of Allen (pp. lxxxv–lxxxvi) probably underestimate the redactor's contribution to his text as well as its Semitic flavour and furthermore fail to do justice to Matthew's ability to write on occasion accomplished Greek (e.g. 17.24–7; cf. Moule, *Birth*, pp. 278–80). Nevertheless, Allen was on target when he wrote of the First Gospel's 'lack of distinction', good or bad. By way of comparison, Luke is known for its impressive preface and its deliberate use of Septuagintisms; and the Second Gospel is characterised by the awkward reproduction of the Semitisms in its sources; and the book of Revelation is notorious for the author's failure to master what was for him a foreign language. But how does one succinctly characterise Matthew? C. F. D. Moule has ventured this evaluation: the evangelist 'was an educated person

[41] Lit.: Allen, pp. xiii–lxv, lxxxv–lxxxvii; Bultmann, *History*, pp. 351–59; Cope; E. von Dobschütz, 'Matthew as Rabbi and Catechist', in Stanton, pp. 19–29, also in German in Lange, *Matthäus*, pp. 52–64; F. V. Filson, 'Broken Patterns in the Gospel of Matthew', *JBL* 75 (1956), pp. 227–31, also in Lange, *Matthäus*, pp. 265–72; Gaechter, *Kunst*; Goulder; Hawkins; Lagrange, pp. lxxviii–cxvii; Luz 1, pp. 19–28, 31–56; Moule, *Birth*, pp. 276–80; Rigaux, *Testimony*, pp. 24–35; Sanders, *Tendencies*; W. Schenk, 'Das Präsens Historicum als Makrosyntaktisches Gliederungssignal im Matthäusevangelium', *NTS* 22 (1976), pp. 464–75; Shuler, pp. 13–35; G. Stanton, 'Matthew as a Creative Interpreter of the Sayings of Jesus', in Stuhlmacher, pp. 273–87; and N. Turner, in MHT 4, pp. 31–44. On the problems of Semitisms in the gospels see, in addition to Lagrange, Moule, and MHT 4, also Beyer; Black; Butler, pp. 147–56; Doudna; Fitzmyer, *Luke* 1, pp. 113–25; and Maloney.

commanding sound Greek with a considerable vocabulary; but he derived many Semitisms, and perhaps some Latin, from his sources; and he also had some feeling for Semitic 'atmosphere', occasionally introducing a Semitism on his own account, though less histrionically than Luke' (*Birth*, p. 280). This summary statement will do well enough, provided one adds that Matthew's 'feeling for Semitic "atmosphere" ' did not come solely from reading the LXX or other Hebraic Greek sources. The author himself knew Hebrew and probably Aramaic (see pp. 32–58). Furthermore, this means that some of the Semitisms in our gospel may not be as artificial as Moule seems to imply, that is, simply sprinkled for good religious effect (much as many religious moderns enjoy punctuating their Sunday speech with the archaic idiom of the King James Version). A number of the Semitisms could instead very well be the natural consequence of thinking in Hebrew or Aramaic. (N.B.: in agreeing with Moule that Matthew had a good command of the Greek language and that he did not have to struggle for the right word, we must hasten to add that this fact does not tell against Matthew's having been a Jew. One should remember that although Josephus' mother tongue was Aramaic, there are few Aramaisms in, for example, the *Jewish War*. Admittedly, Matthew did not have Josephus' education, but the point remains valid: the ability to write good Greek hardly entails that Greek be one's native language. Besides this, we should keep in mind the possibility that Matthew, perhaps a diaspora Jew, grew up in a bilingual or even trilingual environment (Greek, Hebrew, Aramaic).)

(2) *The treatment of Mark*. In his commentary on Matthew, W. C. Allen (pp. xiii–xl) examined in great detail the changes Matthew introduced into his Markan material. Because we agree with Allen concerning the priority of Mark, his observations remain for us valid, and nothing would be added by reproducing his lengthy tables. What follows, therefore, is simply a summary of his most important conclusions:

A. Matthew frequently abbreviates Mark's record (cf. Hawkins, pp. 158–60) by dropping details (e.g. from Mk 1.13, 20, 29; 3.17; 4.38; 5.13; 6.39–40; 9.3; 15.21), and he occasionally abbreviates a whole narrative or section (e.g. Mk 3.7–12; 5.1–43; 6.14–39; 9.14–29).

B. The First Evangelist tends to amplify Markan discourses by adding to them material taken from other sources (cf. e.g. Mt 10 with Mk 6, Mt 13 with Mk 4, Mt 24–5 with Mk 13).

C. Matthew more or less freely alters the order of Mark up to Mt 14.1 = Mk 6.14. After that point, our two gospels follow the same sequence.

D. Matthew has greatly lessened references to Jesus' emotion and ignorance (see pp. 104–5).

E. Our redactor has omitted sayings and incidents that apparently held no meaning for him. There are, for example, no parallels to Mk 9.49–50 ('everyone will be salted with fire', followed by two non-sequiturs); 11.16 ('and he would not permit anyone to carry a vessel through the temple'); and 14.51–2 (the flight of the naked young man). Matthew's faithfulness to his tradition did not include the passing on of incomprehensible matter.

F. Certain words and constructions characteristic of the Second Gospel are avoided or altered. καὶ εὐθύς, πάλιν, the adverbial πολλά, ὅτι following verbs of saying, ἤρξατο + infinitive, and εἶναι with participle—all found frequently in Mark—are often omitted. δέ frequently replaces καί, which makes for better Greek. Mark's ubiquitous historical present is altered about 130 times, and aorists are often substituted for imperfects, which is another improvement (e.g. Mk 1.32 = Mt 8.16; Mk 3.12 = Mt 12.16; Mk 6.20 = Mt 14.5). Redundancy is reduced (see the Matthean parallels to Mk 1.16, 32; 2.20; 6.35; 9.2; 13.19); double negatives sometimes—but not always—dropped (e.g. from Mk 1.44; 3.27; 9.8; 11.14); and the compound verb along with the same preposition irregularly avoided (cf. MHT 4, p. 39). Several times commonplace words supplant uncommon ones (see p. 105); awkward constructions are avoided (see on 3.16; 9.2; 13.8; 23, 32); and one preposition exchanged for another (see with the Matthean parallels Mk 1.10; 9.25; 12.14) or a different case employed after the same preposition (e.g. Mk 2.22 = Mt 9.16; Mk 4.1 = Mt 13.2; Mk 13.9 = Mt 10.18). The effect of all these changes is, in general, improvement upon Mark's narrative. The result may not be highly polished Greek, but the advance over Mark is undeniable (cf. Luz 1, p. 33).

(3) *Favourite words and expressions* (cf. Gundry, *Commentary*, pp. 641–49; Luz 1, pp. 35–53). J. C. Hawkins (pp. 3–10) listed ninety-five words and phrases which he took to be characteristic of Matthew. (He defined 'characteristic' so as to cover items of vocabulary which occur at least four times in Matthew and which are either not found in Mark or Luke or which are found in Matthew twice as often as in Mark and Luke put together). Here is his list:[42]

---

[42] Not all of the words in Hawkins' list are of great importance. Some e.g. are crowded together in sections which might be traditional (M). And still others are almost demanded by the subject matter.

	Matthew	Mark	Luke
ἀνατολή	5	0	2
ἀναχωρέω	10	1	0
ἀνομία	4	0	0
ἀποδίδωμι	18	1	8
ἀργύρια, plural	8	0	0
ἄρτι	7	0	0
ἀστήρ	5	1	0
βασιλεία τῶν οὐρανῶν	32	0	0
βρυγμὸς τῶν ὀδόντων	6	0	1
γάμος	8	0	2
γενηθήτω	5	0	0
γεννάω	45	1	4
γυμνός	4	2	0
δεῦτε	6	3	0
δικαιοσύνη	7	0	1
διψάω	5	0	0
διώκω	6	0	3
δῶρον	9	1	2
ἐγερθείς	8	0	1
εἷς = τις	4	1	0
ἐκεῖθεν in narrative	11	3	0
ἔνδυμα	7	0	1
ἔνοχος	5	2	0
ἐργάζομαι	4	1	1
ἐρρέθη	6	0	0
εὐώνυμος	5	2	0
ζιζάνιον	8	0	0
ἡγεμών	10	1	2
ἡμέρα κρίσεως	4	0	0
θυσιαστήριον	6	0	2
ἰδού after genitive absolute	11	0	1
κελεύω	7	0	1
κερδαίνω	6	1	1
κλαυθμός	7	0	1
κλέπτω	5	1	1
κρίσις	12	0	4
κρύπτω	7	0	3
λαμπάς	5	0	0
λεγόμενος, used with names	13	1	2
λυπέω	6	2	0
μάγος	4	0	0
μεταβαίνω	6	0	1
μετοικεσία	4	0	0
μισθός	10	1	3
μόνον, adverb	7	2	1
μωρός	6	0	0
ξένος	5	0	0
ὅθεν	4	0	1
ὀλιγόπιστος	4	0	1
ὀμνύω	13	2	1

ὁμοιόω	8	1	3
ὁμολογέω	4	0	2
ὄναρ	6	0	0
ὅπως	17	1	7
ὅρκος	4	1	1
ὅσος ἄν or ἐάν	6	2	1
παρθένος	4	0	2
παρουσία	4	0	0
Πατὴρ ἡμῶν, ὑμῶν, σου, αὐτῶν	20	1	3
Πατὴρ ὁ ἐν (τοῖς) οὐρανοῖς	13	1	0
Πατὴρ ὁ οὐράνιος	7	0	0
πληρόω, used of Scriptures	12	1	2
πονηρός, ὁ; πονηρόν, τό	5	0	0
πρόβατον	11	2	2
πρὸς τό + infinitive	5	1	1
προσέρχομαι	52	5	10
προσκυνέω	13	2	3
προσφέρω	14	3	4
ῥηθέν, and once ῥηθείς	13	0	0
Σαδδουκαῖοι	8	1	1
σαπρός	5	0	2
σεισμός	4	1	1
σκανδαλίζομαι ἐν	4	1	1
συλλέγω	7	0	1
συμβούλιον λαμβάνω	5	0	0
συμφέρει	4	0	0
συνάγω	24	5	6
σύνδουλος	5	0	0
συντέλεια	5	0	0
σφόδρα	7	1	1
τάλαντον	14	0	0
τάφος	6	0	0
τηρέω	6	1	0
τί σοι, or ὑμῖν, δοκεῖ;	6	0	0
τότε	90	6	15
τροφή	4	0	1
τυφλός used metaphorically	6	0	0
ὑποκριτής	13	1	3
ὕστερον	7	0	1
φαίνομαι	13	1	2
φονεύω	5	1	1
φρόνιμος	7	0	2
χρυσός	5	0	0
ὥρα with ἐκείνη in narrative	6	0	1
ὥσπερ	10	0	2

There are a number of other words and phrases that, while they do not satisfy Hawkins' criterion for 'characteristic', must nonetheless be regarded as very often editorial. These include the following:

	Matthew	Mark	Luke
ἀγρός	17	9	9
ἀδελφός	39	20	24
ἀκούω + ὅτι	9	3	0
ἄλλος	29	22	11
ἀμήν + γάρ	4	0	0
ἀμὴν (γάρ) λέγω ὑμῖν/σοι	30–1	13	6
ἀπέρχομαι	35	23	19
ἀπό, indicating material source	5	0	2
ἀπό, instrumental	5	0	0–1
ἀπό, temporal	23	2	12
ἀπό . . . ἕως	12	4	2
ἀποκρίνομαι (finite) + participle	6	1	1
ἀποκριθείς/-θέντες + finite verb	46	15	37
ἀπὸ τῆς ὥρας ἐκείνης	3	0	0
ἀπολύω (= divorce) + γυνή	5	1	1
ἁρπάζω	3	0	0
ἀφίημι	47	34	31
βάλλω	34	18	18
βάλλω εἰς τὴν θάλασσαν	4	1	0
βάλλω, of final judgement	9	2	1
βαπτιστής	7	2	3
βασιλεύς	22	12	11
γάρ	123–4	64	97
γέεννα	7	3	1
γεννήματα ἐχιδνῶν	3	0	1
γῆ	43	19	25
γίνομαι ὡς + noun or adjective	4	0	1
γινώσκω + accusative personal pronoun	3	0	0
γραμματεῖς καὶ Φαρισαῖοι	9	1	3
δεξιός	12	7	6
διά + genitive	26	10	13
διὰ τοῦτο	10	3	4
δίκαιος	17	2	11
δυνάμεις = 'miracles'	7	2	2
δύο	40	19	28
ἐάν	64	35	29
ἐὰν μή	10	6	3
ἐὰν/εἰ οὖν	7	0	4
ἐγείρω	36	19	18
ἐθνικός	3	0	0
εἰ + θέλω	6	2	1
εἷς, μία, ἕν	65	37	44
εἰς (τὴν) ζωήν	5	2	0
εἰς (τὸ) ὄνομα	5	0	0
ἐκβάλλω	28	18	20
ἐκεῖ	28	11	16
ἐκείνη + ὥρα	7	1	1
ἐκεῖνος	55	26	33
ἐκκλησία	3	0	0
ἐκτείνας τὴν χεῖρα	4	1	1

ἐλεέω	8	3	4
ἔμπροσθεν	18	2	10
ἔμπροσθεν τῶν ἀνθρώπων	5	0	1
ἐν ἐκείνῃ τῇ ὥρᾳ/ἐν τῇ ὥρᾳ ἐκείνῃ	4	1	1
ἐνθυμέομαι/ἐνθύμησις	4	0	0
ἐξέρχομαι, in nominative participle	18	9	11
ἔργον	6	2	2
ἐρῶ	30	2	19
ἑταῖρος	3	0	0
εὐθέως	11	0	6
ἕως	48	15	28
ἕως ἄν	10	3	3
ἤ	60	33	45
Ἠσαῖας	6	2	2
θέλω	42	24	28
θεραπεύω + πᾶς	5	0	0
θησαυρός	9	1	4
ἰδού	62	7	57
ἰδών/-όντες + δέ + direct object immediately followed by main verb with subject unexpressed	4	0	0
Ἰησοῦς	150	81	89
κάθημαι	19	11	13
κακῶς	7	4	2
καλός	21	11	9
καρπός	19	5	12
κατά + genitive	16	7	6
κόσμος	9	3	3
κρυπτός	5	1	2
λαμβάνω	53	20	22
λέγω, historical present + asyndeton	27	6	0
λέγω = 'call', with names	14	2	2
μαθητεύω	3	0	0
μαθητής	72–3	46	37
μαλακία	3	0	0
μᾶλλον	9	5	5
μέν . . . δέ	20	3	8
μετά + genitive	61	48	51
μεταμέλομαι	3	0	0
μὴ οὖν	5	0	0
ναί	9	1	4
ναός	9	3	4
νόσος	5	1	4
ὁ before Ἰησοῦς	100–3	52	40
ὁράω + μή	4	1	0
ὅς/ὅστις ἄν/ἐάν	37	21	20
ὅστις, ἥτις, ὅτι	29	4	21
οὐδέ	27	10	21
οὐκ/οὐδέποτε ἀνέγνωτε;	6	2	0
οὖν	57	3–5	31
οὐράνιος	7	0	1

οὐρανός	82	18	34
οὐρανός . . . γῆ	10	2	4–5
οὐρανός, after ἐν	33	5	6
οὐρανός, with πατήρ	13	1	1
οὗτος, resumptive	10	4	4
οὗτός ἐστιν	17	5	7
οὕτως	32	10	21
οὕτως + γάρ	3	0	0
ὄχλοι	30	1	13
πάλιν before finite verb	7	2	1
πάντα ταῦτα, or ταῦτα πάντα	12	4	4
παραδίδωμι	31	21	17
παραλαμβάνω	16	6	6
πᾶς + γάρ	6	2	2
πᾶς + οὖν	6	0	1
πατήρ + μου, of Jesus' Father	16	0	4
πεινάω καὶ διψάω	5	0	0
πέμψας	4	0	0
πλανάω	8	4	1
πληρόω	16	2	9
ποιέω + θέλημα + πατρός	3	0	0
πονηρός	26	2	13
πραΰς	3	0	0
πρεσβύτεροι τοῦ λαοῦ	4	0	0
πρός + articular infinitive	5	1	1
προσέχω + ἀπό	5	0	2
προσῆλθα(ο)ν + αὐτῷ οἱ μαθηταί (αὐτοῦ)	4	1	0
προφήτου/-ῶν, διὰ τοῦ/τῶν	13	0	1
πῦρ	12	4	7
σείω	3	0	0
στόμα	11	0	9
συναγωγή/-αί αὐτῶν/ὑμῶν	6	2	1
τέλειος	3	0	0
τυφλός	17	5	8
υἱὸς Δαυίδ	10	4	4
ὑμεῖς, nominative plural	30	10	20
ὑπὸ ἀνθρώπων	4	0	0
Φαρισαῖοι καὶ Σαδδουκαῖοι	5	0	0
φημί	16	6	8
ἔφη αὐτῷ/-οῖς + asyndeton	7	3	0
χωρέω	4	1	0
χριστός	16	7	12
ὡς καί	3	0	0
ὥστε	15	13	4–5

These statistics are not only helpful for determining to what extent a given passage has been moulded by the evangelist. They also highlight certain key Matthean themes. Thus many of the words have to do either with eschatology (βάλλω, of final judgement, βρυγμὸς τῶν ὀδόντων, γέεννα, εἰς (τὴν) ζωήν, ἡμέρα κρίσεως, κλαυθμός, κρίσις, μισθός, παρουσία, πῦρ, συντέλεια) or with ethics (ἀνομία, δίκαιος, δικαιοσύνη, καρπός, ποιέω + θέλημα + πατρός, πονηρός, πραΰς, τέλειος, ὑποκριτής). The statistics also reveal an interest in ecclesiology (ἀδελφός, εἰς (τὸ) ὄνομα, ἐκκλησία), in OT revelation ('Ησαῖας, πληρόω, προφήτου/-ῶν, διὰ τοῦ/τῶν), and in Davidic Christology and the issue of kingship (βασιλεία τῶν οὐρανῶν, βασιλεύς, ἡγεμών, υἱὸς Δαυίδ, χριστός). And that is not all. The frequency of conditional, explanatory, and inferential conjunctions (e.g. γάρ, ἐάν, ὅπως, οὖν, ὡς καί, ὥστε; cf. also διὰ τοῦτο) reflects an orderly mind and implies that Matthew was well versed in the art of argumentation.

(4) *Semitisms*. Like Mark and Luke, our gospel is full of Semitisms, words and constructions which are to be explained through the influence of Hebrew or Aramaic. These Semitisms derive from four different sources—the author's tradition (Mark, Q, M), his imitation of the LXX, his translation of the Hebrew OT, and his own Semitic mind-set. Unfortunately, given that Matthew knew Hebrew and probably also Aramaic (see below), it is in most cases quite impossible to pin down the origin of a particular Semitism. When, for instance, the evangelist wrote that the magi ἐχάρησαν χαρὰν μεγάλην σφόδρα (2.10), was this construction in his source? or was Matthew deliberately imitating the LXX? or was it just natural for one knowing a Semitic language so to express himself? The answer is not forthcoming. And this is typical. Most of the Matthean Semitisms appear in the LXX (which makes it possible to ascribe them to conscious or unconscious imitation), and many were no doubt to hand in his sources. We are, nevertheless, not always in the dark. There are a few non-LXX Semitisms that are presumably to be attributed directly to Matthew and to his knowledge of Hebrew or Aramaic. In the following list (which is representative rather than exhaustive), these are marked by an asterisk (*).

ἄγγελος = 'angel': Mt: 20; Mk: 6; Lk: 25. This usage is widespread in the LXX and in Hellenistic Jewish literature; and '*angĕlê* appears in the targumim.

ἄγγελος θεοῦ: Mt: 6; Mk: 0; Lk: 2. This is a good LXX expression.

ἄζυμα = 'the festival of unleavened bread': Mt: 1 (from Mark); Mk: 2; Lk: 2.

ἄλλα = εἰ μή ('except') : see 20.23 (from Mk 10.40). Compare Mk 4.22. The Aramaic '*illā* = 'but' and 'except'.

ἀμήν: Mt: 30–1; Mk: 13; Lk: 6. In the LXX ἀμήν translates the Hebrew '*āmēn*; but Matthew's predilection for placing it at the beginning of a sentence with λέγω + ὑμῖν/σοι derives from the Jesus tradition (Mk 3.28; 8.12; etc.).

τὸν ἀναβάντα πρῶτον ἰχθύν='the first fish drawn up': so 17.27. Wellhausen, *Einleitung*, p. 19, explained the active with passive meaning as an Aramaism.

ἀναστάς used inchoatively: the one instance of this in Matthew (9.9) is taken from Mark (2.14).

ἄνθρωπος: as a substitute for the indefinite pronominal adjective (cf. Hebrew *'îš*, Aramaic *nāš*): 7.9; 9.32 (redactional); 11.19; 12.11 (redactional); 13.28 (redactional?), 45, 52; 18.23; 21.33; 25.24; 27.32 (redactional), 57 (redactional); = τις: 8.9; 9.9 (redactional); 11.8; 12.43; 13.31, 44; 17.14 (redactional); 21.28; 22.11 (redactional). There are parallels in the LXX, in Mark, and in Luke (Gen 9.5; 41.33; Lev 21.9; Mk 1.23; 3.1; Lk 2.25; 5.18). Discussion in Black, pp. 106–7; Maloney, pp. 131–5. Moule (*Birth*, p 279) observes that in 13.28, 45, 52; 18.23; 20.1; 21.33; and 22.2 ἄνθρωπος is in apposition to a noun, and that all the verses belong to parables Matthew received, so the idiom could be traditional in all those places.

ἀποκριθεὶς εἶπεν: Mt: 42; Mk: 5; Lk: 26. This is a Septuagintism, often for *wayya'an . . . wayyō'mer* (Gen 18.27; 27.37; etc.). See on 3.15.

*ἀπὸ τῆς ὥρας ἐκείνης: this is redactional in 9.22; 15.28; 17.18 (cf. Jn 19.27). The phrase is rabbinic; see Schlatter, p. 318, and Black, pp. 108–12.

ἄρχομαι, pleonastic: it is difficult to decide whether the verb is ever truly pleonastic in the First Gospel. For discussion see J. W. Hunkin, 'Pleonastic ἄρχομαι in the New Testament', *JTS* 25 (1924), pp. 390–402.

αὕτη = τοῦτο: Mt 21.42 = Mk 12.11. αὕτη = *zō't* (see Ps 118.23).

βαριωνᾶς: see on 16.17.

*βασιλεία τῶν οὐρανῶν: Mt: 32; Mk: 0; Lk: 0. This phrase, which never appears in the LXX or in the NT outside Matthew, is to be judged a Semitism in view of rabbinic usage, *malkût šāmayim* (see SB 1, pp. 172–84).

Βεελζεβούλ: Mt: 3; Mk: 1; Lk: 3. See on 10.25.

βλέπεις εἰς πρόσωπον ἀνθρώπων: Mt 22.16 = Mk 12.14. This is probably a pure Semitism because it does not appear in the LXX (for the closest parallel see 1 Βασ 16.7). See Schlatter, p. 645.

γέεννα: Mt: 7; Mk: 3; Lk: 1. See on 5.22.

γραμματεύς = Jewish scribe: Mt: 22; Mk: 21; Lk: 14. See on 2.4.

διάβολος: Mt: 6; Mk: 0; Lk: 5. See on 4.1.

δοξάζω τὸν θεόν: Mt: 2 (9.8, from Mark; 15.31, redactional); Mk: 1; Lk: 8. Compare Exod 15.2; Judg 9.9; Dan 3.51.

ἐγερθείς + imperative: 2.13, 20. Compare *qûm* + imperative. The LXX typically translates the idiom with ἀναστάς + imperative (see on 2.13). Thus if 2.13 and 20 were to be judged redactional (an uncertain issue), we would have two plausible instances of pure Semitisms in redactional material.

ἔθνη = 'Gentiles': 4.15; 6.32; 10.5, 18; 12.18, 21; 20.19, 25. The usage is characteristic of Matthew and the disparaging reference in 6.32 would seem to imply a Jewish author (cf. 5.47; 6.7; 18.17). In the LXX τὰ ἔθνη often corresponds to *gôyim*.

εἰ preceding a direct question: 12.10 (redactional; contrast Mk 3.2); 19.3 (redactional; contrast Mk 10.2). Is this a Septuagintism? Compare Gen

17.17; 44.19; Amos 3.3–6; Lk 13.23; Acts 21.37; 22.25. The Hebrew *'im* can introduce both indirect and direct questions (cf. BDB, s.v., *'im*, 2).

εἰρήνη = *šālôm*: see on 10.13.

εἰς + accusative for the predicate accusative (cf. Hebrew *lĕ*): 21.46 (redactional; cf. 19.5 and 21.42, both reproducing OT texts). See BDF § 157.5 and compare Acts 7.21; 13.22, 47 (Luke imitating LXX style).

εἰς ... οὐ: 5.18 (redactional); 10.29 (Q? contrast Lk 12.6). Compare Mk 8.14 and see BDF § 302.2.

εἰς = τις: see 8.19 (redactional); 9.18 (redactional); 12.11 (contrast Lk 13.15); 18.24 (M); 19.16 (from Mark); 21.19 (redactional); 22.35 (from Mark); 26.51 (redactional); 26.69 (redactional); 27.48 (redactional). This usage, modelled on the Hebrew *'eḥād*, Aramaic *ḥad*, appears in Mk 9.17 and 10.17 as well as in the LXX: 1 Esdr 3.5; 4.18; 2 Macc 8.33. See BDF § 247.2.

εἰς, postpositioning of: see 5.18; 6.27; 9.18; 21.19—all perhaps redactional. Compare Gen 1.5, 9; Exod 10.19. Has the Septuagint here influenced Matthew?

ἐκ κοιλίας μητρός: Mt : 1 (19.12, M); Mk: 0; Lk: 1. Compare Judg 16.17 (A); Job 1.21; Ps 71.6; Isa 49.1 and the rabbinic texts cited by Schlatter, p. 573.

ἐν + dative of the articular infinitive: compare the Hebrew *bĕ* + infinitive. Instances from Matthew include 13.4 (from Mark), 25 (no parallel); 27.12 (no parallel). Compare Mk 4.4; Lk 1.8; 5.1. The construction, which often appears in the LXX, is evidently rare in Aramaic (although note 11QtgJob 30.2; 30.6, following the Hebrew).

ἐν ἐκείνῳ/-ῃ/-αις τῷ καιρῷ/τῇ ὥρᾳ/ταῖς ἡμέραις: often in all three synoptics and the LXX (cf. Exod 32.28; Deut 10.1, 8; Josh 24.33). See BDF § 459.3. Imitation of the LXX seems certain.

ἔμπροσθεν for simple dative or genitive, reflecting the Hebrew *lipnê*: 7.6 (M); 11.26 (Q); 18.14 (redactional). The usage is sufficiently rare in the LXX to make one wonder whether it can be a Septuagintism (but see Isa 45.1).

ἐπαίρειν τοὺς ὀφθαλμούς: Mt 17.8 (redactional). Compare Gen 13.10; 2 Βασ 18.24; 1 Chr 21.16 (all three for *nāśâ* + *'ênê*); Lk 6.20; 16.23; 18.13.

ἔρχομαι as auxilary: 9.18; 15.25; 26.43—all from Mark; 8.14; 9.10, 23; 13.4; 14.12; 16.13—all additions to Mark; 2.8, 9, 23; 4.13; 5.24; 18.31; 20.10; 27.64; 28.13—all M; 8.7; 12.44; 24.46; 25.27—all in Q material. In the LXX the verb, translating *hlk*, is often an auxiliary.

ἐχάρησαν χαρὰν μεγάλην σφόδρα: see on 2.10 and Schlatter, pp. 38–39.

*ηλι ηλι λεμα σαβαχθανι: so 27.46 diff. Mk 15.34. However we explain the differences between the First and Second Evangelists, Matthew obviously believed himself capable of improving upon the transliteration in his source.

καί + nominative pronoun, unstressed: e.g. 8.9; 10.16 (the first from Mark, the second from M); see BDF § 277.2.

καὶ ἐγένετο + finite verb: see 7.28; 8.26; 9.10; 11.1; 13.53; 19.1; 26.1—all redactional. The construction, which is frequent in Luke (Fitzmyer, *Luke* 1, p. 119), is a Septuagintism, as in Gen 19.29; Exod 12.41, 51; 17.11. See further Beyer, pp. 29–62.

καὶ ἰδού: see 3.16; 7.4; 8.29, 32, 34; 9.2, 20; 12.10, 41, 42; 17.3, 5; 19.16; 26.51; 28.2, 9, 20 (often redactional). This is a Septuagintism (Gen

15.17; 24.15; 28.12; Lev 13.5; etc., for *wĕhinnēh*). Luke has also scattered it throughout his gospel for good effect. It is absent from Mark.

καλεῖν + τὸ ὄνομα αὐτοῦ + proper name: 1.21, 23, 25 are instances from Matthew. Compare Lk 1.13, 31. The construction is a Septuagintism (see e.g. Gen 16.11; 25.26, for *qārā̕* + *šēm* + proper name).

κρύπτειν ἀπό: see 11.25 (Q). This is a Septuagintism with classical parallels (BDF § 155.3). Compare Gen 4.14; Deut 7.20; Job 13.20 (for *str* + *min*).

λαμβάνω, as auxiliary: 21.35, 39; 26.26, 27—from Mark; 13.31, 33—from Q; 17.27; 25.1; 27.24, 48, 59—all without parallel. One may detect here the influence of the Hebrew *lqḥ* or the Aramaic *nṣb*; or LXX precedent could be cited (e.g. Josh 2.4; 1 Βασ 6.7).

λέγω = 'saying' after verbs like 'ask' or 'answer': this occurs in every chapter of Matthew. Compare the LXX translation of the MT's omnipresent *lēᵓmōr*.

μαμωνᾶς: see on 6.24 (Q).

*Ναζωραῖος κληθήσεται: this redactional allusion to Scripture depends upon a Hebrew wordplay; see on 2.23.

ὁδόν as a preposition: see on 4.15.

ὀλιγόπιστος: Mt: 5; Mk: 0; Lk: 1. See on 6.30.

ὀμνύω + ἐν: see 5.34–36 and 23.16–22 (both M) (cf. Heb 3.11; 4.3; Rev 10.6). The LXX often has this for *šbʿ* + *bĕ* (e.g. Judg 21.7; Ps 89.35).

οὗ . . . resumptive pronoun: see 3.12 (Q). The resumptive pronoun after a relative also appears in 10.11 D and 18.20 D. One may detect in these cases the influence of the Hebrew *᾿ăšer* + noun with pronominal suffix (cf. Gen 1.11; 24.3; Deut 28.49; Ps 39.5).

οὐ (μή) . . . πᾶς: see 24.22 = Mk 13.20; Lk 1.37. Compare the Hebrew *lōᵓ* . . . *kōl* and note BDF § 302. The idiom appears in Gen 9.11 LXX. See Maloney, pp. 137–39.

οὐ μή: see 16.28; 24.2, 21, 34–35; 26.29, 35—all from Mark; 5.18, 20; 15.5; 16.22; 21.19—all without parallel; 5.26—Q. Although οὐ μή + the aorist subjunctive or the future indicative is classical, it is also very characteristic of the LXX. In the synoptics the mode of expression is confined to the sayings of Jesus and LXX quotations.

ὀφειλέτης = 'sinner'/ὀφείλημα = 'sin': see on 6.12. Matthew also has ὀφειλέτης in 18.24 (M).

πάλιν = 'then': see 4.8 (Luke has καί); 18.19 (M); 22.4 (M?). Compare the Aramaic *tûb*.

πᾶσα σάρξ = 'all living creatures' or 'all people': see 24.22 and compare the Hebrew *kol-bāśār*, as in Gen 6.17; Num 16.22; Jer 12.12. The LXX translates the expression literally.

πάσχα: Mt: 4; Mk: 5; Lk: 7.

*παρεκτὸς λόγου πορνείας: this seems to be the redactor's literal translation of *dĕbar ʿerwâ*. See on 5.32.

ποιεῖν καρπόν: see on 3.8 (Q). Mt: 11; Mk: 0; Lk: 5.

πορευθείς (pleonastic) + finite verb: e.g. 2.8 (M); 9.13 (redactional); 11.4 (Q); 18.12 (M); 25.16 (M); 28.19 (redactional). This is probably a Septuagintism (cf. Gen 27.13; 45.28).

προάγουσιν ὑμᾶς: if Jeremias, *Parables*, p. 125, n. 48, is correct in taking the sense to be exclusive—'they go, but you do not'—, then the phrase would qualify as an Aramaism (cf. *᾿qdm*). See 21.31.

πρὸ προσώπου + genitive: see Mt 11.10, in an LXX quotation (Exod 23.20; Mal 3.1).

πρός with accusative after a verb of speaking: this is redactional in 3.15. See Fitzmyer, *Luke* 1, p. 116.

πρὸς οὐδὲ ἓν ῥῆμα: see 27.14 (redactional). Compare Job 9.3 LXX (no parallel Hebrew construction).

*ῥαββεί: Mt: 4; Mk: 3; Lk: 0. In contrast with the rest of the NT, in 23.8 'rabbi' seems to reflect the late first-century rabbinic usage. See p. 135.

ῥακά: see on 5.22.

σάββατον: Mt: 11; Mk: 12; Lk: 20.

σὰρξ καὶ αἷμα: see 16.17 and compare Ecclus 14.18; 17.31. *bāśār wādām* is found abundantly in rabbinic texts (SB 1, pp. 730–31). See further J. Behm, *TWNT* 1, p. 171. Matthew is the only evangelist to use the expression.

σπλαγχνίζεσθαι: Mt: 5; Mk: 4; Lk: 3. See on 9.36.

τί = 'how': see 7.14 (M). Compare Lk 12.49. The Semitic *mah* explains this; see Black, pp. 121–24.

υἱός used figuratively: see 8.12 (redactional?); 9.15 (from Mark); 13.38 (redactional); 23.15 (M). Compare Gen 6.2; Deut 32.43; Ps 29.1; Lk 5.34; 10.6; 16.8.

υἱὸς τοῦ ἀνθρώπου: Mt: 30; Mk: 14; Lk: 25. See Excursus VII.

ὤφθη + dative = 'he appeared to': 17.3 (cf. Mk 9.4). This is a common Septuagintism (e.g. Gen 12.7; 26.2; Exod 3.2) as well as an early Christian credal element (cf. 1QapGen 22.27; Lk 24.34; 1 Cor 15.4–8).

active impersonal plurals: see 1.23 (M); 5.15 (cf. Mk 4.21; Lk 8.16; 11.33); 7.16 (redactional); 9.2 (cf. Mk 2.3); 9.17 (redactional). The Matthean texts could be credited to unliterary Greek (see Doudna, pp. 66–70), to imitation of the LXX (cf. 1 Βασ 27.5; 3 Βασ 1.2; Jer 16.6), or to a Semitic habit of thought.

asyndeton: Matthew has eliminated this from Mark thirty times; but twenty-one times he has added it (MHT 4, p. 31). Despite Matthew's fondness for particles, asyndeton remains a prominent feature of his Greek. Especially striking is his use of asyndetic λέγει/λέγουσιν/ἔφη; see Black, pp. 55–61.

anacoluthon after interrogative clause: see 7.9–10 (contrast Lk 11.11) and BDF § 469.

anacoluthon after πᾶς: see 7.12 (redactional); 10.32 (cf. Lk 12.8); 12.36 (redactional); 13.19 (redactional). See Schlatter, pp. 247–48, and BDF § 466.3.

*genitive of quality: see 5.22 (γέενναν τοῦ πυρός—probably redactional); 18.9 (the same, redactional). See BDF § 165. Compare Dan 3.6; 3 Βασ 21.31; Lk 16.8; 18.6; Acts 9.15. In discussing the instances in Luke-Acts, Fitzmyer, *Luke* 1, p. 124, confesses that 'since it is difficult in this case to insist on the influence of the LXX, perhaps a "Semitic" genitive should be admitted'.

*genitive + substantivized verbal adjective, of agent with the passive: see 11.11 (γεννητοῖς γυναικῶν); 24.31 (ἐκλεκτοὶ αὐτοῦ); 25.34 (οἱ εὐλογημένοι τοῦ πατρός). The first is from Q, the second is redactional, the third is in M material. See BDF § 183.

partitive genitive as subject or object: see 23.34(Q). Although there are a few classical parallels, the frequency of the usage in the NT is perhaps due to LXX influence (so BDF § 164.2; but note Doudna, pp. 17–18). Compare 1 Βασ 14.45; 2 Βασ 14.11; 4 Βασ 10.23.

positive for comparative or superlative: see 5.19; 11.20 (redactional); 18.8, 9 (from Mark); 21.8 (contrast Mk 11.8); 22.36 (redactional). Although one may cite classical and especially Hellenistic parallels (BDF §§ 60–1), the construct is particularly frequent in Semitic languages, which do not provide for degree at all; compare Gen 49.12; Exod 18.11; Num 12.3; Lam 4.9; etc.

proleptic personal pronoun: 3.4 (redactional): αὐτὸς δὲ ὁ Ἰωάννης. Compare Mk 6.17; 12.36, 37. See Black, pp. 96–100, who finds in this definite Aramaic influence.

*'You will call his name Jesus, for he shall save his people from their sins': this sentence involves a Hebrew wordplay. See on 1.21.

How does one sum up the nature of the Semitisms in Matthew? The grammarian Turner has expressed himself on this issue as follows: 'It would seem . . . that there is very little to choose between the relative Semitism of Mark's and Matthew's style. Neither Matthew nor Luke discloses any significant tendency to avoid the Semitisms of Mark. Mark is not more likely to be an Aramaic translation than Matthew or Luke . . .' (MHT 4, p. 37). These words seem to us fair. Although Matthew's Greek is much better than Mark's, it is not that much less Semitic. Indeed, in some ways (e.g. asyndetic λέγει, the preference for direct speech, increased parallelism, and love of the genitive) the First Gospel is even more Semitic than its less polished source (see further Goulder, pp. 116–21). Furthermore, certain words and expressions, not to mention the formula quotations, strongly imply a knowledge of more than the Greek language. The Matthean Semitisms, therefore, should not be dismissed as affected ornamentation or Septuagintisms. Quite the contrary: they presumably reflect the evangelist's own style of thought.

(5) *The penchant for numbers* (cf. Hawkins, pp. 163–67; Lagrange, pp. lxxxiv–lxxxvi). The First Gospel begins with our evangelist counting: 'So all the generations from Abraham to David were fourteen generations, and from David to the deportation to Babylon fourteen generations, and from the deportation to Babylon to the Christ fourteen generations' (1.17). Moreover, if we are anywhere near the mark in our analysis of Matthew's structure, triads feature prominently in it (see pp. 62–72). It would appear, then, that Matthew was strongly inclined to arrange his thoughts around numerals. In this he would appear to be thoroughly Jewish. The canons of classical rhetoric, as far as we are aware, hardly encouraged a compositional procedure based upon numerical groupings; and the structuring of material according to quantitative concerns would probably have struck the learned Greek or Roman as a highly artificial business.

Not so the learned Jew. Rabbinic texts are full of numbers and numerical schemes. The Mishnah in particular is memorable in this regard. *m.'Abot* 1, for instance, contains many triads, while in *m.'Abot* 5, the numbers ten, seven, and four are named again and again. And *m. Kelim* 24 contains triad after triad—seventeen triads in all. Matthew's penchant for numbers would thus appear to place him squarely in the Jewish world, and perhaps specifically in the world of the rabbis.

a. The triad (cf. Allen, p. lxv; Moffatt, p. 257; Luz 1, p. 20). We have already, in the discussion on Matthew's structure, called attention to many of the Matthean triads, especially those in the five major discourses. The following list, therefore, which includes examples of greater and lesser interest, takes no account of the triads in chapters 5–7, 10, 13, 18, and 24–25.

1.1 three names
1.2–17 three fourteens
1.18–2.23 three stories (1.18–25; 2.1–12, 13–15)
1.18–2.23 three angelic appearances
2.11 three gifts
3.1–17 three sections (3.1–6, 7–12, 13–17)
4.1–22 three stories (4.1–11, 12–17, 18–22)
4.1–11 three temptations (so already Q; cf. Lk 4.1–13)
8.1–9.38 three sections (8.1–22; 8.23–9.17; 9.18–38)
8.1–17 three miracle stories
8.23–9.8 three miracle stories
9.18–34 three miracle stories
11.2–30 three sections (11.2–19, 20–24, 25–30)
11.1–19 three sections (11.2–6, 7–15, 16–19)
11.7–9 three questions with 'go out' + 'to see' (from Q; see Lk 7.24–26)
11.20–24 woes against three cities
11.25–30 three sections (11.25–26, 27, 28–30)
12.1–21 three sections (12.1–8, 9–14, 15–21)
12.22–46 three sections (12.22–37, 38–45, 46–50)
15.21–27 three pleas for help, 'Lord' repeated thrice (contrast Mk 7.24–30)
16.21 three groups (from Mk 8.31)
16.24–28 three γάρ clauses (contrast Mk 8.34–38)
17.1 three disciples (from Mk 9.2)
17.4 three booths (from Mk 9.5)
17.22–23 three actions (from Mk 9.31)
17.25 three questions (no parallel; in M material)
19.12 three classes of eunuchs
20.19 three punishments (contrast Mk 10.34)
21.9 three cries (contrast Mk 11.9–10)
21.28–22.14 three parables (cf. Mk 12.1)
22.15–40 three questions for Jesus (from Mk 12.13–34)
23.8–10 three warnings
23.11 three declarations
23.20–22 three oaths

23.23 three spices and vegetables
23.23 justice, mercy, faith, three weightier matters
26.36–46 three prayers (from Mk 14.32–42)
26.57–68 the high priest speaks three times (cf. Mk 14.55–65)
26.67–27.44 three scenes of mockery (from Mk 14.65–15.32)
26.69–75 three denials of Peter (from Mk 14.53–72)
27.45 three hours (from Mk 15.33)
27.56 three women (from Mk 15.40)
27.55–28.10 three scenes with women (cf. Mk 15.40–16.8)
27.62–66; 28.4, 11–15 three scenes with Roman soldiers (M)

b. The number two. At least three times the redactor has multiplied a Markan figure by two. In Mt 8.28 one demoniac (so Mk 5.2) becomes two demoniacs. Similarly, the blind man of Mk 10.46–52 becomes two blind men in Mt 20.29–34; and in Mt 21.1–11 an ass (so Mk 11.1–10) becomes an ass and her foal. Note also that the redactional creation in 9.27–30 (cf. Mk 10.46–52) features two blind men; and that in 26.57–68 Mark's 'some stood up and bore false witness against him' (14.57) is turned into 'at last two came forward . . .' . Other instances—not all of them significant—of the number two in the First Gospel include the following: 2.16 ('two years old and younger', M); 4.18–20 (two brothers, from Mark); 4.21 (two brothers, from Mark); 6.24 (two masters, from Q); 10.10 (two coats, from Q); 14.17, 19 (two fish, from Mark); 18.8–9 (two hands, two feet, two eyes, from Mark); 18.16–20 (two or three witnesses, M); 20.21, 24 (two sons, redactional; cf. Mk 10.37, 41); 21.1 (two disciples, from Mark); 21.28 (two sons, M); 22.40 (two commandments, redactional; cf. Mk 12.28–33); 24.40–41 (two men in a field, two women at a mill, from Q); 25.14–22 (two talents, M); 26.2 (two days, from Mark); 27.38 (two thieves, from Mark).

c. The number seven. Although this number occurs several times in the First Gospel, it is usually from the tradition, and Matthew does not lend it any significance. See 12.45 (seven spirits, from Q); 15.34–36 (seven loaves, from Mark); 15.37 (seven baskets, from Mark); 16.10 (seven loaves, from Mark); 18.21–22 (seven times, M); 22.25–28 (seven brothers, from Mark); 23.13–33 (seven woes, M? redactional?).

d. Gematria. The key to understanding the emphasis placed upon the number fourteen in 1.2–17 is, in all probability, gematria: the letters in *dwd* (David) add up to fourteen. See further pp. 161–5.

(6) *Thematic thinking* (cf. Luz 1, pp. 19–20). To judge from Mark and Luke, various sayings attributed to Jesus were at one time brought together because they shared common words. For instance, while it is impossible to discern any thematic unity in Mk 9.47–50, the verses do have a catchword connexion—47–48: fire/49: salted with fire/50a: salt/50b: salt. Similarly, in Lk 11.33–36 the saying about lighting a lamp is followed by the saying about the eye being the lamp of the body—and this only because of the common word, lamp. When we turn to Matthew, however, these types of word associations are hardly if ever to be found. In the First Gospel every single saying is in its proper thematic place. This means that Matthew has often rearranged his source materal

so as to bring together sayings on the same theme. And this, incidentally, largely explains why it is so easy to summarize so succinctly the subject matter of the major Matthean discourses— 5.7: law, cult, social attitudes and obligations; 10: missionary instructions; 13: parables on the kingdom of God; 18: community regulations; 24–25: eschatological teaching.

(7) *Repetition*. Matthew, so far from being averse to repeating himself, seems positively to delight in the practice.[43]

a. Repetition of formulas in close succession.
1.2–16: Abraham begat Isaac,
Isaac begat Jacob,
Jacob begat Judah

.
.
.

(thirty-nine times in a row)

5.2–11: Blessed are the poor in spirit, for . . .
Blessed are those who mourn, for . . .
Blessed are the meek, for . . .

.
.
.

(in all nine beatitudes, the last in a slightly different form)

5.21–48: You have heard that it was said to the men of old . . .
but I say to you . . .
You have heard that it was said . . .
but I say to you
It was said . . .
but I say to you . . .
Again, you have heard that it was said to the men of old . . .
but I say to you . . .
You have heard that it was said . . .
but I say to you . . .
You have heard that it was said . . .
but I say to you . . .

6.2–18: When you do x,
do not do y,
as the hypocrites do.
Truly I say to you, they have their reward.

[43] This gives Matthew a special affinity with the OT legal and wisdom traditions. It also harmonizes well with the long-running supposition, to which we are attracted, that Matthew was not a stranger to rabbinic studies. M. Buber says somewhere that repetition was a way of underlining before there was a printing press.

But when you do x,
do z,
and your Father who sees (is) in secret will reward you.
(repeated three times)

13.24–33: Another parable he set before them saying . . .
Another parable he set before them saying . . .
Another parable he spoke to them . . .

13.44–47: The kingdom of heaven is like + dative
Again, the kingdom of heaven is like + dative
Again, the kingdom of heaven is like + dative

23.1–36: Woe to you, scribes and Pharisees, hypocrites . . .
Woe to you, blind guides . . .
Woe to you, scribes and Pharisees, hypocrites . . .
.
.
.
(repeated in all seven times)

b. Repetition of formulas throughout the gospel. These include:
the introduction to the formula quotations; see 1.22; (2.5–6;) 2.15, 17, 23;
4.14; 8.17; 12.17; 13.35; 21.4; (26.54, 56;) 27.9.
'And it happened when Jesus had finished these sayings' (or: parables); see
7.28; 11.1; 13.53; 19.1; 26.1 (at the end of the five major discourses).
the stereotyped passion predictions; see 16.21; 17.22–23; 20.18–19 (from
Mark); compare 17.12; 26.1–2.
the summarizing accounts of Jesus' ministry; see 4.23–25; 8.16–17;
9.35–38; 12.15–16; 14.13–14; 14.34–36; 15.29–31; 19.1–2; 21.14–16.
These have a great deal of vocabulary in common; see Gerhardsson,
Acts, pp. 11–37.
ἀναβαίνω + εἰς τὸ ὄρος, of Jesus; see 5.1; 14.23; 15.29 (Mk: 1; Lk: 1).
ἀποκριθεὶς (δὲ) ὁ Ἰησοῦς εἶπεν αὐτῷ/οἷς; see 3.15; 11.4; 15.28; 16.17; 21.21,
24; 22.29; 24.4.
'there will be weeping and gnashing of teeth'; see 8.12; 13.42, 50; 22.13;
24.51; 25.30 (Mk: 0; Lk: 1).
c. Twofold repetition of similar phrases or constructions in close
proximity.
2.22–23: ἀκούσας δὲ ὅτι
ἀνεχώρησεν εἰς τὰ μέρη τῆς Γαλιλαίας
ἐλθὼν κατῴκησεν εἰς πόλιν λεγομένην Ναζαρέτ
ὅπως πληρωθῇ τὸ ῥηθέν
4.14: ἀκούσας δὲ ὅτι
ἀνεχώρηεν εἰς τὴν Γαλιλαίαν
ἐλθὼν κατῴκησεν εἰς Καφαρναούμ
ἵνα πληρωθῇ τὸ ῥηθέν

3.1: παραγίνεται Ἰωάννης
3.13: παραγίνεται ὁ Ἰησοῦς

4.18: 'They, immediately leaving . . . followed him'.
4.20: 'They, immediately leaving . . . followed him'.

5.13: 'You are the salt of the earth'.
5.14: 'You are the light of the world'.

5.18: λέγω ὑμῖν + ἄν + οὐ μή
5.20: λέγω ὑμῖν + ἐάν + οὐ μή

5.29: 'If your right eye causes you to sin . . .'
5.30: 'If your right hand causes you to sin . . .'

5.39: ὅστις + σέ + verb + object + verb introducing command
5.41: ὅστις + σέ + verb + object + verb introducing command

5.40: τῷ + participle + σοί + imperative.
5.42: τῷ + participle + σέ + imperative

8.1: καταβάντος δὲ αὐτοῦ
8.5: εἰσελθόντος δὲ αὐτοῦ

9.26: καὶ ἐξῆλθεν ἡ φήμη αὕτη εἰς ὅλην τὴν γῆν ἐκείνην
9.31: οἱ δὲ ἐξελθόντες διεφήμισαν αὐτὸν ἐν ὅλῃ τῇ γῇ ἐκείνῃ

11.25: 'in that hour'
12.1: 'in that hour'

15.21: καὶ ἐξελθὼν ἐκεῖθεν ὁ Ἰησοῦς + verb + geographical notice
15.29: καὶ μεταβὰς ἐκεῖθεν ὁ Ἰησοῦς + verb + geographical notice

17.22: συστρεφομένων δὲ αὐτῶν + geographical notice
17.24 ἐλθόντων δὲ αὐτῶν + geographical notice

24.42: 'Watch then, because you do not know in what day . . .'
25.13: 'Watch then, because you do not know the day . . .'

d. Other instances of twofold or threefold repetition of similar or identical words or phrases not in close proximity, excluding doublets:

3.17: 'And behold a voice from the heavens saying,
This is my beloved son, in whom I am well pleased'.
17.5: 'And behold a voice from the cloud saying,
This is my beloved son, in whom I am well pleased . . .'

3.7: 'brood of vipers'
23.33: 'brood of vipers'

4.10: ὕπαγε σατανᾶ
16.23: ὕπαγε . . . σατανᾶ

4.17: 'From that time Jesus began to . . .'
16.21: 'From that time Jesus began to . . .'

5.17: 'Think not that I came to . . .; I came not to . . . but to . . .'
10.34: 'Think not that I came to . . .; I came not to . . . but to . . .'

5.32: παρεκτὸς λόγου πορνείας
19.9: μὴ ἐπὶ πορνείας

7.12: 'This is the law and the prophets'
22.40: 'On these depend all the law and the prophets'

7.21: 'he who does the will of my Father in heaven'

12.50: 'whoever does the will of my Father in heaven'

8.2: 'Behold, a leper came to him and knelt before him, saying . . .'
9.18: 'Behold, a ruler came in and knelt before him, saying . . .'

8.12: 'the sons of the kingdom'
13.38: 'the sons of the kingdom'

9.27: 'Have mercy upon us, Son of David'
15.22: 'Have mercy upon me, O Lord, Son of David'
20.29, 31: 'Have mercy on us, Son of David'/'Lord, have mercy on us, Son of David'

9.4: 'Knowing their thoughts he said . . .'
12.25: 'Knowing their thoughts he said . . .'

9.20: 'the fringe of his garment'
14.36: 'the fringe of his garment'

9.36: 'see' + 'the crowds' + ἐσπλαγχνίσθη
14.14: 'see' + 'the crowd' + ἐσπλαγχνίσθη

10.6: 'the lost sheep of the house of Israel'
15.24: 'the lost sheep of the house of Israel'

12.39: 'A wicked and adulterous generation'
16.4: 'A wicked and adulterous generation'

13.43: 'they will shine like the sun'
17.2: 'shone like the sun'

14.21: 'And those who ate were about 5,000 men, besides women and children'
15.38: 'Those who ate were 4,000 men, besides women and children'

14.33: 'Truly you are the Son of God'
27.54: 'Truly this man was the Son of God'

16.12: 'Then they understood that . . .'
17.13: 'Then the disciples understood that . . .'

16.16: 'You are the Christ, the Son of the living God'
26.63: 'if you are the Christ, the Son of God'

17.6: 'When disciples heard this they . . . were filled with awe'
27.54: 'When the centurion and those with him . . . saw . . . they were filled with awe'

21.36: 'Again he sent other servants'
22.4: 'Again he sent other servants'

e. Doublets due to the overlapping of sources. (Matthew tends to harmonize these more than Luke.)

10.19–20; 24.9, 13: eschatological persecution on account of Jesus (cf. Mk 13.11; Lk 12.11–12)
10.32; 16.27: the Son of man and eschatological retribution (cf. Mk 8.38; Lk 12.8–9)

10.38–39; 16.24–25: following Jesus and denying self (cf. Mk 8.34–35; Lk 14.27; 17.33)

10.40; 18.5: 'he who receives . . . receives me . . .' (cf. Mk 9.37; Lk 10.16)

11.15; 13.9: 'He who has ears to hear, let him hear' (cf. Mk 4.9, 23; Lk 14.35)

12.38–42; 16.1–4: the sign of Jonah (cf. Mk 8.11–12; Lk 11.16, 29–30)

13.12; 25.29: 'He who has to him shall be given' (cf. Mk 4.25; Lk 19.26)

17.20; 21.21: 'If you have faith . . .' (cf. Mk 11.23; Lk 17.6)

f. Doublets due to Matthean redaction.

3.2; 4.17: 'Repent, for the kingdom of heaven is at hand'

3.10; 7.19: 'Every tree that does not bear good fruit . . .'

5.29–30; 18.8–9: On offences

5.32; 19.9: Jesus' saying on divorce

7.16, 20: 'You will know them by their fruits'

9.13; 12.7: mercy, not sacrifice

10.6; 15.24: the lost sheep of the house of Israel

10.15; 11.24: 'It will be more tolerable on the day of judgement . . .'

10.17–22; 24.9–14: eschatological trial

16.19; 18.18: 'Whatever you bind on earth . . .'

19.30; 20.16: the first will be last

g. Similar stories.

8.23–27; 14.22–33: Jesus and the sea (from Mark)

9.27–31; 20.29–34: two blind men healed

9.32–34; 12.22–34: a dumb demoniac healed

14.31–21; 15.32–38: the feeding narratives (from Mark)

h. Miscellaneous examples of repetition:

5.22: ἔνοχος ἔσται—repeated three times

5.34–36: μήτε ἐν (εἰς) + dative + ὅτι clause—repeated four times

6.25–34: μὴ μεριμνᾶτε/-ήσητε—repeated three times

7.7–11: αἰτεῖτε/αἰτῶν/αἰτήσει/αἰτήσει/αἰτοῦσιν

10.26–31: μὴ φοβηθῆτε/-εῖσθε—repeated three times

26.38–41: γρηγορεῖτε/-ῆσαι—repeated three times (from Mark)

(8) *Inclusio*. The discovery of inclusions in Matthew's gospel is inevitably a somewhat subjective endeavour. The repetition of key words or phrases does not always make for a significant enclosure (cf. 5.17 and 10.34, 4.17 and 16.21). Nevertheless there are, especially in the first seven chapters, several undoubted examples of *inclusio*:

1.23: 'God with us'

28.20: 'I am with you always'

4.23–5.2: Jesus goes about teaching in 'their' synagogues and preaching the gospel of the kingdom, and he heals every disease and every infirmity.

9.35: Jesus goes about teaching in 'their' synagogues and preaching the gospel of the kingdom, and he heals every disease and every infirmity.

5.1–2: the crowds, the mountain, Jesus teaching

7.28–29: the crowds, the mountain, Jesus teaching

5.17: the law and the prophets

7.12: the law and the prophets

5.20: περισσεύσῃ

5.47–48: περισσόν

7.16: 'you will know them by their fruits'

7.20: 'you will know them by their fruits'

15.2: 'they do not wash their hands when they eat'

15.20: 'to eat with unwashed hands does not defile a man'

From these examples it can be seen that the Matthean *inclusio* does more than set off discrete units: it also typically gives expression to the major themes of those units.

(9) *Chiasmus*. In the introductory chapter on structure we have observed that several scholars have tried to impose a chiastic outline on the First Gospel. While we have not found their suggestions compelling, the First Evangelist may very well, at points, have consciously arranged his material in chiastic sequences.[44] Possibilities include 1.1, 18; 8.14–15, 23–27, 28–34; 10.1–42; and 23.16–22. See the commentary.

(10) *Headings and conclusions*. The First Evangelist has a habit of placing summarizing or introductory sentences at the head of sections. See, for instance, 1.1, 18; 4.23–5.2; 5.13–16, 17–20; 6.1, 25; 10.16, 26; 11.20; 23.2; 24.3 This is reminiscent of the rabbinic *kĕlāl* (on which see Gerhardsson, *Memory*, pp. 136–41). See further on 6.1. Matthew also sometimes concludes sections with summarizing statements, as in 5.48; 6.34; 7.12; and 18.35.

(11) *Foreshadowing*. In three different ways the first four chapters of our gospel anticipate the fate of Jesus and the outcome of his mission, with the result that the end is foreshadowed in the beginning. First, chapter 2 foreshadows the passion narrative. After Jesus is born, Jerusalem is troubled (2.3), the chief priests and scribes conspire with Herod (2.4–5), and Jesus' life is threatened (2.13). There are also several verbal links between the infancy narrative and the passion narrative. See further p. 254. Secondly, although Jesus does not command his disciples to preach to non-Jews until after the resurrection (28.19), the Gentile mission is anticipated by 1.1 (Jesus is the son of Abraham), by the visit of the Gentile magi (see on 2.1), by the Baptist's saying about God raising up new children to Abraham (3.9), and by Jesus' appearance in 'Galilee of the Gentiles' (4.15). Thirdly, when John

---

[44] On chiasmus in the biblical tradition see esp. N. W. Lund, *Chiasmus in the New Testament*, Chapel Hill, 1942; Talbert, pp. 51–88; and A. DiMarco, 'Der Chiasmus in der Bibel', *LB* 36 (1975), pp. 21–97; 37 (1976), pp. 49–68. Unfortunately, Lund's study lacks methodological sophistication, and we still await an authoritative treatise on chiasmus in ancient Jewish and Christian texts.

is arrested (4.12), this foreshadows Jesus' fate: the true prophet will be 'handed over' (see also 14.1–12).

(12) *Parallelism.* When compared with both Mark and Luke, the sayings of Jesus in Matthew often show a higher degree of parallelism.[45] This is probably due to the influence of Semitic poetry. The following texts may be regarded as typical:

Mt 5.39–40: στρέψον αὐτῷ καὶ τὴν ἄλλην
ἄφες αὐτῷ καὶ τὸ ἱμάτιον

Lk 6.29: πάρεχε καὶ τὴν ἄλλην
καὶ τὸν χιτῶνα μὴ κωλύσῃς

Mt 6.22–23: ἐὰν οὖν ᾖ ὁ ὀφθαλμός σου ἁπλοῦς
ὅλον τὸ σῶμά σου φωτεινὸν ἔσται
ἐὰν δὲ ὁ ὀφθαλμός σου πονηρὸς ᾖ
ὅλον τὸ σῶμά σου σκοτεινὸν ἔσται

Lk 11.34–36: ὅταν ὁ ὀφθαλμός σου ἁπλοῦς ᾖ
καὶ ὅλον τὸ σῶμά σου φωτεινόν ἐστιν
ἐπὰν δὲ πονηρὸς ᾖ
καὶ τὸ σῶμά σου σκοτεινόν

Mt 18.8–9: εἰ δὲ ἡ χείρ σου . . . σκανδαλίζει σε
ἔκκοψον αὐτὸν καὶ βάλε ἀπὸ σοῦ
καλόν σοί ἐστιν . . .
καὶ εἰ ὁ ὀφθαλμός σου σκανδαλίζει σε
ἔξελε αὐτὸν καὶ βάλε ἀπὸ σοῦ
καλόν σοί ἐστιν . . .

Mk 9.43–47: καὶ ἐὰν σκανδαλίζῃ σε ἡ χείρ σου
ἀπόκοψον αὐτήν
καλόν ἐστίν σε . . .
καὶ ἐὰν ὁ ὀφθαλμός σου σκανδαλίζῃ σε
ἔκβαλε αὐτὸν
καλόν σέ ἐστιν . . .

For other examples of this phenomenon compare Mt 6.19–21 with Lk 12.33–4; Mt 7.24–7 with Lk 6.47–9; and Mt 10.24–25 with Lk 6.40.

One might be tempted, at least at first glance, to suppose that if, as this commentary will observe again and again, parallelism is generally more pronounced in Matthew than in Mark or Luke, this is some evidence for Matthean priority, the implicit idea being that the First Gospel most faithfully preserves Jesus' characteristic use of parallelism.[46] But one cannot make the inference without first deciding whether the heightened parallelism of the First

---

[45] Cf. A. Denaux, 'Der Spruch von den zwei Wegen im Rahmen des Epilogs der Bergpredigt', in Delobel, pp. 331–5.

[46] Cf. W. R. Farmer, 'Certain Results reached by Sir John C. Hawkins . . .', in Tuckett, *Studies*, pp. 75–98.

Gospel has a redactional explanation, that is, without knowing whether Matthew himself rewrote his sources in order to enhance this particular feature. And, in fact, given the heightened parallelism of Matthew *vis-à-vis* Mark in both sayings material and narrative portions,[47] those persuaded of Markan priority will inevitably conclude that parallelism must be regarded as a characteristic of the First Evangelist. (This obviously has ramifications for the quest to recover exactly what Jesus said; for even if Jesus, as it would appear, was fond of parallel constructions, the presence of parallelism in the Matthean form of a saying is hardly good evidence for a Semitic original or for Matthew having the most primitive form.)

(13) *Redactional expansions of and additions to the sayings tradition.* The author of Matthew does, in our judgement, deserve the label, 'conservative redactor'. This is because the vast bulk of his book was to hand in the tradition. Despite, however, the heavy dependence upon sources, Matthew must also be considered a creative writer. Not only did he reorder many events found in Mark and further feel free to distribute Q material wherever he willed, but, even more notably, he on occasion expanded dominical sayings and created a few of his own. It is, of course, impossible to determine exactly the extent of the evangelist's creativity, for it is often impossible to decide when a verse should be ascribed to M and when it should be assigned to pure redaction. Nonetheless, as will appear in the commentary, the items in the following list seem to us to belong, in all probability, to the second category:

3.15 Jesus' words to John the Baptist
5.10 'Blessed are those who are persecuted for righteousness' sake . . .'
5.13 'You are the salt of the earth'
5.14 'You are the light of the world'
5.16 'Let your light so shine before men that . . .'
5.20 'Unless your righteousness exceeds . . .'
5.32 'except for the cause of πορνεία'
6.14–15 on forgiveness
7.12 'This is the law and the prophets'

---

[47] The following is one example in which Matthew's narrative exhibits a higher degree of parallelism than Mark's narrative:

Mt 4.18–22: . . . οἱ δὲ εὐθέως ἀφέντες . . .
    ἠκολούθησαν αὐτῷ . . .
. . . οἱ δὲ εὐθέως ἀφέντες . . .
    ἠκολούθησαν αὐτῷ . . .
Mk 1.16–20: . . . καὶ εὐθὺς ἀφέντες . . .
    ἠκολούθησαν αὐτῷ . . .
. . . καὶ ἀφέντες . . .
    ἀπῆλθον ὀπίσω αὐτοῦ.

7.15 'Beware of the false prophets . . .'
9.13 mercy, not sacrifice
10.8 the disciples will raise the dead and heal lepers
10.41 'He who receives a prophet . . .'
11.29 'and learn from me, for I am meek and lowly of heart'
12.7 mercy, not sacrifice
18.10 'See that you do not despise one of these little ones . . .'
18.14 'So it is not the will of my Father who is in heaven . . .'
19.9 'except for πορνεία'
21.41c 'who will give him the fruits in their season'
21.43 'the kingdom of God will be taken away from you . . .'
23.32–34 'Fill up, then, the measure of your fathers . . .'
24.12 love will grow cold
24.20 'or on a sabbath'
24.26 'If they say, "Lo, he is in the wilderness . . ." '

The length of this far from exhaustive list tells us that Matthew had
no qualms about adding to the tradition of what Jesus said. In
order to make the texts fit better his own *Sitz im Leben* (cf. 7.15;
10.41; 21.41c, 43; 24.12, 20, 26), in order to achieve certain literary
ends (cf. 5.10, 13–14; 7.12), and in order to explain events to his
readers and make theological points (cf. 3.15; 5.20, 32; 6.14–15;
9.13; 10.8; 11.29; 12.7; 19.9), Matthew found it did not suffice to be
simply a channel for tradition: he had to become a source.

(14) *Authorial comments.* Matthew has, more regularly than his
predecessors, Mark and Q, inserted into his work explicit editorial
commentary. Included here are the title (1.1), the formula
quotations and their introductions, and a number of parenthetical
asides or explanatory glosses (e.g. 1.23b; 7.29; 9.6; 12.8; 13.34;
22.33; 24.15; 27.8, 15–16, 33, 46; 28.15). Taken together with other
clues these authorial comments make known to the reader what
the literary critic would call the implied author.

Three final remarks concerning the literary characteristics of the
First Gospel are in order. First, most of the characteristics we have
examined are found throughout the book. Clearly the hand of one
man has been active throughout. Secondly, devices such as
foreshadowing, repetition, and *inclusio* show up the impressive
unity of the gospel. The beginning and end hang together, as do the
various parts that make up the whole. And many theological
themes are constantly reiterated. Thirdly, the literary
characteristics are consistent with our conclusions concerning
authorship. Chiasmus and *inclusio*, the use of numbers and of
frequent repetition, and the numerous Semitisms and
Septuagintisms are all evidence of a mind steeped in the OT and
Jewish tradition.

V. THE SOURCES OF MATTHEW

Serious study of the literary relationships among the gospels began in the latter half of the eighteenth century, and the time since then has seen an array of theories propounded. But, in the twentieth century, the majority of scholars have come to accept one or other of two fundamental positions.[48] According to most, Mark was a source for both Matthew and Luke.[49] A minority, however, has postulated the primacy of Matthew.[50] In their view, both Mark and Luke knew and used the First Gospel.[51] Our first question,

[48] The following discussion presupposes the necessity of postulating either the priority of Mark or the priority of Matthew. For other approaches to the synoptic problem see M.-E. Boismard, *Synopse des quatre évangiles en français*, Paris, vol. 2, 1972; idem, 'The Two-Source Theory at an Impasse', *NTS* 26 (1979), pp. 1–17 (an involved proto-Matthew theory); P. Parker, 'A Second Look at *The Gospel Before Mark*', *JBL* 100 (1981), pp. 359–88 (a proto-Matthew, proto-Luke theory); R. Lindsey, *A New Approach to the Synoptic Problem*, Jerusalem, 1969 (defends the primacy of Luke, and Luke's dependence upon two hypothetical sources); L. Vagany, *Le problème synoptique*, Paris, 1954 (a proto-Matthew theory); A. Gaboury, *La structure des évangiles synoptiques*, NovTSup 22, Leiden, 1970 (various sources for Mt 4–13); J. M. Rist, *On the Independence of Matthew and Mark*, SNTSMS 32, Cambridge, 1978 (Matthew and Mark are independent; their common passages derive from oral tradition); M. Lowe and D. Flusser, 'Evidence corroborating a modified Proto-Matthean Synoptic Theory', *NTS* 29 (1983), pp. 25–47; P. Rolland, *Les premiers évangiles*, LD 116, Paris, 1984 (four pre-synoptic documents, one in Hebrew); J. Carmignac, *La naissance des Évangiles synoptiques*, Paris, 1984 (Mark and Matthew are translations from Hebrew; Luke is based on a revised Mark and other Hebrew documents).

[49] The classic statement is Streeter, pp. 149–332. For recent restatements see H. G. Wood, 'The Priority of Mark', *ExpT* 65 (1953), pp. 17–19; G. M. Styler, 'The Priority of Mark', in Moule, *Birth*, pp. 285–316; J. A. Fitzmyer, 'The Priority of Mark and the "Q" Source in Luke', in *Advance*, pp. 3–40; and Tuckett, *Revival*.

[50] If Matthew be considered the most primitive gospel, then either the synoptics were composed in their canonical order, Matthew-Mark-Luke (so Augustine, Schlatter, Zahn, Butler) or in the order, Matthew-Luke-Mark (so Griesbach, Strauss, Farmer, Dungan, Longstaff).

[51] This is the Griesbach hypothesis. Lit.: W. R. Farmer, *Problem*; idem, 'A "Skeleton in the Closet" of Gospel Research', *BR* 9 (1961), pp. 18–42; idem, 'The Two-Document Hypothesis as a Methodological Criterion in Synoptic Research', *ATR* 48 (1966), pp. 380–96; idem, 'A Response to Robert Morgenthaler's *Statistische Synopse*', *Bib* 54 (1973), pp. 417–33; idem, 'Modern Developments of Griesbach's Hypothesis', *NTS* 23 (1977), pp. 275–95; idem, ed., *New Synoptic Studies*, Macon, 1983; idem, *Jesus*, pp. 93–134; idem, 'Certain Results Reached by Sir John C. Hawkins and C. F. Burney which make more sense if Luke knew Matthew, and Mark knew Matthew and Luke', in Tuckett, *Synoptic Studies*, pp. 75–98; B. Orchard, *Matthew, Luke and Mark*, Manchester, 1976; idem, 'The Two-Document Hypothesis or, Some Thoughts on the Revival of the Griesbach Hypothesis', *DownR* 98 (1980), pp. 267–79; idem and T. R. W. Longstaff, eds., *Jacob J. Griesbach. Synoptic and Textual Critical Studies 1776–1976*, Cambridge, 1977; D. L. Dungan, 'Mark—The Abridgement of Matthew and Luke', in *Jesus and Man's Hope*, 1, Pittsburg, 1970, pp. 51–97; idem, 'Reactionary Trends in the Gospel Producing Activity of the Early Church? Marcion, Tatian, Mark', in Sabbe, pp. 188–94; idem, 'The Purpose and Provenance of the Gospel of Mark According to the "Two Gospel" (Griesbach) Hypothesis', in *Colloquy on New Testament Studies*, ed. B. Corley, Macon, 1983, pp. 133–56; C. H. Talbert and V. H.

then, is to determine the direction of borrowing between Matthew and Mark. Did Matthew use Mark or did Mark use Matthew? (We assume, against Rist, that the contacts between the synoptics are too close to be explicable apart from a literary dependence; cf. Farmer, *Problem*, pp. 202–8).

(1) *Mark*. When we began work on the present commentary, both of us were intrigued by the flurry of renewed activity on the synoptic problem. Although we had taken for granted the truth of the two document hypothesis (Matthew and Luke used Mark and Q), we did wonder whether that hypothesis might not be less certain and more susceptible to criticism than many had conceded. Certainly the mushrooming literature on source criticism seemingly indicated difficulties with the majority position. We wished, therefore, to undertake our exegetical task with open minds, and to discover just why the standard theory was suffering so much at the hands of so many. Our expectations, however, have hardly been met. Our conclusions are far more conventional and therefore far less interesting than we had anticipated. Even while admitting that no one solution of the synoptic problem will ever commend itself to all (the data are too ambiguous for that), we are now more than ever firmly persuaded of the priority of Mark, and more than ever puzzled by the followers of Griesbach. As we have examined Matthew verse by verse, the theory of Matthean antecedence has failed to commend itself while the postulation of Markan priority has consistently brought illumination. The sundry reasons for this assertion can, of course, only be fully understood by working through the details of our commentary. Nethertheless, in this chapter we should like summarily to indicate some of the reasons for maintaining that Mark preceded Matthew.

a. *The argument from order*.[52] B. H. Streeter's highly influential statement of the argument from order was as follows: 'the order of

---

McKnight, 'Can the Griesbach Hypothesis be Falsified?', *JBL* 91 (1972), pp. 338–68; G. W. Buchanan, 'Has the Griesbach Hypothesis been Falsified?', *JBL* 93 (1974), pp. 550–72; T. R. W. Longstaff, *Evidence of Conflation in Mark? A Study in the Synoptic Problem*, SBLDS 28, Missoula, 1977; R. H. Fuller, E. P. Sanders, T. R. W. Longstaff, 'The Current Debate on the Synoptic Problem', *PSTJ* 28 (1975), pp. 63–74; A. Fuchs, 'Die Wiederbelebung der Griesbachhypothese oder Wissenschaft auf dem Holzweg', *SUNT* 5 (1980), pp. 139–49; F. Neirynck, 'The Griesbach Hypothesis: The Phenomenon of Order', *ETL* 58 (1982), pp. 111–22; Tuckett, *Revival*, passim; idem, 'The Griesbach Hypothesis in the Nineteenth Century', *JSNT* 3 (1979), pp. 29–60; H.-H. Stoldt, *History and Criticism of the Marcan Hypothesis*, Macon, 1980; B. Reicke, 'Griesbach und die synoptische Frage', *TZ* 32 (1970), pp. 341–59; D. Peabody, 'The late Secondary Redaction of Mark's Gospel and the Griesbach Hypothesis', in Corley, *Colloquy*, pp. 87–132; A. J. Bellinzoni, ed., *The Two-Source Hypothesis*, Macon, 1985.

[52] B. C. Butler, *The Originality of St. Matthew*, Cambridge, 1951, pp. 62–71;

incidents in Mark is clearly the more original; for wherever Matthew departs from Mark's order Luke supports Mark, and whenever Luke departs from Mark, Matthew agrees with Mark' (p. 161). Although many have repeated this observation, it is, as it stands, problematic. The formulation—which has been labelled the 'Lachmann fallacy'[53]—begs the question because it presupposes what it seeks to prove, namely, Markan priority ('Matthew departs from Mark's order ... Luke departs from Mark'). A second difficulty is this: even if the statement were formulated in a more neutral fashion, the agreement in order between Matthew and Mark against Luke and between Luke and Mark against Matthew is consistent with more than one solution to the synoptic problem. As B. C. Butler demonstrated, the circumstance of alternating support for Mark's order requires only that Mark be the middle term. All of the following solutions are consistent with the facts:

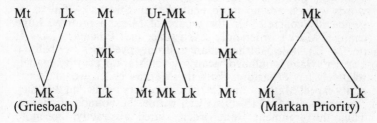

Even many supporters of Markan priority have finally come to admit the inadequacy of Streeter's version of the argument from order.

In resurrecting the Griesbach hypothesis, W. R. Farmer has stood Streeter's proposition on its head:

D. L. Dungan, 'A Griesbachian Perspective on the Argument from Order', in Tuckett, *Studies*, pp. 67–74; W. R. Farmer, 'The Lachmann Fallacy', *NTS* 14 (1968), pp. 441–3; M. Lowe, 'The Demise of Arguments from Order for Markan Priority', *NovT* 24 (1982), pp. 27–36; F. Neirynck, 'The Arguments from Order and St. Luke's Transpositions', *ETL* 49 (1973), pp. 784–815; idem, 'The Argument from Order', in Neirynck, *Agreements*, pp. 291–322; N. H. Palmer, 'Lachmann's Argument', *NTS* 13 (1967), pp. 368–78; E. P. Sanders, 'The Argument from Order and the Relationship Between Matthew and Luke', *NTS* 15 (1969), pp. 249–61; C. M. Tuckett, 'The Argument from Order and the Synoptic Problem', *TZ* 36 (1980), pp. 338–54; idem, *Revival*, pp. 26–40; idem, 'Arguments from Order: Definition and Evaluation', in Tuckett, *Studies*, pp. 197–219; J. B. Tyson, 'Sequential Parallelism in the Synoptic Gospels', *NTS* 22 (1976), pp. 276–308. For an attempt to explain Luke's order on the assumption that he knew and used Mark and Q see F. G. Downing, 'Redaction Criticism: Josephus' *Antiquities* and the Synoptic Gospels', *JSNT* 8 (1980), pp. 46–65; 9 (1980), pp. 29–48.

[53] So Butler, *Originality*. There is doubt as to whether Lachmann himself was guilty of the fallacy; see Tuckett, 'Argument'.

Whenever the order of Mark is not the same as that of Matthew, it follows the order of Luke, that is . . . Mark has no independent chronology.

All that is needed to understand the order of events in Mark is that given in Matthew and Luke. Mark's order shows no independence of Matthew and Luke (excepting the single case of his ordering of the cleansing of the temple). This seems explicable only by a conscious effort of Mark to follow the order of Matthew and Luke.

Only someone writing later who was attempting to combine the two narrative documents has the possibility of preserving what order the second preserved from the first and then, wherever the second departed from the first, following the order of either one or the other ('Developments', pp. 293–4).

It is exceedingly hard to fathom how Farmer believes his affirmations move us beyond Butler's analysis, according to which the phenomenon of relative order proves by itself only the mediating position of the Second Gospel. Moreover, Farmer's words—which are no more neutral than Streeter's—fail to be sufficiently concrete. On the theory of Markan priority, Luke changes Mark's order only seven times (see Fitzmyer, *Luke* 1, pp. 71–72) while Matthew changes it only five times (see below). Farmer's claim is nullified because, given Markan priority, in their relatively few departures from the Markan order, we could not really expect Matthew and Luke to agree very often; and that they concur once (Mk 3.13–19) is well within the bounds of chance. Thus the argument from order, stated abstractly, no more recommends Griesbach than it does Streeter.

The problem with many versions of the argument from order is that they remain abstract. In order to break through the impasse in the discussion, one must inquire which is more credible, the reworking of Mark's order by Matthew and Luke or the reworking of Matthew and Luke by Mark. And it is precisely here that the theory of Markan priority commends itself. Let us consider, because this is a commentary on the First Gospel, what motives Matthew might have had for reordering portions of Mark. From 14.1 on, Matthew agrees with the Markan sequence (Mk 6.14–16.8).[54] Before this, however, there are certain disagreements:

Mt		Mk
1.1–2.23	The infancy narrative	
3.1–12	John the Baptist	1.1–8
3.13–17	Jesus is baptized	1.9–11
4.1–11	The temptation	1.12–13

[54] Mt 15.3–6; 19.4–6; and 21.12–13 are not exceptions because they remain within their Markan contexts.

4.12–17	Jesus in Galilee	1.14–15	
4.18–22	Four disciples called	1.16–20	
4.23–25	Summary report	1.21	
5.1–7.27	The sermon on the mount		
7.28–29	Jesus' teaching	1.22	
8.1–4	A leper healed	1.40–5	1
8.5–13	The centurion		
8.14–15	Peter's mother-in-law	1.29–31	
8.16	Summary report	1.32–4	
8.17	Isa 53.4 cited		
8.18–22	On discipleship		
8.(18,) 23–27	A storm calmed	4.35–41	2
8.28–34	The Gadarene demoniac(s)	5.1–20	
9.1–8	Sins forgiven	2.1–12	3
9.9–13	Tax collectors and sinners	2.13–17	
9.14–17	On fasting	2.18–22	
9.18–26	Two healings	5.21–43	
9.27–31	Two blind men healed		
9.32–34	A demoniac		
9.35–38	Summary report	6.6b	
10.1	The twelve called	6.7	
10.2–4	The twelve named	3.13–19a	4
10.5–8	Mission instructions	6.8–9	
10.9–10	Mission instructions	6.10–11	
10.11–14	Mission instructions		
10.15	The day of judgement		
10.16–42	Mission instructions		
11.1	John's teaching		
11.2–19	John the Baptist		
11.20–24	Woes		
11.25–30	The great thanksgiving		
12.1–8	The Sabbath	2.23–8	5
12.9–14	The Sabbath	3.1–6	
12.15–21	Isaiah fulfilled		
12.22–30	Beelzebub	3.22–7	
12.31–32	On Blasphemy	3.28–30	
12.33–37	On good fruit		
12.38–45	This generation		
12.46–50	The family of Jesus	3.31–5	
13.1–52	Parables	4.1–34	
13.53–58	His own country	6.1–6a	

As the chart reveals, there are five transpositions. Each one is readily explicable (cf. with what follows Allen, pp. xiii–xvii).

1. As we have argued elsewhere, 8.1–22 is structurally parallel

to 8.23–9.17 and 9.18–34 (see p. 67). Each section consists of three consecutive miracle stories + additional material.

8.1–22	8.23–9.17
a leper healed (1–4)	the storm calmed (23–7)
the centurion's son healed (5–13)	the Gadarene demoniac (28–34)
Peter's mother-in-law healed (14–15)	a paralytic healed (9.1–8)
+	+
summary report and words of Jesus (16–22)	call of Levi and words of Jesus (9.9–17)

9.18–34

the ruler and woman with a haemorrhage (18–26)
two blind men healed (27–31)
a dumb demoniac healed (32–4)
+
summary report and words of Jesus (9.35–8)

In order to make this arrangement, Matthew needed three miracle stories immediately after the sermon on the mount. There were to hand in Mk 1: the healing of a demoniac (1.23–8), the healing of Peter's mother-in-law (1.29–31), and the healing of a leper (1.40–5). Matthew moved the last to first place probably because of its command to obey the Law of Moses: this is particularly appropriate coming after a discourse which emphasizes the importance of upholding Torah. Our evangelist then followed with the story of the centurion, substituting this for Mk 1.23–8— presumably because Mark's story was troublesome[55] and because Mt 8.5–13 = Lk 7.1–10 followed upon the great sermon in Q (cf. its position in Luke). After this he continued with the miracle story that stood next in Mark (1.29–31).

2. Mk 4.35–5.20 is brought forward so that Matthew can maintain his thrice repeated pattern, three miracle stories + words of Jesus.

3. The jump from Mk 2.22 to 5.21 is natural. The primary vehicle for Matthean theology in chapters 8–9 is the simple miracle story. In chapter 12 it is the controversy story. Hence, when, at Mt 9.18, our evangelist comes to Mk 2.23ff., which is controversy material, he naturally skips over this (which will be used later) in order to find a miracle story. This takes him to Mk 5.21.

[55] In Mk 1.26, after Jesus speaks, we read, 'the unclean spirit, rending him and crying out with a loud voice, came out of him'. Luke changes this: it 'came out of him, having done him no hurt' (4.35). Matthew's unwillingness to reproduce what Mark wrote is strongly implied by a comparison of Mk 9.20–6 with Mt 17.17–18.

4. 3.13–19a is where it is for thematic reasons: the naming of the twelve nicely serves to open the chapter that reports their commissioning.

5. At 12.1–8 Matthew simply returns to the material now left over from Mk 1.1–6.13 (minus a summary statement, 3.7–12, and a potentially offensive story heading, 3.20–21).

Having explained how the differences between the Markan and Matthean orders are accounted for on the theory of Markan priority, let us now turn the tables. Could Mark be responsible for changing the order up to Mk 6.14 = Mt 14.1? Our conclusions about the structure of Matthew forbid an affirmative response. In his five major discourses and throughout the narrative material up to 14.1, Matthew is very careful to arrange everything in triads. But after 14.1 one hunts mostly in vain for groups of three. Now it can scarcely be coincidence that 14.1 is exactly the point at which Matthew ceases to impose triads on his narrative material and at the same time exactly the point at which the Markan and Matthean orders no longer depart from one another. On the theory of Markan priority, an explanation is to hand: when Matthew composes on his own, he composes in triads; but from 14.1 on, he largely follows Mark, which explains why the triad is not the structural key to the narrative material between Mt 14.1 and 28.20. How does the matter appear from Griesbach's perspective? Mark deviates significantly from Matthew only when the latter composes in triads; but as soon as Matthew quits presenting groups of threes, Mark decides to get in line. What could possibly be the motivation for this? Unless one calls upon coincidence there is none. Certainly Mark cannot be said to have avoided triads (see Neirynck, *Evangelica*, pp. 546–61). We conclude, then, that the argument from order, when considered concretely, favours the theory of synoptic relationships adopted herein.

b. *The tendencies of the synoptic tradition*. Streeter argued that 'a close study of the actual language of parallel passages in the Gospels shows that there is a constant tendency in Matthew . . . to improve upon and refine Mark's version' (p. 162). It is, to be fair to Streeter, roundly conceded that Matthew's style is superior to Mark's; and, on the assumption of Markan priority, one can draw up imposing lists of verses where the First Gospel improved upon the Second (see Allen, pp. xix–xxxi). Still, Streeter failed to ask a fundamental question. Why is it inconceivable that Mark, the abbreviator of Matthew, had less of a command of Greek than his predecessor? On the Griesbach hypothesis, the alleged Matthean improvements of Mark prove nothing. They show only that the author of the Second Gospel was just not the writer Matthew was.

In holding to this view of things, the followers of Griesbach can summon support from the conclusions of E. P. Sanders' *The Tendencies of the Synoptic Tradition*. When the alleged tendencies of the gospel tradition are examined critically, most of them turn out to be phantoms. Was there an established tendency to drop Semitisms? If so, how does one explain codex Bezae; and why, in texts common to the first two gospels, does either Matthew or Mark sometimes have a Semitism where the other does not (see MHT 4. pp. 31–38)? Was there a firm proclivity towards dropping picturesque details (cf. Allen, pp. xvii–xviii)?[56] What then do we make of the adding of specifics, such as the naming of anonymous NT figures in the apocryphal gospels? The alleged tendencies of the tradition so often taken for granted by an earlier generation of scholars have been shown to be largely tendentious—and this includes the issue of style. Would one really wish to maintain that every apocryphal gospel that made use, let us say, of Luke, must necessarily indicate an improvement upon Lukan vocabulary and syntax? If not, who is to say whether Mark is a step down from Matthew or Matthew a step up from Mark?

In view of the preceding considerations, the argument for the priority of Mark that is based upon grammatical and other improvements has, we concede, been somewhat weakened. We nonetheless do not believe it to be utterly without force. When all has been said and done, there remain at least three facts or tendencies which make Mark appear to be earlier than Matthew.

i. The general direction of early Christology cannot be gainsaid. It was from the lesser to the greater. The passing of time incontrovertibly saw a development; there was an enhancing of feelings of reverence, an increase in Jesus' position and status. Hence, because Matthew possesses a higher Christology than Mark, and because he lacks certain details which make Jesus more human, all presumption is against Matthean priority (*pace* Farmer, *Problem*, pp. 230–2, and Dungan, 'Abridgement', p. 65). Consider the following:

Texts in Mark but not Matthew where Jesus experiences emotion.

Mk	1.41:	'moved with anger' (or 'pity'; the text is doubtful)
	1.43:	'he sternly charged'
	3.5:	'he looked around him with anger, grieved'
	6.6:	'he marvelled'
	8.12:	'he sighed deeply in his spirit'
	10.14:	'he was indignant'

[56] See L. R. Keylock, 'Bultmann's Law of Increasing Distinctness', in *Current Issues in Biblical and Patristic Interpretation*, ed. G. F. Hawthorne, Grand Rapids, 1975, pp. 193–210.

10.21: 'he loved him'
14.33: 'greatly distressed and troubled'

Texts in Mark but not Matthew where Jesus experiences inability or exhibits ignorance:

Mk 1.45: 'Jesus could no longer openly enter a town'
    5.9: 'what is your name?'
    5.30: 'who touched my garments?'
    6.5: 'he could do no mighty work there'
    6.38: 'how many loaves do you have?'
    6.48: 'he wanted to pass them by'
    7.24: 'he would not have anyone know it; but he could not be hid'
    8.12: 'why does this generation seek a sign?'
    8.23: 'do you see anything?'
    9.16: 'what are you discussing with them?'
    9.21: 'how long has he had this?'
    9.33: 'what were you discussing?'
    11.13: 'he went to see if he could find anything on it . . . he found nothing'
    14.14: 'where am I to eat?'

Other texts in Mark evidently omitted or altered out of reverence:

Mk 1.32–3: Jesus healed 'many' becomes (Mt 8.16) 'all'
    3.10: Jesus healed 'many' becomes (Mt 12.15) 'all'
    3.21: 'he is out of his mind' (omitted)
    10.18: 'why do you call me good' becomes (Mt 19.17) 'why do you ask me concerning the good?'
    14.58: 'I will destroy' becomes (Mt 26.61) 'I am able to destroy'

To say the least, we find it perplexing to suppose that an early Christian writer with Matthew's text before him would almost systematically set out to highlight Jesus' ignorance and make him a much more emotional figure. But the reverse procedure is quite intelligible.

ii. There are at least twelve verses where Mark has a rare or unusual word or phrase, Matthew a common word or phrase (cf. Allen, pp. xxvi–xxvii)

Mk		Mt	
1.10	σχιζομένους	3.16	ἠνεῴχθησαν
1.12	ἐκβάλλει	4.1	ἀνήχθη
1.16	ἀμφιβάλλοντας	4.18	βάλλοντας ἀμφίβληστρον
2.11	κράβαττον	9.6	κλίνην

Mk			Mt		
	2.21	ἐπιράπτει		9.16	ἐπιβάλλει
	3.28	τοῖς υἱοῖς τῶν ἀνθρώπων		12.31	τοῖς ἀνθρώποις
	9.3	στίλβοντα		17.2	ὡς τὸ φῶς
	10.25	τρυμαλιᾶς		19.24	τρήματος
	11.8	στιβάδας		21.8	κλάδους
	14.68	προαύλιον		26.71	πυλών
	14.72	ἐπιβαλών		26.75	ἐξελθὼν ἔξω
	15.11	ἀνέσεισαν		27.20	ἔπεισαν

How are we to explain this? It would be wholly natural for one writer to replace an uncommon word with a common word. But what would be the motive of someone who did just the opposite—especially someone like Mark, whose literary talents were less than considerable? It is not impossible that this question has a satisfactory answer; but what it might be we cannot guess.

iii. Semitic words. Those who place Mark after Matthew tend to date the former towards the end of the first century or even in the first part of the second century. They also have little doubt that the author was a Gentile writing for Gentiles; none has proposed to find in Mark a 're-Judaizing' of the tradition (contrast many of the commentators on Matthew). How, then, do the proponents of Matthean priority account for the six Semitic expressions found in Mark but not in Matthew: βοανηργές (3.17), ταλιθα κουμ (5.41), κορβᾶν (7.11), βαρτιμαῖος (10.46), ῥαββουνί (10.51), ἀββά (14.36)? The magical papyri and books such as the Testament of Solomon (1st–3rd cent. A.D.) do, to be sure, reveal the possibility of Gentile interest in Semitic names; but are βοανηργές, κορβᾶν, and βαρτιμαῖος really words that would have survived for long in a non-Jewish environment? Related to this question is the problem of Mt 27.46 = Mk 15.34: 'My God, my God, why hast thou forsaken me?' Matthew has this either in Hebrew (at least the first three words) or in Aramaic; Mark has a different text, one in Aramaic (see on 27.46). Now if Mark is prior to Matthew, this makes sense. The author of the First Gospel could read the OT in Hebrew: so we can imagine him (having a knowledge of both Hebrew and Aramaic) thus making the link with Elijah clearer (cf. 27.47). What is the alternative? One is forced to affirm that a Gentile Christian writing for Gentile Christians somehow managed—and for what reason?—to change Hebrew words into Aramaic or Aramaic words into different Aramaic words. Is this credible?

c. *Inconcinnities*. G. M. Styler ('The Priority of Mark') has put forward this argument: several passages in Matthew[57] contain

[57] In addition to what follows see our comments on 3.16; 9.14; 19.16–17; 22.41–5; and 24.3.

logical flaws which are best explained by the hypothesis of Markan priority. We select two of Styler's examples for review.

i. Mk 6.17–29 = Mt 14.3–12, the death of John the Baptist. In Mark's fuller version, all is in order. Herod, we are informed, feared and respected John, knowing him to be righteous and holy; and although the tetrarch had seized John and put him in prison (on account of Herodias, who had a grudge against the Baptist and wished him dead), Herod heard the prophet gladly. When, finally, the Baptist was beheaded, it was because Herodias had forced Herod to act against his will. Turning to Matthew, we get a different picture. In this account Herod arrests John and wants to do away with him; but he cannot because he fears the crowd (14.5). Nothing is said of Herod's admiration for his prisoner. Yet when he is tricked by his sister-in-law into giving her John's head on a platter, Herod is said to grieve (14.9). Nothing has prepared for this remark on the tetrarch's emotion. Because Matthew fails to tell us about Herod's esteem for John, there is no place for grief. It seems to follow that Mt 14.9 betrays a knowledge of Mk 6.20. That is, having revised and abbreviated Mark's introduction but at the same time retained Mark's version of Herod's response to the beheading, Matthew unwittingly disturbs the coherence of Mk 6.17–29.

Matthew also makes a second blunder in 14.3–12. In Mark the story of John's imprisonment and execution is told as a flashback. It is introduced with Herod's declaration, 'John, whom I beheaded, has been raised' (6.16); and after the story is finished the narrative jumps forward in time (cf. 6.30 with 6.13). In the First Gospel, however, the tale is introduced as a flashback but not so concluded. When John is buried, Jesus is told of it, and then he departs—all of which leads to the feeding of the five thousand (14.13–21). So Mt 14.1–12 begins retrospectively yet then flows smoothly into the narrative's present tense. As Styler puts it, Matthew has buttoned his jacket to his waistcoat.

ii. Mk 15.6–10 = Mt 27.15–18, Jesus and Barabbas. In Mark, Pilate, who is aware of the machinations of the Jewish leaders, offers to release Jesus (he does not mention Barabbas). In Matthew, by way of contrast, we find this: 'Pilate said to them, "Whom do you want me to release for you, Barabbas or Jesus who is called Christ?" For he knew that it was out of envy that they had delivered him up'. This makes little sense. 'For he knew, etc.' does not explain why Pilate asked the question, 'Whom do you want me to release for you . . . ?' In fact, 'For he knew, etc.' offers a good reason for Pilate not to ask the crowd for their preference. But all is right in Mark. When Pilate asks, 'Do you want me to release for you the king of the Jews?', he does so because he perceives Jesus' innocence. It is only then that the crowd names Barabbas. In other words, Pilate offers the crowd no choice in Mark but rather seeks to set Jesus free; thus 'For he knew, etc.' fits its context perfectly. Now how do we explain why Matthew has an illogical sequence, Mark a logical one? 'For he knew, etc.' (Mk 15.10 = Mt 27.18) is in harmony with Mk 15.9 but not Mt 27.17; it also goes well with Mk 15.14 = Mt 27.23, where the governor asks, 'Why, for what evil has he done?' This is evidence for Markan originality. Mk 15.10 = Mt 27.18 and Mk 15.14 = Mt 27.23, being in both gospels, must belong to the original story; and because Mk 15.9 but not Mt 27.17 lines up with these two texts, Mark's account is shown to be more original. Matthew, we infer, has imperfectly assimilated Mark's narrative.

d. *The Markan 'additions'*. The passages present in Mark but wholly absent from Matthew and Luke include these: 1.1, 43; 2.27; 3.20–1; 4.26–9; 6.31; 7.2–4, 32–7; 8.22–6; 9.29, 39b, 49–50; 11.11a, 16; 13.33–7; 14.51–2; 15.25, 44; 16.3—some forty verses in all. If, as Farmer claims, Mark had Matthew and Luke for his sources, the texts just cited would give us Mark's additions. But we must ask ourselves, Which is more plausible to imagine, their addition or their subtraction? Surely the latter. On the theory of Markan priority, given that Matthew altogether omits fifty-five verses from Mark, Luke one hundred and eighty seven (Streeter's count), some overlap would be inevitable. Beyond this general consideration, we can perfectly well fathom the reasons for the common omissions. 3.20–1 tells us that Jesus' family thought he was out of his mind. This is potentially embarrassing. So is 8.22–26, which tells us about a healing attempt that did not wholly succeed ('I see men but they look like trees, walking'): Jesus has to try again. As for 9.49–50 ('everyone will be salted by fire', followed by two non-sequiturs); 11.16 ('and he would not permit anyone to carry a vessel through the temple'); and 14.51–2 (the flight of the naked young man), these are among the most mysterious verses in all the gospels, and their meaning escapes us. Why would Mark have added them? We can easily understand why someone might have dropped them. And so it goes. Mk 9.39b ('No one who does a mighty work in my name will be able soon after to speak evil of me') does not agreeably fit with either Mt 7.21–3 (cf. Lk 6.46; 13.26–7), which consigns to perdition outsiders who have taken the Messiah's name to do mighty works, or with Acts 19, the tale about the itinerant Jewish exorcists (cf. also Acts 8 and the story of Simon). Thus we need not be surprised at the absence of Mk 9.39b from Matthew and Luke. The same is also true of the common omission of Mk 1.1 (Matthew and Luke have their own titles); 1.43 (it is scarcely intelligible); 2.27 (see on 12.8); 6.31 (Matthew and Luke are both severely abbreviating); 7.3–4 (Luke omits all of 6.45–8.21, so anything omitted from that section by Matthew would automatically be shared with Luke); 7.32–7 (the same holds true here); 9.29 (in Matthew this is not omitted but rather replaced with a different word of Jesus); 11.11a (neither Matthew nor Luke can reproduce this because their independent condensations and rearrangements of the events surrounding the entrance into Jerusalem leave no room for it); 13.33–7 (13.35 is reproduced in Mt 24.42 and Matthew may otherwise have abbreviated the section because of its parallel in M: Mt 25.13–15; the redactional

Lk 21.34–6 replaces Mk 13.33–7 as the conclusion to Lk 21); and 16.3 (in Matthew the question, 'Who will roll away the stone?', would make no sense (cf. 27.64–6), and Luke is presumably influenced by a non-Lukan source; cf. Taylor, *Passion*, pp. 103–9). The only truly puzzling common omission is Mk 4.26–9. Streeter (p. 171) suggested that neither Matthew nor Luke had it in their copies of Mark: it had dropped out by homoioteleuton (καὶ ἔλεγεν begins both 4.26 and 30). Whatever one's conclusion on this issue (see on 13.24), it cannot overthrow the evidence gleaned from the other alleged Markan 'additions': these surely are best explained as Matthean and Lukan omissions. With all due respect to Griesbach's supporters, who have reminded us that at least Marcion had his reasons for abbreviating and radically revising the gospel tradition, can one seriously envision someone rewriting Matthew and Luke so as to omit the miraculous birth of Jesus, the sermon on the mount, and the resurrection appearances, while, on the other hand, adding the tale of the naked young man, a healing miracle in which Jesus has trouble healing, and the remark that Jesus' family thought him mad?

e. *The minor agreements*.[58] The so-called 'minor agreements' between Matthew and Luke in the triple tradition are generally admitted to be the most serious obstacle in the way of accepting the viewpoint we have taken in this commentary—for they appear to be *prima facie* evidence for literary contact between Matthew and Luke. If, apart from Q, Matthew and Luke agree against Mark, how is this to be explained? Streeter divided the minor agreements into the following four categories: 'irrelevant' (minor agreements due to coincidental editing), 'deceptive' (minor agreements that, despite appearances, are due to coincidental editing), Markan/Q overlap, and textual corruption. For this he has been castigated by Farmer, who holds that the phenomena should not be atomized. If, for example, there are several minor agreements between Matthew and Luke against Mark

---

[58] Lit.: Streeter, pp. 293–331; J. Schmid, *Verhältnisses*; N. Turner, 'The Minor Verbal Agreements of Mt. and Lk. against Mk.', *Studia Evangelica 1*, TU 73, ed. F. L. Cross, Berlin, 1959, pp. 223–34; R. M. Wilson, 'Farrer and Streeter on the Minor Agreements of Mt and Lk against Mk', in ibid., pp. 254–7; A. W. Argyle, 'Agreements between Matthew and Luke', *ExpT* 73 (1961), pp. 19–22; Farmer, *Problem*, pp. 94–152; S. McLoughlin, 'Les accords mineurs Mt-Lc contre Mc et le problème synoptique', in de la Potterie, pp. 17–40; T. R. W. Longstaff, 'The Minor Agreements: An Examination of the Basic Argument', *CBQ* 37 (1975), pp. 184–92; F. Neirynck, *Minor Agreements*; E. W. Burrows, 'The Use of Textual Theories to Explain Agreements of Matthew and Luke against Mark', in *Studies in New Testament Language and Text*, ed. J. K. Elliott, NovTSup 44, Leiden, 1976, pp. 87–99; Tuckett, *Revival*, pp. 61–75; Stoldt, pp. 9–23, 263–80; R. B. Vinson, 'The Significance of the Minor Agreements as an Argument against the Two-Document Hypothesis', unpublished Ph.D. dissertation, Duke University, 1984.

concentrated in one pericope, their cumulative force will not be felt if they are discussed in isolation from each other because they have been assigned to different categories (cf. Farmer, *Problem*, pp. 131–40, on Mk 2.1–12 par.). Farmer, moreover, has registered some other seemingly telling criticisms, such as that Streeter's textual conjectures have not been accepted by modern critical editions of the NT, and that some of his explanations for coincidental editing are far from obvious.

Despite the queries concerning Streeter's approach and conclusions, we have not become convinced that the minor agreements are as devastating to his position as some have made out. Furthermore, because the reasons for Markan priority are compelling, whatever one infers from the minor agreements will have to be consistent with the priority of Mark. With this in mind we offer the following observations.

i. Stoldt (pp. 11–21, 263–80) analyses the minor agreements in this fashion: minor additional details in Mark that extend beyond the texts of Matthew and Luke, including passages where either Mark or Luke is lacking (one hundred and eighty examples);[59] minor additional details in both Matthew and Luke that extend beyond Mark (thirty-five examples);[60] concurrence of Matthew and Luke in expressions and wording, contrary to Mark (thirty-five examples);[61] concurrence of Matthew and Luke in diverging from Mark's word form (twenty-two examples).[62] At first glance, Stoldt's listing of the data appears overwhelming. How can Matthew and Luke independently agree two hundred and seventy-two times? Yet a closer look tells an unexpected story. Stoldt's largest category (minor additional details in Mark that extend beyond the texts of Matthew and Luke, including passages where either Matthew or Luke are lacking) is inflated. Almost half of the one hundred and eighty instances cited touch upon only one gospel and are therefore not really agreements. Beyond this, consider as representative of Stoldt's examples the twelve additional details in Mk 1 not found in the

---

[59] He lists Mk 1.1, 7, 13, 15, 19, 20, 29, 33, 35, 36–7, 41, 43; 2.2, 3, 9, 13, 14, 15, 16, 18, 19, 23, 25, 26, 27; 3.5, 6, 7, 8, 9, 14–16a, 17, 22, 30, 34; 4.1, 2–3a, 7, 8, 10, 12b, 13, 23, 34, 35, 36, 38, 39, 40; 5.5, 6, 13, 20c, 26–7a, 29, 30, 34b, 40c, 41, 42; 6.2, 5–6a, 7, 12–13, 14 (*bis*), 17, 19–20, 21, 23, 24, 25, 26, 27, 30, 31, 37, 38, 39, 40, 41b, 47b, 48b, 52; 7.2–4, 8, 13, 18–19, 24, 26; 8.3b, 12, 14, 15, 17–18, 27, 32, 35; 9.1, 3, 10, 14–16, 25b, 26–7, 28, 29, 33–4, 35, 36, 39, 48, 49, 50b; 10.10, 12, 16, 17, 19, 20, 21a, 24, 29, 32, 38b–9b, 46, 49–50, 52; 11.4, 11b, 13b, 14b, 16, 17, 23, 25, 28; 12.5b, 6, 12b, 13, 14, 15, 21, 27b, 28, 32–4, 37, 41, 42, 43; 13.3, 34b, 35b–7; 14.5, 6, 7, 8a, 13a, 30, 36, 40b, 44, 54, 56b, 59, 65, 68, 72; 15.8, 21, 24, 25, 29, 41, 43, 44–5; 16.1, 3, 4b, 8.
[60] He cites the parallels to Mk 1.5, 8, 40; 2.3, 12, 23, 26; 3.5; 4.10, 15, 36 (*bis*), 38; 5.27; 6.7, 44; 9.2, 7, 19 (*bis*); 10.22, 26; 11.27; 12.3, 7, 12 (*bis*), 28 (*bis*), 38; 13.19; 14.37, 62, 65, 72.
[61] He cites the parallels to Mk 1.10 (*bis*), 13; 2.9, 12, 16, 21, 26; 3.1; 4.41; 5.14, 27; 6.11, 32, 43; 8.31 (*bis*), 34; 9.18; 10.51; 11.2, 7; 12.15, 18, 22, 37; 14.11, 36, 47 (*bis*), 53; 15.1, 20, 39, 43, 46.
[62] He cites the parallels to Mk 2.22; 4.3, 9, 11, 41; 6.7 (*bis*); 8.36; 9.14, 31; 10.20, 28; 11.1 (*bis*), 2, 3, 8; 12.17; 13.2, 25; 14.10; 15.14.

texts of Matthew and Luke. Three can be immediately dismissed because either Luke or Matthew has entirely skipped over the relevant verse or episode (Mk 1.15, 35, 36–7). Two more are not surprising because the Markan text is in one case offensive (1.41—Matthew and Luke probably read, 'moved with anger'), in another hardly intelligible (1.43—see the commentaries). One occurs at a point where Matthew and Luke both turn to Q (Mk 1.13). Three others may be considered insignificant and coincidentally omitted because they are unnecessary details of the type both Matthew and Luke often (on the two source theory) leave out (Mk 1.7, 29, 33). Further, the common omission of Mk 1.1 is not a problem given that Matthew and Luke introduce their respective gospels in their own ways. This leaves only 1.19 ('a little farther') and 20 ('with the hired servants'). But Luke's version of the call of the disciples (5.1–11) is largely drawn from L (it resembles Mark only in a few particulars); only in 5.10–11 is Markan influence manifest, and here, because Luke is condensing, the dropping of details is nothing save inevitable.

Stoldt's second category of minor agreements (additional details in both Matthew and Luke that extend beyond Mark) is much smaller than the first, containing as it does thirty-five illustrations. This is exactly what would be expected on the theory of Markan priority: coincidental omissions should outnumber coincidental additions. Moreover, some of the examples seem less than amazing. The addition of 'region of the Jordan' in Mt 3.5 and Lk 3.3 appears in slightly different contexts, 'Jordan' stands in Mark's text (1.5, 9), and ἡ περίχωρος τοῦ Ἰορδάνου is a LXX phrase (e.g. Gen 13.10–11; 2 Chr 4.17). Mt 3.12 = Lk 3.16 comes from Q on the two source theory, as may Mt 10.1 = Lk 9.1. ἐσθίειν, which appears in both Mt 12.1 and Lk 6.1 but not Mk 2.23, is a wholly natural clarification in view of what follows (see Mk 2.25–6): its addition by two independent writers does not stretch credibility (cf. Streeter, pp. 311–12). And μόνος after εἰ μή in Mt 12.4 = Lk 6.4 (against Mk 2.26) is not exactly unexpected (cf. Mt 17.8; 24.36 = Mk 9.8; Lk 5.21; Phil 4.15; see Streeter, p. 312).

The other agreements in Stoldt's second category are no less explicable:

Mk 1.40: Matthew and Luke often add κύριε (Mt: 33; Mk: 2; Lk: 26–7).

Mk 2.12: ἀπῆλθεν εἰς τὸν οἶκον αὐτοῦ, a common LXX phrase (e.g. Josh 22.4; 1 Βασ 10.26; 2 Βασ 17.23), is added in both Mt 9.7 and Lk 5.25 under the influence of Mk 2.11 (ὕπαγε εἰς τὸν οἶκόν σου) and serves to make the healed man's actions correspond precisely to Jesus' command (cf. Streeter, pp. 299–300).

Mk 3.5: 'your' before and after 'hand' is an obvious addition (cf. 8.15 = Mk 1.31; Mt 15.2 = Mk 7.5; Lk 6.6 = Mk 3.1; Mk 4.10).

Mk 4.10: γνῶναι in Mt 13.11 = Lk 8.10 is moved forward from Mk 4.13 in order to clarify the beginning of the sentence.

Mk 5.27: in Mt 9.20 and Lk 8.44 τοῦ κρασπέδου is brought forward from Mk 6.56, where τοῦ · κρασπέδου τοῦ ἱματίου reappears; see the commentary.

Mk 6.44: the ὡσεί of Mt 14.21 = Lk 9.14 has its parallel in Mk 8.9, which the texts of all three gospels are here very uncertain.

Mk 9.2: 'face' is added because both Matthew and Luke see an allusion to Exod 34.29–35 (cf. 2 Cor 3.7 and Streeter, pp. 315–16).

Mk 9.19: καὶ διεστραμμένη is from Deut 32.5 and could either have been in an early text of Mark (P⁴⁵ has it) or—less probably—it was independently added by Matthew and Luke following the OT.

Mk 13.19: μεγάλη goes with different words in Matthew and Luke.

Only five of the items in Stoldt's second list give one pause: Mk 2.3; 5.27; 14.62, 65, 72. And it may be significant that three of these texts are from the passion narrative. Because we know that both Matthew and Luke had access to passion traditions not found in Mark, the possibility of some overlap between M and L in their parallels to Mk 14–16 cannot be excluded.

What of Stoldt's third category, concurrence of Matthew and Luke in expressions and wording, contrary to Mark? The list of thirty-five cases includes seven where Matthew and Luke have related but not identical words. These should not be counted. Of the remaining twenty-eight cases, many are inconsequential—καλεῖν for λέγειν (Mk 12.37 par.), διὰ τί for ὅτι meaning 'why' (Mk 2.16 par.), μετά for σύν (Mk 2.26 par.), ἀπό for ὑπό (Mk 8.31 par.), δύνασθαι for ἰσχύειν meaning 'be able' (Mk 9.18 par.), ἄγειν for φέρειν [63] (Mk 11.2 par.), πλήν for ἀλλά (Mk 14.36 par.). As for the remainder of the list, plausible elucidations suggest themselves almost instantly. Should we wonder that Mark's harsh εἰς αὐτόν (1.10) was independently changed to ἐπ' αὐτόν (Mt 3.16 = Lk 3.22; cf. Jn 1.32–3)? Or that Matthew and Luke prefer the usual ἀνοίγω with 'heaven(s)' (cf. Isa 24.18; Ezek 1.1; Jn 1.51; Acts 10.11; Rev 19.11) rather than σχίζω with 'heaven(s)' (Mk 1.10)?

Stoldt's final category (concurrence of Matthew and Luke in diverging from Mark's word form) is the least troublesome for defenders of Markan priority. Of the twenty-two examples, three do not count because different forms appear in Matthew and Luke (see the parallels to Mk 6.7; 11.1; 15.14). The rest (including the addition of γε to Mk 2.22, the addition of τοῦ to Mk 4.3, and the converting of the plural to the singular or vice versa in the parallels to Mk 4.11, 41) are indeed minor and average less than two per Markan chapter.

Our conclusion concerning Stoldt's listing of the minor agreements of Matthew and Luke against Mark is this: it is only their sheer number that impresses. When looked at one by one, almost every agreement has an obvious explanation if one assumes that Matthew and Luke independently employed Mark.

ii. Is there, however, strength in numbers? Should the simple fact that Stoldt can cite two hundred and seventy-two minor agreements be itself sufficient to cause us to conclude that Mark must be the late gospel? We are inclined to think not, and for the following reason. Were one to create two lists, one citing every single place Matthew disagrees with Mark, the other citing every single place Luke disagrees with Mark, those lists would contain

[63] On this see J. Fitzmyer, 'The Use of *Agein* and *Pherein* in the Synoptic Gospels', in *Festschrift to Honor F. Wilbur Gingrich*, ed. E. H. Barth and R. E. Cocroft, Leiden, 1972, pp. 147–60.

thousands of entries. In one small pericope alone, Mt 4.18–22 = Mk 1.16–20, where Matthew and Mark are almost as close as they ever get, there are, by our count, at least twenty-one disagreements. This is indicative of how things are throughout. Matthew and Luke are constantly rewriting Mark and going their own ways. The two disagree with Mark in minutiae at every single turn. That they should then agree with each other against Mark in not quite a hundred minor omissions and that they should hit upon the same or similar words or expressions a few dozen times in editing Mark is almost inevitable. There are only so many ways to revise or correct a Greek sentence. When it is added that Matthew and Luke were both recipients of Christian oral tradition, steeped in biblical Greek, and often motivated by similar redactional interests, there is even less cause to question the possibility of their often concurring against a common source. (We should also not wonder that, through chance, these agreements sometimes are clustered at certain points, as at the parallels to Mk 2.1–12 or 6.30–44. This is not, despite Farmer's claims, a stumbling block for the two-source theory).

iii. Only a handful of the minor agreements move us to postulate the workings of more than coincidence. We have already had occasion to suggest that Mt 26.64 = Lk 22.69–70; Mt 26.67–8 = Lk 22.64; and Mt 26.75 = Lk 22.62 might be accounted for by recourse to common passion traditions. This, however, is very far from certain; and some scholars have claimed that some of the minor agreements demand the hypothesis of an Ur-Markus.[64] In our judgement, the theory of a proto-Mark is not as obviously problematic as many have thought. Nonetheless, probably the most satisfactory explanation for the few minor agreements of consequence lies in the history of the manuscript tradition.[65] Despite all the labours of twentieth-century textual critics, we cannot claim to have in our hands a pristine Greek text; and because the earliest papyri and manuscripts attest a very fluid textual tradition, the supposition—following Streeter—that Matthew and Luke had copies of Mark slightly different from what we have is far from impossible. Farmer, to be sure, has

---

[64] So H. Koester, 'History and Development of Mark's Gospel', in Corley, *Colloquy*, pp. 35–57. The theory is much less popular today than it once was; see Moffatt, pp. 191–4; V. Taylor, *Mark*, pp. 68–73.

[65] So also, in different ways, Streeter, pp. 309–31; T. F. Glasson, 'Did Matthew Use a "Western" Text of Mark?', *ExpT* 55 (1944), pp. 180–4; idem, 'An Early Revision of the Gospel of Mark', *JBL* 85 (1966), pp. 231–3; J. P. Brown, 'An Early Revision of the Gospel of Mark', *JBL* 78 (1959), pp. 215–27. See also the review of Burrows, 'Textual Theories'. Harmonization was probably a greater factor in the textual tradition than Nestle-Aland[26] reveals; see J. K.Elliott, 'Textual Criticism, Assimilation and the Synoptic Gospels', *NTS* 26 (1980), pp. 231–42.

countered this point by observing that Streeter's textual conjectures, made to explain certain minor agreements, must be considered special pleading because they have not been adopted by modern textual critics. This is beside the point. We have no reason to believe that either Matthew or Luke knew Mark in its pristine form. Beyond this, while modern critical editions tend to judge a reading or variant by the number and quality of the manuscripts that contain it, Streeter knew that many of his suggestions about the synoptic texts set him against the weight of the manuscript evidence. For him this proved only that the internal evidence (especially a consideration of scribal tendencies) sometimes outweighed the external evidence (the majority of manuscripts and the Fathers; cf. p. 308). So Streeter, were he alive today, would not consider it news to learn that critical editions which rely as heavily on external evidence as, for instance, Nestle-Aland[26], do not support his proposed readings. The question, therefore, is straightforwardly methodological; and, in the end, it may yet be that, even if Streeter exaggerated their number, some of the minor agreements are best resolved by postulating textual corruption. Certainly if the arguments for the priority of Mark and Q are compelling, it is hard to see what is wrong with Streeter's approach; and in any case the handful of troublesome minor agreements do not carry enough weight to establish another view of synoptic origins. Our current Greek texts are not certain enough for that.

iv. A final point. One way of getting around the apparent problem of the minor agreements is to postulate Luke's knowledge of Matthew[66] or Matthew's knowledge of Luke.[67] As proponents of the two-source theory, and for the reasons given immediately below, we resist this alternative. We prefer to solve the riddle of the minor agreements by recourse to coincidental editing, oral tradition, and textual corruption.

[66] For acceptance of Markan priority combined with Luke's knowledge of Matthew see A. Farrer, 'On Dispensing with Q', in *Studies in the Gospels*, ed. D. E. Nineham, Oxford, 1955, pp. 55–88; A. W. Argyle, 'Evidence for the View that St. Luke Used St. Matthew's Gospel', *JBL* 83 (1964), pp. 390–96; W. Wilkens, 'Zur Frage der literarischen Beziehung zwischen Matthäus und Lukas', *NovT* 8 (1966), pp. 48–57; M. D. Goulder, 'On Putting Q to the Test', *NTS* 24 (1978), pp. 218–34; idem, 'The Order of a Crank', in Tuckett, *Studies*, pp. 111–30; H. B. Green, 'The Credibility of Luke's Transformation of Matthew', in ibid., pp. 131–56; J. Drury, *Tradition and Design in Luke's Gospel*, London, 1976; and Gundry, *Commentary*, passim (but he also accepts the standard two-source theory).

[67] So E. von Dobschütz, 'Matthew as Rabbi and Catechist', in Stanton, *Interpretation*, pp. 26–8. See also the scholars named by B. Weiss, p. 25. This is a distinctly minority position.

(2) Q.[68] If, as we have argued, Mark was a source both of Matthew and Luke, what was the source of the so-called double tradition, that is, the non-Markan material common to Matthew and Luke (about two hundred and thirty verses)? There are four basic solutions: (a) Matthew and Luke had in common another source, the document customarily called 'Q'.[69] (b) Matthew and

---

[68] Lit.: C. K. Barrett, 'Q: A re-examination', *ExpT* 54 (1943), pp. 320–3; T. Boman, *Die Jesus-Überlieferung im Lichte der neueren Volkskunde*, Göttingen, 1967, pp. 101–23; F. Bussby, 'Is Q an Aramaic Document?', *ExpT* 65 (1954), pp. 272–5; H. Biggs, 'The Q Debate Since 1955', *Themelios* 6 (1981), pp. 18–28; W. Bussmann, *Zur Redenquelle*, Halle, 1929; C. E. Carlston and D. Norlan, 'Once More—Statistics and Q', *HTR* 64 (1971), pp. 59–78; D. G. Danner, 'The "Q" Document and the Words of Jesus. A Review of Theodore R. Rosché, "The Words of Jesus and the Future of the 'Q' Hypothesis" ', *RestQ* 26 (1983), pp. 193–201; Davies, *SSM*, pp. 366–86; F. G. Downing, 'Towards the Rehabilitation of Q', *NTS* 11 (1965), pp. 169–81; Delobel, ed., *Logia*, passim; M. Devisch, 'Le document Q, source de Matthieu. Problématique actuelle', in Didier, pp. 71–97; Edwards, *Q*; A. Farrer, 'On Dispensing with Q', in *Studies in the Gospels*, ed. D. E. Nineham, Oxford, 1955, pp. 55–88; Fitzmyer, 'Priority'; O. Linton, 'The Q Problem Reconsidered', in *Studies in the New Testament and Early Christian Literature*, Leiden, 1972, pp. 44–59; W. R. Farmer, 'A Fresh Approach to Q', in *Christianity, Judaism and Other Greco-Roman Cults*, ed. J. Neusner, SJLA 12, Leiden, 1975, part one, pp. 39–50; M. D. Goulder, 'On putting Q to the Test', *NTS* 24 (1978), pp. 218–34; D. Guthrie, *New Testament Introduction*, Downers Grove, 1970, pp. 143–57; Harnack; R. Hodgson, 'On the *Gattung* of Q', *Bib* 66 (1985), pp. 73–95; Hoffmann, *Logienguelle*; J. Jeremias, 'Zur Hypothese einer schriftlichen Logienquelle Q', in *Abba*, pp. 90–2; A. D. Jacobson, 'The Literary Unity of Q', *JBL* 101 (1982), pp. 365–89; Kümmel, *Introduction*, pp. 63–76; J. S. Kloppenborg, 'Tradition and Redaction in the Synoptic Sayings Source', *CBQ* 46 (1984), pp. 34–62; idem, 'Bibliography on Q', in *Society of Biblical Literature 1985 Seminar Papers*, ed. K. H. Richards, Atlanta, 1985, pp. 103–26; Lührmann, *Logienquelle*; T. W. Manson, *Sayings*; F. Neirynck, 'Studies on Q since 1972', *ETL* 56 (1980), pp. 409–13; C. S. Petrie, ' "Q" is Only What You Make It', *NovT* 3 (1959), pp. 28–33; Polag; T. R. Rosché, 'The Words of Jesus and the Future of the "Q" Hypothesis', *JBL* 79 (1960), pp. 210–20; Schulz, *Q*; V. Taylor, 'The Order of Q', in *Essays*, pp. 90–4; idem, 'The Original Order of Q', ibid., pp. 95–118; C. M. Tuckett, 'On the Relationship between Matthew and Luke', *NTS* 30 (1984), pp. 130–42; J. M. Robinson, 'Logoi Sophon. On the Gattung of Q', in *TTEC*, pp. 71–113; P. D. Meyer, 'The Community of Q', unpublished dissertation, University of Iowa, 1967; P. Vassiliadis, 'The Nature and Extent of the Q-Document', *NovT* 20 (1978), pp. 49–73; R. D. Worden, 'Redaction Criticism of Q', *JBL* 94 (1975), pp. 532–46. Although there has been debate on the point, 'Q' presumably originated as an abbreviation for the German 'Quelle'. It can be traced back as far as 1890, in a work of J. Weiss. See W. F. Howard, 'The Origin of the Symbol "Q" ', *ExpT* 50 (1939), pp. 379–80; H. K. McArthur, 'The Origin of the "Q" Symbol', *ExpT* 88 (1977), pp. 119–20; L. H. Silberman, 'Whence the *Siglum* Q? A Conjecture', *JBL* 98 (1979), pp. 287–8; J. J. Schmitt, 'In Search of the Origin of the *Siglum* Q', *JBL* 100 (1981), pp. 609–11; F. Neirynck, 'The Symbol Q (= Quelle)', *ETL* 54 (1978), pp. 119–25; idem, 'Once More—The Symbol Q', *ETL* 55 (1979), pp. 382–3.

[69] So most scholars; see esp. Streeter, pp. 223–94 and the works of Taylor, Downing, Fitzmyer, Kümmel, Tuckett, Jacobson, and Danner (as in the previous note).

Luke had in common several additional sources, some perhaps oral, some perhaps written.[70] (c) Luke knew and used Matthew (see n. 62). (d) Matthew knew and used Luke (see n. 63). Solutions (a) and (b) are the most probable. First, as we shall observe again and again in the course of the commentary, sometimes it is the First Evangelist who seems to preserve the more original form of a saying appearing in the double tradition, at other times it is Luke. This is inexplicable if one evangelist is following the other.[71] Secondly, with the exception of the words of John the Baptist and the temptation stories, Matthew and Luke do not agree in the placement of their common material into the Markan framework. Yet surely, if Matthew had used Luke or Luke had used Matthew, their agreement in this respect would be greater. Thirdly, if Luke drew upon the First Gospel it is remarkable that he betrays no knowledge of the obvious Matthean additions to Markan material (e.g. Mt 3.14–15; 9.13a; 12.5–7; 16.2b–3, 17–19; 19.9; 21.10–11; 26.52–4; 27.19, 24, 51b–53). In other words, Luke seems to have known Mark, not Mark as revised by Matthew.

We are left with options (a) and (b), and the following observations move us to believe that most of the double tradition was taken from a common, written source, Q.

i. Oral tradition is unlikely to explain the word for word correspondence in such sections as

Mt	3.7b–10	=	Lk	3.7b–9
	7.3–5	=		6.41–2
	7.7–11	=		11.9–13
	11.4–11	=		7.22–8
	11.21–23	=		10.13–5
	11.25–7	=		10.21–2
	23.37–8	=		13.34–5
	24.45–1	=		12.42b–6

ii. In Luke most of the double tradition appears in either one of two sections, 6.20–8.3 and 9.51–18.14. In Matthew most of it is preserved in six long, redactionally constructed discourses: 5–7; 10; 11; 18; 23; 24.37–25. Despite the different arrangements (which we attribute almost exclusively to the Matthean redaction), the material in Luke and Matthew reflects a common order, as can be seen from the following list (in which agreements in the Matthean

---

[70] So e.g. Bussmann, *Redenquelle*; Ellis, *Luke*, pp. 21–9; Jeremias, *Theology*, pp. 38–41; Wrege, passim.

[71] Farmer's recognition of this fact has led him to postulate the existence of a sayings collection used by both Matthew and Luke ('A Fresh Approach to Q'). Although he does not wish, for obvious reasons, to equate this source with Q, Farmer's collection is not unlike Q.

and Lukan orders are italicized; the parentheses indicate material which some think sufficiently diverse as to be from different sources.)

Luke's order			Matthew's order	
1	3.7–9	John's preaching	3.7b–10	*1*
2	3.16b–17	John's preaching	3.11–12	*2*
3	4.1–13	The temptation	4.1–11	*3*
4	6.20–3	The beatitudes	5.3,6,4,11–12	*4*
5	6.27–36	Love your enemies	5.44,39–40,42; 7.12; 5.46–7, 45,48	*12,10,11* 24,14 *13,15*
6	6.37–42	On judging	7.1–2; 15.14; 10.24–5; 7.3–5	*21,*50 33, *22*
7	6.43–5	On fruits	7.16–20 (cf. 12.33–5)	*26*
8	6.47–9	Hearers and doers of the Word	7.24–7	*28*
9	7.1–10	The centurion's servant	7.28a,8.5–10,13	*29*
10	7.18–23	The Baptist's question	11.2–6	*39*
11	7.24–8	Jesus' answer	11.7–11	*40*
12	7.31–5	Jesus' answer	11.16–19	*42*
13	9.57–60	On discipleship	8.18–22	31
14	10.2–12	The mission charge	9.37–8; 10.7–16	32
15	10.13–15	Woes	11.21–3	*43*
16	10.16	Jesus' representatives	10.40	*38*
17	10.21–2	The Father praised	11.25–7	*44*
18	10.23–4	The blessedness of the disciples	13.16–17	*48*
19	11.2–4	The Lord's Prayer	6.9–13	16
20	11.9–13	On answers to prayer	7.7–11	23
21	11.14–23	Beelzebul	12.12–30	45
22	11.24–6	On unclean spirits	12.43–5	47
23	11.29–32	The sign of Jonah	12.38–42	46
24	11.33–6	On light	5.15; 6.22–3	6, 18
25	11.39–52	Warnings to the Pharisees	23.25–6,23,6–7 27–8,4,29–32, 34–6,13	*59,58,56* *60,55,61* *62,57*
26	12.2–12	Fearless confession	10.26–33	34
27	12.22–34	On earthly care	6.25–33,19–21	20,17
28	12.39–46	On faithfulness	24.43–51	68

29	12.51–3	Why Jesus came	10.34–6	35
30	12.58–9	Agree with your adversary	5.25–6	8
31	13.18–21	The mustard seed and leaven	13.31–3	49
(32	13.23–30	Rejection in the kingdom	7.13–14; 25.10–12; 7.22–3; 8.11–12	25,69 27,30)
33	13.34–5	Lament over Jerusalem	23.37–9	*63*
(34	14.16–21	The great supper	22.2–10	54)
35	14.26–7	Conditions of discipleship	10.37–8	36
36	14.34–5	Parable of salt	5.13	5
(37	15.4–7	The lost sheep	18.12–14	52)
38	16.13	Serving two masters	6.24	19
39	16.16–17	The Torah	11.12–13; 5.18	41,7
40	16.18	On divorce	5.32	9
41	17.3–4	On forgiveness	18.21–2	53
42	17.5–6	On faith	17.20	51
43	17.23–7	The days of the Son of man	24.26–7,37–8	*64,66*
44	17.33–7	The days of the Son of man	10.39; 24.40–1, 28	37,67 65
(45	19.11–28	The parable of the pounds	25.14–30	*70*)

Several observations are to be made. To begin with, the two gospels run parallel through the first four items. Next, all of the material from Mt 15.14 on has Lukan parallels only after Lk 11.36. On the two-source theory, this makes sense: Matthew, having completely used up the first half of Q by the time he comes to the mid-point of his gospel, can draw only from the last half of Q thereafter. Thirdly, Matthew and Luke share four common, large blocks of material:

Luke	Matthew		Luke	Matthew	
1 6.17, 20a	5.1–2	*1*	1 10.2	9.37–8	*1*
2 6.20b–3	5.3,6,4,11–12	*2*	2 10.3	10.16	8
3 6.27–8	5.44	5	3 10.4	10.9–10a	*3*
4 6.29	5.39–40	*3*	4 10.5	10.11–12	*5*
5 6.30	5.42	*4*	5 10.6	10.13	6
6 6.31	7.12	11	6 10.7	10.10b	*4*
7 6.32–33	5.46–47	7	7 10.9	10.7	*2*
8 6.35b	5.45	*6*	8 10.12	10.15	7

Luke		Matthew		Luke		Matthew	
9	6.36	5.48	8				
10	6.37–8	7.1–2	9				
11	6.41–2	7.3–5	10				
12	6.43	7.18	13				
13	6.44	7.16	12				
14	6.46	7.21	14				
15	6.47–9	7.24–7	15				
1	11.39–41	23.25–26	5	1	17.23	24.23	2
2	11.42	23.23	4	2	17.24	24.27	4
3	11.43	23.6–7	2	3	17.26–7	24.37–9a	5
4	11.44	23.27	6	4	17.30	24.39b	6
5	11.45–6	23.4	1	5	17.31	24.17–18	1
6	11.47–8	23.29–30	7	6	17.34–6	24.40–1	7
7	11.49–51	23.34–6	8	7	17.37	24.28	3
8	11.52	23.13	3				

These four blocks appear in the same order in Matthew and Luke, and from them one may infer the existence of a document which contained a programmatic sermon towards its beginning, a missionary discourse and series of anti-Pharisaic denunciations towards its middle, and a collection of eschatological prophecies and warnings at its end.

iii. There is only one true doublet (a text occurring twice) in Mark (9.35 = 10.43–4). Luke, however, has twelve (see Fitzmyer, *Luke* 1, pp. 81–2)—four of which are shared by Matthew:

From Mark						From Q			
Mk 4.25	=	Lk 8.18	=	Mt 13.12		Mt 25.29	=	Lk 19.26	
8.34–5	=	9.23–4	=	16.24		10.38–9	=	14.27; 17.33	
8.38	=	9.26	=	16.27		10.32–33	=	12.8–9	
13.11	=	21.14–15	=	24.9–10		10.19–20	=	12.11–12	

Some of the twice repeated lines may, of course, be explained by an author's special interests (see e.g. on 7.20). But the many doublets in Luke and those shared by Matthew and Luke are best accounted for by the overlapping of sources.[72] This is particularly so because Luke, despite his twelve doublets, demonstrably shows

---

[72] There is reason to think that Q overlapped not only with Mark but also with M; this, at any rate, would go far towards explaining why several passages common to the double tradition (e.g. Lk 14.16–24 = Mt 22.2–10) show wide divergences. Perhaps Matthew sometimes conflated Q and M just as he sometimes conflated Q and Mark. On the overlapping of Mark and Q see B. H. Throckmorton, 'Did Mark know Q?', *JBL* 67 (1948), pp. 319–29; J. P. Brown, 'Mark as Witness to an Edited Form of Q', *JBL* 80 (1961), pp. 29–44; M. Devisch, 'La relation entre l'évangile de Marc et le document "Q" ', in Sabbe, pp. 59–91; Laufen, *passim*; and W. Schenk, 'Der Einflus der Logienquelle auf das Markusevangelium', *ZNW* 70 (1979), pp. 141–65. In our estimation, the evidence does not require that Mark knew Q (so Throckmorton and Laufen, against Schenk).

a tendency to avoid doublets wherever possible;[73] and Matthew too has eliminated them on at least five occasions.[74]

iv. If the Griesbach hypothesis were valid, one would not expect the double tradition to display any theological or literary unity. But it does so when set over against Mark. As A. D. Jacobson ('Literary Unity') has argued, the Q material distinguishes itself by its forms (e.g. the beatitude,[75] the woe,[76] the prophetic threat[77]), by its vocabulary (κρίνω,[78] κρίσις,[79] κριτής,[80] τίς ἐξ ὑμῶν[81]), and by its deuteronomistic interpretation of history.[82] One cannot, therefore, complain that Q is simply an amorphous collection of sayings with no inner unity.

v. There are two very common objections to the Q hypothesis: (1) scholars do not agree in their reconstructions and (2) sometimes Matthew and Luke have different Greek words which are best explained as translation variants, which could not be if they worked with the same Greek source. Neither of these observations is insuperable. The first depends upon the reconstructions compared. C. S. Petrie ('Q'), for instance, examined the seventeen lists printed in Moffatt's *Introduction* and showed that not one verse from Matthew is common to them all.

---

[73] See H. Schürmann, *Untersuchungen*, pp. 279–89. He convincingly argues that the Lukan doublets are due to the overlapping of Luke's sources, not Luke's redactional aims.

[74] Mk 4.9, 23/Lk 8.8c = Mt 13.9/Lk 14.35
Mk 4.21/Lk 8.16 = Mt 5.15/Lk 11.33
Mk 4.22/Lk 8.17 = Mt 10.26/Lk 12.2
Mk 6.8, 10, 11/Lk 9.3, 4, 5 = Mt 10.10–12, 14/Lk 10.4–5+7, 10–11
Mk 12.38–39/Lk 20.46 = Mt 23.6–7/Lk 11.43

[75] From Q: Mt 5.3, 6, 11–12/Lk 6.20, 21, 22–3; Mt 11.6/Lk 7.23; Mt 13.16/Lk 10.23; Mt 24.46/Lk 12.43; perhaps also Lk 11.28. Mark has two beatitudes: 11.9–10. Q consistently has μακάριος; Mark both times has εὐλογέω.

[76] See Mt 11.21/Lk 10.13; Mt 23.25/(Lk 11.39); Mt 23.23/Lk 11.42; (Mt 23.6–7)/Lk 11.43; Mt 23.27/Lk 11.44; (Mt 23.4)/Lk 11.46; Mt 23.29/Lk 11.47; Mt 23.13/Lk 11.52; and perhaps Mt 18.7/Lk 17.1. There are no woes in Mark.

[77] Mt 3.7–10/Lk 3.7–9; Mt 7.21/Lk 6.46; Mt 11.21–4/Lk 10.13–15; Mt 12.41–2/Lk 11.31–2; Mt 23.34–6/Lk 11.49–51; Lk 11.(39), 42–4, 46–7, 52 par.; Mt 10.32–3/Lk 12.8–9; Mt 16.2–3/Lk 12.54–6; Mt 7.22–3/Lk 13.26–7; Mt 8.11–12/Lk 13.28–9; Mt 23.37–9/Lk 13.34–5; Mt 24.37–41/Lk 17.26–7, 34–5. From Mark see only Mk 12.38–40; 8.38.

[78] Q: 3; Mt: 0; Lk 6.37–8 par.; 22.30 par.

[79] Q: 4–6; Mk :0; Lk 10.14 par.; 11.31 par.; 11.32 par.; 11.42 par.; cf. Mt 10.15; 11.24 (cf. Lk 10.12).

[80] Q: 3; Mk : 0; Lk 11.19 par.; 12.58 par. (*bis*).

[81] Lk 12.25 par.; 11.11 par.; 14.5 par.; 15.4/Mt 18.12; cf. Lk 11.33 par.

[82] See Jacobson, 'Q', pp. 383–88, relying upon Steck, *passim*. According to the latter, the deuteronomic tradition contained these elements: Israel's persistent disobedience; God's sending of the prophets; Israel's rejection of the prophets; God's punishment of Israel; a calling to repentance; the promise of redemption for Israel and of punishment for Israel's enemies.

But it is hardly fair to think that the work of Moffatt (who wrote before Streeter's *The Four Gospels*) accurately reflects the current state of the discussion: rather does it represent a period in which research on Q was still in its infancy. And, since Moffatt's time, critical scholarship has come much closer to producing a consensus. If one compares the reconstructions of T. W. Manson, V. Taylor, A. Polag, S. Schulz, P. Hoffmann, H. C. Kee, R. A. Edwards, and J. Fitzmyer, there is a considerable measure of agreement.

As for the second objection, it loses its force because the vast majority of alleged translation variants are naturally explained as due to the redactional tendencies of the evangelists. The proof of this we leave to the commentary. Here we need add only that granted a relatively early date for Q, the possibility of oral tradition influencing Q's Greek recensions must also be admitted (see point vii below). (We do not wish to deny that Q was originally composed in Hebrew or Aramaic—only that, if it was, Matthew and Luke did not use different Greek translations.)

vi. It is impossible to date the Q document (although it must be placed before Matthew and Luke)[83] or to locate the city where it was composed.[84] As for its author's identity, if Papias' remarks about the logia do not apply to Q (see p. 17), then nothing more can be said.

vii. Matthew and Luke in all likelihood knew Q in slightly different forms (Q^{mt}, Q^{lk}). There is no reason to believe that, once written, Q's text was set in concrete. On the contrary, Q, if it existed, circulated during a time when the oral Jesus tradition was still very much alive, and one cannot but suppose that, when Q was copied, editorial changes were made and new material added. Hence, when the exegete is confronted by texts in Matthew and Luke that are to be assigned to Q yet which nevertheless exhibit differences not explicable in terms of redactional motives, there is sometimes good reason to invoke different recensions of Q (see e.g. on 5.3–12).[85]

(3) *M*. If one subtracts from Matthew the material shared with Mark and Luke, the following matter is left:

[83] Streeter dated Q ca. 50. He was followed by T. W. Manson and most modern scholars. Sometimes Lk 11.50–1 = Mt 23.35 has been thought important for the issue; see Kümmel, *Introduction*, pp. 70–1.

[84] Streeter placed Q in Antioch. Most scholars have been content to assign it to Syria or Palestine.

[85] Having inferred this much, we remain doubtful as to whether anyone has successfully reconstructed the whole tradition-history of Q. For a review of attempts see Kloppenborg, 'Tradition'.

1.1 The opening sentence	redactional
1.2–17 The genealogy	partly redactional
1.18–2.23 The infancy stories	
3.14–15 John and Jesus	redactional
4.13–16 Jesus in Galilee	redactional
4.23–5 A summary report (cf. Mk 1.39; 6.6)	redactional
5.1–2 Jesus on the mountain (cf. Lk 6.17,20a)	redactional
5.5 A beatitude	
5.7 A beatitude	
5.8 A beatitude	
5.9 A beatitude	
5.10 A beatitude	redactional
5.13a 'You are the salt of the earth'	redactional
5.14a 'You are the light of the world'	redactional
5.16 'Let your light so shine . . .'	redactional
5.17 'I came not to abolish the law . . .'	
5.19 'Whoever then relaxes one of the least . . .'	
5.20 'Unless your righteousness . . .'	redactional
5.21–4 On murder	
5.27–8 On adultery	
5.31–2 On divorce	partly redactional
5.33–7 On swearing	
5.38–9a On retaliation	redactional
5.41 On going the extra mile	
5.43 On loving the neighbour	redactional
6.1 On righteousness before men	redactional?
6.2–4 On almsgiving	
6.5–6 On prayer	
6.7–9a The introduction to the Lord's Prayer	
6.10b–c,13b Clauses in the Lord's Prayer	redactional?
6.14–15 On forgiveness (cf. Mk 11.25)	redactional
6.16–18 On fasting	
6.34 On worry	redactional
7.6 On casting pearls before swine	
7.12b On the law and the prophets	redactional
7.14 The way to life	
7.15 A warning about false prophets	redactional
7.19–20 Trees for the fire	redactional
7.28–8.1 The conclusion of Mt 5–7 (cf. Lk 7.1)	redactional
8.17 A fulfilment quotation	redactional
9.13 Mercy desired, not sacrifice	redactional
9.26 On Jesus' fame	redactional
9.27–31 Two blind men healed (cf. Mk 10.46–52)	redactional
9.32–4 A dumb demoniac healed (cf. Mk 3.22–30)	redactional
9.35–6 On sheep without a shepherd	redactional
10.2a The names of the twelve	redactional
10.5–8 Jesus' charge to the twelve (cf. Lk 10.2,9)	partly redactional
10.16b Serpents and doves	redactional?
10.23 The coming of the Son of man	
10.25b 'If they called the master Beelzebul . . .'	
10.36 'A man's enemies . . .'	redactional

10.41 On receiving prophets	redactional?
11.1 Conclusion of second discourse	redactional
11.14 John the Baptist is Elijah	redactional
11.20 Jesus rebukes Galilean cities	redactional
11.23b Miracles in Sodom (cf. Lk 10.13)	redactional
11.28–30 Comfort for the heavy-laden	partly redactional
12.5–7 Mercy desired, not sacrifice	redactional
12.17–21 A formula quotation	redactional
12.23 The Son of David (cf. 9.33; Lk 11.14)	redactional
12.36–7 Every evil word	redactional?
12.45d On this generation	redactional
13.18 'Hear then the parable of the sower'	redactional
13.24–30 The parable of the tares	
13.35 An OT quotation	redactional
13.36–43 The parable of the tares interpreted	redactional
13.44–46 Two parables on the value of the kingdom	
13.47–50 The parable of the drag-net	
13.51–52 The conclusion of Mt 13	redactional
14.28–31 Peter walking on the water	redactional
14.33 Jesus as the Son of God	redactional
15.12–13 The Pharisees	redactional
15.23–5 Jesus sent to Israel	redactional
15.30–1 Jesus heals	redactional
16.2b–3 On signs (cf. Lk 12.54–6)	
16.11b–12 The teaching of the Pharisees and Sadducees	redactional
16.17–19 Peter and the keys	
16.22b Peter speaks	redactional
17.6–7 The disciples at the Transfiguration	redactional
17.13 John and Elijah	redactional
17.24–7 The stater in the fish's mouth	
18.3–4 As a little child (cf. Mk 10.15)	redactional
18.10. The angels of the little ones	redactional
18.14 One of these little ones	redactional
18.16–20 On the church	partly redactional
18.23–35 The unmerciful servant	
19.1a The conclusion of Mt 18	redactional
19.10–12 On eunuchs	partly redactional
20.1–16 Parable of the labourers in the vineyard	
21.4–5 A fulfilment quotation	redactional
21.10–11 The entrance into Jerusalem (cf. Mk 11.11)	redactional
21.14 Crowds in the temple	redactional
21.15b–16 The Son of David	redactional
21.28–32 The parable of the two sons (cf. Lk 7.29–30)	
21.43 The kingdom ·	redactional
(21.44 The scribes and Pharisees	textually uncertain)
22.1–14 The parable of the marriage feast (cf. Lk 14.15–24)	
22.33 The crowds	redactional
22.40 On the Law and the prophets	redactional

23.1–3 Moses' seat	partly redactional
23.5 On phylacteries	
23.7b–10 On the one teacher	
23.15–22 Woes	
23.24 Blind guides	redactional?
23.28 Outward appearance/inward state	redactional?
23.32–3 Gehenna	redactional
24.10–12 On false prophets	redactional
24.20 Not on a sabbath	redactional
24.30a The sign of the Son of man	redactional
25.1–13 The parable of the ten virgins	
25.14–30 The parable of the talents (cf. Lk 19.11–27)	
25.31–46 The last judgment	
26.1 A transitional verse	redactional
26.44 A third prayer in Gethsemane	redactional
26.50 Jesus arrested	redactional
26.52–4 The sword	partly redactional
27.3–10 Judas	partly redactional
27.19 Pilate's wife	
27.24–5 Pilate washes his hand	
27.36 The guard	redactional
27.43 Words of mockery	redactional
27.51b–3 Signs and wonders	
27.62–6 The guard at the tomb	
28.2–4 An angelic appearance	
28.9–10 Jesus appears (cf. Jn 20.14–18)	
28.11–15 Soldiers bribed	
28.16–20 Jesus' closing words	partly redactional

Two facts are immediately apparent. First, a great portion of the material found in neither Mark nor Luke is redactional or partly redactional. Secondly, of the remaining, non-redactional matter, all but 17.24–7 (the stater in the fish's mouth) falls into one of five categories. There are (1) the infancy stories (1.18–2.23), (2) parables (13.24–30, 44–6, 47–50; 18.23–35; 20.1–16; 21.28–32; 22.1–14; 25.1–13, 14–30, 31–46), (3) several isolated sayings (5.5, 7, 8, 9—these from Q^{mt}; 5.41; 7.6; 10.23; 11.28–30; 16.17–19), (4) three groups of sayings (5.21–4, 27–8, 33–7; 6.1–18; 23.1–3, 5, 7b–10, 15–22), and, finally, (5) a few traditions about the passion and the resurrection (27.3–10, 19, 24–5, 51b–3, 62–6; 28.2–4, 9–10, 11–15).

It has, from time to time, been argued that, in addition to Mark and Q, Matthew also had at his disposal a third written document, 'M'. Streeter, in fact, thought he could both date this hypothetical source and pin down its place of origin (ca. A.D. 60, in Jerusalem). Of late, however, his conjectures on this matter have not had much of a following—and rightly so, in our judgement. There is no good reason to think of M as a unified composition. Streeter and like-minded scholars were moved to their position in part because they gravely underestimated the extent of the Matthean redaction. For them there was a vast amount of pre-Matthean, non-Markan, non-Q material in the First Gospel, and it was natural to suppose that much or most of it came from a common (written) source. But contemporary interpreters rightly perceive a much larger contribution from Matthew's own hand, so that the amount of material available for incorporation into a hypothetical M source is accordingly much less than it was for Streeter. When to this it is added that the sayings peculiar to Matthew do not readily fall together so as to create a homogeneous and coherent whole, the dismissal of an M document seems to recommend itself.

If M is not to be equated with a particular document, the alternative is to employ the letter as a convenient symbol for a plurality of sources, for those sources behind Matthew—oral and/or written—which cannot be identified with Mark, Q, or Matthean redaction.[86] Unfortunately, any attempt to be more precise, that is, to reconstruct in detail the content and scope of the presumed pre-Matthean sources, necessarily involves indulging in conjecture. There is here no room for certainty. Yet having given caution its due, we tentatively offer the following suggestions concerning M.

i. In addition to a cycle of infancy traditions, a few isolated sayings, and some passion traditions, Matthew may well have been acquainted with a special collection of parables, a collection perhaps resembling the small parable source some have detected behind Mk 4. There are in M ten parables:

13.24–30 The weeds and wheat
13.44–6 The hidden treasure and the pearl of great price
13.47–50 The net
18.23–35 The unfaithful servant
20.1–16 The workers in the vineyard
21.28–32 The two sons
22.1–14 The marriage supper
25.1–13 The ten virgins
(25.14–30 The talents)
25.31–46 The last judgement

Most of these begin in a similar fashion, either with ὁμοία ἐστιν ἡ βασιλεία τῶν οὐρανῶν (13.44, 45, 47; 20.1) or with ὡμοιώθη (or:

---

[86] Our viewpoint prevents us from making too many generalizations about the character of M as a whole. E.g. it will not do to speak of the consistently anti-Pharisaic cast of M or to argue that it is all of Palestinian origin. We thus distance ourselves from the approach of earlier scholars such as Allen, Streeter, and T. W. Manson.

ὁμοιωθήσεται) ἡ βασιλεία τῶν οὐρανῶν (13.24; 18.23; 22.2; 25.1). While these introductory formulas are perhaps redactional (cf. 13.31 diff. Mk 4.30; 13.33 diff. Lk 13.20), they do at least show us that Matthew could conceive of most of the parables in M as treating of the same subject. It is just possible, therefore, that he was familiar with a collection of thematically related parables, parables about the kingdom of God.

ii. In the commentary we have postulated behind Mt 6.1–18 and 5.21–37 respectively a pre-Matthean 'cult-didache' on the one hand and a group of three sayings having the form, ἠκούσατε ὅτι ἐρρέθη . . . ἐγὼ δὲ λέγω ὑμῖν . . . on the other (5.21–4, 27–8, 33–7). There is also good cause to infer the existence of a short sayings collection behind 23.1–22. Certain verses within this section have their counterparts in Q (see Lk 11.43, 46, 52). But 23.1–3, 5, 7b–10, and 15–22 are without parallel. Because they also have to do with the same subject matter, namely, the scribes and Pharisees, they appear to derive from a pre-Matthean discourse, one which may have overlapped to some extent with a portion of Q (cf. Lk 11.39–52).

iii. It is tempting to conclude that the sources behind Mt 6.1–18 and 23.1–22 were knit together in the pre-Matthean tradition. Both have to do with the relation between church and synagogue, and the other similarities are striking indeed.

'Do not be like them' (6.8)	'Do not act according to their deeds' (23.3)
'Do not do your righteousness before men, πρὸς τὸ θεαθῆναι by them' (6.1; cf. 6.2, 5, 16)	'All their deeds they do πρὸς τὸ θεαθῆναι by men' (23.5; the common Greek words occur only two times in the First Gospel)
'φιλοῦσιν to pray standing ἐν ταῖς συναγωγαῖς and in the corners of the streets' (6.5)	'φιλοῦσιν the first seats in the feasts and the first seats ἐν ταῖς συναγωγαῖς' (23.6)
'so as to be glorified ὑπὸ τῶν ἀνθρώπων' (6.2)	'They love to be called "rabbi, rabbi" ὑπὸ τῶν ἀνθρώπων' (23.7)
'hypocrites' (6.2, 5, 16); the theme of hypocrisy is prominent	'hypocrites' (23.13); the theme of hypocrisy is prominent
6.1–18 is built around a triad of subjects (almsgiving, prayer, fasting)	In 23.1–12 there are three woes (13, 15, 16) and three μή + καλέω imperatives (8–10)

'your Father who sees in secret will reward you' (6.4, 6, 18)

'Call no man father on earth, for you have one Father, who is in heaven' (23.9)

These parallels, which encompass both vocabulary and themes, and which are not simply to be put down to Matthean editing, cannot be dismissed as incidental. While, therefore, our proposal remains far from certain, we are inclined to detect behind Mt 6.1–18 and 23.1–22 a strongly anti-Pharisaic source which instructed Jewish Christians on the differences between themselves and the unbelieving members of the synagogues. It told the followers of Jesus to accept the words of the Jewish leaders (23.2–3) but to beware of imitating their hypocritical actions (6.3, 6, 17; 23.3). It called for humility and purity of intention; it stressed that religious consciousness should be focused not on one's fellows but on the Father in heaven (6.1, 3–4, 6, 17–18; 23.8–12).

VI. THE DATE OF MATTHEW[87]

(1) *Scholarly opinion.* The spectrum of opinion concerning the dating of Matthew's gospel may be illustrated as follows:

A.D. 40–50:	H. Grotius
A.D. 50–60:	M. Meinertz, J. A. T. Robinson
A.D. 50–64:	B. Reicke
ca. A.D. 60:	G. Maier
before A.D. 63:	R. H. Gundry
A.D. 60–70:	F. Godet, W. Michaelis
A.D. 65–75:	W. C. Allen
before A.D. 70:	C. F. D. Moule (tentatively), E. E. Ellis
A.D. 70–110:	K. Stendahl, A. Wikenhauser, P. S. Minear
A.D. 70–75:	A. von Harnack
A.D. 70–80:	J. Weiss, W. Sanday, W. R. Farmer
before A.D. 75:	A. Plummer
ca. A.D. 80:	D. Hare

[87] Lit.: Bacon, pp. 90–100; C. H. Dodd, 'The Fall of Jerusalem and the "Abomination of Desolation" ', *JRS* 37 (1947), pp. 47–54; E. E. Ellis, 'Dating the New Testament', *NTS* 26 (1980), pp. 487–502; Gundry, *Commentary*, pp. 599–609; A. von Harnack, *The Date of Acts and of the Synoptic Gospels* (trans. of *Neue Untersuchungen zur Apostelgeschichte und zur Abfassungszeit der synoptischen Evangelien*, 1911), New York and London, 1911; A. H. McNeile, *An Introduction to the Study of the New Testament*, 2nd ed. rev. by C. S. C. Williams, Oxford, 1953, pp. 28, 32–4; Moffatt, pp. 211–17; B. Reicke, 'Synoptic Prophecies on the Destruction of Jerusalem', in *Studies in the New Testament and Early Christian Literature*, ed. D. E. Aune, NovTSup 33, Leiden, 1972, pp. 121–34; J. A. T. Robinson, *Redating the New Testament*, London, 1976.

A.D. 80–100:   E. Renan, T. Zahn (in Greek), F. C. Burkitt, B. W. Bacon, A. H. McNeile, C. G. Montefiore, F. V. Filson, G. Bornkamm, R. Walker, D. Hill, R. H. Fuller, W. Marxsen, W. G. Kümmel, E. Schweizer, J. D. Kingsbury, R. E. Brown

A.D. 80–90:   P. Bonnard, W. Grundmann, J. P. Meier, U. Luz

ca. A.D. 85:   B. H. Streeter

A.D. 85–105:   J. C. Fenton

ca. A.D. 90:   E. Lohse

A.D. 90–100:   E. von Dobschütz, G. D. Kilpatrick

A.D. 90–5:   G. Strecker

ca. A.D. 100:   M. S. Enslin, F. W. Beare

after A.D. 100: F. C. Baur, O. Pfleiderer, H. J. Holtzmann, A. Loisy, H. von Soden

Three inferences are to be drawn. (i) Twentieth-century scholarship shies away from placing Matthew after A.D. 100. (Baur, Pfleiderer, Holtzmann, Loisy, and von Soden all belonged to the nineteenth century or to the beginning of the twentieth century.) (ii) The majority opinion is that the First Gospel was composed in the final quarter of the first century A.D. (iii) There is presently a weighty minority wishing to push the date back before A.D. 70 (J. A. T. Robinson, E. E. Ellis, C. F. D. Moule, B. Reicke, G. Maier, R. H. Gundry).

(2) *Explicit patristic testimony*. Papias, the Bishop of Hierapolis, is seemingly the first witness to refer to Matthew by name (in Eusebius, *H.E.* 3.39): Ματθαῖος μὲν οὖν Ἑβραΐδι διαλέκτῳ τὰ λόγια συνετάξατο, ἡρμήνευσεν δ'αὐτὰ ὡς ἦν δυνατὸς ἕκαστος. (For discussion of these difficult words see pp. 8–17.) Although nothing is here stated about Matthew's date, it is to be observed that *if* Papias understood himself to be referring to our Matthew *then* the time of Papias' writing supplies a *terminus ad quem* for the First Gospel. Usually, on the basis of uncertain inferences and the authority of Philip Sidetes (early fifth century), Papias is thought to have composed his 'Expositions of the Oracles of the Lord' during the latter years of Hadrian's reign, ca. A.D. 130–140.[88] But, as R. H. Gundry has argued, Philip is not a reliable source, and Eusebius, who wrote a hundred years before Philip, affirms that Papias became well known during the time of Ignatius (d. ca. A.D. 107) and Polycarp (ca. A.D. 70–155). Moreover, Eusebius recalls the facts about Papias *before* turning to the persecutions in Trajan's day (A.D. 98–117). Papias *may* therefore,

---

[88] See e.g. J. B. Lightfoot, *Essays on the Work entitled Supernatural Religion*, Cambridge, 1889, pp. 147–50.

have written ca. 100 or before, in which case Matthew would have to be dated even earlier.[89]

With regard to the title of Matthew, ΕΥΑΓΓΕΛΙΟΝ ΚΑΤΑ ΜΑΘΘΑΙΟΝ,[90] no sure conclusion can be reached. 'Gospel according to Matthew' certainly did not belong to the autograph.[91] Among other things, the textual tradition supplies more than one superscription (see n. 90), and the other canonical gospels also have superscriptions with the form, ΕΥΑΓΓΕΛΙΟΝ ΚΑΤΑ + name. Matthew's title must, nevertheless, be early in view of the unanimous attribution of our gospel to Matthew, and a date as early as A.D. 125, although not absolutely demanded by the evidence, is quite reasonable.[92] Thus 'Gospel according to Matthew' reinforces the evidence of Papias: the First Gospel was already known—and considered apostolic—during the first quarter of the second century A.D.[93]

There are several patristic sources that purport to supply more than general information about Matthew's time of composition. (i) According to Clement of Alexandria (in Eusebius, *H.E.* 6.14), Origen (*Comm. in Jn* 6.32), Eusebius (*H.E.* 3.24), and Jerome (*De vir. ill.* 3), Matthew was the first gospel to be penned. Because, however, such a tradition could readily have arisen out of the belief that Greek Matthew is the translation of a primitive, Semitic original (cf. Papias in Eusebius, *H.E.* 3.39) or out of the notion that the order of the gospel collection—Matthew was usually in the first place already in the second century[94]—reflected the order of composition (cf. Irenaeus, *Adv. haer.* 3.1.1; Origen, in Eusebius, *H.E.* 6.25), the Fathers do not command much authority in this matter. (ii) According to Irenaeus, *Adv. haer.* 3.1.1 (= Eusebius, *H.E.* 5.8), Matthew 'issued a written gospel among the Hebrews in their own dialect, while Peter and Paul were preaching at Rome, and laying the foundations of the church'. The source for this

---

[89] Gundry, *Commentary*, pp. 610–11. For a date ca. A.D. 110 see U. H. J. Körtner, *Papias von Hierapolis*, FRLANT 133, Göttingen, 1983.

[90] ℵ B: ΚΑΤΑ ΜΑΘΘΑΙΟΝ. D W *f*[13] Maj: ΕΥΑΓΓΕΛΙΟΝ ΚΑΤΑ ΜΑΤΘΑΙΟΝ (W: ΜΑΘΘ). 1241 *al*: ΑΡΧΗ ΣΥΝ ΘΕΩ ΤΟΥ ΚΑΤΑ ΜΑΘΘΑΙΟΝ ΕΥΑΓΓΕΛΙΟΥ. *f*¹ *al*: ΑΓΙΟΝ ΕΥΑΓΓΕΛΙΟΝ ΚΑΤΑ ΜΑΘΘΑΙΟΝ. L *al*: ΕΚ ΤΟΥ ΚΑΤΑ ΜΑΘΘΑΙΟΝ.

[91] Against Kilpatrick, pp. 138–9, the First Gospel was not originally published as a pseudepigraphon.

[92] So J. H. Ropes, *The Synoptic Gospels*, Cambridge, 1934, pp. 103–4; Kilpatrick, p. 138. Hengel, *Mark*, pp. 64–85, traces the gospel titles back to the end of the first century. Cf. Luz 1, p. 77.

[93] The possibility that our gospel was penned by an unknown Matthew who was later identified with his apostolic namesake is remote. As Luz 1, p. 77 observes, the name 'Matthew' was not overly popular, and the use of 'Matthew' in 9.9 and 10.3 is not likely to be coincidence.

[94] Moffatt, p. 14; K. L. Carroll, 'The Creation of the Four-fold Gospel', *BJRL* 37 (1954), pp. 68–77.

proposition remains uncertain, although it may simply be Irenaeus' own inference, founded upon his conviction that Matthew was written before Mark (see above) and that Mark was composed after Peter's death (cf. *Adv. haer.* 3.1.2 and the Anti-Marcionite Prologues).[95] (iii) Later testimony—such as that of Nicephorus Callistus' (d. 1335) 'Ecclesiastical History', according to which Matthew wrote exactly fifteen years after the ascension—cannot, for lack of early support, be seriously considered.

(3) *Early citations or allusions.* Some scholars (e.g. H. Koester) deny that the earliest of the apostolic Fathers betray certain knowledge of canonical Matthew. We, however, do not find this judgement satisfactory. Leaving aside the possibility that either the author of the Fourth Gospel[96] or the author of 1 Peter[97] knew Matthew, both the writings of Ignatius of Antioch (d. ca. A.D. 107) and the Didache (first half of the second century A.D.?) exhibit dependence upon the First Gospel (see on 2.2; 3.15; 5.38–42; 6.9–15; 15.13).[98] This being so, we have evidence buttressing the inference drawn from Papias' testimony and from the date of Matthew's title: the First Gospel cannot have seen the light of day much later than A.D. 100.

In addition to Ignatius and the Didache, the following authors or documents from the first half of the second century appear to have known Matthew: Polycarp (d. ca. A.D. 156; see on 5.10), the Epistle of Barnabas (ca. A.D. 135?; see on 22.14), the Gospel of Peter (before A.D. 200), and Justin Martyr (ca. A.D. 100–165; see

---

[95] For the possibility of Irenaeus' knowledge of and dependence upon Papias see J. Kürzinger, 'Irenäus und sein Zeugnis zur Sprache des Matthäusevangeliums', *NTS* 10 (1963), pp. 111–12.

[96] We have come to no firm decision on this vexed matter—although we are persuaded that *if* John did know one or more of the synoptics he also had access to independent tradition. Lit.: Dodd, *Tradition*; M. de Solages, *Jean et les synoptiques*, Leiden, 1979; F. Neirynck et al., *Jean et les synoptiques*, BETL 49, Leiden, 1979; J. Muddiman, 'John's Use of Matthew', *ETL* 59 (1983), pp. 333–7; D. M. Smith, *Johannine Christianity*, Columbia, 1984, pp. 97–172.

[97] Luz 1, p. 76 reckons with the possibility that 1 Peter knew and used Matthew. Compare esp. 1 Pet 2.7 with Mt 21.42; 1 Pet 2.12 with Mt 5.16; 1 Pet 3.14 with Mt 5.10; 1 Pet 3.8–9 with Mt 5.39, 44; and 1 Pet 4.14 with Mt 5.11–12.

[98] On Ignatius and Matthew see Massaux, pp. 94–135, and C. Trevett, 'Approaching Matthew from the Second Century', *JSNT* 20 (1984), pp. 59–67; also R. Bauckham, 'The Study of Gospel Traditions Outside the Canonical Gospels: Problems and Perspectives', in Wenham, *Tradition*, pp. 369–403. It should be observed here that even though we are persuaded that both Ignatius and the author of the Didache knew Matthew, this does not entail that they did not also have access to extra-canonical Jesus traditions, including perhaps some of Matthew's special sources (M). (This last possibility is, in the case of Ignatius, occasioned by the fact that most of his parallels to Matthew are specifically to M material; see J. Smit Sibinga, 'Ignatius and Matthew', *NovT* 8 (1966), pp. 263–83).

Dial. 78). Perhaps 2 Clement (before A.D. 150) should be added to this list (see on 7.21 and 10.32).[99]

(4) *Internal evidence and other considerations*. If the external evidence makes firm a *terminus ad quem* ca. A.D. 100, the *terminus a quo* is, obviously, fixed by the last dateable event recorded in the gospel, this being Jesus' death in either A.D. 30 or 33. Beyond this the external evidence will not take us. Other facts must be considered.

A. *The synoptic problem*. The authors of this commentary are fully persuaded—and have argued herein at length—that the First Evangelist knew and used the gospel of Mark. Because they also see no good reason to question the prevalent judgement that the Second Gospel was put together in the 60s or very shortly after the fall of Jerusalem,[100] Matthew, it follows, was almost certainly composed after A.D. 70. It goes without saying, however, that those who hold to the Griesbach hypothesis or who on other grounds reject Markan priority will find the point without force.

B. *Mt. 22.7*. In the middle of the parable of the great supper, Mt 22.1–10 (cf. Lk 14.15–24; Gos. Thom. 64), the redactor has inserted this: 'The king was furious, and sending his troops he killed those murderers and burned their city' (22.7). Most critical commentators have assumed without further ado that this line is *ex eventu*, a clear reference to the destruction of Jerusalem in A.D. 70. But objections have been raised.[101] If the verse is a prophecy after the event, then must we not identify the king with Caesar, thereby making nonsense of the rest of the parable? And does not the τότε of 22.8 make the Gentile mission begin after A.D. 70, in contradiction to 28.16–20, where immediately after Easter the disciples are commanded to go into all the world? Furthermore, Isa 5.24–5 is said to supply the imagery of 22.7, which in any case just reproduces a fixed *topos*; and if Matthew were writing after the horrors of the Jewish wars, why does Mt 24 fail to recite the characteristic features of that war—such as the burning of the temple? In our judgement, all of these questions can be readily answered; that is, none of the objections to the standard interpretation is decisive. The identification of the king of 22.1–10 with Caesar is not at all required (despite Eusebius, *H.E.* 3.5). The Roman ruler is not mentioned, nor is his presence necessarily

---

[99] On Barnabas, 2 Clement, and Polycarp see esp. Massaux, pp. 66–93, 139–64, and 165–87 respectively. Massaux finds all three dependent upon Matthew.

[100] See Kümmel, *Introduction*, p. 98; Pesch 1, p. 14.

[101] So (as cited in n. 87) Dodd, Ellis, Gundry, Reicke, Robinson. See also K. H. Rengstorf, 'Die Stadt der Mörder (Mt 22.7)', in Eltester, pp. 106–29, and S. Pedersen, 'Zum Problem der vaticinia ex eventu (eine Analyse von Mt 21.33–46 par; 22.1–10 par)', *ST* 19 (1965), pp. 167–88.

implied. If one has to think of him at all, perhaps he is to be considered one of the king's (= God's) soldiers. Aside from this, it suffices to remark that more than once Matthew's redactional additions have not made for a perfectly coherent narrative (see e.g. on 27.15–18 and 51–3): so why be troubled if such is the case in 22.1–10? The same consideration also moves us to dismiss the objection based upon τότε: one simply cannot expect perfect coherence at every juncture where tradition and redaction meet. What of Isa 5.24–5? Perhaps it has influenced our text. Yet if it has, the question becomes, why was Matthew led to it in the first place? We cannot say that the plot of the NT parable naturally led to the OT text, for Isa 5 has nothing to do with a wedding feast, nor is there any other obvious connexion between Isa 5.24–5 and Mt 22.1–10. Should we not, in the light of this, entertain the possibility that an extra-textual consideration—the fall of Jerusalem—led the redactor to tell of a king who sent soldiers to kill his enemies and burn their city? In other words, even if Mt 22.7 comes from the OT or reproduces a common prophetic *topos*, we must inquire into the reason for its placement in the parable of the great supper, and for this the events of 70 lie near to hand. Finally, why, especially in chapter 24, are there not more details reminiscent of the calamity of 70? The response to this is two-fold. (i) We must keep in mind Matthew's conservative nature. He was indeed capable of making redactional insertions, but these—especially the longer insertions—typically have some basis in the tradition. So if he did not find in his sources detailed depictions of Jerusalem under siege (cf. Mark 13), we should not really expect to meet with such in his gospel. (ii) The Jewish mind passed indiscriminately from city (Jerusalem) to temple. As far as the ancient literature is concerned, one may speak of the interpenetration or identification of city and temple.[102] So who is to say that when Matthew wrote of the city being burned (22.7), he could not have been thinking of the burning of the temple? In conclusion, when all has been said, Mt 22.7, while it does not demand a date after A.D. 70, does strongly imply one.[103]

C. *Mt 28.16–20*. Scholars have oftentimes sought to assign a relatively late date to Matthew on account of the book's advanced theological development. Its ecclesiology, for example, together with the high Christology of the birth narrative and the seemingly fixed antipathy towards Judaism, are thought to favour a time of composition in the last quarter of the first century. Such arguments are much less compelling than widely assumed. The

[102] See Davies, *GL*, pp. 144–5, 150–4.
[103] Cf. G. W. H. Lampe, 'A.D. 70 in Christian Reflection', in Bammel and Moule, pp. 165–6.

ecclesiology of Matthew is hardly more advanced than what can be reconstructed from the authentic Paulines (see esp. Phil 1.1; 1 Cor 11–14). The closest parallels to Mt 1–2 appear in Acts 3 and 7, in presumably pre-Lukan material. And Matthew's polemic against the Jewish leaders offers nothing that could not have arisen out of the early difficulties believers in Jesus suffered at the hands of non-Christian Jews before A.D. 70 (cf. Acts 4.1–4; 8.1–3; 9.1–2, 13–14, 21; 22.4–5, 19–20; 26.9–12; Gal 1.13, 23; Phil 3.5–6; 1 Th 2.13–16). Yet there is one theological statement in Matthew that we do not feel comfortable placing before 70. In 28.19 Jesus directs his disciples to baptize 'in the name of the Father, and of the Son, and of the Holy Spirit' (we accept the received text; see on 28.19). There are, admittedly, other trinitarian-type formulas in the NT, some even in Paul's letters (1 Cor 12.4–6; 2 Cor 13.14; Tit 3.4–6; 1 Pet 1.2; Jude 20–1). Nonetheless the loaded phrase, 'the name of the Father, and of the Son, and of the Holy Spirit', is, excepting possibly Did. 7, which in any case here depends upon Matthew, without true parallel in first-century Christian literature.[104] It involves a step towards later Trinitarian thought not taken in any other NT writing. We are, therefore, disinclined to place the document to which Mt 28.19 belongs too many years before the beginning of the second century A.D.

D. *The Jewish Background.* Given that our gospel was the work of a Jew who undoubtedly deserves to be considered an 'intellectual', it comes as no great surprise to find that the book has striking connexions with scholastic rabbinism. E. von Dobschütz, in fact, calling attention to our author's fondness for repetition and stereotyped formulas, could contend that Matthew was, like Paul, a 'converted rabbi'.[105] Although this claim outruns the evidence a bit, it could still be correct; and, in any event, it remains the case that the First Gospel is illuminated by rabbinic tradition in a way true of no other gospel. Specifically, and as one of us has argued at length elsewhere (see below), the evangelist appears to have been familiar with rabbinic discussions which presumably took place in the last quarter of the first century A.D. In other words, he appears to have had knowledge of rabbinic Judaism as it sought to emerge like a phoenix from the ashes of 70, that is, knowledge of the critical period of Jewish reconstruction and reconsolidation which, in the rabbinic texts, is pre-eminently

---

[104] See the survey of Schaberg, pp. 11–15.

[105] 'Matthew as Rabbi and Catechist', in Stanton, pp. 19–29. Others have made the same claim—e.g. Bacon (agreeing with von Dobschütz that Matthew might have been a disciple of Johannan ben Zakkai) and F. W. Beare. Of great importance for the question is the commentary of Schlatter, which calls attention to the numerous linguistic parallels between Matthew and rabbinic texts.

associated with the so-called council of Jamnia.[106] The reader is
referred to Davies, *SSM*, pp. 256–315, for full discussion. Here we
shall introduce only four of the links in the chain binding Matthew
to the Jamnian period.

i. Mt 5–7. The sermon on the mount divides itself into three
major sections. The first has to do with the Torah (5.17–48), the
second with the Christian cult (6.1–18), the third with social
attitudes and obligations (6.19–7.12; see pp. 62–3). The
background for understanding this scheme is to be found in
rabbinic discussions after A.D. 70 (cf. Davies, *SSM*, pp. 305–307;
Allison, 'Structure'). Simeon the Just, a rabbi of the Maccabean
period, was purported to have declared, 'Upon three things the
world standeth: upon Torah, upon temple service, and upon acts of
piety' (*m. 'Abot* 1.2). This well-known utterance, whose
correlation with Mt 5–7 is remarkable,[107] was of necessity
reinterpreted after the destruction of Jerusalem because the second
member of the triad—temple service—had become obsolete (cf.
ARN 4). In particular, Johannan ben Zakkai, who left Jerusalem
for Jamnia, seems to have concerned himself with restating
Simeon's three pillars.[108] Now if, as seems to be the case, both the
structure and content of the sermon on the mount do indeed reflect
thoughtful engagement with the saying preserved in *m. 'Abot* 1.2, it
stands to reason that Matthew should be placed at the time when
the rabbis were also concerned with coming to terms with
Simeon's statement of what matters most—which means a date
after A.D. 70.

---

[106] We are fully aware that it is impossible to pin down the developments after
A.D. 70 to the town of Jamnia and the sages there too rigidly. By 'Jamnia' or the
phrase, 'Jamnian period', we mean that movement in its totality which preserved
Judaism after A.D. 70, which, while it was centred, according to the tradition, in
Jamnia, should not be confined to that place. For caution concerning Jamnia see
J. P. Lewis, 'What was "Jamnia"?', *JBR* 32 (1964), pp. 125–32; G. Stemberger,
'Die sogenannte "Synode von Jabne" und das frühe Christentum', *Kairos* 19
(1977), pp. 14–21; and P. Schäfer, 'Die sogenannte Synode von Jabne: Zur
Trennung von Juden und Christen im ersten/zweiten Jh. n. Chr.', *Judaica* 31 (1975),
pp. 54–64, 116–24. Also useful are J. Neusner, 'The Formation of Rabbinic
Judaism: Yabneh (Jamnia) from A.D. 70 to 100', *ANRW* II.19.1 (1979), pp. 3–42,
and in *CHJ*, 4, forthcoming; and S. J. D. Cohen, 'The Significance of Yavneh',
HUCA 55 (1984), pp. 27–53. Pertinent rabbinic texts include *m. Roš Haš.* 4.1–4; *m.
Menaḥ.* 10.5; *m. Bek.* 6.8; *m. Ketub.* 4.6; *m. Sukk.* 3.12; *m. 'Ed.* 2.4.

[107] In addition to Davies, *SSM*, pp. 305–7, and Allison, 'Structure', the parallels
between Mt 5–7 and *m.'Abot* 1.2 have been observed by T. W. Manson, *Ethics and
the Gospel*, London, 1961, following Davies, and P. F. Ellis, p. 37. On the meaning
of the third pillar in Simeon's triad, 'acts of piety' (*gĕmîlût ḥăsādîm*), see esp. J.
Goldin, 'The Three Pillars of Simeon the Righteous', *PAAJR* 27 (1958), pp. 43–56.

[108] Cf. J. Neusner, *Judaism in the Beginning of Christianity*, Philadelphia, 1984,
pp. 95–6.

ii. Hos 6.6 ('I desire mercy, and not sacrifice'). This OT text is quoted only twice in the NT, in Mt 9.13 and 12.7. Both texts are redactional, and both belong to narratives in which Jesus passes judgement on the conduct of the Pharisees. In the first Jesus introduces his quotation by telling his opponents to 'go and learn (cf. *ṣ' + lmd*) what it is'; in the second he says, 'If you had known what it is, "I desire mercy, and not sacrifice" '. In both instances the evangelist, through Jesus, is expressing his judgement that the Jewish leaders have failed to grasp the meaning of Hos 6.6: they do not understand the meaning of 'mercy' (ἔλεος, *hesed*; cf. also 23.23). Now this is so suggestive because Hos 6.6, which is not put on the lips of any rabbi active before A.D. 70, was probably an important watchword of Johannan ben Zakkai in the period following the destruction of the temple (cf. Davies, *SSM*, pp. 306–7; the textual authority is *ARN* 4).[109] With the temple in ruins it was important to come to grips with the cessation of the sacrificial cult, and for this Hos 6.6 was invaluable. One suspects, therefore, that when Hos 6.6 is twice inserted into polemical contexts, the text is being claimed for the church: the meaning of the OT passage is not to be found in its rabbinic application but in the ministry of Jesus. For further discussion see D. Hill, 'On the Use and Meaning of Hosea vi. 6 in Matthew's Gospel', *NTS* 24 (1977), pp. 107–19.

iii. The title, rabbi. It is tempting to see a side-glance at Jamnia in Mt 23.5–10: 'Whatever they (the Pharisees) do is done for show . . . they like to be greeted respectfully in the street and to be addressed as "rabbi". But you must not be called "rabbi"; for you have one Rabbi, and you are all brothers. Do not call any man on earth "father"; for you have one Father, and he is in heaven. Nor must you be called "teacher"; you have one Teacher, the Messiah.' Up to A.D. 70 the term *rabbi* was a mark of courtesy, like 'Sir' or 'Lord' in English. It was at Jamnia that it became a title for ordained scholars authorized to teach (cf. Davies, *SSM*, pp. 271–2). Hillel, Shammai and early Tannaim were not entitled 'rabbi'. The Jamnian usage is revealed in 23.8, where 'rabbi' is understood as 'teacher'. Titular consequence being such a natural weakness, there was possibly much pretentious use of the title rabbi at Jamnia and elsewhere. Not all sages were gentle as Hillel, and some, like the great Gamaliel II himself, were clearly touchy about their dignity. Such consequence as we have referred to seems to have impressed and, perhaps, invaded the Matthean church: some leading members of it may have been tempted to ape it (the aping of the establishment by the sectarian, it might be noted, is not an unfamiliar phenomenon).

[109] Cf. Neusner, ibid.

iv. The *birkat ha-minim*. Some scholars have, in the past, dated Matthew by placing it immediately before or immediately after the *birkat ha-minim*, the petition against heretics.[110] Hummel, for example, has argued that the relationship between church and synagogue reflected in Matthew is still very close: Jewish Christians remain under the jurisdiction of the synagogue and are not yet the object of polemical Jamnian legislation. Kilpatrick, on the other hand, takes the First Gospel's numerous references to persecution to be indicative of more than sporadic mistreatment: they instead imply the promulgation of severe official measures, including the *birkat ha-minim*. In our judgement, the evidence is insufficient to permit a sure conclusion one way or the other. It is not possible to determine whether the tone and content of Matthew disclose a situation effected by the issuance of the benediction against heretics. What we can be relatively sure of, however, is this: Matthew was composed in the general period in which the *birkat ha-minim* was first formulated, that is, the period of Samuel the Small, the last quarter of the first century A.D. (cf. *b. Ber.* 28b).[111] Despite some recent doubts, it seems relatively certain that, as reformulated under Rabban Gamaliel II, the twelfth benediction included within its purview Jewish Christians (*mînîm* and/or *nôṣrîm*) and had a significant impact upon Jewish-

---

[110] An ancient version of the twelfth petition of the eighteenth benedictions was found in a Cairo Genizah in the late nineteenth century by Solomon Schechter. It ran as follows:

For the apostates let there be no hope.
And let the dominion of arrogance be speedily uprooted in our days.
And let the *nôṣrîm* and the *mînîm* perish in a moment.
Let them be blotted out from the Book of life and not be inscribed with the righteous.
Blessed art thou, O Lord, who humblest the arrogant.

See S. Schechter, 'Genizah Specimens', *JQR* 10 (1898), pp. 654–9. The Genizah fragments often preserve Palestinian traditions from Amoraic times, and this seems to be the case here. There is some question, however, as to when, exactly, *nôṣrîm* might have been added to the birkat. The original could have read, simply, 'And let the *mînîm* perish in a moment'; in which case *nôṣrîm* would not belong to the first-century formulation. See the lit. cited in n. 112.

[111] *b. Ber.* 28b–29a: 'Our Rabbis taught: Simeon ha-Paḳuli arranged the eighteen benedictions in order before Rabban Gamaliel in Jamnia. Said Rabban Gamaliel to the sages: Can any one among you frame a benediction relating to the *minim*? Samuel the Lesser arose and composed it. Then next year he forgot it and he tried for two or three hours to recall it, and they did not remove him. Why did they not remove him seeing that Rab Judah has said in the name of Rab: If a reader made a mistake in any of the other benedictions, they do not remove him, but if in the benediction of the *minim*, he is removed, because we suspect him of being a *min*.' From this it would appear that the *birkat ha-minim* functioned originally to exclude Christians from the synagogue service.

Christian relations.[112] It is only natural that the Jewish leaders, occupied with the reconstruction of Judaism after 70, were not unaware of the competition posed by Jewish Christianity, and only natural that they took concrete measures to reduce Christian influence in the synagogue. Moreover—and this is the crucial point—Matthew's gospel fits perfectly into the Jamnian period of Jewish reconsolidation. The First Gospel expresses a personal animus against the Jewish leaders, especially the Pharisees, and this animus—which often presents itself in redactional sentences—is too conscious not to be born of a special, living Matthean concern (see e.g. 5.20; 16.1–12; 23.1–36). This lines up well with the fact that, at Jamnia, official measures against Christianity were adopted by the Pharisees' spiritual descendants. Also suggestive are the notices of persecution in Matthew. These, to be sure, can and have been over-interpreted (see Hare, passim); but our evangelist certainly did have the feeling that he and his Christian friends were being opposed by the Jewish establishment (see esp. on 10.17–23). Even more telling is the apologetic tone and object of Matthew, which is best understood through comparison with two other NT books. Whereas the Epistle to the Romans mounts an apology directed in large part against objections that would be raised firstly by Jewish Christians, and whereas the Gospel of John comes perilously close to dismissing 'the Jews' altogether, Matthew exhibits another tendency. Notwithstanding his positive attitude toward the Gentiles (cf. esp. 28.16–20), Matthew never finds it necessary to polemicize against Jewish-Christians or answer their questions about the Jewish mission. At the same time, he is not so pro-Gentile that he has written off the Jews completely (see pp. 22–4); in fact, we may read between his lines the hope that his grandly conceived apology[113] will not only arm Jewish

---

[112] See esp. W. Horbury, 'The Benediction of the *Minim* and Early Jewish-Christian Controversy', *JTS* 33 (1982), pp. 19–61. Additional lit.: A. T. Herford, *Christianity in Talmud and Midrash*, London, 1903, pp. 125–37; K. G. Kuhn, *Achtzehngebet und Vaterunser und der Reim*, Tübingen, 1950; Davies, *SSM*, pp. 275–6, 296–7; P. Schäfer, *Studien zur Geschichte und Theologie des rabbinischen Judentums*, AGJU 15, Leiden, 1978, pp. 45–55; J. L. Martyn, *History and Theology in the Fourth Gospel*, 2nd ed., Nashville, 1979, pp. 37–62; R. Kimelman, '*Birkat Ha-Minim* and the Lack of Evidence for an Anti-Christian Jewish Prayer in Late Antiquity', in *Jewish and Christian Self-Definition. Volume Two: Aspects of Judaism in the Graeco-Roman Period*, ed. E. P. Sanders, with A. I. Baumgarten and A. Mendelson, Philadelphia and London, 1981, pp. 226–44; L. H. Schiffman, *Who Was a Jew? Rabbinic and Halakhic Perspectives on the Jewish-Christian Schism*, New York, 1985, pp. 53–61; S. Katz in *CHJ*, vol. iv, forthcoming. In view of the inescapable presence of Jewish-Christians at that time one must ask why the *birkat ha-minim* could not have included them.

[113] On the apologetic character of Matthew cf. Moule, *Birth*, pp. 124–7. It strikes us that, in one important respect, the First Gospel is very much like Cardinal Newman's *Apologia Pro Vita Sua:* both books are apologies that take the form of a story.

Christians for their war with Jewish opponents but also, perhaps, turn a few enemies into friends, whether directly (through non-Christian Jews reading the gospel) or indirectly (through informed Christian readers persuading Jews). Certainly the difference between Matthew's depiction of the crowds and his unflattering portrait of their leaders strongly implies that the doors to the Jewish mission have not yet been slammed shut, at least not everywhere (see on 4.18). What all this means is that Matthew must, on the one hand, have been written sometime after Paul because, despite its author's Jewish orientation and conservative mentality, the author and his readers can take the Gentile mission for granted; on the other hand, Matthew appears to be pre-Johannine—and, likewise, pre-Ignatian—in its attitude toward 'the Jews' as a whole. This puts the First Gospel somewhere between the latter part of Paul's career (ca. 60) and the composition of John's gospel (ca. 100). And the middle point of that span is ca. 80, which lies in the Jamnian period, the period which saw the promulgation of the *birkat ha-minim*.

To sum up: Matthew was almost certainly written between A.D. 70 and A.D. 100, in all probability between A.D. 80 and 95.

VII. THE LOCAL ORIGIN OF MATTHEW[114]

Although modern scholarship has tended to place Matthew in Syria, especially in Antioch, other proposals, as the following chart shows, have not been wanting:

Jerusalem or Palestine:	M. Albertz, W. C. Allen, A. Schlatter, T. H. Robinson, J. Schniewind, W. Michaelis, A. Wikenhauser, M. Hengel (tentatively)
Caesarea Maritima:	B. T. Viviano
Phoenicia:	G. D. Kilpatrick, H. B. Green
Alexandria:	S. G. F. Brandon, S. van Tilborg

---

[114] Lit.: S. G. F. Brandon, *The Fall of Jerusalem and the Christian Church*, 2nd ed., London, 1957; W. R. Farmer, 'The Post-Sectarian Character of Matthew and Its Post-War Setting in Antioch of Syria', *PRS* 3 (1976), pp. 235–47; idem, *Jesus*, pp. 134–8; Hill, *Matthew*, pp. 50–2; J. Kennard, 'The Place of Origin of Matthew's Gospel', *ATR* 31 (1949), pp. 243–6; Kilpatrick, pp. 130–4; Meier, *Antioch*; R. E. Osborne, 'The Provenance of Matthew's Gospel', *SR* 3 (1973), pp. 220–35; H. D. Slingerland, 'The Transjordanian Origin of St. Matthew's Gospel', *JSNT* 3 (1979), pp. 18–28; Streeter, pp. 500–23; B. T. Viviano, 'Where Was the Gospel According to Matthew Written?', *CBQ* 41 (1979), pp. 533–46; J. Zumstein, 'Antioche sur l'Oronte et l'Évangile selon Matthieu', *SNTU* A 5 (1980), pp. 122–38.

East of the Jordan (Pella): R. T. Herford, H. J. Schoeps,
                             H. D. Slingerland
Edessa: B. W. Bacon (tentatively), R. E.
                             Osborne
Syria: F. V. Filson, P. Bonnard, G.
                             Strecker, W. Marxsen, D. Hill, N.
                             Perrin, L. Goppelt, M. D. Goulder,
                             E. Lohse, E. Schweizer, G. Künzel,
                             S. Freyne
Antioch: J. Weiss, B. H. Streeter, M. S.
                             Enslin, A. H. McNeile, R. H.
                             Fuller, R. E. Brown, R. H.
                             Gundry, J. P. Meier, J. Zumstein,
                             U. Luz (with reservations)

Given the nature of the available evidence, it is quite impossible to be fully persuaded on the issue at hand. We shall never know beyond a reasonable doubt where the autograph of Matthew was completed. At the same time, it does seem that some of the proposals are more credible than others. In particular, the supposition that Matthew first saw the light of day in Antioch of Syria is quite attractive. Before, however, we set forth the case for Antioch, the status of the other suggested places of composition should be reviewed.

(1) *Alexandria*. This option is associated particularly with S. G. F. Brandon, whose argument has not gained wide acceptance. Perhaps the main reason for doubt is our almost total lack of knowledge about the origins of the Christian community there. Brandon does, admittedly, try to overcome the silence of our sources by reconstructing the history of early Christianity in Alexandria (largely by implausibly placing Matthew, James, Hebrews, Barnabas, and perhaps 2 Clement there); but his reconstruction is more ingenious than convincing. Furthermore, Brandon does not show why the First Gospel contains no traces of the Philonic way of thought (contrast e.g. Hebrews). And when he asserts that Matthew's alleged anti-Paulinism and the story of the flight to Egypt (2.13–23) support his conjectures, one realizes how little solid evidence he has to go on (see further Davies, *SSM*, pp. 317–24, and the references there).

(2) *Jerusalem or Palestine*. This view—represented in the colophons of mss. K 126 174—is traditionally based upon the testimony of the church Fathers as well as the striking Jewish features we find in Matthew (see the Introduction, chap. II., section 5). The supposition is that the most likely place for the composition of a document containing such texts as 23.5 and 24.20

is Palestine, especially if one takes into consideration the conservative attitude shown towards the Jewish Law in the First Gospel (5.17–20).

Some of those who have argued for a Palestinian provenance have also assumed a date before A.D. 70 and rejected the two-source hypothesis (e.g. Schlatter). Their reasoning is understandable. First, it is hard to imagine that a gospel composed in Jerusalem, the centre of early Christianity, would have relied so heavily upon Mark, a Greek document written presumably for Hellenistic Christians, which has hard things to say about the Law (see e.g. 7.15). Secondly, the Jewish war caused major disruptions in both Jewish and Jewish-Christian communities throughout Palestine. Jerusalem was almost completely destroyed and many Jewish settlements throughout Palestine were overrun and depopulated. Modern scholarship estimates that up to one third of the Palestinian population was lost (cf. Josephus, *Bell*. 6.420–34). Whatever the precise numbers, Jerusalem was scarcely a prosperous city after 70, and this ill comports with the evidence that Matthew belonged to a community or church that was relatively prosperous.

It must be admitted that some contemporary scholars would be willing to date Matthew before A.D. 70 and willing likewise to abandon Markan priority. We, however, do not belong to their company. As we have argued elsewhere in this introduction, the two-source theory remains the most illuminating hypothesis of gospel relationships, and a date for Matthew in the last two or three decades of the first century seems assured. Thus the theory of a Palestinian origin is not easy to accept. And there are other difficulties. Although one cannot deny that many first-century Palestinians spoke Greek, the dominant language probably remained Aramaic (cf. Fitzmyer, *Aramean*, pp. 29–56). One would therefore expect a document written for, let us say, the church in Jerusalem, to be in Aramaic. In addition, in 22.7 Matthew seems to refer to the events of 70 (see pp. 131–2 herein). Yet the destruction of Jerusalem is not described or emphasized in such a way as to create the impression that the majority of Matthew's community had experienced the catastrophe first hand. That is, the gospel does not seem to have been written under the immediate impact of that event. Thus Matthew's church probably did not itself undergo the disaster but rather observed it from afar. It is, admittedly, possible, indeed even likely, that some Palestinian Jews and Jewish-Christians took refuge in Matthew's community, wherever it was. And they could have been the source for some of the seemingly Palestinian matter we find in the First Gospel. It is even possible that our author himself was a Palestinian refugee from the educated circles in Jerusalem. Still, the community in which he lived as he wrote his gospel was not, in all probability, in Palestine.

(3) *Caesarea Maritima*. This Palestinian port city has been sponsored by Viviano, who makes these points: Caesarea Maritima (i) was close to Jamnia, and Matthew shows contacts with Jamnian Judaism; (ii) was part of Palestine, and Matthew contains many features that are consistent with a Palestinian birth (e.g. the Semitic words left untranslated, such as *raka*, the religious practices presupposed (cf. 23.2; 24.20), the polemic against Judaism, the Deuteronomic conceptual framework, the use of midrashic techniques); (iii) was an important early Christian centre (cf. Acts 8.40; 9.30; 10.1, 24; etc.), even if we do not know anything about the church there between the last word on the place in Acts and the end of the second century (see Eusebius, *H.E.* 5.22); (iv) was a city that could boast great teachers (Origen, Pamphilus of Berytus, Eusebius) and bishops with a taste for learning; (v) was the home of a Christian school by at least the third centry; and (vi) was the scene of an ongoing dialogue between Jews and Christians (see R. M. de Lange, *Origen and the Jews*, Cambridge, 1976).

Viviano's hypothesis is interesting and has the advantage of being in harmony with patristic tradition, which favours a Palestinian origin. But one suspects that the universal ascription of Matthew to Palestine derives from the difficult tradition about a Semitic original behind the First Gospel. And if so, it could be dismissed as an inference based upon this uncertain tradition. Beyond this, and as Viviano himself observes, Eusebius does not connect the school at Caesarea with Matthew or Matthew's school, and because Eusebius lived there, his silence on this issue is loud indeed. Finally, no less telling is the fact that there was a massacre of Jews in Caesarea in A.D. 66, and Viviano does not supply evidence of Jewish resettlement in the following decades.[115] Since, in our judgement, the First Evangelist himself was a Jew, this makes it difficult to think of him in Caesarea.

(4) *Phoenicia*. According to Kilpatrick, Matthew contains hints which place its genesis near a Mediterranean seaport. (a) The evangelist, in his own composition, describes the Sea of Galilee as τὰ ὕδατα and reserves θάλασσα for the Mediterranean, that is, he

---

[115] See Josephus, *Bell.* 2.266–70, 284–92. Viviano himself cites the following from G. Foerster, 'The Early History of Caesarea', *The Joint Expedition to Caesarea Maritima: Vol. I, Studies in the History of Caesarea Maritima*, ed. C. T. Fritsch, Missoula, 1975, p. 17: 'It would appear that the economic ruin which overwhelmed Judea following the First Revolt, and which took the form of the confiscation of land and various heavy taxes, did not affect Caesarea, since at this time the city contained very few, if any, Jews at all'. Cf. L. I. Levine, *Caesarea under Roman Rule*, SJLA 7, Leiden, 1975, pp. 29–35, 44–5, 63–4.

distinguishes high sea and inland lake (cf. 8.32; 14.28, 29). (b) In the story of the Canaanite woman Mark's Συροφοινίκισσα (Mk 7:26) becomes Χαναναία (a NT *hapax legomenon*) ἀπὸ τῶν ὁρίων ἐκείνων (15:22), that is, τὰ μέρη Τύρου καὶ Σιδῶνος, and whatever the explanation, 'the change was topical and suggests that Matthew was connected in some way with Phoenicia'. (c) The Phoenician ports such as Tyre, Sidon, and Berytus were Greek-speaking while the country-side preserved its Semitic character and speech. This would explain why Matthew, though thoroughly Semitic, is written in Greek.

Against Kilpatrick, it must be stressed that we know very little about Phoenicia in the final quarter of the first century. If there were Christian communities there, they must have been relatively small. Tyre is named in only one passage in Acts (21.3–7). The same is true of Sidon (27.3), and Berytus is not mentioned at all in the entire NT. One is reluctant to assign Matthew to a place about which so little is known and which cannot have been a centre of Christian learning at the time our gospel was composed. There is also the problem of 11.22–3. Would a Phoenician have associated Tyre and Sidon with Sodom? Furthermore, Kilpatrick's assertion that only the maritime areas of Syria had been Hellenized must be doubted; see B. Lifschitz, 'L'hellénisation des Juifs de Palestine', *RB* 72 (1965), pp. 520–38; also Davies, *JPS*, p. 312, n. 28, and the literature cited there. Finally, the claim that Matthew intends a distinction between τὰ ὕδατα and θάλασσα is unacceptable: did Matthew have the distinction proposed in mind would he not have used λίμνη of the Sea of Galilee?

(5) *East of the Jordan*. Probably the most persuasive statement of the case for this possibility has come from Slingerland. He has noted that both 4.25 and 19.1 seem to view Jesus' presence in Palestine as being on the other side of the Jordan. The proposal is intriguing and deserves more discussion than it has up to now generated. Of all the attempts to locate our gospel on the map, this one takes its point of departure from the geography of the text itself. Nevertheless, as we have argued in the commentary, neither 4.25 nor 19.1 is unambiguous, and neither verse demands, in our judgement, an eastern origin for Matthew.

If the implications of 4.25 and 19.1 are uncertain, much less weighty are the arguments of Osborne—who was anticipated by Bacon—in favour of Edessa. (On Bacon's position see W. D. Davies, in *Dictionary of the Bible*, ed. J. Hastings, F. C. Grant, and H. H. Rowley, New York, 1963, pp. 631–3. Bacon urged that while the First Gospel was disseminated in Antioch, it was composed in some eastern locality, possibly Edessa.) One readily grants that there was a well established Jewish community in

Edessa (cf. J. Neusner, *A History of the Jews in Babylon*, vol. 1, rev. ed., Leiden, 1969, p. 95); and this makes it likely that Christianity gained a foothold there very early on.[116] But when Osborne claims that Peter may have been one of the founders of this church, he is indulging in speculation. And the alleged parallels he finds between Matthew's special (M) material and eastern religions do not inspire confidence. According to Osborne, the story of the magi in Mt 2 borrows from Zoroastrianism, while the choice of words in 13.43 (τότε οἱ δίκαιοι ἐκλάμψουσιν ὡς ὁ ἥλιος) reflects the influence of Mithraism (cf. *Yasna* 50.2, 10); and 5.21–48 is to be connected with the 'five precepts' of Buddhism. Moreover, emphasis upon Abraham in Matthew's genealogy would, so it is claimed, be especially meaningful to Jews living in the Osrhoene since Edessa was associated with Abraham (Haran being only thirty miles away); and 19.12 would make sense especially in Edessa, where the citizens were familiar with the cultic practice of castration. Yet all these parallels are not obviously substantial. And even if most of them were, one might just as well conclude that the oriental themes reached Matthew through the medium of Jewish apocalyptic. Osborne himself admits the possibility of detecting eastern influence in some of the Pseudepigrapha.

Probably the greatest obstacle in the way of all those who would put Matthew east of the Jordan is this: the gospel is written in Greek. One would expect a gospel written in, for example, Edessa, to be in Syriac. Almost all inscriptions recovered from Edessa which belong to the first three centuries A.D. are in Syriac, and the earliest full literary texts we have from Edessa are in Syriac, as are the remains of the pre-Christian literature (cf. Meier, *Antioch*, p. 21).

(6) *Antioch in Syria*.[117] The classic statement of the case for Antioch was made by B. H. Streeter in *The Four Gospels* (pp. 500–23). Of his several observations, the following seem most cogent:

a. Although the patristic tradition that Matthew was written in

---

[116] See further H. J. W. Drijvers, 'Jews and Christians at Edessa', *JJS* 36 (1985), pp. 88–102.

[117] On Antioch see esp. these works: C. K. Kraeling, 'The Jewish Community at Antioch', *JBL* 51 (1932), pp. 130–60; B. M. Metzger, 'Antioch-on-the-Orontes', *BA* 11 (1948), pp. 69–88; G. Downey, *A History of Antioch in Syria from Seleucus to the Arab Conquest*, Princeton, 1961; W. Bauer, *Orthodoxy and Heresy in Earliest Christianity* (trans. of *Rechtgläubigkeit und Ketzerei im ältesten Christentum*, 1964), ed. R. Kraft and G. Krodel, Philadeliphia, 1971, pp. 61–76; W. A. Meeks and R. L. Wilken, *Jews and Christians in Antioch in the First Four Centuries of the Common Era*, Missoula, 1978, pp. 1–36; J. Lassus, 'La ville d'Antioche à l'époque romaine d'après l'archéologie', *ANRW* II.8 (1977), pp. 54–102; Meier, *Antioch*.

Palestine cannot be credited (see above), the witness of Papias and Irenaeus has a negative value. 'It proves that Matthew was *not* produced either in Rome or in Asia Minor, but was believed to have originally come from the East'.

b. The ascription of the First Gospel to an apostle must be deemed secondary. Originally, the gospel was anonymous. How, then, did it manage to succeed in being accepted by the Christian community at large? 'Anonymity implies that it was originally compiled for the use of some particular church which accepted it at once as a reliable witness, simply because it knew and had confidence in the person or committee who produced it'. Moreover, the gospel would not have been accepted by other churches as having apostolic authority unless it had been sponsored by one of the great churches—such as Rome, Ephesus, or Antioch.

c. Peter's prominence in Matthew harmonizes well with his undoubted status in Antioch (cf. Gal 2.11; church tradition makes him the first bishop there).

d. Antioch had a very large Jewish population (on post-war immigration into it note Josephus, *Bell*. 7.109). At the same time, the city was the centre of the earliest Christian Gentile mission. This dual feature seems to be mirrored in Matthew, which breathes a Jewish atmosphere and yet looks upon the Gentile mission in a most favourable light.

e. 'Only in Antioch and Damascus did the official stater exactly equal two didrachmae, as is implied in Mt. xvii. 24–7'.[118]

f. The First Gospel has its first external attestation in the epistles of Ignatius, who was bishop of Antioch in the early second century (see esp. *Eph*. 19.1–3, dependent upon Mt 2; *Smyr*. 1.1, dependent upon Mt 3.15; and *Polyc*. 2.2, dependent upon Mt 10.16). And when Ignatius writes of 'the gospel' (*Phil*. 5.1–2; 8.2), one may reasonably identify this with our Matthew.

To Streeter's six arguments—which have considerable cumulative force—, two more may perhaps be added:

g. Our author was, there can be no doubt, some sort of scholar, and when we try to envisage him, we inevitably imagine a 'rabbinic' scribe at his table copying Torah, or someone alone in his study—like Jerome in Albrecht Dürer's famous 1514 engraving. Yet it would be a mistake to think of Matthew as a solitary individual. Even if, against Stendahl (*School*), the formula quotations do not of themselves offer evidence for a Matthean

---

[118] But this has been questioned; see Luz 1, p. 73, n. 184.

School,[119] it is human nature to seek out one's own kind, and all probability favours the notion that Matthew shared his learned and apologetic concerns with other thoughtful Christians. That is, our evangelist was in all likelihood one of several Christian 'scribes' in his area (cf. 13.52), and he and his friends, in a manner reminiscent of the 'rabbinic' academy and the Hellenistic school, will presumably have carried on their common work together. What does all this have to do with Antioch? We do know that, in the third century, Lucian, who was head of a Christian school in Antioch, had a good command of Hebrew and access to several OT textual traditions.[120] And he was not the only Antiochian Christian to know Hebrew. According to Eusebius (*H.E.* 7.32.2), so did a certain Dorotheus. Now we cannot, to be sure, move without further ado from the late third century to the first. Just because the situation of Matthew strikes us as similar to the situation in Antioch when Lucian was presbyter is no reason to postulate a connexion. This one fact, however, does not stand alone. In addition to the several contacts between Matthew's OT quotations and the Lucianic text (see h. below), there is the figure of Theophilus. A bishop of Antioch, he wrote about A.D. 180 (cf. Eusebius, *H.E.* 4.19–20). Modern scholarship has demonstrated that his exegetical methods were primarily those of Jewish haggadah.[121] So long before Lucian and Dorotheus, Antioch was the home of a scholarly Christian with strong links to Judaism.[122] Can we go back even further? Around the time of Matthew, Antioch had a large Jewish population as well as a significant Jewish-Christian population (cf. Ignatius, *Phil.* 6.1; *Magn.* 10.3), and the city was known even among pagans as a centre of learning with an important library (cf. Cicero, *Archia* 3(4)). Thus first-century Antioch is a natural place to locate a document such as Matthew. Its author's learning, his dialogue with Judaism, the probability that he belonged to some kind of Christian school, the relative prosperity of Matthew's community, and the Jewish-Christian elements all fall perfectly into place.

h. There are some points of contact between the Lucianic recension of the Greek Bible and some of Matthew's OT citations

[119] Note B. Gärtner, 'The Habakkuk Commentary (DSH) and the Gospel of Matthew', *ST* 8 (1954), pp. 1–24. Our own judgement is that the formula quotations show every sign of being redactional; and they do not of themselves demand a setting in a school. For refinement of the term, 'school', see R. A. Culpepper, *The Johannine School*, SBLDS 26, Missoula, 1975.

[120] See B. M. Metzger, *Chapters in the History of New Testament Textual Criticism*, NTTS 4, Grand Rapids, 1963, pp. 3–7.

[121] R. M. Grant, *After the New Testament*, Philadelphia, 1967, pp. 136–41.

[122] Given the Matthean penchant for the triad (see pp. 61–72, 86–7), we cannot refrain from mentioning the happy coincidence that Theophilus was apparently the first church Father to label the godhead τριάς.

(see Stendahl, *School*, pp. 38–9, 54–5, 69–72, and Gundry, *OT*, pp. 20–4, 45, 139). The observation interests because Lucian lived in Antioch, and his Greek text is usually thought to be based upon an Ur-Lucianic text.[123] It is, therefore, likely to preserve readings that were known in and around Antioch long before Lucian's time. Thus the agreements between Matthew and Lucian in the texts cited are intriguing and should perhaps be admitted as supplying one more clue in locating Matthew.[124]

Although we have found the evidence for placing Matthew in Antioch to be considerable, we must plainly state that we do not claim for this result a high degree of certainty. We simply know too little about early Christianity, especially between 70 and 100, to be free of all doubt. And beyond this general consideration, we remain a bit uneasy because (i) 4.25 and 19.1 just might betray an origin east of the Jordan (see p. 142) and (ii) patristic tradition places neither our gospel nor the apostle Matthew in Antioch of Syria.[125] So while, in our judgement, the First Gospel was probably

[123] See Metzger (as in n. 111), pp. 30–5; P. Katz, *Lucian's Bible*, Cambridge, 1950; S. Jellicoe, *The Septuagint and Modern Study*, Oxford, 1968, pp. 157–71; and F. M. Cross, 'The Evolution of a Theory of Local Texts', in *Qumran and the History of the Biblical Text*, ed. F. M. Cross and S. Talmon, Cambridge, Mass., 1975, pp. 306–20.

[124] On the whole question of the textual affinities between the NT and Lucian see W. Staerk, 'Die alttestamentlichen Citate bei den Schriftstellern des Neuen Testaments', *ZNW* 35 (1892), pp. 464–85; 36 (1893), pp. 70–98.

[125] According to Hippolytus on the Twelve Apostles (ANF 5, p. 255; date?), the apostle died at Hierees in Parthia. The Acts of Andrew (probably 3rd cent.) places the apostle in the city of Mermidona (see the epitome of the Acts in Gregory of Tours, *Historia* 2.82lff.) while Ambrose (4th cent.) has him in Persia, Paulinus of Nola (4th–5th cent.) in Parthia (cf. E. A. W. Budge, *The Contendings of the Apostles*, Oxford, 1935, pp. 109–14), and Isodore ('Hispalensis', 6th–7th cent.) in Macedonia. Eusebius, *H.E.* 3.24.6, wrote: 'Matthew, who first proclaimed the gospel to the Hebrews, when on the point of going also to other nations, committed his gospel to writing in his native tongue, and thus supplied the want of his presence to them by his writings'. This presupposes the disciple's residence in Palestine followed by missionary work elsewhere. Jerome, *De vir. ill.* 3 has Matthew in Judea. In The Acts and Martyrdom of Matthew (date?), the apostle is slain in Myrna, and The Book of the Bee of Solomon of Basrah (see the edition of E. A. W. Budge, Oxford, 1886, p. 106) has him preach in Phoenicia and die in Antioch of Pisidia. According to Ps.-Dorotheus (PG 92,1071–2; 6th–8th cent.), Matthew was martyred at Hierapolis. In The Apostolic History of Abdias (7.1; 6th–7th cent.) Matthew journeys to Naddaver in Ethiopia and stays there twenty-three years. According to the Hieronymianum (5th cent.) he died in Tarrium (?) in Persia. Finally, the official Martyrologium Romanum puts his death in Ethiopia. See further B. de Gaiffier, 'Hagiographie salernitaine. La translation de S. Matthieu', Another objection *Analecta Bollandiana* 80 (1962), pp. 82–110. The lack of any consistent tradition concerning the apostle Matthew may be due in small part to the fact that he was confused from time to time with Matthias. The one possible link we have found between Matthew and Antioch appears in Eusebius, *Quaest. ad Steph.*, in A. Mai, *Nova. Patr. Bibl.* 4.1.270, following Julius Africanus (ca. 160–ca. 240). According to this, Matthew was a Syrian.

put together for the church of Antioch, this conclusion remains no more than the best educated guess.[126]

VIII. THE TEXT[127]

The Greek text printed in this commentary is based primarily upon two sources: the twenty-sixth edition of the Nestle-Aland *Novum Testamentum Graece* (hereafter NA[26]) and the Huck-Greeven *Synopse der drei ersten Evangelien* (Tübingen, 1981;

---

[126] Another objection might be this: Matthew shows no Pauline influence and there are significant differences between the First Gospel and Ignatius' epistles. But (1) Paul may well have not succeeded in Antioch; (2) Ignatius was a Gentile, Matthew a Jew; and (3) Antioch ca. 100 may well have been a church in transition. See further Meier, *Antioch*. He reconstructs a credible history of early Antiochian Christianity that makes sense of the order, Paul—Matthew—Ignatius.

In view of the connexions which we see between Matthew and Jamnian Judaism (see pp. 133–8), it seems worth observing that there was, according to our sources, traffic between Palestine and Antioch; and Jamnian legislation affected Syria; see Davies, *SSM*, pp. 294–6.

[127] Lit.: K. Aland, *Kurzgefasste Liste der griechischen Handschriften des Neuen Testaments: I. Gesamtübersicht*, AzNTT 1, Berlin, 1963; idem, 'Ein neuer Textus Receptus für das griechische Neue Testament', *NTS* 28 (1982), pp. 145–53; idem, *Studien zur Überlieferung des Neuen Testaments und seines Textes*, AzNTT 2, Berlin, 1967; idem, *Synopsis quattuor evangeliorum locis parallelis evangeliorum apocryphorum et patrum adhibitis*, Stuttgart, 1964; H.-W. Bartsch, 'Ein neuer Textus Receptus für das Neue Testament?', *NTS* 27 (1981), pp. 585–92; R. Champlin, *Family E and Its Allies in Matthew*, Salt Lake City, 1966; E. C. Colwell, *Studies in Methodology in Textual Criticism of the New Testament*, NTTS 9, Grand Rapids, 1969; J. K. Elliott, 'The Citation of Manuscripts in Recent Printed Editions of the Greek New Testament', *NovT* 25 (1983), pp. 97–132; idem, 'An Examination of the Twenty-sixth Edition of Nestle-Aland *Novum Testamentum Graece*', *JTS* 32 (1981), pp. 19–49; idem, 'Textual Criticism, Assimilation, and the Synoptic Gospels', *NTS* 26 (1980), pp. 231–41; E. J. Epp, 'A Continuing Interlude in New Testament Textual Criticism', *HTR* 73 (1980), pp. 131–51; G. D. Fee, 'P[66], P[75] and Origen: The Myth of Early Textual Recension in Alexandria', in *New Dimensions in New Testament Study*, ed. R. N. Longenecker and M. C. Tenney, Grand Rapids, 1974, pp. 19–45; J. Geerlings, *Family 13—The Ferrar Group. The Text According to Matthew*, Salt Lake City, 1961; A. Globe, 'The *Dialogue of Timothy and Aquila* as Witness to a Pre-Caesarean Text of the Gospels' *NTS* 29 (1983), pp. 233–46; D. Holly, *Comparative Studies in Recent Greek New Testament Texts*, Subsidia Biblica 7, Rome, 1983; A. F. J. Klijn, *A Survey of the Researches into the Western Text of the Gospels and Acts*, Utrecht, 1949; idem, *A Survey of the Researches into the Western Text of the Gospels and Acts, Part Two, 1949–1969*, NovTSup 21, Leiden, 1969; Kümmel, *Introduction*, pp. 511–54; S. Larson, 'The 26th Edition of the Nestle-Aland *Novum Testamentum Graece*: A limited Examination of its Apparatus', *JSNT* 12 (1981), pp. 53–68; S. C. E. Legg, *Novum Testamentum Graece. Evangelium Secundum Matthaeum*, Oxford, 1940; C. M. Martini, 'Is There a Late Alexandrian Text of the Gospels?', *NTS* 24 (1978), pp. 285–96; B. M. Metzger, *Annotated Bibliography of the Textual Criticism of the New Testament*, SD 16, Copenhagen, 1955; idem, *Chapters in the History of New Testament Textual Criticism*, NTTS 4, Grant Rapids, 1963; idem, *The Early Versions of the New Testament*, Oxford, 1977; idem, *A Textual Commentary on the Greek New Testament*, London and New York, 1971; idem, *The Text of the New*

hereafter HG).[128] Where these two handbooks agree, we have judged their combined testimony to be truly weighty. Indeed, only a very few times in the entirety of Mt 1–7 have we been moved to dissent from their concurrence (see e.g. on 1.18; 3.15, 16). Where NA[26] and HG do part company, we have indicated this, cited pertinent textual witnesses, and usually given our reasons for following one authority rather than the order. Our notes also contain variant readings which (1) affect significantly the sense of the text; (2) have aroused scholarly interest and discussion; (3) illustrate a tendency in the textual tradition; or (4) have given us cause for considerable doubt. No attempt has been made either to record all significant variants or to give all of the evidence for the different readings. The attempt to reproduce the whole of what already appears in NA[26] and HG would result only in expensive redundancy.

The abbreviations and symbols in the apparatus are those of NA[26], with this exception: instead of the symbol 𝔐 for the Majority text, we have used the abbreviation, Maj.

Testament: Its Transmission, Corruption, and Restoration, 2nd ed., Oxford, 1968; I. A. Moir, 'Can We Risk Another "Textus Receptus"?', *JBL* 100 (1981), pp. 614–18; Neirynck, *Evangelica*, pp. 883–1002; W. L. Petersen, 'Romanos and the Diatessaron: Readings and Method', *NTS* 29 (1983), pp. 484–507; J. R. Royse, 'The Treatment of Scribal Leaps in Metzger's *Textual Commentary*', *NTS* 29 (1983), pp. 539–51; Streeter, pp. 25–148; B. F. Westcott and F. J. A. Hort, *The New Testament in the Original Greek: Introduction and Appendix*, London, 1881; G. Zaphiris, *Le texte de l'Évangile selon saint Matthieu d'après les citations de Clément d'Alexandrie comparées aux citations des Pères et des Théologiens grecs du IIe au XVe siècle*, Gembloux, 1970.

[128] Because of its notorious unreliability, we have not much consulted Legg's critical edition of Matthew (see n. 127). On occasion we have consulted the United Bible Societies' *The Greek New Testament*, 2nd ed., ed. by K. Aland et al., New York and London, 1968.

I

TITLE
(1.1)

(i) *Structure*

The three personal names that appear in 1.1—Jesus Christ, David, Abraham (cf. 1.17)—also appear in 1.2–16, but in reverse order. We thus have in the very first verse of our gospel a triad and the front half of a chiasmus:

   a. Jesus Christ (1.1b)
   b. David (1.1c)
   c. Abraham (1.1d)
   c. Abraham (1.2)
   b. David (1.6)
   a. Jesus Christ (1.16)

(According to J. Chopineau, 'Adam' is the key to the second half of this chiasmus; for the three letters in 'Adam'—', *d*, *m*—stand for, respectively, *'Abrāhām*, *Dāwid*, and *māšîaḥ*.[1] This highly speculative conjecture comes to grief because the name, 'Adam', does not even once appear in Matthew's gospel).

(ii) *Sources*

If one were to judge the genealogy (1.2–16) to be derived from a pre-Matthean source, then there would be reason to suspect that 1.1 belonged to that source. Yet the genealogy is the work of the evangelist (see below), which entails the same conclusion concerning 1.1: it is redactional.

(iii) *Exegesis*

The crux of Matthew's opening line is the second word, γένεσις. Most commentaries and versions translate it as 'genealogy', thereby implying that its function is solely to introduce Mt 1.2–17, the table of the ancestors of Jesus.[2] But it is also possible to render

---

[1] Chopineau (v). For reflection on the significance of the letters of Adam's name see Sib. Or. 3.24–6; 2 En. 30.13; Augustine, *Hom. on Jn.* 9.14; 10.12; Pseudo-Cyprian, *De pascha* 16.
[2] So McNeile, p. 1; Lagrange, p. 3; Lohmeyer, *Matthäus*, p. 4; Lambertz (v), p. 201; Schmid, *Matthäus*, p. 35; Trilling, p. 93; Tatum (v), p. 526.

γένεσις as 'origin' and thus construe 1.1 as introducing 1.2–25[3] or 1.2–2.23[4] or even 1.2–4.16.[5] Yet a third option is to interpret 1.1 as being in the first instance the title for the entire gospel (so Jerome), in which case the the word must mean either 'history' or 'genesis' (='new creation').[6] The view taken here is that, with qualifications, this last alternative is the most probable. The pertinent considerations are these:

(1) βίβλος γενέσεως is hardly an obvious title for a table of progenitors. The phrase occurs only twice in the LXX, at Gen 2.4 and 5.1. In 5.1 it translates *sēper tôlĕdôt* and is followed by a list of descendants (those of Adam), not (as in Matthew) by a list of ancestors. And in 2.4 (where the Hebrew is simply *tôlĕdôt*) the words are not even connected with a genealogy; instead they serve either to conclude the account of the creation of the heavens and the earth in 1.1–2.3 (so most modern commentators) or to open the story of the creation of man and woman in Gen 2 (so the LXX). Further, αὗται αἱ γενέσεις, not βίβλος γενέσεως, is the expression most often used in the LXX to preface genealogies;[7] and while in Genesis genealogies are named after the first entry, this cannot be the case in Matthew.

(2) Not only is βίβλος γενέσεως associated with narrative material in Gen 2.4 (the creation account of P or J), but this is also the case in 5.1 (cf. 6.9). Gen 5.1–32 contains more than genealogical materials. It recounts in addition the creation of Adam and Eve, the ages of the ancients, and the taking up of Enoch. So for those acquainted with the Greek version of Genesis, βίβλος γενέσεως would likely have brought to mind more than the genealogical table of Adam. It would probably have sent thoughts back to the primeval history in general. This in turn suggests that Matthew might have opened his gospel as he did in order to draw a parallel between one beginning and another beginning, between the creation of the cosmos and Adam and Eve on the one hand and the new creation brought by the Messiah on the other.

(3) This proposal gains support from a third consideration, namely, that elsewhere the NT sees the coming of Jesus as the counterpart of the creation account narrated in Genesis. Paul, for instance, speaks more than once of a 'new creation' (2 Cor 5.17; Gal 6.15), and he likens his Lord to a 'last Adam' (Rom 5.12–21; 1 Cor 15.42–50). In addition, special notice should be taken of the prologue of John's gospel (1.1–18), which

[3] So A. Vögtle, 'Die Genealogie Mt 1,2–16 und die matthäische Kindheitsgeschichte', in *Evangelium*, p. 73; Luz 1, p. 88.

[4] So Plummer, p. 1, and Allen, pp. 1–2.

[5] So E. Krentz, 'The Extent of Matthew's Prologue: Toward the Structure of the First Gospel', *JBL* 83 (1964), p. 414, and Kingsbury (v).

[6] So Zahn, pp. 39–44; Klostermann, p. 1; Schniewind, p. 9; Bonnard, p. 16; Davies (v); Gaechter, *Kommentar*, pp. 34–5; Grundmann, p. 61; Frankemölle (v); H. C. Waetjen, 'The Genealogy as the Key to the Gospel according to Matthew', *JBL* 95 (1976), p. 215; Paul (v); Beare, p. 64.

[7] E.g., Gen 6.9; 10.1; 11.10, 27; 25.12, 19; 36.1, 9; 37.2; Num 3.1. Cf. LAB 3.4; 4.17; 5.8.

clearly opens the story of Jesus by setting it against the background of the Genesis creation story (ἐν ἀρχῇ = *bĕrē'šît*; on Mk 1.1 see below).

(4) The title of the first book of the OT in the LXX had already been fixed as 'Genesis' by the time of Matthew. Not only do the earliest mss. of the LXX have Γένεσις,[8] but Justin (ca. 100–ca. 165; see *Dial.* 20.1), Origen (ca. 185–ca. 254; see *Orat.* 23.3; Eusebius, *H.E.* 6.25), Melito of Sardis (d. ca. 190; see Eusebius, *H.E.* 4.26), and the author of Audet's so-called 'Hebrew-Aramaic list of Books of the Old Testament' (from the end of the second century A.D.)[9] knew the book by this name. The NT moreover supplies evidence that at least some of the LXX titles were already current in the first century; see, for example, Acts 1.20 (ἐν βίβλῳ ψαλμῶν); 13.33; Lk 20.42; and perhaps Rom 9.25 and Acts 2.16 (contrast L. Proph. Mal. 3). But the decisive datum comes from Philo of Alexandria (ca. 20 B.C.–ca. A.D. 50). Three times the Alexandrian exegete refers to the first book of Moses as 'Genesis' (*Poster C.*127; *Abr.* 1; *Aet. mund.* 19). Indeed, in *Aet. mund.* 19 he asserts that Moses himself gave the book its name.

That Γένεσις had already before Matthew's time become the standard title of the Greek Torah's first book is obviously rather important for the interpretation of Mt 1.1—perhaps even as important as the occurrences of βίβλος γενέσεως in Gen 2.4 and 5.1. Genesis was a βίβλος, and its name was Γένεσις. One is therefore led to ask whether the introductory use of βίβλος γενέσεως would not have caused Matthew's readers to think of the Torah's first book and to anticipate that some sort of 'new genesis', a genesis of Jesus Christ, would follow. It is difficult to think otherwise. By opening his gospel with another book's title, Matthew almost certainly intended to set up the story of Jesus as a counterpart to the story of Genesis. Beyond this, since 'Genesis' already stood as the title of a particular well-known book, Matthew's appropriation of that word to commence his work seemingly implies a parallel, that is, titular, usage.[10]

(5) If Mt 1.1 be for the moment left aside, it may be said that, throughout the NT, βίβλος means nothing save 'book' (cf. BAGD, s.v.). And as for the patristic period, Lampe's lexicon (s.v.) offers only two meanings for the word: 'papyrus' and 'book'. Now because neither Mt 1.2–17 nor even Mt 1.2–2.23 or 1.2–4.16 could plausibly be labelled a 'book', the βίβλος of 1.1 most naturally encompasses the gospel as a whole.

(6) The question of whether 1.1 is a general title should take into account this consideration: it was a custom in the prophetic, didactic, and apocalyptic writings of Judaism to open with an independent titular sentence announcing the content of the work.[11] Illustrations include the following: Proverbs, Ecclesiastes, Canticles, Hosea, Amos, Joel, Nahum, Tobit, Baruch, the Community Rule, the War Rule, the Testaments of the

[8] B S: Γενεσις; A: Γενεσις Κοσμου (cf. LAB 1.1).
[9] J.-P. Audet, 'A Hebrew-Aramaic List of Books of the Old Testament in Greek Transcription', *JTS* 1 (1950), pp. 135–54.
[10] γένεσις, it is also pertinent to observe, occurs more times in Genesis (16–17) than in any other LXX book. This reinforces the suggestion that Matthew's use of the word would have recalled the OT's first book.
[11] Cf. Lohmeyer, *Markus*, p. 10.

Twelve Patriarchs, Jubilees, 1 Enoch, 2 Enoch (in some mss.), the Testament of Job, and the Apocalypse of Abraham. Even more telling than this, however, is the introductory use of *sēper* or βίβλος or βιβλίον in ancient Jewish and Christian literature. Consider these texts:

a. Nahum 1.1: 'An oracle concerning Nineveh. Book (*sēper*/βιβλίον) of the vision of Nahum of Elkosh'.

b. Tobit 1.1: 'Book (*sēper*/βίβλος) of the acts [or: words] of Tobit the son of Tobiel, son of Ananiel, son of Aduel, son of Gabael, of the descendants of Asiel and the tribe of Naphtali . . .'.

c. Baruch 1.1: 'These are the words of the book (βιβλίου) which Baruch the son of Neraiah, son of Mahseiah, son of Zedekiah, son of Hasadiah, son of Hilkiah, wrote in Babylon . . .'.

d. T. Job 1.1: 'Book (βίβλος) of Job, who is called Jobab'.

e. Apoc. Abraham, title: 'The book (*sēper*?)[12] of the revelation of Abraham, the son of Terah, the son of Nahor, the son of Serug, the son of Roog (Reu), the son of Arphaxad, the son of Shem, the son of Noah, the son of Lamech, the son of Methuselah, the son of Enoch, the son of Jared (Ared)'.

f. 2 Esdras 1.1–3: 'The second book of the prophet Ezra the son of Seraiah, son of Azariah, son of Hilkiah, son of Shallum, son of Zadok, son of Ahitub, son of Ahijah, son of Phinehas, son of Eli, son of Amariah, son of Azariah, son of Meraioth, son of Arna, son of Uzzi, son of Borith, son of Abishua, son of Phinehas, son of Eleazar, son of Aaron, of the tribe of Levi, who was a captive in the country of the Medes in the reign of Artaxerxes, king of the Persians'.

g. Sepher Ha-Razim, preface: 'This is a book (*sēper*), from the Books of the Mysteries, which was given to Noah, the son of Lamech, the son of Methuselah, the son of Enoch, the son of Jared, the son of Mehallalel, the son of Kenan, the son of Enosh, the son of Seth, the son of Adam, by Raziel the angel in the year when he came into the ark (but) before his entrance'.

Beyond a common use of *sēper* or βίβλος or βιβλίον[13], it is noteworthy that several of these openings have an anarthrous βίβλος or βιβλίον (a, b, d) and further that in five out of seven instances a υἱός-formula follows the first mention of the author or subject (b, c, e, f, g). Now because Mt 1.1 likewise opens with an anarthrous βίβλος which is immediately followed by a υἱός-formula and then a genealogy, the texts cited offer firm support for understanding 1.1 as a general title. When the first evangelist began his book with βίβλος, he was evidently following custom.[14]

---

[12] The Apocalypse of Abraham is extant only in Old Church Slavonic, but a Hebrew original may be presumed; see A. Rubinstein, 'Hebraisms in the Slavonic "Apocalypse of Abraham" ', *JJS* 4 (1953), pp. 108–15; idem, 'Hebraisms in the "Apocalypse of Abraham" ', *JJS* 5 (1954), pp. 132–5.

[13] According to Frankemölle, p. 363, whenever βίβλος or its equivalent appears in the superscription of Essene or apocalyptic writings, it invariably means 'book' and covers the entire work.

[14] Also related is the introductory use of *kětāb*; note, e.g., 4Q'Amram[b] 1.1: 'Copy of the book (*kětāb*) of the words of the vision of Amram, son of Qahat, son of Levi . . .'. We should also call attention to the non-Jewish 'Book of Balaam' found at

(7) Judaism conceived of the eschatological redemption and renewal as a new beginning. Not only would the last redeemer (Messiah) be as the first (Moses)[15], but, for the rest, the world would once again be 'as it was in the beginning' (cf. 4 Ezra 7.30; Barn. 6). Matthew was manifestly familiar with this aspect of eschatology (note 19.28: παλιγγενεσίᾳ), and he saw the coming of Jesus in its light. In Mt 19.3–9, Jesus directs his followers back to Gen 1 and 2 and tells them that divorce is (except for the cause of πορνεία) adultery. Thus he announces a return to the initial order of things. Then at the baptism (in 3.16), the Spirit of God descends as a dove to the waters of the Jordan, which is probably intended to bring to mind the picture of Gen 1.2, where the Spirit of God 'hovers' or 'broods' over the face of the waters. And in 8.23–7 Jesus calms the raging sea, thereby showing himself to have the power of the majestic king of creation who, according to the OT, rules the chaotic waves (Job 38.8–11; Ps 89.9; 104.5–7; Prov 8.27–8; Jer 5.22; cf. Gen 1.1–2). Again, in 1.18 and 20 the rôle of the Holy Spirit just may hark back to its activity at the creation: as the Spirit originally moved over material things to bring forth life, so, in the latter days, has it moved once more—this time over a virgin's womb— to bring something new into the world.[16] Note must also be taken of Mt 2.15, according to which the Son of God, like Israel, went down to Egypt and returned therefrom to Palestine, and of those places where Jesus is painted with Mosaic colours (see on 2.16–18 (Herod and the infants); 5.1–2 (Jesus on the mountain); and 17.2–9 (the Transfiguration)); for in the Jewish mind the Exodus was linked with the act of creation.[17] Passages such as these, taken together, demonstrate that an interpretation of Mt 1.1 in terms of a 'new creation' does not place upon that verse an idea foreign to Matthew.[18]

The confluence of the seven points just made constitutes a formidable case for reading 1.1 as a general title: 'Book of the New Genesis wrought by Jesus Christ, son of David, son of Abraham'. It nevertheless remains true that Matthew's first two words are associated with a genealogy in Gen 5.1 and that the second occurrence of γένεσις at 1.18 inclines one to think that βίβλος γενέσεως has special reference to the story of Jesus' origin. What, then, is one to make of the conflicting indicators? Certainty is here unobtainable, but perhaps it would not be rash to conclude that

Deir 'Alla (8th cent. B.C.). It began, apparently, with these words: 'Book (spr) of Balaam, son of Beor . . .'. See J. A. Hackett, *The Balaam Text from Deir 'Alla*, Chico, 1984.

[15] For the evidence see Schoeps, *Theologie*, pp. 87–98, and W. A. Meeks, *The Prophet-King: Moses Traditions and the Johannine Christology*, Leiden, 1967.

[16] Cf. Davies, *SSM*, pp. 70–1, and Barrett, *Spirit*, p. 24.

[17] From the OT see Isa 43.16–20 and Wisd 19 and note the displacement of Rahab, the female monster of chaos, from creation contexts (Job 9.13; 38.8–11) to Exodus contexts (Ps 89.10; Isa 51.9–10). For later evidence see I. R. Chernus, *Redemption and Chaos: A Study in the Symbolism of the Rabbinic Aggada*, Ann Arbor, 1978.

[18] It bears remarking that, in the Eastern liturgy, the reading of the Christmas story from Matthew on Christmas Eve is preceded by a reading of Gen 1.1–13.

our evangelist intended his opening words to have more than one evocation (cf. Leuba (v)). Fenton has put it this way: 1.1 is 'telescopic: it can be extended to include more and more of what Matthew is beginning to write about. First, it can cover *the genealogy* which immediately follows it; then, it can refer to the account of the *birth* of Jesus . . .; thirdly, it can mean "history" or "life story"; finally, it can refer to the whole new creation which begins at the conception of Jesus and will be completed at his second coming'.[19] Such a happy interpretation is not, we think, over subtle; and it has the two-fold advantage of harmonizing conflicting observations and of agreeing with what has been termed Matthew's tendency to cater to different levels of comprehension at the same time.[20] Furthermore, there are other Matthean passages that have at least a double function.[21] To illustrate: 7.12, the golden rule, not only appropriately concludes 7.1–12, a section having to do with attitude towards one's neighbour; it also forms an *inclusio* with 5.17 to mark off the main portion of the sermon on the mount (5.17–7.12). And 28.16–20, which contains the final words of Jesus, is more than just the end of the resurrection narrative (28.1–20). It is also the climax of the entire passion narrative and beyond that the fitting capstone to the entire gospel, containing within itself the message of Matthew in miniature. So nothing prohibits us from urging that 1.1 be assigned more than one function.

βίβλος. Matthew uses the word only here, although it appeared in his Markan source at 12.26 (contrast Mt 22.31). βιβλίον (a near synonym) is found in 19.7 with the meaning of 'certificate'. In the LXX βίβλος always translates *spr*. The primary meaning is 'book', that is, a leather or papyrus roll, scroll, or codex, or the work contained therein; but it (or βιβλίον) could also designate a 'letter' (1 Kgs 21.8) or a 'record' (Gen 2.4; 5.1; Tob 7.13). Constant connexion with the writings of the OT[22] gave the word religious associations in Jewish and Christian circles (cf. BAGD, s.v.), and 'the books' by itself could mean the Scriptures (Dan 9.2; Ep. Arist. 46; Josephus, *Ant*. 1.15). In view of Gen 5.1 and 2.4, it is possible to render Matthew's βίβλος as 'record'; but, considering the evidence already reviewed, 'book' is preferable. For the word in book titles see pp. 151–2.

γενέσεως. This appears here and at 1.18, where 'birth' or 'origin'

[19] Fenton, p. 36. Cf. Bengel 1, p. 50; Gaechter, *Kommentar*, p. 34; Grundmann, p. 61; Beare, p. 64.

[20] R. T. France, 'The Formula Quotations of Matthew 2 and the Problem of Communication', *NTS* 27 (1981), pp. 249–51.

[21] In addition to what follows see Gaechter, *Kommentar*, pp. 34–5; cf. Luz 1, p. 19.

[22] See Josh 1.8; 2 Chr 17.9; Neh 13.1; Dan 9.2; Mk 12.26; Lk 3.4, 17, 20; 20.42; Acts 1.20; 7.42; Gal 3.10.

should be the translation. The basic meaning is 'birth', 'origin', or 'genesis'. 'Life' and 'what has come into being' are derivative meanings, as is 'history'. The LXX frequently connects the word with genealogies.

The γένεσις of 1.1 is probably more inclusive than that of 1.18. That is, it probably includes not only the idea of 'birth' or 'origin' but in addition extends beyond that to the thought of 'creation'. Hence the best translation is transliteration: 'genesis'. Some, to be sure, have claimed that the two occurrences of 'genesis' must be rendered by the same word.[23] But 1.18 marks a new beginning in the story line, not a resumption of 1.1. Further, the alleged necessity for identical translation equivalents has not been evident to the majority of translators (note the AV, the RV, the RSV, and the NEB). One might as well affirm that υἱὸς Δαυίδ in 1.1 (which refers to Jesus Christ) must have exactly the same breadth of meaning as υἱὸς Δαυίδ in 1.20 (where Joseph is the subject). In the one case the phrase connotes 'Messiah', in the other it does not.

We have already noted that the LXX had βίβλος γενέσεως at Gen 2.4 and 5.1. Perhaps, then, it should be added that rabbinic sources contain a special interpretation of these two verses. According to *ARN* 31, Gen 5.1 and 2.4 teach that 'the Holy One, blessed be he, showed Adam all the generations destined to come forth from him, standing and rejoicing before him'. Compare *b. 'Abod. Zar.* 5a; *b. Sanh.* 38b; *Gen. Rab.* on 5.1; and *Pesiq. R.* 23.1. Just possibly this tradition should be taken into account as background for Mt 1.1, if indeed one can believe that 'book of genesis' could hold more than one nuance. In the case of the rabbis, mention of the *sēper tôlĕdôt* of Adam was the opportunity for listing the leaders and sages from the beginning to the present, which perhaps has its parallel in Mt 1.2–17.

Ἰησοῦ Χριστοῦ. 'Jesus' occurs around one hundred and fifty times in the First Gospel. The name, the precise form of which changed over time (*Yĕhôšŭaʿ* > *Yôšŭaʿ* > *Yēšŭaʿ*), was quite popular with Jews before A.D. 70.[24] Despite the wordplay based upon the popular etymology, *Yēšŭaʿ* = 'Yahweh is salvation' (1.21), 'Jesus' is not a christological title in Matthew but a personal name.[25] The compound, 'Jesus Christ' (also in some mss. at 1.18 and 16.21), is on its way to being a personal name as it is elsewhere in the NT (Rom 1.1; Gal 1.1; Jas 2.1; Rev 22.21). Yet 1.17 (where Χριστός appears by itself) and the 'Son of David' in 1.1 warn us that, as in Rom 9.5, Χριστός has messianic content—and this is confirmed by 2.4; 16.16, 20; 22.42; 24.5, 23; 26.63, 68.

[23] This is the argument of Brown, *Messiah*, p. 58.
[24] See G. Foerster, *TWNT* 3, pp. 284–94, and the additional texts referred to by Hengel, *Jesus and Paul*, p. 187, n. 79.
[25] Cf. Kingsbury, *Structure*, pp. 84–5.

If, as we have urged, 1.1 refers firstly not to the genealogy or to the genealogy plus infancy material but rather is a general title for the whole book, then Jesus must be the subject or author of the new genesis. See further Davies, *Setting*, pp. 69–70. To this Mk 1.1 might supply a parallel. This verse, which should probably be taken as Mark's title,[26] may present Jesus Christ as the source (subjective genitive) of the gospel.[27] Compare Rev 1.1: ἀποκάλυψις Ἰησοῦ Χριστοῦ.

'Jesus Christ'—so common in Paul—is not found in Luke. In Mark it occurs only once, at 1.1. This raises the possibility of Markan influence on Mt 1.1, which also has 'Jesus Christ' in the title. Perhaps Mark's ἀρχή hints at this too, in view of the background of Mt 1.1 in Genesis.[28]

υἱοῦ Δαυίδ. This was a standard messianic title for the rabbis (see e.g. *b. Sanh.* 97a–98a), and a titular use *may* already be attested in the first century B.C., in Ps. Sol. 17. Developing out of older expressions such as 'sprout of Jesse' (Isa 11.10) and 'shoot (of David)' (Jer 23.5; 33.15; Zech 3.8; 6.12; 4QPatrBless 3; 4QFlor 1.11–12; 4QpIsa[a] frags. 7–10.11–17), 'Son of David' became the focus of a rich tradition;[29] and, by the time of Jesus, the dominant, although not exclusive, Jewish expectation—no doubt reinforced by the shortcomings of the non-Davidic Hasmoneans—was that the messianic king would be a son of David (cf. 4QPatrBless 2.4; 4QFlor. 1.11–13; 4QpIsa[a] frags. 7–10.22; 4 Ezra 12.32; Jn 7.42). A deliverer was expected who would fulfil the promises made in 2 Sam 7.[30] This largely accounts for the early Christian emphasis on the Davidic lineage of Jesus. Recall especially the confessional statement in Rom 1.3–4 and compare Acts 2.29–36; 13.22–3; 2 Tim 2.8; Rev 5.5; 22.16; Ignatius, *Eph.* 18.2; 20.2.[31]

Of all the NT writers, Matthew lays the most stress on the Davidic ancestry of Jesus. This probably reflects an ongoing dialogue with the synagogue, which looked for the arrival of *ben Dāwid*.[32] 'Son of David' is used nine times in the First Gospel—1.1,

[26] See Pesch 1, pp. 74–5, and A. Feuillet, 'Le "Commencement" de l'Économie Chrétienne d'après He ii. 3–4; Mc i.1 et Ac i.1–2', *NTS* 24 (1978), pp. 166–9.

[27] Cf. Anderson, p. 67, and Gnilka, *Markus* 1, p. 43.

[28] See further M. D. Johnson, *The Purpose of the Biblical Genealogies with Special Reference to the Setting of the Genealogies of Jesus*, SNTSMS 8, Cambridge, 1969, pp. 225–8.

[29] All of the relevant first-century material may be found in Nolan, esp. pp. 158–69.

[30] Cf. 1 Chr 17.11, 14; Isa 9.6–7; 11.1; Jer 23.5; 30.9; Ezek 34.23–4; 37.24–5; Hos 3.5; and (?) Dan 9.25–6.

[31] Jesus, according to some, was not a Davidic. The church only made him such out of theological necessity. Against this see Brown, *Messiah*, pp. 505–12.

[32] Cf. Hummel, pp. 116–22. Lit. on the Son of David in Matthew: Walker, pp. 129–32; J. M. Gibbs, 'Purpose and Pattern in Matthew's Use of the Title "Son of David" ', *NTS* 10 (1964), pp. 446–64; A. Suhl, 'Der Davidssohn im Matthäus-

20; 9.27; 12.23; 15.22; 20.30, 31; 21.9, 15—as opposed to three in Mark and none in Q. The title and its associations are particularly prominent in chapters 1–2. Note 1.1 and 20, the repeated mention of David (1.6; 1.17), and the importance of Bethlehem, the city of David (2.1–8, 16). Clearly Matthew's opening two chapters are intended to demonstrate that Jesus (through his father: 1.16) qualifies as the royal Messiah, the Davidic king (cf. 21.9, 15). This theme was already part and parcel of our evangelist's nativity source (see pp. 190–5)—as is suggested by its independent appearance in Lk 1–2 (see 1.27, 32–3, 69; 2.1–20; cf. 3.31).

Already in Rom 1.3 'of the seed of David' probably qualifies the pre-resurrectional stage of Jesus' history. Something similar may be found in Matthew. Although the disciples never confess Jesus to be the Son of David, and although the title does not appear in the passion narrative after 22.41–56, it comes close to being Matthew's most characteristic appellation for the earthly Jesus.[33]

One should observe that Son of David usage in later chapters probably touches a tradition not directly connected with eschatology. In the OT 'Son of David' refers, with one exception (2 Sam 13.1: Absalom), to Solomon. In addition, Solomon was later renowned as a mighty healer, exorcist, and magician (Josephus, *Ant.* 8.45–9; LAB 60.3; T. Sol. passim; *b. Git.* 68a–b; cf. Wisd 7.17–22; Sepher Ha-Razim, preface; SB 4, pp. 533–5). In fact, 'Solomon' appears often in the magical papyri (e.g. *PGM* 3,3040), and 'David's son' is a name of power on incantation bowls.[34] All of this is significant because Matthew, who unlike Luke (3.31) traces the royal line through Solomon, tends to associate 'Son of David' with healings and exorcisms (9.27; 12.23; 15.22; 20.30, 31). This causes one to suspect that he was familiar with the popular notions about Solomon and saw Jesus in their light. See further on 9.27 and 2.11.[35]

Evangelium', *ZNW* 59 (1968), pp. 67–81; Sand, pp. 162–7; Kingsbury, *Structure*, pp. 99–103; idem, 'The Title "Son of David" in Matthew's Gospel', *JBL* 95 (1976), pp. 591–602; D. C. Duling, 'The Therapeutic Son of David: An Element in Matthew's Christological Apologetic', *NTS* 24 (1978), pp. 392–410; B. D. Chilton, 'Jesus *ben David*: Reflections on the *Davidssohnfrage*', *JSNT* 14 (1982), pp. 88–112. See further on 9.27.

[33] By 'most characteristic appellation' is not meant 'most important appellation'. The presupposition of Kingsbury's study in Christology (*Structure*, pp. 40–127), which is that one christological title—in his case, Son of God—must be pre-eminent, and all other titles subordinate to that one title, has no foundation in the text. Cf. D. Hill, 'Son and Servant: An essay on Matthean Christology', *JSNT* 6 (1980), p. 4. Also relevant is L. E. Keck, 'Toward the Renewal of New Testament Christology', *NTS* 32 (1986), pp. 362–77.

[34] For examples of these last see L. R. Fisher, ' "Can this be the Son of David?" ', in *Jesus and the Historian*, ed. F. T. Trotter, Philadelphia, 1968, pp. 82–97.

[35] LXX mss. have two spellings for David (who in Christian tradition came to be known as 'the grandparent of God'): Δαυείδ and Δαυίδ. This reflects the interchange between ει and ι in the *koiné* (itacism). Josephus has Δαβίδης and Δαυίδης, Philo Δαβίδ. Consult BAGD, s.v. Most modern editors prefer to read Δαυίδ in Matthew, not Δαυείδ (so e.g. NA[26]). But the mss. are divided and one cannot be dogmatic.

υἱοῦ ᾿Αβραάμ. Compare 3.9 = Lk 3.8: τέκνα τῷ ᾿Αβραάμ. 'Son of Abraham' was not a messianic title (although cf. T. Levi 8.15). Rather was it an expression used either of one of Jewish blood (Lk 19.9; Jn 8; Acts 13.26; *m. B. Qam.* 8.6) or of one worthy of father Abraham (4 Macc 6.17, 22; 18.23; Gal 3.7; *b Beṣa* 32b). Here, even though connexion with David is grammatically possible, the reference is to Jesus, and both meanings are appropriate.

Abraham, the 'father of fathers' (T. Jacob 7.22), was the one with whom God made his foundational covenant with Israel (Gen 12; 15), and descent from him was the basis for membership in the people of God (cf. Jub. 12.24; 13.3; 4 Ezra 3.13–15). Hence the significance for Matthew of Jesus being the son of Abraham: as the saviour of Israel, Jesus himself must be a true Israelite, a descendant of Abraham (cf. Jn 4.22; Heb 2.16–17). Beyond this, because the genealogy which follows 1.1 covers the period from Abraham to the Messiah, it is natural to think of Jesus as the culmination, the *telos*, of that history which began with the patriarch. But there is more. 'Son of Abraham', found only here in Matthew, probably also serves to announce the evangelist's interest in the salvation of the Gentiles. Abraham himself was a Gentile by birth, and in the OT it is promised that 'all the nations' will be blessed in him (Gen 12.3; 18.18; etc.). In later Jewish literature Abraham was sometimes portrayed as 'the father of many nations' (Gen 17.5; cf. 44.19; 1 Macc 12.19–21) or the first proselyte (e.g. *b. Ḥag.* 3a); and the promise to Abraham was employed to further the purposes of Jewish mission.[36] When we come to Christianity, we find Paul representing Abraham as the true father of all who have faith, Jew and Gentile alike (Rom 4.1–25; Gal 3.6–29). Matthew may have held a similar conception. In 8.11–12 we read that many (Gentiles) will come from east and west to sit at table with Abraham, Isaac, and Jacob; and in 3.9 the Baptist declares, 'God is able to raise up from these stones children to Abraham'. Matthew, we may think, believed that God had in fact raised up from the Gentiles new children to Abraham and that Jesus as the 'son of Abraham' had brought them their salvation.

The juxtaposition of 'Son of David' with 'son of Abraham' intrigues because outside of Matthew the promises made concerning the 'seed' of David and the 'seed' of Abraham are brought together (see Lk 1.30–3, 55, 69–73; Acts 3.25; 13.23) while the equation of the two seems to lie behind Paul's identification of the 'seed' of Abraham with 'Christ' in Gal 3.16.[37] Moreover, Jer 33.21–2 and the targum on Ps 89.4 conflate or associate

[36] See T. B. Dozeman, '*Sperma Abraam* in John 8 and related Literature', *CBQ* 42 (1980), pp. 343–6. Cf. Hengel, *Judaism and Hellenism* 1, p. 302.

[37] See M. Wilcox, 'The Promise of the "Seed" in the New Testament and the Targumim', *JSNT* 5 (1979), pp. 2–20.

Gen 17.7 (the promise to Abraham and to his seed) with 2 Sam 7.12 (the promise to David and to his seed). Perhaps, therefore, the identification of Jesus Christ in Mt 1.1 as 'Son of David' and 'son of Abraham' reflects the traditional equation, 'seed' of Abraham = 'seed' of David = the Messiah.

Three final points. First, given Matthew's emphasis on righteousness and upholding the Torah (5.17–20), the mention of Abraham is particularly apt, for the patriarch was revered as one who had been perfectly obedient to the commands of the Law. He indeed kept the whole Torah even before it was written.[38] Secondly, there was a tradition that Abraham 'discovered both astrology and Chaldean science' (Ps.-Eupolemus in Eusebius, *Praep. ev.* 9.17; cf. Artapanus in Eusebius, *Praep. ev.* 9.18; the Jewish mystical hymn in Eusebius, *Praep. ev.* 13.12; Josephus, *Ant.* 1.158, 167–8; LAB 18.5; *b. B. Bat.* 16b).[39] It is fitting, then, that the 'son of Abraham' should be honoured by magi from the east (2.1–12). Finally, since the 'son of Abraham' in 1.1 is immediately followed in 1.2 by mention of Isaac, and since, as already suggested, 'son of David' may have had a double meaning for Matthew, referring to Jesus as both the Davidic Messiah and one like Solomon, it is just possible, one might urge, that 'son of Abraham' could also have a double meaning, designating Jesus not only as a descendant of Abraham but as one like Isaac, who carried wood on his back and was willing to give up his life in obedience to God (cf. Rom 8.32?).[40] Yet nowhere else in the First Gospel is Jesus clearly associated with Isaac (although see on 3.17).

(iv) *Concluding Observations*

The 'Jesus Christ' of 1.1 is surrounded by three word pairs, 'book of genesis', 'Son of David', and 'son of Abraham'. These give us the three major points of the title. First, the occurrence of 'genesis', whether dependent upon Gen 2.4 and 5.1 or intended to recall the OT's first book, relates the story of Jesus to the primeval history. This means, according to the principle that the end will be like the beginning (see p. 153), that the gospel concerns eschatology: it recounts the fulfilment of the hope for a 'new creation'.[41] Then, secondly, the phrase 'Son of David' represents Jesus as the king of

---

[38] Ecclus 44.19–21; Prayer of Manasses 8; Jub. 6.19; 16.28; 21.2; 23.10; 2 Bar. 57.2; T. Abr. (A) 1; 4; *m. Qidd.* 4.14; *b. B. Bat.* 17a.

[39] For rejection of this seemingly wide-spread tradition see Jub. 12.15–17; Philo, *De Abr.* 68–71; Sib. Or. 3.218–30; *b. Ned.* 32a. On the whole matter consult Hengel, *Judaism and Hellenism* 2, p. 62, n. 264, and C. R. Holladay, *Fragments from Hellenistic Jewish Authors, Vol. 1: Historians*, Chico, 1983, pp. 180–1.

[40] If, as has sometimes been urged, there was a tradition about the virgin birth of Isaac (see on 1.23), this would certainly buttress such a conjecture.

[41] Philo, *Praem. Poen.* 1: 'The oracles delivered through the prophet Moses are of three kinds. The first deals with the creation of the world, the second with history, and the third with legislation'. This recalls Mt 1–7, which begins with a reference to creation (1.1), moves on to recount 'historical' events (1.18–5.2), and then gives us 'legislation' (5.3–7.27).

Israel, the rightful heir to the Davidic promises. This too pertains to eschatology: the Messiah has come. Lastly, 'son of Abraham' probably implies not only that Jesus is a true Israelite but also— for reasons given above—that with his appearance God's promise to the patriarch has been realized: all the nations of the earth (cf. 28.19) have been blessed.

(v) *Bibliography*

J. Chopineau, 'Un notarikon en Matthieu 1/1. Note sur la généalogie de l'évangile de Matthieu', *ETR* 53 (1978), pp. 269–70.

Davies, *SSM*, pp. 67–70.

O. Eissfeldt, 'Biblos Geneseōs', in *Kleine Schriften III*, Tübingen, 1966, pp. 458–70.

Frankemölle, pp. 360–5.

Kingsbury, *Structure*, pp. 9–11.

M. Lambertz, 'Die Toledoth in Mt 1,1–17 und Lc 3,23bff.', in *Festschrift für Franz Dornseiff*, ed. H. Kusch, Leipzig, 1953, pp. 201–25.

J.-L. Leuba, 'Note exégétique sur Matthieu 1,1a', *RHPR* 22 (1942), pp. 56–61.

A. Paul, 'Matthieu 1 comme écriture apocalyptique. Le récit véritable de la "crucifixion" de l'ἔρως', *ANRW* II. 25.3 (1984), pp. 1952–68.

W. B. Tatum, ' "The Origin of Jesus Messiah" (Matt 1:1, 18a): Matthew's Use of the Infancy Traditions', *JBL* 96 (1977), pp. 523–35.

II

FROM ABRAHAM TO JESUS: THE DAVIDIC MESSIAH'S GENEALOGY
(1.2–17)

(i) Structure

The most notable feature of Mt 1.2–17 is its carefully ordered structure. Fourteen generations fall (inclusively) between Abraham and David, between David and the Babylonian captivity, and—at least according to 1.17—between the Babylonian captivity and Jesus. How does one account for and understand this triadic scheme, which is obviously artificial rather than historical?[1]

(1) It could be pre-Matthean. Such is the position of Strecker, who affirms the traditional character of 1.2–17.[2] But the justified tendency of recent criticism is towards assigning the genealogy, in whole or in part, to the redactor's hand.

(2) Mt 1.17 counts fourteen generations between the captivity and Jesus. This could be tied in with Dan 9.24–7, which prophesies that seven weeks of years ($=490$ years) will pass between the 'going forth of the word to restore and build Jerusalem' and the coming of an anointed one, a king. For if a generation be reckoned to be thirty-five years, the time of Jesus' coming would mark the fulfilment of prophecy, since $35 \times 14 = 490$.[3] But the assumption that the length of a generation should be set at thirty-five years is gratuitous.[4]

(3) The cycle of the moon covers twenty-eight days, fourteen of waning, fourteen of waxing. Perhaps, then, the idea behind 1.2–17 is this: the time between Abraham and David was one of waxing, with David being the climax; next, the period after David was one of waning, the captivity being the low point; finally, there followed

---

[1] See Jeremias, *Jerusalem*, p. 290–7; Brown, *Messiah*, pp. 84–94. On the impossibility of harmonizing Luke's genealogy with Matthew's see Johnson (v), pp. 140–5.

[2] Strecker, *Weg*, p. 38. Cf. Bultmann, *History*, p. 357.

[3] This is the argument of Moore (v).

[4] There was no fixed idea concerning the length of a generation; see D. N. Freedman and J. Lundblom, *TDOT* 3, p. 174.

a time of waxing, the zenith coming with the birth of Jesus. In his *Gnomon*, Bengel already mentioned this interpretation and ascribed it to a certain James Rhenford. In more recent times it has been championed by C. Kaplan.[5] Just such a scheme does, in fact, lie behind *Exod. Rab.* on 12.2.[6] There, however, the cycles of the moon, given as $15 + 15 = 30$, are explicitly cited.

(4) Because seven but not fourteen is a prominent number in the Bible, Matthew's three fourteens can be regarded as the equivalent of six sevens ($3 \times 14 = 6 \times 7$),[7] in which case Jesus would stand at the head of the seventh seven, the seventh day of history, the dawn of the eternal sabbath. A parallel to this could be found in the 'Apocalypse of Weeks' (1 En. 93.1–10; 91.12–17). In this a review of salvation-history divides time into ten weeks, according to the following plan: three before Abraham, seven after Abraham, the seventh being the messianic age (cf. Par. Jer. 3.10).[8] Yet it must be said that Matthew expressly writes of three fourteens, not six sevens.[9]

(5) For H. C. Waetjen, the closest analogy to Matthew's pattern appears in 2 Bar. 53–74, the so-called 'Messiah Apocalypse'.[10] Here history is partitioned into twelve plus two or fourteen epochs of alternating bright and black waters. But it is difficult to see how Matthew's forty-two generations can in any straightforward manner be linked to a division of history into fourteen epochs.

(6) The counting of fourteen generations from Abraham to David was evidently tradition; for, in addition to Matthew, this calculation re-emerges in 1 Chr 1–2; *Exod. Rab.* on 12.2; and perhaps the source behind Luke 3.[11] So one might argue in this

---

[5] Kaplan (v); also Bornhäuser (v).
[6] 'THIS MONTH SHALL BE UNTO YOU THE BEGINNING OF MONTHS: just as the month has thirty days, so shall your kingdom last until thirty generations. The moon begins to shine on the first of Nisan and goes on shining till the fifteenth day, when your disc becomes full; from the fifteenth till the thirtieth day her light wanes, till on the thirtieth it is not seen at all. With Israel too, there were fifteen generations from Abraham to Solomon. Abraham began to shine. . . . When Solomon appeared, the moon's disc was full. . . . Henceforth the kings began to diminish in power. . . . With Zedekiah . . . the light of the moon failed entirely . . .'.
[7] Cf. Farrer, *St. Matthew*, p. 189.
[8] Cf. Bornhäuser (v), pp. 16–20, and SB I, pp. 44–5.
[9] For further criticism see Vögtle, 'Genealogie' (v), pp. 89–90.
[10] Waetjen (v), pp. 207–12; contrast Johnson (v), pp. 193–5.
[11] As it stands, Lk 3.23–8 counts fifteen names (inclusively) from David to Abraham. But the two names, 'Arni' and 'Admin', may have arisen as a result of textual corruption in the pre- or post-Lukan tradition, replacing the one name, 'Ram' (MT) or 'Aram' (LXX). We should also note that the calculation of fourteen names or generations from Abraham to David was only one of several well-known

fashion. Given the traditional reckoning as well as Matthew's penchant for the number three[12] and for order in general, a genealogy of 3×14 generations was the natural result.[13] This proposal is less objectionable than the others already reviewed. It is, nonetheless, not without difficulty. For in view of the repeated mention of the number fourteen in Mt. 1.2–17, it seems likely that our evangelist believed it to hold some sort of intrinsic, symbolic significance.

(7) In *b. Sanh.* 105b and *b. Hor.* 10b, R. Judah (d. 299) in the name of Rab (d. 247) recounts an interpretation of the three sacrifices of Balak and Balaam in Num 23, an interpretation according to which the total number of Balaam's sacrifices was forty-two, this being the product of $3 \times 14 (= 7 \text{ (bulls)} + 7 \text{ (lambs)})$. We do indeed find here the number forty-two and three fourteens, and this fact has been thought significant for Mt 1.2–17.[14] Yet nothing more is involved than a coincidental use of the same numbers. Certainly the subject matter of the gospel text is not in any way treated of in *b. Sanh.* 105b or *b. Hor.* 10b.

(8) Probably the most popular explanation among contemporary scholars makes *gematria* the key. David's name has three consonants, the numerical value of which amounts to fourteen in Hebrew: $d + w + d = 4 + 6 + 4 = 14$.[15] So the suggestion is this: Matthew's genealogy has 3×14 generations because David's name has three consonants whose sum is fourteen. It is not difficult to see why this particular solution has gained wide credence. The other solutions have shortcomings; *gematria* was practised in both Jewish and Christian circles close to Matthew's time;[16] and the numerical interpretation of David's name can

---

reckonings; e.g. the counting of ten periods or generations from Noah to Abraham was traditional (Gen 11.10–32; 4QAges Creat.; *m. 'Abot* 5.3).

[12] In the infancy narrative alone there are, besides three fourteens, three names in the title, three gifts for Jesus, three important places (Bethlehem, Egypt, Nazareth), three angelic appearances to Joseph, and three separate episodes (1.18–25; 2.1–12; 2.13–15); see esp. J. Y. Thériault, 'La Règle des Trois. Une lecture sémiotique de Mt 1–2', *ScEs* 34 (1982), pp. 57–78; also Johnson (v), pp. 211–14, and the introduction to this volume, pp. 85–6.

[13] Cf. Zahn, p. 51; Lagrange, pp. 2–3; Vögtle, 'Genealogie' (v), pp. 90–1.

[14] So Heer (v), pp. 121–2.

[15] See Box (v), pp. 80–1, and those cited by Vögtle, 'Genealogie' (v), p. 90, n. 133. The DSS, it has been observed, have *dwyd* (which is also attested in the MT), implying that this, not *dwd*, might have been the more common form at the time of Jesus. Cf. R. E. Brown, *Messiah*, p. 80, n. 38. This, however, is no decisive objection to the theory of *gematria*, for *dwd* is also found in the DSS; cf. D. N. Freedman, 'The Massoretic Text and the Qumran Scrolls: A Study in Orthography', *Textus* 2 (1962), p. 96.

[16] Rev 13.18; Barn. 9; Sib. Or. 5.12–51; T. Sol. 6.8; 11.6; *b. Yoma* 20a; *b. Makk.* 23b–24a; *b. Ned.* 32a; *b. Sanh.* 22a.

account for both the number three and the number fourteen. Still, objections have been raised. First, the use of *gematria* in Greek documents is customarily accompanied by an explicit statement indicating such. Reference need be made only to Rev 13.18 and Sib. Or. 5.12–51. And even when, as in rabbinic sources, *gematria* is not explicit, it is only because its presence is unmistakable, as in *Num. Rab.* on 5.18 and 16.1. Secondly, the list of fourteen names in 1.2–6a was surely traditional and therefore ought not to be regarded as the product of a numerical play on David's name; see under (6) above.

Must the two aforenamed objections be taken as decisive? The first is not so telling as it initially appears to be. Plays on numbers are not uncommon in Jewish literature,[17] and examination of a passage in Genesis seemingly reveals that *gematria* could play a rôle in the composition of a genealogy and not be explicitly mentioned. In Gen 46.8–27, seven and its multiples are prominent. We read that all the persons of the house of Jacob were seventy, that seven of Judah's descendants went to Egypt, that the sons of Jacob by Rachel were fourteen, and that Bilhah bore to Jacob seven persons in all. Moreover, Gad, whose name has the numerical value of seven ($g + d = 3 + 4 = 7$), is placed in the seventh position and given seven sons. This can scarcely be coincidence.[18] Gen 46 seems to have been constructed so as to put the number seven in relief,[19] and in the process notice has been taken of the value of Gad's name. Here, therefore, we have probable precedent for the inexplicit use of *gematria* in a genealogy.

The second criticism can also be overcome. The appearance of *gematria* usually represents a 'discovery'. Someone, for instance, discovered that the value of the name of Abraham's servant, Eliezer, was the same as the number given in Gen 14.14 (*b. Ned.* 32a), and someone else discovered that HaSaTaN equals the number of days in a year minus one (*b. Yoma* 20a). Mt 1.2–17 may similarly represent a 'discovery'. Knowing that the OT listed fourteen names from Abraham to David and that the value of the latter's name was fourteen, our evangelist may have set himself to looking for other fourteens—only to find them, or numbers close

---

[17] See M. H. Farbridge, *Studies in Biblical and Semitic Symbolism*, New York, 1970, pp. 87–156, and the prolegomenon of H. G. May, pp. xl–xlv; also A. Y. Collins, 'Numerical Symbolism in Jewish and Early Christian Apocalyptic Literature', *ANRW* II.21.2 (1984), pp. 1221–87. There is perhaps an instance of inexplicit *gematria* in Jn 21.11; see J. A. Romeo, 'Gematria and John 21.11—The Children of God', *JBL* 97 (1978), pp. 263–4.

[18] Cf. J. M. Sasson, 'A Genealogical Convention in Biblical Chronography', *ZAW* 90 (1978), p. 181.

[19] Luke's genealogy, interestingly enough, also appears to have been built around sevens; there are seventy-seven names, and God, Enoch, Abraham, and David occupy slots marking multiples of seven.

enough. If such were the case, then *gematria* would have been a factor in the construction of Matthew's genealogy, although not the sole factor.

One last point in this connexion. We suspect *gematria* because David's name has the value fourteen and because in Mt 1.2–16 there are 3×14 generations. But there is an additional observation to be made. David's name is fourteenth on the list. This is telling. In a genealogy of 3×14 generations, the one name with three consonants and a value of fourteen is also placed in the fourteenth spot. When one adds that this name is mentioned immediately before the genealogy (1.1) and twice at its conclusion (1.17), and that it is honoured by the title, king, coincidence becomes effectively ruled out. The name, David, is the key to the pattern of Matthew's genealogy.[20]

(ii) *Sources*

As is evident from the preceding paragraphs, the problem of structure cannot really be considered apart from the discussion of how Matthew composed his proem, and this issue must next be addressed. According to R. E. Brown, two genealogical lists were already in existence in Greek. One covered the pre-monarchical period and resembled the genealogies in 1 Chr 2 and Ruth 4. The other list was a popular genealogy of the royal Davidic line. It contained (with omissions) the names of the kings of Judah and the descendants of Zerubbabel. Matthew noticed that the pre-monarchical list had fourteen names between Abraham and David, and again that there were fourteen names in the monarchical section. Furthermore, the same number appeared for a third time if Joseph and Jesus were added to the post-exilic group of names. So Matthew, with his predilection for numbers, and aware of the numerical value of David's name, produced his genealogy according to a 3×14 pattern.[21]

In our view, Brown's analysis is not above criticism. There is, in the first place, no forceful reason to postulate a pre-monarchical genealogy. As the commentary shows, a redactional use of 1 Chr 1–2 suffices to account for Mt 1.2–6a. In the second place, it is not easy to believe that, if only two names were joined at the end, a 3×14 pattern was already to hand in the pre-Matthean materials. It is more probable that Matthew artificially

---

[20] That the meaning of Matthew's fourteen lies in David's name is supported by this fact: although the Chronicler counted fourteen Aaronite priests from Aaron to Solomon (1 Chr 6.3–11), and although fourteen is a crucial number in 11QTemple's blueprint for the perfect sanctuary (38.8, 10; 41.14; 46.6), and although the rabbis may have named fourteen intermediaries in the transmission of the Torah down to Hillel and Shammai (on this see E. Bickerman, 'La chaîne de la tradition pharisienne', *RB* 59 (1952), pp. 47–8), the number fourteen is not prominent in Jewish tradition. Note that in his *Gnomon* Bengel attributes to a certain Rabbi Bechai (date?) the opinion that David was the fourteenth from Abraham on account of the value of David's name.

[21] *Messiah*, pp. 69–70.

imposed the pattern on his sources, at least in 1.6b–16. For example, the striking omission of three kings between Joram and Uzziah (1.8) is best explained as a way of keeping fourteen names in the monarchical period.

A more plausible theory of composition might move along the following lines. In agreement with Brown, Matthew had at his disposal an originally Jewish list of monarchical and post-monarchical Davidids. This source lies behind what is now Mt 1.6b–16. (The existence although not the accuracy of such a list is made credible by what we otherwise know of Jewish concerns.[22]) Against Brown, Matthew also drew upon 1 Chr 1–3 and knew the traditional reckoning of fourteen generations from Abraham to David (see p. 162). Then, partly out of a fondness for symmetry and partly because fourteen was the value of David's name, and in the conviction that salvation-history could be neatly divided into epochs of equal count,[23] the evangelist imposed the number fourteen upon the list behind 1.6b–16.[24] In order, however, to accomplish this imposition,he had to omit four names from the monarchical period (Ahaziah, Jehoash, Amaziah, Jehoiachim) and add at least two to the post-monarchical period (Joseph, Jesus). If it be objected that Matthew could not have made so much of the 3 × 14 pattern if it were simply the result of his own editing, it suffices to observe that the rabbis tended 'to reduce things and numbers to the very same, when they were near alike'.[25] There is an example of this in *m.* *'Abot* 5.1–6. Here reference is made to the ten sayings by which the world was made, the ten generations from Adam to Noah, the ten generations from Noah to Abraham, the ten wonders wrought for the fathers in Egypt, the ten wonders wrought by the sea, the ten plagues on Egypt, the ten temptations with which Israel tempted God, the ten wonders done in the temple, and the ten things created on the eve of the Sabbath. The manipulation of numbers for edifying ends was an established practice, and we can readily believe that Matthew could have

---

[22] See Jeremias, *Jerusalem*, pp. 275–302; Johnson (v), passim. Pertinent passages include 1 Chr 1–9; Ezek 13.9; Josephus, *Vita* 1–6; *C. Ap.* 1.28–36; *Ant.* 20. 224–51; *m. Yeb.* 4.13; *b. Ketub.* 62b; *b. Qidd.* 76b; *b. Pesaḥ* 4a; Eusebius, *H.E.* 1.7. Genealogies were no doubt sometimes made up; possibilities include Tob 1.1; Jud 8.1; LAB 42.1; *y. Taʿan.* 4.2.68a: *Gen. Rab.* on 49.10; see the commentaries on 1 Chr 6.31–48 and Hood (v), pp. 4–5. Cf. *b. Qidd.* 69a–71a, on false genealogies. For the possibility that a Davidic genealogy was manufactured for Hillel see M. Stern, 'A. Schalit's Herod', *JJS* 11 (1960), pp. 55–6.

[23] Cf. Jub. 47.1; 1 En. 93.1–10; 91.12–17; As. Mos. 1.2; 10.12; 4 Ezra 14.11; 2 Bar. 53–74; Apoc. Abr. 28–9; 2 En. 33.1–2; *b. Sanh.* 97b; *b. 'Abod. Zar.* 9b; and perhaps 4QAgesCreat., for which see J. T. Milik, 'Milkî-ṣedeq et Milkî-reša' dans les anciens écrits juifs et chrétiens', *JJS* 23 (1972), pp. 110–24. Dan 2, following an established tradition (cf. Hesiod, *Op.*), divides world history into four ages. The same scheme may be implicit in Matthew. Cf. Pal. Tg. to Exod. 12.42: there are four nights of history—creation, promise to Abraham, Passover in Egypt, Messiah.

[24] 1 En. 93.5–8 reckons three weeks (inclusively) from Abraham to the building of the temple, and three weeks (inclusively) from the building of the temple to the exile. *Exod. Rab.* on 12.2 reckons fifteen names from Abraham to Solomon, and fifteen from Solomon to the captivity. In both these texts, then, the time from Abraham to David (or Solomon) and from David (or Solomon) to the exile is the same, and there is agreement with Matthew.

[25] Lightfoot 2, p. 15.

been fully aware of the artificiality of his pattern and still at the same time have thought it significant and worthy of attention.

Mt 1.2–17 is, with Luke 3.23–38, evidence for the independence of the First and Third Gospels. If Matthew had had Luke's genealogy before him, he would probably not have constructed one of his own. And if, conversely, Luke had had Matthew's genealogy before him, there would in all likelihood be at least some sign of Matthean influence. But, as throughout the infancy narratives, no such sign exists.[26]

(iii) *Exegesis*

2. With this verse Matthew opens the first section of his genealogy, 1.2–6a, from Abraham to David. It is the sole section showing extensive agreement with Luke's genealogy; see Lk 3.31–4. In fact, there is only one significant difference: between Hezron and Amminadab Matthew has Aram, Luke Arni and Admin. The names in Mt 1.2–6 appear to be taken from the LXX, 1 Chr 1.28, 34; 2.1–15 (cf. Ruth 4.18–22).

If in 1.2 and subsequent verses Matthew is indeed, as we shall urge, drawing upon Chronicles, this is something of an anomaly. Chronicles was not much cited or alluded to by early Christian writers. Perhaps our evangelist's use of Chronicles hints at his scholarly Jewish background.[27]

Ἀβραὰμ ἐγέννησεν τὸν Ἰσαάκ. 'Abraham' (from *'Abrāhām*, 'father of a multitude') is named seven times in Matthew (Mk: 1; Lk: 15). The form, Ἀβραάμ, is the only one known to the LXX and NT; elsewhere Ἀβράμης (see Nicolaus of Damascus in Josephus, *Ant.* 1.159) and Ἄβρα(α)μος (see *Ep. Arist.* 49; Artapanus in Eusebius, *Praep. ev.* 9.18; Josephus, *Ant.* 1.148) are attested. Why does Matthew begin his genealogy with Abraham? Several considerations are relevant. (1) Abraham stands at the beginning of, or at a decisive point in, several schematic accounts of Jewish history (1 Macc 2.51–60; 1 En. 89.10; 93.5; 4 Ezra 6.7–8; 2 Bar. 53.5; 57.1–3; *m 'Abot* 5.2, 3); he also heads the genealogy in *Exod. Rab.* on 12.2. (2) By commencing with the patriarch, the transition from the title (1.1) to the genealogy (1.2) is very neat: 'Abraham begat Isaac' immediately follows 'Jesus, Son of David, son of Abraham'. (3) The placement of Abraham in the initial position makes David's name the fourteenth. (4) There is some evidence that Abraham was regarded as a king (*b. Sanh.* 108b; *Gen. Rab.* on 22.1; according to Justin, *Epit.* 36.2, Trogus Pompeius reported

---

[26] Contra Gundry, *Commentary*, pp. 14–41, who strangely enough sees Mt 1–2 as a 'midrashic' rewriting of Luke's infancy narrative.

[27] Cf. Schlatter, p. 2. For controversy surrounding the interpretation of the genealogies in Chronicles see *b. Pesaḥ.* 62b–63a.

that Abraham was for a time king of Damascus; cf. Josephus, *Ant*. 1.159–60). If Matthew knew this tradition, it may have influenced his decision to begin the royal genealogy with Abraham. Also, the patriarch is the root of David's genealogical tree in *Num. Rab*. on 13.14. (5) Matthew may have believed, as did the author of 2 Bar. 57.2, that, with the advent of Abraham and his sons, 'the unwritten law was named amongst them, and the works of the commandments were then fulfilled, and belief in the coming judgement was then generated, and hope of the world that was to be renewed was then built up, and the promise of life that should come hereafter was implanted' (cf. LAB 4.11). For some, Abraham marked a beginning no less important than that marked by Adam.

In view of the women listed in 1.2–16, the absence in 1.2 of Sarah as well as of Rebekah and Rachel is notable. On Abraham in Matthew see further on 1.1.

With Mt 1.2 compare 1 Chr 1.34 LXX: καὶ ἐγέννησεν Ἀβραὰμ τὸν Ἰσαάκ. The verb Matthew shares with 1 Chronicles, namely, γεννάω, helps make 1.2–17 something other than a dry-as-dust list: events in time, that is, begettings, are the subject. The genealogy is history.

The formula, 'A begat B', is used several times in 1 Chr 1–3, in Ruth 4.18–22, and elsewhere in LXX genealogies. Matthew, for the sake of parallelism and order, prefers to employ it exclusively, at least until 1.16. By using ἐγέννησεν, the evangelist can descend in his enumeration and create a chiastic pattern. Thus 1.1 tells of 'Jesus Christ, Son of David, son of Abraham', while the genealogy gives us, in reverse order, Abraham (1.2), then David (1.6), then Jesus (1.16; cf. on 1.1).

Ἰσαάκ is the standard LXX and NT form (although P[46] and D always have Ἰσάκ; cf. Gen 27.1 LXX A) for *Yiṣḥāq*. Josephus prefers Ἴσακος. Ep. Arist. 49 has Ἴσαχος. Isaac's birth was something of a miracle (Gen 17.15–21; 18.9–15; 21.1–7), so the first begetting in Matthew's genealogy (1.2) has something in common with the last (1.16). On Isaac in Matthew see further p. 159.

Ἰσαὰκ δὲ ἐγέννησεν τὸν Ἰακώβ. Ἰακώβ (= *Yaʿăqōb*) is the form of the LXX and Philo. Josephus has the graecized form, Ἰάκωβος (cf. Ep. Arist. 48), which the NT uses for several people known as 'James' (cf. BAGD, s.v.). In 1 Chr 1.34 the MT has 'Israel', the LXX 'Jacob'. This suggests that Matthew is working with the LXX.

Ἰακὼβ δὲ ἐγέννησεν τὸν Ἰούδαν. Compare Heb 7.14: 'our Lord was descended from Judah' (cf. Lk 3.33). Ἰούδας = Judah the patriarch appears only in 1.2–3 (cf. 2.6: 'land of Judah', 'rulers of Judah'); but the same name belongs to Jesus' brother (13.55) and to Judas the betrayer. On the form see BAGD, s.v. The prophecy in Israel's testament (Gen 49) concerning Judah and his descendants came to be interpreted of the Messiah (so the targums on Gen 49.8–12; cf. 4QPatrBless; Rev 5.5; Justin, *Dial*. 52; Irenaeus, *Adv. haer*. 4.10.2; *b. Sanh*. 98b; *Gen. Rab*. on 49.10). In T. Jud. 1.6 Judah is called a 'king' (cf. 21.2; 22.1–3).

καὶ τοὺς ἀδελφοὺς αὐτοῦ. This phrase is a sign that Matthew's hand is here at work and that we have something more than a traditional genealogy. The brothers of Jacob are named in 1 Chr 2.1–2; but why has Matthew bothered—if only briefly—to note them? (Observe also that Zera is mentioned along with Perez in 1.3 and that 1.11 refers to 'Jechoniah and his brothers'.) Many commentators find here an implicit statement about God's selectivity and providential choice: of the several possible ancestors, Judah alone (like Perez and Jechoniah) was chosen to propagate the royal line (cf. Gen 49.10).[28] Gundry, on the other hand, speaks of Matthew's interest in the people of God as a brotherhood: Judah and his brothers prefigure the church, which is a brotherhood. He also thinks that the same idea explains the reference to the brothers of Jechoniah.[29] According to M. D. Johnson, 'Judah and his brothers' calls to mind the twelve tribes of Israel who will be united once again at the eschatological culmination already inaugurated by Jesus (cf. 19.28; for the regathering of the twelve tribes see 4 Ezra 13.34–50; 2 Bar. 77–86; *m. Sanh*. 10.3).[30] Perhaps the most that can safely be said is this: 'Judah and his brothers' makes plain the character of 1.2–17: it is not just a genealogy but a résumé of salvation-history. Compare the mention of the deportation in 1.11–12.

3. Compare 1 Chr 2.3–9 and Ruth 4.18–19 LXX. Justin, *Dial*. 120, wrote: 'For the seed is divided from Jacob, and comes down through Judah and Phares and Jesse and David. And this was a symbol of the fact that some of your nation would be found children of Abraham, and found, too, in the lot of Christ; but that others . . . would be like sand on the sea-shore, barren and fruitless . . .'.

Ἰούδας δὲ ἐγέννησεν τὸν Φάρες καὶ τὸν Ζάρα.[31] The spellings are those of the LXX. *Pereṣ* and *Zeraḥ* were the twin sons of Judah and Tamar (Gen 38.27–30). On the significance of 'and Zerah' see *supra*.

According to *b. Yeb*. 76b, if David descended from Perez he would be king, for a king breaks—*prṣ* = 'to break'—for himself a way and no one can hinder him, but if he descended from Zerah—*zrh* = 'to shine'—he would be only an important man. Also of

[28] So e.g. McNeile, p. 1, and Hill, *Matthew*, p. 75.
[29] *Commentary*, pp. 14, 17.
[30] Johnson (v), pp. 151–2; cf. Vögtle, 'Genealogie' (v), p. 95.
[31] P¹ B mae, followed by HG, have Ζαρε.

inferest is the rabbinic exegesis which finds in the *happōrēṣ* (= 'the breaker') of Mic 2.13 a prophecy of the Messiah (*Gen. Rab.* on 18.8 and 38.29; *Lev. Rab.* on 24.10). See Davies, *GL*, p. 229.

ἐκ τῆς Θαμάρ. See 1 Chr 2.4 and Ruth 4.12. *Tāmār*, the wife of Er, Judah's eldest son, was probably a Canaanite. After Er died, Judah's other sons failed to fulfil the obligations of levirate marriage to raise up children for their brother, so Tamar deceived Judah, conceiving by him twins (Gen 38). Both Jub. 41.1–2 and T. Jud. 10.1–2 make Tamar a 'daughter of Aram', that is, an Aramean, and both texts explicitly deny her Canaanite ancestry. Matthew may have known this tradition. Tamar is mentioned nowhere else in the NT or in the earliest Christian literature.

Why has the evangelist added 'by Tamar'? This question cannot be raised without asking why Rahab, Ruth, and the wife of Uriah (Bathsheba) are likewise named in the genealogy. Women are not usually named in Jewish genealogies[32] (cf. Lk 3.23–38), and although Tamar and Bathsheba appear in 1 Chr 1–3, the other two women do not. Hence Matthew's citation of four women must signal some special interest.

It might be argued that the four women were sinners.[33] Tamar seduced Judah. Rahab was a prostitute. Bathsheba committed adultery with David. Perhaps Ruth was also guilty of transgression, for Ruth 3.1–18 may imply that she enticed Boaz (see the commentaries and note Josephus' concern with the problem: *Ant.* 5.328–31). Matthew's point would then be a demonstration of God's grace and power: God's purpose for the Davidic line was achieved despite human sin and failure (cf. 1 Cor 1.27–31 and Josephus, *Ant.* 5.337). In other words, God can save his people from their sins (cf. Mt 1.21). Against this, however, early Christian tradition held up Rahab as a model of faith and good works, as did Jewish tradition (see on 1.5); and Gen 38.26 clearly proclaims the righteousness of Tamar (cf. Philo, *Deus Imm.* 136–7; *Virt.* 220–2).[34] One can also cite rabbinic texts that play down the offence of Uriah's wife (see SB I, pp. 28–9); and Ruth 4.11 expresses Ruth's renown. Beyond these facts, 1.2–16 names several male figures whose sins were well-known (e.g., David and Manasseh). Thus the introduction of the women would hardly seem to be a fruitful way of furthering that theme.

A second alternative has been advanced by M. D. Johnson.[35] In his estimation there was an intra-Jewish debate over the ancestry

---

[32] Exceptions include Gen 11.29; 22.20–4; 35.22–6; 1 Chr 2.18–21, 24, 34, 46–9; 7.24; LAB 1–2.

[33] So G. Kittel, *TWNT* 3, pp. 1–3; cf. Jerome, *In Matt.* 9 and Aquinas, *Summa*, 3.31.3 ad 5. For criticism see Spitta (v).

[34] See further SB 1, pp. 15–17, to which add LAB 9.3–6.

[35] Johnson (v), pp. 176–9. See esp. *Ruth Rab.* on 4.2.

of the Messiah. Proponents of a priestly Messiah probably made a point against their rivals by calling attention to the irregularities in the Davidic line. These irregularities—including foreign blood and sinful women—were in turn defended by the Pharisees. Matthew, by putting the women into 1.2–16, would then reveal his Pharisaic bent and his conviction that Jesus had fulfilled the Pharisaic expectation in every respect. This interesting suggestion, which is consistent with our own picture of the evangelist Matthew, does not quite compel, for the necessary evidence concerning Rahab does not exist.

There is probably more truth to the proposal, popular since Luther, that the women in 1.2–16 reflect an interest in the salvation of the Gentiles.[36] Tamar, whether a Canaanite or an Aramean, was certainly a foreigner (cf. Philo, *Virt*. 220–2). Rahab was a Canaanite, Ruth a Moabite, and Bathsheba was (originally) the wife of Uriah, a Hittite. It is true that in some sources Tamar, Rahab, and Ruth are regarded as proselytes;[37] but the knowledge that they were not Jews by birth was not thereby eliminated. Further, Matthew's concern to announce from the outset of his gospel the inclusion of non-Jews in the church is clear from the story of the magi as well probably as from 1.1, where Jesus is 'son of Abraham'.

A fourth suggestion, to which a measure of assent can also be given, finds the common denominator of Tamar, Rahab, Ruth, and Bathsheba to be the nature of their marital unions.[38] These, although irregular and even scandalous, eventuated, in God's providence, in the Messiah's coming. The union of Judah and Tamar was an 'abomination in Israel' (T. Jud. 12.8). Solomon was born because David his father took another man's wife. Ruth was a Moabite. And, although the Bible says nothing about Rahab's marriage to Salmon, she was both a Canaanite and a prostitute. So the occasion for calumny by outsiders was present in each instance. Yet any slanderer would in truth have been depreciating what God had chosen to bless. One can easily see how Matthew might have intended this to prefigure the situation of Mary. The Christian story of Mary's pregnancy involved an extraordinary circumstance which no doubt engendered disbelief and ridicule on the part of those outside the church (and there may have been doubters on the inside, too). But Matthew and his readers could take reassurance from the history of the Davidic line; for those who took offence at Mary would be missing 'the strange

---

[36] See esp. Stegemann (v); cf. Luz 1, pp. 94–5 and the authors cited there.

[37] See SB 1, pp. 16, 20–1, 25.

[38] K. Stendahl, '*Quis et Unde*? An Analysis of Mt 1–2', in Eltester, p. 101, and Brown, *Messiah*, pp. 73–4; also Freed (v), stressing apologetics.

righteousness of God'[39] no less than one might have despised the irregular unions in the royal genealogy.

For γεννάω with ἐκ plus the genitive of the mother see Tob 1.9; 2 Esdr 10.44; Gal 4.23; Josephus, *Ant*. 12.189.

Φάρες δὲ ἐγέννησεν τὸν Ἑσρώμ. Hezron was the eponymous ancestor of a clan of Judah (Gen 46.12; Num 26.21; 1 Chr 4.1). He is to be distinguished from the Hezron who gave his name to a clan of Reuben (Gen 46.9; Exod 6.14; Num 26.6; 1 Chr 5.3). Ἑσρώμ (for *Ḥeṣrôn*) is a LXX form, although some OT mss. have Ἑσερών, Ἑσρών, or Ἁσρών in 1 Chr 2.3, 9.

Ἑσρὼμ δὲ ἐγέννησεν τὸν Ἀράμ. In 1 Chr 2.9 MT the sons of Hezron are three: Jerahmeel, Ram, and Chelubai. The LXX adds a fourth, Aram, and makes him (not Ram) the father of Amminadab. At Ruth 4.19, the LXX has Arran for the son of Hezron. However one unravels the textual confusion, Matthew appears to have followed 1 Chr 2.9 LXX—unless it be supposed that he was acquainted with the lost Hebrew text form beneath the Greek version of 1 Chronicles.

4. Compare 1 Chr 2.10–11 LXX: καὶ Ἀρὰμ ἐγέννησεν τὸν Ἀμιναδάβ, καὶ Ἀμιναδὰβ ἐγέννησεν τὸν Ναασσών . . . καὶ Ναασσὼν ἐγέννησεν τὸν Σαλμών (cf. Ruth 4.19–20).

Ἀρὰμ δὲ ἐγέννησεν τὸν Ἀμιναδάβ. *ʿAmmînādāb* was the father of Elisheba, Aaron's wife (Exod 6.23). Against the LXX and Matthew, Lk 3.33 makes Amminadab a son of the otherwise unknown Admin and a grandson of the otherwise unknown Arni. Josephus has the spelling Ἀμινάδαβος, Philo Ἀμιναδάμ.

Ἀμιναδὰβ δὲ ἐγέννησεν τὸν Ναασσών. *Naḥšôn* was the leader of the tribe of Judah (Num 1.7; 2.3; 7.12, 17; 10.14). 1 Chr 2.10 calls him 'prince of the sons of Judah'.

Ναασσὼν δὲ ἐγέννησεν τὸν Σαλμών. Salmon (*Śalmāʾ*, *Śalmâ*, or *Śalmôn*) occurs in the OT only in genealogies. Ruth 4.20 has Σαλμάν, Luke 3.32, Σαλά. Matthew agrees with 1 Chr 2.11 LXX.

5. Compare 1 Chr 2.11–12 and Ruth 4.21–2 LXX. On why Rahab and Ruth are named see on 1.3.

Σαλμὼν δὲ ἐγέννησεν τὸν Βόες.[40] The LXX has either Βόος (so also some Matthean mss.) or Βόοζ (so also some Matthean mss.) for *Bōʿaz*, the virtuous, righteous Bethlehemite who, according to the book of Ruth, took the Moabitess Ruth for his wife. According to the targum on 1 Chr 4.22, he was master of the scholars in the academy in Bethlehem. The origin of the spelling, Βόες, is obscure. Josephus has Βόαζος and Βοώζης, Luke Βόος.

ἐκ τῆς Ῥαχάβ. Rahab is almost certainly the harlot of Jericho

[39] Schweizer, *Matthew*, p. 25. Cf. Zahn, pp. 63–7; he emphasizes the apologetic force of this.

[40] P[1] ℵ B k DialTimet Aq co read Βοες. Βοοζ (so L *f*[1.13] Maj lat sy[p]) and Βοος (so C *pc* g[1] D[luc]) agree with the LXX.

known from Josh 2 and 6—although the LXX, followed by Heb 11.31; Jas 2.25; and 1 Clem. 12.1–3, has ʿΡαάβ.⁴¹ The χ of ʿΡαχάβ accurately represents the *ḥ* of *Rāḥāb* (cf. Josephus' ʿΡαχάβη and see BDF § 39.3). It may betray the redactor's knowledge of the Hebrew. There is no parallel to the statement that Rahab married Salman and mothered Boaz—which is not surprising since OT chronology separates Rahab and Salman by almost two-hundred years. Maybe we have here the product of Matthean fancy.⁴² In the Talmud Rahab is said to have been the wife of Joshua (*b. Meg.* 14b–15a). For the most part, Rahab received a good report in both Jewish and Christian tradition,⁴³ and the rabbis praised her as a proselyte, a prophetess, and one of the most beautiful women in the world (SB 1, pp. 20–3). It is probably just coincidence that both Rahab and Tamar (1.3) were associated with scarlet cords (Gen 38.28; Josh 2.18).

Ruth Rab. on 1.1 tells us that the Holy Spirit rested upon Rahab before Israel entered the promised land, and several Jewish texts associate Tamar with God's Spirit (e.g. *b. Mak.* 23b; *Gen. Rab.* on 38.15).⁴⁴ So, given that, according to our gospel, Mary conceived by the Holy Spirit, it is possible to think of the women in Mt 1.2–16 as foreshadowing the mother of Jesus in so far as they too were vessels of the Spirit. Most of the sources appealed to are, however, undateable or much too late—such as the medieval midrashim— and make one cautious. Moreover, Sarah and Rebekah were also traditionally associated with the Holy Spirit (Jub. 25.14; *b. Meg.* 14a; *Gen. Rab.* on 16.2), so should they too not have been named?

Βόες δὲ ἐγέννησεν τὸν ᾿Ιωβήδ. 1 Chr LXX A has this spelling for ʿ*Ôbēd*, as does Luke 3.32. Other LXX mss., Ruth 4.17, 21, 22, and late mss. of Matthew have ᾿Ωβήδ (whence our 'Obed'). Josephus has ᾿Ωβήδης.

ἐκ τῆς ʿΡούθ. Our evangelist reproduces the LXX spelling of *Rût*, the Moabitess⁴⁵ after whom the book of Ruth is named. Mt 1.5 contains the only NT reference to her, and she does not often put in an appearance in later Christian literature. Rabbinic

---

⁴¹ See the debate between Quinn (v) and Brown, 'Rahab' (v). The other three women in Mt 1.2–16 are well-known figures, as are all the men in the first two tessaradecads.

⁴² Yet Johnson (v), pp. 164–5, finds evidence that Rahab might have been considered a member of the tribe of Judah by some Jews.

⁴³ Johnson (v), pp. 162–5; A. T. Hanson, 'Rahab the Harlot in Early Christian Theology', *JSNT* 1 (1978), pp. 53–60. Note also Daube, pp. 27–51.

⁴⁴ See Bloch (v). Note esp. Pal. Tg. to Gen 38.25–6.

⁴⁵ In Deut 23.3 (cf. Neh 13.1), Moabites are forbidden to enter the assembly of the Lord until the tenth generation; and the prophets often spoke harsh judgements against Moab (Isa 15; 16; Ezek 25.8–11; Amos 2.1–3). *b. Yeb.* 76b applies the prohibition against Moabites only to males, in order to circumvent an application to David, who was descended from Ruth the Moabitess (cf. *m. Yeb.* 8.3).

tradition made her a proselyte, the mother of kings, and an ancestress of the Messiah (SB 1, pp. 25–7).[46]

'Ιωβὴδ δὲ ἐγέννησεν τὸν 'Ιεσσαί. Matthew agrees with the LXX spelling of *Yišay*. Compare Lk 3.32; Acts 13.22; Rom 15.12. Josephus has 'Ιεσσαῖος. David was known as the 'son of Jesse' (1 Sam 20.27, 30, etc.; Ecclus 45.25), and 'stump' or 'root' of Jesse had a messianic reference (Isa 11.1, 10; Rom 15.12; the Babylonian version of the Eighteen Benedictions, 15; *Midr. Ps.* on 21.2; cf. the targum on Isa 11.1). For Jesse in the OT see 1 Sam 16–17. He lived in Bethlehem.

6. Compare 1 Chr 2.13–15; 3.5, 10; Ruth 4.22 LXX. This is the turning point between the first and second sections of the genealogy. David is the fourteenth on the list and concludes the first period. Solomon is the fifteenth, and between him and Jechoniah (1.11) are again fourteen more names or generations (counting inclusively). On David and Solomon see on 1.1.[47]

'Ιεσσαὶ δὲ ἐγέννησεν τὸν Δαυὶδ τὸν βασιλέα. 'David the king' is from the OT (2 Sam 6.12; 7.18; Prov. 1.1; etc.). Compare 1 Chr 3.4 (ἐβασίλευσεν) and Ruth 4.22 LXX A (τὸν βασιλέα). 1.2–16 is a royal genealogy, and because he is the son of David, the king, Jesus himself is a king. The word 'king', however, must be carefully defined. Jesus is not a king who meets everyone's expectations. His kingship neither involves national sovereignty nor does it restore Israel to good political fortune. Jesus' kingdom is instead one which can be present even in the midst of Roman rule (see on 4.17). The Messiah's first task is to save his people from their sins (1.21), not deliver them from political bondage.

Δαυὶδ δὲ ἐγέννησεν τὸν Σολομῶνα.[48] The gospels and Josephus always, and the rest of the NT usually, have Σολομῶν for *Šělōmōh*. 1 Chr 3.5 LXX has Σαλωμών (Luc.: Σαλομών). See BAGD, s.v. Luke traces Jesus' ancestry through another son of David, Nathan.[49]

ἐκ τῆς τοῦ Οὐρίου. Compare 2 Sam 11.26; 12.10, 15. 1 Chr 3.5 has 'Bathsheba, daughter of Ammiel'. '*Ûrîyyâ* was a Hittite (2 Sam 12.9, etc), so the expression, 'wife of Uriah', is better suited than the simple 'Bathsheba' for calling attention to Gentiles in Jesus' family tree; but it could also evoke the sin of David, who had

---

[46] See further Johnson (v), pp. 165–70.

[47] On the place of David in Judaism see esp. Nolan, pp. 158–215.

[48] C L W Maj lat sy^h insert ο βασιλευς. This increases the parallelism between 6a and 6b ('David the king'/'David the king'), but it disrupts the parallelism between 6 and 11–12, the two break points in the genealogy: David + qualifier (6a)/David (6b) // Jechoniah + qualifier (11)/Jechoniah (12). P¹ ℵ B Γ *f*¹·¹³ 700 *pc* g¹ k vg^mss sy^s.c.p co omit.

[49] For discussion of this and its relation to Matthew see E. Nestle, 'Salomo und Nathan in Mt 1 und Lc 3', *ZNW* 22 (1923), pp. 206–28, and Fitzmyer, *Luke* 1, pp. 496–7.

Uriah killed (2 Sam 11, 12). 1 Kgs 15.5 reads: 'David did what was right in the eyes of the Lord, and did not turn aside from anything that he commanded him all the days of his life, except in the matter of Uriah the Hittite'. For the rabbis on David and Bathsheba see especially *b. Šabb.* 56a, also *b. Qidd.* 43a. Like Rahab, Bathsheba was held to have been exceptionally beautiful (2 Sam 11.2).

7. Compare 1 Chr 3.10.

Σολομὼν δὲ ἐγέννησεν τὸν Ῥοβοάμ. Ῥοβοάμ for *Rĕḥabʿām* is the LXX form. Rehoboam was the first king of Judah after the split of the northern and southern kingdoms. His mother was an Ammonitess, and the OT represents him as upholding pagan practices (1 Kgs 14.21–24; 2 Chr 12.13–14; cf. Josephus, *Ant.* 8.251–5).

Ῥοβοὰμ δὲ ἐγέννησεν τὸν Ἀβιά. Abijah (= ʾĂbîyyâ), also known as Abijam, succeeded his father as king of Judah. The writer of Kings passed a negative judgement on him (1 Kgs 15.1–8), the writer of Chronicles a favourable verdict (2 Chr 13.1–22; cf. Josephus, *Ant.* 8.274–86). Ἀβιά is the LXX spelling in 1 Chr 3.10. Ἀβιού occurs in 3 Βασ 15. Josephus has Ἀβίας and Ὀβίμης.

Ἀβιὰ δὲ ἐγέννησεν τὸν Ἀσάφ. Matthew's Ἀσάφ (cf. D^luc) differs from the Ἀσά of 1 Chronicles.[50] Josephus has Ἄσανος. Matthew or his tradition probably confused the eponymous ancestor or founder of a guild of Levitic temple musicians (the 'sons of Asaph') to whom several Psalms were ascribed (50. 73–83; cf. 2 Chr 29.30; 35.15; Neh 12.46) with ʾĀsāʾ, the good king of Judah (1 Kgs 15.9–24; Josephus, *Ant.* 8.286–315). (A similar confusion concerning two people with the same name occurs in 23.35.) Later scribes corrected the error. In 13.35 Matthew quotes as fulfilled a psalm of Asaph (78.2), and some have found in 5.8 an allusion to another of his psalms, 73.1. So the addition of φ could indicate an interest in the realization of the psalmist's hopes.[51] Note also that Asaph and the sons of Asaph, who were quite important to the Chronicler, were closely associated with David (1 Chr 6.31–2, 39; 1 Esd 1.15; 5.59–60; Asc. Isa. 4.19). According to LAB 51.6, Asaph was a prophet (cf. note 49).

8. Compare 1 Chr 3.10–12.

Ἀσὰφ δὲ ἐγέννησεν τὸν Ἰωσαφάτ. Matthew reproduces the LXX form for *Yĕhôšāpāṭ*, the monarch whose achievements are praised in detail in 2 Chr 17–20 (cf. 1 Kgs 22.41–50; Josephus, *Ant.* 8.393–9.44). Josephus has Ἰωσάφατος, D^luc Ἰωσαφάδ.

Ἰωσαφὰτ δὲ ἐγέννησεν τὸν Ἰωράμ. *Yĕhôrām*, not to be confused with his namesake, the son of Ahab, was the wicked king whose

---

[50] But according to Burkitt, *Evangelion* 2, p. 203, Ἀσάφ became Ἀσά in Greek copies of the OT under the influence of Origen's Hexapla.

[51] Perhaps Asaph was held to have been a prophet; note Eusebius, *Dem ev.* 10.1 and *Gen. Rab.* on 26.34.

reign of eight years is recounted in 2 Kgs 8.16–24 and 1 Chr 21.
The LXX agrees with Matthew's spelling. Josephus has Ἰώραμος.

Ἰωρὰμ δὲ ἐγέννησεν τὸν Ὀζίαν. Ὀζίας is a problem. For
᾽Ăhazyāhû (see 2 Kgs 8.25–9.29 and 2 Chr 22.1–9) in 1 Chr 3.11
most LXX mss. have Ὀχοζία; but B has Ὀζεία, A V Luc Ὀζιάς.
(Elsewhere the LXX generally has Ὀχοζείας) Then in 3.12 there is
confusion over the Greek for king Uzziah ('Uzzîyah or 'Uzzîyāhû;
see 2 Kgs 14.21, 22; 15.1–7; 2 Chr 26). B has Ἀζαρία, A Ἀζαρίας,
Luc. Ὀζίας. (Elsewhere the LXX generally has Ὀζεία.) Matters
are complicated further because Matthew makes Ὀζίας the father
of Jotham (whose father was Uzziah). This has the effect of
striking out three kings between Joram and Uzziah (if Ὀζίας is
Uzziah) or (if Ὀζίας is Ahaziah) between Ahaziah and Jotham.
How is this to be explained?[52]

(1) Someone's eye may have slipped from Ahaziah to Uzziah,
that is, from Ὀχοζία or Ὀζεία or Ὀζίας to Ὀζίας or to some other
spelling of Uzziah (homoioteleuton). Such an accident could be
attributed to the redactional level, to Matthew's source, or to a
copy of the LXX. Yet in view of the evangelist's manifest wish to
have fourteen names between David and the captivity, it is better
to discern design rather than a fortunate accident without which
there would be no 3×14 pattern.

(2) Some have suggested that the omission was intentional, to
rid the genealogy of wicked kings.[53] According to the OT, God
willed the violent deaths of Ahaziah, Joash, and Amaziah (2 Chr
22.1–9; 24.1–25, 28). 1 Kgs 21.21, moreover, places a curse upon
the house of Ahab (cf. 2 Chr 22.7 and 2 Kgs 10.30; Ahab's
daughter Athalia was Joram's wife); and Matthew may have
thought of that curse as extending to the third or fourth generation
(cf. Exod 20.5; Num 14.18) and therefore have dropped three
unworthy names from his genealogy. This second proposal is more
plausible than the first, despite the fact that there are other evil
kings in 1.2–16 (e.g. Joram and Ahaz). In order to maintain his
3×14 pattern, Matthew had to eliminate several kings from the
monarchical section of his genealogy; and he may have decided to
eliminate rulers who were associated with the cursed house of
Ahab.

One should observe that the omission of names from a
genealogy, for one purpose or another, including, apparently,
brevity, was common practice. Examples include Gen 46.21 (cf.
1 Chr 8.1–4); Josh 7.1, 24; 1 Chr 4.1 (cf. 2.50); 6.7–9 (cf. Ezra 7.3);

---

[52] Despite 1.17, which counts only fourteen generations from David to the
captivity, Dˡᵘᶜ syᶜ eth Epiph Th-Mop add three missing kings; cf. 1 Chr 3.11–12.

[53] Cf. Opus Imperfectum, in PL 56, cols. 623–4, and Kuhn (v). But Kuhn himself
admits that Matthew did not eliminate Amon, who also died a violent death.

Ezra 5.1 (cf. Zech 1.1); Josephus, *Vita* 1–5;[54] Apoc. Abr. title. Pertinent also is the rabbinic principle, the sons of sons are sons (*b. Qidd.* 4a).

9. Compare 1 Chr 3.12, 13.

'Οζίας δὲ ἐγέννησεν τὸν 'Ιωαθάμ, 'Ιωαθὰμ δὲ ἐγέννησεν τὸν 'Αχάζ, 'Αχὰζ δὲ ἐγέννησεν τὸν 'Εζεκίαν. The Greek names for *Yôtām*, *'Āḥāz*, and *Ḥizqîyāhû*, three kings who appear nowhere else in the NT, follow the LXX of 1 Chr 3, save that Matthew has μ (cf. also Josephus: 'Ιωάθαμος, 'Ιωθάμης) for the ν in 'Ιωαθάν. The OT portrays Hezekiah as an outstanding king who was faithful to Yahweh (2 Kgs 18–20; 1 Chr 29–32; Isa 36–9; Ecclus 49.4; cf. 2 Bar. 63.1–11): 'there was none like unto him' (2 Kgs 18.5). Jotham also receives a favourable report (2 Kgs 15.32–8; 2 Chr 27). Ahaz (Josephus: 'Αχαζος), however, is thought of as an apostate (2 Kgs 16; 2 Chr 28; Josephus, *Ant.* 9.243–57). This entails that Matthew's concern must be other than the listing of praiseworthy rulers. A rabbinic tradition identified Hezekiah with the Messiah (see *ARN* 25; *b. Sanh.* 94a; *b. Ber.* 28b; cf. *b. Sanh.* 98b–99a), and there may be a bit of Hezekiah typology here and there in the synoptics.[55] An unidentified Joatham appears in Apoc. Zeph. 3.4.

10. Compare 1 Chr 3.13–14.

'Εζεκίας δὲ ἐγέννησεν τὸν Μανασσῆ. *Měnaššeh*—the LXX and Josephus agree with Matthew's spelling—was the most wicked king of Judah (2 Kgs 21.1–18; 2 Chr 33.1–9). It is, nevertheless, impossible to determine whether the evangelist would have thought of him as an unremittingly evil ruler or as one who finally came to repentance. Judaism held conflicting traditions on the point. Contrast 2 Chr 33.10–20; the Prayer of Manasseh; Tob 14.10 LXX B; and Josephus, *Ant.* 10.40–6 with 2 Kgs 21.1–18; 2 Bar. 64.1–65.1; Asc. Isa. 11.41–3; *y. Sanh.* 10.2; and the targum on 2 Chr. 33.13.

Μανασσῆς δὲ ἐγέννησεν τὸν 'Αμώς.[56] 'Αμώς for *'Āmôn*, who 'did what was evil in the sight of the Lord' (2 Kgs 21.19–26; 2 Chr 33.21–5), is attested in LXX mss. (cf. Josephus: 'Αμωσος). But 'Αμών (Luc) or 'Αμνών (B) seems the better reading for 1 Chr 3.14. 'Αμώς (cf. D^luc) may represent a corruption in Matthew's source or in the post-Matthean textual tradition, or perhaps Matthew simply made an error. In the last instance, it might be intentional, a change designed to bring in a note of prophecy—just as the change of Asa to Asaph might hint at an interest in the psalmist's hopes.[57] There are, however, no explicit citations of Amos in Matthew, and

---

[54] On this see Schürer 1, p. 46, n. 3, and Jeremias, *Jerusalem*, p. 214, n. 212.

[55] See D. Daube, *He That Cometh*, London, 1966, pp. 1–6.

[56] K L W *f*¹³ Maj lat sy mae geo correct Matthew's error and substitute 'Amon' for 'Amos'.

[57] Cf. Schniewind, p. 10; Gundry, *Commentary*, p. 16.

allusions are rare; compare, perhaps, Mt 27.45 with Amos 8.9, Mt 10.29 with Amos 3.5.

Ἀμὼς δὲ ἐγέννησεν τὸν Ἰωσίαν. For Yō'šîyāhû, whose lauded reign included commendable reforms and the discovery of the 'book of the law' (2 Kgs 22.1–23.30; 2 Chr 34–5; Josephus, *Ant.* 10.47–80; cf. Ecclus 49.1–4; 2 Bar. 66.1), Matthew, Lucian, and Josephus have Ἰωσίας. LXX mss. contain this spelling and several others.

11. The first tessaradecad, 1.2–6a, concluded with the appearance of king David and the inception of the monarchy; the second, 1.6b–11, concludes, by way of contrast, with a note of disaster, the deportation to Babylon.

Ἰωσίας δὲ ἐγέννησεν τὸν Ἰεχονίαν καὶ τοὺς ἀδελφοὺς αὐτοῦ. In 1 Chr 3.15–16, Josiah has four sons, the second being Jehoiachim, the father of Jechoniah and Zedekiah. Why, then, does Matthew write, 'Josiah begat Jechoniah and his brothers'?[58] Jehoiachin was an alternative name for Jechoniah (2 Kgs 24.8–16/2 Chr 36.9–10); Ἰωακίμ was used for both Jehoiachin (Jechoniah) and Jehoiachim (e.g. 2 Kgs 23.36; 24.8–16); the two names are confused in 1 Esd 1.41 LXX; and both Jehoiachin (Jechoniah) and Jehoiachim apparently had brothers named Zedekiah, which explains why 2 Chr 36.10 erroneously makes king Zedekiah the brother of Jehoiachin instead of Jehoiachim. All this strongly suggests the possibility of a textual or scribal mistake behind Mt 1.11. And yet, without dismissing this option, Yĕhôyākîm/Ἰωακίμ and Yĕkonĕyâ/Ἰεχονίας (which are found in 1 Chr 3.16–17, upon which Matthew's sources presumably drew) are not so close as to be naturally confused. Further, 1 Chr 3.17 calls Jechoniah 'the captive' ('assir/ασιρ),[59] and if this lies behind the association of Jechoniah and the deportation to Babylon in Mt 1.11–12, Ἰεχονίας must there be original. So we should consider the possibility that Matthew deliberately omitted Jehoiachim in order to keep his 3 × 14 pattern from Solomon to the exile.[60] That, however, leaves unexplained the mention of Jechoniah's brothers (1 Chr 13.16 lists only one brother, Zedekiah).[61] Ἀδελφούς might mean more than 'blood brother', perhaps 'kinsmen' (cf. Gen 13.8;

[58] See esp. Vögtle, 'Josias' (v). Is it just coincidence that 1 Esd 1.34 also mistakenly makes Jechoniah the son of Josiah?

[59] There is no definite article in the Hebrew (which originally may have been *hā'assir*), and the LXX and Vulgate translate as a personal name (cf. *b. Sanh.* 37b). Did Matthew have a Greek OT which understood the word differently? Or did he have a right understanding of the Hebrew?

[60] For the telescoping of genealogies see on 1.8.

[61] But *possible* references to the brothers of Jehoiachin have been found in recovered Babylonian tablets (*ANET* 308); see E. F. Weidner, 'Jojachin, König von Juda, in babylonischen Keilschrifttexten', in *Mélanges Syriens offerts à M. René Dussaud*, Paris, 1939, 2, pp. 923–35.

24.48; 29.12) or 'community of co-religionists' or 'fellow
countrymen' (1 Chr 28.2; Rom 9.3). Certainly Jechoniah had
cousins, the sons of king Zedekiah (2 Kgs 25.7), and many of his
fellow Jews went with him to Babylon (2 Kgs 24.10–16). In
addition, 2 Chr 36.10, as already noted, wrongly makes king
Zedekiah the brother of Jehoiachin (Jechoniah) (cf. 2 Kgs 24.17),
which means that if Matthew did not catch this error, it would be
precedent for thinking of the four sons of Josiah as the 'brothers'
of Jechoniah. Against all this, the parallel in 1.2 ('Jacob begat
Judah and his brothers') and the ἐγέννησεν in 1.11 seem to
demand that 'brothers' designates 'blood brothers'. Perhaps the
best explanation for 1.11 is that of Vögtle.[62] He suggests that
Matthew originally wrote, 'Josiah begat Jehoiachim and his
brothers' (1.11) and followed this by 'Jechoniah begat Salathiel'
(1.12). He did this because he could not write, 'After the
deportation to Babylon Jehoiachim begat Jeconiah'—for he knew
that the latter was born before the exile. A later scribe then
changed 'Jehoiachim' to 'Jechoniah' to make the genealogy
uniform. The major drawback to this proposal is its lack of textual
support.

11QTemple 59.13–15 speaks of a king who will not have 'a man sitting
on the throne of his fathers all the days because I will forever cut off his
seed . . .'. If, as seems likely, this refers to Zedekiah, the successor of
Jehoiachin and the last king of Judah, then the Dead Sea Scrolls seemingly
attest the conviction that the Davidic line of anointed ones came to its end
with the exile to Babylon. Mt 1.2–17, by way of contrast, implicitly denies
any break in the kingly succession.

ἐπὶ τῆς μετοικεσίας Βαβυλῶνος. Compare 1.12, 17. For ἐπί with
the genitive of time see BAGD, s.v., I.2. μετοικεσία (cf. Ps.-Clem.
Hom. 16.13) is a NT *hapax legomenon* which has been inserted into
Matthew's source to mark the division between the second and
third sections of the genealogy. It is used of the Babylonian
captivity in 2 Kgs 24.16; 1 Chr 5.22; and Ezek 12.11—each time
for *gōlâ* or *gôlâ*. The classical form is μετοίκησις. Although this is
not developed in depth in first-century Judaism, the exile was not
regarded as historical accident but instead interpreted in
theological categories—God was punishing his people for their
sins or scattering Israel in order to make more proselytes or
accomplishing some other wise purpose (cf. 2 Chr 36.15–21; 2 Bar.
1.1–5; *b. Pesaḥ.* 87b; *b. Sanh.* 37b). Thus 'at the deportation to
Babylon' should perhaps call to mind the hand of divine
providence. μετοικεσία seems in any case better suited to connote
God's activity than αἰχμαλωσία, which has such strong military

[62] In addition to 'Josias' (v) see 'Genealogie' (v), pp. 95–9.

associations. See Davies, *The Territorial Dimension of Judaism*, Berkeley, 1982, pp. 116–17; *JQR* 74 (1983), pp. 105–36.

12. The genealogies of Luke and Matthew converge for Shealtiel and Zerubbabel; but they disagree on the father of the former (Luke: Neri) and the son of the latter (Luke: Rhesa).

μετὰ δὲ τὴν μετοικεσίαν Βαβυλῶνος Ἰεχονίας ἐγέννησεν τὸν Σαλαθιήλ, Σαλαθιὴλ δὲ ἐγέννησεν τὸν Ζοροβαβέλ.[63] The names are in their LXX forms (cf. L. Proph. Zech. 3; D[luc]). Josephus has Ζοροβαβηλος and Σαλαθήλ. According to 1 Chr 3.17–19 MT, *Zĕrubbābel* was the son of Pedaiah.[64] According to 1 Chr 3.17–19 LXX and the rest of the OT, both MT and LXX, he was the son of Shealtiel (whom 4 Ezra 3.1 erroneously identifies with Ezra). See Ezra 3.2; 5.2; Neh 12.1; Hag 1.1; 2.23; 1 Esd 5.5, 48, 56. Perhaps Pedaiah was Zerubbabel's real father but, because Zerubbabel succeeded Shealtiel (of whom no son is recorded) as the head of the family of David or Judah, Zerubbabel was called his son. In any case, either the author of the source behind 1.6b–16 followed the LXX of 1 Chronicles or (less likely) he corrected the Hebrew in the light of other passages.

Zerubbabel, a descendant of David, was, after the exile, the Persian governor of Jerusalem (cf. Josephus, *Ant.* 11.33–78). Messianic hopes came to rest upon him. In Haggai, he is the Lord's 'servant', his 'signet ring' (cf. Ecclus 49.11) and 'chosen' one (2.23). The prophet Zechariah presumably put his hope for a Davidic king in Zerubbabel (Zech 4.6–10; most have followed Wellhausen in supposing that 'Joshua' has replaced 'Zerubbabel' in Zech 6.11–12). The fate of Zerubbabel is unknown, but after him the Persians apparently did not choose governors from the Davidic line. 1 Chr 3.19 gives his descendants, but there is no Abiud among them.

That the second major break point in Matthew's genealogy is the Babylonian captivity gives us a clue to the evangelist's eschatological orientation. The first break point was the establishment of the monarchy while the culmination of the genealogy is Jesus Christ. Is not the reader to infer that the kingdom that was inaugurated with David and lost at the captivity is restored with the coming of Jesus, the Davidic Messiah? In other words, does not the structure of the genealogy mean that the advent of the Messiah marks the beginning of the eschatological restoration of Israel's kingdom?

13. With this verse we enter uncertain territory, for it is no longer possible to show that an OT genealogy is being copied.

---

[63] HG (without apparatus) follows B k, wrongly substituting Σελαθιηλ for Σαλ.

[64] If this is not an error, we could have to do with two Zerubbabels or with a case of levirate marriage.

Because all of the names in 1.13–15 occur in the LXX (see below), some suppose that the LXX has been employed to make up an artificial list,[65] and this is possible.[66] But it is also possible that 1.13–15 gives us a more or less accurate continuation of one part of the Davidic line. In any event, Matthew is using a source.

About five hundred years lie between Zerubbabel (who disappeared from history around 519 B.C.) and Joseph. For this period Matthew has only nine names, excluding Zerubbabel and Joseph (Luke has exactly twice as many: eighteen). Nothing could reveal more clearly the incomplete and inexact character of the evangelist's list of Jesus' ancestors.

Ζοροβαβὲλ δὲ ἐγέννησεν τὸν Ἀβιούδ, Ἀβιοὺδ δὲ ἐγέννησεν τὸν Ἐλιακίμ, Ἐλιακὶμ δὲ ἐγέννησεν τὸν Ἀζώρ. For 'Ăbîhû' (Ἀβιοῦς in Josephus) see Exod 6.23; 24.1, 9; Lev 10.1; Num 3.2, 4; 26.20; 1 Chr 6.3; 8.3; 24.1, 2. The name is not among the five sons of Zerubbabel listed in 1 Chr 3.19–20. For 'Elyāqîm (Ἐλιακίας or Ἐλιάκιμος in Josephus) see 2 Kgs 18.18; 23.34; 2 Chr 36.4; Isa 36.3, 11, 22; 37.2. Of the royal chamberlain of Hezekiah whose name was Eliakim (2 Kgs 18.18, 26, 37; 19.2), Isaiah prophesied, 'I [the Lord] will place on his shoulder the key of the house of David; he will open, and none will shut; and he will shut, and none will open' (22.22; cf. Mt 16.19). For Eliakim, the puppet ruler under Pharaoh Neca, see 2 Kgs 23.34; 2 Chr 36.4. Another Eliakim—the son of Melea—is named in Luke's genealogy (3.31). For 'Azzûr or 'Ēzer see Jer 28.1; Neh 3.19.

14. The source of the names in this verse remains mysterious.

Ἀζὼρ δὲ ἐγέννησεν τὸν Σαδώκ, Σαδὼκ δὲ ἐγέννησεν τὸν Ἀχίμ, Ἀχὶμ δὲ ἐγέννησεν τὸν Ἐλιούδ. Σαδώκ is the most common LXX rendering of Ṣādôq (= 'righteous'), the popular name which is also rendered sometimes by Σαδούκ and Σαδούχ. The best known Zadok was the priest of David, but there was also a Zadok who was the grandfather of the Jotham mentioned in Mt 1.9; and according to Wacholder (pp. 99–229), the founder of the Qumran yāḥad was a certain Zadok, whose dates were roughly 240–170 B.C. Ἀχίμ is unattested. For the similar Ἀχείμ see 1 Chr 11.35 B S; 1 Chr 24.16 B. Ἐλιούδ appears in 1 Chr 12.20 A as the name of a man who deserted David.

15. Ἐλιοὺδ δὲ ἐγέννησεν τὸν Ἐλεάζαρ. 'Ēl'āzar is the name of at least ten different OT figures; only one is closely associated with David (2 Sam 23.9–10; 1 Chr 11.12–14). Mt 1.15 is the only NT

---

[65] So Gundry, *Commentary*, pp. 17–18, who assigns the work to the evangelist. Yet if this were so, why did Matthew not simply follow the LXX of 1 Chr 3, which, unlike the MT, gives eleven generations for Zerubbabel's line?

[66] Esp. since, as Johnson has observed ((v), pp. 179–80), most of the names from Abiud to Matthan are not listed in the *CPJ*.

verse to name an Eleazar. Ἐλεάζαρ is the most common LXX form. Josephus has Ἐλεάζαρος.

Ἐλεάζαρ δὲ ἐγέννησεν τὸν Ματθάν.[67] Ματθάν (= *Mattān*; cf. Jer 45.1 LXX) is attested elsewhere only in 2 Chr 23.17. According to Lk 3.24, the great-grandfather of Jesus was Ματθάτ. Hence many have inferred that the First and Third Gospels agree on the name of Jesus' great-grandfather. Yet Matthew and Luke concur neither on the father of Jesus' great-grandfather nor on his son, so coincidence seems probable. Compare the other appearance of Ματθάτ in Luke's genealogy, at 3.29, and see further Brown, *Messiah*, pp. 86–90.

Ματθὰν δὲ ἐγέννησεν τὸν Ἰακώβ. In Mt 1.16 Jacob (cf. 1.2; 8.11; 22.32) begets Joseph. In the OT too, of course, a Jacob begets a Joseph. Some would take this to be indicative of a Joseph typology in Mt 1–2.[68] Joseph, the father of Jesus, is like the famous Joseph of old in that he (1) has a father named Jacob; (2) goes down to Egypt; (3) has dreams given to him about the future; (4) is chaste and godly (cf. T. Sim. 5.1); and (5) is long-suffering and disinclined to shame others or exhibit their faults (cf. T. Jos. 17.1–2). It is not possible to exclude this proposal. Yet, it must be observed, Jacob's name should presumably be ascribed to Matthew's tradition,[69] and this tradition was not originally connected with what now follows Mt 1.15. Beyond this, several of Joseph's characteristic traits seem to derive from the traditions about Amram, the father of Moses (see pp. 61–2).

Rabbinic tradition occasionally identified Jesus as Ben Pantera or Ben Pandira (names based perhaps upon a corruption or intentional twisting of the Christian title, υἱὸς τῆς παρθένου[70]; see *b. Sanh.* 67a); and Origen asserted that Panther was the surname of Jacob, Jesus' grandfather (*C. Cels.* 1.32–3).

16. Unlike most OT genealogies, in which a genealogy's first name, the progenitor, is the key figure, in Matthew the final entry is the most important.

Ἰακὼβ δὲ ἐγέννησεν τὸν Ἰωσήφ. *Yôsēp* was a popular Jewish name (cf. Ezra 10.42; Neh 12.14; 1 Chr 25.2, 9; Mt 13.55; 27.57; the works of Josephus refer to at least eighteen men by this name). It means, 'he adds' (cf. Gen 30.24 and Philo, *De Ios.* 28). Ἰωσήφ is always the NT spelling. Josephus has Ἰώσηπος, Ep. Arist.

[67] HG reads Ματθαν (cf. Jer 45.1 Qᵐᵍ), which may mark assimilation to Lk 3.24 (if Ματθατ is there original) or to the name, Ματθαιος (see the title and 10.3). On the problem of Ματθ- and Μαθθ- in the NT see A. T. Robertson, *Grammar*, p. 215, and F. C. Burkitt, *JTS* 34 (1933), pp. 387–90.

[68] So e.g. Waetjen (v), pp. 225–7, and Brown, *Messiah*, pp. 111–12.

[69] But Matthew could, perhaps, be making 1.15 parallel to 1.2: 'Jacob begat Joseph' is implicit in the latter ('Jacob begat Judah *and his brothers*').

[70] Cf. Klausner, pp. 23–4.

Ἰωσηφος. Leaving aside the apocryphal gospels, Joseph would be
practically a faceless figure were it not for Mt 1–2. Nowhere else in
the NT is he anything more than a bystander, the husband of Mary
(Lk 1–2), or the father of Jesus (Jn 1.45; 6.42). The First Gospel,
however, purports to tell us a few things about him—he was a
Davidid, upright, a man of visions, and obedient to the Lord. On
whether he is intended to be like the Joseph of the OT see on 1.15.
Matthew seems to go out of his way not to call Jesus the 'son' of
Joseph or Joseph the 'father' of Jesus; and, at least in Mt 2, where
Joseph is the guardian of 'the child and his mother', he avoids
calling Mary the 'wife' of Joseph (note esp 2.13–14, 20–1). The
conjecture that Joseph might be the ultimate source for the
material in Mt 1–2 is problematic given the likelihood—inferred
from his absence from the public ministry—that he died at a time
too early to pass on anything to believers in Jesus. (Although one
cannot rule out the bare possibility that Joseph, before he died,
told his story to someone who then later informed believers of
what had happened.)

τὸν ἄνδρα Μαρίας.[71] Compare 1.19; Mark 10.12 ἀνήρ here

[71] With the exception of Θ and the Ferrar miniscules (f13), all Greek witnesses
read what we have printed. This is also the Greek beneath the various versions,
except the Old Syriac, the Old Latin, and the Armenian; and it has early support in
Tertullian. Another reading is found in Θ and f13: Ιωσηφ ω μνηστευθεισα παρθενος
Μαριαμ εγεννησεν Ιησουν τον λεγομενον Χριστον. Closely related readings are
attested in a (b) c d (k) q syᶜ Ambr Aug Hipp. The publication in 1894 of syˢ, which
for the gospels preserves a text of the late fourth, early fifth century, added another,
much discussed variant. The Greek behind this appears to be, Ιωσηφ, ω εμνηστευθη
παρθενος Μαριαμ, εγεννησεν Ιησουν τον λεγομενον Χριστον Much was made of this
at the time because it seemed to hint at a reading that excluded the virgin birth:
'Joseph . . . begat Jesus'. Furthermore, soon after the recovery of syˢ, F. C.
Conybeare published what purports to be a fifth century dialogue between a
Christian and a Jew, 'The Dialogue of Timothy and Aquila' (in *The Dialogues of
Athanasius and Zacchaeus*, Oxford, 1898); and in one place it preserves not only the
majority Greek text but also this (which is probably a Jewish interpretation of the
so-called 'neutral' text): Ιωσηφ εγεννησεν τον Ιησουν τον λεγομενον Χριστον (fol.
93ʳ). Early in this century there was no unanimity whatsoever over the true text of
Mt 1.16. Allen, p. 8, suggested, Ιωσηφ δε ω μνηστευθεισα ην Μαριαμ παρθενος
εγεννησεν Ιησουν τον λεγομενον Χριστον. W. Sanday, *Outlines of the Life of Christ*,
Edinburgh, 1906, p. 200 proposed this: Ιωσηφ τον ανδρα Μαριας η εγεννησεν
Ιησουν τον λεγομενον Χριστον. Von Soden printed, Ιωσηφ δε, ω εμνηστευθη
παρθενος Μαριαμ, εγεννησεν Ιησουν. . . . Moffatt's translation offered this: 'Jacob
the father of Joseph, and Joseph (to whom the Virgin Mary was betrothed) the
father of Jesus who is called Christ'. McNeile, pp. 4–5; V. Taylor, *The Historical
Evidence for the Virgin Birth*, Oxford, 1920, p. 110; and others remained
noncommittal, refusing to make confident declarations about an uncertain matter.
Of late, however, one particular solution has commended itself to most textual
critics. Assuming that the majority Greek reading is pristine—and the combined
testimony of all Greek witnesses save the Ferrar family is weighty indeed—, it is
possible to explain the reading of Θ and f13: the addition of 'virgin' and the
substitution of 'betrothed' for 'husband' are explicable on doctrinal grounds: Mary
was held to be ever virgin. (Cf. syᶜ, which alters not only 1.16 but also 1.19, 20, 24 in

means 'husband'. The four women named previously in the genealogy were introduced with an ἐκ-construction: 'A begat B ἐκ C'. But we do not read that 'Joseph begat Jesus by Mary'. Mary's case, although to some extent prepared for by the 'holy irregularity' (Stendahl) of earlier unions, stands by itself: it is an anomaly. The break in Matthew's pattern thus reflects a break in the course of history. God is about to do something new.

Μαρία (cf. Josephus, *Bell.* 6.201) occurs several times in the NT for the mother of Jesus (Mt 1.16, 18; 2.11; Mk 6.3; Lk 1.41; 2.19), but the LXX spelling, Μαριάμ (= *Miryām*, etymology disputed, perhaps of Canaanite origin), is more frequent (Mt 13.55; Lk 1.27, 34, etc.; Acts 1.14). Both spellings are also used for Mary the sister of Lazarus. Matthew has Μαρίας for the genitive (1.16, 18; 2.11), Μαρίαν (B L *f*¹) or Μαριάμ (ℵ C D W Z Θ *f*¹³) for the accusative (1.20), and Μαριάμ for the nominative (13.55). For other Marys he has both Μαρία and Μαριάμ (27.56, 61; 28.1). On the name (which was popular in the time of Jesus: the NT alone has seven or eight Marys) and its forms see further BAGD, s.v.; BDF § 53.3. Μαριά(μ)μη is attested in Josephus. Μαρία is not necessarily to be regarded as a Hellenized form, for *Mryh* has been found on inscriptions in Jerusalem (BDF § 53.3).

Because the historical value of the infancy narratives is, to say the least, uncertain, little is known of Mary.[72] In Matthew she has no independent identity: she is the mother of Jesus, the vessel of the Holy Spirit, and the betrothed of Joseph, and Matthew's interest in her (unlike Luke's) ends there.[73]

ἐξ ἧς ἐγεννήθη. Mary now becomes the focus, Joseph being displaced. The 'divine passive' (absent in 1.2–16a) alludes to the activity of the Holy Spirit in Jesus' conception. In 1.2–16a γεννάω

---

order to avoid the words 'man' and 'wife'.) Next, one can without too much trouble account for sy^c and the Old Latin by presuming they go back to a Greek text like that of Θ and *f*¹³. Finally, sy^s can perhaps be explained either as the consequence of a scribal error, that is, a mechanical continuation of Matthew's 'A begat B' pattern, or as a paraphrase of the reading known from sy^c; it might also be an independent, free rendering or mistranslation of the Greek represented by Θ *f*¹³. It is difficult to tell whether this somewhat hazy account of things deserves the widespread favour it currently enjoys. We, unfortunately, can offer none better. Lit.: Burkitt, *Evangelion* 2, pp. 258–66; B. M. Metzger, 'On the Citation of Variant Readings of Mt 1:16', *JBL* 77 (1958), pp. 361–3; idem, 'The Text of Matthew 1.16', in *Studies in New Testament and Early Christian Literature*, ed. D. E. Aune, Leiden, 1972, pp. 16–24; A. Globe, 'Some Doctrinal Variants in Matthew 1 and Luke 2, and the Authority of the Neutral Text', *CBQ* 42 (1980), pp. 52–72.

[72] For discussion see Brown et al., *Mary*.

[73] For possible rabbinic references to Mary by name (*Miryām*) *see b. Ḥag.* 4b (Miriam is a hairdresser, the word for which is *měgaddělā*, which is close to Magdalene,and there may have been confusion between Mary the mother of Jesus and Mary Magdalene; cf. *b. Šabb.* 104b) and *b. Sanh.* 67a (Miriam was the mother of Ben Pandira, who was hanged on Passover eve; she was an adulteress).

(in the active) means 'beget'. In 1.20 (in the passive) it seems to mean 'be conceived'. Here (again in the passive) it could mean either 'be conceived' or (as in 2.1, 4) 'be born'.

It may surprise that the genealogy is followed by a story which denies Joseph's participation in fathering Jesus. But Matthew has in mind legal, not necessarily physical, descent, that is, the transmission of legal heirship; and the idea of paternity on two-levels—divine and human, with position in society being determined by the mother's husband—was familiar in the ancient near east.[74] In addition, the Mishnah relates, 'If a man said, "This is my son", he may be believed' (m. Bat. 8.6; cf. Isa 43.1: 'I have called you by name, you are mine'); and according to Matthew (and presumably his tradition) Joseph gave Jesus his name and thereby accepted the rôle of father. Without force, therefore, is the argument that Matthew's genealogy and that in Luke must have been drawn up by people who, like the later Ebionites (Justin, Dial. 48; Irenaeus, Adv. haer. 3.21.1; Eusebius, H.E. 3.27; Epiphanius, Haer. 30.3.14), believed Jesus to be the actual son of Joseph and Mary. And in point of fact, at least Matthew's genealogy was composed by a believer in the virginal conception, for it was the redactor who expanded a traditional genealogy and linked it with Jesus and Joseph.

Ἰησοῦς ὁ λεγόμενος Χριστός. 'Christ' is here a title (= 'Messiah'), not a reference back to the name in 1.1, 'Jesus Christ' (cf. 4.18; 10.2; 26.14). Matthew likes both ὁ λεγόμενος/ὁ λέγεται (Mt: 14; Mk: 1; Lk: 2) and Χριστός (Mt:17; Mk:7; Lk: 12). Note Josephus, Ant. 20.200: 'James, the brother Ἰησοῦ τοῦ λεγομένου Χριστοῦ'.

17. Two points. First, Matthew likes to summarize (cf. 4.23–5; 9.35–8; 12.15–21; 14.34–6; 19.1–2). Secondly, because the word 'fourteen' is repeated thrice in 1.17, and because 'fourteen generations' has not, unlike the other words and phrases in 1.17, been already used in the genealogy, the number fourteen must be the raison d'être for the verse and must hold some symbolic significance for the evangelist—this being, as already argued, the value of David's name: $d + w + d = 14$ (see pp. 161–5).

πᾶσαι οὖν αἱ γενεαὶ ἀπὸ Ἀβραὰμ ἕως Δαυὶδ γενεαὶ δεκατέσσαρες, καὶ ἀπὸ Δαυὶδ ἕως τῆς μετοικεσίας Βαβυλῶνος γενεαὶ δεκατέσσαρες, καὶ ἀπὸ τῆς μετοικεσίας Βαβυλῶνος ἕως τοῦ Χριστοῦ γενεαὶ δεκατέσσαρες. Compare Demetrius, in Eusebius, Praep. ev. 9.21.18 and Clement of Alexandria, Strom. 1.21.141.1–2. The

---

[74] C. H. Gordon, 'Paternity on Two Levels', JBL 96 (1977), p. 101. Cf. Suetonius, Caes. 6: Caesar's lineage could 'claim both the sanctity of kings, who reign supreme among mortals, and the reverence due to gods, who hold even kings in their power'.

vocabulary of the verse comes largely from 1.2–16 and the rest is unquestionably redactional.[75]

From Abraham to David there are, in fact, fourteen generations, and from David to the deportation to Babylon, another fourteen; but from the deportation to the Christ there appear to be only thirteen generations. Numerous attempts have been made to explain this inconcinnity. Some have proposed that a name has inadvertently dropped out from the third section, or that Mary should be counted in addition to Joseph, or even that Jesus (in his first advent) is the thirteenth, Christ (in his second advent) the fourteenth.[76] A more plausible solution counts David twice, at the end of the first tessaradecad and at the beginning of the second, and makes Josiah conclude the second section, Jechoniah open the third.[77] Yet David alone would then be counted twice, certainly an odd circumstance; and Jechoniah is most naturally included in the second section (cf. 1.11–12 with 1.6). Perhaps it is best, therefore, simply to ascribe a mathematical blunder to Matthew (cf. on 8.1, 4). On this two things may be said, the first being that discrepancies between stated totals and actual totals are not uncommon in biblical and extra-biblical literature; instances can be found in 1 Chr 3.22; Ezra 1.9–11; 2.2–64; Neh 7.7–66; 1 Esd 5.9–41; Cowley 23; LAB 5.8; 10.1. Then, in the second place, Matthew just may have been aware of his error. If the addition of two names (Joseph and Jesus) to his source's post-exilic period resulted in only thirteen names, the evangelist may have been content to suffer the lack of one; for although he may have felt the freedom to omit names he may not have felt the freedom to make them up and add them.

(iv) Concluding Observations

The biblical account of Noah (Gen 5–9) begins with a genealogy (5.1–31). Abraham's story (Gen 11–25) is likewise introduced by a genealogy (11.10–32). And the Chronicler prefaced his account of the kings of Judah with several genealogies. From this it appears that certain OT texts served Matthew as models for his

[75] πᾶς: Mt: 128–9; Mk: 67; Lk: 152. οὖν: Mt: 57; Mk: 5; Lk: 31. ἀπό: Mt: 116; Mk: 47; Lk: 123. ἀπό . . . ἕως (cf. min . . . ‛ad): Mt: 11; Mk: 3; Lk: 2. γενεά: Mt: 13; Mk: 5; Lk: 13. ἕως as a preposition: Mt: 28; Mk: 10; Lk: 13.

[76] A name has been dropped: so McNeile, p. 3, and H. J. Schonfield, *An Old Hebrew Text of St. Matthew's Gospel*, Edinburgh, 1927, pp. 21–3. Mary should be counted: so Filson, p. 53; Argyle, p. 25. Jesus should be counted twice: so Stendahl, 'Matthew', pp. 770–1.

[77] So Schöllig (v) and Schweizer, *Matthew*, p. 23. Cf. Bengel 1, p. 59. Augustine, *Con. ev.* 2.4.10 counts Jechoniah twice.

compositional procedure, which fact in turn probably implies that the evangelist thought of his gospel as a continuation of the biblical history—and also, perhaps, that he conceived of his work as belonging to the same literary category as the scriptural cycles treating of OT figures. Our examination of the title, 1.1, also supports this idea, for it suggests that Matthew set out to compose in some sense a counterpart to Genesis. (On the other hand, it must be admitted that Hellenistic biographies frequently open with genealogies or accounts of a hero's ancestors; see, for example, Isocrates, *Busiris* 10; idem, *Helen* 16; Plutarch, *Alex.* 2; idem, *Brut.* 1; Suetonius, *Caes.* 6; Tacitus, *Agr.* 4; cf. also Josephus, *Vita* 1–6. Discussion in Mussies (v).)

We may now summarize the significance of Mt 1.2–17 under five points.

(1) The section offers proof of the title: Jesus is the son of Abraham and the Son of David. More particularly, because 'the heritage of the king is from son to son only' (Ecclus 45.25), and because Jesus is, through his father, a descendant of king David, in this respect he qualifies as the Davidic Messiah. (Also relevant may be the notion that great men resemble their ancestors; cf. Aristotle, *Rh. Al.* 35.)

(2) Jesus came 'at the right time'. Although the apocalypses of Judaism contain several different outlines of history, Dan 9.24–7; 1 En. 93.3–10; 91.12–17; and 2 Bar. 67.1–74.4 are at one in placing the epoch of the exile immediately before the epoch of redemption. This is significant because Mt 1.2–17 divides history into periods and places the appearance of Jesus at the end of the exilic era. So the time of the Messiah's birth admirably falls in line with a presumably common eschatological calendar. Compare Gal 4.14: Christ came in the fullness of time.

(3) 1.2–17 outlines a story whose surety is God and whose culmination is Jesus Christ. God gave promises to Abraham (Gen 12.2–3; 18.18). He also gave promises to David (2 Sam 7.12–14). Throughout Israel's history these promises often seemed to be in jeopardy, as at the Babylonian captivity. But God remained faithful, despite appearances; and his faithfulness becomes fully and finally manifested in the birth of Jesus, the flower of Judaism and *telos* of salvation-history, in whom the promises to Abraham and David find their yes (cf. Rom 10.4; see Davies, *JPS*, pp. 146–7).

(4) Irregular and potentially scandalous unions, even unions with Gentiles, were blessed by God in establishing and continuing the Davidic line. Thus if the birth of Jesus also involved extraordinary circumstances and brought reproach, that was nothing new. Rather was it foreshadowed in the unions of Joseph

and Tamar, Salmon and Rahab, Boaz and Ruth, David and Bathsheba.

(5) The genealogy implicitly reveals the identity and status of the church (cf. the function of *m. 'Abot* 1.1). Congregations which included both Jews and Gentiles could not find their identity in a shared racial heritage. They found it instead in their common Lord and saviour, who was with them when they gathered together (Mt 18.20). And since he was the Messiah, the Son of David and the son of Abraham, those who adhered to his words and participated in his destiny[78] knew themselves to be heirs to the promises made to Abraham and David. In other words, the history of Jesus was his followers' history, his heritage their heritage (cf. the Pauline 'body of Christ'). Despite its belonging to the rootless Hellenistic world of the first century, the church, by virtue of its union with Jesus, had a secure link with the remote past.

(v) *Bibliography*

E. L. Abel,'The Genealogies of Jesus *Ho Christos*', *NTS* 20 (1974), pp. 203–10.

H. A. Blair, 'Matthew 1,16 and the Matthean Genealogy', *Studia Evangelica 2*, TU 87, Berlin, 1964, pp. 149–54.

R. Bloch, ' "Juda engendra Pharès et Zara, de Thamar" (Matt 1,3)', in *Mélanges bibliques rédigés en l'honneur de André Robert*, Paris, 1957, pp. 381–9.

K. Bornhäuser, *Die Geburts- und Kindheitsgeschichte Jesu*, Gütersloh, 1930, pp. 5–20.

G. H. Box, 'The Gospel Narratives of the Nativity and the Alleged Influences of Heathen Ideas', *ZNW* 6 (1905), pp. 80–101.

R. E. Brown, *Messiah*, pp. 57–95.

idem, '*Rachab* in Mt 1,5 Probably is Rahab of Jericho', *Bib* 63 (1982), pp. 79–80.

Burger, pp. 91–102.

C. T. Davis, 'The Fulfilment of Creation. A Study of Matthew's Genealogy', *JAAR* 41 (1973), pp. 520–35.

Frankemölle, pp. 311–18.

E. D. Freed, 'The Women in Matthew's Geneology', *JSNT* 29 (1987), pp. 3–19.

J. M. Gibbs, 'The Gospel Prologues and their Function', *Studia Evangelica VI*, TU 112, Berlin, 1973, pp. 154–8.

W. Hammer, 'L'intention de la généalogie de Matthieu', *ETR* 55 (1980), pp.305–6.

J. M. Heer, *Die Stammbäume Jesu nach Matthäus und Lukas*, Freiburg, 1910.

---

[78] On the Matthean Jesus as a representative and exemplary figure whose followers are called to participate in his destiny see M. Pamment, 'The Son of Man in the First Gospel', *NTS* 29 (1983), pp. 116–29.

A. D. Heffern, 'The Four Women in St. Matthew's Genealogy of Christ', *JBL* 31 (1912), pp. 68–81.

R. T. Hood, 'The Genealogies of Jesus', in *Early Christian Origins*, ed. A. Wikgren, Chicago, 1961, pp. 1–15.

Jeremias, *Jerusalem*, pp. 275–302.

M. D. Johnson, *The Purpose of the Biblical Genealogies*, SNTSMS 8, Cambridge, 1969.

C. Kaplan, 'The Generation Schemes in Matthew 1.1–17, Luke 3.24ff.', *BSac* 87 (1930), pp. 465–71.

G. Kuhn, 'Die Geschlechtsregister Jesu bei Lukas und Matthäus, nach ihrer Herkunft untersucht', *ZNW* 22 (1923), pp. 206–28.

M. Lambertz, 'Die Toledoth in Mt 1.1–17 und Lc 3.23bff.', in *Festschrift für Franz Dornseiff*, ed. H. Kusch, Leipzig, 1953, pp. 201–25.

E. Lerle, 'Die Ahnenverzeichnisse Jesu', *ZNW* 72 (1981), pp. 112–17.

X. Leon-Dufour, 'Livre de la genèse de Jésus-Christ', in *Études*, pp. 50–63.

J. Masson, *Jésus, Fils de David dans les généalogies de St. Matthieu et de St. Luc*, Paris, 1982.

G. F. Moore, 'Fourteen Generations—490 Years', *HTR* 14 (1921), pp. 97–103.

M. J. Moreton, 'The Genealogy of Jesus', in *Studia Evangelica 2*, TU 87, ed. F. L. Cross, Berlin, 1964, pp. 219–24.

G. Mussies, 'Parallels to Matthew's Version of the Pedigree of Jesus', *NovT* 28 (1986), pp. 32–47.

B. M. Newman, Jr., 'Matthew 1.1–18: Some Comments and a suggested Restructuring', *BT* 27 (1976), pp. 209–12.

D. E. Nineham, 'The Genealogy in St. Matthew's Gospel and its Significance for the Study of the Gospel', *BJRL* 58 (1976), pp. 421–44.

Paul, pp. 9–44.

J. D. Quinn, 'Is "Rachab" in Mt 1.5 Rahab of Jericho?', *Bib* 62 (1981), pp. 225–8.

F. Schnider and W. Stenger, 'Die Frauen im Stammbaum Jesu nach Matthäus: Strukturale Beobachtungen zu Mt 1,1–17', *BZ* 23 (1979), pp. 187–96.

H. Schöllig, 'Die Zählung der Generationen im matthäischen Stammbaum', *ZNW* 59 (1968), pp. 261–8.

P. Seethaler, 'Eine kleine Bemerkung zu den Stammbäumen Jesu nach Matthäus und Lukas', *BZ* 16 (1972), pp. 256–7.

F. Spitta, 'Die Frauen in der Genealogie des Matthäus', *ZWT* 54 (1912), pp. 1–8.

H. Stegemann, ' "Die des Uria": Zur Bedeutung der Frauennamen in der Genealogie von Matthäus, 1,1–17', in G. Jeremias, pp. 246–76.

Strauss, pp. 108–18.

W. B. Tatum, ' "The Origin of Jesus Messiah" (Matt 1:1, 18a): Matthew's Use of the Infancy Traditions', *JBL* 96 (1977), pp. 523–35.

A. Vögtle, 'Die Genealogie Mt 1,2–16 und die matthäische Kindheitsgeschichte', in *Evangelium*, pp. 57–102.

idem. ' "Josias zeugte den Jechonias und seine Brüder" (Mt 1,11)', in *Lex tua Veritas: Festschrift für H. Junker*, ed. H. Gross, Trier, 1961, pp. 307–13.

P. Vogt, *Der Stammbaum bei dem heiligen Evangelisten Matthäus*, Freiburg, 1907.

H. C. Waetjen, 'The Genealogy as the Key to the Gospel according to Matthew', *JBL* 95 (1976), pp. 205–30.

R. R. Wilson, *Genealogy and History in the Biblical World*, New Haven, 1977.

Y. Zakowitch, 'Rahab als Mutter des Boas in der Jesus-Genealogie (Matth. I 5)', *NovT* 17 (1975), pp. 1–5.

EXCURSUS I

The Sources of Mt 1.18–2.23[1]

To the problem of what sources or traditions lie behind 1.18–2.23, three basic solutions have been offered. The section could be a free Matthean composition, the traditional basis being only isolated elements such as the names of Jesus' parents, their residence in Bethlehem, and the virginal conception of Jesus.[2] Or, quite to the contrary, the evangelist's contribution could be minimal, 1.18–2.23 in this case representing for the most part what was already a unified story before Matthew took up pen.[3] The third option lies somewhere between the first two: 1.18–2.23 might be a Matthean synthesis of two or more originally separate pericopae.[4]

Against the first proposal, several observations seem to show that our piece is not a free Matthean creation. For example, 2.22–3 (the move to Nazareth) strikes one as a very artificial addition designed to move Jesus to the place presupposed by 3.13. So 2.19–21 (the return to Israel) is presumably the original—and that suggests pre-Matthean—conclusion. Were the evangelist not passing on tradition in 2.19–21, our narrative would probably have only one geographical thrust and one suitable conclusion, for the contents of 2.19–21 and 22–3 could easily be combined into one small pericope.[5] Internal tensions are also apparent in 2.1–12.

[1] Lit.: R. E. Brown, *Messiah*, pp. 104–21; Bultmann, *History*, pp. 291–4; C. T. Davis, 'Tradition and Redaction in Matthew 1:18–2:23', *JBL* 90 (1971), pp. 404–21; W. L. Knox, vol. 2, pp. 121–8; E. Nellessen, *Das Kind und seine Mutter: Struktur und Verkündigung des 2. Kapitels im Matthäusevangelium*, SBS 39, Stuttgart, 1969; Nolan, pp. 16–22; Soares Prabhu, pp. 294–300; A. Vögtle, 'Die matthäische Kindheitsgeschichte', in Didier, pp. 153–83; idem, *Messias und Gottessohn: Herkunft und Sinn der matthäischen Geburts- und Kindheitsgeschichte*, Düsseldorf, 1971.

[2] So Kilpatrick, p. 55; Goulder, pp. 228–42; Gundry, *Commentary*, pp. 13–41.

[3] So Strecker, *Weg*, pp. 51–5, and Brown, *Messiah*, pp. 104–19.

[4] According to Dibelius, *Tradition*, pp. 128–9, the evangelist brought together the story of the magi and the story of the slaughter of the children; he also composed 1.18–25. According to M. Hengel and H. Merkel, 'Die Magier aus dem Osten und die Flucht nach Ägypten (Mt 2) im Rahmen der antiken Religionsgeschichte und der Theologie des Matthäus', in Hoffmann, *Orientierung*, p. 141, Matthew was the first to join the self-contained 2.1–2.23 to the birth history, 1.18–25.

[5] See further Davis, 'Tradition', pp. 406–9, and Brown, *Messiah*, p. 106.

While the star guides the magi to Bethlehem (2.9), the astrologers from the east are also guided by the words of the chief priests and scribes, who quote Scripture (2.4–6). Here two different modes of revelation come into play, making one redundant.[6] Further, while the magi find Jesus rather easily, Herod, strangely enough, cannot. And 2.1–12 seems overfull of wise men—magi, chief priests, and scribes. Such inconcinnities as these make the presence of traditional pericopae manifest.

There are likewise difficulties with the third option, according to which Matthew brought together several originally isolated stories for the first time. The dream pattern common to 1.20–5; 2.13–14; and 2.19–21 is probably traditional given the pre-Matthean character of 2.19–21 (see above). This supplies evidence that at least the pieces preserved in 1.18–25 and 2.13–21 come from the same pre-redactional source. In addition, when the extensive haggadic parallels to 1.18–2.23 are taken into account (see below), a thematic unity comes into focus, a unity not likely to be the result of a putting together of onetime separate pieces.

We come then to the one option left, namely, that Mt 1.18–2.23 more or less reproduces a pre-Matthean narrative. In order to defend this particular thesis and to trace the history of our hypothetical source we must make several observations.

(1) As most scholars now recognize, the redactor has added the five so-called 'formula quotations'. 1.22–3; 2.5b–6, 15b–c, 17–18, and 23b are 'parasitic'.[7] Beyond the fact that Matthew elsewhere has appended quotations to material which we know came to him from the tradition, as in 4.12–16 and 21.4–5, no difficulty ensues if the paragraphs in chapters 1–2 are read without the scriptural citations. They run as smoothly or even more smoothly without them.[8] When one adds that the formula quotations are in harmony with Matthew's special interests,[9] no doubt about their derivation should remain.

(2) We have already given reason for thinking 2.22–3 to be redactional. The parallel with 4.12–16 supplies confirmatory evidence:

2.22–3: ἀκούσας δὲ ὅτι . . .
    ἀνεχώρησεν εἰς τὰ μέρη τῆς Γαλιλαίας . . .
    ἐλθὼν κατῴκησεν εἰς πόλιν λεγομένην Ναζαρέτ
    ὅπως πληρωθῇ τὸ ῥηθέν. . . .
4.12–16: ἀκούσας δὲ ὅτι
    ἀνεχώρησεν εἰς τὴν Γαλιλαίαν. . . .
    ἐλθὼν κατῴκησεν εἰς Καφαρναούμ . . .
    ἵνα πληρωθῇ τὸ ῥηθέν. . . .
Because 4.12–16 is redactional (see pp. 374–86), 2.22–3 presumably is too.

(3) That which is left after the formula quotations and 2.22–3 are removed still bears the imprint of Matthean style. This, however, is no

---

[6] So also Hahn, *Hoheitstitel*, p. 277.

[7] This has been all but demonstrated by Prabhu, passim. See also the survey of F. van Segbroeck, 'Les citations d'accomplissement dans l'Évangile selon saint Matthieu d'après trois ouvrages récents', in Didier, pp. 107–30.

[8] Cf. M. J. Down, 'The Matthean Birth Narratives: Matthew 1:18–2:23', *ExpT* 90 (1978), pp. 51–2.

[9] See the Excursus after 27.10.

argument for a purely Matthean origin. It is simply a sign of the evangelist's thorough editing. And if the presence of Matthean characteristics seems accentuated in 1.18–2.23,[10] this is perhaps to be put down to the fluid character of the redactor's sources, which were probably oral (cf. Luz 1, pp. 87, 101).[11]

(4) The key to understanding Mt 1.18–2.23 is to be found in the haggadic traditions about Moses.[12] This becomes plain from the following points of resemblance.

a. In Josephus, *Ant*. 2.210–16, Amram, the noble and pious father of Moses, is said to have been fearful, ill at ease, and at a loss as to what to do about his wife's pregnancy, for Pharaoh had commanded every male child to be cast into the Nile. Being in such a state, God then appeared to Amram in a dream and exhorted him not to despair (cf. LAB 9—from the first century A.D.?). In Mt 1.18–21, while Joseph, the just father of Jesus, is contemplating his course of action with regard to his wife's pregnancy, the angel of the Lord appears to him in a dream and bids him not to fear.

b. According to LAB 9.10, the Spirit of God came upon Miriam the sister of Moses and she saw in a dream a man (an angel) who prophesied of her brother to be: 'by him will I do signs, and by him will I save my people'. Compare *Mek*. on Exod 15.20; *b. Soṭa* 12b–13a; and *b. Meg*. 14a.[13] In Josephus, *Ant*. 2.216, the prophecy that Moses 'will deliver the Hebrew nation' is received by Moses' father. In Mt 1.21, Joseph, the husband of Mary, is told by an angel in a dream that his son will 'save his people from their sins'.

c. At the time of Moses' birth, Pharaoh had given the order to do away with every male Hebrew (Exod 1.15–22). The birth of Jesus was accompanied by a like circumstance, Herod's slaughter of the infants of Bethlehem (Mt 2.16–18).

d. According to Jewish tradition, Pharaoh ordered the killing of Hebrew infants because he had learned of the birth of the future liberator of Israel (Josephus, *Ant*. 2.205–9; Tg. Ps.-J. on Exod 1.15). Matthew tells us that Herod killed the Hebrew infants of Bethlehem because knowledge came to the king of the birth of Jesus (2.2–18).

e. Just as Herod learned of the coming saviour from the chief priests (ἀρχιερεῖς) and scribes (γραμματεῖς; Mt 2.4–6), so Pharaoh, it was said,

---

[10] For 1.18–25 see R. Pesch, 'Eine alttestamentliche Ausführungsformel im Matthäus-Evangelium (Schluss)', *BZ* 11 (1967), pp. 81–8.

[11] For the detailed argument that the amount of redactional vocabulary in Mt 2.1–23 is consistent with a pre-Matthean origin see Vögtle, 'Kindheitsgeschichte', pp. 156–65.

[12] Lit.: R. Bloch, 'La naissance de Moïse dans la tradition aggadique', in *Moïse, l'Homme de l'Alliance*, Paris, 1955, pp. 102–18; C. Perrot, 'Les récits d'enfance dans la Haggada antérieure au IIᵉ siècle de notre ère', *RSR* 55 (1967), pp. 481–518; P. Winter, 'Jewish Folklore in the Matthean Birth Story', *HeyJ* 53 (1954), pp. 34–42.

[13] On the traditions about Miriam, the sister of Moses, see R. Le Déaut, 'Miryam, soeur de Moïse, et Marie, mère du Messie', *Bib* 45 (1964), pp. 198–219.

learned of the future deliverer from sacred scribes (ἱερογραμματέων; Josephus, *Ant.* 2.205, 234). (In Tg. Ps.-J. on Exod 1.15, Pharaoh dreams about a lamb and an ewe, and it is only after the dream is interpreted by Janis and Jambres, the chief magicians, that the ruler understands its significance: a son of Israel is about to be born, and he will ruin Egypt.)

f. In Mt 2.13–14 Jesus is providentally taken from the land of his birth because Herod wishes to kill him. Similarly, when Moses was a young man, he was forced to leave his homeland because Pharaoh sought his life (Exod 2.15). And before that, when he was under the shadow of death as an infant, Moses was kept safe only by divinely ordered circumstances (Exod 2.1–10; Philo, *Mos.* 1.12; Josephus, *Ant.* 2.217–27).

g. After the death of Herod, Joseph was commanded by the angel of the Lord to return to Israel, his place of origin (Mt 2.19–20). After the death of Pharaoh, Moses was commanded by God to return to Egypt, his homeland (Exod 4.19). The wording of the two commands is almost identical:
τεθνήκασιν γὰρ   οἱ ζητοῦντες   τὴν ψυχὴν τοῦ παιδίου (Matthew)
τεθνήκασιν γὰρ πάντες οἱ ζητοῦντές σου τὴν ψυχήν (Exodus)
The angel's words in Matthew have clearly been constructed on the basis of the Lord's words to Moses, particularly as the antecedent of the plural in Matthew is the singular, Ἡρῴδου. The OT phrase has been taken over without complete grammatical adjustment.

h. According to Exod 4.20, Moses took his wife and his sons and went back to Egypt. According to Mt 2.21, Joseph took his son and his wife and went back to Israel.

i. One of the central issues of 1.18–2.23 is kingship. Who is the rightful heir to the throne of Israel? Should Herod be the ruler, or should Jesus? Needless to say, for Matthew and his tradition these questions were not open for discussion: Jesus was the king of Israel. This matters because Moses too was made a king in Jewish tradition (see e.g. Philo, *Mos.* 1.334; *Mek.* on Exod 18.14; *Sipre* on Num 10.29; *ARN* 1 (B); *b. Zeb.* 102a; *Exod. Rab.* on 34.27; *Midr. Ps.* on 5.11).

In our view, the parallels just set forth[14] leave little doubt as to the origin of Matthew's infancy material. The haggadic legends surrounding the birth and early life of Moses have determined the content of Matthew's source. The prophecy, given in a dream, of a child who will be Israel's saviour, a wicked king's attempt to destroy that saviour, and the child's safe-keeping under divine providence—these are the primary elements of Mt 1.18–2.23, and they come from the haggadic imagination, from the infancy legends about Moses.

(5) Certain elements of our story must be traditional because they must be historical. These include at least the names of Jesus, Mary, and Joseph,

---

[14] Parallels could also be found in the haggadic traditions about other OT heroes, e.g., Abraham; see G. Vermes, *Tradition*, pp. 90–5, and in general Perrot, 'Les récits'. But Mt 1.18–2.23 finds its closest parallels in the legends about the lawgiver, and the infancy traditions about Noah and Samson and others could have developed under the influence of the Moses materials.

the birth of Jesus in Palestine towards the end of the reign of Herod the Great, and the residence of Jesus' family in Nazareth.[15]

(6) If we now take a look at Mt 1.18–2.23 and substract the redactional contributions, the certainly historical elements, and the items with parallels in the legends about Moses, three particulars remain: virginal conception by the Holy Spirit, birth in Bethlehem, and magi following a star. Significantly enough, each of these can be linked up with a Davidic Christology. The star and the magi, as we shall see, recall Num 24.17, a text applied in pre-Christian Judaism to the Davidic Messiah (see on 2.2). The birth at Bethlehem gains its meaning from Mic 5.2, which foretells the coming forth of a Davidic ruler from the city of David. And the virginal conception is closely related to Isa 7.14, an OT text addressed to the house of David (7.13; see further below on 1.23). (Incidentally, the variant version in Luke of the annunciation of the virginal conception, 1.26–38,[16] contains allusions not only to Isa 7.14 but also to 2 Sam 7.4–17, the prophecy of a Davidid who will be God's son and build the temple.[17])

The preceding observations allow us to draw up a likely history of Mt 1.18–2.23. Three stages are to be differentiated. Stage I painted the picture of Jesus' nativity with Mosaic colours. It told of the annunciation to Joseph in a dream, concerning his son who would deliver the people; it told of the evil machinations of Herod, who learned from his scribes of the birth of the king of the Jews; it told of the futile attempt to kill the newborn king, and (perhaps) of a slaughter of infants (in Nazareth?); and it told of Jesus' successful escape from his would-be murderer, and of his safe return to Israel when Herod the king died. This stage, whose core is roughly represented by 1.18–21, 24–5; 2.13–15, and 19–21, just may have originated in the same group responsible for the early traditions Luke has preserved in Acts 3 and 7. These two chapters draw a number of parallels between Jesus and Moses,[18] and they show familiarity with the haggadic traditions about the infancy and young life of Moses. According to Acts 7.20, Moses was 'beautiful' as an infant (cf. Philo, *Mos.* 1.9, 15; Josephus, *Ant.* 2.224, 231–2); and according to 7.22, he was instructed in all the wisdom of the Egyptians (cf. Philo, *Mos.* 1.23–4; Josephus, *Ant.* 2.230, 236). Christians who regarded Jesus as a new Moses, as the 'last redeemer', as the prophet like Moses (Deut 18.15, 18; Acts 7.37), could quite naturally have used Mosaic traditions to produce an infancy narrative like that in Matthew.[19]

Stage II represents the expansion of the Mosaic narrative in the interests of a Davidic Christology. The story of the virginal conception

---

[15] All of these items also appear in Lk 1–2. For a complete listing of the elements common to Mt 1–2 and Lk 1–2 see Fitzmyer, *Luke* 1, p. 307.

[16] On the parallels between Mt 1.18–25 and Lk 1.5–38 see Perrot, 'Les récit', p. 511, n. 79.

[17] R. Laurentin, *Structure et théologie de Luc I–II*, EB, Paris, 1957, pp. 71–2.

[18] R. F. Zehnle, *Peter's Pentecost Discourse*, SBLMS 15, Nashville, 1971, pp. 44–60, 71–94, 133–7. See also Schoeps, *Theologie*, pp. 87–116, for other pertinent texts.

[19] We recall that the significance of certain rabbis—Hillel, Akiba, Judah—was shown by setting their lives over against that of Moses; for Hillel see I. Elbogen, 'Die Überlieferung von Hillel', in *Festschrift für Leo Baeck*, Berlin, 1938, pp. 68ff.

(cf. Lk 1.26–38) was conflated with the original annunciation to Joseph.[20] The legend of the magi and the star (preserved with additions in 2.1–2, 9b–11)[21] was merged with the story of Herod and the infants.[22] And the geographical outline was modified to include Bethlehem.[23] Stage II could be placed almost anywhere on the map of early Christianity. Interest in the Davidic sonship of Jesus was widespread. It cannot be associated with any one community in particular.

Stage III, which probably marks the transition from the oral to the written sphere, is the redactional stage. This brought the addition of the formula quotations and of 2.22–3, as well as the influx of Matthean style and vocabulary.

One final remark. Because the formula quotations are secondary, and because more was involved in the production of 1.18–2.23 than reflection on Scripture, the narrative is not properly designated 'midrash'—if—and this is debatable—that term be taken to mean that the OT is the constant point of reference.[24] Rather is the infancy narrative a Christian story inspired by popular Jewish haggadic traditions.[25]

[20] Cf. Brown's analysis, *Messiah*, pp. 116–17.

[21] Cf. Davis, 'Tradition', p. 418. The Arabic Gospel of the Infancy 7–9 oddly enough presents first the tale of the magi (7) and then the material about Herod (8–9). While this cannot be due to the retention of primitive tradition, it does reflect the feeling that Mt 2.1–23 intertwines two self-sufficient stories.

[22] Cf. Schweizer, *Matthew*, pp. 36–7, and F. Zinniker, *Probleme der sogenannten Kindheitsgeschichte bei Matthäus*, Freiburg, 1972, p. 167. This explains the internal tensions noted on p. 191. In *b. Sanh.* 101a and *Exod. Rab.* on 1.22, Pharaoh is informed of the birth of Moses by astrologers. The presence of astrologers in some of the infancy legends about Moses could have encouraged the introduction of the magi into stage II. Cf. Brown, *Messiah*, p. 117, n. 46.

[23] Davis, 'Tradition', p. 421, also reconstructs an original narrative in which Bethlehem had no place.

[24] Cf. Perrot, 'Les récits', pp. 514–15.

[25] Cf. Vögtle, 'Kindheitsgeschichte', p. 169: 'haggadisch inspirierte Christusgeschichte'. See Perrot, 'Les récits', pp. 515–18, for the suggestion that the oral tradition behind Mt 1.18–2.23 developed primarily in the synagogue, in Jewish-Christian homiletical reflection. On midrash in general see J. Goldin, in *CHJ*, 4, forthcoming.

III

CONCEIVED OF THE HOLY SPIRIT, BORN OF A VIRGIN, IMPLANTED INTO THE LINE OF DAVID
(1.18–25)

(i) (ii) *Structure, Sources*

1.18–25, the first of three short infancy stories (1.18–25; 2.1–12; and 2.13–23), opens with a general introductory sentence (18a). Then follows first a notice of Mary's circumstance—she is with child of the Holy Spirit—and secondly a statement of Joseph's initial response to that circumstance (18b–19). The next two verses recount the appearance of an angel who (1) commands Joseph not to fear, (2) offers an explanation of what has happened, and (3) utters a prophecy concerning Mary's son (20–1). This angelic message is succeeded by a formula quotation (22–3) and by an account of Joseph's obedient response (24–5).

If one compares 1.18–25 with the other two angelic appearances to Joseph (2.13–15a; 2.19–21), a common pattern emerges:

A. note of circumstance (1.18b–19; 2.13; 2.19)
B. appearance of the angel of the Lord in a dream (1.20a; 2.13; 2.19)
C. command of the angel to Joseph (1.20b; 2.13; 2.20a)
D. explanation of command (γάρ clause; 1.20c; 2.13; 2.20b)
E. Joseph rises (ἐγερθείς) and obediently responds (1.24–5; 2.14–15; 2.21)

But the structure of 1.18–25 is a bit more complicated than the parallels indicated might imply, for the passage also exhibits features common to other angelic annunciation narratives, instances of which appear in Gen 16 (Ishmael), Judg 13 (Samson), and Luke 1 (John the Baptist; Jesus); compare also Gen 17–18; 1 Kgs 13.1–10; 1 Chr 22.9–10; Isa 7.14–17; LAB 9.10; 42. The texts can be analysed in this fashion:

A. description of circumstances (Gen 16.1–7; Judg 13.2; Lk 1.5–10; 1.26; Mt 1.18–20)
B. the angel of the Lord appears (Gen 16.7; Judg 13.3; Lk 1.11; 1.26–8; Mt 1.20)
C. angelic prophecy of birth, including child's future deeds (Gen 16.11–12; Judg 13.3–7; Lk 1.13–17; 1.30–3, 35–7; Mt 1.20–21)

196

D. account of the issue of things (Gen 16.13–16; Judg 13.19–25; Lk 1.18–25; 1.38; Mt 1.24–5)

(For a slightly different outline see Conrad (v).)

Evidently, Mt 1.18–25 represents a conflation of two different patterns, the pattern shared with Mt 2.13–15a and 2.19–21 and the pattern shared with Gen 16, Judg 13, and Lk 1. This is probably to be explained in terms of tradition-history. As argued in Excursus I, stage I in the development of the Matthean infancy narrative, the Mosaic stage, told of a dream in which Jesus' father was commanded to take his wife because her child would deliver Israel. It also told of two other similar dreams in which Joseph was again given commands and explanations—whence the common pattern still preserved in 1.18–25; 2.13–15; and 2.19–21. But when the primitive story line was expanded in the interests of a Davidic Christology (stage II), certain traditions were added, including that of the virgin birth, this last being passed on in the standard angelic annunciation of birth pattern (cf. Lk 1.26–38). The result was the confluence of two once independent structures.[1]

To the traditional story taken up into 1.18–25, Matthew (stage III) added a general introductory statement (18a), inserted a formula quotation (22–3), and rewrote 24–5 in accordance with an OT sentence form (see below). Beyond this, he presumably made minor additions and stamped the language of the entire pericope with his own style.

(iii) *Exegesis*

18. 'Now concerning the Messiah, his origin was thus'. Matthew is writing about *ben Dāwid*, and the events that follow take place in Bethlehem, the city of David—although this is not stated until 2.1. (There are, in fact, no geographical notices at all in chapter 1. This is in striking contrast to chapter 2, where geography is a central theme.)

1.18–25 as a whole serves as a commentary on the last link in the genealogy, albeit in terms of the history of tradition the genealogy was composed last, to introduce the pre-Matthean story of the virginal conception and birth. Note the possible chiastic connexion: the genealogy names, in order, Joseph, Mary, and the Messiah, while 1.18–25 speaks first about the Messiah (18a), then about Mary (18b), and then about Joseph (19–20) (cf. the chiasmus in 1.1–16; see on 1.1).

The juxtaposition of 1.18–25 with 1.1–17 just may have a parallel of sorts in Gen 1–2.[2] In the account of creation in Gen 1,

---

[1] Cf. Brown, *Messiah*, p. 116.

[2] Note Davies, *SSM*, pp. 71–2, and cf. Hamerton-Kelly, pp. 77–8.

we have a catalogic account of the stages of creation which culminates in the appearance of man, whose 'ancestors' are listed. This agrees with Mt 1.1–17, a catalogic account of Jesus' ancestors culminating in the Messiah. Then in Gen 2 we have a different, more detailed account of man's creation 'from the dust of the ground'. In this narrative version man comes first. This corresponds to Mt 1.18–25, the detailed narrative account of Jesus' 'genesis'. That such a parallelism could have been in Matthew's mind is suggested (although far from proved) by the creation motifs in Mt 1—the 'genesis' of 1.1 and the creative Holy Spirit of 1.18 and 20.

τοῦ δὲ Χριστοῦ ἡ γένεσις οὕτως ἦν.[3] The unusual word order (cf. 10.2) links the story introduced in 1.18a with the genealogy concluded by 1.17c, where Χριστοῦ recurs. The repetition of 'genesis' serves a like purpose: it recalls 1.1. οὕτως (only here with ἦν) is a favourite word of Matthew (Mt: 32; Mk: 10; Lk: 21). For another redactional use of this adverb as a predicate with εἶναι see 19.10.

In 1.1 we preferred to transliterate 'genesis'. Here the translation 'origin' or 'birth' is ostensibly demanded by the context (cf. Gen 31.13; 40.20 Ruth 2.11; Lk 1.14). Yet because of the mention in 1.18c of the Holy Spirit, God's creative power (see below), the thought of 'creation', first connoted by the 'genesis' of 1.1, may lie in the background.

μνηστευθείσης τῆς μητρὸς αὐτοῦ Μαρίας τῷ Ἰωσήφ. Compare Deut 22.23; Josephus, *Bell.* 1.508. Matthew, like Mark, commonly uses the genitive absolute to introduce the circumstance of a new pericope. Here the construction is awkward, for no new subject follows (cf. Acts 22.17 and see BDF § 423.4).

---

[3] Ιησου Χριστου has the best attestation, being found in P[1] ℵ C E K L P Δ Θ Π *f*[1] *f*[13] Maj sy [p.h.pal] sa bo arm eth geo Diat Ir Or Did Epiph. Χριστου Ιησου (an assimilation to Pauline usage?) is in B Or[gr.lat] Hier; Ιησου in W 4 74 270 Cyr Max-Conf DialTimetAq; Χριστου in latt sy[c.s] Theoph Ir[lat] Aug Ps-Ath. Most authorities accept the first reading (see Soares Prabhu, p. 177), and it certainly enjoys the great weight of external attestation. The evidence for omission of Ιησου, however, is early (second century); and the majority text could represent assimilation to 1.1 and 1.16; and, despite witnesses at Acts 8.37 and 1 Jn 4.3, the NT probably contains no other instance of the grammatically awkward use of the definite article before Ἰησοῦς Χριστός; and, finally, the addition of Ιησου is easier to explain than its omission, particularly as its position is variable—a fact often indicative of a later insertion. So we are inclined to accept Χριστου as original. Matthew is writing about *ben Dāwid*. γενεσις is also a problem. It is read by P[1] ℵ B C P S W Z Δ Θ Σ *f*[1] sy[h.pal] bo arm Eus Max-Conf Ps-Ath. But the orthographically and phonetically similar γεννησις ('birth') is attested by K L M Γ Π *f*[13] Maj it vg sy[c.s.p] sa Diat Ir Or Did Epiph Aug DialTimetAq. Although the second reading could be pristine, the first an assimilation to 1.1. (cf. Davies, *SSM*, p. 69), γενεσις is to be preferred (so Soares Prabhu, pp. 177–9): it has better external attestation and, as Metzger, p. 8, observes, γεννησις was the common patristic word for the nativity (cf. Lampe, s.v.).

μνηστεύειν (Mt: 1; Mk: 0; Lk: 2) means 'to betroth', 'to woo and win' (cf. *'āraś*). For the word in the passive or middle with reference to Mary see Lk 1.27; 2.5; Mt 1.16 Θ *f*[13] (cf. Deut 22.23–8). To judge from the rabbinic sources (which may be late), betrothal or engagement (*'ērûsîn* or *qiddûšîm*) in ancient Judaism took place at a very early age, usually at twelve to twelve and a half years (*b. Yeb.* 62b; SB 2, p. 374). Following courtship and the completion of the marriage contract (Tob 7.14), the marriage was considered established: the woman had passed from her father's authority to that of her husband. But about a year typically passed before the woman moved from her parents' house to her husband's house (*m Ketub.* 5.2; *m. Ned.* 10.5; *b. Ketub.* 57b). During that time, although the marriage was not yet consummated, the woman was 'wife' (Deut 20.7; 28.30; Judg 14.15; 15.1; 2 Sam 3.14) and she could become a widow (*m. Yeb.* 4.10; 6.4; *m. Ketub.* 1.2) or be punished for adultery (Deut 22.23–4; 11QTemple 61). Thus betrothal was the legal equivalent of marriage, and its cancellation divorce (*m. Ketub.* 1.2; 4.2; *m. Yeb.* 2.6; *m. Giṭ* 6.2). This explains the situation of Joseph (cf. Lk 1.27). Even though he has not yet taken Mary, she is his wife (1.20, 24); thus separation requires a certificate of divorce (1.19).

It is noteworthy that while Mary may be called Jesus' 'mother', Joseph is not called his 'father'. God alone is Jesus' 'father'.[4]

πρὶν ἢ συνελθεῖν αὐτούς. Compare Exod 1.19; Josh 11.33; Isa 7.15; Acts 7.2. συνέρχομαι (Mt: 1; Mk: 2; Lk: 2), whose primary meaning is 'come together', frequently designated sexual relations, as in Wisd 7.2; Philo, *Virt.* 40; Josephus, *Ant.* 7.168; and 1 Cor 7.5 Maj. Evidence that the word was used of the ceremonial coming of the bride to the groom's house is lacking, although in the papyri συνελθεῖν πρὸς γάμον means 'to marry' (BAGD, s.v.; cf. Horsley 3, p. 85). In Mt 1.18 συνέρχομαι probably refers to both domestic and marital relations: 'come together under the same roof as man and wife' (BAGD, s.v.). We are to understand, in accordance with the custom of the time, that Mary and Joseph, although betrothed to one another, have not yet taken up common residence. Matthew's major point, already hinted at in 1.16, is thus made: Mary's conception cannot be by human agency. On πρίν (Mt: 3; Mk: 2; Lk: 2) with the infinitive see BDF § 395.

According to rabbinic sources, the halakah of Galilee differed at certain points from the halakah of Judea, one such being marriage law (*m. Yeb.* 4.10; *m. Ketub.* 1.5; 4.12; *b. Ketub.* 12a). Specifically, in Judea a man could spend a night with his betrothed before the wedding celebration,

---

[4] Despite the prominence of creation motifs in Mt 1 and the possible allusions to Gen 1–2, Matthew does not model Mary on Eve or develop an Eve typology (contrast Justin, *Dial.* 100; Irenaeus, *Adv. haer.* 3.22.4).

something strongly forbidden in Galilee. Now since Mt 1.18–25 is set in Judea, one might argue, as did Harnack,[5] that Mary conceived by Joseph before the wedding ceremony but after the betrothal, and that this circumstance was one catalyst towards belief in the virgin birth. This possibility, though it would fit ill with 1.19, cannot be excluded. But we cannot be certain at what date the Judean custom—which was apparently intended to prevent Roman soldiers from raping betrothed Jewish virgins (cf. *b. Ketub.* 3b; *y. Ketub.* 1.25c)—came into being. It may have arisen as late as A.D. 70 or even 135.

εὑρέθη ἐν γαστρὶ ἔχουσα ἐκ πνεύματος ἁγίου. The aorist passive of εὑρίσκω literally means 'was found'. Here the sense is 'proved to be' or 'turned out to be'. As is sometimes the case with *nimṣā'*, no 'finder' is necessarily implied (cf. Acts 5.39; Rom 7.10; Phil 2.8).

ἐν γαστρί + ἔχειν (= 'to be pregnant') is a fixed expression occurring in Herodotus (3.32), in medical writers after Hippocrates, and commonly in the papyri; it is also frequent in the LXX for *hārâ* or *hāreh* (Gen 16.4, 5; 38.42, 25; Judg 13.5, 7); compare Mt 24.19 parr.; 1 Th 5.3; Rev 12.2. Here the expression anticipates the quotation of Isa 7.14 in 1.23 (ἐν γαστρὶ ἕξει). ἐκ of agency might be regarded as redactional (Mt: 6; Mk: 2; Lk: 2), but it occurs only here in Matthew with πνεῦμα. 'Through the Holy Spirit' (cf. 1.3, 5, 6, 16), a phrase which soon found its way into the creeds ('conceived of the Holy Spirit'), is probably a redactional insertion in anticipation of 1.20; it gives the reader knowledge the main character (Joseph) has not yet received. The omission of the article (cf. Lk 1.35) with God's πνεῦμα is found also in 1.20 and 3.16. But the word is definite from the nature of the case, and the absence of the article before a definite word preceded by ἐκ is well-attested (e.g. 27.38; Lk 9.7; Jn 1.32; 6.58). The Spirit should not be thought of in terms of later trinitarian thought. Rather should it be equated with the creative power of God.[6] Compare the parallelism of Lk 1.35: 'The Holy Spirit will come upon you, and the power of the Most High will overshadow you'.

What led believers in the virginal conception of Jesus to see the Holy Spirit as the agent of that conception? According to R. E. Brown, it was the outcome of a christological process by which the moment of Jesus' divine sonship, first tied to the resurrection, was moved back to the ministry and baptism and then to the conception: because divine adoption at the resurrection and at the baptism was considered the work of the Spirit (Rom 1.4; 1 Tim 3.16; Mk 1.10–11), the Spirit's activity was again

---

[5] A. Harnack, *The Date of Acts and of the Synoptic Gospels* (trans. of *Neue Untersuchungen zur Apostelgeschichte und zur Abfassungszeit der synoptischen Evangelien*, 1911), London and New York, 1911, pp. 149–50. See on Galilean and Judean customs, M. Goodman, in *CHJ*, 3, forthcoming.

[6] See further the discussion of Bultmann, *Theology* 1, pp. 155–7.

naturally invoked when Christians came to believe that Jesus was God's Son at his conception.[7] This thesis, in its essentials already propounded by J. Weiss and A. Harnack,[8] is no doubt simplistic. For not only does the Son of God Christology play a relatively minor rôle in the birth narratives,[9] but the birth of Jesus was an important christological moment from very early times, as is evident from the pre-Pauline materials preserved in Rom 1.3–4 and Gal 4.4–5 (cf. Heb 1.6). In addition, one need not look any further than the prophetic tradition, where election is from the womb (Jer 1.5; Isa 49.1; Gal 1.15), to understand how the conception of Jesus could early on have come to hold christological significance. To find, moreover, as have many, an adoptionist Christology in Mk 1.9–11 or its parallels, one must read too much between the lines, and the motifs of Spirit and sonship in these narratives do not represent a retrojection of resurrection language (see on 3.16–17). Finally, the interpretation of Mary's pregnancy as due to the Holy Spirit can be assigned to the confluence of other factors. (1) The coming of the Messiah constituted a 'new creation' for the early church (see on 1.1) and creation was the work of the Spirit (Gen 1.2; Job 26.13; Ps 33.6; 104.30; Isa 32.15; 2 Bar. 21.4). (2) The Spirit was traditionally understood to be the source of (human) life; see Gen 6.3; Job 27.3; 33.4; Ps 33.6; Isa 32.15; Ezek 37.9–10, 14; Jud 16.14; Jub. 5.8; Sib. Or. frag. 1, 5; Philo, *Op. Mund.* 29–30; cf. Jn 3.5–6; 6.63; 2 Cor 3.6; Rev 11.11. (3) Jesus was believed to be the Davidic Messiah and the suffering servant, and both of these figures were firmly associated with the Holy Spirit: Isa 11.2; 42.1; 61.1; 1 En. 49.1–4; 62.2; T. Levi 18.7; T. Jud. 24.2; Ps. Sol. 17.37. (4) The virginal conception was a miracle, and in both Jewish and Christian texts the Holy Spirit is the power behind miracles (Judg 13.25; 14.6, 19; 15.14; Mt 12.28; Acts 2.4; 1 Cor 12.3–13). (5) Eschatological sonship and the Spirit were closely linked in early Christian thinking (Jn 3.5; Rom 8.9–17; Gal 4.6, 28–9)—as they apparently already were in pre-Christian Judaism (Jub. 1.23–4; T. Levi 18.11–12; T. Jud. 24.3; cf. 1QH 9.32–6). (6) In significant ways, Joseph, the father of Jesus, was modelled on the figure of Amram, Moses' father (see pp. 190–5). Similarly, Mary, Jesus' mother, may have been to some extent thought of as a counterpart to Moses' sister, Miriam.[10] If so, it becomes important to observe that in LAB 9.10 we read that 'the Spirit of God came upon Miriam by night and she saw a dream . . .'. Also, in *Mek.* on Exod 15.20, Miriam's 'standing' (Exod 2.4) is taken to suggest the presence of the Holy Spirit. (7) Given the interpenetration of Hellenism and Judaism, the pagan texts that put down supernatural conceptions to the spirit of a god must be remembered (although note p. 208); see, for instance, Aeschylus, *Supp.* 17–18; Plutarch, *Num.* 4. (8) It was believed that messianic times would see a fresh and full coming of the Holy Spirit (Isa 44.3–4; Ezek 37.1–14; Joel 2.28–9; T. Jud. 24.3; T. Levi 18.11; *Num.*

[7] *Messiah*, pp. 29–32, 140–2.

[8] J. Weiss, *History* 1, pp. 118–23; Harnack (as in n. 3), pp. 143–5.

[9] Cf. R. H. Fuller, 'The Conception/Birth of Jesus as a Christological Moment', *JSNT* 1 (1978), pp. 37–52, esp. p. 40. In our judgement, both Pesch, 'Gottesohn' (v), and Kingsbury, *Structure*, pp. 43–4, have exaggerated the importance in 1.18–25 of Matthew's Son of God Christology.

[10] See R. Le Déaut, 'Miryam, soeur de Moïse, et Marie, mère du Messie', *Bib* 45 (1964), pp. 198–219.

Rab. on 15.25). (9) Lastly, in Lk 1.15 it is said of John that he was 'filled with the Holy Spirit from his mother's womb'. R. E. Brown thinks this line redactional.[11] In the judgement of Fitzmyer, it derives ultimately from a pre-Lukan Baptist source.[12] If Fitzmyer be correct—and we cannot be sure that he is—, then the presence of the Holy Spirit with a hero still in the womb would be attested in ancient Judaism. More than this, given the lines of communication between early Christians and followers of the Baptist, the presence of the Holy Spirit in the infancy narratives of Matthew and Luke could owe something to infancy traditions about the Baptist. In any event, in view of the facts to which we have called attention, it is no surprise that the eschatological appearance of the Messiah and the resultant new creation were interpreted by the faithful as brought about by the Spirit of God.

19. 1.18 maintained the focus established in 1.16 ('Mary, of whom Jesus was born [or: conceived]'). With 1.19, which sets the stage for the angelic appearance (1.20), the focus shifts—to the situation of Joseph, to his response to Mary's pregnancy.

Obviously redactional elements are sparse in 1.19, a sign that the evangelist is taking up tradition.

Ἰωσὴφ δὲ ὁ ἀνὴρ αὐτῆς. Compare 1.16. 'Her man' was a standard expression for husband, common in the LXX for *'îšâ*; see Num 30.8–9, 11–14; Ezek 16.45; 11QTemple 54.3 (cf. Rev 21.2, of a bridegroom).

δίκαιος ὤν. The meaning most naturally attached to the adjective is 'just', 'law-abiding'. The word could, admittedly, include the whole range of right action, but principally it pertained to legal justice.[13] This was particularly so within Judaism, where the whole sphere of righteousness was contained in the Torah. Compare Lk 1. 6: Zechariah and Elizabeth 'were both δίκαιος before God, walking in all the commandments and ordinances of the Lord blameless' (cf. Sus 3). The DSS and rabbinic literature present us with basically the same understanding: those who are properly religious in that they observe the Law of God are *ṣaddîqîm*, 'just'.[14]

Matthew has δίκαιος (a rabbinic loan word) seventeen times, always in a positive sense. Often there is no synoptic parallel.[15] Mt 13.17; 23.29 and 35 reveal an inclination to label as 'righteous' or 'just' the pious of the past who were upright and properly religious

[11] *Messiah*, pp. 244–5, 270–9. Cf. Jeremias, *Lukasevangelium*, pp. 35–6.
[12] *Luke* 1, pp. 316–19. Cf. Schweizer, *Luke*, pp 15, 20.
[13] Cf. G. Schrenk, *TWNT* 2, pp. 184–93.
[14] See Przybylski, pp. 13–52. Relevant passages include CD 4.7; 4QpPs[a] 2.13–15, 22–3; *Sipra* on Lev 18.5 and 20.16. On the rabbinic literature see esp. R. Mach, *Der Zaddik in Talmud und Midrasch*, Leiden, 1957.
[15] For this and what follows see esp. Przybylski, pp. 101–4, and Giesen, pp. 179–96.

(cf. Heb 12.23).[16] In 5.45; 9.13; 10.41; 23.28; and 27.19, 'righteous' refers to contemporaries not necessarily Christian who observe the Law. Only in 13.43, 49; 25.37 and 46—the last two of which may be from the tradition, and all four of which concern the future—is 'righteous' clearly an appellation for the followers of Jesus. Thus δίκαιος should not be understood as Matthew's preferred technical term for true Christian disciples; and in 1.19 the word simply indicates obedience to the Torah (cf. Prot. Jas. 14.1).

Some have proposed that Joseph was 'righteous' in that he had mercy upon his betrothed: 'being just and (*therefore*) unwilling to put her to shame publicly . . .'.[17] The meaning of 'just' would then shade into that of φιλάνθρωπος or ἐπιεικής (compare Deut 6.25), and λάθρα would be stressed. Against this proposal, which was put forth by both Clement of Alexandria and Jerome, it seems better to adopt a sense more in line with Matthew's predominant use of words with the δικ- root (although Luz 1, p. 104, sees no antithesis here). Still others, finding it difficult to suppose that Joseph suspected Mary of unfaithfulness, or finding it hard to think that Matthew so thought, take δίκαιος to imply reverential hesitation or awe: Joseph was afraid he would do wrong if he took Mary for wife, for he might find himself interfering with God's plan (cf. Eusebius in PG 22.884).[18] (On this interpretation, Joseph already knows that Mary's pregnancy is of the Holy Spirit; cf. 1.18.) But if this were so, we should expect to find Joseph in a quandary, at a loss concerning what action to pursue, not determined to divorce his betrothed. Moreover, the information divulged by the angel in 1.20—Mary is with child of the Holy Spirit—is most readily viewed as revelatory; that is, Joseph does not yet know the true cause of his wife's conception. Compare the OT annunciation narratives, in which an angel gives the visionary information he or she does not already have (Gen 16.11–12; Judg 13.3–7; 1 Kgs 13.2; cf. LAB 9.10); and observe that in both 2.13 and 20 the angel of the Lord divulges to Joseph things Joseph does not yet know. So the interpretation already presupposed by Justin and the Protevangelium of James and advanced later by Chrysostom, Ambrose, Augustine, and Luther must be upheld: 'Joseph, the husband of Mary, who at first wished to put away Mary his betrothed, since he supposed her to be pregnant by intercourse with a man, from fornication . . .' (*Dial.* 78).[19]

[16] This reminds one of a similar tendency in rabbinic sources; primarily those who lived long ago before the Tannaim are called 'righteous'; see Przybylski, pp. 42–4.

[17] See esp. Spicq (v). Cf. Klostermann, p. 8; Filson, p. 54; Schweizer, *Matthew*, pp. 30–1; and Pesch, 'Ausführungsformel' (v), p. 91.

[18] So above all Léon-Dufour (v). He cites the support of Eusebius, Ephrem, Pseudo-Basil, and Pseudo-Origen. Cf. Schlatter, p. 13; Krämer, 'Menschwerdung' (v); and Cantwell (v). For a critical review see Giesen, pp. 183–7.

[19] Cf. Language, pp. 11–12; Descamps (v); Hill (v); Bonnard, p. 20;

Is δίκαιος redactional? Perhaps, given Matthew's fondness for the word. Yet the tradition may also have carried such a characterization; for in the haggadic legends about Moses' birth, the father of Moses, Amram, is presented as full of great faith and piety; see e.g., LAB 9.3–8; Josephus, *Ant.* 2.210–18; *Exod. Rab.* on 1.13. Maybe Matthew's source read, 'Joseph, being just, took counsel to divorce her', to which Matthew added, 'not wanting to put her to shame . . . secretly'.[20]

καὶ μὴ θέλων αὐτὴν δειγματίσαι.[21] 'But' or 'and in spite of that' or 'and yet' would be appropriate translations for καί given our interpretation, and the word can (like the Hebrew *w*) be so used (BAGD, s.v. I.1.2.g). From Matthew alone note 3.14; 6.26; 10.29; 12.43; 13.17; 26.20. θέλω (Mt: 42; Mk: 24; Lk: 28) is often redactional. μὴ θέλων (which does not explicate δίκαιος) appears only once in the First Gospel, although the evangelist not infrequently couples μή with a participle, as in 13.19; 18.13, 25; 22.12, 25; 25.29 (all either redactional or without parallel). δειγματίζω, a *hapax legomenon* in the synoptics, is a rare word (absent from the LXX) which occurs elsewhere in the NT only at Col 2.15. The basic meaning is 'to exhibit', 'to bring to public notice' (cf. Asc. Isa. 3.13; Acts of Peter and Paul 33; Eusebius in PG 22.884). The related δεῖγμα ('sample', 'example', 'evidence'; cf. Jude 7) came into Hebrew as a loan word, and *'āśâ dî(ū)gmā'* (= δειγματίζω) is attested in rabbinic literature (Schlatter, p. 14). Furthermore, in *m. 'Ed.* 5.6 and *b. Ber.* 19a, *dî(û)gmâ/ā'* is used in connexion with the public trial of one caught in adultery. This parallels the Greek use of δειγματίζω (BAGD, s.v.),

ἐβουλήθη λάθρα ἀπολῦσαι αὐτήν. ἀπολύω (Mt: 19; Mk: 12; Lk: 13) means 'let go', 'dismiss', here 'divorce', as in Diodorus Siculus 12.18; 1 Esd 9.36; Mur. 115.3–4 (DJD 2, p. 105); Mt 5.31–2; 19.3, 7–9. The stress is on this word, not λάθρα (Mt: 2; Mk: 0; Lk: 0).

The precise procedure for obtaining a divorce in first-century Palestine is not perfectly clear. But judging from Matthew's text, one of two options confronted Joseph. Either he could accuse his betrothed before the public authority and ask for a trial to determine whether she had been forcibly seized against her will or seduced with consent (cf. Deut 22.23–7; 11QTemple 66. 1–8; *b.*

Grundmann, p. 68; Brown, *Messiah*, pp. 127–8; Tosato (v); Broer (v), pp. 251–3; Przybylski, p. 102; and Luz 1, p. 104. According to Giesen, pp. 187–9, Joseph is just not in that he is obedient to the Torah but in that he acts in accord with the demand of God as it is revealed to him.

[20] So Soares Prabhu, pp. 249–50.

[21] For the rare δειγματισαι (so ℵ¹ B Z *f*¹), ℵ*·² C L W Θ *f*¹³ Maj sy^hmg Epiph followed by HG have the more common παραδειγματισαι, which is found in the LXX and Heb 6.6.

Sanh. 57b)[22], or, as with (perhaps) the Jews at Elephantine,[23] he could without further ado draw up a bill of divorce himself (Deut 24.1; *m. Giṭ* 2.5), without a trial (*m. Soṭa 1.5?*),[24] and call upon two or three witnesses to sign the document (*m. Giṭ* 9.4, 8). The former course of action is represented by δειγματίζω. (As no third party is or could be mentioned, the outcome of a trial would have been, we are to assume, complete public disgrace.) The second course, and the one preferred by Joseph, is represented by λάθρᾳ ἀπολῦσαι, the adverb (cf. 2.7) indicating relative quiet, as opposed to the alternative.[25]

In LAB 9, after Pharaoh commands the slaughter of all Hebrew children, the elders of the people conclude that no man should any longer come near his wife (cf. *Exod. Rab.* on 1.15, where even pregnant wives are divorced). But after this decision is made, the pious Amram, reflecting on God's covenantal faithfulness, and recalling the story of Tamar (cf. Mt 1.3), decides that he will go ahead and take a wife: and God blesses him. Should we not find in this yet one more parallel between the infancy traditions about Moses and those about Jesus (see pp. 57–67)? Like Amram, Joseph took his wife despite difficult circumstances.

20. In this verse and 1.24 we learn that the angelic revelation of 1.20 came to Joseph in a dream. This shows us that the evangelist feels perfectly free to inform his readers not just about objective events but also about (what we must regard as) subjective experiences. This is consistent with his stance as an omniscient narrator: his knowledge is not hindered by any circumstance. Thus Matthew informs us about a secret meeting between Herod and the magi (2.7) and about the latter's dream (2.12). He narrates an event at which only Jesus and Satan were present (4.1–11). He gives us the thoughts of the Pharisees (9.3) and the feelings of Herod (14.9). He tells us that Peter was afraid (14.30) and that Jesus was hungry (21.18). He recounts the Pharisees' perceptions

---

[22] 'The bitter waters' (Num 5.11–31) were evidently reserved for those already married (*m. Soṭa* 4.1). There was no agreement on whether divorce was necessary if the betrothed virgin was innocent; see Tosata (v), pp. 549–50. Further, if the woman was guilty, she was not necessarily stoned (Deut 24.1; Jn 18.31; *b. Sanh.* 41a; SB 1, pp. 51–53; contrast Deut 22.24; Jub. 30.4–10 and note Jn 8.2–11).

[23] See R. Yaron, *Introduction to the Law of the Aramaic Papyri*, Oxford, 1961, pp. 53–64; B. Porten, *Archives from Elephantine*, Berkeley, 1968, p. 210.

[24] See further W. Falk, *Introduction to the Jewish Law of the Second Commonwealth*, Part 2. AGJU 11, Leiden, 1978, p. 311. According to Falk, pp. 311–13, the school of Shammai required an appearance in court.

[25] The just Joseph, it is assumed, cannot have Mary because she has, whether willingly or not, been with another; compare Jub. 33.7–9; 41.20; 1QapGen 20.15. According to Tg. Ps.-J. on Deut 22.26, a husband must divorce even an innocent wife if she has slept with another, Joseph seems to be following this halakah. Contrast *m. Soṭa* 4.4.

(21.45–6). He even knows the feelings and convictions that motivated Jesus (9.36; 12.15; 13.58; 14.14).

ταῦτα δὲ αὐτοῦ ἐνθυμηθέντος ἰδοὺ ἄγγελος κυρίου κατ᾽ ὄναρ ἐφάνη αὐτῷ λέγων. Instead of the genitive absolute, one expects the participle in the dative (cf. the variants at 8.1, 5, 28; 21.23). ἐνθυμέομαι (Mt: 2; Mk: 0; Lk: 0) means 'to take something to heart', 'to ponder', 'to consider' (cf. 9.4 diff. Mk 2.8 and Josephus, *Ant.* 11.155). The word occurs for various Hebrew equivalents in the LXX, where it typically refers to God pondering destruction (Gen 6.6, 7; Isa 10.7; Lam 2.17) or to men entertaining wicked thoughts (Josh 7.21; Isa 37.29; Wisd 3.14). In the NT there are no occurrences outside Matthew, although Acts 10.9 has διενθυμέομαι. The mental states of those having important dreams are frequently related in Hellenistic literature (cf. Plutarch, *Brut.* 36.4; Josephus, *Ant.* 11.334; Philostratus, *VA* 4.34). According to Isocrates, *Evagoras* 21, portents, oracles, and visions in dreams foretell supernatural births.

The interjection, ἰδού (= *hinnēh*, Aramaic *hā᾽*), which 'points to a thing unexpected' (Bengel), is a favourite of the redactor (Mt: 62; Mk: 7; Lk: 57). Its occurrence with the genitive absolute (Mk: 0; Lk: 1) is particularly characteristic of him (1.20; 2.1, 13, 19; 9.10, 18, 32; 12.46; 17.5; 26.47; 28.11). A redactional origin is nevertheless uncertain here as at 2.13 and 19. For the word and its Semitic equivalents were traditionally associated with angelic appearances or theophanies and so could have been in Matthew's source; see Gen 18.2; 28.13; Ezek 1.4; Dan 7.13; 1 En. 1.9 = Jude 14; 2 Bar. 22.1; Jos. Asen. 14.1; Par. Jer. 3.2; 6.2, 15; Lk 24.4; Acts 1.10; Rev 19.11. It is also a standard item in annunciation narratives: Gen 16.11; Judg 13.7; Isa 7.14; LAB 42.3; Lk 1.31. For *hinnēh* or *hā᾽* or ἰδού in dreams see Gen 37.9; 41.1–7; Dan 7.2; 1QapGen 19.14; 4Q᾽Amram[b] frag. 1, 10; LAB 9.10. For καὶ ἰδού see on 3.16.

The 'angel of the Lord' is not, as in Gen 16; 21; 22; Exod 3; and Judg 6, a way of speaking of God himself; the angel is rather, in accordance with later Jewish thought, a being with its own identity (cf. Zech 1.8–17; Lk 1.26; and the naming of angels in 1 En. 6.7; 8.3–4; 69.1). The absence of the articles is a Septuagintism reflecting the Hebrew construct state (cf. *maPak YHWH*; 'Lord' without article also represents *YHWH* in Mt 3.3 = Isa 40.3; 21.9 = Ps 118.26; and 23.39 = Ps 118.26). Apart from 28.2, where Matthew interprets Mark's 'young man' as an 'angel of the Lord', ἄγγελος κυρίου is confined to the infancy narratives (1.20, 24; 2.13, 19). In both 1–2 and 28 the angel is a messenger. Given the parallels shared by Mt 1.18–25; Gen 16; Judg 13; LAB 42; and Lk 1.5–23 (see p. 196), it is certainly notable that the 'angel of the Lord' occurs also in Gen 16.7; Judg 13.3; LAB 42.6; and Lk 1.11.

Evidently this figure was traditionally associated with announcing miraculous conceptions and the names of sons.[26]

κατ᾽ ὄναρ = baḥălôm, although the LXX translates with καθ᾽ ὕπνον or ἐν (τῷ) ὕπνῳ, never κατ᾽ ὄναρ. In the NT the phrase appears only here and in Mt 2.12, 13, 19, 22; 27.19. It is unattested before the turn of the era (BAGD, s.v. ὄναρ; cf. Crates, *Ep.* 26). The OT Joseph received revelation in a dream (37.5–11). Maybe then the NT Joseph is meant to be like him. Yet the background is more plausibly to be found in the Moses legends, where the prophecies about the coming deliverer are given in dreams (e.g. LAB 9.10; Josephus, *Ant.* 2.212–17; Tg. Ps.-J. on Exod 1.15). Also, in 4Q'Amram[b], Amram, the father of Moses, has a dream vision in which he sees and converses with angels.[27]

Dreams are frequently vehicles of divine revelation in the OT, especially in Genesis and Daniel, and they remain so in the intertestamental literature.[28] According to Job 33.15–17, 'In a dream, in a vision of the night . . . [God] opens the ears of men, and terrifies them with warnings, that he may turn man away from his deed [LXX: injustice] . . .'. Dreams were also of great importance in the Graeco-Roman world (cf. Origen, *C. Cels.* 1.66), and Matthew's story of Joseph can be profitably compared with the typical dream patterns found in the literature that that world produced.[29] This is particularly true because the standard OT pattern is to state 'X dreamed a dream' and then to give the contents only after the event, after the dreamer awakes (as in Gen 37.5–7, 9; 40; Dan 2; 7); while in the Graeco-Roman materials, on the other hand, the contents of a dream are (as in Mt 1–2 and 1QapGen. 19) usually given concurrently with the dreaming, that is, given as the dream takes place. For rabbinic reflection on dreams see especially *b. Ber.* 55a–b.

Note that the angel of the Lord 'appears'[30] only in order to speak. His sole function is to bring revelatory speech. He does nothing else at all.

᾽Ιωσὴφ υἱὸς Δαυίδ. Compare 1.1, 16. The appellation, 'son of David', probably derives from stage II of the story's history, when

[26] On the angel of the Lord see further G. Kittel, *TWNT* 1, pp. 75–9.

[27] The appearance of an angel in a dream may combine two distinct modes of revelation (although angels do appear in dreams in Gen 31.11; LAB 9.10; and 2 En. 1). This would be in line with our postulated tradition history. The original narrative, based on legends about Moses, perhaps spoke only of dreams (stage I). But this could have changed when the annunciation of the virginal conception, which contained an angel (cf. Lk 1.26), was incorporated, thus resulting in the angel in a dream, 1.20 (stage II). 2.13 and 19 were subsequently brought—either by Matthew or by his tradition—into parallel with 1.20.

[28] See BAGD, s.v., ὄναρ, and A. Oepke, *TWNT* 5, pp. 220–38.

[29] See J. S. Hanson, 'Dreams and Visions in the Graeco-Roman World and Early Christianity', *ANRW* 23.2 (1980), pp. 1395–1427, esp. p. 1421.

[30] φαίνω (Mt: 13; Mk: 1; Lk: 2) here and at 2.13 and 19 may have displaced an original ὤφθη (cf. Judg 13.3; Lk 1.11).

elements from a Davidic Christology were added (cf. Lk 1.27). With this one exception, Matthew reserves 'son of David' for Jesus. The nominative for the vocative is common in the synoptics.

μὴ φοβηθῇς παραλαβεῖν Μαρίαν τὴν γυναῖκά σου.[31] The quelling of human fear is a standard element in OT theophanies;[32] it is also prevalent in intertestamental literature and the NT, where appearances of God are all but non-existent but appearances of angels common (see below). One can make a case for treating 'fear not' (Mt: 8; Mk: 2; Lk: 8) as editorial (it is so in 10.26; 17.7; 28.5, 10). But the comforting appeal turns up also in Luke's infancy narrative (1.13, 30; 2.10) and otherwise frequently in accounts of angelic appearances (Dan 10.12, 19; 1 En. 15.1; Apoc. Abr. 9.3; Jos. Asen. 14.11; 2 En. 1.8; Acts 27.24; Rev 1.17).

There are several 'fear not' formulas in the OT. In one of these the imperative is followed by a motive clause employing kî.[33] See, for instance, Gen 21.17 and 26.24. The angel's utterance in Mt 1.20 displays this form: 'fear not . . . for . . .' (cf. Lk 1.30; 2.10).

παραλαμβάνω is a word Matthew likes (Mt: 16; Mk: 6; Lk: 6) and it occurs often in Mt 1–2 (1.20, 24; 2.13, 14, 20, 21). Joseph should—as he will in 1.24—'take' his wife Mary, that is, take her to his home and thereby turn engagement into marriage; compare Herodotus 4.155; Ct 8.2; Josephus, Ant. 1.302; 17.9; and the rabbinic haknāsâ ('carrying in'), as in b. Ketub. 17a.

Mary, like her son Jesus, is a completely passive character throughout Mt 1–2. It is Joseph who does what needs to be done. This circumstance is partly to be explained by a christological interest: by his actions, Joseph, the Davidid, proves that he has made Jesus his own.

τὸ γὰρ ἐν αὐτῇ γεννηθὲν ἐκ πνεύματός ἐστιν ἁγίου. Compare LAB 9.7. This is the heart of the angelic message. Joseph now knows what the reader knows from 1.18: Mary has conceived miraculously by the Holy Spirit. τὸ ἅγιον πνεῦμα occurs in 28.19, but here and in 1.18 (q.v.) there is no article. In 1.18–25 Matthew's thought is not of a person (as in later Christian thought) but more along the lines of the OT concept of the Spirit as divine power and energy; and because πνεῦμα is neuter in Greek and its Hebrew counterpart feminine, no male principle is involved. The association of the pregnancy of Mary with the Holy Spirit must be from stage II of our narrative's history (cf. Lk 1.35).

21. This prophecy of future greatness, which may be compared

[31] Μαριαμ is found in ℵ C D W Z Θ f[13] Maj Eus, Μαριαν in B L f[1] 1241 pc. Cf. the variants for Rom 16.6.

[32] J. K. Kuntz, The Self-Revelation of God, Philadelphia, 1967, pp. 65–7; Conrad (v).

[33] Cf. L. Köhler, 'Die Offenbarungsformel "Fürchte dich nicht!" im Alten Testament', Schweizerische Theologische Zeitschrift 36 (1919), pp. 33–9.

with those concerning Moses, Buddha, Confucius, Augustus, and many other religious heroes, exhibits a form common to birth annunciation narratives:

Gen 16.11: σὺ ἐν γαστρὶ ἔχεις καὶ τέξῃ υἱὸν καὶ καλέσεις τὸ ὄνομα αὐτοῦ Ισμαηλ, ὅτι. . . .

Gen 17.19: ἡ γυνή σου τέξεταί σοι υἱόν, καὶ καλέσεις τὸ ὄνομα αὐτοῦ ᾿Ισαακ, καί. . . .

Isa 7.14: ἰδοὺ ἡ παρθένος ἐν γαστρὶ λήμψεται (or: ἕξει) καὶ τέξεται υἱόν, καὶ καλέσει(ς) τὸ ὄνομα αὐτοῦ ᾿Εμμανουήλ.

Lk 1.13: ἡ γυνή σου . . . γεννήσει υἱόν σοι καὶ καλέσεις τὸ ὄνομα αὐτοῦ ᾿Ιωάννην. καὶ. . . .

Lk 1.31: συλλήμψῃ ἐν γαστρὶ καὶ τέξῃ υἱὸν καὶ καλέσεις τὸ ὄνομα αὐτοῦ ᾿Ιησοῦν. οὗτος ἔσται. . . .

See also 1 Kgs 13.2 and LAB 42.3.

Stage I of our text's development probably contained only a notice that Joseph's son would deliver Israel.[34] In this Jesus would be like Moses (cf. LAB 9.10; Josephus, *Ant.* 2.216; *b. Soṭa* 12b). Stage II then introduced the formal annunciation of the name, which was perhaps influenced by Judg 13.5 or—more likely—Ps 129.8 LXX (cf. Lk 1.77; Tit 2.14).[35]

τέξεται δὲ υἱόν, καὶ καλέσεις τὸ ὄνομα αὐτοῦ ᾿Ιησοῦν. The future indicative serves as an imperative (cf. 5.43; 21.3; 27.4 and see BDF § 362). Joseph, the son of David, is being instructed by the angel to name Jesus and thereby accept him as his own. Jesus will therefore himself be a Davidid. Compare Isa 43.1: 'I have called you by name, you are mine'.

'As his name is, so is he' (1 Sam 25.25; cf. Mt 16.17–18). 'Jesus' is the Greek for the Hebrew 'Joshua' (*Yēšûa'*), which by popular etymology was related to the Hebrew verb 'to save' (*yšʿ*) and to the Hebrew noun 'salvation' (*yĕšûʿâ*). Thus the saving character of Jesus (cf. 8.25; 9.21–2; 14.30; 27.42) is aptly evoked by his name. Compare Ecclus 46.1; *b. Soṭa* 34b; *Num. Rab.* on 13.16. It is unnecessary to postulate a Hebrew source for this play on words. Matthew offers no clarification for his readers as he does in 1.23, and Philo (*Mut. nom.* 121) proves that the etymology of 'Joshua' was recognized outside Palestine. Beyond this, even Hellenistic Christianity would certainly have preserved the significance of Jesus' name (cf. Justin, *1 Apol.* 33.7; *2 Apol.* 6; Eusebius, *Dem. ev.* 4.10, 17; Epiphanius, *Haer.* 29.4).

[34] So also Bultmann, *History*, p. 292, and R. E. Brown, *Messiah*, p. 109.

[35] While Ps 129.8 LXX has ἀνομία and λυτροῦν, the latter could have become σῴζειν in order to make the etymological pun with 'Jesus' (see below); and the appearance of ἁμαρτία in Isa 53.5, 6, 10 and in primitive confessional statements (1 Cor 15.3; 1 Pet 3.18) may account for its preference, not to mention that ἁμαρτία (Mt: 7; Mk: 6; Lk: 11) is much more appropriate than ἀνομία because the evangelist uses the latter in polemics (7.23; 13.41; 23.28; 24.12).

Those who received their names directly from God were no doubt considered to be particularly important and righteous people; see *Mek*. on Exod. 13.2.

αὐτὸς γὰρ σώσει τὸν λαὸν αὐτοῦ ἀπὸ τῶν ἁμαρτιῶν αὐτῶν. The subject could admittedly be God (cf. Ps 130.8), especially as 'Jesus' might be rendered, 'Yahweh is salvation'. But Matthew will have thought of Jesus, for elsewhere he associates σῴζω with him, not with the Father. Furthermore, αὐτός, being nominative and juxtaposed to 'Jesus', is probably emphatic: 'it is *he* who will save . . . .'.

According to Luz 1, p. 105, 'his people' refers to the OT people of God, that is, Israel. In accordance with this suggestion, throughout our gospel λαός refers to the people of Israel (see on 4.23). Nevertheless, according to 21.43, 'the kingdom of God will be taken from you [the elders of the Jewish nation; see 21.23] and given to a people (ἔθνος) producing the fruits thereof'. So the majority of commentators are probably correct to identify 'his people' with the ecclesia of both Jew and Gentile.

Jesus saves his people 'from their sins'. This underlies the religious and moral—as opposed to political—character of the messianic deliverance. Liberation removes the wall of sin between God and the human race; nothing is said about freedom from the oppression of the governing powers (contrast Ps. Sol. 17). Beyond this, however, our verse is not very illuminating with regard to exactly *how* Jesus saves. The atoning death must be in view; but given the connexion in Matthew's world between sickness and sin (see on 9.2), Jesus' healing ministry could also be thought of as having saved people from their sins. Furthermore, Jesus' revelatory imperatives and abiding presence (18.20; 28.20) are salvific in so far as they encourage and enable believers to obtain the 'better righteousness' (5.20). Perhaps, then, Matthew thought that Jesus saved his people from their sins in a variety of ways.

Although in the OT forgiveness of sins is the prerogative of God alone, the final victory over sin and iniquity was sometimes in Judaism linked to an angelic or human leader, as in T. Levi 18.9 (priestly Messiah); 11QMelch. 2.6–8 (Melchizedek); 1 En. 10.20–2 (Michael the archangel); Tg. Isa on 53.4, 6–7 (the Messiah).

The passion already comes into the picture, for it is at the crucifixion that Jesus pours out his lifeblood εἰς ἄφεσιν ἁμαρτιῶν (26.28). Thus the entire gospel is to be read in the light of its end. In addition, 1.21 makes clear from the outset that, notwithstanding Matthew's insistent demand for human righteousness, salvation is the gift of God.[36] This fact will be reiterated in 20.28 and 26.28.

22. This verse contains the first of Matthew's formula

---

[36] Cf. Przybylski, pp. 106–7.

quotations, on which see the Excursus after 27.9–10. Compare
2.5–6, 15, 17, 23; 4.14; 8.17; 12.17; 13.35; 21.4; 26.54, 56; 27.9.
(There has been debate over exactly how many formula quotations
there really are; the status of 2.5–6 and of 26.54 and 56 is
uncertain.) An almost identical sentence occurs in 21.4, which
proves a redactional origin. Word statistics confirm this.[37]

Matthew's introductory formulas have a few parallels in the
LXX (3 Βασ 2.27; 8.15 = 2 Chr 6.4; 2 Chr 36.21–2) and the
Pseudepigrapha (T. Mos. 5.3) but none, interestingly enough, in
the Dead Sea Scrolls.[38] By way of contrast, πληρόω-formulas are
frequent in the NT, particularly in the gospels and Acts (cf. Mk
14.49; Jn 12.38; 13.18; 15.25; 17.12; 19.24; Acts 1.16). The early
church found in the Scriptures the declared will of divine
providence and believed that the life of Jesus in its every detail
completely fulfilled that will. Thus arose the NT's distinctive sense
of fulfilment and its distinctive πληρόω-formulas.[39]

It is difficult to decide whether Matthew intended the angel's
speech to include 1.22–3.[40] The parallel in 26.56 suggests that he
did (cf. also 2.5–6), as does the perfect tense, which well suits the
point of view of one involved: 'this all has happened'. But the NT
contains aoristic uses of the perfect (BDF § 343), and the parallel
in 21.4–5 as well as in other formula quotations (which are
obviously to be read as editorial remarks) are against extending
the quotation marks of 1.20–1 through 1.23.

τοῦτο δὲ ὅλον γέγονεν. Compare 24.2, 8, 33–4; 26.56; also 1 En.
67.6; Sib. Or. 3.91–2. The 'all' may contain theological content,
alluding to the universal providence of God, who 'knows all things
before they come to pass' (1 En. 9.11) and sees to it that 'everything
shall come and be fulfilled' (1 En. 90.41).

ἵνα πληρωθῇ. This expression (cf. lĕqāyêm) the evangelist took
over from his tradition, as is proved by Mk 14.49 and the parallels
in John (cited above). The passive implies God's activity (cf. Acts
3.18: 'what God foretold by the mouth of the prophets . . . he thus
fulfilled'). ἵνα is, for the evangelist, interchangeable with ὅπως (cf.
2.23; 8.17; 13.35; contrast Soares Prabhu, pp. 50–2).

---

[37] Matthew is fond of (ἵνα) πληρωθῇ (Mt: 9; Mk: 0; Lk: 1), of τοῦτο . . . γέγονεν
ἵνα (Mt: 3; Mk: 0; Lk: 0), of τὸ ῥηθέν (Mt: 12; Mk: 0; Lk: 0), and of διὰ τοῦ προφήτου
and similar constructions (Mt: 13; Mk: 0; Lk: 1).

[38] Lit.: B. M. Metzger, 'The Formulas Introducing Quotations of Scripture in the
New Testament and the Mishnah', JBL 70 (1951), pp. 297–307; J. Fitzmyer, 'The
Use of Explicit Old Testament Quotations in Qumran Literature and in the New
Testament', in Essays, pp. 3–58; Rothfuchs, pp. 27–56; Soares Prabhu, pp. 46–63;
and Moule (as in next note).

[39] Additional discussion in C. F. D. Moule, 'Fulfilment-Words in the New
Testament: Use and Abuse', NTS 14 (1968), pp. 293–320; in Essays, pp. 3–36.

[40] For an affirmative answer see Fenton (v). Cf. Irenaeus, Adv. haer. 4.23.1; Zahn,
p. 80.

τὸ ῥηθὲν ὑπὸ κυρίου διὰ τοῦ προφήτου λέγοντος.[41] For Matthew
the prophets spoke of the latter days, that is, of the time of Jesus
and his church. Note the passive construction (cf. *mah
šenne'ĕmar*). The word is truly spoken by God (ὑπὸ κυρίου). The
prophet is only a channel (διά). For διά (= *bĕyad*) used of the
prophets as intruments of God see Ezek 38.17; Dan 9.10; Ecclus
prologue 1; Lk 1.70. Compare also Lk 18.31; Acts 2.16; Rom 1.2.
The rabbis typically use 'through the hand of the prophet(s)'.

Why is the name of the prophet not mentioned? Contrast 2.17;
4.14; 8.17; 12.17; 13.35; and 27.9.[42] And why is ὑπὸ κυρίου used
here, as in 2.15? According to W. Rothfuchs, Matthew wanted
Isaiah's name associated with the salvific work of Jesus to the lost
house of Israel (cf. 4.14; 8.17; 12.17; 13.35), just as he wished to
associate the opposition of the Jewish authorities against the
Messiah and the resultant rejection with the prophet Jeremiah (cf.
2.17; 27.9). And because Isa 7.14 did not share the same theme as
the quotations in 4.14; 8.17; 12.7; and 13.35, Matthew did not find
it to his purpose to mention Isaiah by name, and, encouraged by
the frequency of κύριος in the infancy materials, chose instead to
write, 'of the Lord'.[43] R. Pesch has offered another solution.[44]
Because both of the scriptural quotations introduced by a formula
with ὑπὸ κυρίου have the word 'son' in them, we have here a
reflection of Matthew's Son of God Christology: the 'son' is the
Lord's Son. Of the two conjectures, that of Pesch seems the more
plausible. Matthew wants 'son' to be associated with God.

23. Although we have here to do with a Matthean insertion, the
evangelist was almost certainly not the first to find the fulfilment of
Isa 7.14 in Mary's conception of Jesus. The OT verse seems to have
influenced Lk 1.26–33; for even if Lk 1.31 has parallels outside of
Isa 7.14 (e.g. Gen 16.11; Judg 13.3), the description of Mary as a
'virgin', of Joseph as belonging to the 'house of David' (cf. Isa
7.13), and of Jesus as reigning 'over the house' (cf. Isa 7.17) make
dependence upon Isaiah's prophecy plain enough.[45]

At least three ends are served by the formula quotation. (1) It
offers scriptural confirmation for the extraordinary history
narrated in 1.18–25. Isaiah's words, which pertain to the house of
David and speak of a virgin, are intended to show that Jesus'
origin was according to the Scriptures. This is so important

[41] D *pc* it sy[s.(c).h] sa[ms] add Ησαιου, in conformity to Matthean usage elsewhere
(4.14; 8.17; 12.17; 13.14); but the omission is explicable in terms of redactional
motive; see above.

[42] The prophet's name is also missing in 2.15; 13.35; and 21.4, but in these texts 'of
the Lord' is missing (contrast 1.21 and 2.15).

[43] Rothfuchs, pp. 40–1.

[44] Pesch, 'Gottessohn' (v).

[45] Cf. Schürmann, *Lukasevangelium* 1, pp. 62–3, and Marshall, p. 66; contrast
Fitzmyer (v), p. 75, n. 89.

because it implicitly identifies and vindicates the church as the continuation of Israel; for if Jesus, whom the church confesses, has fulfilled the Scriptures, then Christians must be the true people of God. (2) The mention of Emmanuel gives Matthew one more christological title with which to work. This is consonant with his desire to open his work by telling us *who* Jesus is. It also permits a sort of *inclusio*. For just as 1.23 speaks of Jesus as 'God *with us*', so the gospel ends with the promise, 'I am *with you* always . . .' (28.20). (3) The notion of promise and fulfilment may to some extent be an apologetic. Matthew may be supplying believers with scriptural ammunition with which to enter into debate with the synagogue (cf. Justin, *Dial.* 43).

The location of 1.22–3 is a bit awkward. Placement after 1.25 would seem more natural. But the present order permits the redactor to conclude with an OT sentence form (see on 1.24–5). Also, coming as it does immediately after the command to name the child, the position of the citation would seem to indicate that Matthew is as interested in Joseph's naming of Jesus as he is in Mary's virginity.

Isa 7.14 was originally addressed to King Ahaz and perhaps prophesied the future coming of a Davidic king. Yet it is not certain that a royal person is in view. The force of the OT text could lie entirely with the name: 'Emmanuel' will be named because Yahweh will soon intervene for salvation and be with his people (cf. the naming of Hosea's children). However that may be, later Judaism apparently did not understand Isa 7.14 messianically; at least we have no positive evidence that it did. What Jewish traditions we do have connect the verse with Hezekiah (Justin, *Dial.* 43; *Exod. Rab.* on 12.29; *Num. Rab.* on 7.48). Thus the application of Isa 7.14 to the Messiah is evidently peculiarly Christian. (Although one should perhaps not forget that Hezekiah is, in some rabbinic texts, regarded as the Messiah; see on 1.9.)

ἰδοὺ ἡ παρθένος ἐν γαστρὶ ἕξει καὶ τέξεται υἱόν, καὶ καλέσουσιν τὸ ὄνομα αὐτοῦ Ἐμμανουήλ.[46] Matthew follows the LXX.[47] He reads ἕξει with א A Q, not λήμψεται as the rest of the LXX or συλλαμβάνει (so Aq., Sym., Theod.). The only other difference is the substitution of καλέσουσιν for καλέσεις (B A) or καλέσει (א). If this does not represent a textual variant no longer extant,[48] the plural could be put down to editorial licence. Matthew may simply have preferred an impersonal plural ('one will call . . .') because of his Semitic mind (cf. 5.15; 7.16; 9.17), or he may have preferred a

---

[46] καλεσουσιν becomes καλεσεις in D *pc* bo^mss Or Eus in order to bring the quotation into line with Isa 7.14 LXX and Lk 1.31.

[47] Stendahl, *School*, pp. 97–8; Gundry, *OT*, pp. 89–91; Rothfuchs, pp. 57–60; Soares Prabhu, pp. 229–53.

[48] So Gundry, *OT*, pp. 89–91. Cf. Brown, *Messiah*, p. 151.

plural because it is not Mary and Joseph but all those saved from their sins (1.21) who will call Jesus 'Emmanuel', the third person plural having for its subject the church (so Frankemölle, pp. 16–18).

παρθένος translates the Hebrew '*almâ* ('young maiden'), a little used word generally carrying the implication of virginity (exceptions in Ct 6.8; Prov 30.19).[49] *bĕtûlâ* is the normal Hebrew term for a virgin, although here too one may cite exceptions (*t. Nid.* 1.6; perhaps Joel 1.8; note the need for further qualification in Gen 24.16). παρθένος, the usual LXX translation of *bĕtûlâ*, stands for '*almâ* only in Gen 24.43 and Isa 7.14. (νεᾶνις, 'young girl', typically represents '*almâ*.) The chastity of the παρθένος, while ordinarily implied (as in Mt 25.1, 7, 11), is not always (Gen 34.3; LSJ, s.v.). Aquila, Symmachus, and Theodotion, who were presumably aware of the Christian reading, have νεᾶνις at Isa 7.14. For early Christian discussion of the meaning of παρθένος see Justin, *Dial.* 43; 77; Irenaeus, *Adv. haer.* 3.21.1 = Eusebius, *H.E.* 5.8.10; Origen, *C. Cels.* 1.34–5; Eusebius, *Dem. ev.* 7.1.

According to the MT, a 'young girl will conceive (or: "is with child"; the tense is ambiguous) and will bear a son'. According to the LXX, 'a virgin will conceive and will bear a son'. The LXX probably means only that she who is now a virgin will later conceive and give birth: no miracle is involved. If the MT be understood similarly, then the OT does not clearly foresee an event like that in Matthew. This, along with the lack of pre-Christian evidence for a messianic interpretation of Isa 7.14, offers some reason for concluding that reflection on Isaiah's prophecy was not a sufficient cause of belief in the virginal conception of Jesus.

If Isa 7.14 does not of itself suffice to explain the Christian story of Jesus' origin, there is no scholarly agreement as to what might. The pagan parallels so often listed—such as the fertilization of the mothers of the Pharaohs by Amon,[50] Io's being quickened by Zeus' breath (Aeschylus, *Supp.* 17–19), the begetting of Dionysus by Zeus (Diodorus Siculus 4.2.1), the supernatural origin of Romulus, son of Mars (Ovid, *Met.* 14.805–28; Plutarch, *Rom.* 2), the conception of Alexander the Great in the womb of his mother before the consummation of marriage (Plutarch, *Alex.* 2), the fathering of Plato by Apollo (Diogenes Laertius 3.2; Origen, *C. Cels.* 1.37)—all of these are of contested worth for a couple of reasons.[51]

[49] Discussion in M. Rehm, 'Das Wort '*almah* in Jes. 7.14', *BZ* 8 (1964), pp. 89–101.

[50] On this see Boslooper (v), pp. 165–7.

[51] See Boslooper (v), pp. 135–86. Contrast Bultmann, *History*, pp. 291–2, and H. Braun, 'The Meaning of New Testament Christology', in *God and Christ: Existence and Providence*, ed. Robert W. Funk and G. Ebeling, New York, 1968, pp. 100–4. In opposition to most of the Hellenistic accounts of miraculous conceptions or births, 'spirit' is neuter in Greek and feminine in Hebrew, and Mt 1.18–25 excludes

Conception without a male element in some form, parthenogenesis in the strict sense, does not seem to be attested. Beyond this, in narratives which breathe such a Jewish atmosphere as do Mt 1 and Lk 1–2, one prefers to seek for analogies in Judaism (even while recognizing it was Hellenized). Here too, however, the proposed parallels are of uncertain meaning. The possibility of impregnation by angels was believed in (1 En. 6–7; 1QapGen. 2; T. Sol. 5.3; Prot. Jas. 14.1), but this notion can have had little to do with our canonical infancy narratives, at least in their present form. The bizarre story of the miraculous conception and birth of Melchizedek at the end of some mss. of 2 Enoch (chapter 71), albeit intriguing, may be of relatively late origin; also, it neither has to do with a virgin nor does it mention a divine agent.[52] A divine begetting of the Davidic Messiah has been read out of 1QSa 2.11–12, but the text contains critical lacunae which can be filled in more than one way, and the context, treating of rules about blemishes and the arrangement of the messianic banquet, scarcely lends itself to a treatment of God's begetting the Messiah.[53] More worthy of consideration is the proposal that Philo's allegorical interpretation of the birth stories of the patriarchs (*Cher.* 40–52) is based upon a Hellenistic-Jewish legend about God's direct begetting of the Patriarchs. And Gal. 4.23 and 29 have been understood to presuppose this legend. Yet the investigation of P. Grelot has demonstrated how uncertain this initially attractive thesis really is, and Rom 9.6–13 hardly permits the required reading of Gal 4.23 and 29.[54] Lastly, D. Daube's brilliant conjecture that the Passover Haggadah interprets Exod 2.25 ('God saw the people of Israel and God *knew*') in a sexual sense (*yāda'* = both 'to know' and 'to have sexual intercourse with') and thereby attributes the conception of Moses to God's direct intervention remains an inviting possibility, despite its quick dismissal by most.[55] Even here, however,

intercourse of any kind and is reticent to offer details; cf. Bonnard, pp. 18–19. To the lists of parallels so often cited, add Apoc. Adam 7.9–12, from Nag Hammadi: 'The third kingdom says of him, "He came from a virgin womb. He was cast out of his city, he and his mother; he was taken to a desert place. He was nourished there. He came and received glory and power. And thus he came to the water' (cf. also 7.13–16 and 31–4).

[52] But note C. H. Talbert, 'The Myth of the Descending-Ascending Redeemer in Mediterranean Antiquity', *NTS* 22 (1976), p. 426, n. 1. He affirms a non-Christian and at least first-century origin. F. I. Anderson, in Charlesworth 1, pp. 96–7, agrees that the story cannot be Christian, but he does not offer to date it.

[53] Discussion in R. Gordis, 'The "Begotten" Messiah in the Qumran Scrolls', *VT* 7 (1957), pp. 191–4; M. Smith, ' "God's Begetting the Messiah" in 1QSa', *NTS* 5 (1959), pp. 218–24; O. Michel and O. Betz, 'Von Gott gezeugt', in Eltester, pp. 3–23; E. F. Sutcliffe, 'The Rule of the Congregation (1QSa) II, 11–12: Text and Meaning', *RevQ* 2 (1960), pp. 541–7; O. Michel and O. Betz, 'Nocheinmal: "Von Gott gezeugt" ', *NTS* 9 (1962–3), pp. 129–30.

[54] P. Grelot, 'La naissance d'Isaac et celle je Jésus: Sur une interprétation "mythologique" de la conception virginale', *NRT* 94 (1972), pp. 462–87, 561–85. Contrast M. Dibelius, 'Jungfrauensohn und Krippenkind. Untersuchungen zur Geburtsgeschichte Jesu im Lukas-Evangelium', in *Botschaft und Geschichte*, Tübingen, 1953, 1, pp. 25–34, and Fuller, *Christology*, pp. 195–6, 202. For the discussion before Dibelius see J. G. Machen, *The Virgin Birth of Christ*, New York, 1930, pp. 297–309.

[55] Daube, pp. 5–9. Cf. Davies, *SSM*, pp. 63–4, 81–2.

reservations must be expressed. The proposed interpretation is not explicit in any extant Jewish source; the genuine paternity of Amram is assumed not only by Josephus (*Ant.* 2. 210–23) but also by the first century Liber Antiquitatum Biblicarum, a source rich in Moses birth legends; and no *virginal* conception could be involved in any event, for Miriam and Aaron were older than Moses.

None of the proposed parallels, either pagan or Jewish, seemingly accounts for the story we find in the NT. Because of this, some have considered the possibility of an historical catalyst. If, for instance, Mary did indeed, as both Matthew and Luke have it, conceive in advance of her marriage to Joseph, this potentially embarrassing fact might have been given a supernatural interpretation, with Isa 7.14 in mind.[56] The story might also have arisen as a response to polemic about Jesus' origins. Or, if one is predisposed to find a genuine miracle in the birth of Jesus, appeal could be made to the idea of a 'family secret': Mary, who 'kept all these things, pondering them in her heart' (Lk 2.19), could be the ultimate source of the account of Jesus' extraordinary entry into history.[57] But this proposal raises difficult problems of its own, even apart from the question of the miraculous (see below).

It is, certainly, the doubtful character and meagre number of the extant sources and the limitations of historical research in general which disallow a final verdict on the issue at hand. The origin of belief in the virginal conception and birth of Jesus remains unclarified. Yet, this being said, it should be plainly stated that to say that no satisfactory mundane explanation has so far procured a critical consensus is not to say that the historical evidence clearly confirms the miraculous conception of Jesus. The apparent silence of most of the NT, particularly Mark and John and Paul, the number of possible even though imperfect parallels in the history of religion, the fact that Mary and her family show no special understanding of Jesus during the ministry, and the non-historicity of so much in the infancy narratives all point rather strongly in one direction: affirmation of the virgin birth entangles one in difficult dilemmas. Hence if the traditional belief be maintained, it will have to be on the basis of strictly theological considerations; historical reasoning offers little support.

(It is important to note that parthenogenesis, that is, the derivation of offspring from a female only, is not unknown among primitive forms of life. Though the birth of a male from a female only raises formidable difficulties, as far as the world of science is concerned, we are here dealing not so much with impossibilities as extreme improbabilities. Parthenogenesis does occur in very small and simple forms of animals and

---

[56] So e.g. M. Smith, *Magician*, pp. 26–7.

[57] This is the opinion of Reicke (v), and many have held it. For critical discussion see Brown, *Messiah*, pp. 525–6, and Vögtle, *Evangelium*, pp. 43–56. Luz 1, p. 102, n. 25, observes that the report of the supernatural begetting of Plato by Apollo was purported to have come from members of Plato's own family (Diogenes Laertius 3.2). For attempts to uphold the basic historicity of the infancy narratives see the works of Laurentin (v); also Schmid, *Matthäus*, pp. 53–5; Stauffer, pp. 13–41; McHugh (v), pp. 3–247; and A. Feuillet, *Jesus and His Mother* (trans. of *Jésus et sa Mère*, 1974), Still River, 1984, pp. 67–78, 140–71.

plants: the highest form on which there is a record of parthenogenesis is the lizard.)

ὅ ἐστιν μεθερμηνευόμενον. This phrase (which is not found in the LXX) may be taken over from Mk 5.41; 15.22 and 34, although Matthew has it only here. Compare Jn 1.41; Acts 4.36; and LAB 6.18 ('And they called that place by the name of Abram, and in the tongue of the Chaldeans Deli, which is, being interpreted, God').

μεθ' ἡμῶν ὁ θεός. These words are from Isa 8.8 LXX (cf. 8.10) and translate the '*immānû ʼēl*(= 'God is with us') of Isa 7.14. For early Christian gematria on the name, Emmanuel, see T. Sol. 6.8; 11.6; 15.11. Matthew's interpretation has been taken in two different ways. Either the evangelist is calling Jesus 'God' (cf. Jn 1.1–5; 20.28), or he is bringing out his significance as one in whom God's active presence, that is, the divine favour and blessing and aid, have manifested themselves. In support of the first alternative these facts may be cited:[58] (1) The presence of Jesus *with* his disciples is a Matthean theme (cf. 18.20; 25.31–46; 28.20).[59] God the Father, by way of contrast, is spoken of as being in heaven (6.9, etc.). (2) If 1.23 matches 28.20, then the ἐγώ of the latter appears to correspond to the θεός of the former. (3) μετά with the genitive in Matthew almost always means 'in the company of' (e.g. 2.11; 5.25; 8.11; 9.15; 12.3; 16.27) and so applies more easily to the Son than to the Father. (4) Irenaeus read Mt 1.23 as making Jesus God (*Adv. haer.* 3.21.4). Despite these arguments, one may do right to follow the other line of interpretation. (1) The NT rarely if ever calls Jesus 'God'.[60] Matthew never does so, if 1.23 be left aside. (2) The evangelist could have believed Jesus to be the fullest embodiment or vehicle of the divine purpose and love and yet have perceived him as less than God (cf. Lk 1.68; 7.16; Mt 11.25–30). (3) If ὁ θεός were a predicate of Jesus, we might expect to read, Ἐμμανουήλ . . . ὁ θεός μεθ' ἡμῶν. What we in fact find is, following the order of the Hebrew, Ἐμμανουήλ . . . μεθ' ἡμῶν ὁ θεός. The μεθ' ἡμῶν is probably adverbial; hence we should translate, 'with us is God', not 'God with us'. (While the passage is not 'Incarnational' in its intent in the sense that it posits a pre-existent being, the Son, who took flesh, it does, in a more general sense, indicate that through the coming of Jesus Christ God's Spirit became uniquely present among men.)

Does Jesus, by being Emmanuel, bring an eschatological

[58] For what follows see Fenton (v).

[59] See esp. Frankemölle, passim, and J. A. Ziesler, 'Matthew and the Presence of Jesus', *Epworth Review* 11 (1984), pp. 55–63, 90–7.

[60] Discussion in Cullmann, *Christology*, pp. 306–14; R. E. Brown, *Jesus God and Man*, New York, 1967, pp. 1–38; B. A. Mastin, 'A Neglected Feature of the Christology of the Fourth Gospel', *NTS* 22 (1975), pp. 32–51.

expectation to fulfilment? According to Jewish tradition, while God had been 'with' his people in the past (e.g. Num 23.21; Deut 2.7), he would, it was hoped, be especially 'with' them in messianic times (Isa 43.5; Ezek 34.30; 37.27; Zech 8.23; 11QTemple 29.7–10; Jub. 1.17, 26; Rev 21.3).

24. This verse and the next constitute a redactional enlargement of what before Matthew may have been only an indefinite notice of the fulfilment of the angelic command ('Joseph then did as the angel commanded'). In any case, in the text before us Joseph (1) rises and (2) does (ἐποίησεν) as the angel of the Lord has commanded (προσέταξεν) him; specifically, he (3) takes Mary his wife (see on 1.20), does not have relations with her until she gives birth to a son, and calls the child's name Jesus. Compare 21.6: the disciples (1) go and (2) do (ποιήσαντες) as Jesus has commanded (προσέταξεν or συνέταξεν) them; specifically, they (3) bring the ass and the colt, put their garments upon them, and then Jesus sits thereon. These two sentences exhibit a form found in the OT.[61] In Exod 7.10, for instance, Moses and Aaron (1) go before Pharaoh and his servants and (2) do (ἐποίησαν) just as the Lord has commanded (ἐνετείλατο) them; specifically, (3) Aaron throws down his rod before Pharaoh and his servants and it becomes a dragon. Matthew, in employing the OT sentence form, wishes to show first Joseph's perfect obedience and secondly the complete fulfilment of the divine words spoken through the angel and through Scripture. Because the angel told him to, Joseph takes his wife, Mary. Because, according to Isa 7.14, a virgin will bear a son, Joseph does not have relations with Mary until she delivers. And, because the angel has given him the name, Joseph calls his child 'Jesus'. The content of 1.20–3 determines the conduct of Joseph in 1.24–5.

ἐγερθεὶς δὲ ὁ Ἰωσὴφ ἀπὸ τοῦ ὕπνου ἐποίησεν ὡς προσέταξεν αὐτῷ ὁ ἄγγελος κυρίου.[62] Compare Judg 16.14 LXX A. Matthew likes ἐγείρω (Mt: 36; Mk: 19; Lk: 18), especially the form ἐγερθείς, which is absent from the LXX (Mt: 8–9; Mk: 0; Lk: 1). The biblical tradition has a habit of observing that visionaries arise or stand up after a divine encounter (e.g. Ezek 2.1–2; Dan 8.27; Lk 1.39; 4 Ezra 10.30; Apoc. Abr. 11.1). On 'the angel of the Lord' see on 1.20.

καὶ παρέλαβεν τὴν γυναῖκα αὐτοῦ. The vocabulary is from 1.20. Joseph no longer fears to take Mary to wife. The angelic annunciation has removed his doubts.

[61] Pesch, 'Ausführungsformel' (v).

[62] εγερθεις appears in ℵ B C* Z 071 f¹ pc Epiph. The substitution of διεγερθεις in C³ D L W 087 f¹³ Maj, which is preferred by HG, breaks the parallel with 2.13 and 19, and the longer word appears nowhere else in the First Gospel. HG is also probably mistaken in not printing the definite article before Ιωσηφ. NA²⁶ prints it on the authority of B C D L W f¹ Maj. It is omitted by ℵ K Z Γ Δ f¹³ 28 565 (700) 1241 al.

25. καὶ οὐκ ἐγίνωσκεν αὐτὴν ἕως οὗ ἔτεκεν υἱόν.[63] This retrospective observation does not necessarily imply that there were marital relations later on, for ἕως following a negative need not contain the idea of a limit which terminates the preceding action or state (cf. Gen 49.10 LXX; Mt 10.23; Mk 9.1). At the same time, had Matthew held to Mary's perpetual virginity (as did the second-century author of Prot. Jas. 19.3–20.2), he would almost certainly have chosen a less ambiguous expression—just as Luke would have avoided 'first-born son' (2.7).[64] See further on 12.46; 13.55–6; and compare Diogenes Laertius 3.1.2 on the father of Plato, who was not an only child: ὅθεν καθαρὰν γάμου φυλάξαι ἕως τῆς ἀποκυήσεως. 'To know' was a euphemism for sexual intercourse in both the Greek and Jewish worlds (Heraclides, *Pol.* 64; Gen 4.1; Lk 1.34; *b. Yeb.* 57a).

Note that the verb τίκτω is in the aorist tense. Contrast 1.21 and 1.23. Promise has become fulfilment.

καὶ ἐκάλεσεν τὸ ὄνομα αὐτοῦ Ἰησοῦν. This repeats verbatim part of 1.21, save that the second person future indicative is now a third person aorist. The correlation between the angel's words and Joseph's obedience is thereby underlined; and, again, promise has become fulfilment.

(iv) *Concluding Observations*

(1) Mt 1 is, as K. Stendahl (v) has rightly argued, largely designed to announce *who* Jesus is. The title (1.1) and the genealogy (1.2–17) proclaim Jesus to be the Messiah, the Son of David, and the son of Abraham—in sum, the *telos* of Israel's history. 1.18–25 continues the piling up of appellations and general descriptions. 'The Messiah is Emmanuel, "with us is God".' He is the bearer of a name given by the angel of the Lord, Jesus, and he shall save his people from their sins. He is a true Davidid, the legal son of a Davidid, and his birth means the fulfilment of the promise made to the house of David in Isa. 7.14. He is, finally, one 'conceived by the Holy Spirit' (1.20; cf. 1.18); in other words, his origin is with God.

(2) This last point, the supernatural conception of Jesus, brings us to what must be regarded as the second major thrust of 1.18–25. Jesus is at once descended from David and conceived of the Holy Spirit. *How* can this be?[65] How can a son of David also be ἐκ θεοῦ (Ignatius, *Eph.* 7.2)? Matthew, obviously, has contemplated this

---

[63] k sy^s omit the clause, 'did not know her until', in order to remove any hint that the couple later had sexual relations. See the discussion in Globe (v), pp. 62–3.

[64] Contra Bulcke (v). Further discussion on Vögtle, 'Mt 1,25' (v).

[65] For the addition of a 'how' to Stendahl's 'what' see Paul, p. 96, and R. E. Brown, *Messiah*, pp. 53–4.

puzzle, and he has an answer. Through his father Jesus is the Son of David. Through his mother and the Holy Spirit he has a more exalted origin. Davidic sonship is a legal sonship which does not demand biological descent. All that is required is that his mother's husband, a Davidid, acknowledge Jesus as his own (cf. *m. B. Bat.* 8.6). This Joseph does when he chooses to remain with Mary and give Jesus his name. Divine sonship comes about in a different way. Jesus has a biological mother but no biological father. He is 'conceived of the Holy Ghost, born of the Virgin Mary'. Therefore his 'genesis' is from above, he is 'fathered' by God himself.

(3) In addition to answering the questions, 'Who?' and 'How?', there must be some justice in the supposition that 1.18–25 has an apologetical intent.[66] All presumption favours assuming that already in Matthew's time Mary's purported virginal conception by the Holy Spirit had been seized upon by outsiders and turned into calumny.[67] Certainly there was slander later on (Acts Pilate 2.3; Origen, *C. Cels.* 1.28, 32; Tertullian, *Spec.* 30; SB 1, pp. 36–43, and Mt 27.62–6; 28.11–15 proves the existence at the end of the first century of Jewish polemic which had Christian tradition as its point of departure.[68] How then did the evangelist respond to the aspersions against Jesus' origin? (We must also not overlook the possibility that some Christians known to Matthew found the story unbelievable or difficult; cf. Justin, *Dial.* 48; Irenaeus, *Adv. haer.* 3.21.1; Eusebius, *H.E.* 3.27.)[69] 1.18–25 musters a two-pronged defence. First, appeal is made to the character of Jesus' father. Joseph was, we are told, a man of strict religious principle. He was, in fact, prepared to divorce his betrothed. If he refrained from so doing, that was only because of divine intervention: it was revealed to him that his wife had done no wrong, that she had conceived by the Holy Spirit. Hence the uprightness of Joseph testifies against an immoral situation. Secondly, appeal is made to the Tanak, which becomes an

[66] According to Soares Prabhu, pp. 16–17, 296, Matthew's source had an apologetical aim but this is something Matthew himself did not develop.

[67] Although the virginal conception is seemingly unattested in the NT outside Matthew and Luke, Ignatius at the beginning of the second century seems to have known it as part of the christological kerygma: *Smyr.* 1.1–2; *Eph.* 18.2–19.1; cf. Bousset, p. 343. This means that the story of Jesus' miraculous birth could have been known to Jews in Matthew's time.

[68] By way of comparison, libel about the descent of the seventeenth-century Jewish Messiah, Sabbatai Ṣevi, circulated already during Ṣevi's own lifetime; cf. Scholem, p. 107. It is possible that non-Christian rumours of the illegitimacy of Jesus' birth circulated even before the Christian story of the virgin birth was generally known.

[69] On the rejection of the virgin birth by Jewish Christians see Schoeps, *Theologie*, pp. 71–8.

apologetic shield for faith. Did not Isaiah prophesy that one from the house of David would be born of a virgin mother? To doubt the story passed on in Mt 1.18–25 would be, in Matthew's eyes, to doubt the authoritative oracles of the OT.

(4) An anti-docetic aim has been discerned in Mt. 1.18–25.[70] In favour of this proposal is the way in which Ignatius, early in the second century, refuted what he took to be the dangers of docetic heresy by calling attention to Jesus' being 'the child of Mary' (e.g. *Trall.* 9.1). On the other hand, there seems to be no anti-docetic apologetic elsewhere in the First Gospel. Neither is such an apologetic likely to have been to the fore in stage I or II of our narrative's history. In these stages other interests predominate.

(5) Matthew, we can be sure, believed in the virginal conception of Jesus. This fact, however, does not tell us whether he thought of his infancy narrative as being solid, sober history. The issue, of course, admits of no straightforward resolution, in part because Matthew's thoughts are not our thoughts: he could hardly have operated with modern ideas of history and fiction. Nonetheless it is worth asking, Did Matthew not recognize the haggadic, indeed the poetic, character of his narrative? The rabbis were quite capable of making up stories when it suited their purposes (cf. *b. B. Meṣ.* 59b; *b. Sanh.* 98a; *b. Ta'an.* 21b–22a; *b. 'Abod. Zar.* 17a); and if our author knew—as he must have—that Jesus' parables, unlike, let us say, the passion narrative, were in no way historical, he would have been able, in at least some rudimentary fashion, to understand the distinction between fact and edifying fiction. But, unfortunately, this is as far as we can go. Whether Matthew was persuaded that his infancy traditions, with their many parallels in the haggadic traditions about Moses, were more poetry than prose, how could one decide? Here words of Josef Pieper are pertinent: 'Anyone who treats the charged expressions encountered in cultural history exclusively from the "historical standpoint" is in that very measure incapable of genuine interpretation.'[71]

(We are aware—and the NT editor of this series, Dr. Cranfield, has reminded us of this—that other competent critical scholars are firmly convinced of the historicity of the Virginal Conception, though not, of course, supposing that it can be conclusively proved by historical-critical methods, and that careful attention should be paid to their discussions of the relevant evidence as well as to the view expressed here.)

---

[70] E.g. Bacon, pp. 149–50, and Wickings (v).
[71] Cited by Ben F. Meyer in *Theological Studies* 47 (1986), p. 382.

(v) *Bibliography*

K. Barth, *CD* I/2, pp. 172–202.

H. Boers, 'Language Usage and the Production of Matthew 1:18–2:23', in *Orientation by Disorientation*, ed. R. A. Spencer, Pittsburgh, 1980, pp. 217–33.

T. Boslooper, *The Virgin Birth*, Philadelphia, 1962.

I. Broer, 'Die Bedeutung der "Jungfrauengeburt" im Matthäusevangelium', *BuL* 12 (1971), pp. 248–60.

R. E. Brown, *Messiah*, pp. 122–64, 517–46.

idem, *The Virginal Conception and Bodily Resurrection of Jesus*, New York, 1973.

M. Bulcke, 'The Translator's Theology. A response to "Taking Theology Seriously in the Translation Task" ', *BT* 35 (1984), pp. 134–5.

L. Cantwell, 'The Parentage of Jesus', *NovT* 24 (1982), pp. 304–15.

E. W. Conrad, 'The Annunciation of Birth and the Birth of the Messiah', *CBQ* 47 (1985), pp. 656–63.

Descamps, *Justes*, pp. 34–7.

A. M. Dubarle, 'La conception virginale et la citation d'Is., VII, 14 dans l'Évangile de Matthieu', *RivB* 85 (1978), pp. 362–80.

M. S. Enslin, 'The Christian Stories of the Nativity', *JBL* 59 (1940), pp. 317–38.

J. C. Fenton, 'Matthew and the Divinity of Jesus: Three questions concerning Matthew 1:20–3', in Livingstone, pp. 79–82.

J. Fitzmyer, 'The Virginal Conception of Jesus in the New Testament', in *Advance*, pp. 41–78.

J. M. Ford, 'Mary's Virginitas Post-Partum and Jewish Law', *Bib* 54 (1973), pp. 269–72.

Frankemölle, pp. 12–21.

R. H. Fuller, 'The Virgin Birth: Historical Fact or Kerygmatic Truth?', *BR* 1 (1956), pp. 1–8.

A. Globe, 'Some Doctrinal Variants in Matthew 1 and Luke 2 and the Authority of the Neutral Text', *CBQ* 42 (1980), pp. 52–72.

J. M. Graystone, 'Matthieu 1:18–25. Essai d'interprétation', *RTP* 23 (1973), pp. 221–32.

H. Hendrickx, *The Infancy Narratives*, London, 1984.

D. Hill, 'A Note on Matthew i. 19', *ExpT* 76 (1964–5), pp. 133–4.

P. P. A. Kotze, 'The Structure of Matthew One', *Neotestamentica* 11 (1977), pp. 1–9.

M. Krämer, 'Die globale Analyse des Stiles in Mt 1, 18–25' *Bib* 45 (1964), pp. 4–22.

idem, 'Die Menschwerdung Jesu Christi nach Matthäus (Mt 1)', *Bib* 45 (1964), pp. 1–50.

S. T. Lachs, 'Studies in the Semitic Background to the Gospel of Matthew', *NovT* 17 (1977), pp. 195–217.

J. Lagrand, 'How was the Virgin Mary "Like a Man" (*'yk gbr*')? A note on Mt. 1.18b and Related Syriac Christian Texts', *NovT* 22 (1980), pp. 97–107.

R. Laurentin, *Les Évangiles de l'Enfance du Christ*, 2nd ed., Paris, 1982.

idem, 'Vérité des Évangiles de l'enfance', *NRT* 105 (1983), pp. 691–710.

X. Léon-Dufour, 'L'annonce à Joseph', in *Études*, pp. 65–81.

J. McHugh, *The Mother of Jesus in the New Testament*, Garden City, 1975, pp. 157–72, 269–329.

A. Milavec, 'Matthew's Integration of Sexual and Divine Begetting', *BTB* 8 (1978), pp. 108–16.

M. Miyoshi, 'Zur Entstehung des Glaubens an die jungfräuliche Geburt Jesu in Mt 1 und Lk 1', *AJBI* 10 (1984), pp. 33–62.

Nolan, pp. 24–8, 58–63, 116–19, 203–4.

Paul, pp. 45–94.

A. Pelletier, 'L'annonce à Joseph', *RSR* 54 (1966), pp. 67–8.

R. Pesch, 'Eine alttestamentliche Ausführungsformel im Matthäus-Evangelium', *BZ* 10 (1966), pp. 220–45; 11 (1967), pp. 79–95.

idem, 'Der Gottessohn im matthäischen Evangelienprolog (Mt 1–2). Beobachtungen zu den Zitationsformeln der Reflexionzitate', *Bib* 48 (1967), pp. 395–420.

idem, ed., *Zur Theologie der Kindheitsgeschichten. Der heutige Stand der Exegese*, München, 1981.

H. Pirlot, *L'analyse littéraire de Mt. I, 18–25*, Louvain, 1966.

J. H. Raatschen, 'Empfangen durch den Heiligen Geist. Überlegungen zu Mt 1,18–25', *TB* 11 (1980), pp. 262–77.

B. Reicke, 'Christ's Birth and Childhood', in *From Faith to Faith*, PTMS 31, ed. D. Y. Hadidian, Pittsburgh, 1979, pp. 151–65.

K. Romaniuk, ' "Joseph, son époux, qui était un homme juste et ne voulait pas la dénoncer . . ." (Mt 1.19)', *Collectanea Theologica* 50 (1980), pp. 123–31.

F. Schnider and W. Stenger, ' "Mit der Abstammung Jesu Christi verhielt es sich so: . . ." ', *BZ* 25 (1981), pp. 225–64.

Soares Prabhu, pp. 176–80, 229–53.

C. Spicq, ' "Joseph, son mari, étant juste . . ." (Mt., I, 19)', *RB* 71 (1964), pp. 206–14.

Stauffer, pp. 15–18.

idem, 'Jeschu ben Mirjam', in E. E. Ellis and M. Wilcox, eds., *Neotestamentica et Semitica*, Edinburgh, 1969, pp. 119–28.

K. Stendahl, 'Quis et Unde? An Analysis of Mt 1–2', in Eltester, pp. 97–105.

V. Taylor, *The Historical Evidence for the Virgin Birth*, Oxford, 1920.

A. Tosato, 'Joseph, Being a Just Man (Matt 1:19)', *CBQ* 41 (1979), pp. 547–51.

A. Vögtle, *Messias und Gottessohn. Herkunft und Sinn der matthäischen Geburts- und Kindheitsgeschichte*, Düsseldorf, 1971.

idem, 'Mt 1,25 und die Virginitas B. M. Virginis post partum', *TQ* 147 (1967), pp. 28–39.

H. F. Wickings, 'The Nativity Stories and Docetism', *NTS* 23 (1977), pp. 457–60.

J. T. Willis, 'The Meaning of Isaiah 7:14 and Its Application in Matthew', *RestQ* 21 (1978), pp. 1–18.

IV

MAGI FROM THE EAST: GENTILES HONOUR THE NEW-BORN KING
(2.1–12)

(i) *Structure*

Mt 2.1–12, the second of the three acts comprising Matthew's infancy drama, begins with the magi's arrival and ends with their departure. For convenience it can be divided into six short scenes.[1]

A. The magi from the east come to Judea, looking for the king of the Jews (2.1–2)

B. Herod, hearing of this, asks and learns from the chief priests and scribes where the Messiah is to be born (2.3–6)

C. Herod divulges the information to the wise men and asks for their co-operation (2.7–8)

D. The magi follow a star to Bethlehem (2.9–10)

E. The magi pay homage to the child and offer him precious gifts (2.11)

F. The magi, being warned in a dream not to return to Herod, leave Bethlehem (2.12)

Scene A finds the magi in Jerusalem, and scenes B and C take place there. Scene D brings them to Bethlehem, and scenes E and F take place there.

It is common to divide chapter 2 into five sections and to claim that each section has as its conclusion a reference to the Scriptures: 2.1–6, 7–12, 13–15, 16–18, 19–23.[2] Such a division is problematic. (1) The allusions to Ps 72.10–11 and Isa 60.6 in 2.11 are hardly comparable with the explicit formula quotations in 2.6, 15, 18, and 23. (2) The unity of 2.1–12 is wrongly obscured when a major break is drawn between verses 6 and 7. (3) Just as 2.1–6 and 7–12, because they both have to do with the magi, naturally go together, so do 2.13–15, 16–18, and 19–23, because they all concern Herod and the threat to infants, constitute one piece. Thus the major break in chapter 2 comes between 2.1–12 and 13–23, and any analysis that does not underline this must be suspect.[3]

---

[1] Cf. Lohmeyer, *Matthäus*, p. 19.

[2] See Fenton, pp. 44–51, following the paragraph divisions of the RSV; Hengel and Merkel (v), pp. 141–2.

[3] Cf. Brown, *Messiah*, pp. 178–9. Although he finds five scenes in 2.1–12 (1–6, 7–12, 13–15, 16–18, 19–23), he rightly divides the section into two acts, 1–12 and

(ii) *Sources*

Concerning sources, elements from the original magi story have been preserved in scenes A, D, and E (2.1–2, 9–11), and scene B (2.3–6) still contains pieces of the story in which Herod was modelled upon Pharaoh (stage I). Scenes C and F (2.7–8, 12) represent expansions necessitated by the joining of stories at stage II. See Excursus I.

(iii) *Exegesis*

1. In chapters 1–2 the evangelist is concerned with events preceding and following the birth of Jesus; that is, he is interested in the circumstances surrounding Jesus' conception and entrance into the Davidic line (1.1–25) and with people's response to the advent of the child Messiah (2.1–23). The birth itself is mentioned only in passing (1.25). This makes for a striking contrast with the later apocryphal infancy narratives.

τοῦ δὲ Ἰησοῦ γεννηθέντος ἐν Βηθλέεμ τῆς Ἰουδαίας. Again Matthew opens with a genitive absolute (cf. 1.18). This permits the word order to link 2.1ff. with the preceding paragraph: Ἰησοῦν/τοῦ δὲ Ἰησοῦ. Compare how 1.18–25 is linked to 1.2–17 by 'Christ'.

The passive γεννηθέντος recalls the passive uses of γεννάω in 1.16 and 20. In the latter two instances the verb denotes 'conception' or 'birth'. Here 'birth' is clearly signified.

'In Bethlehem' (cf. Lk 2.4, 15) is from stage II of the tradition, where Mic 5.2, although not explicitly cited, was presupposed. The close link between Bethlehem and Davidic sonship can be seen from Jn 7.42: 'Does not the Scripture say that the Christ comes from the seed of David and from Bethlehem, the village where David was?'

13–23. Another way of approaching the structure of 2.1–12 is to see it as part of a larger section which has its structural twin in 27.57–28.20:

Joseph	1.18–25	Jesus	27.57–61
Herod	2.1–12	guard	27.62–6
Joseph	2.13–15	Jesus	28.1–10
Herod	2.16–18	guard	28.11–15
Joseph	2.19–23	Jesus	28.16–20

See J. C. Fenton, 'Inclusio and Chiasmus in Matthew', in *Studia Evangelica I*, ed. F. L. Cross, TU 73, Berlin, 1959, pp. 174–9; cf. Nolan, p. 107. One can even add to the structural parallel thematic parallels: the motif of Jewish blindness, the revelation of angels, the worshipping of Jesus. Perhaps the major problem with this analysis is that 2.1–12 is firstly about the magi, not Herod. Herod is in fact altogether absent from 2.9–12. In addition, Jesus is no more closely associated with 27.57–61 (which is about Joseph of Arimathea) than he is with 27.62–6.

Bêt(-)leḥem, where David was brought up and anointed king of Israel (1 Sam 16.1–13; cf. 17.12, 15, 58; 20.6, 28), was a Judean village located about five or six miles (Josephus, *Ant.* 7.312, incorrectly has 20 stades = 2½ miles) south-southwest of Jerusalem. Its importance in the OT, where it is usually called 'the city of David', derives principally from its association with King David. It is also where the story of Ruth (cf. Mt 1.5) is set. The town appears only rarely in later Jewish literature (e.g. Demetrius in Eusebius, *Praep. ev.* 9.21; Asc. Isa. 2.7, 8, 12; 3.1)—perhaps in response to Christian claims for it (cf. Origen, *C. Cels.* 1.51). Despite Mic 5.2; Mt 2.5; and Jn 7.42, it is uncertain to what degree Jewish opinion looked to Bethlehem as the Messiah's birthplace. The targum on Mic. 5.2 mentions the Messiah (cf. Tg Ps.-J. on Gen 35.21), but rabbinic sources generally supply only scanty and late evidence (*y. Ber.* 2.4.5a; *Lam. Rab.* on 1.16), and the Psalms of Solomon fail to mention the city of David. All this, along with Jn 7.27 ('when the Messiah appears, no one will know where he comes from'), makes possible the supposition of C. H. Dodd: 'so far from the Nativity stories in Matthew and Luke having been composed for apologetic purposes, in order to meet a generally held belief that the Messiah must be born in Bethlehem, it was the fact that Jesus was actually born there that revived in Christian circles interest in a prophecy which played little part in contemporary Jewish thought'.[4] On the other hand, only the infancy materials in the First and Third Gospels put Jesus' parents in Bethlehem, and they do not agree on the details. In Luke, Joseph and Mary are visiting the city when Jesus is born. In Matthew they are living there. The rest of the NT may presuppose Nazareth as Jesus' place of birth (Mk 6.1,4; Jn 1.46; 7.41, 52). Further, had Jesus in fact been born in Bethlehem, would not the NT have perhaps got more service out of the prophecy in Micah? Finally, Jewish tradition makes Bethlehem the birth home of the messianic child, Menaḥem b. Hezekiah (*y. Ber.* 2.4.5a). This, as has been suggested, might reflect an old report concerning the rebel leader Menaḥem (Josephus, *Bell.* 2.433–48), a report against the facts, an attempt by someone to validate Menaḥem's messianic credentials.[5] In any case, one must reckon seriously with the possibility that the placement of Jesus' birth in the city of David owes more to apologetics than history.[6]

The purpose of the qualification, 'of Judea' (cf. 2.5), could be to make it quite clear that Bethlehem in the south is meant, not the Bethlehem in Zebulun seven miles north-west of Nazareth (cf. Josh 19.15). But Matthew elsewhere adds the superfluous 'of Galilee' to 'Nazareth' (21.11—there was no other Nazareth), and in Jn 7.42 Bethlehem needs no qualification (cf. Lk 2.4). Perhaps, then, 'of Judea' stresses that the birth of 'the king of the Jews' (τῶν Ἰουδαίων) took place in a city of Judea (τῆς Ἰουδαίας), the land of the tribe of Judah (Ἰούδα; cf. 1.2–3). Or maybe it helps determine

---

[4] *Interpretation*, p. 91. Cf. M. Wilcox, 'Jesus in the Light of His Environment', *ANRW* II.25.1 (1982), pp. 142–3.

[5] So e.g. Jeremias, *Jerusalem*, p. 277.

[6] Further discussion (with bibliography) in Brown, *Messiah*, pp. 513–16.

the outline of the Messiah's movements: from Judea (2.1) to Egypt (2.14) to Israel (2.21) to Galilee (2.22). (For Chrysostom, *Hom. on Mt.* 6.5, Gen 49.10 is being recalled.)[7]

The article before 'Judea' is a remnant from the original adjectival use of the word (cf. Mk 1.5; Jn 3.22; BDF§ 261.4).

ἐν ἡμέραις Ἡρῴδου τοῦ βασιλέως. Compare Lk 1.5, and contrast 1.6, where David is king. Herod reigned from 37–4 B.C. ἐν (ταῖς) ἡμέραις + proper name in the genitive is a biblicism, frequent in the LXX. In the NT it is found in Mt 2.1; Lk 1.5; 4.25; 17.26, 28; and 1 Pet 3.20 (cf. Rev 2.13).

Herod the Great, about whom we learn the most from Josephus, *Ant.* 14–18, probably died shortly before the Passover in 4 B.C.[8] So, according to Matthew (cf. 2.15, 19–20), Jesus must have been born shortly before this, probably between 7 and 4 B.C. Matthew's concern, however, is not with chronology. Herod matters for two reasons. First, in his attempt to slaughter the Messiah he is like the Pharaoh of Jewish tradition, who sought to kill the first redeemer, Moses. Secondly, Herod, although he could boast no royal genealogy, was a king, and our evangelist is interested in contrasting his rule and kingdom with the rule and kingdom of Jesus the Davidic Messiah.

ἰδοὺ μάγοι ἀπὸ ἀνατολῶν. 'Behold' is redactional (see on 1.20) and arouses attention: the magi are extraordinary visitors. μάγος[9] (Mt: 4, Mk: 0, Lk: 0; elsewhere in the NT only Acts 13.6, 8; cf. the rabbinic *māgôš*) designated originally a member of a priestly caste of the Medes and Persians (Zoroastrians) who specialized in

---

[7] As a rule the OT has 'Bethlehem of Judah', *bêt(-)leḥem yĕjûdâ* or Βηθλεεμ (δήμου (τῆς)) Ἰούδα (Judg 17.7, 8; 19.1, 2, 18; Ruth 1.1, 2; 1 Sam 17.12; cf. Asc. Isa. 2.7). This makes one wonder why Matthew (or his source) chose 'of Judea'. No persuasive explanation seems forthcoming. Sometimes the OT has (τῆς) Ἰούδα for 'of *yĕhûdâ*' (as in the aforenamed texts), sometimes τῆς Ἰουδαίας (e.g. 1 Sam 17.1; 27.6, 10; Isa 1.1). Matthew, who, unlike Luke, consistently takes 'Judea' in the narrow sense to refer to the southern division of Palestine, has Ἰουδαία eight times (Mk: 4; Lk: 10). Ἰούδας (= the tribe) occurs only in the quotation in 2.6 (*bis*).

[8] See Schürer 1, p. 326, n. 165, and the literature cited there, to which add: J. Van Bruggen, 'The Year of the Death of Herod the Great', in *Miscellanea Neotestamentica*, NovTSup 48, ed. T. Baarda et al., Leiden, 1978, pp. 1–15; O. Edwards, 'Herodian Chronology', *PEQ* 114 (1982), pp. 29–42; and P. M. Bernegger, 'Affirmation of Herod's Death in 4 B.C.', *JTS* 34 (1983), pp. 526–31.

[9] Lit.: E. J. Bickerman, 'Darius I, Pseudo-Smerdis and the Magi', *Athenaeum* 56 (1978), pp. 239–61; E. Beneveniste, *Les mages dans l'Ancien Iran*, Paris, 1938; J. Bidez and F. Cumont, *Les Mages hellénisés*, 2 vols., Paris, 1938; M. Boyce, *Zoroastrians*, London, 1979 (index, s.v., 'magus', 'priests'); G. Delling, *TWNT* 4, pp. 360–3; G. Messina, *Der Ursprung der Magier und die Zarathušthrische Religion*, Rome, 1930; J. H. Moulton, *Early Zoroastrianism*, London, 1913, esp. pp. 182–253; A. D. Nock, 'Paul and the Magus', in *Beginnings* 5, pp. 164–88; also in Nock's *Essays on Religion and the Ancient World*, 2 vols., ed. Z. Stewart, Oxford, 1972, 1, pp. 308–30; idem, 'Greeks and Magi', in *Essays* 1, pp. 516–26; M. Smith, *Magician*, pp. 71–4.

interpreting dreams (Herodotus 1.120, 128, etc.; Strabo 15.3.15; Plutarch, *Quaest. conv.* 4.5.2; Dio Chrysostom 49.7).[10] Later the word came to be used of those who possessed superior knowledge and ability, including astrologers, oriental sages, and soothsayers in general (Aristotle, frag. 27; Josephus, *Ant.* 10.195, 216); it also became a label for all 'sorcerers' and 'magicians' (Dan 2.2, 10 LXX; T. Reub. 4.9; Philo, *Spec. leg.* 3.93) and, finally, for 'quacks', 'deceivers', and 'seducers' (Sophocles, *OT* 387; Plato, *Rep.* 572e; cf. γόης).

Matthew does not identify his magi. 'From the east' could call to mind (1) Arabia (so Justin, Tertullian, Epiphanius, the Dialogue of Athanasius and Zacchaeus; Arabia is 'east' in the biblical tradition: Gen 10.30; Judg 6.3; Job 1.3; Isa 11.14; Ezek 25.4, 10; Demetrius, in Eusebius, *Praep. ev.* 9.29.3; and in Isa 60.6 gold and frankincense are associated with Midian, Sheba, and Ephah; cf. 1 Clem. 25.1–2); (2) Babylon (so Celsus, Jerome, Augustine; Daniel links Chaldeans and magi in 2.2, 10; the 'land of the east' is Babylon in As Mos. 3.13); or (3) Persia (so Clement of Alexandria, Chrysostom, Cyril of Jerusalem, Cosmas Indicopleustes, the Arabic Gospel of the Infancy, early iconographic tradition).[11] A choice among these three alternatives is impossible, although if 2.11 does allude to Isa 60.6, one would be inclined to opt for Arabia, for that OT text speaks of Midian and Sheba (cf. also Ps 72.10).

Most modern commentators see the undescribed[12] and mysterious magi as representatives of the best wisdom of the Gentile world, its spiritual élite: and while the Jewish leaders reject their Messiah, the Gentiles from outside the Land of Israel are anxious to greet him (cf. Augustine in PL 38, col. 1035). Because, however, μάγος carries an unfavourable sense elsewhere in the NT (Acts 13.6, 8; cf. Did. 2.2 and Acts 8.9, 11), and because the magi appear as sinister figures in early Christian sources (e.g. Ignatius, *Eph* 19.3),[13] and because the parallels with the traditions about

[10] Paul, pp. 104–12, 116–25, identifies Matthew's magi with followers of Zarathustra. This permits one to find in the text a demonstration of the superiority of Christianity over Zoroastrianism.

[11] Full discussion in Brown, *Messiah*, pp. 168–70. If the wise men be thought of as coming from Babylon or Persia, they might represent the overlords of the exile who now prostrate themselves before a Jewish king. But if the magi be supposed to hail from Arabia, perhaps one should recall the strange story in *y. Ber.* 2.4.5a, in which an Arab is the first to know of the Messiah's birth in Bethlehem. Incidentally, Matthew and his source may not have shared the same thought concerning the magi's home.

[12] Contrast Gos. Naz. frag. 28 (in Hennecke 1, p. 151), in which the magi's dress is described in great detail, and their complexion said to be dark.

[13] But the Fathers were interested in opposing astrology—it is telling that the star is dropped in Justin, *Dial.* 78—while the reception of the primitive 'science' in

Moses seem to put the magi on a par with the wise men and sorcerers and charmers of Pharaoh, Matthew could be carrying on a polemic against astrology or at least telling his readers that at the advent of the Messiah the power of the magi (astrologers) was broken.[14] This interpretation, which was maintained by Justin, Tertullian, and Origen, fails for four reasons. To begin with, the magi, unlike the Egyptian sorcerers, do not contend with Jesus. They simply give him gifts and offer worship—and indeed rejoice greatly so to do (2.10). Beyond this, the magi do not co-operate with Herod. They are in fact shown to be of upright character when they are the recipients of a divine warning and respond in obedience (2.12). Thirdly, we might expect, if the proposed interpretation were true, to find in the text 'magi from Egypt'— this being required to drive home the parallelism between Matthew's magi and the magicians who withstood Moses. Lastly, although the sorcerers of Pharaoh became astrologers or magi in some of the later legends about Moses (see p. 195, n. 22), our work in Excursus I has shown that the story of the magi was initially separate from the story of Herod's persecution of the infants. And in the latter, the rôle of the Egyptian wise men was occupied not by astrologers but by 'the chief priests and scribes' or their pre-Matthean counterparts, those who told Herod the whereabouts of the messianic child (2.3). So it will not do to view the magi as adversaries.

If this conclusion is firm, so is its usual partner: the magi are Gentiles (cf. Ps 72.11). Admittedly, some so-called 'magi' were Jews (Acts 8.9–24: Simon; Acts 13.6–11: Elymas; Josephus, *Ant.* 20.142: Atomus). But this observation is in itself scarcely decisive, and 'king of the Jews' would be difficult on the lips of Jews. Moreover, the standard interpretation has the virtue of drawing a sharp contrast between the Jewish élite (represented by Herod and all of Jerusalem and the chief priests and scribes) on the one hand and the Gentile world (represented by the magi) on the other—a contrast which fits Matthew's interest in universal mission and his

certain quarters of Judaism warns us that Matthew need not have shared the concern of later ecclesiastical writers; see Hengel, *Judaism and Hellenism* 1, pp. 236–9, and J. H. Charlesworth, 'Jewish Astrology in the Talmud, Pseudepigrapha, the Dead Sea Scrolls and early Palestinian Synagogues', *HTR* 70 (1977), pp. 183–200. Note *b. Šabb.* 156a: according to Ḥanina b. Ḥama, 'the stars make one wise, the stars make one rich, and there are stars for Israel'. If the Treatise of Shem goes back to ancient times (a disputed issue), it would be an important witness to the impact of astrology on certain Jewish circles; see Charlesworth 1, pp. 473–86. According to Chrysostom, *Hom. on Mt.* 6.4, some Christians inferred from Mt 2 that astrology could be trusted.

[14] So Clark (v); Davies (v); Mann (v).

disappointment in the Jewish people, especially their leaders. Jesus is king not just of Judea (2.6) but of the whole world (28.16–20). The interpretation also nicely fits in with the common rabbinic designation of Gentiles as 'worshippers of the stars' (*b. Sanh.* 59a; *b. 'Abod. Zar.* 3a; *Sipra* on Lev 20.7). Finally, the magi, although they are wise men, do not know the Jewish Scriptures; otherwise they would not have to ask others where the Messiah is to be born (2.2–6).

Magi and astrologers were widely regarded in the Graeco-Roman world as able to recognize the signs of the times, to foretell events of world importance, including the rise of kings. The dreams of King Astyages of Media (6th century B.C.) were, according to Herodotus, taken by magi to mean that his grandson (Cyrus) would usurp the throne (Herodotus 1.107–30). And Persian magi allegedly prophesied on the night of Alexander's birth that one newly born would threaten all of Asia (Cicero, *De div.* 1.23.47). The astrologer Publius Figulus purportedly cried out, when he learned the hour of the birth of Augustus, 'The ruler of the world is now born' (Suetonius, *Aug.* 94). Later, when Augustus was a young man, his destiny was said to have been presaged by yet another astrologer, Theogenes of Apollonia, who flung himself at the feet of the Caesar-to-be (Suetonius, ibid.). Suetonius tells us that, when Tiberius Caesar was still an infant, Scribonius the astrologer prophesied for him an illustrious career and kingship (Suetonius, *Tib.* 14.2). Tiberius' accession to the throne was also reportedly foretold by another, the Chaldean astrologer Thrasyllus (Tacitus, *Ann.* 6.21). An unnamed Chaldean is said to have predicted future greatness for the emperor Pertinax, when Pertinax was yet a babe (*Scrip. hist. Aug. Pert.* 1.3). Also of great interest is the story of the Persian king and magos Tiridates who, arriving in Rome, addressed Nero as 'my God Mithras', offered homage, foretold great things of the Roman king, and then 'returned to . . . [his] own country by another way' (Dio Cassius 63.1–7; Pliny, *H.N.* 30.16–17; Suetonius, *Nero* 13; cf. Mt 2.12 and the story told about Plato in Seneca, *Ep.* 58). It is readily apparent that the magi in the First Gospel play a favourite, well-attested rôle, one they played often in the Graeco-Roman world. They are the mysterious wise foreigners who, having mastered secret lore, are able to recognize who it is that will be king—and in Mt 2 they testify to Jesus.

If the broad background to the story in Mt 2.1–12 is not peculiarly Jewish, it remains true that the text also has a special background in the OT. In Num 22–4, the foreigner Balaam utters a prophecy about a star and a sceptre. This prophecy came in time to have messianic meaning, and it probably lies behind the star that Matthew's magi see (see on 2.2). According to Num 23.7 LXX,

Balaam was ἐξ ὀρέων ἀπ᾽ ἀνατολῶν,[15] and Jewish tradition made him a magos (Philo, *Mos*. 1.276), a prophet for the Gentiles (*Sipre* on Deut 34.10), one of Pharaoh's advisers, and the father of Jannes and Jambres, themselves magi (cf. Numenius of Apamea (2nd cent. A.D.) in Eusebius, *Praep. ev*. 9.8; Tg. Ps.-J. on Exod 1.15 and Num 22.2; Sefer ha-Yashar 61–85; Ambrosiaster, *2 Tim*. on 3.8; SB 3, pp. 660–4).[16] When the evil king Balak tried to enlist Balaam in the cause against Israel, the seer turned around and prophesied the nation's future greatness and the coming of a great ruler. This is rather close to Mt 2.1–12, where the cruel Herod, in his attempt to destroy the king of Israel, employs foreign magi who in the event bring only honour to the new-born deliverer. Hence Matthew probably thought of the magi as 'Balaam's successors' (so Eusebius, *Dem ev*. 9.1) who come to witness the fulfilment of the OT oracle their predecessor uttered so long ago—'A star will come forth (LXX: ἀνατελεῖ ἄστρον) out of Israel' (Num 24.17); 'He will rule many nations' (24.7 LXX). But the magi may be more than witnesses to the fulfilment of prophecy. They may, for Matthew, themselves fulfil OT promises, being 'those from Sheba who will come', who will bring to Jerusalem the wealth of nations, gold and silver, as the glory of the Lord rises upon her (Isa 60.3–6; cf. Ps 72.10–11, 15; see on v. 11).

The very popular magi of later Christian tradition[17] take us well beyond Matthew's text. Matthew tells us neither that the magi were kings nor that they were three. Even greater problems are created by modern presentations—crèches and plays—which have the magi arrive in Bethlehem immediately after the birth of Jesus. In the First Gospel the eastern intellectuals evidently come onto the scene only some time later—and they come not to a cave or a stable (as do the shepherds in Luke) but to the house of Mary and Joseph. So popular imagination has taken quite a few liberties with the canonical story. Yet this matters little, given the presumably non-historical character of the original sources. The meaning of Matthew's narrative does not reside in the faithful recording of historical facts.

ἀπὸ ἀνατολῶν (common in the LXX for several expressions: *miqqedem, mizrāḥ, mimmizrâ, mizrāḥâ;* cf. Mt 8.11; 24.27) goes

[15] According to Num 22.5; 23.7; and Deut 23.4, Balaam lived near the Euphrates valley at Pethor (cf. Josephus, *Ant*. 4.104; LAB 18.2). Num 31.8 and Josh 13.21–2, however, associate Balaam with Midianites; and the ambiguous Greek of Num 22.5 LXX can be read as placing Balaam near 'the river of the land of his [=Balak's] people'. Sefer ha-Yasher 67, moreover, has Balaam dwelling in Egypt.

[16] On Balaam in rabbinic tradition see J. R. Baskin, *Pharaoh's Counsellors*, BJS 47, Chico, 1983, pp. 75–113.

[17] See Kehrer (v); also Marsh-Edwards (v). For the magi's many names see B. M. Metzger, 'Names for the Nameless', in *New Testament Studies*, NTTS 10, Leiden, 1980, pp. 23–43. Their supposed relics are housed in Cologne Cathedral.

with 'magi', not 'came' (cf. 4.25; 21.11; 27.57; Jn 11.1; T. Job 28.6).
It should be seen in the light of Hellenism's superstitious esteem
for eastern sages and prophets: people looked for 'light from the
orient'.[18] Compare 1 Kgs 4.30: 'Solomon's wisdom surpassed
(even) the wisdom of all the people of the east, and all the wisdom
of Egypt' (cf. Jer 49.7; Obad 8). On the meaning of 'east' see
further on 2.2.

παρεγένοντο εἰς Ἱεροσόλυμα. Compare the LXX for Josh 24.11;
Judg 9.31; 18.7; Ruth 1.22; 2 Βασ 10.14; 10.17; 24.6; and 2 Macc
5.25. Presumably the redactor's hand is here evident (cf. 3.1, 13).[19]
Matthew wishes to associate Herod and Jerusalem, for in his eyes
many Jerusalemites share the king's malice and culpability (cf.
2.3–5). In addition, the opposition to Jesus is centred in the capital,
for that is where the leaders are, and Matthew puts the heaviest
blame on them. This is a theme that will surface again and again in
the passion narrative.

παραγίνομαι (Mt: 3; Mk: 1; Lk: 8) is used by Matthew to
introduce the magi, the Baptist (3.1, redactional), and the adult
Jesus (3.13, redactional). As for Ἱεροσόλυμα (Mt: 11; Mk: 10; Lk:
4), Matthew has the usual Greek spelling everywhere save in 23.37
(where he has Ἱερουσαλήμ). Unlike Luke, our evangelist does not
play upon the popular etymology, ἱερός > Ἱεροσόλυμα (cf.
Diodorus Siculus 40.3.3; Josephus, Bell. 6.438; Ant. 7.67;
Eusebius, Praep. ev. 9.34.13).[20]

2. Compare Prot. Jas. 21.1. This is the only sentence the magi
speak. Their general silence enhances the aura of mystery about
them.

λέγοντες· ποῦ ἐστιν ὁ τεχθεὶς βασιλεὺς τῶν Ἰουδαίων; Compare
2.4. The query, 'where?', signals a leading theme of Mt 2. It is
implicitly asked three times, and three different answers are given,
each based upon Scripture. Where was the Messiah born? In
Bethlehem of Judea, for so is it written of him, 'And you, O
Bethlehem, in the land of Judah . . .'. Where did the Messiah go
after his birth? To Egypt and then back to Israel, for the word of
the Lord through the prophet says, 'Out of Egypt have I called my
son'. Where did the Messiah finally settle? In Nazareth, for as the
word through the prophets has it, 'He will be called a Nazarene'.
Scripture thus provides a messianic itinerary.

The use of the verb, τίκτω (Mt: 4; Mk: 0; Lk: 5), which calls
attention to Mary's rôle, rather than γεννάω (cf. 2.1, 4), may mark
dependence upon a source. This is particularly so because when

---

[18] See Hengel, Judaism and Hellenism 1, pp. 210–18.
[19] So also Brown, Messiah, p. 192, who postulates an original, 'came to Judea'.
[20] See further D. D. Sylvia, 'Ierousalem and Hierosoluma in Luke-Acts', ZNW
74 (1983), pp. 207–221.

using an attributive participle with an articular substantive, Matthew prefers the pattern, article + substantive + article + participle + remaining matter, as in 6.4; 7.13, 14; 10.6; 11.21; 18.6; 21.9; 25.41; 26.3, 63; 27.44.[21] Here we find article + attributive participle + substantive, as in 2.7; 3.7 (= Luke 3.7); 17.27; 25.34; and 27.52 (traditional).

Although ὁ τεχθείς might be thought virtually independent (with 'king' as a predicate or another substantive), it is rather an attributive participle (cf. 2.7). The translation is not 'he that is born, the king of the Jews', but 'the (new-) born king of the Jews'.

The phrase, 'king of the Jews', which appears again and again in the passion narratives of all four canonical gospels, is attested in non-Christian sources (Josephus, *Ant.* 14.36, of Alexander Jannaeus; *Ant.* 15.373; 16.311, of Herod the Great). In the NT it occurs only on the lips of Gentiles. Jews say, 'king of Israel' (Mt 27.42; Mk 15.32; Jn 1.49; 12.13).

εἴδομεν γὰρ αὐτοῦ τὸν ἀστέρα. The testimony of the Scriptures (2.5) is supported by the testimony of nature. On the intimate connexion between the natural world and the religious world of human beings see on 5.45; 6.26; 10.29; and 27.51–3. For αὐτοῦ before the noun (rare in the synoptics and in translations of Semitic sources) see Jn 1.27.

The story of the star and of magi from the east seeking a king would not have been foreign to the ancients. In the first place, according to both Suetonius and Tacitus, at the turn of the era there was abroad the expectation of a world-ruler to come from Judea (Suetonius, *Vesp.* 4; Tacitus, *Ann.* 5.13). Whether or not these two historians had read Josephus (*Bell.* 3.399–408; 6.310–15) or one of his sources is uncertain. Nevertheless the account of Tiridates (see above) offers a good parallel to Matthew's tale of men from the east looking for the world's saviour in what was to them the west. And the hopes so elegantly expressed in Virgil's *Fourth Eclogue* probably reflect a general longing for a change in the times and the advent of a divine saviour. In the second place, the association of astronomical phenomena—and other prodigies for that matter (cf. Suetonius, *Aug.* 94)—with the appearance of a new king was not uncommon.[22] Not only did ancient astrologers claim that the conjunction of certain constellations hailed the birth of a king (cf. Ps.-Callisthenes 1.12; Firmicus Maternus, *Math.* 6.1; 8.31), but, in Tacitus' words, 'the general belief is that a comet means a change of emperor'; so 'when a brilliant comet now appeared . . . people speculated on Nero's successor as though Nero were already dethroned' (*Ann.* 14.22). According to Pliny the Elder (*H.N.* 2.28), popular belief held that stars rose with people, bright for the rich, small for the poor, dim for those worn out. At the birth of Alexander Severus (reigned A.D. 222–235) a new

---

[21] For this and what follows see Turner (v).
[22] Heavenly signs were also often associated with a king's death; see on 27.45.

star of great magnitude reportedly appeared in the heavens (*Scrip. hist. Aug. Alex. Sev.* 13.5). A comet and star were said to have appeared in the years of the conception and accession of Mithridates IV Eupator of Pontus (ca. 120–63 B.C.; Justin, *Ep.* 37.2). When the emperor Commodus (reigned A.D. 180–193) was born, the astrologers prognosticated for him and his brother equal horoscopes, and certain celestial signs were associated with his reign (*Scrip. hist. Aug. Comm.* 1.3; 15.1). When we turn to Jewish sources, we read in the late *Sefer ha-Yashar* (chapter 8) of the appearance of a new star in the night sky after Abraham's birth, a star which was taken by astrologers to announce the birth of a great man. And from the Christian Eusebius these words may be cited: 'In the case of . . . remarkable and famous men we know that strange stars have appeared, what some call comets, or meteors, or tails of fire, or similar phenomena that are seen in connexion with great or unusual events. But what event could be greater or more important for the whole universe than the spiritual light coming to all men through the saviour's advent, bringing to human souls the gift of holiness and the true knowledge of God? Wherefore the herald star gave the great sign . . .' (*Dem. ev.* 9.1).[23] Compare *Midr. Ps.* on 148.3: every righteous man has his star and it shines according to the brightness of his deeds.

Even more light is thrown upon our subject when attention is directed to Num 24.17: 'A star will come forth out of Jacob, and a sceptre will rise out of Israel'. The covenanters of Qumran understood 'a star will come forth/rise out of Jacob' to be the expected levitical Messiah (CD 7.18–26).[24] And in T. Levi 18.3, it is said of the priestly Messiah, 'his star will rise in heaven as of a king'. (Here a real star is in view; cf. Ignatius, *Eph.* 19.) In T. Jud. 24.1 (Christian) the verse seems to be applied to the Davidic Messiah. The various targumim on Num 24.17 insert 'king' or 'anointed one'. Already in the LXX a messianic interpretation is presupposed: 'a sceptre' (MT) becomes 'a man'. The same interpretation of the text lies behind the change of Bar Kosiva's name to Bar Kokhba ('son of the star').[25] It is even possible that Num 24.17 (or an interpretation thereof) was the so-called 'equivocal oracle' which, according to Josephus, encouraged the belief in a world ruler from Palestine (Josephus, *Ant.* 6.312).[26] In any case, one can readily see how popular Num 24.17 was and how

[23] A star also reportedly arose on the night of Mohammed's birth; and Islamic tradition gave Moses his own birth star. See Jalalu'ddin Rumi, *Mathnawi* 3.900–2, where we find this: 'Whenever any prophet enters into the womb, his star becomes conspicuous in the sky'. We are dealing here with a world-wide motif. In Chinese tradition, a star fell from the sky the moment Lao-Tze was born, and a great comet coincided with his conception.

[24] The text is also cited in 4QTestimonia and 1QM 11.6.

[25] See P. Schäfer, 'Aqiva and Bar Kokhba', in *Approaches to Ancient Judaism II*, ed. W. S. Green, Ann Arbor, 1980, pp. 117–20.

[26] So Hengel, *Zeloten*, p. 243.

Christians would have understood the star of Bethlehem. It was that star predicted so long ago by Balaam, the Messiah's star, the star of a new king (cf. Rev 22.16). Certainly later Christians saw Num 24.17 as the scriptural key to Mt 2.1–2 (cf. Justin, *Dial.* 106; Irenaeus, *Adv. haer.* 3.9.3; Origen, *C. Cels.* 1.60; Eusebius, *Dem. ev.* 9.1).

Why does Matthew not cite Num 24.17? This question, often raised especially by those wishing to find the source of Mt 2.1–12 in history, not haggadic imagination, has a simple answer. The formula quotations in Mt 2 serve the chapter's geographical orientation and—what cannot be said of Num 24.17—each contains a place name—Bethlehem, Egypt, Ramah, Nazareth.

Mt 2 does not contain the First Gospel's only reference to astronomical phenomena. According to 24.29, the stars will fall from the heavens at the consummation. According to 27.45, the sun became darkened for three hours when Jesus was being crucified. In both cases something terrible is involved: the judgement of the world and the torturing of Jesus. By way of contrast, the birth of Jesus is not something terrible. It is an occasion for joy (2.10) and thus accompanied neither by darkness nor falling stars but by a new star. A happy event on earth has as its correlate a good omen in the sky.

In view of all that has been said it is possible to explain Matthew's star as being something other than historical. One cannot, however, altogether exclude the possibility of some historical basis.[27] Bearing in mind that Matthew undoubtedly took himself to be writing not of a mystery but of a miracle, we may observe that Halley's comet did appear in 12–11 B.C.; and Josephus records the appearance of a notable star and comet sometime before the destruction of Jerusalem (*Bell.* 6.289);[28] and, as modern astronomers now know, Jupiter (the 'star' of kingship) and Saturn (the 'star' of the Jews; cf. Tacitus, *Hist.* 5.4) were in conjunction three times in 7 B.C. It is therefore possible that Christians, after the event, remembered an unusual celestial happening and connected it with Jesus' birth.

The appearance of an unusual star coincident with the birth of a great man is not to be confused with the motif of the lighted house, in which a new born illuminates the place of his birth, as in 1 En. 106.2, 10 (Noah); LAE 21.3 (Cain); *b. Meg.* 14a and *Exod. Rab.* on 2.4 (Moses); and Prot. Jas. 19.2 (Jesus)—and in legends about Hercules, Zoroaster, and Mohammed.[29]

---

[27] Discussion in J. Finegan, *Handbook of Biblical Chronology*, Princeton, 1964, pp. 238–48;Stauffer, pp. 32–5; Brown, *Messiah*, pp. 170–3; Nellessen (v), pp. 117–19; Zinniker (v), pp. 111–15; Boll (v); Rosenberg (v); Hughes (v).

[28] He adds (6.310): 'God cares for mankind and by all kinds of premonitory signs shows his people the way of salvation'.

[29] See further R. Mach, *Der Zaddik in Talmud und Midrasch*, Leiden, 1957, pp. 68–80, and note L. Proph. Elijah 2–3.

ἐν τῇ ἀνατολῇ. This is generally recognized as being here and in 2.9 a technical astronomical phrase, 'at its rising' (cf. Homer, *Od.* 12.4; Plato, *Polit.* 269a; Euripides, *Ph.* 504; T. Levi 18.3; *PGM* 13.1027), not (as in sy⁵) 'in the east', although the absence of αὐτοῦ is unexpected.[30] The points of the compass never take the article (BDF § 253.5), and Matthew has just used the plural without an article for 'east'. The related verb, ἀνατέλλειν, occurs in Num 24.17.

Whether 'at its rising' carries messianic content is uncertain.[31] Both ἀνατολή and ἀνατέλλειν occur in the LXX in messianic prophecies and in passages about redemption: Num 24.17; Ps 72.7; 97.11; Isa 43.19; 45.8; 60.1; Jer 23.5 (for ṣemaḥ = 'shoot' of David); Ezek 29.21; Zech 3.8 (for ṣemaḥ); 6.12 (for ṣemaḥ; cf. Justin, *Dial.* 100.4); Mal 3.20 (cf. T. Naph. 8.2; T. Gad 8.1). The enigmatic Lk 1.78 is also of interest in this connexion: 'when a rising light (ἀνατολή) will dawn upon us from on high'. But one cannot do anything more than call attention to a possibility. 'At its rising' may or may not have conjured up messianic speculation. We do not know.[32]

καὶ ἤλθομεν προσκυνῆσαι αὐτῷ. Compare Ps 71.11 LXX. As in the LXX, the dative after a verb for worship (almost a rule) reflects the Hebrew hištaḥăwâ + lĕ or lipnê. Matthew likes προσκυνέω (Mt: 13; Mk: 2; Lk: 3), especially with (προσ)έρχομαι: 2.2, 8, 11; 8.2; 9.18; 15.25; 20.20; 28.9.

The custom of prostration before kings and high officials was universal in the ancient orient (cf. Herodotus 1.134; Gen 23.7; 27.29; 33.3; 1 Sam 24.8; 1 Kgs 1.16, 47; Esth 3.2; Josephus, *Ant.* 6.285; *Bell.* 1.621; Philo, *Leg. Gai.* 116; Mt 18.26).[33] So one might translate προσκυνέω by 'pay homage' (so the NEB). Yet the child

---

[30] According to Allen, p. 12, αυτου may have dropped out at an early stage because 'at its rising' was misunderstood and thought of as meaning 'east'. More probable is the suggestion that the presence of αυτου just before τον αστερα discouraged its use after ανατολη.

[31] See Davies, *SSM*, pp. 445–6, and note Eusebius, *Dem. ev. 6.18*.

[32] Given the probability of Ignatius' knowledge of Matthew (see on 3.15 and 15.13), Ignatius, *Eph.* 19, almost certainly is based upon Mt 1–2. It reads in part: 'And hidden from the prince of this world were the virginity of Mary and her child-bearing and likewise also the death of the Lord—three mysteries to be cried aloud—the which were wrought in the silence of God. How then were they manifest to the ages? A star shone forth in the heaven above all the stars; and its light was unutterable, and its strangeness caused amazement; and all the rest of the constellations with the sun and moon formed themselves into a chorus about the star; but the star far outshone them all (cf. Sib. Or. 12.30–1); and there was perplexity to know whence came this strange appearance which was so unlike them. From that time forward every sorcery and every spell was dissolved . . .' (trans. J. B. Lightfoot; cf. Clement of Alexandria, *Exc. ex Theod.* 74).

[33] See B. A. Mastin, 'Dan 2.46 and the Hellenistic World', *ZAW* 85 (1973), pp. 80–93.

before whom the magi bow (2.11) is the Son of God. Moreover, ἔρχομαι followed by προσκυνέω denotes a cultic action in the LXX,[34] and Jews tended to think of complete *proskynesis* as properly directed only towards the one God (see on 2.11). So 'worship' is perhaps implied in 2.2 (cf. 28.17 and note Eusebius, *H.E.* 1.8). Almost everywhere else in Matthew such a translation is probably fitting.[35]

Remark should be made of Matthew's relatively free introduction of προσκυνέω into the Jesus tradition. Mark has it two times (5.6: the Gerasene demoniac; 15.19: mocking soldiers). Luke has it three times (4.7–8: the devil wants Jesus to worship him; 24.52: the disciples worship the risen Lord). Matthew has it numerous times, including 2.2, 8, 11 (the magi and Herod); 8.2 (a leper); 9.18 (a ruler); 14.33 (the disciples); 15.25 (the Canaanite woman); 20.20 (the mother of James and John); 28.9 (women at the tomb); 28.17 (the disciples before the risen Lord). Two observations. (1) By introducing προσκυνέω so often into the pre-Easter period, our redactor blurs more than Mark and Luke the distinction between the time before and after the resurrection. (2) By omitting the verb in his versions of Mk 5.1–13 and 15.16–20, Matthew shows a tendency to reserve the word for true worship; he does not want it associated with demons or mocking soldiers.

3. Compare the rough parallel in 2 Sam 4.1 MT: 'When Ishbosheth, Saul's son, heard that Abner had died at Hebron, his courage failed, and all Israel was dismayed'.

ἀκούσας δὲ ὁ βασιλεὺς Ἡρῴδης ἐταράχθη καὶ πᾶσα Ἱεροσόλυμα μετ' αὐτοῦ.[36] Similar constructions appear in 8.10; 14.13; 19.22; Mk 6.16; Lk 18.22; Jn 11.4. Compare also Mt 17.6; 19.25; 20.24 (= Mk 10.41); and 22.33, where the act of hearing precedes a verb of emotion, as in Gen 3.10 and 2 Sam 13.21.

We have in this verse an adverbial participle of cause (cf. Acts 9.36; Col 1.3–4): the hearing is the cause of what follows. The appellation βασιλεύς already given to Herod in 2.1, is not strictly necessary (and is omitted from Prot. Jas. 21.2); but it underlines the theme of kingship. On the name Ἡρῴδης (cf. 2.1) and its form see Schürer 1, p. 294, n. 20. Julius Africanus, in Eusebius, *H.E.* 1.6, finds Herod's foreign blood to be significant in that it betokened that 'the expectation of the nations was at hand, according to prophecy; because with him terminated the regular

---

[34] See J. Schneider, *TWNT* 2, pp. 663–5.

[35] See further Pesch (v), pp. 414–15; H. Greeven, *TWNT* 6, pp. 764–5; and Moule, *Christology*, pp. 175–6.

[36] 'Jerusalem' (see on 2.1) is treated in 2.3 like a feminine singular (cf. Par. Jer. 4.7; 6.24). Everywhere else in the First Gospel (3.5 being questionable) it is a neuter plural. D, by omitting πασα, restores consistency.

succession of governors and princes, from the time of Moses'. ταράσσω is used one other time in the First Gospel, where it is redactional: 14.33 (elsewhere in the synoptics: Mk 6.50; Lk 1.12; 24.38). Here the sense goes beyond 'startled'; it is closer to 'disturbed', 'unsettled' (cf. Gen 41.8; Jn 12.27; Josephus, *Ant.* 16.75; Mart. Polyc. 5.1). Herod thinks his throne to be in jeopardy (cf. Josephus, *Ant.* 17). In this he is like Pharaoh, who 'feared' when he learned of Moses' birth (Josephus, *Ant.* 2.206; cf. Dio Chrysostom 6.53). Prot. Jas. 21.2 omits 'and all Jerusalem with him'.

Matthew, like the other evangelists, likes πᾶς (Mt: 128–9; Mk: 67; Lk: 152). This reflects immersion in the OT, where the omnipresent πᾶς = *kōl* appears approximately 7,500 times. Its use in Mt 2.3 stresses the guilt of the capital, which is here personified: broadly speaking, she 'did not repent' (11.20). Just as the Jews in the Johannine passion narrative are made to declare, 'We have no king but Caesar' (19.15), so in Mt 2 the Jewish leaders are implicit sympathizers and servants of Herod. Instead of acknowledging the Messiah, the son of David born in Bethlehem, for whom they professedly long and pray, they in fact acknowledge as their king one whose kingly credentials are wholly unsatisfactory, a 'half-Jew', Herod (cf. Josephus, *Ant.* 14.8–10, 121, 403).

Perhaps we are to find in 2.1–23 a rejection of Jerusalem as the all-absorbing locus of eschatological expectation. The capital was, according to Jewish tradition, to be the primary scene of the messianic redemption and revelation.[37] So when the Messiah comes not to the centre of Judaism but to a small, obscure village, does this not, at least implicitly, run counter to popular expectation?

Jerusalem is, in the First Gospel, the stronghold of Jewish leadership, and, despite its being 'the holy city' (4.5; 27.53), it represents corrupt political power and corrupt political authority. But Jerusalem does not, it must be underlined, simply represent the Jewish people as a whole. Joseph and Mary are, after all, Jews; and as the gospel proceeds, Jesus will gain twelve Jewish disciples and command the sympathetic attention of large Jewish crowds. Moreover, our evangelist does not lump together the Jewish leaders and the Jewish people: one can detect his sympathy for the latter. So Jerusalem does not stand for the entire Jewish community. Instead she represents those in charge, the Jewish leadership (cf. 2.4). And 2.1–12 does not, accordingly, just play Jewish unbelief off against Gentile faith. The contrast is more nuanced: obdurate Jewish leaders versus open-minded Gentile wise men.

---

[37] Davies, *GL*, pp. 131–50, 234–5.

A related point also deserves consideration. While Jerusalem opposes Jesus in 2.1–12, Bethlehem is the place of his birth and Nazareth becomes his home. Now Jerusalem was the centre of Jewish history and tradition, Bethlehem and Nazareth insignificant hamlets. Yet it is these last which welcome Jesus. One may see in this an example of the redactional tendency to humble the exalted and to exalt the humble. Herod, the Pharisees, the scribes, the chief priests, Pilate, Jerusalem—all are associated with power, all oppose Jesus, and all are rebuked by Matthew. In contrast, Bethlehem and Nazareth, the persecuted parents of Jesus, the twelve disciples—all are lowly, all receive Jesus, and all are exalted by Matthew. In our judgement, scholars in the past have tended to overplay the Gentile/Jew contrast in Matthew and ignore altogether the powerful/powerless contrast. The result has sometimes been the unjustified reading of anti-Judaism into the First Gospel. See further Levine (v).

4. Mt 2.1–12 offers a transmutation of a traditional motif—the superiority of the Jewish hero to foreign wise men. One thinks of Joseph's ability to interpret Pharaoh's dream when the Egyptian magicians and wise men could not (Gen 41), of the duels between Moses and Aaron and the sorcerers and wise men of Pharaoh (Exod 7–10), and of Daniel's success in revealing and interpreting Nebuchadnezzar's dream while the king's own enchanters are reduced to silence (Dan 2). The First Gospel too has a story in which foreigners must acknowledge the superiority of their Jewish counterparts. The magi do not know what is known by the chief priests and scribes, namely, where the Messiah should be born. They thus must seek enlightenment from the Jews. Beyond this, however, the traditional theme is turned on its head. For although the Jews excel in knowledge, they do not put their knowledge to its proper end; it is instead Gentiles who honour Jesus.

καὶ συναγαγὼν πάντας τοὺς ἀρχιερεῖς καὶ γραμματεῖς τοῦ λαοῦ. In Josephus, *Ant.* 2.205, 234, Pharaoh is informed of the coming deliverer by 'sacred scribes' (ἱερογραμματεῖς). Oddly enough, and in contrast with Matthew, Eusebius (*H.E.* 1.8) tells us that Herod learned where Jesus should be born from the magi. The verb συνάγω (Mt: 24; Mk: 5; Lk: 6) is a Matthean favourite. Here it foreshadows 26.57: 'the scribes and the elders had gathered'.

'Chief priests' (ἀρχιερεύς: Mt: 25; Mk: 22; Lk: 15) refers not to the present and past high priests alone but to an established college.[38] It included the current high priest and his predecessors, the captain of the temple, the heads of the weekly courses, the directors of the daily courses,

[38] Lit.: Jeremias, *Jerusalem*, pp. 160–81; Schürer 2, pp. 275–91; G. Schrenk, *TWNT* 3, pp. 265–84.

the temple overseers, and the temple treasurers. Matthew's association of this group with Herod may have been encouraged by his knowledge that the king personally selected several high priests (Josephus, *Ant.* 15.22–41, 319–22). Because the 'chief priests' are found in the synoptic tradition above all in the passion narratives, their presence at the beginning of our gospel foreshadows their rôle at the end. 'The chief priests and scribes' (cf. 16.21 (with elders); 20.18; 21.15; 27.41 (with elders)) designates the religious authorities in Jerusalem. Whether we are to think of a meeting of the Sanhedrin is unclear. It would in any event be historically incredible. Herod opened his reign by massacring its members (Josephus, *Ant.* 14.175; cf. *b. B. Bat.* 3b).

The 'scribes' (= *sōpĕrîm*), later known as the 'sages' (*ḥăkāmîm*), were the 'teachers of the law' (Lk 5.17; Acts 5.34; cf. Ezra 7.6, 11; Neh 8.1), the 'lawyers' who interpreted the legal principles of the Torah, taught the people, and administered justice—functions which at one time in Israel's history belonged to the priests.[39] They were Judaism's spiritual and intellectual leaders (cf. Ecclus 38–9; Josephus, *Ant.* 20.264), its most prominent citizens (cf. Mt 23.6–7; Mk 12.38–9; Lk 20.46). They lived chiefly in Judea, close to the capital (cf. Mt 15.1; Mk 3.22); but there must also have been scribes in Galilee, even before A.D. 70 (cf. Mk 3.22; 7.1; *m. Šabb.* 16.7; 22.3; *b. Šabb.* 146a). It is usual to identify the scribes as a professional class, not a party: thus some of the Pharisees were scribes, not all scribes Pharisees (cf. Mk 2.16; Acts 23.9). Nonetheless a case can be made for identifying the scribes and Pharisees in the first century.[40]

Matthew never criticizes the scribal office as such (cf. 13.51–2; 23.34), only scribal hypocrisy and misplaced priorities (cf. Hummel, pp. 17–18). In fact, our author has eliminated some of Mark's disparaging references to scribes by substituting 'Pharisees' and 'elders' (as in 9.11; 26.47; 27.1; cf. Bonnard, p. 227). Perhaps he himself had been a Jewish scribe at one time. However that may be, after accepting Jesus as the Messiah, he almost certainly joined a group of Christian scribes, a 'school'.[41]

On λαός see on 1.21. Jesus should 'save his people from their sins' and govern his people Israel (2.6). The people, however, led astray by their leaders, have not, at least as a body, recognized their saviour and king. Hence there is a contradiction between the divine intention and the human response. For this reason Matthew contains grim elements of tragedy. His people's rejection of the Messiah so troubles the author that the Christian joy so

---

[39] Lit.: Jeremias, *Jerusalem*, pp. 233–45; Schürer 2, pp. 322–36; Westerholm, pp. 26–39; J. Neusner, 'The Formation of Rabbinic Judaism', *ANRW* II.19.2 (1979), pp. 37–41; *CHJ* 3, forthcoming.

[40] E. Rivkin, 'Scribes, Pharisees, Lawyers, Hypocrites: A Study in Synonymity', *HUCA* 49 (1978), pp. 135–42; idem, 'Scribes and Lawyers in Judaism', *CHJ* 3, forthcoming.

[41] Cf. Stendahl, *School*, passim; Bornkamm, in *TIM*, p. 50, n. 5; Hummel, p. 159; Fenton, p. 230; Zumstein, pp. 156–63. On the Christian scribes of Matthew's community see Suggs, pp. 120–7; E. Schweizer, 'Matthew's Community', in Stanton, *Matthew*, pp. 133–5; van Tilborg, pp. 128–41; Luz 1, pp. 60–1.

prominent throughout the NT—especially in Luke–Acts (e.g. Lk 1.44; 2.10; 6.23; 8.13; 10.17; etc.)—makes itself felt only very rarely (2.10; 13.20, 44; 28.8), and the threat of judgement comes to the fore.

ἐπυνθάνετο παρ' αὐτῶν ποῦ ὁ χριστὸς γεννᾶται. Compare 2 Chr 32.31 LXX. The issue of geography is once again emphasized. πυνθάνομαι (always for *dāraš* in the LXX) appears only here in Matthew (Mk: 0; Lk: 2). The redactor prefers αἰτέω (fourteen times) and ἐπερωτάω (eight times). On the imperfect with verbs of asking see BDF § 328. παρά with the genitive occurs only five or six times in Matthew, three times in Mt 2 (4, 7, 16). It is from Mk 12.11 in Mt 21.42, from Matthew's special source in 18.19, and 20.20 is textually doubtful. For its elimination from sentences taken over from Mark see 16.1 = Mk 8.11 and 21.34 = Mk 12.2. The presence of a source behind 2.4 is indicated.

'Christ' (see on 1.1) = 'the king of the Jews' (2.2). Compare the interchange in the passion narrative (26.63, 68; 27.11, 17, 22, 29, 37) and the intimate link between χριστός and kingship in the LXX (1 Βασ 2.10; 2 Βασ 22.51; Ps 2.2; 17.51) and the Apocalypse (11.15; 12.10; 20.4, 6).

5. Compare Jn 7.42; Prot. Jas. 21.2; Justin, *Dial.* 78; *1 Apol.* 34. Whether 2.5–6 constitutes a formula quotation has been debated. On the one side, the verb, πληρόω, is absent;[42] on the other, how could one expect it, since the quotation is on the lips of Jewish authorities? Whatever the outcome of the issue, it does not affect interpretation of the text.

οἱ δὲ εἶπαν αὐτῷ. There is no spokesman for the scribes; they speak instead as an impersonal unit.

ἐν Βηθλέεμ τῆς Ἰουδαίας. See on 2.1. According to Jerome, *Comm. on Mt.* on 2.5, Bethlehem 'of Judea' is 'an error on the part of the copyist. We believe that, as we read in the Hebrew, "Judah" and not "Judea" was originally written by the evangelist'. This is probably an incorrect reference to the OT text, not a reference to a Hebrew gospel.[43]

οὕτως γὰρ γέγραπται. This expression is appropriate coming from scribes. Compare *kî kēn kātûb* (cf. 1QS 5.15; CD 11.18; 2Q25 1.3; L. Proph. Mal. 2; 1 Cor 15.45).

διὰ τοῦ προφήτου.[44] See on 1.22. The singular is used even though the citation is a conflation of sentences from two different books, Micah and 2 Samuel. Perhaps owing to the conviction that

---

[42] This is not because the fulfilment is yet to be ('who *will* shepherd my people Israel'); for in 1.22 and 21.4 the evangelist employs fulfilment formulas before the events signified have come to pass.

[43] P. Vielhauer, 'The Gospel of the Nazaraeans', in Hennecke 1, pp. 140–1.

[44] 'Micah' is named in a few Syriac and Coptic mss., 'Isaiah' in it[a].

'a single teaching cannot be deduced from different scriptural verses' (*b. Sanh.* 34a), composite or merged quotations are few and far between in rabbinic sources.[45] In the NT they are common (cf. Mt 21.5; 27.9–10; Mk 1.2–3; Rom 11.8–10; 1 Cor 15.54–5). It is difficult to say whether the early church's freedom to mix quotations was encouraged by a similar tendency on the part of Jesus (cf. Mk 10.6–8; 11.17; 14.62; Lk 10.27).[46]

6. The quotation follows neither the LXX nor the MT of Mic 5.2.[47] The differences are in fact sufficient to tempt one to speak of an 'interpretation' instead of a 'quotation' of Scripture. The text has been freely altered by Matthew in order to make it best serve his ends. (Against 2.5–6 being derived from a Christian testimony book, the translation vocabulary seems characteristically Matthean; see below.) For messianic interpretations of Mic 5.2 see the targum on Micah and Tg. Ps.-J. on Gen 35.21.

καὶ σὺ Βηθλέεμ, γῆ 'Ιούδα. The unexpected γῆ 'Ιούδα (one expects the genitive, γῆς) replaces 'Ephrathah' (MT) or 'house of Ephrathah' (LXX). 'Ephrathah' (cf. Gen 35.19; 48.7) would likely have meant little to Matthew's audience. 'Judah', by way of contrast, is full of meaning. It emphasizes the connexion between Jesus and the patriarch Judah (cf. 1.2–3)—so important because the Davidic Messiah was expected to come from the tribe of Judah (Rev 5.5; cf. Gen 49.9–10 LXX; the targums on Gen 49.9–10; T. Jud. 21.2; 24.5; Heb 7.14; *b. Sanh.* 98b). 'Land of Judah' anticipates the 'Judah' from Mic 5.2 which is quoted in the next line (cf. also 1 Sam 17.12). The repeated appearance of γῆ (Mt: 43; Mk: 19; Lk: 25) in Mt 2 (2, 6, 20, 21, always for Palestine) makes one aware of the chapter's geographical orientation.

οὐδαμῶς ἐλαχίστη εἶ ἐν τοῖς ἡγεμόσιν 'Ιούδα.[48] *ṣā'îr lihyŏt bĕ'alpê yĕhûdâ* appears in the MT. The LXX has: ὀλιγοστὸς εἶ τοῦ εἶναι ἐν χιλιάσιν 'Ιούδα. οὐδαμῶς (a NT *hapax legomenon*; in the LXX only in 2, 3, 4 Maccabees) has no basis in either OT text. The OT in fact remarks upon Bethlehem's insignificance. Matthew's denial can only mean that because the Messiah has come into the world at Bethlehem, he has brought the city greatness. ἐλάχιστος (Mt: 5; Mk: 0; Lk: 4) is an independent translation of the Hebrew *ṣā'îr* ('little', 'insignificant'). Compare 5.19; 25.40, and 45, where

---

[45] The *hāraz* method is different: the different biblical texts are separated at least by conjunctions; see E. E. Ellis, *Paul's Use of the Old Testament*, Edinburgh, 1957, pp. 49–51.

[46] On the phenomenon of composite quotations, esp. as it relates to the hypothesis of early Christian testimony collections, see further Fitzmyer, *Background*, pp. 60–89.

[47] Stendahl, *School*, pp. 99–101; Lindars, *Apologetic*, pp. 192–4; Gundry, *OT*, pp. 91–3; Rothfuchs, pp. 60–1; Soares Prabhu, pp. 261–7.

[48] D it Tert Cyp have μη = *non* for οὐδαμως.

other things qualified by 'the least' become important. As for ἡγεμών (Mt: 10; Mk: 1; Lk: 2), the MT has *'alpê* ('thousands', 'clans'; cf. the LXX, χιλιάσιν); but the Hebrew consonants could be pointed to give *'allûpê* = 'princes'. This explains Matthew's reading. He is working with the Hebrew.

ἐκ σοῦ γὰρ ἐξελεύσεται ἡγούμενος. *mimměkā lî yēṣēʾ lihyôt môšēl běyiśrāʾēl* appears in the MT. The LXX reads: ἐκ σοῦ μοι ἐξελεύσεται τοῦ εἶναι εἰς ἄρχοντα ἐν τῷ Ἰσραήλ. 'For' is a logical addition given the previous changes: the 'not at all least' requires clarification. The rational Matthew is explaining. The participial form of ἡγέομαι is the equivalent of the MT's *môšēl* = 'ruler' and the LXX's ἄρχοντα = 'leader'; it is chosen because of its resemblance to ἡγεμών (cf. also perhaps Ps 68.27). Jesus, not those Herod has gathered, should lead Israel.

ὅστις ποιμανεῖ τὸν λαόν μου τὸν Ἰσραήλ. This reproduces 2 Sam 5.2 = 1 Chr 11.2, save 'who will govern' replaces 'you will govern'; otherwise there is agreement with both the LXX and MT: 'you shall shepherd my people Israel'. Matthew's interest in Davidic Christology is here emphasized, for 2 Sam 5.2 and its parallel are addressed in the OT to David (cf. Ps 78.70–1). In addition, Moses was remembered as a shepherd (Isa 63.11; LAB 19.3, 9; *Mek.* on Exod 14.31; *Exod. Rab.* on 2.2), so the quotation nicely fits Matthew's Moses-Messiah typology.

The switch from Micah to Samuel was probably motivated by a desire to underline Jesus' status as the 'Son of David' (so Soares Prabhu, p. 266); and it permits the re-use of a key word already introduced, λαός (1.20; 2.4; cf. Rothfuchs, p. 61).

To a first-century Jew, reference to a ruler come forth to 'shepherd my people Israel' would have conjured up the eschatological expectation of the ingathering of the twelve tribes of Israel (cf. Ezek 34.4–16; Mic 5.1–9; Ps. Sol. 17; 4 Ezra 13.34–50; 2 Bar. 77–86; *m. Sanh.* 10.3), an expectation apparently shared by Matthew (19.28). Israel's blindness would then be only for a season (see on 23.37–9). The alternative is to suppose that for Matthew the church of both Jew and Gentile had already come to supplant once and for all the place of Israel in salvation-history.[49] Yet surely the OT promises of restoration—such as are found in Ezek 37 and Hos 2—would have prohibited this thought. If Paul could write that 'God's wrath has come upon them [the Jews] at last' (1 Th 2.16) and still hold out hope for their final redemption

---

[49] For the view that repentance is no longer a possibility for Israel see Trilling, *Israel,* passim, and L. Gaston, 'The Messiah of Israel as Teacher of the Gentiles', *Int* 29 (1975), pp. 24–40. Contrast G. N. Stanton, 'Aspects of Early Christian-Jewish Polemic and Apologetic', *NTS* 31 (1985), pp. 377–92.

(Rom 11),[50] and if the Qumran sect could think of most Jews as outside the covenant and yet expect to see 'all the congregation of Israel . . . join the Community and walk according to the laws of the sons of Zadok the Priests, and of the men of their covenant' (1QS 1.1–2),[51] the same could have been true for Matthew: the Jewish destiny could still be open. As the prophet foresaw, the Lord will 'say to Not my people, "You are my people" ' (Hos 2.23).

Why does the evangelist not go on to quote the rest of Mic 5.2? Mention of one 'whose origin is from of old, from ancient days' would have admirably suited the purposes reflected by the genealogy; and 5.3 ('until the time when she who is in travail has brought forth') would have been to the point coming after 1.18–25. Maybe the readers are supposed to fill in for themselves.

7. Herod now inquires of the Gentile magi just as he inquired of the Jewish scribes. Putting together the information gathered from both, he can infer what has happened.

τότε Ἡρῴδης λάθρᾳ καλέσας τοὺς μάγους. λάθρᾳ (cf. 1.19; Josephus, *Vita* 388) may carry sinister overtones (cf. Job 31.27; Hab 3.14; 1 Macc 9.60). The later (successful) attempt to do away with Jesus was also clandestine (26.3–5, 14–16, 47–50). Are we to suppose that just as Herod keeps his true devices from the magi, so too does he hide his machinations from the Jewish leaders, who are not privy to what the easterners divulge?

ἠκρίβωσεν παρ' αὐτῶν τὸν χρόνον τοῦ φαινομένου ἀστέρος. Compare 2.16. ἀκριβόω (not in the LXX) occurs in the NT only here and in 2.16. Its meaning is 'ascertain (exactly)' (so BAGD, s.v.). For the related ἀκριβῶς see 2.8. φαινομένου might be considered redactional (φαίνω: Mt: 13; Mk: 1; Lk: 2).

'The time of the appearance of the star' matters because Herod must determine the age of the children to be slaughtered (cf. 2.16). The implicit assumption is probably this: the initial appearance of the star coincided with the birth or conception of the child. The Greek could also, however, be read as pertaining to the star's duration ('time' = 'span of time') or, more precisely, to the length of time it was seen by the magi.

In Matthew as it now stands Herod learns the time of Jesus' birth from the magi. In stage I of our story's history the king probably gained the

---

[50] See Davies, 'Paul and the People of Israel', in *JPS*, pp. 123–52 (pp. 125–7 on the authenticity of 1 Th 2.16), and D. C. Allison, 'Romans 11:11–15: A Suggestion', *PRS* 12 (1985), pp. 23–30. For the Pauline origin of 1 Th 2.16 see further G. Lüdemann, *Paulus und das Judentum*, Münich, 1983, pp. 25–7, and K. P. Donfried, 'Paul and Judaism. 1 Thess. 2.13–16 as a Test Case', *Int* 38 (1984), pp. 242–53.

[51] See further Sanders, *Paul*, pp. 240–57.

information from scribes. Compare Josephus' version of Moses' birth, in which Pharaoh is informed by a 'sacred scribe' that 'at that time' there would be a child born to the Israelites (*Ant.* 2.205).

What the magi told the king is not related (as it probably would have been had Matthew wished to make them sinister figures). But should not the reader infer that Herod cruelly chose an excessively wide margin of safety when he determined to have every Bethlehem infant two years of age and under put to the sword?

8. Herod, having learned the birthplace of the Messiah and the time of his star's appearance (2.5–7), sends the magi 'to make careful search concerning the child', in order that he may learn precisely who the child is and so have him slain.

καὶ πέμψας αὐτοὺς εἰς Βηθλέεμ εἶπεν. πέμψας (Matthew's only form of πέμπω) occurs also in 11.2 (with εἶπεν; cf. Lk 7.19: ἔπεμψεν ... λέγων); 14.10 (diff. Mk 6.27: ἀποστείλας); and 22.7 (redactional).

πορευθέντες ἐξετάσατε ἀκριβῶς περὶ τοῦ παιδίου. The vocabulary is not obviously redactional.[52] For πορευθέντες + aorist imperative see 9.13 (redactional); 11.4 (= Lk 7.22); and 28.19 (redactional). The participle is pleonastic (cf. BAGD, s.v., πορεύομαι, 1).

υἱός fails to appear in Mt 2 except in a formula quotation (2.15). Otherwise παιδίον is used of Jesus (8, 9, 11, 13, 14, 20, 21). This is to be explained, according to R. Pesch, by the evangelist's desire to connect υἱός especially with God, which entails that another word must be employed when God is not in the picture.[53]

ἐπὰν δὲ εὕρητε ἀπαγγείλατέ μοι ὅπως κἀγὼ ἐλθὼν προσκυνήσω αὐτῷ. ἐπάν (cf. Lk 11.22, 34) is a *hapax legomenon* in Matthew (in the LXX it appears only twice) while ὅπως (cf. 2.23) is one of his favourite words (Mt: 17; Mk: 1; Lk: 7). Matthew also likes κἀγώ (Mt: 9; Mk: 0; Lk: 6).

Herod's remark, 'That I too coming may worship him', which restates the magi's goal (2.2), is intended to deceive the magi (but not the reader) and to put Herod on their side. Nothing could make plainer that the magi are free of complicity in the king's scheme: in order to comply, they must be tricked.

9. The wise men go by themselves to find the new-born king. The Jewish scribes, if they know where he is, are not interested in going (cf. Chrysostom, *Hom. on Mt.* 6.6).

οἱ δὲ ἀκούσαντες τοῦ βασιλέως ἐπορεύθησαν καὶ ἰδοὺ ὁ ἀστήρ, ὃν εἶδον ἐν τῇ ἀνατολῇ. The vocabulary of this line has been wholly

---

[52] πορεύομαι: Mt: 29; Mk: 1; Lk: 51. ἐξετάζω (cf. Jn 21.12): Mt: 2 (redactional in 10.11); Mk: 0; Lk: 0. ἀκριβῶς: Mt: 1; Mk: 0; Lk: 1. παιδίον: Mt: 18; Mk: 12, Lk: 13.
[53] Pesch (v), pp. 413–4.

anticipated in 2.1–3 and 8. Recalling an OT idiom (Exod 24.7; Judg 2.20; Jer 35.14; 11QTemple 54.11), it is possible to translate ἀκούσαντες as 'obeying'.[54] But 'hearing' and 'obeying' are carefully distinguished elsewhere in the First Gospel (7.26; 13.19–23); and if the magi do as Herod bids, it is only because they do not support his wily intents, as 2.12 suggests. 'Hearing' is therefore the better translation.

προῆγεν αὐτούς. Compare 14.22; 21.9, 31; 26.32; 28.7. The star appeared once (2.2), then disappeared (2.7: φαινομένου); now it reappears ('behold') and 'goes before' the magi—who, despite the tradition of a daytime light (Ignatius, *Eph.* 19; Chrysostom, *Hom. on Mt.* 6.3; Sib. Or. 12.30–1), must be travelling at night, like Luke's shepherds—to Bethlehem. This raises difficult questions. Even if the 'going before' is not to be conceived of literally but rather labelled 'oriental rhetoric', a way of saying that the star was ahead of the magi and cheered them on, why would one need supernatural guidance (cf. Gosp. Ps.-Mt. 16) to make the six mile trek from the capital to Bethlehem? And how could a heavenly light be perceived as standing over a precise place, seemingly a particular house? Or do these questions stem from an unimaginative and overly literal interpretation of Matthew's text?[55]

Although we must remain very uncertain about the historicity of Matthew's story, it does have parallels in other ancient sources. In Exod 13.21 we read of the Israelites in the wilderness, 'And the Lord went before them (*hōlēk lipnêhem*; LXX: ἡγεῖτο αὐτῶν) by day in a pillar of cloud to lead them along the way, and by night in a pillar of fire to give them light, that they might travel by day and by night' (cf. 40.38; Chrysostom, *Hom. on Mt.* 6.3 cites this parallel). According to Tg. Ps.-J. on Gen 22.3, a cloud was said to have appeared and marked out the place where Abraham should sacrifice Isaac. Clement of Alexandria writes that when Thrasybulus was bringing back exiles from Phyla and wished to elude observation, a pillar became his guide as he marched over a tractless region to Munychia (*Strom.* 1.24.163). In the *Aeneid* (2.692–704), the way of escape for Aeneas is shown by 'a star that drew a fiery train behind'. According to Diodorus Siculus (16.66.3), a comet went before Timoleon of Corinth as he travelled to Sicily.

Some later Christians came to identify the star of Bethlehem with an angel (Arabic Gospel of the Infancy 7), and long before Matthew angels and stars were already intimately associated with each other (Job 38.7; 1 En. 86.1, 3; Rev 9.1; 12.4; T. Sol. 20.14–17; see further on 26.53). So the evangelist could have thought of the guiding star as angelic. But on this the text is silent.

---

[54] Brown, *Messiah*, p. 165. Cf. Gaechter (v), p. 288.
[55] Additional objections to the historicity of Mt 2.1–12 may be found in Strauss, pp. 162–81.

ἕως ἐλθὼν ἐστάθη ἐπάνω οὗ ἦν τὸ παιδίον.[56] In Prot. Jas. 21.3 the
star goes before the magi until it stands over Jesus' head. Compare
the remarks of Chrysostom, *Hom. on Mt.* 6.3: the star 'did not,
remaining on high, point out the place; it not being possible for
them [the magi] so to ascertain it, but it came down and performed
this office. For you know that a spot of so small dimensions, being
only as much as a shed would occupy, or rather as much as the
body of a little infant would take up, could not possibly be marked
out by a star. For by reasons of its immense height, it could not
sufficiently distinguish so confined a spot, and discover it to them
that were desiring to see it'.

10. The births and accessions of kings were typically occasions
for rejoicing (cf. 1 Kgs 1.40). Also of possible relevance for Mt
2.10 is the standard promise of eschatological joy (Isa 65.17–19;
66.14; 1QS 4.7; 1QM 1.9; 12.13; Mt 25.21, 23) and Philo's
understanding of the wise man, the sage, as the one who is truly
capable of experiencing joy (*Mut. nom.* 166–71).

The joy of the Gentiles should be shared by Jerusalem and her
scribes; but the messianic salvation leaves them only troubled
(2.3).

ἰδόντες δὲ τὸν ἀστέρα ἐχάρησαν χαρὰν μεγάλην σφόδρα.
Compare Jos. As. 3.4; 4.2; 7.10; 9.1; 15.12; 24.5. Joy is a prominent
part of Luke's infancy narrative: 1.14, 28; 2.10. For χαίρω (Mt: 6;
Mk: 2; Lk: 12) with the sense of 'rejoice' or 'be glad' see 5.12 (cf. Lk
6.23) and 18.13. In 26.49 (redactional); 27.29 (= Mk 15.18); and
28.9, the word is used as a greeting, 'hail', 'hello'. χαρά (Mt: 6; Mk:
1; Lk: 8) is redactional in 13.44 and 28.8. It was often coupled with
μέγας (e.g. Isa 39.2; Jon 4.6; Lk 2.10; 24.52; Acts 15.3) and χαίρω
(Isa 39.2; Jon 4.6; Jn 3.29; 1 Th 3.9). 'Rejoice (with) great joy' is a
Semitism (cf. 1 Kgs 1.40; Isa 39.2; Jon 4.6; Neh 12.43; BDF
§ 198.6).

Matthew is fond of σφόδρα (7; Mk: 1; Lk: 1). The adverb is
linked with χαίρω in Zech 9.9 ('Rejoice greatly, O daughter of
Zion'), part of which Matthew quotes in 21.5. Note also its use
with fear, the antithesis of joy, in 17.6 and 27.54.

11. The first act of chapter 2 now comes to its climax. The goal
of the magi's journey (stated in 2.2) has been obtained: 'and falling
down they worshipped him'.

As word statistics prove, 2.11 has been cast by Matthew's hand.
The verse must, nonetheless, have some basis in the tradition, for
the pre-Matthean story surely recounted the happy end of the
visitors' travels.

---

[56] D it substitute του παιδιου for ου ην το παιδιον. For εσταθη L W 0233 *f*[13] Maj
ProtJas 21.3 have εστη.

καὶ ἐλθόντες εἰς τὴν οἰκίαν. Compare Lk 2.15–16. καί appears six times in 2.11–12, four times as a consecutive, which adds a Semitic flavour: 'and coming . . . and falling . . . and opening . . . and being warned . . .'. If 'the house' is the house of Jesus and his parents in Bethlehem, this would obviously not harmonize with Luke's account, which explains that Jesus was laid in a feeding trough, 'because there was no room for them in the inn' (2.7).

εἶδον τὸ παιδίον μετὰ Μαρίας τῆς μητρὸς αὐτοῦ. Until now the magi have gazed upon a star. Coming to Bethlehem, their eyes rest on what the guiding star has led to: Jesus. The phrase, 'the child with Mary his mother' recurs (with 'and' for 'with' and without 'Mary') in 2.13, 14, 20, 21. It serves three ends. (1) It puts Joseph out of the picture, thereby reinforcing the impact of 1.16–25: Jesus has no human father. (2) 'The child and his mother' probably harks back to Exod 4.20 (τὴν γυναῖκα καὶ τὰ παιδία), for Exod 4.19 is the basis for Mt 2.20, in which 'the child and his mother' appears again (see below). The Moses typology is thereby furthered. (3) Because 'the child' (see on 2.8–9) is named first, he is shown to be the focus of all the action. Even Mary is in the shadows, for she gains her identity only by being 'his mother'. For μετά + personal name + 'the mother' or 'the father' + personal pronoun see also 4.21 (diff. Mk 1.20).

καὶ πεσόντες προσεκύνησαν αὐτῷ. Compare 2.2. The use of 'falling down' with 'worship' is probably redactional, as 4.9 and 18.26 suggest. The combination was, however, quite common: Ps 72. 11; Dan 3.5–7; Josephus, *Ant.* 7.95; 9.11; Acts 10.25; 1 Cor 14.25; Rev 4.10; 7.11; 22.8. The magi do not simply bend their knees (cf. 17.14; 18.29). They fall down on their faces. This is noteworthy because there was a tendency in Judaism to think prostration proper only in the worship of God (cf. Philo, *Leg. Gai.* 116; *Decal.* 64; Mt 4.9–10; Acts 10.25–6; Rev 19.10; 22.8–9).

καὶ ἀνοίξαντες τοὺς θησαυροὺς αὐτῶν. For ἀνοίγω (Mt: 11; Mk: 1; Lk: 7) with 'treasure' in the LXX see Deut 28.12; Jer 27.25; Amos 8.5. θησαυρός (Mt: 9; Mk: 1; Lk: 4) means 'receptacle for treasure', 'treasure-chest' (cf. Job 38.22; Prov 8.21; 1 En. 97.9; Josephus, *Ant.* 9.163). As the magi seem to know, earthly treasure is to be given up or given to God (2.11; 6.19). Only heavenly treasure matters (6.20–1; 19.21).

προσήνεγκαν αὐτῷ δῶρα. Both προσφέρω (Mt: 15; Mk: 3; Lk: 4) and δῶρον (Mt: 9; Mk: 1; Lk: 2) are Matthean favourites. Their combination (never in Mark or Luke) occurs also in 5.23–4; 8.4; Heb 5.1; 8.3; 9.9. The three gifts are a symbol of loyalty and submission; but the magi are not—as the church Fathers taught (see on 2.1)—giving up the tools of their trade.

χρυσὸν καὶ λίβανον καὶ σμύρναν. λίβανος occurs only one other time in the NT, in Rev 18.13. σμύρνα also occurs only one other time, in Jn 19.39. χρυσός appears four times in Matthew, never in Mark or Luke.

λίβανος, a Semitic loan word (*lĕbōnâ, lĕbônâ*), means either the 'frankincense tree' (as in T. Job 32.11) or (as here) 'frankincense', an odoriferous gum resin from various trees and bushes which had a cultic usage in the ancient world.[57] According to Exod 30.34–8, frankincense was a prescribed ingredient of sacred incense. According to Lev 24.7, it was to be offered with the bread of the Presence (cf. Josephus, *Ant.* 3.143; Jub. 50.10). According to Lev 2.1–2, 14–16; 6.14–18, it was added to cereal offerings (cf. Neh 13.5, 9). In *b. Sanh.* 43a it is said to be an anodyne (cf. Celsus 5.18.6). Whether frankincense was cultivated in Palestine is debated and doubtful; that it was imported from Arabia is certain (cf. Isa 60.6; Jer 6.20; Herodotus 3.107).

σμύρνα = μύρρα (latin *murra*), another Semitic loan word (*mōr, môr*), is 'myrrh', a fragrant gum resin from the 'balsamodendron myrrh' or 'commiphora kataf', trees particularly abundant in south Arabia and north Ethiopia (cf. Herodotus 3.107).[58] It had a variety of uses, being an element in perfumes (Esth 2.12; Ps 45.8; Ct 1.13; LAB 12.9), a component of holy anointing oil (Exod 30.23), and an ingredient in incense (Ct 3.6). It also served as a burial spice (Jn 19.39; cf. Herodotus 2.40, 86) and, like frankincense, as an anodyne (Mk 15.23). For frankincense with myrrh see Ct 3.6; 4.6, 14; Ecclus 24.15; 1 En. 29.2; 1 Clem. 25.2; Herodotus 3.107; Sepher Ha-Razim 1.30, 224; *PGM* 1.62–3, 73–4, 243–7.

What is signified by the gold, frankincense, and myrrh? The most common interpretation in church history appears early: gold for Jesus as king, frankincense for Jesus as God, myrrh for Jesus as the one to die (cf. Irenaeus, *Adv. haer.* 3.9.2; Clement of Alexandria, *Paed.* 2.8.63, 5; Origen, *C. Cels.* 1.60; Theodotus of Ancyra, *Hom.* 1.5; Prudentius in PL 69.904–5; Pseudo-Bede in PL 94.541).[59] This explanation we cannot endorse. Among other things, by changing Mark's 'wine mingled with myrrh' (15.23) to 'wine mingled with gall' (27.34; cf. Ps 68.22 LXX), Matthew has ruined the possible connexion between myrrh and the passion. A better guess as to what the gifts mean is this: the magi's worship and presentation are the firstfruits of the eschatological pilgrimage of the nations and their submission to the one true God. The OT teaches that the great redemption will see the Gentiles come up to Zion, bringing gifts and offering right worship (see on 8.11–12). Especially interesting in this regard is Ps. Sol. 17.31, according to

[57] See W. Michaelis, *TWNT* 4, pp. 268–9, and the lit. cited there; also W. G. van Beek, 'Frankincense and Myrrh', *BA* 23 (1960), pp. 69–95.

[58] See Beek, ibid., and W. Michaelis, *TWNT* 7, pp. 457–8. Myrrh is not to be confused with μύρον, a word which means ointment (Mt 26.7, 12).

[59] According to a legend in *The Travels of Marco Polo*, the three gifts were brought in order to determine who Jesus was. If the new-born prophet took the gold, he would be an earthly king. If he took the frankincense, he would be a god. If he took the myrrh, he would be a healer. Jesus took all three.

which the heathen nations will come from the ends of the earth with gifts in hand to see the glory of the Son of David. Note further 1 En. 53.1, where Enoch foresees the time when all those dwelling on the earth and sea and islands will bring to the Righteous and Elect One, the Son of Man, gifts and presents and tokens of homage. (For later material see SB 1, p. 84, to which add *Gen. Rab.* on 49.10: 'all the nations of the world shall in the future bring a gift to the Son of David'.) Now undoubtedly both Isa 60 and Ps 72 would have been understood by Matthew and his readers in terms of the expected pilgrimage of the nations (cf. Mt 8.11–12)—and these two OT texts, although they are not explicitly cited, are probably alluded to in Mt 2 (cf. Tertullian *Adv. Marc.* 3.13).[60] Isa 60, a thoroughly eschatological passage which has influenced another early Christian text, Rev 21.23–6, contains these words: 'Arise, shine; for your light has come, and the glory of the Lord has risen upon you' (60.1). 'Nations shall come to your light, and kings to the brightness of your rising' (60.3). 'The wealth of nations shall come to you' (60.5). 'They shall bring gold and frankincense and proclaim the praise of the Lord' (60.6). And in Ps 72, which even a few modern interpreters have taken to be messianic,[61] there is this: 'May the kings of Tarshish and of the isles render him tribute, may the kings of Sheba and Seba bring gifts' (72.10); 'May all kings fall down (LXX: προσκυνήσουσιν) before him, all nations serve him' (72.11); 'Long may he live, may gold of Sheba be given to him' (72.15).[62]

Beyond the eschatological theme, a Jesus/Solomon typology may also perhaps be discerned in Mt 2.11. (1) Gold and myrrh were among the gifts brought to king Solomon by foreigners, and gold and frankincense were firmly associated with the temple he built (1 Kgs 10.2, 25; 1 Chr 9.29; 2 Chr 9.24; Neh 13.5, 9; Ecclus 47.18). (2) Ps 72, alluded to in 2.11, is attributed in the OT to Solomon. Moreover, if we are to trust Justin (*Dial.* 34), some Jews at least applied the psalm's words to king Solomon. (3) Leaving aside Ecclus 24.15, frankincense and myrrh appear together only three times in the OT, each time in connexion with Solomon: Ct 3.6; 4.6, 14. (4) The eschatological events (including the eschatological pilgrimage of the nations, foreshadowed or begun in Mt 2) were sometimes conceived as a return to—or a surpassing of—the days of Solomon, the days of the first temple (e.g., Hag

---

[60] So most modern commentators; cf. Brown, *Messiah*, pp. 187–8; Nolan, pp. 44–6.

[61] See the survey of opinion by P. Veugelers, 'Le Psaume LXXII, poème messianique?', *ETL* 49 (1965), pp. 317–43. The targum makes the psalm messianic.

[62] The finding of an implicit citation of Isa 60.6 and Ps 72.10–11, 15 made possible the equation of the magi with kings in Christian tradition. Cf. Isa 49.7. The camels of tradition also come from Isa 60.6.

2.7–9 and T Benj. 9.2). (5) Just as the magi give both gifts and homage to king Jesus, so foreign royalty once rendered both gifts and honour to King Solomon (1 Kgs 10.1–10, 15, 23–5; 2 Chr 9.14; T. Sol. 108)—and in late Jewish tradition the queen of Sheba saw a star as she made her way to David's son.[63] Further, if Matthew thought the magi's home to be Arabia—an option reinforced by Herodotus 3.107: 'Arabia is the only place that produces frankincense and myrrh'[64]—it may be recalled that the most famous visitors Solomon received were also from Arabia (1 Kgs 10.1–5; Mt 12.42; T. Sol. 19.1–3; 21–2). In view of these several points, it is rather tempting to see the Jesus of Mt 2 as one like Solomon, the son of David.

In addition to Isa 60 and Ps 72, could Ps 110.3 also have played some rôle in the formation of Mt 2.1–12, or at least have later been read in terms of the story of the magi? In the LXX we read of a beginning, a birth, a brightness, and of 'the morning-star'. The Hebrew, certainly corrupt, is virtually unintelligible. If, however, someone understood the verse as does the NEB ('At birth you were endowed with princely gifts'), and if the application of Ps 110 to Jesus was presupposed (cf. Mt 22.44 par.; Acts 2.34–5; Heb 1.13), it would have been easy to read the psalm's words as prophesying the events Matthew narrates. Melito, *Hom.* 82 applies Ps 110.3 to Jesus: 'He is the first born of God, begotten before the morning star. He made the light shine and the day be radiant . . .'.[65]

12. This is an addendum from stage II, necessitated by the merging of the magi story with the Herod story.

καὶ χρηματισθέντες κατ' ὄναρ μὴ ἀνακάμψαι πρὸς Ἡρῴδην. The use of χρηματίζω in the passive proves the dream to be divinely given, for a revelation or warning signified by this verb is always of God.[66] See Diodorus Siculus 15.10; Josephus, *Ant.* 3.212; Lk 2.26; Acts 10.22; Heb 8.5; 11.7; 12.25. Bengel (ad loc.) went so far as to affirm that in 2.12 the word signifies an answer, that is, an answer to the magi's prayer for guidance; and indeed the word does often

[63] See Bruns (v), pp. 51–4, citing N. Ausbel, *Jewish Folklore*, New York, 1948, p. 482.

[64] Although strictly inaccurate, the statement is bound to reflect some popular opinion.

[65] Of the many legends that later came to surround the magi and their gifts, one of the most pleasing is found in the so-called Cave of Treasures (6th cent. A.D.). Adam, we are told, had many treasures in paradise, and when he was expelled therefrom he took what he could with him—gold, frankincense, and myrrh (cf. Jub. 3.27?). Upon his death, Adam's sons hid their father's treasures in a cave, where they lay undisturbed until the magi, on their way to Bethlehem, entered the cave to get gifts for the Son of God. In this legend, Matthew's story has become the vehicle for a very Pauline idea: Jesus is the second Adam.

[66] Cf. J. Lindblom, *Geschichte und Offenbarung*, Lund, 1968, pp. 29–30; B. Reicke, *TWNT* 9, pp. 469–71.

refer to the response of an oracle to those who have consulted it. For divine warnings in dreams see Herodotus 3.65; Josephus, *Ant*. 11.327; Mt 27.19. For 'in a dream' see on 1.20. No angel is here alluded to; contrast 1.20; 2.13, 19; Prot. Jas. 21.4; Origen, *C. Cels*. 1.60. Approximately half of the instances of πρός with accusative belong to special Matthean material, and ten times in Matthew the combination is redactional. Oddly enough, the redactional use of πρός + accusative is confined to two clusters, one in chapter 3 (13, 14, 15), one in chapter 26 (12, 18 (*bis*), 40, 45, 57 + 27.14). In Prot. Jas. 21.4, the magi are warned not to return to Judea; Herod is not named.

δι᾽ ἄλλης ὁδοῦ ἀνεχώρησαν εἰς τὴν χώραν αὐτῶν. Compare 1 Kgs 13.9–10. The magi obey the divine warning. The vocabulary of the line is typical of the redactor.[67] 'By another way' recalls the use of *bĕderek ᾽eḥād* (*bis*) in 1 Kgs 18.6. In Dio Cassius 63.7, the magos Tiridates takes leave of Nero 'by another way'. Note that in chapter 2 γῆ is reserved for the land of Israel.

Although we do not know when the magi left, we do know when they received their warning—at night ('in a dream'). On this two points may be pertinent. (1) God spoke to Balaam in the night (Num 22.7–13, 19–20; LAB 18.3–4, 8). (2) According to some rabbinic sources (e.g. *Gen. Rab.* on 20.3), God speaks to the Gentiles only at night.

(iv) *Concluding Observations*

Mt 2.1–12 has the power to fascinate readers and to stay in the memory because it incorporates ever-popular and perennially pleasing characters and motifs: the mysterious magi from the east, the anomalous star coincident wih the birth of a king, the threat to the life of an infant hero, the warning that comes in a dream. These are things to delight and enchant, to entertain and cause wonder. They are also vehicles of truths when contemplated within their literary context in Matthew (see below). In our view, however, they are not the stuff out of which history is made. Rather do they supplement history as history's addendum. As the haggadah fills up the voids in the OT text, so does Mt 2.1–12 close one of the gaps in the Jesus tradition. (But, as the NT editor, Dr. Cranfield, urges, the reader should note that other critical scholars reckon with the possibility that the narratives contained in this section and also in 2.13–23 may have a much more substantial factual basis than is envisaged here.)

[67] διά with the genitive: Mt: 26; Mk: 10; Lk: 13. ἀναχωρέω: Mt: 10; Mk: 1; Lk: 0. For ἀναχωρέω + εἰς + locale see also 2.14, 22; 4.12; 14.13; 15.21.

Having already discussed the special theological tendencies which gave shape to the materials behind Mt 1.18–2.23 (Excursus I), we shall now summarily indicate Matthew's particular concerns as they come to the surface in 2.1–12.

(1) As in Jn 7.40–4, the question of who Jesus is (Mt 1) leads to the question of where he is from (Mt 2). The implicit dialogue is this. Who is Jesus? He is the Messiah. Where is the Messiah to be born? In Bethlehem. Where was Jesus born? In Bethlehem.

(2) Mic 5.2 foretells the advent of a Davidic ruler, and 2 Sam 5.2 is, in the OT, addressed to David. By adding these two scriptural texts to his narrative (in 2.5–6), the evangelist continues the theme of Jesus as the Son of David (1.1–17).

(3) Mt 1.1 opens the gospel by announcing that Jesus is the 'son of Abraham'. This we interpreted to mean that Jesus brings salvation to the Gentiles. The same thought is now found again. In contradistinction to the leaders in Jerusalem, the magi, who are Gentiles, worship Jesus. (The suggested link between the magi and Abraham is the stronger because, according to some, the patriarch was a master of astrology and a teacher of eastern wise men; see on 1.1)

(4) Jesus is the Messiah (1.1, 17, 18), which implies two things. First, it implies his fulfilling messianic Scriptures. Mt 2 accordingly contains explicit and (probably) implicit citations of eschatological texts (Mic 5.2; Isa 60.11; Ps 72.10–11, 15). (Mt 1–2 contains a relatively large percentage of the formula quotations. The reason for this might be that as of yet the Messiah cannot speak for himself.) Secondly, messiahship implies kingship. This explains the apparent allusions to King Solomon (see on 2.11) as well as Herod's actions: the evil and illegitimate king, who will tolerate no threat to his throne, recognizes that he has a rival. Kings are meeting here. (βασιλεύς occurs four times in 2.1–12.)

(5) Mt 2 offers an 'inaugurated eschatology'. The pilgrimage of the nations, foretold in Isa 60 and Ps 72, has commenced. The one destined to shepherd the scattered sheep of Israel, the one who fulfils the words of 2 Sam 5.2, has already appeared. And the promise of a Davidic ruler to be born in Bethlehem, the promise made in Mic 5.2, has been fulfilled. The time of eschatological fulfilment, of the 'new creation' (cf. 1.1), has dawned.

(6) Although he does not add to the parallels, the evangelist must have known that his narrative largely derived its meaning from agreements with the Moses legends (see Excursus I). He will then have seen eye to eye with his source: Jesus the Messiah is like

Moses; the first redeemer is as the last. See further on 5.1 for discussion of the Mosaic typology in Mt 1–5.

(7) In T. S. Eliot's poem, 'Journey of the Magi', the visitors from the east see, on their way to Bethlehem, 'three trees on the low sky', and 'six hands at an open door dicing for pieces of silver'. The three trees stand for the three crosses while the men dicing for silver represent the soldiers casting lots for Jesus' garments and Judas' betrayal of his master for thirty pieces of silver. Thus at Jesus' birth his death is already anticipated (cf. the intermingling between the slaughter at Bethlehem and the passion in Gos. Nicodemus (B) 9). Matthew would have approved of Eliot's interpretation. We have had occasion to observe several of the connexions between Mt 2 and the passion narrative, such as the gathering of the Jewish leaders, the title, 'king of the Jews', and the decision of the ruling authority to do away with Jesus. Matthew wants the end foreshadowed in the beginning.

(8) Leonardo da Vinci's Adoration of the Magi highlights an aspect of Matthew's text that other artists—and some exegetes—have missed: Mt 2.1–12 has not only a foreground but also a background. In da Vinci's painting, behind the magi and Jesus and Mary there are buildings in ruin and horsemen at joust. The meaning is manifest. The world into which the Messiah comes is in chaos and decay; things need to be righted. This is also an element in Matthew's story. When Jesus is born, Jerusalem, instead of being overjoyed, is troubled at the news. And there is upon Israel's throne a wicked and illegitimate ruler. And innocent blood is about to be shed (cf. 2.13–23). In brief, the world is ill. Is it any wonder that the first word of Jesus' public proclamation is, 'Repent!' (4.17)?

(v) *Bibliography*

An asterisk (*) denotes an entry which treats not only 2.1–12 but all of chapter 2.

E. E. F. Bishop, 'Some Reflections on Justin Martyr and the Nativity Narratives', *EvQ* 39 (1967), pp. 30–9.

F. Boll, 'Der Stern der Weisen', *ZNW* 18 (1917), pp. 40–8.

*I. Broer, 'Jesusflucht und Kindermord: Exegetische Anmerkungen zum zweiten Kapitel des Matthäusevangelium', in Pesch, *Theologie* (as in section v. for 1.18–25), pp. 74–96.

Brown, *Messiah*, pp. 165–201.

J. E. Bruns, 'The Magi Episode in Matthew 2', *CBQ* 23 (1961), pp. 51–4.

*Bultmann, *History*, pp. 292–4, 304.

W. K. L. Clark, 'The Rout of the Magi', in *Divine Humanity*, London, 1936, pp. 41–51.

*Davies, *SSM*, pp. 77–83.

A. M. Denis, 'L'adoration des mages vue par S. Matthieu', *NRT* 82 (1960), pp. 32–9.

*J. D. M. Derrett, 'Further Light on the Narratives of the Nativity', *NovT* 17 (1975), pp. 81–108.

*R. T. France, 'The Formula Quotations and the Problem of Communication', *NTS* 27 (1981), pp. 233–51.

*M. A. Friggens, 'The Relationship of the Prophetic Quotations in Matthew ii in the Light of the Triennial Lectionary Cycle', in *Studia Evangelica 7*, TU 126, ed. E. A. Livingstone, Berlin, 1982, pp. 183–8.

P. Gaechter, 'Die Magierperikope (Mt 2.1–12)', *ZTK* 90 (1968), pp. 259–95.

*Goulder, pp. 236–42.

H. Heater, 'Matthew 2:6 and Its Old Testament Sources', *JETS* 26 (1983), pp. 395–7.

*M. Hengel and H. Merkel, 'Die Magier aus dem Osten und die Flucht nach Ägypten (Mt 2) im Rahmen der antiken Religionsgeschichte und der Theologie des Matthäus', in Hoffmann, *Orientierung*, pp. 136–69.

D. Hughes, *The Star of Bethlehem Mystery*, London, 1979.

Hull, pp. 122–8.

H. Kehrer, *Die heiligen drei Könige in Literatur und Kunst.*, 2 vols, Leipzig, 1908–9.

Levine, pp. 42–58.

M. McNamara, 'Were the Magi Essenes?', *IER* 110 (1968), pp. 305–28.

*B. Malina, 'Matthew 2 and Isa 41,2–3: a possible relationship?', *SBFLA* 17 (1967), pp. 290–302.

C. S. Mann, 'Epiphany—Wise Men or Charlatans?', *Theology* 61 (1958), pp. 495–500.

J. C. Marsh-Edwards, 'The Magi in Tradition and Art', *IER* 85 (1956), pp. 1–9.

M. A. V. van der Merwe, 'The Form and Message of MT 2 Based on a Structural Analysis', *Neotestamentica* 11 (1977), pp. 10–18.

*E. Nellessen, *Das Kind und seine Mutter*, SBS 39, Stuttgart, 1969.

*Nolan, pp. 73–91, 131–4.

*Paul, pp. 95–169.

*R. Pesch, 'Der Gottessohn im matthäischen Evangelienprolog (Mt 1–2). Beobachtungen zu den Zitationsformeln der Reflexionzitate', *Bib* 48 (1967), pp. 395–420.

A. J. Petrotta, 'A Closer Look at Matt 2.6 and its Old Testament Sources', *JETS* 28 (1985), pp. 47–52.

H. J. Richards, 'The Three Kings (Mt ii. 1–12)', *Scripture* 8 (1956), pp. 23–38.

*J. Riedl, *Die Vorgeschichte Jesu. Die Heilsbotschaft von Mt 1–2 und Lk 1–2*, Stuttgart, 1968.

R. A. Rosenberg, 'The "Star of the Messiah" Reconsidered', *Bib* 53 (1972), pp. 105–9.

G. Ryckmans, 'De l'or(?), de l'encens et de la myrrhe', *RB* 58 (1951), pp. 372–6.

G. Schmahl, 'Magier aus dem Osten und die Heiligen Drei Könige', *TTZ* 87 (1978), pp. 295–303.

A. Schulze, 'Zur Geschichte der Auslegung von Mt 2.1–12', *TZ* 31 (1975), pp. 150–60.

*Stauffer, pp. 36–43.

*K. Stendahl, '*Quis et Unde?* An Analysis of Mt 1–2', in Eltester, pp. 94–105.

N. Turner, 'The New-Born King (Matthew 2.2)', *ExpT* 68 (1957), p. 122.

*A. Vögtle, *Messias und Gottessohn: Herkunft und Sinn der matthäischen Geburts- und Kindheitsgeschichte*, Düsseldorf, 1971.

*idem, 'Die matthäische Kindheitsgeschichte', in Didier, pp. 153–83.

*idem, 'Das Schicksal des Messiaskindes. Zur Auslegung und Theologie von Mt 2', *BuL* 6 (1965), pp. 246–79.

*F. Zinniker *Probleme der sogenannten Kindheitsgeschichte bei Matthäus*, Freiburg, 1972.

THE MESSIAH'S FLIGHT AND RETURN
(2.13–23)

(i) *Structure*

Mt 2.13–23, the third and final act of Matthew's infancy drama, consists of three scenes, each of which is concluded by a formula quotation (cf. Schmid, *Matthäus*, pp. 45, 49, and Luz 1, p. 125). There are also three dreams in 2.13–23:

A. Joseph is warned by an angel in a dream to flee to Egypt in order to keep Jesus safe from Herod + formula quotation (2.13–15)
B. Herod slaughters the infants + formula quotation (2.16–18)
C. After Herod's death, Joseph brings Jesus and Mary back from Egypt (2.19–23)
    1. A dream and the return to Israel (19–21)
    2. A dream and the move to Nazareth + formula quotation (22–23).

2.22 and 23 create one of the so-called 'broken patterns'[1] of the First Gospel. For while the two verses, considering their content, could easily have been brought into perfect parallelism with 1.18–25; 2.13–15; and 2.19–21, they have not been. The expected words—'the angel of the Lord appeared in a dream to Joseph saying'—do not occur. Why should this be so? Perhaps a fondness for the number three accounts for there being three—and only three—analogous episodes. Or perhaps the evangelist recognized that if 2.19–21 and 22–3 stood in perfect parallel, the tension between them, that is, the superfluity of the command to go to the land of Israel (see p. 190), would be all the more pronounced. Above all, though, the omission of 'the angel of the Lord appeared, etc.' makes it possible to regard 2.19–23 as a unit, to see 2.19–21 and 22–3 not as two separate scenes with two separate angelic appearances but rather as two halves of a single whole, this whole being the account of Jesus' return from exile in Egypt. This in turn makes it possible to divide 2.13–23 into three sections, which is what Matthew wanted.

(ii) *Sources*

Concerning the issue of sources behind 2.13–23 see Excursus I, pp. 190–5.

---

[1] Cf. F. V. Filson, 'Broken Patterns in the Gospel of Matthew', *JBL* 75 (1956), pp. 227–31.

(iii) *Exegesis*

A dramatic contrast is occasioned by the juxtaposition of 2.13–23 with the conclusion of the magi story. The reader is taken from a scene of prostration and gift-giving to a scene of danger and flight. The disparity between the magi's response to the child Messiah and that of Herod could hardly be more pronounced. While the foreigners worship Jesus, the king in Israel threatens his life. (Perhaps this circumstance should be thought of as reflecting the range of possible responses to Jesus or to those preaching him: the people who hear can either embrace the message or react with anger or violence; cf. 10.16–23.)

As seen in Excursus I, the threat to the life of the young Jesus has its counterpart in tales about Moses. But one should also take cognizance of the large number of other legends with which comparison may be made. The peril to the saviour or hero at or soon after his birth is well-nigh a universal theme in world mythology and literature.[2] Names that come to mind include Gilgamesh, Sargon, Zoroaster (who, like Jesus, was allegedly visited by adoring magi), Cyrus, Apollo, Perseus, Hercules, Romulus and Remus, Augustus, John the Baptist (so Prot. Jas. 22–3), and later than our period Pope Gregory the Great and Charlemagne. Recall also Rev 12.1–6. The stories about Cyrus and Augustus in particular are of special interest. King Astyages of Persia (6th cent. B.C.) had dreams about his daughter, Mandane, and these were interpreted by the magi to mean that his daughter's son (Cyrus) would usurp the throne. Astyages therefore commanded his steward to kill Mandane's child as soon as it was born. But fortuitous circumstances then intervened. Cyrus was spared death, to be raised by a shepherd (Herodotus 1.108–13). The life of Augustus was also imperilled when he was an infant. When a public portent warned the Romans that nature was about to provide them with a king, the Senate issued a decree banning the rearing of male children for an entire year. However, a number of senators had wives who were already pregnant, and these men prevented the decree from being filed with the Treasury—for each hoped his own child would gain the kingship (Suetonius, *Aug.* 94).

Frequently hand in hand with the theme of peril is the theme of exile and return. Moses was born in Egypt, then fled to Midian, then returned to Egypt. As an infant, Krishna was forced to suffer exile among the cowherds of Gokula and Brindaban (*Viṣṇu Purāṇa* 5). Zeus, in danger of death at birth, was spirited away to be safely raised in Crete. He later took Chronos' place as king of Olympus (Hesiod, *Th.* 453–506). Perseus, having been enclosed by his father in a wooden ark and cast into the sea, was drawn out by a fisherman and raised in the court of king Polydectes of Seriphos (Apollodorus 2.4). Afterwards he found his way back to the land of his birth and became ruler. Oedipus, after surviving his father's attempt to kill him, was entrusted to the care of a shepherd of the king of Corinth

---

[2] See further Lord Raglan, *The Hero*, London and New York, 1936, pp. 177–89, and O. Rank, *Myth of the Birth of the Hero*, New York, 1959, pp. 3–96.

and brought up there, from whence he eventually returned to become king of Thebes (Apollodorus 3.5–6). And Charlemagne was compelled to flee to Saracen Spain before taking his rightful place on the throne of the Franks. When Jesus goes down to Egypt and returns to Palestine, he recapitulates not only the experience of Israel but also the experience of 'the hero with a thousand faces'.

13. This verse has an almost perfect parallel in 2.19–20. The common structure is: genitive absolute + 'behold' + 'the angel of the Lord appeared in a dream to Joseph saying' + 'rise, take the child and his mother' + command to move to a designated land + an explanatory 'for'-clause.

ἀναχωρησάντων δὲ αὐτῶν ἰδοὺ ἄγγελος κυρίου φαίνεται κατ' ὄναρ τῷ Ἰωσὴφ λέγων. For the construction and vocabulary see on 1.20. The magi were warned of Herod in a dream, but no angel appeared. Because one appears to Joseph, this points to his importance. The opening verb links 2.13–15 to what precedes (cf. on 1.18 and 2.1) and continues the homeophony: ἀνεχώρησαν/χώραν/ἀναχωρησάντων. Does the present tense, φαίνεται (cf. 2.19 but contrast 1.20, which has the aorist), imply simultaneity, that is, does it make the angelic appearance concurrent with the magi's departure?

ἐγερθεὶς παράλαβε τὸ παιδίον καὶ τὴν μητέρα αὐτοῦ. ἐγερθείς (see on 1.24 and cf. 2. 14, 20, 21) + imperative is a Semitism, being the equivalent of *qûm* + imperative. The LXX typically translates the idiom by ἀναστάς + imperative (Gen 13.17; Deut 17.8; Josh 1.2; cf. Lk 17.19; 22.46; Acts 9.11; T. Job 24.10; Par. Jer. 1.3). 1 Chr 22.19 is an exception. παράλαβε recalls 1.20 and 24. Joseph is still the only active character in the family of Jesus. For the imperative of παραλαμβάνω (only in Matthew in the synoptics) see also 2.20 and 18.16. On 'the child and his mother' see on 2.11.

καὶ φεῦγε εἰς Αἴγυπτον. Compare Gen 46.2–4. Almost as soon as he is born, the Son of man, who like Moses will grow up in Egypt, has no place to lay his head (cf. 8.20).

If the faithful followers of Jesus must flee when the tribulations of the latter days fall upon them (10.23; 24.16; cf. 3.7; 23.33), they can take comfort in this, that they are only suffering the same fate as did their master and his family (cf. 10.24–5).

Egypt was the traditional refuge for Palestinian Jews seeking asylum. See, for example, 1 Kgs 11.40 (Jeroboam); 2 Kgs 25.26 and Jer 41.16–18 (Gedaliah's friends who departed from Geruth Chimham 'near Bethlehem'); Jer 43.1–7 (Jeremiah); Josephus, *Ant.* 12.387 (Onias IV); 14.21 ('principal men among the Jews'); 15.46 (a frustrated attempt by Alexandria); Josephus, *Bell.* 7.409–10 (Sicarii); and *b. Sanh.* 107b (Joshua b. Peraḥyah) (cf. also Zech 10.10; Rev 12.4–6).

Little weight is to be placed upon the fact that Jewish sources speak of the travels of Jesus in Egypt (*b.* '*Abod. Zar.* 16b–17a; *b. Sanh.* 107b; *b. Šabb.* 104b; cf. Origen, *C. Cels.* 1.28). This tradition was presumably passed on principally out of a desire to make Jesus' false teachings derive from Egyptian soothsayers, not Jewish rabbis, and it scarcely supplies independent evidence for an historical journey of Jesus' family in Egypt. More plausible but still very improbable is M. Smith's proposal that primitive polemic against Jesus as a magician led to the assertion that he must have gone down to Egypt to learn magic; Christians then responded by having Jesus go to Egypt as an infant, before the time when he could have learned anything.[3]

Some have found in the exile to Egypt a harking back to the story of Jacob, who was persecuted (by Laban) and who (unlike Moses) fled *to* Egypt.[4] Yet given the theme of exile, which *does* have its parallel in the traditions about Moses (not to mention numerous other heroes), and given belief in Jesus' birth in Nazareth or Bethlehem, the sequence, birth in Palestine, exile in Egypt, return to Palestine, was inevitable. When one adds that the other correlations between Mt 1–2 and the legends about Jacob depend mostly upon sources of rather late or uncertain date (such as *Midrash Rabbah*), it becomes difficult to find the background of the Matthean infancy narrative in the stories about the patriarch.[5]

Apoc. Adam 5.78.18–26 from Nag Hammadi reads thus: 'He came from a virgin womb. He was cast out of his city, he and his mother; he was brought to a desert place. He was nourished there. He came and received glory and power. And thus he came to the water.' If this text is indeed from a document wholly unacquainted with the NT (so e.g. G. MacRae in Charlesworth 1, p. 709), the parallels with Mt 1–3 are remarkable.

καὶ ἴσθι ἐκεῖ ἕως ἂν εἴπω σοι. Compare Exod 24.12. The appearance of the angel in 2.19–20 is here prophesied. Both ἐκεῖ (Mt: 28; Mk: 11; Lk: 16) and ἕως ἄν (Mt: 9–10; Mk: 3; Lk: 2–3) are often redactional.

μέλλει γὰρ Ἡρῴδης ζητεῖν τὸ παιδίον τοῦ ἀπολέσαι αὐτό. Compare Exod 2.15 and Mt 16.27 (redactional). The angel who appears to Joseph is reasonable: his imperative is followed by an explanatory clause which makes the command sensible. For μέλλω with the infinitive, used to express imminence, see BDF § 356. Concerning ἀπολέσαι, the genitive articular infinitive may well betray the redactor's hand; see 3.13; 11.1; 13.3 (diff. Mk 4.3); 21.32; 24.45 (= Lk 12.42). Direct purpose is indicated (cf. 13.3): seek in order to kill. Because ἀπολύω also appears in the passion narrative (27.20), it adds to the parallelism between the initial persecution of Jesus and the last days in Jerusalem.

[3] Smith, *Magician*, pp. 47–8, 150–1. But if Smith is right, why did Christians not just simply deny that Jesus went to Egypt in the first place?

[4] D. Daube, 'The Earliest Structures of the Gospels', *NTS* 5 (1959), pp. 174–87; C. H. Cave, 'St. Matthew's Infancy Narrative', *NTS* 9 (1963), pp. 382–90; M. M. Bourke, 'The Literary Genus of Matthew 1–2', *CBQ* 22 (1960), pp. 160–75.

[5] Further discussions and criticism in Vögtle, 'Kindheitsgeschichte' (see p. 256), pp. 165–7; Brown, *Messiah*, pp. 544–5; Nolan, pp. 82–3.

14. Joseph obeys the angel's command to the letter: he rises, he takes, he goes, and he returns, just as instructed. See the remarks on 1.24–5.

The parallel in 1 Kgs 11.40 is interesting: 'Solomon sought therefore to kill Jeroboam; but Jeroboam arose, and fled into Egypt, to Shishak king of Egypt, and was in Egypt until the death of Solomon'. See further Soares Prabhu, pp. 226–7.

Matthew gives none of the details we might expect from other narrators, such as the route Joseph took to Egypt, or how long the family resided there, etc. The evangelist sticks to the barest essentials. If we could somehow recover the pre-Matthean tradition, Mt 2 might show itself to be an abbreviated version. In any event, Matthew's conciseness, his leaving so much unsaid, could not but stimulate later apocryphal fantasy; see, for instance, Eusebius, *Dem. ev.* 6.20; Gosp. Ps.-Mt. 18–25; Arabic Infancy Narrative 9–26.

ὁ δὲ ἐγερθεὶς παρέλαβεν τὸ παιδίον καὶ τὴν μητέρα αὐτοῦ νυκτὸς καὶ ἀνεχώρησεν εἰς Αἴγυπτον. Compare 1.24; 2.13. The vocabulary is taken over from earlier verses.

Why is the time of flight recorded? (The magi, one infers, must also have travelled at night, although Matthew fails to remark on this.) (1) The *Passover Haggadah* puts the exodus at night. Yet if this were pertinent, the note of time should come in 2.21, when the family *leaves* Egypt, not here, when they enter it. (2) Given the other parallels between Mt 2 and the passion narrative, it might not be fanciful to observe that Jesus was later overtaken by his enemies at night (Mt 26). (3) Joseph must escape by night to avoid being seen; he must go under cover of darkness (cf. 28.13). The danger of the situation is thereby made plain. (4) Because Joseph is warned 'in a dream', are we not to think of him getting up in the middle of his sleep to carry off Mary and Jesus without a moment's delay? Again, the danger of things would be the point.

In the passion narrative Jesus will declare that, if he willed it, more than twelve legions of angels would come to his aid: but the time has come for something else, the fulfilment of Scripture (26.53–4). In Mt 2, on the other hand, the time of the crucifixion lies far ahead, and Jesus must be saved for what is to come. This is why the angelic command to flee and Joseph's keeping Jesus safe from harm are for the moment necessary.

15. This verse anticipates 2.19–21: the stay in Egypt will be ended by Herod's death—just as Moses' stay in Midian was concluded when the king of Egypt died (Exod 4.19 LXX).

καὶ ἦν ἐκεῖ ἕως τῆς τελευτῆς Ἡρῴδου. τελευτή (LXX: 26–7) is a NT *hapax legomenon*. Compare Exod 4.19 LXX: 'the king of Egypt died' (ἐτελεύτησεν).

ἵνα πληρωθῇ τὸ ῥηθὲν ὑπὸ κυρίου διὰ τοῦ προφήτου λέγοντος. See on 1.22. The following brief citation of Hos 11.1[6] agrees with the Hebrew: 'out of Egypt have I called my son' (*mimmiṣrayim qārā'tî libĕnî*). The LXX has: 'Out of Egypt I summoned his children' (μετεκάλεσα τὰ τέκνα αὐτοῦ). Unless one posits use of a non-LXX Greek version (cf. Aquila's translation) or a Christian testimony book, Matthew's knowledge of Hebrew here seems evident.

ἐξ Αἰγύπτου ἐκάλεσα τὸν υἱόν μου. Although Hosea was much mined for early Christian testimonies (Dodd, *Scriptures*, pp. 75–78), Matthew was presumably the first to connect Hos 11.1 with the story of Jesus.[7] He was in all likelihood led to it via Num 24.8, which reads, 'God led (ὡδήγησεν) him out of Egypt' (cf. 23.22).[8] A messianic interpretation of this verse already lies to hand in the LXX, for the opening line of 24.7 ('water shall flow from his buckets', so MT) becomes in the LXX, 'a man will come forth from his seed'. This makes 24.7 a potential reference to the Messiah[9]—a possibility strongly reinforced by the fact that other verses in Balaam's oracle were given a messianic interpretation by Jews and Christians (see p. 234). So having been sent to Num 24.7 by the story of the magi and the star, Matthew's attention was then directed to Num 24.8, which seemed a good proof text for the tradition about Jesus' departure to and return from Egypt. That the evangelist then went on to quote the very similar Hos 11.1 and not the verse in Numbers must be put down to the mention of 'son' in the former. (No influence from Gen 46.3–4 is to be detected.)

It is exceptional for a formula quotation to refer forward to an event yet to be narrated, so Matthew's placement of the quotation here rather than after 2.21 has puzzled commentators. Yet Egypt is the geographical focus of 2.13–15, and Hos 11.1 names Egypt. 2.19–21, on the other hand, is oriented towards the land of Israel, and an appropriate scriptural proof at that juncture would have to name Israel or the land. So Hos 11.1 could not go after 2.21. In short, Matthew's placement is determined by the naming of Egypt

[6] Stendahl, *School*, pp. 101–2, Gundry, *OT*, pp. 92–4; Rothfuchs, pp. 62–3; Lindars, *Apologetic*, pp. 216–17; Soares Prabhu, pp. 216–18; Brown, *Messiah*, pp. 219–21.

[7] Dodd, *Scriptures*, p. 103, suggests that the words of Hosea's prophecy might first have been applied by Christians to the deliverance of God's people in Christ for, according to Rev 11.8, the place where Jesus was crucified is spiritually called 'Egypt'. This is highly speculative.

[8] For this and what follows see Lindars, *Apologetic*, pp. 216–17. For those familiar only with the LXX, Matthew's quotation would have seemed closer to Num 24.8 than to Hos 11.1. This explains the scribal note in the margin of א, which ascribes the text to Numbers.

[9] Cf. Lindars, ibid., who also calls attention to the Peshitta ('a mighty man shall proceed from his sons') and Targum Onkelos ('a king shall grow great, who shall be reared from his sons'), both of which appear to him to be independent of the LXX.

in Hosea's prophecy, not by the movement envisaged (cf. Stendahl (v), p. 97). If one further asks why the quotation is not placed after the first mention of Egypt, that is, in 2.13, the answer must be because it would destroy the perfect parallelism between 2.13–14 and 19–21.

The application of Hos 11.1 to Jesus inevitably seems to us gratuitous. In its original context the verse unambiguously refers to Israel: 'When Israel was a child I loved him, and out of Egypt have I called my son'. But three points should give us some sympathy for Matthew's use of this OT Scripture. To begin with, the evangelist was, we are strongly inclined to think, perfectly aware that 'Out of Egypt, etc.' was originally spoken of Israel. He was not naïvely oblivious of the switch in referents when he applied Hos 11.1 to Jesus, not to the people. We think this in part because, in the second place, Christian tradition before Matthew had portrayed Jesus as repeating or recapitulating certain experiences of Israel. See 4.1–11 with our comments. Thus there was Christian precedent for the hermeneutical move behind 2.13–15. Indeed, if Jesus' talk of 'the Son of man' depended in part at least upon a collective interpretation of Daniel's 'one like a son of man' (see the excursus after 8.20), if he viewed his own person and work as the focus or heart of the renewed and restored people of God, it would have been natural for his followers to draw parallels between his story and the story of Israel. Finally, in ancient Jewish sources concerned with eschatological matters, the redemption from Egypt often serves as a type for the messianic redemption, and the prospect of another exodus is held forth: before the consummation, the pattern, exodus/return, will repeat itself (cf. Isa 40.3–4; 42.14–55.13; Ezek 20.33–44; Hos 2.14–15; 1 Macc 2.29–30; 1QS 8.12–18; Mt 24.26; Acts 21.38; Rev 12.6, 14; Josephus, *Ant.* 20.97; *Bell.* 2.259,261; 7.438; SB 1, pp. 85–88). Given this expectation, it would have been no large step for our author to find it foreshadowed in the life of Jesus. In other words, the eschatological exodus and return to the land would be anticipated in the story of Mt 2.

2.15 contains the first appearance in Matthew of the 'Son (of God)' title. Because the present context (Mt 1–2) emphasizes Jesus' rôle as Messiah and king, it is notable that Jewish kings were sometimes called 'sons' (2 Sam 7.14; 1 Chr 17.13; 22.10; 28.6; Ps 2.7; 89.26–27) and that 'Son (of God)' just may—although this is disputed—have been a messianic title in pre-Christian Judaism (cf. 4QpsDanA^a; 4QFlor. 10–14). Also significant is the recurrence of 'Son of God' in 4.3 and 6, where Jesus again repeats the history of Israel. For Matthew, 'Son of God' must have to do in part with Jesus as the personification or embodiment of true, obedient

Israel.[10] If God could call Israel his 'first-born son' (Exod 4.22–3), how much more Messiah Jesus.

16. Compare 22.7.[11] The magi and the family of Jesus have left the stage and attention is now directed towards Herod, whose anger, inflamed by the magi's failure to co-operate, moves the king to act as Pharaoh once acted. The angel's prediction (2.13) comes to pass.

τότε 'Ηρῴδης. The adverb of time (cf. 2.7, 17) occurs in Matthew ninety times (Mk: 6; Lk: 14; often in the LXX for 'āz). The evangelist likes to employ it in an unclassical manner as a connective particle introducing a subsequent event taking place at an unspecified time.[12] In the present instance, an indefinite amount of time has passed since the events of 2.12, enough time to show that the magi are not coming back to the king. 'Herod' marks the unity of chapter 2 almost as much as the geographical place names; see 2.1, 3, 7, 12, 13, 15, 16, 19, 22.

ἰδὼν ὅτι ἐνεπαίχθη ὑπὸ τῶν μάγων. Compare 27.3, also 27.24; Mk 9.25; 12.28; 15.39; Lk 17.15. Save for Lk 14.29 and the present verse, ἐμπαίζω (Mt: 5; Mk: 3; Lk: 3) is used in the NT only in connexion with the passion of Jesus: when he is handed over, he is 'mocked'. Here the word, which reproduces the point of view of Herod, means 'duped', 'deceived' (cf. Jer 10.15). ὑπό + the genitive is redactional in 1.22; 2.15; 3.13, 14; 5.13; 8.24; 14.8, 24; 19.12; 20.23; 22.31; and 27.12.

ἐθυμώθη λίαν. The wise men were exceedingly joyous. Herod, because his plan has been frustrated (by God), is exceedingly angry. θυμόω, although frequent in the LXX (but never with λίαν), is a NT *hapax legomenon*. Here it appears as an ingressive aorist: 'he became angry'. λίαν (Mt: 4; Mk: 4; Lk: 1) is redactional in 4.8; 8.28; and 27.14.

καὶ ἀποστείλας ἀνεῖλεν πάντας τοὺς παῖδας τοὺς ἐν Βηθλέεμ. Compare Exod 2.15: Pharaoh sought to kill (ἀνελεῖν) Moses. Note that the children to be slaughtered are all male children. In Matthew's mind there could be no thought of a female king. Recall also Exod 1.22: 'every male (πᾶν ἄρσεν) born to the Hebrews' is, by Pharaoh's command, to be thrown into the Nile river.

As a matter of historical fact, Herod's reign was marked by the massacres of many innocents (Josephus, *Ant.* 15.5–7, 50–87, 173–8,

---

[10] Cf. T. de Kruijf, *Der Sohn des lebendigen Gottes*, AB 16, Rome, 1962, pp. 56–8, 109. Kingsbury, *Structure*, pp. 40–83, has failed to develop this aspect of Matthew's Son of God Christology.

[11] Soares Prabhu, pp. 257–8, rightly observes that the differences between 2.16 and the redactional 22.7 imply the traditional origin of the former. The inference is supported by the appearance in 2.16 of several words occurring nowhere else in Matthew: ἀναιρέω, διετής, θυμόω, and κατωτέρω.

[12] Cf. A. H. McNeile, 'τότε in St. Matthew', *JTS* 12 (1911), pp. 127–8.

232–6, 247–52, 260–6, 289–90; 16.361–94; 17.42–4, 167, 182–7).
Moreover, As. Mos. 6 says of the ruler, 'he shall slay the old and the
young, and he shall not spare. . . . And he shall execute judgements on
them as the Egyptians executed upon them . . .'.[13] Herod was known as
the slaughterer of young and old alike, and his oppression was such that
the author of As. Mos. 6 was reminded of the difficult days under Pharaoh
in Egypt. Thus the deed reported in Mt 2 would have been in character.[14]
This does not, however, prove the historicity of the event in Matthew. For
although that can hardly be excluded (Josephus might have passed it over
as a minor incident), the agreement with the legends about Moses makes it
possible to see the haggadic imagination rather than the sphere of history
as the source of our tale.[15] (The late legend in *Sefer ha-Yashar* about
Nimrod's slaughter of male children in his attempt to do away with
Abraham is one example of how the Moses traditions could be transferred
to another figure.) And even if one supposes that Herod the Great did in
fact have children in Bethlehem slaughtered, his decision so to do cannot
have come about as Matthew portrays it, for then we would have to accept
as historical the story of the magi and the star and too many other
improbabilities.[16]

καὶ ἐν πᾶσι τοῖς ὁρίοις αὐτῆς. Similar phrases occur in the LXX:
Gen 23.17; Deut 28.40; Ps 104.31. The addition, 'and in all her
regions', makes Herod's deed all the worse. ὅριον (Mt: 6; Mk: 5;
Lk: 0) is redactional in 4.13; 15.22 (but cf. Mk 7.24); 15.39.

ἀπὸ διετοῦς καὶ κατωτέρω. Compare 1 Chr 27.23; 2 Chr 31.16.
The second word is a NT *hapax legomenon*. κάτω appears in 4.6
(= Lk 4.9) and 27.51 (= Mk 15.38); but the comparative appears
only here in the NT.

Some would find in the phrase, 'two years and under', which Justin
drops from his retelling of our story (*Dial.* 78), a pointer to genuine
historical memory (e.g. Soares Prabhu, p. 298). This is perhaps naïve.

[13] Attention was drawn to this text by Stauffer, pp. 35–41. The other source
sometimes appealed to as upholding the historicity of Mt 2.16–18, Macrobius, *Sat.*
2.4.11, is too late (A.D. 400) to be treated as certainly independent of Christian
tradition. According to Macrobius, Herod killed his own son when he killed boys
up to two years old, and this caused Augustus to declare, 'Better is it to be Herod's
pig (ὗς) than his son (υἱός)'.
[14] Cf. A. Schalit, *König Herodes*, SJ 4, Berlin, 1969, p. 648, n. 11.
[15] According to Smallwood, pp. 103–4, not only the story in Mt 2 but also the
report of Herod's killing of prominent Jews at Jericho immediately before his death
(Josephus, *Ant.* 17.174–9, 193) are typical of the 'tyrant legends' which soon grow
up after the death of a hated despot in order to blacken his memory; thus their
historicity is doubtful.
[16] The attempt of R. T. France, 'Herod' (v), 'Massacre' (v), to uphold the
historicity of the massacre of the infants fails in part because he does not prove that
the Mosaic typology is a 'redactional gloss' on an already established narrative. In
our reconstruction, the earliest stage (I), was largely determined by Mosaic legends.
And even if one disputes our tradition-history, when one takes away from Mt 2 all
the items with parallels in the Moses materials, little more than a few lines about
magi remain.

Seemingly inessential details are abundant in apocryphal literature; they arise precisely to create an impression of verisimilitude. Who would be willing to defend as historical reminiscence the fabricated data in, for instance, Jth 2.1; T. Job 22.1; 41.2; L. Proph. Hab. 8–9; Jos. Asen. 1.1; Prot. Jas. 7.1; and Acts Jn. 18? Beyond this, Jesus may well have been born about two years before Herod died, and if Christians knew this (cf. Lk 1.5; 3.1, 23), this would be sufficient to account for the notice in 2.16. So the source of 'two years and under' remains uncertain.

κατὰ τὸν χρόνον ὃν ἠκρίβωσεν παρὰ τῶν μάγων. This refers back to 2.7, from whence the vocabulary derives. κατά + accusative is redactional in 9.29; 16.27; 19.3; 20.17; 23.3; and 25.15. Because it is not clearly stated whether the star seen at its rising by the magi coincided with Jesus' birth or his conception, we have no certain indication of how old Jesus is supposed to be.

17. τότε ἐπληρώθη τὸ ῥηθὲν διὰ Ἰερεμίου τοῦ προφήτου λέγοντος. In addition to the issues raised with reference to the formula quotation in 1.22 (see the discussion there), 2.17 poses two questions. First, why the temporal τότε for the purposive ἵνα? Secondly, why is the prophet Jeremiah named?

τότε also replaces ἵνα in 27.9, where a quotation concludes the story of Judas' betrayal and hanging. Two explanations are equally possible. (1) According to the vast majority of commentators, what 2.17 and 27.9 have in common is this: they both introduce texts attached to stories in which evils are suffered because of opposition to Jesus. Such evils and their cause Matthew cannot attribute directly to the hand of God. Rather, culpability lies with those who seek to do away with Jesus, and they bring judgement on themselves. Thus a distinction is implicitly drawn between what God foresees and permissively wills and what God actively wills and makes come to pass. (2) In most of the formula citations God or Jesus is the author of the indicated action, which action is therefore purposeful, that is, occasioned in order to fulfil Scripture (ἵνα). In 2.16–18 and 27.3–10, Scripture is fulfilled not by the direct action of God or Jesus but by human beings whose motivation cannot have been the carrying out of prophecy, although in the event prophecy was carried out. τότε is therefore appropriate.[17]

In the NT only Matthew mentions Jeremiah by name, and three times at that: 2.17; 16.14; 27.9. The evangelist will also probably have thought of Jeremiah when he wrote of those Jerusalem had stoned (23.37; cf. Heb 11.37). See L. Proph. Jer. 1; Par. Jer. 9; Apoc. Paul 49; Num. Rab. on 5.30. That he introduces Jeremiah in 2.17 (the slaughter of the infants) and 27.9 (the betrayal of Jesus by Judas to the Jewish authorities) must be put down to this:

---

[17] Cf. Rothfuchs, pp. 36–9. He refers to Gnilka, *Verstockung*, pp. 104–5.

Jeremiah was the prophet of doom and sorrow.[18] Appropriate, therefore, is the linking of his name with the tragic circumstances of Jewish opposition to the Messiah. (Incidentally, if this is indeed the truth, does it not betray Matthew's awareness that the Scripture, despite its divine origin, reflects the various personalities of its authors?)

18. As we shall see, this quotation, like those in 2.6 and 15, is closer to the MT than the LXX, and any pre-Matthean application is difficult to imagine. Again we have evidence favouring the evangelist's knowledge of Hebrew.

The clue to the meaning of 2.18 may be found by looking at the context of Jer 31.15. The chapter as a whole is one of hope. It pictures in bright colours the joyous day on which the exiles will return to the land of Israel. That the chapter could be viewed as eschatological must be granted, especially in view of vv. 31–34, which foresee a new covenant and the dwelling of God with his people. Certainly many early Christians thus understood the matter, for they applied the verses to the Messiah's advent and the consummation (Lk 22.20; Jn 6.45; Rom 11.27; 1 Cor 11.25; Heb 8.8–12; 9.15; 10.16–17; see Dodd, *Scriptures*, pp. 44–6). Now if Matthew had read the chapter with the story of Jesus as he knew it in mind, a number of statements and expressions would have caught his attention. The one who returns to Israel is called a 'virgin' (vv. 4, 21; cf. Mt 1.23) and 'my dear son . . . my darling child' (v. 20; cf. Mt 2.15; 3.17; 17.5). In v. 9 God declares, 'I am a father to Israel, and Ephraim is by first-born' (cf. Mt 11.25–7). Among those who return from exile is 'the woman with child' (v. 8; cf. Mt 2.11, 14, 20, 21). We further read that 'the Lord has saved his people' (v. 7; LXX: ἔσωσεν κύριος τὸν λαὸν αὐτοῦ; cf. Mt 1.22), that 'your children shall come back to their own country' (v. 17; cf. Mt 2.19–23), that God fixed 'the stars for light by night' (v. 35; cf. Mt 2.1–12), that those who hunger and thirst will be filled (v. 25; cf. Mt 5.6), and that God will establish a new covenant with his people (vv. 31–3; cf. Mt 26.28). In the light of all this, and given the typological equation of Jesus with Israel (see on 2.15; 4.1–11), the evangelist could readily have seen in Jeremiah's prophecy of Israel's return from the exile and of the new things promised for thereafter a transparent cipher or prototype for the Messiah's return to Israel and subsequent ministry: the words originally spoken of Israel are equally applicable to Israel's Messiah. It would then have been a small step to discover in v. 15 a reference to the slaughter of the infants of Bethlehem, for beyond the

---

[18] Menken (v) even finds in 16.14 a connexion between the rejection of the Messiah and the rejection of Jeremiah. See also F. Vouga, 'Le seconde passion de Jérémie', *LumV* 32 (1983), pp. 71–82. Vouga claims that Matthew's thoughts about Jeremiah can be detected in 7.15–23; 11.28–30; and 23.37–9.

association made possible by the lamentation and weeping for children that are not, Ramah was near to Bethlehem, and Rachel's grave was thought by many to be in the city of David (see below).

What we are suggesting comes down to this. In looking for proof texts for chapter 2, Matthew—who had the OT 'engraved on his soul' (cf. Josephus, *C. Ap.* 2.178)—will have recalled biblical passages dealing with exile and return, Jer 31 being among them. Then remembering or reading sentences which reminded him of events in Jesus' life, he attended to the entire chapter with some care, thence discovering in v. 15 a prophecy or prototypical announcement of the massacre of the innocents which he was happy to quote.

φωνὴ ἐν Ῥαμὰ ἠκούσθη. So LXX B. The MT has: *qôl bĕrāmâ nišmāʿ*. ἐν τῇ ὑψηλῇ or its equivalent is found for *bĕrāmâ* in LXX A א*, the Vulgate, Aquila, and the targum, so Matthew's use of the geographical name may go against the predominant interpretation in Judaism. This is one reason for thinking that 'Ramah' is not without special meaning (cf. Stendahl (v), p. 97).

Like the other three formula quotations in Mt 2, this one includes a geographical term, Ramah. But whereas Bethlehem (v. 6), Egypt (v. 15), and Nazareth (v. 23) are names belonging to both the narrative proper and to the scriptural citations (vv. 5, 13–14, 23a), Ramah appears only in v. 18. It is not part of the story line. What significance then did our author see in it? (1) Jer 31.15 and 1 Sam 10.2 place Rachel's tomb in Benjamin, near the Ramah five miles north of Jerusalem (probably modern er-Ram).[19] Yet according to Gen 35.16–19 and 48.7 (cf. Jub. 32.34) Jacob's wife was buried 'on the way to Ephraph (that is, Bethlehem)'. This second tradition, which identifies Ephraph with Bethlehem (cf. Demetrius in Eusebius, *Praep. ev.* 9.21.10),[20] favoured the traditional site venerated by Christians and Muslims, and it puts Rachel's burial place near Bethlehem on the Jerusalem road. Thus there were two rival reports as to the location of the tomb (cf. *Gen. Rab.* on 35.18 and Jeremias, *Heiligengräber*, pp. 75–76). Matthew speaks for the report found in Gen 35 and 48. This is why he can associate Rachel's weeping in Ramah with the slaughter of infants in Bethlehem. (Curiously, Jacob, Rachel's husband, is associated with Bethlehem in Apost. Con. 7.37.2, which is probably from a Jewish synagogal prayer.) (2) According to Jer 40.1, all the captives of Jerusalem were gathered at Ramah for the march to Babylon (cf. the targum on Jer 31.15). This encourages one to

---

[19] There was more than one Ramah: see Josh 19.8, 29, 36; 1 Sam 1.19.

[20] Perhaps the city of Ephrath was confused with the district of Ephrath(ah) (cf. Ps 132.6?), where Bethlehem was (Ruth 4.11; Mic 5.2). Or, since the clan of Ephrath(ah) settled in or near Bethlehem (Ruth 1.2), the city became known as Ephrath(ah).

draw a typological correlation between Israel and the Messiah. Just as the Jews, amid lamentation and grief, left Ramah to go into exile, so Jesus, amid lamentation and grief, left Bethlehem to go into exile. The departure of the Messiah to Egypt recapitulated the deportation of the people to Babylon—an event to which Matthew, significantly, calls attention thrice in the genealogy (1.11, 12, 17). (3) Three different OT prophecies involve Ramah: Isa 10.29; Jer 31.15; Hos 5.8. All three associate the place with a disaster of one sort or another. When one adds that the exile to Babylon began there (see above), Ramah might be regarded as a city of sadness *par excellence*. (Cf. the way in which the 9th of Ab became the date of disasters *par excellence*; see Davies, *GL*, pp. 71–2.)

κλαυθμὸς καὶ ὀδυρμὸς πολύς.[21] The MT has: *nĕhî bĕkî tamrûrîm* (= 'lamentation and bitter weeping', so RSV). Although the MT's *bĕkî tamrûrîm* should probably be read as forming a nominative construct chain (appositional to *qôl*), the LXX (A, B) finds three separate nouns, puts them in the genitive, and adds two conjunctions: θρήνου καὶ κλαυθμοῦ καὶ ὀδυρμοῦ. That Matthew reverses the order of the Hebrew, putting 'weeping' before 'mourning', might have as its explanation this (unless the order was in his *Vorlage*): in one of his favourite stereotyped phrases, 'the weeping and gnashing of teeth', κλαυθμός (Mt: 7; Mk: 0; Lk: 1) always comes first (8.12; 13.42, 50; 22.13; 24.51; 25.30). The reversal in order also gives rise to an a-b-a-b parallelism: Rachel's weeping and refusal to be consoled in lines 3–5 corresponds to the sequence in line 2: weeping and great lamentation (cf. Gundry, *Commentary*, p. 36).

The quotation in Mt 2.18 reproduces the only gloomy verse in all of Jer 31: the chapter as a whole conveys joy and hopeful expectation. Indeed, the thrust of 31.15 is immediately cancelled by the admonition not to weep and cry, for the lost children will return (v. 16). For this reason a number of scholars have suspected Matthew of hoping that his readers would take cognizance of the context of Jer 31.15 and recognize the implicit promise: exile is to be followed by return, sorrow is to be swallowed up by joy, for the oppression of the tyrant must be broken by God's victory.[22] Whether or not such was Matthew's expectation we have no way to decide—although an affirmative answer would be consistent with Jewish interpretation of the passage (*Mek.* on Exod 12.1; SB 1, pp. 89–90).

[21] θρηνος και (from Jer 38.15 LXX) is added in C D L W 0233 *f*[13] Maj sy[s.c.h.] arm geo Or. According to Lagrange, p. 36, πολυς—which in the LXX never translates *mārar* or its derivatives—has, through textual corruption, replaced an original πικρως (cf. 26.75). For this there is no evidence.

[22] Cf. Bourke (as in n. 4), pp. 171–2.

'Ραχὴλ κλαίουσα τὰ τέκνα αὐτῆς. The MT has: *rāḥēl mĕbakkâ 'al-bānêhā*. LXX B reads: 'Ραχὴλ ἀποκλαιομένη . . . ἐπὶ τοῖς υἱοῖς αὐτῆς. Compare LXX A: 'Ραχὴλ ἀποκλαιομένης ἐπὶ τῶν υἱῶν αὐτῆς. Matthew is closer to the Hebrew. One wonders why the evangelist did not choose υἱοί (LXX) or the plural of παῖς (cf. 2.16) or even the plural of ἄρσην (cf. Exod 1.16, 22)—and Strecker (*Weg*, p. 59) would find here evidence for the pre-Matthean origin of 2.18. But a similar question arises at 22.24, where τέκνα occurs for *bēn* against a united LXX testimony; and in the redactional 27.25 (which may here be anticipated—see below) the Jewish people are made to cry out, 'His blood be upon us and our τέκνα'. κλαίω (Mt: 2; Mk: 3; Lk: 9) is not 'weep' (intransitive) but 'weep for' (transitive), as in Rev 18.9 and Par. Jer. 4.6 (cf. BDF § 148.2).

Rachel—the mother of all Israel in *Gen. Rab.* on 29.31—is mentioned only here in the NT. (She and the other wives of the patriarchs are passed over in Matthew's genealogy). On why she should be associated with Ramah and Bethlehem see above.

In 27.25 the people exclaim to Pilate, 'His blood be upon us and upon our children' (τέκνα). This could be linked up with our present text as follows.[23] To the extent that the Jewish people are seen as supporters of Herod and therefore seen as sharing his guilt (see on 2.3), to that extent are they responsible for the slaughter of the infants of Bethlehem, and to that extent do they bring judgement upon themselves. Thus when they later declare, 'His blood be upon us and upon our children', the tragic and ironic truth for Matthew may be that, by rejecting Jesus, they—acting through their king—have in fact already brought blood and death upon their offspring. But whether this chain of thought occurred to Matthew, who could tell?

καὶ οὐκ ἤθελεν παρακληθῆναι. The MT has: *mēʾānâ lĕhinnāḥēm*. LXX B has this: οὐκ ἤθελεν παύσασθαι (ἐπὶ τοῖς υἱοῖς αὐτῆς). LXX A agrees with Matthew. The MT also adds another 'for her sons', which lines up with the word order of LXX B. At this point Matthew and LXX A may well reflect a better Hebrew text. That the MT is corrupt in the next line seems likely.

ὅτι οὐκ εἰσίν. So LXX A and B. The MT has *kî 'ênennû* ('because he is no more'), which may be corrupt. In the LXX the children 'are not' because they have been exiled from Israel. In Matthew the children 'are not' because they have been killed.

19. The demise of Herod the Great introduces the concluding section of the infancy narrative, Jesus' return from exile to Egypt.

τελευτήσαντος δὲ τοῦ Ἡρῴδου. The verb (Mt: 4, Mk: 2, Lk: 1), which is redactional in 9.18 and 22.25, recalls Exod 2.23: ἐτελεύτησεν ὁ βασιλεύς (Pharaoh). What the angel foresaw before

[23] Cf. Vögtle, 'Kindheitsgeschichte' (see p. 256), p. 173, and Gundry, *Commentary*, p. 36.

Joseph left Israel, namely, the death (τελευτῆς) of Herod (2.15), has now come to pass.

When exactly Herod died is not stated, and the guesses of the commentators as to how long we should think of the family's stay are just that—guesses. The apocryphal gospels supply various reckonings—'no little time' (Gosp. Ps.–Mt. 25), at least one year (Latin Gosp. Thom. 1–3), three years (Arabic Gospel of the Infancy 25–6).

ἰδοὺ ἄγγελος κυρίου φαίνεται κατ' ὄναρ τῷ Ἰωσὴφ ἐν Αἰγύπτῳ. Compare 1.20; 2.13.

20. The first half of this verse—which has its twin in 2.13—depends upon Exod 4.19b and 20a while the second half draws upon Exod 4.19c:

Matthew	Exodus
2.19 But when Herod died, behold, the angel of the Lord appeared in a dream to Joseph in Egypt	4.19 After these many days the king of Egypt died (LXX only). The Lord said to Moses in Midian,
2.20 saying, 'Rising, take the child and his mother and go to the land of Israel. For those seeking the life of the child have died'.	 'Go back to Egypt, for all those seeking your life have died'.
2.21 Rising, he took the child and his mother and went unto the land of Israel.	4.20 Moses, taking his wife and his children, mounted them on asses and returned to Egypt (MT: 'the land of Egypt').

Particularly striking is the plural in Mt 2.20: 'those seeking . . . have died'. Herod is the only immediate antecedent. This might be explained as a 'rhetorical' or 'allusive' plural (BDF § 141), with references to Herod's coactors in 2.3–4. But it is easier to believe that the language of Exod 4.19 has been retained without perfect grammatical adjustment, in order to make the parallel with the sentence from the story of Moses unmistakable.

λέγων· ἐγερθεὶς παράλαβε τὸ παιδίον καὶ τὴν μητέρα αὐτοῦ. So also 2.13.

καὶ πορεύου εἰς γῆν Ἰσραήλ. The verb (Mt: 29; Mk: 1; Lk: 51) replaces the 'flee' of 2.13. The time of flight is ended for Herod has died. Matthew cannot use the ἐπιστρέφω of Exod 4.20 because Joseph, unlike Moses, is not returning to the place he left—his destination is somewhere new, Nazareth.[24]

τεθνήκασιν γὰρ οἱ ζητοῦντες τὴν ψυχὴν τοῦ παιδίου. See above and p. 62. 'To seek the soul' (= *bāqaš* + *nepeš*) of someone means to seek to kill him (cf. 2.13 and Rom 11.3 = 1 Kgs 19.14). It is a good OT idiom (Exod 4.19; 1 Sam 20.1; 22.23; 1 Kgs 19.10; Prov 29.10; Jer 4.30). The RSV rightly renders, 'those who sought', for the present participle can connote antecedent time (cf. Jn 12.17; Acts 4.34; Rom 9.30; Gal 1.23; BDF § 339.3).

21. This is the original conclusion of the pre-Matthean narrative. Again the response of Joseph matches perfectly the angel's command.

ὁ δὲ ἐγερθεὶς παρέλαβεν τὸ παιδίον καὶ τὴν μητέρα αὐτοῦ. So also 2.14. Compare Exod 4.20: 'Moses, taking (ἀναλαβών) his wife and his children (τὰ παιδία) . . .'.

καὶ εἰσῆλθεν εἰς γῆν Ἰσραήλ.[25] 'To go into the land' is a thoroughly biblical phrase with a rich history and a number of possible connotations; see Exod 12.25; Lev 14.34; 19.23; Num 32.9; Deut 4.21.

22. We have already (p. 191) drawn attention to the correlation between 2.22–3 and 4.12ff. and observed that this is one good reason for thinking the conclusion of the Matthean infancy narrative to be redactional.

ἀκούσας δὲ ὅτι Ἀρχέλαος βασιλεύει τῆς Ἰουδαίας ἀντὶ Ἡρῴδου τοῦ πατρὸς αὐτοῦ.[26] Compare 3 Βασ 3.7: ἀντὶ Δαυὶδ τοῦ πατρός μου. From whom Joseph is supposed to have learned of Archelaus we are not told. The situation, however, is similar to that recounted in 1.18–25. (1) Joseph learns a disquieting fact—in the one case that his wife is pregnant, in the other that Archelaus is king. (2) Divine revelation intervenes to make the rightful course of action under the difficult circumstances plain.

In indirect discourse the present tense with verbs of saying takes

[24] 'Land of Israel' is found in the NT only in Mt 2.20 and 21; it does, however, occur in the LXX (Judg 6.5; 1 Βασ 13.19; Ezek 20.38), and *'eres yiśrā'ēl* is a standard designation in rabbinic literature for Palestine, including Galilee (see SB I, pp. 90–1).

[25] א B C 157 *pc* sa have εισηλθεν (so NA[26]). HG prints ηλθεν, following D L W 0233 0250 *f*[1.13] Maj Aug. Although he has sometimes dropped it from his sources, Matthew often has εἰσέρχομαι + εἰς (Mt: 27; Mk: 23; Lk: 31)—and it is occasionally redactional, as in 5.20 and 7.21.

[26] Against א B C* W eth, Ηρωδου is placed before του πατρος αυτου in Maj and C[3] D L 0233 0250 *f*[1.13] latt co Eus Aug. Maj, followed by HG against NA[26], is probably original, for while neither 1.18 (τῆς μητρὸς αὐτοῦ Μαρίας; cf. Mk 11.10) nor 2.11 (Μαρίας τῆς μητρὸς αὐτοῦ) can be proven to reflect a redactional tendency (because Matthew may be influenced by his source in one verse or the other or both), the order in 4.21—Ζεβεδαίου τοῦ πατρὸς αὐτῶν—is certainly editorial (contrast Mk 1.19–20).

up the temporal point of view of the speaker. Similarly here the present tense ('rules') with a verb of perception ('hearing') reflects the temporal point of view of Joseph (BDF § 324). For Ἰουδαία see on 2.1. The genitive is usually used with verbs of ruling (BDF § 177). Matthew likes ἀκούω + ὅτι: Mt: 9; Mk: 3; Lk: 0 (cf. the Hebrew *šāmaʿ* + *kî*).

When Herod the Great died in 4 B.C., his kingdom was divided among Philip, Antipas, and Archelaus, his three sons. Archelaus, who is mentioned nowhere else in the NT, gained charge of Judea proper, Samaria, and Idumea. He was reputed to be the worst of the three brothers. His short reign was marked by scandal, by brutality, by tyranny.[27] Matters got so bad that complaints lodged against him in Rome by a deputation of Jews and Samaritans succeeded in having him deposed and sent into exile in Gaul in A.D. 6.

If Joseph cannot take Mary and Jesus back to Judea, to the house in Bethlehem, this is because, presumably, the identity of the messianic child might somehow become known, and Archelaus' response would be like his father's—he would kill Jesus. It is worth recalling that, according to Josephus (*Ant.* 17.213–18; *Bell.* 2.1–13), Archelaus ordered a massacre immediately after the death of his father.

According to our text, Archelaus 'reigned' (cf. Josephus, *Ant.* 18.93) in place of his father. This is strictly incorrect and reminds one of the similar problem in 14.9 = Mk 6.26, where Herod the tetrarch is called 'king'. Archelaus was an ethnarch (Josephus, *Ant.* 17.317; *Bell.* 2.93; extant coins). The kingship was only a prospect for him, contingent upon his proving himself worthy in the eyes of the emperor. Matthew, however, wishes to continue the theme of the conflict of kings. Thus the son takes the place of his father, and Jesus, the true king, still has a rival.

ἐφοβήθη ἐκεῖ ἀπελθεῖν. In contrast to all that has gone before, human initiative now plays a rôle in Matthew's story. The adverb, ἐκεῖ, here the equivalent of ἐκεῖσε, 'thither', is frequent in the LXX for *šām* or *šammâ* but typically comes after, not before, a verb of motion.

χρηματισθεὶς δὲ κατ᾽ ὄναρ. See on 1.20 and 2.12. This is the third and final dream in 2.13–23, and it is about to be followed by the section's third and final formula quotation.

ἀνεχώρησεν εἰς τὰ μέρη τῆς Γαλιλαίας. Note the three successive uses of εἰς and the progressive geographical restriction: 'into Israel' (2.21), 'into the district of Galilee' (2.22), 'in a city called

---

[27] See Schürer 1, pp. 353–7; E. Gabba in *CHJ* 3, forthcoming; and Smallwood, pp. 102–19. In Smallwood's judgement, Mt 2.22–3 reflects Archelaus' unpopularity towards the conclusion rather than the beginning of his reign (p. 114, n. 37).

Nazareth' (2.23). 'Galilee' (see on 4.12) prepares for 3.13, where Jesus comes to the Jordan from Galilee.

23. The pressure on Jewish Christians to come up with a proof text for Jesus' having lived in Nazareth must have been considerable. The town was of little account and nothing in the OT or Jewish tradition prepared for its connexion with messianic events. To what extent non-Christian Jews turned Nazareth into a reproach we do not know; but early believers in Jesus certainly would have felt a difficulty (cf. Jn 1.46). Moreover, given the belief in the significance of Bethlehem and in Jesus' birth there, the prominence of Nazareth in the gospel tradition would have been all the more puzzling. Mt 2.23 is, therefore, an attempt to come to grips with a difficult fact.

καὶ ἐλθὼν κατῴκησεν εἰς πόλιν λεγομένην Ναζαρέτ.[28] A participial form of ἔρχομαι + κατοικέω—compare 4.13; 12.45—might be labelled a Septuagintism (cf. Gen 13.18; 1 Βασ 31.7; 4 Βασ 16.6; Lk 11.26; Acts 7.4). λεγομένην is typical of Matthew's style (see on 1.16). Luke also calls Nazareth a πόλις (1.26; 2.4, 36). One expects κώμη. But between πόλις and κώμη the NT does not always make a sharp distinction (cf. Mk 1.38 and Swete, p. 27; the LXX occasionally translates 'ir with κώμη). Certainly Luz 1, p. 133, is mistaken when he finds in the use of πόλις in Mt 2.23 evidence for Matthew's ignorance of Palestine.

The small, insignificant Nazareth (cf. Jn 1.46), an agricultural village about fifteen miles straight west of the southern tip of the Sea of Galilee, does not appear in the OT, Josephus, the Talmuds, or the Midrashim. This led some earlier scholars to deny its existence.[29] They argued for invention by Christians, who created a city, 'Nazareth', to correspond to the adjective, 'Nazarene', which adjective originally had other than a patrial meaning. Today few if any would be found supporting such an assessment. Certainly not every single small village in Galilee should be expected to demand record in our extant sources; and in any case *nṣrt* has turned up on a third or fourth century A.D. Jewish inscription of priestly courses found at Caesarea in 1962.[30]

ὅπως πληρωθῇ τὸ ῥηθὲν διὰ τῶν προφητῶν ὅτι. See on 1.22. This introductory formula is marked by two peculiarities. Why is the word not (as elsewhere) 'through the prophet' but rather 'through

[28] C K N W Γ (Δ) 0233ᵛˡ 0250 f(1).13 28 565 *pm* lat co have -ρεθ. P⁷⁰ᵛⁱᵈ has -ρα. -ρετ appears in ℵ B D L 33 700 892 1241 1424 *pm*. The external evidence is rather evenly divided and a decision impossible—unless one prefers as a matter of course the testimony of ℵ and B.

[29] For names and details see Moore (v) and Soares Prabhu, pp. 197–201.

[30] See M. Avi-Yonah, 'A List of Priestly Courses from Caesarea', *IEJ* 12 (1962), pp. 137–9; idem, 'The Caesarea Inscription of the Twenty-Four Priestly Courses', in *The Teacher's Yoke*, ed. E. J. Vardaman and J. L. Garrett, Waco, 1964, pp. 46–57.

the prophet*s*' (plural)? And why is the expected λεγόντων displaced by ὅτι? These two problems are almost certainly to be related to a third, namely, that 'he will be called a Nazarene' cannot be found in the OT. What is the explanation? By writing of 'the prophet*s*' (cf. 26.56; Jn 6.45; Acts 3.18, 21, 24; Rom 1.2), Matthew alerts us to expect something other than the verbatim quotation of one particular Scripture: he is not just reproducing an OT text. The displacement of λεγόντων probably serves the same purpose. For although ὅτι *recitativum* is found in Matthew (e.g. 4.6; 21.16), our author shows a marked tendency to drop it from Mark (cf. Neirynck, *Agreements*, pp. 213–16); and the unexpected replacement of λεγόντων—2.23 is the only formula quotation with ὅτι—must point to an unusual status *vis-à-vis* the other fulfilment citations. 26.54 supports this contention. 'How then would the Scripture*s* be fulfilled, that (ὅτι) thus it is necessary to be?' In this verse ὅτι introduces a remark of scriptural substance, not a sentence found in the OT, and this fact is in part signalled by the unspecified reference to 'the Scripture*s*' (plural). This offers something close to what we propose to find in 2.23: a quotation which rests upon or alludes to more than one OT text ('the prophet*s*') and whose wording does not exactly match any particular Scripture (ὅτι). The alternative is to suppose either that Matthew found 'he will be called a Nazarene' in a source and, not knowing whence it came, satisfied himself with a vague reference to 'the prophets' (so Lindars, *Apologetic*, p. 196) or that the words come from a lost apocryphon (Chrysostom, *Hom. on Mt.* 9.6; Bengel, p. 84). But for reasons soon evident, neither of these options is necessary.[31]

In having no perfect OT parallel although prefaced by words which might be taken to indicate otherwise, Mt 2.23 is not alone. Ezra 9.11–12 quotes a command purportedly delivered to the prophets, but no such command is found in the OT. In the NT, Jn 7.38; Rom 11.8; and Jas 4.5 attribute to Scripture sentences that at best paraphrase the substance of several OT passages. There is also a rabbinic example in *b. Ketub.* 111a.

Ναζωραῖος κληθήσεται. Even though grammatically awkward, the subject of this sentence appears to be Jesus, not Joseph. Compare the conclusion of chapter 1: 'he called his name Jesus'.[32]

---

[31] According to E. Zuckschwerdt (v), p. 70, if Judg 13.5–7 be the text behind Mt 2.23 (see below), then ὅτι might not be part of the introductory formula but instead belong to the quotation (Judg 13.5 LXX B: ὅτι ναζιρ θεοῦ ἔσται). Yet this would leave us with another problem: why no λεγόντων? Still, it is just possible that an early scribe, finding 'through the prophets λεγόντων ὅτι' before him, did not recognize that ὅτι was part of the quotation and therefore omitted λεγόντων as redundant.

[32] Without real reason, Allen, pp. 17–18, supposed that the phrase might be a gloss. Cf. McNeile, p. 22.

Jesus' identity as Ναζωραῖος (so Mt 26.29 v. 1; 26.71; Lk 18.37; Jn 18.5, 7; 19.19; Acts 2.22; 3.6; 4.10; 6.14; 22.8; 26.9) or Ναζαρηνός[33] (so Mk 1.24; 10.47; 14.67; 16.6; Lk 4.34; 24.19; Jn 18.5 D) was already part of the pre-Matthean tradition. Hence our first question does not concern etymology but Matthew's interpretation. Of what OT text(s) are we to think?

(1) Mt 2.23 almost certainly has to do with a play on the word, *nāzîr*.[34] (On the Nazarite, a holy person who consecrated himself or herself to the service of God by taking a special vow which required abstinence from wine and the keeping of uncut hair, see esp. Num 6; Judg 13.5–7; 16.17; Amos 2.11–12; 1 Macc. 3.49–52; Acts 18.18; 21.17–26; *m. Nazir*).[35] To begin with, there is in the LXX an interchange between ναζαραῖος θεοῦ and ἅγιος θεοῦ (see A and B for Judg 13.7; 16.17). This is significant because Jesus was known as 'the holy one of God' (Mk 1.24; Lk 4.34; Jn 6.69; cf. Acts 3.14; 1 Jn 2.20; Rev 3.7). Moreover, in Mk 1.24 we find this: 'What have you to do with us, Jesus of Nazareth (Ναζαρηνέ)? Have you come to destroy us? We know who you are, the holy one of God' (ὁ ἅγιος τοῦ θεοῦ). Here 'Jesus of Nazareth' and 'holy one of God' are in parallel and we clearly have a word play: Jesus, the 'holy one of God' (= *nāzîr*), is from Nazareth.[36] So already before Matthew—indeed, in one of his primary sources—'holy one of God' and 'Nazarite' and 'Nazareth' were associated. Then, secondly, in Luke's infancy narrative words originally spoken of Samuel the Nazarite are spoken of Jesus (cf. 1 Sam 2.26 with Lk 2.52; 1 Sam 2.1–10 with Lk 1.46–55; 1 Sam 2.34 with Lk 2.12). Thus even though Jesus, no ascetic, hardly satisfied the OT requirements for being a Nazarite, this did not prevent his followers from thinking of him in such terms to some extent. Jesus was, after all, consecrated to God's service, a bearer of the Spirit, and a charismatic leader. Beyond this, Jesus took an oath to refrain from drinking wine until the coming of the kingdom of God (Mk 14.25 = Mt 26.29), and shortly thereafter he refused the offer of wine mingled with myrrh (Mk 15.23; cf. Mt 27.48).[37] Thirdly, if

[33] Cf. the variation between Εσσαιος and Εσσηνος in the mss. for Josephus, *Ant.* 13.311 and the different readings in Greek versions of the OT for 1 Chr 5.19 (Αγαρηνοι/Αγαραιοι) and 2 Esdr 1.8 (γ/τασβαρηνου/γανζαμβραιου).

[34] So also McNeile, p. 22; Schaeder (v), p. 883; Schweizer (v); Sanders (v); Zuckschwerdt (v)—citing other authorities in agreement (p. 69, n. 19) and calling special attention to the possible allusion to Judg 13.5 in Mt 1.21b—; Soares Prabhu, pp. 205–7; Brown, *Messiah*, p. 224; Allan (v).

[35] See SB 2, pp. 747–51, and J. C. Rylaarsdam, *IDB* 3, s.v. (with literature).

[36] See F. Mussner, 'Ein Wortspiel in Mk 1,24?', *BZ* 4 (1960), pp. 285–6; Schweizer (v).

[37] On the possibility of connecting Mk 14.25 and 15.23 with a Nazarite vow see M. Wojciechowski, 'Le naziréat et la Passion (Mc 14,25a; 15,23)', *Bib* 65 (1984), pp. 94–6.

Ναζωραῖος is to be related to ναζαραῖος, the precise form of Mt 2.23 can be explained. Isa 4.3 MT reads, 'He will be called holy'.[38] Now we have already noted the interchange between 'Nazarite' and 'holy one of God' in the LXX. If 'Nazarite' is substituted for 'holy' in Isa 4.3, the resulting sentence is, 'he will be called a Nazarite'. This seems too close to Matthew's line to be coincidence. We should probably conclude that before us is an involved word play. 'He will be called a Nazarene' depends upon (a) the equation of 'Nazarite' and 'holy' one of God'; (b) the substitution of 'Nazarite' for 'holy' in Isa 4.3 (cf. the LXX variants in Judges); and (c) the substitution of 'Nazarene' for 'Nazarite'. Although complex, this conclusion is consistent with our interpretation of the introductory formula: the use of ὅτι instead of λεγόντων hints that the following quotation cannot be found word for word in the OT; it is at best a free rendering.[39]

Our conclusion is not to be resisted by the doubt often entertained over the derivation of Ναζωραῖος and its (latinized?) synonym, Ναζαρηνός. It might be remarked that the two words are not naturally derived from nāzîr. But this is to confuse the issue. The etymology of Ναζωραῖος and Ναζαρηνός and the question of what Christians made of the two words are two different problems with not necessarily one answer.

(2) Many have found the key to Mt 2.23 in Isa 11.1: 'A shoot will come forth from the stump of Jesse, and a branch (nēṣer) will grow out of his roots'.[40] An allusion to this verse is favoured by several considerations. First, Isa 11.1 has to do with the Davidic line, a leading theme of Mt 1–2. Secondly, in Mt 1.23 Isa 7.14 is quoted, and the evangelist could readily have identified the 'branch' of Isa 11.1 with the 'Immanuel' of Isa 7.14. Thirdly, Isa 11.1–10 appears to have been a source of early Christian testimonia (Rom 15.12; 1 Pet 4.14; Rev 5.5; Dodd, Scriptures, p. 83); and 11.10 is quoted—albeit in Greek—in 12.21; further, Matthew may have recalled 11.2 ('the Spirit of the Lord will rest upon him') when he wrote of Jesus' baptism. Later Christian writers also interpreted Isa 11.1ff. of Jesus (Justin, 1 Apol. 32; Dial.

---

[38] LXX: 'they will be called holy' (ἅγιοι κληθήσονται).

[39] Most who see nāzîr behind Mt 2.23 wish to see an allusion to Judg 16.17: 'I have been a Nazarite to God from my mother's womb' (so e.g. Soares Prabhu and Brown). This is unnecessary. Isa 4.3 is the only text which needs to be brought into the picture. Judg 16.17 is not the only OT text about Nazarites, and the variation between 'Nazarite' and 'holy one of God' in the LXX tradition occurs in more than one place. Interesting nonetheless is Zuckschwerdt's (v) explanation of the vocalization of Ναζωραῖος: Matthew read the nzr of Judg 13.5, 7 and 16.17 with the vowels of qādôš, 'holy'.

[40] So B. Weiss, pp. 57–8; Schlatter, p. 49; Schniewind, p. 20; SB 1, pp. 93–4; Caspari (v); Gundry, Commentary, p. 40; Rüger (v).

126; Irenaeus, *Adv. haer*. 3.9.3)—and the targum refers it to the Messiah. Fourthly, *ṣemaḥ*, a synonym for *nēṣer*, appears in several OT messianic prophecies: Isa 4.2; Jer 23.5; 33.15; Zech 3.8; 6.12. By way of this second word, Matthew could have thought of the 'branch' as belonging to several prophetic disclosures, whence the plural 'prophets' of 2.23.[41] Fifthly, *nēṣer* was used of the Messiah in Judaism (SB 1, p. 94, to which add *T. Jud*. 24.6 and 4QpIsa^a 3.15–26).[42] Sixthly, *nṣr*, which is vocalized in the MT as *nēṣer*, may have been pronounced as Νάζαρ in first century Hebrew (so Rüger (v), p. 262)—and this is strikingly close to the form for Nazareth in Mt 4.13 and Lk 4.16 (Ναζαρά). Finally, in *b. Sanh*. 43a, in a debate between Jewish judges and five disciples of Jesus, one disciple, by name *Nēṣer*, defends himself by citing Isa 11.1.[43] The judges respond by citing Isa 14.19 ('you are cast out, away from your sepulchre, like a loathed branch'). Although unhistorical and late, this rabbinic tale probably reflects the ease with which 'Jesus the Nazarene' (*Nôṣrî* in the Talmud) or 'the Nazarenes' (*Nôṣrîm* in the Talmud; cf. Acts 24.5) could be associated with Isa 11.1.

Because the evidence for supposing 'Nazarite' and Isa 4.3 to lie behind 'he will be called a Nazarene' is so strong, it is a bit disconcerting to find so many reasons supporting the dependence of Mt 2.23 on Isa 11.1. Perhaps we should speak of a secondary allusion. Might our evangelist have found 'Nazarene' to be coincidentally similar to more than one OT key word or text? This possibility is the more inviting since 'he will be called holy' (Isa 4.3) follows immediately upon a prophecy about the 'branch' (Isa 4.2). (The targum takes the *ṣemaḥ* of Isa 4.2 to be the Messiah.)

Against finding an echo of Isa 11.1 in Mt 2.23, one might, following Jerome, remark that the *ṣādê* (*ṣ*) in *nēṣer* does not match the zeta (ζ) in Ναζωραῖος, so the one cannot be derived from the other. (The Semitic *ṣ* is regularly represented by the Greek sigma (σ).) This observation, even if it were correct, which it is not,[44] simply muddles etymology with the Matthean interpretation. Whatever its origin, Ναζωραῖος was to hand in the tradition; and our initial question, as already stated, is what Matthew made of it, not how the word came into being. Which is to say: even if Ναζωραῖος was not in the first place formed with an eye towards Isa 11.1, the word may well have prompted the gospel writer to think of Isaiah's *nēṣer*. A second objection is also less than decisive. It is this: Isa 11.1

---

[41] Cf. Gundry, *Commentary*, p. 40. Note also the recurrence of another synonym, *šōreš* (cf. Isa 11.1) in Isa 53.2.

[42] *nēṣer* also occurs in non-messianic contexts in the OT: Isa 14.19; 60.21; Dan 11.7. Note should also be taken of its non-messianic yet pregnant usage in 1 Q H 6.15; 7.19; 8.6–10.

[43] Discussion in J. Maier, *Jesus von Nazaret in der talmudischen Überlieferung*, Darmstadt, 1978, pp. 232–5; also Klausner, pp. 28–30.

[44] See Moore (v), pp. 427–9; Schaeder (v), p. 884.

cannot be the key text because while the connexion between *nēṣer* and
Ναζωραῖος appears only to one knowing Hebrew, Matthew is writing in
Greek. Yet this is to overlook Matthew's procedure elsewhere. Already in
Mt 1 he has apparently used gematria based upon the numerical value of
dwd. Likewise, 'you will call his name Jesus, for he will save his people
from their sins' (1.21) depends upon a pun apparent only in Hebrew. So
Matthew was not above scattering items in his Greek text whose deeper
meaning could only be appreciated by those with a knowledge of Hebrew.
Indeed, it might even be that Matthew found authorial delight in hiding
'bonus points'[45] for those willing and able to look a little beneath the
gospel's surface.

(3) Two other passages from Isaiah have merited attention. The
nṣyry of Isa 49.6 is traditionally read as a passive participle. This
results in the sentence, 'It is too light a thing that you should be my
servant to raise up the tribes of Jacob and to restore the preserved
of Israel'. *nṣyry* could, however, be construed as an adjectival form
of *nēṣer* (cf. Isa 11.1) or as a patronymic, 'Nazarene'. In this case,
the verse could be referred to Jesus: 'and a Nazarene to restore
Israel'.

Isa 42.6 might also be pertinent. 'I am the Lord, I have called
you in righteousness; I have taken you by the hand and have kept
you' (*'eṣṣarkā*). The object of this declaration is the servant.

Favouring an allusion to Isa 42.6 and 49.6 are four
observations. The first is Matthew's general interest in the servant
songs of Isaiah.[46] The next is the use of 'call' in both passages
(LXX only for 49.6). A third is the occurrence of 'a light to the
nations' in both 42.6 and 49.6, a phrase used of Jesus in Lk 2.32.
The final fact is the early and well attested Christian interest in the
first few verses of Isa 42 and in all of Isa 49: these passages were
important sources for early Christian *testimonia* (Mt 12.18–21; Lk
2.32; Acts 13.47; 17.24–25; 26.18; 2 Cor 6.2; Gal 1.15; Phil 2.16;
Rev 7.16; 12.12).

Considering these several facts, one can hardly exclude
altogether the possibility of an allusion to Isa 42.6 or 49.6 or both.
Yet having already concluded that Isa 4.3 and perhaps 11.1 lie in
the background, too many texts are beginning to come into the
picture. For this reason we are forced to issue a verdict of
unproven for the dependence of Mt 2.23 on Isa 42.6 and 49.6.

(4) Even less persuasive is the attempt to find the explanation of
our crux in Jer 31.6–7: 'There shall be a day when watchmen
(*nōṣĕrîm*) will call in the hill country of Ephraim, "Arise and let us

---

[45] This is France's phrase; cf. 'Quotations' (v), p. 250. He rightly sees the
possibility for more than one level of meaning.
[46] See esp. D. Hill, 'Son and Servant: An Essay on Matthean Christology', *JSNT*
6 (1980), pp. 2–16. In favour of the influence of Isa 42.6 and 49.6 on Mt 2.23 is
Gärtner (v).

go up to Zion, to the Lord our God". For thus says the Lord, "Sing aloud . . . and say, 'The Lord has saved his people, the remnant of Israel' " '.[47] Although Matthew has already quoted from this chapter (31.15 in Mt 2.18), and although, as we have argued, the evangelist may have seen all of Jer 31 as a typological forecast of the Messiah's advent, and although 'The Lord has saved his people' recalls Mt 1.21, no material connexion obtains between 'watchmen' and Jesus of Nazareth. Contrast Isa 4.3, which appears in a prophecy about the 'branch', and Isa 11.1, which has to do with the offspring of David, and Isa 42.6 and 49.6, which have to do with the servant of the Lord. If Matthew expected his readers to catch an allusion to Jer 31.6, did he not expect too much?

(5) Gen 49.26 reads, 'May they [the blessings of Jacob] be on the head of Joseph and on the brow [or: crown] of him who was separate from [or: a prince (*nzyr*) among] his brothers' (cf. Deut 33.16). *Sipre* on Deut 33.16 and *Gen. Rab.* on 49.26 interpret this to mean that Joseph was a 'Nazarite'. But *nzyr* could be read as 'prince'. A Joseph–Jesus typology could then make Jesus the prince among his brothers, the wearer of the crown (cf. Klausner, *Jesus* p. 230). There is, however, no trace of such a typology in Matthew (Jesus is descended from Judah: 1.3); and Gen 49.26 does not seem to have been interpreted of the Messiah in Judaism.

Having now examined the possible texts upon which Mt 2.23 might draw, we may sum up thus. The primary dependence is upon Isa 4.3, with the substitution of 'Nazareth' for 'holy'. There is perhaps also a secondary allusion to Isa 11.1. Possible but unproven is dependence upon Isa 42.6 or 49.6. Improbable is any allusion to either Jer 31.6–7 or Gen 49.26. (Our examination also renders problematic another interpretation, one which goes back to Jerome and was popular in the nineteenth century and which should be noted for the sake of completeness.[48] Jn 1.46 implies the meanness of Nazareth (cf. perhaps Jn 19.19 and Acts 24.5); and it seems likely that the inhabitants of Nazareth—and therefore Jesus—were looked down upon because of their humble residence. Thus 'Nazareth' might be connected with reproach and in this sense be regarded as the object of prophecy, specifically, those prophecies about the suffering servant who is scorned and despised by men.)

[47] See Zolli, 'Nazarenus' (v) and Albright and Mann, pp. 20–2.

[48] Cf. Zahn, p. 117; Lagrange, p. 39; Tasker, p. 45; Bonnard, p. 30; France, 'Quotations' (v), pp. 247–8. We pass by Eusebius' explanation (*Dem. ev.* 7.2), which links Mt 2.23 with Lev 21.12. For still other accounts of Mt 2.23 see Strecker (*Weg*, pp. 61–3: a Matthean formulation without any OT textual basis), Smith (v) (there is a connexion with Lam 4.7), and Rothfuchs (p. 67: the reference is back to the formula quotations in 2.6, 15, and 18, to the providential hand of God there implied).

Having considered Matthew's interpretation of Ναζωραῖος, it remains to remark briefly on the etymology of the word and its variant, Ναζαρηνός. The most straightforward explanation would seem to be derivation from the name of a town, Nazareth: Ναζωραῖος and Ναζαρηνός = ὁ ἀπὸ Ναζαρέθ (cf. Mt 21.11; Jn 1.45; Acts 10.38). This would fit in with the common Jewish custom of distinguishing individuals according to the place from which they come (as in Mk 15.21 and 43), and it is Matthew's assumption. There is further no difficulty standing in the way of accepting this account for Ναζαρηνός; for Ναζαρά was one form of 'Nazareth' (see on 4.13), and elsewhere in the NT we find Μαγδαληνή for one from Magdala and Γαδαρηνός for one from Gadara (Mt 8.28; 27.56, 61; 28.1; Mk 15.40; etc.). But Ναζωραῖος is problematic. Among other things, the ω does not well match the second α in the various forms of 'Nazareth',[49] and the θ or τ ending in four of the five forms of 'Nazareth' is not represented.[50] Moreover, (a) Ναζωραῖος resembles Σαδδουκαῖος and Φαρισαῖος, names of religious groups, (b) in Acts 24.5 Christians are ἡ τῶν Ναζωραίων αἵρεσις,[51] and (c) there is a similarity between Ναζωραῖος and one of the names of the Mandeans, nāṣōrāyē ('guardians', 'observants')— all of which has led some to think Jesus and perhaps John the Baptist belonged to a pre-Christian sect, the 'Nazarenes' (see n. 29). This, however, is to speculate unduly, for there is no insuperable difficulty in accepting a derivation of Ναζωραῖος from Ναζαρέθ or its Semitic equivalent, as several authorities have demonstrated.[52] So it seems more prudent to accept the simplest solution: Ναζωραῖος = ὁ ἀπὸ Ναζαρέθ. This entails further that any connexion with nāzîr or nēṣer should be regarded not as primary but as secondary, the result of homeophony noticed once Ναζωραῖος and Ναζαρηνός had already come into existence.

(iv) *Concluding Observations*

(1) The special Matthean concerns which run through Mt 2.1–12 (see above, pp. 252–4) are also to the fore in 2.13–23. Even the theme of Davidic sonship continues in so far as stress is laid on Jesus' kingship; and perhaps the notion of Jesus as saviour of the Gentiles is implicit in the move to Galilee (v. 22), for in Matthew Galilee is 'of the Gentiles' (4.15).[53] Particularly prominent in the

[49] Cf. Black, p. 198. But Schaeder (v), p. 882, argues first that the second α in Ναζαρηνός reproduces the 'full' form of a šewa vowel and then gives examples of ω for the šewa simplex, which explains the form, Ναζωραῖος. And according to Rüger (v), pp. 261–2, a parallel to the variation between Ναζωραῖος and Ναζαρηνός may be found in the alternative forms of the place name, dābĕrat/dābôr.

[50] Cf. Kennard, 'Capernaum' (v), p. 131. But nāṣôr for 'Nazareth' may have been known; see Rüger (v).

[51] Syrian Christians adopted this as their self-appellaton. Furthermore, a Jewish-Christian sect descended from John the Baptist's followers reportedly was known as Νασαραῖοι; see Epiphanius, *Haer.* 18.1; 29.1; 29.6–7.

[52] Schlatter, pp. 49–50; Moore (v); Albright (v); Schaeder (v); Rüger (v).

[53] It is questionable whether the references to Egypt further the Gentile theme; cf. Luz 1, p. 129.

second half of chapter 2 is the extension of the geographical interest, an interest which marks all of Mt 2 and which shows up the unity of the chapter. The movements of the messianic family are given in detail and each is reinforced by an appeal to Scripture. (All the formula quotations in Mt 2 include place names; contrast 1.23.) Thus we learn not only the whence and whereto of the Messiah (Bethlehem and Nazareth), but also where he was in between (Egypt) and what Scriptures were thereby fulfilled. The importance of the OT for Matthew could hardly be made more evident. One gains the impression that, in his mind, every significant detail of the Messiah's life and ministry could be found—foretold or foreshadowed—in the OT.

(2) There is in 2.13–23 a Jesus/Israel typology, a typology which will be taken up once again in chapters 3 and 4 (where Jesus passes through the waters of baptism and then enters into the desert). In 2.15, for instance, the 'son' of Hos 11.1, originally Israel, becomes Jesus. And behind the quotation of Jer 31.15 in 2.18 there apparently lies, as argued, a typological equation of Jesus with Israel: in Jeremiah's prophecy of return for the exiles Matthew discerns a cipher for the Messiah's return to Israel. We may say, then, that while Jesus culminates Israel's history in chapter 1, in chapter 2 he repeats it. Jesus is not only the last redeemer who is like the first redeemer, Moses, he is not only the messianic king who is like the great king, David, but he is also like Israel in that he experiences exodus and exile and return; and Scriptures originally pertaining to Israel can be transferred to him.[54]

(3) At the end of Mt 1–2 one is left with the impression that, at least concerning salvation-history, human choice matters little. Rather does all come down to the divine will. The events and movements of 1.2–2.23 are 'determined' by providence.[55] There are, in Mt 1–2, five formula quotations, and these, taken together, seemingly imply that the unprecedented occurrences surrounding the Messiah's advent were 'determined' long before they happened. Moreover, to make sure that all goes according to plan, there is the angel of the Lord, who, when someone is not acting out the script, will intervene to put things right (1.20; 2.12). Our gospel's 'deterministic' interpretation of history also seems manifest in its proem, the genealogy, in which we find the ancestral

---

[54] Brown, *Messiah*, p. 217, observes that the three names in the formula quotations in 2.1–18—namely, Bethlehem, the city of David, Egypt, the land of the Exodus, and Ramah, the mourning place of the exile—evoke the whole history of Israel by calling to mind three decisive moments in her history.

[55] For this and what follows see K. R. R. Gros Louis, 'Different Ways of Looking at the Birth of Jesus', *Bible Review* 1 (1985), pp. 33–40.

line of Jesus neatly divided into 3×14 generations, and in which the movement towards the Messiah appears inevitable. In short, then, one comes away from Matthew's first two chapters with the feeling that history is divinely run from first to last. At the same time, it must be said that the evangelist was nevertheless not naïvely persuaded that 'God's on his throne—all's right with the world'. In 2.16–18 there is a terrible tragedy, the massacre of the infants of Bethlehem; and Matthew, by substituting τότε for ἵνα in 2.17, betrays his reluctance to ascribe suffering or evil outcomes to the Lord God. Beyond this, there runs throughout Matthew's gospel a strong eschatological expectation—a sure sign of dissatisfaction with the world as it is. The conclusion, therefore, is that while history is, for our evangelist, the arena of God's mighty acts, it is also the arena of much else: there is darkness as well as light. God's will is not always done (cf. 6.10b), and this will be true until the end of the age comes.

(v) *Bibliography*

In addition to what follows see section v on pp. 254–6.

W. F. Albright, 'The Names "Nazareth" and "Nazorean" ', *JBL* 65 (1946), pp. 397–401.
G. Allan, 'He shall be called—a Nazirite?', *ExpT* 95 (1983), pp. 81–2.
Black, pp. 197–200.
Brown, *Messiah*, pp. 202–30.
W. Caspari, ' "Ναζωραῖος": Mt 2,23 nach alttestamentlichen Voraussetzungen', *ZNW* 21 (1922), pp. 122–7.
R. T. France, 'The Formula Quotations of Matthew 2 and the Problem of Communication', *NTS* 27 (1981), pp. 233–51.
idem, 'Herod and the Children of Bethlehem', *NovT* 21 (1979), pp. 98–120.
idem, 'The "Massacre of the Innocents"—Fact or Fiction?', in Livingstone, pp. 83–94.
B. Gärtner, *Die rätselhaften Termini Nazoräer und Iskariot*, Uppsala, 1957.
J. S. Kennard, 'Was Capernaum the Home of Jesus?', *JBL* 65 (1946), pp. 131–41.
idem, 'Nazorean and Nazareth', *JBL* 66 (1947), pp. 79–81.
Lindars, *Apologetic*, pp. 194–6.
S. Lyonnet, 'Quoniam Nazaraeus vocabitur: L'interprétation de S. Jérôme', *Bib* 25 (1944), pp. 196–206.
M. J. J. Menken, 'The References to Jeremiah in the Gospel According to Matthew (Mt 2,17; 16,14; 27,9)', *ETL* 60 (1984), pp. 5–24.
G. F. Moore, 'Nazarene and Nazareth", in *Beginnings* 1, pp. 426–32.
Paul, pp. 141–69.
J. Rembry, ' "Quoniam Nazaraeus vocabitur' (Mt 2.23)', *SBFLA* 12 (1961), pp. 46–65.

284　　COMMENTARY ON MATTHEW

Rothfuchs, pp. 65–7.

H. P. Rüger, 'ΝΑΖΑΡΕΘ/ΝΑΖΑΡΑ　ΝΑΖΑΡΗΝΟΣ/ΝΑΖΩΡΑΙΟΣ', *ZNW* 72 (1981), pp. 257–63.

J. A. Sanders, 'Ναζωραῖος in Matt. 2:23', *JBL* 84 (1965), pp. 169–72.

H. H. Schaeder, *TWNT* 4, pp. 879–84.

E. Schweizer, ' "Er wird Nazoräer heissen" (zu Mc 1,24; Mt 2,23)', in Eltester, pp. 90–3; reprinted in *Neotestamentica*, pp. 51–5.

H. Smith, 'Ναζωραῖος κληθήσεται', *JTS* 28 (1926), p. 60.

Soares Prabhu, pp. 184–228, 253–61.

W. B. Tatum, 'Matthew 2.23—Wordplay and Misleading Translations', *BT* 27 (1976), pp. 135–8.

D. B. Taylor, 'Jesus—of Nazareth', *ExpT* 92 (1981), pp. 336–7.

E. Zolli, 'Nazarenus vocabitur', *ZNW* 49 (1958), pp. 135–6.

idem, 'The Nazarene', in *The Nazarene*, London, 1950, pp. 7–60.

E. Zuckschwerdt, 'Ναζωραῖος in Mat 2,23', *TZ* 31 (1975), pp. 65–67.

JOHN THE BAPTIST AND JESUS (3.1–17)

(i) *Structure*

3.1–17, like both 1.2–17 and 1.18–2.23, naturally divides itself into three sections. There is first of all a paragraph introducing John the Baptist (3.1–6). This is followed by 3.7–12, which reports John's words to and encounter with the Pharisees and Sadducees. Finally, 3.13–17 tells of the baptism of Jesus.

I. John the Baptist introduced (3.1–6)
   A. Introductory sentence (3.1–2)
   B. Scriptural text (3.3)
   C. John described (3.4–6)
      1. John's appearance (3.4a–b)
      2. John's diet (3.4c)
      3. John's baptism (3.5–6)

II. John and the Sadducees and Pharisees (3.7–12)
   A. The setting (3.7a)
   B. John's demand for repentance (3.7b–10)
      1. Rhetorical question and exhortation (connected by οὖν; 3.7b–8)
      2. Warning and justification of warning (3.9)
      3. Parable of the axe and tree (3.10)
   C. John's words about the coming one (3.11–12)
      1. John's baptism (3.11a)
      2. The coming one is stronger (3.11b)
      3. John's unworthiness (3.11c)
      4. The coming one's baptism (3.11d)
      5. The coming one's winnowing fork (3.12)
         a. It is in his hand (3.12a)
         b. The coming one will cleanse (3.12b)
         c. The coming one will gather (3.12c)
         d. The coming one will burn (3.12d)

III. The baptism of Jesus (3.13–17)
   A. Jesus arrives from Galilee (3.13)
   B. The conversation between John and Jesus (3.14–15)
   C. The baptism of Jesus (3.16–17)
      1. Jesus leaves the water (3.16a)

2. The heavens are opened and a vision is seen (3.16b–c)
3. A voice is heard from heaven (3.17)

(ii) *Sources*

3.1–12 has largely been formed by adding Q material (3.7–12) to Markan material (3.1–6). Admittedly, on the two-source theory some degree of Markan/Q overlap must be postulated (see on 3.3, 11). This makes matters untidy, and that is not welcome. But the alternatives invite even less. If Luke were dependent upon Matthew for his Q material, we would be at a loss to fathom how he managed to preserve the original wording of Q in one instance or more. (Luke may be original against Matthew in his parallels to Mt 3.7, 8, and 9; and he is almost certainly original as opposed to Mt 3.11–12; see section iii.) Still more does it obfuscate to think of Mark as a conflation of Matthew and Luke, as on the Griesbach hypothesis. Mk 1.5–6 is more primitive than Mt 3.4–5, as the commentary shows. Further, why should the Second Evangelist have dropped almost all the material he found in Mt 3.7–12 and Lk 3.7–17? Mark, it is true, consistently omits all language about the eschatological judgement when it comes to the Baptist, and in that a purpose might be discerned. Yet what properly Markan purpose? Jesus is a figure of judgement for Mark (8.38; 13.26), and the Second Gospel affirms the reality of both the eschatological fire (9.42–50) and of the eschatological harvest (4.26–9; 13.27). Thus the themes of Mt 3.7–12 and Lk 3.7–9, 15–17 could not have troubled Mark. Why then should he have excluded them from the words of John the Baptist?·

Turning to 3.13–17, it is, as the commentary shows, perfectly explicable on the assumption that Mark is the primary, even exclusive, source. (For possible influence from Q see on 3.16.) There is nonetheless nothing to compel this conclusion if our pericope were to be considered in isolation. Mk 1.9–11 could be regarded as dependent upon Mt 3.13–17 because (save for Mt 3.14–15) the differences are only stylistic and can be explained in terms of Matthew's linguistic preferences or those of Mark. Even so, if Matthew be thought of as original *vis-à-vis* Mark, is it not striking that 3.14–15 has left no trace in the Second—or for that matter, the Third—Gospel?

(iii) *Exegesis*

JOHN THE BAPTIST INTRODUCED (3.1–6)

1. Matthew now jumps over many years, passing from Jesus' infancy to his baptism. The intervening period is thus relatively unimportant and does not even merit an allusion. That Matthew inherited no stories about the boy Jesus is strongly suggested by the general paucity of such stories in first-century Christian literature, Lk 2.21–52 being exceptional. Only in the second century did 'novelistic' tales about what Jesus did as a youth begin to multiply and circulate in number, as the later apocryphal gospels testify.

Several scholars have argued that Mt 3.1 does not introduce a new section of the gospel; for them, 1.1–4.16 constitutes the gospel's first major section (cf. Augustine, *Cont. Faust.* 2.1).[1] The reasons for their opinion are several and include the repetition of ἀπὸ τότε ἤρξατο (ὁ) Ἰησοῦς in 4.17 and 16.21, which is said to mark off the three major divisions of Matthew (1.1–4.16; 4.17–16.20; 16.21–28.20), and the continuation in chapters 3–4 of the geographical interest shown in chapters 1–2 (note esp. 3.3; 4.13, 15). It is, however, difficult indeed not to draw a rather heavy line between 2.23 and 3.1. Not only does the story line witness a jump of about thirty years, but there is also the introduction of a totally new subject, John the Baptist, as well as the fact that, with the exception of 'Son (of God)', the christological themes so central to Mt 1–2—Jesus as the son of Abraham, the Son of David, the Messiah of OT prophecy, and the one like Moses—noticeably recede into the background. One should also keep in mind the question of sources. While chapters 3 and 4 come from Mark and Q, chapters 1 and 2 come from a different source, the source reconstructed in Excursus I. Now the switching of sources could not but have encouraged Matthew to think of 1–2 and 3–4 as distinct sections; and in confirmation of this he has done little more than place 1–2 and 3–4 side by side: no close seam has been sewn, no continuity of theme emphasized. Beyond this, the 'in those days' of 3.1 may function not so much as a connective, implying that John the Baptist appeared when Jesus was residing in Nazareth (2.23), but rather primarily as an opening with eschatological content, marking a new point in the fulfilment of salvation-history (see below). Lastly, one hesitates to put the required weight upon ἀπὸ τότε, a phrase which hardly calls attention to itself and which reappears in 26.16. And 4.17 and 16.21 are not the only places where we read that Jesus 'began' to do something (cf. 11.7, 20). It appears, then, that any structural analysis of the First Gospel will have to reckon with a division between 2.23 and 3.1.

All four gospels, in different ways, treat John the Baptist as the beginning of the gospel (cf. Acts 1.22). This circumstance must ultimately derive from Jesus' own estimation of the Baptist. Through John and his ministry Jesus came to perceive the nearness of the kingdom of God and his own relation to it.

[1] E.g. E. Krentz, 'The Extent of Matthew's Prologue', *JBL* 83 (1964), pp. 401–14, and Kingsbury, *Structure*, pp. 7–25. For critical remarks see Meier, *Vision*, p. 56, n. 21, and D. Hill, 'The Figure of Jesus in Matthew's Gospel', *JSNT* 21 (1984), pp. 42–4.

ἐν δὲ ταῖς ἡμέραις ἐκείναις.[2] This is an addition to the Markan narrative, drawn forward perhaps from Mk 1.9. Because 'that day' and 'those days' frequently carry eschatological content in the First Gospel (7.22; 9.15; 10.15; 11.22, 24; 12.36; 24.19, 22, 29, 36, 42, 50; 25.13; 26.29), and because there is OT precedent for such usage (Jer 3.16, 18; 31.33; 50.4; Joel 3.1; Zech 8.23), an eschatological connotation is here quite possible: the time of John and Jesus is the time of eschatological fulfilment, of what the prophets spoke.[3] Perhaps one might also find in the phrase, whose imprecision betrays Matthew's lack of interest in precise chronology (contrast Lk 3.1–2), evidence of an 'historicization', to which Strecker in particular has called so much attention: John and Jesus belong to the unrepeatable past, to 'those days'. And yet, OT texts such as Gen 6.4; Exod 2.11; Deut 17.9; 19.17; 26.3; and Dan 10.2, texts in which the thoroughly biblical expression, 'in those days', occurs without pregnant meaning or eschatological content, warn against reading too much into the first few words of Mt 3.1. Compare also the rabbinic bĕ'ôtô hayyôm (as in b. B. Meṣ. 59b): it is often just a redactional link.[4]

παραγίνεται Ἰωάννης ὁ βαπτιστής. The verb means 'made his appearance'. In the LXX it usually translates bô'. Mark has ἐγένετο. Compare 2.1 and 3.13 (also present tense). The historical present appears to function in 3.1 to help introduce a change of scene (cf. 2.13, 19; 4.5, 8; 9.14; 15.1; 19.10; 20.8; 22.16; 25.19; 27.38); see W. Schenk, 'Das Präsens Historicum als Makrosyntaktisches Gliederungssignal im Matthäusevangelium', NTS 22 (1976), pp. 466–7.

'John the Baptist' is the form always used by Matthew (3.1; 11.11–12; 14.2, 8; 16.14; 17.13); it also appears in Luke (7.20, 33; 9.19) and Josephus (Ant. 18.116). Mark has this (6.25; 8.28) and another form, John ὁ βαπτίζων (1.4; 6.14, 24). This second form puts more stress on the activity of baptism. Our evangelist presumably avoids the secondary, Markan construction in favour of the other form quite simply because in his community John was known as ὁ βαπτιστής. Hence the change does not betoken some

---

[2] One can hardly decide whether δε (cf. Lk 3.1) is original. It is found in ℵ B C W 0233 f[1.13] 33 892 1241 1424 pm lat sy[p.h] sa mae bo[pt] Aug. It is dropped by D E K L N[vid] S Γ Δ Π 28 565 700 1010 pm it sy[s] bo[pt] arm eth Hil followed by HG.

[3] See esp. Kingsbury, Structure, pp. 28–30. It is not clear how this comports with Kingsbury's argument for the unity of Mt 1–4.

[4] Some earlier critics, finding 'in those days' unduly awkward after 2.23, argued that the phrase had its rightful and original place in a pre-Matthean source about the Baptist which narrated particulars about the time before his public appearance (see Strauss, p. 209). Others, including A. Hilgenfeld, 'Friedrich Loofs gegen Ernst Häckel', ZNW 43 (1900), p. 269, supposed that 3.1 originally linked up with 1.17 and that 1.18–2.23 was a later interpolation. For other, similar theses and discussion see B. Weiss, p. 59, and Moffatt, pp. 250–1.

subtle theological interest. (Certainly the lack of background information on John assumes on the readers' part some familiarity with his name and his work.)

In the First Gospel John the Baptist is distinguished by three chief characteristics.[5] First, John is Jesus' forerunner, the messenger sent to prepare Israel for her encounter with the coming one (3.3, 11–12; 11.10); that is, he is Elijah (11.14; 17.11–13), whose task it is to ready God's people for the day of the Lord (Mal 4.5–6). John's proclamation, because it is a call to repentance (3.2) and because it anticipates Jesus' preaching (cf. 3.2 with 4.17), should encourage Israel to embrace her Messiah when he comes. The baptism in the Jordan with its confession of sins (3.6) serves the same purpose. Thus John's person and work are one: by his words and deeds the forerunner prepares his hearers to meet him who will baptize with holy spirit and with fire (3.11).

The second outstanding feature of John the Baptist in Matthew is his utter subordination to Jesus. This subordination, which is particularly apparent in 3.11–12, 14 and 11.2–6, is implicit in John's ministry as forerunner, for it is his assigned task to point towards another (3.11–12). The origin of the theme is largely to be accounted for by the rivalry between Jesus' disciples and those of John. But of this rivalry there is no development in Matthew, and there is no significant polemic against the Baptist or his followers (see 9.14–17; 11.2–6; 14.12; contrast Jn 1). Indeed, side by side with the theme of subordination is—and this is the third major item in Matthew's portrait of the Baptist—a high degree of parallelism between John and Jesus (cf. Lk 1). The two men say similar things (cf. 3.2 with 4.17, 3.7 with 12.34 and 23.33, and 3.10 with 7.19). Both are introduced in similar fashion (cf. 3.1 with 3.13). Both are opposed by the Pharisees and Sadducees (cf. 3.7–10 with 12.34 and 23.33). Both appeal to the same generation to repent (11.16–19). Both act by the same authority, the authority of heaven (21.23–32). Both are taken by the people to be prophets (11.9; 14.5; 21.11, 26, 46). Both are rejected and executed as criminals (14.1–12; 26–27). And both are buried by their own disciples (14.12; 27.57–61). Now how are we to explain all these similarities? As a matter of historical fact, Jesus and John did suffer similar fates; and they were both prophets who knew rejection and suffered a violent end at the hands of the government. Thus their careers lent themselves to similar interpretations. But more than this is going on in Matthew. The First Evangelist alone makes John—like Jesus—proclaim the kingdom of heaven. Why? 11.11–15 places John the Baptist in the days of the kingdom of heaven. Hence John and Jesus belong to the same stage of

[5] Lit.: Trilling (v); Wink, pp. 27–41; J. P. Meier (v).

salvation-history.[6] This is why they proclaim the same kingdom and call upon Israel with the same words. This is also why Matthew feels so free to draw parallels between the two figures. Jesus and John, being sent by God at the same time to the same people, have the same eschatological message to utter (cf. Meier, 'Baptist' (v)).

κηρύσσων ἐν τῇ ἐρήμῳ τῆς Ἰουδαίας. The emphasis falls upon the verb (most frequently in the LXX for *qārā'*) as it is placed before 'in the wilderness' (contrast Mark). Both Mark and Luke also use κηρύσσω of John. For the preaching of Jesus see 4.17, 23; 9.35; 11.1. For the preaching of the disciples and other followers of Jesus see 10.7, 27; 24.14; 26.13. For the preaching of John the Baptist see only 3.1. Unlike Jesus and the disciples, John is not said to preach the gospel (cf. 4.23; 9.35; 24.14; 26.13). The NT's distinctive use of κηρύσσω probably developed in the Greek-speaking mission; there is no Semitic equivalent which can explain it (see Chilton, *Strength*, pp. 75–8).

'In the desert of Judea' refers to the Judean wilderness in the lower Jordan valley, between the Judean plateau and the Dead Sea and lower Jordan river—although the precise location of John's activity is unknown.[7] According to Josephus, between the Sea of Galilee and the Dead Sea the Jordan 'runs a long way over a desert' (ἐρημίαν; *Bell.* 3.515). See also Judg 1.16; 1 Macc 2.29–30; 5.24, 28; 2 Macc 5.27; Jn 11.54; Acts 21.38. The place where John baptized is placed by Jn 1.28 in Transjordan and by 10.40 in Bethany. Perhaps Matthew in his own mind stretched 'Judea' to include part of that area (cf. 19.1?).

The link between John and the desert is strong in early Christian tradition and must be regarded as first of all historical, whatever symbolic significance be attached to it.[8] Some have thought that

---

[6] This is true whether one sees a three-stage scheme for salvation-history in Matthew—so e.g. J. P. Meier, 'Salvation-History in Matthew: in Search of a Starting Point', *CBQ* 37 (1975), pp. 103–15; idem, *Law*, pp. 25–40, arguing for this outline: OT period, period of Jesus (including the Baptist), period of the church—or a two-stage scheme—so e.g. Kingsbury, *Structure*, pp. 25–7; J.-C. Ingelaere, 'Structure de Matthieu et histoire du salut: Etat de la question', *FV* 78 (1979), pp. 10–33; and Donaldson, pp. 209–11, arguing for this outline: period of promise (OT), period of fulfilment (Jesus, Church). (In our judgement it is impossible to come to a firm conclusion as to Matthew's outline of salvation-history—because we have yet to see the evidence that he gave the issue any thought at all.)

[7] For the interesting conjecture that John worked not in Judea but in Peraea see T. W. Manson, *Servant*, pp. 40–1.

[8] On the wilderness tradition see Davies, *GL*, pp. 75–90; Scobie (v), pp. 91–8; U. W. Mauser, *Christ in the Wilderness*, SBT 39, London, 1963, pp. 15–58; S. Talmon, 'The "Desert" Motif in the Bible and Qumran Literature', in *Biblical Motifs*, ed. A. Altman, Cambridge, Mass., 1966, pp. 31–63. The desert was, among other things, a place of refuge (Exod 2.15; 1 Sam 23.14; Jer 48.6; Rev 12.6), the haunting place of demons (4 Macc 18.8; Mk 1.12–13; Mt 12.43), the scene of Israel's wanderings (Exod 13.1ff.; Jer 2.1–2), and the focus of eschatological

John the desert dweller must have had some association with the Dead Sea community,[9] and in fact there are several intriguing similarities between the Baptist and the Qumran sectaries (e.g. the prominence of ritual washings). These, however, prove less than has often been claimed and the connexion with Qumran must remain only an inviting possibility.[10] (Pertinent to the discussion is Josephus, *Vita* 11–12, in which we learn of a certain Banus, who lived alone in the desert, made clothes from trees, ate only food that grew of its own accord, and bathed himself in cold water by day and night. He was not an Essene.) Perhaps we should see John's desert abode as indicative of two things, the first being his eschatological orientation, for a return to the desert was widely anticipated as one of the end-time events. As happened in ancient times, so at the culmination a period in the wilderness would precede the redemption: and there would be a second entry into the land (see on 2.15). Then, secondly, the wilderness, with its barren rocks and bleak landscape, would no doubt have been the appropriate spot in which to preach judgement—especially if Sodom and Gomorrah were in the vicinity.

Given Matthew's identification of John with Elijah (17.10–13) and the Elijah-like traits given to the Baptist (see below), 'in the desert of Judea' just might be consonant with a desire to evoke memory of the Tishbite. Elijah found refuge in and wandered about the desert, and he was taken up in the fiery chariot near the Jordan (1 Kgs 17.3; 19.3–18; 2 Kgs 2.1–12). Also, while the OT has Elijah come from Tishbe of Gilead in the northern kingdom (1 Kgs 17.1), the first century Lives of the Prophets tells us Elijah 'was a Tishbite from the land of the Arabs', that is, from Transjordan, where John reportedly worked.

To 'in the desert' (so Mark and Luke), which anticipates the quotation of Isa 40.3, Matthew has added 'of Judea' (cf. Ps 62 LXX, title; Mk 1.5; Lk 3.1). This takes the reader back to chapter 2 where Judea is a place of danger (1, 5, 22); so John's ministry is set in a hostile place. On ἔρημος (most frequently for *midbār* in the LXX, rarely for *'ărābâ*) see D. Baly, in *CHJ* 1, pp. 18–23.

2. The when ('in those days'), the what ('he made his appearance . . . preaching'), and the where ('in the wilderness of Judea') of John the Baptist were the subjects of 3.1. 3.2 continues

expectation (see on 2.15). For an early attempt to fathom the symbolism of the desert see Eusebius, *Dem. ev.* 9.6. On retreat from society and its meaning in the Greek world see A.-J. Festugière, *Personal Religion among the Greeks*, Berkeley, 1954, pp. 53–67.

[9] E.g. Brownlee (v) and Geyser (v). Additional lit. in Braun, *Qumran*, 2, pp. 1–29.
[10] Cf. the remarks of F. F. Bruce, *Second Thoughts on the Dead Sea Scrolls*, rev. ed., London, 1961, pp. 140–4. M. Smith, *Clement*, pp. 206–7, has even gone so far as to find polemic against John the Baptist in 1QS 3.14ff.

by further unfolding the what ('and saying, "Repent . . ." ').

καὶ λέγων· μετανοεῖτε· ἤγγικεν γὰρ ἡ βασιλεία τῶν οὐρανῶν.[11] This same utterance is also ascribed to Jesus in 4.17. See the comments there. It is certainly redactional. Neither Mark nor Luke puts such an announcement on John's lips, and it must be regarded as one of the deliberate parallels—created on the basis of Mk 1.4 and 15—that Matthew has drawn between the Messiah and his forerunner (see above). On μετανοέω and the subject of repentance see on 3.8. Josephus tells us that John offered moral exhortation (*Ant.* 18.116–19).

In adopting Mk 1.4 and 15 for his summary of the Baptist's preaching, Matthew has dropped (1) 'the forgiveness of sins'; (2) 'the gospel of God' and 'believe in the gospel'; and (3) 'the time is fulfilled'.[12] These phrases have in all likelihood been omitted because it was sensed that they were more appropriately associated with the Christian Lord. Jesus is the one who brought forgiveness of sins (1.21; 26.28), who introduced the gospel (4.23; 9.35; cf. 11.5), and who ushered in the time of fulfilment (1.2–17). Furthermore, if John had preached a baptism for the forgiveness of sins, Jesus' baptism would have been all the more troublesome for Matthew than it is already.

3. The Baptist's ministry is now illuminated by a quotation from the prophet Isaiah.

οὗτος γάρ ἐστιν ὁ ῥηθεὶς διὰ 'Ησαΐου τοῦ προφήτου λέγοντος. Compare 4.14; 8.17; 11.10 (also of John); 12.17; and see on 1.22. Matthew keeps Mark's mention of Isaiah (15.7 offers the only other instance of a non-formula quotation which mentions the prophet); otherwise he alters the introductory formula to bring it into line with his other scriptural prefaces, although the usual ἵνα πληρωθῇ is, for no obvious reason,[13] replaced by οὗτος γάρ ἐστιν ὁ ῥηθείς. The parallels in CD 10.16; 16.15; and (according to van der Woude's reconstruction) 11QMelch. 2.14 are very close. Note also Acts 2.16 and 7.37.

Throughout Matthew Isaiah's name (Mt: 6–7; Mk: 2; Lk: 2) is associated on the one hand with Jesus' ministry to a blind Israel that rejects him and, on the other hand, with the salvation held out to the Gentiles (8.17; 13.14(?), 35(?); 15.7; and 4.14 and 12.17

---

[11] καὶ before λεγων is found in C D L W 0233 *f*[1.13] Maj lat sy but not in ℵ B 28 q eth Hil. In both 4.23 and 9.35 κηρύσσων is followed by καί + another participle. This speaks in favour of retaining the καὶ here.

[12] Matthew never uses πληρόω of time.

[13] According to Gundry, *Commentary*, p. 44, Matthew does not import the verb 'fulfil' because he reserves this for the story of Jesus. This does not explain 2.17, where πληρόω is used in connexion with Herod's slaughter of the infants. Neither 2.17 nor 3.3 has to do with the activity of Jesus; but both are directly related to his coming. We thus cannot see how 'fulfil' would be appropriate in one instance but not in the other.

respectively). Hence Matthew's agreement with Mark in introducing the Baptist by means of a prophecy explicitly attributed to Isaiah is fitting. John rebuffed the Jewish leaders, negated the benefits of Abrahamic descent, and proclaimed God's ability to raise up a new people from stones—for Matthew an allusion to the salvation soon to come to the Gentiles.

φωνὴ βοῶντος ἐν τῇ ἐρήμῳ· ἐτοιμάσατε τὴν ὁδὸν κυρίου, εὐθείας ποιεῖτε τὰς τρίβους αὐτοῦ. The quotation of Isa 40.3, taken over word for word from Mark, agrees with the LXX, save for the substitution of the personal pronoun for τοῦ θεοῦ ἡμῶν, which identifies the Lord as Jesus (contrast Justin, *Dial.* 50.3). The messianic character of the prophecy (see below) is thereby made manifest. (The pronoun might also be explained as resulting from avoidance of the divine name, for in 1QS 8.13 we find, 'to prepare there the way of him', 'him' being God.) The MT has something else altogether: 'make straight in the desert a highway for our God'. The synoptics and the LXX, together with the targum, the OT Peshitta, and the Vulgate, agree in taking 'in the desert' with 'the voice of one crying' (Gundry, *OT*, pp. 9–10). This lessens the geographical impact of the passage (cf. Davies, *SSM*, p. 31). In the MT, 'in the desert' goes with what follows (as is demanded by the parallelism): 'in the desert prepare the way of the Lord'—advice the Dead Sea sect took to heart. The LXX reading made possible the identification of the 'voice' with John, who lived in the desert.

Originally Isa 40.3 spoke to the exiles in Babylon, comforting them with the immediate prospect of return: the highway is even now being prepared for Yahweh, who will soon return to the Land with his people (cf. 40.11). In the gospels all is made new. The voice is not the voice of the Lord or the heavenly council or an unnamed herald but John the Baptist. The Lord is not Yahweh but Jesus. The exile is not in view but the time of the Messiah. Some precedent for this thorough reinterpretation which disregards original context can be found in the Dead Sea Scrolls. In 1QS 8.12–16 (cf. 9.19–20), Isa 40.3 is programmatically applied to the community which prepares the way of the Lord by withdrawing into the wilderness to study there the Law (cf. 1QM 1.3; 4QpPs[a] 3.1; 4QpIsa[a] 2.18). So an eschatological reading of Isa 40.3 with reference to activity around the Jordan—ethical activity preparing for the Lord's coming—just may have been in the air around John's time, and who is to say whether the Baptist himself or his followers were not the first to apply Isa 40.3 to his ministry in the desert?[14] In any case, Mark and his fellow-evangelists were not the

---

[14] Cf. Pesch (v), pp. 116–18. Jn 1.23 probably offers independent testimony to the use of Isa 40.3 to interpret the Baptist; see n. 12. Bultmann, *History*, p. 246, gives no reason for concluding that the idea of the Baptist as a wilderness preacher arose out of a specifically Christian interpretation of Isa 40. On the link between Isa 40.3

only ones to reapply and update the text for an eschatological situation. For additional eschatological interpretations of Isa 40.1–5 see Bar 5.7; Sir 48.24; 1 En. 1.6; As. Mos. 10.4; *Lev. Rab.* on 1.14; *Deut. Rab.* on 4.11; *Pesiq. R.* 29; 30; 33.

Although we know precisely what the evangelists must have made of 'the voice of one crying in the wilderness', the meaning of preparing the way and of making straight the paths is not made explicit. Judging, however, by the Matthean context, two things may be inferred. First, John prepares the way in that he goes before Jesus in order to bear witness to Jesus, the coming one: 3.11–12, 14. Secondly, as Elijah (11.14; 17.11–13), whose task it is to turn the hearts of the father to the son (Mal 4.6; Ecclus 48.10; cf. Lk 1.15), John calls for repentance: 3.8 (cf. 3.10; 11.16–19). Thus when Jesus is manifested, the people should be repentant and looking for the coming one. They should, in other words, be prepared, and Jesus' task should be the easier.

There is an interesting agreement between Matthew and Luke against Mark in the text before us. The first and third evangelists omit the conflation of Exod 23.20 and Mal 3.1 which is joined to Isa 40.3 in Mk 1.2–3. The explanations for this are several. Coincidence could be invoked. Or Mk 1.2 could be an early interpolation (so Taylor, *Mark*, p. 153). Or both Matthew and Luke may have recognized the inappropriateness of attributing to Isaiah sentences found in Exodus and Malachi and therefore decided to omit them. Or, what is no less likely, the Q source may also have included a quotation of Isa 40.3 with reference to the Baptist as well as, in another context, a conflation of Exod 23.20 and Mal 3.1 (see Mt 11.10 = Lk 7.27).[15] In this case, both Matthew and Luke could independently have followed the text of Q in Mt 3.3 = Lk 3.4 and then (again independently) have preferred to reserve the quotation of Exod 23.20 + Mal 3.1 for its Q context. (The placement of 'in the wilderness' before the quotation of Isa 40.3 in both Matthew and Luke might also be explained by the influence of Q.)

---

and Elijah in later Judaism see G. Molin, 'Elijahu der Prophet und sein Weiterleben in den Hoffnungen des Judentums und der Christenheit', *Judaica* 8 (1952), pp. 65–94.

[15] Jn 1.23 is probably evidence for the traditional association of Isa 40.3 with John the Baptist (cf. Dodd, *Tradition*, pp. 252–3; Brown, *John* 1, pp. 50–1); and the association of Exod 23.30 with Mal 3.1 was perhaps traditional in Jewish circles; see *Exod. Rab.* on 32.9; *Deut. Rab.* on 11.9; and Stendahl, *School*, pp. 49–54. So Mt 3.3 = Lk 3.4 and Mt 11.10 = Lk 7.27 could be more or less independent of Mk 1.2–3. On Isa 40.3–5 as an early Christian *testimonium* see K. R. Snodgrass, 'Streams of Tradition Emerging from Isaiah 40:1–5 and their Adaptation in the New Testament', *JSNT* 8 (1980), pp. 24–45, and Dodd, *Scriptures*, pp. 39–41. Does Lk 3.4–6, in which both Isa 40.3 and 40.4–5 are cited, preserve the Q text, Matthew having abbreviated under the influence of Mark? See Schürmann, *Lukasevangelium* 1, p. 161.

4. After learning of the heart of John's message (3.2) and of his biblical rôle as the voice in the wilderness (3.3), we next (3.4) read about his external appearance and habits (3.5–6 will then tell us what John did). The point is not to satisfy simple curiosity or the historian's eye for detail, although as a matter of fact John undoubtedly matched the description given. Rather, John's striking habits mark him off as a prophet, particularly as one like Elijah (see below).

3.4 is taken from Mk 1.6. Matthew has made a few changes, all of them stylistic. There is no parallel in Luke (a gospel in which the Baptist and Elijah are not clearly identified).

αὐτὸς δὲ ὁ Ἰωάννης εἶχεν τὸ ἔνδυμα αὐτοῦ ἀπὸ τριχῶν καμήλου καὶ ζώνην δερματίνην περὶ τὴν ὀσφὺν αὐτοῦ.[16] After ἀπό Matthew follows Mark exactly. The proleptic pronoun is intensive, perhaps even demonstrative ('this John'). According to Black, pp. 96–7, an Aramaism is to be detected here. Matthew usually drops the typically Markan periphrastic imperfect (here, ἦν . . . ἐσθίων). ἔνδυμα (cf. the Hebrew *lĕbûš*) is a Matthean favourite (Mt: 7; Mk: 0; Lk: 1), as is ἀπό used to indicate material source (cf. *min* as in Ct 3.9): Mt: 5; Mk: 0; Lk: 2.

The garment of camel's hair (cf. Justin, *Dial.* 88; Gosp. Eb. according to Epiphanius, *Haer.* 30.13.4–5) is worn even today by Bedouin: it is rough desert clothing (cf. Josephus, *Bell.* 1.480; Rev 6.12). On John the Baptist it had special meaning. John was a noticeably ragged figure of striking, austere appearance, and his haircloth was a sign of his special status as a prophet (cf. Mt 11.7–9 = Lk 7.24–6); see especially Zech 13.4; also Heb 11.37; 1 Clem. 17.1 (which names Elijah); and Asc. Isa. 2.7–11. More than this, once the identification of John with Elijah was made,[17] an eschatological motif must have been read in: Elijah the prophet has returned in the person of the Baptist. According to the most plausible translation of 2 Kgs 1.8, Elijah 'wore a garment of haircloth' (MT: 'îš ba'al śē'ār; LXX: ἀνὴρ δασύς); and in 1 Kgs 19.13, 19 and 2 Kgs 2.8, 13–14 we read of his 'mantle' ('adderet'). The LXX translates this last with μηλωτή, 'rough skin' or 'sheepskin'; and Tg. Ps.-J. to 2 Kgs 2.8 has *šôšîpā*, 'coarse cloak' (Jastrow). The connexion with Elijah is all the more certain

---

[16] 'And a leather girdle around his waist' is absent from Mk 1.6 D a b d ff r¹ t vgᵐˢ, and C. H. Turner (*JTS* 26 (1925) p. 151) argued that the phrase in Mark could be put down to assimilation to Matthew (cf. Gundry, *OT*, p. 131). This is only a remote possibility.

[17] Whether this interpretation goes back to the Baptist himself, to the Baptist's disciples, to Jesus, or to Jesus' disciples, we need not decide here. For discussion see J. A. T. Robinson (v); Richter (v); and Vielhauer (v). In Vielhauer's opinion, while the historical John wore a leather girdle and a garment of camel's hair, these were common dress; only later were they connected with Elijah. Contrast Hengel, *Charismatic Leader*, p. 36, n. 71.

because, in addition to the common mantle, both John and the Tishbite had leather girdles around their waists (cf. Clement of Alexandria, *Paed.* 2.10.112):

2 Kgs 1.8 LXX:	Mt 3.4:
καὶ ζώνην δερματίνην	καὶ ζώνην δερματίνην
περιεζωσμένος	περὶ
τὴν ὀσφὺν αὐτοῦ	τὴν ὀσφὺν αὐτοῦ

Compare Josephus, *Ant.* 9.22. For the MT's equivalent of ζώνην δερματίνην, '*ēzôr 'ôr*, Tg. Ps.-J. has *zarzā' dĕmaškā*', 'garments of hide'.[18]

ἡ δὲ τροφὴ ἦν αὐτοῦ ἀκρίδες καὶ μέλι ἄγριον. For Mark's καὶ ἐσθίων Matthew has substituted 'the food of him was'. This makes for better parallelism between 4a and b. The final four words are from Mark, with the necessary adjustment in case ending. Gosp. Eb. frag. 2 (in Epiphanius, *Haer.* 30.13.4) reads: 'and his food, as it says, was wild honey, whose taste was that of manna, as a cake dipped in oil' (cf. Exod 16.31; Num 11.8). For locusts as food see Lev 11.20–3; Pliny, *Nat. hist.* 6.35; 7.2; 11QTemple 4; *m.Ḥul.* 3.7; *m. Ter.* 10.9; SB 1, pp. 98–100. Even today Bedouin and poorer inhabitants of Arabia, Africa, and Syria have been known to eat raw or roasted or boiled locusts and grasshoppers. There is no need to speculate that 'locusts' might mean something else, such as carob pods or dried fruit (cf. Lampe, s.v.). Compare CD 12.14: 'As for locusts, according to their various kinds they shall plunge them alive into fire or water for this is what their nature requires'.

μέλι ἄγριον is 'wild honey'. On honey (a clean food according to *m. Makš.* 6.4) in Palestine see Gen 43.11; Exod 3.8 ('a land flowing with milk and honey'); Deut 32.13; Judg 14.8; 1 Sam 14.25; Ps 81.16; Ezek 27.17; Ep. Arist. 112; Josephus, *Bell.* 4.469; Eusebius, *Praep. ev.* 8.11 (the Essenes keep bees); SB 1, pp. 100–101. There is insufficient cause for supposing 'wild honey' to be an exudation of certain trees (cf. Diodorus Siculus 19.94; *b. Ber.* 38a; *b. Ketub.* 111b). We are instead to think of the honey of wild bees as opposed to the honey marketed by beekeepers.[19]

If John's dress characterized him for Christians as a prophet and particularly as one like Elijah, his diet pointed to asceticism and

---

[18] In Christian art John's leather girdle is wrongly represented as a leather apron. ζώνη is a belt, as in Mt 10.9; Mk 6.8; Acts 21.11; M. Poly. 13.2. It became a loan-word in rabbinic Hebrew; see Jastrow, s.v. *zônî*.

[19] The account of John's food in the Gospel of the Ebionites (see text) interests because if, as seems probable, Mk 1.12–13 portrays Jesus as a second or last Adam, then the phrase, 'and the angels served him', signifies that Jesus was given the food of paradise, manna. Note also that honey is a paradisiacal food in Jos. Asen. 16 and *Sepher Ha-Razim* 6.1. On honey as a eucharistic food in the second century and later see J. Betz, 'Die Eucharistie als Gottes Milch in früchristlicher Sicht', *ZKT* 106 (1984), pp. 1–26, 167–85.

poverty, to one 'lean and haggard in the eyes of men but beautiful in the grace of the Most High', to quote an ancient description of Daniel (L. Proph. Dan. 3). Compare the saying attributed to Jesus in Q: 'John came neither eating nor drinking' (Mt 11.18 = Lk 7.33; the latter has 'nor drinking wine'). That the Baptist abstained from flesh from which blood had been drained and took no strong drink is implicit in his diet of wild honey and locusts.[20] John was thus, on the one hand, like the Nazarites who, being wholly consecrated to God, refused wine (cf. Num 6.3; Judg 13.4–5, 14; and esp. Lk 1.15; recall also the Rechabites: Jer 35); on the other hand, he was like those holy men in both the Jewish and Graeco-Roman worlds who refused meat (Dan 1.12, 16; Josephus, *Vita* 14; Philo, *Vit. Cont.* 37; Asc. Isa. 2.11; T. Isaac 4.5; L. Proph. Dan. 14; Hist. Rechab. 11.3; 12.4; Philostratus, *VA* 1.8; cf. Rom 14.2, 21).[21] Note also that in not worrying about what to eat or wear, John demonstrated the character of a true disciple of Jesus (cf. 6.25–34; 10.10; 24.45). For parallels with Stoic-Cynic philosophers see Mussies, pp. 35–6. He cites Dio Chrysostom 1.61–2; 4.70; 6.12, 14; 13.10–11; 60.7–8.

5. The reason for John's appellation, 'the Baptist', is now recorded, and the meaning of his baptism now explained.

τότε ἐξεπορεύετο πρὸς αὐτὸν Ἱεροσόλυμα καὶ πᾶσα ἡ Ἰουδαία καὶ πᾶσα ἡ περίχωρος τοῦ Ἰορδάνου. The changes in this line *vis-à-vis* Mark are characteristic of Matthew. τότε (see on 2.16) replaces καί. The rare Ἱεροσολυμῖται (only once in the LXX: Ecclus 50.27; cf. 4 Macc 18.5; twice in the NT: Mk 1.6; Jn 7.25) is dropped and its replacement, Ἱεροσόλυμα (cf. 2.3), moved forward, which puts the emphasis upon the (personified: cf. Gen 41.57) capital. (Given the mention of 'all Judea', 'all the Jerusalemites' [so Mark] or 'Jerusalem' [Matthew] is strictly unnecessary; but the city merits mention as the most conspicuous and important portion of Judea, its quintessence; cf. Isa 1.1; 2.1; 3.1.) 'And all the region about the Jordan' (cf. Gen 13.10, 11; 2 Chr 4.17; Lk 3.3)[22] is added (in parallel to 'all Judea') to increase the geographical impact of John's ministry.[23] There may also be a connexion with 17.11: is it

[20] Against S. C. Davies (v), who thinks John an Essene who simply had to eat off the land when unable to eat food prepared by Essenes (cf. Josephus, *Bell.* 2.143).

[21] On vegetarianism in Judaism see H. Lietzmann, *An die Römer*, HNT 8, Tübingen, 1933[4], excursus on 14.1. For the Greek world see G. Bornkamm, *TWNT* 4, pp. 66–8. In 4 Ezra 9.26 and 12.51 vegetarianism is a temporary state for the seer, one in which he receives visions (cf. Dan 10.2–3). Later Christian tradition may have altered or dropped 'locusts' in the interests of vegetarianism (cf. Epiphanius, *Haer.* 30.13; Tatian has 'milk'). Yet in *m. Ḥull.* 8.1 one who abstains from flesh is permitted to eat fish and locusts (cf. *b. Ḥull.* 65a).

[22] This minor agreement of Matthew and Luke against Mark might be due to Q's account of the Baptist which underlies Mt 3.7–10 = Lk3.7–9; see also on 3.3.

[23] While in Mk 1.5 there just might be an allusion to Mal 3.4 ('Then the offering of Judah and Jerusalem will be pleasing to the Lord . . .'), this cannot be the case in

because John (= Elijah, 11.14) is to restore *all* things that out to him go *all* Judea and *all* the region about the Jordan?[124]

περίχωρος (cf. the rabbinic *pĕrîkôrîn*) could either derive from Q (cf. Lk 3.3) or be redactional (as it is in 14.35). Note that the verb, ἐκπορεύομαι (Mt: 5; Mk: 11; Lk: 3), like the 'baptize' of 3.6, is kept in the (progressive) imperfect. This puts before the reader's eyes a course of events taking place over a period of time.

In the use of 'all' here it is usual to see a note of exaggeration reminiscent of the looseness with which the OT often employs *kōl* (cf. 2.3; 21.10; 27.25): John is being praised. Nevertheless, not only does Mk 11.27–33 presuppose knowledge of John in Jerusalem, but Josephus (*Ant.* 18.116–20) testifies to the Baptist's far-flung impact. And John's fame and influence are confirmed by his undoing at the hands of Antipas: an insignificant preacher would not have brought upon himself the death penalty. Moreover, anyone who has seen the films of Mother Teresa of India in our own day knows that the appearance of the holy person can utterly empty villages and countryside. Historically, John must often have drawn large crowds. He was a sensation (cf. 11.7–9).

This verse and the next should not be passed over in judging Matthew's attitude towards the Jewish people. If in 2.3 'all Jerusalem' is associated with the wicked Herod, and if in 27.25 'all the people' say, 'His blood be upon us and upon our children', in 3.5–6 'Jerusalem and all Judea and all the region about the Jordan' go out to John the Baptist and are baptized by him, confessing their sins. It is unfortunate that this last notice has usually been left out of account in discussions of Matthew's view of Judaism. 3.5–6 is instructive in several respects. (1) If 'all Israel' repents in 3.5–6, in 27.25 'all the people' proclaim their guilt. Clearly we cannot take Matthew's πᾶς at face value. (2) If there are verses which seem to dismiss the Jews, there are others which put them in a positive light. No consistent attitude can be discerned in our text. (3) If the evangelist had believed that the Jewish people as a whole had rejected Jesus, how could he have written 3.5–6? The First Gospel seems to acknowledge that John and Jesus found a favourable reception among many Jews.

6. This verse reproduces Mk 1.5b with one minor change. 'By him' is moved from its position immediately after the verb and placed after 'in the Jordan river', perhaps in order to bring the latter closer to the 'Jordan' of 3.5.

Matthew. The word order is wrong and 'the area around the Jordan' has been added.

[24] Cf. K. Brower, 'Elijah in the Markan Passion Narrative', *JSNT* 18 (1983), p. 87.

καὶ ἐβαπτίζοντο ἐν τῷ Ἰορδάνῃ ποταμῷ ὑπ᾽ αὐτοῦ.[25] Apart from chapter 3, the verb, which in the active means 'to dip', 'to immerse', 'to plunge', occurs only in 28.19. For 'baptize' with 'Jordan' see 4 Βασ 5.14.

The antecedents of John's baptism have been much discussed (see the survey in Beasley-Murray (v), pp. 1–44). Resemblances have been observed with OT ablutions (see Dahl (v)), with Jewish proselyte baptism (see Jeremias (v)),[26] and with the washings of Qumran (Brownlee (v), Geyser (v)). And while some have argued that John's baptism should be seen as part of a much wider baptist movement in first-century Judaism (Brandt (v), Thomas (v)),[27] others have suggested that John's action was more or less novel and based primarily upon certain OT texts (Dahl (v); cf. Thyen, 'βαπτισμα' (v), p. 135). The truth probably lies in more than one solution. Perhaps, for instance, John was influenced by the sectaries at Qumran or other baptists but made his own unique contribution through a novel reapplication of scriptural texts. In this regard Ps 51.6–9; Isa 4.4; 44.3; Jer 4.11–14; Ezek 36.25–27; and Zech 13.1 are worth considering. In any case, John's distinctiveness is clear. His baptism was directed towards the nation as a whole (contrast Qumran), administered once and for all (contrast OT ablutions), and was for Jews only (contrast proselyte baptism). Most important of all, it was eschatological and probably sealed the repentant, marking them as those who would pass through the coming judgement to enter the messianic kingdom.

For 'the river Jordan' see Num 13.29; Josh 4.7; 5.1 LXX; Ep. Arist. 116; Josephus, *Ant.* 20.97. 'River' is strictly superfluous, and in the OT 'Jordan' usually stands on its own (cf. Mt 3.13; 4.15, 25; 19.1). According to *Did.* 7, baptism should preferably be administered in 'living' (= running) water, and the fact that John baptized in a river played a rôle in the later Christian debate as to whether the corresponding Christian sacrament had to take place in a river or stream. Maj. omits 'river', probably for dogmatic reasons. It would, however, be unwise to read into the original text of Mt 3.6 anything about the evangelist's views on Christian baptism. Perhaps 'river' found its way into the tradition simply because washings and baptisms were not usually performed in rivers. The Dead Sea sect, for example, appears to have conducted its washings in rather large cisterns.[28] But see especially Davies, *JPS*, pp. 74–76: water, an agent of cleanliness, purifies the area around it: *Mekilta, Pisḥa* 1 on Exod. 12.1. Prophets are associated with rivers. (Paradoxically (?) the sea is a symbol of chaos.)

[25] ποταμω is dropped in C³ D L *f*¹³ Maj lat mae geo Hil followed by HG. Compare the ms. division at Mk 1.5.
[26] The pre-Christian origin of Jewish proselyte baptism was once almost taken for granted (cf. SB 1, p. 103; Flemington (v), pp. 4–6). This is no longer possible; see Beasley-Murray, pp. 18–31; L. H. Schiffman, 'At the Crossroads: Tannaitic Perspectives on the Jewish-Christian Schism', in *Jewish and Christian Self-Definition*, vol. 2, ed. E. P. Sanders, Philadelphia, 1981, pp. 127–31; D. Smith (v); and contrast K. Pusey, 'Jewish Proselyte Baptism', *ExpT* 95 (1984), pp. 141–5.
[27] See K. Rudolph, 'The Baptist Sects', *CHJ* 3, chapter 5H, forthcoming.
[28] B. G. Wood, 'To Dip or Sprinkle? The Qumran Cisterns in Perspective', *BASOR* 256 (1984), pp. 45–60.

Jewish texts from antiquity have much to say about the Jordan. According to Gen 13.10, before fire and brimstone fell on Sodom and Gomorrah, 'the Jordan valley was well-watered everywhere like the garden of the Lord' (cf. Jub. 16.5–6). According to other OT texts, the river was part of the eastern boundary of Israel and its crossing was the beginning of the Jewish conquest of Palestine (e.g. Num 34.10–12; Josh 3; Jub. 50.4; 1 En. 89.37). According to 1 Maccabees, its strategic significance during the Maccabean wars was considerable (5.24, 52; 9.34, 42, 43, 45, 48). According to LAE 6–8, Adam stood in the Jordan river for forty days doing penance for his sin in Eden.[29] According to Par. Jer. 6.25, the Jordan proved to be a means of testing the exiles from Babylon to see whether they were worthy to enter Jerusalem ('you will prove them by the water of the Jordan'; cf. 8.2–7). Despite all this, ancient Jewish sources know no special veneration of the Jordan (cf. K. H. Rengstorf, *TWNT* 6, pp. 608–23), so that cannot have had anything to do with its being the place of John's baptism. On the other hand, the possibility of a connexion between the Jordan and Eden motifs in the interpretation of John's ministry cannot be altogether excluded. The river is associated with paradise or with Adam in three of the texts just cited, and when to this it is added that John's diet of honey and locusts can also be linked to paradisiacal traditions (see n. 19), one could wonder whether John, like Jesus (Mk 10.2–9), was understood as heralding a return to paradise.

We do not know for certain whether those who came out to John were baptized in groups or as individuals, whether they went into the water and immersed themselves or were led by the hand and immersed by John or John's disciples.

ἐξομολογούμενοι τὰς ἁμαρτίας αὐτῶν. Identical or similar phrases occur in Acts 19.18; Jas 5.16; Did. 4.14; 1 Clem. 51.3; Herm. v. 1.1.3; 3.1.5; s. 9.23–4. The language is not that of the OT. The verb occurs elsewhere in the synoptics only in Mt 11.25 = Lk 10.21 and Lk 22.6.

The relationship between John's baptism and the forgiveness of sins is uncertain. According to Josephus' account the baptism did not put away sins but was for the purification of the body; it was an ablution, and it was undertaken not by the sinful but by the virtuous and pious (*Bell.* 18.116–20). The contrast with the synoptics could hardly be greater. The first three gospels link John's baptism with 'repentance', and Mk 1.4 and Lk 3.3 make it 'for the forgiveness of sins' (Matthew drops this; see below). Given our uncertainty regarding the religio-historical context, the gospel texts are difficult. Because, however, Christians saw Jesus Christ as the source of forgiveness, we may be confident that they did not invent the report that John's baptism was for the forgiveness of sins. Perhaps baptism in the Jordan was originally conceived of as an 'eschatological sacrament' (A. Schweitzer), a vehicle of grace

[29] This may be Christian redaction on a Jewish text; see K. H. Rengstorf, *TWNT* 6, pp. 611–12.

effectual in itself seems implausible. The ineffectiveness of ritual without inward turning had long been emphasized by Jews (Amos 4.4–6; Hos 6.1–6; Zech 7.1–7; 1QS 3.3–12; 5.13–14; *m. Ber.* 2.1; *Num. Rab.* on 19.18).

For his part, Matthew says no more than that those who came to John confessed their sins. He does not use the word 'forgiveness' (contrast Mk 1.4; Lk 3.3). 'Forgiveness' was apparently too central a feature of Jesus' work to be associated with another (cf. 1.23; 26.28). In Matthew's eyes, John only brought people to repentance in order to make them ready for the Messiah. It was then the Messiah's task to bring the world forgiveness.

JOHN AND THE JEWISH LEADERS (3.7–12)

7. Matthew now turns from his Markan source to Q (cf. Lk 3.7–9), and his account is very close to Luke's. Of sixty-three (so Matthew) or sixty-four (so Luke) words, sixty are in common.

The sayings assigned to John in Q are best received as authentic (*contra* Schulz, *Q*, pp. 371–2). Semitisms are present (Black, pp. 144–5). Distinctive Christian elements are absent. The eschatological thrust and strong note of repentance are consistent with what must have been John's orientation (cf. Mt 11.7–19). And the attack against reliance upon baptism without authentic inward repentance has its parallel in 1QS 5.13–14. It is a good guess that disciples of John recalled their former master's words after they became followers of Jesus and that in this way the lines in Q found their way into the Jesus tradition (cf. Acts 10.37; 13.24–5, also Jn 1.35–51).

ἰδὼν δὲ πολλοὺς τῶν Φαρισαίων καὶ Σαδδουκαίων ἐρχομένους ἐπὶ τὸ βάπτισμα αὐτοῦ εἶπεν αὐτοῖς.[30] This is a redactional introduction based on Q. Compare Lk 3.7: 'He said then to the crowds coming out to be baptized by him'. Although there is only one article (τῶν) before 'Pharisees and Sadducees', this is not good reason to suppose that the evangelist did not know the difference between the two groups. See pp. 31–2.

The Pharisees[31]—who numbered over 6,000 according to Josephus, *Ant.* 17.42—comprised a Jewish sect comparable with other Hellenistic philosophical schools. They prided themselves on their rigorous and accurate interpretation and keeping of the Law (cf. the use of ἀκρίβεια in Josephus, *Bell.* 1.108–9; 2.162; *Vita* 191; *Ant.* 17.40–5; Acts 26.5). And for

---

[30] αυτου is absent in ℵ* B 28 sa mae Or against ℵ¹ C D L W 0233 *f*¹·¹³ Maj latt sy^s.c bo. A decision is difficult. Metzger, p. 9, argues that αυτου was easily passed over as unnecessary or inappropriate.

[31] See Schürer 2, pp. 381–403, and the literature cited there; also E. Rivkin, *A Hidden Revolution*, Nashville, 1978; J. Neusner, *CHJ* 3 forthcoming.

thèm the Law consisted of the written plus the oral Torah, both of which they traced back to Moses on Sinai. In the gospels the Pharisees are greatly concerned with purity laws, with Sabbath observances, and with agricultural taboos, and in all this at least the NT seems to be historically correct, for the rabbinic sources about the Pharisees paint a similar picture. Above all, the Pharisees—who, according to J. Neusner, originated as a political party but came, especially after Hillel, to be concerned primarily with religious matters—seem to have sought to observe the ritual purity laws outside the temple: they lived as though they were temple priests. They first appear on the stage of history during the second century B.C., in the time of Jonathan (Josephus, *Ant.* 13.171), and they evidently emerged out of the non-priestly Hasidim known from 1 Maccabees (2.42; 7.13; cf. 2 Macc 14.6). The name, 'Pharisee', probably derives from *pĕrûšîm* = 'separatists', which was interpreted by the Pharisees in a positive sense, by their opponents in a negative sense.[32]

In Matthew[33] the Pharisees are—more so than in Mark and Luke—the real opponents of Jesus, and this may reflect the fact that Matthew's Jewish contemporaries and opponents considered themselves heirs of the Pharisees, in which case our author would see his own enemies in those of Jesus. Certainly there is no better way of explaining Matthew's attitude towards the Pharisees: his words about them evince a special, living concern (see esp. 23.13–36). (This concern seems to us to count against Strecker's claim (in *Weg*, pp. 137–43) that in Matthew Pharisaism is only a *topos* which simply stands for whatever Matthew dislikes.)

The Sadducees[34] were a priestly, aristocratic party whose locus was the temple in Jerusalem and whose influence on the populace was considerably less than that of the Pharisees (Josephus, *Bell.* 2.164–6; *Ant.* 13.171–3, 297–8; 18.11, 16–17). The origin of the name is uncertain. Most take it to derive from the personal name, '*Ṣādôk*', although which Zadok remains in dispute. Others, following Epiphanius, *Haer.* 14.2, would trace it to *ṣaddîq*, that is, 'righteous' (cf. Jerome, *Comm. on Mt.* on 22.13). The sect, which had its beginning sometime after the Maccabean revolt, died out in A.D. 70, and we must reconstruct its convictions from secondary sources. Both the NT and Josephus report that the Sadducees denied the resurrection (Mk 12.18; Acts 4.1–2; 23.8; Josephus, *Ant.* 18.11; *Bell.* 2.164–6). Josephus adds that they rejected every idea of an after-life. Acts 23.8 has them also disbelieving in angels and spirits (which is difficult to accept at face value as angels appear in the OT from Genesis on; perhaps evil angels are meant, or perhaps the report arose from the Sadducees' repudiation of developed angelology). Josephus, *Ant.* 13.173 claims that they believed in Fate, not free will. The notion that the conservative Sadducees embraced as authoritative only the Pentateuch (see the texts in

[32] See esp. A. I. Baumgarten, 'The Name of the Pharisees', *JBL* 102 (1983), pp. 411–28. T. W. Manson connected the Pharisees with Persians, their theology reflecting that of the latter: he has not been followed. See Davies, *Introduction to Pharisaism*, Philadelphia, 1967.

[33] Lit.: Strecker, pp. 137–43; Hummel, pp. 12–17; Van Tilborg, passim.

[34] See Schürer 2, pp. 404–14, and the literature cited there.

Schürer 2, p. 408, n. 24) seems doubtful. Josephus is silent on the point, and the authority of the prophets was firmly established long before the group came into existence. The Sadducees did, however, deny the validity of the Pharisaic oral Torah. In this respect, the characterization of them as reactionary dinosaurs perhaps has its place. See G. Stemberger, *CHJ* 3, forthcoming. (D. Daube, orally, urged that the Sadducees were not conservatives: they took the position they did to be free from the burdens of Pharisaism's oral tradition.)

The lack of interest in the Sadducees in Mark and Luke needs no explanation. But Matthew[35] has redactionally inserted them into his story seven times. How is this to be explained? Does Matthew know Jewish opponents who traced their heritage to the defunct Sadducees? To settle the issue one has to take a second look at the statistics, which are a bit misleading. In 22.34 the reference to the Sadducees refers back to 22.23, and this last is from Mark. In addition, 'Sadducees' is used five times in 16.1–12. This means that there are really only two places in which our evangelist has added the name—in 3.7 and 16.1–12. Thus the situation is completely different from what it is with the Pharisees, and one does not come away from the First Gospel with the impression that its writer was terribly concerned with the Sadducees. Yet why then mention them at all? The question is, we think, unanswerable if Matthew be taken to be a Gentile. A non-Jew would not have thought twice about a small group that passed away with the temple. If Matthew, however, were a Jew, he would have known a few things about the Sadducees and have realized that his Lord must have encountered some of them. So by adding them to his story he adds a note of realism, and Strecker (*Weg*, p. 140) may be correct when he speaks here of 'historicization' (cf. Hummel, pp. 20–1).

The Pharisees and Sadducees (who appear together again only in chapter 16) oppose John the Baptist as they oppose Jesus. This is part of the Jesus/John parallelism in Matthew and is one more sign of Matthew's conviction that it is primarily the Jewish leaders who are responsible for the nation's tragic fall (cf. esp. 21.33–46). Luke, who speaks only of multitudes, could represent the original of Q, but this is far from certain.[36] Historically, John, like Jesus after him, probably gained most of his following from the common people (cf. Mk 11.30–2; Mt 21.32).

In Luke the multitudes come to be baptized. But could Matthew

[35] Lit.: Meier, *Law*, pp. 18–19; Hummel, pp. 18–20; Van Til, passim.

[36] Schürmann, *Lukasevangelium* 1, p. 163; Hoffmann, p. 17; Schulz, *Q*, pp. 366–7; and Wink, p. 34, n. 1 argue for the originality of Luke. If, however, Lk 7.30 is from Q (questionable), then Matthew's version would fit an idea Q has elsewhere. Cf. Mk 11.27–33. It may be that neither Matthew nor Luke has the Q introduction. οἱ ὄχλοι is a favourite of Luke (Jeremias, *Lukasevangelium*, p. 104). Further, 'brood of vipers' would be harsh as an address to the crowd, yet 'brood of vipers' was in Q.

have envisaged his chief villains, the Pharisees, together with the Sadducees, submitting to John's baptism (cf. 21.25)? The NEB has, 'Many of the Pharisees and Sadducees coming for baptism' (cf. sy^p). But perhaps Matthew altered Q precisely in order to avoid this picture. ἐπί could mean 'to' or even 'against' (cf. BAGD, s.v., III.1.a.ε), and one can read the text so that the leaders come 'to the baptism' only for critical observation (cf. Jn 1.24). Admittedly, the Baptist's words would not then hit their mark so well since they seem to be aimed at those seeking some benefit from baptism; but this inconcinnity could be the outcome of imperfect editing.

γεννήματα ἐχιδνῶν. This is a phrase from Q that Matthew likes (cf. 12.34—of the Pharisees; 23.33—of the scribes and Pharisees). It stands over against the self-designation, 'children of Abraham'. The image is of vipers scurrying before dry scrub about to ignite. Acts 28.3, where a viper comes forth from a fire, contains the only other NT use of ἔχιδνα (LXX: 0). We are not here to think of the adder or viper as 'cunning' (cf. Mt 10.16; Rom 16.19; Midr. Cant. on 2.14). The intended reference is rather to an evil and destructive and repugnant character: the serpent is poisonous (cf. Herodotus 3.109; Ps 58.4; Mt 12.34; T. Abr. 19; m. 'Abot 2.10). γεννήματα probably points to the serpent's nature. He is what he is by birth. His poison is in the blood. And so—it is implied—is it with the Sadducees and Pharisees (cf. 23.29–33). (Because Satan was identified as a serpent, as in Wisd 2.24; Rev 12.9; 20.2, 'brood of vipers' could be regarded as equal to 'children of Satan' (cf. Jn 8.44). Yet ἐχιδνῶν is plural.) Matthew has ὄφις in 7.10 (Q); 10.16; and 23.33.

τίς ὑπέδειξεν ὑμῖν φυγεῖν ἀπὸ τῆς μελλούσης ὀργῆς; So also Luke. Compare 23.33, where Jesus takes up the Baptist's words (this adds again to the Jesus/John parallelism). ὑποδείκνυμι means 'show' or 'warn'. For eschatological flight see Zech 14.5; Ps. Sol. 17.25; Mt 24.20; Rev 6.15–16; 12.6; L. Proph. Jer. 12; Ap. Elijah 4.21. ἀπό after 'flee' is Semitic (BDF § 149; cf. Exod 14.25; Amos 5.19; Mt 23.33; Rev 9.6; 20.11). Was 'the coming wrath' a fixed expression (cf. 1 Th 1.10)? ὀργή (cf. Isa 13.9; Zeph 1.15; 2.2; Ezek 7.19; Col 3.6; Eph 5.6) appears only here in Matthew. μέλλω (see on 2.13) here implies not so much purpose as imminence or futurity (BAGD, s.v., 2). The wrath is eschatological. It is unleashed when the great tribulation begins and culminates in the great assize (Lk 21.23; Rev 6.12–17; 16–17). For John God's wrath was yet to manifest itself. For Jesus and the early church the tribulation had already begun (cf. Rom 1.18 and see Allison, passim). On the issue of how exactly God's wrath is to be conceptualized see C. H. Dodd, The Epistle of Paul to the Romans, New York and London, n.d., pp. 20–4; G. Stählin et al., TWNT 5, pp. 382–448; A. J. Heschel, The Prophets, vol. 2, New York, 1962, pp. 59–86; L. Morris, *The Apostolic Preaching of the Cross*, London, 1955, pp. 161–6; and Cranfield, *Romans* 1, pp. 108–9, 214–17.

How are we to understand John's ironic question, 'Who warned you to flee from the wrath to come?' Is the emphasis upon 'who' (implying, Certainly not I) or upon 'you' (implying the hypocrisy of those addressed)? On the lips of the Baptist, the first alternative seems more reasonable while for Matthew the character of his opponents must be to the fore. In either case the question is not really open but is instead rhetorical.

8. This verse, which presupposes 3.7, proclaims that salvation from the coming wrath will only be for those who repent and show the proofs of their repentance.

ποιήσατε οὖν καρπὸν ἄξιον τῆς μετανοίας. So Lk 3.8a, with the plural, 'fruits' (cf. L U Or sy). 'Make fruit' is a Semitism (cf. Gen 1.11, 12; Rev 22.2; Par. Jer. 9.16 and see Black, pp. 138–9). For making or producing or bearing fruit as a metaphor for doing good works or as the proof of repentance or reformation see Mt 3.10 = Lk 3.9; Mt 7.16–20; 12.33; Lk 13.6–9; Jn 15.2, 4, 5, 8, 16. As these texts suggest, the figurative use of 'fruit' in ethico-religious speech meaning 'consequence' or 'act' or 'product' was quite popular with Jesus and perhaps also with the Baptist. Outside the Gospels see Ps 1.3; Prov 1.31; Isa 3.10; Hos 10.1; Ecclus 23.25; Rom 6.22; Jas 3.18; Josephus, *Ant.* 20.48; 2 Bar 32.1; Apoc. Adam 6.1; *b. Qidd.* 40a; and for an example outside of Judaism, the Buddhist text, *Dhammapada* 5. 'Trees are judged not by their roots but by their fruits' (Caird, p. 73). Luke has the plural, 'fruits', and because he exhibits a tendency towards the singular (1.42; 3.9; 6.43, 44 (diff. Mt 7.16–20); 8.8; 13.6–9; 20.10 (diff. Mk 12.21); contrast only 3.8; 12.17), the plural could have stood in Q. On the other side, the plural could be an improvement because it makes for better Greek. It could also be put down to the implicit equation, 'good fruits' = 'good works' or 'deeds'. Matthew, moreover, may preserve a Semitic distributive singular (cf. Jeremias, *Lukasevangelium*, p. 105).

οὖν is not merely transitional, it is illative: if the Pharisees and Sadducees really wish to flee from the wrath to come, *then*. . . .

'Fruit ἄξιον of repentance' means 'fruit corresponding to (or befitting) repentance' (cf. Acts 26.20). John has already declared, 'repent' (3.2). Now substance is given to the injunction. The call to 'repentance', which goes out to all, is uttered in view of the eschatological judgement looming on the horizon. And motivated largely by a fear of their own damnation (cf. Hos 3.5), people are called to be sorry for their transgressions and turn from them wholeheartedly—without delay (cf. Ecclus 5.5–7). The Greek word literally means, 'change of mind'; but it stands for the

Hebrew *šûb*, 'turn around', 'return', and a complete change in conduct, not just a change of opinion, is involved. Alarmed by the prospect of the divine wrath and in response to the warning delivered through his spokesman, John, Israel is called to turn to God and away from sin, to arise in moral earnestness from a sinful slumber and to gain a wakeful heart and sober thought (cf. Isa 55.7; Jub. 21.23; and *m*. '*Abot* 4.11, where repentance is a 'shield against punishment').

Repentance was a central concept in the Judaism of John's time, and the power of repentance was highly valued (cf. *Sipre Deut*. on 33.6; *t. Qidd*. 1.15–16; *b. Yoma* 86a–b).[37] Even the righteous man had need of repentance. Indeed, it (paradoxically) characterized him. Wherein then lay John's distinctiveness? The Baptist called his hearers to turn themselves from being unfruitful trees threatened by the eschatological fire into fruitful trees. Evidently he believed there to be two classes of people, the repentant and the non-repentant. Adopting a prophetic and pessimistic outlook (cf. Amos 3.2; 4.1–13), one not unlike the writer of 4 Ezra, John saw the Jews of his day headed for catastrophe and pleaded with them to make a radical and resolute break with the past. He declared that their salvation was not guaranteed by Abrahamic descent or any other circumstance save true repentance. His was not the opinion put forward in *m. Sanh*. 10.1, according to which only heretics, that is, those who repudiate the covenant, are condemned: 'all Israel has a place in the world to come'. In other words, John denied the validity of what most Palestinian Jews took to be the heart of their faith, namely, 'covenantal nomism' (see Sanders, *Paul*, pp. 33–428). Unlike the Pharisees of his day, John did not think of repentance as primarily a daily affair which served to maintain one's status as a member of the covenant community (cf. T. Asher 1.6; *b. Šabb*. 153a; *t. Yoma* 5.6). Instead it signalled for him the transition from one group of Jews, the chaff facing the fire, to another group, the wheat for the granary (see further below). One is reminded of the rôle of repentance in the Dead Sea Scrolls: it coincides with leaving the impious of Israel and entering the covenant community (CD 4.2; 6.4–5; 8.16; 19.16; 20.17; 1QS 10.20; 1QH 2.9; 14.24; 4QpPs 37 3.1).

That the Day of the Lord will be for Israel darkness and not light, judgement and not salvation, is a theme John took over from the OT (it is particularly prominent in Amos). One might thus regard the Baptist's threat of damnation as less than novel. Yet even the book of Amos, at least in its canonical form, concludes with a passage (admittedly often regarded as a scribal addition to Amos's own words: see Davies *GL*, pp. 38–41) about salvation (9.9–15)—and there is nothing corresponding to this in John. On the other hand, the ubiquity of covenantal nomism in first-century Palestinian Judaism might incline one to suppose that John presupposed its truth; and one might infer that, despite the harshness of John's outlook, he must have believed that Israel would repent in the last

[37] See SB I, pp. 162–72; Moore 1, pp. 323–53, 507–34; C. J. G. Montefiore, 'Rabbinic Conceptions of Repentance', *JQR* 16 (1904), pp. 209–57; Urbach 1, pp. 462–71; J. J. Petuchowski, 'The Concept of "Teshuvah" ', *Judaism* 17 (1968), pp. 175–85; Sanders, *Paul*, s.v. index.

days (cf. Jub. 1.23; As. Mos. 1.18; T. Dan. 6.4; T. Jud. 23.5; *b. Sanh.* 97b). That is, he hoped that his ministry would be effective and prepare the people for what was to come (cf. Rivkin (v), p. 83). Even the Dead Sea sect, which thought of most Jews as outside God's covenant, apparently expected that the Day of the Lord would see all the congregation of Israel join the community and walk according to the law of the sons of Zadok (1QSa 1.1–2). Such an expectation was demanded by the OT (cf. Hos 2.23; Ezek 37) and made credible because it was widely held that repentance itself was God's gift (cf. Ezek 11.19–20; 18.31; Ep. Arist. 188; Ps. Sol. 18.4–6; *y. Ber.* 4.2.7d). Paul too, despite everything, held out hope for all Israel (Rom 11.25–32). Nevertheless, John's words as preserved in the gospels say nothing at all about this; and Mt 3.9 = Lk 3.8, as we shall see, seemingly disallows such an interpretation. It is also seemingly disallowed by the stringency of the Baptist's threats, which would make little sense if traditional covenantal nomism were being presupposed. Our conclusion, then, must be that even if John did expect Israel to repent on or before the Day of the Lord, this in his mind was not connected with covenantal nomism. We are all the more confirmed in this judgement because it goes a long way towards explaining why Jesus, Paul, and other early Christian thinkers broke with the standard Jewish understanding of salvation: in this they were following in John's footsteps.

9. This verse interrupts the flow of thought, and 3.10 is the logical conclusion of 3.8. Thus we probably have here an insertion: two or more sayings of the Baptist have been brought together.

καὶ μὴ δόξητε λέγειν ἐν ἑαυτοῖς. μὴ δόξητε means 'do not suppose' or 'do not presume' (cf. BAGD, s.v. δοκέω, 1.a). The thought is illusory. Luke has ἄρχομαι, 'begin' (which is the only difference between Mt 3.9 and Lk 3.8b). Which aorist imperative appeared in Q? No decision can be reached. In favour of Matthew, Luke likes ἄρχομαι (Mt: 13; Mk: 26; Lk: 31). In favour of Luke, Matthew often drops the frequently occurring ἤρξατο of Mark, and 'begin', being pleonastic, could be explained as a Semitism. 'To say in yourselves' is also a Semitism (cf. Ps 10.6; Est 6.6; Isa 47.8; Rev 18.7). It means 'to think'. For the prophetic habit of quoting only to refute see Isa 24.14–19; Jer 8.9–13; Ezek 11.14–21; Hag 1.2–11.

πατέρα ἔχομεν τὸν Ἀβραάμ. So Luke. Compare Jn 8.39. Abraham, although born a Gentile, was the father or forefather of all Jews (cf. Lk 16.19–31; Rom 4.1; SB 1, p. 116). On Abraham see further on 1.1. To be born a Jew of a Jewish mother was to be born a member of the covenant community, and for many that was enough: Abrahamic descent was not only a necessary condition for salvation but a sufficient condition—unless one denounced the covenant or committed some other deed of apostasy and became a heretic (cf. T. Levi 15.4; *m. Sanh.* 10.1; Justin, *Dial.* 140). The Baptist held a different conception: salvation would come only to those who made a radical, one-time repentance. Abrahamic

descent of itself guaranteed nothing; if anything, perhaps it made
the threat of judgement more real (cf. Amos 3.2). The merit of the
fathers (see Davies, *PRJ*, pp. 270–2) was not enough. With this
judgement the early church soon concurred (Jn 8.39; Rom 9.1–33),
and the concept of 'sons of Abraham' accordingly came to include
Gentiles (Rom 2.28–9; 4.12; Gal 3.16, 29; 4.21–31). We cannot say,
however, whether John gave explicit teaching on non-Jews[38]—
only that, by his fulminating judgements on his contemporaries,
his sceptical view of their favoured status before God, and his
apparent diminution of the Torah as the standard of judgement,
John placed a large question mark over the covenantal nomism of
his day and avowed that those born of Abraham were not by that
fact alone members of the people of God. As Kümmel rightly
remarks of John, 'the relationship of man to God in principle is
defined solely by his being human, and no longer by his belonging
to the Jewish people or to any other human group' (*Theology*,
p. 28). Visible Israel and the people of God are no longer identical.
(For individualizing tendencies within Judaism see Isa 55.7; Ezek
18.21–2; 33.11; Philo, *Praem. Poen.* 152.)

λέγω γὰρ ὑμῖν ὅτι δύναται ὁ θεὸς ἐκ τῶν λίθων τούτων ἐγεῖραι
τέκνα τῷ Ἀβραάμ. So Luke. Although a word-play can be found in
Hebrew or Aramaic—*bānîm* ('sons')/*ʾăbānîm* ('stones') or
běnayyāʾ ('sons')/*ʾabnayyāʾ* ('stones')—, Q has τέκνα ('children'),
and Jeremias (*TWNT* 4, pp. 274–5) has persuasively argued for an
original Aramaic *kêpāʾ* behind λίθων with the sense of 'rock'.

ἐγείρειν ἔκ τινος is a Semitism meaning 'to cause to be born', 'to
cause to bring forth progeny' (Deut 18.15, 18; 2 Sam 7.12; Acts
13.23; *Lam. Rab.* on 5.3). It equals the ἀναστήσει σπέρμα of 22.24.
The figure then is of God giving to rocks the power to bring forth
people (cf. Schlatter, p. 74). The background for this picture is Isa
51.1–2 (so already Chrysostom): 'Look to the rock from whence
you were hewn and to the quarry whence you were digged. Look to
Abraham your father and to Sarah who bore you. For when he
was but one I called him and blessed him and I caused him to
increase' (cf. Gen 12.1–3 and see the reworking of Isa 51.1–2 in
LAB 23.4). From Abraham, a lifeless rock (cf. Gen 17.17;
18.10–14; Rom 4.17), God had miraculously caused to be born
Isaac and descendants as numerous as the stars of heaven. This,
the Baptist declares, God can do again, thereby cutting the ground
out from under those who would stand upon their physical
sonship from Abraham. (By associating Abraham with the new
children the Lord can bring forth, John shows that God will
faithfully fulfil the promises in Genesis. Thus the Baptist is not
overturning the fundamental idea of covenant but rather

---

[38] The soldiers who inquire of John in Lk 3.14 could be Jewish soldiers in the
service of Herod (but note Josephus, *Ant.* 17.198).

repudiating the popular understanding of what the Abrahamic covenant entailed. We might put it this way: John does away not with covenant but with popular covenantal nomism.)

Although we should probably not read a reference to the Gentiles into John's words if we are thinking of their first utterance, matters must be different for Matthew. Given his interest in the Gentile mission and the firm connexions between Abraham and the Gentiles in both Jewish and Christian tradition (see on 1.1), 3.9 must for him imply criticism of the self-assurance of the Jews and the acceptance of non-Jewish Christians. From Matthew's perspective, God has in fact already raised up new offspring to Abraham: the Gentile Christians. Compare Ignatius, *Mag.* 10, long recension: 'those that were of stony heart have become the children of Abraham'.

Our interpretation, which links Mt 3.9 with Isa 51.1–2, is more plausible than that of O. J. F. Seitz (v), who identifies 'these stones' with the twelve stones Joshua set up in the Jordan to commemorate Israel's crossing on dry land (Josh 4): John drew a typological connexion between his baptism and Israel's crossing of the Jordan. Seitz calls attention to Josh 4.9 (where the ṣtones are 'there to this day') and to Josh 5.7 (where we read of 'children which he [God] raised').

10. The imagery of 3.8 is picked up again. The soon to be realized consequences of not making fruit worthy of repentance are now spelled out: unfruitful trees will be cut down and cast into the fire.

ἤδη δὲ ἡ ἀξίνη πρὸς τὴν ῥίζαν τῶν δένδρων κεῖται. Luke adds καί after δέ; otherwise there is agreement. The line, whose content is similar to 3.12, expresses the imminence of the eschatological judgement. Note the emphatic placement of 'already': John the prophet sees what others as yet do not. Similar pictures appear in Isa 10.33–4; Jer 11.19; 46.22; Ezek 31; Dan 4 (cf. 2 Kgs 6.1–4). ἀξίνη (LXX: 7) appears in the NT only in Mt 3.10 par. The use of ῥίζα (cf. *šōreš*) makes plain that not just the branches are to be cut but also the root (contrast Rom 11.17, 24; see Davies, *JPS* pp. 153–163). The choice of δένδρον is particularly apt because John is addressing the Pharisees and Sadducees, and leaders, as well as reputedly righteous people and scholars, were sometimes compared to trees (as in Judg 9.7–16; Ps 1.3; Jer 17.7–8; Dan 4.20–2; 2 Bar. 39.1–8; *m. 'Abot* 3.18; *Pesiq. R.* 60b). Concerning the verb κεῖμαι (never with ἀξίνη in the LXX), God is implicitly the agent of the passive: 'is laid (by God)'.

Lk 13.6–9 preserves a parable about an unfruitful fig tree whose owner, after finding no fruit on his tree for three years, orders his vinedresser to cut it down. The vinedresser, however, pleads for more time. 'Sir, leave it alone this year until I dig around it and put on manure; and if it provides fruit for the future (well and good); but if not, you may cut it down'. The point of this parable is this. The Jewish people have been unfruitful. Yet God, in his mercy, has not rendered immediate judgement; rather, he has granted a period of respite. And if, in that period of respite, Israel repents and becomes fruitful, she will cause God to allay her destruction. It is as if the time for the judgement of the nation has come and as if God, in his unfathomable patience has said, 'Let it pass; wait another year' (cf. Jeremias, *Parables*, pp. 170–1). Now as background for Lk 13.6–9 the presumably well-known tale in *Aḥiḳar* (8.30 in the Arabic) about a fig tree cut down because it has not borne fruit is usually cited, and Jesus is thought to have reversed the traditional ending in order to drive home his point about God's grace. But might it not be that Lk 13.6–9 should also be read against Mt 3.10 = Lk 3.9? If John said that the axe is already laid to the root of the tree (= Israel) and that the unfruitful tree will soon be cut down, and if subsequently Jesus, perhaps encouraged by a delay in the fulfilment of John's prophecy, declared that the time for cutting down the unfruitful tree (= Israel) had been postponed, might this not reflect a conscious modification of John's teaching (cf. Becker (v), pp. 97–8)? Certainly at other points Jesus must have been aware of differing from John (see e.g. Mt 11.16–19 = Lk 7.31–5).

πᾶν οὖν δένδρον μὴ ποιοῦν καρπὸν καλὸν ἐκκόπτεται. So also Luke. The threat of trees being cut down (3.10a) is continued and combined with the theme of making fruit (cf. 3.8). The first 'therefore' in John's speech (3.8) introduced the command to 'make fruit'. The second 'therefore' spells out the consequences of not making fruit. For the prophetic 'therefore' see Isa 8.6–8; Jer 7.16–20; Hos 2.5–6; Amos 3.2; Mic 2.1–3. For the themes of good fruit, bad fruit, and unfruitfulness in Matthew see further 7.16–20; 12.33; 13.8, 26; 21.19, 41, 43. In 7.19 Jesus repeats John's words verbatim (minus the 'therefore'). 'Good fruit' is 'fruit worthy of repentance' (3.8). ἐκκόπτω (Mt: 4; Mk: 0; Lk: 3) is used of trees in Deut 20.19–20; 1 En. 26.1; Josephus, *Ant.* 10.52; *IGA* 2.44b. According to Black (p. 145), an Aramaic word-play could lie behind 'root' = 'qqr and 'hewn down' = 'qr.

καὶ εἰς πῦρ βάλλεται. So Luke. Compare Mt 7.19; Jn 15.5–6; Heb 6.8. For the burning of trees in the judgement of God see Isa 10.15–19; Jer 11.16. Both as a concomitant of the final judgement and as an instrument of punishment of the dead, fire was a traditional eschatological prospect: Isa 66.24; Jdt 16.17; 4 Macc. 9.9; Jub. 9.15; 1QpHab. 10.5, 13; 1 En 10.6; 54.1–2; 90.24–5; 100.9; Ps. Sol. 15.4–5; Sib. Or. 3.53–4; 4 Ezra 7.36–8; 13.10–11; 2 Bar. 37.1; 44.15; 59.2; T. Zeb. 10.3; Apoc. Abr. 31. Compare Joel 2.30 and especially Mal 4.1, where the Day of the Lord burns like an oven and burns both root and branch. (C. Maurer, *TWNT* 6, p. 988, sees the passage from Malachi as the immediate background for the Baptist's utterance.) For John fire appears to have been the outstanding feature of the coming judgement (cf. 3.11–12). As for our evangelist, he is particularly fond of making fire a threat on the lips of Jesus: 5.22; 7.19; 13.40, 42, 50; 18.8, 9; 25.41. (With the exception of 18.8 and 9, these verses are all unique to Matthew.) In 7.19 he even has Jesus repeat John's warning, the words of the present verse. There, as here, the context has to do with false leaders and teachers, those most deserving of punishment.

The three major verbs in 3.10, 'is cut down', 'is laid', and 'is cast' are in the present tense, and in 3.7 the wrath is said to be 'coming'. We should therefore interpret the present tense as implying certainty and immediacy, and this is supported by the use of ἤδη.

11. At this point Luke inserts John's response to three different questions, one asked by the multitudes, one by toll collectors, one by soldiers (Lk 3.10–14). The Baptist's ethical advice could have stood in Q, Matthew omitting it because he wished to focus all of the forerunner's words on the eschatological judgement and/or because he wanted to reserve the rôle of ethical authority to Jesus alone. In favour of this, Lk 3.10–13 is certainly pre-Lukan (cf. Jeremias, *Lukasevangelium*, pp. 105–9), Q included sayings of the Baptist, and nowhere else is the Baptist mentioned in Luke's special sources (L). But in the nature of the case proof is not forthcoming.

3.1–10 has informed us about the Baptist. Now the Baptist informs us about Jesus, making a christological statement (3.11–12). Thus the context for the baptism (3.13–17) is the reader's knowledge of the two participants, John and Jesus.

Mt 3.11 has a parallel not only in Lk 3.16 but also in Mk 1.7–8. According to the two source theory, adopted in this commentary, we have here a Markan/Q overlap, with the Q version being primary (cf. Hoffmann, *Logienquelle*, pp. 19–22, and Fleddermann (v)). (Note the two-fold agreement between Matthew and Luke against Mark: the present tense of βαπτίζω—Mark has the aorist—and the placement of 3.11 before 3.12.) This is the more likely since another, seemingly independent variant appears also in Jn 1.26–7, 33.[39] This suggests that our saying was popular (cf. also Acts 1.5; 11.16). If indeed we do have here to do with an overlap of Matthew's two major sources, then the minor agreements between Matthew and Mark against Luke (ὀπίσω, ὕδατι after the verb) and between Luke and Mark against Matthew (ἔρχεται,[40] λῦσαι, τὸν ἱμάντα) could be evidence of conflation: Matthew and Luke have both

[39] See Dodd, *Tradition*, pp. 253–6, 266–9. For the proposal that the agreements of John with Matthew and Luke over against Mark show the Johannine tradition to be influenced by Q or Q-like material see Buse, 'St John' (v).

[40] If Matthew's ἐρχόμενος is editorial, it can hardly express an Aramaic future tense (against Jeremias, *Eucharistic Words*, p. 179). But it is possible that Mark's ἔρχεται is an historicization (cf. 1.9) which Luke followed. Jn 1.27 agrees with Matthew.

used Mark and Q. Or early textual corruption has manifested itself. It is more difficult to think that Mark has combined Matthew and Luke, for why should he destroy the parallelism of Mt 3.11 = Lk 3.16 by moving 'I baptize you, etc.', and why should he omit Mt 3.12 = Lk 3.17? (Certainly Mark believed that Jesus would come to judge the world: 13.26–7.)

As observed, a number of minor but intriguing differences exist between Mt 3.11 on the one side and both Mk 1.7–8 and Lk 3.16 on the other. Although these are partly explained by Luke's use of Mark or by later textual assimilation, one must also take into account Matthew's purely redactional alterations. His love of parallelism probably explains several changes. Of John we read (3.11a),

$$\text{ἐγὼ μὲν ὑμᾶς βαπτίζω ἐν . . .}$$

Of Jesus we read (3.11d),

$$\text{αὐτὸς ὑμᾶς βαπτίσει ἐν . . .}$$

This parallelism is not so well expressed in Luke or Mark, and in order to achieve it our evangelist has, in 11a, presumably moved ὑμᾶς before βαπτίζω (contrast Mark and Luke), added an ἐν (contrast Mark and Luke), and displaced ὕδατι (contrast Luke).

ἐγὼ μὲν ὑμᾶς βαπτίζω ἐν ὕδατι εἰς μετάνοιαν. Compare Jn 1.26, 31, 33. The statement, 'I baptize you with water (only)', does not contain new information but is simply the reference point by way of which the coming one, through contrast, can be introduced (note the μέν/δέ): he is not like John.

'Unto repentance' (without parallel in the other gospels) may be taken as meaning (1) baptism *effects* repentance (cf. Lohmeyer, *Matthäus*, p. 44) or (2) baptism *demands* or *summons* repentance (so J. Behm, *TWNT* 4, p. 295). It is, however, better to endorse a more nuanced position: (3) baptism presupposes and expresses repentance (cf. 3.7–10) while it also, through the action of God, issues in a true reformation (cf. Beasley-Murray (v), pp. 34–5).

ὑμᾶς betrays the editorial origin of Mt 3.7 ('many of the Pharisees and Sadducees'). 'You' more naturally applies to a large mixed audience that has come out for baptism (cf. Luke), not to Jewish leaders being rebuked.

ὁ δὲ ὀπίσω μου ἐρχόμενος. Whom did John expect? Who was the coming one? The significant alternatives are these. (1) The coming one is God (so Hughes (v)). (2) He is the Son of man (Becker (v), pp. 34–7). (3) He is a disciple of John (Grobel (v); Cullmann (v); Dodd, *Tradition*, pp. 272–4). (4) He cannot be linked to any particular form of Jewish expectation because John's vagueness was deliberate: he refused to align himself with any one messianic figure (McNeile, p. 29; Goppelt, *Theology* 1, p. 38). (5) The coming one is Elijah (Schweitzer, pp. 373–5; Robinson (v); Brown (v), pp. 181–4). (6) He is the Messiah, priestly or Davidic (Manson, *Sayings*, p. 41; this is the traditional Christian interpretation, with the qualification that the Messiah is Jesus).

In favour of (1), God is spoken of as ἰσχυρός in Jer 39.18 LXX and Dan 9.4 LXX; and in Jewish eschatology God is often the eschatological judge who sends fire. Further, if Lk 1.76 originated in Baptist circles (a disputed issue), then John was thought of as the one who would go before the Lord God. Finally, there is evidence that John was regarded as the Messiah (and therefore the forerunner of God), although how early this opinion was reached we cannot say (note Lk 3.15; Ps.-Clem. Rec. 1.54). Against (1), the Baptist would hardly have spoken of God with the relative, 'mightier', and made himself out to be unworthy of undoing God's sandals. Such speech more readily involves comparison between two human figures or at least between two figures less than divine.

(2) musters support from the frequent linking between ἔρχομαι and 'Son of man' in the gospels. Yet this solution falters under the impact of recent work that has thrown so much doubt on the belief that there was a pre-Christian Son of man concept (see Excursus VI).

Supporting (3), ὀπίσω does not typically have a temporal meaning in the NT; with the genitive the word constantly has to do with the followers of the person named by the genitive; and 'to come after someone' is the standard expression for being a disciple of Jesus (Mk 1.20; 8.34; Lk 9.23; Jn 12.19). So John could conceivably have been speaking—and Matthew thinking (cf. Wink, p. 138)—about 'a follower of mine'. Yet this suggestion, while it is quite in accord with the local sense of ἔμπροσθεν in Jn 1.15 and with the fact of Jesus' having emerged from the Baptist's circle, suffers because ὀπίσω *is* used of succession of time in the LXX (3 Βασ 1.6; Neh 3.17; 11.8; cf. the Hebrew '*aḥărê*). Moreover, 'the coming one' receives a messianic interpretation in Mt 11.2–6 = Lk 7.18–23.

(4) probably puts too much of an emphasis upon the silence of our scanty sources.

(5) has much to be said in its favour. 'The one coming after' could allude to Mal 3.1, in which God's messenger (= Elijah) 'comes'. Mt 11.14 also speaks of 'Elijah who is to come' (cf. Mk 9.11–13). Next, in quite a few texts Elijah, like the coming one, is associated with fire: 1 Kgs 18.38; Mal 3.2; Ecclus 48.1; L. Proph. Elijah 2–3; Lk 9.52–6. Finally, if John expected Elijah, and if Christians—some of whom came from the Baptist movement—thought Jesus was the coming one of John's prophecy, this might help account for the gospel traditions in which Jesus possesses Elijah-like traits.[41] Against (5), the notion of the forerunner of a forerunner is perhaps not a happy one.[42] More importantly, if, as we are

[41] From Luke alone note 4.24–6; 7.11–17 (cf. 1 Kgs 17.18–24); and 9.51–6 (cf. 2 Kgs 1.9–16). For John see J. L. Martyn (v), pp. 190–7. Brown (v), p. 183, observes that the equation of the coming one with Elijah could explain Jn 1.30: 'After me is coming one who ranks before me because he existed before me'.

[42] But this presupposes that Elijah was in turn expected to be a forerunner of the Messiah, and this is disputed. See M. M. Faierstein, 'Why Do the Scribes Say that

inclined to think, Mt 11.2–6 = Lk 7.18–23 preserves a genuine historical memory, then Jesus identified himself with John's coming one—but Jesus did not take himself to be Elijah (cf. Mk 9.10–13).

Option (6) has in its favour, among other things, the messianic interpretation of Ps 118[43], a psalm in which we read of 'he who comes' (cf. Mk 11.9–10). And if Jn 1.26 implies that the Baptist believed in a hidden Messiah (so Dodd, *Tradition*, pp. 266–9; Brown, *John* 1, pp. 52–4), this would clinch the argument—unless (as is unlikely) John saw the Messiah and Elijah as one and the same.[44] One final point. For his first followers Jesus was above all the Messiah, and if those who heard John thought the coming one to be the Messiah, the Christian identification of Jesus as the person of John's prophecy would be natural and easy to comprehend. (On 'the coming one' as a messianic title see further on 26.26–9.)

Our choice would clearly seem to be between options (5) and (6). Both are possible. But there are fewer objections to the latter than the former; and as John's coming one is pre-eminently a figure of eschatological judgement, and as there is more precedent for making the office of judgement belong to the Messiah, we regard (6)—the coming one is the Messiah—as the more probable alternative.

Luke has ἔρχεται ὁ ἰσχυρότερός μου, Mark the same with ὀπίσω μου added at the end. Matthew's ὁ ὀπίσω μου ἐρχόμενος (cf. Jn 1.15, 27) comes closer to turning 'the coming one' into a title. No doubt this explains the change.

ἰσχυρότερός μού ἐστιν. Corresponding to the synoptics' 'mightier', John has ἔμπροσθεν (1.15, 30), which he probably interprets as an allusion to pre-existence. But in the tradition before John ἔμπροσθεν could have been employed in the sense of 'higher in rank', which would bring it nearer the synoptic record.

In Matthew the emphasis is on the strength of the coming one ('the one coming after me is stronger'). In Mark and Luke the emphasis is perhaps on the coming itself ('the one stronger than me comes' [after me]). Maybe our evangelist already has 12.29 in mind: Jesus has the strength to bind even the strong man, Satan (cf. Isa 49.25; T. Levi 18.12). ἰσχυρός (most often in the LXX for *gibbôr*, *'ēl*, and *ḥāzāq*) is in Isa 11.1–2 one of the pneumatic endowments of the shoot that shall come forth from Jesse (cf. *b. Sanh.* 93b), and in Isa 53.12 the suffering servant shares the spoil of

---

Elijah Must Come First?', *JBL* 100 (1981), pp. 75–86 and the response to this by D. C. Allison, ' "Elijah Must Come First" ', *JBL* 103 (1984), pp. 256–8; also J. Fitzmyer, 'More about Elijah "Coming First" ', *JBL* 104 (1985), pp. 295–6.

[43] See E. Werner, ' "Hosanna" in the Gospels', *JBL* 65 (1946), pp. 97–122, and Jeremias, *Eucharistic Words*, pp. 256–60.

[44] For the later merging of Elijah and the Messiah see N. Wieder, 'The Doctrine of the Two Messiahs among the Karaites', *JJS* 6 (1955), pp. 14–25. Despite J. Jeremias, *TWNT* 2, pp. 930–43, evidence for their having been identified already in the first century is lacking.

the strong. In 1 En. 49.3 the Elect One has a spirit of strength while in Ps. Sol. 17.37 the Son of David is made mighty by God's Spirit. Thus, while 'the stronger one' may not have been a fixed title, ἰσχύς was associated with messianic figures. (The *gibbôr* of 1QM 12 is probably God, not the Messiah of Israel; cf. Deut 10.17; Jer 32.18.)[45]

οὗ οὐκ εἰμὶ ἱκανὸς τὰ ὑποδήματα βαστάσαι. To judge from Mark, Luke, John, and Acts 13.25, in the pristine form of this saying John said he was not worthy to untie the thong of the coming one's sandals. The background for this is to be found in rabbinic sources: it was the menial task of the non-Hebrew slave to unloosen his master's shoes. See *b. Ketub.* 96a; *b. Qidd.* 22b; *b. Pesah.* 4a; *Sipre* on Num 15.41; SB 1, p. 121 (cf. Plautus, *Trin.* 2.1; Eusebius, *H.E.* 4.15.30). John deems himself unworthy to perform even the slave's task.

Why has Matthew, who is followed by Justin, *Dial.* 49, substituted βαστάζω (Mt: 3; Mk: 1; Lk: 5) for λύω (cf. Exod 3.5; Josh 5.15)? The former could be nothing more than a synonym for the latter, meaning 'remove' or 'untie' (cf. Bretscher, 'Sandals' (v), p. 84). But βαστάζειν can also mean 'to carry', and this is probably the meaning here because the evangelist has dropped τὸν ἱμάντα;[46] also, the verb means 'carry' the other two times it appears in Matthew (8.17; 20.12). The image is thus of a disciple carrying— not untying—the master's shoes. Yet this hardly changes the substance; for the carrying of another's garments was presumably a sign of submission or servanthood (cf. *b. Sanh.* 62b; *b. B. Meṣ.* 41a; *b. 'Erub.* 27b). Note *b. Pesah.* 4a: R. Ḥiyya said to his servant,'Take off my shoes and carry my things after me to the bath'. (Too ingenious, perhaps, is the suggestion of Daube, pp. 266–7, that Matthew was influenced by a rabbinic principle: a disciple should do everything for his teacher a slave would do— save take off his shoes; see *b. Ketub.* 96a. On Daube's reading, the First Evangelist has John adhere to strict principle: he will carry Jesus' shoes but not take them off.)

According to P. G. Bretscher (v), Mt 3.11 and Acts 13.25 are both misinterpreted when the sandals are taken to belong to Jesus. John is instead the subject and the meaning is: 'of whom I am not worthy to wear (my) sandals'. That is, in Jesus' presence John must take off his shoes (cf. Exod 3.5; Josh 5.15). Although just perhaps grammatically possible, one hesitates to endorse Bretscher's position. It puts Mt 3.11 and Acts 13.25 at odds with Mk 1.7; Lk 3.16; and Jn 1.27. Moreover, surely the unambiguous (Mk 1.7; Lk 3.16; Jn 1.27) should be permitted to interpret the ambiguous (Mt 3.11; Acts 13.25).

[45] So also R. E. Brown, 'The Messianism of Qumran', *CBQ* 19 (1957), pp. 58–9.
[46] This stood in both Mark and Q presumably; cf. Jn 1.27.

The early influence of the synoptic tradition on John is probably revealed by the ἱκανός in both Bodmer papyri for Jn 1.24. All other mss. have ἄξιος.

αὐτὸς ὑμᾶς βαπτίσει ἐν πνεύματι ἀγίῳ καὶ πυρί. The pronoun is emphatic. In this clause Matthew and Luke agree. They are therefore following Q. Mark has δέ after αὐτός, ὑμᾶς before ἐν, and nothing corresponding to 'fire' (cf. Jn 1.33). It has been popular in the past to argue that the original utterance included only a reference to 'fire' (so e.g. Bultmann, *Tradition*, p. 246; Taylor, *Mark*, p. 157). John's prophecy of a baptism of eschatological fire, based perhaps upon Mal 3.1, was then interpreted by Christians as pertaining to Christian baptism or to Pentecost (cf. Acts 2.3 ('tongues of fire') and Chrysostom, *Hom. on Mt* 11.4). This done, the expression, 'in holy Spirit' (cf. Acts 2.2, 4), was added. Later, and before the saying came to Mark, 'in fire' was dropped (cf. Jn 1.33 and Acts 1.5; 11.16).

There is nothing implausible in this reconstruction of tradition-history, and no decisive objection can be raised against it. Nonetheless, the premise, namely, that the Baptist did not speak of a Spirit baptism, may, as we shall see, well be doubted.

The OT contains numerous texts in which water, like fire (see on 3.10), is a symbol of calamity (2 Sam 22.5; Ps 18.16; 32.6; 42.7; 69.1–2, 14–15; 124.4–5; 144.7; Cant 8.7; Job 22.11; Isa 8.7; 43.2) or an instrument of judgement (Gen 6.6; Hos 5.10; cf. 1QH 3.12–18). Further, as symbols of judgement, fire and water are closely linked in a number of Jewish sources: Ps 66.10–12; Isa 30.27–28; 43.2; 66.15–16; Sib. Or. 3.689–92; Josephus, *Ant.* 1.70; Lk 17.26–9 (cf. also Num 31.23). Of special importance is this fact: in apocalyptic literature and the Dead Sea scrolls, fire and water are joined to become one symbol. In Dan 7.10: 1QH 3.29–36; 1 En. 67.13; Sib. Or. 2.196–205, 252–4, 3.54, 84–7; 4 Ezra 13.10–11; and T. Isaac 5.21, we read of a river or flood of fire (cf. also the Zoroastrian text, *Bundahis* 30 and passages which have a lake of fire: 1 En. 17.5; Rev 19–21; 2 En. 10.2). Most of these texts have the last judgement in view: a stream of fire comes forth from God and consumes the wicked (cf. Ps 50.3; 97.3). The rabbis also spoke of the eschatological flood of fire (*Mek.* on Exod 18.1; *b. Zeb.* 116a; *Gen. Rab.* on 39.6 and 49.9). When John the Baptist warned of the coming one who would baptize with fire, he almost certainly had in view this fiery stream (cf. Dunn, 'Baptized' (v), pp. 135–6). All would be forced to pass through the river of fire, through the judgement which overcomes the wicked but purifies the righteous (cf. 1 Cor 3.10–15; T. Isaac 5.21–5; T. Abr. 12–13). As it was in the beginning, when God let loose a flood and rained down fire (Gen 6–8; 19), so shall it be in the end.

What then of the Spirit? (The qualification of 'Spirit' by 'holy' in both Luke and Matthew may be due to Markan influence; that is, Q may have had only 'Spirit'.) The joining of water and Spirit was traditional: Isa 32.15; 44.3; Ezek 36.25–6; Joel 2.28–9; 1QS 4.21–2; Jn 3.5; 7.39. But that is just the first point. Spirit is *rûaḥ*, and *rûaḥ*, like fire, was sometimes associated with judgement (Isa 4.4; 40.24; 41.16; Jer 4.11–16; 23.19; 30.23; Ezek 13.11–13; 1QSb 5.24–5) or thought of as a purifying or cleansing element (1QS 4.21). Moreover, two passages in Isaiah reveal the possibilities for linking up fire and *rûaḥ* in prophecies about judgement. In Isa 30.27–8, the name of the Lord comes from afar, burning with anger and rising in thick smoke; his tongue is like a devouring fire; and his breath (*rûaḥ*/πνεῦμα) is like an overflowing stream reaching up to the neck to sift the nations with the sieve of destruction, and to place on the jaws of the people a bridle that leads astray. In Isa 4.4 it is prophesied that the Lord will cleanse Zion and Jerusalem by a spirit of judgement and by a spirit of burning (cf. also Isa 29.6 and Ezek 1.4). Even more telling is 4 Ezra 13.8–11, in which a stream of fire and a flame of breath issue from the Messiah's mouth as judgement. Here is precisely the background requisite for interpreting John's talk of baptism in Spirit and in fire.[47] For the Baptist, fire and Spirit were not two things but one—'fiery breath' (hendiadys). He proclaimed that, at the boundary of the new age, all would pass through the fiery *rûaḥ* of God, a stream which would purify the righteous and destroy the unrighteous.[48] Congruent with this understanding is the following verse (12), in which the one act of harvesting, that is, the judgement, means the salvation of some (wheat) and the damnation of others (chaff).[49]

The influence of the Baptist's conception upon Jesus is almost certainly to be discerned in three different texts: Lk 12.49–51; Mk 10.35–40; and 9.49. In these Jesus interprets his own time as part and parcel of the eschatological tribulation; and he and his disciples will have to undergo the baptism of fire of which John spoke (see Allison, pp. 124–8).

Did Matthew take the baptism of the coming one to be fulfilled in Christian baptism (cf. 28.16–20) or did he think of it as yet outstanding, a feature of the final judgement?[50] The close

[47] Cf. Dunn, 'Spirit-and-Fire Baptism' (v); Allison, pp. 124–5.

[48] The places in the OT where *rûaḥ* is spoken of as being like water (e.g. Isa 32.15; 44.3; Joel 2.28–9) help remove the harshness of 'baptize in spirit'.—Contra Origen, *Hom. in Luc.* 24, who is followed by F. Lange, *TWNT* 6, p. 943, and L. Goppelt, *TWNT* 8, p. 329, the Spirit is not a gift for the righteous, the fire a punishment for the wicked. There is only one 'you' in the text.

[49] We have interpreted Mt 3.11 = Lk 3.16 with Jewish conceptions in mind. For possible Greek parallels see Beare, pp. 95–6, and Glasson (v).

[50] According to Luz 1, p. 149, the disjunction is false. Matthew understood the

connexion in Q with the saying about wheat and chaff (reproduced
by Matthew) will have pointed him in one direction, the Markan
version (which has only 'Holy Spirit') in another (cf. Jn 1.33; Acts
1.5; 11.16). The decisive facts would seem to be these: Matthew
reproduces Q, not Mark, and with the inconsequential exception
of 17.15 (the epileptic who often throws himself into the fire), fire is
in the First Gospel always an eschatological element (3.10, 12;
5.22; 7.19; 13.40, 42, 50; 18.8, 9; 25.41). Matthew will then have
rightly understood the Baptist's prophecy: the future judgement
will be through fire.

12. There is no parallel in either Mark or John to this line,
which closes the proclamation of John with an ominous warning.
οὗ τὸ πτύον ἐν τῇ χειρὶ αὐτοῦ καὶ διακαθαριεῖ τὴν ἅλωνα αὐτοῦ καὶ
συνάξει τὸν σῖτον αὐτοῦ εἰς τὴν ἀποθήκην, τὸ δὲ ἄχυρον κατακαύσει
πυρὶ ἀσβέστῳ. Given its present context, the emphasis probably
comes down not on the gathering of the wheat in the granary but
on the burning of the chaff. Judgement, not salvation, is the theme.
(Contrast Pist. Soph. 3.133, which has the wheat gathered last.)

Lk 3.17 differs from Mt 3.12 in omitting Matthew's first καί, in
having infinitives instead of the future for the first two verbs, in
following ἀποθήκην (a loan word in rabbinic Hebrew, as in Tg.
Yer. I on Gen 24.2 and Deut 32.34) rather than σῖτον with αὐτοῦ
(although Luke's text is here uncertain), and in using διακαθαίρω
(a NT *hapax legomenon* absent from the LXX; καθαίρω: in the NT
only in Jn 15.2) rather than διακαθαρίζω (a word not yet found
elsewhere in Greek literature). The first three differences are to be
put down to Matthew's love of parallelism. Matthew's changes
over against Luke (= Q) make for two perfectly analogous lines—

καὶ διακαθαριεῖ τὴν ἅλωνα αὐτοῦ
καὶ συνάξει   τὸν σῖτον αὐτοῦ—

and the first two future tenses make for agreement with the tense of
the concluding verb and underline the eschatological thrust.

The short parable here recounted, which shares with the
preceding verse the presupposition that the divine judgement is
near, and which the evangelist will have interpreted in accord with
13.36–43, makes four statements. (1) The winnowing fork (πτύον;
cf. Isa 30.23 Sym., translating *zōreh*) is already in the hand of the
coming one (cf. 3.10). The judgement is imminent. (2) The
threshed grain [51] (ἅλων; cf. Job 39.12; Isa 25.10) is about to be

---

baptism of the Spirit to refer to Christian baptism, the baptism of fire to be
eschatological. This possibility cannot be excluded.

[51] The word might also mean 'threshing floor' (= Attic ἅλως, cf. 1 Clem. 29.3), as
in Deut 13.3 and 1 Clem. 56.15. This would not make much difference for
interpretation.

thoroughly (note the διά) cleansed, which means that a separation is near to hand. As grain is winnowed, tossed in the wind in order to be separated from the light and worthless chaff (cf. Ps 1.4), so—it is implied—will it be with people. (3) The sifted wheat will be gathered into the granary (cf. 6.26; 13.30). The meaning is transparent: those with fruits worthy of repentance (3.8) will be preserved. (4) The chaff (ἄχυρον; most often in the LXX for *teben*) will, like the unfruitful trees of 3.10, be consumed (κατακαίω; cf. Mt 13.30, 40) in or by (is the dative locative or instrumental?) unquenchable fire. (The absence of αὐτοῦ after 'chaff' is conspicuous.) Compare the rabbinic parable in *Midr. Ps.* on 2.12: Soon harvest will come and everyone will see and know for certain for whose sake the field was sown. In no time at all, with the coming of harvest, the straw is disposed of in the water, the chaff in the wind, and the weeds in flame, but the wheat is brought in for safe-keeping, and whoever handles it, kisses it. In the time to come, when the day of judgement arrives, the peoples of the earth will be dragged into the Valley of Hinnom, but Israel will remain.

According to Beare, p. 97, in reality the chaff or stubble would simply blow away, so the burning of it is odd. If this were indeed so, then all the more emphasis would fall upon the conclusion, the fire of judgement. But BAGD, s.v., cites Ostraka 2.1168 for the burning of ἄχυρον; and ἄχυρον is the near equivalent of *qaš*, for the burning of which see Exod 15.7; Isa 5.24; 47.14; Obad 18; Mal 4.1; *m. Šabb.* 3.1; *m. Para* 4.3. On the other hand, ἄχυρον never translates *qaš* in the LXX; and if, as G. Schwarz (v) has proposed, 'in unquenchable fire', which turns a true to life parable into something more, is a secondary addition, one could further conjecture (as does Schwarz) that κατακαίω has replaced an original verb which meant 'blow away'. This is the more plausible—although not proven—by the constant connexion between 'chaff' and words like 'wind' and 'blow' in the OT (Job 21.18; Ps 1.4; 35.5; Isa 17.13; 29.5; 41.15–16; Dan 2.35; Hos 13.3; Zeph 2.2). Interestingly enough, the third-century Mart. Pionius 4.14 refers to Mt 3.12 but has the chaff simply carried off by the wind.

For the work of judgement belonging not to God but to a messianic figure see 1 En. 69.27–9; 11QMelch. 2; 2 Bar. 72–4; 4 Ezra 12.31–4; Ps. Sol. 17.21–3. For unquenchable—which is not necessarily eternal—fire see Isa 34.10; 66.24 (οὐ σβεσθήσεται); Jer 7.20; Mk 9.48 (οὐ σβέννυται); Jude 7; LAB 18.10 ('fire which consumeth water'); 63.4; Ignatius, *Eph.* 16.2; *b. Pesaḥ.* 54a. For the image of threshing or winnowing or harvesting as a prophecy of judgement see Ps 1.4; Prov 20.26; Isa 41.14–16; Jer 15.7; 51.33; Hos 6.11; Mic 4.12–13; Joel 3.13; Rev 14.14–20; 4 Ezra 4.30, 38–9; Tg. Ps.-J. on Isa 28.28; from the synoptics: Mk 4.26–9; Mt 9.37–8 = Lk 10.2; Mt 13.24–30; Lk 22.31; Jn 4.35–8. For the wicked as chaff see Job 21.18; Ps 1.4; Isa 17.13; Hos 13.3. Note Tg. Isa. on 33.11: God's *memra* ('word') will destroy just as a whirlwind scatters chaff.

The redundant οὐ . . . αὐτοῦ is probably a Semitism (cf. *'ašer* + noun with pronominal suffix). Compare Gen 1.11; Ps 40.4; Lk 12.43 D; Mk

7.25; Acts 15.17; Rev 7.2, 9; 13.8. For discussion see Robertson, p. 722; Black, pp. 100–1; Doudna, pp. 98–103.

THE BAPTISM OF JESUS (3.13–17)

13. 3.13–17 opens with a sentence which is parallel to 3.1. Its purpose is to announce what Jesus is doing at the Jordan: he, arriving to the tidings of his own coming (3.11–12), appears in order to be baptized by John. This is followed by a redactional interpolation (3.14–15) which tells us why Jesus has to be baptized (to fulfil all righteousness). 3.16 then resumes the narrative flow, quickly passing over the baptism itself to recount what happens immediately thereafter. First (3.16), a heavenly vision (introduced by καὶ ἰδού) is granted. Secondly (3.17), a heavenly voice (also introduced by καὶ ἰδού) sounds forth. God has the last word.

Does 3.13–17 belong to a fixed literary form? According to F. Lentzen-Deis, *Taufe* (v), pp. 195–227, Mk 1.9–11, along with its Matthean parallel, should be classified as a *Deutevision* (a vision interpreted by a voice), such as is found in the targums on Gen 22.10 and 28.12.[52] According to K. Berger, our story is a *Berufungsgeschichte* of a kind quite at home in apocalyptic literature.[53] Neither of these solutions is completely satisfying (see ns. 52–3). Probably the closest parallel to Mt 3.13–17 is Mt 17.1–8 (the transfiguration narrative), where a heavenly voice again follows a visionary experience. Both narratives have this form:

3.13–16a/17.1–2	Setting
3.16b/17.3a	'and behold!'
3.16b–d/17.3	Vision
3.17a/17.5b	'and behold!'
3.17a–c/17.5c–d	Heavenly voice

But there are also differences. In 17.1–8 the voice from heaven does not terminate the episode; and the transfiguration episode contains narrative material (Peter's response: 17.4) between the vision (17.3) and the second 'and behold' (17.5b). Further, 3.13–17 does not give rise to comment from Jesus himself (contrast 17.9–13). We conclude, then, that Mt 3.13–17 does not follow a set scheme. Its component parts—heavenly voice, heavenly vision, καὶ ἰδού—may be traditional, but the whole does not belong to any one *Gattung*.

---

[52] For criticism see A. Vögtle in *BZ* 17 (1973), pp. 115–23.

[53] He is followed by Gnilka, *Markus* 1, p. 53. They cite the following texts: 1 En. 65.4–5; T. Levi 18.6; LAB 53.3–11; Gk. Apoc. Ezra 6.3; 7.13. There is, however, no vision in LAB 53.3–11; 1 En. 65.4–5; or Gk. Apoc. Ezra 6.3; 7.13; and T. Levi 18.6 must be suspected of being influenced by the NT accounts of Jesus' baptism.

τότε παραγίνεται ὁ Ἰησοῦς ἀπὸ τῆς Γαλιλαίας ἐπὶ τὸν Ἰορδάνην πρὸς τὸν Ἰωάννην τοῦ βαπτισθῆναι ὑπ' αὐτοῦ. This prosaic opening is based upon Mk 1.9. Jesus, for the first time, becomes an active character. The parallel with 3.1 (where John the Baptist is introduced) is close: temporal note + παραγίνεται + proper name (+ verb) + place name + verb. τότε (see on 2.16) replaces Mark's 'in those days', which has already been used in 3.1. Perhaps the adverb serves to make 3.13–17 chronologically separate from 3.1–12 (so Kingsbury, *Structure*, p. 14). For παραγίνεται compare 3.1 and the comments there. Mark has καὶ ἐγένετο (which he also has to introduce the Baptist) + ἦλθεν. Matthew retains καὶ ἐγένετο only in 8.26 = Mk 4.39 and 9.10 = Mk 2.15. Contrast the Matthean parallels to Mk 1.9; 2.23; 4.4; and 9.7. With the exceptions of 8.26 and 9.10, Matthew reserves the Semitic καὶ ἐγένετο for the formula, καὶ ἐγένετο ὅτε ἐτέλεσεν ὁ Ἰησοῦς (7.28; 11.1; 13.53; 19.1; 26.1). Given its use in the LXX, perhaps παραγίνεται is intended to sound a note of solemnity or consequence; see Gen 35.9; Exod 19.9; Judg 13.9; 1 Βασ 13.10; 2 Βασ 5.1; Est 5.5.

Mt 2.22 prepared for the geographical notice, ἀπὸ Γαλιλαίας— although Nazareth is, interestingly enough, not here mentioned (contrast Mark). On Galilee in the First Gospel see on 4.12–16. Note the contrast with 3.5: in Chapter 3 Jesus alone comes from Galilee; everyone else is from Jerusalem or Judea or the region around the Jordan.

Instead of ἐπί Mark has εἰς with 'Jordan': 'baptized *in* the Jordan'. Matthew could not be expected to reproduce this because he, unlike the other evangelists, consistently avoids using εἰς in a local sense, as though it were ἐν (BDF § 205). In Mt 3.7 the Jordan becomes a destination: 'Jesus came . . . *to* the Jordan'. For the Jordan see on 3.5–6.

τοῦ βαπτισθῆναι means 'in order to be baptized' (see on 2.13 and compare Lk 3.7). The verb appears six times in Mt 3. Mark has 'and was baptized'. Compare the change at Mk 1.13 = Mt 4.1: 'and he was tempted' becomes 'in order to be tempted'. Jesus is determined and will not be dissuaded by the Baptist's protest; he is determined 'to fulfil all righteousness'. For ὑπ' αὐτοῦ (cf. 3.6) Mark has 'by John'. Matthew has 'by him' to avoid naming John three times in near succession.

Why did Jesus submit to John's baptism? Matthew's answer—'in order to fulfil all righteousness' (3.15)—has scarcely cancelled further discussion. There has been no dearth of conjectures on the query. (1) Jesus went to John in order to repent and find forgiveness (Strauss, pp. 237–9; Hollenbach (v), pp. 198–202). This, rightly or wrongly, sets aside the traditional doctrine of Jesus' sinlessness, which has strong roots in the NT

(Acts 3.14; Jn 8.46; 2 Cor 5.21; Heb 7.26; 1 Pet 1.19).[54] (2) Jesus only wished to join the saved remnant, the new Israel, and saw its formation in the ministry of John, to which he then submitted (cf. Marsh (v), p. 102; T. W. Manson, *Sayings*, p. 149). (3) Jesus, conscious of being the servant of Deutero-Isaiah, had himself baptized in order to identify himself with sinners (cf. Chromatius of Aquileia 329). He had to be numbered with the transgressors (Isa 53.11–12). Baptism was the first step in bearing the sins of the world (Cullmann, *Baptism* (v), pp. 15–22; Cranfield, *Mark*, pp. 51–2). (4) God's call to all Israel had gone out through the Baptist: repent and be baptized. Jesus, humbly and obediently, responded to the call: it was religious duty to be accepted without question (Schlatter, p. 85; Fridrichsen (v)). (5) According to Jerome (*Adv. Pelag.* 3.2), the Gospel according to the Nazaraeans contained this: 'Behold, the mother of the Lord and his brothers said to him: John the Baptist baptizes unto the remission of sins. Let us go and be baptized by him. But he said to them: Wherein have I sinned that I should go and be baptized by him? Unless what I have said is ignorance'. The substantial truth of this report has been upheld (C. J. Cadoux, *The Life of Jesus*, West Drayton, 1948, pp. 44–7). When invited to accept John's baptism, Jesus saw no need for any act of repentance, for he was not conscious of having transgressed God's will. But he shrank from following his conscience because he knew the united teaching of the Scriptures to the effect that no human being is free from sin (cf. Rom 3.10–18). (6) Perhaps as Messiah and Son of Man and therefore as representative person, but in any case as he came to seek and to save those who were lost, Jesus took his stand with the publicans and sinners against the self-righteous. He was thus compelled to join the ranks of those who came to the Jordan confessing their sins and in need of deliverance (cf. Heb 2.17 and see Beasley-Murray (v), pp. 55–62; V. Taylor, *The Life and Ministry of Jesus*, London, 1954, pp. 58–9; Feuillet, 'Personnalité' (v)). (7) According to Justin Martyr, the Jews believed that 'the Messiah is unknown and does not even know himself and has no power until Elijah comes to anoint him and make him manifest to all' (*Dial.* 8.4; cf. 49.1).[55] Maybe, then, Jesus went to the Jordan to be anointed as Messiah by one he took to be Elijah (cf. Mk 9.11–13). But Justin himself could be responsible for the eschatological expectation he attributes to the Jews, for it has no parallel in rabbinic sources.[56] (8) To the traditional answers already listed,[57] we should like to add one more. If, as seems overwhelmingly probable, Jesus interpreted his prospective dark fate in terms of eschatological trial (see Allison, pp. 115–41), and if, as we have

---

[54] See Beasley-Murray (v), p. 47, for like-minded critics. For criticism see Feuillet, 'La personnalité' (v).

[55] For support for Justin's assertion see SB 4, pp. 797–8. The seventeenth-century messianic figure Sabbatai Ṣevi claimed that he had been anointed by Elijah; see Scholem, *Sabbatai Ṣevi*, p. 141; Davies, *JPS*, p. 262.

[56] See M. M. Faierstein, 'Why Do the Scribes Say That Elijah Must Come First?', *JBL* 100 (1981), pp. 85–6.

[57] We pass over the patristic solutions to the problem, such as that Jesus wished to sanctify the waters of baptism, or to give an example to Christians, or to teach submission to priests. Pertinent texts include Ignatius, *Eph.*, 18.2; Justin, *Dial.* 88; Clement of Alexandria, *Paed.* 1.6; Jerome, *Adv. Pelag.* 3.2; Gregory Nazianzen, *Or. Holy Lights* 14; Cyril of Alexandria, *Hom. on Lk.* 11.

argued, John saw his baptism as preparing Israel for the tribulation and judgement of the latter days, then Jesus could have gone to the Baptist not in order to obtain the forgiveness of sins but rather to receive a pledge of ultimate deliverance, a seal of divine protection (cf. Rev 7.4–8; 9.4; Ps. Sol. 15.1–9) from the imminent eschatological flood of fire (cf. Mt 3.11; Mk 10.35–45; Lk 12.49–51).

A prudent choice between the—far from exhaustive—listed alternatives involves intricate and disputed problems, the most fundamental being this: even if we do not subscribe to the conventional doctrine of Jesus' sinlessness, was his historical self-consciousness or sense of mission such as to discourage us from thinking he could submit to a baptism for the remission of sins without further ado?[58] An affirmative response will leave open options (2)–(8), of which (2), (4), (6), and (8), or some combination thereof, appear the most plausible. A negative response will entail (1) as the clear choice. Beyond this inventory of options, however, the historical evidence will not take us, and no firm decision can be reached. We remain in the dark.

14. John somehow recognizes who Jesus is—compare the recognition scenes in Jn 1.29ff. and Suetonius, *Aug.* 94—and thinks it unfitting to baptize him. Now, although in fact the historical Baptist, like later Christian officials, may well have interviewed candidates for baptism, this hardly compels us to accept the historicity of Matthew's dialogue. 3.14–15 is full of redactional vocabulary (see below). It has a very plausible origin in a specifically Christian difficulty. And the declaration, 'I need to be baptized by you, and do you come to me!' (3.14), presupposes a developed Christology and is inconsistent with the doubt exhibited by John in Mt 11.2–6 = Lk 7.18–23.

ὁ δὲ Ἰωάννης διεκώλυεν αὐτὸν λέγων. The verb is a NT *hapax legomenon* (LXX: 2). The imperfect is conative, implying attempted action: 'he tried to hold him back' (cf. BDF § 326).

Because κωλύω appears in connexion with baptism in Acts 8.36; 10.47; 11.17; Gosp. Eb. frag. 4 (Epiphanius, *Haer.* 30.13; this depends upon Mt 3 but the δια- is dropped); as well as Mt 3.14 (cf. also Mk 10.13–16), Cullmann (*Baptism* (v), pp. 71–80) has argued that the word was part of early Christian baptismal ritual. When candidates were brought forward, enquiry was made as to whether the pre-conditions of baptism had really been met: τί κωλύει; His conjecture seems sound, which means that Mt 3.14 has been influenced by Christian ritual.

ἐγὼ χρείαν ἔχω ὑπὸ σοῦ βαπτισθῆναι. The vocabulary is consistent with a redactional origin.[59] If John is not worthy to

[58] Pertinent considerations in J. A. T. Robinson, *The Human Face of God*, Philadelphia, 1973, pp. 88–98.
[59] ἐγώ: Mt:29; Mk:16; Lk:22. χρεία: Mt:6 (redactional in 6.8; 14.16); Mk:4; Lk:7; with ἔχω (cf. Tob 5.7, 11 ℵ; Prov 18.2; Wisd 13.16): Mt:6; Mk:4; Lk:6. ὑπό: Mt:29

carry the Messiah's sandals, how can he baptize him? If John's baptism only foreshadows an eschatological baptism, how can the dispenser of the latter submit himself to the authority of the former? How can the Messiah, who, according to expectation, should, like some of the fathers (cf. As. Mos. 9.4; 2 Bar. 9.1), be pure from sin (Ps. Sol. 17.36; 1QSb5; T. Jud. 24.1; T. Levi 18.9), submit to a baptism which involves the confession of sins (3.6)? Presumably questions such as these were in Matthew's mind, and 3.14–15 gives us the fruit of his ponderings. See further Giesen, pp. 25–9, for a review of suggestions as to what questions 3.13–14 might answer.

καὶ σὺ ἔρχῃ πρός με; Compare Mk 1.9. πρός με parallels the 'to John' of the previous verse. καί here means 'and yet' (see on 1.19). Is there a play on the ἐρχόμενος of 3.11—the 'coming one' comes?

15. This verse contains the first words uttered by Jesus in Matthew, and they show every sign of being editorial (*pace* Strecker, *Weg*, p. 178, and Gaechter, *Kommentar*, p. 100). They are also, we believe, programmatic. πληρόω and δικαιοσύνη are both loaded terms in the First Gospel, and to understand them rightly is to understand a good deal about our evangelist.

ἀποκριθεὶς δὲ ὁ Ἰησοῦς εἶπεν αὐτῷ.[60] This introductory phrase is redactional or at least has no synoptic parallel in 14.28; 15.15; 16.16 (diff. Mk 8.29); 16.17; 17.4 (diff. Mk 9.5); 20.22 (diff. Mk 10.38); 21.21 (diff. Mk 11.22); 21.24 (diff. Mk 11.29); 22.29 (diff. Mk 12.25); 25.26; 26.33 (diff. Mk 14.29); 27.21 (diff. Mk 15.12); 28.5 (diff. Mk 16.6). ἀποκριθείς + εἶπεν is a common Septuagintism (cf. *wayya'an . . . wayyō'mer*) restricted in the NT to the gospels and Acts. For discussion see P. Joüon, 'Respondit et dixit', *Bib* 13 (1932), pp. 309–14, and Jeremias, *Lukasevangelium*, pp. 39–41.

ἄφες ἄρτι. This means 'let it be so now'. It is an idiom of permission (cf. BDF § 364.1–2) not found in the LXX. ἀφίημι occurs with κωλύω in Mk 10.14 in what is perhaps a baptismal context. Gosp. Eb. frag 4 (Epiphanius, *Haer*. 30.13.8) has ἄφες without ἄρτι. ἄρτι (= 'for the moment at least') is a Matthean favourite (Mt:7; Mk:0; Lk:0), and Matthew has the habit of placing adverbs after imperatives (BDF § 474.3; see 5.13; 9.18; 18.16; 19.20; 26.53, 65; 27.42, 43).

(redactional in 1.22; 2.15; 3.14; 5.13; 8.24; 14.8, 24; 20.23; 22.31; 27.12); Mk:12; Lk:30.

[60] B *f*13 *pc* Eus have αυτω for προς αυτον, which is found in P67 ℵ C Ds L W 0233 *f*1 Maj. 0250 sams boms omit the two words and supply nothing in their place. Against HG and NA26, we follow B and *f*13 because there is no other example of ἀποκριθείς . . . εἶπεν πρὸς αὐτόν in the First Gospel while ἀποκριθείς . . . εἶπεν αὐτῷ is well-attested (15.15; 16.17; 19.27; 25.26; 26.33). In addition, there is no other instance of εἶπεν + πρός in the First Gospel.

οὕτως γὰρ πρέπον ἐστὶν ἡμῖν πληρῶσαι πᾶσαν δικαιοσύνην. Gosp. Eb. frag. 4 (Epiphanius, *Haer.* 30.13.8) has, ὅτι οὕτως ἐστὶ πρέπον πληρωθῆναι πάντα. For οὕτως (Mt:32; Mk:10; Lk:21) followed by γάρ see also 2.5; 5.12 (never in Mark or Luke). οὕτως does not (*pace* Lohmeyer, *Matthäus*, pp. 50–1) prove that in the baptism alone Jesus fulfils all righteousness; rather is the baptism an example or instance of Jesus' fulfilling righteousness (cf. Descamps, pp. 114–15). Compare the use of οὕτως by Paul in Rom 11.26; see Davies, *JPS*, p. 347, n. 36. πρέπον ἐστίν means 'it is right, proper, fitting, natural' (cf. BAGD, s.v., and 3 Macc 7.13; 1 Cor 11.13; Ignatius, *Rom.* 10.2; *Phil.* 10.1). Jesus recognizes the will of God and freely obeys. On πρέπω (which appears only here in the synoptics) see M. Pohlenz, 'Τὸ πρέπον. Ein Beitrag zur Geschichte des griechischen Geistes', *Nachrichten der Gesellsch. der Wissenschaften zu Göttingen* (1933), pp. 53–92. It had established itself in the moral vocabulary of the Greek world. ἡμῖν is most naturally understood to refer to John and Jesus—who in Matthew's account are perhaps the only two to see the heavens opened and hear the voice of 3.17—acting together; they both accomplish all righteousness. It is unnecessary to interpret 'us' as a plural of majesty (*pace* Klostermann, p. 25) or as embracing the Jewish people or (cf. Gos. Philip. 72.30–73.1) as inviting Christians to join with Jesus in fulfilling all righteousness (*pace* Giesen, pp. 31–3). As is consistent with a redactional origin, both πληρόω (Mt:16; Mk:2; L:9) and δικαιοσύνη (Mt:7; Mk:0; Lk:1) are special favourites of our evangelist.

How are we to interpret 'to fulfil all righteousness'?[61] (1) It has been proposed that, according to Jewish expectation, it would be the special task of the Messiah as righteous one to bring to fulfilment the total will of God and that the baptism of Jesus was interpreted in this light (cf. Jer 23.5–6; 33.15; Zech 9.9; Ps. Sol. 17.26–34; T. Jud. 24.1; *Pesiq. R.* 36)[62] The evidence from Jewish sources is, however, less than extensive, and even if it were otherwise we should still have to inquire how the expectation relates to the specific act of baptism. There is also the difficulty that Matthew himself does not develop the link between righteousness and messianic expectation. (2) For Cullmann (*Baptism* (v), pp. 18–20), 'all' righteousness is fulfilled because Jesus' baptism typified his death by which he effected 'justice', that is, a general forgiveness (cf. Rom 6 and see Ljungmann (v) and Bartsch (v), pp. 89–90). This suspiciously imports a Pauline idea into the First

[61] For reviews of interpretation see Eissfeldt (v) and Dupont, *Béatitudes*, 3, pp. 224–45.
[62] So M. J. Fiedler, 'Der Begriff δικαιοσύνη im Matthäus-Evangelium', Dissertation Martin Luther Universität, Halle-Wittenberg, 1957, vol. 1, pp. 109–13, according to Przybylski, p. 92.

Gospel. And from Matthew we do not learn that Jesus' baptism was 'for others'. (3) Jesus is giving an example to Christians, who are involved in the 'us': the followers of Jesus should follow in their master's footsteps and fulfil all righteousness by accepting Christian baptism (cf. Strecker, *Weg*, p. 180; Kraeling (v), p. 134; Giesen, pp. 31–3). This, as already indicated, puts too much weight upon the little word 'us'—especially given Matthew's tendency to historicize and the absence of other texts in Matthew where 'us' or 'we' embraces Jesus together with the Christian reader. (4) Every divinely commanded ordinance must be fulfilled; baptism is such an ordinance; therefore Jesus submitted to it (cf. Zahn, p. 144; Klostermann, p. 25). But for Matthew 'righteousness' does not mean formal obedience to the divine commands, which are rather called to mind by the word δικαίωμα (cf. Barth, in *TIM*, p. 138). (5) John 'came in the way of righteousness' (21.33) and demanded righteousness of those who went out to accept his baptism. In going out to the Jordan, Jesus upheld the validity of John's demand and announced his intention to fulfil it completely (cf. Hill, *Matthew*, p. 96; Przybylski, pp. 93–4). On this interpretation, 'righteousness' encompasses more than one act, and the Pauline idea of 'righteousness' as God's gift is rightly not in the picture. The problem with this solution, however, is that it gives insufficient attention to the special Matthean use of δικαιοσύνη. (6) O. Eissfeldt (v) has related Mt 3.14–15 to Mt 17.24–7 (Peter and the half-shekel tax) and to 22.15–22 (paying tribute to Caesar): sometimes the right action is not necessary in itself but expedient in order not to offend and in order to get along in the world. This suggestion fails because in neither Mt 17.24–7 nor 22.15–22 do we find the key word, 'righteousness'. (7) The most convincing approach to the difficult phrase, 'to fulfil all righteousness', has been advanced by Meier, *Law*, pp. 76–80 (cf. Frankemölle, pp. 94–5; Sabbe (v)): it refers to Jesus fulfilling prophecy. πληρόω occurs sixteen times in Matthew, thirteen times in formula quotations or in verses where prophecy or the prophets are the subject (1.22; 2.15, 17, 23; 4.14; 5.17; 8.17; 12.17; 13.35; 21.4; 26.54, 56; 27.9; cf. 13.14, ἀναπληρόω). Of the remaining three instances, one is empty of theological meaning (13.48: a net is filled up) and another (23.32) probably has to do with an ironic fulfilment of prophecy ('Fill up, then, the measure of your fathers'; cf. Gundry, *Commentary*, p. 469). This leaves only 3.15, and it follows that all presumption is in favour of finding in it a reference to OT prophecy. This is seemingly confirmed by 3.17: the voice from heaven, drawing upon Ps 2.7 and Isa 42.1, makes plain that the baptism of Jesus brings to realization scriptural hopes. So when Jesus fulfils all righteousness, he is fulfilling Scripture. This interpretation leaves one free to interpret

'righteousness' in more than one way. It is possible, on the one
hand, to think of moral effort or obedience to God's will: by
fulfilling Scripture, John and Jesus are acting rightly, they are
exhibiting 'righteousness'. Meier, on the other hand, interprets the
word as signifying the saving activity of God. A choice between
these two options is problematic. Yet because, with the possible
exception of 5.6, δικαιοσύνη seems in Matthew to be uniform in
meaning—moral conduct in accord with God's will (cf. Dupont,
Béatitudes 3, pp. 211–384; Strecker, *Weg*, pp. 149–58; Przybylski,
passim)—, we are inclined to define the 'righteousness' of 3.15 as
moral conduct: Jesus, knowing the messianic prophecies of the
OT, obediently fulfils them and thereby fulfils all righteousness.
Because prophecy declares God's will, to fulfil prophecy is to fulfil
righteousness.

In Ignatius, *Smyr.* 1, which was composed before A.D. 115, we read that
Jesus was truly born of a virgin and was baptized by John in order 'that all
righteousness might be fulfilled by him'. Granted our conclusions
concerning the editorial genesis of Mt 3.14–15, this is the earliest firm
evidence pertaining to the date and circulation of our gospel.[63]

τότε ἀφίησιν αὐτόν. John, a model of discipleship, unhesitatingly
obeys. He hears the word of Jesus and does it, thereby setting an
example for Matthew's audience. For the verb see 3.15b. For the
historical present see on 3.1. Here it marks the transition from
3.14–15 to 16–17.

16. Although it is possible we should suppose some influence
from Q (see below), Matthew now returns to his Markan source in
reciting the goal and *raison d'être* of chapter 3.

βαπτισθεὶς δὲ ὁ ᾽Ιησοῦς. Mark has, 'And he was baptized in the
Jordan by John'. Jesus again is named (contrast Mark) because the
subject of the preceding sentence is John the Baptist ('Then he
permitted him'). Introductory aorist participles are common in the
First Gospel, and Matthew names Jesus more often than his fellow
synoptic evangelists (Mt:150; Mk:81; Lk:89).

ἀνέβη εὐθὺς ἀπὸ τοῦ ὕδατος.[64] Compare Acts 8.39; Barn. 11.8, 11;
Herm. s. 9.16. Mark's present participle (ἀναβαίνων) has become
an aorist in accordance with the introductory βαπτισθείς, and his
ἐκ has become ἀπό (an apparently insignificant change also made
in 14.2 = Mk 6.14; 21.8 = Mk 11.8; 24.1 = Mk 13.1; and
24.29 = Mk 13.25; cf. the textual variants in Mt 7.4; 17.9; Mk 16.3).
For water as the site of revelation see Ezek 1.1; Dan 8.2; 10.4; 1 En.

---

[63] According to Koester, *Überlieferung*, pp. 58–61, Ignatius is quoting a
formulation of someone else who had read Matthew. The necessity for this
hypothesis escapes us.

[64] ευθυς ανεβη (cf. Mk 1.10): ℵ B Dˢ W *f*¹ 33ᵛⁱᵈ *pc* lat syP followed by NA²⁶. With
HG we prefer ανεβη ευθυς, the word order attested in C L (0233) *f*¹³ Maj d h syʰ.

13.7–8; *Mek.* on Exod 12.1; 3 Bar. title; see also Davies, *JPS*, p. 76.

In Mark εὐθύς[65] goes with εἶδεν; here it goes with ἀνέβη. Matthew has usually dropped the word (Mt:7; Mk:42; Lk:1) and retains it only for temporal expression whereas Mark frequently employs it as though it were the equivalent of καὶ ἰδού. In the present instance Matthew's usage makes little sense: 'Jesus at once came out of the water; and behold, the heavens opened . . .'.[66] Why would anyone ever *stay* in the water? But Mark is intelligible: 'he was baptized in the Jordan by John. And immediately, having come out of the water, he saw the heavens rent . . .'. Because it is Mark's habit to write sentences with the form, εὐθύς + participle + verb qualified by εὐθύς (e.g. 1.18; 2.8; 11.2; 14.43), we must suspect Matthew of being secondary. In rewriting his source he has erroneously joined the adverb to the wrong verb.

Jesus' emerging from the water and climbing the bank—which connects the heavenly vision and voice not with an action of John but with an action of Jesus—recalls at least two related images. (1) In Judaism creation was thought of as emergence from a watery chaos (Gen 1.3; Isa 43.16–20)—an important observation since, as we shall see, other creation motifs are present in our story. (2) Israel was adopted and became God's 'son' at the exodus from Egypt, at the crossing of the Red Sea, and some scholars have found a new exodus motif in the story of Jesus' baptism: when Jesus comes out of the waters, new Israel is born (cf. Davies, *SSM*, pp. 34–45).

καὶ ἰδού. This redactional insertion (see on 1.20) draws attention to the first dramatic climax of 3.1–17. It is the equivalent of the Hebrew *wĕhinnēh*, the Aramaic *wĕhā'* (cf. Gen 1.31; 1QapGen 20.30; 22.27; 4QEn[e] 1.22.1) and is a Septuagintism (Gen 1.31; 15.17; 29.2; Deut 9.13; etc.).

ἠνεῴχθησαν οἱ οὐρανοί.[67] Matthew differs from Mark in putting

---

[65] See G. Rudberg, 'ΕΥΘΥΣ', *ConNT* 9 (1944), pp. 42–6, and D. Daube, *The Sudden in Scripture*, Leiden, 1964, pp. 46–60.

[66] For this and what follows see Kümmel, *Introduction*, p. 61, and D. Daube, 'Zukunftsmusik', *BJRL* 68 (1985), pp. 55–6.

[67] αυτω after the verb is omitted by ℵ* B vg[mss] sy[s.c] sa geo[B] Ir Hil CyrJ Vig PsAmbr. This testimony is weighty and we follow it (against NA[26] and HG). Metzger, p. 11, suggests that the word was omitted as unnecessary and misunderstood. The omission of αυτω could also mark assimilation to Luke. But more probable, we think, is alteration by a scribe wanting to bring Matthew's version of the baptism (where things are public or semi-public) into line with Mark's: 'to him' would then make Jesus alone the one who sees the heavens open (cf. Mk 1.10). Cf. the addition of προς αυτον by some witnesses in 3.17 ('saying *to him*'). That tension was felt to exist between Mt 3.16–17 and Mk 1.10–11 and that attempts were made to establish harmony is demonstrated by *Gosp. Eb.* frag. 4, where the heavenly voice first speaks to Jesus alone in the words of Mk 1.11 and then again to John in the words of Mt 3.17.

'heavens'—the plural is Semitic (Maloney, pp. 190–2)—in the nominative and by changing the verb to the passive of ἀνοίγω (see on 2.11). Both modifications probably signal assimilation to Ezek 1.1: ἠνοίχθησαν οἱ οὐρανοί, καὶ εἶδον ὁράσεις θεοῦ. Compare also Isa 63.19 LXX; Acts 7.56; Rev 4.1. That Luke has ἀνεῳχθῆναι τὸν οὐρανόν (3.21) can scarcely be taken as the firm sign of a common source, particularly in view of OT usage (cf. Gen 7.11; Isa 24.18; Mal 3.10; 3 Macc 6.17). Nevertheless, because Q contained an account of the Baptist's preaching shortly followed by a temptation narrative which presupposes Jesus' divine sonship, it is likely that between the material behind Mt 3.7–12 = Lk 3.7–9, 15–17 and Mt 4.1–11 = Lk 4.1–13 there was a notice of the baptism.[68]

The splitting of the heavens in connexion with God's judgment was an eschatological expectation (Job 14.12 LXX; Ps 102.26; Isa 64.1; Hag 2.6, 21; Sib Or. 3.82; 8.233, 413; Mt 24.29; 2 Pet. 3.10; Rev 6.14). But the pertinent texts for comparison are those in which Jewish or Christian seers receiving revelation see heaven opened: Ezek 1.1; Jn 1.51; Acts 7.56; 10.11; Rev 11.19; 19.11; 2 Bar. 22.1; T. Abr. 7; Herm. v. 1.1.4; Apocryphon John 1 (cf. 3 Macc 6.18; Jos. Asen. 14.2). The reception of heavenly mysteries or divinely bestowed knowledge was often conceived of in terms of the heavenly world above drawing back its 'curtain' or 'garment' (cf. Job 14.12; Ps 104.2; Isa 40.22; b. Meṣ.59a) to allow a person in the earthly world below to see secrets. See Lentzen-Deis, 'Motiv' (v). (A distinction is to be drawn between this type of revelation and that in which heaven opens in order to allow the seer to journey into the upper regions, as in Rev 4.1; T. Levi 2.6; 5.1.)[69] In the present pericope, the heavens open not only to signal the forthcoming of revelation but also to make it possible for the Spirit to descend. (The text may presuppose the mythopoeic cosmology common to the ancient near east: the sky is a solid firmament beyond which is the highest heaven, and beyond that is the abode of the gods or God.)

The opening of the heavens at the baptism of Jesus is a prominent feature of both T. Levi 18 and T. Jud. 24 (both must be Christian in their present form).[70] Justin interestingly enough omits mention of it in his

[68] So Harnack, p. 254; Streeter, p. 188; Flemington (v), p. 26, n. 1; Schürmann, *Lukasevangelium*, 1, p. 197; Luz 1, pp. 150–1; against Fitzmyer, *Luke* 1, p. 479.

[69] Cf. Rowland, pp. 52–8. On the splitting of (the) heaven(s) see further W. C. van Unnik, 'Die"geöffneten Himmel" in der Offenbarungsvision des Apokryphons Johannes', in *Apophoreta*, ed. W. Eltester, Berlin, 1964, pp. 269–80, and Lentzen-Deis, 'Motiv' (v). The former draws attention to the non-Jewish parallels in Ovid, *Fast.* 3.370ff.; Virgil, *Aen.* 9.20; Cicero, *Div.* 1.43.97.

[70] So M. de Jonge, 'Christian Influence on the Testaments of the Twelve Patriarchs', *NovT* 4 (1960), pp. 99–117, and M. A. Chevallier, *L'Esprit et le Messie*

otherwise full account (*Dial.* 88). He does, however, recount how a fire was kindled in the Jordan. This fire or light also appears in the Old Latin mss. a and g¹ at Mt 3.15 as well as in the Gospel according to the Ebionites (Epiphanius, *Haer.* 30.13), Tatian's *Diatessaron*, the Preaching of Paul (so Ps.-Cyprian, *Tractatus de rebaptismate*); Sib. Or. 7.82–5; and the Syriac liturgy of Severus. Perhaps in these places we are to think of the Shekinah, or maybe the fire makes Jesus experience the baptism of the coming one ('Holy Spirit' and 'fire'), or possibly the baptism and the transfiguration scenes are being brought even closer together, or just perchance we should recall the rabbinic texts which conceive of the Holy Spirit as a light or fire (e.g. *b. Mak.* 23a; see Davies, *PRJ*, p. 187). There might also be influence from Ezek 1.4 ('a stormy wind came out of the north, and a great cloud, with brightness round about it, and fire flashing forth continually'); for this follows a vision which is seen by one standing by a river and is accompanied by the heavens opening (1.1). For further texts and discussion see W. Bauer, *Das Leben Jesu im Zeitalter der neutestamentlichen Apokryphen*, reprint ed., Darmstadt, 1967, pp. 134–9.

καὶ εἶδεν τὸ πνεῦμα τοῦ θεοῦ καταβαῖνον ὡσεὶ περιστεράν.[71] Matthew has displaced εἶδεν so that it now comes after the opening of the heavens. This makes the event more public because the occurrence in the sky is no longer qualified by 'he saw' but instead narrated as a straightforward fact: 'and behold! the heavens opened . . .'. Similarly, the alteration in 3.17 of Mark's 'You are my Son' to 'This is my Son' serves the same purpose: the voice is not speaking to Jesus alone. Seemingly, therefore, and despite the singular form of the verb, εἶδεν, at least two people, Jesus and John, are privy to the events recounted (cf. Philoxenus, *Comm. on Mt.* folio 4, where John too sees the dove). (The question of whether *only* two witnesses are involved—so Kingsbury, *Structure*, p. 14—is probably moot; nevertheless, that there is no remark on the amazement or awe of others present is noteworthy.) Mark's account, by way of contrast, is readily understood as relating the experience of one individual, a θεωρία νοητή (Origen, *Comm. in Jn.* on 1.31; cf. *C. Cels.* 2.71). In Jn 1.29–34 it is evidently John alone who sees the Spirit rest upon Jesus. In Luke matters are ambiguous. While the opening of the heavens is recounted as an objective event, and while 'in bodily form' has been added, the voice is addressed to Jesus alone ('You are my Son . . .'; cf. Acts 22.9?).

Matthew makes three other changes in his Markan source. (1) He adds τοῦ θεοῦ in order to qualify Mark's oddly unqualified

---

dans le Bas-Judaïsme et le Nouveau Testament, Paris, 1958, pp. 125–30; against A. Hultgard, 'The Ideal "Levite", the Davidic Messiah and the Saviour Priest in the Testaments of the Twelve Patriarchs', in *Ideal Figures in Ancient Judaism*, SBLSCS 12, ed. J. J. Collins and G. W. E. Nickelsburg, Chico, 1980, pp. 93–110.

[71] το and του are omitted by ℵ B (which makes for a closer parallel with Gen. 1.2).

and un-Semitic τὸ πνεῦμα (although note 1QS 4.6). For the Spirit as God's Spirit in Matthew see also 10.20; 12.18, 28, none of which has a precise synoptic parallel. Note also Isa 42.1; Gen 1.2. (2) Matthew reverses the order of 'like a dove' and 'descending' (cf. Lk 3.22; Jn 1.32). The effect of this is to allow the addition of another participle, ἐρχόμενον (see below). (3) Mark's ὡς becomes ὡσεί as in Mt 9.36 = Mk 6.34. Note also the insertion of ὡσεί in 14.21 = Mk 6.44. The same alteration between ὡς and ὡσεί frequently occurs in the LXX and NT ms. traditions (see e.g. the variants for Gen 31.2; Exod 16.31; Lk 1.56; Jn 1.32; 19.14). D Iren Eus have ὡς in our present verse. It is difficult to discern any difference in meaning (cf. 9.36 with 10.16). See Davies, *JPS*, p. 378, n 60.

It is not coincidence that ὡς occurs most often in the NT in Revelation (about 70 times). The frequency of the particle reflects the visionary character and symbolic content of apocalyptic literature (cf. Ezek 1.4, 5, 7, 13, 16, 22, 24, 26–8; Dan 7.13). For word-plays between καταβαίνω and ἀναβαίνω see Gen 24.16; 28.12; Jn 1.51; 3.13; Rom 10.6–7; Eph 4.9–10 (and note Daube, pp. 111–12). For the association of water with the giving of the Spirit see Ezek 36.25–6; 1QS 4.21; Jn 3.5; 7.37–9; *Mek.* on Exod. 14.12 and on 15.1 (in these last the subject is the exodus from Egypt).

What are we to make of the dove? Various suggestions have been made.[72]

(1) Some nineteenth century rationalists argued that a thunderstorm broke when Jesus was being baptized and that a dove, frightened by lightning, fluttered around the Messiah's head (e.g. K. H. Venturini according to Schweitzer, p. 45; cf. J. H. Bernard, *A Critical and Exegetical Commentary on the Gospel According to St. John*, Edinburgh, 1929, 1, p. 49). Although history does present strange occurrences, comment on such flights of fancy is happily no longer necessary.

(2) The dove symbolizes wisdom in Philo (*Rer. div. her.* 126–7; cf. *Mut. nom.* 248). This observation, however, does not help because other wisdom motifs are absent from the baptismal story.

(3) The Gospel according to the Hebrews, according to Jerome, *Comm. on Isa.* on 11.2, has the Spirit without the dove (cf. Jn 1.32 sy^s) and Odes Sol. 24 has the dove without the Spirit. This circumstance, according to S. Gero (v), shows that Spirit and dove were originally two separate motifs which Mark conflated. (The dove originally symbolized Jesus as Messiah.) Such an argument is, to say the least, rather speculative given the presumed priority of Mark over both of the sources Gero cites; and Odes Sol. 28.1 presupposes the Spirit as dove tradition ('As the wings of

---

[72] Reviews of the discussion may be found in Telfer (v); Seethaler (v); Keck (v); and Gero (v). On dove symbolism in Judaism see, in addition to what follows, Goodenough 8, pp. 41–6.

doves over their nestlings . . . so also are the wings of the Spirit over my heart').

(4) Noah's dove (Gen 8.8–12) could be recalled, indicating that the time of judgement is past, that the kingdom of God has come (cf. Dunn, *Baptism* (v), p. 27, n. 13). This is particularly plausible as John's baptism in part symbolized the eschatological flood and as the deliverance of Noah was compared with baptism (1 Pet 3.20–1). On the other hand, prior to Tertullian (*Bapt.* 8) and even later in the east Noah's dove and the dove at the Jordan were not thought of together (not even in Justin, *Dial.* 138, where Noah is a type of Christ).

(5) According to P. Garnet (v), the dove belongs to Son of Man imagery because Noah was associated with Son of Man ideas. His argument is too circuitous to carry conviction. For instance, Enoch's having been thought of as the Son of Man says nothing about Noah even though Enoch and Noah were closely associated.

(6) In Genesis Noah's dove has an olive branch in its mouth, and the branch was a messianic cipher (see on 2.23). So the dove at the baptism could signal Jesus' messiahship (cf. Apoc. Elijah 3.2–4). Yet the gospels do not tell us that the dove had a branch in its mouth, and the argument made against (4) applies here too.

(7) The *bat qôl* is said in rabbinic sources to be like the cooing of a dove (*b. Ber.* 3a); and in Tg. Cant. on 2.12, 'the voice of the turtle dove' becomes 'the voice of the Spirit of salvation'. This interests because in the gospels the dove precedes a heavenly voice. Yet the relevant rabbinic sources are of rather late date, and in the gospels the Spirit and the voice are two different motifs.

(8) A frequent motif in fairy tales is the choice of a king by a bird that selects the one from the many. Bultmann, *History*, pp. 248–9, dismissed the pertinence of this because, in his view, the choice of Jesus as messianic king was never a question for the early church. (But what of Jesus?) For the same reason Bultmann also set aside as relevant background the choice by the dove-goddess (Ishtar in Babylon or Atargatis in Syria) of her son or lover. Yet notice should be taken of Prot. Jas. 9.1: 'Joseph received the last rod and behold! a dove came out of the rod and flew on to Joseph's head. And the priest said to Joseph, "Joseph, to you has fallen the good fortune to receive the virgin of the Lord . . ." ' Here is a second century text in which a dove makes the divine selection, and as this passage must be suspected of being influenced by the story of the baptism, it could presuppose a similar understanding of the dove of the gospel tradition (cf. also Eusebius, *H.E.* 6.29). Further, εὐδοκέω is the language of election[73] and this nicely fits the theme of choice.

(9) Bultmann himself (*History*, p. 250) affirmed that Persian mythology supplies the answer: the divine power which fills the king is symbolized by a bird. This takes one too far afield. As we shall see, a background in Judaism lies near to hand.

(10) Attempts have been made to achieve clarity by postulating an early scribal error, perhaps confusion between *yônâ* (dove) and *yānûaḥ* (rest; cf. Isa 11.2). Such 'solutions' only skirt the issue; and in John's account both a dove and a motif of rest are present (1.32).

---

[73] See G. Münderlein, 'Die Erwählung durch das Pleroma', *NTS* 8 (1962), p. 266.

(11) Israel is a dove in Hos 7.11; LAB 21.6; 39.6; and Tg. Ps. 68.14 (additional texts in SB 1, pp. 123–4), and one might think Jesus' emergence from the waters to be the emergence of renewed Israel (cf. T. A. Burkill, *Mysterious Revelation*, Ithaca, New York, 1963, pp. 17–19; cf. Lentzen-Deis, *Taufe* (v), pp. 265–70). Favouring this thesis are passages in the *Mekilta*. In *Mek.* on Exod 14.13, the Holy Spirit rests upon Israel as she crosses the Red Sea, Israel is compared to a dove, and Israel is granted a heavenly vision (cf. Davies, *SSM*, pp. 40–4). In addition, *Mek.* on Exod 15.2 has the Holy Spirit call from heaven when the Red Sea is crossed. So here are almost all the elements of Mk 1.9–11 and its parallels. Moreover, the proposed interpretation gains credence because Matthew associates 'son' with 'Israel' (see on 2.15), and 'son' occurs in the next verse. Still, it must be remarked that it is the Spirit, not Jesus the Son, with which the dove is identified in the gospels.

(12) In LAB 23.7 prophets are likened to turtle-doves, so one might see in Mt 3.16 a return of the Spirit of prophecy. But the simile in LAB 23.7 is, as far as we have been able to determine, without parallel.

(13) In *b. Ḥag.* 15a the hovering or brooding of the Spirit of God over the face of the waters (Gen 1.2) is represented as the fluttering of a dove. (In other versions of this tradition other birds are named; see Rowland, pp. 323–31). This has led to the suggestion that ὡσ(εὶ) περιστεράν was originally adverbial: it referred not to the Spirit's form but to its manner of descent; see Keck (v); Jeremias, *Theology* 1, p. 52; Rowland, p. 361. (Lk 22.43–4 may be compared: 'his sweat as [ὡσεί] drops of blood falling on the ground'. The phrase, 'as drops of blood', should probably be taken with the verb, not with 'sweat'.) On this reading the dove of Mt 3.16 almost certainly recalls Gen 1.2; for there it is said that the Spirit of God 'hovered' (like a bird; cf. Deut 32.11) over the face of the waters, and meditation upon Gen 1.2 lies in the background of *b. Ḥag.* 15a. Compare Odes Sol. 24.1, where, if the Syriac *prḥt* be pointed in the pael,[74] we read that 'the dove *fluttered* over the head of our Lord Messiah'. Yet, having said all this, it seems more natural to regard 'as a dove' as adjectival, this because 'he saw the Spirit' almost requires some stated concretion for the Spirit (which would otherwise remain a blank; cf. Richter (v)). Certainly our earliest interpreters understood things thus: Lk 3.21 ('bodily as a dove'); Justin, *Dial.* 88; Gosp. Eb. frag. 4.

(14) According to M. Smith, *Magician*, pp. 96–100, the baptism should be understood as a magical ritual whereby Jesus sought to gain for himself the power of a spirit. Smith can, admittedly, find texts in the magical papyri that associate birds with spirits (*PGM* 1.54ff.; cf. 4.154–221) and in which the Holy Spirit, sonship, and deification are brought together (*PGM* 4.154–221). But he cites no initiation text in which doves appear.

(15) For representing the coming of the Spirit from heaven only a bird would be appropriate; and given that a particular bird is to be specified, only the dove could be considered in view of the fulness of its positive associations in the OT and in the ancient world in general. Thus no particular symbolic meaning is to be attached to the dove. This is the

---

[74] So J. H. Charlesworth, *The Odes of Solomon*, SBLTT 1, PS 7, Missoula, 1977, pp. 98–9.

position adopted by Pesch (1, pp. 91–2; cf. H. Greeven, *TWNT* 6, p. 68); and given the lack of a consensus upon the issue under review, it is inviting. We nonetheless cannot accept it because of the evidence which favours the final option to be considered.

(16) Even though ὡσ(εί) probably does not introduce an adverbial phrase, Gen 1.2 remains the most obvious text offering elucidation of the dove (cf. Abrahams 1, pp. 49–50; Taylor, *Mark*, p. 161; Barrett, *Spirit*, pp. 38–9; Cranfield, *Mark*, p. 54). 'The Spirit of God was hovering over the face of the waters'. We have here three elements which reappear in the baptism story: the Spirit of God, water (the LXX has τοῦ ὕδατος), and the image of a bird. Concerning this last, and as noted already, it remains suggestive that the hovering of the Spirit is likened to the hovering of a dove in *b. Ḥag.* 15a. (See also Tg. Cant. 2.12 for the equation of Spirit and dove.) Moreover, we may observe that the theme of Jesus as bringer of the new creation was at home in the early church (see on 1.1) and could be no more appropriately located than at the baptism, the beginning of the ministry (cf. Justin, *1 Apol.* 61.1). In addition, the Fathers tended to think of Gen 1 when writing about the baptism of Jesus or Christians (see e.g. Tertullian, *De bapt.* 1–4; Theodotus, *Excerpta* 7; Cyril of Jerusalem in PG 33.433A; Didymus the Blind in PG 39.692C). We are, accordingly, encouraged to conclude that the Spirit as dove originally meant— and meant also for Matthew—that the events of Gen 1 were being recapitulated or repeated in the Messiah's life: the eschatological creation had commenced. (In Tg. Ps.-J. on Gen 1.2 the Spirit of God is the Spirit of the Messiah. Cf. *Gen. Rab.* on 1.2.) (Exodus and creation motifs often conjoin, see above p. 153, below p. 344.)

ἐρχόμενον ἐπ' αὐτόν.[75] Compare 3.7; Acts 1.8. This replaces Mark's much harsher εἰς αὐτόν (cf. Gosp. Eb. frag. 4; Mt 3.16 D Eus Iren; Lk 3.22 D Eus vg), perhaps because Mk 1.10 just might be taken to imply that hitherto the Spirit had not dwelt within Jesus (Gosp. Eb. frag. 4: εἰσελθούσης εἰς αὐτόν), or maybe because in the OT ἐπί is typically used when the coming of the Spirit is being recounted (Judg 11.29; 14.6, 19; 15.14; 1 Sam 10.6, 10; 11.6; Isa 11.2; 32.15 (with ἐπέρχομαι); 44.3; 61.1). There could also be influence from Isa 42.1 (quoted in Mt 12.18): ἔδωκα τὸ πνεῦμά μου ἐπ' αὐτόν. The coincidental use by both Matthew and Luke of ἐπί (so also John) is probably just that, coincidental: both have independently corrected Mark.

The significance of the vision of the Spirit is found in this phrase: the Spirit comes upon Jesus. This cannot, of course, mean any sort

[75] NA,[26] following ℵ² C D L W 0233 *f*^1.13 Maj f l vg^cl sy, print και (in brackets) before ερχομενον. ℵ* B lat bo Ir Hil Aug omit (so also HG). A firm decision seems impossible.

of adoption, for already at his birth Jesus was of the Holy Spirit
(1.18–25). It does, however, serve to reveal or confirm Jesus'
already existing status and worthiness[76] as the eschatological
bearer of God's Spirit and therefore as the servant of the Lord (cf.
12.18). It also marks a turning point in salvation-history, for only
after the Spirit comes does the Messiah's ministry begin (cf. Acts
10.38); and it sets Jesus in line with certain national leaders of the
OT—Gideon (Judg 6.34), Samson (15.14), Saul (1 Sam 10.6)—
upon whom the Spirit came and with the prophets. So at the
Jordan the messianic office is taken up. The promises made
concerning the Messiah and the Spirit have begun to be realized
(cf. Isa 11.2; Joel 2.28–9; 4QpIsaᵃ col. 3; Ps. Sol. 17.37; 18.7; 1 En.
49.3; 62.2; T. Levi 18; T. Jud. 24). The quenched Spirit has
returned.[77]

17. Here the Lord 'declares to man what is his thought' (Amos
4.13); and a second witness, a heavenly voice, adds its testimony to
that of the Spirit (cf. Rev 14.13).

καὶ ἰδού. Matthew again adds ἰδού (see on 1.20). What follows is
the culmination and highlight of 3.1–17. For 'behold' with a
heavenly voice see 1 Kgs 19.13; Mt 17.5; Rev 4.1; 1 En. 13.8;
4 Ezra 14.38; 2 Bar. 13.1; Par. Jer. 9.12.

φωνὴ ἐκ τῶν οὐρανῶν. So Mark, with the textually doubtful
ἐγένετο after 'voice'. It is natural to link the voice from the heavens
with the rabbinic bat qôl[78] ('daughter of a voice') because this
vehicle of revelation sometimes quoted Scripture (e.g. b. Soṭa 21a;
b. Sanh. 104b), often came to declare God's favourable estimation
of a righteous individual or to settle disputes (e.g. t. Soṭa 13.3–4; b.
Soṭa 48b; b. Sanh. 11a; b. B. Meṣ. 59b; b. Taʿan. 24b), was often
spoken of as being from the heavens (e.g. b. Ḥag. 14b; b. Sanh.
11a;—but note also Deut 4.36; Dan 4.31), and could be thought of
as the voice of God himself (e.g. b. Meg. 3a; b. Sanh. 94a). Caution
is nevertheless required. The distance between the rabbis and the
evangelists can be seen in this, that while for the former—perhaps
in response to Christianity?[79]—the bat qôl is generally an inferior
substitute for the Holy Spirit (t. Soṭa 13.2; b. Yoma 9b), for the
latter the voice accompanies a new coming of God's Spirit, and it is

[76] Hillel the Elder was said to have been worthy to receive the Holy Spirit, but his
generation was not; see t. Soṭa 13.3; b. Soṭa 48b; discussion in Davies, PRJ,
pp. 207, 209.
[77] On the Spirit as an eschatological hope in Judaism see Davies, PRJ,
pp. 177–226; Jeremias, Theology, 1, pp. 80–2; J. S. Vos, Traditionsgeschichtliche
Untersuchungen zur paulinischen Pneumatologie, Assen, 1973, pp. 46–64; and W.
Bieder and E. Sjöberg, TWNT 6, s.v. πνεῦμα.
[78] On this see S. Lieberman, Hellenism in Jewish Palestine, New York, 1950,
pp. 193–9, and O. Betz, TWNT 9, pp. 281–3; also SB 1, pp. 125–34.
[79] So A. Guttmann, 'The Significance of Miracles for Talmudic Judaism', HUCA
20 (1947), pp. 363–406.

no 'echo': in the gospels God speaks directly, without intermediary, to his Son. Hence specifically rabbinic conceptions of the *bat qôl* offer as much of a contrast as a comparison with regard to Mt 3.16, and we cannot claim that the voice at the Jordan is just the Christian equivalent of the rabbinic 'daughter of a voice'. We must instead be content with observing the frequency with which heavenly voices occur not only in rabbinic literature but also in the OT and in early Christian and non-rabbinic Jewish texts; see Gen 21.17; 22.11, 15; Exod 19.19; Deut 4.10–12; 1 Kgs 19.13; Dan 4.31; 1 En. 65.4; Jn 12.28; Acts 9.4; 10.13–15; 11.7–9; 2 Pet 1.18; Rev 1.10; 4.1; 10.4 (φωνὴν ἐκ τοῦ οὐρανοῦ λέγουσαν); 11.12; 14.13; Josephus, *Ant.* 13.283; *Bell.* 6.300; 2 Bar. 13.1; 22.1; LAB 53.3–5; T. Abr. 10.12; 14.13 (φωνὴ ἐκ τοῦ οὐρανοῦ λέγουσα); Par. Jer. 9.12 (καὶ ἰδοὺ φωνὴ ἦλθε λέγουσα); Gk. Apoc. Ezra 6.3; 7.13; Act of Peter BG 136.17–137.1; Ep. Pet. Phil. 8.134.13–14. The Apophthegmata Patrum (in PG 65) is filled with heavenly voices speaking to hermits and monks.

Of interest for comparison with our text is *b. Ta'an* 24b: R. Judah reported Rab as saying, 'Every day a *bat qôl* issued forth from Mt. Horeb and proclaimed, "The whole world is sustained on account of Ḥanina my son; but Ḥanina my son is satisfied with one kab of carob from one Sabbath eve to another" ' (cf. *b. Ber.* 17b; *b. Ḥul.* 86a).

λέγουσα.[80] The voice itself (personified? cf. Rev 1.12; Ladder of Jacob 3; Apoc. Abr. 9) speaks (cf. Ezek 43.6; Rev 4.1; 10.8). λέγουσα replaces Mark's ἐγένετο (cf. Acts 7.31; Rev 11.15, 19), if that is original. Compare the addition to 17.5 = Mk 9.7. Matthew is particularly fond of λέγω in its participial form meaning 'saying' (Mt 118; Mk 36; Lk 94). *'mr* often follows *bat qôl* in rabbinic sources (e.g. *b. B. Meṣ.* 59b; *b. Sanh.* 94a; *b. B. Bat.* 74b; *b. 'Erub.* 13b).

The quotation—or is it more properly an allusion?—here introduced from Mark is widely thought to be a conflation of Isa 42.1 and Ps 2.7. Some, however, would deny any allusion to Isa 42.1,[81] others any allusion to Ps 2.7.[82] Here are the texts:

Ps 2.7 LXX

υἱός μου εἶ σύ
ἐγὼ σήμερον
γεγέννηκά σε

---

[80] πρὸς αυτον is added after λεγουσα in D a b g¹ h sy^{s.c}? Cf. the addition to 3.16.
[81] So Vielhauer, pp. 205–6, and Gnilka, *Markus* 1, p. 53.
[82] So Fuller, *Mission*, pp. 86–9; Cranfield, *Mark*, p. 55; Pesch 1, p. 92.

Mk 1.11

σὺ εἶ ὁ υἱός μου
ὁ ἀγαπητός
ἐν σοὶ εὐδόκησα

Isa 42.1 LXX

Ἰακωβ ὁ παῖς μου
ἀντιλήμψομαι αὐτοῦ
Ἰσραηλ ὁ ἐκλεκτός μου
προσεδέξατο αὐτὸν
ἡ ψυχή μου

Mt 3.17

οὗτός ἐστιν ὁ υἱός μου
ὁ ἀγαπητός
ἐν ᾧ εὐδόκησα

Isa 42.1 in Mt 12.18

ἰδοὺ ὁ παῖς μου
ὃν ᾑρέτισα
ὁ ἀγαπητός μου
εἰς ὃν εὐδόκησεν
ἡ ψυχή μου

Isa 42.1 MT

hēn 'abdî
'etmāk-bô
bĕḥîrî
rāṣĕtâ
napšî

Firstly, we observe the lack of any link between Isa 42.1 LXX and the voice at the baptism. Secondly, the text closest to Mark's first line is Ps 2.7 LXX: the differences are minor, primarily a change in word order which stresses that it is Jesus who is the Son. Furthermore, while there are no additional similarities between Mk 1.11 and Ps 2.7,[83] a number of early references to the baptism cite Ps 2.7 more or less fully (e.g. Lk 3.22 D; Justin, *Dial.* 88; 103; Clement of Alexandria, *Paed.* 1.6.25; Apost. Const. 2.32; Gosp. Eb. frag. 4). Thirdly, Mark's ὁ ἀγαπητός has—if we leave aside for the moment suggestions of influence from Gen 22.2, 12, 16 and Exod 4.22–3—its only parallel in Isa 42.1 as this is quoted in full in Mt 12.18. Now the ὁ ἀγαπητός of 12.18 could be put down to influence from the story of the baptism (cf. Gundry, *OT*, p. 112). It must be conceded, however, that it is a possible translation of *bāḥîr*, especially as 'beloved' (*'itre'ê*) appears in the targum on Isa 42.1 and as 'beloved' is elsewhere attested as an epithet of the servant (cf. Isa 44.2 LXX; Mart. Poly. 14; Ep. Diog. 8.9–11). Fourthly, ἐν σοὶ (ᾧ) εὐδόκησα, which has no counterpart in Ps 2.7 or Isa 42.1 LXX, evidently represents an independent translation of the Hebrew of Isa 42.1. In fact, both Theodotion and Symmachus so translate (cf. Mt 12.18). Fifthly, the parallels between Mt 3.17 and 12.18 all but prove that the First Evangelist

[83] Although in the Aramaic targum to Ps 2.7 we find *ḥābîb*, the equivalent of ἀγαπητός. But this may represent a Jewish response to Christian claims; see E. Lohse, *TWNT* 8, p. 363.

heard Isa 42.1 in the voice at the Jordan, and the same is shown to be probably true for Luke by his insertion of ἐκλελεγμένος in the parallel 9.35: this probably comes from Isa 42.1.

The most natural explanation of the five facts cited would seem to be that of common opinion: the first line of our text is from or has been influenced by Ps 2.7 (LXX?) while the next two lines are derived from a non-LXX version of Isa 42.1. How then is this circumstance to be explained? To begin with, the most primitive reading in Jn 1.34 appears to be ὁ ἐκλεκτός, which recalls Isa 42.1 LXX (so Brown, *John* 1, p. 57; Schnackenburg, *John* 1, pp. 305–6). Thus, the independent[84] version of the baptism in John seemingly contains as its theme Jesus as *'ebed Yahweh*. Ps 2.7 plays no rôle. Next, the context of Mk 1.11—the descent of the Spirit—reproduces a motif found in Isa 42 ('I have put my Spirit upon him', v. 1). Provided, then, that the heavenly voice refers to the fulfilment of Scripture, Isa 42.1, not Ps 2.7 (where no Spirit is found), must be in mind. Lastly, Ps 2.7 was originally applied in early Christianity to the resurrection of Jesus (cf. Acts 13.33; Heb 1.5; 5.5).[85] This is important because if, as we shall argue, the story of the baptism rests upon primitive tradition, and if the voice is an integral part of that story—and it is hard to imagine otherwise—, it is highly unlikely that Ps 2 would have been quoted. It follows that the allusion to Ps 2.7 is secondary.[86] When was it added? Some have conjectured that υἱός has displaced an original παῖς (= *'ebed*). Because παῖς is ambiguous ('servant' or 'son'), and because Hellenistic Christianity avoided the title, παῖς θεοῦ, the substitution would be natural.[87] But this introduction of a hypothetical Greek stage with παῖς fails to explain the precise form of the first line of Mk 1.11. σὺ εἶ is not from Isa 42.1. It does, however, recall Ps 2.7. So it seems best to suppose that the entire first line has been taken over from Ps 2.7 (with contextual modification) and that the voice at the baptism is a conflation of texts. In other words, at some time in the history of the tradition, a quotation of Isa 42.1 was altered in order to gain an allusion to Ps 2.7 (cf. Lindars, *Apologetic*, pp. 139–40). (In accordance with our conclusion concerning the anteriority of the reference to Isa 42.1,

[84] See Dodd, *Tradition*, pp. 259–61; Brown, *John*, 1, pp. 65–6.

[85] See Lindars, *Apologetic*, pp. 140–3, and E. Lövestam, *Son and Saviour*, CN 18, Lund, 1961, pp. 15–37. (Against Lindars, pp. 144–52, there is no good reason for supposing that Isa 42.1 was originally applied to the resurrection.)

[86] So also, among others, Bousset, p. 97, n. 70; Cullmann, *Christology*, pp. 66–7; Jeremias, *TWNT* 5, pp. 699–70; and Hahn, *Hoheitstitel*, pp. 281–2, 340–2. For a different view see Marshall (v).

[87] The παῖς in Lk 7.7 is the same as the υἱός of Jn 4.47. Note also the closeness of the two words in Wisd 2.13 and 18. On the use of παῖς in post-NT texts see A. von Harnack, 'Die Bezeichnung Jesu als "Knecht Gottes" und ihre Geschichte in der alten Kirche', *SPAW* 28 (1926), pp. 212–8.

the targum to Isaiah several times uses 'I am well pleased' in connexion with the servant (41.8–9 (here in a direct, solemn address); 43.10, 20; 44.1–2); and in 43.10 it identifies the servant and the Messiah; cf. Chilton, *Rabbi*, pp. 129–30.)

Whatever one concludes about the tradition history of Mk 1.11, we may be confident that Matthew saw in Mt 3.17 a confirmation of the truth of Jesus' divine sonship as proclaimed in Ps 2 and the truth of his being the Spirit-endowed servant of Deutero-Isaiah. (Elsewhere Isa 42.1–4 is fully quoted (12.18–20).)

Ps 2 may have been interpreted in a messianic sense in pre-Christian Judaism, but this is far from certain.[88] Isa 42.1ff., on the other hand, probably did receive a messianic reading, at least in some circles, although this too is not guaranteed and has in fact been vigorously debated.[89]

οὗτός ἐστιν.[90] Compare Jn 1.34 and Mk 9.7 par. This answers to Mark's σὺ εἶ. The replacement of a personal address (cf. Ps 109.4 LXX; 1 En. 71.14) by a formula of identification[91] makes the event more public (cf. on 3.16) and permits assimilation to 17.5 = Mk 9.7. οὗτός ἐστιν appears more often in Matthew than in either Mark or Luke (Mt:18; Mk:6; Lk:11).

ὁ υἱός μου. So Mark. The declaration of sonship does not reveal new truth to the readers. It only confirms and emphasizes with the voice of God himself the fact already expressed in 1.18–25 and 2.15. On the other hand, it may be significant that it is God himself who first openly proclaims by revelation (cf. 16.16–17) Jesus as 'the Son of God'. This could explain the absence of 'Son of God' from 1.1, the gospel's title (so R. Pesch, 'Der Gottessohn im matthäischen Evangelienprolog (Mt 1–2)', *Bib* 48 (1967), p. 416).

For Matthew, 'Son (of God)' is a key christological title, occurring in such consequential passages as 3.17; 11.27; 16.16; 17.5; 26.63; and 28.19. This is not to say, as Kingsbury has said, that all the other christological titles are to be subsumed under this one. Rather is it closer to the truth to say that the other major appellations—Messiah, Son of David, Son of Man, Servant, Lord—and their attendant themes, taken along with the story in 1.18–23 and Jesus' words and deeds, give content to 'Son of God'.

[88] See Fitzmyer, *Aramean*, pp. 105–7. For the rabbinic evidence see SB 3, pp. 675–7. For Ps 2 in early Christian testimonia see Dodd, *Scriptures*, pp. 31–2, 104–5.

[89] For a positive evaluation of the evidence see Jeremias, *TWNT* 5, pp. 685–98. For the other side see M. Hooker, *Jesus and the Servant*, London, 1959, pp. 53–61. See further on 8.17.

[90] συ ει appears in D a sy[s.c] Ir under the influence of Mk 1.11 and Ps 2.7 LXX. Given the deliberate parallelism between 3.17 and 17.5, 'this is', which occurs in 17.5, is probably original there. Cf. Allen, p. 30.

[91] Cf. K. Berger, 'Die königlichen Messiastraditionen des NT', *NTS* 20 (1973), p. 28, n. 108.

The title also receives meaning from the Jesus/Israel typology found in chapter 1–5. And that is not all. It would be a mistake—one which Kingsbury has made—to restrict our eyes to Matthew's gospel. 'Son of God' was a very pregnant title with various associations in Judaism and in the ancient world in general.[92] Should we not think that to some extent all of these associations, in so far as they were known to Matthew and thought of by him in a positive fashion, were considered by the evangelist to have been fulfilled or brought to perfection in the person of Jesus?

Mt 3.16–17, which was interpreted by later Christian theology as depicting the supreme manifestation of the Trinity, is only one of several NT baptismal texts in which the Father, Son, and Holy Spirit are present; see Mt 28.16–20; Jn 1.33–4; Acts 2.38–9; 10.38; 1 Cor 6.11; Tit 3.4–6; 1 Pet 1.2 (this last heading what may well have been originally a sermon to the newly baptized). Why the NT should contain so many triadic baptismal texts is far from obvious. But the ultimate cause could be the story of Jesus' baptism by John, in which God the Father speaks to his Son and the Holy Spirit comes upon him.

ὁ ἀγαπητός. So Mark, against Luke. Compare Mk 9.7; 12.6; Eph 1.6 D*; Col 1.13; 2 Pet 1.17; Barn. 3.6; 4.3, 8. This is probably an adjective, not a second title,[93] although in 12.18 'my beloved' stands on its own. Half of the time in the LXX the word translates yāḥîd, 'only' (e.g. Gen 22.2, 12; Judg 11.34; Jer 6.26) and is thus equivalent to μονογενής (cf. Philo, Ebr. 30; see Turner (v), Souter (v)). This is probably not its meaning here (cf. 1 Cor 4.17; 2 Tim 1.2; Philem 1, 16; 2 Pet 3.15; 3 Jn 1; Herm. s. 5.2.6). ἀγαπητός matches εὐδόκησα. Both are words of emotion. For 'beloved' in messianic contexts see Asc. Isa. 1.4; 3.13; etc.; T. Benj. 11. (Full discussion in J. A. Robinson, St. Paul's Epistle to the Ephesians, rev. ed., London, n.d., pp. 229–33.) For other significant uses see Jdt 9.4 (with 'sons'); 3 Macc 6.11 (cf. 6.28); Par. Jer. 7.24 (υἱέ μου

---

[92] Lit.: Dodd, Interpretation, pp. 250–62; Fitzmyer, Aramean, pp. 85–113; P. Pokorný, Der Gottessohn, Zürich, 1971; W. von Martiz, G. Fohrer, E. Lohse, E. Schweizer, and W. Schneemelcher, TWNT 8, pp. 334–402; G. Delling, 'Die Bezeichnung "Söhne Gottes" in der jüdischen Literatur der hellenischtisch-römischen Zeit', in God's Christ and His People, ed. J. Jervell and W. A. Meeks, Oslo, 1977, pp. 18–28; M. Vellanickal, The Divine Sonship of Christians in the Johannine Writings, An Bib 72, Rome, 1977, pp. 1–52; M. Smith, Magician, pp. 100–4; Vermes, Jew, pp. 192–213; M. Hengel, The Son of God, Philadelphia, 1976; W. Schlisske, Gottessöhne und Gottessohn im Alten Testament, Stuttgart, 1973; Dunn, Christology, pp. 12–64. 'Son of God' just may have been a messianic title in pre-Christian Judaism; cf. Cullmann, Christology, pp. 272–5, and S. Gero, ' "My Son the Messiah": A Note on 4 Esdr 7.28–9', ZNW 66 (1975), pp. 264–7. For doubts see Fitzmyer, Aramean, pp. 90–4, 102–7.

[93] See G. D. Kilpatrick, 'The Order of Some Noun and Adjective Phrases in the NT', NovT 5 (1962), pp. 112–13. sy^s and sy^c, however, have 'my Son and my beloved'. Compare 2 Pet 1.17.

ἀγαπητέ, Jeremiah's address to Baruch); *m.* '*Abot* 3.15 ('Beloved are Israel in that they are sons of God'); Gk. Apoc. Ezra 5.12; 6.3, 16; 7.1, 13 (in 6.3 and 7.13 Ezra is addressed by a voice from heaven as 'my beloved (one)'); 2 En. 24.2 (of Enoch); T. Isaac 2.7 ('your beloved son Jacob'; cf. 6.33); 6.23 ('my beloved ones, the saints'); T. Jacob 1.13 ('my beloved son', Jacob speaking of Joseph; cf. 4.3; 7.17). Some have found behind the gospels' 'beloved Son' an Isaac typology (cf. Gen 22.2, 12, 26; T. Abr. 4, 7, 15; so already T. Levi 18.6 and Irenaeus, *Adv. haer.* 4.5.4), others an Israel typology (cf. Exod 4.22–3), and Jer 38.20 LXX has even been cited as a key to our passage.[94] None of these suggestions can be excluded altogether. But 'beloved' and 'son(s)' were commonly tied together (*supra*),[95] and as Isaiah's servant was known as 'beloved' (*supra*), and as Isa 42.1 has certainly influenced our text, any allusion to Isaac or Israel or Jer 38.20 LXX could only be secondary at best.

ἐν ᾧ εὐδόκησα. Compare 17.5. Mark has σοι for ᾧ.[96] Mt 12.18 has εἰς ὃν εὐδόκησεν, Gosp. Eb. frag. 4 ἐφ' ὃν ηὐδόκησα. Jesus' relationship to God is right and therefore the Spirit rests upon him. For the sense of εὐδοκεῖν see 2 Sam 22.20;[97] Ps 44.3; 149.4; 151.5 LXX; Isa 62.4; Hab 2.4; Mal 2.17. The aorist, which renders a Hebrew stative perfect (Black, pp. 128–9), is only 'a vivid way of saying, "I am well pleased" ' (so Burton, p. 29).

According to Kingsbury, *Structure*, p. 50, εὐδόκησα does not apply to Jesus as the servant *per se*. Rather does it connote God's choice, referring to Jesus as the Son of God, that is, as the one in whom God brings his rule to mankind. It is difficult to register agreement. He cites 1.23; 4.17, 23; 9.35; 12.18; 24.14; 28.18b–20. But unless one is already prepared to grant Kingsbury's dubious claim that each of these verses is especially linked to a Son of God Christology (a good case can be made only for 1.23 and 28.18b–20), the texts prove nothing. Beyond this, one may doubt whether Son of God in Matthew designates Jesus as the one in whom God's eschatological rule draws near to his people. The only 'evidence' adduced for this claim is the doubtful equation of 'God with us' (1.23) with 'Son of

---

[94] For the Isaac typology see Best, *Temptation*, pp. 169–72; Vermes, *Tradition*, pp. 222–3; J. Daniélou, 'La typologie d'Isaac dans le Christianisme primitif', *Bib* 28 (1947), pp. 363–93; R. J. Daly, 'The Soteriological Significance of the Sacrifice of Isaac', *CBQ* 39 (1977), pp. 68–71. For Israel see Bretscher, 'Voice' (v) and Feuillet, 'La personnalité' (v). For Jer 38.20 LXX see E. Schweizer, *TWNT* 8, p. 355. Even the figures of Adam and Abraham have been thought to be recalled by 'My beloved Son'; see Lentzen-Deis, *Taufe* (v), pp. 228–43, who is followed by Pesch 1, p. 93. In T. Abr. 4, Isaac is called 'my beloved son' and the Holy Spirit is sent upon him.

[95] Note also Tob 3.10 S, where 'beloved' goes with 'daughter', as well as 1 Cor 4.14, 17; Eph 5.1; 2 Tim 1.2; 1 Jn 3.2.

[96] The influence of Matthew upon Mark's textual history can be seen in the variant reading ᾧ, which appears in the textual tradition of Mk 1.11.

[97] E. Schweizer, *TWNT* 8, pp. 369–70, who claims that this verse supplies the closest parallel to Mark's εὐδόκησα.

God'. Wrongly moved by a desire to make one christological title, Son of God, 'preeminent', Kingsbury has read into εὐδόκησα what is not there.

Perhaps at this juncture we should consider whether it is possible to go behind the accounts of the baptism and say something about an historical event in the life of Jesus. Some have doubted that anything more can be said than that John baptized Jesus (Bultmann, *History*, p. 247; cf. Strauss, p. 246). Some have doubted even that.[98] And even those who seek to reconstruct an historical event must confess to being on uncertain ground. The following points are to be made. (1) To judge from Lk 10.18,[99] Jesus, like Peter and Paul after him (cf. Acts 10.9–16; 2 Cor 12.1–10), had at least one visionary experience about which he spoke. (2) In Matthew Jesus' baptism is set forth as a public or semi-public event, and Luke's account hints at this. But in Mark, the earliest record, the experience at the Jordan can be interpreted as a private, visionary experience. Could this not reflect an originally first person account (cf. Rowland, p. 360)? (3) Despite repeated reiteration, nothing in our accounts demands a Hellenistic milieu (Keck (v); Pesch 1, p. 94). (4) In Mk 1.9–10 Jesus' baptism does not appear to be an etiological cult legend, the basis of the corresponding Christian rite. At least the details of the gospel story and its language do not much reflect baptismal practice. (5) If there were no good reason for so doing, we cannot easily see why early Christians made Jesus' baptism by John the beginning of the gospel and the moment of a decisive christological event. What was there in the simple fact of Jesus' baptism by John that would have led believers to create out of it the tale of an experience crucial for Jesus' mission?[100] (6) According to the unanimous testimony of the canonical gospels, Jesus' public ministry commenced soon after his meeting with John (cf. Acts 1.22; 10.38). If this is correct (and we have no reason to doubt it), and if Jesus, like other prophets before him, received a call or commissioning, are we not strongly impelled to place the event of that call or commissioning at the Jordan (cf. Fuller, *Christology*, p. 116; Jeremias, *Theology*, pp. 55–6; Goppelt, *Theology* 1, pp. 41–2)?

Assuming the answer to this last question to be in the affirmative,[101] we are still in no position to describe what Jesus experienced at his baptism. But we can indeed say something about Jesus' *interpretation* of his experience, whatever this last was. (As Flemington (v), p. 29, rightly remarks, if Jesus ever recounted the story of his baptism, he must have told what it meant to him.) First, Jesus will have thought of himself as

---

[98] E.g. Enslin (v) and Haenchen, pp. 58–63. The latter, from the different theological conceptions of Jesus and John, infers that the two could not have been closely associated. But Haenchen exaggerates the distance between the Baptist and Jesus; and in any case why could Jesus not have accepted John's baptism and then gone on to preach his own distinctive message?

[99] On Lk 10.18 see U. B. Müller, 'Vision und Botschaft', *ZTK* 74 (1977), pp. 416–48.

[100] Cf. Kümmel, *Theology*, p. 74. According to Vögtle (v), Christians manufactured the story in order to exalt Jesus over John. But only in John—where the baptism is not recounted!—can we find clear polemic against the Baptist or his followers.

[101] See further the discussions of Dunn, *Spirit*, pp. 62–5; Hill, *Prophecy*, pp. 48–50; and Feuillet, 'Vocation' (v).

becoming especially endowed with God's Spirit and will have grasped this
conviction within eschatological categories: the new creation has begun.
Then, secondly, as early as his baptism Jesus will have associated his work
of restoration with the prophecies of Deutero-Isaiah. The first proposal is
consistent with Jesus' exalted self-consciousness (note Mt 12.28 = Lk
11.20 and Mt 11.2–6 = Lk 7.18–23), with his belief that the Spirit of God
was specially at work in him (see Mt 12.28; Mk 3.28–9 parr.; Lk 4.18–19),
and with his teaching that eschatology was in the process of realization
(note Mk 2.19; 3.27; Mt 12.28 = Lk 11.20; Mt 12.41–2 = Lk 11.31–2; Lk
10.18; 17.21). The second is consistent with W. Grimm's recent
demonstration that Jesus interpreted his ministry in terms drawn from
Deutero-Isaiah,[102] and it fits nicely such possibly dominical passages as Lk
4.18–19; Mt 5.3–6 = Lk 6.20–1; and Mt 11.2–6 = Lk 7.18–23.[103]

(iv) *Concluding Observations*

(1) The primary purpose of Mt 3.1–12 is to set the stage for Jesus'
baptism. To this end the person and ministry of the Baptist are
succinctly summarized (we have only a silhouette). Thus John is
no independent figure. He is viewed only from a Christian
perspective. As the voice of Isa 40, as one like Elijah, as a baptizer,
and as a preacher, John only prepares for Jesus. His words and
deeds point away from himself to one incomparably greater.

In addition to introducing us to John the Baptist and putting his
work in perspective, 3.1–12 gives expression to at least two major
Matthean themes. (A) Who are the people of God? In Matthew's
eyes, Israel has been divided ever since the Messiah's advent (cf.
10.21–2, 34–6). While some have come to belief in Jesus, others
have not. Now because the number of these last is so large and
includes the leaders (cf. 3.7), the nation as a whole has, at least for
the time being, forfeited her privileged status. The kingdom is now
in the custody of the church (21.43; cf. Rom 11.17–24). As John
prophesied, God has raised up new children to Abraham, and
judgement has begun to fall upon Israel. (B) The Baptist's division
of his listeners into two categories, fruitful and unfruitful, wheat
and chaff, gives us the first taste of a strong 'dualism' that runs
throughout Matthew. With the clarity characteristic of many
moral visionaries, and despite his awareness of the need to qualify
or to temper absolutes (cf. 5.32; 18.15–22 and 13.30), our
evangelist often writes as though matters were black or white.
There are good fish and bad fish (13.47–50). There are sheep and

---

[102] Grimm, passim. Also important for this question are the following: W.
Manson, passim; A. Oepke, W. Zimmerli, J. Jeremias, *TWNT* 5, pp. 636–713;
Chilton, *Rabbi*, pp. 57–147, 199–200.

[103] On these texts see, in addition to the appropriate sections of Grimm's book,
Chilton, *Strength*, pp. 123–77; Dunn, *Spirit*, p. 53–62; and our own commentary
on the verses from Matthew.

goats (25.31–46). There are those on the right hand and those on the left hand (25.31–46). There are wise men who build their houses upon rock and foolish men who build their houses upon sand (7.24–7). There are people for Jesus and people against him—and seemingly none in between (12.30). In all this the First Gospel exhibits an outlook reminiscent of the Dead Sea scrolls and such ancient Jewish apocalypses as 4 Ezra and 2 Baruch. For the Qumran covenanters and the apocalyptic seers, as for Matthew, it was the nearness of the eschatological assize, at which only two sentences, salvation and damnation, would be passed, that made the existing world appear to be composed solely of the sons of light on the one hand and the sons of darkness on the other.

(2) There are four major Matthean themes to be discerned in 3.13–17: Jesus as Son, Jesus as servant, Jesus as the inaugurator of the new exodus and new creation, and Jesus as the one who fulfils all righteousness. We need not repeat what has already been said on the first theme, Jesus as Son; see on v. 17. With regard to the second, Jesus is the one in whom God is pleased, that is, he is the servant. In that capacity he not only brings OT prophecy to fulfilment, receiving the Spirit (3.17; 12.18), taking up infirmities (8.17), and giving his life as a ransom for many (20.28)—he is also the paradigm of the righteous sufferer.[104] Thus he humbly accepts from God both the good portion and the portion of the chastised, and he meekly sides with the weak and powerless while being delivered over into the hands of the mighty and powerful. Jesus came not to be served but to serve (20.28), and this idea presents itself at every turn of our gospel. From this we learn that sonship largely consists in choosing to take up the ministry of the suffering servant.

As for the third theme, although we have not found in the dove or in 'Son' evidence of a new exodus motif, it would be wrong to exclude the idea altogether from Matthew's story of the baptism. This is because 3.13–17 is followed immediately by the temptation narrative, in which Jesus the Son repeats the experience of Israel in her desert wanderings. In other words, 3.13–17 is coloured by what comes after, and this suggests, as we shall see, new exodus. Like the Israel of old, the Son comes out of the waters to enter the desert

---

[104] On the righteous sufferer as a standard figure in Judaism see L. Ruppert, *Der leidende Gerechte*, FzB 5, Würzburg, 1972; idem, *Der leidende Gerechte und seine Feinde*, FzB 6, Würzburg, 1973; G. W. E. Nickelsburg, *Resurrection, Immortality, and Eternal Life in Intertestamental Judaism*, HTS 26, Cambridge, Mass., 1972, esp. pp. 48–92; idem, 'The Genre and Function of the Markan Passion Narrative', *HTR* 73 (1980), pp. 155–63. For Jesus as righteous sufferer in Matthew see esp. B. Gerhardsson, 'Gottes Sohn als Diener Gottes', *ST* 27 (1973), pp. 73–106, and idem, 'Jesus livré et abandonné d'après la passion selon Saint Matthieu', *RB* 76 (1969), pp. 206–27.

and suffer temptation.[105] If this be so, then probably the idea of new creation is also present, for in Jewish thought exodus motifs and creation motifs were intertwined with one another and with eschatological expectation (see on 1.1). Further, Matthew probably saw in the dove a harking back to Gen 1.2. (In Christian tradition, the baptism of Jesus, like the temptation, has sometimes been interpreted as a reversal of Adam's fall: paradise was closed to Adam and remained closed until the heavens opened to Jesus; cf. Gregory of Nazianzus in PG 36, col. 353.)

Finally, concerning righteousness, this is what the followers of Jesus are called to seek (5.6; 6.33). Indeed, their righteousness is to exceed that of the scribes and Pharisees (5.20). But in what does righteousness consist? 3.14–15 holds a partial answer. In his own deeds Jesus 'fulfilled all righteousness'. This means: what believers are called to perform, Jesus has fulfilled. Thus there is implicit in the First Gospel an *imitatio Christi*. In seeking to fulfil the gospel's demand for righteousness, the believer has an example in his Lord.

(v) *Bibliography*

E. Bammel, 'The Baptist in Early Christian Tradition', *NTS* 18 (1971), pp. 95–128.

K. Barth, *CD* IV/4, pp. 52–68.

H.-W. Bartsch, 'Die Taufe im NT', *EvTh* 8 (1948), pp. 75–100.

G. R. Beasley-Murray, *Baptism in the New Testament*, London, 1962.

J. Becker, *Johannes der Täufer und Jesus von Nazareth*, Neukirchen, 1972.

S. Bénétreau, 'Baptêmes et ablutions dans le Judaïsme. L'originalité de Jean-Baptiste', *FoiVie* 80 (1981), pp. 96–108.

D. A. Bertrand, *Le baptême de Jésus. Histoire de l'exégèse aux deux premiers siècles*, BGBE 14, Tübingen, 1973.

E. Best, 'Spirit-Baptism', *NovT* 4 (1960), pp. 236–43.

O. Böcher, 'Johannes der Täufer in der neutestamentlichen Überlieferung', in *Kirche in Zeit und Endzeit*, Neukirchen-Vluyn, 1983, pp. 70–89.

W. Brandt, *Die jüdischen Baptismen*, Giessen, 1910.

H. Braun, 'Entscheidende Motive in den Berichten über die Taufe Jesu von Markus bis Iustin', *ZTK* 50 (1953), pp. 39–43.

P. G. Bretscher, 'Exodus 4:22–23 and the Voice from Heaven', *JBL* 87 (1968), pp. 301–11.

[105] On the new exodus motif in the baptism and temptation narratives see, in addition to Davies, *SSM*, pp. 34–45, also Buse, 'Isaiah LXIII' (v) and Feuillet, 'Le baptême' (v). Buse finds the background of Mk 1.9–11 to be in Isa 63 and 64.1. In this section of Scripture the exodus from Egypt is mentioned (63.11) along with the Holy Spirit (63.11, 14) and the fatherhood of God (63.16); and 64.1 reads, 'Oh that thou wouldst rend the heavens and come down'. In our estimation these parallels are interesting not because they entail the reliance of Mk 1.9–11 upon Isa 63–4 but because they show up a natural cluster of themes; cf. T. Levi 18 and *Mek*. on Exod 14.13 and 15.2.

idem, ' "Whose Sandals"? (Matt 3:11)', *JBL* 86 (1967), pp. 81–7.

S. Brock, 'The Baptist's Diet in Syriac Sources', *OCP* 54 (1970), pp. 113–24.

R. E. Brown, 'John the Baptist in the Gospel of John', in *Essays*, pp. 174–84.

W. H. Brownlee, 'John the Baptist in the New Light of Ancient Scrolls', in Stendahl, *Scrolls*, pp. 33–53.

I. Buse, 'The Markan Account of the Baptism of Jesus and Isaiah LXIII', *JTS* 7 (1956), pp. 74–5.

idem, 'St John and "the First Synoptic Pericope" ', *NovT* 3 (1959), pp. 57–61.

F. D. Coggan, 'Note on St Matthew iii. 15', *ExpT* 60 (1948/49), p. 258.

C. E. B. Cranfield, 'The Baptism of Our Lord—A Study of St Mark 1.9–11', *SJT* 8 (1955), pp. 55–63.

O. Cullmann, *Baptism in the New Testament*, London, 1950.

idem, 'Ο ΟΠΙΣΩ ΜΟΥ ΕΡΧΟΜΕΝΟΣ', *ConNT* 11 (1947), pp. 26–32.

N. A. Dahl, 'The Origin of Baptism', in *Interpretationes ad Vetus Testamentum pertinentes Sigmundo Mowinckel septuagenario missae*, Oslo, 1955, pp. 36–52.

S. L. Davies, 'John the Baptist and Essene Kashruth', *NTS* 29 (1983), pp. 569–71.

Davies, *SSM*, pp. 26–45.

Davies, *JPS*, pp. 72–83.

M. Dibelius, *Die urchristliche Überlieferung von Johannes dem Täufer*, FRLANT 15, Göttingen, 1911.

J. D. G. Dunn, *Baptism in the Holy Spirit*, London, 1970.

idem, *Spirit*, pp. 62–5.

idem, 'Spirit-and-Fire Baptism', *NovT* 14 (1972), pp. 81–92.

Dupont 3, pp. 225–45.

O. Eissfeldt. 'Πληρῶσαι πᾶσαν δικαιοσύνην in Matthäus 3, 15', *ZNW* 61 (1970), pp. 209–15.

M. S. Enslin, 'John and Jesus', *ZNW* 66 (1975), pp. 1–18.

J. Ernst, 'Öffnet die Türen dem Erlöser. Johannes der Täufer—seine Rolle in der Heilsgeschichte', *TG* 74 (1984), pp. 137–65.

A. Feuillet, 'Le baptême de Jésus', *RB* 71 (1964), pp. 321–52.

idem, 'La personnalité de Jésus entrevue à partir de sa soumission au rite de repentance du Précurseur', *RB* 77 (1970), pp. 30–49.

idem, 'Le symbolisme de la colombe dans les récits évangéliques du baptême', *RSR* 46 (1958), pp. 524–44.

idem, 'Vocation et mission des prophètes. Baptême et mission de Jésus: Étude de christologie biblique', *NV* 54 (1979), pp. 22–40.

H. Fleddermann, 'John and the Coming One (Matt. 3:11–12//Luke 3:16–17)', in *Society of Biblical Literature 1984 Seminar Papers*, ed. K. H. Richards, Chico, 1984, pp. 377–84.

W. F. Flemington, *The New Testament Doctrine of Baptism*, London, 1948.

A. Fridrichsen, ' "Accomplir toute justice". La rencontre de Jésus et du Baptiste (Mt 3.15)', *Congrès d'histoire du Christianisme, Jubilé Alfred Loisy*, ed. P. L. Couchoud, Paris, 1928, vol. 1, pp. 167–77.

A. Fuchs, 'Die Überschneidungen von Mk und "Q" nach B. H. Streeter und E. P. Sanders und ihre Wahre Bedeutung (Mk 1.1–8 PAR)', in

Wort in der Zeit, ed. W. Haubeck and M. Bachmann, Leiden, 1980, pp. 28–81.

idem, 'Intention und Adressaten der Busspredigt des Täufers bei Mt 3.7–10', in *Jesus in der Verkündigung der Kirche*, ed. A. Fuchs, SNTSU series A, 1, Freistadt, 1976, pp. 62–75.

P. Garnet, 'The Baptism of Jesus and the Son of Man Idea', *JSNT* 9 (1980), pp. 49–65.

S. Gero, 'The Spirit as Dove at the Baptism of Jesus', *NovT* 18 (1976), pp. 17–35.

A. S. Geyser, 'The Youth of John the Baptist', *NovT* 1 (1956), pp. 70–5.

Giesen, pp. 21–41.

F. Gils, *Jésus Prophète*, Louvain, 1957, pp. 49–73.

T. F. Glasson, 'Water, Wind and Fire (Luke iii 16) and Orphic Initiation', *NTS* 3 (1956), pp. 69–71.

Goppelt, *Theology* 1, pp. 32–42.

K. Grobel, ' "He That Cometh After Me" ', *JBL* 60 (1941), pp. 397–401.

L. Hartman, 'Taufe, Geist und Sohnschaft', in *Jesus in der Verkündigung der Kirche*, ed. A. Fuchs, SNTU, series A, 1, Freistadt, 1976, pp. 89–109.

Hoffmann, pp. 15–33.

P. W. Hollenbach, 'The Conversion of Jesus: From Baptizer to Healer', *ANRW* II.25.1 (1982), pp. 196–219.

J. Hughes, 'John the Baptist: the Forerunner of God Himself', *NovT* 14 (1972), pp. 191–218.

J. Jeremias, *Theology*, pp. 43–56.

idem, 'Der Ursprung der Johannestaufe', *ZNW* 28 (1929), pp. 312–20.

L. E. Keck, 'The Spirit and the Dove', *NTS* 17 (1970), pp. 41–67.

C. H. Kraeling, *John the Baptist*, New York, 1951.

Laufen, pp. 93–125.

F. Lentzen-Deis, 'Das Motiv der "Himmelsöffnung" in verschiedenen Gattungen der Umweltliteratur des Neuen Testaments', *Bib* 50 (1969), pp. 301–27.

idem, *Die Taufe Jesu nach den Synoptikern*, Frankfurt am Main, 1970.

J. Lindeskog, 'Johannes der Täufer', *ASTI* 12 (1983), pp. 55–83.

Ljungmann, pp. 97–126.

E. Lohmeyer, *Das Urchristentum, 1: Johannes der Täufer*, Göttingen, 1932.

idem, 'Zur evangelischen Überlieferung von Johannes dem Täufer', *JBL* 51 (1932), pp. 300–19.

C. C. McCown, 'The Scene of John's Ministry and its Relation to the Purpose and Outcome of his Mission', *JBL* 59 (1940), pp. 113–31.

T. W. Manson, 'John the Baptist', *BJRL* 36 (1954), pp. 395–412.

H. G. Marsh, *The Origin and Significance of New Testament Baptism*, Manchester, 1941.

I. H. Marshall, 'Son of God or Servant of Yahweh?', *NTS* 15 (1969), pp. 326–36.

J. L. Martyn, 'We have found Elijah', in *Jews, Greeks, and Christians*, ed. R. Hamerton-Kelly and R. Scroggs, SJLA 21, Leiden, 1976, pp. 181–219.

J. P. Meier, 'John the Baptist in Matthew's Gospel', *JBL* 99 (1980), pp. 383–405.

H. Merklein, 'Die Umkehrpredigt bei Johannes dem Täufer und Jesus von Nazaret', *BZ* 25 (1981), pp. 29–46.

F. Neirynck, 'Une nouvelle théorie synoptique (À propos de Mc., I, 2–6 et par.). Notes critiques', *ETL* 44 (1968), pp. 141–53.

P. Nepper-Christensen, 'Die Taufe im Matthäusevangelium', *NTS* 31 (1985), pp. 189–207.

E. Pickelmann, 'Zu Mt 3,4 und Mk 1,6', *BZ* 23 (1935/36), pp. 190–1.

R. Pesch, 'Anfang des Evangeliums Jesu Christi', in *Die Zeit Jesu*, ed. G. Bornkamm and K. Rahner, Freiburg, 1970, pp. 108–44.

D. Plooij, 'The Baptism of Jesus', *Amicitiae Corolla*, ed. H. G. Wood, London, 1933, pp. 239–52.

I. de la Potterie, 'L'onction du Christ: Étude de théologie biblique', *NRT* 80 (1958), pp. 225–52.

P. Proulx and L. A. Schökel, 'Las sandalias del Misias Esposo', *Bib* 59 (1978), pp. 1–37.

B. Reicke, 'Die jüdischen Baptisten und Johannes der Täufer', in *Jesus in der Verkündigung der Kirche*, ed. A. Fuchs, SNTSU series A, 1, Freistadt, 1976, pp. 62–75.

G. Richter, 'Zu den Tauferzählungen Mk 1,9–11 und Joh 1,32–34', *ZNW* 65 (1974), pp. 43–56.

E. Rivkin, 'Locating John the Baptizer in Palestinian Judaism: the Political Dimension', *SBL 1983 Seminar Papers*, ed. K. H. Richards, Chico, 1983, pp. 79–85.

J. A. T. Robinson, 'Elijah, John and Jesus: An Essay in Detection', *NTS* 4 (1958), pp. 263–81.

J. M. Robinson, L. Vaage, and U. Luz, 'The Preaching of John: Work Sheets for the Reconstruction of Q', in *Society of Biblical Literature 1984 Seminar Papers*, ed. K. H. Richards, Chico, 1984, pp. 365–76.

Rowland, pp. 358–64.

M. Sabbe, 'Le baptême de Jésus', in de la Potterie, pp. 184–211.

Sand, pp. 128–33.

A. Schlatter, *Johannes der Täufer*, ed. W. Michaelis, Basel, 1956.

H. Schlier, 'Die Verkündigung der Taufe Jesus nach den Evangelien', in *Geist und Leben* 28 (1955), pp. 414–19.

C. H. H. Scobie, *John the Baptist*, London, 1964.

R. Schütz, *Johannes der Täufer*, AThANT 50, Zürich, 1967.

Schulz, *Q*, pp. 366–78.

G. Schwarz, 'τὸ δὲ ἄχυρον κατακαύσει' *ZNW* 72 (1981), pp. 264–71.

P. Seethaler, 'Die Taube des heiligen Geistes', *BuL* 4 (1963), pp. 115–30.

O. J. F. Seitz, ' "What Do These Stones Mean"?', *JBL* 79 (1960), pp. 247–54.

J. Sint, 'Die Eschatologie des Täufers, die Täufergruppen und die Polemik der Evangelien', in *Vom Messias zum Christus*, ed. K. Schubert, Vienna, 1964, pp. 55–163.

D. Smith, 'Jewish Proselyte Baptism and the Baptism of John', *RestQ* 25 (1982), pp. 13–32.

A. Souter, 'ΑΓΑΠΗΤΟΣ', *JTS* 28 (1927), pp. 59–60.

W. R. Stegner, 'The Baptism of John and the Binding of Isaac', in *The Answers Lie Below*, ed. H. O. Thompson, New York, 1984, pp. 331–48.

Strecker, *Weg*, pp. 178–81.

W. Telfer, 'The Form of a Dove', *JTS* 29 (1928), pp. 238–42.

J. Thomas, *Le mouvement baptiste en Palestine et Syrie*, Gembloux, 1935.

H. Thyen, 'βάπτισμα μετανοίας εἰς ἄφεσιν ἁμαρτιῶν (Mk 1,4 = Lk 3,3)', in *The Future of Our Religious Past*, ed. J. M. Robinson, New York, 1971, pp. 131–68.

idem, *Studien zur Sündenvergebung im Neuen Testament und seine alttestamentlichen und jüdischen Voraussetzungen*, FRLANT 96, Göttingen, 1970, pp. 131–45.

W. Trilling, 'Die Täufertradition bei Matthäus', *BZ* 3 (1959), pp. 271–89.

C. H. Turner, 'Ο ΥΙΟΣ ΜΟΥ Ο ΑΓΑΠΗΤΟΣ', *JTS* 27 (1926), pp. 113–29.

R. E. H. Uprichard, 'The Baptism of John', *IBS* 3 (1981), pp. 187–202.

P. Vielhauer, 'Tracht und Speise Johannes des Täufers', in *Aufsätze*, pp. 47–54.

A. Vögtle, 'Die sogennante Taufperikope', in *Evangelisch-Katholischer Kommentar zum Neuen Testament*, Vorarbeiten Heft 4, Zürich, 1972, pp. 105–39.

H. Windisch, 'Die Notiz über Tracht und Speise des Täufers Johannes', *ZNW* 32 (1933), pp. 65–87.

Wink, pp. 27–41.

VII

THE BEGINNING OF THE MINISTRY
(4.1–22)

(i) *Structure*

4.1–22 falls between the Baptist material (3.1–17) and the sermon on the mount (which is introduced by 4.23–5.2). Its broad structure is manifest. It consists of three pericopae which recount events associated with the opening of Jesus' ministry:

1. The temptation (4.1–11)
2. The return to Galilee (4.12–17)
3. The calling of four disciples (4.18–22)

(ii) *Sources*

Little can be said for taking Mk 1.12–13 as an abbreviation of what we find in Mt 4.1–11 and Lk 4.1–13 (cf. Pokorný (v), pp. 116–17). As we shall see, the story in Mark, although brief, has its own integrity, and its proper interpretation shows it to have a point which cannot be easily derived from Matthew or Luke. This makes dependence hard to imagine. If the Griesbach theory be correct, either Mk 1.12–13 is the free composition of the Second Evangelist, or he has used some source other than Matthew or Luke.

W. Wilkens (v) has recently argued that, as opposed to the Q hypothesis, Mt 4.1–11 is largely a redactional product, and that Lk 4.1–13 is dependent upon Matthew.[1] We must, by way of reply, confess that the themes of Mt 4.1–11 are indeed not foreign to the First Evangelist, and one can also find characteristic Matthean style and vocabulary. Yet, in carrying out an exegesis of the text, we have found reasons for thinking that Matthew is not always original *vis-à-vis* Luke, that Luke sometimes represents a more primitive or original wording (see e.g. on vv. 2, 3, 4, 7). Thus we are forced back into thinking of a common source. Was the source written? The differences between Mt 4.1–11 and Lk 4.1–13 are considerably greater than those between Mt 3.1–11 and Lk 3.1–17. Yet the said differences belong for the most part to the narrative proper: the speeches are not excessively disparate. This is exactly what we would expect to find since (in our view) Matthew and Luke have treated Mark the same way, that is, they have felt freer to revise the Markan narrative

[1] See also his earlier study, 'Die Versuchungsgeschichte Lukas 4,1–13 und die Komposition des Evangeliums', *TZ* 30 (1974), pp. 262–72.

framework than the Markan words of Jesus. So a written source is plausible. Should we then speak of Q? P. Hoffman (p. 56) thinks not. It is atypical for Q to quote Scripture, and Q contained mostly sayings. But these arguments are far from decisive. Scripture is cited in Mt 11.10 = Lk 7.27 and Mt 23.39 = Lk 13.35, texts which are usually assigned to Q; and Q certainly had some narrative material (e.g. Mt 3.7 = Lk 3.7; Mt 8.5–13 = Lk 7.1–10; Mt 12.22–30 = Lk 11.14–23). Further, it has not been shown that the themes of Mt 4.1–11 and its parallel are foreign to the theology of Q. We in fact think Streeter hit the nail on the head a long time ago: the baptism and temptation narratives belong together. They were placed at the beginning of Q and regarded as the 'call' of the prophet Jesus, a call like to those which sometimes open OT prophetic books (Isa 6.1–13; Jer 1.1–19; Ezek 1.1–3.11).[2] In addition, a place in Q seems plausible in view of the other Q passages in which Jesus, the bringer of the eschatological crisis, struggles with the prince of demons and speaks of unclean spirits: Mt 12.22–30 = Lk 11.14–23 and Mt 12.43–5 = Lk 11.24–6.[3]

How does Mt 4.12–22 bear on the synoptic problem?[4] The evidence favouring the priority of Mark is weighty. (1) Mt 4.22 can be explained as a redactional alteration of Mk 1.20. One has trouble imagining the reverse (see on 4.22). (2) As we shall see, Matthew has consistently accentuated the parallelism between 4.18–20 and 4.21–2. On the theory of Matthean priority, we are forced to think of Mark as destroying, for no good reason, much of this parallelism. (3) Mark's version does not contain vocabulary or style typical of Matthean redaction (e.g. δύο ἀδελφούς, τὸν λεγόμενον Πέτρον). (4) It is natural to suppose that Matthew made stylistic improvements upon Mark's text (e.g. περιπατῶν παρά for παράγων παρά (4.18), αὐτοῦ for Σίμωνος (4.18), οἱ δέ for καί (4.20, 22), the omission of the unnecessary γενέσθαι (4.19)).

(iii) *Exegesis*

THE TEMPTATION OF JESUS (4.1–11)

Mt 4.1–11 is most naturally analysed in this fashion:

Introduction (4.1–2)
  1. The first temptation (4.3–4)

[2] Streeter, p. 291. The interest of Q in prophets and prophecy cannot be denied; see A. D. Jacobson, 'The Literary Unity of Q', *JBL* 101 (1982), pp. 365–89. For Jesus as a prophetic figure in Q see esp. Mt 11.20–4 = Lk 10.13–15; Mt 12.40 = Lk 11.30; Mt 23.37–9 = Lk 13.34–5.

[3] On the eschatological crisis in Q see Davies, *SSM*, pp. 366–86. For the possibility of Mt 4.1–11 par. being a later addition to Q see Zeller (v).

[4] In addition to what follows see esp. Pesch (v), pp. 4–5. For the independence of Matthew and Luke see C. M. Tuckett, 'On the Relationship between Matthew and Luke', *NTS* 30 (1984), pp. 131–2; against M. D. Goulder, 'On Putting Q to the Test', *NTS* 24 (1978), pp. 221–2.

2. The second temptation (4.5–7)
3. The third temptation (4.8–10)
  Conclusion (4.11)

Three observations are to be made. First, one is reminded of 26.36–46, where Jesus withdraws from his disciples three times, and of 26.69–75, where Peter denies his Lord thrice. Secondly, the three temptations exhibit a spatial progression, from a low place to a high place. The first takes place in the desert, the second on a pinnacle in the temple, the third on a mountain from which all the kingdoms of the world can be seen. This progression corresponds to the dramatic tension which comes to a climax with the third temptation. Thirdly, in each temptation Jesus quotes from Deuteronomy, from Deut 8.3 in 4.4, from Deut 6.16 in 4.7, and from Deut 6.13 in 4.10. This is the key to the narrative: we have before us a haggadic tale which has issued forth from reflection on Deut 6–8. Jesus, the Son of God, is repeating the experience of Israel in the desert (cf. Tertullian, *De bapt.* 20). Having passed through the waters of a new exodus at his baptism (cf. 1 Cor 10.1–5), he enters the desert to suffer a time of testing, his forty days of fasting being analogous to Israel's forty years of wandering. Like Israel, Jesus is tempted by hunger. And, like Israel, Jesus is tempted to idolatry. All-important for a right understanding of our pericope is Deut 8.2–3: 'And you shall remember all the way which the Lord your God has led you these *forty* years *in the wilderness*, that he might humble you, *testing you* to know what was in your heart, whether you would keep his commandments, or not. And he humbled you and let you *hunger* . . .';

Form-critically, the closest parallels to our narrative are to be found in rabbinic sources. It requires little labour to find debates in which two rabbis throw biblical passages back and forth—and that is more or less what we have here: Jesus and the devil confront each other by quoting various Scriptures (cf. *b. Sanh.* 97b). Moreover, there is one rabbinic text in which Satan and Abraham (whom God 'tested with many trials', *b. Sanh.* 89b) enter into debate by citing texts against the other's purpose. The passage deserves to be quoted in full.

On the way Satan came towards him and said to him, '*If we assay to commute with thee, wilt thou be grieved?* . . . *Behold, thou hast instructed many, and thou hast strengthened the weak hands. Thy words have upholden him that was falling, and thou hast strengthened the feeble knees. But now it is come upon thee, and thou faintest*' (Job 4.2–5). He replied, '*I will walk in my integrity*' (Ps 26.2). '*But*', Satan said to him, '*should not thy fear be thy confidence?*' (Job 4.6). He retorted, '*Remember, I pray thee, whoever perished, being innocent?*' (Job 4.6). Seeing that he would not listen to him, he said to him, '*Now a thing was secretly brought to me* (Job 4.12); thus have I heard behind the curtain, "the lamb for a burnt offering but not Isaac for a burnt offering" '. He replied, 'It is the penalty of a liar, that should he even tell the truth, he is not listened to' (*b. Sanh.* 89b).

The similarities between this and Mt 4.1–11 hardly need remark.

If, indeed, Mt 4.1–11 is what it appears to be, namely a haggadic tale spun largely out of Deut 6–8 and akin to rabbinic disputations, presumably its author was a sophisticated Christian scribe. B. Gerhardsson (v) has even gone so far as to argue that the temptation narrative is haggadic midrash, the production of a converted rabbi of no mean talent. He finds the telling fact to be the rabbinic interpretation of the *Shema* which appears in *m. Ber.* 9.5 and *Sipre Deut.* on 6.5. According to these texts, 'with your whole heart' means with both the good and evil inclinations—which links up nicely with the craving for food in Mt 4.2. 'With your whole soul' means even if God takes your life—which recalls the temptation to jump off the temple. 'With your whole might' means with all your property—which has its corollary in the devil's offer to give Jesus all the world as his possession. Thus, according to Gerhardsson, we have in Matthew an insightful haggadic exposition of the *Shema*. Whether in all this he is correct, we must express some doubt. While the suggested interpretation is certainly brilliant, it is somewhat speculative, especially because one has doubts about the other places in Matthew where Gerhardsson finds allusion to the *Shema* (see on 6.1 and 13.1–23).

1–2. In these two verses there are five points of agreement between Matthew and Luke against Mark: the naming of Jesus, the use of διάβολος rather than σατανᾶς, the remark that Jesus fasted or did not eat anything, the placement of 'forty' before (instead of after) 'days', and the word, ἐπείνασεν. From this, it may be inferred, Q's introduction to the temptation related how Jesus fasted forty days, became hungry, and encountered the devil. Probably further details were also mentioned, but the Markan/Q overlap prevents their discovery.

τότε ὁ Ἰησοῦς ἀνήχθη εἰς τὴν ἔρημον ὑπὸ τοῦ πνεύματος. Mark's εὐθύς is, as often, dropped. Its replacement, τότε, is a Matthean favourite. Matthew, as opposed to Mark and Luke, is fond of the sentence structure, τότε + subject (+ participial phrase) + verb; see 2.7, 16; 4.1; 12.29; 13.43; 16.24; 21.1; 22.13; 23.1; 26.56, 65; 27.27, 58. The construction is common in the LXX only in 1 Esdras, 2 Esdras, and Daniel. Mark does not name Jesus. Luke does name him but without the article (so also Mt 4.1 B Δ 700 *pc*).

Instead of ἀνήχθη, which means 'was brought up', 'was led up' (cf. T. Abr. A 14.8; BAGD, s.v., 1),[5] Mark has the active, present ἐκβάλλει (cf. Gen 3.24?), Luke the passive, imperfect ἤγετο. As

---

[5] According to Mauser (v), p. 145, Matthew's 'led up' seems to reflect a knowledge of the mountainous plateau of the Judean desert.

·Luke likes ἄγω (Mt: 4; Mk: 3; Lk: 13) and as ἀνάγω (Mt: 1; Mk: 0; Lk: 3) is found only here in the First Gospel, Matthew's word probably comes from Q. There is, however, room for uncertainty. ἀνάγω is comparatively frequent in Luke–Acts (Lk: 3; Acts: 17), so if it appeared in Q we might have expected Luke to retain it (cf. Jeremias, *Lukasevangelium*, p. 90). In any case, Luke's ἄγω has its parallel in Deut 8.2 LXX. Perhaps Matthew's ἀνήχθη should recall the exodus from Egypt, to wit: just as God led Israel out of Egypt and through the waters and into the desert (Num 20.5; 1 Βασ 12.6; Ps 80.1 LXX; etc., all using ἀνάγειν), so does the Spirit of God lead Jesus into the desert after he is baptized.

εἰς τὴν ἔρημον: Mark also has this, Luke a dative construction, ἐν τῇ ἐρήμῳ (cf. Deut 8.2, where the Hebrew is *midbār*). For the 'desert' see on 3.1. Although the exact location of the wilderness is not specified, the connexion with chapter 3 causes one to think of a place near John's activity, that is, the region around the Jordan. Yet the important fact is another: God's son Israel was 'tested' in the desert after the exodus, and that history is being recapitulated. Also, in Jewish and Christian belief, as in Persian and Egyptian religion, the wilderness was the haunt of evil spirits, a dangerous zone outside the boundaries of society; see Lev 16.10; Tob 8.3; 1 En. 10.4–5; 4 Macc. 18.8; 2 Bar. 10.8; Mt 12.43 = Lk 11.24; Tg. Yer. I to Deut 32.10.[6] The Christian desert Fathers, it will be remembered, professedly retired into the desert to combat demons.

ὑπὸ τοῦ πνεύματος: the absolute use of τὸ πνεῦμα is common in the NT save the gospels. In the present instance, as at Mt 12.31 (cf. 12.28); Lk 4.14 (cf. 4.1); and the parallels to Mt 4.1, it is anaphoric, referring back to the Spirit which descended upon Jesus after his baptism.[7]

To be led by God's Spirit has as its result perfect subjection to and performance of God's will, as Jesus will soon prove. For possible parallels see 1 Kgs 18.12; 2 Kgs 2.16; Ezek 3.14; Acts 8.39; Rom 8.14; Gal 5.18. In Matthew's eyes, the victory of 4.1–11 will have been just as much a 'fulfilling of all righteousness' as the submission to John's baptism in chapter 3.

[6] See further Böcher, pp. 28–30; Davies, *GL*, pp. 86–90; and S. Talmon, 'The "Desert Motif" in the Bible and in Qumran Literature', in *Biblical Motifs*, ed. A. Altman, Cambridge, Mass., 1966, pp. 43–4. This belief has parallels around the world; see J. Campbell, *The Hero with a Thousand Faces*, Bollingen Series 17, 2nd ed., Princeton, 1968, pp. 77–89. For the wilderness as a place of testing see esp. Stegner (v).

[7] The Gospel According to the Hebrews contained this statement: 'Even so did my mother, the Holy Spirit, take me away on to the great mountain Tabor'; see Origen, *Com. on Jn*. 2.12.87; *Hom. on Jer*. 15.4; Jerome, *Com. on Mic*. on 7.7; *Com on Ezek*. on 16.13; *Com. on Isa*. on 40.9. This probably introduced a version of the temptation story, not a version of the transfiguration.

The Spirit of God was held to have been particularly active among the Israelites during the exodus and the wilderness wanderings, and this helps account for its mention here. See Num 11.17, 25, 29; Neh 9.20; Ps 106.33; Isa 63.10–14; Tg. Yer. to Exod 15.2; *Mek.* on Exod 14.13 and 15; *b. Soṭa* 30b; *Num. Rab.* on 11.17; *Exod. Rab.* on 15.1.

πειρασθῆναι ὑπὸ τοῦ διαβόλου. In Mark and Luke Jesus is apparently tempted during the period of forty days (cf. Ps.-Clem. Hom. 11.35; 19.2). In Matthew temptation clearly comes afterwards. For fruitless attempts at harmonization see Strauss, pp. 256–8.

Both the Second and Third Gospels have πειραζόμενος. On Matthew's telic infinitive see on 3.13 (also with ὑπό). Outside the present context, πειράζω (always for *nāsâ* in the LXX; see further below) is used in the synoptics exclusively of the Jewish teachers who ask difficult questions in order to discredit Jesus; for Matthew see 16.1; 19.3; 22.18, 35. For the devil or Satan as 'tempter' outside the gospels see 1 Cor 7.5 and Rev 2.10. Note also Heb 2.18, where the sentence, 'he himself (Jesus) has suffered and been tempted', is preceded by mention of the devil (2.14). A tradition related to the synoptic accounts of Jesus' temptation seems to lie in the background (cf. Heb 4.15, where Jesus is 'Son of God').

There are three 'testing' stories in Matthew which bear comparison with 4.1–11 (cf. Wilkens (v), p. 481–8). In 16.1; 19.3; and 22.34–5, Jewish leaders 'test' Jesus by asking him questions. A form of πειράζω is used in each instance. And in each case Jesus answers by alluding to or quoting Scripture. The similarities with 4.1–11 are obvious.

The Son of God has already been 'tempted' in a sense by John the Baptist, who initially tried to prevent Jesus' baptism; and even though there are great differences, 3.14–15 has been called 'a prelude to the temptation' (so Wilkens (v), p. 481, who lists the parallels between 3.13–14 and 4.1–11).

ὑπὸ τοῦ διαβόλου: so also Luke. Mark has ὑπὸ τοῦ σατανᾶ (cf. Mt 4.10). The διάβολος (4.1, 5, 8, 11; 13.39; 25.41; so the LXX for the MT's *śāṭān*, except in 3 Βασ 11, where 'Satan' is used; it is absent from Josephus) is the same as 'Satan' (4.10; 12.26; 16.23) and Beelzebul (10.25; 12.24, 27). He is 'the enemy' (13.39), the 'evil one' (6.13), who is destined to be defeated and thrown with his angels into eternal fire (25.41). In tempting Jesus, he only acts as he does towards all (cf. 6.13; 26.41), even though a personal appearance is extraordinary.[8] (As T. Job 3.6 puts it, it is 'the power of the devil by which human nature is deceived'.) His power can be broken by the recalling and heeding of the Bible (4.1–11) or by

[8] Yet not absolutely unprecedented; see e.g T. Job 6–8; *b. Sanh.* 89b.

prayer (6.13; 26.41). And because the Messiah has appeared and bound him (12.29), the devil and his host of evil demons, who seek nothing other than the destruction of humanity and its alienation from God (cf. 12.22 and 17.14–21), are subject to the name of Jesus (cf. 7.22; 10.1, 8).

In the OT Satan is an accuser in the heavenly court, one of the sons of heaven, and he incites the deity to test people; see 1 Chr 21.1; Ps 109.6; Job 1–2; Zech 3.1–10; also 1 Kgs 22.19 (discussion in von Rad, *TWNT* 2, pp. 71–4). By the time we reach the NT there has been a metamorphosis. Satan, known by a variety of names, has become a demonic, wholly evil figure, bent on the destruction of Israel and every other good thing. Among the more significant texts are 1 En. 54; Jub. 10.1–14; 11.5; LAE 12–17; T. Ash. 1.8–9; T. Job 6–8; 16–27; 4 Macc. 18.8; 4Q'Amram^b, frag. 2; CD 4.12–13; 1QS 3.13–4.26.[9] See further on 4.10.

καὶ νηστεύσας. There is no parallel in Mark. Luke has καὶ οὐκ ἔφαγεν οὐδέν, which might be influenced by Exod 34.28 or Deut 9.9. What Matthew has may be redactional: the introductory aorist nominative participle is characteristic of our evangelist, Matthew is alone in offering detailed instruction on 'fasting' (6.16–18), and the modification of Mk 2.18–20 in Mt 9.14–15— 'mourn' replaces 'fast'—points to considered opinion on the subject of fasting. Hence Matthew may have chosen νηστεύω, the proper cultic term (cf. 6.16–18; Did. 7.4), in order to help his readers make the connexion between the Christian practice of fasting (6.16–18; 9.14–15) and the precedent of Jesus (4.1). On fasting in Judaism see on 6.16. For fasting in connexion with exorcism see Böcher, pp. 113–17. For fasting as the prelude to a visionary experience see 1 Sam 28.20; Dan 10.3; 4 Ezra 5.20; 2 Bar. 20.5–6; *y. Ter.* 8.10.46b; *Eccl. Rab.* on 9.10.

Although Mark does not explicitly tell us that Jesus went without food, this seems implicit in his account. In Mk 1.12–13 Jesus is probably the last Adam (cf. Rom 5.12–21; 1 Cor 15.42–50; Justin, *Dial.* 103; Gosp. Philip 71.16–21; Irenaeus, *Adv. haer.* 5.21.2).[10] He, like the first Adam, is tempted by Satan. But unlike his anti-type, he does not succumb, and the result is the recovery of paradise (cf. T. Levi 18.10): the wild beasts are tamed and once again a man dwells with angels and is served by them (cf. Gen 1.19–20; Isa 11.6–9; 65.25; Hos 2.18; Jub. 3.27–9; 2 Bar. 73.6–7; LAE 4; 33.2; Apoc. Mos. 10–11; 24; T. Naph. 8.4; Apoc. Sed. 5; *ARN* 1).

[9] Lit.: SB 1, pp. 136–49; T. H. Gaster, *IDB* 4, pp. 224–8; W. Foerster and K. Schäferdiek, *TWNT* 7, pp. 151–64; W. Foerster, *TWNT* 2, pp. 69–71, 74–80; J. Ernst, *Die eschatologischen Gegenspieler in den Schriften des Neuen Testaments*, BU 3, Regensburg, 1967, pp. 269–80; and P. J. Kobelski, *Melchizedek and Melchireša'*, CBQMS 10, Washington, D.C., 1981, pp. 75–98.

[10] See Davies, *PRJ*, pp. 42–3; J. Jeremias, *TWNT* 1, p. 141; E. Fascher, 'Jesus und die Tiere', *TLZ* 90 (1965), pp. 561–70; P. Pokorný (v), pp. 120–1; Pesch 1, pp. 95–6; Mahnke (v), pp. 28–38.

Furthermore, the word for 'serve', διακονεῖν, here means 'to give to eat' (cf. Mk 1.31; Lk 12.37; Jn 12.2), a sense which lines up nicely with the tradition that Jesus' temptation involved fasting (so Q). So the angels feed Jesus (cf. 1 Kgs 19.5–8); and this means that we are presumably to think of the food of angels, that is, manna—the food which Adam ate in paradise (Ps 78.25; LAE 2–4; 2 Esdr. 1.19; b. Sanh. 59b; ARN 1). But if so, then the points of commonality between the accounts of the temptation in Mark and Q are greater than is generally imagined. For according to Deut 8.3, manna was thought of as bread (cf. Num 21.5; Neh 9.15; Ps 78.24–5; Wisd 16.20; Jn 6.31–4); and because this OT text is cited in Mt 4.4 = Lk 4.4, both Mk 1.12–13 and its relative in Q have to do with manna or bread in the desert. This forcefully suggests that Mk 1.12–13, in which Jesus is the last Adam, and the story in Q, in which Jesus is the Son of God and new Israel, ultimately derive from two different interpretations of the same story or parable. The one employed the original cluster of themes—desert, temptation, fasting, Satan, bread or manna—in order to portray Jesus in the colours of Adamic myth. The other took up the same motifs to link them up with traditions about Israel in the desert.[11]

Although such a conclusion must remain, in the nature of the case, hypothetical, we should observe that, if the story of the temptation depends at all upon dominical tradition, the original telling could not have taken the form of either Mk 1.12–13 or Mt 4.1–11 = Lk 4.1–13. Jesus did not make himself out to be a new Adam—that was left to the church. Nor did he plainly announce in so many words his identity as 'Son of God', as Q would require; and even if this were otherwise, the narrative behind Mt 4.1–11 and its parallel is clearly the work of a Christian scribe working with Deut 6–8, as Gerhardsson has made so plain. Nevertheless, having said all this, if Jesus did speak—in a parabolic fashion—of a time of testing and fasting in which he believed he had gained a victory over the devil, the genesis of our hypothetical original would thereby be elucidated. We would besides this be able to give a satisfactory account for both Mk 3.27—Jesus is the strong man who has bound Beelzebul and plundered his goods—and Lk 10.18—'I saw Satan fall like lightning from heaven'.[12] Moreover, Jesus' proclamation of the presence of the kingdom in his own person and work and his radical call for a restoration of paradisiacal principles (e.g., in Mk 10.2–9) are perhaps best explained by a conviction that Satan had been confronted and conquered. Finally, Mk 8.33 and Lk 22.31–2 show us that Jesus perceived behind opposition to himself and his work the face of Satan. Would he not have seen the same face during a period of solitary trial and struggle?[13]

[11] Against A. B. Lord, 'The Gospels as Oral Traditional Literature', in W. O. Walker, p. 63; Feuillet (v); and the supporters of Griesbach, Mk 1.12–13 is not an abbreviation of the longer Q account. And against Brown, Essays, pp. 263–4, Q's version is not an expansion of what we now find in Mk 1.

[12] A few scholars, among them C. J. Cadoux (pp. 65–6) and Jeremias (Parables, pp. 122–3), have supposed one or both of these texts to refer back to Jesus' victory in the wilderness. For other concordances between the temptation narratives and Jesus' teaching on evil see Dupont (v), pp. 119–26.

[13] For other attempts to find an historical nucleus behind the canonical temptations see esp. T. W. Manson, Servant-Messiah, pp. 55–8; Jeremias, Theology, pp. 68–75; and Dupont (v), pp. 36–9, 75–130.

There is no real contradiction between the statement that Jesus fasted (Mt 4.2) and Mk 2.19 and Mt 11.19 = Lk 7.34, according to which the disciples did not fast and Jesus came 'eating and drinking'. The latter passages simply preserve the memory of the overall impression left by Jesus: he was no ascetic. This cannot, however, rule out the occasional practice of religious disciplines such as fasting. Fasting is a means of self-abnegation, which Jesus, like most great religious teachers, took to be an imperative; and if Jesus had not kept the general days of fasting (especially the fast for the Day of Atonement, which is commanded in Lev 16.29), would this not have left some deposit in our sources?[14]

ἡμέρας τεσσεράκοντα καὶ τεσσεράκοντα νύκτας.[15] The 'and forty nights' is a Matthean addition, no doubt primarily prompted by Exod 34.28 and Deut 9.9, where we read that Moses ate nothing for forty days and forty nights (cf. also 1 Kgs 19.8 and Irenaeus, *Adv. haer.* 5.21.2: 'fasting forty days, like Moses and Elijah'). Compare the change at Mt 12.40: the Son of man will be three days *and three nights* in the heart of the earth. The addition of 'and three nights' makes the parallel with Jonah perfect (cf. Jon 1.17).

The period of forty days is an important one in Scripture and Jewish tradition. It is most often, as the church Fathers observed, associated with hardship or affliction or punishment (cf. Origen, *Com. on Deut.* on 25.3, and Augustine, *Con. ev.* 2.4.8–9). The flood in Noah's day lasted that long (Gen 7.4, 12, 17; 8.6). So did the fasting of Moses (Exod 24.18; 34.28; Deut 9.9, 11, 25; 10.10) and the fasting of Elijah (1 Kgs 19.8)—as also the penitential fasting of Adam in LAE 5–6 and the fasting of Abraham in Apoc. Abr. 12.1–2. (This last reads: 'And we went, the two of us alone together, forty days and nights. And I ate no bread and drank no water, because (my) food was to see the angel who was with me, and his discourse with me was my drink'; cf. Jn 4.34.) Forty days was the length of time Ezekiel lay on his right side symbolizing the punishment of the house of Judah (Ezek 4.6). Jonah prophesied, 'Yet forty days and Nineveh will be destroyed' (Jon 3.4). According to Jub. 3.9, Adam was placed in Eden forty days after he was created. According to LAB 61.2, the people of Israel feasted forty days in the wilderness when they received the law. In Acts, forty days elapse between Jesus' resurrection and his ascension (Acts 1.3). For forty days as a round number see 1 Sam 17.16; Jub. 5.25; 50.4; Ep. Arist. 105; 4 Ezra 14.23, 42–5; 2 Bar.

---

[14] Cf. J. Behm, *TWNT* 4, p. 932. On fasting see, in addition to the works cited in the commentary on 6.16, SB 4, pp. 77–114; J. A. Montgomery, 'Ascetic Strains in Early Judaism', *JBL* 51 (1932), pp. 183–213; and V. MacDermot, *The Cult of the Seer in the Ancient Middle East*, Berkeley, 1971, pp. 39–43, 322–32.

[15] ℵ D 892 eth Aug: τεσσερακοντα νυκτας (so HG). This is the word order in Exod 24.18 and 3 Βασ 19.8 and is therefore probably original. The words are reversed in B C L W 0233 *f*[13] Maj sy[h] followed by NA[26]. *f*[1] *pc* sy[c] Ir omit 'and forty nights', perhaps under the influence of the Lukan parallel.

76.4; L. Proph. Dan. 9; Acts 4.22; 7.23; 23.13, 21. For forty days as a time of fasting see, in addition to the texts already cited, Diogenes Laertius 8.40 and T. Isaac 4.4. Because, in the temptation narrative a Jesus/Israel typology obtains, the most important consideration is this: Israel wandered for forty years in the desert (cf. Tertullian, *De bapt.* 20). See Exod 16.35; Num 14.33; Deut 2.7; 8.2, 4; 29.5; Josh 5.6; Neh 9.21; Ps 95.10; Amos 2.10; Acts 7.36. In most of these texts the period in the wilderness is a time of testing. Especially significant in this regard is Deut 8.2–3: 'your God has led you these *forty* years in the *wilderness* that he might humble you and *test* you . . . and he humbled you and let you *hunger* . . .'. The resemblance to Mt 4.1–2 is striking, and it would be all the stronger if one pointed '*nh* ('to humble') so as to mean God caused Israel to fast (cf. Lev 23.27, 29, 32; Ps 35.13). Moreover, in Num 14.34 and Ezek 4.5–6 the period of forty days symbolizes forty years. It therefore appears that we should understand the forty days from the life of Jesus to correspond to the forty years during which Israel was tested in the desert.

The tradition of Jesus' forty day fast must lie behind the Easter fast of forty days which was already assumed to be common practice at Nicaea (see the fifth canon). The parallels with other religions—for instance, the forty day fast of Buddha and the forty days of stillness observed by the yogi in *Samādhi*—are to be explained not in terms of dependence but in terms of natural coincidence. Religious heroes typically fast for great lengths of time, and forty days is simply a common, round figure. On the indifference of the ancients to absolute chronology see E. J. Bickermann, in *CHJ* 1, p. 69.

ὕστερον ἐπείνασεν. This notice provides the introduction to the first temptation. Luke has only the verb. ὕστερον (cf. '*aḥărê*) means 'then', 'thereafter', or 'finally'. The adverb, which occurs in Matthew more times than in all the rest of the NT put together (Mt: 7; Mk: 0; Lk: 1), is redactional. See further BDF § 62

In Matthew all temptation appears to come only after the fast; in Luke Jesus is tempted during the forty day period. Matthew's version, in which the forty days go with the fasting, is closer to Exod 32.28.

3. What follows is, with the exception of 4.11b, taken entirely from Q.

καὶ προσελθὼν ὁ πειράζων εἶπεν αὐτῷ.[16] The first two words are redactional. Compare the differences between 8.19, 25; 13.10; 14.12; 15.23; 16.1 and their synoptic counterparts. Note also 21.28; 25.20; 28.2, and 18: these have no synoptic parallels. For

[16] ℵ B W *f*[1.13] 33 700 892[vid] *al* aur ff[1] vg sy[p] mae bo: ο πειραζων ειπεν αυτω. C L 0233 Maj f (k) sy[h] have a different order: 4,1–3 (so HG). The order, 4,1–4, appears in (D it) sy[s.c] sa?

προσέρχομαι with πειράζω see 16.1 and 19.3.

Matthew's excessive use of προσέρχομαι (Mt: 52; Mk: 5; Lk: 10) may serve the function of emphasizing Jesus' majesty. Of its fifty-two occurrences, fifty involve people or spirits—friend and foe alike—making approach to Jesus. (In 28.18 the resurrected Jesus is the subject, in 17.7 the transfigured Jesus.) The linking with προσκυνέω (8.2; 9.18; 20.20; 28.9) and the use of the word in Judaism in connexion with the cult, with the worship of God, and with approaching kings and entering courts (e.g. Lev 9.5; Num 18.4; Deut 25.1; Jer 7.16; Heb 10.1; 1 Pet 2.4; Josephus, *Ant.* 12.19) should perhaps tell us that the verb implies reverence and circumspection. In our present passage, 4.1–11, presumably even the devil and the angels (vv. 3, 11) approach Jesus with some diffidence.

ὁ πειράζων is the equivalent of Luke's ὁ διάβολος (probably Q). The title, which names the devil's chief characteristic (cf. 1 Cor 7.5; Rev 2.10), reappears in the NT only in 1 Th 3.5. It is not found in the LXX. There developed over time in Judaism a tendency to view Satan rather than God as the source of temptation (cf. 2 Sam 24.1 against 1 Chr 21.2; Jub. 17.16 against Gen 22.1; Jub. 48.2 against Exod 4.24; also Eusebius, *H.E.* 5.20.1; Ps.-Clem. Hom. 3.55.2). And in Jas 1.13 we find this: 'God cannot be tempted by evil and he himself tempts (πειράζει) no one'. In the NT in general God typically only 'tries' or 'tests' (πειράζω = *nāsâ* or δοκιμάζω = *bāḥan*), and that with hope for a good outcome (cf. 1 Th 2.4; 1 Tim 3.10; Heb 11.17). The devil typically 'tempts' (πειράζω, never δοκιμάζω) with nothing but an evil end in view (cf. 1 Cor 7.5; 1 Th 3.5; Rev 2.10). As for Mt 4.1 and 3, the activity of the Spirit and the presence of Satan give the verb πειράζω a double connotation: Jesus is at the same time being 'tested' by God and 'tempted' by the devil (cf. Gundry, *Commentary*, p. 55). That is, the hostile devil, 'that slinking prompter who whispers in the heart of men' (*Koran* 114), is here the instrument of God. Recall again Deut 8.2. In this text Israel's time of testing is brought on by God himself. The same must be true in the gospels. As God once tested Israel in the wilderness (Exod 20.20), so now does the Spirit lead Jesus into the desert in order that he might face the ordeal with Satan: the confrontation is initiated by God.

εἰ υἱὸς εἶ τοῦ θεοῦ. Compare 4.6 = Lk 4.9; also Mt 27.40. Luke has exactly what Matthew has, which points to a common written source. The reference is to the voice at the baptism,[17] so the temptation may be to abandon the mission of the servant. At the

[17] According to Luz 1, p. 110, the temptation story preserved in Q may very well have been originally composed as the sequel to the baptism, where Jesus' sonship is proclaimed. If so, Q not only contained a notice of Jesus' baptism but also, in that connexion, referred to Jesus as God's Son.

same time, 'Son of God' is appropriate not only in view of 3.17 but
also because it is the title Jesus shares with Israel (Exod 4.22–3;
Deut 1.31; 32.5, 6, 18–20; Hos 11.1). Compare especially Deut 8.5:
'Know then in your heart that as a man disciplines his son, so the
Lord God disciplines you'. Note that the introductory εἰ expresses
a real condition ('since'; cf. BAGD, s.v., I.1). Jesus' status as 'Son
of God' is not questioned; rather it is the presupposition for the
devil's temptation.[18]

For the insertion of a form of the verb 'to be' between a noun
and its genitive qualifier see 5.35; 12.8, 27; 23.31; 27.43. For 'Son of
God' without the article as a definite christological title see Mt
14.33; Mk 15.39; Jn 10.36; 19.7.

εἰπὲ ἵνα. This means 'command that' (cf. 20.21—redactional; Lk
10.40). ἵνα functions as an infinitive. Luke has ἵνα elsewhere:
'command this stone *that* it become bread'.

οἱ λίθοι οὗτοι ἄρτοι γένωνται. Compare Ps.-Clem. Hom. 2.32.
Luke has a dative singular as the indirect object of εἰπέ: τῷ λίθῳ
τούτῳ. For Gundry, the plurals in Matthew should be associated
with the stone*s* of 3.9 and the loave*s* of 16.10–12, to wit: in 3.9 the
Pharisees and Sadducees are being addressed, and in chapter 16 we
have talk of 'the leaven of the Pharisees and Sadducees' (v. 11); so
in 4.3 Satan is allegedly a type of the Jewish leaders (*Commentary*,
pp. 55–6). Now undoubtedly, in view of 16.1; 19.3; and 22.34–5,
Satan and the Jewish leaders play similar rôles in Matthew (see on
4.1). But the proposed explanation of the differences between Mt
4.3 and Lk 4.3 is scarcely perspicuous. It is much easier to content
oneself with the observation that Matthew frequently has plurals
where Mark and/or Luke have singulars; see, for example, 8.26
diff. Mk 4.39; 13.2 diff. Mk 4.1; 13.5 diff. Mk 4.5; 13.11 diff. Mk
4.11; 26.15 diff. Mk 14.11. Or one might urge that Luke changed
'stones' to 'stone' in order to create a more realistic picture (so
Dupont (v), p. 53). After all, one does not need a desert full of
loaves to feed one person. In any event, Gundry's proposal is
oversubtle and unnecessary.[19]

Jesus is not being tempted to perform, as the second Moses, a
messianic miracle and thereby prove his messiahship (cf. Mk
6.30–44; Jn 6.1–15).[20] If this were the case, we should expect
onlookers. There are none. Besides, it is Jesus who is hungry, not a

[18] Less than little can be said for the interpretation of Theodore of Mopsuestia:
the devil, although he has heard a voice from heaven, does not yet believe Jesus is
the Son of God, so he is testing him to find out (cf. Clement of Alexandria, *Strom.*
1.9.44). See Kesich (v).

[19] According to Gerhardsson (v), p. 52, n. 53, *if* the plural is significant, it simply
underlies the demand for a superfluity of food.

[20] So many, including T. W. Manson and Jeremias. It is usually assumed, on this
interpretation, that the temptation narrative preserves the memory of Jesus'
struggle with political messianism. See, however, Hoffmann (v), who instead finds

crowd, and if Q had only 'this stone' (see above), a multiplication miracle would be out of the question. Nor is Jesus being tempted to doubt his sonship. On the contrary, Jesus has fasted and is hungry, and the devil is asking him to use his divine powers—these are presupposed—to act on his own instead of solely in response to the Father's will.[21] Israel, when hungry in the desert, had murmured against the Lord and Moses (Exod 16; Num 11). The devil now finds Jesus in a similar situation, and he wishes to make him become groundlessly anxious about his physical needs (cf. 6.34). The temptation is to make the Son of God demand the food he craves (cf. Ps 78.17–18). The devil's aim is to break Jesus' perfect trust in his Father's good care (cf. 6.24–34) and thereby alter the course of salvation-history.[22]

Perhaps attention should be called to T. Job 22–5, where Satan disguises himself as a breadseller and tempts Job's wife, as she is begging food for her hungry husband.

4. Although the experience of God's people of old—hunger in the desert—is being re-experienced by him, Jesus does not respond by murmuring against God. Instead he takes up 'the sword of the Spirit which is the word of God' (Eph 6.17). As did Michael the archangel when he contended with the devil (Jude 9), Jesus quotes Scripture, and to the effect 'that food will not keep a man alive, unless God says that he is to live; and if God says that he is to live, he will live, whether he has food or not' (Plummer, p. 40). God wills his Son to live. How then can Jesus take matters into his own hands? The Messiah does not command or compel God. He obeys. The means to the good end are not to be dictated but received. And

---

the community's rejection of Zealot ideology. There is admittedly some evidence from Jewish sources that the Messiah would repeat the miracle of the manna; see on 14.13–21. And for the desert as the site of the Messiah's manifestation one might refer to Mt 24.26 and Acts 21.38 among other texts. But the manna to be produced by the Messiah like Moses is always bread from heaven, never bread from stones; cf. Davies, *SSM*, pp.46–7; Gerhardsson (v), p. 44. Against the messianic interpretation of the temptation see esp. Schlatter, pp. 95–112; Luz 1, pp. 161–3; and our comments on 4.5–6 and 8–9. The title, 'Messiah', is, tellingly, absent from 4.1–11. We also reject the proposal that 4.1–11 sets forth the three messianic offices of Jesus—prophet, priest, king (cf. Mahnke (v), pp. 122–4). As Luz 1, p. 161, n. 14 rightly observes, there is no real link between the second temptation and priestly messianism.

[21] Cf. Schürmann, *Lukasevangelium* 1, p. 209, and Marshall, pp. 170–1. Is there implicit also a disassociation of Jesus from magicians and wonder workers? So Bultmann, *History*, p. 257, and M. Smith, *Magician*, pp. 104–6. Note Gk. Apoc. Ezra 4.27, where we read of Antichrist, 'he . . . made stones bread and water wine'. Schulz, *Q*, pp. 186–7, discerns in 4.1–11 par. a polemic against a θεῖος ἀνήρ Christology.

[22] Gerhardsson (v), p. 52, wonders whether the frequent rabbinic association between stones and the evil inclination might not be somewhere in the background of 4.3–4.

concern with righteousness first will be accompanied by the meeting of all needs (6.25–33; cf. Deut 28.1–14; Job 5. 17–27; Ps 33.18–19; 37.19; 104.27–8; 146.5–7).

Matthew quotes Deut 8.3b LXX (cf. Jn 4.34; *m. 'Aboth* 6.7), as does Luke. The latter, however, at least according to the best mss., has only 'man shall not live by bread alone'. This was probably the extent of the quotation in Q. In accordance with his interest in obedience to the Torah, Matthew has added 'but by every word that proceeds from the mouth of God'.[23] The LXX's closing words, ζήσεται ὁ ἄνθρωπος, have been left off as repetitious.

The quotation faithfully follows the LXX save in one particular, or perhaps two. LXX B (diff. A F Luc) has τῷ after ῥήματι. This was probably not in Matthew's Greek OT. Further, if—as some have argued—'every word of God' is the original reading, the evangelist has abbreviated by dropping ἐκπορευομένῳ διὰ στόματος. See n. 24.

The context of Deut 8.3b in the OT must be carefully considered. Again we need to quote 8.2: 'And you shall remember all the way which the Lord your God has led you these forty years in the wilderness, that he might humble you and test you to know whether you would keep his commandments or not'. Here are three elements of our gospel story: the number forty, the wilderness, and testing. Then, in 8.3a, mention is made of hunger, and in 8.5 Israel is spoken of as a son, and in 8.9 we even find stones. Clearly an awareness of Deut 8.1–10 as a whole provides the presupposition for grasping the meaning of the devil's temptation and Jesus' response: in his own person, Jesus is recapitulating the experience of Israel. The OT context of the NT quotation thus defines its meaning. Without a knowledge of Deut 8.1–10, the point of Mt 4.4 is necessarily lost.

ὁ δὲ ἀποκριθεὶς εἶπεν. This may be redactional. Compare 12.39, 48; 13.11, 37; 15.3, 13, 24, 26; 16.2; 17.11; 19.4; 21.29, 30; 24.2; 25.12; 26.23. The expression, which is common in the LXX, occurs only twice in Mark (6.37; 10.3), only thrice in Luke (8.21; 10.27; 15.29), never in John. Luke's introduction is also redactional (Jeremias, *Lukasevangelium*, p. 116), although Q must have had something similar (cf. Lk 4.12 diff. Mt 4.7).

γέγραπται. Luke has γέγραπται ὅτι (cf. CD 9.5: *kātûb kî*; Mk 7.6; 11.17; Acts 23.5; Rom 3.10; 4.17; 8.36; Gal 3.10; 4.22; 1 Pet 1.16). Given Luke's occasional avoidance of ὅτι-*recitativum* (see BDF § 470.1) and the conjunction's undoubted presence after γέγραπται in Q (Mt 4.6 = Lk 4.10), Matthew has apparently dropped it, as he will in 21.13 diff. Mk 11.17. On 'it is written' as a formal

---

[23] The MT does not have 'word'. The targums do; see Gundry, *OT*, pp. 66–7. Against Mahnke (v), pp. 60–1, Lk 4.22 hardly shows that Matthew's long text belonged to Q.

introduction to scriptural quotations see Fitzmyer, *Background*, pp. 8–10.

οὐκ ἐπ' ἄρτῳ μόνῳ ζήσεται ὁ ἄνθρωπος. So Luke. Deut 8.3 MT has: *lōʾ 'al-hallehem lĕbaddô yihyeh hāʾādām.*

ἀλλ' ἐπὶ παντὶ ῥήματι ἐκπορευομένῳ διὰ στόματος θεοῦ.[24] This is a redactional addition from Deut 8.3 LXX. The MT reads: *kî 'al-kol-môṣāʾ pî-yhwh yihyeh hāʾādām.* For sustenance as something other than normal food see also Prov 9.1–5; Wisd 16.26 ('it is not the production of crops that feeds man, but . . . thy word preserves those who trust in thee'); Ecclus 24.19–21; Jn 6.35; Apoc. Abr. 12.1–2 (quoted on p. 358).

5–6. The order of the last two temptations in Matthew is reversed in Luke. Most scholars have thought this circumstance to be Luke's doing, the primary reasons being these: (1) in Matthew the two Son of God temptations are together, and this seems original;[25] (2) the most blatant temptation ('worship me') is most naturally put off until the end, where it has the most dramatic effect; (3) Luke's interest in the temple and Jerusalem[26] could have moved him to turn the scene in the temple into the climax.[27] Although these points admittedly fall short of proof, they nevertheless persuade because no better argument has yet been offered as to why Matthew might have engineered the change in sequence (see further Donaldson, pp. 88–90, 97).

τότε παραλαμβάνει αὐτὸν ὁ διάβολος εἰς τὴν ἁγίαν πόλιν. For τότε see on 2.16. For the verb see on 2.13. For the present tense see on 3.1. 4.8 is very similar. Luke has ἤγαγεν δὲ αὐτόν. Whether we are to think of a visionary experience (so Theodore of Mopsuestia in PG 66.721a and other Antiochene theologians) or of a miraculous teleportation (cf. Acts 8.39–40; 2 Bar. 6.3; Apoc. Zeph. frag. in Clement of Alexandria, *Strom.* 5.11.77; L. Proph. Hab. 4–7; and the Catholic stories of bilocating saints, such as those about St. Martin de Porres) is unclear (cf. 2 Cor 12.2!), although 4.8 ('and he showed him all the kingdoms of the world') may argue for the former possibility. Compare Luke's 'in a moment of time' (4.5).

[24] D (with a b g¹) drops the three words after ῥήματι, and because D typically contains expanded readings, G. D. Kilpatrick, *JTS* 45 (1944), p. 176, thinks it here preserves the original text.

[25] It could even be that originally the two Son of God temptations formed a unit, the third temptation being added later; see O. Linton, 'Coordinated Sayings And Parables In The Synoptic Gospels', *NTS* 26 (1980), p. 140.

[26] On this see esp. J. B. Chance, 'Jerusalem and the Temple in Lucan Eschatology' (unpublished dissertation, Duke University, 1984).

[27] Cf. Dupont (v), p. 33; Fitzmyer, *Luke* 1, pp. 507–8. For the opposite opinion see Schürmann, *Lukasevangelium* 1, p. 218. For full discussion of the issue see A. Feuillet, 'Le récit lucanien de la tentation', *Bib* 40 (1959), pp. 613–31. He concludes that Matthew preserves the original order. If Gerhardsson ((v), pp. 71–83) be correct in linking up our narrative with a rabbinic interpretation of the *Shemaʿ* (see above, p. 353), the order in Matthew would have to be original.

Origen, *De prin.* 4.3.1 sees in Mt 4 prime proof of the folly of taking Scripture literally.

The devil is mentioned at the beginning of Luke's second temptation, not at the beginning of the third. Matthew names him in both places. See further on 4.1. 'Holy city' is almost certainly redactional (cf. 27.53). For the same or similar expressions see Isa 48.2; 52.1; Neh 11.1; Dan 9.24; 2 Macc 3.1; Ecclus 49.6; Tob 13.9; Rev 11.2; 21.2, 10; 22.19; Ps. Sol. 8.4; Josephus, *C. Ap.* 1.31; Par. Jer. 1.6; *b. Sanh.* 107b; *b. B. Qam.* 97b. Luke, no doubt following Q, has 'to Jerusalem' (cf. the Zion Gospel edition, variant to Mt 4.5, in Hennecke 1, p. 147). See cols. 45–7 of 11QTemple (where the city is really an extension of the temple) for what it meant for some Jews to think of Jerusalem as holy. See also *ARN* 35; *m. Šabbath*; and Davies, *GL*, pp. 131–54.

καὶ ἔστησεν αὐτὸν ἐπὶ τὸ πτερύγιον τοῦ ἱεροῦ. Luke drops αὐτόν. It is restored in some mss., presumably under Matthean influence. Otherwise there is agreement with Matthew. The meaning of πτερύγιον (diminutive of πτέρυξ, 'wing') is uncertain.[28] The word occurs only here in the NT and its sense ranges from 'peak' to 'turret' to 'horn' (LSJ, s.v.; cf. Dan 9.25–7 Theod[29]). Intended here perhaps is the pinnacle of the στοὰ βασιλική, south of the outer court,[30] or the reference might be to a balcony in the temple wall (cf. *y. Pesaḥ.* 35b), or perhaps the lintel of the temple gateway is in view. Gerhardsson (v), p. 59, has also claimed to find some allusion to the 'wings' of Ps 91.4. The devil will quote Ps 91.11–12 in the next verse (Mt 4.6), and Ps 91.4 reads, 'He will cover you with his pinions, and under his wings (πτέρυγας) you will find refuge . . .'. However one resolves the issue, one neglected point should be kept in mind. According to Jewish tradition,[31] the temple was at the centre of Jerusalem (Josephus, *C. Ap.* 1.196–8; *b. Yoma* 54a–b; *Tanḥuma Qidd.* 10), and Jerusalem, in turn, was thought of as being the *umbilicus mundi* (Ezek 5.5; 38.12; Jub. 8.19; 1 En. 26.1; Sib. Or. 5.248–50). So when Jesus is taken up to the πτερύγιον of the temple, he is standing precisely at the centre of the world. We may also note the rabbinic view that the temple was the highest point on the earth: *b. Qidd.* 69a.

According to Hegesippus (in Eusebius, *H.E.* 2.23.11), James the Lord's brother was cast down to his death from τὸ πτερύγιον τοῦ ναοῦ (cf.

---

[28] Discussion in J. Jeremias, 'Die "Zinne" des Tempels (Mt 4.5; Lk 4.9)', *ZDPV* 59 (1936), pp. 195–208; N. Hyldahl (v); and D. Baldi, *Enchiridion locorum sanctorum*, Jerusalem, 1955, pp. 228–37.

[29] Goulder, p. 246, speculatively supposes that the parallel with Dan 9.25–7 Theod. makes Mt 4.4–5 a messianic temptation.

[30] Josephus wrote (*Ant.* 15.411–12) that from the στοὰ βασιλική one could barely see the bottom of the valley below, and that to look made one giddy.

[31] Which tended to ignore geographical actualities; cf. Davies, *GL*, p. 9, n. 10, p. 10, n. 12.

'2 Apoc. Jas. 61.20–7). This report may, obviously,.be influenced by the gospel tradition, even though the gospel has ἱεροῦ, not ναοῦ. According to the Narrative of Joseph of Arimathea (Tischendorf, *Evangelica Apocrypha*, Leipzig, 1876), the πτερύγιον fell when the earth quaked at Jesus' crucifixion (3.4).

For the roof of the temple proper and the stairs leading to it see *m. Mid.* 4.5 and b. *Ta'an.* 29a. For the temple as the special place of God's protection see Exod 21.12–14 and Ps 61.4–5; 91.

καὶ λέγει αὐτῷ· εἰ υἱὸς εἶ τοῦ θεοῦ. So Luke, with εἶπεν for λέγει. The present tense (cf. 4.5) is probably Matthew's doing. See further on 4.3.

βάλε σεαυτὸν κάτω. Luke adds ἐντεῦθεν (Mt: 0; Mk: 0; Lk: 2) before κάτω. Jesus responded to the first temptation by declaring his trust in God, and this is the point the devil now works from: if you really trust God. . . .

γέγραπται γὰρ ὅτι. So Luke. Jesus answered the first temptation by quoting Scripture. The devil himself responds in kind. But he twists the Scripture's meaning so as to make it appear that what he is asking accords with God's revealed will. Did not the psalmist confidently write about God's deliverance of the righteous? 'I will rescue him' (Ps 91.15).

For 'for it is written' (*kî kātûb*) as a formula for the introduction of Scripture see 4.10; 26.31; Lk 4.10; Acts 1.20; 23.5; Rom 12.19; 14.11; 1 Cor 1.19; 3.19; Gal 3.10; 4.27; CD 11.20; Philo, *Post. C.* 102; 176; 179; 1 Clem. 36.3.

τοῖς ἀγγέλοις αὐτοῦ ἐντελεῖται περὶ σοῦ. This agrees with Ps 90.11a LXX and with Luke. The latter adds, in agreement with the Greek Bible, τοῦ διαφυλάξαι σε, 'to guard you'. The addition may be redactional: the use of τοῦ with the infinitive of the verb of intention is typical of Luke (Jeremias, *Lukasevangelium*, p. 117), and Luke likes φυλάσσω and related words. The 'in all your ways' of the psalm is omitted by both Matthew and Luke, for no clear reason. But it is just barely possible to see the omission as an interpretative key (so Tasker, pp. 53–4): 'in all your ways' could be taken to mean that God keeps the faithful safe wherever their way leads—provided there is obedience to the divine will. By omitting the phrase, the devil would be subtly distorting Scripture (cf. Gen 3.1).

καί. Both this and Luke's καὶ ὅτι perhaps reflect the dropping of a few words from the OT.

ἐπὶ χειρῶν ἀροῦσίν σε, μήποτε προσκόψῃς πρὸς λίθον τὸν πόδα σου. So Ps 90.12 LXX and Luke. For Israel being 'borne up on wings' in the desert see Exod 19.4 and Deut 32.10–12 and compare Deut 1.31 and Isa 63.8–9.

Many commentators have interpreted the challenge to leap off the temple as a messianic temptation: the devil is asking Jesus to perform a spectacular public miracle, to give the people a sign, and thus reveal his identity to Israel (cf. 1 Cor 1.22; Mk 8.11).[32] In line with this, there is some evidence—albeit late—of an expectation that the Messiah would manifest himself in the temple (*Pesiq. Rab.* 36; SB 1, p. 151). And why is Jesus taken from the desert to the temple, if not to gain an audience? There were cliffs enough in the desert. On the other hand, no spectators are mentioned, and if the royal colonnade is in view, the picture may be of Jesus standing over the Kedron Ravine alone, far from the court. There are moreover no texts in which the Messiah manifests himself by being hurtled from the temple;[33] and Ps 91 did not receive a messianic interpretation in Judaism.[34] For these reasons, the devil's words are best interpreted without reference to Messianic expectation.[35] The question instead is, How should Jesus exercise his powers as Son of God? The answer given is, In obedience to God. The Father in heaven is not to be compelled; rather should every deed be an obedient reaction to what he has willed, a submissive response to the divine initiative. To use divine energy in order to gain self-assurance or to prove what is known to faith or to make display is to 'tempt' God. This Jesus cannot do. Any peril he must face—and he will face the cross—and any miracle he is to do—and he will do plenty—must arise solely from obedient service to God's purpose. When the time comes, the Son will put his life on the line and the holy city will see miracles. But the time is not yet.[36]

[32] Recall the attempts of some during the Jewish War of A.D. 70 to force the hand of God: Josephus, *Ant.* 20.97ff., 169ff.; *Bell.* 2.261ff.; cf. *Ant.* 18.85ff.

[33] Cf. SB 1, pp. 151–2. Neither Mt 26.52 nor the tradition about the flight of Simon Magus (Ps.-Clem. Rec. 3.47; Acts Pet. 4) is evidence to the contrary. The tale of Balaam's flight (Tg. Ps.-J. on Num 31.8) is also irrelevant.

[34] The psalm is not clearly referred to in the NT outside the present passage, although Lk 10.19 (which, interestingly enough, follows a sentence about the downfall of Satan) has been thought to recall Ps 91.13 ('You will tread on the lion and the adder, the young lion and the serpent you will trample under foot'). So e.g. K. H. Rengstorf, *Das Evangelium nach Lukas*, NTD 3, 9th ed., Göttingen, 1962, ad loc. Others have sought some association between Psalm 91 and the wild beasts of Mk 1.13; so e.g. Schweizer, *Mark*, p. 42.

[35] Cf. Heydahl (v), pp. 119–20. If the background for leaping off the temple is not to be found in messianic expectation, then perhaps we should see a creative conjoining of Exod 19.4 or Deut 32.10–12 with Ps 91, with a view towards making the devil tempt the Son of God to repeat an experience which Israel had in the wilderness. See also the discussion of Strauss, pp. 261–2.

[36] In T. Adam 4.1 (fourth century A.D.?), we read that the heavenly powers 'carry our Lord Jesus the Messiah and bear him up'. This novel picture may reflect an interpretation of Q's temptation narrative. Although Jesus had refused to turn stones into bread and to receive all the kingdoms of the world, Christians believed that he had later on miraculously produced food and that he had received all authority in heaven and in earth. So what the devil offered Jesus in the first and third temptations became his in time. Why not then also the promise of the second temptation, that the angels would bear him up?

˙**7.** Just as he will in 26.53–4, Jesus rejects the proposal to call on angelic aid.

Deut 6.16 is cited not in order to dispute the truth of Ps 91.11–12. Jesus rather refutes the devil's erroneous application of a biblical text. One should indeed trust in God's providence, as Psalm 91 teaches; but this should not be taken as implying the propriety of putting God to the test. On the offence of tempting God see Gerhardsson (v), pp. 28–31.

ἔφη αὐτῷ ὁ 'Ιησοῦς. Luke has ἀποκριθεὶς εἶπεν αὐτῷ ὁ 'Ιησοῦς, which presumably represents Q since Luke generally avoids this phrase (Jeremias, *Lukasevangelium*, pp. 39–41, 117) while Matthew likes it (see on 3.15). For the redactional ἔφη αὐτῷ in Matthew see 17.26; 19.21; 22.37; 25.21, 23; 26.34. For Matthean examples of asyndetic ἔφη without synoptic parallels see 4.7; 19.21; 25.21, 23; 26.34; 27.65. Compare the Aramaic *'āmar/'ămĕrîn*.

πάλιν γέγραπται. Compare the introductory formula in 4.4. Because Luke studiously avoids πάλιν—Mt: 17; Mk: 28; Lk: 3—it could here come from Q. Yet Matthew has sometimes added it to parallel material: 22.1, 4; 27.50. Probably Luke's ὅτι εἴρηται brings us closer to Q than Matthew's words. Luke would presumably have kept 'it is written' had it stood in Q (he shows no tendency to drop it) and the addition of this formula to Matthew's account creates a neat threefold parallelism among 4.4, 7, and 10. For 'again' before the citation of Scripture see Jn 12.39; Rom 15.10–12; 1 Cor 3.20; Heb 1.5; 2.13; 4.5; 10.30. Here 4.4 is in mind.

οὐκ ἐκπειράσεις κύριον τὸν θεόν σου. So Luke and Deut 6.16 LXX. The latter continues, 'just as you tested him in the temptation' (πειρασμῷ). The Hebrew in its entirety reads, 'You (plural) shall not put the Lord your God to the test, as you tested him at Massah'. In its original setting the verse refers to the time when Israel found fault with Moses because there was no water. The rebellious people put the Lord to the proof only to see water come forth from a rock struck by Moses (Exod 17.1–6; Num 20.2–13). The incident is recalled for a hortatory end in Ps 95.7–9: 'O that today you would hearken to his voice! Harden not your hearts as at Meribah, as on the day at Massah in the wilderness, when your fathers tested me and put me to the proof although they had seen my work' (cf. 1 Cor 10.9; Heb 3.7–4.13). The same hortatory application of the incident is presupposed in the text before us, as it is in Heb 3.7–4.13 and *b. Sanh.* 98a. For Matthew, Jesus sees himself as being tempted to do what Israel did at Massah; he sees himself being asked to put God to the test. But the murmuring Israel is his type, and unlike the fathers in the wilderness (Num 14.22; Ps 78.17–20, 40–2, 56–7; 106.6–15; *m. 'Aboth* 5.4; *ARN* 34) he will not test the Lord. Being himself full of faith, he need not try God's faithfulness. It is not necessary for him to challenge God, to make God demonstrate his fidelity.

Texts for comparison include Isa 7.12: 'I will not ask, I will not put the Lord to the test'; Ecclus 3.26: 'the one loving danger will perish by it'; and *b. Šabb.* 32a: R. Jannai said: 'A man should never stand in a place of danger and say that a miracle will be wrought for him, lest it is not. And if a miracle is wrought for him, it is deducted from his merits'.

Some of the older commentators took 'You shall not tempt the Lord your God' to be a command addressed by Jesus to the devil, who is tempting 'the Lord God', that is, Jesus. But Matthew would never simply have equated Jesus with 'the Lord God', and Jesus is clearly distinguished from ὁ θεός in 4.3, 4, 6, and 10.

8–9. The third and final temptation in Matthew is the second temptation in Luke. See on 4.5. The differences between the First and Third Gospels are here greater than in the other two temptations. Luke's hand seems particularly evident.

πάλιν παραλαμβάνει αὐτὸν ὁ διάβολος. For the same phrase (with τότε for πάλιν) see 4.5 (redactional). Luke has καὶ ἀναγαγὼν αὐτόν (cf. Lk 4.9), which is probably redactional given that the third evangelist introduces a participle forty times in cases where Mark has two verbs co-ordinated with καί (cf. Jeremias, *Lukasevangelium*, p. 116). We could explain both Matthew and Luke if Q had, καὶ ἀνήγαγε (or: ἀνάγει) αὐτὸν καὶ ἔδειξεν (or: δείκνυσιν) αὐτῷ, but one expects an εἰς-phrase before the second καί (cf. 4.5 = Lk 4.9).

In 4.8 πάλιν seems to have the sense of the Aramaic *tûb* ('then'; cf. MHT 4, p. 32); compare 18.19 and 22.4 (both without synoptic parallels).

εἰς ὄρος ὑψηλὸν λίαν. This is probably redactional. There is no parallel in Luke.[37] Matthew will add a mountain in 5.1; 8.1; 15.29; and 28.16; and he likes λίαν (see on 2.16). For ὑψηλός (Mt: 2; Mk: 1; Lk: 1) with ὄρος (Mt: 16; Mk: 11; Lk: 12) see 17.1 (from Mark; cf. Gen 7.19–20; Deut 12.2; Jth 7.4; Isa 2.14; 14.13; Jer 3.6; Ezek 40.2). The 'high mountain'—perhaps suggested by Q's ἀνάγω— seems to be the counterpart of the mountain in 28.16. Whereas Jesus, after his death and resurrection, will stand on a mountain and declare that he has received all authority in heaven and earth, here in the temptation narrative the devil takes him up to a mountain top and offers him the kingdoms of the world. Jesus must, of course, reject the devil's proposal. Only after the passion,

---

[37] Yet some have found Luke's 'then he took him up' to be cryptic, the result of omitting the mountain; so Conzelmann, *Luke*, p. 29, and Dupont (v), p. 55. According to the former, in Luke the mountain is 'the place of prayer, the scene of secret revelations, of communication with the unseen world. No temptation can take place on it nor any public preaching'.

and then only from the Father in heaven, can Jesus accept all authority. There is no getting around the crucifixion. The Scriptures must be fulfilled (26.54).

Although Moses went up to the top of Pisgah, looked in all directions, and saw the land he would not enter (Deut 3.27; 34.1–4; *Mek.* on Exod 17.14–16), one does not know whether the third temptation should recall this OT scene and thereby add to the Moses/Jesus parallelism in Matthew.[38] There are also other parallels. 2 Bar. 76.3 reads: 'Go up therefore to the top of that mountain, and then will pass before you all the regions of that land, and the figure of the inhabited world, and the tops of the mountains, and the depths of the valleys, and the depths of the seas, and the number of the rivers that you may see what you are leaving, and where you are going'. 1 En. 87.3–4 reads, 'And those three that had last come forth grasped me (Enoch) by my hand and took me up, away from the generations of the earth, and raised me up to a lofty place, and showed me a tower raised high above the earth, and all the hills were lower. And one said to me, "Remain here till thou seest everything that befalls those elephants, camels, and asses, and the stars and the oxen, and all of them" '. Rev 21.10 reads: 'And in the Spirit he carried me away to a great, high mountain, and showed me the holy city Jerusalem coming down out of heaven from God'. See also Ezek 40.2; T. Abr. 9; and 1QapGen. 21.8–14 (quoted below). There is even a parallel in Dio Chrysostom 64.14: 'If someone should raise me aloft and transport me through the sky, either, as it were, on the back of some Pegasus or in some winged car of Pelops, offering me the whole earth and its cities . . .'.

For mountains as haunts for demons see Mk 5.5 and Böcher, pp. 30–1. In the biblical tradition mountains and high places are often associated with idolatry (e.g. Lev 26.30; 2 Kgs 12.3; Isa 65.7, 11). For temptation on a mountain see Gen 22 and Apoc. Abr. 12–13.

καὶ δείκνυσιν αὐτῷ. Luke has ἔδειξεν αὐτῷ. Does δείκνυμι here mean more than just 'to show' or 'to point out'? Perhaps. The word elsewhere seems to have the significance of trying to explain or demonstrate or convince (e.g. Deut 4.5; Mt 16.21; Acts 10.28; cf. Burnett, pp. 146–8). Moreover, the act of showing the kingdoms of the world seems to be a legal one—to see is to possess; see D. Daube, *Studies in Biblical Law*, Cambridge, 1947, pp. 24–39. Consider Gen 13.14–15: 'The Lord said to Abram . . . "Lift up your eyes and look from the place where you are, northward and southward and eastward and westward, for all the

---

[38] Those who think it should include Gerhardsson (v), pp. 62–4; Dupont (v), pp. 296–7; and Wilkens (v), p. 485. Schlatter, p. 108, draws attention to *Sipre Deut.* § 357: on Nebo God showed Moses 'all the world'.

land which you see I will give to you and to your descendants forever" '. In 1QapGen. 21 these words are quoted and followed by this: 'the next day I climbed up to Ramath-Hazor and I saw the land from this height, from the river of Egypt unto Lebanon and Senir, and from the great sea unto Hauran and all the land of Gebal unto Kadesh, and all the great desert which is east of Hauran and Senir unto the Euphrates. And he said to me, "To your descendants I shall give all this land, and they will inherit it forever" '.

πάσας τὰς βασιλείας τοῦ κόσμου. Luke has τῆς οἰκουμένης (cf. T. Abr. A 9.8). Matthew's phrase, which does not appear in the LXX, may be original. Luke shows no fondness for κόσμος (Jeremias, *Lukasevangelium*, pp. 209–10) but likes οἰκουμένη (Mt: 1; Mk: 0; Lk: 3; Acts: 5). The notion that Satan has the authority to give Jesus the kingdoms of the world—κόσμος (Mt: 9; Mk: 3; Lk: 3) means 'world', 'earth', not just Rome and her empire or Palestine—accords with the pessimism abroad in late antiquity. Satan was thought of as 'the god of this world' (2 Cor 4.4), 'the ruler of this world' (Jn 12.31; 14.30; 16.11), the κοσμοκράτωρ (Eph 6.12; Irenaeus, *Adv. haer.* 1.5.4). In Lk 4.6 the devil declares, 'I will give to you all this authority and glory, for it has been delivered to me (cf. T. Job 8.1–3; 16.2) and I give it to whom I will'.[39] Compare 1 Jn 5.19: 'the whole world lies in the power of the evil one' (cf. Mk 16.14 W). Nevertheless, as our gospel unfolds, we shall learn that Satan's position in the world has been dramatically lessened since the advent of the Son of God: the demonic hosts have been routed (12.22–30), and God has chosen to give to Jesus authority over the earth (9.6–8; 10.1; 11.27; 28.16–20).

Luke's 'in a moment of time' seems to be a redactional addition (χρόνος: Mt: 3; Mk: 2; Lk: 7).

καὶ τὴν δόξαν αὐτῶν. This means 'and their magnificence', their 'splendour'. Compare Rev 21.24, 26. The words make the offer more attractive. Luke has the same phrase in 4.6: Satan says he will give Jesus τὴν δόξαν αὐτῶν. This must be displaced. In Matthew αὐτῶν makes good sense after βασιλείας; in Luke it hangs in the air.

9. Having, without a word, shown Jesus the kingdoms of this world and their glory, the devil now speaks: all this is yours, if you will worship me. The subtlety of the earlier temptations is absent. Jesus is clearly being asked to break the first commandment of the Decalogue. Note that what is evil is not the end—after all, as the

---

[39] On this see esp. H. Kruse, 'Das Reich Satans', *Bib* 58 (1977), pp. 44–50. T. W. Manson, *Sayings*, p. 44, suggested that Matthew might have dropped this line because he thought it false and blasphemous. But the evidence points to its being not from Q but from Luke's pen; see Schulz, *Q*, pp. 180–1, and Gundry, *Commentary*, p. 58; against Schürmann, *Lukasevangelium* 1, pp. 211–12.

Son of Ps 2, Jesus will inherit the nations and possess the ends of the earth. The problem is the means, servitude to Satan.

'If (since) you are the Son of God' is dropped because the request is no longer for an act of power but for subjection to one who is not Jesus' Father; see J. Bieneck, *Sohn Gottes als Christusbezeichnung der Synoptiker*, Zürich, 1951, p. 64, n. 18.

καὶ εἶπεν αὐτῷ. So Luke, who appends 'the devil'. Compare 4.3.

ταῦτά σοι πάντα δώσω. This must be close to Q. All four words are reflected in Luke's expanded version, σοι δώσω τὴν ἐξουσίαν ταύτην ἅπασαν. ἐξουσία is Lukan (cf. Donaldson, p. 102). In Rev 13.2 the devil (= the dragon) gives his power and throne and great authority to another, the beast.

ἐὰν πεσὼν προσκυνήσῃς μοι. Compare Rev 13.4, 8, 12, 15. προσκυνεῖν (see on 2.2) is the equivalent of the hithpael of šāḥâ. Matthew has added 'falling' (see on 2.11) and Luke has changed μοι to a more Semitic ἐνώπιον ἐμοῦ (ἐνώπιον: Mt: 0; Mk: 0; Lk: 23). In the wilderness Israel was guilty of idolatry, of bowing down before false gods (Exod 32). Jesus is being tempted to act similarly. For the equation of idolatry with Satan worship see Gerhardsson (v), p. 65.

10. τότε λέγει αὐτῷ ὁ Ἰησοῦς. This formula is redactional (cf. 26.31, 52; 27.31; 28.10). Luke has καὶ ἀποκριθεὶς ὁ Ἰησοῦς εἶπεν αὐτῷ, which lays better claim to reproduce Q (cf. 4.4 = Lk 4.4).

ὕπαγε σατανᾶ.[40] This is probably a Matthean addition. The words attribute the devil's departure (4.11) to the authoritative command of Jesus. They are found again in Mk 8.33 = Mt 16.23. (But 'behind me' is left out as inappropriate: the devil does not follow behind Jesus as a disciple.) Matthew likes the imperative of ὑπάγω (Mt: 17; Mk: 12; Lk: 2). Yet possibly 'Begone, Satan!' was found in Q. As Luke moved the last temptation to second place, he could not have retained the repudiation.

'Begone, Satan!' points to more than a verbal link with 16.21–3. In both places Jesus is choosing the path of duty: the end ordained by the Father is to be achieved by the manner ordained by the Father, namely, the cross. And any opposition to this is satanic. To reject the way of the cross is to be on the side of the devil.

σατανᾶς (see W. Foerster and K. Schäferdiek, *TWNT* 7, pp. 151–64) is a name for ὁ διάβολος. It does not certainly appear in the LXX (although note Ecclus 21.27 and Job 1.6 Aq.). In the NT it is found in the four gospels, the Pauline literature, and Revelation. The appellation, which became quite popular around the turn of our era (Jub. 10.11; 23.29; 50.5; 1 En. 54.6; T. Job 3.6; 6.4; 7.1; T. Dan 3.6; 5.6; 6.1), derives from the Hebrew śāṭān (= σατάν), 'adversary' (cf. 1 Kgs 11.14, 23). By the time of

---

[40] Under the influence of 16.23 = Mk 8.33, οπισω μου is added after υπαγε in C² D L Z Maj b h 1 sy^{c.h**} sa^{mss} bo^{mss} arm eth geo Ju Ath Aug.

Jesus the idea of Satan as a fallen angel was firmly implanted in many Jewish minds (cf. Wisd 2.24; Rev 12.7–12; LAE 14–16; 2 En. 29.4–5; *Pirqe R. El.* 13.14).

γέγραπται γάρ. See 4.6 and the remarks there. Luke does not have the conjunction. Matthew has probably added it (cf. 2.5 and 26.31 diff. Mk 14.27), although for γάρ with 'written' in Q see Mt 4.6 = Lk 4.10.

κύριον τὸν θεόν σου προσκυνήσεις καὶ αὐτῷ μόνῳ λατρεύσεις. So Lk 4.8 א B D *f*[1.13] lat sy[p.h]; the first verb is moved to the front in A Θ Maj. Deut 6.13 LXX (= Deut 10.20) agrees with Matthew save in two particulars. (1) Following the MT, φοβηθήσῃ appears instead of 'worship'. (2) The synoptics' 'only' (cf. 1 Sam 7.3 MT) has no basis in Deuteronomy.[41] These differences are readily explicable. προσκυνήσεις comes in to make the scriptural response line up with the tempter's temptation ('if you . . . worship me'). And 'only', which serves to bring out what is implicit in the original (cf. the LXX addition at Gen 3.11), emphasizes that none but God should receive divine honours. It is also not surprising that 'and swear by his name', the conclusion of Deut 6.13, is omitted: it is not precisely pertinent.

The original context of the OT text is instructive. It pertains to idolatry and takes the reader back to the incident with the golden calf. In the NT Jesus the Son of God does not follow the folly of Israel. He turns down the devil's offer of the kingdoms of the world and their glory, rejecting the proposed condition.[42] The one true God alone is to be served and worshipped. What would it profit to gain the whole world without acknowledging God's lordship (cf. 16.26; Ignatius, *Rom.* 6.1)?[43]

11. The first half of this verse, which concludes the temptation story, is taken from Q, the second half from Mark.

τότε ἀφίησιν αὐτὸν ὁ διάβολος. For τότε see on 4.1 and 5. For the verb see on 3.15. Luke has the substance of Matthew's sentence (ὁ διάβολος ἀπέστη ἀπ' αὐτοῦ) plus redactional additions ('and having ended every temptation', 'until an opportune time').[44]

---

[41] LXX A (with 'worship' and 'only') has probably been assimilated to the NT. But this has been disputed by S. E. Johnson, 'The Biblical Quotations in Matthew', *HTR* 36 (1943), p. 145.

[42] And not because, as in Ps.-Clem. Hom. 8.21.4, he knows everything and therefore sees through the devil's designs.

[43] The parallel in Vendidad 19.8 is worth noticing: Zarathustra is tempted in the wilderness by Būiti, who has been sent by Ahriman, the devil. He responds, 'I shall not renounce the good religion of the worshippers of Mazda, not though life, limb, and soul part asunder'.

[44] Conzelmann, *Luke*, pp. 27–9, found in Lk 4.13 the idea that the time of Jesus (up until 22.3) was free of Satan. While this cannot be correct (see 11.14–16 and 22.28), it is true that all three synoptics make the time of Jesus one of great victory over Satan and his demons.

ἀφίστημι—Mt: 0; Mk: 0; Lk: 4—appears to be Lukan as does ἀπό (cf. Lk 1.38; 2.15; 9.33; 24.31, 51; Acts 1.9; 12.10). Perhaps Q had, καὶ ἀφῆκε αὐτόν ὁ διάβολος. Matthew's present tense may signify the provisional nature of Satan's departure (so Hill, *Matthew*, p. 102). Perhaps we should translate, 'leaves (for a time)' (cf. Luke).

καὶ ἰδοὺ ἄγγελοι προσῆλθον καὶ διηκόνουν αὐτῷ. Compare Jn 1.51; Heb 1.14. To sound a note of solemnity Matthew adds ἰδού (see on 1.20) and προσῆλθον καί (see on 4.3). διηκόνουν means 'minister' or 'serve' and here includes the sense 'to give to eat' (cf. 8.15; 25.44; Lk 22.27; Jn 12.2; Acts 6.2; Josephus, *Ant.* 11.163, 166 and see Schnackenburg (v), pp. 105, 121–2). Compare 1 Kgs 19.5–8, where Elijah is fed by an angel and then goes forty days without sustenance. We are probably to think of angel food, manna (see on 4.2), and the point seems to be this. Jesus did not turn stones into bread. Nor did he force God to send angels. Instead he trusted the Father in heaven—and all his needs were met (cf. 6.25–34). In time food was given him, and angels appeared (cf. our remarks on T. Adam 4.1 under 4.6). As God once miraculously gave Israel manna in the desert, so now he feeds his Son—his Son who, unlike Adam, did not succumb to temptation and so received the food which the first man ate in paradise before the fall. Perhaps we should also think of the tradition according to which God sent the angels to guard Adam and pay him homage (LAE 12–17, 33; Apoc. Sed. 5; Gk. Apoc. Ezra 2; cf. Heb 1.14). What Adam forfeited by his disobedience, namely, the ministration of angels, Jesus regained by his obedience (cf. Phil 2.5–11?; Heb 1.6). (Eden was on a mountain according to some Jewish texts (see on 5.1). This would fit in with seeing Jesus as the counterpart of Adam. So too would the identification of Adam as 'son of God'; see Philo, *Virt.* 203–5; Lk 3.38; Sophia of Jesus Christ 3.105.22–3).

JESUS' FIRST PREACHING IN GALILEE (4.12–17)

4.12–17 is, in typical Matthean fashion, triadic (cf. Luz 1, p. 168). It begins with (1) a recapitulation of Jesus' return to Galilee and his move to Capernaum (12–13). This is followed by (2) a formula quotation (14–16) which recalls 2.1–6, 13–15, 16–18, and 22–3, passages in which fulfilment quotations containing place names explicate what has preceded. The quotation is in turn succeeded by (3) a succinct programmatic summary of Jesus' preaching about the kingdom of heaven (17). Thus in the brief span of six verses we are rapidly taken from Judea (4.1–11) to Galilee to Nazareth to Capernaum, we are informed that Jesus' movements were in accordance with messianic prophecy, and we are given the central content of Jesus' public proclamation. The compression of the narrative is remarkable.

12. This is a redactional version of the cryptic Mk 1.14 (cf. Lk 4.14). Jn 4.1–3 preserves a parallel but apparently independent tradition.[45]

ἀκούσας δὲ ὅτι 'Ιωάννης παρεδόθη ἀνεχώρησεν εἰς τὴν Γαλιλαίαν.[46] For ἀκούω + ὅτι see on 2.22. The verb turns John's arrest into the proximate cause of the withdrawal to Galilee: the handing over of John is the divine cue for Jesus to proclaim the kingdom (cf. Lohmeyer, *Matthäus*, p. 63). On the parallel with 2.22 see p. 191. Although Matthew does not rename Jesus as the subject of the sentence (we must go back to 4.10 for this), there is no real connexion with what has preceded, and, in accord with Matthew's chronological indifference, the span of time between the temptation and John's arrest is unspecified.[47] Are we to think of John's disciples sending word to Jesus (cf. 14.12; so Gaechter, *Kommentar*, p. 120)?

'Ιωάννης: Matthew has changed Mark's accusative into a nominative to make it fit the sentence structure and, against Mark, has no article with the name (cf. 11.18; 21.32). This agrees with 2.22 and 20.30: after ἀκούω + ὅτι our evangelist does not put articles before names.[48]

παρεδόθη: the aorist passive of this verb appears elsewhere in Matthew only in 11.27 (Q). Mark has the aorist infinitive passive. It is important to note that the verb which is here used of John the Baptist is elsewhere bound up with the passion of Jesus. παρεδόθη thus highlights the parallelism between the Messiah and his herald,[49] the 'divine passive' showing John's sad end to be, like that of Jesus, the outcome of a divinely commissioned ministry (cf. Isa 53.6; Rom 4.25; 8.32; 1 Cor 11.23). John, as will be spelled out in 11.2 and 14.3–12, suffers the fate of the true prophet (cf. 5.12; 11.9;

[45] See C. H. Dodd, *Tradition*, pp. 236–8. He finds Mt 4.12 to be closer to Jn 4.1–3 than Mk 1.14 because in both the First and Fourth Gospels and not in the Second a motive for the move to Galilee is cited. Yet perhaps Matthew has only made explicit what is implicit in Mark: John's arrest was the occasion (and therefore reason) for Jesus' withdrawal.

[46] ο Ιησους is added after δε in C² L W Θ 0233 *f*¹·¹³ Maj it vg^cl sy^c.p.h. bo^pt Hil Epiph.

[47] For the good possibility that between his baptism and his return to Galilee Jesus was, as the Fourth Gospel has it, active in the south, see Dodd, *Tradition*, pp. 223–47, and Grundmann, pp. 107–9.

[48] Thus, against Chilton, *Strength*, p. 99, the unqualified 'John' is not evidence of pre-Matthean, non-Markan tradition.

[49] Perhaps, in the pre-Markan source behind Mk 1.14–15, παραδίδωμι implied John's death, not simply his arrest. See Pesch 1, pp. 100–1. Chilton, *Strength*, pp. 99–100, thinks the aorist passive indicates a non-Markan source behind Mt 4.12. The aorist, however, is from Mark, and the passive of παραδίδωμι (cf. Isa 53.12) is dictated by the (redactional) sentence form, ἀκούσας δὲ ὅτι 'Ιωάννης. . . .

23.29–37; see further Schlatter, pp. 112–13, and Chilton, *Strength*, pp. 65, 70–1). The fate of the forerunner foreshadows the fate of the coming one.

ἀναχωρέω means 'withdraw', 'take refuge' (BAGD, s.v.). It here replaces Mark's ἦλθεν and is redactional. See on 2.22, where fear for one's life provides the motivation for a scripturally attested move. In 4.12 are we to think that Jesus' life is already in danger in the south, so that he takes what will later be his own advice (10.23) and flees (cf. 12.15), it not being time for him to be delivered up (cf. Jn 7.6)? Or does ἀναχωρέω lack the connotation of fear and flight (cf. 9.24; 27.5; Acts 26.31; Josephus, *Vita* 151; so Soares Prabhu, pp. 124–6, who interprets 4.12 not as a flight but as a challenge)? A decision seems impossible. On the one hand, 12.15, where Jesus flees because of a plot laid against him, favours the first option. On the other hand, 4.12 involves no change of jurisdiction, for Herod Antipas, who laid hands on John, also had charge of Galilee. However one decides the issue for the redactional level, it seems historically plausible that Jesus, a follower of John the Baptist, became cautious or even went into hiding after John was arrested;[50] and he may have felt safer in Galilee. Mk 6.14 = Mk 14.1 shows clearly enough that the tradition recognized at least a short interlude between the time of John and the time of Jesus (cf. Wink, p. 96). Moreover, John's arrest was certainly one of the significant factors which allowed Jesus to gain public attention: with John gone there was a vacancy to be filled (cf. Jn 3.30).

4.12 has a close parallel not only in 2.22 but also in 14.13, where we are told that Jesus, upon hearing (ἀκούσας) of John's demise, withdrew (ἀνεχώρησεν). In both 4.12 and 14.13 a turn of events in the life of John makes for a turn of events in the life of Jesus. When John is handed over, Jesus opens his public ministry in Galilee (4.12); and when John is finally put to death, it is the beginning of the end of Jesus' public ministry (14.13). Thus John and Jesus are linked in salvation-history. What happens to the eschatological Elijah makes known to the Messiah what to do next (cf. 17.9–13).

13. This is a redactional sentence which transfers Jesus from Nazareth (2.23) to Capernaum (8.5; cf. Mk 1.21) and which provides the elements on which to hang the scriptural citation of the following verses.

καὶ καταλιπὼν τὴν Ναζαρά.[51] Compare 16.4 (diff. Mk 8.13) and

---

[50] This is not irrelevant for judging the historical value of the passion predictions which appear later in the gospel. Jesus was conscious from the beginning of the possibility of a violent end.

[51] Ναζαρετ: B² L Γ 209 346 565 700 892 1010 1241 1424 *pm* aur Epiph. These witnesses are relatively late and assimilation to 2.22 is to be suspected (cf. the readings of these witnesses in 21.11). ραθ: C P Δ *pc*. ρεθ: ℵ* D K W Θ 0233 *f*¹.¹³ 28 *pm* lat sa bo Or^pt Eus. ρα: ℵ¹ B* Z 33 k mae Or^pt. This last is the *lectio difficilior*. See the discussion in Soares Prabhu, pp. 130–1.

21.17 (diff. Mk 11.11), which argue for a redactional origin. According to 2.23, Jesus spent his youth in Nazareth. But according to Mark, a source Matthew regards as authoritative, Jesus began his ministry in Galilee. Thus, to make all harmonious, a move is required (cf. Strecker, *Weg*, p. 65, who sees in Matthew's editorial work evidence of *Historisierung*). Is there, nevertheless, cause to suppose the influence of tradition here? Intriguingly enough, both Matthew and Luke agree against Mark in having Jesus, after his temptation, return to Ναζαρά (a spelling found in the NT only in Mt 4.13 and Lk 4.16). Only later does Jesus go to Capernaum. From this, it has been inferred, and with some degree of plausibility, that after the temptation scene Q contained at least a transitional sentence which named Ναζαρά (cf. Streeter, pp. 206–7; Schürmann, *Untersuchungen*, p. 77; Soares Prabhu, pp. 130–2; Luz 1, p. 168).

Ναζαρά (cf. Lk 4.16; is this the Aramaic spelling? see Chilton, *Strength*, pp. 311–13) is textually uncertain (see note 51). Assuming it to be original, the different spellings in 2.23 (Ναζαρέτ) and 21.11 (Ναζαρέθ) are striking—and all the more so as all three verses are primarily redactional. Whatever the explanation, we should observe the similar phenomenon in Luke-Acts, which has Ναζαρέτ in the infancy narrative (1.26; 2.4, 39, 51), Ναζαρά after the temptation (4.16), and Ναζαρίθ in the construction, Jesus + article + ἀπό + 'Nazareth' (Acts 10.38; cf. Mt 21.11).[52]

ἐλθὼν κατῴκησεν εἰς Καφαρναούμ. Compare 2.23 and see p. 191. The construction (cf. Gen 13.18; 1 Βασ. 31.7; 4 Βασ 16.6) is redactional. In writing that Jesus 'dwelt' (cf. Isa 8.23 LXX) in Capernaum, Matthew goes beyond Mark, although it can be argued that this is implicit in the second gospel; so G. D. Kilpatrick, 'Jesus, His Family, and His Disciples', *JSNT* 15 (1982), pp. 3–19. Luke says simply, Jesus 'went down' (κατῆλθεν) to Capernaum (4.31). For other instances of auxilary 'come' (a Semitism; cf. Hebrew *ylk*, Aramaic *'zl*) see p. 82. 'Capernaum' (= *kĕpar naḥūm*, 'village of Nahum') is brought forward from Mk 1.23 (cf. Jn 2.12). The city does not appear in the OT. In the NT it occurs only in the gospels, including John. Josephus knew of it (*Vit.* 403; *Bell.* 3.519), as did the rabbis (SB 1, pp. 159–60).[53] It was located on the north-west shore of the Sea of Galilee, in the territory of Naphtali (cf. Josh 19.32–9), about two miles west of the Jordan. It was within the territory of Herod Antipas and

[52] If the common spelling of 'Nazareth' in Mt 4 and Lk 4 is not coincidence, Matthew's unmotivated καταλιπών (4.12) could presuppose the outcome of Lk 4.16–30 (see Lk 4.31) or some parallel tradition; cf. Schürmann, *Lukasevangelium* 1, pp. 241–4, who goes so far as to argue that Lk 4.16–30 comes from Q (an intriguing possibility).

[53] Some would add the *Kefar-Aḥim* of b. Menaḥ. 85a and the *Kefer-Ahus* of *t. Men.* 9.2. The Καφορναούμ of Josephus, *Bell.* 3.519 is a fountain in Gennesaret.

should be identified not with Khan Minyeh (*pace* G. A. Smith, p. 295) but with the ruin Tell Ḥum (Ḥum recalling Naḥum). The city—it is a πόλις in the gospels[54]—may have had a population as high as 12,000,[55] although most estimates are much lower than this. Fishing, agriculture, and trading were undoubtedly its mainstays, and it was near the trade route that ran between Damascus and Ptolemais (Accho). If we trust the gospels, the place housed a Roman garrison and a customs station (Mt 8.5–13; 9.9–10; 17.24). A synagogue of the fourth and fifth centuries A.D. (which might be located on the same spot as the first-century synagogue; see Mk 1.21–8; Lk 7.4–5) has been excavated. No first-century public buildings have yet been uncovered.[56]

The centre of Jesus' ministry according to the synoptic gospels, Capernaum was the home of Peter and Andrew (Mk 1.29).[57] In Matthew the place is mentioned four times: 4.13; 8.5; 11.23; 17.24. Its significance is evident from the first two references.[58] In 4.13 it is not only Jesus' dwelling place (of no other place is this said), it is also associated with an OT prophecy. And in 8.5 it is the setting for a string of wonder stories. Further, in 9.1 Capernaum, although not mentioned by name, is clearly designated 'his [i.e.Jesus'] own city'. (According to *m. B. Bat.* 1.5, dwelling in a city for twelve months made one a citizen.) Perhaps one might suppose, especially in view of *Eccl. Rab.* on 1.8, which connects *minim* with Kephar Naḥum, that Matthew knew of a Christian community there (cf. Acts 9.31). But *Ecclesiastes Rabbah* is not an early source, and the evidence is not otherwise compelling (Freyne, p. 361). We may safely infer that Capernaum was simply an important place in Matthew's tradition and that the evangelist emphasized it because of its location in the territory named in Isaiah's prophecy (Isa 9.1–2).

[54] So also Ptolemy, *Geog.* 5.16.4. Josephus has κώμη, 'village'.

[55] So E. M. Meyers and J. F. Strange, *Archaeology, the Rabbis, and Early Christianity*, Nashville, 1981, p. 58. They estimate the total size to have been about 300,000 square metres.

[56] Lit.: G. Orfali, *Capharnaum et ses Ruines*, Paris, 1922; G. Dalman, *Sacred Sites and Ways* (trans. *Orte und Wege Jesu*, 1924), London, 1933, pp. 133–59; E. L. Sukenik, *Ancient Synagogues in Palestine and Greece*, London, 1934, pp. 7–21; E. F. F. Bishop, 'Jesus and Capernaum', *CBQ* 15 (1953), pp. 427–37; S. Loffreda, 'The Late Chronology of the Synagogue at Capernaum', *IEJ* 23 (1973), pp. 37–42; idem, *A Visit to Capharnaum*, 6th ed., Jerusalem, 1978; J. F. Strange, 'Capernaum', *IDBSup*, pp. 140–1. See further on 8.14.

[57] See J. Blinzler, 'Die Heimat Jesu', *BK* 25 (1970), pp. 14–20, for arguments against the implausible suggestion made by H. Stegemann (1969 inaugural lecture at the University of Bonn) that Jesus' home was always Capernaum. For the unconvincing argument that Jesus was not as much of an itinerant as often thought see F. H. Borsch, 'Jesus—the Wandering Prophet?', in *What About the New Testament?*, ed. M. Hooker and C. Hickling, London, 1975, pp. 45–63.

[58] There are still a handful of scholars who think Matthew the apostle penned our gospel (Tasker, Stonehouse, Petrie, Gundry). For them, of course, Matthew's interest in Capernaum would be obvious: it was his home town (cf. 9.9).

τὴν παραθαλασσίαν ἐν ὁρίοις Ζαβουλὼν καὶ Νεφθαλίμ. Although παραθαλάσσιος, a good LXX word (Jer 47.7; 2 Chr 8.17 (εἰς τὴν Αἰλὰθ τὴν παραθαλασσίαν); Ezek 25.9; 1 Macc 7.1; 11.8; 2 Macc 8.11; cf. Josephus, *Bell*. 1.257), is a NT *hapax legomenon*, this is not evidence of pre-Matthean tradition. The word prepares for the quotation of Isa 9.1 in 4.15 ('land of Zebulun and land of Nephtalim, toward the *sea*'). In addition, the call of Simon and the others in 4.18–22 takes place on the shore of the Sea of Galilee (παρὰ τὴν θάλασσαν). For ὅριον (= 'territory', 'region'; cf. *gĕbūl*) see on 2.16. For the absence of the article see the anarthrous γῇ of 4.15. Luke always uses λίμνη ('lake') for the Sea of Galilee; Matthew, Mark, and John invariably have θάλασσα ('sea') or τὰ ὕδατα. Incidentally, the present remark betrays Matthew's knowledge of Palestinian geography: he knows Capernaum is in the territory of Naphtali, and this is not a fact he could have gleaned either from the OT or from Mark or Q.

Thompson (p. 19) has observed how the place names in 4.13 form a chiastic pattern with names in 4.15:

> a. Galilee
>   b. by the sea ⎫
>   –. the territory of Zebulun and Naphtali ⎬ Jesus
>   c. the land of Zebulun and the land of Naphtali ⎫
>   b. towards the sea ⎬ the OT
> a. Galilee

This interlocking scheme underlines the providential correlation between the scriptural prophecy from Isaiah and an event in Jesus' life.

14. ἵνα πληρωθῇ τὸ ῥηθὲν διὰ Ἠσαΐου τοῦ προφήτου λέγοντος. See on 1.22 for this introductory formula. On Isaiah in Matthew see on 1.22 and 3.3. Matthew typically associates the prophet with Jesus' work for the Gentiles, as in the present instance.

The quotation which follows may be in part an attempt to make an asset out of a liability (cf. Klostermann, p. 30). The stumbling block which Jesus' associations with Galilee could have caused are known from John's gospel: 'No prophet is to rise from Galilee' (7.52; cf. Jn 1.46; 7.41–2). For confirmation from the Jewish sources see Davies, *GL*, pp. 221–35, 425–9. Matthew counters by calling on Isaiah.

15–16. The function of these verses is to offer scriptural warrant for a geographical fact of Jesus' ministry, namely, his presence in Galilee. This recalls the similar function of the four redactional fulfilment texts in Mt 2, each of which is attached to a geographical place name. Now there would seem to be two different possible approaches to 4.14–16. Either Matthew has some special vested theological interest in Galilee,[59] or he has simply tried to vindicate the geographical particulars of Jesus' ministry against the weight of Jewish objections. The latter alternative is to be preferred. Neither the work of Davies (*GL*, pp. 211–43) nor that of Freyne (pp. 360–4) uncovers a Galilean idyll in the First Gospel. Indeed, the region's undoubted significance is qualified by several facts, among them the passage of doom in 11.20–4, the rejection of Jesus by his own in 13.53–8, and the universal dimension of the gospel which transcends any concept of a messianic holy land (cf. 28.19). Note also that from the quotation in 4.15–16 Matthew has dropped the OT's 'and later he will make glorious'. Thus one can overstress the importance of Galilee for our evangelist. It is perhaps no more to be emphasized as a holy place than the places around which chapter 2 and the formula quotations there revolve. In short, Matthew makes of Galilee a good simply because of its firm place in the tradition and the need, spurred by Jewish calumny, to find for it scriptural support.[60]

The quotation itself is from Isa 9.1–2 and, as we shall see, agrees neither with the LXX nor the MT.[61] What we probably have before us is an independent rendering of the Hebrew with influence from the LXX. In any case there are agreements with the LXX against the MT and agreements with the MT against the LXX.

In its original context the passage concerns a broken people who have suffered Assyrian attack and deportation (cf. 2 Kgs 15.29; 1 Chr 5.26); to them is promised deliverance: a son from the house of David will bring salvation (9.6–7). In Matthew the prophecy is taken up and applied to the ministry of the Messiah, whom the evangelist undoubtedly took to be the son of Isa 9.6–7. Hence there is a shift from literal destruction and political plight to moral and spiritual darkness; compare S. L. Edgar, 'Respect for Context in Quotations from the OT', *NTS* 9 (1962), p. 58; also Luz 1, pp. 172–3.

Many have thought the quotation to come from an early Christian testimony collection; so McNeile, p. 44; Strecker, pp. 63–6; Lindars,

---

[59] In this connexion the following works deserve special mention: R. H. Lightfoot, *Locality and Doctrine in the Gospels*, New York, 1937; E. Lohmeyer, *Galiläa und Jerusalem*, Göttingen, 1936; Marxsen; L. E. Elliott-Binns, *Galilean Christianity*, SBT 16, London, 1956; and N. Wieder, *The Judean Scrolls and Karaism*, London, 1962. For critical discussion of these works see Davies, *GL*, and the appendix to this by G. Stemberger.

[60] There is no evidence of a first century Jewish eschatological expectation centering on Galilee; see Davies, *GL*, pp. 221–35. Matthew's choice of Isa 9.1–2, however, will have been impressive given its 'messianic' context in the OT.

[61] Lit.: Stendahl, *School*, pp. 104–10; Gundry, *OT*, pp. 105–8; Lindars, *Apologetic*, pp. 196–9; Rothfuchs, pp. 67–70; Soares Prabhu, pp. 86–104; and H. D. Slingerland, 'The Transjordanian Origin of St. Matthew's Gospel', *JSNT* 3 (1979), pp. 24–5.

Apologetic, pp. 197–9; and R. Hodgson, 'The Testimony Hypothesis', *JBL* 98 (1979), p. 367. Their reasons include the following: (1) Isa 6.1–9.7 was a primary source of early Christian testimonies;[62] (2) our verses could originally have had another application—for example, to the birth of Jesus (so Lindars); (3) Jn 7.52 and 8.12 may preserve an apologetic use of Isa 9.1–2 (so Lindars), and Lk 1.79 clearly depends upon these verses; and (4) the peculiar textual reading could witness to a lost text type. In our estimation, all of these reasons, while consistent with the testimony hypothesis, are far from convincing. Moreover, the alterations in 4.15–16 *vis-à-vis* the OT suit Matthew's context perfectly (see below). Given this and our findings with regards to the redactional origin of the formula quotations in Mt 1–2, we are not inclined to suppose that Mt 4.15–16 comes from a testimony collection.

γῆ Ζαβουλὼν καὶ γῆ Νεφθαλίμ. Compare 4.13. The LXX, in which Zebulun and Naphtali are vocatives, has χώρα for the first γῆ, lacks the καί, and adds the feminine article to the second γῆ. Matthew is closer to the MT, which reads: ʾarṣâ zĕbulûn wĕʾarṣâ naptālî. (Here Zebulun and Naphtali are in the accusative; they are objects of verbs Matthew has omitted.) The only evidence for the use of the LXX is in the μ-ending for Naphtali. (Josephus, *Ant.* 2.181 has Νεφθάλις while *Ant.* 1.305 has Νεφθάλεις.) Anarthrous γῆ + proper name is characteristic of our redactor (Mt: 7; Mk: 0; Lk: 0).

The evangelist has dropped the first part of Isa 9.1 and certain portions of the second half, including the verbs. This makes Zebulun and Naphtali and their apparent qualifiers ('towards the sea', 'beyond the Jordan') functionally equivalent to Galilee: they are in apposition to Γαλιλαία.

Of interest is an old Jewish-Christian interpretation of Mt 4.12–16 reported by Jerome in his commentary on Isaiah (*Comm. on Isa.* on 9.1):

The Hebrews who believe in Christ interpret these passages as follows: 'Of old these two tribes of Zebulun and Naphtali were taken captive by Assyrians and were led away into a strange country, and Galilee was deserted; but as the prophet said, they should be relieved by him [Christ], who should bear the sins of the people'. Afterwards not only the two tribes, but the remnant who dwelt beyond the Jordan and in Samaria, were likewise led away into captivity. And this they [the Judeo-Christians] affirm the Scripture to say, 'in the selfsame region whose population had been led captive and had started to serve the Babylonians, and which was first tormented by the darkness of error, that same land should be the first to see the light of the preaching of Christ' (PL 24.127).

[62] Dodd, *Scriptures*, pp. 78–82. For Matthew's use of this section see 1.23 (cf. Isa 7.14; 8.10) and 21.42 (cf. Isa 8.14).

It is possible that Matthew held a similar view. Zebulun and Naphtali were two of the first tribes to go into exile (2 Kgs 15.29), and it would be appropriate for the kingdom to be restored first where it was initially dissolved. For support, one could observe that our quotation is followed by an announcement of the advent of the kingdom of God.[63] On the other hand, Matthew has omitted the words from Isa 9.1–2 that would foster this interpretation. 'In the former time he brought into contempt . . . but in the later time he will make glorious' is omitted (see further Davies, GL, p. 227.).

ὁδὸν θαλάσσης. So LXX A Q אc.a (under Hexapla influence? see Gundry, OT, 105–6; Soares Prabhu, p. 93) for derek hayyām. The surprising accusative is probably adverbial. The meaning is, 'towards the sea', that is, 'on the coast', as if κατά had been used (cf. BDF § 161.1). This is not good Greek style and depends upon the prepositional use of derek, as in 1 Kgs 8.48 (see BAGD, s.v., ὁδός). The phrase probably equals the (otherwise unmotivated) παραθαλασσίαν of 4.13, although one could conceivably think of the west coast of Galilee, 'toward the (Mediterranean) Sea' (so Zahn, pp. 164–9). In this case, Galilee, equated with Zebulun and Naphtali, might be pictured as between the sea and the Jordan (see below).

Matthew, following Mark, uses the thoroughly Semitic θάλασσα (Black, p. 133) for the lake of Gennesaret (so also John). Luke uses λίμνη, which is more accurate (so also Josephus; Pliny, Nat. hist. 5.15.71: lacus). See further on 4.18. θάλασσα is perhaps preferred in Matthew and Mark because of its OT connotations—chaos, threat, danger; these Jesus overcomes when he walks on the sea, rebukes the waves, and so on. See E. S. Malbon, 'The Jesus of Mark and the Sea of Galilee', JBL 103 (1984), pp. 363–77.

πέραν τοῦ Ἰορδάνου. So the LXX for ʿēber hayyardēn. Compare 4.25; 19.1; also Josephus, Ant. 7.198; 12.222; 14.277. Matthew has omitted as irrelevant for his purposes several words which occur in the LXX and MT. He is intent (as in chapter 2) on geographical concerns—land of Zebulun, land of Naphtali, beside the sea, beyond the Jordan, Galilee of the Gentiles. All else is dropped.

H. Dixon Slingerland, 'The Transjordanian Origin of St Matthew's Gospel', JSNT 3 (1979), pp. 18–28, has proposed that the geographical perspective of this verse (along with 19.1 and perhaps 4.25) points to east of the Jordan as the place of Matthew's composition. This is because 'beyond the Jordan' qualifies what precedes, namely, land of Zebulun and Naphtali. The perspective is thus of one standing in the east and seeing

---

[63] Cf. A. S. Geyser, 'Some Salient NT Passages on the Restoration of the Twelve Tribes of Israel', in Lambrecht, Apocalypse, p. 307.

Galilee on the other side of the Jordan.[64] Contrast the LXX, where there is a καί before the πέραν; this makes 'beyond the Jordan' not a point of reference but a place like Zebulun and Naphtali and Galilee. So the LXX has a western perspective: Galilee is on its author's side of the Jordan, that is, in the west.

Slingerland has undoubtedly made an intriguing observation, one which should henceforth be seriously considered in attempts to locate the origin of Matthew. We offer, however, three caveats. First, 'beyond the Jordan' could be thought of as standing on its own (cf. 4.25) and mean either the transjordanian region or Peraea, as in Isa 8.23 LXX (so BAGD, s.v., πέραν, and Soares Prabhu, p. 97; cf. *m. Šeb.* 9.2). In this case, 'Galilee of the Gentiles' would be conceived of as a theological term encompassing more than the normal boundaries of Galilee.[65] Secondly, and more importantly, there are several agreements between Mt 4.15–16 and the MT; and the MT (with the OT Peshitta) shares Matthew's geographical perspective: Galilee is to the west. Perhaps, then, Matthew has in this particular just followed the MT. The slip, if such it be, is not unthinkable. Lastly, our gospel may have been written in Antioch on the Orontes, and if one looks at a map and extends the north-south line created by the Jordan river, Antioch appears east of that line. Thus it might have been natural for Matthew to think of Galilee as on the other side of the Jordan.

Γαλιλαία τῶν ἐθνῶν. So the LXX. The MT has *gĕlîl*[66] *haggôyim*. Matthew's 'Galilee of the Gentiles' is the key to and reason for the quotation of Isaiah's text. The originally pejorative phrase has been given new content so that its connotations are positive.

The Messiah's work for the Gentiles has heretofore only been foreshadowed. 1.1 declared Jesus to be the son of Abraham. There were Gentiles in the genealogy. Foreign magi worshipped Jesus the infant. John the Baptist proclaimed God's ability to raise up new sons to Abraham. Now Jesus himself goes to 'Galilee of the Gentiles' and there preaches the kingdom of heaven (v. 17).

Was Galilee in fact 'the land of the Gentiles'? And, closely related to this question, how did Galilean Judaism differ from Judaism in the south? These are difficult issues, and we can only offer the outlines of an answer. According to Judg 18.7 and 28 a significant portion of the population of Zebulun and Naphtali was made up of Canaanites and Sidonians. From 2 Kgs 15.29 and 17.24–7 we learn about the influx of foreigners after the deportation of the Jewish populace. In Isa 9.1–2 *gĕlîl haggôyim* probably

---

[64] Cf. the remarks of G. Stemberger, 'Galilee—Land of Salvation?', in Davies, *GL*, p. 420. For nineteenth century proponents of the view see B. Weiss, p. 17. For an endorsement of Slingerland's conclusions see G. Theissen, 'Lokalkoloritforschung in den Evangelien' *EvT* 45 (1985), pp. 492–3.

[65] Cf. Lohmeyer, *Matthäus*, p. 64; Grässer, p. 30; and M. Black, *The Scrolls and Christian Origins*, London and New York, 1961, p. 81. But see the criticism of Stemberger, 'Galilee—Land of Salvation?', in Davies, *GL*, p. 420. For Josephus' account of the boundaries of Galilee see *Bell.* 3.35–40.

[66] This word is difficult. According to BDB, s.v., it means 'circuit', 'region', and always has reference to the northern borders of Palestine.

reflects the then common conviction as to the mixed population of the north (so R. E. Clements, *TDOT* 2, p. 427). In 1 Macc 5, second century Galilee is still depicted as predominantly heathen. According to Strabo 16.2.34, Egyptians, Arabians, Phoenicians, and Greeks (cf. Josephus, *Vit.* 67) lived in Galilee. All of this points rather strongly in one direction. On the other hand, the Jewish element in Galilee was probably never completely eliminated, and a recent study (Freyne, pp. 41–50) has called into question the widely-received notion that the Hasmoneans (Aristobulus 1 or John Hyrcanus) Judaized the north.[67] Further, scholars have probably made far too much of the differences between Judea and Galilee, especially when it comes to piety.[68] There are indeed texts that portray Galileans as lax in the observance of the Torah (e.g. *y. Šabb.* 16.15d); and the halakah of Galilee differed at certain points from the halakah of Judea (see on 1.18). Moreover, before A.D. 70, the Pharisaic population in Galilee, there is reason to believe, was not very large (cf. M. Smith, *Magician*, p. 157; Freyne, pp. 305–23; and Cohen, p. 226). Nevertheless, regional differences as a rule almost inevitably breed popular prejudice, and all sweeping statements as to the character of piety in Galilee should be received critically. First, it is impossible to speak of Galilee as if it were a monolithic entity. Diversity must have characterized the north just as it did the south. In this connexion, it is important to remark that a case has been made for the conservatism of the Jewish population in Upper Galilee as opposed to Lower Galilee (where Jesus apparently remained): the north was more isolated and less urbanized, this last circumstance perhaps reflecting resistance to cultural change.[69] One should also carefully distinguish between attitudes before A.D. 70 and attitudes after that date, although this is difficult given the extant sources. Secondly, Josephus does not write about an assimilated Judaism in Galilee. He pictures the Jews there as observant and Torah-abiding, and one cannot doubt that the pilgrimage to Jerusalem was the focus of Galilean religious practice.[70] A third consideration is this: the migration of Judean Jews to northern Palestine after A.D. 70 and their ready integration there make great discontinuity unlikely. (See M. D. Goodman in *CHJ* 3.)

The facts as outlined in the previous paragraph lead one to conclude that by 'Galilee of the Gentiles' Matthew did not mean to imply that Galilee was occupied primarily by non-Jews, or even that Jesus ministered there to Gentiles (an idea which would contradict 10.5–6 and 15.24). Rather, as Luz 1, p. 171 puts it,

[67] According to Schürer 1, pp. 217–18, Galilee was first judaized by Aristobulus (104–103 B.C.). According to G. A. Smith, p. 270, this took place under Hyrcanus (135–114 B.C.).

[68] For lit. on this theme see Davies, *GL*, p. 235, n. 30. See also now Freyne, passim.

[69] See E. M. Meyers, 'The Cultural Setting of Galilee: The Case of Regionalism and Early Judaism', *ANRW* II.19.1 (1979), pp. 686–702.

[70] See Freyne, pp. 259–334; F. X. Malinowski, 'Torah Tendencies in Galilean Judaism According to Flavius Josephus', *BTB* 10 (1980), pp. 30–6; and idem, 'Galilee in Josephus' (unpublished Ph.D. dissertation, Duke University, 1973). For some issues there is even evidence of a stricter halakah in Galilee; see Oppenheimer, pp. 213–15. On Galilee during the first revolt see Cohen.

'Galilee of the Gentiles' has 'fiktiven Charakter'. There was no literal sense in which Galilee was for Jesus Gentile territory. But that matters not for the evangelist since his interest is wholly theological: he wants a scriptural text linking the Messiah and the Gentiles. And he wants this in 4.14–16 so that the end will be foreshadowed in the beginning: although Jesus must minister only to the lost sheep of the house of Israel, the kingdom will eventually embrace the Gentiles (21.43).

ὁ λαὸς ὁ καθήμενος ἐν σκοτίᾳ.[71] The LXX reads: ὁ λαὸς ὁ πορευόμενος ἐν σκότει. The MT has: hāʿām hahōlĕkîm baḥōšek. The verb (see Davies, *GL*, pp. 27–8) may be altered under the influence of the τοῖς καθημένοις in 4.16b (so Rothfuchs, p. 69). Or perhaps Matthew's OT had καθήμενος (cf. Lk 1.79: 'to shine on those sitting in darkness, and in the shadow of death'). Or maybe Ps 107.10 or Isa 42.7 has been influential: καθημένους ἐν σκότει (yōšbê ḥōšek; cf. Schlatter, p. 115). Compare 2 Bar. 59.2: 'At that time the lamp of the eternal law shone on all those who sat in darkness . . .' (cf. 46.2). For κάθημαι as meaning 'to reside' or 'settle' see BAGD, s.v., 1b. For the possibility that λαός in Matthew has been influenced by the Deuteronomic idea of God's faithfulness to his unfaithful people see Frankemölle, pp. 193–200. Origen, *C. Cels.* 6.66, wrongly equates λαός with 'the Gentiles'.

'Darkness' as a symbol of moral and spiritual bankruptcy is common in the writings of the NT (Lk 1.79; Jn 1.5; 3.19; 8.12; Rom 2.19; 13.12; Eph 5.8, 11; Col 1.13; 1 Th 5.4–5; 1 Pet 2.9; 1 Jn 2.9, 11). This is our best guide as to what Matthew thought by Galilee sitting in darkness. Yet it could be that the darkness/light paradigm has to do with Jesus as revealer: the Messiah reveals what has been hidden (cf. Stendahl, *School*, pp. 117, 141–2).

φῶς εἶδεν μέγα. The LXX has: ἴδετε φῶς μέγα. The MT has: raʾû ʾôr gādôl. LXX אᶜ Luc C have εἶδεν. Matthew might have had an Ur-Lucianic text in front of him, but the several disagreements between Matthew and Lucian here make this doubtful (see Gundry, *OT*, p. 107). Has then Lucian been influenced by Matthew? Or is the common εἶδεν the result of independent considerations? In favour of this last option, Matthew requires a past tense (the prophecy has been fulfilled), and Lucian might have found ἴδετε awkward after ὁ λαός. Note Matthew's word order: the light (= the person, words, and deeds of Jesus) comes first.

καὶ τοῖς καθημένοις ἐν χώρᾳ καὶ σκιᾷ θανάτου. The LXX lacks a καί (but not A) and has the nominative plural οἱ κατοικοῦντες;

---

[71] א* C L Θ *f*.¹·¹³ Maj Eus read σκοτει (so N²⁶). This probably marks assimilation to Isa 9.1 LXX and/or Lk 1.79. א¹ B D (σκοτεια) W Orᵖᵗ followed by HG have: σκοτια. Chilton, *Strength*, p. 301, suggests that this second reading could represent assimilation to Mt 10.27 or to the ending of σκια in 4.16c. This seems less likely than revision to gain harmony with the LXX.

otherwise there is agreement. The MT has: *yōšbê bĕ° ereṣ ṣalmāwet*.
Matthew's 'and' is either epexegetical or makes a hendiadys (BDF
§ 422.9, 16). καὶ σκιᾷ θανάτου in both the LXX and Matthew
appears to require dependence of the latter upon the former. But
Gundry (*OT*, p. 107) has argued that our MT may be a corruption
of an original *we'* + *ṣelem* + *māwet*, in which case the LXX and
Matthew could be independent renditions of the same Hebrew
text. It is also just possible, though unlikely, that the LXX has been
corrupted by the First Gospel or that a common interpretation of
ṣalmāwet as σκιᾷ θανάτου (see Ps 107.10 LXX) gave rise to
common translations.

φῶς ἀνέτειλεν αὐτοῖς. φῶς λάμψει ἐφ' ὑμᾶς appears in the LXX,
'ôr nāgah 'ălêhem in the MT. Matthew agrees with the MT against
the LXX with the third person αὐτοῖς; and his aorist is closer to the
Hebrew perfect than the LXX's future, although ἀνέτειλεν is a
rather free translation of the Hebrew *nāgah* (the one is never used
for the other in the LXX). Matthew has nothing corresponding
either to *'al* or ἐπί. ἀνέτειλεν recalls Lk 1.79, which alludes to Isa
9.1, and this may indicate a common non-LXX Greek text. The
verb might also be influenced by Num 24.17 or Mal 4.2 (so
Lindars, *Apologetic*, p. 198; cf. T. Sim. 7.1) or by its association
with messianic expectation (see on 2.2). Further, 'to dawn' better
fits the beginning of Jesus' ministry than the LXX's 'to shine'.

A few pertinent points: (1) In Deutero-Isaiah the servant brings
light to the nations. (2) In Matthew's infancy narrative the advent
of Jesus is heralded by a heavenly light (see on 2.2). (3) The theme
of Jesus bringing light to a dark world is a key theme in John's
gospel: 1.9; 8.12; 12.35, 46. (4) The rabbis knew of the light of the
Messiah (see SB 1, pp. 161–2).[72]

17. Having inserted unparalleled material after 4.12 = Mk
1.14a–b, Matthew now returns to Mark and offers a revised
edition of Mk 1.14c–15. Whether the Markan version preserves a
saying of Jesus we may well doubt. V. Taylor was probably closer
to the truth when he wrote that Mark offers us 'a summary of what
Jesus proclaimed', a summary which 'rightly catches the
eschatological note in the preaching of Jesus'.[73]

That beginning with 4.17 we have a new division of the gospel is held by
Kingsbury.[74] Largely because ἀπὸ τότε ἤρξατο ὁ Ἰησοῦς + infinitive

[72] See also O. Michel, 'Das Licht des Messias', in *Donum Gentilicium*, ed. E.
Bammel, C. K. Barrett, and W. D. Davies, Oxford, 1978, pp. 140–50.

[73] *Mark*, p. 165. Cf. Gnilka, *Markus* 1, p. 65. Further discussion in Ambrozic (v);
Beasley-Murray, pp. 71–5; Chilton (v); Mussner (v); Pesch (v); Schlosser (v).

[74] *Structure*, pp. 1–39. Cf. Lohmeyer, *Matthäus*, p. 264; McNeile, pp. 45, 244; E.
Krentz, 'The Extent of Matthew's Prologue', *JBL* 83 (1964), pp. 409–14; Kümmel,
Introduction, p. 105; T. B. Slater, 'Notes on Matthew's Structure', *JBL* 99 (1980),
p. 436. For discussion and criticism see F. Neirynck, 'Le rédaction matthéenne et la
structure du premier évangile', in de la Potterie, pp. 56–8.

occurs in both 4.17 (where the public ministry begins) and 16.21 (where the passion begins), he sees 1.1–4.16 as the opening section. We have already (see on 3.1) criticized this analysis, observing, among other things, that ἀπὸ τότε recurs not only in 16.21 but also in 26.16, and that ἤρξατο is again used of Jesus in 11.7 and 20 (this last with τότε). We may here add a few more criticisms. First, the division of Matthew into three major sections does not adequately take into account the five-fold repetition of the words that close the five great discourses (7.28–9; 11.1; 13.53; 19.1–2; 26.1–2). These seem even more prominent and more deserving of the tag 'formula' than the ἀπὸ τότε ἤρξατο ὁ Ἰησοῦς of 4.17 and 16.21. Secondly, as Gundry (*Commentary*, p. 10) has rightly observed, 4.17 and 16.21 serve to mark turning points in Jesus' life but not so much in Matthew's gospel. Thirdly, the compositional and thematic unity of Mt 1–2 is patent (see on 3.1), as is the compositional and thematic unity of Mt 5–7. These two facts strike us as far more forceful and impressive than the words common to 4.17 and 16.21. We are therefore strongly disinclined to find the gospel's first major division in the middle of chapter 4. We have much more sympathy for those who would divide Mt 1–7 in this fashion:[75]

1–2: the genealogy and infancy of the Messiah Son of God
3–4: the beginning of the gospel
5–7: the sermon on the mount

ἀπὸ τότε ἤρξατο ὁ Ἰησοῦς. This is a redactional formula (cf. 16.16). For τότε see on 2.16. For ἀπὸ τότε in the LXX see 2 Esdr 5.16; Eccles 8.12; and Ps 93.2. In the NT see, outside of Matthew, only Lk 16.16. For redactional uses of ἄρχομαι see 12.1; 14.30; 18.24(?); 20.8(?). The verb is not pleonastic here (a new beginning is in fact being made) or perhaps anywhere else in Matthew. The same cannot be said of Mark or Luke. Because ἀπὸ τότε links what follows with what precedes (cf. 16.21; 26.16; against Soares Prabhu, pp. 120–2), it is probably in Jesus' preaching above all that the light has dawned on those in darkness (cf. Jerome's comment quoted above, p. 381).

κηρύσσειν καὶ λέγειν. See on 3.1. Compare Ezra 6.11; Jon 3.4. The verbs are both from the Markan parallel, Mk 1.14–15. The redundant use of the verb λέγειν also follows the verb 'to preach' in 3.2 and 10.7.

There are several significant differences between the summary account of Jesus' preaching in Mt 4.17 and that in Mk 1.14–15. Matthew lacks any mention of 'the gospel of God', omits 'the time is fulfilled' (cf. LAB 28.9; 59.1; 62.2), and drops 'believe in the gospel'—all found in Mark. Why?[76] Matthew wished to make the

---

[75] Cf. Gaechter, *Kommentar*, pp. 5, 81; Guy, p. 29; Green, p. vii; Hill, *Matthew*, p. 44; Meier, *Vision*, p. vi.
[76] We reject Chilton's attempt (*Strength*, pp. 116–21) to find the source of Mt 4.17b in Greek-speaking mission apologetic. The supposition of a redactional modification of Mk 1.14–15 seems to us more probable (see text) and is certainly less hypothetical.

words of John in 3.2 and those of Jesus in 4.17 identical: the two heralds preach the same kingdom. But it was not possible to put the words of Mk 1.14–15 on the lips of the Baptist without modification (see on 3.2). 4.17, then, is abbreviated *vis-à-vis* Mk 1.14–15 because it conforms to 3.2. In other words, we can explain the form of 4.17 by explaining the form of its parallel, 3.2. Note also that Matthew never uses πληρόω of time (5.18 has γίνομαι); that the note of fulfilment has already been rung in 4.14; that Mark's πιστεύετε ἐν τῷ εὐαγγελίῳ refers to Mk 1.14, a verse with no parallel in Matthew; that Matthew has Jesus preaching 'the gospel of the kingdom' in 4.23; that Matthew never uses 'the gospel' without qualification (cf. 4.23; 9.35; 24.14; 26.13); that our evangelist has also dropped 'the gospel' from his Markan source at 16.25 and 19.29; and that elsewhere Markan repetition and redundancy have been avoided (Allen, pp. xxiv–xxvi) while certain sayings of Jesus have been abbreviated (cf. with their Matthean parallels these verses from Mark: 2.19; 4.30; 6.4; 10.27; 12.27). (Matthew has not dropped the notice of fulfilment because he thinks the kingdom only future (cf. 12.28). Even so, Matthew may have found Mark's πεπλήρωται ὁ καιρός to be overstatement: only in the παλιγγενεσία (19.28) will all be fulfilled.)

μετανοεῖτε.[77] The imperative, being before the indicative (ἤγγικεν κ.τ.λ.), receives the emphasis (contrast Mark).

Although the correlation between 4.17 and 3.2 is to be put down to Matthean redaction, as a matter of historical fact both John and Jesus did demand repentance of their hearers.[78] Furthermore, the two meant by it much the same thing, namely, a radical change of heart and mind, a 'rebirth' of sorts. See on 3.2 and note Mt 11.21 = Lk 10.13 and 12.41 = Lk 11.32 (both from Q).

In Matthew's gospel repentance is less than a key theme. μετάνοια occurs only twice (3.8, 11), both times in traditional verses, both times on the lips not of Jesus but of John the Baptist. μετανοέω occurs five times. In 3.2, where it is John who calls for repentance, Mk 1.15 is the source. Jesus himself speaks of repentance only four times: 4.17 (from Mk 1.15); 11.20 (redactional); 11.21 (= Lk 10.13 Q); and 12.41 (= Lk 11.32 Q). To judge from these texts the evangelist has not introduced any change, fundamental or otherwise, into the concept of repentance. Perhaps this is to be explained by the fact that Matthew thought of

---

[77] μετανοειτε (along with the following γαρ) is missing from k sy^c.s (Ju) Cl Eus Or^pt Cyr. For discussion see Chilton, *Strength*, pp. 302–10, who accepts retention.

[78] We do not accept the proposal of Romaniuk (v). He supposes that the theme of repentance was introduced by the church into the preaching of Jesus from the catechesis of John the Baptist. On the reservations of Sanders (*Jesus*, pp. 106–13) about the rôle of repentance in the preaching of Jesus see D. C. Allison, 'Jesus and the Covenant: A Response to E. P. Sanders', *JSNT* 29 (1987), pp. 57–78.

repentance primarily as associated with entrance into the Christian community, in which case it would be applicable principally to outsiders and thus not prominent in a book addressed above all to believers.

ἤγγικεν γὰρ ἡ βασιλεία τῶν οὐρανῶν. Compare 3.2 and 10.7. For the historical Jesus the kingdom of God, which was at the heart of his proclamation and thus fairly belongs to a summary statement, primarily signified not the territory God rules or will rule—it was not just a place, like Shangra La—but God's eschatological activity as ruler. In its fullness, this rule, whose creator is indicated by the genitive, was still unrealized, and its arrival (conceived of partially as a judgement) would mark the end or transformation of the world, the restoration of an idyllic, paradisial state in which God's will would be perfectly realized. Note especially Mt 6.10a = Lk 11.2a; Mt 8.11 = Lk 13.28–9; and Mk 14.25. For discussion and literature see Allison, pp. 101–41; idem, 'A Millennial Kingdom in the Teaching of Jesus?', *IBS* 7 (1985), pp. 46–52; Beasley-Murray; B. Chilton, ed., *The Kingdom of God*, Issues in Religion and Theology, London, 1984; and Sanders, *Jesus*, esp. pp. 123–56. See also on 5.5 and 8.11.

Yet God's rule was also spoken of by Jesus as already present, and this claim, although not unique, was at least distinctive.[79] Especially important is Mt 12.28 = Lk 11.20, a statement whose meaning is explicated in the synoptic tradition by sundry images. Satan has already been cast out of heaven (Lk 10.18) and bound (Mk 3.27). There is new wine (Mk 2.22). In the midst of Israel is something greater than Solomon or Jonah (Mt 12.41–2 = Lk 11.31–2). Even today the sons of Abraham can open their eyes and see what the prophets and righteous only longed to see (Mt 13.16–17 = Lk 10.23–4).

Now the conjunction of statements about the presence of the kingdom with statements about its future coming appear to entail a dilemma, one horn of which has been grasped by some ('consistent eschatology'), the other horn by others ('realized eschatology'). But it seems best to strive for harmony. Only overly sceptical dissection or misinterpretation can remove from Jesus' preaching of the kingdom either its future or its present elements. Assuming, then, that neither 'realized eschatology' nor 'consistent eschatology' is in itself quite adequate, perhaps the best solution involves the idea of an extended time. Not unlike the program in

[79] On 'realized eschatology' in the teaching of Jesus see esp. Dodd, *Parables*, passim; E. Linnemann, 'Zeitangabe und Zeitverstellung in der Verkündigung Jesu', in Strecker, *Jesus Christus*, pp. 237–63; and Merklein, pp. 59–91. Although the works of both Dodd and Linnemann are rather one-sided, they do call attention to an important aspect of Jesus' eschatological message. On 'realized eschatology' in Judaism see Allison, pp. 17–19, 83–100, 104–6, 148–9.

Deutero-Isaiah—a section of Scripture which presumably influenced Jesus—the advent of God's kingdom did not, for Jesus, belong to a moment but constituted a series of events that would cover a period of time (cf. Gaston, p. 414). A similar conception is present in Jubilees 23, in which the age of blessedness enters the stage of history a step at a time (cf. Allison, pp. 17–19). And in the so-called Apocalypse of Weeks, 1 En. 93+91.12–17, the eschatological transition is a protracted process.[80] So the seeming contradiction between the presence of the kingdom and its futurity is dissolved when one realizes that Jewish thinking could envision the final events—the judgement of evil and the arrival of the kingdom of God—as extending over time, and as a process or series of events that could involve the present. When Jesus announces that the kingdom of God has come and is coming, this means that the last act has begun but not yet reached its climax: the last things have come and will come.

If we have rightly understood Jesus' proclamation of the kingdom, it follows that Matthew's views are in line with those of his Lord (and of much of the early church in general), for, as we shall see throughout this commentary, Matthew thinks in terms of a complex of prophesied events, some of which have taken place (e.g., the Messiah has appeared and there have been resurrections), some of which are taking place (see, e.g., 10.16–23), and some of which will take place in the near future (see, e.g., the parables of chapter 25). But here we must pause and ask how all this is reflected in Matthew's diction. Our evangelist usually writes about the 'kingdom of heaven' while 'kingdom of God', the expression so often found in Mark and Luke, occurs only in 12.28; 19.24; 21.34, 43; and textually doubtful is 6.33. Matthew does not explain 'kingdom of heaven'; it is used as though the readers are expected to know what it means. Most scholars assume that 'kingdom of heaven' is the equivalent of 'kingdom of God', 'heaven' being a periphrasis for God, perhaps under rabbinic influence.[81] More than one scholar, however, has argued otherwise: 'kingdom of heaven' does not equal 'kingdom of

---

[80] J. Licht, 'Time and Eschatology in Apocalyptic Literature and in Qumran', *JJS* 16 (1965), pp. 178–9.

[81] For 'kingdom of heaven' in the rabbis see SB 1, pp. 172–84. On rabbinic avoidance of the divine name see Moore 1, pp. 424–32. 'kingdom of heaven' does not appear in Jewish literature before the statement attributed to Yoḥanan ben Zakkai in *y. Qidd.* 1.2.59d. Jesus himself almost certainly spoke of 'the kingdom of God'; see Jeremias, *Theology*, p. 97. For Jewish and Christian examples of avoidance of the divine name see Dan 4.26; 1 Macc 3.50; Mt 5.12; 6.20; 16.19; 18.18; Mk 10.21; Lk 15.18, 21; SB 1, pp. 172–84, 862–5; 2, pp. 308–11. Also relevant is G. Howard, 'The Tetragram and the New Testament', *JBL* 96 (1977), pp. 63–83. For 'heaven' as a substitution for 'god' or 'the gods' outside the biblical tradition see Horsely 3, p. 49.

God'.[82] On this view, especially as propounded at length by M. Pamment, 'kingdom of heaven' refers to a wholly future and imminent reality while 'kingdom of God' denotes God's sovereignty which can be experienced in the present. Should this distinction be upheld? The futurity of 'kingdom of heaven' certainly seems well-founded; but a present reference cannot be altogether omitted from 11.11 and especially 11.12 (see the commentary). Moreover, only by special pleading can a future reference be eliminated from all the 'kingdom of God' sayings, 6.10 and 21.31 being decisive. Also particularly troublesome for the proposal under review is 19.23–4. Here 'kingdom of heaven' and 'kingdom of God' stand in what most commentators take to be parallel sentences. 'How difficult is it for the rich man to enter into the kingdom of heaven' (v. 23). 'It is easier for a camel to go through the eye of a needle than for a rich man (to enter) into the kingdom of God' (v. 24). What could be the distinction between 'kingdom of God' and 'kingdom of heaven' in these two verses?[83] Finally, it should be noted that Matthew uses not only 'kingdom of heaven' and 'kingdom of God' but also 'kingdom of my Father', 'kingdom of the Son of man', and the absolute, 'the kingdom'. We are not told by proponents of the view under scrutiny how all of these expressions are to be related to one another; and the absolute use of 'the kingdom' in particular seems perplexing and misleading if Matthew were making the distinction proposed.

If we are not persuaded that a difference exists between 'kingdom of God' and 'kingdom of heaven', neither are we satisfied with Gundry's account of Matthew's fondness for the latter. For Gundry the term stresses the majesty of God's universal dominion (cf. Dan 4.1–37); it also prevents Matthew's readers from wrongly thinking that God the Father rules to the exclusion of the Son: 'heaven' encompasses them both.[84] In our judgement this account leaves unexplained the several occurrences of 'kingdom of God' and particularly the eight occurrences of 'kingdom of my Father'. Perhaps what needs to be injected into the discussion is this: the variation between 'kingdom of heaven' and 'kingdom of God' in Matthew is simply one instance of a phenomenon wider than the First Gospel. The Gospel of Thomas uses 'kingdom of heaven' alongside 'kingdom of the Father' and 'the kingdom', and no distinction in meaning is apparent (see e.g. 3, 20, 22, 54, 57, 76, 114). Similarly, while Mark almost always has 'kingdom of God', also attested are the synonyms 'my kingdom'

---

[82] E.g. Allen, pp. lxvii–lxxi, and M. Pamment, 'The kingdom of Heaven according to the First Gospel', *NTS* 27 (1981), pp. 211–32.

[83] On Pamment's reading, v. 23 pertains to the future, v. 24 to the present pursuit of righteousness. This, however, is to read into the text what is not there.

[84] *Commentary*, p. 43. Cf. Schweizer, *Matthew*, p. 47.

and 'the kingdom of our father David'. And Luke, who uses 'kingdom of God' thirty-two times, sometimes writes of 'his kingdom' (once of Jesus, once of the Father), 'the kingdom', 'your kingdom' (once of Jesus, once of the Father), and 'my kingdom' (twice of Jesus). Note also the variation between 'kingdom of God' and 'kingdom of heaven' in the Testament of Jacob (2.25; 7.11, 19, 20, 23, 27; 8.3) and the Testament of Isaac (1.7; 2.8; 8.5–6). Further, in all three synoptic gospels we find 'heaven' sometimes but not always used as a periphrasis for God (e.g. Mt 3.17; Mk 11.31; Lk 11.16); and it seems safe to claim that Jesus himself did not shrink from speaking of God yet also frequently used periphrasis (cf. Jeremias, *Theology*, pp. 9–14, 97). All this leads us to think of 'kingdom of heaven' as nothing more than a stylistic variation of 'kingdom of God'. For the most part, Matthew used periphrasis; but no more than with Jesus was this usage inflexible. So 'kingdom of heaven' equals 'kingdom of God'. Both denote God's rule, present and coming.

ἐγγίζω is used of the kingdom of heaven in 3.2; 4.17; and 10.7. The meaning is probably, 'on the point of arrival', 'at the door'. The kingdom is imminent but not yet present.[85] Thus 12.28, where the kingdom has already come, means something different.

JESUS CALLS FOUR DISCIPLES (4.18–22)

This pericope contains two parallel stories, 4.18–20 and 21–2. Both exhibit the same structure:
   (1) The appearance of Jesus (vv. 18, 21)
   (2) Remark on the disciples at work (vv. 18, 21)
   (3) The call to discipleship (vv. 19, 21)
   (4) The obedient response to the call (vv. 20, 22)
That this is a fixed and significant form appears from Mk 2.14, the story of Levi's call, which can be analysed thus:
   (1) Jesus appears
   (2) Levi is at work, sitting at the tax office
   (3) Jesus calls Levi to follow him
   (4) Levi obediently follows
The explanation for this common form would appear to lie in the OT, in 1 Kgs 19.19–21, Elijah's call of Elisha, which can be set forth as follows:
   (1) Elijah is travelling (v. 19)
   (2) He finds Elisha, who is ploughing with oxen (v. 19)

[85] Lit.: Dodd, *Parables*, pp. 28–30; J. Y. Campbell, ' "The kingdom of God has come" ', *ExpT* 48 (1936), pp. 91–4; K. W. Clark, ' "Realized Eschatology" ', *JBL* 59 (1940), pp. 367–83; Kümmel, *Promise*, pp. 19–25; Cranfield, *Mark*, pp. 67–8; R. F. Berkey, 'ΕΓΓΙΖΕΙΝ, ΦΘΑΝΕΙΝ, and Realized Eschatology', *JBL* 82 (1963), pp. 177–87.

(3) Elijah puts his mantle on Elisha, which is a sign of the call to prophetic office (v. 19)
(4) Elisha, who responds, ἀκολουθήσω ὀπίσω σου, asks to kiss his parents first, and he slaughters oxen for a sacrifice (vv. 20–1)
(5) Elisha follows (ἐπορεύθη ὀπίσω) Elijah (v. 21)

The agreements between 1 Kgs 19.19–21 and the NT accounts are obvious (cf. Chrysostom, *Hom. on Mt* 14.3), and Matthew must have recognized them. Just as obvious, however, is an outstanding difference, namely, the request of Elisha to say farewell to parents and the sacrificial act. The difference is the more outstanding since, as opposed to what appears to have been the narrative's original intent, in the LXX and Josephus, *Ant.* 8.354 (which presumably represent a prevalent interpretation) Elijah grants Elisha permission to kiss his father and mother. In the NT, by way of contrast, family and possessions are forsaken on the spot: there is no parallel to 1 Kgs 19.20–1a. Yet how could it be otherwise? Mt 8.21–2 = Lk 9.59 tells of a disciple who asked, 'Lord, let me first go and bury my father'. Jesus' answer was, 'Follow me, and leave the dead to bury their own dead'. We may presume that when the stereotyped stories recounting the calls of Peter and Andrew, James and John, and Levi were constructed, the hard word of Jesus entailed that there be no farewell to family. So while Elijah's call of Elisha was the OT model for the NT call stories, the model was modified under the memory of Jesus' radical demand, and we learn that the Messiah required more of his disciples than Elijah required of Elisha.

18. Matthew follows Mark in placing the call of the first four disciples immediately after the summary of Jesus' proclamation. He does not, however, continue with Mk 1.21ff. After the summary statements in 4.23–5 we are given the sermon on the mount. Thus what is held together in Mk 1 is divided in Matthew. The explanation is this. Matthew wishes to place the great sermon at the beginning of Jesus' public ministry (and thus before the events in Capernaum are recounted). At the same time, since 5–7 is teaching for the disciples as well as the crowds, the evangelist must place the call of Peter and the others before 5.1: 'the disciples came to him'. In short, the function of 5–7 demands that the Matthean equivalent of Mk 1.16–20 be sundered from the Matthean equivalent of Mk 1.21ff.

The story preserved in Mt 4.18–22 = Mk 1.16–20 has been widely labelled an 'ideal scene', one spun out, in all probability, from the traditional metaphor, 'fishers of men'.[86] This judgement would seem to be reinforced by the parallels with 1 Kgs 19.19–21 and Mk 2.19 as well as by the implicit paraenesis. There are, nonetheless, good reasons for supposing an historical foundation. First, the synoptics and John agree that Peter and Andrew were followers of Jesus during the ministry in Galilee. Secondly, to judge by Mt 8.19–22 = Lk 9.57–62, Jesus did not gain disciples as did the rabbis (cf. *m. 'Abot* 1.6: 'Choose a teacher and get thee a companion'). Rather, as a charismatic, prophetic figure, one like Elijah, he chose his disciples: they did not choose him. Mk 1.16–20 par. fits in with this. It is also noteworthy that 1 Kgs 19.19–21, the literary model for Mk 1.16–20, hardly plays any rôle in rabbinic literature. Thirdly, the words of Mk 1.17 involve not only following ('Come, follow me!') but *sending* ('I will make you fishers of men'). Now Jesus was undoubtedly gripped by a sense of mission. He had a message to promulgate. And everything argues for his having chosen a number of men to aid him in his missionary task (see on 10.1ff.). Fourthly, the structure of the saying attributed to Jesus in Mk 1.17 (imperative + καί + future tense) is recognizably Semitic, and a translation into Hebrew or Aramaic is possible.[87] This in itself is not decisive for authenticity, but for this other considerations speak loud enough (see on 19). So Mk 1.17 contains a genuine saying of Jesus. This matters because 'Come, follow me, and I will make you fishers of men' is difficult to imagine as an isolated logion. The words indeed almost demand some context such as the story in which they are now embedded. Note particularly that the stress in 'I will make you fishers of men' lies on the last word, men: those who are now fishers (of fish) are to become fishers *of men*. That is, it is only the object of their catch which is changed: the disciples remain fishers. But this means that the saying of Jesus presupposes a context in which fishermen have already been mentioned. For this reason, saying and story belong together, and the dominical origin of the former strongly implies some historical basis for the latter. Fifthly, we scarcely need doubt that Peter and Andrew and James and John were fishermen. We should also notice that the mention of Andrew is striking: he plays no significant rôle in the synoptic tradition (contrast John's gospel). His presence thus perhaps raises the question of history.

In view of the preceding considerations, above all the fourth, and despite its structural dependence upon 1 Kgs 19.19–21, it seems probable that Mk 1.16–20 = Mt 4.18–22 has a foothold in historical reminiscence. At the least, Jesus called Peter and Andrew and James and John to be fishers of men, and probably while they were working at their daily tasks near Capernaum.

Whether Mk 1.16–20 par. should be harmonized with Jn 1, that is, whether we should think that the disciples' call to be fishers of men came after an earlier encounter with Jesus, we cannot say for sure. Mark's story certainly by-passes all the psychological factors; and its impact would in

---

[86] Bultmann, *History*, p. 28. According to Dibelius, *Tradition*, pp. 111–12, Mark himself created our narrative; before him nothing more than the word with which Jesus called the fishermen was known. This is doubtful, as our argument will show. See also Pesch (v).

[87] See Beyer, p. 252, and Hengel, *Charismatic Leader*, pp. 76–77.

fact be greatly diminished if it were preceded by contact between Jesus and the fishermen. Nonetheless, this hardly eliminates the possibility of historical tradition behind Jn 1 (Dodd, *Tradition*, pp. 302–12). As many of the older commentators thought, Jesus' call may well have come to those who already knew of him.[88]

περιπατῶν δὲ παρὰ τὴν θάλασσαν τῆς Γαλιλαίας. Compare Job 9.8; Mt 14.25–6, 29. Mark begins with καὶ παράγων, otherwise there is agreement. περιπατέω is also redactional in Mt 14.29 and 15.31. Matthew has retained παράγω in 9.9 = Mk 2.14 but dropped it here and in 27.32 = Mk 15.21. It is redactional in 9.27 and 20.30. It seems to mean 'depart' in 9.9, 27; and 20.30 (cf. Gundry, *Commentary*, p. 61). This helps account for its absence at this point, as does the awkward iteration in παράγων παρά (on this see Allen, pp. xxv–xxvi, and MHT 4, p. 39).

'By the Sea of Galilee' picks up on 4.13 and 15. There is no note of time. The location is presumably near Capernaum (cf. 4.13). Peter and Andrew, who, according to Jn 1.44, lived in Bethsaida (='house of the fisher'), had apparently moved. For παρὰ τὴν θάλασσαν elsewhere see Mk 2.13; 4.1 (=Mt 13.1); 5.21; and Mt 15.29 (redactional). In the Lukan story of the call of Peter and the others we read that Jesus was ἑστῶτα παρὰ τὴν λίμνην (5.2; cf. Gosp. Eb. in Epiphanius, *Haer*. 30.13.2–3).

The so-called Sea of Galilee was also known by the names Gennesaret (1 Macc 11.67; Lk 5.1; Josephus, *Bell*. 3.506), Tiberias (Jn 6.1; 21.1; cf. Josephus, *Bell*. 4.456; so often in the rabbis: SB 1, p. 185), and Taricheae (Pliny, *Nat. hist*. 5.15.71). It is actually an inland, fresh-water lake, about thirteen miles long and eight miles wide at one point, not a sea as we think of such. The translation of θάλασσα (which like *yām* can mean either sea or lake) by 'sea' (cf. the Latin *mare*) derives from Wycliffe and Tyndale. Literature: G. A. Smith, pp. 284–300; N. Glueck, *The Jordan River*, New York, 1968, pp. 1–59; and Baly, pp. 196–8.

In Matthew, the full name, 'Sea of Galilee', occurs only twice (4.17; 15.29); everywhere else it is just ἡ θάλασσα, 'the sea'. On its symbolic significance see on 4.15 and 8.23–7.

εἶδεν δύο ἀδελφούς. Mark has simply εἶδεν. Matthew likes both δύο (Mt: 40; Mk: 19; Lk: 28) and ἀδελφός (Mt: 39; Mk: 20; Lk: 24). He also adds δύο ἀδελφούς in 4.21, which increases the parallelism between 4.18–20 and 21–2. Note further the substitution of 'two brothers' for Mark's 'James and John' in Mt 20.24 = Mk 10.41, and the similar replacement in Mt 26.37 = Mk 14.33 ('two sons of Zebedee' for 'James and John').

[88] We cannot here consider the connexion between Mk 1.16–20 on the one hand and the similar accounts in Lk 5 and Jn 21 on the other, except to state our conviction that if primacy is to be ascribed to one story, it must be that in the Second Gospel.

It is Jesus who sees Simon and Andrew, not Simon and Andrew who see Jesus (cf. Lk 5.2). Hence the initiative lies with the master. He is choosing them, not they him. This recalls the story of Elijah calling Elisha (1 Kgs 19.19–21) and contrasts with rabbinic practice, where the disciple chose his rabbi. Compare Jn 15.16: 'You did not choose me, but I chose you . . .'.

Σίμωνα τὸν λεγόμενον Πέτρον. Compare 10.2. Matthew has added 'the one called Peter'. 'Simon', which also appears in the call stories in Lk 5 and Jn 1, occurs five times in Matthew, being redactional or at least without a synoptic parallel in 16.16–17; and 17.25. Our evangelist much prefers Πέτρος (Mt: 23; Mk: 19; Lk: 18). For Peter's place in Matthew see the excursus after 16.13–20. Here we observe only that, as in Mark, Peter is the first disciple to be mentioned and the first (along with his brother) to respond to the call of Jesus. On τὸν λεγόμενον, which is typically Matthean, see on 1.16.

Σίμων is a good Greek name (cf. BAGD, s.v.) which stands for the Semitic Simĕʿôn (from šāmaʿ + ʾēl/yāh = 'God has heard', cf. Gen 29.33). It was very popular among Jews during the Roman period; see Fitzmyer, *Background*, pp. 105–12. The Semitic variant Συμεών appears in the LXX (over forty times), in Josephus (e.g. *Bell*. 4.159), and in the NT (for five different people: Lk 2.25; 3.30; Acts 13.1; 15.14; 2 Pet 1.1; Rev 7.7).

Πέτρος, attested only in post-Christian sources apart from the NT, stands for the Aramaic *kepāʾ*, 'rock', 'stone' (see 11Qtg Job 32.1; 33.9; 4QEnᵉ 4.3.19; 4QEnᶜ 4.3; 4QEnᵃ 1.2.8). *Kepāʾ* seems to occur only once as a name in pre-Christian times, in a document from Elephantine; see Fitzmyer, *Advance*, pp. 112–24.

καὶ ʾΑνδρέαν τὸν ἀδελφὸν αὐτοῦ. Compare 4.21. So Mark, with Σίμωνος for αὐτοῦ. Andrew (a good Greek name missing from the LXX) is named again only in 10.2, where he is once more said to be 'his [that is, Peter's] brother' (cf. Lk 6.14; Jn 1.40; 6.8). His name has been dropped from Mt 8.14 (= Mk 1.29) and from the introduction to the discourse in Mt 24 (contrast Mk 13.3). He is not a significant character in our gospel. According to Jn 1.35–49, Andrew was from Bethsaida and was at one time a disciple of John the Baptist. For another Jew with his name Dio Cassius 68.32.1.

βάλλοντας ἀμφίβληστρον. Matthew replaces Mark's ἀμφιβάλλοντας, a NT *hapax legomenon* (cf. Hab 1.17 LXX for *rûq*), with another *hapax legomenon* (cf. Ps 140. 10; Hab 1.15–17; Eccles 9.12) + βάλλω (Mt: 34; Mk: 18; Lk: 18). The ἀμφίβληστρον was a circular casting net (BAGD, s.v.). To its edges were tied stones which caused the net to sink rapidly, encompassing fish. When the net was lifted by a rope tied to the middle, the stones would be gathered together and keep the fish entrapped; see F. Dunkel, 'Die Fischerei am See Gennesareth und das Neue

Testament', *Bib* 5 (1924), pp. 375–90.

In 1 Kgs 19.19–21, the story of Elijah calling Elisha, the latter's engagement with his occupation is recorded: Elisha 'was ploughing'. Compare Mk 2.14: Levi was 'sitting at the tax office'. Note also Judg 6.11–12; 1 Sam 11.5; Amos 7.14–15. By making Jesus' call come to one engaged in his livelihood, our text underscores the break with everyday affairs.

εἰς τὴν θάλασσαν. Compare Exod 10.19 LXX and Jon 1.15 LXX. All three times that Mark has ἐν τῇ θαλάσσῃ (Mk 1.16; 4.1; 5.13) Matthew has changed it; and our evangelist elsewhere avoids Mark's ἐν + dative (see the parallels to Mk 5.2, 25; 9.41; 14.6). On the interchange between ἐν and εἰς see Robertson, pp. 584–6, 591–4; BDF § 205; and for Matthew, Allen, pp. xxvii–xxviii. Given the condensed narrative we cannot tell whether Peter and Andrew are supposed to be on shore or in a boat (cf. 4.21–2). Nets were thrown from both.

ἦσαν γὰρ ἁλιεῖς. So Mark. Compare Lk 5.2. The common phrase is evidence of literary dependence, one way or the other. For the spelling of ἁλιεύς see BDF.§ 29.5. For the fish in the Sea of Galilee—mostly mullet—see Josephus, *Bell.* 3.508. Peter and Andrew and James and John appear to have belonged to a fishing partnership which included Zebedee and a number of hired servants (Mk 1.16–20; Jn 21.1–3); and if Lk 5.1–11 be accurate, they had at least two boats. Perhaps, then, these followers of Jesus were, if it be legitimate to speak in such terms, from the (lower) middle class.[89]

19. Having been informed as to what Jesus saw, we next learn what he said.

καὶ λέγει αὐτοῖς. Mark has εἶπεν and names the subject, ὁ Ἰησοῦς, at the end. Concerning the first difference, Matthew's historical present places emphasis upon Jesus' command (cf. 4.10 diff. Lk 4.8; 8.22 diff. Lk 9.60) and perhaps more readily encourages the reader to apply the following words to himself. Concerning the second, Jesus has just been named (4.17), so he need not be named again.

δεῦτε ὀπίσω μου. So Mark and 2 Kgs 6.19 LXX (MT: *lĕkû ʾaḥăray*). Jesus' words, which contain no why, are not invitation. They are unconditional demand. (Hengel, *Charismatic Leader*, p. 17, claims that in the OT it is ultimately God himself who issues the prophetic call (1 Kgs 11.31ff.; 19.15–21; 1 Sam 16.1ff.) while in the NT the authority resides with Messiah Jesus.)

---

[89] Cf. Wuellner (v), pp. 45–61, and B. T. Viviano, *Study as Worship*, SJLA 26, Leiden, 1978, pp. 173–4. On the question of a middle class in ancient Galilee see Hoehner, pp. 70–3, and Sherwin-White, pp. 139–42. Contrast Chrysostom, *Hom. on Mt.* 14.3: 'So exceeding great was their poverty, that they were mending what was worn out, not being able to buy others'.

On 'coming after' as an expression for discipleship, for sharing in Jesus' unique work and perilous destiny, see on 3.11; see also 8.19, 22; 9.9; 10.38; 16.24; 19.21. δεῦτε (Mt: 6; Mk: 3; Lk: 0) is an exclamation in the plural ('come'!) and is used as an imperative, being the functional equivalent of ἀκολουθεῖτε (see 8.22; 9.9; 19.21 and BDF § 364). ὀπίσω (see on 3.11) occurs three times in 1 Kgs 19.19–21, the paradigmatic call story. Compare also 1 Macc 2.27: 'Let everyone zealous for the Law and supporting the covenant come out after me' (ἐξελθέτω ὀπίσω μου). In rabbinic sources, 'follow after' (hlk 'ḥry) is typically employed only in connexion with real wandering and travelling (e.g. t. Pesaḥ. 1.27; Mek. on Exod 31.12; ARN 4), and the phrase is less loaded with meaning than it is in the NT (see further Hengel, Charismatic Leader, pp. 50–7).

καὶ ποιήσω ὑμᾶς ἁλιεῖς ἀνθρώπων. So Mark, with γενέσθαι after 'you'. The expression, 'fishers of men', occurs in the NT only here and in Mk 1.16. It has no real parallel in rabbinic or Hellenistic literature. This speaks for an origin with Jesus. The Semitic syntax of the sentence in which it is found (see on 4.18) is consistent with this. Moreover, 'fishers of men' may have had a negative ring to it, causing one to think of deceit or persuasion, of those who 'trap' people (cf. Jer 16.16; Prov 6.26b; Eccles 9.12; 1QH 2.29; 3.26; 5.8; CD 4.15–16; T. Dan. 2.4; cf. Ezek 26.5; 1QpHab 5–6—in which case the words would have been provocative or at least paradoxical, which would fit what we know to have been characteristic of Jesus. Lastly, there is an independent variant in Lk 5.10. (This last has ζωγρέω, perhaps to lessen the connotation of deceit.)

We argued above that the call to be 'fishers of men' is bound up with its historical context, the call of Galilean fishermen. But an allusion to Jer 16.16 cannot be altogether dismissed (cf. Tertullian, Adv. Marc. 4.9): 'Behold, I am sending for many fishers, says the Lord, and they will catch them; and afterwards I will send for many hunters, and they will hunt them from every mountain and every hill, and out of the clefts of the rocks'. A glance at Ezek 47.10 or Amos 4.2 or Hab 1.14–17 seems less likely. One should observe, however, that these OT passages, along with 1QH 5.7–8 and Mt 13.47–50 (the sorting of good and bad fish), all have to do with judgement. This may tell us that the metaphor, 'fishers of men', was formulated with the eschatological judgement in view, that in the face of the great judgement the disciples were selected as heralds of Jesus' message (cf. Smith (v)). Compare 9.37–8: with the harvest at hand, Jesus needs labourers. In any event, in being called by Jesus, the disciples were not being invited to study Torah or practise it. Rather were they being called to rescue the lost, to help in the work of announcing and preparing for the kingdom of God.

Perhaps Matthew thought of the Gentiles as included in the ἀνθρώπων (cf. 5.16; 10.22; 12.41). For Jesus as a fisherman see Gosp. Thom. 8. In early Christian art, of course, the fish is a symbol of Jesus and of Christians; and on ancient Christian sarcophagi the fisherman becomes a symbol of baptism.

20. The conclusion to the call story of Peter and Andrew ends with a remark on their sacrificial obedience.

οἱ δὲ εὐθέως ἀφέντες τὰ δίκτυα ἠκολούθησαν αὐτῷ. Mark agrees with Matthew save for the first three words, for which Mark has καὶ εὐθύς. Matthew often drops Mark's adverbial, vulgar εὐθύς (see on 3.16). He prefers the more archaic εὐθέως (Mt: 12; Mk: 0; Lk: 6). Compare 4.22 diff. Mk 1.20; 8.3 diff. Mk 1.42; 13.5 diff. Mk 4.5; 14.22 diff. Mk 6.45; 20.34 diff. Mk 10.52; 26.49 diff. Mk 14.45; 26.74 diff. Mk 14.72 and note 14.31; 24.29; 25.15; 27.48. On εὐθύς and εὐθέως see BDF § 102.2 (lit.). Matthew replaces the Markan καί with δέ about sixty times.

In 3 Βασ 19.20 Elisha says to Elijah, ἀκολουθήσω ὀπίσω σου. Compare Lk 5.11; Josephus, *Ant.* 8.354 (Elisha καταλιπὼν τοὺς βόας ἠκολούθησεν 'Ηλίᾳ; cf. *Ant.* 5.127); Diogenes Cyn. *Ep.* 38.5; Diogenes Laertius 2.48 (Socrates to Zenophon: ἕπου τοίνυν καὶ μάνθανε); 6.36 (ἐκέλευσεν ἀκολουθεῖν); 7.2–3. The word, δίκτυον, which in the LXX translates *rešet* and *śĕbākâ*, occurs in the synoptics only in Mk 1.16–20 = Mt 4.18–22 and the Lukan parallel (cf. Jn 21.6, 8, 11). For the metaphorical usage of ἀκολουθέω (to follow = to be a disciple) see 8.19, 22; 9.9; 10.38; 16.24; 19.21, 27, 28. For the literal usage see 4.25; 8.1, 10; 9.19, 27; 14.13–14; 19.2; 20.29, 34; 21.9; 26.58; 27.55. 8.23 is ambiguous. Note that the metaphorical usage consistently involves at least two things: (1) Jesus is the speaker—he issues the summons to follow—and (2) cost is involved: discipleship entails sacrifice.[90]

Matthew could readily have written, οἱ δὲ ἠκολούθησαν αὐτῷ. He has, however, followed Mark: 'they followed him' is qualified by 'immediately' and by 'leaving the nets'. The adverb makes the disciples act according to the word of 8.22. When the authoritative call of Jesus comes, there is not even time to say farewell to one's father (contrast 1 Kgs 19.19–21). Peter and Andrew no longer belong first to kith and kin. They belong from here on to Jesus (cf. Mt 10.37 = Lk 14.26). 'Leaving the nets' highlights the disciples' radical commitment. Renouncing their old life, not even taking time to bring in nets (and boat?), they leave all and follow Jesus (cf. 19.27; also 6.25–34; 8.20; Lk 14.33). Their call is to homelessness.

[90] Our analysis follows J. D. Kingsbury, 'The Verb *Akolouthein* ("To Follow") as an Index of Matthew's View of His Community', *JBL* 97 (1978), pp. 56–73. Further discussion in G. Kittel, *TWNT* 1, pp. 210–16. Strecker, *Weg*, pp. 230–1, is mistaken in stating that in Matthew 'to follow' consistently has a metaphorical meaning.

They are being ordered to deny self, to suffer the loss of their own lives and livelihood (cf. Mk 8.34–5). Perhaps, for Matthew, a contrast with common rabbinic practice is intended. Unlike the affluent or those who practised trades to support themselves (cf. Paul the tentmaker and see SB 2, pp. 745–6), the disciples of Jesus must give full time and all energy to their work (cf. Hengel, *Charismatic Leader*, pp. 32–3). On the other hand, one may well doubt whether the rabbinic injunctions to combine work with study developed before the middle of the second century A.D.; see E. E. Urbach, 'Class-Status and Leadership in the World of the Palestinian Sages', *Proceedings of the Israeli Academy of Sciences and Humanities*, Jerusalem, 1968, 2, pp. 38–74. Moreover, the idea of renouncing property for a religious cause has parallels not only in the Graeco-Roman world (the Stoics and Cynics) but also within Judaism. In Jos. Asen. 13, when Aseneth turns to the true God, she casts away all her fine food and clothing. And according to Philo, *Omn. prob. lib.* 76–7, 85; *Vit. con.* 25–31; and Josephus, *Bell.* 2.122; *Ant.* 18.20, the Essenes and the Therapeutae held something approaching an ideal of poverty (cf. 1QS 1.11–13; 6.20–3).

21. καὶ προβὰς ἐκεῖθεν. Compare 9.9 and 1 Kgs 19.19 (καὶ ἀπῆλθεν ἐκεῖθεν). So Mark, with ὀλίγον instead of ἐκεῖθεν. The former never appears in Matthew and Mark in parallel material. 'And going on from there' leaves the impression that, after calling Peter and Andrew, Jesus walked along the shore a short distance until he encountered two more fishermen. This may just be a pictorial way of making one episode out of two incidents which were historically separate. (According to Lohmeyer, *Matthäus*, p. 71, and Wuellner (v), p. 71, two independent traditions have been combined. This is doubtful because, as it is, the second half of our story depends so completely upon the first half. Mk 1.19–20 could not stand on its own. Further, the formulation of 1.19–20 so clearly resembles that of 1.16–18 that a common origin seems assured.)

εἶδεν ἄλλους δύο ἀδελφούς. Mark has only the verb. The redactional addition, 'two other brothers', enhances the parallelism between 4.18–20 and 21–2. See further on 4.18.

Ἰάκωβον τὸν τοῦ Ζεβεδαίου. So Mark. Only in 10.2 and 17.1 is this James again mentioned by name, but in 20.20; 26.37; and 27.56 we read of 'the sons of Zebedee'. In Mark, James is named nine times (although never by himself; it is always 'Peter and James and John' or 'James and John'). A comparison of Mk 16.1 with Mt 27.56 seems to imply that Matthew believed that Zebedee was married to Salome. Interestingly enough, James the son of Zebedee and his brother are nowhere mentioned by name in the Fourth Gospel. In Jn 21.2, however, οἱ τοῦ Ζεβεδαίου occurs in a list of disciples, and the two are fishing. 'Zebedee' (Mt: 6; Mk: 4; Lk: 1) is from the Aramaic *zabday* or Hebrew *zĕbadyâ*, words which mean 'gift of Yah'. Ζαβδαίας appears in 1 Esdr 9.35 and Ζαβδ(ε)ία in 2 Esdr 8.8; 10.20. A synagogue column in Capernaum and dated to ca. A.D. 200 preserves the name of a certain son of Zebidah. Josephus, *Ant*. 5.33 names another son of Ζεβεδαίου. For rabbis with the name see SB 1, p. 188.

καὶ Ἰωάννην τὸν ἀδελφὸν αὐτοῦ. So Mark. John, whose name occurs in Mark ten times (Mt: 3), is always in Matthew 'his [i.e. James'] brother' (cf. 10.2; 17.1). The formulation, 'James and John his brother', has a primitive sound, for while the former was killed in A.D. 43 (Acts 12.1–3), the latter was one of the so-called 'pillars' (Gal 2.9). Contrast the order of the names in Lk 8.51; 9.28; Acts 1.13. That James and John (the younger presumably) were with their father probably shows that they could not have been very old. (Matthew even introduces their mother in 20.20.)

ἐν τῷ πλοίῳ. So Mark. Matthew has omitted as unncessary Mark's Semitic καὶ αὐτούς. 'In the boat' parallels the 'casting a net into the sea' of 4.18. James and John, like Peter and Andrew and Elisha of old, are called to discipleship in the midst of their daily activity. They leave one occupation for another.

μετὰ Ζεβεδαίου τοῦ πατρὸς αὐτῶν. This is Matthean redaction (cf. 2.11). It sets the stage for the next verse, where the sons of Zebedee leave their father. The theme is stressed because of Jesus' words in 8.22; 10.35–7; 19.29; and 23.9. Matthew is being consistent.

καταρτίζοντας τὰ δίκτυα αὐτῶν. Matthew has added the possessive to give 'their nets' and 'their father' the same character: the disciples are giving up what they own. For δίκτυον see 4.20. καταρτίζω occurs again in 21.16, a redactional citation of Ps 8.3 LXX, where the meaning seems to be, 'prepare' or 'create'. Here 'mend' (cf. 2 Cor 13.11) and/or 'put in order' ('fold'?) must be intended (cf. BAGD, s.v.). The mention of nets furthers the parallelism between 4.18–20 and 21–2. No symbolic significance is to be discerned. (Fenton, pp. 73–4, uncautiously speculates that casting a net into the sea may prefigure evangelistic work, while mending the nets prefigures pastoral work within the church. This is surely overdone.)

καὶ ἐκάλεσεν αὐτούς. 'And he called them' succinctly summarizes the content of 4.19, which is not repeated. Mark has this plus εὐθύς after καί. See on 4.20. In the OT καλέω is used of Wisdom's pleas (Prov 1.24). Most significantly, in Deutero-Isaiah it comes close to meaning ἐκλέγω: to call is to choose; see 43.1; 45.3; 46.11; 48.15; 50.2; 51.2. This seems to be the meaning in Mt 4.21 (cf. Rom 1.1; 1 Cor 1.1; Gal 1.15; CMC 18.12–13; 64.18). For Jesus as the one who 'calls' see also 9.13. In Paul's epistles it is God typically who 'calls' (e.g. Rom 9.24; 1 Cor 1.9; 7.15; Gal 1.15; 1 Th 2.12).

22. This verse is clearly secondary compared with Mk 1.20. If Matthew were original, we would be at a loss to explain Mark's destruction of the parallelism between Mt 4.20 and 22 or the addition of the obscure reference to hired servants.

οἱ δὲ εὐθέως ἀφέντες τὸ πλοῖον καὶ τὸν πατέρα αὐτῶν. Matthew's first three words are taken from 4.20 and substituted for Mark's καί. Jesus' authoritative call—perhaps 'command' would be a better word—produces instant obedience. Compare the call stories about Jeremiah and Paul: Jer 1.1–10; Acts 9.1–19; 22.3–21; 26.9–23. Mark has 'leaving Zebedee their father in the boat with the hired servants'. Compare Lk 5.11 (ἀφέντες πάντα). Matthew has used Mark's words but altered their order to make them line up with 4.20. See our comments there. James and John leave behind not only their means of livelihood but also give up personal, family ties (contrast Peter and Andrew). Perhaps the dissimilarity at this point with 4.20 betrays the knowledge that Peter did not forsake his family; as 1 Cor 9.5 states, he travelled with a wife; and as Mk 1.29–31 recounts, he lived with his mother-in-law.

Mark's 'with the hired servants' (added to soften the harshness of leaving the father alone?) is omitted as adding nothing. 'Zebedee their father' becomes 'their father' to avoid repetition (Zebedee is named twice in the previous verse). 'Boat' comes before 'father' because this is the order in 4.21. 'In the boat' becomes 'the boat' (object of ἀφέντες) to stress the element of sacrifice (cf. the double use of αὐτῶν in 4.21).

In 1 Kgs 19.19–21 Elisha asks permission to kiss his father before he follows Elijah (see p. 392). By way of contrast, in Mk 1.19–20 = Mk 4.21–2 Zebedee is left without further ado. Compare Mt 8.18–22. Is this breaking of family ties to be regarded as an eschatological motif? See Mt 10.34–6 and the parallels cited there.

ἠκολούθησαν αὐτῷ. This replaces Mark's ἀπῆλθον ὀπίσω αὐτοῦ. Again the motivation is conformity to 4.20.

(iv) *Concluding Observations*

On 4.1–11—

(1) Jesus, as the personification or embodiment of obedient Israel, repeats the experience of Israel of old: having passed through the waters, he enters the desert to suffer a time of testing (cf. Deut 8.2). What does this signify? Why is the parallel important? 4.1–11 leads through 4.12–17 to 4.18–22, this last being the calling of the first disciples; and this means that the baptism

and temptation of Jesus inaugurated the renewal of the people of God. Just as Israel was born in the first exodus, so is the church born in a second exodus. By repeating or recapitulating in his own person the exodus and the events thereafter, the Son of God brings a new people into being.

(2) Satan and his evil legions appear not infrequently in Matthew (4.23; 8.16, 28; 9.32; 12.22; 13.39; 15.22; 17.18). Whenever they do they always wear the faces of defeat. To illustrate: when the devil first appears and tempts Jesus, he is wholly ineffectual and in the end is vanquished. And when demons afflict suffering souls in Israel (as they do so often from chapter 4 on) they are readily cast out by the Son of God. And when Peter in 16.22 gives utterance to a word of Satan, he is rebuked and must fall into place behind his master. We have then in Matthew, as in early Christianity in general, recognition of the limitations of the powers of iniquity. These are strictly circumscribed, and they fail completely in the presence of the Son of God and those members of his community who are full of faith (cf. 17.14–21).

(3) In the first century A.D. Hellenistic Jewish romance, Joseph and Aseneth, the conversion of the heroine, Aseneth, is followed by a series of trials. Conversion leads to harassment, to inner conflict and external opposition. And the point of the book is in part to show potential or recent converts the dangers ahead and to offer encouragement by illustrating how they can be overcome.[91] We recall this because implicit in 4.1–11 is a parable about the life of the Christian disciple (cf. Luz 1, p. 162: 'indirekt paränetischen Charakter'). Revelatory experiences, encounters with the divine realm, and the joy of repentance are inevitably trailed by trials and temptations. There is no getting around these. If they came to the Son himself, they will certainly come to his followers. Trials are to be expected (cf. Acts 14.22). But if there is no way around, there is a way through. Using Jesus as a model (cf. Zeller, *Kommentar*, pp. 24–5), the disciple is called to the religious discipline of fasting, which breeds self-denial and thereby narrows the devil's foothold in the soul (6.16–18). The disciple is also to know and use Scripture as a light for his path, a guide-book which, rightly understood, leads down the right way (cf. 13.52?). Lastly, and most importantly, the disciple is to emulate his Lord by exercising trust in God's faithfulness. This is the prerequisite of obedience, and to him who exercises such trust, all will be added (cf. 6.24–34).

[91] See H. C. Kee, 'The Socio-Cultural Setting of Joseph and Aseneth', *NTS* 29 (1983), pp. 394–413.

(4) The mountain in Mt 4.8–9 forms an *inclusio* with the mountain in Mt 28.16–20 (cf. Lange, *Erscheinen*, pp. 404–5; Donaldson, pp. 101–2). On the first mountain in Matthew the devil offers to *give* Jesus *all* the kingdoms of the world and their glory on the condition that he *worship* him. On the last mountain, where Jesus is *worshipped* by others, Jesus declares that he has been *given all* authority in heaven and earth. It is hard not to think the correlation intentional. The two texts mark the beginning and end of Jesus' labours: he rejected the devil's temptation (4.8–9), choosing instead to travel the hard road of obedient sonship, which in the end brought fitting and everlasting reward (28.16–20).

On 4.12–22—

(1) On the literary level the functions of 4.12–17 are (a) to signal the beginning of the public ministry (v. 12), (b) to move Jesus from Nazareth (2.23) to Capernaum (v. 13), and (c) to introduce in summary fashion the content of Jesus' proclamation. On the theological level, the passage carries forward three outstanding Matthean themes: (a) the fulfilment of Scripture (vv. 14–16), (b) the salvation of the Gentiles (v. 15), and (c) the coming of the kingdom of God (v. 17). The last (c) calls the most attention to itself. This is because it repeats verbatim a line already spoken by John the Baptist (3.2) and because the ingressive aorist (ἤρξατο) conjures in the mind's eye the image of a man uttering the same words again and again. In fact, just as 1.1 stands over the rest of the gospel as a descriptive title (see on 1.1), so does 4.17 stand over the entire public ministry of Jesus: 'Repent, for the kingdom of heaven is at hand'.

(2) 4.18–22, the story of the calling of Peter, Andrew, James, and John, serves an aetiological function, for it recounts the act whereby Jesus began to make men into missionaries. This means that we have before us the birth of the Christian mission. Also before us is the birth of the church, the decisive moment when people first threw in their lot with the cause of Jesus. But we may not be wrong in guessing that Matthew's interest in Jesus' call of the fishermen was primarily paraenetic. Are not the disciples who left their nets and boats and all else to follow Jesus good models of Christian commitment and discipleship? All who follow Jesus, not just Peter and Andrew and James and John, are called to leave behind the past. All must obediently respond to the call, 'Follow me'. Granted this, however, how was this act of renunciation understood by Matthew and his readers? Was the call to

discipleship for them too a call to do away with material goods and to give up home and family? Probably not.[92]

In the first place, there are, as has been pointed out by others, indications that the evangelist lived in an urban environment. Matthew was obviously an educated man and he had a fairly good Greek vocabulary—qualities which, while not out of the question for a rural man, are perhaps more natural in a city dweller. One should also consider the significance of the fact that the evangelist, sometime before the end of the first century, managed to acquaint himself with Mark, with Q, and with the various traditions conventionally lumped together under the letter 'M'. Where else but in a significant Christian centre was the opportunity for this likely? Perhaps even more telling are the statistics on πόλις: whereas the word occurs only eight times in Mark, it appears twenty-six times in the First Gospel. Secondly, Matthew has tempered the tradition's portrait of Jesus as an itinerant. Thus Capernaum becomes the place where Jesus 'dwelt' (4.13), his 'own city' (9.1). Thirdly, as compared with Mark and Luke, Matthew shows knowledge of a wide range of money;[93] and while gold and silver are seldom mentioned in the other gospels, in the First Gospel they appear often (χρυσός: Mt: 5; Mk: 0; Lk: 0; ἀργύριον: Mt: 9; Mk: 1; Lk: 4). Fourthly, Matthew's strong warnings about wealth (e.g. 6.19–21; 19.16–22) do not of themselves imply that he objected to people with plenty of money. Philo, for one, was quite well-to-do and yet had very harsh things to say about wealth. Finally, as compared with the other gospels, Matthew appears less strident in his attitude to the rich or those of means. This appears from several Matthean texts, such as 5.3 ('the poor *in spirit*', contrast Lk 6.20) and 27.57 (Joseph of Arimathea becomes both a disciple and a rich man). From this point of view, it is not surprising that the story of the widow's mite (Mk 12.41–4 = Lk 21.1–4) has been dropped and that it is Luke, not Matthew, who hands on a woe aimed at the wealthy (Lk 6.24).

Considerations such as those just introduced imply that Matthew was more prepared than the other evangelists to accommodate the tradition to his apparently more wealthy congregation or community and that, like many rabbis and unlike many radical Christian enthusiasts, he may have been more or less

---

[92] In addition to what follows see Kingsbury, as in n. 80. We have largely drawn upon his arguments. For a different position see Schweizer, 'Matthew's Community', in Stanton, *Matthew*, pp. 129–55. There were undoubtedly early Christian itinerants who could have taken sayings like Mt 8.22 = Lk 9.60 quite literally; see G. Theissen, *Sociology*. But for caution about our knowledge of early Christian itinerants and questions about Theissen's work see A. E. Harvey, review of Theissen, *Sociology*, in *JTS* 30 (1979), pp. 279–83.

[93] Details in Kilpatrick, pp. 124–5, and Kingsbury, as in n. 90.

at home with the well-to-do. This in turn implies that he could hardly have expected or wished all of his readers to imitate Peter and the others in forsaking property and livelihood.[94] It follows, then, that 4.18–22, at least within its context in Matthew, must be interpreted not as setting forth a rigid precedent but as being illustrative of the general nature of discipleship. That is, 4.18–22 offers simply an example of whole-hearted obedience to the cause of Jesus. The implicit demand is to be like the disciples in so far as they were unreservedly obedient to the word that came to them, even to the point of great sacrifice. There is not, however, any general call to be rid of wealth or to forsake kin.

(Perhaps Matthew's views with regard to riches may be profitably compared with those of the wisdom teacher Ben Sira, who inveighed against ill-gotten gain and warned of the dangers of loving gold (18.32; 31.5; 34.20–2) yet simultaneously praised the rich man who was devout (13.24; 31.8; 40.18). Recall also that the rabbis did not advocate rejecting wealth but rather using it in accordance with the demands of the Torah.)

(3) Our conclusions anent 4.18–22 bear on the discussion of 'historicizing' in Matthew. On our interpretation, Peter and Andrew and James and John are not to be perfectly imitated: their act is not necessarily to be repeated by later disciples. 4.18–22 thus belongs to the unrepeatable past, to the time of the earthly Jesus. It would, nevertheless, be an error to leave matters at that, for the call that came to the Galilean fishermen—'Follow me, and I will make you fishers of men'—must equally be heard by others. It is in fact timeless. All disciples are to follow Jesus; as the church Fathers recognized, 'the footsteps of Christ are a road to heaven' (Clement of Alexandria, *Paed.* 3, hymn). Further, missionary activity cannot be confined to the pre-Easter circle around Jesus: Matthew's readers know that they too are to be fishers of men. Hence 4.18–22 offers us both 'historicization' and 'typification', this last meaning that there is a rough correlation between the pre-Easter followers of Jesus and the members of the Christian community of Matthew's day. What is true of the former pertains to the latter. This, indeed, is what is found throughout the First Gospel. Alongside the 'historicization' which, as Strecker has

[94] In our sentence the qualification, 'all of', may be important. Matthew could have thought greater sacrifice appropriate or even compulsory for certain Christian 'offices', such as that of travelling missionary. On the other hand, the distinction between leaders of the community and others is not pronounced in Matthew, not even in chapter 18. Cf. U. Luz, 'The Disciples in the Gospel According to Matthew', in Stanton, *Matthew*, p. 110. He notes among other things the equation between 'little one' and 'disciple' in 10.42. On the problem of whether there are two levels of demand in Matthew see Davies, *SSM*, pp. 209–15, and the commentary on 5.48 and 19.16–22.

shown, is unquestionably present, there is also, as U. Luz has persuasively argued,[95] a typification (he uses the word, 'Transparenz') of the disciples, without which the 'historicization' would reduce the relevancy of the narrative. What Jesus once asked of Peter, Andrew, James, and John, he asks afresh of those reading Matthew's gospel.

(v) *Bibliography*

Ambrozic, pp. 3–31.

M. E. Andrews, 'Peirasmos—A Study in Form-Criticism', *ATR* 24 (1942), pp. 229–44.

Barrett, *Spirit*, pp. 46–53.

K. Barth, *CD* IV/4, pp. 360–4.

Best, *Temptation*.

O. Betz, 'Donnersöhne, Menschenfischer und der davidische Messias', *RevQ* 3 (1961), pp. 41–70.

Bultmann, *History*, pp. 28, 254–6.

Chilton, *Strength*, pp. 27–95.

P. Doble, 'The Temptations', *ExpT* 72 (1960), pp. 91–3.

Donaldson, pp. 87–104.

A. J. Droge, 'Call Stories in Greek Biography and the Gospels', in *Society of Biblical Literature 1983 Seminar Papers*, ed. K. H. Richards, Chico, 1983, pp. 245–57.

J. Dupont, *Les tentations de Jésus au désert*, Bruges, 1968.

A. Feuillet, 'L'épisode de la Tentation d'après l'Évangile selon saint Marc', *EstBib* 19 (1960), pp. 49–73.

J. T. Fitzgerald, 'The Temptation of Jesus: The Testing of the Messiah in Matthew', *RestQ* 15 (1972), pp. 152–60.

B. Gerhardsson, *The Testing of God's Son (Matt 4:1–11 & Par.)*, CB, NT 2/1, Lund, 1966.

E. Graham, 'The Temptation in the Wilderness, *CQR* 162 (1961), pp. 17–32.

Hengel, *Charismatic Leader*, pp. 76–8.

P. Hoffmann, 'Die Versuchungsgeschichte in der Logienquelle: Zur Auseinandersetzung der Judenchristen mit dem politischen Messianismus', *BZ* 13 (1969), pp. 207–23.

N. Hyldahl, 'Die Versuchung auf der Zinne des Tempels (Matth 4,5–7 = Luk 4,9–12)', *ST* 15 (1961), pp. 113–27.

Jeremias, *Theology*, pp. 68–75.

H. A. Kelly, 'The Devil in the Desert', *CBQ* 26 (1964), pp. 190–220.

V. Kesich, 'The Antiocheans and the Temptation Story', in *Studia Patristica 7*, TU 92, ed. F. L. Cross, Berlin, 1966, pp. 496–502.

P. Ketter, *Die Versuchung Jesu nach dem Berichte der Synoptiker*, NTAbh 6/3, Münster, 1918.

Kingsbury, *Structure*, pp. 7–21.

J. A. Kirk, 'The Messianic Role of Jesus and the Temptation Narrative: A Contemporary Perspective', *EvQ* 44 (1972), pp. 11–29, 91–102.

---

[95] Luz, as in n. 94. The German original appeared in *ZNW* 62 (1971), pp. 141–71.

K. P. Köppen, *Die Auslegung der Versuchungsgeschichte unter besonderer Berücksichtigung der Alten Kirche*, BGBE 4, Tübingen, 1961.

H. G. Leder, 'Sündenfallerzählung und Versuchungsgeschichte', *ZNW* 54 (1963), pp. 188–216.

E. Lohmeyer, 'Die Versuchung Jesu', *ZST* 14 (1937), pp. 619–50.

H. Mahnke, *Die Versuchungsgeschichte im Rahmen der synoptischen Evangelien: Ein Beitrag zur frühen Christologie*, Frankfurt am Main, 1978.

J. Mánek, 'Fishers of Men', *NovT* 2 (1958), pp. 138–41.

U. W. Mauser, *Christ in the Wilderness: The Wilderness Theme in the Second Gospel and its Basis in the Biblical Tradition*, SBT 39, London, 1963.

F. Mussner, 'Gottesherrschaft und Sendung Jesu nach Mk 1,14f', in *Praesentia Salutis*, Düsseldorf, 1967, pp. 81–98.

F. Neugebauer, *Jesu Versuchung. Wegentscheidung am Anfang*, Tübingen, 1986.

L. Panier, *Récit et commentaires de la tentation de Jésus au désert*, Paris, 1984.

R. Pesch, 'Anfang des Evangeliums Jesu Christi. Eine Studie zum Prolog des Markusevangeliums', in *Die Zeit Jesu. Festschrift für Heinrich Schlier*, ed. G. Bornkamm and K. Rahner, Freiburg, 1970, pp. 108–44.

idem, 'Berufung und Sendung, Nachfolge und Mission. Eine Studie zu Mk 1, 16–20', *ZKT* 91 (1969), pp. 1–31.

P. Pokorný, 'The Temptation Stories and Their Intention', *NTS* 20 (1973–4), pp. 115–27.

Polag, pp. 146–51.

B. Przybylski, 'The Role of Mt 3:13–4:11 in the Structure and Theology of the Gospel of Matthew', *BTB* 4 (1974), pp. 222–35.

H. Riesenfeld, 'Le caractère messianique de la tentation au désert', in *La venue du Messie*, RechB 6, Bruges, 1962, pp. 51–63.

J. A. T. Robinson, 'The Temptations', in *Twelve Studies*, pp. 53–60.

K. Romaniuk, 'Repentez-vous, car le Royaume des Cieux est toute proche (Matt 4.17 par)', *NTS* 12 (1966), pp. 259–69.

Schlosser 1, pp. 91–109.

R. Schnackenburg, 'Der Sinn der Versuchung Jesu bei den Synoptikern', *TQ* 132 (1952), pp. 297–326. Also in *Schriften*, pp. 101–28.

Schulz, *Q*, pp. 177–90.

C. W. F. Smith, 'Fishers of Men', *HTR* 52 (1959), pp. 187–203.

F. Smyth-Florentin, 'Jésus, le Fils du Père, vainqueur de Satan: Mt 4,1–11; Mc 1,12–15; Lc 4,1–13', *AsSeign* 14 (1973), pp.56–75.

Soares Prabhu, pp. 84–134.

F. Spitta, 'Steine und Tiere in der Versuchungsgeschichte', *ZNW* 8 (1907), pp. 66–8.

W. Stegemann, 'Die Versuchung Jesu im Matthäusevangelium. Mt 4,1–11', *EvT* 45 (1985), pp. 29–44.

W. R. Stegner, 'Wilderness and Testing in the Scrolls and in Mt 4:1–11', *BR* 12 (1967), pp. 18–27.

M. Steiner, La tentation de Jésus dans l'interprétation patristique de Saint Justin à Origène, Paris, 1962.

A. B. Taylor, 'Decision in the Desert: The Temptation of Jesus in the

Light of Deuteronomy', *Int* 14 (1960), pp. 300–9.

G. H. P. Thompson, 'Called—Proved—Obedient: A Study in the Baptism and Temptation Narratives of Matthew and Luke', *JTS* 11 (1960), pp. 1–12.

W. Wilkens, 'Die Versuchung Jesu nach Matthäus', *NTS* 28 (1982), pp. 479–89.

W. Wuellner, *The Meaning of 'Fishers of Men'*, Philadelphia, 1967.

G. R. Wynne, 'Mending their Nets', *Expositor*, 7th series, 8 (1909), pp. 282–5.

D. Zeller, 'Die Versuchungen in der Logienquelle', *TTZ* 89 (1980), pp. 61–73.

VIII

INTRODUCTION TO THE SERMON ON THE MOUNT
(4.23–5.2)

(i) *Structure*

4.23–5.2 is a literary unit which closes one door and opens another: it concludes Mt 3–4 and at the same time introduces Mt 5–7 (cf. Gaechter, *Kommentar*, p. 135). It consists of two parts. The first, 4.23–25, is to be analysed thus:

4.23a	Jesus goes about all Galilee
4.23b	teaching
4.23c	preaching
4.23d	healing

4.24a	The report of this goes out to all Syria and
4.24b	people bring to Jesus the sick, that is,
4.24b	the diseased, and the tormented, that is,
4.24c	demoniacs, epileptics, and paralytics
4.24d	Jesus heals them

4.25	Great crowds follow Jesus from Galilee
	the Decapolis
	Jerusalem
	Judea
	beyond the Jordan

Once again Matthew's fondness for the triad seems evident. In 4.23 Jesus does three things. In 4.24a, b, c, three things happen. And in 4.24c three types of sufferers are named. As for 5.1–2, it may be set forth in this fashion:

5.1a	Seeing the crowds	(participle)	
5.1b	he went up on the mountain,	(main verb)	Jesus
5.1c	and with him sitting down,	(participle)	
5.1d	his disciples came to him,		the disciples
5.2a	and opening his mouth	(participle)	
5.2b	he taught them,	(main verb)	Jesus
5.2c	saying	(participle)	

The vocabulary of 4.23–5.2 is of great help in determining how

410

many major discourses the First Gospel contains (cf. Keegan (v)).
This is because several of its key words or phrases recur in
9.35–10.1, 5; 13.1–3; 18.1–3; and 24.3–4 (as well as in 13.36–7, this
being the middle point of a major discourse, marking the
transition from exoteric to esoteric teaching). That is, the
introduction to the sermon on the mount has its closest parallels in
the introductions to chapters 10, 13, 18, and 24–5. This is good
cause for holding there to be five and only five major Matthean
discourses. Consider the following chart, which illustrates the
elements common to the introduction of the major discourses.

	4.23–5.2	9.35–10.1, 5	13.1–3	13.36–37	18.1–3	24.3–4
ὄχλος/οι	X	X		X		
ὄρος	X					X
καθίζω/κάθημαι	X		X			X
προσῆλθα(ο)ν αὐτῷ οἱ μαθηταὶ αὐτοῦ	X			X	X	X
μαθηταί	X	X		X	X	X
λέγω/εἶπεν	X	X	X	X	X	X
disciples ask a question				X	X	X
change of scene	X	X	X	X		X

(ii) *Sources*

4.23–5.2 is not particularly helpful for solving the synoptic problem. As
the commentary shows, the hypothesis that Matthew's text is based upon
Mark and Q has nothing against it. At the same time, our passage and its
parallels do not supply any reason to reject the Griesbach hypothesis or
any other serious theory of synoptic relationships. See further on 5.1.

(iii) *Exegesis*

23. Compare the almost identical 9.35. The two verses together
create a sort of *inclusio*: between them Jesus first teaches (5–7) and
then heals (8–9). Afterwards, in chapter 10—and this constitutes a
climax in the narrative—Jesus instructs and sends out the disciples
for mission. The logic behind the arrangement should not be
missed. When Jesus instructs his missionaries, he is telling them to

do exactly what he has done, for they too are to teach and heal. This accounts for the parallelism between 4.17 and 10.6 as well as between 4.24 and 10.1:

4.17 Jesus preaches, 'The kingdom of heaven has drawn near'

10.6 The disciples preach, 'The kingdom of heaven has drawn near'

4.24 Jesus healed every disease and infirmity

10.1 The disciples are to heal every disease and every infirmity

Missionary activity is part of the *imitatio Christi*.

4.23 and the following two verses constitute a redactional summary which draws on Mk 1.39 and 3.7–12 (cf. also 1.14–15, 21, 28, 32–4; 6.6). It is the first of several such summaries, the others being 8.16(–17); 9.35(–38); 12.15–16(–21); 14.13–14; 14.(34–)36; 15.29–31; 19.1–2; 21.14(–16); and one might consider 10.1,(5–)7–8 and 11.(2–)4–6 'quasi-summaries' (so Gerhardsson, *Acts*, pp. 20–1). Observe that, in addition to the introductory summary, 4.23–5, there are at least two typifying résumés between each of the five great Matthean discourses (cf. Theissen, *Stories*, p. 205). These do not primarily just 'summarize' what has gone before or what will come after; instead do they supply narrative continuity, lengthen narrative time, expand the geographical setting, create a picture of movement (Jesus goes from here to there), highlight central themes, and tell us that the material in Matthew represents only a selection (cf. Jn 20.30; 21.5).[1] Note further that the activity spelled out in 4.23–5 characterizes not only Jesus' early work but his entire ministry. 4.23–5, along with 9.35, outlines 'the *programme* of Jesus' active ministry' (Gerhardsson, *Acts*, p. 23).

καὶ περιῆγεν ὁ Ἰησοῦς ἐν ὅλῃ τῇ Γαλιλαίᾳ.[2] The sources for this phrase, which places all initiative with Jesus, appear to be Mk 1.39 (καὶ ἦλθεν κηρύσσων εἰς τὰς συναγωγὰς αὐτῶν εἰς ὅλην τὴν Γαλιλαίαν) and 6.6b (καὶ περιῆγεν τὰς κώμας κύκλῳ διδάσκων). Compare also Lk 4.40–1, 44; 8.1.

The verb, περιάγω (here in the imperfect: the action—of unspecified duration—is continuous) also occurs in another redactional summary, 9.35. It makes Jesus, unlike the typical prophets of Israel and rabbis but not certain Hellenistic philosophers, an itinerant wanderer (cf. 23.15). Perhaps it sets an

---

[1] Cf. C. W. Hedrick, 'The Role of "Summary Statements" in the Composition of the Gospel of Mark', *NovT* 26 (1984), pp. 289–311. Although Hedrick's observations are on Mark, many of them apply equally well to Matthew.

[2] ο Ιησους is present (although in different positions) in ℵ C D W *f*[1.13] 33 892 Maj lat bo Eus. B (k) sy^c sa mae NA^26 omit (cf. Mk 1.39; 6.6b; Lk 4.44; 8.1, all of which lack ο Ιησους).

example for Christian evangelists (cf. 10.23; 28.19). On Galilee see on 4.12. On ἐν (cf. Amos 2.10) for εἰς see on 4.18. Is the universalism of the gospel (26.13; 28.19) foreshadowed in Jesus' preaching in '*all*' of Galilee, the land of the Gentiles (4.15)?

Of special interest for comparison (and contrast) with the synoptic summary narratives is Empedocles frag. 112:

I (Empedocles) go about you all an immortal god, mortal no more, honoured as is my due and crowned with garlands and verdant wreaths. Whenever I enter the prosperous townships with these my followers, men and women both, I am revered; they follow me in countless numbers, asking where lies the path to gain, some seeking prophecies, while others, for many a day stabbed by grievous pains, beg to hear the word that heals all manner of illness.[3]

διδάσκων ἐν ταῖς συναγωγαῖς αὐτῶν. See also Mk 1.21; Lk 4.15–30; 6.6; 13.10; Jn 6.59; 18.20, all of which have Jesus in a synagogue. This part of the tradition seems well established. In contrast to John the Baptist, who evidently spoke only to those who went out to him in the desert, Jesus sought out listeners.

'Teaching' is the first of three parallel participles: 'teaching', 'preaching', 'healing'. Coming in the first place (as also in 9.35), it betrays Matthew's overriding interest. It is no coincidence that the sermon on the mount precedes the mighty acts recounted in chapters 8–9.

In Matthew the synagogue is associated with three themes. First, it is a place where Jesus preaches and teaches the gospel (4.23; 9.35; 13.54). Secondly, it is a locus of opposition and persecution (10.17; 12.9–14; 23.34). Thirdly, it is a showcase for Jewish hypocrisy (6.2, 5; 23.6). Taken together, these three facts appear to mirror a three-stage history. I. Through the proclamation of Jesus and his faithful followers, the gospel of the kingdom came to the synagogue. II. That gospel was largely rejected and its bearers typically ill-treated. III. This led to uniquely Christian services and caused many, among them Matthew, to view the non-Christian synagogues as fostering a hypocritical and inadequate piety. We nonetheless remain unsure as to the precise relationship between our evangelist's community and the synagogue of his day. αὐτῶν qualifies 'synagogue(s)' in both Mark (1.23, 39) and Luke (4.15); but from Matthew there are six instances of the construction: 4.23; 9.35; 10.17; 12.9; 13.54; 23.34 (this last with ὑμῶν; contrast 6.2, 5; 23.6). The fixed nature of the expression is shown by 4.23; 12.9; and 13.54, where 'their' has no proper grammatical antecedent. What are we to infer? There could be an implicit distinction between 'their synagogues' and 'our synagogues'— just as 'their scribes' in 7.29 functions to differentiate Jewish scribes from

[3] Trans. of G. S. Kirk and J. E. Raven, *The Presocratic Philosophers*, Cambridge, 1957, pp. 354–5. For summary statements in Philostratus' *Life of Apollonius* see Hedrick, as in n. 1.

Christian scribes (cf. 13.52). In other words, there could have been Christian synagogues—this perhaps having come about because of Jewish consolidation after A.D. 70 or because of the *birkat ha-minim* (cf. Kilpatrick, p. 111; he unconvincingly argues that 'their' is not original in Mk 1.23, 39; Lk 4.15). On the other hand, 'their synagogues' might reflect a situation in which Christians no longer attended 'synagogues' of any sort (so Hummel, p. 29, equating 'your synagogues' with the synagogues of Pharisaic Judaism; so Walker, pp. 33–5, equating, 'your synagogues' with the synagogues of Israel in general; the former argues that, even though the Christians did not participate in synagogue worship, they remained under the synagogal jurisdiction). A decision between the two stated alternatives is difficult. While Jas 2.2, where the 'synagogue' is apparently a place of Christian worship (cf. BAGD, s.v., 2b), supports the first option, the second is hardly thereby excluded. So the question is best left open; and the attempt to fathom the relationship between Matthew's church and the synagogue will have to be founded upon something more solid than the references to 'their synagogues'.[4]

καὶ κηρύσσων τὸ εὐαγγέλιον τῆς βασιλείας. Compare 4.17. κηρύσσω (see on 3.1) occurs in Mk 1.39 and with 'the gospel of God' in Mk 1.15. 'Gospel of the kingdom' is found in the NT only in Matthew. It could well evoke Isa 52.7 where, in a messianic passage (cf. SB 3, pp. 282–3), the LXX has both εὐαγγελίζομαι and βασιλεύω.

εὐαγγέλιον (= 'joyous news'; cf. *běśôrâ*, as in Tg. Isa 52.7 and 53.1)[5] appears just four times in Matthew as compared with seven in Mark (Lk: 0; the corresponding verb occurs in Matthew only in 11.5, quoting Isa 61.1). It is qualified in 4.23 and 9.35—these two verses framing Mt 5–9 and implying that the sermon on the mount contains 'the gospel of the kingdom'—by the genitive τῆς βασιλείας, in 26.13 by τοῦτο, and in 24.14 it draws both qualifiers. In all four places it is the object of κηρύσσω. This is characteristic for Matthew. Jesus' speech (which cannot be sundered from his deeds: the latter incarnate the former) constitutes the gospel. That is, the Messiah's revelatory words and commands and their complete realization in his deeds and person (cf. 26.13) announce and tell about God's activity (the kingdom) and are good news.

[4] On the Jewish synagogue—which originated in Egypt? so J. G. Griffiths, 'The Legacy of Egypt in Judaism', *CHJ* 4 (forthcoming)—see Schürer 2, pp. 423–63 and the lit. cited there; also J. Gutmann, ed., *The Synagogue: Studies in Origins, Archaeology and Architecture*, New York, 1975; W. Schrage, *TWNT* 7, pp. 798–850; F. H. Hüttenmeister and G. Reeg, *Die antiken Synagogen in Israel*, 2 vols. (Wiesbaden, 1977); J. Gutmann, ed., *Ancient Synagogues*, BJS 22, Ann Arbor, 1981; also J. G. Griffiths, *JTS*, n.s., 38 (1987) pp. 1–15.

[5] On the Semitic background of εὐαγγέλιον see P. Stuhlmacher, *Das paulinische Evangelium. I: Vorgeschichte*, FRLANT 95, Göttingen, 1968. Strecker, *Weg*, p. 128, rightly observes that while the absolute εὐαγγέλιον is a *terminus technicus* in Mark, in Matthew it has the unspecified sense of 'good news'. This is why it is always qualified; it never stands by itself.

Further, it is extremely difficult to distinguish between Jesus'
preaching and his teaching, although some have thought
otherwise.[6] Both have as their content the Messiah's words and
deeds, and this is why they are so closely joined in 4.23; 9.35; and
11.1 (cf. Burnett, pp. 283–91). Moreover, preaching is bound up
with the kingdom (see above), and because the announcement of
this last is coupled with repentance (4.17), preaching can hardly
avoid making a demand on people. Thus teaching and preaching
appear nearly synonymous.[7] For the equation between preaching
and teaching in Mark compare 3.14–15 with 6.30.

καὶ θεραπεύων πᾶσαν νόσον καὶ πᾶσαν μαλακίαν ἐν τῷ λαῷ.
Compare Deut 7.15; T. Jos. 17.7; Mt 9.35; 10.1; Justin, *1 Apol.* 31.
The phrase, loosely dependent upon Mk 1.34, is full of redactional
vocabulary: θεραπεύω + πᾶσαν (cf. Acts 5.16): Mt: 5; Mk: 0; Lk: 0;
νόσος with πᾶς (cf. Exod 15.26; Deut 7.15; Ps 102.3 LXX): Mt 3;
Mk: 0; Lk: 0; μαλακία (cf. Isa 53.3 LXX): Mt: 3; Mk: 0; Lk: 0
(nowhere else in the NT; with πᾶς in Deut 7.15; 28.61).

4.23 and the verses around it set Mt 5–7 within the framework of
mercy. Before being confronted by the rigorous demands of the
higher righteousness, Israel hears the good news of the gospel and
receives the Messiah's healing, all this as a free gift (cf. Davies,
SSM, p. 96). See further section (iv).

In 9.35 we again read that Jesus was 'healing every disease and
every infirmity'. (Nothing like this is said of the Baptist.) Only a
few verses later we read that the twelve disciples were authorized to
act likewise, 'to heal every disease and every infirmity' (10.1). The
common phrase binds the pre- and post-Easter periods together.
What Jesus practised the twelve practised; therefore the church is
called to the same. Note furthermore that the disciples, like Jesus,
are to preach (10.7) and to teach (28.20).

Given the firm connexion between sin and sickness in Judaism and early
Christianity (cf. Jn 5.14; 9.2; 1 Cor 11.29–30; T. Sol. passim; SB 1,
pp. 495–6; 2, pp. 193–7), Jesus' healing ministry may be viewed as a
saving of his people from their sins (cf. 1.21). On the absence of sickness

[6] E.g. Bornkamm, 'End-Expectation', in *TIM*, p. 38, n. 1, finds preaching to
refer to God's kingdom—it has a missionary function; teaching, on the other hand,
pertains to the exposition of the Law. For Schlatter, p. 121, teaching speaks of
what man must do, preaching of what God will do. Schweizer, *Matthew*, p. 77,
draws a distinction between teaching in the synagogue and preaching. In 4.23,
however, preaching is preceded by 'teaching in the synagogues' and followed by
another activity, healing, which also took place there (see 12.9–14).

[7] So also Bonnard, p. 51; Strecker, *Weg*, pp. 126–8; Burchard, p. 58; Kingsbury,
Structure, pp. 20–1; Luz 1, pp. 181–3 (different accent, same substance); cf.
Gerhardsson, *Acts*, p. 23, n. 8. On the false distinctions often made by scholars
between *kerygma* and *didache* see J. I. H. McDonald, *Kerygma and Didache*,
SNTSMS 37, Cambridge, 1980, pp. 4–7, and J. J. Vincent, 'Didactic Kerygma in
the Synoptic Gospels', *SJT* 19 (1957), pp. 262–73.

and disease as an eschatological or messianic hope see Isa 29.18; 35.5–7; Jub. 23.28–30; 2 Bar. 73.2–3; 4 Ezra 8.53.

According to J. A. Comber, 'The Verb *Therapeuō* in Matthew's Gospel', *JBL* 97 (1978), pp. 431–4, while Jesus throughout the pre-Easter period carries on a healing ministry to the Jews, his teaching and preaching to them ceases at 11.1. This seems strained. In 13.54 Jesus is still teaching in a synagogue, and in 21.23 he is teaching in the temple (cf. 26.55). If Jesus' rôle as teacher of Israel does, nonetheless, decline somewhat in the last half of the public ministry, this is simply because Matthew, following Mark, gives more and more space to esoteric instruction (e.g. 13.34–52; 16.5–12; 17.9–27; 18.1–35; 24.1–25.46). This is wholly natural. As death approaches, the master must concentrate on instructing his true followers.

24. The summary list of troubles, which is historically suggestive in that Jesus' fame was undoubtedly largely due to his powers as a wonder-worker (cf. Jn 6.2), is rather sizeable. But then, as M. Smith has remarked, 'through all antiquity no other man is credited with so many [miracles]' (*Magician*, p. 109).

The Markan summaries tend to describe Jesus' activity as twofold—Jesus preaches and he casts out demons (1.39; 3.14–15; 6.12–13 with v. 7). This dual emphasis is reflected in the gospel as a whole. In Matthew there is a different accent. Jesus' work is more aptly summed up as teaching and preaching and *healing in a more general sense* (cf. D. C. Duling, 'The Therapeutic Son of David', *NTS* 24 (1978), pp. 393–9). Perhaps in this Matthew has been influenced by Q (cf. Mt 11.4–6 = Lk 7.22–3). In any event, it seems that our evangelist is concerned to present Jesus as the Messiah who heals every disease and infirmity, and that this concern has to do with a desire to see Scripture fulfilled. See 8.16–17, quoting Isa 53.4, and 11.4–6 quoting or alluding to Isa 26.19; 29.18–19; 35.5–6; 42.18; 66.1. It would not have been so easy to find proof texts for exorcisms, for the OT (excluding the apocrypha) is completely silent on the subject of casting out demons (although note 1 Sam 16.14–16; 18.10; 19.9).

καὶ ἀπῆλθεν ἡ ἀκοὴ αὐτοῦ εἰς ὅλην τὴν Συρίαν. Compare Est 9.4 MT. Mk 1.28 (ἐξῆλθεν δὲ ἡ ἀκοὴ αὐτοῦ εὐθὺς πανταχοῦ εἰς ὅλην τὴν περίχωρον τῆς Γαλιλαίας) is probably the inspiration for this line. The aorist (ἀπῆλθεν) here and in 4.25 contrasts with the imperfect in 4.23 but harmonizes with the tense in the healing summaries in 8.16; 12.15; 14.14; 14.35–6; 15.30; 19.2. For Matthew replacing ἐξέρχομαι with ἀπέρχομαι see Mt 9.7 diff. Mk 2.12 and Mt 28.8 diff. Mk 16.8. For ἀκοή (cf. *šĕmu'â*) with the objective genitive see Nah 1.12 and Jer 6.24. Only Jesus' fame goes out; he himself stays in Galilee. This accords with the biblical prophecy (4.14–16). For ὅλη see on 4.23. Συρία (usually for *'ărām* in the LXX) occurs only here in the First Gospel. Many have suggested

that the redactional mention of Syria (*sûrĕyāʾ* in the rabbis) is a
hint that Matthew's home was there (e.g. Kilpatrick, p. 131; cf.
Luz 1, p. 181, n. 16). Whether or not this be so, the evangelist
likely had in mind not the Roman province, that is, the vast region
from the lands of the Euphrates to the Mediterranean and from
the Syro-Arabian desert to Cilicia (cf. Lk 2.2; BAGD, s.v.) but
rather—as in the Mishnah[8]—a narrower territory, exclusive of
and to the north-northeast of Palestine, perhaps extending
approximately from Damascus to Antioch and on to the east; see
Gal 1.21–3; Josephus, *Bell.* 7.43.[9] If so, and even though Syria had
a large Jewish population, we are probably to think of Syria as
including Gentiles (contra Trilling, p. 135), so that while Jesus
remained in Galilee ministering to the Jews (cf. 10.5–6; 15.24),
news of him reached non-Jewish ears. (On our interpretation,
Syria in 4.24 is not a general term embracing the places in 4.25; it
instead simply expands the geographical impact of Jesus' ministry
beyond the locales named in 4.23 and 25; cf. Guelich, pp. 48–9).[10]

καὶ προσήνεγκαν αὐτῷ. Compare Mk 1.32. προσφέρω is a
Matthean favourite (see on 2.11). For προσήνεγκαν αὐτῷ (Mk: 0;
Lk: 0) see also 2.11; 8.16; 9.32; 12.22; 14.35; 22.19. The subject is
here unspecified. Are Galilean Jews in view (4.23)? Are those from
Syria included? Are the crowds of 4.25 anticipated? Whatever the
answer, the picture is of Jesus as the centre around which
everything happens.

πάντας τοὺς κακῶς ἔχοντας ποικίλαις νόσοις. κακῶς ἔχειν (Ezek
34.4; *P. Oxy.* 935.15), the antithesis of καλῶς ἔχειν (Mk 16.18), is
to be ill or sick. For νόσος see on 4.23. In the synoptics ποικίλος
('manifold') occurs only here, in Mk 1.34, and in Lk 4.40. πάντας
τοὺς κακῶς ἔχοντας is a phrase Matthew takes over from Mk 1.32;
he uses it again in 8.16 and 14.35. κακῶς ἔχοντας ποικίλαις νόσοις
appears also in Mk 1.34. Matthew has apparently conflated Mk
1.32 with 1.34.

καὶ βασάνοις συνεχομένους. This means 'and those suffering
severe pains'. The first meaning of the noun is 'torture, torment'

[8] *Dem.* 6.11; *B. Qam.* 7.7; *Roš. Haš.* 1.4; *ʿEd.* 7.7; *ʿAbod. Zar.* 1.8; *Šeb.* 6.2, 5, 6;
Maʿas. Š. 5.5; *Ḥal.* 4.7, 11; *ʿOr.* 3.9; *Ohol.* 18.7.
[9] So Zahn, p. 172, n. 24, against Trilling, p. 135. If Matthew read Mark's τὴν
περίχωρον τῆς Γαλιλαίας as 'the country around Galilee', not 'throughout Galilee',
then it could be regarded as the impetus for Matthew's naming of Syria. For lit. on
Syria see BAGD, s.v. and H. D. Betz, *Galatians*, Hermeneia, Philadelphia, 1979,
p. 80, n. 221. On the impact of rabbinic legislation on Jews in Syria note Davies,
SSM, p. 296. This has been questioned by H. Macoby, in *TLS*, July, 1983, p. 702,
col. 5.
[10] According to the well-known legend in Eusebius, *H.E.* 1.13, the report of Jesus'
wonder-working powers reached even king Abgar who reigned over the nations
beyond the Euphrates. Perhaps Mt 4.24 is partly responsible for the genesis of this
tale. For Jesus' reputation as a miracle worker in Jewish sources see *t. Ḥull.* 2.22–3;
b. Sanh. 43a; *y.Šabb.* 14d.

(BAGD, s.v.; cf. Lk 16.23, 28). Compare 1 Macc 9.56; 2 Macc 9.5; Philo, *Abr.* 96. συνέχω, which underlines the severity of the ailment, is a *hapax legomenon* in Matthew. Compare 4 Macc 15.32: ταῖς τῶν υἱῶν βασάνοις συνεχομένη.

δαιμονιζομένους καὶ σεληνιαζομένους καὶ παραλυτικούς.[11] The participial form of δαιμονίζομαι (cf. Ps 90.6 Aq.) is relatively frequent in Matthew (see 4.24; 8.16, 28, 33; 9.32; 12.22; cf. Mk 1.32; 5.15–16; Lk 8.35; D; Jn 10.21). For the casting out of demons as an eschatological sign see 12.22–32. σεληνιάζομαι appears only twice in the NT, in Mt 4.24 and 17.15. The rare word literally means 'be moon-struck' and seems to refer to epilepsy (cf. the description in Mt 17.15), which the ancients must have supposed was caused by the moon (cf. Ps 121.6; the English 'lunacy' is from the Latin *luna*, and many moderns, it is worth observing, still believe that violence increases during a full moon). Given the possible connexion between epilepsy and demons (cf. 17.15; *b. Giṭ.* 70a), it may be that the first two items in our list (bodily diseases and pains) are followed by two illnesses caused by supernatural influences (demon-possession and epilepsy); so Ross (v). This requires retaining the textually doubtful καί before δαιμονιζομένους. The alternative is to omit καί and view demon-possession and 'moon-struckness' and paralysis as instances of disease and pain (so RSV, NEB). This last is preferable because the distinction between mundane and supernatural illness was scarcely hard and fast in antiquity. For παραλυτικός (LXX: 0) coupled with 'epileptic' (ἐπιληπτικός) see *P.Mon.Gr.* inv. 123, lines 16–17.

καὶ ἐθεράπευσεν αὐτούς. This means 'he healed them' (cf. Wisd 16.12), not 'he treated them medically'. Compare Mk 1.34. See on 4.23 for the verb, which in the gospels usually connotes mercy and compassion. ἐθεράπευσεν αὐτούς occurs only once in Luke (4.40), never in Mark, five times in Matthew: 4.24; 12.15; 15.30; 19.2; 21.14 (always in summary material). Later the evangelist will tell us that Jesus' acts of corporal mercy fulfilled messianic expectation; see 8.16–17 and 11.2–6, both quoting Isaiah.

25. Compare 12.15. The few general agreements between Mt 4.25–5.2 and Lk 6.17–20a imply that, in the introduction to Q's great sermon (Lk 6.20–49 par.), mention was made not only of Jesus' disciples but also of an ὄχλος or ὄχλοι (cf. Schürmann, *Lukasevangelium* 1, p. 323); so our verse owes something to Q. But then Markan influence also seems apparent. Indeed, both Mt 4.24–5.2 (the introduction to the sermon on the mount) and Lk 6.17–20a (the introduction to the sermon on the plain) seem to draw upon Mk 3.7–13a (cf. Mt 5.1 with Mk 3.13a, Mt 4.25a with

[11] א C² D W *f*¹ Maj latt sa mae followed by NA²⁶ add a καί before δαιμον., against B C* *f*¹³ 892 *pc* (so HG).

Mk 3.7b–8, Lk 6.17 with Mk 3.7–8). This similar use of Mark at the same point is, assuming the independence of the First and Third Gospels, somewhat surprising; but see further on 5.1.

καὶ ἠκολούθησαν αὐτῷ ὄχλοι πολλοὶ ἀπὸ τῆς Γαλιλαίας. Compare Mk 3.7 and Lk 6.17. On the verb (which here does not connote discipleship) see on 4.20. ἠκολούθησαν αὐτῷ ὄχλοι πολλοί (cf. Mk 5.24) occurs again in 8.1 and 19.2; similar phrases appear in 12.15; 14.13; 20.29; 21.9. ὄχλος was a rabbinic loan word (see R. Meyer, *TWNT* 5, p. 585); and Matthew, unlike Mark but like the rabbis, liked the plural (ὄχλοι: Mt: 30; Mk: 1; Lk: 13). Against Keegan (v), one hesitates to find a theological meaning in the plural that is not present in the singular (cf. 13.1–2). 'Many crowds' seems simply Matthew's way of saying 'a great crowd' (cf. MHT 4, p. 43). The article before Galilee seems also to define the other regions immediately named (cf. Lk 5.17; Acts 2.9; BDF § 276.1). ἀπό is thus not repeated (see BDF § 479).

The crowds in Matthew serve several functions. First and foremost, they follow Jesus wherever he goes and thereby show him to be a charismatic figure, indeed a sensation (e.g., 4.25; 8.1, 18; 11.7; 12.46; 15.30; 17.14; 19.2). Secondly, as an audience they are open and receptive, for they respond to the Messiah with amazement, astonishment, and reverential fear (e.g. 9.8; 12.23; 15.31; 22.23). They in fact hold Jesus to be, like John the Baptist (14.5; 21.26), a prophet (21.11, 46), and they bless him when he enters the holy city (21.9). Thirdly, they are contrasted with the Pharisees (9.33–4; 15.1–10; 23.1). Jesus condemns the Jewish leaders, but he has compassion on the multitudes (9.36; 14.14; 15.32). Fourthly in 13.36 and 14.22–3 the crowd is clearly distinguished from the disciples, and there are places in Matthew where Jesus delivers esoteric teaching (e.g. 16.21–8, 18; 24–5). The crowd, then, cannot represent the church. Finally, the crowd is implicated in Jesus' death: 26.47, 55; 27.20, 24. An ὄχλος comes out with Judas against Jesus (26.47, 55), and the ὄχλος asks Pilate for Barabbas (27.20, 24). Yet this last point is softened by several considerations. The disciples also failed to follow Jesus when darkness came; and in 26.47 and 55 the crowd is 'from the chief priests and the elders of the people', while in 27.20–4 the people fail to ask for the prisoner Jesus only because they succumb to the persuasion of the Jewish leaders.

Generalizing from the data cited, the crowds are more than neutral background, more than a Greek chorus. They are presented in a more or less positive light. To be sure, the ὄχλοι are not true followers of Jesus; yet they are also not in the same league with Jesus' opponents, the chief priests, the elders, the Pharisees. The crowds fall somewhere in between. This is because they are thought of as being, above all, 'the lost sheep of the house of Israel'.[12] They have not yet found faith in the Messiah, but they are not uniformly opposed to him. Many of them even hold Jesus to be a prophet. If this is the extent of their faith, the blame is to be laid squarely at the feet of their misguided leaders, Matthew's intellectual

[12] Matthew may presuppose a Gentile presence among the crowds, but he does not emphasize this.

counterparts. Thus the appropriate attitude towards the multitudes is compassion. This implies, in our view, that for Matthew the mission to Israel, despite Jewish opposition, is—and this is very important for understanding our gospel—still open.[13]

καὶ Δεκαπόλεως καὶ Ἱεροσολύμων καὶ Ἰουδαίας καὶ πέραν τοῦ Ἰορδάνου. Compare 3.5. Note the absence of Samaria (cf. 10.5) and of Tyre and Sidon (which are named in Mk 3.7–8). Matthew is limiting himself in this verse (contrast 4.24) to the Jewish populace, presumably because Jesus' ministry is to Israel (10.5–6; 15.24). The Decapolis,[11] the group (league?) of ten Hellenistic cities east of the Jordan (with the exception of Scythopolis) and south of the Sea of Galilee, probably received its name sometime in the first century B.C. It is mentioned only once in Matthew, only twice in Mark (5.20; 7.31), and nowhere else in the OT or NT. The ten cities— Damascus, Philadelphia, Raphana, Scythopolis, Gadara, Hippos, Dion, Pella, Galasa, Canatha, according to Pliny, *Nat. hist.* 5.74; Ptolemy, *Geog.* 5.14.22 adds nine more: Heliopolis, Abila, Saana, Hina, Abila Lysanius, Capitolias, Edrei, Gadora, Samulis— belonged to the Roman province of Syria. Within the context of Matthew's gospel, are we to think of it as the home of Gentiles? Probably not. As Trilling (p. 135) has stated, in Matthew's mind 'the land of Israel' (2.20–1) could consist of all the places named in 4.25. This would be consistent with rabbinic geography; see A. Neubauer, *Geographie du Talmud*, Amsterdam, 1965, pp. 5–24. On Jerusalem (here a neuter plural) see on 2.3. On Judea see on 3.1. For the order, Jerusalem and Judea (contrast Mk 3.7–8), see on 3.5. If πέραν τοῦ Ἰορδάνου (cf. *'ēber hayyardēn*, on which see BDB, s.v., *'ēber*, 1, A–B) presupposes a point of view west of the Jordan, that is, if it is, as in Isa 9.1 and Josephus, *Ant.* 12.222, the equivalent of Perea (see on 4.15; according to Josephus, *Bell.* 3.46–7, Perea extends in length from Machaerus to Pella, in breadth from Philadelphia to the Jordan), Matthew manages to cover the compass—Galilee (NW), the Decapolis (NE), Judea (SW), Transjordan (SE)—as well as name the centre of the world, Jerusalem.

5.1. This verse and the next, which are of a piece with 4:23–5,

---

[13] On the crowds in Matthew see further van Tilborg, pp. 142–65, and P. Minear, 'The Disciples and the Crowds in the Gospel of Matthew', *ATR* Supplement Series 3 (1974), pp. 28–44. We reject Minear's attempt to identify the disciples with church leaders, the crowd with the Christian laity. We also cannot follow J. A. Baird, *Audience Criticism and the Historical Jesus*, Philadelphia, 1969. He divides the crowd into two parts, 'the disciple crowd' and 'the opponent crowd'.

[14] Lit.: G. A. Smith, pp. 397–408; Schürer 2, pp. 125–7; I. Benzinger, *PW* 4.2415–17; H. Bietenhard, 'Die Dekapolis von Pompejus bis Trojan', *ZDPV* 79 (1963), pp. 24–58; S. T. Parker, 'The Decapolis Revisited', *JBL* 94 (1975), pp. 437–41.

are redactional. The evangelist, to be sure, has made use of Mk 3.13 and Q's introduction to the sermon on the plain. But he has reworked them so thoroughly that 5.1–2 is truly his own.

It is odd that Luke, like Matthew, draws upon Mk 3 in creating the setting for the sermon on the mount/plain. While Lk 6.20a, which introduces Luke's sermon, must be influenced by Q (cf. Mt 5.1–2), Lk 6.12–16, the appointment of the twelve, corresponds to Mk 3.13–19, and Lk 6.17–19, which tells of Jesus healing great crowds from various places, corresponds to Mk 3.7–12 (cf. Mt 4.23–5). What led both Matthew and Luke to Mk 3? For defenders of the Griesbach hypothesis, Luke has simply followed Matthew: there is no problem. For those who believe in the independence of Matthew and Luke, the answer is less obvious. According to Marshall (p. 241), if the great sermon was already, in Q, associated with a mountain, then Matthew and Luke could independently have turned to Mk 3 because of the mountain there. Schürmann (*Untersuchungen*, pp. 281–2; *Lukasevangelium* 1, p. 319) proposes something a bit different: in Q the sermon on the plain was prefaced by the equivalent of Lk 6.12–16. This would mean that Q as well as Mark included a story about Jesus going up to a mountain to select there his twelve disciples; and it would be natural, given the Markan/Q overlap, for both Matthew and Luke to have turned to Mk 3 as they composed their introductions to the sermon on the mount/plain. Perhaps the best solution to the problem created by the common use of Mk 3 comes from Donaldson (pp. 106–11). Accepting Schürmann's case that the agreements of Matthew and Luke against Mark in their accounts of the appointment of the twelve (see on 10.1) are evidence of a non-Markan tradition, and also accepting the claim that in Q the great sermon was introduced by a list of the twelve (cf. Luke), Donaldson argues that both Mt 5–7 and Lk 6 have been brought into relationship with Mk 3.13–19 simply because the sermon in Q was prefaced by the call of the twelve, and this naturally led both Matthew and Luke to Mk 3. Against Schürmann, Q's introduction to the sermon did not mention a mountain. Mk 3.13a suffices to explain the mountain in both Mt 5.1 and Lk 6.12.

ἰδὼν δὲ τοὺς ὄχλους. Compare 8.18 and 9.36 (both redactional). Lk 6.17 has: 'And coming down with them he stood on a level place, with a great crowd (ὄχλος) of his disciples and a great multitude of people . . .'. Matthew has ἰδών/ἰδόντες + δέ + direct object immediately followed by main verb with subject unexpressed in 2.10; 3.7; 5.1; and 9.36, and each time the construction—which is not found in the LXX—appears to be redactional. On the crowd see on 4.25.

ἀνέβη εἰς τὸ ὄρος. Compare 14.23 (diff. Mk 6.46) and 15.29 (diff. Mk 7.31). The phrase may be taken from Mk 3.13. The impression created by this and the previous clause is that Jesus, having seen the crowds, goes up the mountain[15] to get away from them (cf. Jn

---

[15] τὸ ὄρος means 'the mountain', not 'the hill country' or 'the mountain range'; see Donaldson, pp. 9–11.

6.3).[16] Yet in view of 7.28–8.1, we must think of the crowds as overhearing the discourse. So there are two circles around Jesus, an inner circle (disciples) and an outer circle (the crowds).

Lk 6.17 has Jesus deliver the sermon on a plain (ἐπὶ τόπου πεδινοῦ). This is likely to preserve Q. (1) πεδινός appears only once in Luke-Acts (it is indeed a NT *hapax legomenon*) and (2) the mountain is easily ascribed to Matthew. For the plain as a place of revelation see *Mek*. on Exod. 12.1, citing Ezek. 3.22. Against those who have harmonized Luke's plain with Matthew's mountain and argued that Jesus delivered his sermon on a flat ridge on the side of a mountain, it suffices to observe that the sick would hardly be carried up to such a place (see Lk 6.17–19) and that the 'coming down' of Lk 6.17 naturally involves leaving the mountain of 6.12. See further Strauss, pp. 334–5. John Calvin (1, pp. 258–9) made the essential point long ago; the sermon is 'a brief summary of the doctrine of Christ . . . collected out of his many and various discourses'.

'The mountain', which Christians have sometimes identified as Karn Hattin near Tiberias or Tabghah near Capernaum, cannot be located on a map of Palestine any more than the mountain of 17.20 ('If you have faith as a grain of mustard seed, you will say to this mountain, "Move from here to there", and it will move'). This is because its significance is not geographical but mythological.[17] How so? If it was believed that God did not speak to any random individual but only to men or women properly prepared and specially chosen, so too was it often thought that not every place was appropriate for divine revelation, and also that some places were particularly appropriate.[18] And mountains, like rivers (see on 3.11), were held to be fitting places; see Jub. 1.2–4; T. Levi 2; T. Naph. 5.1; 2 Bar. 13.1; Apoc. Abr. 9, 12; 3 Bar. title; Apoc. Zeph. 3.1–4; Ep. Pet. Phil. 134.9–18; 1st Apoc. Jas. 30.18–20; CMC 52–5. Why?[19] The mountain was a symbol of power (Ps 97.5; Jer 51.25; Dan 2.45; Zech 4.7; 1 En. 52.2, 6–7; T. Sol. 23.1; *b. Sukk*. 52a) and the site of numerous theophanies (Gen 22.14; Exod 3.1; 4.27; 18.5; Deut 4.11; 5.4; 9.15; 1 Kgs 19.11–14). And mountains were said to have been created at the beginning of creation (Prov 8.25; Job 15.7), were spoken of as though they would endure forever (Gen 49.26; Ps 125.1; Hab 3.6), and had played an important rôle in salvation-history, as the names Moriah, Horeb, Sinai, Zion, and Carmel attest. (Eden was also a mountain according to Ezek 28.13–16; 1 En. 24; 87.3; Jub. 4.26.) Moreover, in Semitic mythology—as in mythology the

---

[16] This verse could conceivably betray a knowledge of Matthew: ἀνῆλθεν δὲ εἰς τὸ ὄρος Ἰησοῦς καὶ ἐκεῖ ἐκάθητο μετὰ τῶν μαθητῶν αὐτοῦ. See also 6.2, which recalls Mt 4.25: ἠκολούθει δὲ αὐτῷ ὄχλος πολύς.

[17] Cf. Stendahl, 'Matthew', p. 798, commenting on 28.16.

[18] For rabbinic discussions of this see Davies, *JPS*, pp. 72–83.

[19] Lit.: S. Talmon, *TDOT* 3, pp. 427–47; W. Foerster, *TWNT* 5, pp. 475–86; A. Strobel, 'Der Berg der Offenbarung (Mt 28,16; Apg 1,12)', in *Verborum Veritas*, ed. O. Böcher and K. Haacker, Wuppertal, 1970, pp. 133–46; McCurley (v); Donaldson, pp. 25–83.

world over for that matter— the mountains were thought to be close to the gods, indeed they were the dwelling places of gods (*CTA* 2.1.19–21; Gen 28.10–22; 1 Kgs 20.23–8; Isa 14.13; Philostratus, *V.A.* 3.13; recall also the Greek's Mount Olympus).[20] When one adds to all this the natural correlation between knowledge and a place from which great expanses can be surveyed, the locating of divine revelation on a mount in so many ancient texts is easily grasped.

The mountain in Mt 5.1 is to be understood partly against the background detailed in the previous paragraph. When Jesus 'goes up the mountain', he is seeking a place befitting his weighty words. That is, the revelatory character of the discourse demands a site consistent with its content. The 'mount of the beatitudes' is, therefore, a symbolic mountain, 'the mount of revelation'.

Is it also the case that Mt 5.1 should recall the momentous events at Sinai and the giving of the Torah? Is Jesus here made out to be a new Moses? Although many have affirmed this (e.g. Bacon, pp. 165–86; Lohmeyer, *Matthäus*, p. 76; Gundry, *Commentary*, p. 66; Luz 1, pp. 197–8), others have been cautious (e.g. Wellhausen, *Matthaei*, p. 12; Schmid, *Matthäus*, p. 74; Davies, SSM, p. 99). Why the hesitation? For one thing, we might expect the allusions to OT texts about Moses to be bolder and more fully developed. 'Mountain' by itself scarcely suffices, even when it is added that Mt 5 treats of the Torah. In other words, one feels that if the allusion to Sinai were indeed present in 5.1–2 it should not be so quiescent. Furthermore, any alleged comparison with Moses is dwarfed by the ways in which Mosaic categories are transcended (cf. Davies, *SSM*, pp. 93–108). Jesus is, among other things, the Son of God, the Messiah, and Lord—titles to which Moses could make no claim. It would thus be a grave injustice to think of him who utters the great sermon as simply a new Moses: Jesus is much more. Thirdly, the mountain of Mt 5 differs from Sinai in not being a place of divine theophany and secret revelation to one man alone. Lastly, Donaldson (v) has put forward an interesting case for thinking that Matthew's mountains are to be explained primarily in terms of a Zion—not Sinai—typology.

Notwithstanding the seemingly sound reasons for doubting the presence of a Mosaic motif in Mt 5.1–2, we are moved, in view of three facts, to accept it. (1) Matthew writes that Jesus 'went up on the mountain'. In the LXX, ἀναβαίνω + εἰς τὸ ὄρος occurs twenty-four times, and of these, fully eighteen belong to the Pentateuch, and most refer to Moses: Exod 19.3, 12, 13; 24.12, 13, 18; 34.1, 2(A), 4; Num 27.12; Deut 1.24, 41, 43; 5.5; 9.9; 10.1, 3; 32.49; the other occurrences are in Ps 24.2; Isa 2.3; Mic 4.2; Hag 1.8; 1 Macc

---

[20] Bengel, *Gnomon, ad loc.*: 'A mountain, as a lofty part of the earth, nearer to heaven, is suited to the most holy actions'.

5.54; 7.33. This inclines one to associate Matthew's phrase with the OT law-giver. (2) In Deut 9.9 (a text which might be alluded to in Mt 4.2), Moses speaks these words, 'When I went up the mountain to receive the tables of stone, the tables of the covenant which the Lord made with you, I remained on the mountain forty days and forty nights; I neither ate bread nor drank water' (RSV). The word translated 'remained' is wā'ēšēb. BDB, s.v., lists, as the second and third meanings of yāšab, 'remain' and 'dwell' respectively. But the first meaning given for the verb is 'sit', and in b. Meg. 21a we find this: 'One verse says, "And I sat in the mountain" (Deut 9.9), and another verse says, "And I stood in the mountain" (Deut 10.10). Rab says: He Moses stood when he learnt and sat while he went over (what he had learnt). R. Ḥanina said: He was neither sitting nor standing, but stooping. R. Joḥanan said: "Sitting" here means only "staying", as it says, "And ye stayed in Kadesh many days" (Deut 1.46). Raba said: The easy things (he learnt) standing and the hard ones sitting'. This rabbinic text, which is also found in b. Soṭa 49a, proves that Deut 9.9 could be taken to mean—and was by at least some rabbis taken to mean—that Moses sat on mount Sinai (see also Pirqe R. El. 46). We cannot, of course, move from this to Mt 5.1–2 without further ado, for the rabbinic text and the tradition contained therein cannot be dated with any certainty. (Ḥanina and Rab flourished in the early third century, Joḥanan and Raba even later.) Still, b. Meg. 21a and b. Soṭa 49a plainly reveal the ambiguity of the verb in Deut 9.9 and raise the possibility of a Jewish tradition about Moses sitting on Sinai. This is all the more significant given that Matthew not only knew the Hebrew text of the OT but was also probably acquainted with Jewish exegetical tradition. (3) If in chapters 1–2 the events of Jesus' childhood have their parallels in the childhood events of Moses (see pp. 190–5), in chapters 3–4 there is a new exodus: Jesus emerges from the waters to enter the wilderness. Can it then be coincidence that soon after this Jesus goes up on a mountain and there speaks of the Law? See further section iv and Allison (v).

καὶ καθίσαντος αὐτοῦ. Compare 15.29: 'And he went up on the mountain and sat down there'. For teaching in a sitting position—something emphasized by our evangelist—see Ezek 8.1; Mt 13.1, 2; 15.29; 23.2; 24.3–4; 26.55; Lk 4.20–7; 5.3; Acts 16.13; Eusebius, H.E. 5.20; m. 'Abot 1.4; 3.2, 6; ARN 6; SB 1, p. 997. (Yĕšîbâ, the Hebrew word for 'school'—so already Ecclus 51.23, 29—means 'seat'; see Hengel, Judaism and Hellenism 1, p. 79; 2, p. 54, n. 165; Schürer 2, p. 419, n. 31). Perhaps sitting implies honour or dignity in Matthew; see also 19.28; 20.21, 23; 25.31; 26.64 and compare Augustine, De serm. mont. 1.2. In Lk 6.17—as in Q?—Jesus stands. The superfluous genitive pronoun αὐτοῦ is a Semitism; for other examples see Sanders, Tendencies, pp. 167–8, 184.

In Matthew Jesus sits or is said to have sat six times (5.1; 13.1, 2; 15.29; 24.3; 26.55; when he sits in the future it will be on a throne: 19.28; 25.31; cf. 20.21, 23). Only once (15.29) does he sit without teaching. And three times—twice on a mountain—a major discourse is introduced with Jesus sitting (5.1; 13.1–2; 24.3).[21]

προσῆλθαν αὐτῷ οἱ μαθηταὶ αὐτοῦ. προσῆλθα(ο)ν + (αὐτῷ/τῷ Ἰησοῦ +) οἱ μαθηταὶ (αὐτοῦ) occurs seven times in Matthew: 5.1; 13.36; 14.15; 18.1; 24.1, 3; 26.17. Three of these verses appear at the beginning of major discourses (5.1; 18.1; 24.3), and a fourth (13.36) in the middle of another. The only major discourse lacking the phrase is 10.1ff., but here Jesus calls the disciples to himself (10.1).

Until this point, the word 'disciple' has not been used, and only four followers have been called (4.18–22). Moreover, at this juncture it is difficult indeed to identify the disciples with the twelve because at least one of them, Matthew the tax-collector (see 10.3), does not meet Jesus until 9.9. Who then are the disciples of 5.1? The redactor, one might argue, thought of the sermon on the mount as being addressed directly to only four disciples—those named in 4.18–22, Peter and Andrew, James and John. This, however, would be to read too much into the text. The problem of 5.1 simply warns us that our evangelist was not overly interested in informing his readers as to who exactly was on the mountain when Jesus spoke. In 5.1, the unspecified disciples, who must be a group larger than the four of 4.18–22, are—and this is the key point— contrasted with the crowd and so represent the church. The disciples, in other words, stand for the faithful; they are transparent symbols of believers. So the sermon on the mount is spoken directly to Matthew's Christian readers.[22]

2. καὶ ἀνοίξας τὸ στόμα αὐτοῦ ἐδίδασκεν αὐτοὺς λέγων. The opening of the discourse is deliberate and solemn. Compare Job 3.1–2 and Dan 3.25 LXX. The redactional nature of 5.2—which exhibits Semitic redundancy—is probably indicated by the fact

---

[21] According to S. T. Lachs, 'Rabbinic Sources for New Testament Studies—Use and Misuse', *JQR* 74 (1983), p. 171, Jesus probably did not teach in a sitting position. He cites *b. Meg.* 21a, where, in a baraita, it is said that from the days of Moses up to Rabban Gamaliel (the Elder), the Torah was learned only while standing. When Rabban Gamaliel died, feebleness descended upon the world and they learned the Torah while seated. But this hardly settles the matter. (1) The talmudic text may deal only with the reading and learning of the Torah, not with teaching. (2) Already in Ecclus 51.23 and 29, the Jewish school is called yĕšîbâ (see above). (3) Even if it was the practice of Pharisees at Jesus' time to stand while they taught, this scarcely entails that non-Pharisaic teachers followed suit. (4) What guarantees do we have that *b. Meg.* 21a preserves an accurate chronological observation?

[22] Strecker's argument that Matthew 'historicized' the disciples and consistently identified them with the twelve alone fails to make sense of 5.1 as well as of 8.21. For further criticisms see Luz, in Stanton, *Matthew*, pp. 98–128.

that ἀνοίγω + στόμα (cf. *pātaḥ + peh*, about forty times in the OT, never with 'to teach') occurs three times in Matthew (5.2; 13.35; 17.27), never in Mark, once in Luke. Note also the *inclusio* created by 5.2 and 7.29: ἐδίδασκεν αὐτούς/διδάσκων αὐτούς. (Does the αὐτούς in 5.2, like that in 7.29, include not just the disciples but also the crowds?).

Mk 1.22 ('And they were amazed at his teaching, for he was teaching them as one having authority, and not as the scribes') is the Markan text which gave Matthew the opportunity to introduce the sermon on the mount. Lk 6.20a ('And he lifted up his eyes on his disciples and said') is probably redactional (cf. Lk 16.23; 18.13).

Before turning to the sermon on the mount, perhaps we can at this point shed some light on how Matthew has prepared his readers for Mt 5–7 by considering a rabbinic text. *m. Ber.* 2.2 reads: R. Joshua ben Korcha said, 'Why does the *Shemaʿ* precede the (paragraph that begins with) *wĕhāyâ im šāmōʿaʿ*? In order that one should first acknowledge the sovereignty of the Almighty and then recognize the obligation of the commandments'. A similar line of thought apparently undergirds the structure of Mt 1–7. Before Jesus speaks a word, before he utters his commands, the reader has been informed—by OT prophecy, by John the Baptist, by God, and by the devil—who Jesus is: the Messiah, the Son of David, and the Son of God; he is the fulfiller of prophecies, the bearer of the Spirit, and the healer *par excellence*. This Jesus, therefore, by virtue of his identity, must speak with authority and make sovereign demands (cf. 7.29). So the obligation to obey the commands of Mt 5–7 is grounded in Christology, in the person of Jesus; and Matthew has set up his gospel so that one may first confess Jesus' unique status and then recognize the obligation of his commandments (cf. Kennedy, p. 104).

Assuming this conclusion to be sound, one wonders whether it is not primarily as Messiah that Jesus takes up his rôle as teacher. The question, which unfortunately cannot be definitely answered, is occasioned by two facts. The first is the prominence of the title, 'Messiah', and associated themes in Mt 1–4 (see 1.1–17; 2.2, 4, 6; 3.11). The second is the connexion in Jewish eschatological expectation between messianic figures on the one hand and wisdom, instruction, and Torah on the other. See, for example, Isa 42.1–4 (on this see Davies *SSM*, pp. 133–7); CD 6.11; 7.18; 4QFlor 1.11; 4QMess ar; 11QMelch 2.18–21; 1 En 49.3–4; 51.3; Ps. Sol. 17.26–32, 42–3; 18.7–10; T. Levi 18.2–6; Tg. Gen. on 49.10; Tg. Isa. on 53.5, 11; *Midr. Qoh.* on 2.1 and 11.8; *Yal.* on Isa 26.2. Significant too is Mt 11.2–6, where John the Baptist is supposed to be able to recognize Jesus as 'the coming one' by, among other things, Jesus' words (11.4: 'what you *hear*'; 11.6: 'the poor have good news *preached* to them').

(iv) *Concluding Observations*

(1) 4.23–5.2, which gives us in brief an overview of Jesus' ministry to Israel (he preached, he taught, he healed), introduces the sermon on the mount. It tells us that the disciples were not the only ones to hear Jesus. So did the crowds. What crowds? Those who were healed by Jesus. 'And he went about all Galilee, teaching in their synagogues and preaching the gospel of the kingdom and healing every disease and every infirmity among the people. So his fame spread throughout all Syria, and they brought to him all the sick, those afflicted with various diseases and pains, demoniacs, epileptics, and paralytics, and he healed them . . .'. Before the crowds hear the Messiah's word they are the object of his compassion and healing. Having done nothing, nothing at all, they are benefited. So grace comes before task, succour before demand, healing before imperative. The first act of the Messiah is not the imposition of his commandments but the giving of himself. Today's command presupposes yesterday's gift.

(2) If the opening of the sermon on the mount be linked up with Sinai (see p. 423), then Mt 1–5 in all its parts reflects a developed exodus typology. The gospel opens with events recalling the birth and childhood of Moses. Then there is Jesus' baptism, which parallels Israel's passing through the waters. There follows next the temptation, in which Jesus re-experiences the desert temptations recounted in Deuteronomy. Finally, there is 4.23–5.2, where Jesus, like Moses, sits on the mountain of revelation. In other words, every major event in Mt 1–5 apparently has its counterpart in the events surrounding Israel's exodus from Egypt. Moreover, the order of the events in Matthew—childhood of Jesus, temptation, mount of revelation—lines up with the chronological order of events in the Pentateuch—childhood of Moses, exodus from Egypt, entry into the wilderness, Sinai. The typology is thus extensive and consistently thought through. So when Jesus goes up on the mountain to utter the sermon on the mount, he is speaking as the mosaic Messiah and delivering messianic Torah.

(v) *Bibliography*

D. C. Allison, 'Jesus and Moses (Mt 5.1–2)', *ExpT* 98 (1987), pp. 203–5.

Donaldson, pp. 105–21.

Gerhardsson, *Acts*, pp. 20–37.

T. J. Keegan, 'Introductory Formulae for Matthean Discourses', *CBQ* 44 (1982), pp. 415–30.

Kingsbury, *Structure*, pp. 56–8.

G. Lohfink, 'Wem gilt die Bergpredigt? Eine redaktionskritische

Untersuchung von Mt 4.23–5.2 und 7.28f', *TQ* 163 (1983), pp. 264–84.

J. Mánek, 'On the Mount—On the Plain' (Mt. v 1–Lk. vi 17)', *NovT* 9 (1967), pp. 124–31.

F. R. McCurley, *Ancient Myths and Biblical Faith*, Philadelphia, 1983, pp. 122–82.

IX

THE BEATITUDES (5.3–12)

(i) Structure

A number of scholars have argued that the Matthean beatitudes should be divided into two sets of four.[1] The first set—'Blessed are the poor (πτωχοί) in spirit', 'Blessed are those who mourn (πενθοῦντες)', 'Blessed are the meek (πραεῖς)', and 'Blessed are those who hunger (πεινῶντες) and thirst after righteousness'—is held together by two features, the letter π and the subject matter, which is the persecuted (passive) condition of the disciples (cf. esp. Michaelis (v)). The second set—'Blessed are the merciful', 'Blessed are the pure in heart', 'Blessed are the peacemakers', and 'Blessed are those who are persecuted for righteousness' sake'—is said to be a unit because it uniformly treats of the ethical (active) qualities leading to persecution. Moreover, while beatitudes 1–4 contain thirty-six words, there are also thirty-six words in beatitudes 5–8.

A second analysis of Matthew's arrangement comes from N. J. McEleney (v), who finds a chiastic pattern in 5.3–10. He too thinks 5.3–6 and 7–10 divide themselves into two units:

Matt. 5.3   inclusory formula: 'because theirs is the kingdom of heaven'

     5.4   divine passive: 'because they shall be comforted'

     5.5   future active with object: 'because they shall inherit the earth'

     5.6   divine passive: 'because they shall be satisfied'

     5.7   divine passive: 'because they shall receive mercy'

     5.8   future middle with object: 'because they shall see God'

     5.9   divine passive: 'because they shall be called sons of God'

     5.10   inclusory formula: 'because theirs is the kingdom of heaven'

McEleney's proposal is reinforced by the acknowledged presence of chiasmus elsewhere in the First Gospel.

[1] See Schweizer, *Matthew*, p. 82; Gundry, *Matthew*, p. 73; Guelich, p. 93; Meier, *Matthew*, p. 39; Lambrecht, *Sermon*, p. 61.

Whether either of the two preceding analyses should be embraced it is difficult to say. Each, although aesthetically pleasing, is open to certain objections. For instance, while the first has to explain why Matthew permitted 'and thirst' to disrupt the π pattern and why in vv. 7–10 there is no unifying letter as in vv. 3–6, the second runs into difficulty because the key word, 'righteousness', occurs in vv. 6 and 10 and therefore does not fall into the chiastic pattern; and both schemes questionably put vv. 11–12 completely to one side. In addition, the fact that there are two distinctly different ways of neatly dividing up the beatitudes, each of which seems plausible on the surface, only goes to show that every attractive analysis need not be correct. It is in the nature of things that, given sufficient time and effort, several patterns could probably be discerned in Mt 5.3–12. For this cause, then, we remain hesitant over the issue.

There are, however, two further remarks to be made. To begin with, the beatitude in vv. 11–12 should not be, as it sometimes is (e.g. by Suggs, pp. 121–7), excluded from the total number of beatitudes and joined not with 5.3–10 but with 5.13–16. 5.11–12 is, admittedly, different in form from the preceding beatitudes—it is much longer, it contains imperatives, and it is addressed directly to the reader (the second person is used). Yet these facts do not tell the whole story. The eight other beatitudes all begin with μακάριοι, and the appearance of this word at the beginning of v. 11 most naturally indicates a continuation of the series. It would be strange indeed if 5.11–12 introduced a new section. Beyond this, as D. Daube (pp. 196–201) has noticed, there is good precedent for making the last member of a series much longer than the preceding members and for the abrupt switch from the third to second person. Both things can be found in Jewish prayer texts, in the Bible, and even in English literature (cf. Isa 63.10–14; Ecclus 47.12–22; 48.1–11; Mt 1.2–16; 23.13–36; Lk 1.68–79; 6.37–8). Hence 5.11–12, which is thematically so closely related to 5.10 (both concern persecution), should not be separated from 5.3–10.

The second additional remark concerning the structure of 5.3–12 is this: there are, to all appearances, nine beatitudes (cf. 2 En. 42), for μακάριοι appears nine times. (Betz, *Essays*, p. 24, is perhaps alone in counting ten beatitudes; he finds two in 5.11–12.) Is this number significant? According to our tradition-history, the evangelist inherited eight beatitudes (see pp. 434–6). He has therefore added only one—'Blessed are those who are persecuted on account of righteousness, for theirs is the kingdom of heaven' (5.10). Why was Matthew moved to add this line? In section (iii) on 5.10, we shall argue that it is difficult to account for the verse on grounds of content alone: it really adds little if anything at all. (If one were to combine 5.3b and 5.11a, the result would be very close to 5.10.) But there is an explanation when the structure of the sermon on the mount as a whole is considered. Mt 5–7 is built around triads; threes are almost everywhere (see pp. 62–4). It seems a good guess, then, that 5.10 has been inserted in order to bring the total number of beatitudes to a multiple of 3.

(ii) *Sources*

On the bearing of Mt 5.3–12 on the synoptic problem, see pp. 434–6.

EXCURSUS II

THE BEATITUDES (Mt 5.3–12; Lk 6.20–3)

(1)   Beatitudes.[2] μακάριος is first found in the work of Pindar (b. 522 or 518 B.C.). The word basically means 'free from daily cares and worries', 'prosperous', and was used of the blessed state of the gods, who neither toiled nor suffered (cf. Homer, *Od.* 5.7; Socrates, *Ep.* 6.4). It frequently turns up in the formula, μακάριος ὅσ(τις), as in Pindar, *Pyth.* 5.46; Menander, frag. 114; and Euripides, frag. 256. But this was only one of many forms the beatitude took on Greek soil. ὄλβιος ὅσ(τις) was also used (Hesiod, *Theog.* 95, 954–5; Theocritus 12.34; Pindar, *Olymp.* 7.11), as were expressions employing τρισμακάριος (Aristophanes, *Ach.* 400; Philemo 93.1) and other words. Among the objects evoking the beatitude in Greek literature are praiseworthy children, virtue, piety, wisdom, and fame.

The OT also has its beatitudes or blessings, in which *'ašrê* or *bārûk* are the key words. The difference between these two is probably to be found in the fact that the former, which is never applied to God (although note Philo, *Sacr.* 101; 1 Tim 1.11; 6.15), is less sacred and solemn. Also, 'the desire for happiness is different from the blessing in that it demands that the believer do certain things'[3] (cf. Ps 41.2; 65.4; 84.4–5; 127.5; 137.8).[4] In

---

[2] Lit.: G. L. Dirichlet, *De veterum macarismis*, Giessen, 1914; G. Bertram and F. Hauck, *TWNT* 4, pp. 365–73; C. Keller, 'Les "Béatitudes" de l'Ancien Testament', in *Hommage à W. Vischer*, Montpellier, 1960, pp. 88–100; W. F. Beardsley, *Literary Criticism of the New Testament*, Philadelphia, 1971, pp. 36–9; W. Janzen, ' "Asre" in the Old Testament', *HTR* 58 (1965), pp. 215–16; A. George (v); Schweizer (v); Lipiński (v); H. Cazelles, *TDOT* 1, pp. 445–8.

[3] Cf. Cazelles, ibid., p. 446.

[4] Note how the distinction between *'ašrê* and *bārûk* is maintained in *b. Ḥag.* 14b: 'R. Joḥanan b. Zakkai rose and kissed him on his head and said: Blessed (*brwk*) be the Lord God of Israel . . . Happy (*'šryk*) art thou, O Abraham our father, that R. Eleazar b. 'Arak came forth from thy loins'. Cf. Ps. Sol. 5.18, 22; 6.1, 9.

any event, in the LXX μακάριος only translates 'ašrê, so the significance of the bārûk formulas (usually translated by εὐλογητός) for understanding the background of Mt 5.3–12 = Lk 6.20–3 must be minimal.

In accordance with probable Egyptian influence,[5] the OT μακάριος formulas appear first in wisdom literature or in literature influenced by wisdom, in sentences praising the wise man and holding him up as a model.

'Blessed am I! For the women will call me blessed' (Gen 30.13).

'Behold! Blessed is the man whom God reproves' (Job 5.17).

'Blessed is the man who walks not in the counsel of the wicked, nor stands in the way of sinners, nor sits in the seat of scoffers; but his delight is in the law of the Lord, and on his law he meditates day and night' (Ps 1.1–2).

'Blessed is he who lives with an intelligent wife, and he who has not made a slip with his tongue, and he who has not served a man inferior to himself' (Ecclus 25.8).

See also Ps 2.12; 32.1–2; 34.8; 41.1; 84.12; 119.1; 127.5; Prov 3.13; Wisd 3.13–14; Ecclus 14.1–2, 20; 26.1; 28.19; 31.8; 34.15; 48.11; 50.28; Tob 13.14.

Later the beatitude begins to appear in eschatological contexts, particularly in apocalyptic writings.

'Blessed is he who waits and comes to the three thousand three hundred and thirty-five days' (Dan 12.12).

'How blessed are those who love you. They will rejoice in your peace. Blessed are those who grieved over all your afflictions, because they will rejoice for you upon seeing all your glory, and they will be made glad for ever' (Tob 13.14).

'Blessed are you, righteous and elect ones, for glorious is your portion. The righteous ones shall be in the light of the sun . . .' (1 En. 58.2–3).

'Blessed be they that shall be in those days, in that they shall see the good fortune of Israel which God shall bring to pass in the gathering together of the tribes' (Ps. Sol. 17.44).

See also Ps 72.17; Isa 30.18; 31.9 LXX; Ecclus 48.11; 1 En. 81.4; 82.4; Ps. Sol. 18.6; 2 Bar. 10.6–7; 2 En. 42.6–14; 52.1–14. The eschatological makarism, it is important to observe, is usually addressed to people in dire straits, and the promise to them is of future consolation. So in contrast to the wisdom beatitude, where moral exhortation is, despite the declarative form, generally the object, assurance and the proffering of hope are the goal: eyes become focused on the future, which will reverse natural values and the present situation; fulfilment is no longer to be found in this world but in a new world. The dismal status quo of those addressed is taken as a given for the present and is only to be altered by the eschatological intervention of God.

---

[5] J. Dupont, ' "Béatitudes" égyptiennes', Bib 47 (1966), pp. 185–222. On the original setting for the beatitude in Israel see the lit. cited by Guelich, p. 64.

Sometimes in Jewish literature, and in anticipation of what we find in Mt 5 and Lk 6, different beatitudes are brought together to form a pair or series of blessings. Ecclus 25.8–10 reads:

'Blessed is he who lives with an intelligent wife, and he who has not made a slip of the tongue, and he who has not served a man inferior to himself; happy is he who has gained good sense, and he who speaks to attentive listeners'.

Compare Ecclus 14.1–2:

'Blessed is the man who does not blunder with his lips and need not suffer grief for sin. Blessed is he whose heart does not condemn him, and who has not given up his hope'.

See also Ps 32.1–2; 84.4–5; 119.1–2; Tob 13.14–15; and 2 En. 52.1–14. The beatitude series is not, apparently, found in Greek literature; and while in wisdom literature the pair but not the series is used, both are to be found in eschatological or apocalyptic texts.

Another noteworthy development in the history of the biblical makarism is the eschatological woe, which is the counterpart of the eschatological blessing (cf. Deut 27.15–28.14; Eccles 10.16–17; Isa 5.8–23; Lk 6.24–26). Consider these two texts:

'Woe unto you sinners who are dead! When you are dead in the wealth of your sins, those who are like you will say of you, "Happy are you sinners!" ' (1 En. 103.5).

'Cursed (*'rwr*) be Belial in his hostile scheme, and damned be he in his guilty domination. Cursed be all the spirits of his lot in their wicked scheme. . . . Cursed be you, Angel of the Pit, and spirit of Abaddon in all the schemes of your guilty inclination. . . . And cursed be all who execute their wicked schemes and conform your evil purpose . . .' (4Q286 10 ii 2–13).[6]

See also 1 En. 99.10–15; 2 Bar. 10.6–7. In 2 En. 52.1–14 we find both a series of blessings and a series of woes:

'Happy is he who opens his heart for praise, and praises the Lord. Cursed is he who opens his heart to insults, and to slander against his neighbor. Happy is he who opens his lips, both blessing and praising the Lord. Cursed is he who opens his lips for cursing and blasphemy, before the face of the Lord. Happy—is he who glorifies all the works of the Lord. Cursed is he who insults the creatures of the Lord. Happy is he who organizes the works of his hand, so as to raise them up. Cursed—who looks to obliterate the works of others. Happy—who preserves the foundations of his most ancient fathers, made firm from the beginning. Cursed—he who breaks down the institutions of his ancestors and fathers. Happy—who cultivates

---

[6] Trans. and restoration of P. J. Kobelski, *Melchizedek and Melchireša'*, CBQMS 10, Washington, D.C., 1981, pp. 43–4.

the love of peace. Cursed—who disturbs those who are peaceful by means of love. Happy (is he who) even though he does not speak peace with his tongue, nevertheless in his heart there is peace toward all. Cursed—who with his tongue speaks peace, but in his heart there is no peace (but a sword)'.

Turning to the NT, μακάριος occurs fifty times, thirteen in Matthew, fifteen in Luke, two in John, two in Acts (neither a beatitude), seven in the Pauline corpus (only three of which are beatitudes), two in James, two in 1 Peter, seven in Revelation. The word is used almost exclusively of religious joy. (The related noun, μακαρισμός, appears three times, in Rom 4.6, 9; Gal 4.15, the verb, μακαρίζω, twice, in Lk 1.48 and Jas 5.11.) ὄλβιος and εὐδαίμων do not make an appearance. With regard to form and function, the NT makarisms exhibit diversity and display all of the features heretofore noted in Jewish literature. There are beatitudes belonging to the sapiential tradition (Rom 14.22) and beatitudes belonging to the eschatological tradition (Rev 19.9; 20.6; 22.7, 14). There are isolated beatitudes (Jn 13.17; 20.29; Rom 14.22; Jas 1.12) and beatitudes in series (Mt 5.3–12; Lk 6.20–2; 11.27–8; 14.14–15; cf. Rev 20.7, 14). The NT also contains eschatological woes (Mk 13.17; Lk 6.24–6; Rev 8.13; 9.12; 11.14; 12.12; 18.10, 16, 19).

From the brief survey of the previous paragraphs, it is immediately obvious that the beatitudes in Mt 5.3–12, with their parallels in Lk 6.20–3, are in many ways typical. The form, μακάριος + subject + ὅτι clause, is attested (Gen 30.13; Tob 13.16; Mt 16.17; Par. Jer. 4.10), and there are parallels for the eschatological content and for the grouping of beatitudes (and woes), as well as for the third person and second person forms in Matthew and Luke respectively (for the latter—which is rarer—see Deut 33.29; Ps 128.2; Eccles 10.17; Isa 32.20; 1 En. 58.2; Mt 16.17; Lk 14.14; Jn 13.17; b. 'Erub. 53b). Probably the only exceptional formal characteristic of the synoptic beatitudes is their succinctness: those blessed are, especially in Luke, described with the utmost brevity—'the poor', 'those who hunger', 'those who mourn'. Hence if anything beyond this sets apart the beatitudes of the sermon on the mount/plain it cannot be their form but only their content on the one hand and their context in the proclamation of Jesus and the theology of the evangelists on the other.

(2) Tradition-history. Of Matthew's nine beatitudes, four, because of their Lukan parallels, are to be ascribed to Q: 5.3–4, 6, and 11–12. Of the remaining five, only one is, on the basis of word statistics, to be assigned to redaction (v. 10; see the commentary). This leaves four beatitudes to be accounted for: 5.5, 7, 8, and 9. All four are probably to be assigned to Q^mt, for the following two reasons:

  i. Mt 5.5, 7, 8, and 9 do not display typical Matthean vocabulary or interests and therefore cannot easily be ascribed to Matthew's hand.[7]

  ii. Mt 5.7, 8, and 9 link up, through both catchword and theme, with passages which are to be assigned to Q's sermon on the mount/plain. This entails that the three makarisms were added to make the opening section of the sermon (the beatitudes) correlate with its main contents.

---

[7] Contra Frankemölle (v); with Guelich (v); Strecker (v); and Luz 1, p. 200.

Mt 5	Lk 6
The *merciful* will obtain mercy (v. 7).[8]	Be *merciful*, even as your Father is *merciful* (v. 36).
The pure in *heart* will see God (v. 8).	The good man out of the treasure of his *heart* brings forth the good (v. 45).
The peacemakers will be called *sons of God* (v. 9).	Those who love their enemies and do good to them will be *sons of the Most High* (v. 35; cf. Mt 5.45).

Two of these links exist only when Mt 5.7, 8, and 9 are compared with Lk 6 and not when they are compared with Mt 5. This fact is weighty evidence indeed for a Q source.[9]

On the basis of the above considerations the following reconstruction of the tradition-history of the beatitudes may be offered:

Stage I: Jesus utters three paradoxical beatitudes: blessed are the poor, blessed are those who mourn, and blessed are those who hunger. The theme is that of eschatological reversal. (The reversal motif does not occur in many of the other beatitudes.)

Stage II: The three dominical beatitudes are, after translation into Greek, joined to what is now Lk 6.27–38 and to at least part of what is now Lk 6.39–49. The result is an early form of the sermon on the mount/plain. And probably to make the transition from the beatitudes to the section on the love of enemies, a fourth beatitude, that on persecution (Mt 5.11–12 = Lk 6.22–3), is added or composed. It links up verbally with both the previous beatitudes and with the pericopae that follow it.[10]

Lk 6.20–1 μακάριοι
6.22–3 μακάριοι . . . μισήσωσιν ὑμᾶς
6.27–38 μισοῦσιν ὑμᾶς

Stage III: Q next takes two different forms, Q^lk and Q^mt.[11] In Q^lk, four woes corresponding to the four beatitudes are composed.[11] In Q^mt, 'Blessed are the meek . . .' is added to explain the potentially misleading 'Blessed

---

[8] Matthew has ἐλεήμονες and ἐλεηθήσονται, Luke οἰκτίρμονες and οἰκτίρμων. But use of the ἐλε-root is probably due to Matthew; Q^mt probably had οἱ οἰκτίρμονες (see the commentary).

[9] It is also a most weighty objection to the Griesbach hypothesis, which must dubiously brand the parallels between Mt 5.7–9 and Lk 6 as of no account. For if the parallels are acknowledged to be substantial, their explanation can only lie in the independent use of a common source. The parallels also negate Agourides' attempt (v) to revive the old theory that Mt 5–7 and Lk 6 go back to different sermons preached by Jesus. For additional difficulties the Griesbach hypothesis has with the beatitudes see Tuckett (v), who observes, among other things, that Matthew's fifth, sixth, and seventh beatitudes would have been congenial to Luke.

[10] Cf. Guelich (v), pp. 420–1. Our tradition-history leaves open the question of whether 5.11–12 goes back to Jesus. According to Boring, pp. 138–41, the saying was first spoken by a Christian prophet.

[11] On the woes see Dupont 1, pp. 299–342; Schürmann, *Lukasevangelium* 1, pp. 336–41. They are to be judged community productions. It is just possible that Q^mt contained the woes too and that Matthew omitted them (so Schürmann, *Lukasevangelium* 1, pp. 339–41; Frankemölle (v), pp. 64–5; and Crossan (v),

are the poor . . .' (which was not yet qualified by 'in spirit')[12], and three more beatitudes are composed in order to establish a correlation between the beatitudes and what follows. The result is eight beatitudes.[13]

Stage IV: Matthew and Luke now edit their different versions of Q, the former adding a beatitude of his own making (v. 10), which results in nine makarisms.

Of the several questions still left unanswered by this reconstruction, perhaps the most perplexing is the disagreement in order between the second and third common beatitudes. (On Luke's second person address versus Matthew's third person see on 5.3.) Matthew has, 'Blessed are those who mourn . . .' before 'Blessed are those who hunger . . .'. Luke has the opposite order. According to Guelich (v), p. 427, Matthew altered his source's arrangement in order to accentuate the parallels between 5.3 and 4 and Isa 61.1–2: the poor now come immediately before the mention of the mourners in the beatitudes just as they do in Isaiah. But against Guelich, Matthew has, as we shall see, done nothing to underline the parallels between Mt 5 and Isa 61, so this suggestion is improbable. According to Dupont (1, pp. 271–2), Matthew's order is original, and Luke moved things around because he associated hunger with poverty. This too is an uncertain proposition, being very far from self-evident. We prefer to confess ignorance.

(3) Isa 61. The Matthean beatitudes exhibit a number of parallels with Isa 61, some less certain than others:

Mt 5	Isa 61
'Blessed are the poor (πτωχοί) in spirit, for theirs is the kingdom of heaven' (v. 3).	'The Spirit of the Lord is upon me, because the Lord has anointed me, to preach good news (εὐαγγελίσασθαι) to the poor' (πτωχοῖς) (v. 1; the connexion is all the surer since, in the synoptic tradition, 'to preach good news' or 'good news' is so closely bound to the kingdom of God).

---

pp. 169–70). Why? (1) Matthew is more aware perhaps of the audience than is Luke and realizes how disruptive and inappropriate Luke 6.24–6 would be in a sermon directed above all to disciples. (2) In Matthew the beatitudes are antithetically correlated with the warnings in 7.13–26, and the woes would not fit into this scheme.

[12] Cf. Guelich (v), pp. 424–6; *pace* Dupont 1, pp. 252–3, who wrongly considers 5.5 to be a doublet of 5.3 (the two translating '*anāwîm* with two different words).

[13] Concerning the order of Mt 5.7–9 in Q[mt], Guelich (v), pp. 422–3, suggests that there is an eschatological sequence: the saints receive mercy on the last day (5.7), then see God (5.8), and then becomes his sons (5.9). While this is not obviously persuasive, nothing better has yet been offered. Cf. Schürmann, *Lukasevangelium* 1, pp. 326–7, and Frankemölle (v), pp. 60–1.

Mt 5	Isa 61
'Blessed are those who mourn (πενθοῦντες) for they shall be comforted' (παρακληθήσονται) (v. 4)	'to comfort all who mourn' (παρακαλέσαι πάντας τοὺς πενθοῦντας) (v. 2).
'Blessed are the meek (πραεῖς), for they shall inherit the earth' (κληρονομήσουσιν τὴν γῆν) (v. 5).	'to preach good news to the poor' (MT: *'ănāwîm*, which is, in the LXX, usually translated by πραεῖς) (v. 1); κληρονομήσουσιν τὴν γῆν (v. 7).
'Blessed are those who hunger and thirst after righteousness, for they shall be satisfied' (v. 6)	'Righteousness' occurs three times in Isa. 61, in vv. 3, 8, and 11; and in v. 6, God's people will 'eat the wealth of nations'.
'Blessed are the merciful, for they shall receive mercy' (v. 7)	no parallel
'Blessed are the pure in heart (καθαροὶ τῇ καρδίᾳ), for they shall see God' (v. 8)	'to heal the brokenhearted' (συντετριμμένους τῇ καρδίᾳ) (v. 1)
'Blessed are the peacemakers, for they shall be called sons of God' (v. 9)	no parallel
'Blessed are those that have been persecuted for righteousness' sake, for theirs is the kingdom of heaven' (v. 10)	'Righteousness' occurs three times in Isa. 61, in vv. 3, 8, and 11; and 'kingdom of heaven' can be related to the preaching of 'good news' (see the first parallel)
'Blessed are you when men revile you and persecute you and utter all kinds of evil against you falsely on my account; rejoice and be glad (ἀγαλλιᾶσθε), for your reward is great in heaven, for so men persecuted the prophets who were before you' (vv. 11–12).	'Let my soul be glad (ἀγαλλιάσθω) in the Lord' (v. 10; cf. v. 11).

According to W. Grimm (pp. 68–77), the connexion with Isa 61—a jubilary text; see Lev 25; 11QMelch 2—was strongest at the beginning of the tradition (with Jesus); it gradually weakened over time (cf. Schürmann, *Lukasevangelium* 1, pp. 326–7). R. Guelich (v), pp. 427–31, has put forward precisely the opposite thesis: Matthew has increased the parallelism between Isa 61 and the beatitudes (cf. Frankemölle (v), pp. 60–1). Grimm has the better of the argument. The most persuasive allusions to Isa 61 occur in 5.3, 4, and 5[14], and in these three verses (from Q

---

[14] The rest of the allusions or parallels are hardly striking and should be considered fortuitous.

or Q^{mt}) the links with Isa 61 do not appear in the redactional contributions of Matthew (see for details the commentary on the individual verses). Moreover, since the allusion to Isa 61.1 in v. 5 (from Q^{mt}) is weaker than the allusions in vv. 3 and 4[15], the strongest links with Isa 61 are to be assigned not to Q^{mt} but to an earlier stage of Q. So the farther back we go, the greater the impact of Isa. 61 seems to be. The implication? If, as seems overwhelmingly probable, the core of the beatitudes (5.3, 4, 6) be dominical, Jesus must have formulated them with Isa 61.1–3 in mind (cf. Mt 11.5 = Lk 7.22; Lk 4.18–19). Conversely, Matthew has not done much if anything to accentuate the connexions between Isa 61 and Mt 5.3–12.

Two observations confirm the conclusions just reached. First, Matthew cannot be said to have drawn upon Isa 61 independently of his tradition. Apart from the beatitudes and 11.5 (both from Q), there are no allusions to the chapter in his book. Which is to say: the first evangelist shows no special interest in Isa 61. Secondly, 11.5 = Lk 7.22 ends by clearly borrowing from Isa 61.1 ('and good news is preached to the poor'), and this is immediately followed by a beatitude: 'And blessed is he who is not offended at me'. Now can this second association of Isa 61.1 with a beatitude be treated as the fruit of coincidence? Probably not. 11.5–6 = Lk 7.22–3 seemingly shows us that Jesus associated the makarism form with the OT text about good news for the poor. Hence 11.5–6 = Lk 7.22–3 bolsters our claim that the influence of Isa 61 upon the beatitudes should be located at the fount of the tradition.[16]

The exegetical significance of the association between the dominical beatitudes and Isa 61 should not be missed. (i) In the NT Isa 61 is applied to messianic or eschatological events (Mt 11.5 = Lk 7.22; Lk 4.18–19; Acts 10.38). It is the same in ancient Jewish texts. For instance, 11QMelch, in its portrayal of Melchizedek's eschatological liberation of captives, draws frequently upon Isa 61.1–3 (2.4, 6, 9, 13, 17, 20); see M. P. Miller, 'The Function of Isa 61.1–2 in 11 Q Melchizedek', *JBL* 88 (1969), pp. 467–9. Other examples of the eschatological interpretation of Isa 61 include Tg. Ps.-J. to Num 25.12 and *Midr. Ekhah* on Lam. 3.50; for discussion see J. A. Sanders, 'From Isaiah 61 to Luke 4', in *Christianity, Judaism, and other Graeco-Roman Cults*, SJLA 12, ed. J. Neusner, Leiden, 1975, vol. 1, pp. 75–106. When Jesus employed Isa 61 in order to bless the poor who heard him speak and promise them participation in God's eschatological kingdom, he was using the text as others had before him. (ii) But this is not the whole story. The implicit Christology of the beatitudes is remarkable. Isa 61.1–2 reads: 'The Spirit of the Lord God is upon me, because the Lord has anointed me to bring good tidings to the poor; he has sent me to bind up the brokenhearted, to proclaim liberty to the captives, and the opening of the prison to those who are bound; to proclaim the year of the Lord's favour, and the day of vengeance of our God; to comfort all who mourn'. The comforting of mourners and the bringing of good tidings to the poor are themselves, according to Isa 61.1–2, eschatological events. Moreover, they are the work of the figure who speaks in the first person. Thus, if Jesus did utter the beatitudes, he must have done so conscious of being the

---

[15] 'The meek shall inherit the earth' (v. 5) is closest not to Isa 61.7 but to Ps 37.11.

[16] We have not offered a full listing of the parallels with Ps 37; for this see Buchanan (v). Most of these must also, *pace* Buchanan, be regarded as insignificant.

eschatological herald who had been anointed by God and given the Spirit. And those who heard him would not have missed this. (iii) Interpreted against the background of Isa 61. 1–2, Mt 5.3, 4, and 6 with their Lukan parallels constitute a paradigmatic example of 'eschatology in the process of realization'. On the one hand, salvation is not yet. The hungry *will* be satisfied. Those who weep *will* laugh. The poor *will* enter the kingdom of God (see on 5.3). On the other hand, the anointed, Spirit-bearing herald of Isa 61 has already appeared. He has already brought good tidings to the poor. He has already comforted those who mourn. Prophecy has been fulfilled. Eschatology has entered the present.

(4) Entrance requirements or eschatological blessings? Matthew has, according to many authorities, 'ethicized' the beatitudes, that is, turned what were once straightforward blessings (so Lk 6.20b–3) into entrance requirements for the kingdom of God (so Windisch, pp. 26–7, 87–8; Dodd (v); Dupont 1, pp. 254–8; Strecker (v); for a dissenting voice see Guelich (v)). On this view, the Lukan beatitudes, which fit rather well in the eschatological or apocalyptic tradition, have in Matthew been modified along wisdom lines: the 'poor in spirit' and 'the meek' have become ideal characters to be imitated (cf. the function of Ps 1); they are no longer those directly addressed (this being supposedly emphasized by the shift from the second to third person address). So Mt 5.3–12 and Lk 6.20–3 serve different ends.

There is no denying the initial plausibility of this view, indeed its element of truth. After hearing 'the peacemakers' and 'the pure in heart' praised and promised salvation, the reader cannot avoid the implicit imperative: be pure in heart, be a peacemaker. This is all the more indubitable given the correspondences between certain beatitudes and imperatives elsewhere in the sermon (cf. 5.6 with 20, 5.7 and 5.9 with 43–8). Nevertheless, do Matthew's makarisms really function primarily as imperatives? Has the ethical thrust come to overshadow the elements of consolation and promise? Several reasons suggest otherwise.

(i) The very form of the Matthean beatitudes speaks against the theory that the evangelist has 'ethicized' them. Above all, and to state the obvious, there are no explicit imperatives—save in 5.11–12, where the reader is called to rejoice and be glad. Moreover, the eschatological content in the second member of each beatitude is crystal clear, which inclines one to place 5.3–12 not in the wisdom stream but rather in the apocalyptic tradition, where consolation is the priority.[17]

(ii) It is striking that the qualities upheld in the beatitudes appear very infrequently in NT virtue lists, these being 2 Cor 6.6–7; Gal 5.22–3; Eph 6.14–17; Col 3.12–14; Phil 4.8; 1 Tim 3.2–3; 6.11; Tit 1.7–8; Jas 3.17; 2 Pet 1.5–7.

(iii) According to our hypothetical tradition-history, so far from Matthew having created links between the beatitudes and other material in his sermon, he seems to have dissolved several that existed in Q[mt]. This is inconsistent with his supposed attempt to offer paraenesis.

(iv) In 5.10–12 those who are persecuted are blessed. Yet persecution is hardly a virtue in itself, and it certainly cannot be attained on one's own. If

[17] Although, it must be conceded, the eschatological makarisms in Revelation are mostly paraenetic.

one is being persecuted, it is because someone else is persecuting. So 5.10–12 does not fall in line with any alleged tendency to 'ethicize' 5.3–12.

(v) The last two beatitudes (5.10–12) presuppose the reader's present state of suffering and persecution and supply consolation. Thus the reader is directly addressed and given promises. No change in behaviour is envisaged.

(vi) The beatitudes which usually lead scholars to the assertion which is being disputed here (namely, 5.5, 7, 8, 9) are without parallel in Luke. But they are not redactional. Their origin is in Q^{mt}, and Matthew has made little revision of them. If, therefore, the tendency to 'ethicize' be detected, it should probably be traced not to our evangelist but to his special tradition.

(vii) If, as Betz (*Essays*, pp. 27–30) has urged, the setting for the beatitudes was originally initiation into the Christian cult (cf. Jos. Asen. 16.7–8), then Mt 5.3–12 would be reminder more than imperative. (But Betz himself, pp. 34–5, finds an ethical thrust in Mt 5.3 because of the addition, 'in spirit'; in his opinion, this calls for the virtue of self-abasement.)

(viii) Lastly, our examination of the structure of the sermon on the mount is highly relevant. The beatitudes are sandwiched between 4.23–5.2 and 5.13–16. The former serves to put the Messiah's words within the context of grace: before speaking, Jesus heals. The latter is the heading for what follows. The disciples are to be salt and light—what this means being spelled out in 5.17–7.12. Structurally, therefore, 5.3–12 comes before the detailed paraenesis of the sermon proper. That is, being before 5.13–16, it is separated from the main corpus of imperatives. Is this not because its function is to put grace before imperative, greeting before confrontation, blessing before demand? and because it is only after having heard the comforting words of 5.3–12, words which point to the priority of God's grace, that one is confronted by the Messiah's demands?

In conclusion, it would be foolish to deny the imperatives implicit in 5.3–12: there is no going around this. (This is also true of the woes in Mt 23, which, although not primarily exhortation, offer such implicitly, even to Matthew's Christian readers.) But the question is whether the primary function of the Matthean beatitudes is moral, and whether a moral dimension excludes a promissory or conciliatory dimension. The answer in both cases is negative. 5.3–12 serves firstly to bless the faithful as they are now. When Jesus speaks, the drudgery and difficulties of day-to-day life fade away and the bliss of the life to come proleptically appears. Time is, however briefly, overcome, and the saints are refreshed.

(5) Mt 5 and Mt 23. In his *Gnomon*, Bengel called attention to some possible parallels between the beatitudes of Mt 5 and the seven woes of chapter 23. The two antithetical series have in common several words:

'kingdom of heaven' (5.3; 23.13)
'mercy' (5.7; 23.23)
'purity' (5.8; 23.25–6)
'persecution' (5.10–12; 23.34)
'prophets' (5.12; 23.34)

Adding force to these parallels are three facts: (a) they occur in exactly the same order in both chapters; (b) whereas 5.3–12 opens a Matthean discourse, 23.13–39 closes another; (c) both 5.3–12 and 23.13–39 conclude with the theme of the martyrdom of the prophets. Nonetheless, we are not willing to make much of all this, despite its being intriguing. The evangelist may, just possibly, have intended to open his first discourse with blessings and to close a later one with woes, but beyond this it would not be safe to go. For, quite simply, the observed parallels are not sufficiently extensive to rule out coincidence. Would there not be more points of contact between 5.3–12 and 23.13–39 if one had been composed with an eye towards the other?

(6) The Gospel of Thomas. There are ten beatitudes in the Gospel of Thomas. Seven of them are isolated:

(i) 'Blessed is the lion which the man eats and the lion will become man; and cursed is the man whom the lion eats and the lion will become man' (7).

(ii) 'Blessed are the solitary and elect, for you shall find the kingdom; because you came from it, you will go there again' (49).

(iii) 'Blessed is the man who knows in which part the robbers will enter, so that he will rise and collect his (. . .) and gird up his loins before they enter' (103).

(iv) 'Blessed is he who will take his place in the beginning; he will know the end and will not experience death' (18).

(v) 'Blessed is he who came into being before he came into being' (19).

(vi) 'Blessed are the poor, for yours is the kingdom of heaven' (54).

(vii) 'Blessed is the man who has suffered and found life' (58).

Three of the beatitudes in Gos. Thom. appear in a series:

(viii) 'Blessed are you when you are hated and persecuted, and no place will be found where you have been persecuted!'

(ix) 'Jesus said, Blessed are those who have been persecuted in their heart. These are they who have known the Father in truth!'

(x) 'Blessed are the hungry, so that the belly of him who desires will be filled' (68–9).

Although, as we have argued in the commentary on 5.3, 6, 10, and 11, it is not necessary to postulate direct dependence upon the synoptic gospels for any of these beatitudes, there must be some connexion. While (i)–(v) have next to nothing in common with the beatitudes in Mt 5 and Lk 6, (vi) recalls Mt 5.3 = Lk 6.20b, (viii) and (ix) recall Mt 5.11 = Lk 6.22 and the redactional Mt 5.10, and (x) recalls Mt 5.6 = Lk 6.21a. What is the explanation? Perhaps the decisive observation is this: Gos. Thom. contains no beatitude which, according to our reconstruction of the tradition history, belonged to Q^{mt}. Rather does the Coptic document supply variants only for three makarisms which appeared in an early form of the sermon on the mount/plain (see pp. 434–6). Moreover, there are also parallels to (viii) and (ix) in Mt 5.10; 1 Pet 3.14; and an agraphon preserved in Clement of Alexandria, *Strom.* 4.6. A very tentative account, therefore, of this state of affairs might run as follows. Gos. Thom. reflects knowledge of an early (oral?) form of the sermon on the mount/plain, from which three beatitudes ((vi), (viii), (x)) were drawn and then modified under the influence of another tradition (cf. Clement of

Alexandria, *Strom.* 4.6). Then one of these (viii) was expanded—by the author of Gos. Thom.?—to create a second beatitude on persecution (ix).

The tradition-history just suggested must remain, we eagerly confess, tenuous. But of other things we can be more certain, and the following three, miscellaneous observations should be registered.

(i) It has always been thought odd that Luke's beatitudes contain both the second and third person—'Blessed are *the poor*, for *yours* is the kingdom of God'. Without here going into the question of whether this form is to be judged original (see on 5.3), we note that at least Gos. Thom. 49 has the same construction: 'Blessed are *the solitary and elect*, for *you* shall find the kingdom . . .'.

(ii) It has also been thought odd that Matthew has eight beatitudes in the third person (5.3–10), one in the second person (5.11–12). Gos. Thom. 68–9, which contains three consecutive beatitudes, preserves a similar irregularity. The first beatitude (viii) is in the second person, the next two ((ix), (x)) in the third person.

(iii) Gos. Thom. 7 contains a beatitude followed by a woe. The same pattern, only expanded, appears in Lk 6.20–6. Yet there is no reason to make much of this, for the beatitude/woe combination is, of course, to be found in a number of other ancient sources.

(iii) *Exegesis*

3. μακάριοι οἱ πτωχοὶ τῷ πνεύματι. Compare Ps Sol. 10.1 Syr. This religious makarism overturns a popular secular sentiment: 'Blessed are the rich'. Compare Jas 2.5 and Polycarp, *Ep.* 2.3 (see on 5.10). Lk 6.20b lacks 'in spirit'. Three inquiries are to be made. (1) Is 'in spirit' redactional? (2) What is meant by 'poor'. (3) What does 'in spirit' signify?

(1) 'In spirit' is probably redactional, and for four reasons. First, in another Q passage, Mt 11.5 = Lk 7.22, 'poor' occurs without qualification. Next, the qualification disrupts what would otherwise be perfect parallelism in Q: μακάριοι οἱ πτωχοί, μακάριοι οἱ πεινῶντες, μακάριοι οἱ κλαίοντες. Thirdly, Lk 6.24, the first woe, has 'the rich' without qualification, which probably implies an unqualified 'the poor' in at least Q[lk]. Lastly, Matthew has a habit of tacking on qualifying phrases (as in 5.6a, 32; 6.13b; 13.12b; and 19: 9).

(2) πτωχός means 'one who is poor, needy, dependent on others, a beggar'.[18] The word occurs one hundred times in the

[18] Lit.: F. Hauck and E. Bammel, *TWNT* 6, pp. 885–915; Percy, pp. 40–108; H.-J. Kandler, 'Die Bedeutung der Armut im Schrifttum vom Chirbet Qumran', *Judaica* 13 (1957), pp. 193–209; Guelich, pp. 67–72; L. E. Keck, in IDBSup, s.v. 'Poor'; idem, 'The Poor Among the Saints in the New Testament', *ZNW* 56 (1965), pp. 100–37; 57 (1966), pp. 54–78; E. Lohse, 'Das Evangelium für die Armen', *ZNW* 72 (1981), pp. 51–64; and E. Bammel, 'The Poor and the Zealots', in Bammel and Moule, *Politics*, pp. 109–28.

LXX, thirty-nine times for *'ānî* (= 'poor', 'afflicted', 'humble'), twenty-two times for *dal* (= 'low', 'weak', 'poor', 'thin'), eleven times for *'ebyôn* (= 'needy', 'poor'). The primary reference is to economic poverty (Prov 13.8; Mk 12.42; 14.7; Lk 21.3; Jn 12.5; Josephus, *Bell*. 5.570; T. Job 10.6–7; 12.1; this is the exclusive meaning in Greek literature outside the Jewish and Christian traditions; cf. LSJ, s.v.). But already in the OT, especially in the Psalms, the Greek word and its Hebrew equivalents refer to those who are in special need of God's help (Ps 12.5; 14.6; 22.24; 37.14; 69.29; 70.5; 86.1; 88.15; Isa 61.1)[19], and in time 'poor' came to be a self-designation for the meek, humiliated, and oppressed people of God (Isa 10.2; 26.6; Ps. Sol. 5.2, 11; 10.6; 15.1; 18.2; 5 Apoc Syr. Ps. 2.18; 1QpHab. 12.3; 1QM 14.7; 1QH 5.13–14; 4QpPs[a] 2.9–10; Jerusalem is 'the poor one' in Isa 54.11).[20] This is the sense in which πτωχός is used in the beatitudes (cf. also Mt 11.5; Lk 4.18; 7.22). Yet it must be stressed that the religious meaning of 'poor' does not exclude the economic meaning (cf. the apparent self-designation of the Jerusalem community: Gal 2.10; Rom 15.26). Rather do the two go together. With probably the majority or at least many of Jesus' audience, the religious state of poverty was matched by an outward condition: they suffered literal poverty or at least experienced first-hand economic inequities. They knew the meaning of need because they were poor in spirit and poor in fact (cf. Ps. Sol. 15.1–3).

This interpretation is confirmed by the ties between Isa 61.1–2 and Mt 5.3 and 4 (see above and Eusebius, *Dem. ev.* 9.10). In the OT prophetic passage, the oppressed people of God are promised salvation: 'The Spirit of the Lord God is upon me, because the Lord has anointed me to bring good tidings to the poor; he has sent me to bind up the brokenhearted, to proclaim liberty to the captives, and the opening of the prison to those who are bound; to proclaim the year of the Lord's favour, and the day of vengeance of our God; to comfort all who mourn'. Both Jesus himself and his followers saw the earthly ministry as a fulfilment of this prophecy (Mt 11.5; Lk 4.16–21; 7.22); and presumably they understood rightly that the text promises salvation for those who face oppression and poverty in the world and in their need turn to God. Thus when the eschatological reversal (περιπέτεια) takes place, the sick are made well, the humble are exalted, and the poor are made rich.

(3) It follows that Matthew's 'in spirit' does not pervert the

---

[19] In Ps 35.10; 37.14; 40.17; 70.5; 86.1; 109.22, πτωχὸς καὶ πένης is a fixed expression used of the attitude of one in prayer.

[20] Recall also that in the OT God is the special protector of the poor; see esp. the laws in Exod 21–3; cf. 2 Sam 22.28; Ezek 22.29; Ps 72.2, 4, 12, 13; 132.15.

meaning of the original, unqualified 'poor'. The addition does, admittedly, shift the emphasis from the economic to the religious sphere (see below).[21] But the religious dimension was not altogether lacking in the pre-Matthean tradition, as the argument just made proves. Moreover, the religious meaning should also be read into Luke, despite the third evangelist's several simple contrasts between the rich and poor (as in 12.13–21; 14.7–14; and 16.19–31). For in the Third Gospel the rich have little sense of need for God (see 12.16–21; 16.19–31) while the poor depend upon him (1.46–53; 14.25–33); so the words 'rich' and 'poor' cannot be purely economic. Luke does not hold forth salvation for the poor simply because they are poor.

Despite its secondary nature, 'the poor in spirit' has a Hebrew equivalent in 1QM 14.7: *'nwy rwḥ*.[22] Unfortunately, the Hebrew, like Mt 5.3, can bear several senses. It could refer to the 'fainthearted'[23], or to the 'spiritually poor' (= 'humble')[24], or to those who have voluntarily made themselves poor.[25] In trying to solve the issue, it seems best to settle upon a meaning which satisfies both 1QM 14.7 and Mt 5.3. This would appear to eliminate the notion of voluntary poverty since this would not fit in well with Matthew's redactional viewpoint; for him, the renunciation of all goods is not a blanket command (see on 19.21), so to make this the object of the first makarism would narrow beyond reason the scope of the first beatitude. Also difficult to endorse is the interpretation, 'fainthearted', for Légasse (v), p. 340, has shown its inappropriateness as a translation in 1QM 14.7. This leaves us with the sense, 'spiritually poor', which fits 1QM 14.7 and Mt 5.3 and has to commend it the vast majority of exegetical opinion.[26] It also allows 'poor in spirit' to find an antonym in 1QS 11.1: 'the haughty of spirit'.

The 'in heart' of 5.8 and the 'meek and lowly in heart' of 11.29 argue that the spirit is the sphere of poverty. The emphasis is not simply on external conditions but on internal disposition (cf. Dupont 3, pp. 386–99). For similar phrases see Ps 24.4 ('pure in heart'); 34.18 ('crushed in spirit'); Prov 29.23 ('lowly of spirit'); 7.8 ('proud in spirit'); Ps 11.2 ('upright in heart').

[21] Yet the economic realm is not altogether out of view; for the coming of the kingdom of heaven (5.3, 10) will certainly eliminate the evils that cause poverty in the present. Against πνεῦμα being God's Spirit see Luz 1, pp. 205–6.

[22] Context: 'He has taught war (to the hand) of the feeble and steadied the trembling knee; he has braced the back of the smitten. By the poor in spirit . . . the hard of heart, and by the perfect way all the nations of wickedness have come to an end: not one of their mighty men stands' (Vermes).

[23] So E. Best (v). He thinks that the demands of the sermon create faintheartedness. 'Conscience doth make cowards of us all'.

[24] See Légasse (v). He finds internal poverty the appropriate meaning for both 1QM 4.7 and Mt 5.3.

[25] See Schubert, 'Sermon', p. 122. Cf. Ps.-Clem. Rec. 2.28 and Lohmeyer, *Matthäus*, pp. 82–3. See also those cited by Luz 1, p. 207, n. 60.

[26] Exhaustive survey in Dupont 3, pp. 385–471. He agrees with the conclusion reached here. Flusser, 'Poor' (v), offers a novel interpretation: 'the poor' are those who are enriched by the Holy Spirit.

In Isa. 61.1 πτωχοί translates '*ānāwîm*. But because it has mostly a religious nuance, the LXX usually translates '*ānāwîm* with πραεῖς. It can thus be argued that if Matthew knew the Hebrew as well as the OT Greek, he might have added 'in spirit' in order to bring out more than the LXX the religious dimension of the original Hebrew. But whether the evangelist paid much attention to Isa. 61 is, as we have seen, doubtful, and the desire to clarify πτωχοί can be understood without reference to Isa 61.

ὅτι αὐτῶν ἐστιν ἡ βασιλεία τῶν οὐρανῶν. So also 5.10b. 'Theirs is the kingdom of heaven'—the meaning is neither that the poor now possess the kingdom (it is God's possession) nor that the kingdom consists of the poor; rather are we to think, 'To the poor will be given the kingdom of heaven'. The outcome of the last judgement is here proclaimed. The world will be turned upside down; 'those who are on top here are at the bottom there, and those who are at the bottom here are on the top there' (*b. Pesaḥ.* 50a; cf. Mt 19.30; 20.16).

Lk 6.20c has the second person plural, ὑμετέρα, instead of the third person plural (cf. Gos. Thom. 54; Polycarp, Ep. 2.3), and 'of God' (cf. Polycarp, Ep. 2.3) instead of 'of the heavens' (here Gos. Thom. 54 agrees with Matthew). The latter is surely due to Matthew's hand (see on 3.2 and 6.10). What of the former? There has been a plenitude of scholarly discussion as to whether Matthew's third person or Luke's direct address—'you'—is more original (see Dupont 1, pp. 272–96; he thinks Matthew original). No agreement has been reached. The observation that beatitudes in both Greek and Jewish literature are usually in the third person can cut both ways. On the one hand, it could be argued that the third person, being the standard form, must have been original and that it was changed in order to make the beatitudes better fit their present context in Q or Luke. On the other hand, if the less usual second person form were primary, it could, arguably, have been altered towards the common form. No more helpful is the claim that Matthew's more aphoristic form must be secondary because he has 'ethicized' the beatitudes. This does not persuade because the premise—Matthew 'ethicized' the beatitudes—is to be disputed (see pp. 439–40).

Are there other arguments which might take us beyond the inconclusiveness of the two just introduced? (1) If the Gospel of Thomas be independent of Matthew and Luke, then it supports the priority of the latter, for Gos. Thom. 54 reads, 'Jesus said, "Blessed are the poor, for yours is the kingdom of heaven" '.[27] Many, however, would not concede the independence of Thomas. Moreover, the beatitudes in Thomas appear with both the second and third person forms (see 68–9), and this might simply betray flux in the oral tradition. (2) One might infer from Luke's editing of Mark in Lk 5.30, 34; 6.2; 21.16, 19 that the Third Evangelist had a tendency to introduce the second person address into his material. But,

---

[27] This saying might also be important for other reasons. It stands by itself as a solitary beatitude, preceded by a saying on true circumcision (Gos. Thom. 53) and followed by the equivalent of Mt 10.37 = Lk 14.26 (Gos. Thom. 55).

as Gundry has observed, at these points the Lukan formulations have been affected by the use of the second person in surrounding material or the evangelist has changed the referent altogether—neither of which applies to the beatitudes.[28] (3) The Lukan woes (6.24–6), in both their first and second lines, have the second person plural. The beatitudes in Lk 6.21–3, by way of contrast, have the second person only in the second line ('Blessed are *the poor*, for *yours* is the kingdom of God', etc.). Now since the woes are, by common consent, secondary constructions, they show that the 'you' form was adopted at least by Luke or by someone before him. In addition, it could be argued that the Lukan beatitudes, influenced by the form of the woes, have been imperfectly rewritten—which is why the first and second lines are not in perfect harmony. And yet, it has also been affirmed that the awkward juxtapositioning of the third person and second person in Luke cannot be put anywhere save at the tradition's fount: it is too odd (so Gundry, *Commentary*, p. 68). Once again, therefore, the argument is indecisive.

Unfortunately, none of the other reasons for favouring Luke's form over against Matthew's or vice versa is any more persuasive than the five just examined. This means that the clouds of doubt still hang over the issue: we still await a decisive observation. This does not, however, matter much for the interpretation of the beatitudes. The difference between Matthew and Luke is stylistic and does not greatly affect the sense.

The present tense, 'is' ('because theirs *is* the kingdom of heaven'), stands in contrast to the future tenses in the second members of all the other beatitudes ('because they shall be comforted', 'because they shall inherit the earth', etc.). It is usually—and in our opinion rightly—judged to be a futuristic or proleptic present (see BDF § 323), expressing vividness and confidence (cf. 11.3; 24.43). But perhaps the present also hints at the fact that the kingdom is already in some sense present (see on 4.17) and therefore a blessing enjoyed even now.[29] In either case, there would have been no verb in the Semitic original.

According to Goppelt 1, p. 68, 'As a single ray of light passing through a prism is broken into the colourful spectrum of the rainbow, so too what the kingdom brings finds colourful development in the promises of the Beatitudes'. In other words, 4b, 5b, 6b, 7b, 8b, and 9b explicate the meaning of 'theirs is the kingdom of heaven'. Thus Mt 5.3–12 falls nicely under the summary in 4.23: Jesus preached the good news of the kingdom of heaven. For the idea that there will be no poverty in the next age,

[28] *Commentary*, p. 68. On the favouring of the second person plural in Luke see H. J. Cadbury, *The Style and Literary Method of Luke*, HTS 6, Cambridge, Mass., 1920, pp. 124–6.

[29] So Guelich, pp. 76–7. Thurneysen, p. 32: 'the kingdom of heaven is here, but it is here as future'. For the claim that the beatitudes (at least on the lips of Jesus) referred primarily to the presence of the kingdom of God see P. Hoffmann and V. Eid, *Jesus von Nazareth und eine christliche Moral*, QD 66, Freiburg, 1975, pp. 29–39.

see Sib. Or. 3.378; T. Jud. 25.4; *b. Pesaḥ.* 50a; and contrast *b. Šabb.* 15lb and *Sipre* on Deut. 15.11. Perhaps the repeated αὐτῶν in the second clause in each of the Matthean beatitudes has an antithetical effect, indicating 'these' people rather than 'those'—in which case the groups emerge in 5.17–7.12 as the Christians and the Jewish leaders.

According to G. Schwarz (v), the first beatitude originally read, 'Blessed are the poor, for they will be rich' (cf. Sib. Or. 8.208: οἱ πτωχοὶ πλουτισθήσονται). Such a reconstruction has the advantage of (a) making the original three beatitudes (5.3, 4, 6) perfectly parallel, (b) providing an exact antithesis of 'poor', and (c) producing a saying which could be reflected in Jas 2.5 ('Has not God chosen those who are poor in the world to be rich in faith . . .?'). Further, it is easy to understand why someone might have wished to change the potentially misleading 'they will be made rich', and easy to see why 'theirs is the kingdom of heaven' was substituted—in the NT 'riches' are associated with salvation (1 Cor 1.5; 2 Cor 6.10; 9.11). Nonetheless, all of these points do not create firm conviction. The basic presupposition of the argument, namely, that the first three beatitudes must at one time have been perfectly parallel, is not established and in the nature of the case cannot be.

4. Compare 1QH 18.14–15 (fragmentary, alluding to Isa 61.1–2) and 11QMelch 2.20. The beatitude in Matthew is about mourners who will be comforted; it corresponds to the third beatitude in Luke, which promises laughter for those who now weep. The order in the First Gospel corresponds to Isa. 61.1–2: 5.3 alludes to 61.1, 5.4 to 61.2.[30]

μακάριοι οἱ πενθοῦντες. πενθέω is redactional in 9.15. Luke has οἱ κλαίοντες (which is probably redactional; κλαίω: Mt: 2; Mk: 3; Lk: 10) + νῦν. The verb in Matthew is probably from the Q source (cf. Luz 1, p. 200, n. 9); for it has its counterpart in the third Lukan woe: 'Woe to you that laugh now, for you shall *mourn* and weep' (Lk 6.25, alluding to Ps 126.2–6? cf. also Mk 16.10; Jas 4.9; Rev 18.11, 15, 19). On the other hand, if, as Guelich supposes, the evangelist sought to connect the first few beatitudes with Isa 61.1–3, then because 61.2 speaks of comfort for those in mourning, 'those who mourn' could be redactional. But it may also be that neither Matthew nor Luke has preserved the wording of Q.

---

[30] 5.5 comes before 5.4 in D 33 vg syᶜ boᵐˢ Cl Or Eus Hil Ephr Chr Bas GrNy Hier Aph. The traditional order is supported by ℵ B C K W Δ Θ Π syᵖˑˢˑʰ sa bo eth arm geo Tert Chr Sche Ps-Chr Diatᵃˑᵖ. According to Metzger, p. 12, 'if verses 3 and 5 had originally stood together, with their rhetorical antithesis of heaven and earth, it is unlikely that any scribe would have thrust ver. 4 between them. On the other hand, as early as the second century copyists reversed the order of the two beatitudes so as to produce such an antithesis and to bring πτωχοί and πραεῖς into closer association'. —ℵ¹ 33 892 *pc* aur vgᵐˢˢ saᵐˢ eth bo Chr add νυν, under Lukan influence.

Why do the people of God mourn? The clue is to be found—this against most of the church Fathers—not in the fact that they are guilty sinners[31] but rather in Isa 61.1–3, which is alluded to here (v. 2: παρακαλέσαι πάντας τοὺς πενθοῦντας; cf. v. 3 and Barn. 14.9). In the OT text Israel is oppressed at the hands of her heathen captors; her cities are in ruins (v. 4); and her people know shame and dishonour (v. 7). In sum, God's own are on the bottom, the wicked on the top. So mourning is heard because the righteous suffer, because the wicked prosper, and because God has not yet acted to reverse the situation. It is the same in the NT text. The people of God have yet to see the kingdom of God in its fullness. They are still persecuted (5.10–12). They do not see the twelve on twelve thrones judging the twelve tribes of Israel (19.28). The Son of man has not come in his glory (24.29–31). God's will is not done on earth as it is in heaven (6.10). And for the present the wicked hold the upper hand against the righteous (2.1–23; 5.10–12; 7.15–22; 13.53–8; 21.12–13; 26.1–27.66). The righteous therefore cannot but mourn. Until the eschatological reversal takes place, it is not possible to be content with the status quo. To those who understand the truth about the present aeon, grief cannot be eliminated: 'this world is to them a strife and a labour with much trouble' (2 Bar. 15.8).

There is some discrepancy between 5.4 and 9.15. In this last Jesus declares that the wedding guests (= his disciples) cannot mourn (diff. Mark, who has 'fast') as long as the bridegroom (= Jesus) is with them. So the text of Matthew both addresses the disciples as those who mourn (5.4) and at the same time excuses them for not mourning while Jesus is with them. The seeming contradiction, however, is only one aspect of the tension created by the fact that the kingdom of God is both present and coming in the gospel tradition (see on 4.17). And while in 5.4 the weight comes down on the future coming of the kingdom, in 9.15 the presence of the kingdom is being proclaimed.

ὅτι αὐτοὶ παρακληθήσονται. Compare Gen 37.35; 1 Chr 7.22; 1QH 15.14–15; and Rev 7.17. For παρακαλέω as meaning 'comfort' see also 2.18. Ecclus 48.24 ('By the spirit of might he [Isaiah] saw the last things and comforted those who mourned in Zion') shows that 'comfort' and 'mourn' in combination were catchwords associated with Isaiah's name.

Six points should be noted: (1) The passive is a 'divine passive': *God* will comfort the mourners. (2) The comfort here promised is not any consolation which can be known in the world (contrast 2 Cor 1.4) but is rather the other-worldly joy and satisfaction and

---

[31] According to Augustine, *De serm. mont.* 1.5, the saints mourn the loss of the earthly things they gave up when becoming Christians.

fulfilment brought about only by the coming of the Son of man in his kingdom. (3) As Albright-Mann, p. 46, have written, 'The favour of God does not rest upon the state of mourning *as such*, but upon those who lament the sin which mars God's choice of Israel' (cf. above). (4) It is difficult to see how Mt 5.4 can be understood as paraenesis. The evangelist can hardly be encouraging his readers to mourn (contrast Jas 4.9). Their present situation of mourning is presupposed as the given which is the basis for hope announced. 5.4a is indicative, not imperative. (5) There is some NT and rabbinic evidence for the Messiah's having been thought of as a 'comforter' or as bearing this name (*měnahēm*); see Lk 2.25; SB 1, p. 66; 2, pp. 124–6. (6) The theme of God turning sorrow into joy is common in the Jewish tradition (see, e.g., Isa 60.20; 66.10; Jer 31.13; Bar 4.23; Ps 126.2–6; Rev 21.4).

5. If the tradition-history outlined on pp. 434–6 be correct, this line, which is based upon Ps 37.11 and which has no parallel in Luke, was added by an editor of Q^{mt} in order to explicate the first beatitude (which it at one time immediately followed). The word, πραΰς, usually translated 'meek', was intended to make plain the religious dimension of 'poor' (this before Matthew's qualification, 'in spirit'). Hence 5.3 and 5.5 are in synonymous parallelism. No real difference in meaning between the two is to be discerned.

μακάριοι οἱ πραεῖς. Compare 2 En. 50.2 ('In patience and meekness spend the number of your days so that you may inherit endless life'). πραΰς occurs only four times in the NT, three times in Matthew (5.5; 11.29; 21.5) and once in 1 Peter (3.4). The praise of mildness and gentleness was known in both the Greek and Jewish worlds; see Plato, *Crit.* 120E; *Rep.* 375C; Lucian, *Somnium* 10; Ep. Arist. 257, 263; Philo, *Vit. Mos.* 2.279; Josephus, *Ant.* 19.330; *m. Soṭa* 9.15; *ARN* 7; *b. Soṭa* 40a, 49b; *b. Šabb.* 30b; *b. Ned.* 38a; F. Hauck and S. Schulz, *TWNT* 6, pp. 645–9. But, as Schweizer, *Matthew*, pp. 89–90, has suggested, in Matthew 'the powerless' may be a better translation. The πραεῖς are not so much actively seeking to avoid hubris (an attitude) as they are, as a matter of fact, powerless in the eyes of the world (a condition).

In both 11.29 and 21.5 Jesus himself is, like Moses before him (Num 12.3), called πραΰς: he bowed the neck of his soul and body. This makes him in 'meekness', as in so much else, the model (cf. also 12.19). The Messiah's life gives content to his words.

Ps 37.11 is quoted in 4QPs^a 2.9–11 and interpreted in this fashion: 'It concerns the congregation of the poor, who will accept the appointed time of affliction (or: fasting), and they will be delivered from all the traps of Belial'.

ὅτι αὐτοὶ κληρονομήσουσιν τὴν γῆν. Compare Deut 4.1. The 'meek' or 'powerless' will possess 'the earth'; they will be set over much (cf. 25.21, 23). This is eschatological reversal: the world is turned upside down. 'He who humbles himself will be exalted'. Compare Ps 37.11: οἱ δὲ πραεῖς κληρονομήσουσιν γῆν (= waʿănāwîm yîrĕšû ʾāreṣ; cf. vv. 9, 22, 34, and esp. 29: 'the δίκαιοι will inherit the land'). There is no definite article before 'earth' in the MT or LXX; but Matthew's τήν does have a counterpart in the targum on Ps 37.11 as well as in Isa 61.7 (κληρονομήσουσιν τὴν γῆν). On the possession of the land as an eschatological hope see Isa 60.21–2; 61.7; 11QTemple 59.11–13; 4QpPsᵃ 2.9–12; 1 En. 5.7 ('to the elect ones there shall be light, joy, and peace, and they shall inherit the earth'); Jub. 32.18–19; m. Qidd. 1.10. For additional NT allusions to Ps 37 see Acts 7.54 (cf. 37.12); Heb 11.7 (cf. 37.29); and Heb 11.40 (cf. 37.13). For its use in rabbinic literature see SB 1, pp. 199–200. For 'possession' as an eschatological promise in the NT see also Mt 19.29; 25.34; 1 Cor 6.9–10; 15.50; Gal 5.21; Heb 1.14; Jas 2.5; 1 Pet 1.4; Rev 21.7. The usual sense in Greek of κληρονομεῖν is 'to inherit', but in the LXX the verb translates yāraš and so it comes to mean 'to possess' or 'to acquire'.

'They shall inherit [or: possess] the earth'—or should we translate, 'the Land'? That is, does the promise of 5.5 have reference to the Land of Israel,[32] or is γῆ more general: all land? (discussion in Davies, GL, pp. 361–2)—or do we have here nothing more than a symbol for inheriting the spiritual kingdom of heaven? (The Apocalypse of Paul puts the 'land' of the third beatitude in the pre-existent new earth that is to appear in the latter days; see 21.) One might argue from 8.11 and 19.28 that our evangelist looked forward to a time when the Son of man would set up his throne within the boundaries of Israel. But 19.28 seems to promise a cosmic renewal (ἐν τῇ παλιγγενεσίᾳ), and throughout Matthew nationalistic hopes—which are otherwise absent from 5.3–12—are undone. This speaks against the simple equation, τὴν γῆν = the Land of Israel, and two additional considerations bolster this inference. First, with the possible exception of the ambiguous 27.45 (darkness over all τὴν γῆν), the unqualified γῆ appears in Matthew to refer not to Palestine but to the earth (as in 5.13, 18, 35; 6.10, 19; 9.6; 11.25; 12.42; 16.19; 18.18–19; 23.9; 24.30; 28.18). Secondly, because the kingdom is already in some sense present (see on 4.17), the βασιλεία is necessarily spiritualized and divorced from geography. It would seem to follow, then, that in Mt 5.5 'to inherit the land' has been spiritualized, and 5.5b is no more concrete than any of the other promises made in the

---

[32] Cf. the Latin version of Did. 3.7: esto autem mansuetus, quia mansueti possidebunt sanctam terram. Ps 37 certainly pertains to the land of Israel; and 'to inherit the land' recalls the entry of the Jews into Palestine (cf. Deut. 4.1; 16.20; also Gen 17.8).

beatitudes. It is just another way of saying, 'The one who humbles himself will be exalted (in the kingdom of God)'.

In Isa 61.7 LXX, those who are addressed in 61.1–3 as the 'poor' and 'those who mourn' are told that they κληρονομήσουσιν τὴν γῆν. Given the other allusions to Isa 61 in the other beatitudes, perhaps 5.5 should recall Isa 61.7 even though 5.5 clearly quotes Ps 37.11—especially since both Matthew and Isaiah agree, against the psalm, in having the definite article before γῆν (see above).

Does Did. 3.7 betray a knowledge of the First Gospel? ἴσθι δὲ πραΰς, ἐπεὶ οἱ πραεῖς κληρονομήσουσι τὴν γῆν. One might consider this to be a quotation of Ps 37.11 and therefore uninfluenced by the Jesus tradition. Yet the article before 'earth' agrees with Matthew over against the LXX, and this shifts the balance slightly in favour of some connexion between the two texts. What sort of connexion? Because 5.5 was added to the beatitudes by an editor of Q^{mt}, one is almost compelled to conclude either that the author of the Didache knew Matthew or that he knew Q^{mt} (as opposed to Q^{lk}).

6. This modified Q beatitude is the Matthean equivalent of Lk 6.21a: 'Blessed are those who hunger now, for you shall be satisfied'. Compare 2 Bar. 29.6: 'those who are hungry will enjoy themselves'.

μακάριοι οἱ πεινῶντες καὶ διψῶντες τὴν δικαιοσύνην. Compare Ps 107.5–9; Isa 49.10; 55.1–2; 65.13; Jn 6.35; Rev 7.16. Righteousness is to be earnestly and habitually sought, as though it were meat and drink. Matthew has inserted 'and thirst after righteousness', as can be seen from a comparison with Lk 6.21a and the First Gospel's awkward Greek (the accusative after 'hunger and thirst' and the lopsided correspondence of χορτάζω with πεινάω but not διψάω). Also, καὶ διψῶντες breaks the π alliteration in the first beatitudes: πτωχοί, πενθοῦντες, πραεῖς, πεινῶντες.

Those who hunger and thirst after righteousness are the same as those who 'seek above all else the kingdom and his righteousness' (6.33). For 'hunger' and 'thirst' with reference to religious longing see Ps 42.2; 63.1; 143.6; Amos 8.11. The meaning here is not passive longing but active seeking (cf. Ecclus 24.21–2; Philo, Poster C. 172; Fug. 139). Compare b. Sanh. 100a: 'Him who starves himself for the sake of the study of Torah in this world, the Holy One, blessed be He, will fully satisfy in the next'.

The addition of 'righteousness' serves two or perhaps three ends. (1) It clarifies the object of 'hunger', which in Q remained unspecified. (It does not, however, simply spiritualize a physical need. Even in Luke = Q 'the hungry are men who both outwardly and inwardly are painfully deficient in the things essential to life as God meant it to be, and who, since they cannot help themselves, turn to God on the basis of his promise'.)[33] (2) It brings the beatitudes into closer connexion with the rest of the sermon on the mount, in which 'righteousness' is a prominent theme (5.10, 20; 6.1, 33). (3) Given the use of the first few verses of Isa 61 in the first three beatitudes, it is perhaps to be noted that 'righteousness' occurs in Isa 61.3 LXX (κληθήσονται γενεαὶ δικαιοσύνης; see also 61.8, 11). Those who think Matthew responsible for the links between Isa 61 and the beatitudes will find this significant.

Isa 32.6 reads, 'For the fool speaks folly, and his mind plots iniquity: to practise ungodliness, to utter error concerning the Lord, to leave the craving of the hungry unsatisfied, and to deprive the thirsty of drink'. The targum explains that those who hunger and thirst are 'the righteous who desire teaching even as a hungry man bread, and words of the Law, which they (desire) as a thirsty man water'. Although a bit different, this reminds one of Matthew's editorial work in 5.6, where the images of hunger and thirst are interpreted with reference to righteousness.

What is meant by 'righteousness' in 5.6? Przybylski, p. 96, has listed the alternatives (cf. Giesen, pp. 95–8). (1) It is justification, the gift of God, given to those who ask for it (so SB 1, p. 201, and Bultmann, *Theology* 1, p. 273). (2) It is the eschatological vindication of the elect: those who hunger and thirst after righteousness are seeking the overthrow of the ungodly, the salvation of the saints, and, in general, the establishment of divine justice.[34] (3) 'It is the fulfilment by man of God's will *and* the fulfilment by God of His own purposes of grace and mercy'.[35] (4) It is the right conduct which God requires, as in 6.33. The thought of gift is not involved (so the Fathers; cf. Sand, p. 202; Przybylski, pp. 96–8; Luz 1, p. 210).

Of these options, the fourth commends itself. To begin with, those who argue that 'righteousness' must be a gift and that those who are satisfied are given righteousness, just as those who show mercy are given mercy (5.7), overlook the fact that a direct correspondence between character and reward does not obtain in most of the beatitudes (cf. Przybylski, p. 97). The meek are not given meekness. The pure in heart are not given purity. The

---

[33] L. Goppelt, *TWNT* 6, p. 18. Yet according to Origen (*De prin.* 2.11.2), some Christians used Mt 5.6 to buttress their belief in the literal fulfilment of messianic prophecies: the hungry will be able to satisfy their desires and eat and drink to heart's content (cf. Irenaeus, *Adv. haer.* 5.9.3–4). See further Davies, *JPS*, pp. 267–8.

[34] So C. H. Dodd, *The Bible and the Greeks*, London, 1935, p. 55 (wrongly presupposing an Aramaic original); Bonnard, p. 57; Schweizer, *Matthew*, pp. 91–2; Gundry, *Commentary*, p. 70; and Reumann, pp. 127–8.

[35] T. W. Manson, *Sayings*, p. 48. Cf. H. Günther, 'Die Gerechtigkeit des Himmelreiches in der Bergpredigt', *KD* 17 (1971), p. 123; Beare, p. 130; Guelich, pp. 84–7; and Giesen, pp. 98–103.

peacemakers are not given peace. It is therefore far from obvious that those who hunger and thirst for righteousness gain righteousness. And even if this were not so, the righteousness to be given would not need to be identified with justification or vindication; it could simply be interpreted as the righteousness that is to prevail in the new aeon, in which all will follow the Law of God without deviation. But the deciding factor is this: the righteousness of 5.6 should probably be construed in terms of the word's usage elsewhere in the sermon on the mount, in 5.10, 20; 6.1, 33. And since in these places we shall find righteousness to be the right conduct required by God, such is probably the meaning here. Particularly weighty is 5.10: 'Blessed are those persecuted for righteousness' sake'. Righteousness cannot, in this verse, have anything to do with divine vindication, nor can it mean justification or be God's gift. It is, rather, something disciples have, and they are persecuted because of it. Hence it is recognizable behaviour of some sort.

It is worth observing that 5.6 does not congratulate those who are as a matter of fact righteous; instead it lifts up those who are hungering and thirsting for conformity to the will of God. The distinction is a matter of some remark. Righteousness, it is implied, must be ever sought, must always be a goal which lies ahead: it is never in the grasp. Recall Lk 18.9–14, the parable of the Pharisee and the tax collector—which, as Luke has it, was addressed by Jesus to 'those who trusted in themselves that they were righteous'. In this tale, the man who thinks himself righteous is in fact not, while the one who knows his own shortcomings 'went down to his house justified'. Those who hunger and thirst after righteousness are blessed, not those who think they have attained it.

ὅτι αὐτοὶ χορτασθήσονται. Compare Ps. 37.19; 132.15; 4QpPs^a 3.2–5. Again the future tense is the eschatological tense and the passive is the 'divine passive': 'Because they shall, on the last day, be satisfied by God'.[36] In Luke there is no personal pronoun and the verb is in the second person plural. Precisely how or with what religious reward the saints will be satisfied is not explicitly stated (cf. Par. Jer. 9.20). It could be the vision of God, as in Ps 17.15,[37] or the messianic banquet (cf. Ps 107.1–9; Isa 25.6–8; 49.10–13; 1 En. 62.14; 1QSa; Mt 8.11), or—most probably—a world in which righteousness dwells (cf. Isa 32.1, 16–17; 1 En. 58.4; T. Levi 13.5;[38] 2 Pet 3.13).

[36] Contrast Acts of Thomas 94: 'Blessed are you who hunger for the Lord's sake, because for you is rest preserved *and from now on your souls rejoice*'.

[37] 'But I in righteousness will behold thy face, I will be satisfied (χορτασθήσομαι) in beholding thy glory'.

[38] 'Do righteousness on earth, in order that you might find it in heaven'. In Prov 21.21 MT those who pursue righteousness and kindness find life and righteousness.

Gos. Thom. 69b reads: 'Blessed are those who hunger, so that the belly of the one wanting will be filled'. This verse cannot be considered good evidence of dependence upon Matthew, for it lacks precisely the redactional traits of 5.6. ('thirst after righteousness'). Neither is it at all necessary to see Gos. Thom. 5.6 as a reworking of Lk 6.21a. Indeed, one might even argue that the version in Thomas is the most primitive, and that 'the belly of the one wanting will be satisfied' was dropped in the pre-synoptic tradition because it did not so easily lend itself to a spiritualizing interpretation.

7. This and the next three beatitudes are from Q^mt and were added to create correlations between the beginning of the sermon on the plain and the material after it (see pp. 434–6). There are no parallels in Luke. With v. 7 compare Mt 18.33: 'Should you not have had mercy on your fellow servant, as I had mercy on you?'; Ps 18.25–6: 'With the loyal thou dost show thyself loyal; with the blameless man thou dost show thyself blameless; with the pure thou dost show thyself pure . . .'; and *b. Šabb.* 151b: 'Whoever has pity on people will obtain pity from heaven'. The sentiment is also paralleled in Mt 6.12–15; 7.1–5; 18.21–35; Mk 11.25; and *t. B. Qam.* 9.30: 'As long as you are merciful, the Merciful One is merciful to you'. Note further the agraphon preserved in 1 Clem. 13.2: 'Be merciful in order that you might receive mercy' (also in Polycarp, *Ep.* 2.3).

μακάριοι οἱ ἐλεήμονες. ἐλεήμων, which appears only twice in the NT, in Mt 5.7 and Heb 2.17 (cf. T. Sim. 4.4; Josephus, *Ant.* 10.41; Did. 3.8),[39] means 'merciful' (with the emphasis upon pardon?). In the LXX the word usually translates *ḥannûn*. Q^mt probably had οἱ οἰκτίρμονες (cf. Lk 6.36), which Matthew changed because of his fondness for the ἐλε-root. Further, it is almost certain that Q had the following sentence in the sermon on the plain: 'Be merciful (οἰκτίρμονες) even as your heavenly Father is merciful' (οἰκτίρμων). This means that, in Q^mt, 5.7 was verbally correlated with 5.44–8 = Lk 6.27–36.

Matthew's gospel has a great deal to say about mercy. It is a fundamental demand (cf. 9.13; 12.7; 23.23) which is fleshed out both by Jesus' words (5.43–8; 18.21–35; 25.31–46) and by his example (9.27–31; 15.21–8; 17.14–18; 20.29–34). In much of this there is strict continuity with the OT and Jewish tradition, for the disposition towards mercy—both an outward act and an inward feeling—was, of course, acknowledged as a human virtue as well as a divine attribute (1 Sam 23.21; Ps 72.13; Prov 14.21; Mic 6.8; T. Zeb. 5.1, 3; 7.1–8.6; Philo, *Spec. leg.* 4.72, 76–7; rabbinic texts in

---

[39] In Did. 3.8 the word may be due to Matthean influence because Did. 3.7 probably depends upon Mt 5.5 ('Blessed are the meek, for they shall inherit the earth').

SB 1, pp. 204–5).[40] Matthew's Jesus, however, gives the demand
for mercy renewed emphasis and vividness by placing it at the
centre of his proclamation (9.13; 12.7; 23.23; 25.31–46) and by
making it plain that mercy should be shown to all (contrast *b. Ber.*
33a; *b. Sanh.* 92a), including not only those on the fringes of
society but even enemies (5.43–8; cf. Lk 10.29–37). Furthermore, it
may be that our evangelist's use of 'mercy' has been affected by a
polemical stance over against the rabbinate of his time.[41] In 9.13;
12.7; and 23.23, ἔλεος connotes the idea of loyalty within a
relationship. (9.13 and 12.7 cite Hos 6.6, in which *ḥesed* = ἔλεος
clearly involves covenant loyalty.) In each instance the Pharisees
are being criticized. Hence, it would seem, the evangelist was
persuaded that while Jesus and his followers, in their acts of mercy
and loving-kindness, were demonstrating their loyalty to God and
his Messiah, the Pharisees had failed to remain faithful. 'Justice
and mercy and faith'—these were 'the weightier matters of the law'
neglected by Matthew's opponents. So perhaps throughout
Matthew (including 5.7) 'mercy' and its cognates imply that
merciful action is the concrete expression of loyalty to God, and
that what God demands is not so much activity directed Godward
('I desire . . . not sacrifice') but loving-kindness benefiting other
people ('I desire mercy').

ὅτι αὐτοὶ ἐλεηθήσονται. Compare Prov 17.5 LXX (ὁ δὲ
ἐπισπλαγχνιζόμενος ἐλεηθήσεται) and Jas 2.13 ('Judgement is
without mercy to one who has shown no mercy; yet mercy
triumphs over judgement'). For the hope of receiving mercy at the
last judgement, which is what is envisaged here, see also 2 Tim
1.18; Jude 21; 1 Clem. 28.1. Note that if mercy is known in the
future, it has also been known in the past. As 18.21–35 proves,
disciples are able to show mercy because God has first shown them
mercy (cf. Lk 6.36).

8. This is the sixth beatitude. It has no parallel in Luke and, as
argued above (pp. 434–6), derives not from the redactor but from
Qᵐᵗ.

μακάριοι οἱ καθαροὶ τῇ καρδίᾳ. Compare 11.29: Jesus is 'lowly in
heart'. 'Pure in heart' is probably from Ps 24.3–4: 'He who has
clean hands and a pure heart (LXX: καθαρὸς τῇ καρδίᾳ), who does
not lift up his soul to what is false, and does not swear deceitfully,
he will receive blessing (LXX: εὐλογίαν) from the Lord, and
vindication from the God of his salvation. Such is the generation
of those who seek him, who seek the face of the God of Jacob' (cf.

---

[40] The Stoics, identifying ἔλεος with an emotion which entailed partiality, did not
regard it as a virtue. See Bultmann, *TWNT* 2, p. 475.
[41] For what follows see D. Hill, 'On the Use and Meaning of Hosea vi. 6 in
Matthew's Gospel', *NTS* 24 (1977), pp. 107–19.

Jas 4.8).[42] But in addition compare Gen.20.5–6 (where ἐν καθαρᾷ καρδίᾳ appears); also Isa. 61.1; T. Naph. 3.1 (ἐν καθαρᾷ καρδίᾳ); T. Jos. 4.6 (ἐν καθαρᾷ καρδίᾳ); 1 Tim 1.5; 2 Tim 2.22; and Heb 10.22.

In the biblical tradition, the heart (= *lēb*, *lēbāb*) is the real or true self, the psyche at its deepest level; it is the seat of emotions (Deut. 28.47; Prov 27.11; Isa 35.4; Acts 14.17), volition (Prov 6.18; Jer 3.17; 23.20; Dan 1.8), and the intellect (Gen 27.41; Judg 5.16; T. Gad. 5.3; 1QH 4.21; Mk 2.6; *m. Ber.* 2.1), as well as the internal sphere in which the divinity is encountered (Ps 27.8; Eph 3.17). See further on 6.21.

The meaning of 'pure (or: clean) in heart'—which presupposes as its counterpart external, ceremonial purity (cf. 23.25–6)—is given full body by several pericopae in the sermon on the mount. 5.27–30 demands that the heart be pure from adulterous thoughts. 6.1–18 portrays a piety which is concerned not with outward show but with the private encounter with God; in other words, what matters is what goes on in the heart. 6.21 declares that one's heart is to be in heaven, where one's treasure is. And 7.16–20 propounds the strict correlation between observable behaviour and the true, internal self. So purity of heart must involve integrity, a correspondence between outward action and inward thought (cf. 15.8), a lack of duplicity, singleness of intention (cf. Augustine, *De serm. mont.* 1.8: *cor simplex*), and the desire to please God above all else. More succinctly: purity of heart is to will one thing, God's will, with all of one's being. (In this any contrast with Judaism comes not in the demand for purity of heart but in the failure to put any weight on cultic purity; the emphasis in the NT is much more one-sided. Still, one cannot detect in Mt 5.8 any criticism of the Jewish cult as such. Cf. Luz 1, pp. 211–12.)

Black (p. 158, n. 2) has tentatively suggested that, in Aramaic, 'pure in heart' would be *dky lb*, and that this is significant because *dky lb* is very close to *dkyky lb*, which in turn equals the *nišbĕrê-lēb* ('broken-hearted') of Isa 61.1. But the beatitudes that are on either side of 5.8 are from the same source as 5.8 (Q[mt]), and neither alludes to Isa 61. One therefore does not anticipate an allusion to that OT text here, and the fact that Mt 5.3 and 4 do allude to Isa 61 is scarcely solid reason to emend Mt 5.8.

ὅτι αὐτοὶ τὸν θεὸν ὄψονται. To see God[43] is to know him, and in Judaism the promise of the future was associated with the

---

[42] Other uses of Ps 24 in the NT include 1 Cor 10.26 (quoting 24.1) and perhaps 1 Tim 1.1 (alluding to 24.5?) and Jas 4.8 (alluding to 24.4?).

[43] Despite Philoxenus, *Matt.* p. 143 (ed. Fox) and Gundry, *Commentary*, p. 71, God, not Jesus, is the object of sight. Jesus may be, for Matthew, 'God with us' (1.23), but he is never simply called 'God'.

knowledge or vision of God[44]—privileges the angels enjoy even
now (18.10); see Isa 52.6; 60.16; Jer 24.7; 31.31–4; 1 Cor 13.12;
Heb 12.14; 1 Jn 3.2 (probably with reference to God, as the
Eastern Fathers understood it); Rev 22.4; 4 Ezra 7.98; b. B. Bat.
10a; SB 1, pp. 212–14. For other texts which connect sight with the
eschatological events see Mk 13.26; 14.62; Rev 1.7; b. Sanh. 98b.
Whether to 'see God'—which may or may not imply that God has
a body—is intended to have cultic significance (cf. Exod 23.17
LXX; Ps 42.2; 63.2) cannot be determined, although the context of
Ps 24.4 might suggest this. In any event, Mt 5.8 has to do with the
eschatological future; the possibility of attaining the beatific vision
in the present life—something taken for granted by medieval
theologians—is not implied.

There are two biblical traditions about 'seeing' God. One seems
to put this out of the realm of possibility (Exod 3.6; 19.21; 33.20,
23; Jn 1.18; 1 Tim 6.15–16; Sipre on Num 12.8), the other to make
it a blessed goal (Ps 11.7; 17.15; Job 19.26; Philo, Vit. cont. 11–12;
Abr. 57–9; Mut. nom. 81–2; Rev 22.4). Perhaps the ancients
harmonized things in this way: the former texts have in mind
physical sight, the latter inner or spiritual sight; or perhaps they
thought one to pertain to this world, the other to the world to
come. See further the discussions in Origen, C. Cels. 7.33–4, and
Augustine, Civ. Dei 22.29.

9. In Q^mt this verse linked up, on verbal and thematic grounds,
with 5.38–48 = Lk 6.27–30, 32–6 (on turning the other cheek and
loving enemies). In its present context in Matthew the verse is also
nicely illustrated by 5.21–6 (on setting aside anger and making
friends with enemies).

μακάριοι οἱ εἰρηνοποιοί. Compare 2 En. 52.11–15.
'Peacemaker', not 'pacifist' or 'peaceful', is the right translation of
εἰρηνοποιός, for a positive action, reconciliation, is envisioned: the
'peacemakers' seek to bring about peace (see Dupont 3,
pp. 635–40). The word is a LXX and NT hapax legomenon,[45] and
the theme of 'peace' is not prominent in the First Gospel.[46] Both of
these facts supply evidence for a pre-Matthean origin. The verbal
equivalent of 'peacemaker' occurs in Prov 10.10 LXX ('He who
boldly reproves makes peace') and Col 1.20. Compare Jas 3.18:

[44] There is a wealth of material in K. E. Kirk, The Vision of God, London, 1931;
see also A. R. George, Communion with God in the New Testament, London, 1953,
pp. 93–105.

[45] In Graeco-Roman lit. it is often used of kings who establish peace, as in Dio
Chrysostom 72.15.5. See further Windisch (v).

[46] Gundry, Commentary, p. 72, who argues for the Matthean genesis of 5.9,
suggests that the evangelist (1) has introduced peacemakers in order to supply a
contrast with the haters of 5.10–12, (2) has drawn upon Mk 9.50c (which he later
omits because of 5.9), and (3) may be alluding to Hos 1.10. None of this is
convincing.

'The harvest of righteousness is sown in peace by those who make peace'. See also Ps 34.14; Mk 9.50; *m. 'Abot* 1.12 ('Be disciples of Aaron, making peace and pursuing peace'); *m. Pe'a* 1.1; *Mek.* on Exod 20.25; and the texts cited in SB 1, pp. 215–18. Because there is no qualification for 'peacemakers', it would be wrong to delimit precisely the sphere to which the 'peacemakers' bring peace (see Schnackenburg (v)), although in view of the consistent social dimension in the texts just quoted above, religious peace ('peace with God') is probably not the subject. (Origen's inclusion of those who reconcile contradictory Biblical texts among the 'peacemakers' (*Philocal.* 6.1) is only a curiosity which evokes a smile.) Perhaps our beatitude was first formulated during the Jewish war or shortly thereafter and reflects the conviction that revolution against Rome was the wrong course to take. For Jesus as the bringer of peace see Lk 2.14; 19.38; Acts 10.36; Rom 5.1; Eph 2.14–18; Col 1.2; Heb 7.2 (cf. Isa 9.5–6; Zech 9.10). In being a peacemaker, the disciple is imitating his Father in heaven, 'the God of peace' (Rom 16.20; cf. T. Dan. 5.2; Rom 15.33; Phil 4.9; 1 Th 5.23; 2 Th 3.16; Heb 13.20).

How 5.9 is to be harmonized with 10.34 ('Do not suppose that I came to cast peace on the earth; I did not come to cast peace but a sword') is not revealed by our evangelist. But the tension created by the two texts is not extraordinary but actually typical: Matthew's gospel has more than its fair share of inconcinnities; compare 16.6 with 23.3, 8.12 with 13.38, 9.13 with 10.41. This fact indicates that Matthew was a faithful preserver of tradition as well as a creative redactor-theologian. (Ps-Clem. Rec. 2.29 establishes artificial concord between 5.9 and 10.34 by referring 5.9 to fellow-believers, 10.34 to heretics.)

ὅτι αὐτοὶ υἱοὶ θεοῦ κληθήσονται.[47] 'Sons of God' occurs only here in Matthew. 'Sons of your Father in heaven' occurs in 5.45 (cf. Lk 6.35). The unexpressed subject of κληθήσονται is God ('shall be called (by God)'); and it is assumed that to be called something by God is to be that something.

In harmony with the Johannine and Pauline traditions (Jn 1.12; Rom 8.14–15; Gal 3.26–7; 4.5; Eph 1.5), believers in Jesus are, in Matthew, already children or sons of God (5.45), whom they call Father (6.9). At the same time, there is in our gospel an expectation that the people of God will *become* sons in the future, in the

---

[47] ℵ C D *f*[13] *pc* it vg[cl.st] sy[p] geo[b] Did Aug Hil omit αυτοι, B W Θ 0133 0196 *f*[1] Maj f k vg[ww] sy[s.c.h] co followed by NA[26] retain it. The true reading cannot be determined. If the first were original (and this cannot be ruled out, since Matthew does not always maintain perfectly parallel constructions; contrast e.g. 5.31a with 5.21, 27, 33, 38, and 43), the second would inevitably have arisen (cf. HG, p. 30). And if, on the contrary, the second were original, the first could be explained as a scribal slip.

eschaton; compare Ps. Sol. 17.27; Sib. Or. 3.702; Lk 20.36; Rom 8.19, 23; 9.26; Rev 21.7. What is hoped for and symbolized by the notion of eschatological sonship is twofold—(1) a degree of intimacy with God heretofore not experienced and (2) a likeness to him (cf. 5.48).

Only in Mt 5.9 and 5.44–5 = Lk 6.35 are eschatological sonship and peace-making brought together. This supports the hypothesis of their linkage in Q^mt. In the OT sonship and peace-making are brought together in 1 Chr 22.9–10: 'Behold, a son [Solomon] shall be born to you [David], and he will be a man of *peace*. I will give him *peace* . . . I will give *peace* and quiet to Israel in his days. . . . He shall be my *son*, and I will be his father . . .'. *m. Pe'a* 1.1 associates the making of peace with benefit in the world to come.

10. There is no counterpart to this in Luke, and no evidence that the verse ever stood in Q. All signs, including word statistics, betray a redactional genesis (so Beare, p. 133; Guelich, p. 93; and many others). But why has Matthew added 5.10? Not in order to gain a beatitude about persecution. 5.11–12 satisfies that requirement. Nor in order to give 'righteousness' a home in the beatitudes, for it has already been named in 5.6. Nor even to connect persecution and righteousness, for the evangelist could easily have added 'and righteousness' at the end of 5.11. No, the explanation for 5.10 lies not in its content but instead in a formal consideration: without it there would be only eight beatitudes. Our evangelist has carefully arranged his material throughout chapters 5–7 so as to generate numerous triadic groupings: the number three is the key to the structure of the sermon on the mount. But if so, then the addition of 5.10 makes excellent sense. Matthew wanted the number of the beatitudes to be a multiple of three. So, having received eight beatitudes, he created one more.

μακάριοι οἱ δεδιωγμένοι ἕνεκεν δικαιοσύνης.[48] For the persecution of the righteous see especially Wisd 1.16–5.23; also Mt 23.34–5. There is in the OT no blessing of the persecuted. The verb, διώκω (Mt: 6; Mk: 0; Lk: 3), may refer to physical violence or to verbal abuse or to both. The perfect tense entails that persecution is a fact of the past and of the present. ἕνεκεν most naturally implies that 'righteousness' is the occasion or cause of persecution, although it has been suggested (by e.g. Hare, p. 131) that 'on account of' simply identifies the persecuted ('Blessed are the persecuted righteous'). For δικαιοσύνη (here without the article; contrast 5.6) see on 5.6. 'Righteousness' can here only be

---

[48] HG prints the Attic ενεκα. See, however, BDF § 35.3. Clement of Alexandria, *Strom.* 4.6 has this: μακάριοι, φησίν, οἱ δεδιωγμένοι ἕνεκεν δικαιοσύνης ὅτι αὐτοί υἱοὶ θεοῦ κληθήσονται· ἤ, ὡς τινὲς τῶν μετατιθέντων τὰ εὐαγγέλια, μακάριοι, φησίν, οἱ δεδιωγμένοι ὑπὲρ τῆς δικαιοσύνης, ὅτι αὐτοὶ ἔσονται τέλειοι· καί, μακάριοι οἱ δεδιωγμένοι ἕνεκα ἐμοῦ, ὅτι ἕξουσι τόπον ὅπου οὐ διωχθήσονται.

something people have, namely, their obedient, righteous conduct; 'justification' and 'vindication' are both excluded. So in 5.10 'righteousness' has demonstrably to do with God's demand, not God's gift.[49] This is important for interpreting the other occurrences of δικαιοσύνη in Matthew which are more ambiguous (see further Przybylski, pp. 98–9).

According to S. Lachs (v), pp. 101–3, the original of 5.10 had not 'righteousness' but 'just one': ṣaddîq was mistaken for ṣedeq. Two objections overthrow this conjecture. First, 5.10 does not derive from a Semitic original: it is redactional and was first composed in Greek. Secondly, 5.10 makes perfect sense as it stands, so there is no real need to postulate a different original.

1 Pet 3.14 reads: 'But if you do suffer because of righteousness, (you are) blessed'. If 1 Peter be dated, with many, ca. 90–5, this verse could supply the earliest external attestation to Matthew's gospel (cf. Luz 1, p. 76). If, on the other hand, one is persuaded that 1 Peter should be dated to an earlier time, the resemblances between 1 Pet 3.14 and Mt 5.10 would have to be (1) put down to coincidence or (2) taken as a reason for questioning the redactional origin of the latter or (3) construed as evidence that in creating 5.10 Matthew drew upon traditional material or (4) thought to argue for a very early dating of the First Gospel.

Polycarp, *Ep.* 2.3 reads: 'Blessed are the poor and οἱ διωκόμενοι ἕνεκεν δικαιοσύνης, because theirs is the kingdom of God'. If there is doubt about the implications of 1 Pet 3.14, there is none about this text: it betrays a direct dependence upon Matthew, probably quoted from memory and perhaps with Lukan influence·('poor' lacks 'in spirit' and Polycarp agrees with Luke in having 'kingdom of God', not 'kingdom of heaven').

ὅτι αὐτῶν ἐστιν ἡ βασιλεία τῶν οὐρανῶν. This repeats 5.3b. An *inclusio* is thus formed between the first and eighth beatitudes. Its function is to mark the beginning and end of the formally similar beatitudes, that is, beatitudes 1–8, which are then followed by a ninth that is much different in form. The *inclusio* also implies that the promises in beatitudes 2–7 are all different ways of saying the same thing, namely, 'theirs is the kingdom of heaven', the promise of the first and eighth beatitudes. Yet if 5.10, through the device of repetition, is bound to what precedes it, the verse also points forward by virtue of its subject matter, persecution, to 5.11–12, for persecution is also the subject matter of these two verses. Thus 5.10 is a bridge or transition to 5.11–12.

11. This verse and the next constitute the ninth and concluding beatitude. In Q it served as a bridge between the beatitudes and the

---

[49] So also Barth, in *TIM*, p. 139; Fenton, p. 81; Gundry, *Commentary*, p. 72; Luz 1, p. 214; Przybylski, pp. 89–9; Strecker, *Weg*, p. 154; Reumann, p. 127; and Ziesler, p. 142. But see Giesen, pp. 103–22, for a different opinion. He finds the 'gift character' of righteousness even in 5.10.

teaching on love of enemies: 'Blessed are you when men hate you
. . .' was immediately followed by '. . . do good to those who hate
you . . .'.

In Lk 6.22 persecution takes four forms: the disciples are hated,
excluded, reviled, and their name is cast out as evil. In Mt 5.11
there are only three forms: the disciples are reviled, persecuted,
and spoken against. Probably Matthew's love of the triad is again
in evidence.

μακάριοί ἐστε ὅταν ὀνειδίσωσιν ὑμᾶς.[50] Contrast Luke's last woe,
6.26. Lk 6.22a reads: 'Blessed are you whenever men hate you and
when they exclude and reproach you'. The change in Matthew
from the third person in 5.3–10 to the second in 5.11–12 has two
possible explanations between which it is impossible to choose. (1)
The evangelist could simply be reproducing Q, which juxtaposed
several beatitudes in the third person with a final beatitude in the
second person. In this case, the problem would be pushed back a
stage and would probably best be accounted for in terms of
different sources: Mt 5.11–12 = Lk 6.22–3, which was first
formulated in the second person, originally circulated in isolation
and only later came to be joined to other beatitudes, which had
been formulated in the third person. (2) If Matthew be responsible
for the third person form of 5.3–10 (an issue admitting of no
resolution), the question would then become, Why did he not also
alter 5.11–12? The response to this is probably two-fold. Either he
wished to smooth the transition to 5.13–16 (which is in the second
person: 'You are the salt of the earth', etc.), or he thought it would
be climactic to switch from the third to the second person: 'You
rejoice' and 'you be glad'. Whatever the solution, it must be
admitted that the irregular, long form of 5.11–12 as compared with
5.3–10 makes the change from third to second person less
awkward than it otherwise would be.

Matthew has dropped Q's 'when men hate you (cf. Isa 66.5; Mt
10.22; 24.9; Jn 17.14) and when they exclude (excommunicate?)
you'. This is because, presumably, he wants to keep 'revile' (cf. Isa
51.7 LXX), use a favourite word, διώκω (cf. 5.9, 12), and retain a
reference to speech ('utter all kinds of evil'); and since all this
results in three verbs, and since three is his preferred number, Q's
'hate' and 'exclude' must go. As for his dropping of the subject,
'men' (which in Q may have made a word-play with 'Son of man'),
this leaves an unspecified 'they', which must be the Jewish leaders,
as the rest of the sermon on the mount and Matthew puts beyond
doubt. (Cf. Davies, *SSM*, p. 289, who observes that the RSV
wrongly introduces a subject, 'men'.)

---

[50] οι ανθρωποι is, in conformity to Luke, inserted after 'whenever' in 0133 (aur g[l]
q vg[s]) sy[s.c.].

καὶ διώξωσιν. This is Matthew's preferred word for persecution. See on 5.10. It occurs three times in 5.10–12.

καὶ εἴπωσιν πᾶν πονηρὸν καθ᾽ ὑμῶν ψευδόμενοι ἕνεκεν ἐμοῦ.[51] Lk 6.22c has this: '*and* cast out *your* name as evil *on account of* (ἕνεκα) the Son of man'. (The words in italics are those common to Matthew and Luke.) Despite the great differences between these two verses, we are not required to postulate different sources. Luke, with the exception of the Attic form, ἕνεκα (cf. Lk 6.22; Acts 19.32; 26.21), presumably reproduces Q; for behind 'cast out your name as evil', which is so awkward in Greek, there probably lies a Semitic expression, 'to cause an ill name to go out' (see Black, pp. 135–6). Compare Deut 22.14 (*wĕhôṣîʾ ʾālêhā šēm rāʿ*); 22.19; *m. Ṣoṭa* 3.5; Yer. Tg. on Gen 34.30. In addition, the word-play, man/Son of man, probably appeared in Q. Matthew, it follows, has, in the interests of clarity, simply rewritten Q's awkward, literal translation of a Semitic idiom and, in order to make for conformity with 10.18, 39; and 16.25, changed 'on account of the Son of man' to 'on account of me' (cf. the change in 16.21 = Mk 8.31).[52] Word statistics are consistent with this supposition.[53]

Chrysostom, *Hom. on Mt.* 15.7, wrote: 'Lest thou shouldest think that the mere fact of being evil spoken of makes men blessed, He hath set two limitations; when it is for His sake, and when the things that are said are false: for without these, he who is evil spoken of, so far from being blessed, is miserable.' If, by our gospel's time, Christians had, as 10.17; Jn 9.22; 16.22; and the story of Paul in Acts require, already been denounced in synagogues, this may have been what Matthew's readers thought of when they read of the uttering of all kinds of evil and the delivering of reproaches. Yet the language of 5.11 admittedly remains quite general and could be applied to a wide range of situations, from being the butt of religious jokes to facing accusers in court (cf. 10.15). Furthermore, if something as definite as the synagogue ban were intended, we might have expected Matthew to

[51] 'Falsely', although omitted by D it sy͜s geo Diat͜v Tert Or Eus Did Hil Lcf Aug, is probably original given Matthew's fondness for ψευδο-words (Mt: 9; Mk: 5; Lk: 2). See further Holmes (v). —As in 5.9, HG prints ενεκα.

[52] So also Schulz, *Q*, p. 453; Lührmann, p. 55; Higgins, *JSM*, pp. 119–21; Tuckett (v), p. 203; and Hoffmann, *Logienquelle*, p. 148. This wrecks the generalization of Jeremias, according to whom 'Son of man' is always secondary when it appears in a synoptic text which has a parallel in which a pronoun is used instead of the christological title; see 'Die älteste Schichte der Menschensohn-Logien', *ZNW* 58 (1967), pp. 159–72. On persecution 'for my sake' see Satake (v).

[53] εἶπον + non-personal accusative: Mt 8–9 (without exact parallel in 5.11; 12.32; 17.9; 21.3; 23.3; 26.44); Mk: 5; Lk: 11. κατά + genitive: Mt: 16; Mk: 7; Lk: 6. ψευδο-words: Mt: 9; Mk: 5; Lk: 2. ἕνεκεν (cf. 5.10) + ἐμοῦ: Mt 4 (redactional in 10.39); Mk: 3; Lk: 1.

retain Q's ἀφορίζω (exclude, excommunicate).[54]

In Gos. Thom. 68 'Jesus says: "Blessed are you when they hate you and persecute you. And there will not be found a place in which you have been persecuted in it" '. The common use of the verb, διώκειν, is insufficient reason to postulate influence from Matthew, although such cannot be excluded with certainty. Clement of Alexandria, *Strom.* 4.6 preserves this: 'Blessed are those who have been persecuted (δεδιωγμένοι) on account of me, because they will have a place where they will not be persecuted'. The connexion with Gos. Thom. 68 is evident, but so is the connexion with Matthew ('on account of me'). Perhaps what Clement preserves is a version of the saying preserved in Gos. Thom. 68 which has been slightly modified by knowledge of the First Gospel. 1 Pet 4.14 has: εἰ ὀνειδίζεσθε ἐν ὀνόματι Χριστοῦ, μακάριοι. This does not necessarily reflect Matthew or Luke or Q: it could derive from independent oral tradition, especially since Mt 5.11–12 = Lk 6.22–3 may have circulated in isolation at one time.

12. This verse, which consists of three parts, contains the only two imperatives in the beatitudes: 'rejoice' and 'be glad'. The thought is: since the disciples are being ill-treated just as the prophets of old were, they too must be God's servants;[55] therefore they will have a great reward and, knowing this, can even now rejoice and be glad. (McNeile: 'The joy is to be, not in spite of, but because of persecution'.) So although the kingdom in its fullness has not arrived, thought of its future blessing transforms the present and makes suffering bearable. One is reminded of Jas 5.10–11: 'As an example of suffering and patience, brethren, take the prophets who spoke in the name of the Lord. Behold we call those happy (μακαρίζομεν) who were steadfast'. Compare Betz, *Essays*, p. 26: 'One must read the argument [of 5.12] in reverse, so to speak. The historical verdict rendered in v. 12c leads to the dogmatic judgment in 12b, and both together constitute the basis for the macarism in v. 12a'.

χαίρετε καὶ ἀγαλλιᾶσθε. Compare Tob 13.13; Rev 19.7; Par. Jer. 6.20. Lk 6.23a has: χάρητε ἐν ἐκείνῃ τῇ ἡμέρᾳ καὶ σκιρτήσατε. Note the difference in tenses: Matthew has the present imperative, Luke the aorist imperative. 'In that day' (which has eschatological sense) is probably traditional (cf. Jeremias, *Lukasevangelium*, p. 139). Either Matthew dropped it for reasons we know not or he did not find it in Q^mt. The classical σκιρτάω (= 'leap for joy') is

---

[54] See the detailed discussion in Hummel, pp. 28–33; Hare, pp. 114–21; and Davies, *SSM*, p. 297. None finds that 5.11–12 provides solid evidence for the excommunication of Christians from synagogues.

[55] Against Stendahl, 'Matthew', p. 776; Schweizer, *Matthew*, p. 97; Suggs, p. 121–2; and many others, the disciples are no more called prophets here than are James' readers in Jas 5.10–11 (see text). Speculative is Steck's assertion (p. 283) that for the so-called 'Q community', 5.12 applied only to Christian prophets.

probably Lukan, Matthew's ἀγαλλιάομαι (cf. Isa 61.10 LXX and see BDF § 307) probably from Q. That both words are translation variants of the Aramaic *dûṣ* (so Black, pp. 158, 193) is an unnecessary hypothesis. On joy in suffering see Jdt 8.25; 2 Macc 6.28–30; Acts 5.41; Rom 5.3–5; Phil 4.10–13; Jas 1.2, 12; 1 Pet 1.6; 4.13–14; 2 Bar 48.48–50; 52.5–7; *b. Sanh.* 101a (discussion in W. Nauck, 'Freude im Leiden', *ZNW* 46 (1955), pp. 68–80). According to Montefiore, the exhibition of joy in hardship is 'distinctive of Christianity and of its saints and apostles and martyrs. And doubtless many thousands of humble sufferers have risen superior to their troubles and afflictions through the memory and influence of the beatitudes' (*Gospels* 2, p. 44; but *b. Šabb.* 88b does speak of rejoicing in suffering).

In contrast to Luke, for whom joy and rejoicing are major motifs (1.14, 47; 2.10, 13, 20; 10.20; 15.5, 7, 10, 24, 32; 24.41, 52), Matthew rarely writes of them (although note 2.10 and 13.44). This reflects not only his solemn character but his combative environment. The gospel was written by a man making urgent argument.

ὅτι ὁ μισθὸς ὑμῶν πολὺς ἐν τοῖς οὐρανοῖς. Compare Gen 15.1 and recall the maxim, 'the more enemies the greater the glory'. So Luke, with ἰδοὺ γάρ (Mt: 0; Mk: 0; Lk: 5) rather than ὅτι and the singular 'in the heaven' (a reverential circumlocution meaning 'with God').[56] Both differences may be ascribed to Luke,[57] which permits the inference that Matthew has just reproduced Q. Luke/Acts has 'heaven' fifty-three times, 'heavens' only six times (cf. Jeremias, *Lukasevangelium*, p. 113). On the concept of μισθός (= 'reward', not 'good repute' or 'glory') see on 6.21. 'Reward' signals what matters most, this being divine approval.

οὕτως γὰρ ἐδίωξαν τοὺς προφήτας τοὺς πρὸ ὑμῶν. Compare 23.31, 36; Acts 7.52. Mt 23.31 raises the possibility that the 'scribes and Pharisees' are the unexpressed subjects of 5.11–12, for in 23.31–6 they are named as the sons of those who murdered the prophets. Lk 6.23c has: 'For so (κατὰ τὰ αὐτά) their fathers did to the prophets'. The expression in parenthesis may or may not be Lukan. While it occurs only three times in the NT, and all three times in Luke (6.23, 26; 17.30), it could be characteristic not of Luke but of the pre-Lukan tradition (so Jeremias, *Lukasevangelium*, p. 139; against Marshall, p. 254). In any case, οὕτως (Mt: 32; Mk: 10; Lk: 21) and διώκω (Mt: 6; Mk: 0; Lk: 3) are Matthean. 'Their fathers' must be ascribed to the hand of Luke (so

[56] Discussion in Dalman, *Words*, pp. 206–8. According to M. Pamment, 'Matthew and the kingdom of heaven', *NTS* 27 (1981), p. 214, Matthew's 'in the heavens' means 'in the kingdom of heaven'.

[57] Yet ἰδού also appears in Jas 5.10–11, which could draw upon a variant of Mt 5.11–12 = Lk 6.22–3.

also Dupont 1, pp. 246–9) for, in addition to Luke's dislike of impersonal subjects, the plural of πατήρ with the meaning of 'forefathers' or 'ancestors' is used twice in Matthew, never in Mark, six times in Luke, and nineteen times in Acts. Whether Matthew's πρό + ὑμῶν reproduces Q it is impossible to say. It is not, however, likely to be a mistranslation of *qādāmêhôn* (= 'before them') read as *qādāmêkôn* ('before you'; against Black, pp. 191–2; cf. Hare, pp. 174–5).

Highly implausible is the claim of K. Schubert[58] that the prophets of Mt 5.12 were Essenes. The members of the Dead Sea sect were, we can have no doubt, the recipients of abuse. But that they would be pre-eminently called to mind by the phrase, 'the prophets before you', is without foundation.

The mention of those who killed the prophets puts Mt 5.12 in the line of a well-established tradition.[59] Already in the OT itself we find the notion that true prophets are put to death by the disobedient people of Israel. The earliest text is Neh. 9.26: 'Nevertheless they were disobedient and rebelled against thee and cast thy law behind their back and killed thy prophets, who had warned them in order to turn them back to thee, and they committed great blasphemies. Therefore thou didst give them into the hand of their enemies . . .'. Other OT passages reflecting this theme or contributing to it include the following: 1 Kgs 18.4, 13; 19.10, 14; 2 Chr 24.20–1; 36.15–21; Jer 2.30; 26.20–4.

In intertestamental sources, the link between prophet and martyrdom becomes almost fixed; and 'the fate of the prophet' is typically violent death. Martyrdom is indeed a proof or badge of the prophetic office. See especially the Lives of the Prophets; also Jub. 1.12; 4QpHos[a] 2.3–6;[60] Josephus, *Ant.* 10.38; Asc. Isa. 2.16; 5.1–14; Par. Jer. 9.21–32; Tg. on Isa 28.1. The NT picks up where these Jewish sources leave off; see Mt 13.57; 21.35–6; 22.6; 23.29–32, 34–7; Mk 6.4; 12.2–5; Lk 4.24; 11.47–51; 13.33–4; Jn 4.44; Acts 7.51–2; Rom 11.3; Heb 11.32–8; Jas 5.10–1; Rev 11.6–7; 16.6; 18.24. Particularly noteworthy is 1 Th 2.14–16: 'For you, brethren, became imitators of the churches of God in Christ Jesus which are in Judea; for you suffered the same things from your own countrymen as they did from the Jews, who killed both the Lord Jesus and the prophets, and drove us out, and displease God and oppose all men by hindering us from speaking to the Gentiles that they may be saved—so as always to fill up the measure of their sins. But God's wrath has come upon them at last.' Here the motif of the prophets' martyrdom is connected not only with the rejection of Jesus but also with the persecution of Jesus' followers, in this case Paul and his co-workers. This is not far from Mt 5.12, in which the

---

[58] In Stendahl, *Scrolls*, pp. 118–28. Note the criticism of Braun, *Qumran* 1, p. 14.

[59] See O. Michel, *Prophet und Märtyrer*, BFTh 37, 2, Gütersloh, 1932; Schoeps, *Zeit*, pp. 126–43; H. A. Fischel, 'Martyr and Prophet', *JQR* 37 (1946–7), pp. 265–80, 363–86; Steck, passim; B. H. Amaru, 'The Killing of the Prophets: Unraveling a Midrash', *HUCA* 54 (1983), pp. 153–80.

[60] On this see D. C. Carlson, 'An Alternative Reading of 4QpHos[a] 2.3–6', *RevQ* 11 (1983), pp. 417–21.

disciples of Jesus are persecuted as were the prophets of old. In both texts the rhyme and reason for the persecution of Christians are illumined by reference to the past persecution of God's special messengers, the prophets.

(iv) *Concluding Observations*

(1) We have argued (pp. 439–40) that the beatitudes are first of all blessings, not requirements. So by opening the sermon on the mount they place it within the context of grace, and their function is very similar to the function of 4.23–5.2: just as healing comes before imperative, so does blessing come before demand. The precedence of grace could not be plainer. The hard commands of Mt 5–7 presuppose God's mercy and prior saving activity.

(2) According to Mt 5.3–12, the kingdom of God will bring eschatological comfort, a permanent inheritance, true satisfaction, the obtaining of mercy, the vision of God, and divine sonship. In brief, it will in every way bring the *telos* of the religious quest. Thus the word 'kingdom' serves to foretell the eventual realization in human experience of the fullness of God's bounteous presence. 'Kingdom' is indeed almost a surrogate for God, and it is rightly considered the *summum bonum* of Matthew's gospel. No other subject, then, could more fittingly lead off the sermon on the mount, Matthew's first and most important discourse.

(3) The dependence of 5.3–12 upon Isa 61.1–3 (see pp. 436–9) implicitly reveals the identity of the one who proclaims the sermon on the mount. In the OT text the person who brings good tidings to the poor and comforts those in mourning is an anointed one and bearer of the Spirit. So when Jesus blesses the poor and those in mourning, one cannot resist the conclusion: Jesus is the anointed one upon whom the Spirit of God rests. He is the Messiah. Moreover, he and his ministry are the fulfilment of OT prophecy. This supplies the sermon on the mount with an eschatological framework and makes Jesus an eschatological figure. What follows? First, the words of Jesus are the result of a divine commissioning for the purpose of bringing OT promise to fulfilment. This fact sets Jesus apart from all other teachers (cf. 7.28–9) and makes intelligible the authority with which he speaks. Secondly, we have discerned a Mosaic motif in 5.1–2 and found that 5.3–12 sets 5.13ff. in an eschatological context. These facts are so important because a lengthy discourse treating of the law (5.17–48), the cult (6.1–18), and social issues (6.19–7.12), and uttered in an eschatological situation by an anointed one like Moses, is naturally thought of as being 'messianic Torah'.

(4) Jesus was himself meek (11.29; 21.5). Jesus mourned (26.36–46). Jesus was righteous and 'fulfilled all righteousness' (3.15; 27.4, 19). Jesus showed mercy (9.27; 15.22; 17.15; 20.30–1). And Jesus was persecuted and reproached (26–7). So the beatitudes are illustrated and brought to life by Jesus' actions. He embodies his own words and thereby becomes the standard or model to be imitated (cf. Origen in PG 13.152).

(5) In so far as the beatitudes bring consolation and comfort to Jesus' heavy-laden followers, they function as a practical theodicy. Although 5.3–12 does not explain evil or human suffering, the verses do, by putting into perspective the difficulties of the present, lessen pain and anguish and effect encouragement (cf. 10.26–30). This happens through an exercise of the imagination (cf. on 9.12). Eschatological promises for the poor, the meek, and the persecuted reveal that all is not what it seems to be. That is, the truth, like the kingdom, is hidden (cf. 11.25; 13.33, 44). Only the future—with its rewards and punishments—will bring to light the true condition of the world and those in it (cf. 25.31–46). Those who use the eye of the mind in order to foresee and live for the future promised by the beatitudes will, with their faith, possess a secret vision and hope that makes powerlessness and suffering bearable. See further section (iv) for 7.13–29.

(v) *Bibliography*

S. Agouridès, 'La tradition des béatitudes chez Matthieu et Luc', in Descampes, *Mélanges*, pp. 9–27.
B. W. Bacon, 'The Blessing of the Peacemakers', *ExpT* 41 (1929), pp. 58–60.
K. Barth, *CD* 4/2, pp. 289–92.
I. W. Batsdorf, *Interpreting the Beatitudes*, Philadelphia, 1966.
Beasley-Murray, pp. 157–69.
E. Best, 'Matthew V.3', *NTS* 7 (1961), pp. 255–8.
H. D. Betz, 'Die Makarismen der Bergpredigt (Matthäus 5,3–12)', *ZTK* 75 (1978), pp. 3–19; translated and reprinted in *Essays*, pp. 17–36.
M. Black, 'The Beatitudes', *ExpT* 64 (1953), pp. 125–6.
F. Böhl, 'Die Demut (*'nwh*) als höchste der Tugenden. Bemerkungen zu Mt 5.3,5', *BZ* 20 (1976), pp. 217–23.
M. E. Boring, 'The Criteria of Authenticity: the Lukan Beatitudes as a Test Case', *Forum* 1/4 (1985), pp. 3–38.
G. Braumann, 'Zum traditionsgeschichtlichen Probleme der Seligpreisungen Mt v 3–12', *NovT* 4 (1960), pp. 253–60.
I. Broer, *Die Seligpreisungen der Bergpredigt*, BBB 61, Bonn, 1986.
G. W. Buchanan, 'Matthean Beatitudes and Traditional Promises', in Farmer, *Studies*, pp. 161–84.
H. Bürki, 'Die geistlichen Armen', in *Abraham unser Vater*, AGSU 5, ed.

O. Betz, M. Hengel, and P. Schmidt, Leiden, 1963, pp. 58–64.

C. H. Cave, 'The Sermon at Nazareth and Beatitudes in the Light of the Synagogue Lectionary', in *Studia Evangelica*, vol. 3, ed. F. L. Cross, Berlin, 1964, pp. 231–5.

Crossan, *Aphorisms*, pp. 168–71.

Davies, *GL*, pp. 359–63.

C. H. Dodd, 'The Beatitudes: A form-critical study', in *MNTS*, pp. 1–10.

W. J. Dumbrell, 'The Logic of the Role of the Law in Matthew v 1–20', *NovT* 23 (1981), pp. 1–21.

Dupont, I, II, III, passim.

idem, 'Les πτωχοὶ τῷ πνεύματι de Matthieu 5,3 et les *'nwy rwh* de Qumrân', in *Neutestamentliche Aufsätze*, ed. J. Blinzler, O. Kuss, and F. Mussner, Regensburg, 1963, pp. 53–64.

idem, 'Introduction aux béatitudes', *NRT* 98 (1976), pp. 97–108.

D. Flusser, 'Blessed are the Poor in Spirit . . .', *IEJ* 10 (1960), pp. 1–13.

idem, 'Some Notes on the Beatitudes (Matthew 5:3–12, Luke 6:20–6)', *Immanuel* 8 (1978), pp. 37–47.

H. Frankemölle, 'Die Makarismen (Mt 5,1–12; Lk 6,20–3): Motive und Umfang der redaktionellen Komposition', *BZ* 15 (1971), pp. 52–75.

Friedlander, pp. 11–23.

A. George, 'La "forme" des béatitudes jusqu'à Jésus', in *Mélanges bibliques A. Robert*, Paris, 1957, pp. 398–403.

Giesen, pp. 79–122.

Goulder, pp. 252–69, 272–9.

R. Guelich, 'The Matthean Beatitudes: "Entrance Requirements" or Eschatological Beatitudes?', *JBL* 95 (1976), pp. 415–34.

Grimm, pp. 68–77.

W. Grimm, 'Die Hoffnung der Armen. Zu den Seligpreisungen Jesu', *TB* 11 (1980), pp. 100–13.

Hare, pp. 114–21, 174–5.

Hoffmann, *Logienquelle*, pp. 182–7.

P. Hoffmann, ' "Selig sind die Armen . . .". Auslegung der Bergpredigt II (Mt 5,3–16)', *BuL* 10 (1969), pp. 111–22.

M. W. Holmes, 'The Text of Matthew 5.11', *NTS* 32 (1986), pp. 283–6.

R. Kieffer, 'Weisheit und Segen als Grundmotiv der Seligpreisungen bei Matthäus und Lukas', in *Theologie aus dem Norden*, SUNT A2 (1977), pp. 29–43.

W. Kirchschläger, 'Die Friedensbotschaft der Bergpredigt. Zu Mt 5,9.17–48; 7.1–5', *Kairos* 25 (1983), pp. 223–37.

K. Koch, *The Growth of the Biblical Tradition* (trans. of *Was ist Formgeschichte?*, 1967), New York, 1969, pp. 6–8, 16–18, 28–9, 39–44, 59–62.

S. Légasse, 'Les pauvres en esprit et les "volontaires" de Qumran', *NTS* 8 (1962), pp. 336–45.

E. Lipiński, 'Macarismes et psaumes de congratulation', *RB* 75 (1968), pp. 321–67.

C. C. McCown, 'The Beatitudes in the Light of Ancient Ideals', *JBL* 46 (1927), pp. 50–61.

N. J. McEleney, 'The Beatitudes of the Sermon on the Mount/Plain', *CBQ* 43 (1981), pp. 1–13.

H. Merklein, *Die Gottesherrschaft als Handlungsprinzip*, FB 34,

Würzburg, 1978, pp. 48–55.

C. Michaelis, 'Die π-Alliteration der Subjektsworte der ersten 4 Seligpreisungen in Mt v 3–6 und ihre Bedeutung für den Aufbau der Seligpreisungen bei Mt., Lk., und in Q', *NovT* 10 (1968), pp. 148–61.

T. Y. Mullins, 'Ascription as a Literary Form', *NTS* 19 (1973), pp. 194–205.

B. M. Newman, 'Some Translational Notes on the Beatitudes. Matthew 5.1–12', *BT* 26 (1975), pp. 106–20.

Percy, pp. 40–108.

Przybylski, pp. 96–9.

M. J. Rife, 'Matthew's Beatitudes and the Septuagint', in *Studies in the History and Text of the New Testament*, ed. B. L. Daniels and M. J. Suggs, Salt Lake City, 1967, pp. 107–12.

V. Rodzianko, 'The Meaning of Matthew 5, 3', in *Studia Evangelica*, vol. 3, ed. F. L. Cross, Berlin, 1964, pp. 229–35.

A. Satake, 'Das Leiden der Jünger "um meinetwillen" ', *ZNW* 67 (1976), pp. 4–19.

Schlosser 2, pp. 423–50.

R. Schnackenburg, 'Die Seligpreisung der Friedensstifter (Mt 5,9) im matthäischen Kontext', *BZ* 26 (1982), pp. 161–78.

Schulz, *Q*, pp. 76–84, 452–7.

G. Schwarz, ' "Ihnen gehört das Himmelreich"? (Matthäus v. 3)', *NTS* 23 (1977), pp. 341–3.

E. Schweizer, 'Formgeschichtliches zu den Seligpreisungen Jesu', *NTS* 19 (1972), pp. 121–6. Also in *Gemeinde*, pp. 69–77.

Steck, pp. 20–7.

W. Stegemann, *The Gospel and the Poor* (trans. of *Das Evangelium und die Armen*, 1981), Philadelphia, 1984.

G. Strecker, 'Die Makarismen der Bergpredigt', *NTS* 17 (1971), pp. 255–75.

C. M. Tuckett, 'The Beatitudes: A Source-Critical Study', *NovT* 25 (1983), pp. 192–207. There is a reply on pp. 208–16 by M. D. Goulder.

N. Walter, 'Die Bearbeitung der Seligpreisungen durch Matthäus', in *Studia Evangelica*, vol. 4, TU 102, ed. F. L. Cross, Berlin, 1968, pp. 246–58.

H. Windisch, 'Friedensbringer—Gottessöhne', *ZNW* 24 (1925), pp. 240–60.

Wrege, pp. 5–34.

W. Zimmerli, 'Die Seligpreisungen der Bergpredigt und das Alte Testament', in *Donum Gentilicium*, ed. E. Bammel, C. K. Barrett, and W. D. Davies, Oxford, 1978, pp. 8–26.

Zumstein, pp. 283–308.

X

SUMMARY STATEMENT OF THE TASK OF THE PEOPLE OF GOD IN THE WORLD (5.13–16)

(i) *Structure*

Although 5.13–16 contains three parables (on salt, on the high city, on the lamp), it most naturally divides itself into two sub-sections, one headed by 'You are the salt of the earth' (5.13), the other by 'You are the light of the world' (5.14–16).

  I. A parable: on salt (13)
    A. Descriptive affirmation: 'You are . . .' (13a)
    B. Question: 'If salt . . .' (13b)
    C. Answer: 'It is good for nothing . . .' (13c)
  II. Two parables (14–16)
    A. Descriptive affirmation: 'You are . . .' (14a)
    B. First parable: 'A city . . .' (14b)
    C. Second parable (15–16)
      i. Negative generalization: 'They do not . . .' (15a)
      ii. Positive generalization: 'But on a lampstand . . .' (15b)
      iii. Application/imperative: 'Let your light . . .' (16)[1]

(ii) *Sources*

What are the sources of 5.13–16? The following offers an overview of the parallels:

  5.13a—no parallel (redactional)
    13b—cf. Lk 14.34b (Q); Mk 9.50
    13c—cf. Lk 14.35a (Q)
    14a—no parallel (redactional)
    14b—cf. Gos. Thom. 32; *P. Oxy.* 1.7
    15—cf. Lk 11.33 (Q); Mk 4.21; Lk 8.16; Gos. Thom. 33b
    16—no parallel (redactional)

---

[1] Suggs (v) offers a different analysis. Comparing 16.17–19, which has a benediction ('Blessed are you, Simon Bar-Jonah!. . . .), the bestowal of a name ('I tell you, you are Peter . . .'), and a commissioning ('I will give you the keys of the kingdom of heaven . . .'), he divides Mt 5.11–16 thus: benediction (11–12), bestowal of names (13–15), commission (16). The problem with this is that 5.11–12 is best linked up with 5.3–10; see p. 430 herein. 5.13–16, not 5.11–16, is the unit to be analysed.

If one assumes the priority of Mark and the Q hypothesis, three conclusions are irresistible. (1) The unity of Mt 5.13–16 is secondary. The section is made up of two sayings drawn from different sections of Q (see Lk 14.34–5 and 11.33) and a third logion (5.14b) derived from another source (M).[2] (2) Since 5.13 = Lk 14.34–5 and 5.15 = Lk 11.33 have imperfect parallels in Mk 4.21 and 9.50, since the verses in Matthew and Luke appear in non-Markan contexts, and since Lk 11.33 is a doublet of Lk 8.16 = Mk 4.21, it is necessary to postulate Markan/Q overlap for the sayings on salt and light. (3) Matthew's redactional sentences come precisely at the beginning of each paragraph (5.13a, 14a) and at the end of the entire section (5.16).

Against the Griesbach hypothesis, three queries may be directed. (1) Is it not odd that, on the thesis of Matthean priority, there is no Markan or Lukan parallel to the three clauses or verses which most clearly stem from Matthew's hand, namely, vv. 13a, 14a, and 16? (2) Is it not striking that, if Mark used Matthew and Luke, he chose to replace the μωρανθῇ of Mt 5.13 = Lk 14.34 with ἄναλον γένηται (9.50), and that the Hebrew (and Aramaic) *tpl* means both 'to be foolish' and 'to become saltless'? If ever there were good candidates for translation variants these would seem to qualify. (3) Is it not true that, as shall be argued in section iii, the Markan and Lukan parallels to Mt 5.13–16 sometimes seem more likely to preserve the more primitive reading *vis-à-vis* Matthew (see on 5.13 and 15)?

(iii) *Exegesis*

13. This and the following verses serve as the heading for 5.17–7.12. In 5.13 would-be disciples are told that they are the salt of the earth, in 5.14–16 that they are the light of the world. The statements are quite general. The reader is not told how to become salt or light. This is because 5.13–16, as a general description or superscription, stands above the detailed paraenesis proper. It is a transitional passage in which the speaker moves from the life of the blessed future (5.3–12) to the demands of life in the present (5.17–7.12), in which the theme switches from gift to task, and in which those who live as 5.17–7.12 will direct are summarily characterized. In short, in 5.13–16 descriptive names are bestowed upon those who live as the sermon on the mount demands.

'You are the salt of the earth' and 'you are the light of the world' would probably have struck most Jewish ears as being at least implicitly polemical. For it is not the Torah or the temple or Jerusalem or Israel or some group within Israel (such as the Pharisees) that is the salt or light of the world (cf. Isa 60.1–3; Bar

---

[2] Luz 1, p. 220, however, assigns 14b to Q^{mt}.

4.2; LAB 11.1; L. Proph. Hab. 10; *Pesiq. Rab. Kah.* 21.5; *b. Ber.* 28b; SB 1, p. 237) but Jesus' followers (the 'you' is emphatic).[3] Moreover, Jesus' followers are not the salt and light of *Israel* (contrast T. Levi 14.3) but of the whole *world* (the passage thus presupposes the Gentile mission).

ὑμεῖς ἐστε τὸ ἅλας τῆς γῆς. This is redactional (cf. v. 14a). The second person address follows smoothly upon the second person verbs and pronouns in vv. 11–12. ἅλας is the common LXX and NT form; otherwise it is rare. Note the article: the disciples' rôle is theirs alone (cf. BDF § 273.1). γῆ (= 'all those dwelling on the earth', as in Gen 11.1; 18.35; Mt10.34[4]) is a Matthean favourite (Mt: 43; Mk: 19; Lk: 25). Within its context, 'you are the salt of the earth' is strikingly paradoxical: the world is saved precisely by those it persecutes (see 5.10–12).

As to what is meant in this passage by salt, the options are many. The following considerations are pertinent. (1) In Lev. 2.13 and Ezek. 43.24 salt is prescribed as an element to be added to sacrifices (cf. Ezra 6.9; Jub. 21.11; 11QTemple 20; *m. Mid.* 5.3). (2) In Num 18.19 and Lev 2.13 the 'salt of the covenant' is mentioned (cf. 2 Chr 13.5; Jub. 21.11; 11QTemple 20.13; *Sipra* on Num 18.19). (3) In 2 Kgs 2.19–23 Elisha performs a miracle and uses salt in order to purify bad drinking water. The connexion between salt and purity is also found in Exod 30.35 (the salt mixed with incense is called 'pure and holy') and perhaps Ezek 16.4 (where infants are rubbed with salt; cf. *b. Šabb.* 129b). (4) In Job 6.6 salt is a condiment for food (cf. Plutarch, *De garrul.* 23, 514–15; Col 4.6; *b. Ber.* 34a). (5) In Ignatius, *Magn.* 10 salt is a preservative. Compare Diogenes Laertius 8.1.35: salt 'should be brought to table to remind us of what is right; for salt preserves whatever it finds, and it arises from the purest sources, sun and sea'. Note also *b. Ketub.* 66b and *ARN* 17: 'the salt of money' is 'diminution' (that is, charity preserves wealth). (6) In Ecclus 39.26 we find this: 'Basic to all the needs of man's life are water and fire and iron and salt . . .'. Compare Pliny, *Nat. hist.* 31.102: 'there is nothing more useful than salt and sunshine' (cf. 31.88). In these two texts salt is a necessity. (7) In Ezra 4.14 those who eat the salt of the palace cannot be witnesses against the king. To eat salt with someone is therefore a sign of loyalty (cf. the 'salt of the covenant'). (8) In Mk 9.50 salt is linked with peace: 'Have salt in yourselves and be at peace with one another'. Salt and friendship are also associated in Philo, *Som.* 2.210. (9) Col 4.5 reads: 'Let your speech always be gracious, seasoned with salt, so that you may know how you ought

[3] On the lips of Jesus, however, the saying on salt could have been uttered as a warning to Israel (cf. Lk 14.25–35). For the suggestion that Qumran may lie in the background see Davies, *SSM*, pp. 249–50, 457.

[4] Contra Dumbrell (v), who equates 'earth' with the land of Israel.

to answer every one'. (10) In rabbinic texts salt is sometimes associated with wisdom, as in *m. Soṭa* 9.15: 'the wisdom of the scribes will become insipid'.[5] (11) In the Greek tradition salt is 'beloved of the gods' (Homer, *Il*. 9.214; Plato, *Tim*. 60E) and often spoken of as being the 'spice' (= wit) of conversation (Plutarch, *Mor*. 514 F; Dio Chrysostom, *Or*. 18.13).

Given the various uses for salt (cf. Pliny, *Nat. hist*. 31.73–92, 98–105) and its several symbolic associations, it is quite impossible to decide what one characteristic is to the fore in Mt 5.13. Thus, while it would make sense to affirm that the disciples are, for example, the world's wisdom, it would also be reasonable to think that the pure in heart (5.8) purify the world, or (as Origen, *C. Cels*. 8.70 has it) that Jesus' followers preserve the world, or that they are willing to sacrifice themselves (cf. Schnackenburg (v), pp. 195–6). But, as is implied by two facts, the ambiguity of 'salt' need not trouble; for salt was probably equivocal and multivocal for our evangelist. First, 5.13 is part of the introduction or superscription of 5.17–7.12, and this last is comprehensive, covering as it does the law, the cult, and social issues. 5.13 should also, therefore, be comprehensive. Secondly, 'you are the salt of the earth' stands in parallel to 'you are the light of the world', and in 5.14–16 the light is understood very broadly, being associated with good deeds in general. It would appear, then, that salt is, like light, a symbol which should not be delimited to any one referent. The disciples, like salt, have several characteristic qualities, qualities without which they would cease to be what they are and instead become useless.

Luther (p. 54) wrote: 'salt is not salt for itself, it cannot salt itself'. So also is it with the disciples: what they are they are for the world, not for themselves.

ἐὰν δὲ τὸ ἅλας μωρανθῇ ἐν τίνι ἁλισθήσεται; So Mk 9.50, with ἄναλον γένηται for μωρανθῇ and αὐτὸ ἀρτύσετε for ἁλισθήσεται. So Lk 14.34, with ἀρτυθήσεται for ἁλισθήσεται. As an introductory declaration, both Mark and Luke have 'salt is good', which Matthew has replaced with 'you are the salt of the earth'.

There has been much discussion as to whether or not salt—which was gathered from evaporation pools or from the edge of the Dead Sea (Ezek 47.9–11; Zeph 2.9; Josephus, *Ant*. 13.128)—can in fact lose its savour (see Marshall, pp. 595–7). But the question about salt may simply be hypothetical hyperbole, or—more probably, as 5.13c is about salt being thrown out—it should be explained by the indisputable fact that salt can be so mixed with impurities as to become useless (cf. Pliny, *Nat. hist*. 31.82).

[5] See further Nauck (v), who argues that the metaphorical equation of salt with wisdom is the key to Mt 5.13. For light as wisdom see H. Conzelmann, *TWNT* 9, pp. 314–6.

Matthew and Luke agree against Mark in having μωρανθῇ, literally, 'becomes foolish'. Mark has ἄναλον γένηται. The explanation for this difference is probably to be found in the Hebrew or Aramaic *tpl*, which means both 'to be foolish' (Job 1.22; 24.12; Jer 23.13) or 'to be ἄναλος' (Job 6.6; cf. Ezek 13.10 Aq.); see Black, p. 166; Jeremias, *Theology*, p. 28. So we appear to have translation variants. The supposition is supported by the possibility of a word-play in Aramaic: 'if salt has lost its taste (*tāpēl*), how shall it be seasoned (*tabbĕlunneh*)'?

εἰς οὐδὲν ἰσχύει ἔτι εἰ μὴ βληθὲν ἔξω καταπατεῖσθαι ὑπὸ τῶν ἀνθρώπων.[6] There is nothing corresponding to this in Mk 9.50. Lk 14.35, however, reads: 'It is fit neither for the land (εἰς γῆν) nor for the dunghill; men throw it away (ἔξω βάλλουσιν—into the street). He who has ears to hear, let him hear'. This Lukan text demonstrates that Mt 5.13 = Lk 14.34–5 derives firstly from Q, not Mk 9.50. We are thus led to postulate a Markan/Q overlap: both Mark's source and Q had the saying about salt becoming bad, Mark in an abbreviated version.

With regard to the reconstruction of Q, Luke seems more original (so also Schulz, *Q*, p. 471, and Jeremias, *Lukasevangelium*, p. 243). Thus εἰς οὐδὲν ἰσχύει summarizes Luke's 'it is fit neither for the land nor for the dunghill'. Nevertheless, the vocabulary of 5.13a is not obviously redactional—with the exception of ὑπὸ ἀνθρώπων (Mt: 4; Mk: 0; Lk: 0; the expression is rare in the LXX; see Ecclus 3.17; 45.1; 2 Macc 7.14; 4 Macc 18.3). εἰ μή here means 'but' (cf. 12.4; Lk 4.26, 27; Gal 1.19). 'Throw out' perhaps hints at the last judgement (cf. 8.12; 22.13; 25.30). καταπατέω appears only twice in the synoptics, here and in Mt 7.6 (cf. 2 Macc 8.2). The word can mean 'treat with disdain' (BAGD, s.v.).

If, as 5.13a implies, Israel is no longer the salt of the earth, then likewise the church, as 5.13b–c implies, can lose its savour and suffer rejection: there are no guarantees of privileged status.[7]

14. The saints are the locus of God's activity in the world; and

---

[6] D W it sy^{s.c.p} Cyp omit ετι. For βληθεν εξω—so ℵ B C*f*¹ 33 892 *pc* Or—βληθηναι εξω και appears in D K W Δ Θ Π *f*¹³ Maj latt sy^{p.h.} arm geo Diat.

[7] It may be that *b. Bek.* 8b preserves a rabbinic response to Jesus' saying about salt. R. Joshua b. Ḥaninia purportedly said: 'There was once a mule which had a foal. On this was hung a chain with the inscription that it should raise 100,000 Zuz from its father's family. He was asked: Can then a mule bear offspring? He said: These are fables. He was then asked, When salt loses its savour, wherewith shall it be salted (*mylḥ' ky sry' bm'y mlḥy lh*)? He answered: With the young of a mule. He was then asked: Does then the unfruitful mule have young? He answered: Can salt lose its savour?' T. W. Manson (*Sayings*, p. 132) commented: 'The natural interpretation of this is that in the Rabbi's view Israel is a salt that does not become insipid, and therefore stands in no need of seasoning, least of all by Jesus' disciples'. Yet one cannot be certain that *b. Bek.* 8b betrays a knowledge of the Jesus tradition. It may rather indicate only that Mt 5.13 parr. incorporates a proverbial sentence, an observation of common wisdom. Cf. Luz 1, p. 222, n. 29.

God, who is and gives off light (Job 29.2–3; Ps 4.6; 18.28; 31.16; 2 Cor 4.6), shines through them as he shone through Jesus (4.16). As St John of the Cross would later put it, the followers of Jesus are to be windows through which the divine light enters the world. For people as lights—a very common metaphor—see Isa 42.6; 49.6; Dan 12.3; Ecclus 48.1; 1 En. 104.2; 2 Bar. 77.13–16; T. Levi 14.3–4; T. Job 31.5; Mt 4.16; Mt 6.22–3 par.; Acts 13.47; Rom 2.19; Eph 5.8–9; Phil 2.15; Par. Jer. 9.14; Apoc. Adam 83.3–4; b. Sanh. 14a; b. B. Bat. 4a; ARN 25.

ὑμεῖς ἐστε τὸ φῶς τοῦ κόσμου. This is redactional (cf. 5.13a), although 'the light of the world' (cf. nēr šel 'ôlām) was a traditional phrase (cf. Isa 49.6; Jn 8.12; Apoc. Abr. 9.3; b. B. Bat. 4a; ARN 25). There is no parallel in either Mark or Luke. Both φῶς (Mt: 7 (redactional in 5.16 and 17.2); Mk: 1; Lk: 7) and κόσμος (Mt: 9; Mk: 2; Lk: 3) are words Matthew likes. Cicero, Cat. 4.6, describes Rome as 'a light to the whole world'.

οὐ δύναται πόλις κρυβῆναι ἐπάνω ὄρους κειμένη.[8] This intrusive line probably reproduces a traditional wisdom saying. Compare Gos. Thom. 32 = P. Oxy. 1.7: 'Jesus said: A city being built on a high mountain, made strong, can neither fall nor be hidden'.[9] κρύπτω (Mt: 7; Mk: 0; Lk: 3), ἐπάνω (Mt: 8; Mk: 1; Lk: 5), and ὄρος (see on 5.1) can be considered Matthean favourites. For κεῖμαι with πόλις see 2 Macc 4.33.

Since Gerhard von Rad (v) made the suggestion, it has been common to think of the city set on a mountain as the new Jerusalem (cf. Campbell (v); Donaldson, p. 117). And, it must be conceded, there are texts supporting this conjecture. The new Jerusalem was to be raised to a great height and shed its light throughout all the world (cf. Isa 2.2–4; 60.1–22; Mic 4.1–3; Sib. Or. 5.420–3; Rev 21.10–11). In the words of Pesiqta de Rab Kahana, 'Jerusalem is destined to be a beacon for the nations of the earth, and they will walk in its light' (20.7). Yet one hesitates. 5.14b is perfectly understandable if any city is meant, and there is no definite article. Furthermore, the force of 5.14b lies in 'hidden', not in 'city', as 5.15 (the lamp under a bushel) proves. The parallel 5.15 also belies the proposed interpretation because the lamp in that verse is no particular lamp: any lamp would fit the bill.[10]

15. The function of a lamp—a small terra cotta oil lamp is

[8] For κειμενη sy[s.c] Hil Ps.-Clem. Hom 3.67.1 Diat have ωκοδομημενη, P. Oxy. 1.7 οικοδομημενη (sic).

[9] Ahikar 68 (Lindenberger, p. 159): 'A man of (fi)ne character and a happy disposition is like a mighty c(it)y which is bu(ilt) on a h(ill)'.

[10] Against Derrett, 'Lamp' (v) and 'Light' (v), the Hanukkah lamp is not in the picture. For speculation of the older commentators as to what particular high city of Galilee Jesus supposedly pointed to as he spoke of the city on a hill see Alford 1, p. 41.

envisioned[11]—is to give light to those around it. What one should therefore do with a lamp is set it on a lampstand, where it best fulfils its function. One would certainly not put it under a container. Likewise is it with the disciples of Jesus. Their unselfish purpose is to bring God's light to the world around them. So they must be in the world for the world. To hide themselves away would be a betrayal of God's purposes for them.

In its pre-Easter *Sitz im Leben*,[12] the parable of 5.15 probably compared Jesus the prophet or his prophetic message (light = teaching in many texts, such as Prov 6.23; Par. Jer. 6.12; *b. Ta'an.* 7b) with a lamp in order to bring home the point that one or the other or both had to be manifested before the world despite all opposition and danger.[13] In Mark the reference is to Jesus or the gospel, in Gos. Thom. 33 to the gospel. In Luke the inner light (cf. 11.34–6) is apparently the theme, although this is far from certain. In Matthew the parable is applied to the disciples.

οὐδὲ καίουσιν λύχνον. Lk 11.33 has: οὐδεὶς λύχνον ἅψας (cf. Lk 8.16). Matthew's third person plural, which functions as a passive (cf. 9.2; 17.27), might be an Aramaism (see Jülicher 2, pp. 80–1; Black, pp. 126–7) and therefore judged original, Luke having improved upon the Greek. Yet because Matthew shows a fondness for οὐ, οὐδέ . . . οὐδέ (Mt: 18; Mk: 3; Lk: 11), and because Luke does not like asyndeton (Jeremias, *Lukasevangelium*, pp. 60–1), certainty eludes us. ἅπτω (Mt: 9; Mk: 11; Lk: 13) is surely Lukan. καίω (Mt: 1; Mk: 0; Lk: 2; the word implies less the act of lighting than the attempt to keep something burning; so BAGD, s.v.) cannot readily be assigned to Matthew's hand; and of all the NT writers, only Luke uses ἅπτω with the sense of 'light' or 'kindle'. For his part, Matthew has added δέ, which links vv. 14 and 15. Mk 4.21 has: μήτι ἔρχεται ὁ λύχνος. Between this and Q (= Matthew's version without δέ), the former, with its interrogative form[14], may well be original. In addition, ἔρχεται could be a mistranslation of

---

[11] See R. H. Smith, 'The Household Lamps of Palestine', *BA* 27 (1964), pp. 2–31, 101–24; 29 (1966) 2–27; R. W. Funk and I. Ben-Dor, in *IDB* 3, s.v., 'Lamp'; and V. Sussman, *Ornamental Jewish Oil-Lamps from the Destruction of the Second Temple Through the Bar-Kokhba Revolt*, Jerusalem, 1982.

[12] Most scholars have favoured authenticity; see e.g. Pesch 1, p. 249. Bultmann, however, affirmed that the verse might contain a secular proverb which was turned into a dominical word (*History*, p. 102).

[13] Further discussion in Jeremias, *Parables*, pp. 99–102; idem, *Abba*, pp. 99–102; and Schneider (v), pp. 192–4. Jeremias finds the original point to be in the contrast between lighting and extinguishing. Schneider, more persuasively, thinks the point is this: one who puts a lamp under a *modius* does not allow that lamp to fulfil its proper function.

[14] On the primacy of this see Schneider (v), p. 187. Cf. Lk 6.39 = Mt 15.14. Schneider documents a tendency in the synoptic tradition to change questions to statements or imperatives. Cf. Bultmann, *History*, p. 93.

the aphel or ittaphal of 'ṭ' (which was originally intended as a passive, 'brought').[15]

καὶ τιθέασιν αὐτὸν ὑπὸ τὸν μόδιον. Compare Lk 11.33: εἰς κρύπτην τίθησιν οὐδὲ ὑπὸ τὸν μόδιον. Matthew's third person plural again probably reproduces Q, as does his parataxis. But what of εἰς κρύπτην (= 'in a cellar', 'in a dark and hidden place' or 'grotto'; cf. Josephus, Bell. 5.330)? κρύπτη (LXX: O) is a NT hapax legomenon and so not obviously from Luke. Yet its secondary if not Lukan character is perhaps indicated by the circumstance that cellars were far more common outside Palestine (Jeremias, Parables, p. 27, n. 9).

Mk 4.21 reads: ἵνα ὑπὸ τὸν μόδιον τεθῇ ἢ ὑπὸ τὴν κλίνην. One may doubt whether 'under the bed' (or: bench?) first stood in this saying. It destroys the parallelism of Mk 4.21 and, on Jesus' lips, the presence of beds in his hearers' houses would not have been taken for granted (cf. Jülicher 2, p. 81).

What is meant by *modios* (Mt: 1; Mk: 1; Lk: 1, nowhere else in the NT)? The word, which is absent from the LXX, is Latin (*modius*) and was a loanword into both Greek and rabbinic Hebrew (*môdyā*). It means a 'peck-measure', that is, a grain measure holding sixteen sextarii, then a measure in general (BAGD, s.v.; Jastrow, s.v.). For the extinguishing of a lamp by the placing of a dish or vessel over it see *m. Šabb.* 16.7 and *b. Beṣ* 22a.[16]

ἀλλ' ἐπὶ τὴν λυχνίαν. So Lk 11.33 (cf. 8.16, which lacks the article and has the genitive in P75 A B L W Ξ f1.13 Maj). Mk 4.21 reads: οὐχ ἵνα ἐπὶ τὴν λυχνίαν τεθῇ; Again the interrogative form is probably original (see above). The λυχνία (= *mĕnôrâ* in the LXX) is not a candlestick (so KJV) but a lamp stand (of pottery or metal), on which lamps were set (cf. Exod 25.31–40; Philo, *Spec. leg.* 1.296). The article is probably generic.

καὶ λάμπει πᾶσιν τοῖς ἐν τῇ οἰκίᾳ. There is nothing corresponding to this in Mark. Lk 11.33 has: ἵνα οἱ εἰσπορευόμενοι τὸ φέγγος βλέπωσιν (cf. Lk 8.16). Although λάμπω (Mt: 3; Mk: 0; Lk: 1) might be thought Matthean, the First Gospel probably reproduces Q in that it (1) contains parataxis and (2) presupposes the typical, one room Palestinian peasant's dwelling while Luke seems to have in his mind's eye a vestibule or entrance passage.[17] Also, the substantive plural participle, 'those coming in', appears in the NT only in Luke's double work, in Lk 8.16; 11.33; Acts 3.2; 28.30.

[15] Doudna, p. 106. But did Mark interpret 'the lamp coming' as referring to Jesus' coming? See Gnilka, *Markus* 1, p. 180, and Lane, pp. 165–6.

[16] See further Dupont-Sommer (v) and Schneider (v), p. 189, n. 29.

[17] Cf. C. H. Dodd, 'Changes of Scenery in Luke', *ExpT* 33 (1921), pp. 40–1, and Dupont, 'La lampe' (v), p. 48, n. 17.

T. W. Manson, *Sayings*, p. 93, proposed that there is a significant point of difference between Luke's 'they which enter in may see the light' and Matthew's 'it shines unto all in the house'. Whereas the latter contemplates a reformation within Judaism, the former has in view conversions from outside. However that may be, a missionary concern is certainly evident in both texts.[18]

16. This redactional verse, which lacks a synoptic parallel, is the only directly hortatory line in 5.13–16, and it clearly states the meaning of 5.14–15 (as well as of 5.13): Jesus' disciples are to live in the world so that the world will see them and be moved to glorify God. Closet Christianity and self-directed service are excluded. Compare 25.14–30: talents must be turned into talents; to hide them away is to lose everything. Note that, in being lights, the disciples are imitating Jesus, who was a light to those sitting in darkness (4.15–16).

οὕτως λαμψάτω τὸ φῶς ὑμῶν ἔμπροσθεν τῶν ἀνθρώπων.[19] οὕτως, a Matthean favourite (see on 2.5), links v. 16 to vv. 14 and 15: like a city set on a hill, like a lamp on a lampstand. . . . 'Shine' is taken from v. 15, 'light' from v. 14. 'Before men' is a characteristic Mattheanism (see on 6.1). In the present text, 'men' refers to Jews and Gentiles outside the church. The universal mission (28.19) is presupposed.[20]

ὅπως ἴδωσιν ὑμῶν τὰ καλὰ ἔργα.[21] The disciples are on display. But their being seen is not an end in itself (see 6.1–18; 23.5). Instead is it a means by which the Father in heaven may be known: Jesus' followers are to be transparent, making the heavenly manifest in the earthly.

'Good works'—with καλός or ἀγαθός—is common in the NT, occurring about thirty times. Compare the rabbinic *maʿăśîm*

---

[18] Gos. Thom. 33b: 'For no one lights a lamp and puts it under a bushel, nor does he put it in a hidden place, but he sets it on the lampstand so that all who have entered and will go out may see its light'. This almost certainly betrays acquaintance with the Third Gospel (cf. Schrage, pp. 81–5). In common with Luke and against the other synoptic gospels are several items which we have traced to Lukan redaction or to Luke's special tradition, these being, 'put it in a hidden place' (cf. Luke's εἰς κρύπτην), 'who (have) entered', and 'see its (the) light'. In view of this, the author of Gos. Thom. or a contributor to his tradition must have seen the gospel of Luke.

[19] There is a remarkable Buddhist parallel to Mt 5.16 in the Maha-Vagga: 'O bhikkhus, must you so let your light shine before the world that you, having embaced the religious life according to so well-taught a doctrine and discipline, are seen to be forbearing and mild . . .'.

[20] Mt 5.16 seems to have been known to Jews in touch with the Rabbis. In *b. Šabb.* 116b the wife of R. Eliezer, in a discussion with R. Gamaliel, declares, 'Let thy light shine forth like a lamp' (*nhwr nhwryk kšrg*). R. Gamaliel responds: 'An ass came and knocked over the lamp!'

[21] The vocabulary is redactional: ὅπως: Mt: 17; Mk: 1; Lk 7; ἔργον: Mt: 6; Mk: 2; Lk: 2; καλός: Mt: 21; Mk: 11; Lk: 9.

ṭôbîm. In context, the 'good works' of 5.16 are to be identified with the acts commanded in 5.17–7.12.

καὶ δοξάσωσιν τὸν πατέρα ὑμῶν τὸν ἐν τοῖς οὐρανοῖς. This, the final clause of 5.13–16, expresses the disciples' true end. Compare Jn 15.18 ('By this my Father is glorified, that you bear much fruit, and so prove to be my disciples') and 1 Pet 2.12 ('maintain good conduct among the Gentiles, so that in case they speak against you as wrongdoers, they may see your good deeds and glorify God in the day of visitation'). This last could be reminiscent of Mt 5.16. On 'your Father in heaven' see on 6.1.

(iv) *Concluding Observations*

The summary description of the disciples as salt and light, a description which fits those who live as 5.21–7.12 will detail, has the whole world (γῆ, κόσμος) as its backdrop. This implies that the Gentile mission is presupposed. The followers of Jesus are salt and light for all, for Jew and Gentile the world over. So Matthew's universalism is once more apparent. No less apparent is the evangelist's exalted estimation of the ecclesia's rôle in the religious life of humanity. If the church does in fact consist of those who are 'the salt of the earth' and 'the light of the cosmos', then the church must be the primary locus of God's activity in and for all people. 'What the soul is in a body, this the Christians are in the world' (Diognetus, *Ep.* 6.1).

(v) *Bibliography*

P.-R. Berger, 'Die Stadt auf dem Berge: Zum kulturhistorischen Hintergrund von Mt 5.14', in *Wort in der Zeit*, ed. W. Haubeck and M. Bachmann, Leiden, 1980, pp. 82–5.

K. M. Campbell, 'The New Jerusalem in Matthew 5.14', *SJT* 31 (1978), pp. 335–63.

O. Cullmann, 'Que signifie le sel dans la parabole de Jésus?', *RHPR* 37 (1957), pp. 36–43.

E. P. Deatrick, 'Salt, Soil, Savour', *BA* 25 (1962), pp. 41–8.

J. D. M. Derrett, 'The Lamp which must not be hidden (Mark 4.21)', in *Law*, pp. 189–207.

idem, 'The Light under a Bushel: The Hanukkah Lamp?', *ExpT* 78 (1966), p. 18.

Dodd, *Parables*, pp. 108–114.

W. J. Dumbrell, 'The Logic of the Role of the Law in Matthew V 1-20', *Novt* 23 (1981), pp. 1–21.

J. Dupont, 'La lampe sur le lampadaire dans l'évangile de saint Luc (8.16; 11.33)', in *Au service de la parole de Dieu*, Gembloux, 1969, pp. 43–59.

idem, 'La transmission des paroles de Jésus sur la lampe et la mesure dans Marc 4, 21–5 et dans la tradition Q', in Delobel, pp. 201–36.

A. Dupont-Sommer, 'Note archéologique sur le proverbe évangélique: Mettre la lampe sous le boisseau', in *Mélanges Syriens*, Paris, 1939, pp. 78–94.

K. Grayston, 'Matthew 5.16: An Interpretation', *Epworth Review* 6 (1979), pp. 61–3.

F. Hahn, 'Die Worte vom Licht Lk 11.33–6', in Hoffmann, *Orientierung*, pp. 107–38.

Jeremias, *Abba*, pp. 99–102.

idem, *Parables*, pp. 168–9.

Jülicher 2, pp. 79–91.

Klauch, pp. 280–6.

M. Krämer, ' "Ihr seid das Salz der Erde . . . Ihr seid das Licht der Welt" ', *MTZ* 28 (1977), pp. 133–57.

S. Légasse, 'Les chrétiens "sel de la terre", "lumière du monde". Mt 5.13–16', *AsSeign* 36 (1974), pp. 17–25.

W. Nauck, 'Salt as a Metaphor in Instructions for Discipleship', *ST* 6 (1953), pp. 165–78.

Ogawa, pp. 228–34.

R. Schnackenburg, *Schriften*, pp. 177–200.

G. Schneider, 'Das Bildwort von der Lampe', *ZNW* 61 (1970), pp. 183–209.

Schulz, *Q*, pp. 470–2.

G. Schwarz, 'Matthäus 5.13a und 14a', *NTS* 17 (1970), pp. 80–6.

J. B. Souček, 'Salz der Erde und Licht der Welt', *TZ* 19 (1963), pp. 169–79.

Suggs, pp. 122–7.

G. von Rad, *The Problem of the Hexateuch and Other Essays* (trans. of *Gesammelte Studien zum Alten Testament*, 1958), New York, 1966, pp. 232–42.

Wrege, pp. 27–34.

Zumstein, pp. 422–8.

XI

JESUS FULFILS THE LAW (5.17–20)

(i) *Structure*

5.17–20 begins with three interlocking verses which are (1) structurally similar in that each exhibits antithetical or synonymous parallelism and (2) thematically connected in that each upholds the abiding authority of the Torah. 5.20 then follows and introduces a second but related theme, the better righteousness. Schematically—

17	First general statement: Jesus fulfils the law
17a	Thesis rejected: Think not that
	I have come to abolish the law and the prophets;
17b	Thesis affirmed:
	I have come not to abolish but to fulfil.

18	Supporting thesis: The abiding validity of the Torah
18a–c	Basic assertion: For truly, I say to you,
	until heaven and earth pass away,
	not one iota, not one dot will pass from the law,
18d	Qualification: until all is accomplished.

19	Application: Keep the law
19a–b	First inference: Whoever then relaxes one of the least
	of these commandments
	and teaches men so
	shall be called least in the kingdom of heaven.
19c–d	Second inference: But whoever does them
	and teaches them
	shall be called great in the kingdom of heaven.

20	Second general statement: The better righteousness
20a	Condition: Unless your righteousness
	exceeds that of the scribes and Pharisees,
20b	Result: you will not enter the kingdom of heaven.

5.17–20 is primarily *prokatalepsis*, that is, an anticipation of objections. As the introduction or preamble to 5.21–48 (cf. the function of 6.1 *vis-à-vis* 6.2–18) it is intended to prevent the readers of the First Gospel from making two errors. First, it plainly states that the six subsequent paragraphs are not to be interpreted—as they have been so often by so many—as 'antitheses', 'antitheses' that, in at least two or three instances, set aside the Torah. Instead

481

Jesus upholds the law, so that between him and Moses there can be no real conflict (see further on 5.18). Then, secondly, and despite the concord declared by 5.17–19, 5.20 tells us that what Jesus requires of his followers surpasses what has traditionally been regarded (by the scribes and Pharisees) as the requirements of the Torah. So although there is continuity with the past, the Messiah also brings something new, and it does not surprise when 5.21–48 goes beyond the letter of the law to demand even more.

(ii) Sources

For arriving at a solution to the synoptic problem 5.17–20 is not very enlightening. If the Griesbach hypothesis be embraced, Mark's omission of the passage might be put down to a different attitude towards the law; and perhaps—although less plausibly—one might also explain Lk 16.17 as a Lukan rewriting of Mt 5.18. On the other side, and as the commentary shows, it is not difficult to account for Mt 5.17–20 and Lk 6.17 assuming the priority of Mark and Q.

(iii) Exegesis

17. The genesis of this verse, which is without parallel in Mark or Luke, cannot be pinned down. A pre-Easter *Sitz im Leben* is not out of the question. Jesus may well have wished to defend his loyalty to the Torah against those who made him out to be an antinomian (cf. Davies, *COJ*, pp. 34–7, 47–52; Banks, pp. 236–40; McEleney (v), pp. 563–7). And yet, in view of the great debates in the early church over the status of the Mosaic law, 5.17 could easily have been composed as a response to what was perceived as cultic or moral laxness on the part of the so-called Hellenists (cf. Acts 6.13–14), on the part of Paul and his disciples, or on the part of uncircumcised Gentile Christians (Bultmann, *History*, pp. 138, 163). 5.17 could also conceivably have originated as a Jewish-Christian reply to Jewish aspersions about Jesus being an opponent of the law of God (cf. Acts 6.11; 21.28; Justin, *Dial.* 108), an eschatological deceiver or pseudo-prophet (cf. Dan 7.25; 1 Macc 1.44–9; T. Levi 16.3; *b. Sanh.* 43a).

μὴ νομίσητε ὅτι ἦλθον. Compare the construction in Pap. Eg. frag. 1, recto: μὴ δοκεῖτε ὅτι ἐγὼ ἦλθον κατηγορῆσαι ὑμῶν πρὸς τὸν πατέρα μου. Note also 2 Macc 7.19; 4 Macc 2.14; 9.7. The same words occur also in 10.34 (diff. Lk 12.51) and appear to be redactional there as well as here.[1] This does not imply that 5.17 is

---

[1] So also Trilling, p. 171; Hummel, p. 66; Meier, *Law*, pp. 65–70; against Banks, pp. 204–5, and Guelich, p. 136.

purely Matthean, a redactional creation *ex nihilo* (contrast Luz
(v)). Just as 10.34 is not a redactional creation but rather the
redactional version of a traditional logion (cf. Lk 12.51), so too
may 5.17 be an old saying made new (see further below).

Concerning the verb νομίζω (Mt: 3; Mk: 0; Lk: 2), it is always in
the First Gospel followed by ὅτι (cf. Acts 21.29; the construction
does not appear in the LXX). Here, with μή, the negative
imperative does more than supply a rhetorical wall off which to
bounce a positive statement. 'Do not think . . .' rebuts a real
misunderstanding: somebody thinks that Jesus came to abolish
the law. See further p. 501, n. 54.

The synoptics contain a number of 'I came' sayings.[2] They are all
sometimes dismissed as post-Easter products because they seem to look
'back to the historical appearance of Jesus as a whole'.[3] Such a conclusion
is hardly demanded by the evidence. In Lk 12.49 'Jesus is clearly speaking
of his ministry as still in process and of his tension until it is completed'
(Fuller, *Christology*, p. 128); and there is in any case no solid reason for
disputing that Jesus had a *Sendungsbewusstsein*, especially as such can be
attributed to the Teacher of Righteousness at Qumran.[4] Furthermore, (1)
the case for the authenticity of at least the 'I came' saying in Mt 10.34 = Lk
12.51 is very strong;[5] (2) Josephus, according to his own testimony, could
address Vespasian in this manner: ἐγὼ δ' ἄγγελος ἥκω σοι μειζόνων,[6] and
(3) if Jesus spoke of his purpose in coming into the world, this would be
consistent with his self-conception as a prophetic figure and his conviction
that his commissioning was of heavenly origin (cf. Jer 20.18; 49.14; Obad
1; 2 Bar. 3.1).

καταλῦσαι τὸν νόμον ἢ τοὺς προφήτας. Compare Clement of
Alexandria, *Strom.* 3.9.63, quoting the Gospel of the Egyptians: 'I
came to destroy the works of the female'. Compare also
Epiphanius, *Haer.* 30.16.5, quoting the Gospel of the Ebionites: 'I
am come to do away with sacrifices'. καταλύω (Mt: 5; Mk: 3; Lk: 3)
is used of the destruction of the temple in 24.2; 26.6; and 27.40.
Here it probably means 'abolish' or 'annul' (cf. 2 Macc 2.22; 4.11;

[2] Lit.: A. von Harnack, ' "Ich bin gekommen": Die ausdrücklichen
Selbstzeugnisse Jesu über den Zweck seiner Sendung und seines Kommens', *ZTK*
22 (1912), pp. 1–30; Bultmann, *History*, pp. 150–63; W. Manson, pp. 67–71;
Fuller, *Christology*, pp. 127–8; Arens, passim; J. A. Bühner, *Der Gesandte und sein
Weg im vierten Evangelium*, WUNT II.2, Tübingen, 1977, pp. 138–52.

[3] So Bultmann, *History*, p. 155. Cf. Beare, pp. 141–2, who writes that Mt 5.17
has the sense, 'I came down to earth'.

[4] On this see G. Jeremias, *Der Lehrer der Gerechtigkeit*, SUNT 2, Göttingen,
1963, pp. 334–6.

[5] See F. Mussner, 'Wege zum Selbstbewusstsein Jesu', *BZ* 12 (1968), pp. 165–7;
Allison, pp. 118–19.

[6] On this see O. Michel, ' "Ich komme" (Jos. Bell. III, 400)', *TZ* 24 (1968),
pp. 123–4.

4.Macc 5.33; Philo, *Som.* 2.123; Josephus, *Ant.* 16.35; 20.81). Compare Jn 10.35: 'Scripture cannot be broken' (λυθῆναι). Paul was evidently accused of taking the position our clause rejects; see Rom 3.31; Acts 18.13; 21.28.

'The law and/or the prophets' (Mt: 4 (redactional in 7.12 and 22.40); Mk: 0; Lk: 2) was a traditional phrase (2 Macc 15.9; 4 Macc 18.10; Ecclus prologue; Jn 1.45; Rom 3.21; *t. B. Meṣ.* 11.23) meaning 'the Scriptures'. νόμος refers to the Pentateuch (cf. 4 Macc 1.34; 2.5–6, 9; 9.2; Mt 12.5; Josephus, *Ant.* 17.151) and οἱ προφῆται refers to the rest of the Bible (cf. Lk 16.29, 31). For full discussion see Sand, pp. 33–45, 183–93. The phrase, which could here have been suggested by its appearance in Lk 16.16 Q (Lk 16.17 = Mt 5.18), forms an *inclusio* with 7.12 ('this is the law and the prophets') between which lies the core of the sermon on the mount. See further on 7.12; Davies, *JPS*, pp. 1–26, esp. 6f.

The disjunctive ἤ instead of the expected, conjunctive καί, is redactional and probably due to the negative form of the sentence (so Bonnard, p. 61). The evangelist typically employs the particle to add a noun to one in his tradition, usually with insignificant result (cf. 5.18 = Lk 16.17; 12.25 = Mk 3.25; 16.14 = Mk 8.28; 18.8 = Mk 9.43). But here there must, we fancy, be an important motive. And it is probably this: for Matthew, who has seen in the coming of Jesus Messiah the fulfilment of the OT prophecies, not only is the prophetic portion of the Scripture no less important than the five books of Moses, but 'the law and the prophets' together constitute in his eyes a united prophetic witness: 'the prophets and the law prophesied until John' (11.13). So Matthew cannot simply let it be said that Jesus fulfilled the law or that Jesus fulfilled the prophets: he must tell us that he fulfilled both.

The phrase, 'to abolish the law or the prophets', is evidence for 5.17 not being wholly redactional. 'To abolish the law' makes sense, and no doubt the charge was levelled against both Jesus and his post-Easter followers. But 'to annul the prophets' does not make so much sense, and one wonders whether such an accusation was ever brought against Christians or their Lord. The implication, seemingly, is that 'or the prophets' is a redactional addition which has made for an awkward construction.[7] That is, 'to abolish the law' was the perfectly understandable sentence received by Matthew, who then changed it to 'to abolish the law or the prophets'.

οὐκ ἦλθον καταλῦσαι ἀλλὰ πληρῶσαι. This clause repeats and re-emphasizes that Jesus did not come to abolish the law and the

---

[7] So also Allen, p. 46; McNeile, p. 58; Guelich, pp. 142–3. We thus reject the hypothesis of a redactional genesis for 5.17, as proposed by Bacon, p. 273; Schweizer, *Matthew*, p. 106; Gundry, *Commentary*, p. 78; Luz (v); and others. Dalman, *Jesus-Jeshua*, p. 62, is unjustified in excising the phrase.

prophets and adds another claim: he came to fulfil them. Compare
Rom 8.4; 13.8; Gal 5.14; Acts 6.14. For οὐκ ἦλθον + infinitive +
ἀλλά + infinitive see also 9.13 = Mk 2.17; 20.28 = Mk 10.45; and
Mt 10.34. The crux of this clause—and of all of v. 17—is the
meaning of πληρόω (Mt: 16; Mk: 3; Lk: 9), which is usually
translated, 'fulfil'. Unfortunately, the gamut of possible
interpretations is quite long. (1) The Greek could be a translation
of 'ôsîp (= 'to add to'). Jesus originally said, as b. Šabb. 116a–b has
it, 'I did not come to destroy the law of Moses nor did I come to
add to the law of Moses'.[8] (2) πληρόω is the equivalent of the
Aramaic qûm, with the meaning 'establish', 'make valid', 'bring
into effect' (see Jastrow, s.v.).[9] According to Schlatter, pp. 153–4,
qûm might also mean 'to do', 'to execute' (cf. SB 1, p. 341). (3)

[8] So Schoeps (v) and Jeremias, *Theology*, pp. 83–85. Cf. Deut 4.2; 12.32; Rev
22.18–19. *b. Šabb.* 116a–b reads: 'Imma Shalom, R. Eliezer's wife, was R.
Gamaliel's sister. Now, a certain philosopher lived in his vicinity, and he bore a
reputation that he did not accept bribes. They wished to expose him, so she brought
him a golden lamp, went before him, (and) said to him, "I desire that a share be
given me in my (deceased) father's estate." "Divide", ordered he. Said he (R.
Gamaliel) to him, "It is decreed for us, Where there is a son, a daughter does not
inherit." (He replied,) "Since the day that you were exiled from your land the law of
Moses has been superseded and another book given, wherein it is written, "A son
and a daughter inherit equally." The next day, he (R. Gamaliel) brought him a
Libyan ass. Said he to them, "Look at the end of the book, wherein it is written, I
did not come to destroy the law of Moses nor (so codex. B; codex M: rather) did I
come to add to the law of Moses, and it is written therein, A daughter does not
inherit where there is a son." Said she to him, "Let thy light shine forth like a lamp."
Said R. Gamaliel to him, "An ass came and knocked the lamp over!" ' On this text
see E. B. Nicholson, *The Gospel According to the Hebrews*, London, 1879,
pp. 145–7; R. T. Herford, *Christianity in Talmud and Midrash*, London, 1903,
pp. 146–54; Klausner, pp. 44–6; K. G. Kuhn, 'Giljonim und sifre minim', in
Eltester, p. 54, n. 100; Jeremias, *Theology*, pp. 83–4. Kuhn assigns the text to the
third century A.D. According to Jeremias, that Jesus originally said, 'I came to add
to', is buttressed by Ps.-Clem. Rec. 1.39.1 ('But when the time began to draw near
that what was wanting in the Mosaic institutions should be supplied') and a Jewish-
Christian source revised by a Moslem ('I did not come to diminish but, on the
contrary, to complete'); see S. Pines, *The Jewish Christians of the Early Centuries of
Christianity According to a New Source*, Jerusalem, 1966, p. 5. He could have added
Did. 4.13: 'Do not forsake the commandments of the Lord, but guard what you
have received, neither adding to them nor taking away from them'. But there are
objections to the interpretation of Schoeps and Jeremias. (1) One would expect
yĕsap to be translated by προ(σ)τιθέναι, esp. if the allusion to Deut. 4.2 and 12.32
were original. (2) Except for the ambiguous testimony of the Didache, all of the
sources appealed to are relatively late, and they could have been formulated under
the influence of Deut 4.2 and 12.32. For further discussion and criticism see Légasse
(v).
[9] So Branscomb, pp. 226–8; Dalman, *Jesus-Jeshua*, pp. 56–8; Daube, pp. 60–1.
Cf. Riesner, pp. 456–60. Against this, (1) the LXX does not render forms of *qûm*
with πληρόω and (2) we would expect, if the sense were 'establish' or 'bring into
effect', to find instead the word ἵστημι. For additional criticism see Ljungman (v).

πληρόω means 'obey', as in Rom 8.4.[10] (4) Jesus 'fulfils' the law by observing it perfectly and completely in his own person and ministry.[11] (5) Jesus 'fulfils' or 'completes' the law by bringing a new law which transcends the old.[12] (6) The Torah is 'fulfilled' when Jesus, explaining God's original intention, brings out its perfect or inner meaning or expands and extends its demands.[13] (7) Jesus 'fulfils' the law because, through his coming, he enables others to meet the Torah's demands.[14] (8) When Jesus 'fulfils' the law or the prophets, he does it by bringing the new righteousness, which is the new spirit of love: love is the fulfilling of the law.[15] (9) The 'fulfilment' is eschatological: the *telos* which the Torah anticipated, namely, the Messiah, has come and revealed the law's definitive meaning. Prophecy has been realized (cf. As. Mos. 10.8; Clement of Alexandria, *Strom.* 3.6.46; Eusebius, *Dem. ev.* 8.2, p. 387).[16]

In our judgement, the best interpretation of πληρόω combines elements of options 5 and 9. (For criticism of the other alternatives see footnotes 8–11, 13–15). It is at once clear from 5.21–48 that Jesus proffers new demands, as (5) recognizes: so πληρόω must at least be consistent with a transcending of the Mosaic law. At the same time, the verb almost certainly has prophetic content, for (i) Matthew uses πληρόω most frequently to express the fulfilment of an OT prophecy by Jesus (the formula quotations); (ii) 'and the prophets' has been added to 'the law' in 5.17, which proves that the

[10] So Zahn, pp. 212–13. On this interpretation, καταλύω would, presumably, equal 'disobey', but the Greek seems much stronger than that; cf. Gundry, *Commentary*, p. 81.

[11] So Descamps, *Justes*, pp. 127–31. Cf. Ljungman (v), pp. 58–61; Thurneysen, p. 48; Hill, *Matthew*, p. 117; and Guelich, pp. 138–42. The difficulty with this view is that in 5.17–20 and the following verses, Jesus' teaching, not his behaviour, is under consideration. This fact also speaks against interpretation 3. Cf. Calvin 1, p. 178: in 5.17–20 Jesus 'treats of doctrine, not life'.

[12] So Davies, *COJ*, pp. 33–4. There is, as we shall see, truth in this proposal.

[13] So Allen, p. 45 (on the pre-Matthean meaning); Plummer, p. 76; Lagrange, pp. 93–4; McNeile, p. 58; Dupont 1, pp. 138–44; Green, pp. 36, 65; Burchard, p. 73; Lambrecht, *Sermon*, p. 84. However, in the following paragraphs Jesus' words are much more than exegesis.

[14] So Schniewind, p. 54. Cf. Chrysostom, *Hom. on Mt.* 16.3. This certainly seems to be eisegesis.

[15] So Giesen, pp. 143–6. Cf. Schweizer, *Matthew*, p. 108. The problem with this is that the continuity between 5.17 on the one hand and 5.18–19 on the other is not smooth: what can jots and tittles and 'the least of these commandments'—which cannot be identified with anything in the teaching of Jesus—have to do with the commandment to love?

[16] So, in different ways, Banks, pp. 207–10; Meier, *Law*, pp. 73–82; Goppelt, *Theology* 1, p. 104; Hahn (v), p. 44–5; B. S. Jackson, 'Legalism', *JJS* 30 (1979), pp. 3–4; and Moo (v), pp. 24–5. Gundry, *Commentary*, p. 81, applies πληρῶσαι to the accomplishment of prophecies (but not the Torah), καταλύω to antinomianism (but not to the prophets). Melito, *Hom.* 34: 'The gospel is the explanation and fulfilment of the law, and the Church is the place where the law comes true'.

evangelist is thinking of prophecy; (iii) in 11.13 a verse from Q is edited with the result that the Torah prophesies ('the prophets and the law prophesied until John'), and this implies that the Torah could be fulfilled just as the prophets could;[17] and (iv) ἕως ἂν πάντα γένηται (5.18) probably, as we shall see, refers to all predicted or prophesied events (cf. 24.34–5 and the NEB on 5.18: 'until all that must happen has happened')—which once again shows Matthew's concern with prophecy in 5.17–20. So when Jesus declares, 'I came . . . to fulfil', he means that his new teaching brings to realization that which the Torah anticipated or prophesied: its 'fulfiller' has come.

What does this mean for understanding the law? First, he who fulfils the law and the prophets displaces them in so far as he must become the centre of attention: the thing signified (Jesus) is naturally more important than the sign (the law and the prophets) pointing to it. This is why Matthew's book is firstly about Jesus, not about the law and the prophets. Secondly, if the law is fulfilled, it cannot on that account be set aside. Fulfilment can only confirm the Torah's truth, not cast doubt upon it. And while Jesus' new demands may surpass the demands of the OT, the two are not contradictory (see on 5.21–48; 9.14–17; 12.1–14; 15.1–20; 19.3–9). Rather do the words of the Torah remain the words of God (cf. 15.4), their imperatival force undiminished (cf. 5.18; 23.23).

In favour of the position just taken, one additional observation may be made. Matthew, as 17.5 implies, understood Jesus to be the eschatological prophet like Moses (Deut 18.15–20; cf. Acts 3.22). For him, then, not only was Jesus' coming in fact prophesied by the Pentateuch ('I will raise up for them a prophet'), but the Pentateuch itself anticipated that God would speak anew ('I will put my words in his mouth, and he shall speak to them all that I command him'; see also Acts 26.22–3). Matthew, like Luke (Jervell, *Paul*, pp. 122–37), would have thought of Moses as a prophet and of the Pentateuch as a prophetic book (cf. n. 17); hence the 'fulfilment' of the law is a concept congenial to Matthean theology.

18. This verse belongs to a group of synoptic logia that exhibit the same basic literary structure: (ἀμὴν) λέγω ὑμῖν + οὐ μή + ἕως (ἄν).[18] See

---

[17] In this connexion one should recall that Moses was considered a prophet: Deut 18.15, 18; As. Mos. 3.11; 11.16; Justus of Tiberias, quoted in Eusebius, *Chron.*, *apud* George Syncellus, *Chronicle*, p. 122.3–10 ed. Dindorf (Moses was 'the first of all the prophets'); 2 Bar. 59.4–11; Philo, *Quaest in Gen.* 1.86; 4.29.

[18] Lit.: W. Kelber, 'Kingdom and Parousia in the Gospel of Mark' (Dissertation University of Chicago, unpublished, 1970), pp. 88–95; D. Peabody, 'A Pre-Markan Prophetic Sayings Tradition and the Synoptic Problem', *JBL* 97 (1978), pp. 391–409; Berger, *Amen*, pp. 73–4; B. Crawford, 'Near Expectation in the Sayings of Jesus', *JBL* 101 (1982), pp. 225–44.

Mk 9.1 = Mt 16.28 = Lk 9.27; Mk 13.10 = Mt 24.34 = Lk 21.32; Mt 10.23; 5.18 = Lk 16.17; Mt 5.26 = Lk 12.59; Mt 23.39 = Lk 13.35; Mk 14.25 = Mt 26.29 = Lk 22.16, 18; cf. Jn 13.38. It has been urged that the form common to these logia goes back to early Christian prophets and that therefore none of the verses cited has a pre-Easter *Sitz im Leben*.[19] Yet the reasons for assigning much of the Jesus tradition to Christian prophets are far from persuasive (see Aune, pp. 233–45), and at all events the lumping together of the several (ἀμὴν) + λέγω ὑμῖν + οὐ μή + ἕως (ἄν) sayings into one category hides as much as it reveals. For there are in fact three different kinds of sentences which exhibit this common structure. The first consists of eschatological sayings that announce or presuppose the nearness of the end: Mk 9.1 = Mt 16.28 = Lk 9.27 ('some standing here will not taste death'); Mk 13.30 = Mt 24.34 = Lk 21.32 ('this generation will not pass away'); Mk 14.25 = Mt 26.29 = Lk 22.16, 18 ('I will no longer drink of the fruit of the vine'); and Mt 10.23 ('You will not have gone through all the towns of Israel'). Actually, since Mk 9.1; 13.30; and Mt 10.23 are in all likelihood variants of one original utterance (see on 10.23), we are here dealing in essence with only two words, one on the eschaton's imminence, the other on drinking wine in the kingdom of God. Both may well go back to Jesus (see on 10.23 and 26.29).

The second category has only one member, 23.39 = Lk 13.35: 'For I say to you, you will not see me from now on until you say, "Blessed is he who comes in the name of the Lord" '. Unlike the sayings in the first category, this saying—which may or may not come from Jesus—does not state or imply the nearness of the kingdom of God. Instead it declares the end's pre-condition, namely, the acceptance by Israel of Jesus Messiah.[20] A traditional form which survives in the rabbinic literature has been taken up: (a) statement about the messianic advent with adverbial particle of negation attached; (b) conditional particle ('*ad*); (c) condition to be met (in Israel) for the fulfilment of the messianic advent. See, for example, *b. Sanh.* 98a: Ze'iri said in R. Ḥanina's name: 'The Son of David will not come until there are no conceited men in Israel'. See further on 23.39.

The third category includes those sayings which do not directly pertain to eschatology: Mt 5.26 = Lk 12.29 ('you will not get out until you have paid the last penny') and Jn 13.38 ('the cock will not crow until you have denied me three times'). Except for the prefatory 'I say to you', these verses could simply be classed with the host of *lō'* (or: '*ên*) . . . '*ad*/οὐ (or: μή) . . . ἕως formulas scattered throughout Jewish literature, such as in Gen 19.22; 29.8; Ezra 2.63 (LXX: εἶπεν . . . αὐτοῖς + μή + ἕως); 11QTemple 58.18; 1 Cor 4.5; *m. Ber.* 7.5; *b. Soṭa* 48b.

Mt 5.18 belongs to the third type. It neither declares the consummation to be near nor states its pre-condition; rather is it about the Torah. But unlike most of the other sayings introduced in the previous paragraph, in 5.18 the (ἀμὴν) λέγω ὑμῖν + οὐ μή + ἕως (ἄν) form appears to belong to the redactional level (see below). Thus, although the (ἀμὴν) λέγω ὑμῖν +

---

[19] See esp. Crawford, ibid. According to Boring, pp. 173–4, Mt 5.18 is the product of Christian prophecy.

[20] For the following see on 23.29 and D. C. Allison, 'Matt. 23:39 = Luke 13.36 as a Conditional Prophecy', *JSNT* 18 (1983), pp. 75–84.

οὐ μή + ἕως (ἄν) form probably was used by Jesus himself, its appearance does not itself guarantee a dominical birth. Lk 16.17 reads: 'It is easier for heaven and earth to pass away than for one dot of the law to become void'. Matthew has rewritten this sentence so as to give it a traditional form familiar to him from the Jesus tradition.

ἀμὴν γὰρ λέγω ὑμῖν. Compare John's frequent, 'Amen, amen, I say to you'. There is no parallel in Lk 16.17 and therefore Matthew has evidently added the phrase, as he has elsewhere (cf. Gundry, *Commentary*, p. 79). Here it adds solemnity. γάρ follows 'amen' four times in the First Gospel (5.18; 10.23; 13.17; 17.20; Mk: 0; Lk: 0). In the present clause the conjunction shows that 5.18 establishes the basis for 5.17.

ἀμήν (= 'āmēn, 'certainly'), which occurs seven or eight times in the LXX, is, in its introductory placement, usually thought of as being characteristic of Jesus' speech.[21] This is because, with few exceptions,[22] in Jewish and Christian sources 'amen' is always used responsively (cf. Deut 27.15; Neh 8.6; Ps 106.48; *m. Soṭa* 2.5). This is in striking contrast to the canonical sayings of Jesus, in which 'amen' is never used responsively but always as a fixed introductory formula.

V. Hasler has nonetheless put forward the thesis that 'Amen I say to you' derives from the liturgy of the Hellenistic church and that its presence in the Jesus tradition is secondary (criticism in Jeremias, *Theology*, p. 36, n. 2); and K. Berger similarly thinks that the prefatory 'amen' originated in the post-Easter period as part of a legitimation formula for eschatological asseverations (cf. the homophonic ἦ or εἶ μήν; in T. Abr. 8.7 ἀμήν replaces the ἦ μήν from Gen 22.17). Yet another hypothesis has been put forward by B. Chilton. Accepting Berger's claim that the introductory 'amen' was not a known Aramaic idiom, he postulates that Jesus originally addressed his hearers with 'in truth' (= Aramaic bĕqûšĕṭā'). This idiom, which is attested in Aramaic literature (1QapGen. 2.5; the targum on Isa 37.18; 45.14–15; cf. *b. Ber.* 55a), was then translated into Greek as 'amen'. But despite Hasler, Berger, and Chilton, it is prudent to stick with a more conventional opinion, for there are sound reasons for holding to the authenticity of many of the synoptic sayings

---

[21] Lit.: SB 1, pp. 242–4; H. Schlier, *TWNT* 1, pp. 339–42; Jeremias, *Prayers*, pp. 112–15; idem, *Theology*, pp. 35–6; idem, 'Zum nichtresponsorischen Amen', *ZNW* 64 (1973), pp. 122–3; Daube, pp. 388–93; Berger, *Amen*; idem, 'Zur Geschichte der Einleitungsformel "Amen, ich sage euch" ', *ZNW* 63 (1972), pp. 45–75; V. Hasler, *Amen. Redaktionsgeschichtliche Untersuchung zur Einführungsformel der Herrenworte 'Wahrlich, ich sage euch'*, Zürich, 1969; Aune, pp. 164–5; B. Chilton, ' "Amen"—an Approach through Syriac Gospels', *ZNW* 69 (1978), pp. 203–11; Riesner, pp. 379–82.

[22] A seventh-century B.C. potsherd in Hebrew (?); T. Abr. recension A 8.7; 20.2 (under Christian influence?); and perhaps Rev 7.12 and 22.20. For discussion see Berger, *Amen*, pp. 1–3; J. Strugnell, ' "Amen, I Say Unto You" in the Sayings of Jesus and in the Early Christian Literature', *HTR* 67 (1974), pp. 177–82; and Fitzmyer, *Luke* 1, p. 536.

that carry an introductory 'amen'. Moreover, because, as the DSS prove, the Hebrew 'amen' was a living word in Jesus' time (4QDib.Ham 1.7; 1QS 1.20; 2.10, 18), its use in his speech is credible, whether parallels to its consistent prefatory placement can be found or not.[23]

'Amen I say to you' is, in the canonical gospels, the functional equivalent of 'I say to you' (cf. Aune, pp. 164–5). Both phrases presuppose the superior status of the speaker over against those being addressed (cf. Prov 24.38; Jub. 36.11; T. Gad. 5.2; 1 En. 92.18; 94.1; 99.13; T. Job 37.1; Mt 3.9; Acts 5.38; Rom 11.13; 1 Apoc. Jas. 5.32.9). Hence '(Amen) I say to you'—which even without the 'amen' is rare in non-Christian Greek sources—reflects at least Jesus' implicit claim to be God's prophetic spokesman, and one should compare the OT legitimation formula, 'Thus says Yahweh' (Manson, *Teaching*, p. 207). That 'amen' has anything to do with Jesus' avoidance of oaths seems unlikely.

ἕως ἂν παρέλθῃ ὁ οὐρανὸς καὶ ἡ γῆ. Lk 16.17 has: εὐκοπώτερον δέ ἐστιν τὸν οὐρανὸν καὶ τὴν γῆν παρελθεῖν. Compare also Ps 148.6 LXX; Mk 13.31; Mt 24.35; Lk 21.33; Gos. Thom. 11; 2 Bar. 19.2 ('heaven and earth will stay forever'). Luke almost certainly preserves Q. Both ἕως as a conjunction (Mt: 20; Mk: 5; Lk: 15) and ἕως with ἄν (Mt: 9; Mk: 3; Lk: 3) are readily ascribed to Matthew while εὐκοπώτερον (Mt: 2; Mk: 2; Lk: 3) cannot be said to be characteristically Lukan.

'Until heaven and earth pass away' is not just hyperbole, the equivalent of 'until mules bear offspring' (although note Philo, *Vit. Mos.* 2.14). Mt 5.18b, like 24.35 par., envisions the end of heaven and earth (without stating the manner of their passing). See on 5.18d. The law—in contrast to Jesus' words (cf. 24.35 and see Luz (v), pp. 417–18)—therefore only endures until the heavens and the earth are gone. It is not eternal (cf. *b. 'Abod. Zar.* 9a; *b. Sanh.* 97a–b; *b. Nid.* 61b).

ἰῶτα ἓν ἢ μία κεραία οὐ μὴ παρέλθῃ ἀπὸ τοῦ νόμου.[24] On the perpetuity of the law—a common sentiment—see Bar 4.1; 4 Ezra 9.37; 2 Bar. 77.15 and Moore 1, pp. 269–80. Lk 16.17 reads: ἢ τοῦ νόμου μίαν κεραίαν πεσεῖν. Matthew has presumably added the reference to 'one iota' (only here in the NT), changed πίπτω (Mt: 19; Mk: 8; Lk: 17) to παρέρχομαι (cf. 5.18), and rearranged the elements of his sentence to fit the 'Amen I say to you' + 'not' + 'until' form (cf. esp. 24.34). The postpositioning of 'one' in the

---

[23] Concerning Chilton's thesis, two objections arise immediately. First, if the prefatory 'amen' reflects a prefatory 'in truth', and if this latter was a known idiom, why does prefatory 'amen' appear in the NT only in the Jesus tradition? Secondly, would we not, if Chilton were correct, expect to find ἀληθῶς or something similar introducing synoptic logia? (In Lk 9.27; 12.44; and 21.3, ἀληθῶς is redactional.)

[24] Θ 565 *f*[13] *al* Ir[lat] arm Diat[P] add καὶ τῶν προφητῶν, which increases the parallelism between 5.17 and 5.18.

redactional 'one iota' is Semitic (BDF § 247.2; cf. 6.27; 21.19). The double negative, οὐ μή, is a Septuagintism (MHT 4, p. 33). κεραία,[25] traditionally translated 'tittle', is literally 'horn' (cf. Josephus, Bell. 3.419). The exact meaning of the word in Mt 5.18 has yet to be established beyond doubt, although the general connotation—smallness, insignificance; compare iota, the smallest Greek letter—is palpable. Perhaps 'horn' refers to scribal ornaments (SB 1, pp. 248–9), or to the small serifs or strokes that differentiated certain very similar Hebrew and Aramaic letters (*h* and *ḥ*, *b* and *k*, *y* and *w*, *r* and *d*), or to accents and breathings (cf. *IG* 2.4321.10; Plutarch, *Mor.* 1100A), or to the smallest Hebrew or Aramaic letter, *yod* (cf. *y. Sanh.* 11.6.20c and Schlatter, p. 156), or to the Semitic equivalent of 'and', the ubiquitous *waw* (*w*). Compare Philo, *In Flacc.* 131: τὰ γράμματα κατὰ συλλαβὴν μᾶλλον δὲ καὶ κεραίαν ἑκάστην. Note that within the context of Matthew it is only the written Torah itself that is being upheld. The rabbinic fence around the law (cf. *m. 'Abot* 1.1), that is, the added scribal casuistry, is out of the picture (cf. 15.1–20).

According to T. W. Manson (*Sayings*, p. 135), 5.18 = Lk 16.17, in its original form, was bitter irony. Referring to the decorative additions to the law made by the scribes, Jesus criticized unbending conservatism: 'It is easier for heaven and earth to pass away than for the scribes to give up the smallest bit of that tradition by which they make the Law of none effect'. While brilliant, this conjecture is far less than certain. For one thing, we cannot be sure that 'tittle' stands for scribal, ornamental penstrokes. Beyond this, Manson assumed a pre-Easter *Sitz im Leben*, and though in this he might be correct, the saying might also be a community product, in which case it would be plausible to think of the formulation as stemming from conservative Jewish Christians who wished to uphold the law.[26] Thirdly, Manson must suppose that both Matthew and Luke misunderstood what Jesus said.

Turning to Matthew's understanding of 5.18, it is to be asked how he could have thought even the minutiae of the written Torah to be valid until the consummation. If Jesus had, among other things, forbidden oaths (5.33–7), dismissed the eye for eye principle (5.38–42), defended his disciples for plucking grain on the Sabbath (12.1–8), and sent his disciples into the Gentile world without so much as mentioning circumcision (28.16–20), how could the Jewish Torah still be thought of as inviolate? Several considerations are relevant. First, as we shall see in the exegesis of the pertinent texts, Matthew's gospel is much less radical than has sometimes been made out. The evangelist has toned down some of the more sweeping statements about the law in Mark (note, for instance, the omission of Mark 7.19c), and we cannot think that he believed the teachings of 5.21–48 to contradict the Torah. In other words, in Matthew's eyes the tension between Jesus' teaching and the Mosaic commandments was much less than in the eyes of many modern scholars.

Secondly, and despite the doctrine of the immutability of the Torah, there are not only Jewish texts that teach that the Torah will be better understood in the future than in the present (1 Macc 4.46) but also texts, such as *b. Šabb.* 151b; *Lev. Rab.* on 7.11–12 and 11.2; *Yal.* on Prov. 9.2; and *Midr. Ps.* 146.7, which 'reveal an awareness that, even though the Torah was immutable, nevertheless modification of various kinds, at least in certain details, would be necessary' (Davies, *SSM*, p. 161). Despite this, in none of the passages cited is the continuing validity of the Torah questioned: the changes envisaged by the rabbis were not deemed by them to diminish the Torah's authority. Similarly, we cannot think that 11QTemple, which frequently offers a revised version of Pentateuchal laws, was thought by the Dead Sea sectarians to call into question the authority and perpetuity of the Mosaic Law; and when Hillel introduced the prozbul (*m. Šeb.* 10.3–4), legislation which does not harmonize perfectly with Scripture, he did not intend to attack Moses; and when the rabbis argued, against Exod 20.7 and Deut 5.11, that one who took the Lord's name in vain could become guiltless (through atonement; see *Mek.* on Exod 20.7), they did not dream of taking anything away from the Torah; and the fact that, after A.D. 70, sacrifices were no longer offered in the temple did not diminish the rabbis' faith in the law's abiding validity. And so likewise must it have been for Matthew. Even if he did sense some tension between Jesus' sayings and the Torah, he could only, as 5.17 makes plain, have thought in terms of fulfilment.

In the third place, and if we may be permitted to generalize, three different attitudes about the Mosaic law existed in first-century Jewish Christianity. There were first of all the so-called 'Judaizers' who apparently expected Gentiles to become Jews and uphold the Torah (cf. Acts 15.1, 5; 21.21; Gal 6.13; Justin, *Dial.* 47.3). There were, secondly, those who believed the law had been set aside so that neither Jew nor Gentile had to submit to its yoke (Stephen?; John's Gospel; Epistle of Barnabas). Then, thirdly, and somewhere between the two extremes, were those who recognized the relative freedom of the Gentiles and yet at the same time believed that those born as Jews should remain within the law and Jewish tradition (so James, and Cephas, and John according to

Gal 2; also probably Paul (see 1 Cor 7.18; 9.19–21; Gal 5.3); cf. Justin, *Dial.* 47). Matthew, we should like to think, belonged to this third group. For him, the law was still to be observed by Jewish Christians (5.17–20; 23.3), but such was not necessary for the Gentiles. (Despite the opportunity permitted by texts such as 28.16–20, the circumcision of Gentiles is never mentioned, a circumstance which can only be explained if Matthew saw no need for it.)[26] It would, therefore, be no problem for the evangelist to affirm the perpetuity of the Torah and yet embrace the mission to the uncircumcision. Perhaps he thought that the law required of the Gentiles only fulfilment of the Noachic commandments (cf. Jub. 7.20; Sib. Or. 4.24–34; Acts 15.20; *b. 'Abod. Zar.* 64b; *b. Sanh.* 56a–b); and the Paul of Acts, who does not require circumcision for the salvation of the Gentiles and yet himself submits to Jewish tradition (Acts 16.3; 18.18; 21.23–6) might be a figure not altogether unlike Matthew. See Davies, *GL*, p. 402; *SSM*, pp. 325–326.

Fourthly and finally, when Paul writes in Gal 6.2 of τὸν νόμον τοῦ Χριστοῦ, the implied contrast with the traditional phrase, τὸν νόμον Μωϋσέως, proves that, whether or not speculation about a messianic Torah had clearly emerged already in first-century Judaism,[28] at least one Christian could think of Jesus Christ as bringing his own law.[29] Matthew too may have thought in this fashion. This does not, we hasten to add, entail that he recognized no strain between old and new. He certainly did. But for this an explanation was to hand: the course of salvation-history may affect the Torah. To illustrate: in 19.3–9, where Jesus prohibits divorce, the problem is that the Torah itself appears to have two different teachings; for while in Gen 1–2 marriage is an indissoluble union, in Deut 24.1–4 provisions are made for obtaining a certificate of divorce. The problem is resolved by recognizing that Gen 1–2 refers to a paradisiacal state while Deut 24 applies to a period in which people are hard-hearted; and Jesus, by siding with Gen 1–2 against Deuteronomy, is presupposing the *Urzeit = Endzeit* equation (see on 1.1) and declaring that

---

[27] Although it must be admitted that, according to some scholars, some religious Jews (even in Palestine) ignored circumcision; see Philo, *Migr. Abr.* 89–93; Josephus, *Ant.* 20.34–48; *ARN* 26; *y. Pesah.* 33b; but see L. H. Schiffman, *Who was a Jew? Rabbinic and Halakhic Perspectives on the Jewish-Christian Schism*, New York, 1985, p. 25.

[28] See esp. Davies, *Torah*; idem, *SSM*, pp. 109–90. The whole question needs to be reopened in the light of 11QTemple. Wacholder, pp. 1–32, e.g., believes the Qumranic Torah was intended to be a new Torah superseding the canonical Pentateuch.

[29] See esp. H. Schürmann, ' "Das Gesetz Christi" (Gal. 6.2)', in Gnilka, *Kirche*, pp. 282–300.

eschatological time has entered the arena of history. So Deut 24.1–4 is not contradicted but instead recognized as delimited by the inbreaking of unique circumstances and a new time. Only in so far as the Mosaic law contains concessions to the post-paradisiacal condition[30] will it not directly apply to the eschatological restoration of paradise.

ἕως ἂν πάντα γένηται. This is obviously a redactional addition. Against Lohmeyer, *Matthäus*, p. 108 (cf. Hübner, pp. 16–19), one need not postulate, because of the repetition in 5.18, that the verse is a conflation of two originally separate lines—'until heaven and earth pass away not one jot or tittle will pass away' and '(one tittle) will not pass away from the law until all is accomplished'. On ἕως ἄν[31] see above. Against γίνομαι (see on 6.10) here meaning 'be done' see Meier, *Law*, pp. 53–4.

Many have believed that this phrase further qualifies 5.17–18 and sets a limit for the inviolability of the Torah that has already been met—by Jesus' obedience,[32] by his death,[33] or by the destruction of the temple in A.D. 70.[34] The natural objection to all three options is this: 'until heaven and earth pass away' (so 18a) most naturally suggests that there is still a long period of time to elapse before the law passes away. Others have affirmed that the law remains in effect because it has been fulfilled by Jesus, who brought a new commandment containing the whole law[35] or

---

[30] On the idea of concession in Jewish law see D. Daube, 'Concessions to Sinfulness in Jewish Law', *JJS* 10 (1959), pp. 1–13, and H. Hübner, 'Mark vii.1–23 und das "jüdisch-hellenistische" Gesetzesverständnis', *NTS* 22 (1976), pp. 319–45.

[31] Against Schweizer, 'Matth. 5,17–20' (v) and 'Noch einmal' (v), ἕως is not telic. See Meier, *Law*, p. 48, n. 23.

[32] Yet one can hardly translate ἕως ἂν πάντα γένηται as 'until all (the law) has been observed'; see Meier, *Law*, pp. 53–4, 61–2.

[33] Davies (v); Jeremias, *Sermon*, p. 24; Meier, *Law*, pp. 30–5; idem, *Vision*, pp. 229–34. The advantages of this proposal are several. (1) The NT elsewhere associates cancellation of the law with death (e.g. Rom 7.1; Gal 2.19). (2) Early Christianity and Matthew himself saw Jesus' passion as an eschatological event, so the passing away of heaven and earth could be referred to the passion and/or resurrection of Jesus. (3) In 28.11 ἅπαντα τὰ γενόμενα refers to circumstances surrounding Jesus' resurrection. On the other side, (1) Matthew nowhere explicitly relates changes in the Torah to Jesus' passion or resurrection; (2) 'until heaven and earth pass away' remains a bit awkward; we might, on the proposed interpretation, have expected Matthew to have written: 'Truly I say to you, not one jot or tittle will pass from the law until all is accomplished'; and (3) the 'fulfilment' of 5.17–20, a passage which after all introduces the rest of Mt 5, is more naturally interpreted as referring to the teaching of the earthly Jesus rather than to salvific events at the end of the ministry. We might also observe that Davies at least at one time considered 'until all is accomplished' to be possible on Jesus' lips; but the phrase is almost certainly redactional.

[34] A Feuillet, 'La synthèse eschatologique de Saint Matthieu', *RB* 57 (1950), pp. 62–91, 180–211.

[35] So Schweizer, 'Matth. 5,17–20' (v); idem, 'Noch einmal' (v).

because his teaching about the kingdom of God incorporates the truth of the Torah.[36] For these scholars, obviously, the 'law' has been redefined.[37] But this is to read too much into the text. It is best to equate νόμος with the OT law and to view 'until heaven and earth pass away' and 'until all things are accomplished' as standing in synonymous parallelism: both refer to the outstanding consummation (so Klostermann, p. 51). This is supported by 24.34: 'Truly I say to you that this generation will not pass away ἕως ἂν πάντα ταῦτα γένηται'. Here 'all these things' are the eschatological events prophesied in chapter 24. So in 5.18 ἕως ἂν πάντα γένηται means, as the NEB translates, 'until all that must happen has happened' (cf. 1.22; 21.4; 26.54–6). The objection that this makes for unnecessary redundancy fails because 'until all things are accomplished' adds two things: it (1) introduces the idea, absent from the preceding ἕως clause, of God's prophetic promises and redemptive purposes (so Moo (v); cf. the mention of 'prophets' in v. 17 and the prophetic use of πληρόω) and (2) eliminates the possibility of interpreting 'until heaven and earth pass away' as being the rhetorical equivalent of 'never': rather is a definite end to the law set forth.

19. Compare Did. 4.13; Barn. 19.11. The vocabulary of this verse—a so-called 'sentence of holy law', in which the human action in the protasis correlates with a divine action in the apodosis[38]—is largely Matthean, and the antithetical parallelism of 19a–b and 19c–d could also be considered characteristic of the redactor. But 5.19, which has no synoptic parallel, might nevertheless be a redactional version of a traditional line. Indeed, 5.19 may take up a pre-Matthean application of 5.17–18, in which case the sources of 5.17–20 would be two—Q^mt (17–19) and Matthean redaction (20).[39] Moreover, if this be correct, and if 5.17 and 18 are based upon words of Jesus, 5.19 probably preserves a post-Easter interpretation aimed at perceived libertine tendencies. In any case 5.19 certainly fails to find an echo elsewhere in the authentic words of Jesus.[40] Elsewhere in the gospels 'greatness' is

[36] So Banks, p. 218. For Banks, Jesus' commands replace the OT, which continues only in so far as it is taken up by Jesus.

[37] But surely 'iota' and 'tittle' direct the reader's mind to the traditional Torah.

[38] Lit.: Käsemann, *Questions*, pp. 66–81; K. Berger, 'Zu den sogenannten Sätzen des heiligen Rechts', *NTS* 17 (1970), pp. 10–40; D. Schmidt, 'The LXX *Gattung* "Prophetic Correlative" ', *JBL* 96 (1977), pp. 517–22.

[39] For 5.19 as belonging to Q see Schürmann (v) and Meier, *Law*, pp. 101–3. As to the stage before Q^mt, some form of 5.17 and 19 may have circulated together, 5.18 being inserted between them sometime later.

[40] As. Mos. 12.10–11 supplies a Jewish parallel: 'Those who fulfil the commandments of God will flourish and will finish the good way, but those who sin by disregarding the commandments will deprive themselves of the good things which were declared before'.

defined only in paradoxical terms: to be great one must be last, or be a servant, or be a child, etc.

Within the present context in Matthew, 5.19 follows well upon 5.18: if the law remains valid even down to its jots and tittles, then it must be practised and taught in its entirety.[41] A liberal attitude towards the law is not in order; all antinomian tendencies are excluded.[42]

ὃς ἐὰν οὖν λύσῃ μίαν τῶν ἐντολῶν τούτων τῶν ἐλαχίστων. There is with this line—whose vocabulary is characteristic of Matthew[43]—a change of subject. 5.17–18 has to do with Jesus while 5.19–20 has to do with his followers.

'The least of these commandments' adverts back to 5.18 and therefore to the commandments of the Mosaic Torah,[44] not ahead to 5.21ff. and the words of Jesus.[45] The οὖν and the flow of thought are decisive. Beyond this, where is the Matthean parallel to applying 'lesser' and 'greater' to the sayings of Jesus?,[46] or to calling Jesus' words ἐντολαί (although this last is common in John and the Apostolic Fathers; see BAGD, s.v.)? And does not the λύω in 5.19 take the reader's mind back to the καταλύω in 5.17, where the Torah is indisputably the subject?

If 5.19, as just argued, does indeed connect up with 5.17–18, this is almost decisive reason for not interpreting 5.18's 'until all things are accomplished' as delimiting a period now ended. If jots and tittles have in fact fallen away, how can 5.19 enjoin the keeping of even the least of the commandments? 5.19 presupposes that the

[41] Jas 2.10: 'Whoever keeps the whole law but fails in one point has become guilty of all'. Although it was recognized that total obedience was not possible, the importance of doing not part of the law but all of it was a commonplace in ancient Judaism, as was the distinction between 'heavy' and 'light' commandments; see *m. 'Abot* 2.1; 4.2; *b. Ned.* 39b; *b. Šabb.* 70b; SB 1, pp. 249, 901–5.

[42] Kilpatrick's suggestion, pp. 25–6 (cf. McNeile, p. 60), that v. 19 originally followed v. 41 is based only upon the lack of a clear antecedent for 'the least of these commandments'. The antecedent, however, is implicit or indirect (cf. 3.9; 25.40, 45): 'one jot or tittle' and 'the least of these commandments' are conceptually very close. (Augustne, *De serm. mont.* 1.8.20, identifies them.) Furthermore, there is no textual warrant for Kilpatrick's proposal.

[43] ὅς/ὅστις ἐάν/ἄν: Mt 37; Mk 21; Lk 20; with λύω: Mt 3; Mk 0; Lk 0. λύω with theological content: Mt 5; Mk 0; Lk 0. ἐντολή (redactional in 22.38): Mt 7; Mk 6; Lk 4. ἐλάχιστος: Mt 5; Mk 0; Lk 4.

[44] Johnston (v) unconvincingly suggests that the law of the bird's nest (Deut. 22.6–7) should be called to mind, for in *y. Qidd.* 1.61b.58 and *Deut. Rab.* 6.2, it is called the least of the commandments.

[45] Contra Lohmeyer, *Matthäus*, pp. 110–12; Banks, p. 223; and Schweizer, *Matthew*, pp. 108–9. Schlatter, pp. 157–8, interprets 'the least of these commandments' as referring to the ten commandments. Cf. Dibelius (v).

[46] According to Betz, *Essays* pp. 47–8, 'the least of these commandments' = Jesus' commandments only in an ironic sense: the Pharisaic emphasis on 'heavy' commandments is being rejected.

time of the law's demise, the time prophesied by 5.18, has not yet come to pass.

καὶ διδάξῃ οὕτως τοὺς ἀνθρώπους. When Matthew thinks of those he is opposed to, he thinks of their leaders, that is, their teachers. Only here and in 28.20 is Jesus not the subject of διδάσκω (Mt: 14; Mk: 17; Lk: 17). The evangelist is fond of οὕτως (Mt: 32; Mk: 10; Lk: 21).

ἐλάχιστος κληθήσεται ἐν τῇ βασιλείᾳ τῶν οὐρανῶν. The punishment fits the crime. 'As we treat the word of God, so does God treat us' (Bengel, ad loc.). Those who have not kept the least of the commandments will be called—by God at the great assize—least in the kingdom of heaven. 'Kingdom of heaven' (Mt: 32; Mk: 0; Lk: 0) is typical of the redactor. ἐλάχιστος occurs for the second time in our verse and creates paronomasia (cf. BDF § 488.1). καλέω (Mt: 26; Mk: 4; Lk: 43) is here in the passive and is the functional equivalent of 'to be': to be called something by God is to be that something.

Does 'least in the kingdom of heaven' entail utter exclusion from the final state of the blessed?[47] Perhaps not (cf. As. Mos. 12.10–13). The idea of rank in heaven and of degrees of reward is found not only in rabbinic writings but also in the gospel of Matthew (5.12; 10.41–42; 20.23; SB 1, pp. 249–50; 4, pp. 1138–43).

It has, from time to time, been urged that Mt 5.19 adverts to Paul, who in one place called himself 'the least of the apostles' (1 Cor 15.9; the Latin *paulus* = small).[48] Now there is no doubting the polemical tone of 5.19: the verse was obviously formulated with laxness towards the law in view. And we cannot exclude the possibility that Paul was originally the intended target. But this possibility remains far outside the bounds of certainty. There were many besides Paul who, at least in the eyes of others, sat loose to the law. Moreover, the phrase, 'the least in the kingdom of heaven', may simply have been suggested by the preceding 'the least of these commandments'. And in any case one cannot be certain that Paul was actually known as 'the least', and certainly one cannot confidently claim Matthew's familiarity with 1 Corinthians.

ὃς δ' ἂν ποιήσῃ καὶ διδάξῃ.[49] 5.19c–d parallels 5.19a–b, but only imperfectly. 'Shall be called least' matches 'shall be called great';

[47] So Chrysostom, *Hom. on Mt.* 16.5; Bonnard, p. 62; Schweizer, *Matthew*, p. 105; and Luz (v), p. 410; against Meier, *Law*, pp. 92–5; Mohrlang, p. 18; and Betz, *Essays*, p. 49.

[48] So Weiss, *History*, p. 753; Manson, *Sayings*, pp. 25, 124; Betz, *Essays*, pp. 21–2, 49, 56, n. 54; cf. Streeter, pp. 256–7, and Bultmann, *Theology* 1, p. 54. For a differing view see Barth, in *TIM*, pp. 159–64; Davies, *SSM*, pp. 334–6; and Sand, pp. 99–100.

[49] ℵ* D W bo^ms omit this and the rest of 5.19, probably because of homoioteleuton: a scribal eye passed from the first occurrence of 'will be called in the kingdom of heaven' in 5.19 to the second occurrence of the same phrase.

but there is no 'greatest of these commandments' corresponding to 'the least of these commandments'. Perhaps 5.19c–d is a redactional expansion made to Matthew's source, a balancing addition required to make 5.19 better fit its context as an introduction to the doing of the better righteousness.

ἄν replaces the ἐάν of 5.19a (see BDF § 107). The verb, ποιέω, which is here the antithesis of λύω, occurs twenty-two times in the sermon on the mount and underlines the necessity of *doing* the will of the Father in heaven (see esp. 7.17–26). 'Do' and 'teach' occur in combination only here in Matthew, although 23.3 and 28.20 supply near parallels (cf. also Acts 1.1). The order, doing before teaching, may indicate Matthew's agreement with the Shammaites who, as opposed to the Hillelites, placed doing over studying (cf. *m. 'Abot* 1.15, 17; 3.10; *Sipre* on Deut 11.13; *y. Ber.* 1.5.3b). In any event, those who do and teach are imitating Jesus, who upheld the law in his own person (5.17).

οὗτος μέγας κληθήσεται ἐν τῇ βασιλείᾳ τῶν οὐρανῶν.[50] Compare T. Levi 13.9: πᾶς ὃς ἂν διδάσκει καλὰ καὶ πράττει σύνθρονός ἐσται βασιλέων. See 20.26 for the disciples' greatness, 18.1 for greatness in the kingdom of heaven, and 11.11 for the least/great(er) contrast in connexion with the kingdom of heaven. Observe that 'great' contrasts not with 'less' but with 'least'. Does this reflect the circumstance that Hebrew and Aramaic have no comparative form for adjectives? Did our Semitic evangelist find juxtapositioning of the positive degree with the superlative degree less awkward than we do?

As 5.20 teaches, one can only enter the kingdom of heaven if one's righteousness exceeds that of the scribes and Pharisees; and 'if mere entrance requires so much, greatness requires even more, i.e., obedience to all the least commandments, too' (Gundry, *Commentary*, p. 82).

20. This redactional verse (cf. Meier, *Law*, pp. 108–19), which is quoted first by Justin, *Dial.* 105, is the transition between 5.17–19 and 5.21–48. Jesus came to 'fulfil' the law, which must therefore be upheld by his followers. Moreover, because, as 5.21–48 leaves not in doubt, the Messiah's words are even more demanding than Moses' words, those who obey the Messiah will inevitably find that their 'righteousness' exceeds that of the scribes and Pharisees. (It could be, however, that the contrast in 5.20 between two types of righteousness has as much or more to do with doing than with teaching. The previous verse, 5.19, is about doing, and when Jesus elsewhere speaks of the scribes and Pharisees, he

---

[50] Resumptive οὗτος: Mt 10; Mk 4; Lk 4. μέγας: Mt 20 (often redactional); Mk 15; Lk 26.

typically refers to their 'hypocrisy' (e.g. 15.7; 22.18; 23.13–15, 28). The slur presupposes that they really do know better. So in Matthew the main problem with the Jewish leaders is not that they do not know the difference between right and wrong, it is instead simply that, knowing what they should do, they do something else. In view of this, 5.20 may not so much anticipate unique teaching as enjoin readers to do, to act, to be. The better righteousness is the righteousness of action—based, of course, on the words of Jesus.)

5.20 is structurally very similar to 5.18. Both have in common λέγω ὑμῖν + ἐάν/ἄν + μή. Thus, in composing 5.20, the redactor has been influenced by 5.18.

For N. J. McEleney (v), Mt 5.17–19 introduces 5.21–48 while 5.20 introduces 6.1–7.12. Against this, we should expect 5.20 to be where 6.1 now is and we should expect 6.1 not to be at all if McEleney were right. Also, 5.20 links up with 5.21–48 both by catchword (περισσεύσῃ, 5.20; περισσόν, 5.47) as well as by theme (the disciples must do more than the scribes and Pharisees and more than the Torah requires). We must also reject Broer's suggestion. He holds ((v), p. 73) that 5.17a is the heading for 5.18–20 and 5.17b the heading for 5.21–48. Among other things, it is all but impossible not to think of 5.21–48 as illustrating the better righteousness of 5.20.

λέγω γὰρ ὑμῖν ὅτι.[51] See on 5.17. The switch from the third person singular (in 5.19) to the second person plural (in 5.20) is to be put down to the stereotyped expression, 'I say to you'.

ἐὰν μὴ περισσεύσῃ ὑμῶν ἡ δικαιοσύνη πλεῖον τῶν γραμματέων καὶ Φαρισαίων.[52] The word 'righteousness', which is here 'elegantly omitted' before 'the scribes and Pharisees' (Bengel, ad loc.), expresses the essence of the sermon on the mount (cf. on 7.12). On the abbreviated comparison see BDF §185.1. The addition of a second comparative (πλεῖον) heightens the contrast (BDF § 246).

The meaning of 'righteousness' in 5.20 is determined by the paragraphs that follow. 'Righteousness' is therefore Christian character and conduct in accordance with the demands of Jesus—right intention, right word, right deed. Hence 'righteousness' does not refer, even implicitly, to God's gift. The Pauline (forensic, eschatological) connotation is absent. This conclusion is confirmed by the mention of the scribes and Pharisees. For they

[51] D omits 5.20, probably because of homoioteleuton: the words between οὐρανῶν at the end of 5.19 and οὐρανῶν at the end of 5.20 were inadvertently skipped.
[52] ἐάν: Mt 64; Mk 35; Lk 29; with μή: Mt 10; Mk 6; Lk 3. περισσεύω: Mt 5; Mk 1; Lk 4. πλείων: Mt 7; Mk 1; Lk 9. 'Scribes and Pharisees' (in this order): Mt 9; Mk 1; Lk 3.

too have a righteousness, but it is of a sort insufficient to enable them to enter the kingdom of heaven. So what they have is clearly not the gift of God; instead their want of righteousness is a failure in their conduct.

One may compare 5.47: 'And if you salute only your brethren, what more are you doing than others?' The greater righteousness is a doing more. It is therefore a quantitative advance. Yet this is not to deny that, in Matthew's eyes, there is also a qualitative advance. After all, love cannot be quantified. Further, in following Jesus' example and obeying his commandments, the disciples are to obtain 'perfection'; see on 5.48.

On the 'scribes' and 'Pharisees' see on 2.4 and 3.7 respectively. Together the two groups are transparent figures representing the Jewish leaders of Matthew's world. (According to most, even the phrase itself, 'the scribes and the Pharisees', reflects the post A.D. 70 situation, in which the Pharisaic scribes came to dominate Judaism, for, before 70, many scribes did not belong to the Pharisaic party. But we must exercise caution in this regard. Ellis Rivkin has made a strong case for identifying the scribes and Pharisees.)[53]

The appearance of the scribes and Pharisees in 5.20 creates tension with 5.17–19, for while this last seems to be directed against liberal or antinomian tendencies, 5.20 suddenly mentions the Jewish leaders, and they remain in the picture as far as 6.18 (note also 7.29). Probably we should think of Matthew as fighting on two fronts, against a Christian laxity towards the law on the one hand and against the rabbinic rejection of Christianity on the other (cf. Chrysostom, *Hom. on Mt.* 16.3). (It is interesting that, despite Matthew's serious differences with the scribes and Pharisees and the harsh *ad hominem* dunderhead-bashing in chapter 23, in 5.20 they receive a backhanded compliment: their achievement in righteousness marks out the goal to be surpassed by Christians. Compare Chrysostom, *Hom. on Mt.* 16.6: 'were they not doing well, he would not have said they have a righteousness'.)

οὐ μὴ εἰσέλθητε εἰς τὴν βασιλείαν τῶν οὐρανῶν. The non-Markan 18.3 contains this identical phrase. Compare also 7.21; 23.13. Although the threat in 5.20 is the converse of the promise in 5.19, in both verses eschatology provides the motivation for proper behaviour.

---

[53] For a brief statement of his views see *IDSup*, s.v. 'Pharisees'. For a fuller treatment see his book, *A Hidden Revolution* (Nashville, 1978), and idem, 'Scribes, Pharisees, Lawyers, Hypocrites: A Study in Synonymity', *HUCA* 49 (1978), pp. 135–42.

Despite the redactional origin of Mt 5.20, Jesus himself surely spoke of 'entering into the kingdom' (Mk 9.47; 10.15; Jn 3.5, 6; there is no exact rabbinic parallel; see SB 1, pp. 252–53). The background for the expression is to be found in the OT, in the idea of entering the promised land (Num 20.24; Judg 18.9; As. Mos. 2.1). What happens at the end is like what happened at the beginning of Israel's history: God's people enter the eschatological land, paradise (cf. 5.5).

(iv) *Concluding Observations*

In denying the suspicion that Jesus abolished the Torah, 5.17–20 looks forward, not backward, for surely from what has gone before (5.3–16) no such suspicion could be generated (Chrysostom, *Hom. on Mt.* 16.1). Hence the verses anticipate and therefore introduce 5.21–48, setting the reader right beforehand: the so-called 'antitheses' are not to be interpreted as antitheses, for Jesus does not overturn the Pentateuch. If Jewish or Christian opponents[54] think or say otherwise, they are simply wrong. Consequently, 5.17–20, by upholding the law, has a twofold effect. It defends Jesus and Matthew (1) from the accusation, no doubt made by non-Christian Jews, that they had dismissed the Torah[55] and (2) from the claim, certainly made by some early Christians, that Jesus had set his followers free from the law. For our evangelist the OT has not been drained of its ancient life. It is not just a precious cemetery. It is still the living, active word of God.

5.17–20 not only rebuts in advance a wrong interpretation of the so-called 'antitheses', it also supplies the reader with a clue as to the right interpretation. 5.20, in announcing that the righteousness of Jesus' followers must exceed that of the scribes and Pharisees, anticipates that Jesus' words in the subsequent paragraphs will require even more than the Torah itself requires. Thus the tension between Jesus' teaching and the Mosaic Law is not that those who

---

[54] According to Zumstein, pp. 171–200, and others, Matthew was fighting on two fronts—against Christian antinomians and against Jewish accusers. Against this, Strecker, *Weg*, p. 276, and Walker, pp. 135–6, fail to discern a specific set of opponents behind the First Gospel. In our judgement, our evangelist was undoubtedly troubled by a real Jewish objection to Christianity, namely, Christians reject Moses. Matthew also must have known—if only because he had read Mark—that some Christian groups had gone too far in relativizing the Torah. We hesitate, however, to affirm that he had a concrete group of Christian antinomians in his mind's eye as he wrote: for this the evidence is insufficient.

[55] For some of the evidence see G. N. Stanton, 'Aspects of Early Christian-Jewish Polemic and Apologetic', *NTS* 31 (1985), pp. 377–92. He considers the evidence of the Testaments of the Twelve Patriarchs, Justin Martyr, and Marcion's addition at Lk 23.2 (καὶ καταλύοντα τὸν ναὸν καὶ τοὺς προφήτας).

accept the former will transgress the latter; rather is it that they will achieve far more than they would if the Torah were their only guide. As the πλεῖον of 5.20 and the περισσόν of 5.47 imply, Christian righteousness means doing more. It means, in fact, as 5.48 plainly states, a quest for 'perfection'; and such a quest was not, in Matthew's eyes, equally enjoined by Moses.

(v) *Bibliography*

Arens, pp. 99–116.

W. Auer, 'Iota unum aut unus apex non praeteribit a lege (Mt 5,18)', *BK* 14 (1959), pp. 97–103.

Banks, pp. 203–26.

R. Banks, 'Matthew's Understanding of the Law: Authenticity and Interpretation in Matthew 5:17–20', *JBL* 93 (1974), pp. 226–42.

Barth, *TIM*, pp. 58–164.

Berger, *Gesetzauslegung*, pp. 209–27.

H. D. Betz, 'The Hermeneutical Principles of the Sermon on the Mount', *JTSA* 42 (1983), pp. 17–28; reprinted in *Essays*, pp. 37–54.

I. Broer, *Freiheit vom Gesetz und Radikalisierung des Gesetzes*, SBS 98, Stuttgart, 1980.

Davies, *COJ*, pp. 31–66.

F. Dibelius, 'Die Kleinsten Gebote', *ZNW* 11(1910), pp. 188–90.

Giesen, pp. 122–46.

R. Guelich, ' "Not to Annul the Law, Rather to Fulfill the Law and the Prophets": An Exegetical Study of Jesus and the Law in Matthew with Emphasis on 5.17–48' (Hamburg Dissertation, unpublished, 1967).

Guelich, pp. 134–74.

F. Hahn, 'Mt 5,17—Anmerkungen zum Erfüllungsgedanken bei Matthäus', in *Die Mitte des Neuen Testaments*, ed. U. Luz and H. Weder, Göttingen, 1983, pp. 42–54.

R. G. Hamerton-Kelly, 'Attitudes to the Law in Matthew's Gospel: A Discussion of Matthew 5:18', *BR* 17 (1972), pp. 19–32.

A. Harnack, 'Geschichte eines programmatischen Wortes Jesu (Matt. 5,17) in der ältesten Kirche', *SPAW* (1912), pp. 184–207.

C. Heubült, 'Mt 5:17–20. Ein Beitrag zum Theologie des Evangelisten Matthäus', *ZNW* 71 (1980), pp. 143–9.

A. Honeyman, 'Matthew 5.18 and the Validity of the Law', *NTS* 1 (1954–5), pp. 141–2.

Hübner, pp. 15–39, 230–6.

Hummel, pp. 64–75.

R. M. Johnston, ' "The Least of the Commandments": Deuteronomy 22.6–7 in Rabbinic Judaism and Early Christianity', *Andrews University Seminary Studies* 20 (1982), pp. 205–15.

W. G. Kümmel, 'Jesus und der jüdische Traditionsgedanke', *ZNW* 33 (1934), pp. 105–30.

S. Légasse, 'Mt 5,17 et la prétendue tradition paracanonique', in *Begegnung mit dem Wort*, ed. J. Zmijewski and E. Nellessen, Bonn, 1980, pp. 11–22.

Ljungman, pp. 7–75, 91–6.

U. Luz, 'Die Erfüllung des Gesetzes bei Matthäus', *ZTK* 75 (1978), pp. 398–435.

McConnell, pp. 6–58.

N. J. McEleney, 'The Principles of the Sermon on the Mount', *CBQ* 41 (1979), pp. 552–70.

Marguerat, pp. 110–41.

Meier, *Law*, passim.

Meier, *Vision*, pp. 222–39.

J. D. Moo, 'Jesus and the Authority of the Mosaic Law', *JSNT* 20 (1984), pp. 3–49.

Ogawa, pp. 138–45.

Przybylski, pp. 80–7.

Riesner, pp. 456–60.

L. Sabourin, 'Matthieu 5,17–20 et le rôle prophétique de la Loi (cf. Mt 11,13)', *ScEs* 30 (1978), pp. 303–11.

H. J. Schoeps, *Zeit*, pp. 212–20.

H. Schürmann, 'Wer daher eines dieser geringsten Gebote auflöst . . . ', *BZ* 4 (1960), pp. 238–50; reprinted in *Untersuchungen*, pp. 126–36.

G. Schwarz, 'ἰῶτα ἓν ἢ μία κεραία (Matthäus 5,18)', *ZNW* 66 (1975), pp. 268–9.

E. Schweizer, 'Noch einmal Mt 5,17–20', in *Das Wort und die Wörter*, ed. H. Balz and S. Schulz, Stuttgart, 1973, pp. 69–73; reprinted in *Gemeinde*, pp. 78–85.

idem, 'Mt 5.17–20. Anmerkungen zum Gesetzesverständnis des Matthäus', in *Neotestamentica*, pp. 399–406.

H. Simonsen, 'Die Auffassung vom Gesetz im Matthäusevangelium', in *Theologie aus dem Norden*, *SNTU* A 2, ed. A. Fuchs, Freistadt, 1976, pp. 44–67.

Strecker, *Weg*, pp. 143–53.

Suggs, pp. 115–27.

E. F. Sutcliffe, 'One Jot or Tittle, Mt 5,18', *Bib* 9 (1928), pp. 458–60.

Trilling, pp. 167–86.

D. Wenham, 'Jesus and the Law: an exegesis on Matt. 5.17–20', *Themelios* 4 (1979), pp. 92–6.

Wrege, pp. 35–46.

XII

THE BETTER RIGHTEOUSNESS
(5.21–48)

(i) *Structure*

5.21–48 divides itself into two triads, 5.21–32 and 5.33–48. This is evident from the following facts. (1) Vv. 20 and 27 begin with 'You have heard that it was said', v. 31 with 'it was said'. And then comes v. 33, the opening line of the fourth unit in the series. It begins: '*Again* you have heard that it was said'. Why the adverb? (It occurs nowhere else in the sermon on the mount.) The word's presence, which in no way affects the content of the surrounding material but which does break the rhythm of chapter 5, becomes explicable only if Matthew wished to indicate that with v. 33 he was in some sense making Jesus start over or begin a new series. That is, 'again' marks an editorial dividing line. Jesus first speaks to three issues, murder (5.21–6), adultery (5.27–30), and divorce (5.31–2). He then ('again') moves on to consider three more issues, oaths (5.33–7), retaliation (5.38–42), and love (5.43–8). So the evangelist is thinking in terms of triads. (2) In 5.21–32 the three-fold 'But I say to you' is in each instance followed by ὅτι. In 5.33–48 this construction does not occur. (3) The full phrase, 'You have heard that it was said to the men of old' appears only in 5.21 and 5.33, in the two verses which head the two triads. (4) While in 5.21–32 'But I say to you that' prefaces a legal ordinance form which employs πᾶς ὁ, in 5.33–48 'But I say to you' prefaces straightforward imperatives. (5) 5.21, 27, and 31 open with citations of or allusions to OT texts that appear in Deuteronomy (although not exclusively in Deuteronomy), and 5.33, 38, and 43 open with citations of or allusions to OT texts that appear in Leviticus (although not exclusively in Leviticus). The evangelist just may have thought of 5.21–32 as offering contrasts with laws in Deuteronomy and of 5.33–48 as offering contrasts with laws in Leviticus.

(ii) *Sources*

With regard to the sources of 5.21–48, most scholars have accepted Bultmann's analysis: 5.21–6, 27–30, and 33–7 incorporate pre-Matthean 'antitheses' while the other 'antitheses' are redactional (*History*, pp. 134–6; so also Guelich, 'Antitheses' (v) and Luz 1, p. 246). But the traditional nature of all six so-called 'antitheses' has also been defended (e.g. Jeremias, *Theology*, pp. 251–3, and Wrege (v)), as has indeed their exclusively redactional origin (Suggs, pp. 109–15; Gundry, *Commentary*, pp. 82–4; Broer, 'Antithesen' (v)). Certainty on the issue is unobtainable. But it does seem to us that general probabilities encourage one to embrace Bultmann's position. The material in 5.21–48 has, as a matter of history, given rise to the conviction that Jesus contradicted pieces of Mosaic legislation. Such an erroneous understanding was anticipated by the evangelist: the first function of 5.17–20 is to state unequivocally that Jesus came not to abolish the Torah. This raises a question. Is it more likely that Matthew created the ἠκούσατε . . . δέ form and that he, anticipating the resultant problems, placed 5.17–20 before 5.21–48? Or is it easier to imagine that before Matthew took up his pen certain sayings now preserved in 5.21–48 had already been interpreted in a fashion disagreeable to the evangelist and that he in turn responded with 5.17–20? The latter alternative appears to us the more plausible. Matthew would hardly have created a formula knowing full well in advance—as 5.17–20 implies—that it would only lead to misunderstanding. Since, moreover, 5.31–2, 38–42, and 43–8 appear in Luke but in a different form from that in Matthew (and are therefore to be assigned to Q), presumption favours the inference that only in 5.21–6, 27–30, and 33–7 should the ἠκούσατε . . . δέ form be assigned with any confidence to tradition.[1]

The conclusion just drawn is, because it assumes the existence of Q, not consistent with the Griesbach hypothesis and would therefore be rejected by proponents thereof. But 5.21–48 contains material that seems to support defenders of the traditional two-document hypothesis. For example, 5.29–30 appears to be secondary over against its doublet in 18.8–9 (note the redactional γάρ, the editorial συμφέρει . . . ἵνα (Mt: 3; Mk: 0; Lk: 0) and the omission for the sake of context of the saying about the foot); and when 18.8–9 is in turn compared with Mk 9.45–7, Matthew seems to have a secondary version (see on 18.8–9). In addition, and as we shall argue in section iii, Luke appears to be more original than Matthew in Lk 6.29–30 = Mt 5.39, 42; in Lk 6.35 = Mt 5.45; and in Lk 6.36 = Mt 5.48.

EXCURSUS III

THE INTERPRETATION OF MT 5.21–48

Because interpretations of the six paragraphs in Mt 5.21–48 have been so various, we shall refrain from reviewing previous work and instead set forth what we think are the four primary conclusions to be reached.

---

[1] Albertz, pp. 146–9, argued that the three traditional 'antitheses' were joined before Matthew. He reconstructed a source consisting of 5.17, 21–2a, 27–8, 33–4a, 37. This remains an attractive possibility; cf. Taylor, *Formation*, pp. 94–100. See Luz 1, p. 249, for the argument that at least the first two 'antitheses' go back to Jesus. We endorse his conclusions.

1. 5.21–48 does not set Jesus' words over against Jewish interpretations of the OT; rather is Jesus' 'But I say to you' intended to mark a point of contrast with the OT itself (cf. Schlatter, pp. 165–6; Luz 1, pp. 247–9).

a. 5.17–20, which introduces 5.21–48, denies that Jesus came to abolish the law and the prophets (= the OT). Thus what 5.17–20 anticipates is someone concluding that Jesus' words contradict the Torah. This probably shows that the primary point at issue is Jesus and the OT. In other words, 5.17–20 moves the reader to think in terms of Jesus and the Torah, not in terms of Jesus and Jewish opinion. (Some might respond that the point is not valid because there was no perceived distinction between the written and the oral Torah; cf. Hahn, *Worship*, p. 16. Against this it suffices to recall the position of the Sadducees (Josephus, *Ant.* 13.297) and NT texts such as Mt 15.2, 3, 6.)

b. The content of 5.21, 27, 31, 33, 38, and 43 can be derived in every instance from the OT (as we shall show in the commentary proper). It is not necessary to rifle extracanonical literature for parallels.

c. 'You have heard' is past tense, 'I say to you' present tense. Why the distinction in tenses if Jesus' disagreement is with current Jewish interpretation? The past/present dichotomy most naturally involves—although it admittedly does not necessitate—two authorities separated in time (Jesus and Moses; cf. Ogawa, p. 122).

d. In Rom 9.12 and Gal 3.16 ἐρρέθη is used of the speech of God in the OT (cf. the rabbinic *ne'ĕmar*).

e. 5.17–48 is set not in the synagogue (where exegetical points were debated) or addressed to the learned; it is instead delivered to a crowd on a mountain.

f. Because 5.21–48 does not offer us Jesus' *interpretation* of the law (see points 2 and 3), the Torah's interpretation by others cannot be in view.

g. It is possible to construe the introductory phrase, 'You have heard that it was said to the men of old', as more or less reproducing a rabbinic formula used to contrast the different interpretations of two rabbis (Daube (v); Smith (v)). But the parallel between Matthew and the rabbinic texts breaks down upon the implicitly christological ἐγώ and the fact that Jesus does not support his supposed interpretations by appeals to Scripture. Furthermore, 5.27 ('You shall not commit adultery'), 5.31 ('Whoever divorces his wife, let him give her a certificate of divorce'), and 5.38 ('Eye for eye, tooth for tooth') in particular resist being labelled 'interpretation'.

2. Although Jesus' words are contrasted with the words of Torah, the two are not contradictory (cf. Irenaeus, *Adv. haer.* 4.12.1, on Marcion's followers).

a. We have already, in the commentary on 5.18, supplied reasons for holding that the first evangelist did not believe his Lord to have opposed the Mosaic law.

b. If, as seems most probable, ἐρρέθη is a divine passive (='God said'; see on 5.21), then an interpretation that sets what was said to the ancients in contradictory antithesis to Jesus' 'But I say to you' would inevitably make Jesus disagree with God, an obvious impossibility.

c. Those who find the Torah contradicted in 5.21–48 must confess that this is only a possibility for the third, fourth, fifth, and sixth paragraphs. Yet if any sort of consistency is to be ascribed to the redactor, he must have understood each paragraph having the 'You have heard . . . but I say to you' form to have had the same general import. So if the first and second paragraphs do not on any reckoning overturn the law, we do not expect this from the other paragraphs.

d. In Matthew, δέ, unlike ἀλλά, does not always signal a strong antithesis or contrast (see on 1.19 and note 16.18: κἀγὼ δέ σοι λέγω.) Besides 'but', the particle can also mean 'and yet' or even 'and'; and the continuative function of δέ is well attested: 6.29; 8.10–11; 12.5–6; see further Levison (v). We would translate the so-called 'antitheses' this way: 'You have heard that it was said to the men of old . . . but I (in addition) say to you . . .'. The contrast involves not contradiction but transcendence.

e. The OT does not command divorce or the taking of oaths (cf. 19.3–9). (The pertinent legislation is provisional; that is, it takes for granted divorces and oaths and proceeds from there). Thus 5.31–2 and 33–7 cannot be said to overthrow OT *commandments*. See further Sanders, *Jesus*, pp. 256–7.

f. Anyone who followed the words of Jesus in 5.21–48 would not find himself in violation of any Jewish law.[2]

---

[2] This has led to the proposal that 5.21–48 in fact supplies a 'hedge' about the Torah (cf. *m.* '*Abot* 1.1). See Holtzclaw (v) and Przybylski, pp. 81–3. Cf. Harvey, p. 56, n. 93. Chrysostom, *Hom. on Mt.* 16.4 wrote: each command 'is filled up and put in greater security' (cf. Clement of Alexandria, *Paed.* 2.6.51). One hesitates to accept this approach because (1) it involves reading a great deal into 5.38–47 (see Przybylski, p. 82) and (2) Matthew has nothing equivalent to the rabbinic *sĕyāg* = 'fence'. There may nonetheless be some truth in a related point. In *m. Ber.* 1.1 we read, concerning when the *Shemaʿ* is to be read in the evening, 'In all cases where the Sages say, Until midnight, the obligation referred to may be carried out till dawn. . . . If this be so, why did the Sages say, Until midnight? In order to keep a

3. 5.21–48 probably does not offer us Jesus' interpretation of the law. 5.21–6 and 27–30 can, admittedly, be thus understood, for they could perhaps be said to intensify or deepen the law by drawing out implicit principles. There are, however, two difficulties with this approach. First, the third, fourth, and fifth paragraphs are not susceptible to the proposed interpretation. In particular, the labelling of remarriage as adultery is not easily construed as in any way an interpretation or extension of OT law. It is simply a new pronouncement that goes beyond the OT. Secondly, Jesus' 'But I say to you' would seem to locate the authority of his declarations in his own person, so although the Torah supplies him with a point of departure, it does no more than this. Hence the category of interpretation is inadequate.

4. If 5.21–48 does not give us an interpretation or extension of the Torah, and if it does not intend to contradict the Torah, and if it does not polemicize against Jewish interpretations of Scripture, what does it do? Its primary function is, quite simply, two-fold: to show, through six concrete examples, (i) what sort of attitude and behaviour Jesus requires and (ii) how his demands surpass those of the Torah without contradicting the Torah. Concerning the first point, Jesus' followers are to strive for purity of intention (5.21–30), for obedience to God's will with as little concession to human sin as possible (5.31–7), and for unselfish love of friend and foe alike (5.38–48). In other words, the disciples are to be perfect (5.48). Concerning the second point, strict obedience to the commandments of the Torah is not enough, for the Torah does not communicate all the imperatives that must be fulfilled. And in line with this, although 5.21–48 does not oppose specific interpretations of the Torah, it does implicitly downplay a casuistic or legalistic approach or attitude (although see the discussion of 5.32). The letter of the law does not give life. All things lawful may not be helpful. One may refrain from murder and still hate, refrain from committing adultery and still lust in the heart, and it is possible to follow the OT's provisions with regard to divorce and oaths and yet be found in sin. Hence, in order to attain perfect conformity to God's will (5.48), one must be animated by something that cannot be casuistically formulated—things such as 'purity of heart' (5.8) and the thirst for peace (5.9).

man away from trangression' (cf. *b. Mak*. 22b). It may be that while the strict keeping of all of the commands in Mt 5.21–48 is not a real possibility, their radical formulation has in fact accomplished more than a balanced, casuistic formulation ever could have. If people are asked to give everything, they may not give it, but they will probably give more than if they had been asked to give less than everything. Recall Wordsworth, *Ecclesiastical Sonnets* 3.43: 'Give all thou canst; high Heaven rejects the lore of nicely-calculated less or more'.

God demands more than justice. This is why, despite the fact that he transforms 'the pre-messianic Torah into the messianic Torah' (Gerhardsson, *Memory*, p. 327), Jesus is not for Matthew a legislator or rule maker in any usual sense, and why the evangelist has Jesus put so much emphasis upon love of God and love of neighbour, things which are unquantifiable. Obedience to rules, even to the Torah, does not automatically produce the spirit that Jesus requires of those who would follow him. Or to put it another way: purely legal norms, such as those cited in Mt 5.21, 27, 31, 33, 38, and 43, can never convey how life is to be lived by those who are genuinely poor in spirit, pure in heart, and full of mercy (5.3, 7, 8). So while Jesus does not abolish legal norms (to do so would be foolish and unthinkable) and himself submits to legal observances, he does demand more. And this more is the 'better righteousness' announced by 5.20 and delineated in 5.21–48.

(iii) *Exegesis*

ON MURDER (5.21–6)

According to Moses, those who commit murder will suffer punishment. According to Jesus, those who direct anger towards a brother and speak insulting words should or will suffer punishment. It is thereby stated that it is not sufficient for followers of Jesus to refrain from the act of murder. They must do more. They must go to the source and root out all anger. In this way will the violent impulse to murder not arise in the first place (cf. T. Gad. 4.1–7). Furthermore, by making the punishment for anger the same as that for murder (a clear hyperbole), anger and harsh words are made out to be not two human shortcomings among others but grievous sins to be exorcised at all costs. Compare 1 Jn 3.15: 'Anyone who hates his brother is a murderer' (cf. Tg. Ps.-J. and Tg. Onq. on Gen. 9.6; *Der. Er. Rab.* 11.13).

5.21–6 is to be analysed thus:

21–2	I. First contrast: on murder	
21	A. Traditional teaching	
21a	1. Command: do not kill	
21b	2. Punishment for infraction: liable to the local court	
22	B. Jesus' teaching	
22a	1. First assertion, introduced with 'I say to you'	
	a. Infraction: being angry with a brother	
	b. Punishment: judgement by the local court	

22b   2. Second assertion
                     a. Infraction: uttering *raka*
                     b. Punishment: judgement by sanhedrin
22c   3. Third assertion
                     a. Infraction: uttering *more*
                     b. Punishment: judgement in Gehenna

23–4   II. First application/illustration
23   A. Situation: 'If you are offering your gift . . .'
24   B. Action commanded
24a   1. Leave gift and go
24b   2. Be reconciled
24c   3. Then offer gift

25–6   III. Second application/illustration
25a   A. Command: 'Make friends quickly . . .'
25b   B. Result of not obeying
                     1. Handed over to judge
                     2. Handed over to guard
                     3. Be put in prison
26   C. Concluding observation: 'You will not get out
                     . . .'

Matthew's love of triadic forms is once again in evidence. There
are three subsections in 5.21–6, and each subsection is in turn
divided into two or three parts, the second of which is in each
instance triadic. Observe also that the structure of the next
paragraph, 5.27–30, has the form, (1) summarising contrast
(5.27–8), (2) first application/illustration (5.29), (3) second
application/illustration (5.30).

One wonders whether Mt 5.21–6 was intended by the evangelist
to allude to the story of Cain (which is alluded to elsewhere: 18.22;
23.35). To readers steeped in the OT the mention of murder in
conjunction with hating one's brother could readily call to mind
Gen 4, particularly as the enmity between Cain and Abel grew out
of God's rejection of Cain's sacrificial gift (δῶρον), and the
offering of a δῶρον is the situation described in 5.23–4 (cf.
Cyprian, *Unity of the Church* 13; *Lord's Prayer* 23).

21. ἠκούσατε ὅτι ἐρρέθη τοῖς ἀρχαίοις. Compare 5.33. ἀκούω
followed by ὅτι (cf. *šāma'* + *kî*, as in Gen 42.2; 43.25; Num 14.13)
here probably refers to the OT and to its being read in the
synagogues (cf. Jn 12.34; Rom 2.13). Although one could compare
the rabbinic *šm'* formulas in which 'hear' means 'receive as
tradition' (*m. Sanh.* 11.2; *m. 'Ed.* 5.7; SB 1, p. 253), 5.21–48 deals
with the OT, not with the oral law or Jewish misinterpretation (cf.
Guelich, pp. 181–2).

In both Jewish and Christian writings, 'it (was) said (by God)' is common for introducing OT quotations (Fitzmyer, *Background*, pp. 10–12). This supplies the necessary background for understanding ἐρρέθη. The passive is divine. The rabbinic *'itmar* (= 'it was taught as tradition'; see SB 1, pp. 253–4) is an inexact parallel. Matthew is concerned with the Torah, not with tradition (cf. Guelich, pp. 181–2). If ἐρρέθη had a human subject, he or they would be named (cf. Schlatter, p. 165).

ἀρχαῖος (cf. *zĕqēnîm*; *dôrôt hāri'šônîm*) in the plural means 'men of olden times' (cf. Ecclus 39.1; Lk 9.8, 19; Josephus, *Ant.* 7.171; 12.413; Did. 11.11; SB 1, pp. 253–4). Here the generation in the wilderness is pre-eminently in view (cf. Percy, pp. 123–4). Compare the use of πρεσβύτεροι in Josephus, *Ant.* 13.292: ἀκούομεν παρὰ τῶν πρεσβυτέρων. The dative refers to those spoken to ('it was said to'; so Chrysostom, *Hom. on Mt.* 16.7; RSV, NEB), not to those who spoke ('it was said by'; so KJV; cf. SB 1, p. 254); see Meier, *Law*, p. 133, n. 20. If we had here a dative of agency it would be only one of two questionable NT examples (the other being Lk 23.15; see BDF § 191). In addition, the ἐρρέθη τοῖς ἀρχαίοις of 5.21 is parallel to the λέγω ὑμῖν of 5.22, and in this last the function of the dative is manifest.

οὐ φονεύσεις. The command is from the decalogue, Exod 20.13 = Deut 5.17, and agrees with the LXX. Compare 19.18; Mk 10.19; Rom 13.9.

ὃς δ' ἂν φονεύσῃ ἔνοχος ἔσται τῇ κρίσει. This addition to 'Thou shalt not kill', although not found in the OT or in extant Jewish literature, is a fair summary of the legislation set forth in Exod 21.12 = Lev 24.17; Num 35.12; and Deut 17.8–13; it is, therefore, not to be labelled rabbinic interpretation. For the sentence form compare Exod 21.17. ἔνοχος (LXX: 21, for several Hebrew words) is a legal term meaning 'liable', 'answerable', 'guilty' (BAGD, s.v.; cf. *ḥûb*). κρίσις, a word Matthew likes (Mt: 12; Mk: 0; Lk: 4), occurs here in the dative with uncertain meaning. 'Trial', 'penalty', 'judgement', 'legal proceedings', 'judicial sentence', and 'the court' are all possibilities (cf. the range of *mišpāṭ*).[3]

22. Jesus now goes beyond the teaching of the sixth commandment to demand an end to anger and hateful speech. On the triadic structure of the verse see pp. 509–10. On the subject of intention in Jewish law see B. S. Jackson, 'Liability for Mere Intention in Jewish Law', in *Essays in Jewish and Comparative Legal History*, SJLA 10, Leiden, 1975, pp. 202–34. Relevant texts include Gen 6.5; 1 Sam 16.7; 1 Kgs 8.18–19; Josephus, *C. Ap.* 2.215, 217; Tg. Ps.-J. on Deut 5.21; *m. 'Abot* 4.21; *b. Qidd.* 39b. An

---

[3] On local Jewish courts see Josephus, *Ant.* 4.214–18; SB 1, pp. 257–75; Schürer 2, pp. 225–6; J. S. Kennard, Jr., 'The Jewish Provincial Assembly', *ZNW* 53 (1962), pp. 25–51; and Westerholm, pp. 40–50.

instructive text from the Roman world is Cicero, *De Finibus Bon. et Mal.* 3.9.32: 'As it is a sin to betray one's country, to use violence to one's parents, to rob a temple, where the offence lies in the result of the act, so the passions of fear, grief, and lust are sins, even when no extraneous result ensues'.

ἐγὼ δὲ λέγω ὑμῖν ὅτι. See on 5.18a and 20a. Compare Lk 6.27a: ἀλλὰ ὑμῖν λέγω τοῖς ἀκούουσιν. This may have influenced Matthew's formulation in 5.21–2, 27–8, 31–2, 33–4, 38–9, 43–4. For the δέ see p. 507. The 'I' in first position is emphatic—almost perhaps defiant—and puts Jesus side by side not with 'the men of old' but with Moses, through whom God spoke (cf. 15.4 and the ἐξουσία of 7.29). The implicit Christology is remarkable. The 'you' also contains an implicit contrast: the church versus Israel.

πᾶς ὁ ὀργιζόμενος τῷ ἀδελφῷ αὐτοῦ ἔνοχος ἔσται τῇ κρίσει.[4] This would seem to blur the clear distinction sometimes made in Christianity between mortal and venial sins. Less and more in the matter of anger are not to be calculated.

The πᾶς, together with the thrice-repeated 'whoever' of 5.21 and 22 and the passage's concluding words, 'the last penny', show the universal and uncompromising character of the demands made in our pericope. For other prohibitions of anger—one of the seven deadly sins in Christendom—see Prov 6.34; 14.17, 29; 15.1; 16.14; 19.19; 27.4; Ps 4.4; Eph 4.26, 31; 6.4; Col 3.8; 1 Tim 2.8; Jas 1.19–20; *b. Ned.* 22b; *b. Pesaḥ.* 66a–b; note also 1QS 6.26; 7.2–4. One wonders how anger can be judged by a human court. Perhaps '*should* be liable to judgement' is implicit. Or perhaps the parallelism with 5.21 is more important than logical consistency. Or perhaps we should simply accept the difficulty as demonstrating that Jesus is uttering a parable and not describing a true-to-life situation. One in any case cannot solve the problem by thinking of divine judgement, for then the ἔνοχος ἔσται τῇ κρίσει of 5.22 would mean something altogether different from the ἔνοχος ἔσται τῇ κρίσει of 5.21 (cf. SB 1, pp. 275–6).

Even though there is in Matthew—as in early Christianity in general (see BAGD, s.v., ἀδελφός)—a very strong tendency to use the word 'brother' of a spiritual relative, a 'Christian brother (or: sister)' (Jeremias, *Parables*, p. 109, n. 82), one certainly should ask whether this limiting usage should be read into 5.21. If the verse has to do with fellow believers in a Christian community (cf. 18.15–20), as it must if 'brother' means 'Christian brother', it is a bit awkward for the evangelist to go on to mention the sanhedrin

---

[4] ℵ² D K L W Δ Θ Π 0233 *f*[1.13] Maj it sy sa bo goth arm geo Ir[lat] Or[pt] Cyp Cyr Chr Bas PsAth Lcf insert εικη = 'without cause' after αυτου, no doubt to allow room for righteous indignation (cf. Eph 4.26). Jerome, *C. Pelag.* 2.7: 'in plerisque codicibus antiquis sine causa additum non est'.

(5.22), the altar (5.23–4), and the prison (5.25–6): these are not peculiarly Christian things. And does not the spirit of 5.38–48 demand that the Christian be reconciled with believer and non-believer alike? Nevertheless, the equation of 'brother' with 'neighbour' or 'fellow Israelite' (cf. Jer 22.18; Lk 6.41–2; Barn. 19.4; SB 1, p. 276) is not free of difficulty. Apart from Matthew's typical equation of 'brother' with 'Christian', 5.21–6 recalls in certain respects the community regulations of 1QS 6.24–7.14, and this encourages a communal interpretation of Matthew's text (see Davies, *SSM*, pp. 236–9; for 'brother' = co-religionist in the Scrolls see CD 7.1–2; 1QS 6.10, 22; cf. Josephus, *Bell*. 2.122). We leave the question unresolved. For the use of 'brother' in Greek fraternities see H. F. von Soden, *TWNT* 1, p. 146.

ὃς δ' ἂν εἴπῃ τῷ ἀδελφῷ αὐτοῦ ῥακά, ἔνοχος ἔσται τῷ συνεδρίῳ. This clause and the next condemn external manifestations of evil. In this way both the inner emotion of hatred (5.22a) and its outworkings (5.22b–c) are rejected. It follows that the evangelist is not concentrating on drawing distinctions between outward acts and internal dispositions. On the punishments for harsh words spoken against fellow sectarians in 1QS see Davies, *SSM*, pp. 237–9. For unkind or careless words see also Mt 12.36–7; 15.11. τῷ ἀδελφῷ αὐτοῦ is repeated from the previous clause but absent from the next. ῥακά[5] occurs only here in the NT. Among the various explanations offered for this word, two deserve consideration. (1) *Raka* is derived from the Aramaic *rêqāʾ/rêqâ*, a word which was employed as a contemptuous insult: 'empty-head', 'good for nothing', 'fool' (cf. Neh 5.13 and the κενέ of Jas 2.20 and see SB 1, 278–9, also Jastrow, s.v.).[6] This is the most probable solution—in which case Matthew's failure to translate the term might suggest an audience familiar with an oriental word of abuse, although it is also possible that the evangelist could leave *raka* untranslated because its field of meaning was roughly indicated by the *mōre* in 5.22c.[7] (2) *Raka* could be a vocative form of the derogatory ῥαχᾶς, which is found in one of the Zenon papyri: Ἀντίοχον τὸν ῥαχᾶν (see Preisgke, *Sammelbuch* 5, 7638.7). For further discussion see Horsley 2, p. 97.

[5] Lit.: Köhler (v); E. C. Colwell, 'Has Raka a Parallel in the Papyri?', *JBL* 53 (1934), pp. 351–4; M. Smith, *JBL* 64 (1945), pp. 502–3; J. Jeremias, *TWNT* 6, pp. 973–6; Bussby (v).

[6] The first α (rather than the expected η for *ê*) can be explained by the influence of the Syriac *raqa* (cf. Chrysostom, *Hom. on Mt.* 16.7). (And Matthew, we have argued, lived in Syria.)

[7] So G. Mussies, 'The Use of Hebrew and Aramaic in the Greek New Testament', *NTS* 30 (1984), pp. 424–5. Mussies also proposes that *raka* 'escaped translation because its emotional value could not be rendered exactly'.

τῷ συνεδρίῳ[8] substitutes for 'the court' in the previous clause and means either 'the high council, the Sanhedrin' (*sanhedrîn*) in Jerusalem (the definite article argues for this) or a local court, as in 10.17 = Mk 13.9; *m. Makk.* 1.10; *m. Sanh.* 1.6; *t. Sanh.* 7.1. Those who have argued that 'sanhedrin' refers to a church body responsible for discipline of church members (so Weise (v), p. 117; Wrege, pp. 59–60; cf. 1QS 8.1) face the difficulty that this meaning for the word is not attested in NT times (additional objections in Guelich, p. 187).

ὃς δ' ἂν εἴπῃ μωρέ, ἔνοχος ἔσται εἰς τὴν γέενναν τοῦ πυρός. Like the previous clause, this makes concrete and vivid the general principle of 5.22a. The line might be redactional and added to give 5.22 a triadic structure. Certainly the vocabulary is typical of the editor: μωρός (a word beloved by Sirach): Mt: 6–7; Mk: 0; Lk: 0; γέεννα (LXX: 0): Mt: 7; Mk: 3; Lk: 1; with πυρός (a traditional association: Sib. Or. 1.103; 2 Clem. 5.4; *PGM* 4.3072): Mt: 2; Mk: 0; Lk: 0.

μωρέ is usually translated, 'you fool' (cf. Socrates, *Ep.* 14.6; Epictetus, *Diss.* 2.16.13; 3.13.17; Philo, *Cher.* 75; LXX: Deut 32.6; Ps 93.8; Isa 19.11). Some, however, have equated it with the Hebrew *môreh* (= 'rebel'; cf. Deut 21.18, 20),[9] or argued that it is the proper Greek translation of *rêqā'/rêqâ* (e.g. Köhler (v), Moule (v)). Against this last opinion, μωρός does not translate the root *ryq'* in the LXX; and against the meaning, 'rebel', *môreh* only becomes a term of abuse under the influence of the Greek loan word *môrôs/môreh* = μωρός (cf. Guelich, 'Mt 5²²' (v), pp. 40–2). From this it follows that μωρέ = 'you fool', and it presumably translates either *mrṣ* or—more probably—the Aramaic *šty'*. This conclusion means in turn that *raka* and *môre* are practically indistinguishable; both could be translated by 'fool' or 'idiot'.

'Gehenna'[10] (= Aramaic *gêhinnām*) is, in the NT, the place where the wicked dead suffer fiery torments (cf. 1 En. 90.24; 2 Bar. 85.13; Rev 19.20; 20.14–15) either immediately after death or after the last judgement (cf. 1 En. 27.2–3(?); 54.1(?); 4 Ezra 7.36 Lat.; 2 Bar. 59.10; Sib. Or. 1.103; 2.292; 4.186; *t. Sanh.* 13.3; *b. Ber.* 28b; *b. 'Erub.* 19a; in *b. Pesaḥ.* 54a it is pre-existent; cf. Mt 25.41). Why the place of torment came to have this name, the name of the valley south of Jerusalem, *gê-hinnōm* (Josh 18.16 LXX: Γαιεννα), now

[8] See the lit. cited by E. Lohse, *TWNT* 7, pp. 858–69; also E. Rivkin, *What Crucified Jesus?*, Nashville, 1984, pp. 27–36; idem, 'Bet-Din, Boulé, Sanhedrin: A Tragedy of Errors', *HUCA* 46 (1975), pp. 181–99; Schürer 2, pp. 199–226.

[9] So, e.g., F. Schulthess, *ZNW* 21 (1922), p. 241, and Manson, *Sayings*, pp. 155–6.

[10] Lit.: J. Montgomery, 'The Holy City and Gehenna', *JBL* 27 (1908), pp. 24–47; J. Jeremias, *TWNT* 1, pp. 657–8; M. Gaster, *IDB*, s.v.; L. Bailey, *IDBSup*, s.v.; W. J. P. Boyd, 'Gehenna—According to J. Jeremias', in Livingstone, pp. 9–12.

Wādier-rabābi, is uncertain. The standard view, namely, that the valley was where the city's garbage was incinerated and that the constantly rising smoke and smell of corruption conjured up the fiery torments of the damned, is without ancient support, although it could be correct. Perhaps the abode of the wicked dead gained its name because children had there been sacrificed in fire to the god Molech (2 Chr 28.3; 33.6), or because Jeremiah, recalling its defilement by Josiah (2 Kgs 23.10; cf. 21.6), thundered against the place (Jer 7.31–2; 19.2–9; 32.35), or because it was believed that in the valley was the entrance to the underworld home of the pagan chthonian deities (cf. *b. 'Erub.* 19a).

There was no one Jewish opinion as to how long the unrighteous would suffer in the netherworld. (In Persian religion the wicked are consumed by fire; they do not suffer in it—an idea which may be distinctively Jewish). R. Akiba reportedly affirmed punishment would be for only twelve months while R. Joḥanan b. Nur said torment would last only from Passover to Pentecost (*m. 'Ed.* 2.9–10; cf. *t. Sanh.* 13.3; *b. Roš. Haš.* 17a). Matthew, by coupling αἰώνιος with 'fire' (18.8; 25.41; cf. 25.46), seems to show agreement with those who believed the damned would suffer for ever (cf. Dan 12.2; 1QS 2.8; *t. Sanh.* 13.3; *t. Ber.* 6.7; Isa 66.24 is ambiguous). The wicked will be ever dying, never dead.

Because there is an ascending order of punishments in 5.22— local court, sanhedrin, Gehenna—one expects a corresponding ascent in the severity of the crimes listed. It does not obtain. Anger, rebuking a fellow with *raka*, and insulting another by calling him *more*—one is not more obviously heinous than the others. The difficulty thus created has been solved in several ways—by arguing that *more* is more odious than *raka* and that the uttering of either is worse than anger (cf. Augustine, *De serm. mont.* 1.9.24, and Schweizer, *Matthew*, p. 119); or by claiming that κρίσις, συνέδριον, and γέεννα are functionally similar, each being three different ways of referring to the death penalty (J. Jeremias, *TWNT* 6, p. 975); or by emending or rearranging the text;[11] or by seeing 22a as a general statement which is then illustrated by two concrete examples (so Luz 1, p. 253); or by inferring that the incongruity is intentional and serves as an ironic commentary on or parody of scribal exegesis: as all wrongs against one's neighbour are equally wrong, it is foolish to make casuistic distinctions with regard to degrees of punishment.[12] We should like to add another

[11] See the discussion in Allen, pp. 48–9. Many have argued that originally the word of Jesus ended with 5.22a; so e.g. Manson, *Sayings*, p. 155.

[12] So Zahn, p. 228. Cf. E. von Dobschütz in Stanton, *Matthew*, p. 24; Guelich, p. 188; and Meier, *Vision*, pp. 244–5.

possibility. As spoken by Jesus,[13] the saying consisted only of 5.21–2b and affirmed, in hyperbolic fashion, that anger and insulting words were as deserving of punishment as murder; and, originally, the Aramaic or Hebrew words behind κρίσις and συνέδριον were roughly synonymous or of similar import, both referring to judicial trials. Problems arose only when Matthew, in order to clarify *raka* and to create a triad, tacked on the final clause. His choice of *more* created no difficulty; but 'into the Gehenna of fire' (cf. 18.9 diff. Mk 9.47), which he no doubt felt justified in adding to underline the severity of the named offences, created the possibility of apprehending an ascending order of punishments.

23. This and the next verse offer the first concrete illustration/application of 5.21–2. There is a second concrete illustration/application in 5.25–6. Reconciliation replaces hatred. For the structure of the section see p. 510.

5.23–4, although full of redactional vocabulary, probably preserves a traditional (oral) piece. Bultmann (*History*, p. 132) indeed thought it to be a more original form of the saying preserved in Mk 11.25 ('And whenever you stand praying, forgive, if you have anything against any one; so that your Father also who is in heaven may forgive you your trespasses'; cf. Mt 6.12, 14–16). Whether this be so or not, 5.23–4 would appear to be pre-Matthean, and possibly even dominical. For (1) the continuing existence of the sacrificial system in Jerusalem may be presupposed, and this suggests composition before A.D. 70 (while Matthew was composed later); (2) the elevation of brotherly reconciliation above sacrifice is consistent with Jesus' strong emphasis on loving one's neighbour; and (3) 5.23–4 is also perfectly in accord with the fifth clause of the Lord's Prayer, which puts forgiveness of others before God's forgiveness of oneself. Whether 5.23–4 had already come to be linked with 5.21–2 in the pre-Matthean tradition one cannot decide, but the connexion is in any case secondary.

Did. 14.2 reads: πᾶς δὲ ἔχων τὴν ἀμφιβολίαν μετὰ τοῦ ἑταίρου αὐτοῦ μὴ συνελθέτω ὑμῖν, ἕως οὗ διαλλαγῶσιν, ἵνα μὴ κοινωθῇ ἡ θυσία ὑμῶν. Although we believe that the author of the Didache had read Matthew, this particular text does not clearly exhibit any knowledge of the First Gospel. It should probably be considered an independent variant of the logion in Mt 5.22–3 and thus evidence for the non-redactional genesis of Matthew's text.

ἐὰν οὖν προσφέρῃς τὸ δῶρόν σου ἐπὶ τὸ θυσιαστήριον. What follows is more a parable than a prosaic description of a real life possibility. For discussion of gift and altar see 23.18–19. For the legal form, conditional particle + (οὖν +) present subjunctive + imperative see also 6.2, 5, 16. Compare further *m. Pesaḥ.* 3.7: 'If a man was on the way to slaughter his Passover-offering or to

---

[13] For arguments favouring the dominical origin of 5.21–2 see Guelich, 'Mt 5²²' (v); Merklein, *Botschaft*, pp. 105–11; Luz 1, pp. 254–6.

circumcise his son or to eat the betrothal meal at his father-in-law's house and he remembered that . . .'. The οὖν naturally ties our verse to 5.21–2, and it is implied that disciples must not only root out their own anger but, in simplicity and innocence (cf. Irenaeus, *Adv. haer.* 4.18.1), do all they can to lessen the anger of a brother, above all when they are themselves guilty of offending him. προσφέρω (we are to envisage the gift being handed over to the priest; cf. 8.4) is a Matthean favourite: Mt: 15; Mk: 3; Lk: 4. So too is its combination with δῶρον: Mt: 4 (2.11; 5.23, 24; 8.4); Mk: 0; Lk: 0. (προσφέρω + δῶρον occurs often in Leviticus LXX, usually for *qārab + qorbān* (cf. T. Iss. 5.3).) 'If then you are (in the process of) offering' are words describing an act that should, according to Matthew, presuppose repentance—which is why the offended brother must first be appeased. Sacrificial expiation is conditioned by the spiritual and moral state of the one making sacrifice (cf. Hos 6.6; Ecclus 7.8–9; 34.18–19). The switch to the second person singular (the second person plural appears in 5.21–2) probably reflects the secondary connexion between 5.21–2 and 23–4. Both ἐπί with the genitive (Mt: 35; Mk: 21; Lk: 27) and θυσιαστήριον (= the altar of burnt offering in Jerusalem, the *mizbēaḥ*; Mt: 6; Mk: 0; Lk: 2) are sometimes redactional.

κἀκεῖ μνησθῇς ὅτι ὁ ἀδελφός σου ἔχει τι κατὰ σοῦ. Before one seeks forgiveness from God one must seek forgiveness from one's brother (cf. 6.12, 14–15). The word, 'brother', makes the connexion between 5.22 and 23 not only thematic but also verbal. The question whether, for Matthew, 'brother' means Christian brother or not (see on 5.22) remains a problem, although the vast majority of the Fathers certainly favoured the equation. Cyril of Jerusalem, in fact, took the reconciliation of 5.23–24 to refer to the congregational kiss of peace (*Cat.* 5.3).

It is not immediately clear whether it is the offender (as in 5.24–6) or the offended (cf. 6.14–15) who is to make reconciliation. If the latter, this would certainly surpass traditional Jewish teaching. But two points favour the former option. (1) In Rev 2.4, 14, 20 the 'have (something) against' idiom is used of Jesus having something against failing Christians. In this case, the subject of ἔχω is clearly the innocent party. Compare Mk 11.25. (2) 5.21–6 and 5.27–30 are structural twins: each consists of (i) summarizing contrast; (ii) first application/illustration; (iii) second application/illustration. Now in 5.27–30 the two illustrations or applications are in synthetic parallelism. One therefore expects the same to hold true in 5.21–6; and because in the second illustration/application in 5.21–6 the imperative is directed towards the offender, the imperative in the first illustration/application (5.23–4) is most naturally read as likewise addressed to the offender.

518 COMMENTARY ON MATTHEW

24. There is close parallelism between this verse and 5.23:

    5.23   verb + 'your gift on   the altar and there'
    5.24   verb + 'your gift before the altar and'

ἄφες ἐκεῖ τὸ δῶρόν σου ἔμπροσθεν τοῦ θυσιαστηρίου καὶ ὕπαγε.[14]
The need to be reconciled to an offended brother takes priority over the sacrifice for (unwitting)[15] sins. The action depicted by Matthew's words is all the more arresting because one cannot really imagine someone doing it. Could one, without causing offence or disturbance, really leave a sacrifice in the hands of the priest or on the altar and go (perhaps to Galilee) and make search for a brother and then, some time later, return to the temple and pick up where one left off, with everything in order and the priest waiting?

πρῶτον διαλλάγηθι τῷ ἀδελφῷ σου. πρῶτον could connect up with the earlier imperative, 'go'; but the sense demands that we read, 'first be reconciled . . . then coming offer your gift'. The emphasis is upon reconciliation. διαλλάσσομαι (followed by dative: 1 Βασ 29.4; 1 Esdr 4.31; Josephus, Ant. 16.125, 335) appears only here in the NT. On the importance of reconciliation in the rabbinic texts see SB 1, pp. 283–7. The theme is certainly prominent in Matthew: 5.21–6; 6.14–15; 18.21–35. See further on 6.15 and 9.2.

καὶ τότε ἐλθὼν πρόσφερε τὸ δῶρόν σου. This concluding line shows that 5.23–4 is far from being an 'open declaration of war on the cult' (Hahn, *Worship*, p. 25; contrast Hummel, p. 80). Participation in the sacrificial system is presupposed ('offer your gift'); and the demand for making reconciliation with others before offering sacrifice does not diminish temple worship but is rather simply another example of the conviction that the formal observance of religion without genuine personal piety or proper ethical behaviour is empty and inefficacious (cf. 1 Sam 15.22; Hos 6.6; T. Isaac 4.18–22, 39; *m. B. Qam.* 9.12; *b. Yoma* 87a; SB 1, pp. 287–8). Recall 23.23: 'These you ought to have done, without neglecting the others'. Bengel, *ad loc.*, was correct: 'The meaning is, Whatever you are doing, even if you have already undertaken the best and most holy and most necessary matter, leave everything till you have been reconciled with your brother'. Compare *m. Yoma* 8.9: 'For transgressions that are between man and God the Day of Atonement effects atonement, but for transgressions that are between a man and his fellow the Day of Atonement effects atonement only if he has appeased his fellow'.

[14] Every significant word in this clause appears more often in Matthew than in Mark or Luke: ἀφίημι: Mt: 47; Mk: 34; Lk: 31; ἐκεῖ: Mt: 28; Mk: 11; Lk: 16; δῶρον: Mt: 9; Mk: 1; Lk: 2; ἔμπροσθεν: Mt: 18; Mk: 2; Lk: 10; θυσιαστήριον: Mt: 6; Mk: 0; Lk: 2; ὑπάγω: Mt: 19; Mk: 15; Lk: 5.
[15] See Davies, *PRJ*, pp. 254–8.

25. The second illustration/application of 5.21–2 stresses, like the first illustration/application (5.23–4), the importance of reconciliation. But whereas 5.23–4 may demand only reconciliation between Christian brothers, 5.25–6 seems to demand irenic relations between Christians and those outside the church, including opponents or enemies (cf. 5.38–48). (ἀντίδικος can mean not only 'opponent in a law suit' but also 'enemy'; see BAGD, s.v., and SB 1, pp. 288–9, on *anṭîdiqôs*). Hence 5.23–4 and 25–6, taken together, demand that the Christian make peace with all. For the passage's structure see p. 510.

5.25–6 has a parallel in Lk 12.58–9 and would therefore appear to derive from Q. Originally the parable probably gained its meaning from its eschatological context in the preaching of Jesus (cf. Lk 12.49–57): you are shortly to appear before the great judge! Settle your accounts beforehand! Be reconciled with your opponent! (cf. Dibelius, *Tradition*, pp. 248–9). In Matthew, this eschatological urgency has obviously receded to some extent and homiletical or common sense paraenetic motives have come forward.

Nothing stands in the way of tracing 5.25–6 = Lk 12.58–9 to Jesus. (1) The conditions reflected, especially the role of the κριτής, point to Jewish territory;[16] (2) the urgent eschatological orientation of the parable (see above) is consistent with Jesus' outlook; and (3) there is no good reason for doubting the passage's unity.

ἴσθι εὐνοῶν τῷ ἀντιδίκῳ σου ταχὺ ἕως ὅτου εἶ μετ' αὐτοῦ ἐν τῇ ὁδῷ. Compare Lk 12.58: 'For as (ὡς) you go with your accuser (μετὰ τοῦ ἀντιδίκου σου) before the magistrate, on the way (ἐν τῇ ὁδῷ) make an effort to be reconciled with him'. It is here impossible to reconstruct Q word for word, for the vocabulary and syntax of neither Mt 5.25a nor Lk 12.58a are sufficiently Matthean or Lukan to make the redactional contributions manifest.

εὐνοέω (LXX: 3: Est 8.13; Dan 2.43; 3 Macc 7.11) appears only here in the NT. The imperative means 'make friends', and it is here placed at the front of the sentence in order to make plain the main theme. ταχύ (which appears with ὁδός in Exod 32.8; Deut 9.16; and Judg 2.17 LXX), might be considered redactional (Mt: 3; Mk: 1; Lk: 1). In any case, the rapidity of the narration in the next three clauses reinforces the lack of time expressed by ταχύ. 'In the way' means 'on the way to court'.

μήποτέ σε παραδῷ ὁ ἀντίδικος τῷ κριτῇ. The judge (cf. the κρίσει of 5.21) is perhaps a symbol for God. Lk 12.58 has: μήποτε κατασύρῃ σε πρὸς τὸν κριτήν. Matthew has presumably altered Q in order to make 5.25b line up with 5.25c: 'the accuser' matches

---

[16] See Sherwin-White, pp. 133–4. He writes: the 'judge' of the gospels 'corresponds to nothing in Roman usage or in the magisterial hierarchy'.

'the judge', and 'to the judge' matches 'to the guard', and the verb in 25b, παραδῷ, is to be read into 25c (contrast Luke, where two different verbs are used). This is consistent with the fact that Luke's κατασύρῃ is a NT *hapax legomenon* and thus probably not Lukan.

καὶ ὁ κριτὴς τῷ ὑπηρέτῃ. So Lk 12.58, with σε παραδώσει after 'the judge' and τῷ πράκτορι (= bailiff?) instead of τῷ ὑπηρέτῃ. The First Evangelist has evidently dropped the verb because of its appearance in the previous clause, and perhaps used the more common ὑπηρέτης instead of the less common πράκτωρ. Against the assertion that because he thought in Hellenistic categories, Luke changed ὑπηρέτης (a synagogue official) to πράκτωρ (a Roman official), it should be observed that the former could designate in the Hellenistic world the officer who executed a judge's sentence; see Rengstorf, *TWNT* 8, p. 540.

καὶ εἰς φυλακὴν βληθήσῃ. Compare Jn 3.24. Lk 12.58 reads: 'and the bailiff throws you εἰς φυλακήν'. The sentence of prison (cf. the rabbinic *pîlaqî*) for debtors is not attested in Jewish law. So we have either hyperbole or a reference to non-Jewish law.[17]

While the reason for seeking reconciliation in 5.23–4 is because God condemns enmity, in 25–6 one seeks peace in order to avoid punishment. There is no getting around the conclusion that this makes for an awkward paragraph: 5.25–6 is really not an apt illustration of 5.21–2 (cf. Allen, p. 50). The cause of this, however, is understandable. Matthew does not compose freely. He rather feels obliged to take up tradition, and it is inevitable that traditional pieces sometimes do not fit perfectly into their new, Matthean contexts.

26. This sentence concludes 5.21–6 with a note of judgement. Compare Did. 1.5: 'Woe to him that receiveth; for, if a man receiveth having need, he is guiltless; but he that hath no need shall give satisfaction why and wherefore he received, being put in confinement he shall be examined concerning the deeds that he hath done, and οὐκ ἐξελεύσεται ἐκεῖθεν, μέχρις οὗ ἀποδῷ τὸν ἔσχατον κοδράντην'. This is much closer to Mt 5.26 than to Luke 12.59; but since, at the points of disagreement between Matthew and Luke, the former is closer to Q, dependence upon Matthew is not here a necessary inference.

ἀμὴν λέγω σοι. On this introduction and the sentence form see 5.18. Although Matthew has sometimes added 'amen' (Mt: 30–1; Mk: 13; Lk: 6) to his sources, Luke has sometimes dropped it from Mark so that we cannot be certain whether or not it was here in Q.

---

[17] According to Irenaeus, *Adv. haer.* 1.25.4, the Carpocratians took the 'prison' of Mt 5.25 to be the body and 'thine adversary' to be the devil (so also Clement of Alexandria), and they interpreted the entire passage in terms of reincarnation (cf. Pist. Soph. 3.113; Test. Truth 30.17).

οὐ μὴ ἐξέλθῃς ἐκεῖθεν. So also Lk 12.59. This agreement, along with the agreement of the previous two words and one more following, points to a common written source, Q. According to Jeremias, we should, keeping in mind the Semitic avoidance of passives, translate, 'you will not be released from there' (*Parables*, p. 180).

ἕως ἂν ἀποδῷς τὸν ἔσχατον κοδράντην. Compare 18.34 and Sextus, *Sent.* 39. No doubt Matthew thought of this clause as alluding to punishment in Gehenna (cf. 5.22). Lk 12.59 has: ἕως καὶ τὸ ἔσχατον λεπτὸν ἀποδῷς. Matthew has added ἄν (ἕως ἄν: Mt: 10; Mk: 10; Lk: 3) and dropped Q's καί (after ἄν only in 24.43). Luke has moved the verb to the end and, in order to achieve an even smaller amount, presumably substituted 'lepta' (according to Mark 12.42 a quadrans = 2 lepta) for the smallest Roman coin, the 'quadrans' (cf. the omission of this word—another rabbinic loan word—by Luke at Mk 12.42 = Lk 21.2). Matthew's final word, 'quadrans', indicates that the point at issue between accuser and accused is money. As in 18.23–35 (cf. Lk 7.41–3), the debtor stands for the sinner.

In equating anger with murder, in making reconciliation a prerequisite for participation in the cult, and in demanding irenic relations with all people, the Jesus of Mt 5.21–6 does not introduce anything new into Judaism. This the parallels we have cited make plain. How then does one account for the antithetical form? What justifies its use? Several observations are pertinent. First, while the equation of hatred with murder can be found in the Jewish tradition, it is not clearly present in the OT itself. Secondly, the antithetical form itself contains meaning: life in strict accord with legal ordinances is not enough. God demands a radical obedience that cannot be casuistically formulated (see further Luz 1, pp. 254–6). Thirdly, by setting his words in contrast to a text belonging to Judaism's most sacred document (the Pentateuch), Jesus was being deliberately provocative. The effect would be at least two-fold. Not only would the utterance not easily be forgotten (a pedagogical plus), but people would be impelled to ask about Jesus' identity: what kind of a man speaks like this? Finally, and in contrast to later Christian interpretation (on which see Luz 1, pp. 256–7), Jesus does not make allowance for justified anger, for 'holy hate' (such as hate of demons or evil thoughts), or for the wrath of the state. As it stands, Jesus' prohibition of anger is unqualified (contrast Eph 4.26). This fact would seem to take Jesus one step beyond the wisdom tradition and may well have struck his contemporaries as novel. (For justified anger or hatred in Judaism see Jer 6.11; 15.17; Ecclus 1.22; 1 Macc 2.44; 2 Macc 10.35; Philo, *Spec. leg.* 3.31; *b. Meg.* 6b.)

ON ADULTERY (5.27–30)

27. 5.27–28, which has no synoptic parallel, contrasts the OT prohibition of adultery with Jesus' prohibition of lust. Between the two injunctions there is no contradiction: one who does not lust after a woman will certainly not commit adultery with her. At the same time, Jesus, who wishes to instil holiness, does demand more than the decalogue. (Compare Methodius, *Leprosy* 6.45: Jesus 'counsels to root out not the fruit of adultery but the seed'). Thus 5.27–30 at once upholds and supplements the law. For the structure see p. 510.

As the following passages imply, Jesus was probably not the first to equate lust with adultery. Indeed, Mt 5.27–8, assuming it to be dominical, could belong to the deposit of traditional wisdom materials which Jesus mined for his own purposes. Compare T. Iss. 7.2 ('I have not had intercourse with any woman other than my wife, nor was I promiscuous by lustful look'); *Mek.* of R. Simeon 111 ('He is not to commit adultery . . . either by the eye or by the heart' (cf. Jub. 20.4)); T. Isaac 4.53 ('Do not look at a woman with a lustful eye'); Sextus, *Sent.* 233 ('Know that you are an adulterer even if you merely think of committing adultery'); and *Pesiq. R.* 24.2 ('Even he who visualizes himself in the act of adultery is called an adulterer'). See also Job 31.1; Ecclus 23.4–6; 26.9–11; Ps. Sol. 4.4–6; T. Benj. 8.2; Herm. v. 1.1: SB 1, pp. 298–301. There is also a parallel in Epictetus, *Diss.* 2.18.15.

ἠκούσατε ὅτι ἐρρέθη. This is a shortened version of the formula in 5.21.

οὐ μοιχεύσεις. This is the seventh of the ten commandments as found in the LXX at Exod 20.14 and Deut 5.18. What follows presupposes the literal validity of the OT prohibition. There is no 'antithesis'. That is, Jesus does not do away with the Torah's injunction against adultery.

28. ἐγὼ δὲ λέγω ὑμῖν ὅτι. See p. 507 and on 5.22a.

πᾶς ὁ βλέπων γυναῖκα πρὸς τὸ ἐπιθυμῆσαι αὐτὴν ἤδη ἐμοίχευσεν αὐτὴν ἐν τῇ καρδίᾳ αὐτοῦ.[18] As the Christian ascetics would later put it, it is through the imagination that demons and sinful impulses enter the hearts and minds of men. In addition to the texts already cited for comparison, see also Ep. Arist. 133: 'even if a man should think of doing evil . . . he would not escape detection'; T. Gad. 5.5: 'Being concerned not to arouse the Lord's anger, he is completely unwilling to wrong anyone, even in his thoughts'; Ps.-Phoc. 52: 'It is each man's intention that is examined' (cf. 2 Pet. 2.14; T. Jos. 17.3; Sextus, *Sent.* 178, 181). Contrast *b. Qidd.* 39b: 'Evil intention is not combined with deed';

---

[18] The first αυτην, which is grammatically awkward, is not found in P⁶⁷ ℵ* *pc* Ter Cl Cyr. αυτης appears in ℵ¹ *f*¹ *al.*

that is, there is no punishment for intention alone. In holding that intention is to be judged as deed the Jesus of Matthew is closer to the school of Shammai than to the house of Hillel. See the discussion in *b. Qidd.* 43a.

πᾶς ὁ unites the first three paragraphs of 5.21–48 (cf. 5.22, 32). πᾶς ὁ βλέπων (in Judg 19.30 LXX for *kol-hārō'eh*) functions as a conditional (BDF § 333.2). πρός + articular infinitive could be redactional (Mt: 5; Mk: 1; Lk: 1) and should perhaps be considered a Semitism (BDF § 402.5 cites as a parallel the participle-like Hebrew infinitive preceded by *lĕ*). The infinitive after πρός represents result and implies that the sin lies not in the entrance of a thought but in letting it incite passion (cf. Evagrius, *Praktikos* 51). The addition of ἤδη intensifies the thought of the sentence.

ἐπιθυμέω (cf. *'āwâ* and *ḥāmad*) appears in Exod 20.17: 'You shall not covet—ἐπιθυμήσεις—your neighbour's wife'. Is this commandment being used to interpret the commandment against adultery? In other words, does Mt 5.28 combine Exod 20.14 and 17 in order to make perfectly clear the sort of conduct consonant with the Creator's intention? (Cf. Mk 10.6–9, where two other texts are combined.)

Although we have followed a different line of interpretation, αὐτήν could just possibly be the subject of ἐπιθυμῆσαι (so Haacker (v)). In this case, consideration of the woman would be to the fore: 'Whoever looks at a woman so that she desires, has already misled her to adultery in his heart'.

29. In 5.29 and 30, verses which vividly demand radical sacrifice for the purpose of avoiding occasions of sin, Matthew probably draws upon Mk 9.42–7,[19] a passage he will again employ at the beginning of chapter 18. Here he puts the saying about the eye before the saying about the hand because the link is with the lustful gaze in 5.28. Observe that the 'enter into life' of 18.8–9 (cf. Mk 9.43–7) is absent. This places all the emphasis upon the judgement of Gehenna.

Col 3.5 reads: 'Put to death τὰ μέλη τὰ ἐπὶ τῆς γῆς.' This imperative might be based upon the *skandalon* sayings of Jesus. If so, it is significant that it is immediately followed by mention of fornication, impurity, passion, and evil desire (ἐπιθυμίαν κακήν). Matthew, by referring the *skandalon* sayings to sexual sins, may have been following tradition.[20]

---

[19] So also Kilpatrick, pp. 18–19, and Gundry, *Commentary*, pp. 88–9. Cf. Thompson, pp. 117–18: Mt 19.8–9 and 5.29–30 must in any case derive from the same source, 18.8–9 being the more original form. Dupont 1, pp. 121–3, thinks 5.29–30 to be a doublet. Pesch 2, p. 115, assigns 5.29–30 to Q. So also Luz 1, p. 261.

[20] On the rabbinic parallel in *Gen. Rab.* on 2.3 see on 18.8.

εἰ δὲ ὁ ὀφθαλμός σου ὁ δεξιὸς σκανδαλίζει σε. So 18.9, with καί, not δέ, and without δεξιός. So also Mk 9.47, with καὶ ἐάν and σκανδαλίζῃ and without δεξιός. ὀφθαλμός connects up with the verb of sight in the previous verse; it also signals a theme taken up later in the sermon on the mount: 5.38; 6.22–3; 7.3. LSJ, s.v., σκανδαλίζειν (= 'to cause to stumble, sin') gives no example of a transitive use of this verb outside the NT (cf. also 1 Cor 8.13, which no doubt betrays Paul's knowledge of the Jesus tradition). Ps. Sol. 16.7 (where the context is, interestingly enough, adultery) may be the only instance attested in pre-Christian times. A Semitic background for the use of the verb in the NT seems likely, 'atqal being a good possibility (see Jastrow, s.v., tĕqal).

As with the references to external acts in 5.22b–c, the references to eye and hand in 5.29–30 show that Matthew's concern is not with any contrast between action and intention.

'Right' is perhaps inserted to enhance the parallelism with the 'right hand' in 5.30. For 'right eye' see 1 Sam 11.2 ('gouge out all your right eyes'); Zech 11.17 ('May the sword smite his arm and his right eye'); and Josephus, Ant. 6.69–72 ('he cut out the right eyes'; 'their right eyes would be put out'). Note also b. Šabb. 88b: 'R. Samuel b. Naḥmani said in R. Jonathan's name, What is meant by, "Thou hast ravished my heart, my sister, my bride: Thou hast ravished my heart with one of thine eyes"? In the beginning with one of thine eyes; when thou fulfillest, with both thine eyes'. Here one eye involves perception alone (which is what Mt 5.27–30 is about) while two eyes means physical contact. (According to Num. Rab. on 32.1, the good inclination dwells on the right, the evil inclination on the left. This idea cannot have anything to do with our text—else it would be the left eye that is cut out.)

ἔξελε αὐτὸν καὶ βάλε ἀπὸ σοῦ. So Mt 18.9. Mk 9.47 has: ἔκβαλε αὐτόν. The closest OT text is 2 Sam 20.6: wĕhiṣṣîl 'ênēnû (= 'and snatch away our eyes'). The imperative is not to be taken literally (cf. Ps.-Clem. Rec. 7.37; Origen, Comm. on Mt. 15.1), despite the story of Origen's castration (Eusebius, H.E. 6.8) and the fact that hands and eyes were sometimes cut off or plucked out to punish criminal offenders (Deut 25.11–12; Judg 16.21; Josephus, Vita 171–3, 177; Bell. 2. 642–4; b. Pesaḥ. 57b). Jesus and the NT writers knew well enough that amputation would scarcely curb the passions since the problem is not with the body itself but, as Paul put it, with 'sin that dwells in me' (Rom 7.17, 20; cf. Sextus, Sent. 12–13). 1 Cor 9.27 adequately conveys the sense behind the hyperbole in Mt 5.29–30: 'I pommel my body and subdue it, lest after preaching to others I myself should be disqualified'. The lustful eye is not to be mutilated but brought into custody. As Origen wrote, the Christian 'amputates the passions of the soul without touching the body' (Comm. on Mt. 15.4). Note that 5.29b would keep its meaning were βάλε, the second imperative, absent. But it adds force and vividness: the eye plucked out is not to be held in the hand but is to be immediately tossed away.

συμφέρει γάρ σοι ἵνα ἀπόληται ἓν τῶν μελῶν σου καὶ μὴ ὅλον τὸ σῶμά σου βληθῇ εἰς γέενναν. The truth of this statement is self-evident. Mt 18.9 reads: 'It is better (καλόν) for you to enter into life one-eyed than, having two eyes, to be thrown (βληθῆναι) into the Gehenna of fire'. So also Mk 9.47, with minor variations. The differences between Mt 5.29 and Mt 18.9 = Mk 9.47 do not really affect the sense and are probably due to Matthean redaction, as the word statistics hint.[21]

The phrase, 'your whole body', apparently refers to the resurrection of the just and unjust (cf. Jn. 5.28–9; T. Benj. 10.8; Sib. Or. 4.181–92; contrast Ps. Sol. 3.11–12). The language implies that the body is raised exactly as it was buried.[22] If a limb has been cut off, then it is missing in the resurrection. But it is improbable that either Jesus or Matthew took such language literally; see on 18.8. For 'your eye . . . all your body' see also 6.22–3, which may have influenced the composition of the present text. The appearance again of βάλλω (βάλε . . . βληθῇ) makes for a word-play: if you do not throw away your eye, you will be thrown away. Perhaps 18.9 is a bit closer to the Markan source than is 5.29 because in 18.9 the evangelist has Mk 9.47 before him while here he is drawing upon his memory. For 'Gehenna' see on 5.22.

Mt 5.29 exhibits the so-called 'Tobspruch' or 'better . . . than' form. In the OT it is signalled by the appearance of *ṭôb . . . min* (Prov 15.16; Eccles 7.2) or just *ṭôb* (as in Eccles 8.13). In the LXX the form is most often κρείσσων/ἀγαθόν . . . ἤ/ὑπέρ, in the NT, καλόν/κρεῖττον . . . ἤ (Mk 9.42–7; Mt 18.8; 1 Cor 7.9; 1 Pet 3.17). (For extra-biblical parallels see Diogenes Laertius 4.49 and Seneca, *On Anger* 3.8.8.) Matthew's συμφέρει σοι . . . καὶ μή (5.29, 30; cf. 18.6), which has a very close parallel in Jn 11.50 (συμφέρει ὑμῖν . . . καὶ μή), appears closest to the rabbinic *nôḥa lô . . . wĕʾal* (as in b. Šabb. 56b and b. Ketub. 67b).[23]

30. καὶ εἰ ἡ δεξιά σου χεὶρ σκανδαλίζει σε.[24] The parallelism with 5.29 is perfect, save that 'and' naturally replaces δέ. 18.8 reads: 'But if your hand or your foot scandalizes you'. 'Foot' may be omitted in 5.30 because the evangelist is thinking of onanism. The

---

[21] συμφέρω: Mt: 4; Mk: 0; Lk: 0. μέλος: Mt: 2; Mk: 0; Lk: 0. ὅλον τὸ σῶμα: Mt: 4; Mk: 0; Lk: 1.

[22] So too some rabbinic texts; see Moore 2, pp. 380–1.

[23] For further discussion see W. Zimmerli, 'Zur Struktur der alttestamentlichen Weisheit', *ZAW* 51 (1933), pp. 192–4, and G. F. Snyder, 'The *Tobspruch* in the New Testament', *NTS* 23 (1976), pp. 117–20. Note also Beyer 1, p. 78, n. 1.

[24] This and all of 5.30 are omitted, probably through homoioteleuton, in D *pc* vg^ms sy^s bo^ms.

subject of the paragraph is, after all, lust. Compare *m. Nid.* 2.1:
'The hand that oftentimes makes examination [of the private
parts] is, among women, praiseworthy, but among men—let it [the
hand] be cut off' (because of onanism). See further the lengthy
discussion in *b. Nid.* 13a–b. Mk 9.43 has: καὶ ἐὰν σκανδαλίζῃ σε ἡ
χείρ σου. The right hand is, in part because most people are right
handed, usually considered more valuable than the left (Gen
48.14; *b. Ber.* 62a; see also on 6.3). This accounts for its mention
here. The more important hand is to be sacrificed. Compare Ps
137.5: 'If I forget you, O Jerusalem, let my right hand wither!'

ἔκκοψον αὐτὴν καὶ βάλε ἀπὸ σοῦ. So 18.8, with the masculine
instead of the feminine pronoun (αὐτόν agreeing with ὁ πούς). Mk
9.43 has this: ἀπόκοψον αὐτήν. Compare also Plato, *Smp.* 205e.
For the principle that the punishment should fit the crime, that is,
that the offending member which commits the act should be
punished, see *b. Nid.* 13b.

συμφέρει γάρ σοι ἵνα ἀπόληται ἓν τῶν μελῶν σου καὶ μὴ ὅλον τὸ
σῶμά σου εἰς γέενναν ἀπέλθῃ.[25] This repeats 5.29 exactly except for
the last word: 'go' (cf. Mk 9.43) replaces 'thrown' and is moved to
the end.

Because 5.29–30 proclaims punishment for sins of eye and hand,
it is impossible to disclaim responsibility for the deeds of one's
bodily members. One cannot say, 'Twas not my mind that swore:
my tongue committed a little perjury on its own account'
(Aristophanes). The parts of the body, being united, are judged as
one accountable individual. Actions are psycho-somatic.

1QSa 2.8–9 reads: 'No man smitten in his flesh, or paralysed in
his feet or hands, or lame, or blind . . . shall come to hold office
among the congregation of the men of renown, for the Angels of
Holiness are [with] their [congregation]'. If the notion reflected in
this passage—that physical disabilities have serious spiritual
consequences—be at all representative of a significant portion of
first-century Judaism (see also Lev 21.17–23; 1QM 7.4–6), then
Jesus' words about cutting off hand and plucking out eye may have
had disputatious or ironical undertones we no longer catch (cf.
Davies, *SSM*, p. 227, n. 2).

Chrysostom, *Hom. on Mt.* 17.3, argued that the bodily members of
5.27–30 should be equated with people, in particular with church
members: 'Why did he [Jesus] mention the right eye, and add the hand? To
show thee that not of limbs is he speaking, but of them who are near to us'.
This interpretation cannot be summarily dismissed. Paul conceived of the
church as a body, and in Mt 18.8–9 Jesus' sayings about doing away with

[25] βληθη εις γεενναν (cf. 5.29; 18.9; Mk 9.45, 47) appears in (L) W Θ 0233 *f*13 Maj f
vg^ms sy^p.h sa. εις γεενναν απελθη appears in ℵ B *f*1 33 892 *pc* (lat) sy^c (mae) bo.

bodily parts occur in a context whose theme is ecclesiology. Nevertheless, ecclesiology is not the theme of Mt 5.27–30, and so we hesitate to follow Chrysostom.

ON DIVORCE (5.31–2)

31. If 5.27–30 offered a representation of adultery as lust, 5.31–2, which closes the first half of 5.21–48,[26] follows up with a second reinterpretation: divorce (and remarriage) = adultery. The passage is presumably based chiefly upon Q (cf. Lk 16.18).[27] This is because, against Mk 10.11–12 = Mt 19.9, both Mt 5.31–2 and Lk 16.18 have in common the phrase, 'everyone who divorces his wife', and both address the issue of a man marrying a divorced woman.

ἐρρέθη δέ. The complete formula found in 5.21 and 33 is here abbreviated.[28] See on 5.21 and p. 507.

ὃς ἂν ἀπολύσῃ τὴν γυναῖκα αὐτοῦ δότω αὐτῇ ἀποστάσιον. This legal prescription is a brief summary of the procedure set forth in Deut 24.1–4, where the main issue is not divorce but remarriage. There is no synoptic parallel. ἀπολύω meaning 'to divorce' (cf. 1.19; Mur. 115.3–4; Josephus, *Ant.* 15.259) followed by γυνή (in the accusative) should probably be regarded as redactional (Mt: 5; Mk: 2; Lk: 1). In any case, the formulation, like that in Lk 16.18, assumes that the man is divorcing his wife. The possibility of a woman divorcing her husband (as in Mk 10.12, in concession to non-Palestinian circumstances) is passed over, in accordance with usual Jewish custom.[29]

32. This saying, with its parallel in Lk 16.18, apparently circulated in isolation. For variants see Mk 10.11–12 and 1 Cor 7.10.

Mal 2.14–16, in which faithfulness is demanded towards the wife of one's youth and in which God declares, 'I hate divorce', takes us a long

---

[26] Against Schmal (v), p. 290, 5.31–2 is a separate and third unit, not a continuation of 5.27–30.

[27] So most commentators; for the unlikely opinion that 5.31–2, like 19.9, derives from Mk 10.11–12, see G. Delling, 'Das Logion Mark X. 11', *NovT* 1 (1956–57), pp. 265–7.

[28] Against Grundmann, pp. 158–9, and Gundry, *Commentary*, p. 89, this is no reason to conclude that 5.31–2 is an appendix to 5.27–30. On the contrary, it suggests a third item. Cf. Guelich, p. 197.

[29] In much Jewish tradition the woman is often spoken of as though she were her husband's chattel or property; cf. Exod 20.17; Num 30.10–14; Ecclus 23.22–7. For exceptional cases in which a woman could sue for divorce see *m. Ketub.* 5.5; 7.2–5, 9–10; SB 1, pp. 318–19; and B. Brooten, 'Konnten Frauen im alten Judentum die Scheidung betreiben?', *EvT* 42 (1982), pp. 65–80. For Jewish divorce bills (quite a few of which have been uncovered in the Elephantine papyri) see *m. Giṭṭin*, the mishnaic tractate on certificates of divorce; also *DJD* 2 (1961), pp. 104–9 (no. 19).

way towards Jesus' equation of divorce (and remarriage) with adultery. But other anticipations of Jesus' attitude are hard to document. Some, to be sure, have found divorce prohibited in 11QTemple 57.17–19 and CD 4.12–5.14; the former, however, concerns polygamy, not divorce, and it is in any case legislation for the king (=high priest?), not necessarily commoners; and the latter text remains ambiguous.[30] On the whole, and despite the few rabbinic texts which mourn divorce (cf. *b. Giṭ* 90b), the impression one gains from ancient Jewish sources is that divorce was relatively easy and was not considered a grave misdeed.

ἐγὼ δὲ λέγω ὑμῖν ὅτι πᾶς ὁ ἀπολύων τὴν γυναῖκα αὐτοῦ παρεκτὸς λόγου πορνείας ποιεῖ αὐτὴν μοιχευθῆναι. On the introductory formula see on 5.21. πᾶς ὁ ἀπολύων τὴν γυναῖκα αὐτοῦ occurs also in Lk 16.18, which bespeaks an origin in Q. Lk 16.18 has, after αὐτοῦ, this: 'and marries another commits adultery'. Given Luke's fondness for ἕτερος (Mt: 9; Mk: 0; Lk: 32), this could be Lukan redaction under the influence of Mk 10.11–12, in which case Matthew's 'makes her to commit adultery' could represent Q (so Schulz, *Q*, p. 117). This possibility is buttressed by the fact that, in chapter 19, the Matthean formulation follows Mk 10.11 and does not conform to 5.32. We thus appear to have two slightly different traditions. In Mark the husband commits adultery (because he remarries) while in Q (= Matthew) the husband causes the woman to commit adultery (because she, it is assumed, will remarry). Which of the two formulations is the more original cannot be determined (*pace* Guelich, pp. 200–2, who favours Mark).

παρεκτός, which is usually translated 'except' (but see below), translates *zûlātî* in Deut 1.36 Aq (LXX: 0). Given the similar qualifying phrase in 19.9 (μὴ ἐπὶ πορνείᾳ), which is certainly redactional, we have here in all probability an editorial addition. Certainly παρεκτὸς λόγου πορνείας cannot be dominical: it has no parallel in Mk 10.11–12; Lk 16.18; or 1 Cor 7.10. If so, that is, if παρεκτὸς λόγου πορνείας is in fact Matthean, then we have more evidence for Matthew's knowledge of Hebrew, for, as we shall argue, the phrase appears to be based on the *'erwat dābār* of Deut 24.1 (the LXX has ἄσχημον πρᾶγμα).[31]

ποιεῖ αὐτήν means 'causes her'. The unstated assumption is that the woman will remarry (because the widow's plight was desperate; cf. Ruth 1.20–1; Ps 94.6; Isa 1.23; 10.2; 54.4); and as 5.32b implies, the real problem is perhaps not divorce in itself but its inevitably leading to remarriage. This is what subverts the ideal

[30] See the doubts of McNamara, p. 147. G. Vermes, 'Sectarian Matrimonial Halakhah in the Damascus Rule', in *Studies*, pp. 50–6, interprets CD 4.12–5.14 as prohibiting only polygamy.

[31] Against Guelich, p. 208, there is no certain evidence for Matthew having used the LXX in formulating 5.31–2.

of monogamy (cf. 19.1–9). Thus, although 5.31–2, in contrast to Mk 10.2–12 and Lk 16.18, might appear to characterize divorce itself—not divorce and remarriage—as adultery, this is not necessarily the case, so the texts may not be as far apart as they first seem.

While μοιχεύω (cf. 5.27, 28) appears in 5.32a, its synonym, μοιχάομαι (cf. 19.9; Mk 10.11, 12), appears in the second half of 5.32. μοιχάομαι may originally have appeared also in the first half. Matthew could have changed 5.32a (= Q) in order to gain a verbal link with 5.27–30 and an allusion to the seventh commandment. Luke, who has μοιχεύω in 16.18, may also have altered an original μοιχάομαι, his purpose being the use of a more common word (cf. Guelich, pp. 199–200).

According to Erasmus and most Protestant scholars since his time, Matthew allows the innocent party to divorce and remarry in the event of adultery. According to the almost universal patristic as well as Roman Catholic opinion, Matthew permits only separation for adultery, not remarriage (cf. 1 Cor 7); see, for example, Chrysostom, *Hom. on Mt*. 17.4, and for full discussion H. Crouzel, *L'Église primitive face au divorce*, Paris, 1971. In our judgement, the issue cannot, unfortunately, be resolved on exegetical grounds: Matthew's words are simply too cryptic to admit of a definitive interpretation. The question of freedom after a lawful divorce is just not addressed, and we cannot wring from the text what it will not give. See further on 19.1–10.

πορνεία has generally been understood to have one of three meanings—'fornication', 'incest', 'adultery'. The first of these is the least likely to be correct. 5.31–2 most naturally presupposes a marital context. The translation 'fornication' would also seem to make sex before marriage worse than adultery (because only the former would be grounds for divorce). Choosing between the two remaining alternatives—'incest' or 'adultery'—is nearly impossible, and if we favour the translation, 'adultery', it is only with great hesitation.

In support of the translation, 'incest', at least four points may be made. (1) This meaning is clearly attested in 1 Cor 5.1. (2) μοιχεύω and μοιχάομαι are words the evangelist uses for 'commit adultery' (5.27, 28, 32; 19.9, 18), and in 15.19, μοιχεία and πορνεία are clearly two different sins. So πορνεία is not likely to mean 'adultery' (cf. Did. 2.2; 5.1; Barn. 19.4). (3) In Acts 15.20, 29; 21.25, the council of Jerusalem declares that Gentiles are to abstain 'from what has been sacrificed to idols and from blood and from what is strangled and from πορνεία'. These four proscribed things are thought by many scholars to be taken from the Holiness code in Lev 17–18, which lays down rules not only for Israelites but for 'strangers that sojourn among them' (see the list of names in

Fitzmyer (v), p. 106, n. 52). And if this be so, πορνεία in Acts would have to refer to sexual intercourse with near kin (cf. Lev 18.6–18). (Matthew, it should be remembered, may even have known the contents of the so-called 'apostolic decree'; according to Acts it was published abroad.) (4) If Matthew's Christian community was, as seems most likely, a mixed body of Jews and Gentiles, the evangelist could easily have faced a situation in which Gentiles entering the community were found to be, because of marriages made before their conversions, in violation of the Levitical incest laws (cf. 1 Cor 5). (Incest was much more common among Gentiles than among Jews.) The exception in 5.31–2 could then be taken as the Jewish-Christian response to this situation: the marriage is invalid. (Mt 5.31–2 might, on this reading, be regarded as more strict than the usual Jewish response to incest, if this is reliably reflected in *b. Sanh.* 57b–8b and *b. Yeb.* 22a, for in these passages certain concessions concerning Lev 18 are made for Gentile converts to Judaism.)

Despite the forceful points just made, the following considerations move us to accept the equation, πορνεία = 'adultery'. (1) There is no patristic support for the translation, 'incest'. (2) πορνεία does not appear in Lev 17–18, and it is not at all certain that the so-called 'apostolic decree' does in fact allude to the Holiness code. (3) λόγου πορνείας would seem to be related to the *'erwat dābār* of Deut 24.1, which the Shammaites, in opposition to the Hillelites, who no doubt represented the dominant Jewish view (cf. Philo, *Spec. leg.* 3.30; Josephus, *Ant.* 4.253), interpreted as *děbar 'erwâ*, that is, as unchastity on the part of the woman within marriage (see *m. Giṭ.* 9.10; *b. Giṭ.* 90a–b; *Sipre* on Deut 24.1). Given Matthew's other links with rabbinic tradition, it is tempting to interpret 5.31–2 as, more or less, a Christian statement of the Shammaite position. This is especially true because if Matthew's λόγου πορνείας reflects Deut 24.1, his word order agrees with neither the OT nor the Hillelites but with the interpretation of the Shammaites (*děbar 'erwâ*). (The difference between Matthew and the Shammaites could then be that whereas the latter permitted remarriage after a lawful divorce, this is not allowed by Matthew. And yet, it may not be necessary to seek for a difference between Matthew and Shammai. We remain uncertain as to whether our text permits remarriage; and if, as seems probable, Matthew wrote when the school of Shammai was in decline and of little influence (the Hillelites being in the process of gaining the ascendancy), a reassertion of Shammai's position on divorce would perhaps have been sufficiently isolated as to be considered much more strict than general Jewish opinion (cf. Mt 19.11). It could therefore be viewed as part of the righteousness that exceeds that of the scribes and Pharisees. In other words, Matthew, given his post-70 environment, could have believed a restatement of the Shammaite position to be radical.) (4) 'Adultery' is a well-attested meaning for πορνεία (BAGD, s.v.; Lampe, s.v.; Lövestam (v)). (5) It can be urged that the less specific πορνεία and not the more specific μοιχεία appears in the exceptive clause because the OT phrase upon which that clause is based (Deut 24.1) is general, not specific ('erwat dābār). Furthermore, Bauer (v) has shown that in biblical Greek the μοιχ-root tends to be used of men, the πορν-root of women. (6) It is not absolutely necessary to interpret 'except for the cause of adultery' as contradictory to Mk 10.9–10 and Lk 16.18. Jesus' prohibition of divorce may have taken for granted that sexual irregularity cancelled a marriage (cf. Deut 22.13–30; Jer 3.8)—or at least Matthew may have thought that such was assumed (cf. Hill, *Matthew*, pp. 124–5). Or, and much less plausibly, as B. Vawter (v) and R. Banks, pp. 155–9, have argued, παρεκτὸς λόγου πορνείας might be a preterition, παρεκτός being closer to 'apart from' rather than 'except' (cf. 2 Cor 11.28; Did. 6.1; T. Zeb. 1.4). From this would result the translation: 'I say to you, whoever dismisses his wife—the permission of Deut 24.1 notwithstanding—makes her commit adultery'. (On this reading, the Shammaite position would be overthrown; but Vawter and Banks have real problems with the μὴ ἐπί of 19.9; see the commentary). (7) If it is possible to find a setting in Matthew's community for 'except for incest' (see above), it is also possible to find in Matthew's gospel itself the reason for the evangelist having added 'except for adultery'. In chapter 1, Joseph, the righteous father of Jesus, is resolved to give Mary a certificate of divorce because he suspects her of unfaithfulness during the time of betrothal (see on 1.18–25). If, then, Matthew had failed to tack on the 'except clause' in chapters 5 and 19, Joseph's resolution might invite the thought that the father of Jesus did not act in accord with Jesus' command about divorce. So 5.32 and 19.9 may be influenced by the desire to remove any question as to the consistency between a righteous man's action and the words of Jesus.

In addition to the meanings, 'fornication', 'incest', and 'adultery', we should observe that πορνεία might also be a term with general import. It might refer, that is, to sexual irregularity of any kind ('unchastity'; cf. BAGD, s.v.). But this would not result in an interpretion of 5.31–2 very different from that implied by the equation, πορνεία = 'adultery'. For sexual 'unchastity' within marriage is more or less the same as 'adultery'. (Augustine, *De serm. mont.* 1.16.46 understands πορνεία 'as general and all-embracing' and includes within its scope unbelief, covetousness, and idolatry; but this is the result of trying to harmonize Matthew with 1 Cor 7.)

καὶ ὃς ἐὰν ἀπολελυμένην γαμήσῃ μοιχᾶται.³² Whereas 5.32a
states that divorce (and remarriage?) save for πορνεία makes for
adultery, 5.32b—which seems implicitly to exclude polygamy (cf.
Wenham (v), pp. 96–7)—states that he who marries a divorced
woman commits adultery. The mind thus conjures up a situation
with three parties: a man divorces his wife and she remarries
another, with the result that all three—the husband who divorces
his wife, the former wife, and her new husband—are guilty of
adultery. Apparently the divorce bill (Deut 24.1; Mt 5.31), which
according to *m. Giṭṭin* had as its essential formula, 'Lo, thou art
free to marry any man', has not in reality cancelled anything. Lk
16.18 reads: καὶ ὁ ἀπολελυμένην ἀπὸ ἀνδρὸς γαμῶν μοιχεύει. There
is no Markan parallel. It is impossible to reconstruct Q exactly, for
while, on the one hand, ὅς/ὅστις ἄν/ἐάν (Mt: 37; Mk: 21; Lk: 20)
could readily be ascribed to our evangelist (cf. 5.31), Luke, on the
other hand, is fond of replacing relative sentences with participles
(cf. Lk 8.8, 21; 20. 27b; and 23.49 with their Markan counterparts).
To make a man who marries a divorced woman guilty of adultery
is quite foreign to Jewish law and introduces a rigidity alien to it.
    Why does he who marries a divorced woman commit adultery?
The key is 5.32a. If a woman has been divorced because of πορνεία,
then she is an adulteress and it would clearly be wrong to marry
her. If, on the other hand, the cause for her divorce was something
else, then she was, according to 5.32a, unlawfully divorced (as
πορνεία is the only valid reason for divorce); therefore she cannot
be free to marry another.
    One last observation. Jesus' saying about divorce was, when
first delivered, probably intended to be more haggadic than
halakhic; that is, its purpose was not to lay down the law but to
reassert an ideal and make divorce a sin, thereby disturbing then
current complacency (a complacency well reflected in Hillel's view
that a woman could be divorced even for burning food: *m. Giṭ.*
9.10). Jesus was not, to judge by the synoptic evidence, a legislator.
His concern was not with legal definitions but with moral
exhortation (cf. 5.27–30). If, however, all this be so, then Matthew
must be found guilty of misunderstanding Jesus; for the 'exception
clause' betrays a halakhic interpretation: it turns the Lord's logion
into a community regulation. Very relevant is C. E. B. Cranfield,
The Bible and Christian Life, Edinburgh, 1985, pp. 229–234.

ON OATHS (5.33–7)

The OT permits oaths in everyday speech—provided they are
neither false nor irreverent. But with the followers of Jesus there

---

³² So ℵ(*) K L W Δ (Θ) Π 0250 *f*¹·⁽¹³⁾ Maj lat? sa? goth arm mae bo. D *pc* a b d k Or?
omit. B *pc* geo sa? have και ο απολελυμενην γαμησας μοιχαται. See Metzger,
pp. 13–14.

should be no need for such oaths. Why? While the presupposition behind the taking of oaths is that there are two types of statements, one of which demands commitment (the oath), one of which does not (the statement unaccompanied by an oath), Jesus enjoins commitment to every statement, that is, invariable honesty and integrity (cf. Josephus, *Bell.* 2.135). This makes the oath superfluous. When the truth reigns, 'that mighty god, the oath' (Stobaeus, *Eclogae* 1.41.44) is dethroned, being without utility.

33. πάλιν ἠκούσατε ὅτι ἐρρέθη τοῖς ἀρχαίοις. The adverb and the repetition of the full formula, 'You have heard that it was said to the men of old' (so also 5.21), prove that 5.33 begins a new section. Thus 5.21–48 is divided into two triads, the first consisting of 5.21–6 + 27–30 + 31–2, the other of 5.33–7 + 38–42 + 43–8. See further p. 504.

As it now stands, 5.33–7 appears to be composite. 'Do not swear at all' (34a) makes 34b–6 ('neither by heaven, etc.') redundant. In addition, 'keep your ὅρκους with the Lord' (33b) *may* stand in tension with 'Do not make a false oath' (33a)—if ὅρκος means not oath but vow (see below); and 5.36 breaks the sentence pattern established in 5.35 (see below). When to all these observations we add that the subtraction of 33b and 34b–6 leaves a perfectly coherent piece, it is inviting to conclude that the original unit consisted only of 5.(33a) + 34a + 37.[33] (The addition, 34b–6, is, in turn, composed of at least two parts—34b–5 + 36—that were added at different stages. This is shown by the change from the plural in 34b–5 to the singular in 36, by the change in structure (ὅτι + noun + ἐστίν + genitive in 34b–5 but not 36), and by the reintroduction of the verb 'to swear' in 36. Gundry, *Commentary*, p. 92, puts forward the suggestion that while 'heaven' and 'earth' were in the tradition, Matthew added the references to 'throne' and 'footstool' (cf. Jas 5.12).)

Jas 5.12 ('Do not swear, either by heaven or by earth or by any other oath; but let your yes be yes and your no no, lest you fall under condemnation'), which gives no evidence of dependence upon the First Gospel, is testimony to the pre-Matthean origin of the core of 5.33–7.[34] Moreover, if the tradition-history offered in the previous paragraph be correct, Jas 5.12 already reflects a secondary, 'gemaric' stage in the tradition, a stage in which qualifications ('by heaven or by earth or by any other oath') have already been added.

οὐκ ἐπιορκήσεις ἀποδώσεις δὲ τῷ κυρίῳ τοὺς ὅρκους σου. This presumably summarizes OT teaching as found in such places as Exod 20.7; Lev 19.12; Num 30.3–15; Deut 23.21–3; Ps 50.14; Zech

---

[33] Cf. Bultmann, *History*, pp. 134–5; Manson, *Sayings*, p. 158; Davies, *SSM*, p. 240; Guelich, pp. 214–16.

[34] See Dibelius, *James*, pp. 250–1; F. Mussner, *Der Jakobusbrief*, HTKNT 12, 3rd ed., Freiburg, 1975, pp. 214–15; S. Laws, *A Commentary on the Epistle of James*, London and San Francisco, 1980, pp. 222–4.

8.17; Wisd 14.28 (cf. 11QTemple 53–4; T. Asher 2.6; Sib. Or. 2.68; Ps.-Phoc. 16). ἐπιορκέω (a NT *hapax legomenon*) can mean either 'to break an oath' (as in 1 Esd 1.46) or 'to swear falsely' (as in T. Asher 2.6; cf. Wisd 14.28). The latter is more likely here, for Lev 19.12 (MT—*wĕlōʾ tiššābĕʿû bišmî laššāqer*; the LXX has, οὐκ ὀμεῖσθε τῷ ὀνόματί μου ἐπ᾿ ἀδίκῳ) seems to lie in the background. In Did. 2.3 the word is ambiguous (οὐκ ἐπιορκήσεις, in a list of prohibitions).

Ps 49.14b LXX ('and give (ἀπόδος) to the Most High your vows (εὐχάς)'; cf. 1 Clem. 52.3) or its counterpart in the MT (Ps 50.14b) could well be the basis for Mt 5.33b. If so, then the evangelist or his tradition has changed 'Most High' to 'Lord' (cf. 8.29 diff. Mk 5.7) and εὐχάς to ὅρκους. What is one to make of this last change, if such it be? One could, despite the fact that εὐχή (cf. *nēder*, *nēzer*) is the usual word for vow, equate ὅρκος (almost always for *šbʿ* in the LXX) with vow (cf. Num 30.3; Deut 23.21–3) and regard the substitution as infelicitous yet intelligible: 5.33a refers to oaths between people, 5.33b to vows before God. But this may be to read too much into the passage. Because the confusion between 'oaths' and 'vows' was widespread,[35] the replacement of εὐχή may not have been significant: it might just mark assimilation to ἐπιορκήσεις. Or—and this seems the best guess—if the distinction between 'oath' and 'vow' was in fact known to the author of 5.33b, the change can be put down to a desire to make both 5.33a and 33b refer consistently to oaths.[36] The meaning of 5.33 would then be: 'You have heard that it was said to the men of old, "All your oaths are to be true." '

34a. The same imperative appears in Jas 5.12a. Understood literally, it would have been difficult in Judaism—despite the reservations expressed towards vows and oaths in Eccles 5.4–5; 9.2; Ecclus 23.9; Philo, *Decal.* 84; *m. Dem.* 2.3; *b. Ned.* 22a. The Essenes, to be sure, are said by Josephus to have avoided oaths (*Bell.* 2.135; cf. Philo, *Omn. prob. lib.* 84); but the Dead Sea Scrolls are ambiguous on the issue (see 11QTemple 53–4; CD 7.8; 9.9–12;

---

[35] See Davies, *SSM*, p. 240, citing S. Lieberman, *Greek in Jewish Palestine*, New York, 1942, pp. 115–43.

[36] Lit. on oaths and vows: SB 1, pp. 321–37; S. Blank, 'The Curse, Blasphemy, the Spell and the Oath', *HUCA* 23 (1950), pp. 73–95; Lieberman (as in previous note); J. Mann, 'Oaths and Vows in the Synoptic Gospels', *AJT* 21 (1917), pp. 260–74; H. Silving, 'The Oath', *Yale Law Journal* 68 (1959), pp. 1329–90; J. Schneider, *TWNT* 5, pp. 458–67; Z. W. Falk, *Introduction to Jewish Law of the Second Commonwealth*, AGJU 11, Leiden, 1972, pp. 129–32; G. Giesen, *Die Wurzel šbʿ 'schwören': Eine semasiologische Studie zum Eid im Alten Testament*, BBB 56, Königstein, 1981. Guelich, pp. 212–14, suggests that 5.33 reflects the rabbinic distinction between 'assertive oaths' (oaths about past actions; so 5.33a) and 'promissory oaths' (oaths about future actions; so 5.33b). This subtlety does not illumine the text.

15–16; 1QS 5.8; 6.27).[37] Perhaps the Essenes required only an entrance oath (cf. Josephus, *Bell*. 2.139, 142). They certainly did not, in any case, forbid all oaths. For aversion to oaths in the non-Jewish world see Sophocles, *OC* 650; Cicero, *Pro Balbo* 5; Plutarch, *Quaest. Rom*. 2.127d; *Mor*. 46A; Epictetus, *Ench*. 33.5; Marcus Aurelius Antoninus 3.5; Diogenes Laertius 8.22; Iamblichus, *Vit. Pyth*. 47. Note that when Jesus, in 26.63, is charged to speak under oath (ἐξορκίζω), he refuses. He says simply, 'You have said so'.

ἐγὼ δὲ λέγω ὑμῖν μὴ ὀμόσαι ὅλως. The problem of how the OT can picture God and the saints as swearing (Gen 14.22; 22.16; Exod 6.8; etc.) is not addressed (contrast Philo, *Leg. all*. 3.203–8; *Sacr. AC*. 91–6). Perhaps the conflict hints at the need for a less than literal interpretation (see below). One also wonders whether Deut 23.22 ('But if you refrain from vowing, it shall be no sin in you'; cf. 11QTemple 53.12) was felt to lessen the tension between Jesus' words and the OT. For 'But I say to you' see on 5.22. Here the introduction, as in 5.39 and 44, prefaces an imperative (contrast 5.22, 28, 32). ὅλως (= 'at all') occurs only here in the synoptics.

Although one may well doubt whether Jesus[38] intended his words about oaths to be an absolute rejection of all oaths instead of a polemic against 'the evil habit of swearing incessantly and thoughtlessly about ordinary matters' (Philo, *Decal*. 92) or a memorable way of requiring total honesty in every situation, it must be admitted that Mt 5.33–7 has been taken from early times—and is still taken by some Quakers and many Anabaptists in our own day—as a blanket prohibition. See, for example, Justin, *1 Apol*. 16.5; Irenaeus, *Adv. haer*. 2.32.1; Tertullian, *Idol*. 11; Origen, *De princ*. 4.3.4; Eusebius, *Praep ev*. 1.4; Acts of Pilate 2.5; Photius, *Ep*. 1.34; Basil, *Ep*. 199; Chrysostom, *Hom. on Mt*. 17.5; and Didymus in PG 39.1688. Contrast Augustine, *De serm. mont*. 1.17.51: 'let a man restrain himself as much as he can, since he understands that swearing is not to be counted among the things that are good, but as one of the things that are necessary'. Tolstoy, *My Religion*, New York, 1885, pp. 27–37, went so far as to affirm that Jesus' words require the abolition of courts. As Augustine recognized, however, the NT itself does not show any aversion to oath taking (cf. Lk 1.73; Acts 2.30; Rom 1.9; 2 Cor 1.23; Gal 1.20; Phil 1.8; Heb 6.13–20; Rev 10.6; discussion in Stählin (v)). It comes as no surprise to learn that most Christian

---

[37] Discussion in Davies, *SSM*, pp. 241–5, and L. H. Schiffman, *Sectarian Law in the Dead Sea Scrolls*, Chico, 1983, pp. 111–54.

[38] On the authenticity of at least part of 5.33–7 see Dibelius, *James*, p. 251, and Westerholm, pp. 104–13. Perhaps the original is to be found in 34a + 37a.

interpreters have not taken the prohibitions of Mt 5.33–7 to be
absolute (see Luz 1, pp. 286–8). For early non-canonical texts in
which swearing is not rejected see Prot. Jas. 4.1; Acts John 28;
Clement of Alexandria, *Strom.* 7.8; and M. Smith's 'Secret Gospel
of Mark', folio 1, verso 1.12.[39]

Against interpreting 5.33–7 as excluding in casuistic fashion all
oaths, the following observations are pertinent. (1) As Jeremias,
Theology, p. 220, has affirmed, the examples given in Mt 5.34–6
are perhaps 'not forms of oath used in court, but the oaths with
which the oriental constantly underlines the truthfulness of his
remarks in everyday speech (cf. 23.16–20). Jesus' disciples have no
need of this expedient, because Jesus expects unconditional truth
of them . . .'. (Compare the 39th article of religion of the Anglican
Church.) (2) N. J. McEleney, 'Sermon', pp. 557–8, has rightly
remarked that 'if Jesus is not presenting us with new *halaka* in his
correlative reduction of speech to "yes, yes," "no, no," he should
not be thought to do so in the hyperbole by which he tells us not to
swear at all. Hyperbole matches hyperbole'. (3) Mt 23.16–22 seems
to presuppose the validity of certain oaths (see commentary). (4)
As already observed, in both the OT and NT God and pious
people swear.

34b–5. In the Mishnah, oaths by heaven, by earth, and by one's
own head are all viewed as not binding by at least some rabbinic
authorities (cf. *m. Šebu.* 4.13; *m. Ned.* 1.3; *m. Sanh.* 3.2; SB 1,
pp. 332–4). This may account for their being cited here (so already
Augustine, *De serm. mont.* 1.17.52). If it was claimed by some
Christians that oaths by heaven or earth or Jerusalem or one's
head were, because not binding, not covered by Jesus' prohibition
of swearing, 5.34b–5 counters by linking heaven and earth and
Jerusalem to God, thereby making the oaths binding (cf. the
argument in 23.20–2; also CD 15–16; *m. Šebu.* 4.13). Any casuistic
attempt to circumvent 34a is excluded; appeal to non-binding
oaths—such as the rabbis specified—is rejected. (According to
Deut 6.13 and 10.20 oaths should be in God's name. But by the
first century that name could no longer be pronounced. So one of
the unstated assumptions behind 5.34b–6 is the Jewish conviction
that God's name itself could not be named and that, therefore,
when one takes an oath, a substitution for God's name must be
employed.)

μήτε ἐν τῷ οὐρανῷ ὅτι θρόνος ἐστὶν τοῦ θεοῦ, μήτε ἐν τῇ γῇ, ὅτι
ὑποπόδιόν ἐστιν τῶν ποδῶν αὐτοῦ, μήτε εἰς Ἱεροσόλυμα, ὅτι πόλις
ἐστὶν τοῦ μεγάλου βασιλέως. The neat triadic structure of these

---

[39] On Clement of Alexandria's ambiguous attitude towards swearing see Smith,
Clement, pp. 53–4.

perfectly parallel clauses argues for 5.36 being a later addition, for 5.36 breaks the pattern of 5.34b–5.

The LXX usually has ἐν after ὀμνύω. Jas 5.12 instead has the accusative, which is a classical construction. εἰς, which is here usually translated 'by', could conceivably mean 'toward'. 'The great king' (cf. 2 Kgs 18.19; Ps 47.2; 48.2; 95.3; Mal 1.14) appears only here in the synoptics. It is just possible, as Kennedy, p. 56, has suggested, that the ὅτι clauses should be interpreted not as giving Jesus' argument but rather as reporting the swearer's excuse: 'Do not swear by your head, alleging that you cannot make the hair white or black'.

The value and meaning of heaven, earth, and Jerusalem reside not in themselves but in their creator and sustainer, God. For heaven as God's throne and the earth as his footstool see Isa 66.1 (quoted in Acts 7.49; cf. Ps 11.4; 99.5; Lam 2.1). For swearing by heaven and earth see Philo, *Spec. leg.* 2.5; *m. Šebu.* 4.13; *b. Šebu.* 35a; Disc. 8–9 6.63.15–18. For the principle that people must swear by a greater than themselves see Heb 6.16. For Jerusalem as the city of the great king see Ps 48.2. For Jerusalem in vows see *m. Ned.* 1.3; *t. Ned.* 1.3.

36. Because this verse destroys the triadic structure of the qualifications in 5.34–6, and because Matthew loves triads, 5.36 is not likely to be assigned to his hand. This is consistent with the word statistics.[40]

μήτε ἐν τῇ κεφαλῇ σου ὀμόσῃς ὅτι οὐ δύνασαι μίαν τρίχα λευκὴν ποιῆσαι ἢ μέλαιναν.[41] Compare 6.27; 10.31. The sentiment expressed in the last half of the line was probably proverbial. Here the idea is: one cannot swear by one's own head because even over it one has no power; only God can make hair black (= young?) or white (= old? cf. Wisd 2.10). For swearing by one's head—which is common in modern Arabic—see 1 Chr 12.19 MT; *m. Sanh.* 3.2; and V. Rogers, 'The Use of *r*'s in an Oath', *JBL* 74 (1955), p. 272.[42]

37. The negative imperatives of 5.34–6 now give way to a concluding, positive imperative.

ἔστω δὲ ὁ λόγος ὑμῶν ναὶ ναί, οὒ οὔ.[43] Compare 2 Cor 1.17–18: 'Was I vacillating when I wanted to do this? Do I make my plans like a worldly man, ἵνα ᾖ παρ' ἐμοὶ τὸ ναὶ ναὶ καὶ τὸ οὒ οὔ; As surely as God is faithful, our word (λόγος) to you has not been yes and no'. The meaning of Matthew's clause seems to be, let your yes be

---

[40] Only κεφαλή (Mt: 12; Mk: 8; Lk: 7) and ἤ (Mt: 60; Mk: 33; Lk: 45) might be considered Matthean favourites. μέλας is a synoptic *hapax legomenon*.

[41] So ℵ B (L) W Θ 33 892 *pc* lat. Maj syʰ move the verb to the end. 0250 *f*¹³ 700 h place it before λευκήν. *f*¹ k GrNy have the verb before μίαν.

[42] For an amusing use of Mt 5.36 in connexion with the problem of whether Christian women should dye their hair see Tertullian, *De cultu fem.* 2.6.

[43] B 700 *pc* have εσται.

true and your no be true (cf. *b. B. Meṣ.* 49a) or, let your yes be only
yes (not yes and an oath) and let your no be no (not no and an
oath). Jas 5.12; Justin, *1 Apol.* 16.5; Clement of Alexandria, *Strom.*
5.99.1; 7.67.5; Const. Apost. 5.12.6; Ps.-Clem. Hom. 3.55; 19.2;
Eusebius, *Dem. ev.* 3.3; Epiphanius, *Haer.* 19.6.2; and 2 Jehu 43 all
differ from Matthew in that they have 'let your yes be yes and your
no no', with the definite article before the first 'yes' and the first
'no' (cf. 2 Cor 2.17). The broad attestation of this formulation,
which is probably closer to what Jesus said than is Mt 5.37, shows
its persistence in the oral tradition.

'Yes yes' and 'no no' are proper oath formulas in *b. Šebu.* 36a
and 2 En. 49.1–2 J;[44] but, against Dibelius, *James*, p. 250, and
others, in Matthew one type of oath is not being substituted for
another. Rather, all oaths are prohibited (5.34a; cf. Luz 1,
pp. 285–6).

τὸ δὲ περισσὸν τούτων ἐκ τοῦ πονηροῦ ἐστιν. This line is probably
editorial, as is indicated by its placement (at the end), by its
vocabulary,[45] by the lack of a parallel in Jas 5.12, and by the use of
a favourite Matthean expression ('the evil one'; see on 6.13). The
line is first cited in Justin, *1 Apol.* 16.5. The 'more' is perhaps the
oath that is not to be sworn (cf. Chrysostom, *Hom. on Mt.* 17.5).
'The evil one' is associated with an oath in 1 En. 69.15, and Jn 8.44
associates falsehood with the devil, 'the father of lies'.

DO NOT RESIST EVIL (5.38–42)

The structure of this section is simple:

5.38   1. OT teaching ('You have heard . . .')
5.39–42   2. Jesus' teaching
5.39a   A. Introductory formula ('But I say to you . . .')
5.39a   B. General principle ('Do not resist . . .')
5.39b–40   C. First pair of illustrations
5.39b   i. ὅστις σε ῥαπίζει . . .
5.40   ii. καὶ τῷ θέλοντι . . .
5.41–42   D. Second pair of illustrations
5.41   i. ὅστις σε ἀγγαρεύσει . . .
5.42   ii. τῷ αἰτοῦντι . . .

There are four brief scenes: the disciple is (1) personally insulted
then (2) taken to court then (3) impressed to do a soldier's bidding
then (4) asked to help one in need of funds.

[44] 2 En. 42.1–2 J may, however, be under NT influence. 2 En. 42.1–2 A lacks the
relevant parallel.
[45] περισσεύω/περισσός (see BDF § 60.3): Mt: 7 (redactional in 5.47); Mk: 2; Lk:
13. πονηρός: Mt: 26; Mk: 2; Lk: 13.

Since, in Q, the material in Lk 6.27–36 formed a unit,[46] Matthew has broken up what once went together. The result is the creation of two separate units dealing with two separate themes—meekness in 5.38–42 and love of enemy in 5.43–8. The evangelist has been motivated by the desire to obtain a second triad in the last half of chapter 5.

In Did. 1.4–5 there are several lines that are crucial for determining the relationship between the Didache and Matthew and Luke: 'If any man give thee a blow on thy right cheek, turn to him the other also, and thou shalt be perfect; if a man impress thee to go with him one mile, go with him twain; if a man take away thy cloak, give him thy coat also; if a man take away from thee that which is thine own, ask it not back, for neither art thou able. To every man that asketh of thee give, and ask not back; for the Father desireth that gifts be given to all from His own bounties'. There are at least six possible conclusions concerning the source(s) of this passage, to wit: (1) it is independent of Matthew and Luke; (2) it is dependent upon Matthew only; (3) it is dependent upon Luke only; (4) it is dependent upon Matthew and Luke; (5) it is dependent upon Matthew and a second, unknown source; and (6) it is dependent upon Luke and a second, unknown source. The relevant considerations which allow us to make a decision between the stated options may be illustrated thus:

A. Agreements between Matthew and the Didache against Luke:
   i. ῥάπισμα/ῥαπίζω, not τύπτω
   ii. εἰς, not ἐπί
   iii. 'right' cheek, not cheek
   iv. στρέφω, not παρέχω
   v. αὐτῷ in Mt 5.39 and Did. 1.4
   vi. 'and you will be perfect' (cf. Mt 5.48)
   vii. 'and if someone [or: whoever] compels you to go one mile . . .'
   viii. τῷ before αἰτοῦντι

B. Agreements between Luke and the Didache against Matthew:
   i. αἴρω ('whoever takes'/'from the one taking'), not κρίνω
   ii. ἱμάτιον before χιτῶνα
   iii. ἀπαίτει, not ἀποστρέφω
   iv. παντί before 'who asks'
   v. δίδου, not δός

We may immediately eliminate options (2) and (3): the agreements with Matthew *and* Luke make them impossible. Option (1) is also eliminated because, as we shall argue in the commentary, A ii, v, and vi are, in Matthew, redactional elements. The Didache therefore depends in part upon the First Gospel—a conclusion which also cancels out option (6), which posits no dependence upon Matthew. We are left, then, with (4) and (5). (4), however, suffers because, of the five elements shared between *Did.* 1.4–5 and Luke, none can be ascribed to Lukan redaction (see the commentary). So (5) is the clear choice: Did. 1.4–5 draws upon an unknown source but also shows Matthean influence.

---

[46] See Schürmann, *Lukasevangelium* 1, pp. 345–7, and Lührmann (v), pp. 413–16; against Dupont 1, p. 191. Yet the extent to which Luke reproduces the exact order of Q is debated. According to Zeller, *Kommentar*, pp. 26–7, the order was this: 6.29–30, 31, 27b, 28b, 35, 32–3 (followed by 6.36).

This is an inference one might have anticipated. There are, as argued elsewhere in this commentary, compelling reasons for thinking that the author of the Didache used the Gospel of Matthew. At the same time, the basic source behind Lk 6.27–36 was not only taken up by Q but continued to exist as an independent piece on into the second century,[47] and, evidently, the compiler of the Didache knew it as such. But, when he set it down on paper, his composition was influenced by Matthew's text, which he knew so well. (This account of things may also hold true for Justin, *1 Apol.* 16.1, where the influence of both Matthew and other traditions seems to be in evidence.)

38. ἠκούσατε ὅτι ἐρρέθη. See on 5.21.

ὀφθαλμὸν ἀντὶ ὀφθαλμοῦ καὶ ὀδόντα ἀντὶ ὀδόντος. So the LXX (without 'and') at Exod 21.24; Lev 24.20; and Deut 19.21—whence the accusative case. The third text could be foremost in mind (so Guelich, p. 220): the setting is the courtroom, the case is about false accusation, and both ἀνθίστημι and τὸν πονηρόν appear in the immediate context (cf. Mt 5.39).

The *lex talionis*, which appears in the ancient code of Hammurabi, is to be found not only in Jewish texts outside the OT (11QTemple 61.10–12; Jub. 4.31–2; LAB 44.10; SB 1, pp. 337–41)[48] but also in early Christian texts (cf. Apoc. Pet. 7–17).[49] It in fact lies behind the NT's so-called 'sentences of holy law'. 1 Cor 3.17 reads, 'If anyone destroys God's temple, God will destroy him'; and in Mk 8.38 Jesus is recorded as having said, 'Whoever is ashamed of me and of my words . . . of him will the Son of man be ashamed'. There is, however, no genuine contradiction between the rejection of the *lex talionis* and a belief that eschatological punishment will fit the crime. What Jesus rejects is vengeance executed on a personal level. He still assumes that God, the only wise and capable judge, will, in the end, inflict fitting punishment on sinners (cf. Rom 12.14–21). So the law of reciprocity is not utterly repudiated but only taken out of human hands to be placed in divine hands. Compare Rom 12.19:

---

[47] The evidence is presented in D. C. Allison, 'The Pauline Epistles and the Synoptic Gospels: The Pattern of the Parallels', *NTS* 28 (1982), pp. 11–12, 18–19; E. Best, 'The Synoptic Tradition in 1 Peter', *NTS* 16 (1970), pp. 95–113; and R. Glover, 'Patristic Quotations and Gospel Sources', *NTS* 31 (1985), pp. 234–51.

[48] Although the extent to which the *lex talionis* was literally followed in ancient Judaism is difficult to make out (cf. *b. B. Qam.* 83b–84a), financial reimbursement seems to have been acceptable to many; see Josephus, *Ant.* 4.280; SB 1, pp. 337–41; and J. Bowker, *Jesus and the Pharisees*, Cambridge, 1973, pp. 72–4. Furthermore, already in Exod. 21.18–27 the eye for eye principle seems to be replaced by that of proportionate compensation. But according to *m. Mak.* 1.6 and *Meg. Ta'an.* 7.3, the Sadducees and Boethusians accepted a literal interpretation. Cf. Judg 1.6–7; 2 Macc 5.10; Jub. 4.31; T. Gad. 5.10.

[49] On this see D. Fiensy, '*Lex Talionis* in the *Apocalypse of Peter*', *HTR* 76 (1983), pp. 255–8.

'Beloved, never avenge yourselves, but leave it to the wrath of God'.

39. Compare Lev 19.18; Deut 32.35; Prov 20.22; 24.29 ('Do not say, "I will do to him as he has done to me; I will pay the man back for what he has done" '); Isa 50.6; Lam 3.30; 1QS 10.18–19 ('I will pay to no man the reward of evil; I will pursue him with goodness. For judgement of all the living is with God and it is He who will render to man his reward'); 1 Pet 2.20–3; Sent. Syr. Menander 126–32; Sextus, *Sent.* 15–17; 2 En. 50.4. It may be observed that the spirit or attitude required by 5.39–42 is implicit in the beatitudes. How could the meek, the merciful, the peacemakers, and those who are happy to suffer for the right cause strike back at their opponents?

ἐγὼ δὲ λέγω ὑμῖν. See on 5.22. The import of the following sentences is lost if one attempts to take them literally.[50] Jesus often resorted to extreme exaggeration in order to drive home his points and to get his hearers to ask questions and see their world from a new perspective.[51] The command to turn the other cheek cannot be understood prosaically. Rather is Jesus calling for an unselfish temperament, for naked humility and a will to suffer the loss of one's personal rights. He is declaring that two wrongs do not make a right, that revenge is poison. He is telling us 'to requite evil with good' (*Koran* 41.34). Love of God and of neighbour are always to be one's motivating force. Personal vengeance, pride, and anger (cf. 5.21–6) must be cut out of the heart. In other words, one must, as Luke puts it, take up the cross daily (9.23). Or, as Paul has it, one must exhibit a love that 'bears all things . . . endures all things' (1 Cor 13.7). Compare the teaching in *b. Šabb.* 88b: 'Our rabbis taught: Those who are insulted but do not insult, hear themselves reviled without answering, act through love and rejoice in suffering, of them the Writ saith, "But they who love Him are as the sun when he goeth forth in his might" ' (cf. Mt 5.44). Compare also Plutarch, *Pericl.* 5, where the story is told of how Pericles accepted in silence for an entire day a hooligan's abuse and reviling and, afterward, when darkness fell, commanded his servants to take a torch and escort the man home. (Plutarch attributes Pericles' serenity to his unbounded admiration for Anaxagoras.) Epictetus also advised turning the other cheek: 'you will be gentle with the man who reviles you' (*Ench.* 42). For additional examples see Basil, *To the Young* 7, and the review of Schottroff (v).

---

[50] For what follows see esp. Vermes, *World*, p. 53; Tannehill, 'Focal Instance' (v); and Crossan (v).

[51] Perrin, *Language*, p. 52, writes that 5.38–42 challenges 'the hearer, not to radical obedience, but to radical questioning'. We would prefer: the passage challenges 'the hearer, not only to radical obedience, but also to radical questioning'.

Because 5.38–42 is not an edict about physical abuse but instead teaching about personal rights and honour (cf. Daube, pp. 254–65), it is perhaps hazardous to draw from Jesus' words—as did Tolstoy—easy inferences concerning the proper course of state institutions. This is especially true because (1) as already argued, Jesus is exaggerating, using hyperbole, (2) only two private parties are involved, and (3) the *lex talionis* is not being wholly rejected—it will be applied by God at the final judgement—but simply branded as inappropriate for personal relations. For the same reasons it is difficult to see that 5.38–42 involves a contradiction between the OT and the NT.[52] While in the Pentateuch the *lex talionis* belongs to the judiciary process, this is not the sphere of application in Matthew. Jesus, to repeat, does not overthrow the principle of equivalent compensation on an institutional level—that question is just not addressed—but declares it illegitimate for his followers to apply it to their private disputes. (Also pertinent is the circumstance that, in its OT context, the *lex talionis* is probably intended to restrain vendettas: once equivalent compensation has been extracted, the matter is ended. If, then, Jesus goes on to prohibit revenge, where is the acute contradiction? Compare Augustine, *De serm. mont.* 1.19.56.)[53]

Even if 5.38–42 is not to be taken literally, and even if it concerns not affairs of state but discipleship, it is hardly possible, given the Jewish situation in the first century, to empty the passage altogether of political meaning. The issue of violent resistance against Rome was a burning one both before and after 70; and both Jesus and Matthew believed that the road to revolution had for its inevitable destination only tragedy (Mt 22.15–22; 26.52; Lk 19.41–42; 23.31).[54] So, on the lips of Jesus, 5.38–42 could not but have had pacifistic implications. And, from Matthew's perspective, 5.38–42 must, at the very least, reflect ideological distance from the cause of the dead and buried zealots.

[52] So rightly Gundry, *Commentary*, p. 94, and Moo (v), p. 22; *pace* Barth, in *TIM*, p. 94; Jeremias, *Theology*, p. 207; Meier, *Law*, p. 157; and Guelich, p. 251. Even if Matthew did perceive tension between Mt 5.38–42 and the Mosaic Law, he could only have interpreted that tension in terms of salvation-history. See on 5.18. Unlike many modern scholars, our author would never have affirmed that Jesus' words 'overthrow' or 'contradict' the Torah.

[53] On the history of the interpretation of 5.38–42 see Luz 1, pp. 298–302. His own theological conclusion seems to us unavoidable: the text should not be interpreted literally or casuistically but is rather exemplary. It is to be creatively applied by the Christian imagination according to the situation.

[54] The attempt to make Jesus into a revolutionary will not bear critical scrutiny; see Bammel and Moule; Borg; Cadoux, pp. 163–74; G. B. Caird, *Jesus and the Jewish Nation*, London, 1965; Davies, *GL*, pp. 336–54; M. Hengel, *Was Jesus a Revolutionist?* (trans. of *War Jesus Revolutionär?*, 1970), FBBS, Philadelphia, 1971; J. H. Yoder, *The Politics of Jesus*, Grand Rapids, 1972.

(On political responsibility in the NT, see Cranfield, *Bible*, pp. 48–68.)

μὴ ἀντιστῆναι τῷ πονηρῷ. This is the general principle illustrated in the subsequent verses. There is no parallel in Luke. We could translate: 'Do not resist an evil person' (so RSV; cf. Deut 19.19–21) or, 'Do not resist the evil one' (= Satan; so Origen, Chrysostom; cf. Jas 4.7), or 'Do not resist evil' (so the AV; cf. Jos. Asen. 29.3). The first option seems the most probable.

ἀνθίστημι, which recalls the ἀντί of 5.38, could, although this is not mentioned by BAGD, s.v., have a forensic meaning: 'Do not oppose in court' (cf. Deut 19.18; Josephus, *C. Ap.* 2.23 uses the word of adversaries in battle; cf. *Bell.* 7.246).

1 Th 5.15 ('See that none of you repays evil for evil, but always seek to do good to one another and to all'), taken together with Rom 12.9–21, probably shows us that Paul was familiar with the dominical words preserved in Mt 5.38–42 = Lk 6.29–30.

ἀλλ' ὅστις σε ῥαπίσει εἰς τὴν δεξιάν σου σιαγόνα στρέψον αὐτῷ καὶ τὴν ἄλλην.[55] Compare Lk 6.29: τῷ τύπτοντί σε ἐπὶ τὴν σιαγόνα πάρεχε καὶ τὴν ἄλλην. The First Evangelist has presumably added ἀλλά (Mt: 37; Mk: 44; Lk: 37; it is absent from Did. 1.4), ὅστις (cf. 5.41; it is absent from Did. 1.4), δεξιός[56] (Mt: 12; Mk: 7; Lk: 6; cf. 5.29–30 and Did. 1.4), σου (which occurs twenty-two times in 5.21–48; it is absent from Did. 1.4), and perhaps αὐτῷ (cf. 5.40 and Did. 1.4; it is strictly superfluous). Matthew's ῥαπίζω and στρέφω (both in Did. 1.4) probably reproduce Q, Luke's τύπτω (Mt: 2; Mk: 1; Lk: 4; Acts: 5) and παρέχω (Mt: 1; Mk: 1; Lk: 4; Acts: 5) being redactional. If so, Luke would preserve Q except in his choice of verbs.

In trying to refute Celsus' argument that Jesus sometimes contradicted the OT, Origen, *C. Cels.* 7.25, appropriately cited as an OT parallel to turning the other cheek this verse: 'let him give his cheek to the smiter, and be filled with insults' (Lam 3.30). For striking the cheek with the open hand as a gross insult see Job 16.10; Ps 3.7; 1 Esdr 4.30 (cf. Aristophanes, *Ra.* 149–50). Matthew evidently mentions the right cheek in order to make plain that the reference is to the backhanded insult (cf. *m. B. Qam.* 8.6; to strike the right cheek with the right hand, one must hit backhandedly). (Another interpretation might be offered: having been hit on the

---

[55] ℵ B W 33 700 1424 *pc* followed by NA[26] have ραπιζει. D L Θ *f*[1.13] Maj Ad Bas Eus followed by HG have ραπισει. A firm decision between these two alternatives is impossible. K L Δ Θ *f*[13] 28 565 700 1424 *pm* have δεξιαν σου σιαγονα (so HG). B and NA[26] have δεξιαν σιαγονα σου. ℵ W *f*[1] 33 544 892 1010 1241 1689 *pm* a f (h) Or Ad Cyr PsBas Epiph omit σου. D k sy[s.c] Ephr omit δεξιαν.

[56] Fitzmyer, *Luke* 1, p. 638: 'Luke's fondness for the "right" hand/ear . . . makes it difficult to think that he would have suppressed the adjective here, if it were in his source'.

right cheek by the weaker left hand, the disciple offers his left cheek
to be hit by the even stronger right hand.)[57]

There are a number of intriguing parallels between Mt 5.38–42 = Lk
6.29–30 and Isa 50.4–9. In the OT passage the suffering servant is heard to
say, 'I gave my back to the smiters, and my cheeks to those who pulled out
the beard; I hid not my face from shame and spitting'. Also, the
vocabulary common to the NT and OT (LXX) passages is notable:
ἀνθίστημι (Isa 50.8; Mt 5.38), δίδωμι (Isa 50.4, 6; Mt 5.42), σιαγών (Isa
50.6; Mt 5.39), ῥαπίζω (Isa 50.6; Mt 5.39), ἀποστρέφω (Isa 50.6; Mt 5.42),
κρίνω (Isa 50.8; Mt 5.40), ἱμάτιον (Isa 50.9; Mt 5.40). Maybe, when Jesus
first spoke about turning the other cheek,[58] he had the passage from the
prophets in mind (so W. Manson, pp. 30–2) or, perhaps, in the
subsequent transmission of the material, Mt 5.38–42 = Lk 6.29–30 was
assimilated to Isaiah's text. There is also a third possibility, namely, that
Matthew himself is responsible for the parallels, and this is supported by
the fact that, of the seven correlations in vocabulary just noted, only three
appear in Luke. In addition, Matthew draws upon Isa 50.6 in composing
26.67 (see the commentary).

According to Jeremias the blow to the right cheek is given to the
disciples as heretics. What is envisioned is not 'reaction to a general insult,
but . . . outrage suffered as a consequence of following the suffering
saviour' (*Sermon*, p. 29). In favour of this reading is the fact that
everywhere else in the synoptic tradition persecution and dishonour are
associated only with discipleship. Against it, however, is the absence from
the text of any specification as to why Jesus' hearers are suffering insults.
All we can say with certainly is that innocence is presupposed.

40. Compare 1 Cor 6.7 ('why not rather suffer wrong?'). Jewish
males typically wore two garments, an inner garment (a shirt or
tunic of linen or wool worn next to the skin; cf. Jn 19.23; Josephus,
Ant. 17.136; Dio Chrysostom 13.61) and an outer garment (a robe
or cloak; cf. the Roman *toga* and see 1 Sam 28.8, 14; Mt 9.20–1;
26.65)—the χιτών (= *kĕtônet/kuttônet*) and ἱμάτιον (= *beged* or
śimlâ) respectively (cf. *b. B. Meṣ*. 78b). (The two can be seen in
many of the Dura-Europas synagogue paintings; see, e.g., the west
wall, the panel of Mordecai and Esther.) See further J. M. Meyers,
IDB 1, s.v., 'Dress', and C. Respond, 'Le costume du Christ', *Bib* 3
(1922), pp. 3–14. Because, according to Exod 22.26–7 and Deut
24.12–13, a man's outer cloak—which was also used as a sleeping
blanket or coverlet—could not be taken away from him by
another in pledge for any length of time (cf. *m. B. Qam*. 8.6), Jesus'
hearers are being asked to give up their lawful rights. Compare *b*.

---

[57] Origen, *De prin*. 4.3.3, uses Mt 5.40 to argue against literal interpretations of
Scripture: unless one suffers from a defect, one naturally strikes the left cheek with
the right hand, so the saviour's words are incredible on a literal level.

[58] On the authenticity of 5.38–42 par. see Bultmann, *History*, p. 105; Perrin,
Rediscovering, pp. 146–9; Lührmann (v); and Crossan (v).

B. Meṣ. 113b: 'R. Ishmael and R. Akiba: For we learnt: If one was a debtor for a thousand *zuz*, and wore a robe a hundred *manehs* in value, he is stripped thereof and robed with a garment that is fitting for him. But therein a Tanna taught with the authority of R. Ishmael and R. Akiba: All Israel are worthy of that robe'. Despite the differences between the two rabbinic opinions, there is agreement on one point: a person will in all cases be left with a robe. It is not permitted to take from a debtor all his clothing.

As the literal observance of Mt 5.40 would land one in prison for exposure, it is manifest that we have in the command to give away inner and outer garments the arresting illustration of a principle, not a rule to be literally and rigidly followed (so Augustine, *De serm. mont.* 1.20.62–8; contrast Chrysostom, *Hom. on Mt.* 18.2; χιτῶνα becomes μαφόριον in Ps.-Clem. Hom. 15.11, perhaps to avoid the offence of nudity). Crossan (v) fittingly speaks of 'case parody'.

καὶ τῷ θέλοντί σοι κριθῆναι καὶ τὸν χιτῶνά σου λαβεῖν, ἄφες αὐτῷ καὶ τὸ ἱμάτιον.[59] The anacoluthon (without relative clause) following an introductory participle is Semitic (BDF § 466.4). Lk 6.29 has: καὶ ἀπὸ τοῦ αἴροντός σου τὸ ἱμάτιον καὶ τὸν χιτῶνα μὴ κωλύσῃς. The σου before the noun is non-Lukan (cf. Jeremias, *Lukasevangelium*, pp. 142–3), and ἀπό with κωλύω is a Semitism or Septuagintism (cf. LXX Gen 23.6; 2 Βασ 13.13; Ecclus 46.7).

καὶ τῷ θέλοντι (absent from Did. 1.4) is Matthean redaction (cf. 5.42b; θέλω: Mt: 42; Mk: 24; Lk: 28; in the present instance the participle opens the clause as *casus pendens*, and one should compare the Hebrew substantival participle). λαμβάνω (Mt: 53; Mk: 20; Lk: 22) and ἀφίημι (Mt: 47; Mk: 34; Lk: 31) might also be editorial. κριθῆναι—which has a forensic meaning: 'to hale you before a court' (cf. Job 9.3; 13.19; Acts 23.6; 1 Cor 6.1)—is likewise redactional if the evangelist is increasing the allusions to Isa 50.4–9 (contrast Did. 1.4). For evidence of Romans requisitioning clothing from civilians see *P. Oxy.* 285, 394.

In Luke the order of 'tunic' and 'garment' is opposite to that of Matthew. Why? Matthew, in thinking of a court scene, has the defendant give the inner garment first because the outer garment cannot be legally requisitioned (cf. Exod 22.25–7; Deut 24.12–13). But then the disciple is to relinquish even more—the outer, more valuable (cf. Mk 13.16; *b. B. Meṣ.* 78b) garment, the garment the law declares cannot be taken away. In Luke, on the other hand, a disciple is being robbed. Naturally his outer garment is the first to go (cf. BAGD, s.v., ἱμάτιον). (Perhaps Matthew is more original in

---

[59] There is a very interesting parallel to Mt 5.40 in Aramaic Ahikar, saying 77 (Lindenberger): 'If a wicked man grasps the fringe of your garment, leave it in his hand. Then appeal to Šamaš; he will take what is his and will give it to you'.

having the text treat of legal action. Luke, for the sake of his Hellenistic readers, who would not have understood the act of seizing a garment for a pledge (cf. Exod 22.25–7; Deut 24.10–13; Amos 2.8), may have changed the scene so as to make it one of robbery and violence. In favour of this, the apostle Paul, who knew the collection behind Lk 6.29–38, offers in 1 Cor 6.1–8 advice which may reflect Jesus' teaching on non-resistance, and the context is Christians and the court.)

Is not the imitation of Christ implicit in 5.39–40? Jesus himself was struck and slapped (26.67: ῥαπίζω), and his garments (27.35: ἱμάτια) were taken from him. If his followers then turn the other cheek and let the enemy have their clothes, will they not be remembering their Lord, especially in his passion?

41. As with the commands in 5.39–40, and 42, no motive is given for acting in the peculiar manner Jesus desires. We are not told, for instance, that turning the other cheek will save the wicked. This means that the question of whether or not the world will be transformed by such actions is just not addressed (contrast T. Benj. 4.1–5.4). That is, no pragmatic motive is invoked; it is simply the case that those who do Jesus' bidding will go the extra mile. Apparently it is sufficient that they are asked by their Lord to do it (cf. Zeller, *Kommentar*, pp. 31–2). (One may also infer that Jesus is not concerned with what to do with the guilty—if he were, one could not circumnavigate the objection that Jesus ignored the differences between good and evil people—but with rooting out the spirit of personal vengeance and self-pity from his followers.) See further on 5.45.

καὶ ὅστις σε ἀγγαρεύσει μίλιον ἕν, ὕπαγε μετ' αὐτοῦ δύο.[60] There is no Lukan parallel. Did. 1.4 agrees with Matthew save for the first four words (ἐὰν ἀγγαρεύσῃ σέ τις). ἀγγαρεύω (a loanword from the Persian—cf. Herodotus 8.98—which also appears in rabbinic literature; see *m. B. Meṣ.* 6.3; *b. Yoma* 35b; Horsley 2, p. 77; Deissmann, *Studies*, pp. 86–7) means 'press into service' or 'requisition' (cf. Josephus, *Ant.* 13.52; in the passion narrative the Romans ἀγγαρεύουσιν Simon of Cyrene to carry Jesus' cross). On the responsibility of occupied peoples for the transportation of Roman soldiers see Horsley 1, pp. 36–45. μίλιον (a rabbinic loanword, from the Latin *mille*) is a NT *hapax legomenon*.[61] The appearance of *mille* is especially appropriate in 5.41 given the context—Roman requisitioning; and ἀγγαρεύω, it should be added, also has a Latin equivalent: *angariare*. Against Gundry,

---

[60] D it vg^cl sy^s add ετι αλλα before δυο. lat sy^c Ir^lat add αλλα only. See Zahn, p. 251, n. 27.

[61] Other Latinisms in Matthew include κῆνσος (17.25; 22.17, 19; cf. Mk 12.14); κουστωδία (22.65–6; 28.11); and (?) συμβούλιον λαβεῖν (27.1, 7). See further Lagrange, p. cxvii.

Commentary, pp. 94–5, the vocabulary does not move us to claim redactional composition; further, Luke may have omitted 5.41 because of his general tendency to exonerate the Romans. Or perhaps 5.41 comes from Q[mt]. In any event, the parallelism between 5.39b and 41 could well be in part due to Matthew: ὅστις + σέ + verb + object + verb introducing command is the construction in both places.

5.41—which would be impossible on the lips of a Zealot or political revolutionary—presumably envisions a situation in which civilians are compelled by Roman soldiers to do their bidding and carry their equipment (cf. Mk 15.21). We may thus compare Epictetus, *Diss*. 4.1.79: 'If there is a requisition and a soldier seizes it (your ass), let it go. Do not resist or complain, otherwise you will be first beaten, and lose your ass after all'. In the gospels, however, prudent considerations are not mentioned. As T. W. Manson wrote, 'the first mile renders to Caesar the things that are Caesar's; the second mile, by meeting opposition with kindness, renders to God the things that are God's' (*Sayings*, p. 160).

42. Compare Exod 22.25; Lev 25.36–7; Deut 15.7–11; Prov 28.27; Ecclus 4.1–10; 29.1–2; Tob. 4.7; T. Job. 9.1–12.4; T. Zeb. 7.2; Heb 10.34. Mt 5.42 = Lk 6.30 was originally no doubt isolated. It does not really fit its present context well, which is about revenge and love of enemies; and in 5.42 the disciple is no longer a victim. Furthermore, there is an independent variant in Gos. Thom. 95, and it is bound to nothing before or after: 'If you have money, do not lend at interest, but give to the one who will not be able to give it back'.

τῷ αἰτοῦντί σε δός.[62] This and the next line are in synonymous parallelism and for Matthew constitute only one example, not two (cf. Lührmann (v), p. 418). Observe the parallelism between 5.42 and 40; both have in common τῷ + participle + σοί/σέ + main verbal command. Did. 1.5 has: παντὶ τῷ αἰτοῦντί σε δίδου. So also Lk 6.30, without the article. As Luke does not like πᾶς + participle without article (Jeremias, *Lukasevangelium*, p. 144), it must come from Q. Matthew then dropped the παντί because it would detract from the parallelism between 5.40 and 42 and because it would seem to imply an indiscriminate giving, a mindless benevolence that would do more harm than good (cf. Did. 1.6; Basil, *Ep*. 150.4). In line with this last point, Matthew's aorist ('give') is more cautious than Luke's present tense ('continue giving'). (Augustine, we may observe, avoided the implication of indiscriminate giving by remarking how the text says not to give everything asked for

---

[62] So ℵ B D W *f*[13] 892 *pc* C1. διδου—due to assimilation to Lk 6.30?—is found in L Θ *f*[1] Maj.

but only to give to everyone who asks; *De serm. mont.* 1.20.67.)[63]

.καὶ τὸν θέλοντα ἀπὸ σοῦ δανίσασθαι μὴ ἀποστραφῇς. Compare Lk 6.30: καὶ ἀπὸ τοῦ αἴροντος τὰ σὰ μὴ ἀπαίτει. καὶ τὸν θέλοντα is redactional (cf. 5.40). For the spelling of δανίζω (which differs in various mss.) see BDF § 23. The word probably comes from Q, for it occurs three times in Lk 6.34–35, a passage which presumably looked back in Q to Mt 5.42 = Lk 6.30 (so Schürmann, *Lukasevangelium* 1, pp. 348, 354).

According to Albright and Mann, pp. 69–70, 5.42 has to do with usury (on which see SB 1, pp. 346–53) and should be translated, 'Give to him who asks you for a loan, and do not refuse one who is unable to pay interest' (cf. Hill, *Matthew*, pp. 128–9). Now lending and borrowing may be the subject of our text (or of an earlier version). Support for this can be gathered from Gos. Thom. 95 (quoted above). But the rendering, 'one who is unable to pay interest', requires inserting without manuscript support a μή before θέλοντα ('the one unable to pay interest on sums borrowed'), and on this point at least Albright and Mann cannot be commended.

LOVE YOUR ENEMY (5.43–8)

Following the opening verse, 5.43, in which both an OT commandment (Lev 19.18) and a possible or alleged understanding of it ('Hate your enemy') are set forth, the remainder of 5.43–8 is, like 5.39–42, marked by pairs and a high degree of parellelism. There are two summary commandments ('Love your enemy', 'Pray for those who persecute you'; 5.44). There are two things the Father does (he makes the sun rise and he makes the rain fall; 5.45). There are two classes of people to be considered (the good and the bad, the just and the unjust; 5.45). And there are two rhetorical questions ('If you love those who love you . . .', 5.46a; 'If you salute only your brothers . . .', 5.47a)—to which two answers, in interrogative form, are returned ('Do not also the toll collectors . . .', 5.46b; 'Do not also the Gentiles . . .', 5.47b). The structure would appear to be this:

1. Old injunctions: Love your neighbour and
                      hate your enemy
2. New injunctions: Love your enemy and
                      pray for those who persecute you
3. Reason: So that you may be sons of your Father who is in
   heaven, for

---

[63] It should be noted that there are rabbinic texts—e.g. *b. Ketub.* 68a—in which the sages are encouraged to give even to deceivers.

> he makes his sun to rise on the evil and the good and
> sends rain on the just and the unjust
4. Discussion: For if you love those who love you . . .?
              Do not even the toll collectors do the same?
              And if you salute only your brethren . . .?
              Do not even the Gentiles do the same?
5. Concluding injunction: You therefore must be perfect. . . .

The general structure, injunction/reason/discussion, seems to have
been a common literary form; see, for instance, Rom 13.8–10; T.
Jud. 16; and T. Y. Mullins, 'Topos as a New Testament Form',
JBL 99 (1980), pp. 541–7.

43. The evangelist has chosen to save until the end, as the sixth
and last of the paragraphs introduced by 5.17–20, the material on
love of one's enemy. The section is thus the climactic section, and it
contains the most important—and surely most difficult—
command (cf. 7.12). This is why 5.43–7 issues in 5.48, the
exhortation to be perfect as the heavenly Father is perfect.

ἠκούσατε ὅτι ἐρρέθη. See on 5.21 and compare 5.38. This and the
remainder of 5.43 are redactional.

ἀγαπήσεις τὸν πλησίον σου καὶ μισήσεις τὸν ἐχθρόν σου. 'Love
your neighbour'—called the 'royal law' in Jas 2.8—comes from
Lev 19.18 LXX (cf. 19.34); it is cited again in Mt 19.19 and 22.39
(both times with 'as yourself' added[64]); note also Rom 13.9–10;
Gal 5.14. Lev 19.18 MT has this: *wĕʾāhabtā lĕrēʿăkā kāmôkā*. The
meaning of μισέω (cf. Lk 6.22, 27) may well be 'not love' or 'love
less' (cf. Gen 29.33; Deut 21.15–17; Prov 13.24; Mt 6.24).
Concerning ἐχθρός (cf. Lk 6.27, 35), in the OT the word is used
equally of personal and national foes; see H. Ringgren, *TDOT* 1,
pp. 212–18 (on *ʾôyēb*).

'Hate your enemy' is not found in the OT, although similar
sentiments appear there: Deut 7.2; 20.16; 23.4, 7; 30.7; Ps 26.5;
137.7–9; 139.19–22 (cf. *Sipra* on Lev 19.18). From outside the
Jewish tradition see Polybius 18.37.7; Hesiod, *Op.* 342–3 ('call
your friend to a feast but leave your enemy'; cf. 352–6); Solon,
frag. 1.3–5 (Diehl) (γλυκὺν φίλοισ', ἐχθροῖσι πικρόν); Plato, *Tim.*
17d–18a; *Rep.* 375c; *Meno* 71e; and Tacitus, *Hist.* 5.5–6. The
closest parallels to 'hate your enemy' belong to the Dead Sea
Scrolls, where we read that the sons of light are 'to hate' (*lśnwʾ*) all
the sons of darkness, each according to his guilt at the time of

---

[64] According to Spicq 1, p. 12, the omission of 'as yourself' is significant. But
Furnish (v), pp. 50–1, observes that in 5.43 the omission of 'as yourself' simply
permits perfect parallelism to obtain between 'love your neighbour' and 'hate your
enemy'.

God's vengeance' (1QS 1.10–11; cf. 1.4; 9.21–3; Josephus, *Bell.* 2.139: μισήσειν δ' ἀεὶ τοὺς ἀδίκους). Because of this, some scholars have urged that Mt 5.43–8 is a polemical barb aimed right at the Essenes. But this would make 5.43–8 anomalous. As we have argued, although at points reminiscent of Essene belief and practice, none of the preceding paragraphs is (presently) directed against the Essenes—or against the belief or practice of any other particular group in Judaism. Rather do they reproduce OT commandments and show how Jesus moves beyond them to make even greater demands. Should not such be the case here?

In our estimation, what Matthew has done is take the key words, 'hate' and 'enemy'—words which were to hand in Q (cf. Lk 6.22, 27, 35)—and turn them into a negative qualification in order to bring home the limitation of an OT directive in contrast with the all-encompassing nature of a word of Jesus. Lev 19.18 declares, 'You shall love your neighbour as yourself'. With this Jesus does not find fault. The text, however, understands neighbour as fellow-Israelite (cf. Ecclus 18.13?; CD 6.20–7.1), and this is the point at which Jesus surpasses the OT teaching. The command to love one's neighbour, although it is not in itself being criticized, is not sufficient for Matthew's Jesus because it permits[65] one not to love those who are not neighbours. That is, Lev 19.18 leaves open the possibility that one will, as is all too natural, confine love to neighbour narrowly defined (cf. *Mek.* on Exod 21.35) or even—as did the Essenes and probably other Jews—define 'neighbour' in opposition to 'enemy'. (The effect of 'and hate your enemy' is to make 5.43a mean, 'Love your neighbour only'.) By way of contrast, the command to love one's enemy redefines neighbour in the broadest possible terms (cf. Lk 10.29–37, the story of the good Samaritan). Hence what is required, as part of the 'better righteousness' (5.20), is a love that is not restricted.

44. 'Hate your enemies' becomes 'love your enemies'. What does 'love' mean? For Jesus it 'is no longer primarily a quality of relationships within the fold, within the walls which hold the dark and threatening powers at a distance; it is something which must prove itself in the engagement with that which is inimical and threatening' (Riches, p. 135). This is why Jesus can seek out the toll collectors and the sinners.

ἐγὼ δὲ λέγω ὑμῖν. The expression is here redactional, despite the parallel in Lk 6.27 (ἀλλὰ ὑμῖν λέγω τοῖς ἀκούουσιν). For even if this last be pre-Lukan (see Jeremias, *Lukasevangelium*, pp. 140–1), it is perfectly explicable in terms of its present context; that is, it does

---

[65] Jeremias, *Theology*, p. 213, n. 3, interprets μισήσεις as a permissive imperfect—'you need not love your enemy'.

not seem to be a vestige of the formula preserved in Matthew (cf. Guelich, pp. 224–5).

ἀγαπᾶτε τοὺς ἐχθροὺς ὑμῶν. So Lk 6.27. Despite the singular 'enemy' in 5.43 (which is to be put down to the requirements of parallelism: the 'neighbour' of Lev 19.18 is in the singular), Matthew here follows Q and switches to the plural. 'Enemies' are defined by what follows as those who persecute Christians (cf. Furnish (v), pp. 47–8). This means that one is to love not only personal opponents but God's opponents, the enemies of God's people. 'Love'—Matthew uses not the future indicative (cf. 5.43) but the present—is also defined by what follows: one must pray for enemies (5.44b), do good to them (5.45), and salute them (5.47b); action, not emotion, is being called for. The verb, ἀγαπάω, unlike the corresponding noun, ἀγάπη, is well attested in pre-Christian secular Greek (LSJ, s.v.). Beginning in the fourth century B.C. it became more and more popular while φιλέω—because it developed sexual connotations?—suffered decline (R. Joly, *Le vocabulaire chrétien de l'amour est-il original?*, Bruxelles, 1968). Despite the distinctive place given to ἀγαπάω and ἀγάπη in the NT and the new associations they gain there, it would be unwise to place too much weight on the difference between ἀγαπάω and φιλέω. The former can mean familial, reciprocal love (Mt 5.46; Col 3.19), the latter divine, unreciprocated love (Jn 16.27; Rev 3.19).

If in Matthew the love commandment refers firstly to persecutors of the church (above all hostile Jews and perhaps Roman officials), when Jesus originally spoke his hearers would undoubtedly have thought of the Romans in Palestine (cf. Cadoux, pp. 171–2; Piper (v), pp. 98–9; Borg, p. 130). So far from fomenting hatred and wreaking vengeance upon the occupying forces, Jesus was asking his hearers to display a spirit of love and tolerance (cf. 5.41). He was among those who sought to halt the Gadarene march towards A.D. 70.

Jesus' call to love one's enemies is reflected in many early Christian writings. It is in fact one of the most cited and influential dominical words in early Christian literature; see Lk 23.34; Acts 7.60; Rom 12.14, 17–20; 1 Cor 4.12–13; 1 Th 5.15; 1 Pet 3.9; Polycarp, *Ep.* 12.3; Irenaeus, *Adv. haer.* 3.18.5; Ps.-Clem. Hom. 3.19; Ep. Apost. 18; 2 Clem. 13.4 (independent of the synoptics?); Justin, *1 Apol.* 14.3; Athenagoras, *Supp.* 12.3 (in these last three texts love of enemy is regarded as peculiarly characteristic of Christianity); discussion in W. Bauer, 'Das Gebot der Feindesliebe und die alten Christen', *ZTK* 27 (1917), pp. 37–54. For OT anticipations see Exod 23.4–5; 1 Sam 24.17–19; 2 Sam 19.6 (LXX: τοῦ ἀγαπᾶν τοὺς μισοῦντάς σε); 1 Kgs 3.11; Job 31.29 (on which note Eusebius, *Dem. ev.* 1.6); Ps 7.3–5; Prov 24.17–18 (quoted in *m.* '*Abot* 4.19); 24.29; 25.21–2; Jer 29.7; Jon 4.10–11. Other Jewish parallels include Ep. Arist. 207, 227, 232; Philo, *De virt.* 116–18; T. Gad. 6.1–7; T. Zeb. 7.2–4; T. Iss. 7.6; T. Benj. 4.2–3; 2 Bar. 52.6 ('Why do you look to the decline of your enemies?'); 2 En. 50.4 ('If ill-requitals befall you, return them not either to neighbour or enemy'; cf. 44.4, 5); *m.'Abot* 1.12; 2.11; 4.3; SB 1, pp. 368–70. See also Epictetus, *Diss*. 3.22.54 (the Cynic 'must needs be flogged like an ass, and while he is being flogged he must love the man who flogs him, as though he were the father or brother of them all'); Diogenes Laertius 8.1.23 (behave 'so as . . . to turn enemies into friends'); Seneca, *De beneficiis* 7.30.2, 5; Marcus Aurelius Antoninus 2.1; Origen, *C. Cels*. 8.35; J. Moffatt, *Love in the New Testament*, London 1929.

Despite all the parallels just listed, the succinct, arresting imperative, 'Love your enemies', is undoubtedly the invention of Jesus' own mind, and it stands out as fresh and unforgettable.[66] 'Love your enemies' is not advice for the Stoic who must remain even tempered in the face of a fickle world. Nor is it prudent wisdom, to the effect that, just as it takes water, not fire, to put out a fire, so it takes love, not hate, to overcome hate. Jesus does not promise that love will turn enemies into friends. He is instead calling for a 'love which does not depend upon some thing' (*m. 'Abot* 5.16). Jesus' words also do not simply constitute a call to give up vengeance, for they go far beyond that to require positive action. In short, 'Love your enemies' seems to contain what may have been a novel demand: do good to the enemy, despite the circumstances and the results.[67]

Gregory Vlastos, in an article on 'Socrates' Contribution to the Greek Sense of Justice', *ARCHAIOGNOSIA* 1 (1980), pp. 301–23, has asserted that classical Greece was deficient in its sense of justice in two large areas. (1) The application of moral norms was grossly discriminatory in conduct towards personal enemies. (2) The same was true with regard to the treatment of social inferiors, especially slaves. Socrates, according to Vlastos, is to be given credit for managing to overcome the first defect: he repudiated the *talio* in dealing with personal enemies (see *Crito* 49B 8-C 8). The great philosopher did not, however, remedy the second deficiency. The extant records nowhere hint that Socrates protested against discriminatory forms of conduct directed at social inferiors. If Vlastos is correct, it would seem that Jesus took a step Socrates did not. For not only did Jesus reject the application of the *talio* to personal relations, he also universalized the love command. This follows above all from the fact that when Jesus spoke of the 'enemy', he was referring to non-Jews, to Roman soldiers (see above). In other words, the imperative to love was not to be confined to one's own kind, that is, one's Jewish neighbours (cf. Mt 5.46–7). Love was to extend beyond the boundaries erected by class and ethnic differences. Compare Lk 10.29–37.

[66] The dominical origin of 5.44–8 or of most of its elements is almost universally accepted; cf. Bultmann, *History*, p. 105; Lührmann (v); Piper (v), pp. 44–99.

[67] For Buddhist parallels see E. A. Burtt, *The Teachings of the Compassionate Buddha*, London, 1955, pp. 42–3, 52, 79. For extensive discussion of the Jewish and Hellenistic parallels see Piper (v), pp. 19–49.

καὶ προσεύχεσθε ὑπὲρ τῶν διωκόντων ὑμᾶς.[68] Compare Lk 23.34 and Acts 7.60. Bengel, *ad loc.*, wrote: 'obtain by your prayer blessings for those who wrest blessings from you'. Lk 6.28 has περὶ τῶν ἐπηρεαζόντων ὑμᾶς after 'pray' (cf. Justin, *1 Apol.* 15.9) and no introductory 'and'. Luke is probably closer to Q. διώκω may well be Matthean redaction (Mt 6; Mk 0; Lk 3).

Parallels to Mt 5.44c include 1QapGen. 20.28–9 (Abraham prays for the healing of the king of Egypt, the king who has taken Abraham's wife: 'I prayed for that [perse]cutor' (Fitzmyer's reconstruction)); T. Jos. 18.2 ('If anyone wishes to do you harm, you should pray for him, along with doing good, and you will be rescued by the Lord from every evil'); Polycarp, *Ep.* 12 ('Pray . . . for those who persecute and hate you, and for the enemies of the cross . . . that ye may be perfect in him'; dependence upon Matthew here seems plausible); *P. Oxy.* 1224 fol 2r° col. 1 ('pray for your enemies'); Sextus, *Sent.* 213 ('Pray that you will be able to do good to your enemies'); *b. Ta'an.* 23b (more divine favour is shown to one who prayed that robbers in her neighbourhood might repent than to one who prayed that they might die; cf. *b. Ber.* 10a; *b. Sanh.* 37a). Sent. Syr. Men. 128–32 ('If you have an enemy, do not pray for him that he may die, for when he is dead he is delivered from his misfortunes; instead pray for him that he may become poor, so that he will live on and perchance cease from his evil practices') is a dubious parallel.

In Luke the commands to love one's neighbour and to pray for persecutors are joined to two additional commands: 'Love your enemies, do good to them that hate you, bless those who curse you (cf. Gen 12.3; 27.29), and pray for those who abuse you . . .' (6.27–8). Contra Fitzmyer, *Luke* 1, p. 637, the pre-Lukan origin of the two middle clauses is to be inferred from four facts. (1) The vocabulary and syntax are not typical of Lukan redaction (Jeremias, *Lukasevangelium*, pp. 141–2). (2) Did. 1.3, which is independent of Luke (see pp. 538–40), also has four imperatives: 'Bless those that curse you and pray for your enemies (cf. *P. Oxy.* 1224 fol. 2r° col. 1), fast for those persecuting you . . . love those who hate you . . .' (cf. Justin, *1 Apol.* 15). (3) Luke's 'Bless those who curse you'—which appears to be without precise Jewish parallel—seems to have been known by Paul (Rom 12.14: 'bless those who persecute you'; 1 Cor 4.12: 'being reviled we bless'). (4) The μισέω of Lk 6.27 probably linked up in Q or Q[lk] with the μισέω in the woe in Lk 6.22 (so Schürmann, *Lukasevangelium* 1, pp. 345–6). Why the two clauses are missing from Matthew cannot be determined (*pace* Gundry, *Commentary*, p. 97)—unless it was to further the dyadic structure of 5.43–8 (see p. 548).

---

[68] D K L W Δ Θ Π *f*[13] 28 Maj lat sy[(p).h] Cl Eus Chry ApostConst arm geo: ευλογειτε τους καταρωμενους υμας (υμιν D* *pc*; omit ε. τ. κ. υ.: 1230 1242* *pc* lat) καλως ποιειτε τοις μισουσιν υμας (omit κ. π. τ. μ. υ.: 1071 *pc* Cl Eus) και (omit: W) προσευχεσθε υπερ των επηρεαζοντων υμας (omit κ. π. υ. τ. ε. υ. D *pc*) και διωκοντων υμας. The text we have printed appears in ℵ B *f*[1] *pc* k sy[c.s] sa bo eth Ad Eus Theo Ir[lat] Or Cyp. The long text is probably an expansion under the influence of Lk 6.27–8 or oral tradition.

45. 'To return evil for good is the devil's way: to return good for good is man's way: to return good for evil is God's way' (Hunter, p. 58). Note the connexion between 5.45 and 5.9, the seventh beatitude: 'Blessed are the peacemakers, for they shall be called sons of God'.

ὅπως γένησθε υἱοὶ τοῦ πατρὸς ὑμῶν τοῦ ἐν οὐρανοῖς. Compare *b. Quid.* 36a: 'When you behave as sons, you are sons'. Lk 6.35 has this: 'you shall be sons of the Most High' (cf. Ps 82.6; Ecclus 4.10). This is undoubtedly closer to Q, as the word statistics indicate.[69] On sonship in Matthew see on 5.9.

Since Matthew's 'show yourselves (now) to be sons' (cf. 10.16; 24.44) seems to be redactional and since Luke has an unambiguous future—that is, eschatological—tense, our evangelist has evidently introduced an element of 'realized eschatology'. Believers in Jesus not only will be sons of God in the messianic age or the age to come but are already such now.

In Eph 5.1–2, love, the *imitatio Dei*, and sonship are brought together in a way reminiscent of Mt 5.44–5: 'Be imitators of God, as beloved children. And walk in love . . .'. These three themes are also intimately linked in 1 Jn 4.7–12 ('let us love'; 'he who loves is born of God'; 'if God loved us, we also ought to love one another') and likewise in 1 Pet 1.13–25 ('as obedient children . . . as he who called you is holy, be holy yourselves', 'love one another earnestly from the heart. You have been born anew'). Apparently there is embedded in Mt 5, Eph 5, 1 Pet 1, and 1 Jn 4 a paraenetic pattern common to early Christian moral teaching: as God's children, imitate him in his love. Presumably the pattern derives from the teaching of Jesus.

ὅτι τὸν ἥλιον αὐτοῦ ἀνατέλλει ἐπὶ πονηροὺς καὶ ἀγαθοὺς καὶ βρέχει ἐπὶ δικαίους καὶ ἀδίκους. One is reminded of Ps 145.9: 'The Lord is good to all, and his compassion is over all that he has made'. Compare also Seneca, *De beneficiis* 4.26.1, and 1 Jn 4.7–8 (where the command to love is grounded in the declaration that 'God is love'). Contrast *Ahiqar* 49 (Lindenberger): 'Whoever takes no pride in his father's and mother's name, may *Šamaš* [the sun god] not shine on him, for he is an evil man'. Lk 6.35d, the counterpart of Mt 5.45b, reads: 'because he is good to the ungrateful and the evil'. The concrete imagery of Matthew over against Luke's generalization seems more characteristic of Jesus. On the other hand the contrasts between 'the evil and the good' and between 'the just and the unjust' are likely to be editorial because, while word statistics do not prove Matthean activity,[70]

---

[69] ὅπως: Mt: 17; Mk: 1; Lk: 7. οὐρανός with πατήρ: Mt: 13; Mk: 1; Lk: 1.

[70] πονηρός: Mt: 26; Mk: 2; Lk: 13; with ἀγαθός: Mt: 7; Mk: 0; Lk: 2. δίκαιος: Mt: 17 Mk: 2; Lk: 11. ἄδικος: Mt: 1; Mk: 0; Lk: 4.

also editorial are the contrasts between 'good' fish and 'bad' fish in 13.48 and between 'evil' and 'good' in 22.10.

McNeile, p. 72, observed that *ṣmḥ*, which is translated by ἀνατέλλω in the LXX, can, in Aramaic, mean 'to shine', so perhaps the presumably Semitic original referred to sunshine. For the personal, active use of βρέχω see the LXX for Gen 19.24 and Ps 77.24 (cf. BDF § 129). Observe that the order, evil/good—just/unjust, is chiastic.[71] Popular Jewish opinion held that, at the time of the feast of booths, God determined the amount of rain that should fall over the course of the coming seasons (cf. *b. Roš. Haš.* 17b; *y. Roš. Haš.* 1.3.57b).

As elsewhere in Matthew, and as often in the wisdom literature, mankind seems to be divided into two classes. Shades of grey are missing. The rabbis in a similar fashion sometimes contrast the *ṣaddîk* and the *rāšāʿ*; but there is always room in the rabbinic texts for 'average' persons (the *bênônîm*; cf. *b. Ber.* 61b). Matthew, with his concern for decision for or against Jesus, has no use for the category. (See on the *rāšāʿ* Davies and Sanders, *CHJ* 3 forthcoming; E. P. Sanders, *Jesus and Judaism*.)

God who, in his cosmic fatherhood, exercises providence over all in mercy (Wisd 15.1), even over those outside the covenant, is full of long-suffering (cf. 2 Bar. 12.1–4; 24.1–4; Irenaeus, *Adv. haer.* 2.22.2), and thus for the present—but not necessarily the future; see *Midr. Ps.* on 22.1—he gives good gifts to all, even to the wicked. Now since God's sons are to be like him—a well-attested Jewish idea—, that is, share his moral character, they too must show mercy to all, even to their enemies. Jewish parallels to the flow of thought include Lev 19.2; *Mek.* on Exod 15.2 ('Be like Him! Just as He is gracious and merciful, so be thou also gracious and merciful'); *Sipre* on Deut 11.22; *b. Soṭa* 14a; *b. Šabb.* 133b; *b. Sukk.* 30a. For discussion see A. Marmorstein, 'The Imitation of God (*Imitatio Dei*) in the Haggadah', in *Studies in Jewish Theology*, London, 1950, pp. 106–21; Abrahams 2, pp. 138–82; and Schoeps, *Zeit*, pp. 286–301. Note also Seneca, *De beneficiis* 7.30.2 ('Do as the gods . . . They begin to give benefits to him who knows them not and persist in giving them to those who are ungrateful') and 4.26 ('If you are imitating the gods, you say, "then bestow benefits also upon the ungrateful; for the sun rises also upon the wicked, and the sea lies open to pirates" '; cf. Heraclitus, *Ep.* 5.1; 9.7).

God makes his sun to rise and he makes it rain—natural processes are, in accordance with the biblical tradition, directly assigned to the hand of God; compare Gen 2.5; Job 38.12–41; Ps

[71] In Origen, *De prin.* 1.3.7; 2.4.1, and Ps. Clem. Hom. 3.57 the order is good/evil—just/unjust.

104; Isa 5.6; Amos 4.7; Mt 6.26, 30; 2 Cor 9.10; *b. Taʿan.* 23b; *Sipre* on Deut 32.1. This way of looking at nature (*creatio continua*) makes it easy to draw inferences about God's character from the natural order. For if the natural realm on the one hand and the moral and spiritual on the other both have God as their author and sustainer, there must be genuine affinity between the two (cf. also Ps 19; Rom 1.19; 1 Cor 11.13–16; for further discussion see on 6.26–30 and Davies, *JPS*, pp. 293–5, 398–9). Recall that the death of Jesus—a religious event—is accompanied by events in the natural world—darkness and an earthquake.

Jesus' words on love are not based upon any prophesied outcome. Unlike the counsel in Diogenes Laertius 8.1.23 (your good behaviour will turn enemies into friends; cf. Thucydides 4.19.1–4; Did. 1.3; Ep. Apost. 18), love is not being required because it will set the world right. Instead one's motivation to love arises out of a desire to be like God: *imitatio Dei* (cf. 18.23–35). This means the energy for love will not be exhausted if the conversion of the wicked does not result. Mt 5.43–8 is not pragmatic advice ('love works'). It is a command to love disinterestedly.[72]

Several rabbinic texts affirm that God is good to the just and unjust; see, for instance, *b. Taʿan.* 7a ('R. Abbahu said: the day when rain falls is greater than the Revival of the Dead, for the Revival of the Dead is for the righteous only whereas rain is both for the righteous and the wicked'); *Mek.* on Exod 18.12 ('The Holy One, blessed be He, . . . gives to every one his wants and to everybody according to his needs. And not to good people alone, but also to wicked people and even to people who are worshipping idols'); and *Pesiq. R.* 48.4 ('In all your life have you ever seen rain come down upon the field of So-and-So who is righteous, but not upon the adjacent field of So-and-so who is wicked? Of course the sun shines upon those in Israel who are righteous, but it also shines upon those who are wicked . . .'). Despite texts such as these, Klausner, pp. 379–80, affirmed that Jesus introduced a new idea into Judaism when he in effect made sinners and non-sinners alike or of the same value in God's eyes. It is, however, dubious whether so much can be read into Mt 5.43–8. The distinction between just and unjust is presupposed, not eradicated; and Jesus is saying only that, for the present, God showers gifts even upon sinners—which is surely not a novel notion for Judaism (cf. 2 Bar. 12.1–4; 24.2; *b. Sanh.* 111a). It may even have been proverbial.

46. This verse and the next, which may at one time have circulated in isolation (cf. Bultmann, *History*, p. 88), and which

---

[72] It should be remembered that, for Matthew, the love of God has been revealed above all in Jesus, so to imitate God in his love is to imitate Jesus in his love. Cf. Irenaeus, *Adv. haer.* 3.18.5: 'The Word of God, who said to us, "Love your enemies and pray for those that hate you", Himself did this very thing upon the cross . . .'.

require disciples to do more than toll collectors and Gentiles, illustrate the theme of the greater righteousness (5.20): the righteousness of the Christian is to be of a surpassing, extraordinary character.

The three-fold structure of 5.46 is repeated in 5.47:

5.46a If you . . .
   46b   what reward have you?
   46c   Do not also . . .?

5.47a And if you . . .
   47b   what are you doing that is remarkable?
   47c   Do not also . . .?

5.45 offered the first reason for obeying the command to love enemies: the imitation of God. 5.46 and 47 now offer a second reason: if disciples love only those who love them, they are hardly doing anything out of the ordinary, much less surpassing the righteousness of the scribes and Pharisees.

ἐὰν γὰρ ἀγαπήσητε τοὺς ἀγαπῶντας ὑμᾶς, τίνα μισθὸν ἔχετε; Compare Lk 6.32: 'And if you love (ἀγαπᾶτε: so also Did. 1.3 and 2 Clem. 13.4) those who love you, what credit is that to you?' 'Only' (cf. 5.47) should be read into the Matthean text: 'For if you love (only) those who love you . . .'. Is μισθός redactional? Three observations render an affirmative answer probable. First, Matthew likes μισθός (Mt: 10; Mk: 1; Lk: 3). Secondly, the combination of μισθός + ἔχετε in Mt 6.1 has often been judged redactional. Thirdly, Luke's 'what credit is that to you' has a parallel in Did. 1.3 (cf. 1 Pet 2.20), and dependence of the Didache upon Luke has yet to be established. On the other hand, χάρις, which had its place in philosophical discussions about doing good to others (van Unnik (v)), is often redactional in Luke and Acts (Mt: 0; Mk: 0; Lk: 8; Acts: 17). So caution is in order. On the concept of reward see on 6.19–21. The injunction, 'Do good to those who do good to you', which makes fine common sense, was a *topos* of Greek philosophy; see Hesiod, *Op.* 352; Aristotle, *Rh. Al.* 144b; Xenophon, *Mem.* 4.4.24; Epictetus, *Diss.* 2.14.18; discussion in van Unnik (v).

οὐχὶ καὶ οἱ τελῶναι τὸ αὐτὸ ποιοῦσιν;[73] Compare 5.47b. Lk 6.32 has: καὶ γὰρ οἱ ἁμαρτωλοὶ τοὺς ἀγαπῶντας αὐτοὺς ἀγαπῶσιν. Matthew has turned a statement into a question (cf. 6.25 diff. Lk 12.23) and substituted 'do the same' (cf. Lk 6.33) for 'love those who love them'. Both of these changes enhance the parallelism between 5.46 and 47b. Luke has probably turned 'toll collectors'

---

[73] Instead of το αυτο (cf. Lk 6.33), D Z 33 h k Lcf sy^{s.c} geo eth have ουτως. *f*[1] *pc* lat mae have τουτο (which is explicable as an error of sight or sound). The same variants appear in the second half of 5.47.

(Mt 8; Mk 3; Lk 10) into 'sinners' (Mt: 5; Mk: 6; Lk: 17) (so Marshall, p. 263).

τελῶναι are not 'tax collectors', that is, the gabbā'îm, the state officials who collected poll and land taxes (publicani) but rather either Hellenistic tax farmers or the despised môkĕsîn, Jewish tax farmers and their agents who, having purchased the toll collecting concessions, collected indirect taxes for the Romans.[74] The latter were infamous for their abuses of the system and were generally denied Jewish civil rights (cf. m. Sanh. 3.3; b. B. Qam. 94b; b. Sanh. 25b). t. B. Meṣ. 8.26 ('For shepherds, tax collectors, toll collectors, it is difficult to make repentance'; cf. b. B. Qam. 94b) expresses what was no doubt a common sentiment.

To judge by the gospel evidence,[75] Jesus extended the right hand of fellowship to toll collectors (Mt 9.10–11; 10.3; 11.19; 21.31–2; Lk 18.9–14; 19.1–10). It is therefore odd to see them referred to in Mt 5.46 (and 18.17) in such a disparaging, off-handed manner. There would seem to be three explanations for the apparent inconsistency: (1) One might hold, with W. O. Walker, that the tradition is wrong in presenting Jesus as the frequent friend of toll collectors (see n. 75). (2) 5.46 and 18.17 might not be dominical, at least in their present form (a strong possibility; 18.17 in particular is not likely to go back to Jesus; see the commentary). (3) There is no real contradiction: Jesus could simultaneously have disapproved of toll collectors' behaviour yet still have reached out to them. The apostle to the Gentiles, we may recall, could speak of 'Gentile sinners' (Gal 2.15).

47. καὶ ἐὰν ἀσπάσησθε τοὺς ἀδελφοὺς ὑμῶν μόνον, τί περισσὸν ποιεῖτε; Compare Lk 6.33: 'And if ever you do good [cf. 6.35] to those who do good to you, what credit is that to you?' Again Luke probably reproduces Q (cf. Jeremias, Lukasevangelium, p. 145). Concerning ἀσπάζομαι (redactional in 10.12), as BAGD, s.v., observes, in its present context the word means more than 'greet'—it implies a desire for God's blessing and peace. (In Exod 18.7 and Judg 18.15 A the verb translates šā'al lĕšālôm.) The redactional use of ἀδελφός (see on 5.22) shows that Matthew is calling Christians to love not only Christians but also those outside the community. μόνον is probably Matthean (Mt: 7; Mk: 2; Lk: 1). τί περισσὸν ποιεῖτε is best translated, 'what are you doing

[74] Lit.: L. Goldschmid, 'Les impôts et droits de douane en Judée sous les Romains', REJ 34 (1897), pp. 192–17; O. Michel, TWNT 8, pp. 88–106; J. R. Donahue, 'Tax Collectors and Sinners: An Attempt at Identification', CBQ 33 (1971), pp. 39–61; W. R. Farmer, 'Who Are the "Tax Collectors and Sinners" in the Synoptic Tradition?', in From Faith to Faith, ed. D. Y. Hadidian, Pittsburgh, 1979, pp. 167–74; F. Herrenbrück, 'Wer waren die "Zöllner"?' ZNW 72 (1981), pp. 178–94.

[75] W. O. Walker, 'Jesus and the Tax Collectors', JBL 97 (1978), pp. 221–38, has argued at length that, if the gospels are examined critically, we are free to believe that Jesus did not associate closely with toll collectors. But (1) the apparent implications of Mt 11.18–19 = Lk 7.33–4 are hard to evade and (2) the story about Levi in Mk 2.15–17 has its grounding in history (see Pesch 1, pp. 167–8).

that is remarkable' (so BAGD, s.v., περισσός). Compare Justin, *1 Apol*. 15: τί καινὸν ποιεῖτε; Since περισσόν recalls the περισσεύσῃ of 5.20, this is another argument for taking 5.20 to be part of the heading for 5.21–48, not for 6.1–7.12.

There are rabbinic texts which urge the saluting of all men: *m*. *ʾAbot* 3.13 ('Be swift (to do service) to a superior, and kindly to the young, and receive all men cheerfully'); ibid. 4.15 ('Be first in greeting every creature'); *b*. *Ber*. 17a ('It was related of R. Joḥannan b. Zakkai that no man ever gave him greeting first, even a heathen in the street'); *m*. *Giṭ*. 5.9 ('Greetings may be offered to Gentiles in the interests of peace').

οὐχὶ καὶ οἱ ἐθνικοὶ οὕτως ποιοῦσιν;[76] Compare 5.46b and Auth. Teach. 5.33.27–31: 'even the pagans give charity'. Lk 6.33b has: 'Even the sinners do the same'. Compare Did. 1.3: οὐχὶ καὶ τὰ ἔθνη τὸ αὐτὸ ποιοῦσιν; If the interrogative form be redactional, Did. 1.3 might at this point depend upon Matthew; but the issue cannot be decided. Luke is no doubt responsible for 'sinners' (cf. Lk 6.32 diff. Mt 5.46; for the equation of 'sinners' with 'Gentiles' see Ps 9.17; 1 Macc 2.48; Ps. Sol. 2.1–2; cf. Mk 14.41; Gal 2.15). ἐθνικός (Mt: 3; Mk: 0; Lk: 0) is usually rendered in modern English translations by 'Gentile'. 'Non-Christian pagan' is also a possibility (see on 6.7). But the fact that L W Θ *f*[13] Mai h sy[p] arm Cyp substitute 'toll collectors' betrays the potential offensiveness of 'do not the ἐθνικοί act thus?' We find in this yet one more reason to think our author Jewish. 'Toll collector' and ἐθνικός are again paired in 18.17 (redactional).

It is odd to find in Matthew condescending words against the ἐθνικοί. How can 5.47; 6.7; and 18.17 be harmonized with such verses as 28.19, which commands Jesus' followers to preach among the Gentile nations? Whether the explanation is wooden, conservative editing, a genuine ambivalence towards the Gentile world, or some other unknown fact, the paradox is not unique to the First Gospel. In the Testaments of the Twelve Patriarchs, which in their present form are Christian, the salvation of the Gentiles is a prominent theme. See T. Sim. 7.2; T. Levi 4.4; 18.9; T. Jud. 22.2; 24.6; T. Zeb. 9.8; T. Dan 6.7; T. Naph. 8.3–4; T. Asher 7.3; T. Benj. 10.9–10. And yet, at the same time, the readers are not to take Gentile wives (T. Levi 14.6) and should not become involved in 'revolting Gentile affairs' (T. Jud. 23.2). See further T. Levi 9.10; T. Dan 5.8; T. Naph. 3.3; 4.1.

---

[76] So K L Δ Θ 565 1010 Maj h sy[c.h] bo geo[1] Bas[1] followed by HG. το αυτο appears in ℵ B D W 28 *f*[1.13] 700 *pm* Cyp Lcf arm geo[2] eth followed by NA[26]. τουτο appears in 1604 sy[p] sa[mss] Bas[1]. The second reading was probably born under the influence of Mt 5.46 and/or Lk 6.33 and in time gave rise to the third.

48. This verse belongs firstly to the unit that begins in 5.43—as is shown by the motif of the *imitatio Dei*, which takes the reader back to 5.45. Simultaneously, 5.48 is the fitting culmination of all of 5.21–48, for each of the six paragraphs in the section calls for 'perfection', that is, each makes an absolute demand which cannot be surpassed. What more, for example, can be done about lust than to drive it out of the heart (5.27–30)? And who else is left to love after one has loved the enemy (5.43–48)? That Mt 5.48, with its call for perfection, was associated not just with the command to love one's enemy is demonstrated by Did, 1.4. where 'and you will be perfect' is associated with the command to turn the other cheek (cf. also Eusebius, *Dem. ev.* 3.3 = 104d).

ἔσεσθε οὖν ὑμεῖς τέλειοι. Lk 6.36 has: γίνεσθε οἰκτίρμονες (cf. Justin, 1 Apol. 15.13). Did. 1.4, drawing upon Matthew, has καὶ ἔσῃ τέλειος (cf. 6.2). Compare Gen 17.1 Aq. (γίνου τέλειος); Jub. 10.17; 15.3 (God to Abraham: 'Be thou perfect'); 23.10; 1 Cor 14.20; Col 4.12; Jas 1.4; Apoc. Pet. 7.71.15–16 ('Peter, become perfect'); Testim. Truth 9.44.18. Lev 19.2 ('You shall be holy; for I the Lord your God am holy') probably lies behind the original saying of Jesus, which is best represented by Luke's text. Matthew is responsible for assimilating the line to Deut 18.13 ('You shall be blameless [LXX: τέλειος] before the Lord your God'). (If, as we have tentatively suggested, the first three paragraphs in 5.21–48 take up teaching from Deuteronomy while the second three paragraphs cite texts from Leviticus, it is satisfying to discover in the final verse of 5.21–48 the influence of both Leviticus and Deuteronomy.) ἔσεσθε appears in Lev 19.2, and the possibility of assimilation to this OT text is raised by the several other possible correlations between Lev. 19 and Mt 5.21–48: compare Lev 19.12 with Mt 5.33, Lev 24.20 with Mt 5.38, Lev 19.18 with Mt 5.43, and Lev 19.34 with Mt 5.44.

The appearance of the particle, οὖν, in Mt 5.48, is particularly apposite, coming as it does at the end of a major section (cf. 1.17; 7.12, 24; Rom 3.1; 7.25; 8.31). As for ὑμεῖς, which is strictly unnecessary, it is again emphatic, as so often throughout the sermon (cf. esp. 5.13–14). τέλειος, which is redactional in 19.21 (also in connexion with the love commandment), is used in Deut 18.13 LXX (for *tāmîm*), and this in part explains its appearance here—along with the fact that 'merciful' (so Q) would not so clearly have signalled the conclusion of 5.17–48.

Because the originality of Luke's 'Be merciful' is consistent with the word statistics for both Matthew and Luke,[77] and because it is favoured by Matthew's redactional insertion of 'perfect' in 19.21 (diff. Mk

[77] τέλειος: Mt: 3; Mk: 0; Lk: 0. οἰκτίρμων: Mt: 0; Mk: 0; Lk: 2 (both in 6.36).

10.21 = Lk 18.22) as well as by Tg. Ps.-J. on Lev 22.28 ('My people, children of Israel, as our Father is [or: as I am] merciful in heaven, so shall you be merciful on earth'; cf. *y. Meg.* 4.9.75c; *y. Ber.* 5.3.9c; *Sipre* on Deut 11.22),[78] we cannot (*pace* Black, p. 181) postulate a word-play in the underlying Aramaic between 'salute' and 'perfect'. (Because Tg. Yer. I. on Lev 22.27 refers to the virtue of the perfect man, and because this immediately precedes the words, 'As our Father is merciful in heaven, so shall you be merciful on earth', Matthew may have been influenced by a targumic tradition; cf. Gundry, *OT*, p. 74.)

'Be merciful even as also your Father is merciful' can, notwithstanding the Jewish parallels, be received without much hesitation as a genuine dominical imperative, since it fits so well with Jesus' typical elevation of mercy above holiness (holiness being interpreted by his contemporaries as separation from all things unclean; cf. 11QTemple 51.5–10; *Sipra* on Lev 11.44; on 20.7; on 20.26; *Mek.* on Exod 19.6). See especialy the declarations in Mt 12.11–12; Lk 13.15–16; and 14.5; discussion in Borg, pp. 51–199. By taking up Lev 19.2 ('Be holy . . .') and substituting 'merciful' for 'holy', Jesus subordinated or redefined 'holiness' and thereby gave expression to one of his most characteristic convictions.

What precisely is meant by τέλειος?[79] The word can be used of things (= what is perfect or complete) or of people. In the latter instance it may signal maturity or adulthood, that is, completed growth (1 Cor 14.20; Eph. 4.13; cf. Philo, *Agric.* 2), initiation into mysteries (Philo, *Somn.* 2.234; Phil 3.15?; Col 1.28?), perfection in kind (1 Clem. 55.6: 'perfect in faith'; Ignatius, *Polyc.* 1.3: 'a perfect athlete'; note the discussion in Ps.-Dionysius, *De div. nom.* 13.1), or, lastly, moral perfection (cf. Mt 19.21; Jas 3.2; Did. 1.4; 6.2). Without doubt, 'moral perfection' is the meaning in 5.48a; yet this only opens the discussion, for which the following points are pertinent. (1) In the LXX τέλειος usually translates *šālēm* or *tāmîm* and means 'unblemished', 'undivided', or 'whole'—as in 'undivided heart' (3 Βασ 8.61; 11.4, 10; 15.3, 14; 1 Chr 28.9; cf. T. Jud. 23.5) or 'unblemished offering' (Exod. 12.5). And in Gen 6.9; Deut 18.13; 2 Βασ 22.26; and Ecclus 44.17, where undivided loyalty to God is the meaning, 'blameless' would be a good translation. (In the LXX *tāmîm* is frequently translated by ἄμωμος). (2) In the Dead Sea Scrolls reference is made to a 'house of perfection' (1QS 8.9; cf. 9.6), to 'men of perfection' (1QS 8.20; CD 20.2, 5, 7), and to 'perfection of way' (1QS 5.24; cf. 1.9, 13; 2.2;

---

[78] Because Luke is not likely to have borrowed from the targum and because the targum is not likely to have borrowed from Luke, we should assign Lk 6.36 to pre-Lukan (Semitic) tradition.

[79] Lit.: Davies, *SSM*, pp. 209–15; G. Delling, *TWNT* 8, s.v.; P. J. Du Plessis, ΤΕΛΕΙΟΣ: *The Idea of Perfection in the New Testament*, Kampen, 1959; R. N. Flew, *The Idea of Perfection in Christian Theology*, Oxford, 1934; D. Peterson, *Hebrews and Perfection*, SNTSMS 47, Cambridge, 1982; K. Prümm, 'Das neutestamentliche Sprach- und Begriffsproblem d. Vollkommenheit', *Bib* 44 (1963), pp. 76–92.

8.1, 10, 26; 9.2, 5, 6, 8, 9, 19; 10.21; 11.2; 1QM 14.7; 1QH 1.36). 1QS 8.1 is especially instructive: 'perfect in all that has been revealed of the law'. For the covenanters, 'perfection' was full obedience to the norm revealed to the community, and failure to observe *all* the rules of the sect meant exclusion from fellowship (see Davies, *SSM*, pp. 210–15; *kōl* is ubiquitous in the scrolls).[80] This is particularly noteworthy for us, given the 'legal' context of 5.48 (5.17–48 is about the Torah) and Matthew's concern that Christians obey *all* of Jesus' commandments (cf. 28.20). Beyond this, Mt 19.16–22, the only other synoptic passage to use the term, 'perfect', *may* introduce a distinction between the merely good and the perfect (see the commentary and Did. 6.2), and it has been proposed that this has a parallel of sorts in the Dead Sea Scrolls, where the initiates, the full members, are distinguished from the novitiates (cf. 1QS 1.11–12; 5.2 and see Davies, *COJ*, pp. 121–2, and *SSM*, pp. 210–15). Different degrees of perfection are evident in 1QS 5.24, for instance: 'And so that they shall have an examination of their spirit and their works year by year, so as to elevate each one according to his understanding and the perfection of his way' (cf. 1QS 9.2; 10.21). (3) 'Perfect' has been closely associated with wisdom (Luck, pp. 30–3). Wisd 9.6 reads: 'Even if one is perfect among the sons of men, yet without the wisdom that comes from thee he will be regarded as nothing'. In 1QS 11, perfection, Torah, and wisdom are brought together while in 1 Cor 2.6 Paul writes that he speaks wisdom 'among the perfect'. 'Perfection' and wisdom also appear side by side in Col 1.28 and Jas 1.4–5 (cf. 1 Cor 14.20). Now if, as Suggs has argued, Matthew's thought was greatly influenced by wisdom motifs, we cannot rule out wisdom associations in 5.48: Jesus, because he is wisdom and dispenses wisdom, can demand of his followers perfection. On the other side, one may well doubt the extent to which Matthew's thought is under the influence of wisdom; see M. D. Johnson, 'Reflections on a Wisdom Approach to Matthew's Christology', *CBQ* 36 (1974), pp. 44–64. (4) The immediate context of 5.48 is the most important key to its understanding. The tradition demanded love of neighbour, but Jesus demands love of enemy, which means, in effect, love of all (cf. Augustine *De serm. mont.* 1.21.69). To obey Jesus' words, his law,[81] is, therefore, to love utterly: no more can be asked. And in

---

[80] One is also reminded of the *Shema*': 'You shall love the Lord your God with *all* your heart, and with *all* your soul, and with *all* your might'.

[81] Guelich, pp. 234–46, tries to separate the 'perfection' of 5.48 from any 'legal' understanding: τέλειος involves first of all a new relationship with God. We do not find this view convincing. It requires that too much be read into the text and wrongly presupposes an antithesis between law and grace which Matthew did not share.

this lies perfection: love of unrestrained compass lacks for nothing. It is catholic, all-inclusive. It is perfect.[82] (On our interpretation, εἶναι + τέλειος might be regarded as the near equivalent of the rabbinic verb, gĕmar, a word which can mean, among other things, 'to complete', 'to be perfect', or 'to be fully developed'; see Jastrow, s.v., and C. C. Torrey, *Our Translated Gospels*, New York, p. 1933, pp. 12, 291.)

ὡς ὁ πατὴρ ὑμῶν ὁ οὐράνιος τέλειός ἐστιν. God is the measure of man. Lk 6.36 has this: καθὼς (καὶ) ὁ πατὴρ ὑμῶν οἰκτίρμων ἐστίν. Luke has added καθώς (Mt: 3; Mk: 8; Lk: 17). Matthew has changed 'merciful' to 'perfect' and added 'heavenly'. Nowhere in the OT or in the Dead Sea Scrolls is God called tāmîm or τέλειος. For Jesus as being 'perfect'—something Matthew assumes but never says—see Heb 2.10; 5.9; Ignatius, *Smyr.* 4.2; Gos. Truth 1.20.39; Clement of Alexandria, *Strom.* 4.21.

The motivation for being 'perfect' in love is grounded in the Father's 'perfect' love, in his giving without measure. (The emphasis is upon God's deeds, not his nature).[83] God gives good gifts to the just and to the unjust, and this from love of both.

Whether or not it be coincidence, in 19.21 'perfect' occurs at the end of a list of commandments whose order—taken from Mk 10.19; contrast Lk 18.20—is paralleled in 5.21–48:

5.21–48	19.16–22
On murder	Do not kill
On adultery	Do not commit adultery
On divorce	
	Do not steal
Do not swear at all	Do not bear false witness,
Turn the other cheek	Honour your father and mother
Love your enemies	Love your neighbour as yourself
The call to perfection	The call to perfection

Neither 5.21–48 nor 19.16–22 follows the order of the ten commandments.[84]

How is one to harmonize Matthew's passage on love of enemies with the vituperations so frequently hurled at the Jewish leaders? Several explanations have been offered. All remain conjectural, for the evangelist never bothered to address the issue. (i) Jesus himself could be, for the

---

[82] Mt 5.48 cannot be, as it sometimes has been, used as a proof for the possibility of Christians' achieving sinlessness in this life. As 6.12 and the performance of the twelve imply, Matthew would have agreed with the author of 1 Jn 1.8—'If we say we have no sin we deceive ourselves'.

[83] According to Origen, *De prin.* 4.4.10, Mt 5.48 demonstrates that in God all the virtues exist for ever.

[84] On the possible connexion between the order of the paragraphs in Mt 5.21–48 and the order of the six divisions of the Mishnah see Davies, *SSM*, pp. 300–2.

evangelist, above the commandment to love because he is the judge. (ii) The scribes and Pharisees have, by rejecting the Messiah, shown themselves to be God's enemies, and the command to love encompasses one's personal enemies but not God's enemies (so Sand, p. 81). (iii) The contradiction is real and cannot be eradicated (see Montefiore, *Rabbinic Literature*, pp. 103–104). (iv) Matthew may have thought his harsh rebukes necessary for correcting error and in this sense he was motivated by love and concern: criticism leads to correction. This is all the more plausible given that the Jewish leaders were, for Matthew, leading their followers astray. (v) Matthew attacks ideas and abuses but not individuals; his rebukes are general, not personal (Manson, *Sayings*, p. 53).

(iv) *Concluding Observations*

(1) 'Men more often require to be reminded than informed.' Matthew, as a Jew and a Christian steeped in both Scripture and tradition, in the revelation that was ever ancient, ever new, would have understood and sympathized with Samuel Johnson's well-known statement. At the same time, our evangelist would have added that, with the advent of Jesus, the Messiah, something truly new had entered the world, something about which people needed to be not reminded but informed. Jesus had brought a new genesis (1.1), new wine (9.17), and a new covenant (26.28, 29). He had also uttered new and surprising words (cf. 5.21–48; 13.54). And although these words were never intended to render old words superfluous (5.17–19), in Matthew's judgement Jesus' speech was revelatory (11.25–7). Jesus himself, who spoke from his reading of the law and the prophets, from his understanding of the book of nature, and from his intuitive grasp of God's will in its nakedness (see Davies, *SSM*, pp. 429–33), was thus like the scribe of 13.52— with the old he brought forth the new. It follows that, when Matthew in his great sermon on the mount reproduced Jesus' 'I say to you', he was not simply reminding his readers of what good people should already know. He was not just putting old wine into new bottles or giving a new and fresh sense to the old. He was instead passing on revelation. He was informing, not just reminding.

(2) Whenever there is a claim to revelation there inevitably is created tension with the past and with what is taken for granted. Such tension is usually relaxed by downplaying the novelty of the new or by undermining the authority of the past. And it might be contended that if the former option was that taken by second century Jewish Christianity, the second was chosen by second century Gentile Christianity. But what of Matthew? He refused to acknowledge any antithesis. As the fulfilment quotations, 5.17–19, and the tone of his entire gospel show us, he was equally

committed to the old and to the new, to Jewish tradition and to the new revelation perceived in Jesus. He therefore did his best to hold together things others let fall apart. This is why 5.21–48 has 5.17–20 for its preface. Jesus did in fact have many new things to say, things which should enable his followers to obtain a righteousness greater than that exhibited by the custodians of the past. And yet Jesus did not set out to overthrow the past (cf. on 7.28). He did not negate the Torah but fulfil it; he began not with a *tabula rasa* but, if we may so put it, with a *tabula Torah*. The new was engrafted upon the old (cf. Rom 11.17–24). Revelation upheld tradition, even when surpassing it.

(3) Because the words of 5.21–48 go beyond OT teaching, because they are revelatory, and because they proceed from the mouth of the Messiah, it is natural to think of the section as part of a 'messianic Torah'. The two most forceful reasons for resisting this inference have been (a) 5.21–48 is only interpretation of the Mosaic Torah and therefore cannot be a new Torah and (b) the evidence for Jewish speculation about a messianic or eschatological Torah is relatively late. We must, however, reject the first point as based upon a false reading (see p. 508); and concerning the second, 11QTemple has completely re-opened the question of a messianic Torah (cf. Wacholder, pp. 1–32); and beyond that, the νόμος τοῦ Χριστοῦ in Gal 6.2 removes any doubt as to whether a first-century Jewish Christian could think of there being some sort of Christian counterpart to the νόμος Μωϋσέως (see on 5.18). Moreover, the sermon on the mount was, evidently, intentionally set within the context of Mosaic motifs (see on 5.1–2). In our judgement, then, Mt 5–7 transforms 'the pre-messianic Torah into the messianic Torah' (Gerhardsson, *Memory*, p. 327).

(4) Mt 5.21–48 gives us insight into Matthew's understanding of ethical motivation. There is in 5.21–48 an appeal to imitate God's benevolence and perfection in nature (5.45, 48). There are commands to do good lest one suffer eschatological retribution (5.22–6, 28–30). There are also appeals to reason, at least of a sort (5.34–6). Yet the overriding factor in 5.21–48 seems to be nothing other than obedience to a sovereign Lord ('I say to you'). This in turn means that the 'righteousness' of 5.20 is in the first place radical submission. One should strive for purity of intention (5.21–30), for obedience to God's will with as little concession to human sin as possible (5.31–7), and for unselfish love of friend and foe alike (5.38–48), not because one is persuaded by reason to do so or even because one loves others. Rather should one faithfully follow the way of the sermon on the mount because the voice in it speaks with divine authority (cf. 11.25–7; 28.18–20). (Compare the

rabbinic idea that God even gave some arbitrary commandments in order to instil unquestioning obedience: *Sipre* on Deut 32.4; *b. Yoma* 67b.)

(5) One objection often raised about Mt 5–7, and about 5.21–48 in particular, is that Jesus' injunctions are in reality impractical because incapable of being accomplished. Klausner wrote: Jesus' words contain 'too high an ideal for ordinary mankind, and even too high for the man of more than average moral calibre' (pp. 392–3). Jesus preached an 'extremist morality' (p. 395), not a 'practical religiousness' (p. 371), and his teaching 'has not proved possible in practice' (p. 397). The same criticism has been sounded by others, who have found in Jesus' 'extremism' something essentially foreign to Judaism and to simple common sense (cf. e.g. P. Goodman, *The Synagogue and the Church*, London, 1908, p. 282). An exceptional English jurist in the last century claimed that the sermon on the mount is 'not only imprudent but unjust' (*TLS*, Nov. 1948, N. 662). The point seems to be exactly that made by Dostoevsky's Grand Inquisitor: Jesus 'judged men too highly' for 'man was created weaker and lower than Christ thought'. We, however, think matters should be understood differently.[85] Mt 5.21–48 does, without question, contain absolute and impractical commands, and their literal observance would land one in hopeless confusion. But then one must ask, What is the passage all about? In our estimation, 5.21–48 contains (with the exception of 5.32) not a foolproof scheme of rules but general directions, not laws for society but an ethic for those within the Christian community. In accordance with this, and as Matthew has made quite plain (5.17–20), the enduring validity of OT legislation is presupposed; the Torah remains valid. So old legislation is not being annulled and replaced by new legislation. What is being added over and above the tradition is something altogether different—a new attitude, a new spirit, a new vision. This is why 5.21–48 is so poetical, dramatic, and pictorial, and why a literal (mis)interpretation creates absurdities. The text functions more like a story than a legal code. Its primary character is to instil principles and qualities through a vivid inspiration of the moral imagination. What one should come away with is not a grossly incomplete set of irrevocable statutes or bloodless abstractions but an unjaded impression of what is right and wrong, a challenging moral ideal. That ideal may, in truth, forever exceed human grasp. Yet it is precisely because it is always before us and never within reach that our gospel's window on the ideal, like a guiding star, ever beckons the faithful to move forward.

[85] In addition to what follows see C. H. Dodd, *Gospel and Law*, New York, 1951, pp. 46–53.

(v) *Bibliography*

H. Baltensweiler, *Die Ehe im Neuen Testament*, Zürich, 1967.

idem, 'Die Ehebruchsklausel bei Matthäus. Zu Matth. 5.32; 19,9', *TZ* 15 (1959), pp. 340–56.

Banks, pp. 182–203.

Barth, in *TIM*, pp. 95–105.

G. A. Barton, 'The Meaning of the "Royal Law"', Matt. 5:21–48', *JBL* 37 (1918), pp. 54–65.

H. W. Basser, 'The Meaning of "Shtuth"', Gen. R. 11 in Reference to Matthew 5.29–30 and 18.8–9', *NTS* 31 (1985), pp. 148–51.

J. B. Bauer, 'Die matthäische Ehescheidungsklausel (Mt 5,32 und 19,9)', *BLit* 38 (1964–5), pp. 101–6.

idem, 'Bemerkungen zu den matthäischen Unzuchtsklauseln (Mt 5,32; 19,9)', in *Begegnung mit dem Wort*, ed. J. Zmijewski and E. Nellessen, Bonn, 1980, pp. 23–33.

O. Bayer, 'Sprachbewegung und Weltveränderung. Ein systematischer Versuch als Auslegung von Mt 5, 43–8', *EvT* 35 (1975), pp. 309–21.

Berger, *Gesetzesauslegung*, pp. 508–75.

Borg, pp. 127–34.

M. Bouttier, 'Hésiode et le sermon sur la montagne', *NTS* 25 (1978), pp. 129–30.

Broer, pp. 75–113.

idem, 'Die Antithesen und der Evangelist Matthäus', *BZ* 19 (1975), pp. 50–63.

H. Bruppacher, 'Was sagte Jesu in Matthäus 5:48?', *ZNW* 58 (1967), p. 145.

Bultmann, *History*, pp. 134–6.

F. Bussby, 'A Note on raka (Matthew v. 22) and battalogeō (Matthew vi. 7) in the Light of Qumran', *ExpT* 76 (1964), p. 26.

G. B. Caird, 'Expounding the Parables: I. The Defendant (Matthew 5.25f.; Luke 12.58f.)', *ExpT* 77 (1965), pp. 36–9.

D. R. Catchpole, 'The Synoptic Divorce Material as a Traditio-Historical Problem', *BJRL* 57 (1974), pp. 92–127.

H. Clavier, 'Matthieu 5:39 et la non-résistance' *RHPR* 37 (1957), pp. 44–57.

K. Condon, 'A propos of the Divorce Sayings', *IBS* 2 (1980), pp.40–5.

J. D. Crossan, 'Jesus and Pacifism', in *No Famine in the Land*, ed. J. W. Flanagan and A. W. Robinson, Missoula, 1975, pp. 195–208.

H. Crouzel, 'Le texte patristique de Matthieu v. 32 et xix. 9', *NTS* 19 (1972), pp. 98–119.

S. D. Currie, 'Matthew 5:39a—Resistance or Protest?' *HTR* 57(1964), pp. 140–5.

Daube, pp. 55–62, 254–65.

D. Daube, 'Concerning the Reconstruction of "the Aramaic Gospels" ', *BJRL* 29 (1946), pp. 69–105.

G. Dautzenberg, 'Ist das Schwurverbot Mt 5, 33–7; Jak 5,12 ein Beispiel für die Torakritik Jesu?', *BZ* 25 (1981), pp. 47–66.

Davies, *SSM*, pp. 209–14, 235–49, 300–2.

Derrett, *Studies* 1, pp. 32–47.

A. Descamps, 'Essai d'interprétation de Mt. 5,17–48', in *Studia Evangelica I*, TU 73, ed. F. L. Cross, Berlin, 1959, pp. 156–73.

idem, 'Les textes évangéliques sur le mariage', *RTL* 9 (1978), pp. 259–86; 11 (1980), pp. 5–50.

C. Dietzfelbinger, *Die Antithesen der Bergpredigt*, Munich, 1975.

idem, 'Die Antithesen der Bergpredigt im Verständnis des Matthäus', *ZNW* 70 (1979), pp. 1–15.

Dodd, *Parables*, pp. 105–8.

M. J. Down, 'The Sayings of Jesus about Marriage and Divorce', *ExpT* 95 (1984), pp. 332–4.

D. L. Dungan, *The Sayings of Jesus in the Churches of Paul*, Philadelphia, 1971, pp. 102–31.

P. J. Du Plessis, 'The Ethics of Marriage according to Matt 5:27–32', *Neot* 1 (1967), pp. 16–27.

idem, 'Love and Perfection in Matt. 5.43–8', *Neot* 1 (1967), pp. 28–34.

J. Dupont, 'L'appel à imiter Dieu en Matthieu 5,48 et Luc 6,36', *RivB* 14 (1966), pp. 137–58.

idem, *Mariage et divorce dans l'Évangile*, Bruges, 1959.

idem, ' "Soyez parfaits" (Mt V, 48), "Soyez miséricordieux" (Lk VI, 36)', in *Sacra Pagina*, BETL 12–13, Paris, 1959, vol. 2, pp. 150–62.

P. Fiebig, 'Jesu Worte über die Feindesliebe im Zusammenhang mit dem wichtigsten rabbinischen Parallelen erläutert', *TSK* 91 (1918), pp. 30–64.

Fitzmyer, *Advance*, pp. 79–111.

R. N. Flew, *The Idea of Perfection in Christian Theology*, Oxford, 1934.

Furnish, pp. 45–54.

Giesen, pp. 122–43.

Goppelt 1, pp. 98–101.

H. Greeven, 'Ehe nach dem Neuen Testament', *NTS* 15 (1969), pp. 365–88.

R. A. Guelich, 'The Antitheses of Matthew v. 21–48: Traditional and/or Redactional?', *NTS* 22 (1976), pp. 444–57.

idem, 'Mt 5.22: Its Meaning and Integrity', *ZNW* 64 (1973), pp. 39–52.

K. Haacker, 'Der Rechtssatz Jesu zum Thema Ehebruch (Mt 5,28)', *BZ* 21 (1977), pp. 113–16.

V. Hasler, 'Das Herzstück der Bergpredigt. Zum Verständnis der Antithesen in Matth. 5,21–48', *TZ* 15 (1959), pp. 90–106.

B. Holtzclaw, 'A Note on Matthew 5,21–48', in *Festschrift to Honor F. W. Gingrich*, ed. E. H. Barth and R. E. Cocraft, Leiden, 1972, pp. 161–3.

U. Holzmeister, 'Die Streitfrage über die Ehescheidungstexte bei Matthäus 5.32, 19.9', *Bib* 26 (1945), pp. 133–46.

H. Hommel, 'Herrenworte im Lichte sokratischer Überlieferung', *ZNW* 57 (1966), pp. 4–8.

Hübner, pp. 40–112, 230–6.

A. Isaksson, *Marriage and Ministry in the New Temple*, Lund, 1965.

J. Jensen, 'Does *Porneia* Mean Fornication? A Critique of Bruce Malina', *NovT* 20 (1978), pp. 161–84.

Jeremias, *Abba*, pp. 103–7.

idem, *Parables*, pp. 43–4, 180.

idem, *Theology*, pp. 251–3.

J. J. Kilgallen, 'To What Are the Matthean Exception-Texts (5,32 and 19,9) an Exception?', *Bib* 61 (1980), pp. 102–5.

K. Köhler, 'Zu Mt 5:22', *ZNW* 19 (1919), pp. 91–5.

E. Kutsch, 'Eure Rede aber sei ja ja, nein nein', *EvT* 20 (1960), pp. 206–18.

Laufen, pp. 343–60.

J. Levison, 'A Better Righteousness. The Character and Purpose of Matthew 5.21–48', *Studia Biblica et Theologica* 12 (1982), pp. 171–94.

O. Linton, 'St. Matthew 5,43', *ST* 18 (1964), pp. 66–79.

Ljungman, pp. 76–96.

E. Lövestam, 'Divorce and Remarriage in the New Testament', *JLA* 4 (1981), pp. 47–65.

G. Lohfink, 'Der ekklesiale Sitz im Leben der Aufforderung Jesu zum Gewaltverzicht (Mt 5, 39b–42/Lk 6, 29f)', *TQ* 162 (1982), pp. 236–53.

E. Lohse, 'Ich aber sage euch', in *Der Ruf Jesu und die Antwort der Gemeinde*, ed. E. Lohse, Göttingen, 1970, pp. 189–203.

D. Lührmann, 'Liebet eure Feinde', *ZTK* 69 (1972), pp. 412–38.

McConnell, pp. 59–100.

A. Mahoney, 'A New Look at the Divorce Clauses in Mt 5,32 and 19,9', *CBQ* 30 (1968), pp. 29–38.

Marguerat, pp. 142–67.

Meier, *Law*, passim.

idem, *Vision*, pp. 240–62.

Merklein, *Botschaft*, pp. 114–24.

P. Minear, 'Yes or No: The Demand for Honesty in the Early Church', *NovT* 13 (1971), pp. 1–13.

J. Moingt, 'Le divorce "pour motif d'impudicité" (Matthieu 5,32; 19,9)' *RSR* 56 (1968), pp. 337–84.

F. J. Moloney, 'Matthew 19,3–12 and Celibacy. A Redactional and Form Critical Study', *JSNT* 2 (1978), pp. 42–60.

Montefiore, *Synoptic Gospels* 2, pp. 55–93.

D. J. Moo, 'Jesus and the Authority of the Mosaic Law', *JSNT* 20 (1984), pp. 17–23.

C. F. D. Moule, 'Uncomfortable Words I. The Angry Word: Matthew 5.21f.', *ExpT* 81 (1969), pp. 10–13.

J. R. Mueller, 'The Temple Scroll and the Gospel Divorce Texts', *RevQ* 10 (1980), pp. 247–56.

U. Nembach, 'Ehescheidung nach alttestamentlichen und jüdischen Recht', *TZ* 26 (1970), pp. 161–71.

Ogawa, pp. 118–23.

J. J. O'Rourke, 'A Note on an Exception: Mt 5:32 (19:9) and 1 Cor 7:12 Compared', *HeyJ* 5 (1964), pp. 299–302.

Percy, pp. 123–64.

J. Piper, *'Love your enemies.' Jesus' love command in the synoptic gospels and the early Christian paraenesis*, SNTSMS 38, Cambridge, 1979.

J. Rausch, 'The Principle of Nonresistance and Love of Enemy in Mt 5,38–48', *CBQ* 28 (1966), pp. 31–41.

B. Rigaux, 'Révélation des Mystères et Perfection à Qumran et dans le Nouveau Testament', *NTS* 4 (1958), pp. 237–62.

L. Sabourin, 'The Divorce clauses (Mt 5:32, 19:9)', *BTB* 2 (1972), pp. 80–6.

idem, 'Why is God called "perfect" in Mt 5:48?', *BZ* 24 (1980), pp. 266–8.

H. Sahlin, 'Traditionskritische Bemerkungen zu zwei Evangelienperikopen', *ST* 33 (1979), pp. 69–84.

Sand, pp. 46–56.

idem, 'Die Unzuchtsklausel in Mt 5.31,32 und 19.3–9', *MTZ* 20 (1969), pp. 118–29.

J. Sauer, 'Traditionsgeschichtliche Erwägungen zu den synoptischen und paulinischen Aussagen über Feindesliebe und Wiedervergeltungsverzicht', *ZNW* 76 (1985), pp. 1–28.

B. Schaller, 'Die Sprüche über Ehescheidung und Wiederheirat in der synoptischen Überlieferung', in *Der Ruf Jesu und die Antwort der Gemeinde*, ed. E. Lohse, Göttingen, 1970, pp. 226–46.

G. Schmahl, 'Die Antithesen der Bergpredigt', *TTZ* 83 (1974), pp. 284–97.

Schnackenburg, *Moral Teaching*, pp. 73–81, 132–43.

idem, 'Die Vollkommenheit des Christen nach den Evangelien', *GuL* 32 (1959), pp. 420–33.

G. Schneider, 'Jesu Wort über die Ehescheidung in der Überlieferung des Neuen Testaments', *TTZ* 80 (1971), pp. 65–87.

L. Schottroff, 'Non-Violence and the Love of One's Enemies', in Fuller, *Love*, pp. 9–39.

J. Schottenmann, 'Jesus and Pythagoras', *Kairos* 21 (1979), pp. 215–20.

P. Schruers, 'La paternité divine dans Mt. V. 45 et VI, 26–32', *ETL* 36 (1960), pp. 593–624.

Schulz, *Q*, pp. 116–49, 421–4.

O. J. F. Seitz, 'Love Your Enemies', *NTS* 16 (1969), pp. 39–54.

M. Smith, 'Mt v, 43: Hate thine Enemy', *HTR* 45 (1952), pp. 71–73.

Spicq I, pp. 8–16, 124–53.

G. Stählin, 'Zum Gebrauch von Beteuerungsformeln im Neuen Testament', *NovT* 5 (1962), pp. 115–43.

W. Stenger, 'Zur Rekonstruktion eines Jesusworts anhand der synoptischen Ehescheidungslogien (Mt 5,32; 19,9; Lk 10,11f; Mk 10,11f)', *Kairos* 26 (1984), pp. 194–205.

A. Stock, 'Matthean Divorce Texts', *BTB* 8 (1978), pp. 24–33.

G. Strecker, 'Die Antithesen der Bergpredigt (Mt 5.21–48 par.)', *ZNW* 69 (1978), pp. 36–72.

idem, 'Compliance—Love of one's Enemy—The Golden Rule', *ABR* 29 (1981), pp. 38–46.

Suggs, pp. 109–115.

idem, 'The Antitheses as Redactional Products', in Fuller, *Love*, pp. 93–107.

Tannehill, pp. 67–77.

idem, 'The "Focal Instance" as a Form of New Testament Speech: A Study of Matthew 5:39b–42', *JR* 50 (1970), pp. 372–85.

W. Trilling, 'Ehe und Ehescheidung im Neuen Testament', *TG* 74 (1984), pp. 390–406.

van Unnik, vol. 1, pp. 111–26.

E. Vallauri, 'Le clausole matteane sul divorzio: tendenze esegetiche recenti', *Laurentianum* 17 (1976), pp. 82–112 (extensive bibliography).

B. Vawter, 'Divorce and the New Testament', *CBQ* 39 (1977), pp. 528–42.

idem, 'The Divorce Clauses in Matt. 5,32 and 19,9' *CBQ* 16 (1954), pp. 155–67.

B. N. Wambacq, 'Matthieu 5,31–32', *NRT* 104 (1982), pp. 34–49.

M. Weise, 'Mt 5.21f.—ein Zeugnis sakraler Rechtsprechung in der Urgemeinde', *ZNW* 49 (1958), pp. 116–23.

P. Wernberg-Møller, 'A Semitic Idiom in Matt. v. 22', *NTS* 3 (1956), pp. 71–73.

Westerholm, pp. 104–113.

B. Witherington, 'Matthew 5.32 and 19.19—Exception or Exceptional Situation?', *NTS* 31 (1985), pp. 571–75.

W. Wolpert, 'Die Liebe zum Nächsten, zum Feind und zum Sünder', *TG1* 74 (1984), pp. 262–82.

Wrege, pp. 57–94, 124–9.

E. Yarnold, 'τέλειος in St. Matthew's Gospel', in *Studia Evangelica 4*, TU 102, ed. F. L. Cross, Berlin, 1968, pp. 269–73.

Zeller, *Mahnsprüche*, pp. 55–67, 101–13, 124–5.

Zumstein, pp. 309–26.

XIII

THE CHRISTIAN CULT: INSTRUCTIONS FOR ALMSGIVING, PRAYER, AND FASTING
(6.1–18)

(i) *Structure*

Mt 6.1–6, 16–18, which has no parallel in Mark or Luke, consists of an introduction (6.1)+three separate but closely related paragraphs, the first on almsgiving, the second on prayer, the third on fasting (cf. Betz (v), pp. 446–51).

6.1	I.	General, introductory paraenesis
6.2–6, 16–18	II.	Specific paraenesis
6.2–4		A. Almsgiving
6.2a		1. Declaration of subject
6.2b–e		2. Prohibition of wrong practice
6.2b		a. negative imperative
6.2b–c		b. description of the wrong practice
6.2d		c. statement of improper intention or goal
6.2e		d. statement of the result of the wrong practice in the form of an 'Amen I say to you' sentence
6.3–4		3. Instruction for proper practice
6.3a		a. declaration of subject
6.3b		b. description of proper practice
6.4a		c. statement of proper intention or goal
6.4b		d. theological grounding of instruction and promise of eschatological reward
6.5–6		B. Prayer
6.5a		1. Declaration of subject
6.5b–e		2. Prohibition of wrong practice
6.5b		a. negative imperative
6.5c		b. description of the wrong practice
6.5d		c. statement of improper intention or goal
6.5e		d. statement of the result of the wrong practice in the form of an 'Amen I say to you' sentence

6.6	3. Instruction for proper practice
6.6a	a. declaration of subject
6.6b	b. description of proper practice
	(c. statement of proper intention or goal—implicit?)
6.6c	d. theological grounding of instruction and promise of eschatological reward
6.16–18	C. Fasting
6.16a	1. Declaration of subject
6.16b–e	2. Prohibition of wrong practice
6.16b	a. negative imperative
6.16b–c	b. description of the wrong practice
6.16d	c. statement of improper intention or goal
6.16e	d. statement of the result of the wrong practice in the form of an 'Amen I say to you' sentence
6.17–18	3. Instruction for proper practice
6.17a	a. declaration of subject
6.17b	b. description of proper practice
6.18a	c. statement of proper intention or goal
6.18b	d. theological grounding of instruction and promise of eschatological reward

(ii) *Sources*

What is the origin of this neat scheme, which is interrupted by 6.7–15? There are two options. Either it is redactional,[1] or Matthew has passed on a traditional 'cult-didache' (to use H. D. Betz's apposite expression).[2] The major reason for choosing the former option is the high number of Mattheanisms—typical Matthean vocabulary and syntax—in 6.1–6, 16–18. This, however, appears to us to be a consideration less than decisive. The Mattheanisms prove at best only that any tradition taken up into 6.1–6, 16–18 has been thoroughly recast by the editor's hand; they do not prove Matthew to have created *ex nihilo*. Moreover, there are six other

---

[1] So Goulder, p. 196, and Gundry, *Commentary*, pp. 101–11. Guelich, pp. 316–20, also attributes the scheme to Matthew, but he argues that the evangelist expanded three traditional sayings: the positive admonitions of the second person singular in 6.3–4, 6, and 17–18. In our judgement, Guelich does not adequately explain the apparently secondary character of 6.7–15. But his reconstruction of Matthew's contribution may come close to describing accurately the procedure of the pre-Matthean author of 6.1–6, 16–18. He perhaps did base his composition upon three sayings of Jesus.

[2] So Gerhardsson, 'Opferdienst' (v); Schweizer (v); Betz (v); Lambrecht, *Sermon*, pp. 38–9; Dietzfelbinger (v); and Luz 1, p. 321. Luz thinks of a written source, one that could have been linked, in the pre-Matthean tradition, with the first, second, and fourth 'antitheses' of chapter 5.

facts to be contemplated. First, and as already noted, 6.7–15 breaks the scheme of 6.1–6, 16–18. This is difficult to explain unless 6.7–15 be a secondary insertion.[3] Why would an author take such pains to devise and execute the production of three perfectly parallel paragraphs and then insert into their midst another paragraph that wrecks the otherwise perfect symmetry? Is it not more reasonable to think of 6.7–15 as having been inserted into the already existing piece, 6.1–6, 16–18? (An affirmative answer is the more attractive since the author of 6.7–15 clearly sought to assimilate its structure to that of the surrounding material but accomplished his task only imperfectly.) Secondly, the parallel with Rom 2.28–9 (see on 6.1) and the existence of a dominical word behind at least 6.3 (see on 6.3) show that Matthew was to some extent working with traditional material. Thirdly, the possibility of a Semitic original has been raised by Black (pp. 176–8). According to him, paronomasia characterizes 6.1–8 if it be retranslated into Aramaic. Of course, the suggestion cannot be demonstrated; but it should perhaps be given some weight. Fourthly, not all of the vocabulary of 6.1–6, 16–18 is readily ascribed to the redactor. ἐλεημοσύνη is found in Matthew only in 6.2–4; and σαλπίζω (6.2), ῥύμη (6.2), ἀριστερός (6.3), σκυθρωπός (6.16), and ἀλείφω (6.17) are *hapax legomena* for Matthew; and ἐν τῷ κρυπτῷ does not appear outside of 6.1–6, 16–18. Fifthly, given the high degree of parallelism between 6.2–4, 5–6, and 16–18, the variation in the exhortations between the second person singular and the second person plural must be secondary, and is probably to be put down to imperfect assimilation to the interpolated material in 6.7–15 (see on 6.5). Finally, 6.1–6, 16–18 does not require its Matthean context: it is a coherent unity unto itself and can easily be imagined as serving a catechetical function.[4] A pre-Matthean *Sitz im Leben* is therefore plausible.

Since we find the evidence for the existence of a pre-Matthean 'cult-didache' persuasive, the question naturally arises, How did it come into being? Unlike 6.7–8, 9–13, and 14–15, verses which are well grounded in the pre-Easter tradition, 6.1–6, 16–18 do not appear to be a particularly good source for the teaching of Jesus (although note Luz 1, p. 322). As Dietzfelbinger (v), pp. 197–201, has argued, a paradoxical, dominical word does, to be sure, probably lie beneath the left hand/right hand saying (6.3), others may be embedded in 6.16–17[5] and perhaps in 6.6, and the spirit or attitude of the whole is consonant with what Jesus taught (cf. 25.31–46; Mk 8.34–7). (These facts explain why the piece could be

---

[3] Cf. Wellhausen, *Matthaei*, p. 25; Bultmann, *History*, p. 133; Betz (v), p. 451; Dietzfelbinger (v), p. 184; and Lambrecht, *Sermon*, pp. 127–8.

[4] Bultmann, *History*, p. 133, n. 1: 'the composition is much more like a Church catechism'.

[5] According to Mk 2.18–20, Jesus and his disciples did not fast as did the disciples of the Pharisees and those of John the Baptist. Does this not disallow finding a dominical word behind Mt 6.16–18, which gives instruction for fasting? Not necessarily. If Jesus and his followers did not practise voluntary weekly fasts (cf. Lk 18.12; *b. Taʿan.* 12a), they almost certainly kept the public days of fasting enjoined by Jewish tradition (cf. Lev 16.29, 31; 23.27, 29, 32; Num 29.7). So a paradoxical saying about hiding one's fast could have been spoken by Jesus, especially as the theme of the joy of repentance was part of his proclamation; cf. Jeremias, *Theology*, pp. 157–8.

attributed to Jesus.) Yet the finely balanced structure of 6.1–6, 16–18 and their patently catechetical character make a post-Easter origin almost certain: the 'cult-didache' was created for Christians. Further, we may think of Jewish Christians in particular. For almsgiving, prayer, and fasting were typical Jewish concerns; the polemic against the hypocrites appears to be intramural; a knowledge of what is done in the synagogues is presupposed—otherwise the illustrations in 6.2 and 5 would be inappropriate; and if 6.1–6, 16–18 were the product of Gentile Christians, we should expect references not to 'hypocrites' but to 'Jews'. But farther than this we cannot go. We do not know when the 'cult-didache' was composed, whether before A.D. 70 or after. We do not know whether it was originally composed in Greek. We do not know what the attitude of the original author was towards the temple cult.[6] We cannot know whether or not 6.7–13 was attracted to 6.1–6, 16–18 before Matthew took up his pen or whether the evangelist himself is responsible for inserting the Lord's Prayer into its present context. Lastly, we cannot even explain with any degree of certainty the sequence, almsgiving, prayer, fasting. The three disciplines were almost certainly traditionally associated with one another, but there does not appear to have been a conventional ordering. Tob 12.8 has the order, prayer, fasting, almsgiving. Mt 6.1–18 has almsgiving, then prayer, then fasting. 2 Clem. 16 has the order, almsgiving, fasting, prayer; and in Gos. Thom. 6 the disciples ask Jesus first about fasting, then about prayer, and finally about almsgiving. The order in Matthew might mirror a ranking of difficulty: almsgiving is more difficult than prayer, prayer more difficult than fasting (cf. 2 Clem. 16, where 'fasting is better than prayer, but almsgiving than both').[7] Or perhaps almsgiving is first because its practice was, because of tough economic circumstances, the most needful at the time 6.1–6, 16–18 was composed.[8] But here we are only in the realm of speculation.

For introductory questions concerning 6.7–15 see the Excursus on the Lord's Prayer, pp. 590–99

(iii) *Exegesis*

1. This verse announces, through a negative formulation, the major theme of 6.2–6, 16–18: δικαιοσύνη is not to be done before others in order to be seen by them. True piety is not for show. Right deeds must be accompanied by right intention (cf. the

---

[6] *Pace* Betz (v), p. 456, according to whom the concentration on private piety in 6.1–18 probably involves a criticism of the public cult.

[7] So Gerhardsson, 'Opferdienst' (v), p. 74, who asserts that this was the rabbinic opinion. Gerhardsson also connects almsgiving, prayer, and fasting with the *Shemaʿ*: almsgiving goes with 'all your might, mammon', prayer with 'all your heart', and fasting with 'all your soul' (cf. *Sipre Deut.* on 11.13; *t. Peʾa* 4.19; *b. Sukk.* 49b; *b. Taʿan.* 2a). Yet, as Gerhardsson himself confesses, we should then expect the order, prayer, fasting, almsgiving, this order corresponding to heart, soul, and strength.

[8] See further Davies, *SSM*, p. 308. He refers to the depression of Jewry after A.D. 70.

rabbinic *kawwānâ*, as in *b. Meg.* 20a). The Father in heaven rewards only those whose motives are pure, who care not for what others think but only for what is right before heaven. The key is intention. Even a good deed brings no reward if it springs from the desire for self-aggrandizement. One must rather seek to bring glory to the Father in heaven (cf. 5.16, which in no way contradicts the present passage, as Augustine, *De serm. mont.* 2.1.2, rightly argued). The pride of show is a malignant growth on religion which leads to counterfeit goodness. One must always remember that 'the Lord sees not as man sees; man looks on the outward appearance, but the Lord looks on the heart' (1 Sam 16.7). God sees what goes on in the dark, even within hearts, and that is what matters (cf. Ecclus 17.15; 23.19; 39.19). Recall Boethius, *de Consolatione* 1.4: 'For as often as a man receives the reward of fame for his boasting, the conscience that indulges in self-congratulation loses something of its secret merit'.

The notion of a private piety coupled with disdain for external appearances was well known to ancient Jews. At this point the NT offers nothing new. It is a Pharisee who in Lk 18.9–14 stands alone in the temple and prays in silence. We can hardly suppose that Jesus and his followers were the first to harp on a religious hypocrisy bound up with the public exhibition of piety. Anyone who had read the OT knew that a true son of Abraham would seek not the glory that comes from others but the glory that comes from God (Jn 5.44), would seek to please God, not men (Gal 1.10). Nevertheless, we cannot conclude that the teaching of Mt 6.1–6, 16–18 sets up only straw men for the attack. Human nature being what it is, the temptation to make a good show of oneself to impress others has been ever present in every religion, and both the ancient synagogue and the early church will have had among their members individuals who were anxious to gain recognition for their religious deeds. This is why both the NT and Jewish texts (see below) warn against ostentation.

Of special interest for Mt 6.1–6, 16–18 is Rom 2.28–9: 'For he is not a real Jew who is one outwardly, nor is true circumcision something external and physical. He is a Jew who is one inwardly (ἐν τῷ κρυπτῷ), and real circumcision is a matter of the heart, spiritual and not literal. His praise is not from men but from God.' These two verses show that the central theme of Matthew's text had some currency in the early church. The contrasts between what is inward and what is outward, between the heart and that which is external, and between receiving praise not from men but from God are precisely those which appear again in the section in Matthew. Note also the occurrence of the rare phrase, ἐν τῷ κρυπτῷ, in both Matthew and Romans. These parallels do not, of course, require a direct link between the two passages. (Paul gives no real evidence of having known the pre-Matthean 'cult-didache'.) Yet the similarities do show us that the convictions expounded in Mt 6.1–6, 16–18 belonged to common Christian tradition and were expressed in a similar fashion in different communities. No doubt this was the case because those same convictions were held by pious Jews; that is, we are dealing with a point at which Jewish tradition entered the Christian church. See further Schweizer (v), who has shown the dependence of both Mt 6.2–6, 16–18 and Rom 2.28–9 upon the OT and later Jewish tradition.

προσέχετε δὲ τὴν δικαιοσύνην ὑμῶν μὴ ποιεῖν ἔμπροσθεν τῶν ἀνθρώπων πρὸς τὸ θεαθῆναι αὐτοῖς· εἰ δὲ μή γε μισθὸν οὐκ ἔχετε παρὰ τῷ πατρὶ ὑμῶν τῷ ἐν τοῖς οὐρανοῖς.[9] Compare Ep. Arist. 168: 'practise righteousness before all men, being mindful of God'. Word statistics strongly suggest the redactional origin of Mt 6.1;[10] so if the pre-Matthean 'cult-didache' (6.2–6, 16–18) which it introduces had an introduction, the evangelist has reworked it thoroughly.[11]

For δικαιοσύνη in the introduction to a section see 5.20. The word is here defined by the paragraphs that follow as almsgiving in secret, prayer in secret, and fasting in secret. Hence the simple equation of δικαιοσύνη (= ṣĕdāqâ) with 'almsgiving' (see SB 1, p. 387) has been left behind: 'righteousness' is in Mt 6.1 a much broader term, the equivalent of right religious observance. The concessive εἰ δὲ μή γε (cf. 9.17) without a verb (= 'otherwise') was a fixed expression; see P. Oxy. 1159.6; Josephus, Ant. 17.113; Lk 5.36–7; 10.6; 13.9; 14.32; 2 Cor 11.16. μισθὸν οὐκ ἔχετε looks forward to the great assize (cf. 5.4–9; 6.19–21). πρὸς τὸ θεαθῆναι αὐτοῖς, with its dative instead of the genitive (cf. 1.20; 17.3; 23.28) might be a Semitism (see Schlatter, p. 200). For ποιέω + δικαιοσύνη see 1 Jn 2.29; 3.7, 10; Rev 22.11. Comparable is the Hebrew ʿāśâ + ṣĕdāqâ (Gen 18.19; 2 Chr 9.8; etc.) and the use of ἐργάζομαι with δικαιοσύνη (Acts 10.35; Heb 11.33; Jas 1.20). For δικαιοσύνη coupled with prayer and fasting and almsgiving see Tob 12.8.

Mt 6.1 is to be labelled a kĕlāl, that is, a general statement of

---

[9] δε appears in ℵ L Z Θ f¹ 33 892 1241 1424 al g¹ syp.h bo. It is omitted by B D W 0250 f¹³ Maj lat syᶜ mae boᵐˢˢ. The original reading is uncertain, but the particle fits well if Matthew is opening a new section of his sermon. δικαιοσυνην becomes ελεημοσυνην (cf. 6.2, 3) in L W Z Θ f¹³ Maj f k syp.h mae arm Cl Ath. This change may presuppose the identification of δικαιοσυνη with ṣĕdāqâ; and the reading could have arisen as the gloss or marginal interpretation of some scribe who wrongly took 6.1 to be not an introduction to 6.1–18 but a part of 6.2–4. For discussion see Nagel (v), who unpersuasively argues for the originality of ελεημοσυνην.

[10] προσέχω: Mt: 6 (always with ἀπό save here); Mk: 0; Lk: 4. δικαιοσύνη: Mt: 7; Mk: 0; Lk: 1. ἔμπροσθεν + ἀνθρώπων (a combination never found in the LXX): Mt: 5; Mk: 0; Lk: 1. πρός + articular infinitive: Mt: 5; Mk: 1; Lk: 1. πρός + θεαθῆναι + dative plural occurs again without a parallel in 23.5. μισθός: Mt: 10; Mk: 1; Lk: 3. 'The (your, my, our) Father in heaven': Mt: 13; Mk: 1; Lk: 1. παρά + dative occurs in Matthew without a parallel in 6.1; 8.10; 21.25; 22.25; and 28.15.

[11] So also Strecker, Weg, p. 152; Schweizer (v), p. 116; Guelich, pp. 274–5; and Luz 1, p. 321; against Gerhardsson, 'Opferdienst' (v), pp. 69–70, and Betz (v), pp. 546–57.

principle that heads a section consisting of various particular cases (*pĕrāṭôt*; cf. *m. B. Qam.* 8.1; *m. 'Ed.* 3.1; *b. Ḥag.* 6a–b; Daube, pp. 63–6). Compare the structure of Gen 5.1–32; Lev 18.1–23; Ecclus 3.1–9; 1QS 3.13–4.26; Barn. 18–20; and especially Mt 5.17–48. This last parallel is particularly important because of the additional similarities between 5.17–48 and 6.1–18 (cf. Klostermann (v)). Both sections have a general introduction employing 'righteousness' (5.17–20; 6.1) which is followed by specific examples (six in 5.21–48, four in 6.2–18). The examples in both are formulated as contrasts, with the negative statements—which take up Jewish tradition or Jewish practices—preceding the positives. And while the positive statements in 5.21–48 are introduced with 'But I say to you', those in 6.2–18 are introduced with 'Amen, I say to you'. These similarities between 5.17–48 and 6.1–18 support our division of the sermon on the mount, according to which 5.17–48 and 6.1–18 are separate but parallel sections having to do with, respectively, the law and the cult.

ALMSGIVING (6.2–4)

2. Two observations. (1) The giving of alms is not at all called into question (that would be unthinkable given Jewish tradition and such OT texts as Deut 15.11). What is being criticized is its misuse for self-glorification. The problem is not whether but how, not the thing but the intent (Chrysostom, *Hom. on Mt.* 19.2). (2) Mt 6.2–4 clearly addresses an audience which can afford to make charitable contributions (although, it must be admitted, according to later rabbinic legislation even the poor were allowed to give alms; *b. Giṭ.* 7b). The readers have the wherewithal to give away money; they are not of the poorest class (contrast Peter in Acts 3.6).

ὅταν οὖν ποιῇς ἐλεημοσύνην. If 6.1 is redactional, the οὖν must be editorial because it makes 6.2 depend upon 6.1. For ὅταν οὖν (Mt: 3; Mk: 0; Lk: 0) see also 21.40; 24.15 (both redactional). ἐλεημοσύνη[12] means 'alms', 'charitable giving' (cf. Diogenes Laertius 5.17; Ecclus 29.8; Tob 4.7, 16; Acts 3.2–3; T. Job. 9.8; cf. the rabbinic *ṣĕdāqâ* and *miṣwâ*, as in *m. 'Abot* 5.13; *m. B. Qam.* 10.1; Tg. Yer. II for Deut 7.10; note also the use of ἔλεος in Ps.-Phoc. 23). The word is not found in Josephus or Philo. For ποιέω + ἐλεημοσύνη (= *'āśâ* + *ṣĕdāqâ* or *miṣwâ*; cf. *b. Giṭ.* 7a) in the LXX see Ps 102.6; Tob 1.3, 16; 12.8; Ecclus 7.10 (cf. Acts 9.36;

[12] See R. Bultmann, *TWNT* 2, pp. 474–83. The Greeks had no word for alms. For almsgiving in ancient Judaism see Moore 2, pp. 162–79; SB 4, pp. 436–58; Montefiore and Lowe, pp. 412–39; and Jeremias, *Jerusalem*, pp. 126–34. For the early church see R. M. Grant, *Early Christianity and Society*, San Francisco, 1977, pp. 124–45 (lit. on pp. 202–3).

10.2; 24.17). For other exhortations concerning almsgiving see Ecclus 12.1–3; 29.8; Sib. Or. 2.78–80; Did. 1.6; *m.* '*Abot* 5.13.

μὴ σαλπίσῃς ἔμπροσθέν σου. σαλπίζω is a good LXX word (usually for *tāqaʿ*) found only here in the gospels and only here in the NT with a non-eschatological function. The meaning is probably figurative (as in Achilles Tatius 8.10.10; Cicero, *Ad. fam.* 16.21.2; Juvenal 14.152; Tertullian, *De virg. velandis* 13; cf. Isa 58.1), although there were trumpets in the synagogues (cf. *b. Šabb.* 35b). To blow a trumpet is probably just a picturesque way of indicating the making of an announcement or the calling of attention to oneself. Compare Chrysostom, *Hom. on Mt.* 19.2: οὐχ ὅτι σάλπιγγας εἶχον ἐκεῖνοι ἀλλὰ τὴν πολλὴν αὐτῶν ἐπιδεῖξαι βούλεται μανίαν τῇ λέξει τῆς μεταφορᾶς ταύτης. Yet it should be observed that trumpets were blown on fast days (Joel 2.15; *m. Taʿan.* 2.5), when alms were asked for (cf. *b. Ber.* 6b; *b. Sanh.* 35a), so it is just possible that some unknown custom is being protested. For trumpets in connexion with sacrificial ceremonies see Josephus, *Ant.* 3.294.

G. Klein, 'Mt 6.2' (v), long ago proposed that 6.2 originally had to do not with trumpets but with the 'sophar chests' which were set up in the temple and in the provinces (*m. Šeqal.* 1.3; 2.1; 6.1–5; *t. Šeqal.* 2.16), and an uninformed translator did not understand the meaning of 'sophar' and turned it into the verb for 'trumpet'. Despite the support of S. T. Lachs, 'Sermon', pp. 103–5, this suggestion has not met a favourable reception, and rightly so. Speculation about a mistranslation should be countenanced only if the text as it stands is problematic, which is not true of Mt 6.2. On the other hand, some connexion with the sophar chests cannot be excluded. Perhaps Jesus—or whoever first formulated Mt 6.2— was making a pun or some sort of word-play. If the trumpet-shaped receptacles (cf. Danby, p. 153, n. 10) for alms could be made to resound when coins were thrown into them, thereby calling attention to the giver, our verse may have been a polemical barb at the practice and a call for silent and inconspicuous giving (cf. the interpretation of McEleney (v)).

Mt 6.2 has numerous parallels in Jewish texts. Consider, for example, *b. B. Bat.* 9b: R. Eleazar said: 'A man who gives charity in secret is greater than Moses our teacher.' *b. B. Bat.* 10a–b is similar: charity saves from death if the giver does not know to whom he is giving and the receiver does not know from whom he receives. In T. Job. 9.7–8 Job arranges things so that those who come to his house seeking alms need not see him (otherwise they might be ashamed). In *b. Yeb.* 79a and elsewhere charity, mercy, and modesty are linked together as the distinguishing characteristics of Israel. In *m.* '*Abot* 5.13 we read that there is one type of almsgiver 'who wishes that he should give and that others should not give'; perhaps this is because he wants all the credit for himself; in any case he is said to have the evil eye. R. Yannai is purported to have said to a man who gave money to a poor man in public, 'It had been better that you had given him nothing than that you should have given him and put him to shame' (*Eccl. Rab.* on 12.14; cf. *b. Ḥag.* 5a). According to *m. Šeqal.* 5.6, 'There were two chambers in the temple: one the chamber of secrets and the other the chamber of utensils. Into the chamber of secrets the devout used to put their gifts in secret and the poor of good family received support therefrom in secret. The chamber of utensils—whosoever made a gift of any article used to cast it therein, and every thirty days the treasurers opened it; and any article which they found of use for the temple fund they left there; and the rest were sold and their price fell to the chamber of the temple fund.' Compare *Sipre* on Deut. 15.10 and *t. Šeqal.* 2.16. For further references to secret almsgiving see SB 1, pp. 391–2. First-century Jews were at one with Christians in thinking that 'whoso makes great his name loses his name' (*m. 'Abot* 1.13; cf. 6.5).

ὥσπερ οἱ ὑποκριταὶ ποιοῦσιν ἐν ταῖς συναγωγαῖς καὶ ἐν ταῖς ῥύμαις. ὥσπερ (Mt: 10; Mk: 0; Lk: 2) is almost certainly redactional. Perhaps ὡς was in the source (cf. 6.5, 16). ὑποκριτής (= Hebrew *ḥānēp*, Aramaic *ḥanpā*'; see SB 1, pp. 388–9) is a Matthean favourite (Mt: 13; Mk: 1; Lk: 3). In Ecclus 31.11 we read that the assembly will relate the acts of charity done by the perfect rich man; and according to *y. Hor.* 3.48a, one who gave an exceptionally large gift was permitted to sit on the *bêmâ* with the rabbis. Clearly there were concrete practices which made Mt 6.2–4 quite relevant. The synagogue was where alms were collected on the Sabbath (cf. Justin, *1 Apol.* 67; *b. Šabb.* 150a). ἐν ταῖς ῥύμαις appears also in Isa 15.3 LXX and Ecclus 9.7 ℵ (cf. Prov 31.23 ℵ). ῥύμη (= *rĕḥōb* in Isa 15.3), which appears only once in the First Gospel, probably here means 'street'.

In classical Greek usage ὑποκριτής[13] (LSJ: 'one who answers', 'interpreter', 'actor', 'one who recites', 'pretender'—this last meaning yet unattested in secular, pre-Christian Greek) did not by itself have a negative connotation; but in the LXX (for *ḥānēp* = 'godless') the word gained—for reasons not altogether vivid—a pejorative sense: the ὑποκριτής is the ungodly man (as in Job 34.14; 36.13; Ecclus 1.29; 35.15; 36.2; 4 Macc. 6.15, 17). Compare Philo, *Jos.* 67; *Som.* 2.40; *Omn. prob. lib.* 99; Josephus, *Bell.* 2.587. In the NT it is the same. Perhaps we must, however, be a bit cautious with regard to the usual translation, 'hypocrite', a word which by definition involves false pretense, conscious deception. This idea of a conscious lack of integrity, of being two-faced, is not necessarily suggested by ὑποκριτής (cf. the LXX usage). Further, from Mt 23.23–8 one might conclude that the

---

[13] See U. Wilckens, *TWNT* 8, pp. 558–71; Albright and Mann, pp. cxv–cxxiii; van Tilborg, pp. 8–26; Garland, pp. 91–123; and I. J. W. Oakley,' "Hypocrisy" in Matthew', *IBS* 7 (1985), pp. 118–38.

'hypocrite' may not always know that he is in the wrong. Nevertheless, in view of 6.2, 5, and 16, one should probably associate ὑποκριτής not only with ἀνομία, the antithesis of righteousness, but also with duplicity, as Augustine already recognised when he associated 'hypocrite' with θεαθῆναι (cf. 'theatre') and spoke of actors and pretenders (*De serm. mont.* 2.2.5). Note also that the word is connected with lying or deceit in 2 Macc 6.25; T. Benj. 6.4–5; and perhaps Ps. Sol. 4.6–8. Mt 6.2 thus appears to reflect both Jewish and Hellenistic ways of thinking (cf. Giesen, pp. 151–7).

Because 'hypocrite' appears in Mark, Q, M, and L, it has been suggested that Jesus himself used the Greek word (so A. W. Argyle, ' "Hypocrite" and the Aramaic Theory', *ExpT* 75 (1963–4), pp. 113–14, and A. Stock, 'Jesus, Hypocrites, and Herodians', *BTB* 16 (1986), pp. 3–7), If so, he almost certainly used it with reference to actors in the Greek theatre, for the ancient Hellenistic theatre uncovered in 1931 by L. Waterman at Sepphoris—a city very near Nazareth—may have been standing in the first century A.D. See R. A. Batey, 'Jesus and the Theatre', *NTS* 30 (1984), pp. 563–74.

In Matthew the 'hypocrites' are usually identified with the scribes and Pharisees (15.7; 22.18; 23.13, 14, 15, 23, 25, 27, 29). This suggests that the scribes and Pharisees are the implicit subject of 6.2–6, 16–18 (as well as of 24.51; contrast only 7.5).[14] But why are they 'hypocrites'? Because they say one thing and do another (23.3), and because their hearts are wrong even when they outwardly do observe Torah (23.23–8). Now this polemical censuring—for which Christians today must feel some embarrassment—can hardly be taken as the conclusion of an objective, detached observer. Rather were Matthew's harsh generalizations the product of his conviction that the Jewish rejection of Jesus was not an honest error or innocent mistake but instead the consequence of a spiritual blindness, an inner defect, a moral failing, an inclination to disobey God's will (cf. 15.3–9). Further, the evangelist—probably a Jewish convert who thought of Judaism without Messiah—Jesus as hollow, as lacking its centre—was apparently persuaded with Plato that ἐσχάτης ἀδικίας εἶναι δοκεῖν δίκαιον μὴ ὄντα (preserved in Basil, *Hom.* 13). Given this, the synagogue's appearance of godliness—we should remember that church and synagogue closely resembled each other—was what must have led the evangelist to level his charge of 'hypocrisy'—a charge which is in any case a commonplace of polemics; see As. Mos. 7; Josephus, *Bell.* 2.587; 1 Tim 4.2; Did. 8.1; Herm. s. 8.6.5.

ὅπως δοξασθῶσιν ὑπὸ τῶν ἀνθρώπων. ὅπως (cf. 6.4, 15, 16, 18) is often redactional in Matthew (Mt: 17; Mk: 1; Lk: 7). δοξάζω (Mt: 4; Mk: 1; Lk: 9) everywhere else in Matthew is used only of glorifying God (5.16; 9.18; 15.31), so here people are putting

---

[14] Cf. Hummel, p. 29. But Zahn, p. 22, and others think that 5.21–48 is directed against the scribes, 6.1–18 against the Pharisees (cf. Fitzmyer, *Luke* 1, pp. 628–9).

themselves in God's place. ὑπὸ τῶν ἀνθρώπων (cf. Ecclus 49.16: ἐν ἀνθρώποις ἐδοξάσθησαν) occurs also in 5.13; 19.12; and 23.7. Note b. B. Bat. 10b: R. Eliezar said: 'all the charity and kindness done by the heathen is counted to them as sin, because they only do it to magnify themselves'.

ἀμὴν λέγω ὑμῖν, ἀπέχουσιν τὸν μισθὸν αὐτῶν. This line is a refrain, appearing as it does again in 6.5 and 16. For the introductory formula see on 5.18. The plural, ὑμῖν, which conflicts with the surrounding occurrences of the singular, is due to the stereotyped formula, 'Truly I say to you' (plural). ἀπέχω (Mt: 5; Mk: 2; Lk: 4) is used also in 6.5 and 16, both times with 'reward' (a pairing that fails to appear in the LXX). The word was used as a technical expression regularly pertaining to drawing up a receipt (Deissmann, Light, pp. 110–12; Studies, p. 229). For the thought see b. Sanh. 101a: R. Akiba said: 'As long as I saw that my master's wine did not turn sour, nor was his flax smitten, nor his oil putrefied, nor his honey become rancid, I thought, God forbid that he may have received all his reward in this world [leaving nothing for the next]; but now that I see him lying in pain I rejoice [knowing that his reward has been treasured up for him in the next]'. Further examples in SB 1, pp. 390–1, to which add Tg. Neof. on Deut 7.10 and Tg. Ps.-J. on Gen 15.1. Those who give alms in order to be glorified by others 'receive their pay then and there, and they receive it in full . . . God owes them nothing. They were not giving, but *buying*. They wanted the praise of men, they paid for it, and they have got it. The transaction is ended and they can claim nothing more' (Plummer, p. 91). Compare Sextus, Sent. 341: 'Whomever you serve for glory (δόξης), you have served for pay' (μισθοῦ).

3. Being a call for humility (cf. m. 'Abot 4.4) and self-forgetfulness (cf. Plato, Apol. 21B; 1 Cor 4.4), 6.3 contains the positive, antithetical corollary to the negative admonition in 6.2.

Some, remarking on the Arabic use even today of the left hand to denote a close friend, think the exhortation is to hide one's good works from one's neighbours (Manson, Sayings, p. 165). Others think more literally: to use one hand is to be discreet, to use two is to call attention to oneself (Gundry, Commentary, p. 102). But most commentators are probably correct to suppose that Mt 6.3 exhorts one not to think too highly of one's own almsgiving—which of course also implies leaving others in ignorance. Compare Chrysostom, Hom. on Mt. 19.2: 'If it can be for thyself not to know it, let this be the object of thine endeavour; that, if it were possible, it may be concealed from the very hands that minister'.[15]

[15] According to Augustine, De serm. mont. 2.2.6–7, the left hand was variously interpreted: some took it to refer to unbelievers, others to enemies, still others to their own wives.

σοῦ δὲ ποιοῦντος ἐλεημοσύνην. This harks back to 6.2a (q.v.). The σοῦ is emphatic and sets the followers of Jesus over against the 'hypocrites' in the synagogue. Note the unclassical genitive absolute with its pleonastic yet emphatic pronoun (σοῦ δὲ ποιοῦντος; cf. BDF § 423.3).

μὴ γνώτω ἡ ἀριστερά σου τί ποιεῖ ἡ δεξιά σου. γινώσκω + τί (Mt: 2; Mk: 0; Lk: 2) is the equivalent of yādaʿ + mah, as in Prov 27.1; Eccles 8.7. For almsgiving being done with the hand see Deut 15.3, 7, 8, 11 and Ps.-Phoc. 23. Because it is the right hand which gives ('what your right hand is doing'), the superiority of the right side to the left side, a notion common to both ancient and modern cultures (cf. Eccles 10.2; Mt 25.31–46; 2 Bar. 54.13; b. Šabb. 88b; Koran 90; cf. the Latin, sinister), is perhaps assumed. In Jon 4.11 ignorance is indicated by the phrase, 'who do not know their right hand from the left'. Could there be a side glance at this text in Mt 6.3?

There probably lies behind Mt 6.3 a paradoxical or hyperbolic dominical word (cf. Dietzfelbinger (v), pp. 197–201). Especially noteworthy in this connexion is Gos. Thom. 62: 'What thy right will do, let not thy left know what it does'. This is an isolated saying unconnected with almsgiving; and as a general statement the meaning might be: all of one's good deeds should be done in humility; and so far from making them known to others, one should prevent even one's own self from glorying in them (cf. Theophilus, Autolycus 3.14). There is a good parallel in Mt 25.37–40, where the righteous do not remember when they took care of the hungry, the thirsty, the naked, strangers, and prisoners (and the right hand/left hand motif is also found). Self-forgetfulness, which arises out of genuine love of one's neighbour, seems to have been characteristic of Jesus' proclamation. Compare Mk 8.35: he who loses his life will save it.

4. Mt 6.4a explicates 6.3: to do alms in secret is to make the left hand not know what the right hand is doing. 6.4b then supplies motive for the envisioned action: the Father who sees in secret will reward the pious giver. This concludes the paragraph. On the concept of reward see on 6.21.

ὅπως ᾖ σου ἡ ἐλεημοσύνη ἐν τῷ κρυπτῷ. Compare Rom. 2.29. Prov 21.14 refers to a 'gift in secret'.

καὶ ὁ πατήρ σου ὁ βλέπων ἐν τῷ κρυπτῷ ἀποδώσει σοι.[16] So also 6.6 and 18, the latter probably with κρυφαίῳ. The unseen Father sees and gives reward to those who care not about receiving reward from men. The καί is consequential, which might point to a Semitic

---

[16] D W f¹ (700) Maj h q syᵖ·ʰ followed by HG insert αυτος before αποδωσει. After σοι K L W Δ Θ Π 0250 Maj it sysᵖ·ʰ goth arm eth geo Or Chr insert εν τω φανερω (cf. Mk 4.22; Lk 8.17). See Metzger, p. 15. According to Augustine, De serm. mont. 2.2.9, the addition was found in many Latin mss. but not in (earlier) Greek copies.

'and' (Black, pp. 66–7). ὁ πατήρ σου, which puts the concept of reward within the context of a father/son relationship, appears in 6.4, 6 (bis), 18 (bis), and nowhere else in the First Gospel (or in Mark or Luke for that matter; the rabbinic 'ābîkā is also rare; see m. 'Abot 5.20). It thus belongs to the pre-Matthean triptych behind 6.1–18. Only in 6.4, 6, and 18 does Matthew use βλέπω of God (cf. 4 Βασ 2.19). 'In secret' (cf. 6.4a) more likely goes with 'seeing' than with the main verb (cf. the addition in many mss. of ἐν τῷ φανερῷ, which goes with 'will reward'). Apart from 6.4, 6, and 18, ἀποδίδωμι (Mt: 18; Mk: 1; Lk: 8) has to do with receiving eschatological reward only in 16.27 (from the Son of man; redactional) and in 20.8 (M, the householder standing for God); compare Rom 2.6. Because the reward of almsgiving in the open is praise by men, perhaps the reward for almsgiving in secret is God's praise (cf. 25.21, 23; Rom 2.29; 1 Cor 4.5).

Ancient Jewish sources are replete with references to God's ability to see into dark and secret places, including human hearts (Moore 1, pp. 368–74). Nothing is hid from his all-surveying eyes; see for instance Ps 90.8; Philo, Prov. 35; Josephus, Ant. 9.3 (with κρύφα and βλέπει); 2 Bar. 83.3; Mek. on Exod 12.33; b. Soṭa 3a, 9a; Sepher Ha-Razim 4.49–50. Compare Mt 10.26 ('Nothing is covered that will not be revealed, or hidden that will not be known') and T. Gad 5.3 ('The person who is just and humble is ashamed to commit an injustice, not because someone else will pass judgement on him but out of his own heart, because the Lord considers his inner deliberations').

According to Black, pp. 177–8, if 6.4 be translated into Aramaic, paronomasia results, for 'secret' = ḥăšaʾy, 'see' = ḥăzî, and 'repay' = gĕzê.

PRAYER (6.5–15)

5. Compare 23.5–7. The switch from the second person singular in 6.2–4 to the second person plural in 6.5 (contrast 6.6) perhaps has for its explanation conformity to the traditional plurals, προσευχόμενοι and προσεύχεσθε, in 6.7 and 9. It would be hazardous to find here evidence of a new source.

καὶ ὅταν προσεύχησθε.[17] καὶ ὅταν στήκετε προσευχόμενοι appears in Mk 11.25. Perhaps 'when you pray' presupposes the three hours of prayer—morning, afternoon (3 p.m.), and evening (cf. Dan 6.10; Acts 3.1; 10.3, 30; Did. 8.3; t. Ber. 3.6). In view of the mention of trumpets in 6.2, it should be remarked that at the time of the afternoon sacrifice, when trumpets were blown (cf. Ecclus

---

[17] sy^s omits this and the rest of the verse. The singular προσευχη ουκ εση, found in (א*) D L W Θ f^13 Maj k q sy^c.p.h, is probably secondary. It makes for agreement with the συ . . . προσευχη in 6.6 (cf. 6.2–4).

50.16; *m. Sukk.* 5.5; *m. Tamid.* 7.5), all were to put down what they were doing and pray.[18]

Matthew's gospel, we may observe, never instructs the believer to pray to Jesus (contrast Jn 14.14). It seems rather everywhere to presuppose that prayer should be directed to God the Father. Perhaps the evangelist would have approved of Origen's formulation: prayer is *to* the Father *through* the Son (*De orat.* 10ff.).

οὐκ ἔσεσθε ὡς οἱ ὑποκριταί. See on 6.2 and compare 6.16 (with μὴ γίνεσθε). For rabbinic exhortations for sincerity in prayer see *Sipre* on Deut 11.13; *m. Ber.* 5.1; *b. Ta'an.* 8a; *b. Ber.* 30b; *t. Ber.* 3.18; *Midr. Ps.* on 108.1.

ὅτι φιλοῦσιν ἐν ταῖς συναγωγαῖς καὶ ἐν ταῖς γωνίαις τῶν πλατειῶν ἑστῶτες προσεύχεσθαι.[19] Behind the ὅτι (cf. the γάρ in 6.16) there could be an ambiguous Aramaic *dî* (cf. the Vulgate's *qui*; see Black, p. 72). For φιλέω (Mt: 5; Mk: 1; Lk: 2) + infinitive—a classical construction found only here in the NT—see Isa 56.10 and Josephus, *Ant.* 18.60. ἵστημι (usually for *'āmad* in the LXX) may allude to the *'ǎmîdâ* or *tĕpillâ*, daily prayer which required standing. Does the perfect tense imply lengthy prayer? Perhaps, but the emphasis must be on the locations, which are public places. Jews regularly prayed while standing (1 Sam 1.26; Neh 9.4; Jer 18.20; Mk 11.25; Josephus, *Ant.* 10.255; SB 1, pp. 401–2). Typically they bent their knees or prostrated themselves only on solemn occasions or during times of trouble (cf. 1 Kgs 8.54; Ezra 9.5; Mk 14.32–5; Acts 20.36; 21.5); see D. R. Ap-Thomas, 'Notes on Some Terms Relating to Prayer', *VT* 6 (1956), pp. 225–34. The specific practice of having the *šālîaḥ ṣibbûr* (= 'messenger of the congregation') lead prayer in the synagogue is probably not under attack here; if it were, the mention of street corners would be out of place. Rather, the synagogues are indoors, the streets are outdoors, so what is in view is ostentatious prayer in every public place, prayer uttered with the intent of enhancing one's reputation, prayer addressed not so much to God as to those looking on. No condemnation of public worship or public prayer as such is to be discerned in Mt 6.5–6. Certainly the early church engaged in corporate prayer.

---

[18] On prayer in Judaism see Moore 2, pp. 212–36; SB 1, pp. 396–402; Montefiore and Loewe, pp. 342–81; N. B. Johnson, *Prayer in the Apocrypha and Pseudepigrapha*, JBLMS 2, Philadelphia, 1948; Jeremias, *Prayers*, pp. 66–81; J. Heinemann, *Prayer in the Talmud*, SJ 9, Berlin and New York, 1977; and Petuchowski and Brocke (v).

[19] H. Sahlin, 'Emendationsvorschläge zum griechischen Text des Neuen Testaments I', *NovT* 24 (1982), pp. 161–2, conjectures that εν ταις συναγωγαις is not a particularly apt parallel to εν ταις γωνιαις των πλατειων. The original was εν ταις αγοραις. This was unconsciously altered by a copyist who, in 6.2, had just written, εν ταις συναγωγαις. We are unpersuaded.

ὅπως φανῶσιν τοῖς ἀνθρώποις.[20] Compare 6.2d, 16c (with added participle); 23.28. For the dative see on 6.1. φανῶσιν is the equivalent of 6.1's θεαθῆναι. The motive of the 'hypocrites' is vainglory. Note Sextus, *Sent.* 285: 'Consider it shameful to be praised in public'.

ἀμὴν λέγω ὑμῖν ἀπέχουσιν τὸν μισθὸν αὐτῶν. So also 6.2e (q.v.) and 16d.

6. The synoptic tradition, it is interesting to observe, portrays Jesus as one who prayed in solitude: Mk 1.35; 6.46; 14.32–42; Lk 5.16; 6.12; 9.18, 28–9. See also 2 Kgs 4.33–4 (quoted below) and *b. Taʿan.* 23b (R. Mani). According to Philo, *Vit. cont.* 25, the Therapeutae hid themselves away in private rooms. In T. Jos. 3.3, the patriach Joseph prays after retiring to his own quarters; and in T. Jacob 1.9 we learn that 'Jacob had a secluded place which he would enter to offer his prayers before the Lord in the night and in the day'.

σὺ δὲ ὅταν προσεύχῃ. Note the switch back to the singular and the emphatic placement of the pronoun (cf. 6.3a). A similar change between the second person singular and plural occurs between 6.1 and 2.

εἴσελθε εἰς τὸ ταμεῖόν σου καὶ κλείσας τὴν θύραν σου. Compare Isa 26.20 LXX (εἴσελθε εἰς τὰ ταμίειά σου ἀπόκλεισον τὴν θύραν σου) and 4 Βασ 4.33 (εἰσῆλθεν Ελισαιε εἰς τὸν οἶκον καὶ ἀπέκλεισεν τὴν θύραν . . . καὶ προσηύξατο πρὸς κύριον). For the imperative of εἰσέρχομαι + εἰς see 10.5; 25.21, 23 (these last two also have εἴσελθε + εἰς + accusative + genitive). εἰσέρχομαι + εἰς + ταμεῖον was a common expression: Gen 43.30; Exod 8.3; Judg 15.1; 3 Βασ 21.30; Isa 26.20; T. Jos. 3.3. ταμεῖον (= innermost or secret room or storeroom; cf. Gen 43.30; Exod 8.3 LXX, both for *ḥeder*; 1 Clem. 50.4; *ṭamyôn* is a loanword in rabbinic Hebrew) appears in Matthew here and in 24.26 (v.l. ταμιεῖον, the older form), where the subject is the location of false Christs. Augustine, *De serm. mont.* 2.3.11, wrongly identifies the 'inner room' with the heart and cites Ps 4.4 in support.

The command to go into one's innermost room and lock the door and then pray is clearly hyperbolic (cf. 6.3). Even if there were no sessions of public prayer at Khirbet Qumran (a disputed issue; see Wacholder, pp. 88, 253, n. 333), in Mt 6.5–6 public prayer is not being banned (cf. Mt 11.25; Mk 6.41; Lk 11.1; Jn 11.41–2), only its vainglorious use; otherwise temple cult and synagogue service would here be abolished. The point is this: prayer is for God alone; it requires no human audience. The soul in prayer must be turned only towards God. One who went into the inner room

---

[20] Although ἄν nowhere else comes after ὅπως in Matthew, it is here inserted by HG on the authority of W Δ Θ 28 565 700 1010 1241 Maj.

only making sure beforehand that others knew where he was to be
and what he was to do would be no better off than one who prayed
for show on the street corners (cf. Chrysostom, *Hom. on Mt.* 19.3).

πρόσευξαι τῷ πατρί σου τῷ ἐν τῷ κρυπτῷ. See on 6.4 and compare
6.18. It is unclear whether the Father is in secret (so RSV, NEB) or
whether the expression is elliptical and requires a verb ('who *sees* in
secret'; cf. 6.4b, 6c, 18b) or whether the second τῷ should be
omitted ('pray in secret to your Father'; so D *f*[13] latt arm; cf. Ps.-
Clem. Hom. 3.55). 2 Apoc. Jas. 5.48.22–4 follows the last line of
interpretation: 'I [James] am the brother in secret, who prayed to
the Father . . .'.

καὶ ὁ πατήρ σου ὁ βλέπων ἐν τῷ κρυπτῷ ἀποδώσει σοι.[21] So 6.4b
(q.v.) and 18b (which is why we here have 'seeing'). Above and
beyond the reward prayer itself works in the present, the last
judgement will add further blessings to those who have acted in
accordance with Mt 6.6.

7. The vocabulary of this verse and the next, verses which
together introduce the Lord's prayer, does not necessarily prove a
redactional origin.

προσευχόμενοι δέ. See on 6.5a. The addition to 6.5–6 of a
command not to pray as the Gentiles is intended to make the
Christian way of prayer distinct: it is different from both Jewish
prayer and Gentile prayer. Perhaps this reflects Matthew's
'concept of Christians as a third race, set over against both Jews
and Gentiles' (Meier, *Matthew*, p. 59).

μὴ βατταλογήσητε. The verb, absent from the LXX, occurs only
here in the NT, save for Lk 11.2 D. It presumably means 'to
babble' and is clarified here by πολυλογίᾳ. The Greek lexicon
traditionally ascribed to Suidas implausibly explains βατταλογέω
by reference to Battus, the stammering Libyan king (see
Herodotus 4.155). According to BAGD, s.v., the word appears
outside of the NT—save for literature influenced by Matthew—
only in *Vita Aesopi* (ed. of A. Westermann, 1845, c. 19, p. 47; it is
absent from the edition of Eberhard I, c. 26, p. 289, 9) and in
Simplicius, *Comm. in Epict. Ench.* 37. At least three explanations
of its etymology have been offered. It is impossible to decide
between them. (1) It might be a hybrid form, deriving from the
Aramaic *bāṭēl* ('empty, inane') + λόγος (cf. BDF § 40, citing Blass;
see sy[s.h.]). *bāṭēl* appears in an Aramaic papyrus from Murabbaʿt
with the meaning of ineffectual; see Mur 25a 1.7. Also from the
Semitic sphere is the Hebrew *bāṭāʾ* = 'speak rashly, thoughtlessly'
(Lev 5.4; Ps 106.33). (2) According to Schlatter (p. 206), the non-
literary word refers to the futility of gathering bramble twigs and
thus to futile exertion in general. βάτος = 'bramble' and λέγειν can

---

[21] K L W Δ Θ *f*[13] Maj it sy[p.h] goth arm eth geo Diat add εν τω φανερω.

mean 'to gather'. (3) In the opinion of G. Delling (*TWNT* 1, p. 598) βατταλογέω was simply formulated on the analogy of the better known βατταρίζω (= 'stammer, stutter') in connection with -λογεῖν.

Jesus was not the first to advise that in prayer the tongue should not go before the heart: the criticism of long-winded prayer or of the profane repetition of prayer was known in Judaism. Already in Eccles 5.2 we find this: 'Be not rash with your mouth, nor let your heart be hasty to utter a word before God, for God is in heaven, and you upon earth; therefore let your words be few'. Compare Isa 1.15; Ecclus 7.14; and *b. Ber.* 61a, which reads: 'A man's words should always be few towards God'. According to *Mek.* on Exod 15.25, the prayer of the righteous is short. In 2 Bar. 48.26, Baruch is commended for having prayed 'simply'. See further *m. Ber.* 3.5; 4.4; *b. Ber.* 32b–3b; SB 1, pp. 403–5. Contrast *y. Ber.* 4.7b: 'He who multiplies prayer will be heard'. With regard to prayer in the Gentile world, the magical papyri put us in touch with a piety which believed in incantations and in the beneficial effect of mechanical repetition; and Seneca could speak of *fatigare deos* (*Ep.* 31.5; cf. the material parallel in 1 Kgs 18.20–9); and one Roman emperor thought it expedient to offer this exhortation: 'A prayer of the Athenians: "Rain, rain, O dear Zeus, upon the ploughed fields of the Athenians and their plains". Either pray not at all, or in this simple and frank fashion' (Marcus Aurelius Antoninus 5.7). It is possible that the polytheism of non-Jews, which required naming the names of many different gods, is relevant for understanding Mt 6.7.

We can be certain that the making of long prayers—which is often evidence of anxiety or superstition—was common. This much Mt 6.7–8 and the rabbinic evidence make plain. How could it be otherwise? Stillness of the mind is never easily achieved; and it is no more easy to be silent before God than it is before one's fellows. Furthermore, the temptation to hope that the deity will hear if supplication be sufficiently lengthy is probably built in to human nature—whence the necessity to be reminded that before God words are neither efficacious in themselves nor in any sense magical. (It is truly ironic that the Lord's Prayer came to be used as a mechanical, magical formula, as is shown by its frequent appearance on amulets; e.g. *PGM* 2.P17; 2.P9; see Horsley 3, pp. 104–5.)

One could set Mt 6.7–8 within the context of prescribed public prayer. The good Jew had to pray the eighteen benedictions thrice daily, recite the *Shema*ʿ twice, and utter blessings before, during, and after meals. But it is not certain that these practices are here being discredited, that an anti-liturgical note is being struck, although as a matter of history the church did come to give up the Jewish hours of prayer. Perhaps originally—and still for Matthew—all that was involved was the practice of private prayer: supplication for private needs should be to the point.

In the synoptics, Jesus, although he often repeats himself (as in Gethsemane) and spends long hours in prayer, consistently utters terse prayers; and his model prayer, the Lord's prayer, is noticeably brief and compact compared with most of the standard Jewish prayers that have come down to us. Only in John do we find lengthy petitions addressed to God (e.g. Jn 17).

ὥσπερ οἱ ἐθνικοί.[22] Compare 6.2, 5, 16, and 32, and see on 5.47. Because the word ἐθνικοί almost certainly means 'heathen, Gentile' (BAGD, s.v.; cf. Lampe, s.v.), or at least 'non-Christian pagan', it is hard to think that the author of this sentence was not Jewish. To avoid this conclusion, one might suggest that 6.7 is traditional, and that therefore it is illegitimate to draw from it inferences about Matthew's ethnic background. Yet surely the evangelist had enough redactional freedom to choose another word (like οἱ λοιποί; cf. Lk 11.2 D) or to add an adjective (like ἄνομοί) if he was not perfectly comfortable with the implications of a traditional sentence.[23]

δοκοῦσιν γὰρ ὅτι ἐν τῇ πολυλογίᾳ αὐτῶν εἰσακουσθήσονται. δοκέω + ὅτι occurs again only in 26.53 (redactional). πολυλογία (LXX: 1, for rōb dĕbārîm in Prov 10.19) is a NT hapax legomenon (although cf. Lk 11.2 D). Chrysostom, Hom. on Mt. 19.5, wrote: 'neither should we make our prayers long; long, I mean, not in time, but in the number and length of the things mentioned'. This must be the right interpretation if we are to judge by Matthew's gospel itself; for in 26.36–46 Jesus prays very few words, but the time involved seems considerable. εἰσακούειν (very often in the LXX for šāmaʿ) appears only once in Matthew (cf. Heb 5.7). The type of popular thinking addressed by Mt 6.7 is well expressed in Sepher Ha-Razim 5.37 (3rd–4th cent. A.D.): 'and walk in humility and prayer, and make your prayers and supplications long, and devote your heart to the fear of heaven, and you will succeed'.[24]

8. Compare Isa 65.24 ('Before they call I will answer, while they

---

[22] B 1424 syᶜ mae have ὑποκριται for the offensive εθνικοι.

[23] Black, pp. 176–7, has argued that, if 6.7 goes back to Jesus, we can scarcely imagine him exhorting his hearers not to pray as the Gentiles: for this there was no need. So taking his cue from the οἱ λοιποί in Lk 11.2 D, he suggests the original was šarkāʾ dî ʾănāšāʾ (= οἱ λοιποὶ τῶν ἀνθρώπων, as in Rev 9.20). Matthew's text thus represents a later, Jewish interpretation: 'the rest of men' has become 'the Gentiles'. Black's conjecture cannot, in the nature of the case, be proved or disproved; but we have two reservations. First, we are not so sure that a reference to wordy Gentile prayers would have been inappropriate on Jesus' lips. Secondly, the variant in Lk 11.2 D might be not an independent translation of the Semitic original but an attempt to obviate the implicit depreciation of Gentiles.

[24] Did the author of Apoc. Sed. 14.10 have Mt 6.7 in mind when of lapsed believers he wrote: 'they stand (cf. Mt 6.5) and do not prostrate themselves in fear and trembling but they pronounce long words which neither I nor my angels accept'?

are yet speaking I will hear')²⁵ and *Exod. Rab.* on 14.15 ('Before a man speaks, God knows what is in his heart'). The followers of Jesus, unlike others, keep their prayers short because of their confidence in God. Their Father in heaven—who is omniscient—knows what they need and will give it to them (cf. 6.32).²⁶ So prayer, the purpose of which is not to exercise the tongue, does not inform or remind God of anything; it is instead worship, and it serves to cleanse the mind, purify the heart, and align one's will with God's will (cf. 6.10); it recalls to the supplicant who God is and what his purposes are. Compare Chrysostom, *Hom. on Mt.* 19.5: 'Wherefore must we pray? Not to instruct Him, but to prevail with Him; to be made intimate with Him, by continuance in supplication; to be humbled; to be reminded of thy sins'.

μὴ οὖν ὁμοιωθῆτε αὐτοῖς. In its present form this phrase is redactional. μὴ οὖν (Mt: 5; Mk: 0; Lk: 0) appears again without parallel in 6.31, 34; 10.26, 31. And Matthew likes ὁμοιόω (Mt: 8; Mk: 1; Lk: 3).

οἶδεν γὰρ ὁ πατὴρ ὑμῶν ὧν χρείαν ἔχετε πρὸ τοῦ ὑμᾶς αἰτῆσαι αὐτόν. This line closely resembles 6.32b, which is from Q. Either Matthew created 6.8 under the influence of the Q saying, or he revised tradition from M. Proof one way or the other is lacking. (6.32b, with its parallel in Lk 12.30, is no less full of Matthean vocabulary than is 6.8, but the former is not redactional. This should warn us against being too quick to move from the presence of Mattheanisms to the conclusion that a verse is a wholly redactional product).

In Matthew αἰτέω often means 'pray to'; see 6.8; 7.7–11; 18.19; 21.22; elsewhere in the synoptics see only Mk 11.24 and Lk 11.9–13 (cf. also Isa 7.11; Zech 10.1; Jn 11.22; 14.13–14).

EXCURSUS IV

THE LORD'S PRAYER (Mt 6.9–13 = Lk 11.2–4)

(1) *Sources.* Mt 6.9–13 could be from Q or M, or it could be a redactional composition. And Lk 11.2–4 could be from Q or from L, or, as on the Griesbach hypothesis, it could depend upon Matthew. The problem posed by these alternatives is not easily sorted out, and certainty is

---

²⁵ Isa 65.24 is an eschatological text, and Luz 1, p. 331, raises the possibility that Jesus' words about prayer being heard had to do with the Jewish expectation that in the new world God will answer prayers even before they are uttered. Cf. SB 4, p. 926.

²⁶ Cf. Xenophon, *Mem.* 1.3.2: Socrates prayed simply, 'Give me that which is best for me'—for he knew that the gods know best what good things are.

unobtainable. Yet there seem to be four major options (of which only the last can be reasonably excluded):[27]

A. Both Mt 6.9–13 and Lk 11.2–4 are from Q. On this supposition, the differences between the two texts are to be ascribed to the redactional tendencies of the two evangelists. The advantage of this hypothesis is that, as we shall see, no objection can be raised on the basis of word statistics or stylistic considerations. Indeed, such phrases as 'Our Father who art in heaven' and 'on earth as it is in heaven', phrases which appear in Matthew but not in Luke, contain distinctively Matthean vocabulary. Furthermore, where the Matthean version is deemed by most scholars to be original, as in having the aorist tense in vv. 11 (δός) and 12 (ἄφες), the secondary character of the Lukan version can without difficulty be attributed to the third evangelist's editorial activity. There is, however, a drawback to thinking that both Mt 6.9–13 and Lk 11.2–4 come from Q: many scholars find it reasonable to assume that when the evangelists came to the Lord's Prayer, a known liturgical piece, they would have reproduced the version known and used in their own church services. See further Luz 1, pp. 334–5.

B. Mt 6.9–13 is from M, Lk 11.2–4 from L. The objection to A is the major reason for favouring B. (While we do not at all exclude this possibility, one version of it must be rejected, namely, that according to which M and L represent different translations from the Hebrew or Aramaic original. This simply will not explain the great similarities between the two texts, especially the common word order. And what is above all decisive in this regard is the common ἐπιούσιος. This word, which occurs nowhere else in Greek literature save in texts influenced by the NT, is forceful testimony to the ultimate derivation of Mt 6.9–13 and Lk 11.2–4 from the same Greek translation of the Lord's Prayer, which perhaps was close to this:[28]

πάτερ
ἁγιασθήτω τὸ ὄνομά σου
ἐλθέτω ἡ βασιλεία σου
τὸν ἄρτον ἡμῶν τὸν ἐπιούσιον
δὸς ἡμῖν σήμερον
καὶ ἄφες ἡμῖν τὰ ὀφειλήματα ἡμῶν
καὶ γὰρ αὐτοὶ ἀφήκαμεν τῷ ὀφείλοντι ἡμῖν
καὶ μὴ εἰσενέγκῃς ἡμᾶς εἰς πειρασμόν.)

C. Either Mt 6.9–13 or Lk 11.2–4 derives from Q, the other from M or L. How could one ever raise a decisive objection against this possibility?

D. Lk 11.2–4 depends upon Mt 6.9–13 (the Griesbach hypothesis and Goulder). The problem with this is four-fold. First, there are no

[27] In what follows we leave to one side the proposal, going back to Origen, that Jesus delivered the Lord's Prayer in two slightly different forms on two different occasions.

[28] According to Jeremias, *Prayers*, p. 93, and many others, while Luke is more original with respect to length, Matthew is more original with respect to wording. This generalization holds up except for the address and Mt 6.12b = Lk 11.4b, in which line neither Matthew nor Luke preserves the pristine wording.

undisputed Mattheanisms in Luke. In fact, Luke omits precisely those lines which, on the basis of word statistics, have the highest claim to being Matthean. 'Our Father who art in heaven', 'thy will be done, on earth as it is in heaven', and 'deliver us from the evil one' are all absent from the Third Gospel. This is telling. Secondly, those who feel the force of the objection to option A—Luke would have reproduced the Lord's Prayer as he prayed it—will be unconvinced. Thirdly, the version of the Lord's Prayer in Did. 8.2, which follows Matthew very closely (see p. 597), shows us what we should expect if Mt 6.9–13 had been the text before Luke. Fourthly, genuinely convincing reasons for Luke's omission of Mt 6.10b, c, and 13b have yet to be brought forward; and it is much easier to think of additions accruing to the sacred text over time or being added by Matthew than of lines being dropped for no evident reason. (In the Lukan textual tradition, the tendency was certainly towards expansion in conformity to Matthew, as a glance at a textual apparatus will show.) The short text thus commends itself as the more original, so we reject the Griesbach hypothesis. (Incidentally, in so doing, we also reject the proposal of Goulder (v) and van Tilborg, 'Form-Criticism' (v), who take Mt 6.9–13 to be a Matthean composition. Lk 11.2–4 is independent of Mt 6.9–13, so the Lord's Prayer must have been a traditional piece.)

(2) Structure. Mt 6.9–13 is a subunit of 6.7–15, the structure of which can be set forth thus (cf. Betz (v), pp. 451–2):

6.7–15	Instruction concerning prayer and forgiveness	
6.7–13	A. Prayer	
6.7a–8a	1. Prohibition of the wrong practice	
6.7a		a. negative imperative
6.7a		·b. description of the wrong practice and comparison with non-Jewish prayer
6.7b		c. the erroneous theology of non-Jews
6.8a		d. warning: do not be like them
6.8b–13	2. Instruction for proper practice	
6.8b		a. theological grounding
6.9a		b. command to prayer
6.9b–13		c. citation of the Lord's Prayer as authoritative standard
6.9b		i. address
6.9c–10		ii. the three 'Thou' petitions
6.11–13		iii. the three 'we' petitions
6.14–15	B. The forgiveness of sins	

From this outline it is easy to see how the preface to the Lord's Prayer has been constructed so that the structure of 6.7–15 resembles the structure of 6.1–6, 16–18 (see section i). Thus, although 6.7–15 is an intrusion, an attempt has been made—by Matthew?—to maintain the traditional arrangement of the received 'cult-didache'.

(3) Authenticity. We have already dismissed the proposal of Goulder and van Tilborg, who attribute the composition of the Lords' Prayer to Matthew. But with this objection out of the way, what is to be said in favour of a dominical origin? First, although they have not agreed on the details, the Semitic specialists have had no difficulty in putting Mt

6.9–13 = Lk 11.2–4 back into good Hebrew or Aramaic (see below). Secondly, as the commentary should make most manifest, the Lord's Prayer coheres well with what we otherwise know of Jesus' proclamation. For example, he spoke of God as Father, announced the coming of the kingdom, and was much concerned with the forgiveness of sins. These concerns were, admittedly, shared by others; but they were at the very heart of what Jesus was all about and therefore are particularly appropriate in a short prayer composed by him. Thirdly, the church prayed for the coming of its Lord, not for the coming of the kingdom (1 Cor 16.22; Rev 22.20; Did. 10.6). These three reasons, although they do not put the issue beyond all cavil, do carry the day and justify the current critical consensus because over against them stands no truly weighty objection.

(4) Original language. Although retranslation of the Greek of Mt 6.9–13 = Lk 11.2–4 into Hebrew is relatively easy, the great majority of scholars to address this problem since Gustav Dalman have defended an Aramaic original. So, in addition to Dalman, C. F. Burney, C. C. Torrey, E. Lohmeyer, K. G. Kuhn, M. Black, and J. Jeremias. J. Carmignac, however, has rejected the common opinion, and his reconstruction of a Hebrew original, which owes much to the Hebrew of the Dead Sea Scrolls, is worthy of serious consideration (*Recherches* (v), esp. pp. 29–52; 'Hebrew Translations' (v)). Even if Jesus, as most scholars seem to think, usually spoke in Aramaic (Fitzmyer, *Aramean*, pp. 29–56), we can readily imagine him uttering prayers in Hebrew, the sacred language. Nevertheless, we must, for three reasons, cast our vote with those who have favoured an Aramaic original. To begin with, and against Carmignac, we are persuaded that the simple 'Father' of Luke is primary, Mathew's 'Our Father who art in heaven' secondary (see on 6.9b); and since we see no reason to question the prevalent judgement as to what stands behind the unqualified 'Father' in the prayers of Jesus, namely, the Aramaic *'abbā'* (cf. Mk 14.36), we infer that Jesus' model prayer opened with the Aramaic *'abbā'*, not the Hebrew *'ābînû*. Next, in our discussion of 6.11, we shall see that it is easier to presume an Aramaic rather than a Hebrew phrase behind ἐπιούσιον . . . σήμερον. Lastly, the Aramaic *ḥôbā'* seems the most likely Semitic candidate for a word which means both 'debt' and 'sin' (cf. Harner (v), p. 134, n. 30; for *ḥôbā'* as 'debt' see Tg. Yer. to Deut 19.15; for *ḥôbā'* as 'sin' see *y. Ḥag.* 2.77d). For these reasons, then, we cannot follow Carmignac—although, at the same time, we acknowledge that his work has made us less certain than we otherwise would be.

(5) Interpretation. Recent discussion has focused on the extent to which the Lord's Prayer is an eschatological prayer. Many have affirmed that Mt 6.9–13 par. is, from beginning to end, concerned with the last things (cf. the prayer in 2 Bar. 21.19–25). See especially Jeremias, *Theology*, pp. 193–203, and R. E. Brown (v). On this view, 'Hallowed be thy name', 'thy kingdom come', and 'thy will be done on earth as it is in heaven' entreat God to reveal his eschatological glory and usher in his everlasting reign. In the petition for bread, what is longed after is the heavenly manna, the bread of life, and the morrow is the great tomorrow, the consummation. 'Forgive us our debts as we also have forgiven our

debtors' is prayed in the face of the coming assize, when sins will be judged. And 'do not put us to the test' refers to the coming time of trouble, to the 'messianic woes'. πειρασμόν does not so much refer to the trials or temptations of everyday life as to the final time of tribulation which will precede the renewal: one prays for preservation from evil or apostasy in the great tribulation (cf. Rev 3.10).

It cannot be denied that the thematic unity given to the Lord's Prayer by the eschatological interpretation speaks much in its favour, as does the eschatological orientation of so many ancient Jewish prayers (see Heinemann, as in n. 18, pp. 34–6, and note as an example the Alenu). It has not, however, satisfied everyone (see esp. Schweizer, *Matthew*, pp. 146–59; Vögtle (v)). Some scholars, for example, while agreeing that the 'Thou' petitions do indeed have to do with the eschatological future, have held it to be otherwise with the three 'we' petitions. These, they affirm, must refer to life in this world, to present experience. The disciples ask God to take care of the daily need for sustenance; they seek God's forgiveness in the present; and they request God's help in trying situations. This interpretation, which is more in line with what Christians have usually understood to be the meaning of the Lord's Prayer, is supported by the many Jewish prayers in which everyday needs are the proper object of petition, and it has the merit of making the Lord's Prayer comprehensive, a prayer which, as Cyprian says somewhere, 'omits absolutely nothing but includes all'.

A decision concerning the issue under review is, in our judgement, exceedingly hard to render, and there is no room for certainty. We are, however, inclined to agree with those who see the Lord's Prayer as thoroughly eschatological. For the eschatological interpretation gives the text a pleasing thematic unity, and the objections raised against that interpretation are far from decisive. Schweizer, for instance, has put the case against an eschatological understanding of the petition for bread as follows:

first, Jesus paid close attention to earthly needs and their alleviation; second, the next petition, and probably the one following, refer unambiguously to this world, where men wrong each other and must find again the path of reconciliation; and third, if the plea were eschatological the word 'our' would be out of place. Furthermore, wine and fat meat—not bread—are characteristic of the eschatological banquet (*Matthew*, p. 154).

But the first point is hardly determinative, the second is disputable, and the thrust of the third we miss entirely. The fourth is more to the point; yet given the equation of manna with bread (see on 6.11) and the belief that the new age would bring manna again, the last criticism also has little weight.

Perhaps the most common objection to the eschatological interpretation is this: against the final clause of the Lord's Prayer having to do with the 'messianic woes', why do the texts have πειρασμόν, not τὸν πειρασμόν? This question can, however, be satisfactorily answered (see on 6.13a); and as this is the case, we conclude that the arguments for the eschatological interpretation are slightly stronger than those opposed.

(6) Jewish parallels. In his book on the gospels, the Jewish scholar, I. Abrahams, gathered together lines from different Jewish prayers in order to produce the following composite (2, pp. 98–9):

> Our Father, who art in Heaven. Hallowed be Thine exalted Name in the world Thou didst create according to Thy will. May Thy Kingdom and Thy lordship come speedily, and be acknowledged by all the world, that Thy Name may be praised in all eternity. May Thy will be done in Heaven, and also on earth give tranquillity of spirit to those that fear Thee, yet in all things do what seemeth good to Thee. Let us enjoy the bread daily apportioned to us. Forgive us, our Father, for we have sinned; forgive also all who have done us injury; even as we also forgive all. And lead us not into temptation, but keep us far from evil. For thine is the greatness and the power and the dominion, the victory and the majesty, yea all in Heaven and on earth. Thine is the Kingdom, and thou are lord of all beings for ever. Amen.

This artificial prayer underlines perhaps more than anything else could the extent to which the Pater Noster reflects typical Jewish concerns. It should nonetheless be stated clearly that for all the parallels, the Lord's Prayer as it was uttered by Jesus distinguishes itself *vis-à-vis* most other Jewish prayers of antiquity by three characteristics: (1) the simple and intimate address; (2) brevity and succinctness in general; and (3) its eschatological orientation. Further, the Lord's Prayer, we must suppose, tells us what Jesus of Nazareth thought to be the most appropriate or urgent concerns for personal prayer, and this is something the Jewish parallels do not teach us.

In addition to the significant parallels to Jewish prayers in general, two Jewish prayers in particular require mention, the first being the Kaddish, which was prayed in the synagogue after the sermon. Its earliest form was perhaps close to the following:

> Exalted and hallowed be his great name
>> in the world which he created according to his will.
> May he let his kingdom rule
>> in your lifetime and in your days and in the lifetime
>> of the whole house of Israel, speedily and soon.
> Praised be his great name from eternity to eternity.
>> And to this say: Amen.

See I. Elbogen, *Der jüdische Gottesdienst in seiner geschichtlichen Entwicklung*, 3rd ed., Frankfurt am Main, 1931, pp. 92–8, and L. A. Hoffman, *The Canonization of the Synagogue Service*, London, 1979, pp. 56–65. The first two petitions of the Lord's Prayer, the two 'Thou' petitions, were, one strongly suspects, formulated under the influence of the Kaddish prayer—if, indeed, that prayer was already well known in the first-century A.D. (an uncertain point).

The second Jewish prayer of special interest is the Tefillah, the Eighteen Benedictions (see SB 4, pp. 211–14, giving both the Palestinian and Babylonian versions; also Schürer 2, pp. 455–63)—although it is not certain this existed in Jesus' time in its present form.[29] Still, there remain some intriguing similarities which may be more than coincidental. The sixth benediction reads, 'Forgive us, our Father; for we have sinned against thee; blot out our transgression from before thine eyes. Blessed art thou, O Lord, who forgivest much'. Compare Mt 6.12a = Lk 11.4a. The ninth benediction, which asks God to fill the world with produce, supplies a distant parallel to Mt 6.11 = Lk 11.3. Moreover, while in the gospels the prayer for bread marks the transition from the first half (the 'Thou' petitions) to the second half (the 'we' petitions) of the Lord's Prayer, in the Shemoneh'Esreh, the ninth benediction is a hinge; for while benedictions 4–8 concern the needs of God's people (cf. the 'we' petitions), benedictions 10–15 are in substance different ways of asking for the coming of God's Kingdom (cf. the 'Thou' petitions).[30] Some have also observed a similarity of rhythm and rhyme between the Lord's Prayer and the Amidah (see Davies, *SSM*, pp. 310–11, referring to Kuhn).

Given the parallels of content just noted between the Lord's Prayer and the Eighteen Benedictions, can we infer a parallel of function? With regard to Jesus himself, the Lord's Prayer was probably delivered in accordance with the tradition that a Jewish teacher should give his followers a characteristic form of prayer (cf. Lk 11.1). But with regard to Matthew, it has been urged that the evangelist thought of the Lord's Prayer as the Christian counterpart of the Shemoneh'Esreh—specifically, of the abbreviated eighteen (see *m. Ber.* 4.3; *b. Ber.* 29a)—which was being reformulated at Jamnia (cf. Davies, *SSM*, pp. 309–13; Bahr (v)). This is a real possibility, one which is particularly inviting because of what we find in *b. Ber.* 29a:

What is meant by 'an abbreviated eighteen'? Rab said: An abbreviated form of each blessing; Samuel said: Give us discernment, O Lord, to know Thy ways, and circumcise our heart to fear Thee, and forgive us so that we may be redeemed, and keep us far from our sufferings, and fatten us in the pastures of Thy land, and gather our dispersions from the four corners of the earth, and let them who err from Thy prescriptions be punished, and lift up Thy hand against the wicked, and let the righteous rejoice in the building of Thy city and the establishment of the temple and in the exalting of the horn of David Thy servant and the preparation of a light for the son of Jesse Thy Messiah; before we call mayest Thou answer; blessed art Thou, O Lord, who hearkenest to prayer.

This version of the abbreviated eighteen (the Palestinian Talmud has a shorter version) is of comparable length with the Pater Noster, being only slightly longer. In addition, it is marked by a simple address ('O Lord') and by three concurrent petitions that are strikingly close to Mt 6.9–13:

[29] Josephus does not mention it. According to P. Billerbeck, 'Ein Synagogengottesdienst in Jesu Tagen', *ZNW* 55 (1964), p. 148, only benedictions 1–3 and 16–18 existed in the first half of the first century A.D. Contrast SB 1, pp. 407–8, and Heinemann, as in n. 18, pp. 21–3, 42–69, 219–21.

[30] Benedictions 1–3 are introductory and have a hymnic character while benedictions 16–18 are thanksgivings.

'forgive us so that we may be redeemed, and keep us far from our sufferings, and fatten us in the pastures of Thy land'. Forgiveness, deliverance, and nourishment: these are precisely the subjects of the three 'we' petitions. If the quoted version of the abbreviated eighteen or something like it was known in the latter half of the first century A.D., the Jewish Matthew must have known how close the Lord's Prayer was to what some Jews prayed morning, afternoon, and evening, and this may well have led him (and others before him) to use Jesus' model prayer instead of—or perhaps after (cf. *b. Ber.* 16b–17a)—the Jewish Amidah. Certainly Matthew's form of the Lord's Prayer, with its accentuated parallelism and liturgical elaborations, would have been appropriate for such usage, even though it has no *berakah* formula; and while, according to rabbinic tradition, the Tefillah was to be recited thrice daily (*m. Ber.* 4.1), in Did, 8.3 Christians are commanded to recite the Lord's Prayer three times daily (cf. Apost. Const. 7.24). This may well have been the practice of Matthew's community. (Also, in Apost. Const. 7.44, the Lord's Prayer is to be prayed, like the Amidah, standing up.) But farther than this we cannot go, for the three 'we' petitions also appear in Luke and indeed are to be traced back to Jesus himself, so they cannot be used as evidence for the particular *Sitz im Leben* of Matthew's gospel.

(7) Did. 8.2 reads:

πάτερ ἡμῶν ὁ ἐν τῷ οὐρανῷ, ἁγιασθήτω τὸ ὄνομά σου. ἐλθέτω ἡ βασιλεία σου. γενηθήτω τὸ θέλημά σου ὡς ἐν οὐρανῷ καὶ ἐπὶ γῆς. τὸν ἄρτον ἡμῶν τὸν ἐπιούσιον δὸς ἡμῖν σήμερον. καὶ ἄφες ἡμῖν τὴν ὀφειλὴν ἡμῶν, ὡς καὶ ἡμεῖς ἀφίεμεν τοῖς ὀφειλέταις ἡμῶν. καὶ μὴ εἰσενέγκῃς ἡμᾶς εἰς πειρασμόν, ἀλλὰ ῥῦσαι ἡμᾶς ἀπὸ τοῦ πονηροῦ. ὅτι σοῦ ἐστιν ἡ δύναμις καὶ ἡ δόξα εἰς τοὺς αἰῶνας.

Is this dependent upon Matthew? Despite some recent scholars who have answered in the negative,[31] we find an affirmative answer irresistible. First, there are only three differences between Did. 8.2 and Mt 6.9b–13, and each is minor: the singular τῷ οὐρανῷ in the address for Matthew's plural; τὴν ὀφειλήν for τὰ ὀφειλήματα in the line about forgiveness; and ἀφίεμεν for ἀφήκαμεν in the same line (but this last is attested as a textual variant in Matthew). The Didache also adds a doxology. To avoid the conclusion of the Didache's knowledge of Matthew, one must suppose that Mt 6.9b–13 owes next to nothing to the redactor's hand. For instance, 'Our Father who art in heaven', 'thy will be done on earth as it is in heaven', and 'deliver us from the evil one' must be regarded as pre-Matthean. But all this is very far from certain. Secondly, Mt 6.9a is almost surely redactional, and it is recalled by the Didache's introduction: οὕτως προσεύχεσθε (contrast Lk 11.2a). Thirdly, those addressed by the Didache are to pray as the Lord ἐκέλευσεν . . . ἐν τῷ εὐαγγελίῳ αὐτοῦ. Is

---

[31] So. J.-P. Audet, *La Didaché: Instructions des Apôtres*, Paris, 1958, pp. 166–86; Lohmeyer (v), p. 16; and R. Glover, 'The Didache's Quotations and the Synoptic Gospels', *NTS* 5 (1958), pp. 12–29. Contrast Streeter, p. 508: 'an interpretation according to the letter, but in flagrant discord with the spirit, of the Sermon on the Mount'.

the gospel referred to not Matthew?[32] Finally, the Pater Noster in Matthew is preceded by two paragraphs which instruct one not to pray as do the hypocrites or the Gentiles; and it is followed by a paragraph on fasting. Corresponding to all this, in Did. 8.1 there is instruction for fasting which strongly recalls Mt 6.16–18 (αἱ δὲ νηστεῖαι ὑμῶν μή/ὑποκριτῶν/νηστεύουσι γάρ/ὑμεῖς δὲ νηστεύσατε); and Did. 8.2 begins, μηδὲ προσεύχεσθε ὡς οἱ ὑποκριταί. One could hardly hope for more evidence of direct literary borrowing.

(8) Jn 17. More than one observer has thought that the words of the high priestly prayer recall the Lord's Prayer (Brown, *John* 2, p. 747; Dodd, *Tradition*, pp. 333–4). But W. O. Walker, Jr. (v) has gone so far as to argue that Jn 17 represents a sort of 'midrash' on the Lord's Prayer, specifically on the Lord's Prayer as known in Matthew and the Didache. And Walker has, in his opinion, found probable, although not certain, indications of literary dependence between Matthew and John. What is the evidence? Walker calls attention to these parallels, among others:

Mt 6.9–13	Jn 17
'Our Father who art in heaven'	πάτερ opens the prayer (v. l; cf. vv. 5, 11, 21, 24, 25; Jesus' looking to heaven in v. 1 could recall 'who art in heaven')
'Hallowed be thy name'	Cf. the mention of the 'name' in vv. 6, 11, 12, and 26; the use of δοξάζειν and δόξα in vv. 1, 4–5, 10, 22, 24; and the use of ἅγιος or ἁγιάζειν in vv. 11, 17, and 19.
'thy kingdom come'	'the hour has come' (v. 1)
'thy will be done on earth as it is in heaven'	Jesus has accepted the work the Father gave him (v. 4), and work = will of God (cf. Jn 5.30; 6.38–40); and Jesus glorified God 'on earth' (v. 4)
the petition for bread	Jesus speaks of eternal life (vv. 2–3), which is earlier identified with Jesus and with the bread of life (6.32–58); and note that 6.34 ('Lord, give us this bread always') may show John's familiarity with the Lord's Prayer.
the petition for forgiveness	the sanctification of the disciples (vv. 17, 19) is their purification (cf. 15.3)
the petition for deliverance	ἵνα τηρήσῃς αὐτοὺς ἐκ τοῦ πονηροῦ (v. 15)

In our judgement, the case upheld by these correlations is rather weak,

---

[32] According to Audet (as in n. 31), the 'gospel' referred to is not our Matthew but a collection of ethical sayings.

and we can conclude no more than that Jn 17 may or may not borrow from the Lord's Prayer: the evidence one way or the other is not decisive. But of one thing we are fairly sure. Jn 17 gives no firm indication of having known the First Gospel. The only real reason for thinking otherwise is the last parallel cited. 'That thou shouldest keep them from the evil one' does recall Mt 6.13b, which has no Lukan parallel. But what is thereby implied? Jn 17.15 also recalls other passages, including Prov 7.5 (ἵνα σε τηρήσῃ ἀπὸ γυναικὸς ἀλλοτρίας καὶ πονηρᾶς); Isa 25.4 LXX; 2 Th 3.3 (φυλάξει ἀπὸ τοῦ πονηροῦ); 2 Tim 4.18 (ῥύσεταί με ὁ κύριος ἀπὸ παντὸς ἔργου πονηροῦ); 2 Pet 2.9 (οἶδεν κύριος εὐσεβεῖς ἐκ πειρασμοῦ ῥύεσθαι); and Did. 10.5 (ῥύσασθαι αὐτὴν ἀπὸ παντὸς πονηροῦ). Thus we may have here just a common type of expression. Moreover, it seems to us that the correspondence between 2 Th 3.3 and Mt 6.13b is particularly impressive; and since we are not inclined to argue that 2 Thessalonians is pseudepigraphical and post-Matthean, and that 2 Th 3.3 in particular betrays knowledge of Mt 6.13b, we hesitate to find in Jn 17.15 borrowing from Matthew. Or to put it another way: if 2 Th 3.3 is not an allusion to the Lord's Prayer, neither probably is Jn 17.15. But if 2 Th 3.3 is indeed a genuine allusion to the Pater Noster, it is probably best taken not as evidence for dependence upon the First Gospel but as evidence for the pre-Matthean origin of Mt 6.13b. So likewise Jn 17.15. Finally, and to expand on the last point, because it is almost impossible to determine the extent of Matthean redaction in the Lord's Prayer, and because 6.13b may or may not be an editorial addition, John could have known the Lord's Prayer pretty much as it is in Matthew without having known Matthew. So Walker's argument falls short of proving its conclusion.

9. Having told the readers of Matthew how not to pray (6.5–8), Jesus now tells them how they should pray. For the pattern, Do not do that, instead do this, see 6.2–4, 5–6, 16–18, 19–21; 10.5–6.

οὕτως οὖν προσεύχεσθε ὑμεῖς. This is presumably redactional, although οὕτως οὖν appears only here in Matthew. Did. 8.2, introducing the Lord's Prayer, has: οὕτως προσεύχεσθε (cf. Origen, *On Prayer* 18.2). The adverb οὕτως (Mt: 32; Mk: 10; Lk: 21) means 'in this manner'. It probably implies that what follows is more an example of how to pray instead of a formula to be mechanically repeated (cf. Zahn, pp. 269–70; McNeile, p. 77; Lohmeyer (v), p. 21)—and this must have been Jesus' intent, to judge from the fact that the prayer has not come down to us exactly as he uttered it. In addition, the church Fathers could speak of it as an *outline* (Tertullian, *De orat.* 1; Origen, *On Prayer* 18.1). (It is worth recalling that the Amidah, which, like the Our Father, was a congregational prayer, also had no fixed form and was treated by many as an outline; see *t. Ber.* 3.5; *m. Ber.* 4.4; *m. 'Abot* 2.13; *Sipre* on Num 12.13; *Mek.* on Exod 15.25; *b. Ber.* 29b, 34a; Bahr (v)). Note that the ὑμεῖς sets the disciples over against both the Jews (6.5) and the Gentiles (6.7).

The Lord's Prayer appears to be an epitome, like the 'fountain' (*mēʿên*) of the rabbis, an abbreviated version of the Eighteen Benedictions (cf. *m. Ber.* 4.3). This could explain why Tertullian recommends adding private petitions after saying the Pater Noster (*De orat.* 10). According to the rabbinic sources, it was the custom of some to add personal prayers after completing the Eighteen Benedictions (see *b.* ʿ*Abod. Zar.* 7b).

πάτερ ἡμῶν ὁ ἐν τοῖς οὐρανοῖς. So Did 8.2, with the singular 'heaven'. Luke has the unqualified πάτερ, behind which, according to the modern consensus, lies the simple '*abbāʾ*. The qualification, 'Our . . . who art in the heavens', certainly bears all the hallmarks of being Matthean (see on 6.1); yet many have wondered whether the evangelist would have had the freedom to alter what was undoubtedly a sacred, liturgical text;[33] and it may also be observed that Matthew has only once introduced into Markan material the phrase, '(My, our, your) Father in (the) heavens' (12.50 = Mk 3.35). Nevertheless, given Matthew's frequent expansions of other words of the Lord and indeed his implied ascription of redactional creations to Jesus himself (as in 6.34), the objections are not so weighty as they at first seem. We leave the issue open.

Even if we cannot demonstrate that the address in Matthew is redactional, its secondary character *vis-à-vis* Luke is likely. Some, to be sure, have found in Luke's short address a form for the convenience of Gentiles. On their view, the long form would not have arisen if Jesus had commanded his disciples to pray the simple '*abbāʾ*; and Mk 11.25 and Mt 7.11 = Lk 11.13 show that Jesus himself probably spoke of the 'Father in heaven' (so Carmignac, *Recherches* (v), pp. 74–6). But against this opinion, Matthew's form is quite easily explained as being influenced by the Jewish liturgy; for while the unqualified 'Father' is as yet unattested on Palestinian soil, 'our Father' (= '*ābînû*) was popular (Isa 63.16; 64.8; Tob 13.4; Rom 1.7; 1 Cor 1.3; 2 Cor 1.2; Phil 1.2; 4.20; 1 Th 1.3; Shemoneh 'Esreh, petitions 4, 6) as was 'our Father in (the) heaven(s)' (at least from the time of Joḥanan b. Zakkai; see *m. Soṭa* 9.15; *m. Yoma* 8.9; etc.). Further, the simple '*abbāʾ* behind Mk 14.36 almost certainly reflects Jesus' usage (cf. Rom 8.15; Gal 4.6); and only unsure theological reasons could cause one to affirm without hesitation that Jesus would not have invited his disciples to address God as he did, that is, as '*abbāʾ*.[34]

---

[33] On the other hand, one might argue that the words of the Our Father were not absolutely fixed until they were set down in writing. Although we do not want to push the parallel too much, study of the Lo Dagaa of Ghana and of their Invocation to the Bagre has shown how even a very short sacred prayer known by all can remain fluid in oral tradition; see J. Goody, *The Domestication of the Savage Mind*, Cambridge, 1977, pp. 118–19. One also calls to mind the variants in the NT accounts of the institution of the Lord's Supper.

[34] Contra Marchel (v), who thinks the church's use of '*abbāʾ* derives not from an injunction of Jesus so to pray but from later reflection upon the believer's union with Christ. Even so, there still remains the difficult question of whether Jesus ever joined with his disciples in saying, 'our Father'. The synoptic distinction between 'my Father' and 'your Father' (cf. Jn 20.17)—firmly upheld by Matthew—may

Concerning the injunction to pray to God as Father and the related concept of the believer's sonship in Matthew, two points are to be made. (1) 'Your Father' and 'Our Father' include the disciples but not the populace at large. This is because sonship depends upon Jesus, the Son of God. Specifically, those who obey the will of God and follow his Son themselves become sons of God (cf. 5.9, 45). This idea is found elsewhere in the NT, as in Gal 3.26 and 1 Jn 5.1. (2) Given the eschatological orientation of most if not all of Mt 6.9–13, note should be taken of the fact that sonship was often set forth as an eschatological hope (Mt 5.9; Lk 6.35; 20.36; M. Vellanickal, *The Divine Sonship of Christians in the Johannine Writings*, AnBib 72, Rome, 1977, pp. 9–68). Perhaps, then, the privilege of praying the Lord's Prayer involves an element of 'realized eschatology'.

In his famous article, 'Abba', J. Jeremias argued that 'there is as yet no evidence in the literature of ancient Palestinian Judaism that "my Father" is used as a personal address to God', and that 'we can say quite definitely that there is no *analogy at all* in the whole literature of Jewish prayer for God being addressed as Abba'.[35] He further affirmed that, since '*abbā*' was a mark of the everyday language of the family, 'it would have been disrespectful and therefore inconceivable to address God with this familiar word' ('Abba', p. 62). So Jesus' address to God was, according to Jeremias, strikingly new and unique, and it betrays a very special relationship with God.

Because Jeremias' researches have been so influential, we here record our reservations. (1) G. Vermes has affirmed that 'one of the distinguishing features of ancient Hasidic piety is its habit of alluding to God precisely as "Father" ' (*Jesus the Jew*, p. 210). He cites *m. Ber.* 5.1: 'The ancient Hasidim spent an hour (in reflection before praying) in order to direct their hearts towards their Father in heaven'.[36] He also calls attention to the following fascinating story in *b. Ta'an.* 23b: 'When the world was in need of rain, the rabbis used to send school-children to him [Ḥanan, Ḥoni the circle-drawer's grandson and cousin of Abba Hilkiah],

---

have had its roots in Jesus' own speech. See further H. F. D. Sparks, 'The Doctrine of Divine Fatherhood in the Gospels', in *Studies in the Gospels*, ed. D. E. Nineham, London, 1955, pp. 241–66, and R. Hamerton-Kelly, *God the Father*, Philadelphia, 1979, pp. 78–81.

[35] Jeremias, 'Abba', in *Prayers*, pp. 29, 57. Additional literature on the problem: Jeremias, *Theology*, pp. 61–8; Marchel (v); G. Kittel, *TWNT* 1, pp. 4–6; Vermes, *Jesus the Jew*, pp. 210–11; idem, *World*, pp. 39–43; Hamerton-Kelly, as in previous note, pp. 52–81; Dunn, *Spirit*, pp. 21–6; idem, *Christology*, pp. 26–8; G. Schelbert, 'Sprachgeschichtliches zu "abba" ', in *Mélanges Dominique Barthélemy*, ed. P. Casetti et al., Göttingen, 1981, pp. 395–447; M. Wilcox, 'Semitisms in the New Testament', *ANRW* II.25.2 (1984), pp. 995–8; J. Fitzmyer, '*Abba* and Jesus' Relation to God', in *À cause de l'Évangile: Études sur les Synoptiques et les Actes offertes au P. Jacques Dupont*, LD 123, Paris, 1985, pp. 15–38.

[36] Some editions have, instead of 'their Father in heaven', *hamāqôm* (= 'the Place, the Existence, the Lord').

who seized the train of his cloak and said to him, Abba, Abba, give us rain! He said to God: Lord of the universe, render a service to those who cannot distinguish between the Abba who gives rain and the Abba who does not'. (2) There are texts in which pious Israelites who clearly have an intimate relationship with God are called sons or children of God (Wisd 2.13, 18; 5.5; 2 Macc 7.34; Jub. 1.24; Ps. Sol. 13. 9; *m. Ta'an.* 3.8; etc.); and in Wisdom circles God was addressed 'as "Father" with a degree of intimacy which in Aramaic could well have been expressed by "Abba" (Wisd 14.3; Sir 23.1, 4; 51.10; III Macc 6.3, 8)'; so Dunn, *Christology,* p. 27. Note also Apoc. Sed. 3.3, which may come from a Jewish source (so S. Agourides in Charlesworth 1, pp. 606–7): 'the son (Sedrach) does have a complaint against his Father (God)'. (3) Morton Smith, underlining the fragmentary nature of our sources, has suggested that *'abbā'* could come from lowerclass Palestinian piety (review of Dunn, *Jesus and the Spirit,* in *JAAR* 44 (1976), p. 726). Although his conjecture cannot be proven, it does point up the uncertainty of Jeremias' argument, which to some extent is an argument from silence. (4) As Jeremias himself admits, *'abbā'* was not only spoken by children; it was retained in adulthood, and it was sometimes used as a term of affection in conversations with old men. This makes one wonder how much stress is to be laid upon *'abbā'* being a word like 'daddy'.

Where does all this leave us? Against Jeremias, we cannot claim that Jesus' use of *'abbā'* was without question unique or that it necessarily expressed a unique sense of divine sonship. Yet it does remain probable that we have here both a characteristic and a distinctive usage. Compared with the extant Jewish prayers of the period, those of Jesus are marked by a simple address. Furthermore, in Rom 8.15–16 and Gal 4.6–7 (cf. 1 Pet 1.17), Paul implies that the use of *'abbā'* in prayer was something special, a sign of unprecedented intimacy with God. But the apostle could not have thought this if *'abbā'* had been widely in use in Jewish prayers (cf. Luz 1, p. 340). Thus, despite legitimate reservations about uniqueness, it appears that when Jesus addressed his prayers to *'abbā'*, he was to some extent differentiating himself from common practice; and perhaps many if not most Jews would have found it awkward and even perhaps verging on the impious to address God simply as *'abbā'*.

ἁγιασθήτω τὸ ὄνομά σου. So Luke and Did. 8.2. This is not a doxology added because of the mention of God—as though Jesus said: 'Father—hallowed be thy name—, thy kingdom come . . .'. Rather, 'Hallowed by thy name' is an independent petition. ἁγιάζω (rare outside the Greek Bible) occurs often in the LXX for a form of *qdš*. For the aorist imperative in prayer see 26.39 and BDF § 337.4. Against Augustine, *De serm. mont.* 2.5.19, and Cyril of Jerusalem, *Myst. Cat.* 5.12, the passive is probably divine. God is being called upon to act: he will hallow his own name (cf. Ezek 36.23; Schlosser 1, pp. 251–2; but note Luz 1, pp. 342–4). ἁγιάζειν τὸ ὄνομα must be regarded as a traditional formula; see Lev 22.32; Isa 29.23; Ezek 36.23; 1 En. 61.12; *b. Yeb.* 79a; the Kaddish prayer ('magnified and hallowed [*wĕyitqaddēš* = ἁγιασθήτω] be his great name'). Contrast the antithetical formula, βεβηλοῦν τὸ ὄνομα, as in Lev 18.21; Ezek 36.20; and Herm. s. 8.6.2. 'Thy name' is a typical and round about way of reverently referring to God's person (cf. Jn 12.28; Rom 9.17); and as God has revealed himself in his name (Exod 3.13–14), to know his name is to know him (cf. Gen 32.28–9; Isa 52.6). But only when the kingdom comes in its fullness will God be wholly honoured and glorified as is his due; only then will he be acknowledged by all (cf. Ezek 36.20–3).[37] Thus the supplication has to do with eschatology—although he who prays it must of course even now act to bring about the realization of God's will within his own sphere of influence (cf. Isa 29.23 and see p. 605 below). That there is a connexion between hallowing God's name and the address, 'Father', as though the first petition is a prayer for God to manifest his character as father to all, is doubtful. But perhaps Matthew will have thought of 'the name of the Father and of the Son and of the Holy Spirit' (28.19).[38]

10. This is the second 'Thou' petition. Note *b. Ber.* 40b: 'Any benediction in which *malkût* does not appear is no benediction'.

ἐλθέτω ἡ βασιλεία σου. So Luke and *Did.* 8.2. Both the line before this and that after have the same construction: aorist imperative + article + subject + σοῦ. This reflects the common content, as does the fact that 'on earth as it is in heaven' could fittingly be subjoined to each.[39] The coming of the kingdom, the hallowing of God's name, and the doing of God's will on earth as in heaven are in essence all one: each looks at the *telos* of history, each refers to the fitting culmination of God's salvific work. So whether 'thy kingdom come' be interpreted as a prayer for others—those outside the circle of Jesus' followers—to experience the coming of the kingdom or as a petition for the present experience of the disciples to come to consummation or as both of

---

[37] A number of parallels have been thought to exist between Ezekiel 36 and the Lord's Prayer; cf. Ezek 36.23 with 'hallowed be thy name', Ezek 36.24 with 'thy kingdom come', Ezek 36.26–7 with the variant reading in Lk 11.2 ('may thy Holy Spirit come upon us and cleanse us'), Ezek 36.26, 29a with the petition for deliverance from evil, Ezek 36.28a with Matthew's 'on earth as it is in heaven', Ezek 36.29b–30 with the petition for bread, and Ezek 36.31, 33a with the petition for forgiveness. Klein, 'Gestalt' (v), pp. 45–6, took these parallels to indicate that the Lord's Prayer was in fact based upon Ezekiel 36, and in this he was followed by Friendlander (pp. 163–5; cf. Swetnam (v)). We are unconvinced. While one should not exclude the bare possibility that Mt 6.9c = Lk 11.2c, 'hallowed be thy name', draws upon Ezekiel 36, the rest of the Lord's Prayer does not show Ezekiel's influence.

[38] *b. Ber.* 40b: 'Any benediction in which "the Name" does not occur is no benediction'.

[39] Indeed, some have argued that the phrase does qualify the first three petitions; so Origen and the Opus imperfectum in Matthaeum; see Nestle, 'Vaterunser' (v); Thompson (v); and Beasley-Murray, pp. 151–2. This is unlikely, especially if 10b–c be secondary, as seems most probable.

these, the petition looks to the future, implicitly acknowledges its magnificence, and asks God to bring it now.

For the kingdom of God and its coming in the teaching of Jesus and in Matthew see on 4.17. According to Norman Perrin, Jesus was not an apocalyptic forecaster who uttered specific, concrete predictions; for, among other reasons, in the phrase 'thy kingdom come', 'kingdom' is a 'tensive-symbol', that is, it has 'a set of meanings that can neither be exhausted nor adequately expressed by any one referent'.[40] Now there is undoubtedly some truth in what Perrin is arguing, but the implications must be carefully unfolded. It is also true that 'kingdom' is not here redefined, so it is natural to suppose that its connotations are pretty much those which it had in pre-Christian Judaism; see As. Mos. 10.1; Sib. Or. 3.46–8, 767; Ps. Sol. 17.3; 1QSb 4.25–6; 1QM 6.6; 12.7; Tg. Zech. 14.9; Tg. Obad 21. One can plausibly urge that 'kingdom' is not defined or circumscribed simply because its meaning(s) can be taken for granted.

In *b. B. Meṣ* 85b, we read of how Elijah always made sure that Abraham, Isaac, and Jacob never awoke to pray at the same time; for he knew that if they were so to do, God would be forced to bring the kingdom prematurely. The presupposition of this tale is that prayer can speed up the coming of God's kingdom, and this same presupposition appears in Lk 18.1–8, the parable of the unjust judge, in which the eschatological act of salvation is represented as an answer to the cry for justice: for the sake of the elect who cry out to him day and night, God will act speedily, will hasten the day of salvation (cf. Mk 13.20). Mt 6.10 should probably be read along these same lines (cf. R. Asting, *Die Heiligkeit im Urchristentum*, FRLANT 29, Göttingen, 1930, pp. 81–4, and Cadoux, p. 201). Despite the tension generated by 6.8 (why pray if God already knows all?), every other petition in the Lord's Prayer is uttered in the hope that the Father in heaven hears and answers the requests of his people. So does not the instruction to pray, 'thy kingdom come', presuppose that the coming of God's kingdom is, like bread, forgiveness, and deliverance, a proper object of petition? Should not those who utter the words hope that God will indeed incline his ear and hasten the redemption? In short, does not Mt 6.10 imply that the supplication of the saints can reach God and help induce him to act?

'Kingdom of God' as the subject of 'come' is unattested in the OT, in ancient Jewish texts, and in the NT outside the gospels (Schlosser 1, pp. 261–2). How, then, are we to explain the usage? The most reasonable answer lies in the old Jewish tradition about the 'coming' of God. Representative texts include Isa 35.4; 40.9–10; Zech 14.5; 1 En. 1.3–9; 25.3; Jub. 1.22–8; T. Levi 5.2; As. Mos. 10.1–12; Tg. to Zech 2.14–15 (discussion in Schlosser 1,

---

[40] N. Perrin, 'Eschatology and Hermeneutics', *JBL* 93 (1974), p. 11. The unspecified content of 'thy kingdom come' is underlined by Beare's comment, p. 173: 'It carries no implication of "realized eschatology", or of any significant role of Jesus in the coming of the kingdom; it does not even imply that the kingdom is at hand'. Perhaps significant is the omission of any nationalistic sentiment.

pp. 268–83; rabbinic texts in SB 1, p. 164; 4, pp. 966, 981). It was natural for Jesus, for whom kingdom = God (as ruler) (cf. Tg. on Isa 24.23; 31.4; 52.7; and see Jeremias, *Theology*, p. 102), to speak of the 'coming' of the kingdom because, in essence, he was speaking about the 'coming' of God.[41]

γενηθήτω τὸ θέλημά σου. So Did. 8.2. Compare Lk 22.42; Acts 21.14. There is nothing corresponding to this, the third 'Thou' petition, in Luke, and again we are faced with the problem of whether Matthean redaction explains the variation or whether the line belonged to the Lord's Prayer as his church prayed it. The word statistics are consistent with a redactional origin,[42] as are those for 6.10c; and the evangelist has introduced the exact words 'thy will be done' in the story of Gethsemane (26.42: cf. 12.50). Nevertheless, for the reasons cited when considering the genesis of 9b, many would remain hesitant to assign 10b–c to Matthew (see esp. Schlosser 1, pp. 287, 289–90). Would the evangelist have changed a received liturgical prayer?

'Thy will be done' seems to be the passive formulation for ποιέω + θέλημά σου (cf. 7.21; 12.50; Mk 3.35; Jn 4.34); see Schlosser 1, pp. 286–7. In the NT the passive of ποιέω is very rare (see BDF § 315).

For Jewish parallels to 'thy will be done' see *t. Ber.* 3.7; *b. Ber.* 29b; *b. Meg.* 27b; and *b. Yoma* 53b. *m. 'Abot* 2.4 reads: 'Annul your will in the face of his will'. Matthew may have understood 'thy will be done' in an ethical, rabbinic manner: the kingdom comes whenever a human being takes upon himself the yoke of the kingdom of God to do it (cf. Chrysostom, *Hom. on Mt.* 19.7; Manson, *Sayings*, p. 169; note 7.21). Most modern interpreters, however, have taken the line to refer primarily to the eschatological realization of heaven on earth: God's will is done when his salvific purpose—a triumph of grace—is fully accomplished. Yet perhaps it is wrong to see here any antithesis. In the biblical tradition God's will is usually accomplished through

[41] In Luke the following variant is found for 'thy kingdom come': ελθετω το πνευμα σου το αγιον εφ ημας και καθαρισατω ημας; so (162) 700 (Mcion GrNy). Tertullian, *Adv. Marc.* 4.26: ελθετω το πνευμα σου το αγιον εφ ημας και καθαρισατω ημας. ελθετω η βασιλεια σου. Although, according to some scholars, the prayer for the Holy Spirit is original—it does fit Lukan interests, and the tendency to assimilate Luke to Matthew might explain the majority reading—it is more likely due to liturgical contamination, the prayer for the Holy Spirit being incorporated into the Lord's Prayer during the laying on of hands or baptismal ceremonies (cf. Acts Thom. 27; Apost. Const. 7.4); see further Metzger, pp. 154–6, and Freudenberger (v); literature in Marshall, p. 458.

[42] The aorist passive imperative of γίνομαι is redactional in 8.13; 9.29; 15.28: and 26.42. It does not appear in Mark or Luke. θέλημα: Mt: 6 (always of the Father's will); Mk: 1; Lk: 4.

his people. So do not the eschatological and ethical interpretations go hand in hand? See further Luz 1, pp. 344–5.

ὡς ἐν οὐρανῷ καὶ ἐπὶ γῆς. So Did. 8.2. Compare Ps 135.6 ('Whatever the Lord pleases he does, in heaven and on earth'); Mt 28.18 (the resurrected Jesus has all authority in heaven and on earth); b. Yoma 29b ('Do thy will in heaven above'); b. Ber. 17a ('May it be thy will, O Lord our God, to establish peace in the upper family and in the lower family'); b. Ber. 29b ('Do thy will in heaven and give rest of spirit to them that fear thee beneath'; cf. t. Ber. 3.7). Although ὡς . . . καί appears only here in the First Gospel, this hardly eliminates the possibility of a redactional origin for the clause in which it is found.[43] For καί with the force of οὕτως see BDF § 453.1. οὐρανῷ and γῆς are definite without the articles (cf. Schlatter, p. 210). Note that οὐρανῷ creates an *inclusio* with the οὐρανοῖς of 9b and thus separates the first half of the prayer from the last half.

Is heaven God's sphere where his rule is already realized, so that we should translate, 'on earth as it is in heaven'? That is, is heaven the standard for earth? Or should we render, 'both in heaven and on earth', heaven being a sphere in which rebellion is as much present as on the earth (cf. Eph 6.11–12; Col 1.20; 1 En. 21.1–6; b. Ber. 16b–17a)? A decision is difficult, but we are inclined towards the former option in view of the positive connotation of 'heaven' in 9b and because heaven is consistently an untarnished place throughout the First Gospel; see especially 5.34: heaven is God's throne. This decided, are we to think of the heavenly hosts (so Didascalia 11; Augustine, *De serm. mont.* 2.6.20, citing Mt 22.30; Cyril of Jeusalem, *Myst. Cat.* 5.14; Chrysostom, *Hom. on Mt.* 19.7; cf. Ps 103.21) or of the heavenly bodies which obediently follow their assigned courses day after day (Ecclus 16.28; 43.6–9; Ps. Sol. 18.10–12; 1 En. 2.1; 41.5; T. Naph. 3.2)? Or, as angels and stars were sometimes identified (see on 2.2 and 26.53), is the antithesis false? Unfortunately, the text is mute. All we can say is this: heaven is the sphere in which God's will is now done. See further Hartman (v). But one fact is plain: the eventual unity of creation is presupposed. Heaven and earth have the same destiny under God. The kingdom of God will in the end embrace everything and all.

According to Gundry, since the doing of God's will in Matthew always applies to the present (see especially 7.21 and 26.42), the eschatological interpretation is incorrect, at least as regards the Matthean viewpoint. Further, since 6.10b–c concerns the present, so must 6.9c–10a. Thus none of the 'Thou' petitions looks towards

[43] ὡς: Mt: 40; Mk: 21; Lk: 51. οὐρανός: Mt: 82; Mk: 18; Lk: 34. οὐρανός . . . γῆ: Mt: 10; Mk: 2; Lk: 4–5.

the future (*Commentary*, p. 106). Against this, three points should be made. First, perhaps Gundry does not give sufficient force to the aorists, which seemingly imply a one time act, an *Einmaligkeit* as the Germans would put it. Secondly, the eschatological interpretation and that of Gundry are not necessarily antagonistic; indeed, the former entails the latter. For if one sincerely prays for the realization of certain eschatological hopes, the present cannot but be implicated: one must live in accordance with that ideal future for which one prays and prepare oneself and others for it. Thirdly, we cannot believe that Matthew was ignorant of the original eschatological thrust of the Lord's Prayer, especially since he must have known the Jewish parallels. Recall the line from the Kaddish: 'May he let his kingdom rule in your lifetime and in your days and in the lifetime of the whole house of Israel, speedily and soon'. Pertinent also is Davies, *PRJ*, pp. 316–7.

11. This is the first 'we' petition.[44] For God as the source of food see Ps 107.9; 146.7; Prov 30.8–9. For daily bread or rations see 2 Kgs 25.29–30; Ezra 6.9; Jer 37.21; extra-biblical parallels in Yamauchi (v), pp. 149–56.

τὸν ἄρτον ἡμῶν τὸν ἐπιούσιον δὸς ἡμῖν σήμερον. So Did. 8.2. Luke has the present δίδου (cf. the difference between Mt 6.12b and Lk 11.4b) and, instead of σήμερον (Mt: 8; Mk: 1; Lk: 11), τὸ καθ' ἡμέραν (cf. Exod 16.5). This last is surely Lukan (κατά + ἡμέρα: Mt: 1; Mk: 1; Lk: 5).

One of the great unresolved puzzles of NT lexicography is the derivation and meaning of ἐπιούσιος, upon which hinges the interpretation of the present verse. The word has not, despite assertions to the contrary, been found outside the gospels, save in literature influenced by them (cf. Origen, *De orat.* 27.7); see Metzger (v) and Hemer (v). On the references sometimes made to ἐπιούσιος in the margin of the LXX for 2 Macc 1.8 see Stendahl (v), p. 81, n. 17, and Hadidian (v). Following BAGD, s.v. (with extensive literature), the four most important interpretations are these: (1) 'necessary or needful for existence' (from ἐπί + οὐσία; so Origen, Jerome, Cyril of Alexandria, the Peshitta; see Bourgoin (v); cf. Prov 30.8 and the story of the manna in Exod 16: the bread for the day is what is needful; that the ι in ἐπί is not dropped, as is usually the case, is not decisive; see W. Foerster, TWNT 2, p. 590, n. 21); (2) 'for the current day' (from ἐπὶ τὴν οὖσαν scil. ἡμέραν; so BDF § 123.1; cf. Thucydides 1.2.2: τῆς καθ' ἡμέραν ἀναγκαίου

---

[44] On the meaning of the first person plural in this clause and throughout the Lord's Prayer see Calvin, *Inst.* 3.20.38, where he writes: 'Let the Christian . . . so regulate his prayers as to make them common, and embrace all who are his brethren in Christ; not only those whom at present he sees and knows to be such, but all men who are alive upon the earth'.

τροφῆς); (3) 'for the coming or following day' (from ἡ ἐπιοῦσα scil. ἡμέρα, a good LXX phrase; note Acts 7.26; 16.11; 20.15; 21.18; Josephus, *Bell.* 2.441; *Ant.* 10.170 and cf. περιούσιος, on which see BDF § 113.1; see Origen's discussion of this option and his rejection of it in *De orat.* 27) meaning either 'tomorrow' (as in an evening prayer) or 'today' (as in a morning prayer) or 'tomorrow' in the sense of 'the future' or 'the great tomorrow, the eschaton' (*māhār* stood in the Gospel of the Hebrews according to Jerome,[45] and Athanasius explained ἄρτος as the bread of the world to come); (4) 'that which belongs to it' (from ἐπιέναι; 'come to' > 'that comes to it' > 'that belongs to it'). The Fathers generally accepted meaning (1) or (3). The majority of modern scholars have opted for (3).

The problem of interpretation is unfortunately compounded by the quest to find the Semitic equivalent. The proposals have been many: *děyōmā'* (Dalman, Aramaic); *(dên) wěyōmāḥěrā'* (= 'of tomorrow'; so Black, Aramaic); *lěyōmā'* (K. G. Kuhn, Aramaic); *dělimḥar* (Jeremias, Aramaic); *lěmāḥār* (Carmignac, Hebrew); *děbar yôm* (Starckey, Hebrew); *sěkôm yôm* (Grelot, Aramaic). In our judgement, the most plausible solution will have to take into account the implicit allusion to the story of the gathering of the manna in Exod 16, where God is the source of food, specifically bread (= manna), where several phrases employing ἡμέρα are found (vv. 1, 4, 5, 22, 26, 27, 29, 30), and where δίδωμι is used (vv. 8, 15, 29; cf. Ps 77. 24 LXX; Jn 6.32). Already Tertullian saw the story of the manna as an interpretative key to ἐπιούσιος (*Adv. Marc.* 4.26.4), and Exod 16.4, which is alluded to elsewhere in the NT (Jn 6.32; 1 Cor 10.3; cf. Rev 2.17), runs, 'Behold, I will rain bread from heaven (*leḥem min-haššāmāyim*) for you; and the people shall go out and gather a day's portion every day' (*děbar yôm běyômô*). This last expression was variously translated (τὸ τῆς ἡμέρας εἰς ἡμέραν, Exod 16.4; τὸ καθ' ἡμέραν εἰς ἡμέραν, Lev 23.37; τὸ τῆς ἡμέρας καθ' ἡμέραν, Dan 1.5 Theod.; καθ' ἑκάστην ἡμέραν, Dan 1.5 LXX), and if one presupposes a Hebrew original for the Pater Noster, ἐπιούσιον could readily be considered the equivalent of *děbar yôm*, σήμερον (and Luke's τὸ καθ' ἑκάστην) of *běyômô* (so Starckey (v), p. 401). If, on the other hand, one presupposes an Aramaic original it becomes necessary to recover the equivalent of *děbar yôm běyômô*. For this task one may turn to the targumim, and two expressions then come into consideration, the first being *pitgām yôm běyômeh* (Tg. Onq. for Exod 5.19; 16.4; Lev 23.37), the second being *sěkôm yôm běyômeh/běyômâ/běyômayyâ* (Tg. Neof.1 for Exod 5.13; 6.19; 16.4; Lev 23.37). ἐπιούσιον could paraphrase *pitgām yôm* or *sěkôm yôm*, σημέρον (and τὸ καθ' ἑκάστην) *běyômeh*.

In choosing between the Hebrew and the Aramaic, the scales seem to be tipped in favour of the latter, for, as Grelot ('Quatrième Demande' (v)) has observed, the non-existence of a Hebrew phrase permitting the

---

[45] In Evangelio quod appellatur 'secundum Hebraeos' pro 'supersubstantiali pane' reperi Mahar, quod dicitur crastinum—ut sit sensus 'Panem nostrum crastinum', id est, futurum, 'da nobis hodie'.

separation of the two elements in the idiom, *děbar yôm běyômô*, is a point for the Aramaic hypothesis. This is because one prefers an original whose order corresponds to the Greek order of the gospels, where ἐπιούσιον is directly followed by the verb. We are thus inclined to see behind Mt 6.11 an Aramaic line which, alluding to Exod 16.4 and the gathering of manna, asked God to feed his people—who find themselves in a new exodus? see Cyster (v)—now just as he did in the past.

Fitzmyer, *Luke* 2, p. 905, objects to the solution we have proposed because, among other things, *sěkôm* is unattested in what he labels 'Middle phase Aramaic'. The objection, while it should rightly caution, is scarcely decisive. First, our knowledge of first-century Palestinian Aramaic is quite limited; and as G. Vermes has observed (*World*, p. 78), 'Aramaic speakers of New Testament times used many more words than those attested in the extant literary and inscriptional remains'. Then, secondly, even if *sěkôm* be rejected because unattested early on, no such problem faces *pitgām*, which appears already in Ezra 6.11 and the Elephantine papyri. Hence nothing stands in the way of supposing that ἐπιούσις translates the Aramaic equivalent of *děbar yôm*, this being perhaps *pitgām yôm*, as in Tg. Onq. on Exod 16.4.

If in this we are justified, interpretation (3) appears to be correct: ἐπιούσιος means 'for the following day' in the sense of 'today' (as in a morning prayer).[46] For in Exod 16 the manna is given in the morning for the day to come. But does this not then exclude the eschatological interpretation, which requires us to think of the 'great tomorrow'? Not necessarily. Bread was equated with manna (Exod 16.4, 8, 12, 15, 22, 32; Ps 77.25 LXX; 105.40; LAB 10.7; Jn 6.25–34), and in Jewish texts the final redemption will see the manna return: 2 Bar. 29.8; Sib. Or. frag. 3, 49; 7.149; *Mek.* on Exod. 16.25; (cf. Sib. Or. 3.746 (with Exod. 16.31); LAB 19.10; Rev 2.17). Note also Lk 14.15: 'Blessed is he who shall eat bread in the kingdom of God'. So one could easily think, especially in view of the eschatological orientation of the three preceding petitions and the circumstance that in Jesus' ministry table fellowship was an anticipation of the eschatological banquet (note Mt 8.11; Lk 22.28–30), that the material bread which God gives today transparently symbolizes and foreshadows and causes one to desire the spiritual, eschatological bread, which will bring lasting satisfaction. (One might also just possibly think in particular of the gathering of manna for the sabbath (Exod 16.22–30), for the sabbath came to be a symbol of the new age: Heb 4.1–10; Barn. 15). Our interpretation is not far from that of Jeremias: 'For Jesus, there was no opposition between earthly bread and the bread of life, for in the realm of the *basileia* all earthly things are hallowed.

---

[46] We have come to this conclusion through an examination of the possible Semitic background. For the same conclusion drawn from an examination of the Greek evidence see esp. Hemer (v).

The bread that Jesus broke when he invited publicans and sinners to his table, the bread that he gave to his disciples at the Last Supper, was earthly bread and yet at the same time the bread of life. For the disciples of Jesus, every meal, and not only the last one, had deep eschatological significance. Every meal with Jesus was a salvation meal, an anticipation of the final feast. At each meal he was the host, as he would be at the consummation'.[47]

We see no contradiction between the proposed reading of Mt 6.11 and 6.34. The injunction, μὴ μεριμνήσητε, does not exclude thought or prayer for the future—'take no thought for the morrow' is a misleading translation—but only the wrong kind of prayer or thought (see on 6.34). So 6.11 and 34, so far from contradicting one another, are complementary: because God supplies the needs for which one prays, anxiety should gain no foothold.

There is nothing in Mt 6.11 itself to prove that Matthew—like the later Fathers—associated the petition for bread with the Lord's Supper or the Eucharist. Yet we should keep in mind the possibility that the Our Father was already in Matthew's time recited in connexion with the Eucharistic service. Indeed, δίδωμι with ἄρτος appears again only in 26.26 and 14.19 (this last alluding probably to the Last Supper); and in the Didache the instruction to pray the Lord's Prayer appears in a chapter (8) which is preceded by a chapter on baptism and followed by one on the Eucharist (cf. Cyril of Jerusalem, *Myst. Cat.* 4–5).

12. The second 'we' petition. The Eighteen Benedictions also has a prayer for forgiveness, but no condition is attached. Contrast Ecclus 28.2–5 ('Forgive your neighbour the wrong he has done, and then your sins will be pardoned when you pray. Does a man harbour anger against another, and yet seek healing from the Lord? Does he have no mercy toward a man like himself, and yet pray for his own sins? If he himself, being flesh, maintains wrath, who will make expiation for his sins?') and *b. Šabb.* 151b: ('He who is merciful to others, mercy is shown to him by Heaven, while he who is not merciful to others, mercy is not shown to him by Heaven'). Other parallels include T. Zeb. 5.3; 8.1–2; T. Jos. 18.2; Mt 5.21–6; Mk 11.25; Col 3.13; Polyc. 6.2; *m. Yoma* 8.9; *t. B. Qam.* 9.29; and *b. Meg.* 28a. The parable of the unforgiving servant, Mt 18.23–35 (M), is especially instructive for understanding the present verse; it is indeed the parabolic equivalent of 6.12; and its conclusion makes plain Matthew's conviction that 'if you do not forgive your brother from your heart', God will not forgive you. The meaning of this is not that forgiveness can be earned (cf. Lk 7.41–2; 17.10). The point has to do not with deserts but with desire:

---

[47] *Theology*, p. 200. Carmignac, *Recherches* (v), has also argued for a multiplicity of meanings for 'bread' (physical food, the word of God, and the Eucharist); also, he suggests that 'manna' would be an appropriate translation. Cf. Dewailly (v).

God's forgiveness, although it cannot be merited, must be received, and it cannot be received by those without the will to forgive others.

For other synoptic words with the form of a two-part pronouncement in which the first clause states an activity of man and the other an eschatological act of God, and in which the same verb is used in each clause, see Mt 5.7; Lk 6.37–8; Lk 14.11 = 18.14 = Mt 23.12; Mt 10.32–3 = Lk 12.8–9. There is no compelling reason to brand Mt 6.12b = Lk 11.4b a secondary accretion.

καὶ ἄφες ἡμῖν τὰ ὀφειλήματα ἡμῶν.[48] So Luke, with ἀμαρτίας (ἀμαρτία: Mt: 7; Mk: 6; Lk: 11) for τὰ ὀφειλήματα (ὀφείλημα: Mt: 1; Mk: 0; Lk: 0); so Did. 8.2, with the singular ὀφειλήν. Compare 1 Macc 15.8, the only place in the LXX where ἀφίημι and ὀφείλημα appear together. ὀφείλημα (LXX: 3) usually means 'what is owed, one's due, debt' (as in Deut 24.10; 1 Macc 15.8; Rom 4.4); but as a religious term 'debt' takes on the meaning of 'sin' because sin makes one indebted to God (cf. 11 Qtg Job 34.4; Lk 7.41–3; Col 2.13–14; m. 'Abot 3.17). The different words in the First and Third Gospels could be translation variants of the Aramaic ḥôbā', Matthew being more literal than Luke (Black, p. 140). But as the many similarities between Mt 6.9–13 and Lk 11.2–4 favour ultimate derivation from the same Greek original, it is preferable to think that Luke chose for his non-Jewish readers the easier word—a proposal supported by the retention of ὀφείλοντι in Lk 11.4b.[49] Matthew could retain 'debt' because he could assume his readers' knowledge of the equation, 'sin' = 'debt'.

ὡς καὶ ἡμεῖς ἀφήκαμεν τοῖς ὀφειλέταις ἡμῶν.[50] So Did. 8.2, with the present tense, ἀφίεμεν. Luke has: καὶ γὰρ αὐτοὶ ἀφίομεν παντὶ ὀφείλοντι ἡμῖν. Matthew's ὡς could be redactional (ὡς καί: Mt: 3; Mk: 0; Lk: 0); and one might argue that Matthew conformed 12b to 12a (both have the aorist tense, both end in ἡμῶν, and τοῖς ὀφειλέταις better parallels τὰ ὀφειλήματα than does Luke's παντὶ ὀφείλοντι). Moreover, while with ἀφίημι Matthew generally has either ἀμαρτία (9.2, 5, 6; 12.31) or παραπτώματα (6.14, 15), τὴν ὀφειλήν . . . ἀφῆκά σοι does occur in 18.32, which belongs to M material. So the case for redactional activity in Mt 6.12b is, on the whole, strong. This suggests that Did. 8.2 depends upon the First Gospel.

[48] το οφειλημα appears in the text of the Lord's Prayer in the Antinoopolis Papyrus (*P. Ant.* 2 (1960), 54, verso); see Bammel, 'New Text' (v); idem, 'Vater-unser Text' (v).

[49] Although Gundry, *Commentary*, p. 108, suggests that Matthew changed 'sins' to 'debts' in order to create a parallel with 'debtors'.

[50] So ℵ* B Z f¹ *pc* vg^st syʳ·ʰ GrNyᵖᵗ Ephr. D (L) W Δ Θ 565 *pc* have αφιομεν. αφιεμεν appears in ℵ¹ f¹³ Maj Did Cl. Certainty is here unobtainable; see Metzger, p. 16.

Given the aorist tenses and eschatological orientation of the rest of the Pater Noster, 6.12 probably has the future—the last judgement—in view. Yet Jesus proclaimed the reality of God's forgiveness in the present (Mk 2.5; Lk 7.48), so such a dimension cannot here be excluded (cf. Lohmeyer (v), p. 179). For the connexion between the forgiveness of sins and the judgement see 5.23–6; 18.32–5; Lk 6.37. For God forgiving in his capacity as Father see Ps 103.10–14; Mt 18.35; Lk 15.11–32. Implicit in the Lord's Prayer is the fundamental obligation to recognize the need of God's forgiveness.

Jeremias has raised the possibility that behind Matthew's aorist— which could be 'an unconscious substitute for the Hebrew Stative perfect' (MHT 4, p. 33; cf. 23.2)—and Luke's present tense—which implies a continual readiness to forgive—there lies 'the Aramaic *šĕbāqnān*, which is meant as a *perfectum coincidentiae* and is therefore to be translated: "as *herewith* we forgive our debtors" '. In the original prayer, the second half of the second 'we' petition was 'a declaration of readiness to pass on God's forgiveness' (*Theology* p. 201). This conjecture cannot, of course, be proved or disproved.

According to Lachs (v), there is in Mt 6.12 an implicit rejection of Hillel's Prosbul: the author of the saying believed that debts were to be remitted in accordance with God's forgiveness of human sin. The problem with this is that the equation of 'debt' with 'sin' in religious contexts had already established itself before Jesus' time (as 11 Qtg Job 34.4 and the rabbinic use of *ḥôbā'* imply); so one could have spoken about forgiving another's 'debt' without turning thoughts to economic matters.

13. The sixth petition, the third 'we' petition. If, as seems most likely, 6.10b–c and 13b are secondary expansions (of either Matthew or the tradition before him), the Our Father must originally have ended on a jarring note. Following the address, the two parallel 'Thou' petitions, and the two 'we' petitions, there was appended an unpaired, terse conclusion, a petition formulated, unlike the others, in the negative. Perhaps the discordance of the line was intended to evoke the serious and troublesome nature of the subject matter. In any case the petition underlines the frailty of human nature by excluding the self-confident desire to face temptation. There is to be no thought of praying, like Clement of Alexandria's true gnostic, 'O Lord, put me to the test' (*Strom.* 4.7.55).

καὶ μὴ εἰσενέγκῃς ἡμᾶς εἰς πειρασμόν. So Luke and Did. 8.2. Compare *b. Ber.* 60b: 'Bring me not into the power of sin, and not into the power of guilt, and not into the power of temptation, and not into the power of anything shameful'. This line also occurs in the so-called morning prayer. Compare also Ps 17.30 LXX; Ecclus 33.1; 2 Pet 2.9 (ἐκ πειρασμοῦ ῥύεσθαι; this might allude to the

Lord's Prayer in its Matthean form); Rev 3.10; Polycarp, *Ep.* 7.2; for other parallels see SB 1, pp. 422–3. πειρασμός means 'test, trial' (as in 1 Pet 4.12) or 'temptation' (as in Lk 4.13; cf. the Hebrew *massâ*).

The statements in Jas 1.13—God tempts no one—and *b. Ber.* 60b (just quoted) suggest that God is not the active agent behind πειρασμός. Rather does μὴ εἰσενέγκῃς, reflecting perhaps a Semitic causative, have permissive force: 'Do not let us fall victim'.[51] Temptations will come; they are inevitable (cf. Mk 9.49; Acts 14.22; 1 Th 3.1–5; Jas 1.2–4; and Tertullian, *De bapt.* 20.2: 'No man can obtain the kingdom of heaven unless he has passed through temptation'). Yet as Mt 6.13b rightly interprets, temptations to sin are from 'the evil one'. God himself may 'test' his children, but he does not 'tempt' them (see on 4.3); he instead helps his own when they are in straits (cf. Tertullian, *On Prayer* 8). As 1 Cor 10.13 has it, 'God is faithful, and he will not let you be tempted beyond your strength, but with the temptation will also provide the way of escape, that you may be able to endure it'.

The main problem with regard to Mt 6.13a is whether it has to do with eschatological affliction, with *heblô šel māšiḥa*, the 'messianic woe' (cf. Mk 13.8; Mt 24.8; Rev 3.10: the hour of the πειρασμοῦ is the great tribulation). The NEB translates: 'And do not bring us to the test'. Several scholars have asserted that the absence of τόν is decisive: anarthrous πειρασμόν refers to tribulation in general, not to the great tribulation in particular (so e.g. Carmignac, *Recherches* (v), pp. 244–5, 340–1, and Vögtle (v), p. 355). Yet many Greek words are, as is well known, definite from the nature of the case and do not require the definite article even when it would be fitting (as 'heaven' and 'earth' in 6.10c). Beyond this, a general application of the sixth petition to all affliction would necessarily include the final affliction. And more to the point: Jesus and the church after him—including Matthew—interpreted their present in terms of the 'messianic woes' (Mt 10.34–6 = Lk 12.51–3; Mt 11.12–13 = Lk 16.16; Mk 10.38–9; 13.5–13; Lk 12.49–50; Rom 8.18; 1 Cor 7.26; Col 1.24; 2 Th 2.7; Rev 7.9–17). For them, therefore, every individual test or trial would inevitably be conceived as belonging to the eschatological

---

[51] Cf. Jeremias, *Theology*, pp. 201–2. For the problems with this see Moule, 'Temptation-Clause' (v). Carmignac, *Recherches* (v), pp. 236–304, 437–45, citing 4QFlor 1.8 and other texts, argues that the first three words of Mt 6.13a should be translated not 'Do not cause us to go' but 'cause us not to go'. See also Carmignac, 'Fais que nous n'entrions pas dans la tentation' (v). (The petition, we assume, has to do not with people tempting or trying God but with people being tried, this against Houk (v) and G. F. Allan, 'Man's Need of God', in *The Modern Churchman* 45 (1955), pp. 177–8.)

drama (cf. perhaps 2 Pet 2.9).[52] Hence Mt 6.13a = Lk 11.4b is a request for God's aid in the present crisis, a plea for divine support so that one may not succumb to the apostasy which characterizes the last time of trouble (cf. Mt 24.5, 9–14). (This interpretation has the advantage of explaining Matthew's aorist: a specific occasion and a specific evil are in view.[53])

Albert Schweitzer (p. 364), assuming the eschatological interpretation of πειρασμόν, affirmed that Jesus encouraged his disciples to pray in the hope that the 'messianic woes' might be averted altogether; compare his *Reich Gottes und Christentum*, ed. U. Neuenschwander, Tübingen, 1967, pp. 131–2. Although this view could muster support for itself by citing 2 Bar. 32.1; 40.2; 71.1; 4 Ezra 9.7–8; 13.48–50; *Mek.* on Exod 16.25; *b. Sanh.* 98b; *b. Šabb.* 118a; and *b. Ketub.* 111a, it should be rejected. Jesus and his followers, as we have already indicated, believed themselves to be suffering already in the eschatological tribulation; and there is no sense in asking to be spared altogether from what one is already experiencing. Schweitzer's reading also goes against the force of the gospel texts cited in the previous paragraph.

ἀλλὰ ῥῦσαι ἡμᾶς ἀπὸ τοῦ πονηροῦ. So Did. 8.2. Luke omits. Compare *b. Ber.* 16b ('Rabbi, on concluding his prayer, added the following: May it be thy will O Lord our God . . . to deliver us from . . . the destructive Accuser') and the other texts cited on p. 599; also Est. 14.17z LXX; 11QPs^aPlea 19.15–6; and Ap. Jas. 4.28–31. Our line recognizes that deliverance from τοῦ πονηροῦ is not within humanity's grasp: for this the power and grace of God are needed.

Because 'the evil one' (see below) is a favourite expression of Matthew, he may either have added the entire line, thus giving a new couplet increasing the parallelism of the Lord's Prayer, or he may have changed the last word—although all this is far from certain, since the appellation was common.

Mt 6.13b has, in the West, traditionally been translated, 'deliver us from evil' (assuming the neuter; cf. Lk 6.45; Rom 12.9; Did. 5.2; 10.5). For a defence of this interpretation see Potwin (v). But ὁ πονηρός is clearly 'the evil one' (masculine) in 13.19 and 38, and this could be the meaning in 5.37, so we are inclined to follow the Eastern liturgies: the line means 'deliver us from the evil one' (cf. Chrysostom, *Hom. on Mt.* 19.10; Cyril of Jerusalem, *Myst. Cat.* 5.18). Compare Jn 17.15: 'I pray . . . that thou shouldst keep them

---

[52] Cf. Dodd, *Parables*, p. 132, n. 1. On the background of πειρασμός see esp. K. G. Kuhn, 'New Light on Temptation, Sin, and Flesh in the New Testament', in Stendahl, *Scrolls*, pp. 94–113.

[53] And yet, because, in Jewish and Christian sources, the final affliction includes many different trials and temptations (cf. Mk 13.3–23), the πειρασμόν of Mt 6.13 must embrace various sorts of tribulation. So μὴ εἰσενέγκῃς κ.τ.λ. remains comprehensive even on the eschatological interpretation.

from the evil one' (τοῦ πονηροῦ; cf. 1 Jn 2.13–14; 3.12; 5.18–19; also Eph 6.16; 2 Thess 3.3; Barn. 2.10; M. Polyc. 17.1). Note also the parallel in Lk 22.28–32, where ἐν τοῖς πειρασμοῖς (cf. Mt 6.13a) is immediately followed by the mention of Satan. Might we not on the alternative explanation of Matthew's τοῦ πονηροῦ expect a qualifying παντός (cf. 5.11; 2 Tim 4.18; Did. 10.5)? (If we have indeed interpreted πονηροῦ correctly, this is reason to think Mt 6.13b a secondary addition, for no dominical word speaks of 'the evil one'. Mt 13.19 is redactional, and the expression has no parallel in Mt 13.38. In addition, 'the evil one' never equals Satan in Hebrew or Aramaic literature. On the other hand, 'the evil one' does belong to the vocabulary of the church.)[54]

14–15. Compare 5.7, 23–6; 18.23–5; and the texts cited on p. 610. See also our comments on 6.11. We have here four lines, each of which is built around ἀφίημι. The first two lines are positive, the second two negative. This creates an antithetical parallelism, to which a chiastic element is added by the use of 'trespasses' in 14a and 15b:[55]

1	For if you			forgive	men their trespasses
2		your heavenly Father		will also forgive you	
3	But if you do not			forgive	men
4	Neither will your		Father	forgive you	your trespasses

[54] There is no doxology in ℵ B D Z 0170 *f*¹ *pc* lat mae bo^pt Tert CyrJ. οτι σου εστιν η βασιλεια και η δυναμις και η δοξα εις τους αιωνας αμην (cf. 1 Chr 29.11–13; Auth. Teach. 6.35.19–22) or something very close to it appears in L W Θ 0233 *f*¹³ Maj f g¹ k q sy sa bo^pt Did. Given Jewish custom (cf. *m. Ber.* 1.4), it seems difficult to think that Jesus formulated a prayer without a doxology. The habit was already established in OT times (cf. Ps 41.13; 72.18–19; 89.52; 106.48; 115.18). And yet, to judge by the weight of the textual evidence, 'deliver us from the evil one' was the original conclusion of the Lord's Prayer in Matthew. This is confirmed by the Lukan text, which likewise had no doxology. In addition, while 6.14–15 is striking enough following 6.13, it would be even stranger coming after a doxology. Perhaps the best solution has been stated by Jeremias: 'In Judaism there were two ways of ending a prayer, a fixed conclusion and a conclusion formulated freely by the supplicant, called the *hᵃ tîmā* ("seal"). Originally the Lord's Prayer was a prayer with a "seal", i.e. with a freely formulated conclusion' (*Theology*, p. 203). Cf. Tertullian, *On Prayer* 10: private prayers are to be subjoined to the Lord's Prayer. Of great interest is the fact that, traditionally in the Eastern liturgies, the congregation utters the Lord's Prayer without the doxology; this is left for the priest to utter by himself. How far back this practice goes is unknown. It is possible, however, that in early Christian worship services the doxology was left for the leader to formulate; and when, after a period of time, one doxology came to be the standard, it then entered the textual tradition of Matthew. For further discussion see Davies, *SSM*, pp. 451–3, and Metzger, pp. 16–17.

[55] Because Mt 6.14–15 is redactional, and because it has the form of a 'sentence of holy law', the appearance of this form is by itself no indication of a prophetic origin; cf. Boring, p. 207. Indeed, as Matthew, who shows some anti-charismatic tendencies, displays a special fondness for 'sentences of holy law', one must wonder whether such 'sentences' were to any notable extent associated particularly with Christian prophets.

By placing the negatives (3, 4) after the positives (1, 2), the evangelist shows that for him the stress lies on the warning of judgement rather than on the promise of forgiveness (cf. 7.24–7). Note also the plurals, which underline the communal setting.

ἐὰν γὰρ ἀφῆτε τοῖς ἀνθρώποις τὰ παραπτώματα αὐτῶν, ἀφήσει καὶ ὑμῖν ὁ πατὴρ ὑμῶν ὁ οὐράνιος. ἐὰν δὲ μὴ ἀφῆτε τοῖς ἀνθρώποις, οὐδὲ ὁ πατὴρ ὑμῶν ἀφήσει τὰ παραπτώματα ὑμῶν.[56] The vocabulary of our two verses is in large part readily ascribed to Matthew. In fact almost every word or expression in 6.14–15 occurs more frequently in Matthew than in Mark or Luke.[57] What we appear to have is a redactional adaptation and expansion of Mk 11.25 (which Matthew omits in his parallel to Mk 11.20–5): καὶ ὅταν στήκετε προσευχόμενοι ἀφίετε εἴ τι ἔχετε κατά τινος ἵνα καὶ ὁ πατὴρ ὑμῶν ὁ ἐν τοῖς οὐρανοῖς ἀφῇ ὑμῖν τὰ παραπτώματα ὑμῶν.[58] 'Whenever you stand praying' is omitted as unnecessary because of the context and perhaps because it would make the disciples resemble the 'hypocrites' of 6.5; and 'if you have anything against any one' (cf. 5.23) is dropped because 6.14 is assimilated to 6.12, which does not use the expression.

Why did Matthew place 6.14–15 in its present location, after the Lord's Prayer, rather than elsewhere (as after 21.22)? Did he simply wish to expand the second 'we' petition because it was his favourite? These questions are seldom asked in the commentaries, and the answers are far from obvious. But light is shed on the problem by some other synoptic texts (cf. Stendahl (v)). The saying on which Mt 6.14–15 is based, that is, Mk 11.25, also occurs within a context of prayer. It follows immediately the saying about faith moving mountains (11.23) and that about receiving whatever one asks in prayer (11.24). Similarly, in Lk 17.3–6 (Q?), the saying on faith moving a sycamore tree into the sea (17.5–6) is preceded by a call to forgive one's brother, even seven times in one day, if he so asks (17.3–4). And Mt 18.23–35, the parable of the unforgiving servant, is prefaced by the equivalent of Lk 17.3–4, the exhortation to forgive one's brother seven times (18.21–2); and this in turn follows 18.15–20, which has to do largely with brothers agreeing

---

[56] τα παραπτωματα αυτων is added at the end of 15a by B L W Θ 0233 *f*[13] Maj (b) f g[2] q sy[c.h] sa arm bo[pt] PsChr. It is omitted by ℵ D *f*[1] 892* *pc* lat sy[p] mae bo[pt]. As the addition interferes with the chiastic structure, it is probably secondary.

[57] ἐάν: Mt: 64; Mk 35; Lk: 29. γάρ: Mt: 123–4; Mk: 64; Lk: 97. ἀφίημι: Mt: 47; Mk: 34; Lk: 31. ἄνθρωπος: Mt: 113; Mk: 56; Lk: 95. παράπτωμα: Mt: 2; Mk: 1; Lk: 0. οὐρανός with πατήρ: Mt: 13; Mk: 1; Lk: 1. ἐάν μή: Mt: 10; Mk: 6; Lk :3. οὐδέ: Mt: 27; Mk: 10; Lk: 19.

[58] Against this being a scribal addition under Matthean influence see Stendahl (v), pp. 76–7. On the other hand, Mk 11.26 ('But if you do not forgive, neither will your Father who is in heaven forgive you your trespasses') does not appear in the best mss.; it comes from Matthew and was added because of the resemblance between Mt 6.14–15 and Mk 11.25.

together in their requests to the Father in heaven. What we thus
have in Mt 6.14–15; 18.15–35; Mk 11.20–5; and Lk 17.3–6 is a
connexion between prayer—omnipotent prayer in all but Mt
6.14–15—and the forgiveness of one's brother, and it is this—
surely traditional—connexion which explains the placement of Mt
6.14–15. The right of the eschatological community to utter the
Lord's Prayer depends, as does the efficacy of the prayer, upon
communal reconciliation. Hence the Lord's Prayer must be prayed
by a church whose members have forgiven one another. (As
Stendahl (v), p. 83, n. 20 observes, this interpretation of 6.14–15
implies that, despite the use of ἀνθρώποις, the ὀφειλέται in the
Lord's Prayer are thought of primarily as members of the
Christian community.)

FASTING (6.16–18)

16. See Isa 58, in which the prophet declares that God does not
delight in sackcloth and ashes but in the fast which looses the
bonds of wickedness, frees the oppressed, brings bread to the
hungry, shelters the poor, and covers the naked. What counts is
not external show but humility; a person's attention should be
directed towards others in order to help them, not in order to learn
what good things others think about him. Compare Jer 14.12;
Zech 7.5–7. For other criticisms of insincere fasting or for
exhortations to sincerity in fasting see Ecclus 34.26; T. Asher 2.8;
Apoc. Elijah 1.18–19; m. Taʿan. 2.1; t. Taʿan. 1.8; b. Taʿan. 16a (the
power of fasting lies in repentance and good works, not in
sackcloth and abstention from food); SB 4, p. 107; Abrahams 1,
pp. 121–8; and S. Lowy, 'The Motivation of Fasting in Talmudic
Literature', JJS 9 (1958), pp. 19–38. For fasting as characteristic
of Judaism in the eyes of non-Jews see Suetonius, Aug. 76 and
Petronius, frag. 37; compare Chrysostom, Hom. adv. Jud. 1.1 (PG
48.844); 8.5 (PG 48.934–5). Nowhere is fasting mentioned in the
Pauline corpus, which was addressed first to Gentiles.[59]

ὅταν δὲ νηστεύητε. The δέ makes for better Greek than the καὶ
ὅταν of 6.5. Public fasting is probably not the subject of this verse.
Only voluntary private fasting (as in Neh 1.4; Dan 9.3; Mk 2.18;
and Lk 18.12) provided special opportunity to call attention to
oneself.

For the problem of 6.16 and the following verses on the lips of

[59] On fasting in Judaism see Moore 2, pp. 55–69, 257–66; Abrahams 1,
pp. 121–8; SB 4, pp. 77–114; J. Behm, TWNT 4, pp. 925–35 (marked by an
unnecessary denigration of Judaism). Some Greek philosophers recommended
fasting; see e.g. Porphyry, Abst.

Jesus see on 4.2. For fasting coupled with prayer, as in Mt 6.7–18, see 1 Sam 7.5–6; Neh 1.4; Tob 12.8; Philo, *Spec. leg.* 2.203; Acts 13.3; Polycarp, *Ep.* 7; Apoc. Zeph. 7.6; T. Jacob 7.17. Nothing in our text reveals whether Matthew thought there to be any deep connexion between prayer and fasting. Did he think of the latter as preparation for the former? Did he, like Nilus the Ascetic, believe that fasting 'transmits prayer to heaven; like a wing it causes it to ascend' (PG 79.1145B)?

μὴ γίνεσθε ὡς οἱ ὑποκριταὶ σκυθρωποί. See 6.2 and 5 and our comments there. σκυθρωπός, which means 'with a sad, gloomy, sullen, or dismal look' (cf. Lk 24.17; T. Sim. 4.1; Josephus, *Bell.* 1.80; *Ant.* 1.59; 11.54), occurs in the LXX for *rāʿ* (Gen 40.7; Neh 2.1) and in Dan 1.10 Theod. for *zāʿap* (in connexion with fasting). In the NT the word appears only in Mt 6.16 and Lk 24.17.

ἀφανίζουσιν γὰρ τὰ πρόσωπα αὐτῶν ὅπως φανῶσιν τοῖς ἀνθρώποις νηστεύοντες. Fasting was often accompanied by external signs, such as sackcloth, ashes, and the rending of clothing (Dan 9.3; Jon 3.5; Jdt 8.5; 1 Macc 3.47; Josephus, *Bell.* 20.89). For ἀφανίζω (most often in the LXX for a form of *šmd* or *šmm*) see on 6.19 and compare T. Zeb. 8.6 (πρόσωπον ἀφανίζει) and Joel 2.20 (ἀφανιῶ τὸ πρόσωπον αὐτοῦ); still useful is the discussion of Alford 1, p. 64. The word literally means 'make disappear'. Here it means 'render unrecognizable' (BAGD, s.v., citing *P. Oxy.* 294.15). As 6.17–18 shows, what is envisaged is the unnatural—compare Seneca, *Ep.* 5—uncleanliness of the head and face; the squalor hides the countenance (although not the identity, or the criticism would miss its mark).

Note that the first two verbs create an oxymoron: the 'hypocrites' make themselves unrecognizable (ἀφανίζουσιν) in order to be recognized (φανῶσιν). Recall that when Jesus fasted (4.2) he was alone.

According to *b. B. Bat* 60b (cf. *t. Soṭa* 15.10; *t. Taʿan* 2.12), after the destruction of the temple by the Romans in A.D. 70, 'large numbers in Israel became ascetics, binding themselves neither to eat meat nor to drink wine'; but the more sober rabbis opposed the extremes into which private fasting sometimes fell. Is this the context within which to read 6.16–18? See Davies, *SSM*, pp. 283–4, 313–14.

According to Did. 8.1, Christians should fast not as the 'hypocrites' do, on Mondays and Thursdays,[60] but rather on Wednesdays and Fridays.

[60] Cf. *m. Taʿan.* 1.4–7; 2.9; also Lk 18.12 ('I fast twice a week'). But in *b. Taʿan.* 27b it is related that, during the second temple period, private fasting was practised on Mondays, Tuesdays, Wednesdays, and Thursdays. According to Büchler (v), Lk 18.12 'refers to the exceptional fasts during October-November, when severe pietists fasted on Mondays and Thursdays if rain failed'. He also thinks this true of Mt 6.16–18 and Did. 8.3.

We cannot determine whether Matthew and his fellow believers followed the practice of the Didache or whether they still observed the Jewish fast days.

ἀμὴν λέγω ὑμῖν ἀπέχουσιν τὸν μισθὸν αὐτῶν. See on 6.2 and 5.
17. σὺ δὲ νηστεύων. The pronoun is emphatic, as in 6.3 and 6.
ἄλειψαί σου τὴν κεφαλήν. Compare Jdt 16.8; Mt 26.7; Lk 7.46. Instead of ashes, oil should be on the head. The inner state should not be advertised by artificial signs. Humility demands secrecy. ἀλείφω (= *sûk*; for the middle see Josephus, *Bell.* 5.565) appears only here in Matthew.

Anointing the head with oil may be a sign of rejoicing (Ps 23.5; 104.15), in which case 6.17 becomes a paradoxical saying: rejoice in the affliction of fasting! But because anointing the head and washing the face were everyday practices (2 Sam 14.2; SB 1, pp. 426–8), it is more likely that the disciple is simply being told to appear as usual. (Against the impression left by SB 1, p. 426, the rabbinic texts do not forbid anointing on every occasion of fasting; see esp. *m. Taʿan.* 1.4–5. Thus the contrast between Mt 6.16–18 and the Sages should not be unduly exaggerated.)

καὶ τὸ πρόσωπόν σου νίψαι. This is ironic because washing the face is usually preparatory to eating (as in Gen 43.41; cf. Mt 15.2).
➣ **18. ὅπως μὴ φανῇς τοῖς ἀνθρώποις νηστεύων.** This is the antithesis of 6.16c. The words of both are the same and appear in the same order. The only difference is the addition of μή and the change in the verbal forms.

ἀλλὰ τῷ πατρί σου τῷ ἐν τῷ κρυφαίῳ.[61] Compare 6.6b. The classical κρυφαῖος, if original, occurs only here in the NT (LXX: 4, twice for *mistār*).

καὶ ὁ πατήρ σου ὁ βλέπων ἐν τῷ κρυφαίῳ ἀποδώσει σοι. See on 6.4b and 6c.

It appears that some early Christians, encouraged by Jesus' words about the bridegroom (Mk 2.18–20), gave up fasting altogether (cf. Apoc. Elijah 1.13–22; Gos. Thom. 14). The Gospel of Thomas in fact contains this strange passage: 'Jesus said to them, if you fast (νηστεύω) you will give rise to sin for yourselves; and if you pray, you will be condemned; and if you give alms (ἐλεημοσύνη) you will do harm to your spirits' (14). This sentence is the polar opposite of Mt 6.1–18. While Matthew gives instruction on almsgiving, prayer, and fasting, the Gospel of Thomas rejects the three practices, naming them in an order precisely opposite to that of the First Gospel. If on other grounds one finds the Gospel of Thomas independent of our gospel, Gos. Thom. 14 could be regarded as

---

[61] L W Θ 0233 0250 *f*¹³ Maj have τω κρυπτω in this clause and the next. It could be original. τω κρυφαιω appears in ℵ B Dᶜ *f*¹ *pc.* εν τω φανερω (cf. Mk 4.22; Lk 8.17) is added by Δ 0233 1241 *pm* it geo eth. See on 6.4, 6.

evidence for the existence apart from Matthew of the 'cult-Didache' preserved in Mt 6.1–18.

(iv) Concluding Observations

(1) After expounding the messianic Torah (5.17–48) Matthew next delivers guidelines for the Christian cult (6.1–18). In great measure what the evangelist is attempting to accomplish in all this is to explain what exactly is characteristic of the community of believers in Jesus the Messiah; that is, he is attempting to show us what is new. This is why the Christian practices of almsgiving, prayer, and fasting are contrasted with the practices of others, with the 'hypocrites' in the synagogues and with the Gentiles. The followers of Jesus are, in Matthew's mind, different from the surrounding world. They have their own law and their own religious practices. They are distinct.

(2) When writing of the 'hypocrites' who sound trumpets before themselves, Jerome (*Ep.* 22.27, 32) applies the words to vain Christians who make a show in the churches. That is, he does not contrast Jewish practice with Christian practice but wrong Christian practice with right Christian practice. Origen does the same (*Comm. on Mt.* 11.15). Why this common interpretation? The two Fathers are not concerned with writing authoritative foundation documents, and rival religious institutions are not so much within their purview. It is otherwise with our evangelist. By drawing upon the words of Jesus himself, he is seeking to establish the legitimacy of Christianity over against the synagogue; hence for him the Jews of 6.2, 5, and 16 are not transparent symbols for misguided Christians but concrete counter-examples, and the positive commands in 6.3–4, 6, and 17–18 present that which is peculiar to the Christian cult. In other words, 6.1–18 is not simply exhortation. It is also meant to supply a partial definition of the nature of the church.

(3) The communal dimension of the Lord's Prayer (cf. Origen, *On Prayer* 33; Cyprian, *Lord's Prayer* 8; Apost. Const. 2.36; 3.18) should be obvious from the plurals in 6.7–16, especially the 'Our Father' address. This is all the more true as the traditional 'cult-Didache' behind 6.1–6, 16–18 was largely formulated with singulars. But why should this social dimension be emphasized? 6.14 and 15, the two parallel clauses on forgiveness, supply the answer. Matthew believes that the new law and the new cult do not count for everything. To have true power they must be practised by a community free of divisions, by a community whose members live in forgiving harmony with one another. In the church's struggle to attain its identity over against Judaism, mutual

reconciliation among Christians is a prerequisite. The brothers must present a united front to the world.[62]

(4) While the subject of 5.21–48 is Jesus and the Torah, in 6.1–18 the cult becomes the subject. There is, however, a more fundamental difference between the two passages. 5.21–48 has to do primarily with *actions*, 6.1–18 primarily with *intentions* (cf. Luz 1, pp. 328–9). One might even argue that 6.1–18 is a sort of commentary on what precedes it. If 5.21–48 tells the disciple *what* to do, the little 'cult-didache' tells him *how* to do it. It is not enough to obey the letter of the commandments, even Jesus' commandments. One must also be 'pure in heart' (5.8). Good deeds are to be done for the glory of God (5.16). 'The intention of a man's heart, its direction and its aim, is what is to be regarded. For if he who wishes his good works to be seen of men, sets before men his own glory and advantage, and seeks for this in the sight of men, he does not fulfil either of those precepts which the Lord has given as touching this matter; because he has at once looked to "doing his righteousness before men to be seen of them"; and his light has not so shined before men that they should see his good works, and glorify his father which is in heaven' (Augustine, *Serm.* 4(54).3, in NPNF 6, pp. 271–2). For Matthew, ethical imperatives are grounded in the divine command, and they are to be carried out for the divine glory. Neither society's recommendations nor its commendations should be the motivation for doing 'good works'.[63]

(v) *Bibliography*

Abrahams 2, pp. 94–108.

G. J. Bahr, 'The Use of the Lord's Prayer in the Primitive Church', *JBL* 84 (1965), pp. 153–9.

E. Bammel, 'Ein neuer Vater-Unser Text', *ZNW* 52 (1961), pp. 280–1.

idem, 'A New Text of the Lord's Prayer', *ExpT* 73 (1961), p. 54.

K. Barth, *CD* 3/4, pp. 102–6.

idem, *The Christian Life*, Edinburgh, 1981, pp 47–270.

Beasley-Murray, pp. 147–57.

H. D. Betz, 'Eine judenchristliche Kult-Didache in Matthäus 6,1–18', in Strecker, *Jesus Christus*, pp. 445–57; translated and reprinted in *Essays*, pp. 55–69.

[62] Disunity had been especially destructive for Judaism. Some sages urged that Jerusalem had fallen because of 'hatred without cause' among the Jews. Was Matthew aware of the dangers of such disunity? See *b. Šabb.* 32b.

[63] Worth comparing is Epictetus, *Diss.* 4.8.17: 'I long endeavored to conceal my embracing the philosophic life; and it was of use to me. For . . . I knew that whatever I did right I did not for spectators, but for myself. I ate in a seemly manner, for my own approbation. I preserved composure of look and manner, all for God and myself'.

J. Blenkinsopp, 'Apropos of the Lord's Prayer', *HeyJ* 3 (1962), pp. 51–60.

P. Bonnard, J. Dupont, and F Refoulé, *Notre Père qui es aux cieux*, Paris, · 1971.

F. J. Botha, 'Recent Research on the Lord's Prayer', *Neotestamentica* 1 (1967), pp. 42–50.

H. Bourgoin, '*Epiousios* expliqué par la notion de préfixe vide', *Bib* 60 (1979), pp. 91–6.

P. F. Bradshaw, *Daily Prayer in the Early Church*, New York, 1982.

F.-M. Braun, 'Le pain dont nous avons besoin, Mt 6,11; Lc 11,3', *NRT* 100 (1978), pp. 559–68.

R. E. Brown, *Essays*, pp. 275–320.

A. Büchler, 'St Matthew VI 1–6 and Other Allied Passages', *JTS* 10 (1909), pp. 266–70.

J. Carmignac, 'Fais que nous n'entrions pas dans la tentation. La portée d'une négation devant un verbe au causatif', *RevB* 72 (1965), pp. 218–26.

idem, 'Hebrew Translations of the Lord's Prayer: An Historical Survey,' in *Biblical and Near Eastern Studies*, ed. G. A. Tuttle, Grand Rapids, 1978, pp. 18–79.

idem, *Recherches sur le 'Notre Père'*, Paris, 1969 (with lengthy bibliography).

F. H. Chase, *The Lord's Prayer in the Early Church*, Cambridge, 1891.

R. F. Cyster, 'The Lord's Prayer and the Exodus Tradition', *Theology* 64 (1961), pp. 377–81.

G. Dalman, *Die Worte Jesu 1*, 2nd ed., Leipzig, 1930, pp. 283–365.

Davies, *SSM*, pp. 309–13, 451–3.

L.-M. Dewailly, ' "Donne-nous notre pain": quel pain? Notes sur la quatrième demande du Pater', *RSPT* 64 (1980), pp. 561–88.

C. Dietzfelbinger, 'Die Frömmigkeitsregeln von Mt 6:1–18 als Zeugnisse frühchristlicher Geschichte', *ZNW* 75 (1984), pp. 184–200.

E. von Dobschütz, 'The Lord's Prayer', *HTR* 7 (1914), pp. 293–321.

M. Dorneich, ed., *Vater-Unser Bibliographie*, Freiburg, 1982.

Dupont 3, pp. 260–72.

idem and P. Bonnard, 'Le Notre Père: notes exégétiques', *Maison-Dieu* 85 (1966), pp. 7–35.

C. F. Evans, *The Lord's Prayer*, London, 1963.

F. C. Fensham, 'The Legal Background of Mt VI 12', *NovT* 4 (1960), pp. 1–2.

P. Fiebig, *Das Vaterunser*, Gütersloh, 1927.

A. Finkel, 'The Prayer of Jesus in Matthew', in A. Finkel and L. Frizzell, eds., *Standing Before God*, New York, 1981, pp. 131–70.

W. Foerster, *TWNT* 2, pp. 587–95.

J. Massyngberde Ford, 'The Forgiveness Clause in the Matthean Form of the Our Father', *ZNW* 59 (1968), pp. 127–31.

idem, 'Yom Kippur and the Matthean Form of the Pater Noster', *Worship* 41 (1967), pp. 609–19.

R. Freudenberger, 'Zum Text der zweiten Vaterunserbitte', *NTS* 15 (1969), pp. 419–32.

A. George, 'La justice à faire dans le secret (Matthieu 6,1–6 et 16–18)', *Bib* 40 (1959), pp. 509–98.

B. Gerhardsson, 'Geistiger Opferdienst nach Matth 6,1–6.16–21', in

Neues Testament und Geschichte, ed. H. Baltensweiler and B. Reicke, Tübingen, 1972, pp. 69–77.

idem, 'The Matthean Version of the Lord's Prayer (Matt 6:9b–13)', in Weinrich, pp. 207–20.

Giesen, pp. 146–66.

M. D. Goulder, 'The Composition of the Lord's Prayer', *JTS* 14 (1963), pp. 32–45.

Grässer, pp. 95–113.

P. Grelot, 'L'arrière-plan araméen du "Pater" ', *RB* 91 (1984), pp. 531–56.

idem, 'La quatrième demande du "Pater" et son arrière-plan sémitique', *NTS* 25 (1979), pp. 299–314.

D. Y. Hadidian, 'The Meaning of ἐπιούσιος and the Codex Sergii', *NTS* 5 (1958), pp. 75–81.

P. B. Harner, *Understanding the Lord's Prayer*, Philadelphia, 1975.

L. Hartman, ' "Your Will Be Done on Earth as It is in Heaven" ', *AfTJ* 11 (1982), pp. 209–18.

C. Hemer, 'ἐπιούσιος', *JSNT* 22 (1984), pp. 81–94.

B. Hemmerdinger, 'Un Elément Pythagoricien dans le Pater', *ZNW* 63 (1972), p. 121.

D. Hill, ' "Our Daily Bread" (Matt 6.11) in the History of Exegesis', *IBS* 5 (1983), pp. 2–10.

C. B. Houk, 'ΠΕΙΡΑΣΜΟΣ, The Lord's Prayer, and the Massah Tradition', *SJT* 19 (1966), pp. 216–25.

Jeremias, *Prayers*, pp. 82–107.

idem, *Theology*, pp. 193–203.

G. Klein, 'Mt 6,2', *ZNW* 6 (1905), pp. 203–4.

idem, 'Die ursprüngliche Gestalt des Vaterunsers', *ZNW* 7 (1906), pp. 34–50.

E. Klostermann, 'Zum Verständnis von Mt 6.2', *ZNW* 47 (1956), pp. 280–1.

K. G. Kuhn, *Achtzehngebet und Vaterunser und der Reim*, WUNT 1, Tübingen, 1950.

S. T. Lachs, 'On Matthew VI.12', *NovT* 17 (1975), pp. 6–8.

E. Lohmeyer, *'Our Father': An Introduction to the Lord's Prayer* (trans. of *Das Vater-Unser*, 1963), London and New York, 1965.

N. J. McEleney, 'Does the Trumpet Sound or Resound? An Interpretation of Matthew 6,2', *ZNW* 76 (1985), pp. 43–6.

J. Magne, 'Le Pater—Mt. 6, 9–13', *Bib* 39 (1958), pp. 196–7.

T. W. Manson, 'The Lord's Prayer', *BJRL* 38 (1955–6), pp. 99–113, 436–48.

W. Marchel, *Abba, Père! La prière du Christ et des chrétiens*, AnBib 19, Rome, 1963.

B. M. Metzger, 'How many times does ἐπιούσιος occur outside the Lord's Prayer?', *ExpT* 69 (1957), pp. 52–4.

Moule, *Essays*, pp. 278–86.

idem, 'An Unsolved Problem in the Temptation Clause in the Lord's Prayer', *RefTheoRev* 33 (1974), pp. 65–76.

W. Nagel, 'Gerechtigkeit—oder Almosen? (Mt 6,1)', *VC* 15 (1961), pp. 141–5.

E. Nestle, 'Matth 6:16', *ZNW* 15 (1914), p. 94.

idem, 'Zum Vaterunser', *ZNW* 6 (1905), pp. 107–8.

B. Orchard, 'The Meaning of *ton epiousion* (Mt 6:11—Lk 11:3)', *BTB* 3 (1973), pp. 274–82.

Perrin, *Kingdom*, pp. 191–8.

J. J. Petuchowski and M. Brocke, eds., *The Lord's Prayer and Jewish Liturgy*, London and New York, 1978.

W. Powell, 'Lead us not into Temptation', *ExpT* 67 (1956), pp. 177–8.

Potwin, pp. 84–104.

R. D. Richardson, 'The Lord's Prayer as an Early Eucharist', *ATR* 39 (1957), pp. 123–30.

Schlosser 1, pp. 247–322.

J. A. T. Robinson, *More Studies*, pp. 44–64.

H. Schürmann, *Das Gebet des Herrn*, Freiburg, 1958.

Schulz, *Q*, pp. 84–93.

G. Schwarz, 'Matthäus VI.9-13/Lukas XI.2–4: Emendation und Rückübersetzung', *NTS* 15 (1969), pp. 233–47.

E. Schweizer, ' "Der Jude im Verborgenen . . . , dessen Lob nicht von Menschen, sondern von Gott kommt". Zu Röm 2,28f und Mt 6,1–18' in Gnilka, *Kirche*, pp. 115–24; reprinted in Schweizer, *Gemeinde*, pp. 86–97.

E. F. Scott, *The Lord's Prayer*, New York, 1951.

G. Smith, 'The Matthaean "Additions" to the Lord's Prayer', *ExpT* 82 (1970), pp. 54–5.

J. Starcky, 'La quatrième demande du Pater', *HTR* 64 (1971), pp. 401–9.

K. Stendahl, 'Prayer and Forgiveness', *SEÅ* 22 (1957), pp. 75–86; reprinted in *Meanings*, pp. 115–26.

G. Strecker, 'Vaterunser und Glaube', in *Glaube im Neuen Testament*, ed. F. Hahn and H. Klein, Neukirchen-Vluyn, 1982, pp. 11–28.

J. Swetnam, ' "Hallowed be Thy Name" ', *Bib* 52 (1972), pp. 556–63.

M. H. Sykes, 'And do not bring us to the Test', *ExpT* 73 (1962), pp. 189–90.

Tannehill, pp. 78–88.

G. H. P. Thompson, 'Thy Will be done in Earth, as it is in Heaven (Matthew vi, 10)', *ExpT* 70 (1959), pp. 379–81.

van Tilborg, pp. 8–13.

idem, 'A Form-Criticism of the Lord's Prayer', *NovT* 14 (1972), pp. 94–105.

A. Vögtle, 'Der "eschatologische" Bezug der Wir-Bitten des Vaterunser', in Ellis, *Jesus*, pp. 344–62.

W. O. Walker, Jr., 'The Lord's Prayer in Matthew and John', *NTS* 28 (1982), pp. 237–56.

Wrege, pp. 94–109.

E. M. Yamauchi, 'The "Daily Bread" Motif in Antiquity', *WTJ* 28 (1966), pp. 145–56.

Zeller, *Mahnsprüche*, pp. 71–4, 133–5.

XIV

GOD AND MAMMON
(6.19–34)

(i) *Structure*

Mt 6.19–34 readily divides itself into four paragraphs: 6.19–21, 22–3, 24, and 25–34. These paragraphs are held together first of all by a common theme. Each has to do with earthly treasure—19–21 with not storing it up, 22–3 with being generous, 24 with serving God, not mammon, and 25–34 with not being anxious about food and clothing. The four paragraphs are in addition related by structure. 6.22–3 and 24 both open with a thesis statement (22a/24a). This is then followed by two observations expressed in antithetical parallelism (22b–3b/24b–c). There is finally a concluding observation addressed directly to the reader (23c–d/24d). Further, while 6.19–20 does not have an opening thesis statement, it does contain two commands formulated in antithetical parallelism (19–20), and these are followed by a concluding remark that confronts the reader directly (21). In sum, 6.19–21, 22–3, and 24 are formally quite similar.

6.25–34 may also be related to the structural scheme shared by 6.19–21, 22–3, and 24. 6.25–34 consists of (1) an introduction (25) followed by (2) two supporting observations exhibiting compound parallelism (26–30, interrupted briefly by 27) followed by (3) concluding observations (31–4). Given this fact, one might wish to analyse the structure of 6.19–34 in this fashion:

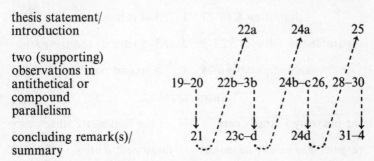

thesis statement/ introduction		22a	24a	25
two (supporting) observations in antithetical or compound parallelism	19–20 22b–3b	24b–c	26, 28–30
concluding remark(s)/ summary	21 23c–d	24d	31–4

It would, however, be inadequate to leave matters at that. The true

625

key to discerning the arrangement of 6.19–34 is to be discovered in the resemblances the section shares with 7.1–12.

6.19–7.12 begins with an exhortation to gather treasures not on the earth but in heaven (6.19–21). This is followed by a parable about the eye (6.22–3) which is in turn followed by a second parable, that of the two masters (6.24). These three relatively short units are then followed by 6.25–34, an extended section which offers encouragement by reference to the care of the Father in heaven: despite what 6.19–24 might imply, there is no need to worry or be anxious about food or drink or clothing. What then of 7.1–12? It is the structural twin of 6.19–34. It, like 6.19–34, opens with an exhortation: do not judge (7.1–2). Then, continuing the theme, there is, as in 6.22–3, a parable about the eye, 7.3–5: why do you see the splinter that is in your brother's eye and not the log in your own? Next comes a second parable, that about giving holy things to dogs and casting pearls before swine (7.6). 7.1–6 is then succeeded by 7.7–11, a passage which, like 6.25–34, offers encouragement by reference to the care of the Father in heaven; ask and you will receive. 7.7–11 and 6.25–34 are also alike in that (1) both are based on arguments *a minori ad maius* ('If God so clothes the grass of the field . . . will he not much more clothe you'; 'If you, then, being evil, know how to give good gifts to your children, how much more will your Father in heaven give good gifts to those who ask him'); (2) both have been constructed around key words that are repeated five times (μεριμνάω in 6.25, 27–8, 31, and 34; αἰτέω in 7.7, 8, 9, 10, and 11); and (3) both use two major illustrations to make their respective cases (the birds of the air and the lilies of the field, the son who asks his father for bread and the son who asks his father for fish). The structure of 6.19–7.12 may, it follows, be set forth thus:

Instruction

exhortation 6.19–21	1	7.1–2 exhortation
parable (on the eye) 6.22–3	2	7.3–5 parable (on the eye)
second parable 6.24	3	7.6 second parable

Encouragement

the heavenly Father's care 6.25–34	the heavenly Father's care 7.7–11
(argument *a minori ad maius*)	(argument *a minori ad maius*)

7.12—the golden rule

Two additional comments are in order. (1) 6.25–34 and 7.7–11
distinguish themselves from the rest of the sermon on the mount.
Between the opening beatitudes (5.3–12) and the closing warnings
(7.13–27) the disciples are constantly bombarded by
uncompromising demands. Respite comes only in two places, in
6.25–34 and 7.7–11—these two places being also the only two to
break Matthew's triadic patterns. Admittedly, even in 6.25–34 and
7.7–11 there are imperatives. But μὴ μεριμνᾶτε really means, as the
context shows, 'You need not worry at all'. Similarly, αἰτεῖτε does
not hang heavy upon the readers' shoulders; instead it introduces
good news: 'it shall be given you'. So 6.25–34 and 7.7–11 proffer
encouragement. They are inserted because of Matthew's pastoral
concern. He knows how hard the instruction delivered in Mt 5–7
really is and therefore how much need there is to be reminded of
the Father in heaven who gives good gifts to his children.

(2) If one asks about the theme common to 6.19–34 and 7.1–12,
an answer is easily returned. The issue of 6.19–34, What should I
do with and about wealth?, and that of 7.1–12, How should I treat
my neighbour?, are both about life in the temporal, 'secular'
world. This means that 6.19–7.12 deals with what may be called
'social issues'. The appropriateness of this cannot be missed.
Having received in 5.17–48 instruction on the Torah and in 6.1–18
on the cult, the true disciple next learns in 6.19–7.12 how to behave
in the world at large. The comprehensive nature of the sermon on
the mount is thereby indicated.

(ii) *Sources*

All of the material in Mt 6.19–34 (save the redactional 34) appears in
Luke.

Matthew	Mark	Luke
6.19–21	—	12.33–4
6.22–3	—	11.34–6
6.24	—	16.13
6.25–33	—	12.22–31
6.34 (redactional)	—	—

Three explanations for the data present themselves. (1) Matthew and
Luke depend upon a common source, oral or written (Q). (2) Luke has
used Matthew (the Griesbach hypothesis). (3) Matthew has used Luke.
The third option is hardly to be endorsed because of the utter dearth of
Lukanisms in Mt 6.19–34 and the lack of evidence in general for
Matthew's employment of Luke. The Griesbach hypothesis is likewise to
be rejected. While Mt 6.19–21 does seem to be more original over against
Lk 12.33–4, vocabulary statistics and other considerations show, as we
shall see, that Luke is more original for much of the remaining parallel

material (see e.g. on 6.22–3, 26, 33). In addition, with the exception of the word, 'little faith', in Mt 6.30 = Lk 12.28, Luke contains nothing that could be considered characteristically Matthean. Particularly noteworthy in this connexion is the absence in Lk 12.31 of Matthew's πρῶτον and δικαιοσύνην and the absence in Lk 12.24 and 30 of Matthew's ὁ πατὴρ ὑμῶν ὁ οὐράνιος. Mt 6.19–34, it follows, is not the source of Lk 11.34–6; 12.22–34; or 16.13. Does this then mean that both Matthew and Luke here depend upon Q? Or are we to think of several common sources? One's answer will probably depend upon whether one thinks that the arguments for the literary unity of Q are sufficiently strong. Three observations may, nevertheless, be made. (1) The verbal agreement between Mt 6.24 and Lk 16.13 is nearly perfect. Twenty-seven out of twenty-eight words are shared, and they appear in precisely the same order. This would seem to indicate a common, written source. (2) In the verse-by-verse commentary we have had no difficulty explaining the differences between Matthew and Luke as redactional modifications of the same source. (3) The disagreement in order between the material shared by Matthew and Luke does not disallow a common use of Q. The Lukan order could be that of Q, the Matthean order completely secondary and to be accounted for by Matthew's desire to bring together in his great sermon programmatic statements regarding earthly goods (so V. Taylor, *Essays*, pp. 95–118). On the other hand, perhaps neither Matthew nor Luke preserves the order of Q. This is the position of D. R. Catchpole ('Q and "the Friend at Midnight" ', *JTS* 34 (1983), pp. 407–24). In his judgement, one section of Q ran this way:

Matthew	Luke
6.7–8	—
6.9–13	11.2–4
7.7	11.5–9
7.8	11.10
7.9–11	11.11–13
6.25–33	12.22–31

There is, of course, no proving this conjecture. Yet Catchpole does raise the possibility that Luke's order, no less than Matthew's, was dictated by redactional interests.

(iii) *Exegesis*

TREASURE ON THE EARTH/TREASURE IN HEAVEN (6.19–21).

19. Jas 5.2–3, which may well be based upon the saying preserved in Mt 6.19–21, reads: 'Your riches have rotted (σέσηπεν) and your garments are motheaten (σητόβρωτα). Your gold and silver have rusted (κατίωται) and their rust (ἰός) will be evidence against you and will eat your flesh like fire. You have laid up treasure (ἐθησαυρίσατε) for the last days'. Note also Ecclus 29.10–11: 'Lose your silver for the sake of a brother or a friend, and do not let it rust (ἰωθήτω) under a stone and be lost. Lay up your treasure (θὲς τὸν θησαυρόν) according to the commandments of the Most High, and it will profit you more than gold'.

μὴ θησαυρίζετε ὑμῖν θησαυροὺς ἐπὶ τῆς γῆς. According to Clement of Alexandria, *Strom.* 3.12, some early Christians understood treasuring up treasure on earth to refer to procreation. For θησαυρίζω . . . θησαυρούς see Mic 6.10 LXX. θησαυρός (usually for *'ôṣār* in the LXX) is, according to Jastrow, s.v., *tisbārā'*, of Semitic origin. Note that instead of ὑμῖν one expects the reflexive, but Hebrew and Aramaic pronominal suffixes do not allow the distinction between personal and reflexive (cf. *MHT* 4, p. 36).

The word statistics[1] might lead one to believe that 6.19a, which has no Lukan parallel, is redactional. The issue is more complex. 6.19 is the antithesis of 6.20 ('Treasure up treasure in heaven . . .'), and 6.20, as we shall argue below, is more original *vis-à-vis* Lk 12.33. This means that the vocabulary of 6.19a was already present in the tradition, in 20a. Further, in material Matthew has taken over from Mark, he has not constructed any new antithetical parallelisms. There is, then, reason to believe that 6.19a, indeed all of 19, stood in Q.

ὅπου σὴς καὶ βρῶσις ἀφανίζει. Like the happiness it brings, earthly treasure is only for a season; it is destined to pass away. ὅπου serves to indicate that the true value of any treasure can be determined by its location: is it in heaven or on earth? ἀφανίζω (Mt: 3) occurs elsewhere in the NT only in Acts 13.41. See further on 6.16. διαφθείρει (cf. Lk 12.33) may have stood in Q (although see on 6.20). σής (Mt: 2; Lk: 1; nowhere else in the NT) is the 'moth', whose larvae eat clothing (BAGD, s.v.; cf. the biblical and rabbinic *sās*, which sounds so similar). In the biblical tradition the moth destroys that which is feeble: Job 4.19; 13.28; Isa 33.1 LXX; 50.9; 51.8; Hos 5.12; Ecclus 19.3; 42.13. βρῶσις (Mt: 2; Mk: 0; Lk: 0; usually for a form of *'kl* in the LXX) is a problem. Although typically it means 'eating' (Rom 14.17) or 'food' (Jn 6.27), 'decay' is also an attested meaning (Galen 6.422; 12.879). So many, encouraged by the parallel in Jas 5.2–3 (where moth and rust (ἰός) appear together), have here translated 'rust' (e.g. Tyndale, RSV, NEB). Still, the issue is not resolved so readily. In Mal 3.11 LXX A, the word means 'grasshopper'. And in Ep. Jer. 10 v.1., βρῶσις is found with ἰός and hendiadys is doubtful (so BAGD, s.v., βρῶσις).

[1] θησαυρίζω: Mt: 2; Mk: 0; Lk: 1. θησαυρός: Mt: 9; Mk: 1; Lk: 4. ἐπὶ (τῆς) γῆς: Mt: 11; Mk: 10; Lk: 5.

Thus Mt 6.19 may have to do with two different insects. If so, costly textiles are in view (cf. 6.28–30). Gos. Thom. 76, which here does not appear to depend upon the synoptics, offers confirmation: 'Do you also seek for the treasure which fails not, which endures, there where no moth (*jooles*) comes near to devour and no worm (*fnt*) destroys'. Note also LAB 40.6, which links the destructive moth with the spoiling worm.

καὶ ὅπου κλέπται διορύσσουσιν καὶ κλέπτουσιν. Compare Lk 12.33. Destruction by nature (19b) is now joined to destruction by human beings (19c), with the result that treasures treasured upon the earth are assailed from every direction. The picture is of a thief breaking through the mud brick wall of a house (cf. Ezek 12.5, 7; Mt 24.43) in order to steal the wealth there vainly hidden for safe-keeping. If such is the fate of earthly treasure, if it can be destroyed or taken away, how can the wise individual rely upon it? Can it ever be really owned? Money is 'a matter insecure' (Menander, *Dyskolos*, frag.); 'prosperity is unstable' (Ps.-Phoc. 27); or, as Epictetus would have put it, wealth is an 'external' over which we do not have control. Fortune, the wheel of chance, is fickle, so 'it will never be sufficient just to notice what is under one's nose: prudence calculates what the outcome of things will be' (Boethius, *de Consolatione* 2.1). This is the prudence which Jesus, from an eschatological perspective, is demanding. Compare 1 En. 94.8; 97.8–10; 100.6; Lk 12.13–21.

The command not to store up treasure on earth should not be understood to entail the renunciation of all possessions. In the first place, the subject of 6.19 is 'treasure', not earthly goods in general. In the second place, the verb, 'to treasure', refers to accumulation, not simple possession. Finally, Matthew's attitude elsewhere is not one of unremitting hostility towards wealth (see on 4.18–22 and 6.24).

20. Compare Justin, *1 Apol.* 15. This sentence stands in perfect parallelism with 6.19:

Do not lay up for yourselves treasure on the earth			6.19a
but	lay up for yourselves treasure in	heaven	6.20a
where	moth and worm consume		6.19b
where neither moth nor worm consumes			6.20b
and where thieves	break in and steal		6.19c
and where thieves do not break in and steal			6.20c

We have already offered some evidence for supposing Mt 6.19–20 to be closer to Q than Lk 12.33. Our case is greatly reinforced by this fact: Lk 12.33 contains recognizably Lukan vocabulary.[2] We believe, then, that there is little reason to conjecture that Mt 6.19–20 and Lk 12.33 derive from different sources or are independent logia. Lk 12.33 is rather a redactional reformulation in line with Luke's characteristic praise for the sharing of possessions and wealth. See further W. Pesch (v).

θησαυρίζετε δὲ ὑμῖν θησαυροὺς ἐν οὐρανῷ, ὅπου οὔτε σὴς οὔτε βρῶσις ἀφανίζει καὶ ὅπου κλέπται οὐ διορύσσουσιν οὐδὲ κλέπτουσιν. Compare Mk 10.21 = Mt 19.21 = Lk 18.22. Luke has 'in the heavens'. This comes from Q since the Third Evangelist prefers the singular, 'heaven' (Lk: 29; Acts: 24) to the plural (Lk: 4; Acts: 2). Matthew, who is more fond of the plural, has here chosen the singular to underline the parallel with 'on the earth' (cf. 6.10). For heaven as a place without corruption see T. Job 33.4–5.

The notion of a heavenly treasure, beyond the reach of corruption, was a common eschatological concept in Judaism. See Koch (v). The righteous on earth do not yet possess it, for it belongs to the future; nevertheless they can now add to it. Typical texts include Tob 4.8–9 ('If you have many possessions, make your gift from them in proportion; if few, do not be afraid to give according to the little you have. So you will be laying up a good treasure (θησαυρίζεις) for yourself against the day of necessity'); Ps. Sol. 9.5 ('He that does righteousness layeth up (θησαυρίζει) for himself life with the Lord'); and 2 Bar. 24.1 ('For behold! the days come and the books shall be opened in which are written the sins of all those who have sinned, and again also the treasures in which the righteousness of all those who have been righteous in creation is stored'). Compare Ecclus 29.10–13; Philo, *Praem.* 104; Col 2.3; 4 Ezra 7.77; 2 Bar. 14.12; *m. Pe'a* 1.1; SB 1, pp. 430–1. In *b. B. Bat.* 11a these are the words of King Monobaz: 'My fathers stored up below and I am storing above. . . . My fathers stored in a place which can be tampered with, but I have stored in a place which cannot be tampered with. . . . My fathers stored something which produces no fruits, but I have stored something which does produce fruits. . . . My fathers gathered treasures of money, but I have gathered treasures of souls. . . . My fathers gathered for this world, but I have gathered for the world to come . . .'. In T. Job 33, Job, who has nothing on earth left to his name, is nonetheless content because his throne—that is, his treasure—is 'in the heavens'. Allen (p. 61) cited a Buddhist parallel: 'Let the wise man do righteousness; a treasure that others cannot share, which no thief can steal; a treasure which passeth not away'.

For διορύσσουσιν Luke has ἐγγίζει, and this may well be original. Compare Gos. Thom. 76: 'where no moth comes near' (*thno ehoun*). If Luke is in fact original, it is the more likely that assonance characterized the Semitic original, for 'draw near' could be *qěrēb*, 'moth' could be *rûqbā*, 'destroy' could be *rěqāb*, and 'worm' could be *raqqābā*. (Does one interpretation of *rqb'* = 'worm' or 'rust' stand behind Jas 5.2–3, another behind the synoptics?)

---

[2] ὑπάρχοντα: Mt: 3; Mk: 0; Lk: 8. διαφθείρω: Mt: 0; Mk: 0; Lk: 1; the related διαφθορά occurs six times in Acts, nowhere else in the NT. ἐλεημοσύνη: Mt: 3; Mk: 0; Lk: 2; Acts: 8. βαλλάντιον: Mt: 0; Mk: 0; Lk: 3.

Both heaven and the kingdom of God could be spoken of as treasure (cf. Mt 13.44; Gos. Thom. 109; T. Job. 26.3); and no doubt for Matthew as for Jesus before him, treasure stood not for specific rewards for specific acts but rather conjured up the kingdom of God and all its blessings (see further on 6.21).

Although there is in 6.19–21 no explanation of how to store up treasure in heaven, this lack is more than made up by the broader context, Mt 5–7. Those who are rewarded by the Father in heaven are those named by the beatitudes (5.3–12), those who practise their piety in secret (6.1), those who give alms in secret (6.4), those who pray in secret (6.6), those who fast in secret (6.18), and those who love their neighbour as themselves (7.12). Such people know that 'Whatever is now is nothing, but that which shall be is very great' (2 Bar. 44.8).

21. ὅπου γάρ ἐστιν ὁ θησαυρός σου, ἐκεῖ ἔσται καὶ ἡ καρδία σου.[3] In Lk 12.34 ὑμῶν replaces σου, and ἔσται is placed at the end. Matthew may have used σου, despite the plural imperatives in 19 and 20, because σου is what he has used in the surrounding verses (17, 18, 22, 23)—even though the same argument could be used to explain the ὑμῶν in Luke (cf. 12.30, 31, 32, 35, 36, 37). Matthew probably moved the verb forward to enhance the parallelism between 21a and b:

ὅπου . . . ἐστιν   ὁ θησαυρός σου
ἐκεῖ   ἔσται καὶ ἡ καρδία σου

The meaning of 6.21, which supplements 6.19–20 by focusing upon the source of one's deeds, 'the heart' (see on 5.8), becomes evident when it is reversed: where your heart is, there will your treasure be also. To have one's heart or mind[4] set on the things above, not on the things below (cf. Col 3.2), is to store up treasure in heaven, where neither moth nor worm destroys and where thieves do not break in and steal. A heart or mind directed towards heaven, and therefore acting in accordance with heaven's will, shall find its reward in heaven (cf. 5.8). In this way one's treasure tells the tale of one's heart. A person is worth what the object of his heart is worth. Compare Sextus, *Sent.* 316 (ὅπου σου τὸ φρονοῦν ἐκεῖ σου τὸ ἀγαθόν) and Epictetus, *Diss.* 2.22.19 (ὅπου γὰρ ἂν τὸ

---

[3] Under Lukan influence and because of the verb forms in 6.19 and 20 (second person plural), L W Θ 0233 *f*¹·¹³ Maj f sy bo^pt have twice substituted υμων for σου.—Despite the very weak attestation (B bo^ms), the omission of καί before ἡ καρδία is conceivable. καί slightly disrupts the parallelism between 6.21a and b. On the other hand, καί could easily have been accidentally omitted after ἔσται.

[4] In the biblical tradition, as in Buddhism, the heart and mind are not distinct realities. The heart is a knowing vessel. Cf. Exod 7.23; 28.3; Deut 4.9; 7.17; 1 Kgs 3.9; 2 Bar. 20.3. Note that, in their versions of Mt 6.21, Justin, *1 Apol.* 15, and Clement of Alexandria, *Strom.* 7.12, have substituted 'mind' for 'heart' (cf. Auth. Teach. 6.28.22–6).

ἐγὼ καὶ τὸ ἐμόν, ἐκεῖ ἀνάγκη ῥέπειν τὸ ζῷον). For further discussion of parallels see W. Pesch (v), pp. 361–6.

Concerning ὅπου . . . ἐκεῖ, the where/there form is common in the Jewish wisdom tradition; see W. Zimmerli, 'Zur Struktur der alttestamentlichen Weisheit', *ZAW* 10 (1933), p. 185, and note Job 39.30; Mt 18.20; 24.28. On γάρ as a connective see BAGD, s.v., 4.

The origin of 6.21 is uncertain. Bultmann, *History*, p. 84, judged it to be an independent gnomic saying which was not originally attached to 6.19–20 (cf. Schweizer, *Matthew*, p. 162). Admittedly, Jas. 5.2–5 does allude only to 6.19–20: there is no parallel to 6.21. Still, we hesitate to follow Bultmann's judgement. Without 6.21, 6.19–20 is hardly memorable. In itself it only expresses a commonplace, as the parallels collected above demonstrate. Hence it makes more sense to see 6.19–20 as preparatory, as having its focus on 6.21, which would therefore be original in this context (cf. W. Pesch (v), pp. 368–9; Guelich, p. 328). What, then, of the authenticity of 6.19–21 as a whole? (1) There is evidence of a Semitic original (see on 6.20). (2) The verses express an attitude towards wealth consistent with what we know of Jesus (see on 6.24). (3) 6.19–21 presupposes an eschatological view of things: this earth is passing away, so it only makes sense to treasure up treasure in heaven. This coheres with the eschatological orientation of Jesus' proclamation. (4) Jesus was apparently fond of antithetical parallelism (cf. Jeremias, *Theology*, pp. 14–20). (5) The component parts of 16.19–20 have parallels in traditions widely regarded as dominical. For the folly of trusting wealth see Lk 12.16–21. For thieves in illustrations and parables see Mk 3.27; 11.17; Lk 10.30, 36. For heavenly treasure see Mk 10.21; Lk 12.21; 16.11.

Although, in view of the five considerations listed, we should return an affirmative answer to the issue of authenticity (see also W. Pesch (v), pp. 369–71), we cannot, unfortunately, now determine whether 6.19–21 was first spoken to insiders (as in Matthew and Luke) or towards would-be disciples.

6.19–21 and the Lukan parallel seem clearly to involve the idea of a reward: there is treasure in heaven. It has recently been argued that the concept of reward had no place in the teaching of Jesus (so Breech, pp. 46–9; for this reason alone he dismisses the authenticity of 6.19–21). Jesus' view was allegedly like that of the Sufic mystic, Rabi'a, who prayed, 'If I worship Thee in fear of hell, burn me in hell. And if I worship Thee in hope of Paradise, exclude me from Paradise; but if I worship Thee for Thine own sake, withhold not Thine everlasting beauty'.[5] What are we to make of this view, which was popular with some in a nineteenth-century Germany under Kantian influence? Despite the possible parallel supplied by the maxim of Antigonos of Socho ('Be not like servants who serve the master on condition of receiving a gift, but be like servants who serve the master not on condition of receiving'; *m. 'Abot* 1.3), it is hardly satisfactory. It involves supposing, first, that Jesus' opinion on this matter was grotesquely misrepresented by the early church, for the synoptic

[5] As found in A. Huxley, *The Perennial Philosophy*, London, 1945, p. 102.

tradition is full of eschatological promises and their corollary, eschatological threats; secondly, that texts such as Mt 6.19–21, which would otherwise be considered dominical, are in fact not; and, thirdly, that even though Jesus rejected the almost universally accepted concept of eschatological reward, he apparently did not make his novel and controversial view explicit: for we do not find any synoptic saying which clearly excludes thinking in terms of rewards and punishments. All this is highly implausible. No, Jesus was neither a unitive mystic[6] nor an anticipatory disciple of Kant. He did not proclaim that the good should be done simply for its own sake, without thought or consequence. He did not preach: *Virtus sibi ipsi praemium*. Jesus the Jew was to this extent a realist: he acknowledged the human hope for happiness and promised its fulfilment in the kingdom of God; and he took human fear for granted and made it serve his proclamation, confronting his hearers with the possibility of a hellish hereafter. For him the issue was not whether there would or should be reward. For him the issue was: whose reward matters—man's or God's? Having, however, argued this much, we must hasten to add that in the synoptics the notion of reward is far from being a mathematical conception. Reward is in no way calculable, and it leaves no room either for religious egotism or for a claim on God. There is no thought of individual rewards for individual acts and no mechanical *do ut des*. Since love, which is the basis of reward (cf. Mt 25.31–46), is not quantifiable, judgement is not made with a scale or balances (contrast the picture in T. Abr. A 12–14). Indeed, the eschatological rewards or gifts are gratuitous, as the parable of the labourers in the vineyard (20.1–16) shows so well. Moreover, disciples are exhorted not to let their left hand know what their right hand is doing (Mt 6.3); and at the last judgement, the righteous will be taken by surprise, for when they clothed the naked and fed the hungry, they gave no thought to themselves (Mt 25.31–46). So despite his words about reward and punishment, Jesus discouraged people from measuring their religious achievements and calculating divine rewards. Lastly, the kingdom, which is itself reward (cf. Mt 25.34), is the kingdom *of God*. It cannot possibly be isolated from the deity. Indeed, as Bo Reicke especially has demonstrated, what is held forth as reward under different images—'kingdom', 'life', 'treasure'—is nothing other than communion with God and service before him; see 'The New Testament Concept of Reward', in *Aux sources de la tradition chrétienne*, Neuchâtel/Paris, 1950, pp. 195–206.[7]

[6] Despite the work of R. C. DeLamotte, *The Alien Christ*, Lanham, 1980.

[7] Also important for the subject of reward in the teaching of Jesus are the following: G. Bornkamm, *Der Lohngedanke im Neuen Testament*, Lüneburg, 1947; Cadoux, pp. 208–19; Jeremias, *Theology*, pp. 214–18; O. Michel, 'Der Lohngedanke in der Verkündigung Jesu', *ZST* 9 (1931), pp. 47–54; W. Pesch, *Der Lohngedanke in der Lehre Jesu*, Munich, 1955; H. Preisker and E. Würthwein, *TWNT* 4, pp. 699–736; Schnackenburg, *Moral Teaching*, pp. 151–60. For the rabbis see A. Marmorstein, *The Doctrine of Merits in the Old Rabbinical Literature*, London, 1920; Montefiore and Loewe, pp. 202–32; and Urbach 1, pp. 436–44. For Matthew see Mohrlang, pp. 48–71.

THE EYE IS THE LAMP OF THE BODY (6.22–3)

6.22–3 is where it is because Matthew has understood ὀφθαλμὸς ἁπλοῦς and ὀφθαλμὸς πονηρός to be related to the 'good eye' and the 'evil eye' of Jewish tradition. Those who have the former are generous (see on 6.22). Those who own the latter have not a generous bone in their bodies (see on 6.23 and 20.15). They are servants of mammon. They store up treasure only for themselves, and only on the earth.

22. ὁ λύχνος τοῦ σώματός ἐστιν ὁ ὀφθαλμός. Lk 11.34 adds σου, which may or may not be original. Pre-modern people tended to believe that the eyes contain a fire or light, and that this fire or light is what makes sight possible (see Allison (v)). Ancient Jews were no exception. They spoke of 'the light of the eyes' (Prov 15.30 MT; Tob 10.5; 11.13 א), of eyes becoming dimmed or darkened (Gen 27.1; 48.10; Deut 34.7; Lam 5.17; T. Benj. 4.2; Josephus, *Ant.* 8.268; *b. Ber.* 16b), and of God 'enlightening' or 'brightening' the eyes (Ezra 9.8; Bar 1.12; cf. 1 Sam 14.24–30 MT; T. Gad. 5.7; *b. Yeb.* 63a; *b. Meg.* 12b). They imagined that the eye was like the sun, both being senders of rays (2 Sam 12.11; Ecclus 23.19; 3 Bar. 8; Jos. Asen. 14.9), and they told stories in which the light or fire of the eyes actually became so intense that it was visible (Dan 10.6; Rev 1.14; 2.18; 19.12; 1 En. 106.2, 5, 10; 2 En. 1.5; 3 En. 1.7–8; 9.4; 25.2–3, 6–7; Par. Jer. 7.3; *b. B. Meṣ.* 59b; *b. Šabb.* 33b).

For the eye as a lamp, see Empedocles, frag. 84 (= D.-K. I, 342.4–9 [31 B 84]); Dan 10.6; Zech 4; T. Job. 18.3; 2 En. 42.1 A; 3 En. 35.2; *b. Šabb.* 151b. (cf. Theocritus, *Idylls* 24.18–19; Theophrastus, *De sensu* 26, quoting Alcmaeon; Aristotle, *De sensu* 437a 22–6).

The vast majority of commentators have understood Mt 6.22–3 to mean that the eyes are like a window: light enters the body through the eye. This interpretation is anachronistic. It wrongly takes for granted a modern understanding of vision. Only since about A.D. 1500 in the West has the intromission theory of vision been universally adopted; and the usual reading of our text cannot be correct, for the following reasons. (1) Not only do ancient Jewish texts reflect the conviction that the eye contains its own light, but in T. Job 18.3 this notion is brought into connexion with the eye/lamp simile.[8] (2) A lamp is not a medium through which light from another source is channelled to an otherwise dark place. A lamp is rather its own source of light. From this alone it follows that the eye/lamp comparison would be natural only for one holding an extramission theory of vision. In line with this, in the

---

[8] We accept the emended text of R. A. Kraft, *The Testament of Job*, Missoula, 1974, p. 40: οἱ ἐμοὶ ὀφθαλμοὶ τοὺς λύχνους ποιοῦντες ἔβλεπον. Kraft translates: 'My eyes, acting as lamps, searched out'. Cf. Allison (v), p. 82, n. 27.

six Jewish texts which liken the eye to a lamp, namely, in Dan 10.6; Zech 4; T. Job 18.3; 2 En. 42.1A; 3 En. 35.2; and *b. Šabb.* 151b, the comparison never has to do with the eye conveying light to the inward parts. On the contrary, *in all six instances it is used to create the picture of a light coming forth from the eye.* This is telling. (3) If Mt 6.22–3 be interpreted as it usually is, the paraenetic conclusion, 'So watch, lest the light within you be darkness!' (so Q), makes little sense. On the intromission theory, what one sees depends solely upon the eye, whether it be good or bad, whether it lets light in or not; the light of day is a given, a constant. Yet in our paraenetic conclusion, there is no exhortation to keep or produce an ὀφθαλμὸς ἁπλοῦς or to avoid gaining an ὀφθαλμὸς πονηρός. The eye is not mentioned at all. Concern is instead expressed about the light within. Thus this, and not the eye, must be the crucial factor—as it would be on the extramission theory of vision. (4) Lk 11.36 appears to be an early addition to the parable about the eye as lamp; it may even have been added before translation into Greek (see Allison (v)). As it stands, the Greek of this verse is most vexing, and one has difficulty seeing the point. But C. C. Torrey made sense of the words by arguing for an Aramaic original that was imperfectly translated into Greek. According to him, Jesus himself said, 'If however your whole body is lighted up with no part dark, then all about you will be light, just as the lamp lights you with its brightness' (*Four Gospels*, p. 309). The key to this reconstruction is the supposition that ἔσται φωτεινὸν ὅλον 'renders (incorrectly) *nahīr leh'we kōllā.* This last word, rendered correctly as the adjective in the first clause, is here unquestionably the noun, "the whole, everything". The man who is full of light lights the world about him' (ibid). Now it is hardly possible to show beyond reasonable doubt that Torrey—who was followed by T. W. Manson (*Sayings*, pp. 93–4)—was correct in his conjecture. Nevertheless the result is a sentence which recalls other lines in the Jesus tradition (e.g. Mt 5.14–16 and Gos. Thom. 24). So Torrey may very well have been on the mark. If so, then at least the earliest interpreter of the saying about the eye as lamp, that is, the author of Lk 11.36, understood Jesus' words in terms of the extramission theory of vision. This is so because it is natural to judge the sentence, 'If however your whole body is lighted up with no part dark, then all about you will be light . . .', as an extension of the eye as lamp metaphor. Just as the healthy, good eye sends light into the world, so too do the righteous, filled with the light of God, dispel the shades around them. They are like a lamp that gives light to its environment. Which is to say: *the picture is not of light coming in but of light going out.* (5) Clement of Alexandria seems to have read our passage as involving the extramission theory of vision. In *Paed.* 3.11.70 there is this: 'the lamp of the body is the eye, Scripture says, δι' οὗ καταφαίνεται τὰ ἔνδον φωτὶ τῷ φαινομένῳ καταυγαζόμενα'. These words appear in the context of a discussion about lust, and the specific subject is how one's eye can affect others by its appearance.

ἐὰν οὖν ᾖ ὁ ὀφθαλμός σου ἁπλοῦς ὅλον τὸ σῶμά σου φωτεινὸν ἔσται.[9] Lk 11.34b–c (ὅταν ὁ ὀφθαλμός σου ἁπλοῦς ᾖ καὶ ὅλον τὸ σῶμά σου φωτεινόν ἐστιν) is probably closer to Q. Matthew shows a greater fondness for ἐάν than the other synoptic writers (Mt: 65; Mk: 34; Lk: 29) while at the same time he has sometimes dropped ὅταν, as in 13.19–20 = Mk 4.15–16; 13.32 = Mk 4.32; 17.9 = Mk 9.9; and 22.20 = Mk 12.25. Beyond this, ἐὰν οὖν is unique in the synoptics to Matthew (5.19, 23; 6.22; 24.26). As to whether Matthew's ἔσται or Luke's ἐστίν reproduces Q, it is impossible to say.

Most commentators assume without reflection that Matthew's ἐάν and Luke's ὅταν introduce a supposition which implies nothing as to the fulfilment of that supposition, and further that, as with most conditional sentences, the realization of the protasis would entail the realization of the apodosis. On this reading, an ὀφθαλμὸς ἁπλοῦς makes the body full of light. Is this true? The proposed interpretation harmonizes nicely with the common understanding of Mt 6.22–3, according to which the eyes are a channel for and therefore, in a sense, a source of, the light that enters the body. We have, however, already seen that this interpretation cannot be upheld. So what are we to make of the statement, 'When your eye is ἁπλοῦς, your whole body is full of light'?

There is a type of conditional sentence in which the causal condition is found not in the protasis but in the apodosis, and in which the protasis names the effect. One example of this sentence type is the saying attributed to Jesus in Mt 12.28: 'But if I by the Spirit of God cast out demons, then the kingdom of heaven has come upon you'. It is, obviously, not Jesus' exorcisms which have caused the arrival of the kingdom of God. On the contrary, the arrival of the kingdom of God explains the striking success of Jesus' battle against the demonic hordes. The exorcisms are a sign, a pointer. A paraphrase makes the logic of Mt 12.28 evident: 'But if I by the Spirit of God cast out demons, then this is because the kingdom of heaven has come upon you'. Instead of 'this is because', one could also insert, 'it shows that'. What we have before us is a sentence in which the protasis states not a true condition but an effect that depends upon and hence implies or shows to be true what the apodosis expresses. Other instances

[9] ουν is omitted by ℵ *pc* lat sy^c mae bo^{ms} Aug.

include Num 16.29; 1 Kgs 22.28; Prov 24.10 MT; Mt 12.26; Jn 9.41; Rom 7.20; 8.9b; and 14.15.

Mt 6.22–3 = Lk 11.34–6 offers one more illustration of this type of sentence. 'When your eye is ἁπλοῦς your whole body will be full of light' does not mean, a good eye creates inner light. This could only be the case if an intromission theory of vision were being presupposed. It is not. 'When your eye is ἁπλοῦς your whole body will be full of light' means, a good eye is evidence of inner light; when there is a good eye, this is because there is light within; to have a good eye is to be full of light, for the condition of the former is the existence of the latter. As in Mt 12.28 = Lk 11.20, in Mt 6.22–3 = Lk 11.34–6 the state signalled by the apodosis accounts for the state signalled by the protasis.

ἁπλοῦς has several possible meanings. For our purposes these fall into basically two categories: the ethical and the physical. If ἁπλοῦς be an ethical term, as in Job 1.1 Aq.; Barn. 19.2; T. Levi 13.1; and Ps.-Phoc. 50, then it means 'single' (= 'single-minded', 'sincere', 'undivided')[10] or—and this is more probable, as ὀφθαλμὸς ἁπλοῦς is the antithesis of ὀφθαλμὸς πονηρός, a fixed expression for a grudging or selfish spirit—it means 'generous',[11] and the Jewish notion of a 'good eye' (ʿayin ṭôbâ) probably lies in the background.[12] If, on the other hand, ἁπλοῦς be taken to refer to a physical state, as in Damascius, Isid. 16, ὀφθαλμὸς ἁπλοῦς must signify an eye that functions properly or is in good health (so BAGD, s.v.). Are we compelled, however, to choose between an ethical and a physical signification?

The question is not resolved by supposing that the Aramaic original must have been less ambiguous. According to both SB 1, p. 431, and E. Sjöberg (v), p. 97, ἁπλοῦς in all likelihood translates šĕlîm. Now this word was used of unblemished animals, of animals without defect, of animals ready for sacrifice, and the dictionaries include as one of its meanings 'uninjured', 'healthy'. But this same word was also sometimes employed to describe a virtuous man, as in b. Meg. 23a (see further BDB, s.v.; Jastrow, s.v.). Thus ʿayin šĕlîmâ might equally have referred to a healthy eye or, recalling the 'good eye', to a generous, upright disposition. The ambiguity remains. (The objection that, if the meaning were generous, the antithesis of ʿayin rāʿă, we should expect only ὀφθαλμὸς ἀγαθός, fails because usage was flexible. For example, in b. Šabb. 74a, ʿayin yâpâ = 'beautiful eye' is found with the meaning of generous).

---

[10] This interpretation may lie behind Gos. Thom. 61: 'When he is the same he will be filled with light, but if he is divided, he will be filled with darkness'.

[11] See esp. Cadbury (v). For ἁπλοῦς and its cognates meaning 'generous' see Rom 12.8; 2 Cor 8.2; 9.11; Jas 1.5.

[12] For this see Prov 22.9; T. Iss. 3.4; m. 'Abot 2.19; m. Ter. 4.3; b. Soṭa 38b. In Prov 22.9, 'he that has a good eye' (MT) becomes, in the LXX, 'he that pities the poor'.

We have already seen how the opening statement, 'The eye is the lamp of the body', makes perfect sense as a picturesque way of expressing a pre-modern theory of vision, and we have also been able to comprehend the second clause as a statement about the physical eye. But Mt 6.22–3 undoubtedly has an ethical thrust, as its conclusion proves. Moreover, in 6.22c, ὀφθαλμὸς πονηρός certainly comes from the moral vocabulary of Judaism. So Mt 6.22–3 appears to be a cleverly constructed riddle which can be read on two different levels (cf. Gregory Nazianzen, *Epist.* 41). One first hears a (proverbial) statement which is taken to apply to the physical eye; but by the time the closing words ring out, one realizes that one has heard a statement about higher truths. So the listener is led to backtrack, to listen to the saying anew, to rethink the whole of what has been said. 'The eye is the lamp of the body' now becomes a spiritual truth: one's moral disposition correlates with a religious state, with the darkness or light within. And 'when your eye is ἁπλοῦς, your whole body will be full of light' now means: singleness of purpose or generosity requires inner light.[13]

What exactly is meant by φωτεινόν? In the OT God is said to dwell in light (Ps 104.2; Dan 2.22; Hab 3.3–4; cf. 1 En. 38.4: LAE 28.2; Jos. Asen. 6.3; LAB 12.9), to have light as his countenance (Ps 44.3; 89.15; 90.8; cf. Hab 3.4), and to give light to his people (Job 29.2–3; Ps 4.6; 18.28; 48.3; cf. 1QS 11.3; 2 Cor 4.6; 2 Bar. 38.1). Furthermore, although light is an eschatological hope (Isa 60.20; cf. Rev 21.23; 22.5), God's children are even now illuminated by the light of life (Ps 56.13). They have the light of wisdom (Hos 10.12 LXX). And they possess wisdom, which is light (Eccles 8.1; Wisd 7.10, 26). Indeed, the righteous are sometimes even called light (Isa 42.6; 49.6; cf. Mt 5.14; 1 En. 104.2; T. Levi 14.3; LAB 51.6; T. Job 31.5; 53.3)—and it is light which determines the direction of all their activities. They 'walk in the light of the Lord' (Isa 2.5). Compare T. Naph. 2.10: 'For if you bid the eye to hear, it cannot; so neither while you are in darkness can you do the works of light'. Right intent proceeds from the light within (cf. Augustine, *De serm. mont.* 2.13.45–6). Thus the person whose body is full of light or lighted up (φωτεινόν) shares the divine life and knows salvation (cf. Ps 27.1): God is with him. To be in darkness, on the other hand, is to be separated from God, to have one's soul darkened (cf. Job 18.5–6; 38.15; T. Job 43.5–6; T. Sol. 26.7). This is why hell, despite its fire, is a dark place (1QS 2.8; 1 En. 103.7; Mt 8.12; 22.13).

23. ἐὰν δὲ ὁ ὀφθαλμός σου πονηρὸς ᾖ, ὅλον τὸ σῶμά σου σκοτεινὸν ἔσται. Compare T. Benj. 4.2. Matthew has probably inserted 'your eye' to make the parallel with 22b all the closer. His ἐάν is also probably secondary and should be explained in like

---

[13] We have translated σῶμα as 'body'. But it, like the Aramaic *gûp* which lies behind it, could be translated, 'self'. Cf. Manson, *Sayings*, p. 93.

manner. It reinforces the parallel with 22b (where, as argued, ἐάν is presumably redactional). Luke's ἐπάν lays higher claim to originality (Mt: 1; Mk: 0; Lk: 2; Acts: 0). Matthew has affixed ὅλον, again to enhance the parallelism with 6.22.

'When your eye is bad, your whole body will be full of darkness' is true, on the extramission theory of sight, because when there is darkness within, there can be no vision. A 'sick eye'[14] is the result of an inner darkness. But there is more here than this. ὀφθαλμὸς πονηρός is recognizably an ethical term. Ancient Jewish texts often mention the 'impudent eye', the 'beguiling eye', and the 'evil eye': Deut 15.9; Prov 23.6; 28.22; Tob 4.7; Ecclus 14.8; 26.11; *m.* '*Abot* 2.9, 11; 5.19; SB 1, pp. 833–5. In all these places 'eye' seems to signify 'intent', and the three expressions in quotation marks mean much the same thing. What is involved is the antithesis of generosity: selfishness, covetousness, an evil and envious disposition, hatred of others. Compare Mt 20.15: 'Am I not allowed to do what I choose with what belongs to me? Or is your eye evil because I am good?' This last means, as the RSV translates, 'Or do you begrudge my generosity?' Mt 6.23a–b, accordingly, tells us that just as a 'good eye', a proper disposition towards others, is an effect of the light within, so similarly is a bad eye, that is, a selfish,ungenerous, miserly spirit, the companion of inner darkness. Or, to put it another way, while inner light leads to loving one's neighbour, inner darkness leads to illiberality and niggardliness. Compare 1QS 4.9–11, where the sons of darkness are said to have greedy minds and blindness of eye.

εἰ οὖν τὸ φῶς τὸ ἐν σοὶ σκότος ἐστίν, τὸ σκότος πόσον. If one is not filled with divine illumination, a vacuum is created; light, having left, leaves only empty darkness. Compare T. Gad 5.1: 'Hatred . . . turns light into darkness . . .' (cf. Job 10.22; Asc. Isa. 8.21).

Luke also has τὸ φῶς τὸ ἐν σοὶ σκότος ἐστίν. But whereas in Matthew there is an exclamation (εἰ οὖν . . . τὸ σκότος πόσον), in Luke there is an admonition (σκόπει οὖν μή . . .). Luke probably preserves Q. (1) Matthew uses εἰ (ἐάν) + οὖν more than any other synoptic author (Mt: 7; Mk: 0; Lk: 4). (2) The word count for 'darkness' points weakly towards the first evangelist: Mt: 6; Mk: 1; Lk: 4. (3) πόσος (Mt: 8; Mk: 6; Lk: 6) is redactionally inserted in 10.25 and 12.12.

'If then the light within you is darkness, how great is that darkness!' With this paradoxical exclamation the parable passes from the theoretical to the personal: γνῶθι σεαυτόν. The listener is called to self-examination. Am I filled with light or with darkness? Is my eye good, or is it bad? These queries, raised by the paraenetic

---

[14] For πονηρός used of a sick eye see BAGD, s.v., citing Plato, *Hipp. Min.* 374D. For the meaning 'ill' see Plato, *Prot.* 313A.

conclusion of Mt 6.22–23, make it evident that our passage belongs to a distinct class of synoptic logia, the class of those sayings that move one to ponder the relation between outward acts and inward states. See Lk 6.43–4 = Mt 7.16–20; 12.33; Lk 6.45 = Mt 12.34–5; Mt 23.27 (cf. Lk 11.44); Mk 7.15–23. The proof of right religion resides in deeds, for that which is within is the source of that without ('faith without works is dead'). This is why the ὀφθαλμὸς ἁπλοῦς and inner light are found together and why the ὀφθαλμὸς πονηρός and inner darkness entail one another.

Mt 6.22–3 = Lk 11.34–5 is undoubtedly an authentic saying of Jesus, for five good reasons. (1) Retranslation into Aramaic or Hebrew is possible (see Sjöberg (v), Allison (v)). (2) The passage contains nothing distinctively Christian. Clear signs of post-Easter influence are wholly absent. There is no Christology, either explicit or implicit. (3) Reflections upon the correlation between inner disposition and outward acts must be regarded as characteristic of Jesus. (4) Mt 6.22–3 is at the same time a riddle and a parable, and Jesus, needless to say, sometimes spoke in riddles and liked parabolic forms. (5) As already observed (section (i)), 6.24 and 6.22–3 have precisely the same formal structure. Granted the dominical origin of the former (see below), one must incline to accept the dominical origin of the latter.

SERVING TWO MASTERS (6.24)

24. The Greek of Lk 16.13 (which concludes the parable of the shrewd manager) agrees perfectly with Mt 6.24, except that Luke, after οὐδείς, has οἰκέτης (a synoptic *hapax legomenon*; cf. Acts 10.7). If this word is a Lukan insertion, then the Gospel of Thomas would appear to show dependence (whether direct or indirect) upon the Third Gospel, for it has: 'It is impossible for a servant to serve two masters' (47). But if one believes, on other grounds, that the Gospel of Thomas is independent of the synoptics, this would imply that Luke has preserved Q and that Matthew or Q^{mt} dropped the word, 'servant'.

The parable in Mt 6.24—which is the foundation text for Origen, *C. Cels.* 8—is admirably suited to its present context, for the two masters can be closely related to the two eyes of 6.22–3 and to the two treasures of 6.19–21. Those who serve God lay up treasure in heaven and will certainly have a good eye (= be generous). Those who serve mammon store up treasure only on the earth and will have a bad eye (= be ungenerous).

οὐδεὶς δύναται δυσὶ κυρίοις δουλεύειν. Compare Rom 6.16. This statement is not, strictly speaking, true. For instances of one person serving two masters see Acts 16.16; Dio Chrysostom 66.13; *m. Pesaḥ.* 8.1; *m. Giṭ.* 4.5; *t. Yeb.* 9.2. But the point is really another, namely, that one cannot serve two masters well, giving each his due, because their demands will not always be compatible. This is true above all when the masters are God and mammon. For God, who demands self-sacrifice, commands an exclusive allegiance and obligation which must transcend all other claimants for a person's soul; while mammon, once it has its hooks in human flesh, will drag it where it wills, all the time whispering into the ear dreams of self-aggrandizement. The marching orders of God and of mammon are in entirely different directions.

In Gos. Thom. 47, 'No servant can serve two masters' is prefaced by this: 'It is impossible for a man to mount two horses and to stretch two bows . . .'. In this particular Thomas is not likely to be primitive, for the remainder of the saying in both the synoptics and Thomas presupposes only 'No servant can serve two masters'. Horses and bows do not link up with what follows.

The import of 6.24a is hardly novel, as the following texts, Jewish and non-Jewish, show: Plato, *Rep.* 8.555C ('It is impossible for the citizens of a city to honour wealth and at the same time acquire a proper amount of temperance; because they cannot avoid neglecting either the one or the other'); Philo, frag. 2.649 (see SB 1, p. 435: 'It is impossible for love of the world to coexist with the love of God . . .'); Poimandres 4.6b ('It is not possible, my son, to attach yourself both to things mortal and to things divine. . . . And he who wills to make his choice is left free to choose the one or the other. It is not possible to take both'); T. Jud. 18.6 (δυσὶ γὰρ πάθεσιν ἐναντίοις δουλεύειν καὶ θεῷ ὑπακοῦσαι οὐ δύναται). Also of interest is *Ruth Rab.* on 3.14: 'Man, while he lives, is the slave of two masters: the slave of his Creator and the slave of his inclination. When he does the will of his Creator he angers his inclination, and when he does the will of his inclination, he angers his Creator. When he dies, he is freed, a slave free from his master' (cf. *b. Ber.* 61a; *b.'Erub.* 18a).

ἢ γὰρ τὸν ἕνα μισήσει καὶ τὸν ἕτερον ἀγαπήσει. εἷς . . . ἕτερος is a Semitism (Black, p. 108). For 'love' and 'hate' as comparatives see Gen 29.30, 33; Deut 21.15; Mal 1.2–3; Mt 5.43; Lk 14.26; Jn 12.25. 'Love' and 'hate' refer not so much to emotions as to faithful labour: to love = to serve (cf. Jer 8.2). The synthetic parallelism is chiastic and triadic:

a. No one can *serve* two masters.
  b. For either he will *hate* the one
    c. and will *love* the other,
    c. or he will *be devoted to* the one
  b. and will *despise* the other.
a. You cannot *serve* God and mammon.

ἢ ἑνὸς ἀνθέξεται καὶ τοῦ ἑτέρου καταφρονήσει. ἀντέχομαι (lit., 'cling to'; NT: 4: Mt 6.24; Lk 16.13; 1 Th 5.14; Tit 1.9) here means 'be devoted to' (so BAGD, s.v.). Instead of ἀντέχομαι and καταφρονέω (which are never contrasted in the LXX), Gos. Thom.

47 has τιμάω and ὑβρίζω. ἀντέχομαι and τιμάω could be translation variants of *sĕbar*, καταφρονέω and ὑβρίζω of *bāsar* (note the resulting assonance).

οὐ δύνασθε θεῷ δουλεύειν καὶ μαμωνᾷ. This is the personal application of the parable, and the implication is patent: tear the mind away from worldly enticements and fix all attention on the Father in heaven. δουλεύω occurs in Matthew only here. μαμωνᾶς (Mt: 1; Lk: 3, nowhere else in the NT) is personified as a rival lord. The Greek transliterates *māmôn* or *māmônā*ʾ; see Ecclus 31.8 Hebrew; 1QS 6.2; 1Q27 a ii 5; CD 14.20; 11QtgJob on 27.17; Kahle's Cairo Genizah *Tg*. C on Gen 34.23; 1 En. 63.10; *m. ʾAbot* 2.12; *m. Sanh.* 4.1; *b. Ber.* 61b. The etymology is uncertain, although it is usually explained as deriving from ʾ*mn* = 'to trust', 'to believe in'. (Favouring this, there could be a pun in Lk 16.10–13 between mammon and πιστός and πιστεύω.) The word signifies 'resources', 'money', 'property', 'possessions' (cf. οὐσία, τὰ ὑπάρχοντα). It had, according to some scholars, already gained a pejorative connotation in first-century Judaism (so F. Hauck, *TWNT* 4, p. 391), but this is far from established (see Rüger (v)). 'Perhaps the early church left this Semitic loan-word untranslated because they regarded it almost as the name of an idol: the service of mammon is idolatry' (Hengel, *Property*, p. 24). According to Augustine, *De serm. mont.* 2.14.47, μαμωνᾶς (= *lucrum*) was Punic, and it is just possible that the doubled *m* in the Latin *mammona* (whence the English, 'mammon') is to be explained by Punic influence. The claim of a few nineteenth century scholars that mammon was a known (Syrian) deity (cf. Milton, *Paradise Lost* 1.679–80) has been roundly rejected.

Bultmann (*History*, pp. 87, 105) argued that Jesus himself could have uttered the proverbial 6.24a ('No one can serve two masters') but that the remainder of the saying must be regarded as secondary (cf. Schulz, *Q*, p. 460). There is little reason to agree. (1) 6.24 as a whole coheres well with the proclamation of Jesus (cf. Mk 10.17–22; Lk 12.13–21). (2) Signs of a Semitic original are present outside 24a ('mammon', εἷς . . . ἕτερος, the possibility of a translation variant in the Gospel of Thomas). (3) The manner in which mutually exclusive alternatives are set forth in hyperbolic fashion recalls other dominical sayings (e.g. Mk 8.35; 9.42–7).

Although we cannot herein present any systematic reflection on the problem of property and wealth in the teachings of Jesus, the following observations should be kept in mind.[15] (1) Many first-century Jews,

[15] Lit.: E. Bammel, *TWNT* 6, pp. 894–915; Goppelt 1, pp. 78–84; F. Hauck and W. Kasch, *TWNT* 6, pp. 318–32; Hengel, *Property and Riches* (with lit. on pp. 89–92); W. G. Kümmel, *Heilsgeschichte und Geschichte*, Marburg, 1965, pp. 271–7; Percy, pp. 89–106; Schnackenburg, *Moral Teaching*, pp. 121–32. On the economic situation in which Jesus found himself see S. Applebaum, 'Economic Life in Palestine', *CRINT* I/2, pp. 631–700; Freyne, pp. 155–207; F. C. Grant, *The*

including sages, no doubt believed prosperity to be a good thing (cf. Prov 10.15; 14.20; 19.15; Ecclus 10.30; 31.8), even a sign of divine favour (cf. Job 1.10; 42.10–17; T. Job 44.5; *b. Ned.* 38a). Yet (2) the criticism of riches had already been heard in the OT, especially in Amos: 2.6; 4.1; 5.10–12; 6.5–6; 8.4–8 (cf. Isa 1.22–3, 3.14–16, 24; 5.8–10; 10.1–3; 13.3–4; 31.5). Later, the apocalyptic tradition made vehement threats against the upper class (as in 1 En. 92–105); and at Qumran, where membership in the community required signing over all property (1QS 1.11–13; cf. 6.17, 22; Philo, *Omn. pro. lib.* 77), the wiles of money were well-known (CD 4.17; 6.15). (3) Individual charismatics or holy men who gave up possessions for religious reasons were not unknown in first-century Judaism. In having nowhere to lay his head (Mt 8.20), Jesus was scarcely alone. We need only recall John the Baptist and Josephus' account of the hermit Bannus (*Vita* 11). Even more telling are the traditions about the first-century Galilean, Ḥanina ben Dosa. He was reported to own next to nothing (*b. Ta'an.* 24b–25a), and, according to words attributed to R. Eleazar of Modi'im, Ḥanina was one of those who hated his own mammon, and even more the mammon of others (*Mek.* on Exod 18.21). It should further be remembered that many Greek and Hellenistic philosophers considered poverty an ideal. These words were put on Socrates' lips by Plato: 'I am in infinite poverty for the service of God' (*Apol.* 23C; cf. Xenophon, *Mem.* 1.2.1). See also Epictetus, *Diss.* 3.22.45–9 (on the true Cynic); Diogenes Laertius 4.16–17 (on Polemo); 6.13 (on Antisthenes). Apollonius of Tyana purportedly prayed, 'Oh Gods, give me to have little and to need nothing' (Philostratus, *VA* 1.33). (4) Jesus' free attitude towards possessions no doubt partly explains the sharing of possessions in the primitive Christian community (Acts 2.44; 4.32–5); and it is also plausible, as Theissen (*Sociology*) in particular has argued, that certain early Christians—itinerant charismatics from rural Syria-Palestine—, following their master's example, took Jesus' hard sayings about poverty, homelessness, and the rejection of family ties quite literally (cf. Eusebius, *H.E.* 6.3). (5) Despite, however, his harsh words about wealth and the radicalism of some early Christians, it is difficult to formulate for Jesus any law-like generalization as to what one must do with wealth. Over against the story of the rich young man in Mk 10.17–23, we find Jesus accepting the hospitality and support of those with wealth (Mk 2.13–17; 14.3–9, 12–16; Lk 7.36; 8.3; 10.38–42; 14.1) and drawing the criticism that he was a glutton and wine-bibber (Mt 11.19 = Lk 7.34). Moreover, his teaching as recorded in Mt 6.2–4; 25.31–46; and Lk 10.30–37 presupposes not the renunciation of all possessions but their proper use; and the parables of Jesus, so many of which have as their major characters landlords and landowners, masters and stewards, slaveowners and slaves, never once engage in polemic against the injustices of the economic system. So Jesus did not, apparently, set himself

---

Economic Background of the Gospels, Oxford, 1926; M. Hengel, 'Das Gleichnis von den Weingärtnern Mc 12:1–12, im Lichte der Zenonpapyri und der rabbinischen Gleichnisse', *ZNW* 59 (1968), pp. 1–39; Hoehner, pp. 65–79; Jeremias, *Jerusalem*, pp. 87–144; Klausner, pp. 174–92; H. Kreissig, *Die sozialen Zusammenhänge des judäischen Krieges*, Berlin, 1970.

to abolish private property or to redistribute wealth (cf. Mk 14.7), nor did he even demand that all who accepted his message share their goods in common (contrast Qumran). He did not proclaim, πᾶσι τὰ κτήματα ἁμαρτήματα (Ps.-Clem. Hom. 15.9). He did not affirm that all wealthy individuals must be rotten to the core with vices of all sorts. He did not teach that it is 'the possession of property as such that is the obstacle'— but rather 'only wealth that is becoming an idol' (Schnackenburg, *Moral Teaching*, p. 125). Voluntary poverty remained with him an earnest religious counsel delivered in the shadow of the eschatological crisis, not a blanket command. Perhaps Martin Hengel has best summed up Jesus' attitude towards poverty and riches: 'Jesus was not interested in any new theories about the rightness or wrongness of possessions in themselves, about the origin of property or its better distribution; rather he adopted the same scandalously free and untrammelled attitude to property as to the powers of the state, the alien Roman rule and its Jewish confederates. The imminence of the kingdom of God robs all these things of their power *de facto* . . .' (*Property*, p. 30).

THE HEAVENLY FATHER'S CARE (6.25–34)

According to Riesenfeld (v), the sayings contained in 6.25–33 were, in Q, adjacent to the sayings about treasuring up treasure (cf. Lk 12.22–34). This resulted in the bringing together of two themes, the first being the gathering of earthly treasure, the second the countering of anxiety. This is significant because, as Riesenfeld observes, the joining of these two themes occurs elsewhere in early Christian paraenesis, as in Mk 4.19; 1 Tim. 6.6–11; and Herm. v. 4.2.4–6 (cf. 1 Cor 7.31–3). Perhaps, then, the Q unit, Lk 12.22–34, was informed by a traditional association.

25. The sense of this and the following verses, which reaffirm a strong faith in providence, is well expressed by 1 Pet 5.7: 'Cast all your anxieties upon him, for he careth for you'. Note also Ps 127.2; Isa 32.17; Heb 13.5 ('Be content with what you have; for he has said, "I will never fail you nor forsake you" '). The idea of trusting God for everyday provisions is already to hand in the OT Jubilee legislation, where Israel is called to depend upon Yahweh's catering hand during the sabbath year fallow (Lev 25.18–24). Further, despite the scanty OT evidence, keeping of the sabbatical year, in which the fields were left uncultivated, was apparently widespread at the turn of the era (1 Macc 6.49, 53–4; 1QS 10.7–8; 1QM 2.6; Josephus, *Ant.* 11.338–43; 14.202–10; *m. Šebuʿot*),[16] so the notion of relying upon God for sustenance would have been quite familiar to ancient Jews. Compare Philo, *Spec. leg.* 2.198:

[16] Cf. S. Safrai, 'The Rechov Inscription', *Immanual* 8 (1978), pp. 48–57, and B. Z. Wacholder, 'The Calendar of Sabbatical Cycles during the Second Temple and the Early Rabbinic Period', *HUCA* 44 (1973), pp. 98–116.

'We have gladly received and are storing the boons of nature, yet we do not ascribe our preservation to any corruptible thing, but to God the Parent and Father and Saviour of the world and all that is therein, who has the power and right to nourish and sustain us by means of these or without these'. In *b. Beṣa* 16a, Hillel is purported to have quoted Ps 68.19 ('Blessed be the Lord, day by day') in support of his conviction that God would provide something worthy for the Sabbath. Significant too are the exodus traditions according to which Israel followed Moses into the wilderness without asking, How can we go into the desert without having provisions for the journey? The people simply believed in Moses and followed him; *Mek.* on Exod 14.15 and 15.22.

διὰ τοῦτο λέγω ὑμῖν. So Luke, where the connexion is with the parable of the rich fool (12.16–21). In Matthew the link is with 6.19–24, to wit: foreseeing a possible objection from the reader, namely, How can I eat and clothe myself if I whole-heartedly serve God and am relatively indifferent to mammon? (cf. the words of R. Simeon b. Yoḥai in *Mek.* on Exod 16.4), the appropriate response is now supplied. God looks after those who look to God, so those who serve him and not mammon need have no anxiety about life's basic necessities. 6.25–34 is a sort of gemara on 6.19–24.

'I say to you' (cf. 6.29), the many imperatives in 6.25–34, and the phrase, 'who among you', have been thought reason enough to assign the last part of Mt 6 to an early Christian prophet who drew upon wisdom traditions in exhorting his congregation (Schulz, *Q*, p. 153). But 'I say to you' was used by Jesus (Aune, pp. 164–5) as was 'who among you' (see on 6.27), and the presence of imperatives is hardly decisive evidence for a prophetic origin (cf. Boring, p. 168). It seems safer to regard 6.25–34 as preserving sayings of Jesus (26–30, 33), traditional proverbs (34a, 34b), and edifying expansions (25?, 31, 32?).

The διὰ τοῦτο shared by Matthew and Luke must come from Q, although the antecedent cannot now be determined with certainty. According to Catchpole's reconstruction (see section (i)), 6.25–33 originally followed 7.11, which ends with, 'how much more will your heavenly Father give good things to those who ask him'.

μὴ μεριμνᾶτε τῇ ψυχῇ ὑμῶν τί φάγητε μηδὲ τῷ σώματι ὑμῶν τί ἐνδύσησθε.[17] So Luke, minus the pronouns. Although the words, 'Do not be anxious', which stand over the rest of the chapter, contain an imperative, they are above all intended to soothe the

---

[17] η (or: καὶ) τι πιητε after φαγητε has strong attestation: B L Θ W *f*¹³ 33 0233 Maj it sa^mss syᵖ·ʰ mae bo goth arm geoⁱ Or. Despite this, the reading is probably secondary, having been added to improve the rhetorical correlation between 6.25 and 6.31 (cf. Lk 12.29). Jerome attests the reading, 'or what you will drink', with these words: he found it in 'some copies'. The phrase—which is omitted by HG and put in brackets by NA²⁶—is absent from ℵ *f*¹ 892 *pc* a b ff¹ k l vg syᶜ sa^mss Ju Cl Chr Aug. Compare Gos. Thom. 36 and *P. Oxy.* 665.

troubled soul: there is, as the following verses will verify, no need for faithful disciples to fret overmuch about food and clothing. The heavenly Father takes care of his earth-bound children.

In view of the reflexive use of ψυχή = *nepeš* in Semitic languages (see BDB, s.v., 4b), μὴ μεριμνᾶτε τῇ ψυχῇ might be a Semitism: 'do not concern yourself' (cf. 11.29; 26.38; and the substitution of ἑαυτόν in Lk 9.25 for the τὴν ψυχὴν αὐτοῦ of Mk 8.36; discussion in Maloney, pp. 118–21). But ψυχή can also mean '(earthly) life', '(earthly) existence' (cf. 2.20; 20.28). And this is the more fitting sense here as the word is immediately used thus in the next line.[18] So we should translate: 'Do not be anxious about your life' (RSV). On this reading ψυχή does not stand in opposition to σῶμα (as in 'body' and 'soul'); rather do the two stand in parallel. For μὴ μεριμνᾶτε see Phil 4.6–7. The command enjoins something like what the Stoics called αὐτάρκεια (cf. 1 Tim 6.6; Clement of Alexandria, *Paed.* 1.12.98). Compare Horace, *Odes* 2.11.4–5: 'Do not be anxious for life's needs; it requires little'.

If it is true, as Hillel purportedly said, that 'the more possessions, the more care' (*m. 'Abot* 2.7), it is also true that the less possessions the more care. No matter what one's economic state, anxiety is near to hand. The natural human tendency to worry about money is shared by rich and poor alike. This is a sure indicator that money in itself cannot cast out anxiety. Thus in order to escape fretfulness one must look elsewhere; and according to Mt 6.25–34, the elsewhere is upwards—towards the heavenly Father. It is faith that has the power to exorcize anxiety. And just as one must serve either God or mammon, so must one either be sustained by anxiety or by faith.

μεριμνᾶτε (see esp. Bultmann, *TWNT* 4, pp. 593–8) betokens the key theme of 6.25–34 (μεριμνάω occurs five times, in 6.25, 27, 28, 31, and 34). The word refers primarily to an attitude, to mental anxiety (cf. 6.27; 10.19; Par. Jer. 6.15; Dupont 3, pp. 286–7); but it is just possible that originally Jesus was telling his disciples not to put forth an effort, not to work save in preaching the gospel (cf. Mk 6.8; 1 Cor 9.14; so Schlatter, pp. 225–7; Jeremias, *Parables*, pp. 214–15). One could, perhaps, combine the two meanings: do not make worried efforts (cf. Guelich, p. 336). In any event, the main point for Matthew is not in doubt. The wise believer will focus attention on the Father in heaven; and notwithstanding the inevitable troubles and frailties of human existence (cf. Ecclus 40.1–11; Ps.-Phoc. 116–21), he will cast aside all earthly cares. The disciple will let nothing interfere with finding the one pearl of great

---

[18] Thorough discussion in Dautzenberg, pp. 92–7. According to Betz, *Essays*, pp. 106–7, ψυχή is intentionally ambiguous, as is σῶμα (= 'body' or 'person'). This forces the reader to make up his own mind as to what is unwarranted and what might be warranted anxiety.

price (cf. 13.46). Compare As. Mos. 12.3; T. Iss. 4; and T. Job 49.1, where Job's daughter has her heart changed so as μηκέτι ἐνθυμηθῆναι τὰ κοσμικά (cf. 48.2; 50.2). All mental concentration will be aimed at spiritual matters (cf. Col 3.1–2), thus freeing one from bondage to the world (cf. 6.24; Ecclus 31.1).

Matthew could readily have thought of μεριμνάω as related to μερίζω and thus have connected anxiety with division within the self. This would link 6.25 well with the ἁπλοῦς in 6.22 and with the theme of serving two masters in 6.24.

For contentment with food and clothing, necessities which all must have, see 1 Tim 6.8 (cf. Ps.-Phoc. 6). Perhaps our evangelist will have thought of the Lord's Prayer and the petition for bread. Having prayed the prayer of Jesus, how could one remain anxious?

οὐχὶ ἡ ψυχὴ πλεῖόν ἐστιν τῆς τροφῆς καὶ τὸ σῶμα τοῦ ἐνδύματος; Instead of οὐχί, which turns the sentence into a question, Luke has γάρ. Otherwise there is agreement. Matthew also has οὐχί where Mark or Luke do not in 5.46 diff. Lk 6.32; 5.47 diff. Lk 6.33; 13.56 diff. Mk 6.3; and 18.12 diff. Lk 15.4; and οὐχί introduces a question in 12.11, which is redactional, as well as in 13.27 and 20.13, which belong to special material. So the first evangelist has probably changed the declaration in Luke (= Q) into a question.

As with the vast majority of questions in the Jesus tradition, this one is closed, rhetorical, not open. The implied argument is *a minori ad maius*, a form of argumentation common in rabbinic texts (*qal wāḥômer*). Will not God, having given the greater thing (ἡ ψυχή), supply the lesser things such as food and clothing?

26. Along with the following verses, 6.26, which calls attention to a fact of everyday experience (cf. 5.45; 6.27, 28; 7.8–10; 10.29–30), encourages one to accept the admonition in 6.25. That which is seen (the birds of the air) makes credible faith in the unseen (God's cosmic fatherhood).

ἐμβλέψατε εἰς τὰ πετεινὰ τοῦ οὐρανοῦ. Luke has κατανοήσατε τοὺς κόρακας. ἐμβλέψατε εἰς (so Isa 51.1, 2, 6 and Ecclus 2.10 for *habbîṭû 'el*) is original. The verb appears only twice in Matthew while Luke is fond of κατανοέω (Mt: 1; Mk: 0; Lk: 4; Acts: 4). On the other hand, 'the ravens' (κόραξ is a NT *hapax legomenon*) is from Q. Not only does the OT associate God's providence with the feeding of ravens (Job 38.41; Ps 147.9), but Matthew preferred 'the birds of the air' (= '*ôp haššāmayim*) (1) because of its liturgical or biblical ring (it occurs often in the LXX) and (2) perhaps because the raven was considered unclean (Lev 11.15; Deut 14.14; Barn. 10.1, 11). Maybe on the lips of Jesus the point was this: 'if God cares even for the raven, an unclean, worthless bird, how much more . . .'. For the paronomasia between 'ravens' and 'feed' in Palestinian Syriac see Black, p. 179. Note that between the sky of 6.26 and the fields of 6.30, heaven and earth are encompassed.

The call to learn spiritual truths by considering the world's creatures (cf. Epictetus, *Diss.* 1.16) can be heard in the OT (e.g. Job 12.7–8; Prov 6.6–11; cf. 1 En. 2.1–5.10; 101). Further, despite its dedication to the revelation of Torah, the Jewish mind apparently saw little problem with the concept of 'natural revelation' (cf. Acts 14.17; Rom 1–2; 2 Bar. 54.18; and Davies, *PRJ*, pp. 325–8). Josephus even tells us that Abraham was the first to embrace monotheism because he inferred its truth from observing land and sea and sun and moon (*Ant.* 1.155–6). And of Jesus C. H. Dodd could write: he held the 'conviction that there is no mere analogy, but an inward affinity, between the natural order and the spiritual order; or as we might put it in the language of the parables themselves, the Kingdom of God is intrinsically *like* the processes of nature. . . . Since nature and super-nature are one order, you can take any part of that order and find in it illumination for other parts' (*Parables*, p. 10). As Wordsworth put it, God 'rolls through all things'. Compare 5.45 and 10.29–31 = Lk 12.6–7. Recall also the intertwining of nature and human affairs in the narrative of the magi and the star (2.1–11) and in the story of Jesus' passion, in which the earth quakes (27.51–3). These accounts reflect belief in a cosmic piety. Because God is the Lord of nature no less than of humanity, no sphere is morally neutral and beyond the pale of religion. Indeed, so much is this the case that religious truths can be— with the help, of course, of the scriptural revelation—read out of man's environment.[19] 'The whole earth is a fruit-bearing witness' (Heraclitus, *Ep.* 4.5).

6.26 might, as Betz holds (*Essays*, p. 108), reflect the widespread notion that human culture and civilization emerged from the animal kingdom, and that, while humankind has become degenerate, the animals have maintained their primal behaviour and harmony with their surroundings. Because, however, the comparison between *plants* and human beings in 6.28–30 must be independent of this consideration, the point is uncertain.

The argument of Mt 6.26 has an interesting parallel in *m. Qidd.* 4.14: R. Simeon b. Eleazar says: 'Hast thou ever seen a wild animal or a bird practising a craft? Yet they have their sustenance without care and were they not created for naught else but to serve me? But I was created to serve my Maker. How much more then ought not I to have my sustenance without care? But I have wrought evil, and forfeited my [right to] sustenance [without care]' (variants in SB 1, pp. 436–7). The point here is rather different from that made in the gospels, but the method of argumentation is identical. See further on 6.30. The Koran also offers a parallel: 'There are countless beasts that cannot fend for themselves. Allah provides for them and for you' (29.60).

ὅτι οὐ σπείρουσιν οὐδὲ θερίζουσιν. So Luke. 'The elaborate structures of care in which we are involved are absent, and yet life goes on' (Tannehill, p. 63). Compare Dio Chrysostom 6.21–2.

---

[19] It should be noted, however, that if the Jesus of the synoptics assumes that there is a real and clear revelation of God in the created world, he also fully recognizes that sinful human beings typically fail to perceive what is right under their eyes; cf. 11.20–4; 12.38–42; 13.13; etc.

οὐδὲ συνάγουσιν εἰς ἀποθήκας. 'Gathering into barns' is the third step of farming, after sowing and reaping. Luke, who has οἷς οὐκ ἔστιν ταμιεῖον οὐδὲ ἀποθήκη, is original. Matthew shows great fondness for συνάγω (Mt: 24; Mk: 5; Lk: 6); his love of parallelism will have moved him to find a verbal phrase to line up with 'toil' and 'reap'; and συνάγω + ἀποθήκη (a combination not found in the LXX) was already to hand in Q (3.12 = Lk 3.17) and is redactional in 13.30.

καὶ ὁ πατὴρ ὑμῶν ὁ οὐράνιος τρέφει αὐτά. Although the Father is in heaven, his hand is not shortened: he graciously stretches down to care for those on the earth. 'Will not that one (God), who created him, create for him his food?' (*Pesiq. R. Kah.* 91a). Luke's simple ὁ θεός reproduces Q and shows that the Third Evangelist is not using the First Gospel. Matthew's αὐτά corresponds to τὰ πετεινά, Luke's αὐτούς to τοὺς κόρακας. The καί means 'and yet' (see on 1.19). 'Your heavenly Father' occurs again in 6.32.

Belief in the care of the heavenly Father for all creatures is thoroughly Jewish. See, for example, Job 12.10 ('In his hand is the life of every living thing and the breath of all mankind'); 38.41 ('Who provides the raven its prey, when its young ones cry to God, and wander about for lack of food?'); Ps 147.9 ('He gives to the beasts their food, and to the young ravens which cry'); Ps. Sol. 5. 9–10 ('Birds and fish dost Thou nourish (τρέφεις), in that Thou givest rain to the steppes that green grass may spring up, (so) to prepare fodder in the steppe for every living thing; and if they hunger, unto Thee do they lift up their face'). Note also the whole of Ps 104. For the rabbis see SB 1, p. 437, and *y. Šeb.* 9.1.38d: 'A bird, unless Heaven wills it, is not caught, how much more a human being!' (cf. *Gen. Rab.* on 33.18).

οὐχ ὑμεῖς μᾶλλον διαφέρετε αὐτῶν; This rhetorical question forestalls a possible protest: perchance mankind, unlike the animals, is outside God's care. Lk 12.24 reads: πόσῳ μᾶλλον ὑμεῖς διαφέρετε τῶν πετεινῶν. πόσῳ μᾶλλον probably derives from Q (cf. 6.30 = Lk 12.28; Mt 7.11 = Lk 11.13). Matthew chooses οὐχ to add to the growing number of negative particles in 6.25–34. Luke's πετεινῶν may or may not be redactional.

As in the previous verse, the argument is *a minori ad maius*, from birds to people. 'Since God provides food for birds who do not even take part in the process of raising, harvesting, and storing food, how much more so will he provide for his valued own who do' (Guelich, p. 338). For the greater value of human beings see 10.31 and 12.12. For God as the source of food see Prov 30.8–9 and recall Mt 4.1–11, where Jesus fasts and waits in faith upon God.

Perhaps the call to live like the birds of heaven had its inspiration in eschatological thinking, in the conviction that the end would be like the beginning (see on 1.1). In paradise Adam did not have to toil for food; indeed, according to 2 Esdr 1.19; LAE 2–4; and *b. Šabb.* 59b, the angels fed Adam manna. Now because elsewhere Jesus seems to seek the recovery of paradisiacal conditions (see on 19.3–9), the call for a carefree existence should perhaps be thus understood. To live without worry for the things of this world would be to live in the new age. (In *m. Qidd.* 4.14, man does not live like the wild animals or birds precisely because he lives after the fall.)[20]

27. Lk 12.25 differs in two respects from Mt 6.27: it has no ἕνα (this could very well be Matthean) and (at least according to the text of NA[26]) it places προσθεῖναι after αὐτοῦ.

6.27 is, on form-critical grounds, to be judged an insertion into Q. As T. W. Manson observed long ago, Mt 6.26–30 = Lk 12.24–8 exhibits compound parallelism if 6.27 = Lk 12.25 is removed (*Teaching*, p. 56):

I.   Consider the ravens,   (a)
          They do not sow or reap;   (b 1)
          They have no barn or storehouse;   (b 2)
              And God feeds them: (d)
          How much better are you than the birds!   (f)

II.   Consider the lilies, how they grow: (a)
          They do not toil or spin;   (b)
          Yet I tell you that not even Solomon in all his
              glory was arrayed like one of these.   (c)
          But if God so clothes the grass   (d)
              Which to-day is in the field   (e 1)
              And to-morrow is cast into the oven; (e 2)
     How much more you, oh ye of little faith?   (f)

Schematically:
I. a, b 1, b 2, d,   f.
II. a, ·b,   c, d, e 1, e 2, f.

Because such compound parallelism has high claim to have had a home in the discourse of Jesus (cf. Mk 9.43–7; Lk 11.31–2; 17.26–30), and because Mt 6.27–8a = Lk 12.25–6 does not fit the scheme, it appears to be intrusive, a secondary addition, probably

---

[20] In *m. Ber.* 5.3 we find this: 'If a man said (in his prayer), "To a bird's nest do thy mercies extend"; or "May thy name be remembered for the good (which thou has wrought)"; or "We give thanks, we give thanks", they put him to silence'. The import of this passage is puzzling; for discussion see Urbach 1, pp. 383–5, and A. F. Segal, *Two Powers in Heaven*, SJLA 25, Leiden, 1977, pp. 98–108. But the double thanksgiving could pertain to ditheism, of which Jews sometimes accused Christians. If so, is it not just possible that the sentiment about the bird's nest also has to do with Christians, who justified some conviction by quoting the gospel text on God's care of birds?

attracted by catchword (μεριμνάω). In accordance with this conclusion, 6.27–8a is about the fruitlessness of worrying while 6.26, 28b–30 has a slightly different thrust, reliance upon the Father in heaven.

According to Bultmann (*History*, pp. 102–3), Mt 6.27 is one of 'the secular *meshalim* which have been made into dominical sayings in the tradition'. He does not offer any real evidence for this assertion; and as Jesus elsewhere speaks of what people cannot accomplish (Mk 10.23–7), the question of authenticity should not be considered closed.

Imagination only is the source for Albright and Mann's proposed reconstruction of the original (p. 82): 'Who can add a cubit to his land, or a day to his life?'

τίς δὲ ἐξ ὑμῶν. This is the equivalent of *mî bākem* (cf. Isa 42.23; 50.10; Hag 2.3). The expression, which introduces a second rhetorical question, and which also occurs in 7.9 = Lk 11.11; Mt 12.11 = Lk 14.5; and Lk 11.5; 14.28; 15.4; and 17.7, has been supposed characteristic of Jesus because without contemporary parallel.[21] Especially striking is its frequent connexion with a *qal wāḥômer* argument (e.g. Mt 12.11–12). Its force is in any case evident: 'Can you imagine that any of you . . .' (so Jeremias, *Parables*, p. 158).

μεριμνῶν δύναται προσθεῖναι ἐπὶ τὴν ἡλικίαν αὐτοῦ πῆχυν ἕνα; Anxiety is foolish and accomplishes nothing (cf. 6.34) except to put God out of the picture (cf. 6.32). It is therefore self-destructive, and so far from adding it takes away. (Ironically enough, doctors now tell us that worrying actually shortens life.) In Aramaic there could have been a word-play between 'worry' (*yĕṣēp*) and 'add' (*yĕsap*); so Black, p. 179.

Although one could render ἡλικίαν αὐτοῦ 'his stature' (cf. Herodotus 3.16; Ezek 13.18; Lk 19.3; Josephus, *Ant.* 2.230; see Potwin (v)), the first meaning of ἡλικία is 'age', 'time of life' (BAGD, s.v.), and this is the predominant usage in the LXX and it fits best here: 'Who . . . can add one πῆχυς to his span of life?' 'Stature' is incorrect because (1) while the addition of a cubit would be no desirable thing, the context implies something wished for; (2) Luke explicitly labels the addition of a πῆχυς a 'small thing' (12.26)—something he could not do if a man were growing a cubit; (3) Matthew's ἕνα presumably means '*even* one', but a cubit with reference to height is hardly insignificant; and (4) the context has to do with food and clothing, which are designed to prolong life, not add height.

[21] So Jeremias, *Parables*, p. 103, citing H. Greeven, ' "Wer unter euch . . . ?" ', *Wort und Dienst* 3 (1952), pp. 86–101. For Hellenistic parallels see K. Berger, 'Zur Frage des traditionsgeschichtlichen Wertes apokrypher Gleichnisse', *NovT* 17 (1975), pp. 58–76.

The noun, πῆχυς, occurs in the synoptics only in this Q saying. The meaning is 'forearm', then 'cubit' (about 18 inches; cf. *'ammâ* and Rev 21.17). It was also used metaphorically of time (see BAGD, s.v.) and is so used in the present context (which justifies the translation of BAGD, s.v.: 'hour'). For a measurement of space being employed with reference to time see Ps 39.5. The postpositioning of ἕνα is a Semitism (BDF § 247.2).

Because the application of 'cubit' to 'span of time' is a bit unusual, the way is opened for conjecturing that the Greek misrepresents Jesus' Aramaic. According to Schwarz (v), Jesus said this: *min běkôn yāṣêp yôsêp 'al garmêh garmîta' ḥădā'* ('who among you can by worrying add one small bone to himself?'). *garmita'* ('bone') was later mistaken to be *garmîdā'* ('arm', 'cubit'). While this surmise, which creates a sentence full of assonance, is certainly intriguing, it must remain highly speculative. The unusual was usual with Jesus, and given this, what we have in the gospels makes perfect sense.

28. We now come to verses which address the problem of anxiety by a call to reflect upon the 'flowers of the field'. The argument, as T. W. Manson saw, is related to a traditional motif. In the OT the comparison of human being to flower or grass is often employed to underline the brevity and fragility of life: 'All flesh is grass, and all its beauty is like the flower of the field. The grass withers, the flower fades . . .' (Isa 40.6–7; cf. Job 8.12; 14.2; Ps 37.2; 90.5–6; 102.11; 103.15–16; Isa 37.27; Jas 1.9–11). In the gospels, however, things are turned around. The brave show of the flora is not taken to express the fleeting, transitory nature of all life but instead makes this point: 'God lavishes infinite pains on these things, brief though their span of life is: how much more will He care for His children' (*Sayings*, p. 113). This novel twisting of an old motif may well have been deliberate and intended to catch the hearer off guard. This is particularly true when the parallel in 6.26 is considered. Although the rabbinic literature contrasts the carefree life of animals with the burdens of humanity, in the gospels the birds of heaven, who neither sow nor reap nor gather into barns, serve to show God's providential care; hence human beings need not be anxious (see on 6.26). So here again a traditional theme seems to be turned on its head. Perhaps, therefore, the double saying preserved in Mt 6.26–30 was, when first uttered, more provocative than now appears. Perhaps an element of irony was involved, Jesus drawing conclusions which contradicted those theretofore drawn from scrutiny of the birds of the air and the flowers of the field.

6.28–30 really repeats the content of 6.26, but the repetition is not redundancy. It rather adds force, which is required because the text is addressing an anxiety that is deeply rooted in human nature.

καὶ περὶ ἐνδύματος τί μεριμνᾶτε; Lk 12.26 continues the subject of the previous verse with this: 'If then you are unable to do as small a thing as that, τί περὶ τῶν λοιπῶν μεριμνᾶτε?' Matthew's second, fourth, and fifth words, being shared by Luke, derive from Q. Overall, Luke's wording may stand a better chance of reproducing what was in the common source. Certainly Matthew's ἐνδύματος must be suspected of being redactional (ἐνδύμα: Mt: 7; Mk: 0; Lk: 1).

καταμάθετε τὰ κρίνα τοῦ ἀγροῦ πῶς αὐξάνουσιν.[22] Luke has κατανοήσατε (see on 6.26). Matthew's imperative might be redactional. Although it is a NT *hapax legomenon* (LXX: 9, for several Hebrew words), the word harmonizes with our author's emphasis upon discipleship as an act of learning (cf. 13.52; 28.19–20). τοῦ ἀγροῦ (ἀγρός: Mt: 17; Mk: 8; Lk: 9), which recurs in 6.30, has been added to reinforce the parallel with 6.26 ('birds *of the air*'; cf. Gen 3.18; Ps 103.15). Luke does not have it. Matthew is the only NT writer to use the adjectival τοῦ ἀγροῦ: 6.28, 30; 13.36. αὐξάνω (often for *pārâ* in the LXX) is in the singular in Luke. This is, as the scribal corrections to Matthew witness, more proper grammatically and therefore may be Luke's improvement, though Matthew might have made αὐξάνω and the following verbs plural to match the plural verbs in 6.26.

What flower (or flowers) κρίνα denotes (κρίνον occurs over twenty times in the LXX, most often for *šôšannâ*; for the rabbinic *qĕrînôn*, a loanword, see Jastrow, s.v.) is uncertain (lit. in BAGD, s.v.). If it is the purple anemone, the image of Solomon's purple robes could be in mind (cf. the following verse). Other possibilities include the gladiolus, the crocus, some variety of poppy, the white Madonna lily, or Galilean flowers in general. This last option is now widely favoured: Jesus was speaking not of one particular flower but of the several beautiful flowers which bloom in abundance between January and May. (Cf. the generic 'birds' of 6.26.)

οὐ κοπιῶσιν οὐδὲ νήθουσιν. Again Luke has the singular. Perhaps behind the words for 'toil' (man's work) and 'spin' (woman's work) there lies an Aramaic word-play: *'ămal/'ăzal*.

Because it seems odd to speak of flowers as neither toiling nor spinning, and because 'birds of the air' and 'beasts of the field' naturally go together (cf. Job 35.11; Ezek 29.5; Dio Chrysostom 10.16), some have inferred that

[22] So (with minor variations) ℵ¹ B Θ f¹ 33 latt sy^c.p.h sa bo eth geo Hil. ου ξενουσιν (= ξαινουσιν) (followed by ουδε νηθουσιν ουδε κοπιωσιν) appears in ℵ*vid Äth Chr. αυξανει (followed by ου κοπια ουδε νηθει) is found in K L W Δ Π 0233 f¹³ Maj goth arm Bas (cf. Lk 12.27). It is possible that the original was ου ξαινουσιν (followed by ουδε νηθουσιν) and that, through corruption, this became αυξαινουσιν (which then required an addition, this being ουδε κοπιωσιν). See further Skeat (v); Katz (v); Glasson (v); and Brunner (v).

at one time in the tradition the Greek was τὰ θηρία τοῦ ἀγροῦ (a good LXX phrase): 'the beasts of the field . . . neither toil nor spin'. Through corruption θηρία became λείρια ('lilies'). 'Lilies' was then glossed by κρίνα, and the statements about 'Solomon in all his glory' and 'the grass of the field' were then added (see Powell (v)). This reconstruction does not satisfy, in part because it is too involved, in part because it destroys the compound parallelism between 6.26 and 28b–30, which must surely be original.

29. λέγω δὲ ὑμῖν ὅτι οὐδὲ Σολομὼν ἐν πάσῃ τῇ δόξῃ αὐτοῦ περιεβάλετο ὡς ἓν τούτων. Luke agrees with this except that he has no ὅτι. Does the text imply a slight disparagement of Solomon? For his proverbial splendour and kingdom see 1 Kgs 9.26–10.29; 2 Chr 9.13–28; Eccles 2.1–11; 1 Esdr 1.5; Josephus, *Ant.* 8.39–41. Solomon 'exceedingly plumed himself upon his riches' (Clement of Alexandria, *Paed.* 2.10.102).

30. This verse presupposes an affirmative response to the question posed in 6.26, 'Are you not of more value than they?' God, who by clothing the grass of the field with splendid colours and finely worked designs thereby displays his providential care for even small things, must care much the more for human beings, who are created in his image.

εἰ δὲ τὸν χόρτον τοῦ ἀγροῦ. Lk 12.28, following Q, has ἐν ἀγρῷ immediately after δέ. Matthew has possibly reworked the phrase in order to produce an LXX locution (Gen 2.5; 3.18; 4 Βασ 19.26; Jer 12.4) to stand in parallel to 'birds of the air' and 'flowers of the field' (cf. 13.36). χόρτος, 'grass' (which is even of less account than the birds), must include or be identical with κρίνα ('flowers')— unless we are to think of the last as the clothing of the former. The εἰ means 'since (as has been made plain in 6.28–9)' (cf. 4.3, 6; Lk 11.19; Phil 2.1; BDF § 372.1a).

σήμερον ὄντα καὶ αὔριον εἰς κλίβανον βαλλόμενον ὁ θεὸς οὕτως ἀμφιέννυσιν. In Luke the order of the first two words is reversed and the main verb—once again in the singular (see on 6.28)—is different: ἀμφιέζω (a NT *hapax legomenon*; LXX: 4). Perhaps Matthew placed the participle after 'today' because the next participle, βαλλόμενον, follows 'tomorrow'. ἀμφιέννυμι occurs again in the NT only in Mt 11.8 = Lk 7.25. It is difficult to explain why Luke has ἀμφιέζω ('a new Hellenistic formation' according to BDF § 73), Matthew the related ἀμφιέννυμι. The two verbs mean the same thing, 'to clothe'. For God clothing people see Gen 3.21. For the 'here today, gone tomorrow' construction see *b. Ber.* 32b; *Pesiq. R.* 122b. Grass was one of the fuels used in baking ovens. For the κλίβανος (= *tannûr*; LXX: 12; Mt: 1; Mk: 0; Lk: 1, nowhere else in the NT; cf. κρίβανος) see Herodotus 2.92 (on the cooking of papyrus-reed in Egypt).

οὐ πολλῷ μᾶλλον ὑμᾶς, ὀλιγόπιστοι; Luke has ποσῷ for οὐ πολλῷ and probably reproduces Q (see on 6.26). ὀλιγόπιστος appears five times in Matthew, once in Luke, and nowhere else in the earliest Christian literature save Sextus, *Sent*. 6 (where it equals ἄπιστος). The word has no Greek antecedent and appears to derive from *qĕṭannê 'ămānâ* (see SB 1, pp. 438–9). Compare *Tanḥuma*, Beshallaḥ 117b: 'R. Elazar of Modi'im said: If a man has food for the day, but says, "What shall I eat tomorrow?" such a one is deficient in faith. R. Eliezer the Great said: He who has yet bread in his basket, and says, "What shall I eat tomorrow?" belongs to those of little faith' (*qĕṭannê 'ămānâ*). In Matthew ὀλιγόπιστος is always addressed to believing disciples; it therefore does not imply an absence of faith but a broken or insufficient faith. It means either a doubting of God's providential protection (6.30; 8.26?) or a failure to accept Jesus' miraculous power or word (8.26?; 14.31; 16.8; 17.20). The word always appears in a trying situation. (Cf. Sextus, *Sent*. 200: 'a terrible situation reveals the man of faith'.) In the present context the reader is encouraged to overcome 'little faith' by reflecting upon the lessons drawn from nature in 6.26–30 and by hearing afresh Jesus' promises in 6.32–3. See further on 8.10 and the discussion Held, in *TIM*, pp. 291–6, and Frankemölle, pp. 152–4.

The use of the rare ὀλιγόπιστος might be considered evidence for Luke's knowledge of Matthew, for besides Lk 12.28, the word is confined in the NT to the First Gospel. This possibility, however, is slim in the light of our arguments for Luke's faithfulness to Q in the rest of the verse.

P. Oxy. 655 contains an interesting variant of the tradition preserved in Mt 6.25–32 and Lk 12.22–30: '[Jesus says, "Be not solicitous f]rom morning un[til evening, nor] from eve[ning until mo]rning either [for y]our [sustenance], what [you will] eat, [or] for [your] clo[thing], what you [will] put on. [You] are worth [far] more than [the lili]es whi[ch g]row but do not s[pi]n, a[nd] have n[o] clo[th]ing. And you, what do [you lack?] Who of you can add to his stature? He will [g]ive you your clothing" ' (trans. of Fitzmyer, *Semitic Background*, pp. 406–7). Compare Gos. Thom. 36: 'Do not be anxious from morning to evening and from evening until morning about what you shall put on'. Five observations are to be made. (1) The last line of *P. Oxy*. 655, αὐτὸ[ς δ]ώσει ὑμεῖν τὸ ἔνδυμα ὑμῶν, is either an adaptation of Mt 6.30 = Lk 12.28 or it is an independent, possibly authentic saying of Jesus (cf. Jeremias, *Unknown Sayings*, pp. 86–7). (2) Gos. Thom. 36 seems to be an abbreviated form of what is found in *P. Oxy*. 655. (3) The tradition in *P. Oxy*. 655 must be largely secondary and abbreviated over against Mt 6.25–32 and Lk 12.22–30 if we are correct in regarding the compound parallelism of Q as original (see on 6.27). (4) Nevertheless there is no clear sign of dependence upon the canonical gospels. (5) The use of the singular, ν[ήθ]ει, in *P. Oxy*. 655 offers some support for our claim that the singular verbs in Lk 12.27 are original and that the corresponding plurals in Matthew are redactional.

31. With this verse, which resembles the opening 6.25, an *inclusio* is formed, and what follows (6.31–4) summarizes and draws out the implications of 6.25–30 (note the οὖν).

μὴ οὖν μεριμνήσητε λέγοντες. Compare 6.34a. Luke has καὶ ὑμεῖς μὴ ζητεῖτε, which is no doubt closer to Q. Matthew likes to use οὖν for introducing an exhortation or consequent command, and the statistics on μὴ οὖν are telling (Mt: 5; Mk: 0; Lk: 0). For the paraenetic οὖν see W. Nauck, 'Das οὖν-paraneticum', *ZNW* 49 (1958), pp. 134–5. The main verb, which is in the second person plural following the ὑμεῖς of Q (= Luke), has been chosen to recall 6.25. Matthew has thus eliminated the antithetical parallelism of Q: μὴ ζητεῖτε . . . ζητεῖτε (so Luke). Why the change? (Matthew is quite fond of parallel constructions). Our evangelist wants to place the key imperative, μὴ μεριμνᾶτε/μεριμνήσητε, at the beginning (25), middle (31), and end (34) of the section on earthly cares.[23] (Cf. the similar threefold 'Do not fear' of 10.26–31—again at the beginning, the middle, and the end.)

τί φάγωμεν; ἤ· τί πίωμεν; ἤ· τί περιβαλώμεθα; Compare the discussion in Epictetus, *Diss.* 1.9. For food, drink, and clothing as the necessities for human existence see Ecclus 29.21 and Epictetus, *Enchr.* 33 (cf. 1 Tim 6.8 and Jas 2.15). Luke has καί's for the ἤ's, second person plurals for the first two verbs, and μὴ μετεωρίζεσθε for 'What shall we wear?' The ἤ's are probably Matthean (Mt: 60; Mk: 33; Lk: 45), and our evangelist may have substituted a third question for Luke's 'do not be anxious', thereby creating a closer parallel with 6.25. Earlier Matthew changed declarations into questions (see on 6.25–6). As for the first person plural, it turns an indirect quotation into a direct quotation, which is perhaps more in line with Matthew's style (cf. 1.20–1; 2.2, 5, 8).

32. Compare Lk 12.30. This verse supports the exhortation just made by urging this point: you need not seek food or clothing in the manner of those who lack faith, for your heavenly Father knows your needs. Implicit is the thought that if God knows, he will act, because he, the treasury of good gifts and giver and life, cares for his children.

πάντα γὰρ ταῦτα τὰ ἔθνη ἐπιζητοῦσιν. In Luke the words on either side of 'for' are reversed and τοῦ κόσμου qualifies ἔθνη. Matthew generally prefers ταῦτα before πάντα (4.9; 13.34, 51, 56; 23.36; 24.2), yet as the opposite order is redactional in 24.8, 33, and perhaps 34, no firm decision can be reached on the order of the two

---

[23] The change from the present imperative in 6.25 (μεριμνᾶτε) to the aorist in 6.31 and 34 (μεριμνήσητε) is not easily explained. But two points may be made. First, the μὴ μεριμνᾶτε of 6.25 is from Q (cf. Lk 12.22), but Q had aorists in 6.26 = Lk 12.24 and 6.28 = Lk 12.27, and these last may have influenced the formulations in 6.31 and 34. Secondly, it may be relevant to observe that the imperative in 6.25 is perhaps more general than those in 6.31 and 34 (see BDF § 335–7).

words at this point in Q. Luke's τὰ ἔθνη τοῦ κόσμου (= 'ummôt hā'ôlām; see SB 2, p. 191) appears nowhere else in Luke and almost certainly comes from Q (see Jeremias, *Lukasevangelium*, pp. 209–10, 218).

As in 6.7, the non-Jewish pagans represent the misguided, those who, because they know not the God of the OT, fail to exhibit the proper religious behaviour. Just as they ignorantly heap up empty phrases when they pray, so too do they fail to trust God's providence; they anxiously ask the questions of 6.31. On the meaning of ἔθνη in Matthew see on 5.47.

Concerning ἐπιζητεῖν, 'the preposition [ἐπί] does not in the least signify *addition* but rather perhaps *direction*. It seems to fix the verb upon a definite object. . . . The preposition is not *intensive*, but *directive* (if the word may be allowed). It prepares us to expect the limitation of the verb to a particular object'; so J. A. Robinson, *St. Paul's Epistle to the Ephesians*, 2nd ed., London, n.d., p. 249.

ἐπιζητεῖν appears two more times in Matthew, in 12.39 and in 16.4. Neither occurrence has a parallel. Both have to do with the vain seeking of signs. In 6.32, the seeking is surprisingly for nourishment and shelter from the elements. This is disconcerting. Concern over food, drink, and clothing unavoidably belongs to the natural order of things, so how can it be wrong? Is irresponsibility being inculcated? Is Mt 6.25–34 not in truth bordering on enthusiastic fantasy? Is it not just one more religious flight from solid reality? The questions, although they inevitably arise, do not have to receive an affirmative answer. Our passage is, obviously, not filled to overflowing with level-headed common sense. But then faith and worldly wisdom often go their separate ways. 6.32b acknowledges that 'your heavenly Father knows that you need all these things'. This is the presupposition of all that follows. Further, 6.32 is not complete in itself. It leads directly into 6.33, where those who seek first the kingdom and righteousness are promised that they will have 'all these things'. Clearly, food and clothing are not illegitimate needs; on the contrary, those who serve God, not mammon, will have adequate food and clothing. The point must be this: compared with God's kingdom, 'all these things' are of secondary import. They should consequently not be anxiously sought as some seek them—for such anxious seeking will not permit full attention to be given to the demands of the kingdom. Nevertheless, as 'all these things' are necessary, they *will*—and this is where unbelieving prudence will demur— somehow, in the providence of almighty God, be graciously supplied or take care of themselves—provided one seeks above all else the kingdom of God and his righteousness. 'God does not need anything, and the believer needs only God' (Sextus, *Sent.* 49). It follows, then, that the answer to our question, Is irresponsibility being inculcated?, depends entirely upon whether one shares Jesus' belief in an active and loving providence. In other words, the issue is whether one can hold the world view of our passage, whether one can acknowledge providence to be like a caring parent. We must further add that, whatever one makes of Mt 6.25–34, Jesus' words could never have encouraged anyone in any sort of laziness. If Jesus—who may have lived out of a common fund (cf. Jn 12.6; 13.29)—appeared to belittle the consuming tasks of obtaining food and clothing, it was only because he had something even more arduous in mind, namely, seeking the kingdom of heaven. And certainly he did not have many illusions about an easy world. The bird will fall to the ground (Mt 10.29), and the righteous will inevitably suffer (cf. 5.10–12; 10.16–23; etc.).[24]

οἶδεν γὰρ ὁ πατὴρ ὑμῶν ὁ οὐράνιος ὅτι χρῄζετε τούτων ἁπάντων. Compare 6.8; 7.11. Over against Luke, Matthew has introduced γάρ (Mt: 123–4; Mk: 64; Lk: 97), added 'heavenly' to 'Father' (cf. 6.26), tacked on a concluding 'all' (the τούτων ἁπάντων in 32b matches the πάντα ταῦτα in 32a), and moved the main verb to the front (which permits γάρ to stand in its necessary, second place). In its present context, χρῄζω may be intended to send thoughts back to the introduction of the Lord's Prayer: 'Your Father in heaven knows what you need before you ask him' (6.8).

33. This verse succinctly wraps up the major theme of 6.25–34. Those who seek first the kingdom and righteousness, who serve God and not mammon, will find their legitimate needs met: they shall be satisfied. As the Lord's Prayer implies, the Father takes care of his own (cf. Lk 22.35). The righteous will not go begging (cf. Ps 37.4, 25; Wisd 7.11). Providence is benevolent to the faithful (Rom 8.28).

6.33 exhibits a structure that permeates the Jesus tradition (see Aune, p. 166):

    a. Seek above all the kingdom of God and his righteousness,
    b. and all these things shall be added unto you.

Line a is in the present tense, line b in the future tense. Line a expresses a condition to be met, line b the reward to be gained. Usually this form reflects the antithesis, this world/the world to come. The present saying is an exception.

---

[24] In coming to terms with 6.25–34 one must keep in mind that, on Jesus' lips, the words were probably not uttered to people in general but to his closest followers in particular. In Matthew the words are aimed at all believers without distinction. This is of hermeneutical significance. Words first addressed to itinerant missionaries in the company of Jesus cannot, without reinterpretation, be directly applied to others in a different situation, with a different calling.

ζητεῖτε δὲ πρῶτον τὴν βασιλείαν τοῦ θεοῦ.[25] Luke substitutes
πλήν (Mt: 5; Mk: 1; Lk: 15) for δέ, thereby enhancing the contrast
between this positive command and the previous negative
warnings (cf. Mt 23.26 = Lk 11.41). αὐτοῦ for τοῦ θεοῦ might also
be Lukan (cf. Lk 1.33). For his part, Matthew adds πρῶτον (cf.
5.24; 13.30; 23.26). The word is here emphatic, meaning 'above all
else', not 'first in a series' (cf. BAGD, s.v., 2c; Guelich, pp. 341–2).
Against Lambrecht, Sermon, pp. 167–70, its effect is not to temper
radicalism and let seeking for other things come in by the back
door, as though the kingdom is not the only thing sought, just the
most important thing (see further below).

'To seek the kingdom'—a phrase which seems to have no precise
Jewish parallel and which has good claim to go back to Jesus—has
been interpreted in several different ways. The problem is that
both 'seek' (cf. 7.7, 8, 14) and 'kingdom' are not free of ambiguity.
(1) According to Dupont (3, pp. 293–95) and others, the kingdom
is in 6.33 purely eschatological. It belongs solely to the future, and
what is enjoined is the attempt to meet the entrance requirements.
(2) Others have affirmed that because ζητέω can mean 'ask for',
'request' (cf. 7.7–8; 1 Cor 4.2), the reader is being called to pray for
the coming of the kingdom, as in the Lord's Prayer (Tasker, p. 78).
(3) 'To seek the kingdom' could mean to strive to bring in the
kingdom through missionary work or at least to prepare for the
coming of the kingdom by such activity. This would leave no time
for the gathering of food and clothing (Jeremias, Parables,
pp. 214–15). (4) Perhaps the thought is this: the kingdom, being
God's sovereign rule which will reach its climax at the
consummation, is already present (in Jesus) and one should make
it his first concern to belong to it in the here and now, to come into
its sphere of working. (This would make Mt 6.33 resemble the
rabbinic call to take upon oneself the malkût of heaven, to do the
will of God as it is revealed in Torah; see Urbach 1, pp. 400–19).

Which of these four approaches is most appropriate for
Matthew? The first suffers because the kingdom is not solely future
in the First Gospel (see 11.11–12; 12.28, 21.43). The second fails
because ζητέω is not most naturally understood as signalling
prayer (especially in view of its relation to the ἐπιζητέω of 6.32).

[25] So K L W Δ Θ Π 0233 f[1.13] Maj lat sy mae arm Aug Cyr. του θεου is omitted by ℵ
B (with δικαιοσυνην before βασιλειαν) (k) 1 sa bo Eus. The omission might be
pristine, for the addition would have been altogether natural, and we might have
expected Matthew to use his favourite, των ουρανων (so 301 Chr), instead of του
θεου (βασιλεια του θεου appears, if 6.33 be discounted, only four times in the First
Gospel). See further Gundry, Commentary, p. 119. And yet, the divine βασιλεία is
unqualified in the First Gospel only in six places, and in every such instance it is in
the genitive and used as a qualifier (τὸ εὐαγγέλιον τῆς βασ.: 4.23; 9.35; 24.14; οἱ υἱοὶ
τῆς βασ.: 8.12; 13.38; τὸν λόγον τῆς βασ.: 13.19). Furthermore, αυτου is a bit
awkward without a preceding του θεου.

The third interpretation can be criticized because it is only plausible as a conjecture about what Jesus himself might have meant by the words; it has no real foothold in the present, Matthean context. We are left with the fourth interpretation, which is supported by two facts. (1) The kingdom is both present and future in Matthew. (2) The possibility for righteousness belongs to the present (see below), and 'all these things' can also be had now. So the future does not seem to be the sphere of application.

καὶ τὴν δικαιοσύνην αὐτοῦ. This is a redactional addition which helps settle 6.25–34 firmly into the sermon on the mount. For 'righteousness' coupled with 'kingdom (of God)' see 5.20; Rom 14.17.

Does 'his righteousness' refer to God's activity, specifically to his eschatological vindication of the saints? Are the disciples being exhorted to seek divine justice (cf. 1QS 10.11 and some interpretations of Mt 5.6)?[26] Or does 6.33 have to do with right conduct, with the righteousness that God requires (cf. Jas 1.20; T. Dan. 6.10)?[27] In our judgement, the first interpretation seems to require what is otherwise doubtful, namely, that the kingdom is here future. Moreover, the interpretation of δικαιοσύνη as the righteousness that God requires better fits Matthean usage elsewhere (see on 5.20). So God's righteousness is here the norm for human righteousness, just as in 5.48 God's perfection is the norm for human perfection (cf. Przyblylski, pp. 89–91). In addition, and against many commentators, 'righteousness' is only God's demand. The notion of gift can only be read into the text (*pace* Reumann, pp. 130–2, and Guelich, p. 347). ('All these things will be added unto you' refers to food, drink, and clothing, not to the kingdom and righteousness; cf. 6.32 and see below.)

To seek God's righteousness and God's kingdom amounts to the same thing. Righteousness is the law of the realm, the law of God's kingdom; and to participate even now in God's eschatological rule one must strive for the better righteousness of 5.20. Righteousness is the narrow gate that leads to the life of God's kingdom. Thus to seek the kingdom is to seek righteousness and to seek righteousness is to seek the kingdom.

καὶ ταῦτα πάντα προστεθήσεται ὑμῖν. Compare Prov 3.2 and Mk 4.24. So Lk 12.31, minus πάντα (which Matthew has added; cf. 6.32). Note the theological passive: it is God who adds 'all these things'. (This is one reason for taking πρῶτον as 'above all else'. Permission is not being given for people to seek food and drink

[26] So Schlatter, pp. 234–5; McNeile, p. 89; Schniewind, p. 94; Gundry, *Commentary*, p. 118.
[27] So Dupont 3, pp. 303–4; Strecker, *Weg*, p. 155; Hill, *Greek Words*, p. 129; Przyblylski, pp. 89–91; Guelich, p. 346.

after they have sought the kingdom; rather, God himself supplies these things.)

What are 'all these things'? The words clearly link up with the ἐπιζητοῦσιν of 6.32, where the subject is food, drink, and clothing. The thought seems to be: if one seeks above all the kingdom and righteousness, God will graciously see to it that life's necessities are met. To include the kingdom and righteousness as subjects of 'will be added' disturbs the whole train of thought by bringing in a distracting and irrelevant idea.

Origen, *De orat.* 2.2; 14.1; *Selecta in psalm.* 4 attributes to 'the Saviour' the following saying: αἰτεῖτε τὰ μεγάλα καὶ τὰ μικρὰ προστεθήσεται ὑμῖν καὶ αἰτεῖτε τὰ ἐπουράνια καὶ τὰ ἐπίγεια ὑμῖν προστεθήσεται. In Clement of Alexandria, *Strom.* 1.24.158, and Eusebius, *Ps.* on 16.1 (LXX) only the first part is preserved, and some have thought this to be a dominical saying. Whatever be made of such a conclusion, both the structure and content of the logion are very close to Mt 6.33.

34. There is in Luke no counterpart to this verse, which is probably redactional. It is—against Matthew's usual practice—linked to its context more by catchword than by theme.[28]

μὴ οὖν μεριμνήσητε εἰς τὴν αὔριον, ἡ γὰρ αὔριον μεριμνήσει ἑαυτῆς· ἀρκετὸν τῇ ἡμέρᾳ ἡ κακία αὐτῆς. ἀρκετός,[29] οὖν,[30] and γάρ are Matthean. Further, μὴ οὖν μεριμνήσητε also occurs in 6.31, αὔριον in 6.30, and μεριμνήσει—odd with the genitive (see BDF § 176.2)—repeats the key verb of 6.25–34. κακία (= *rā'â*, 'trouble') is a *hapax legomenon* in the synoptics. For εἰς τὴν αὔριον (= *lĕmāḥār*) see Est 5.12; 3 Macc 5.38. Perhaps the meaning is, 'for the future' (*māḥār* can mean 'in future time'; see BDB, s.v.).

Both 6.34a and 34b appear to have been drawn from the well of common wisdom and probably go back ultimately to Egyptian proverbs (see Griffiths (v)). Compare the following: The Eloquent Peasant 183: 'Do not prepare for tomorrow before it is come. One knows not what evil may be in it'; Instruction of Amen-em-Opet 19.11–13: 'Do not spend the night in fear of the morrow. At dawn what is the morrow like? One knows not what the morrow is like'; Prov 27.1: 'Do not boast about tomorrow, for you do not know what a day may bring forth'; *b. Sanh.* 100b/*b. Yeb.* 63b: 'Do not fret over tomorrow's troubles, for you know not what a day may bring forth. Tomorrow may come and you will be no more and so you will have grieved over a world that is not yours'; *b. Ber.* 9b: ' "I am that I am" '.

---

[28] Lk 12.32 ('Fear not, little flock, for it is your Father's good pleasure to give you the kingdom') follows Mt 6.33 = Lk 12.31 in the Third Gospel. It may or may not have belonged to Q[lk]. It in any case is not redactional.

[29] A rare word. LXX: 0. NT: 3: Mt 6.34; 10.25; 1 Pet 4.3. Cf. T. Job. 24.6–8.

[30] Mt: 57; Mk: 3–5; Lk: 31. For this particle as introducing a sentence that concludes a section or subsection of the sermon on the mount see also 5.48; 7.12, 24.

The Holy One, blessed be He, said to Moses, Go and say to Israel, I was with you in this servitude, and I shall be with you in the servitude of other kingdoms. He said to Him, Lord of the universe, sufficient is the evil in the time thereof (*dayyâ lĕṣārâ bĕša'tâ*). See further Jas 4.13–14; Ps.-Phoc. 116–21; and Sent. Syr. Men. 385–6; also Sophocles, *Oed. C.* 567–8; Seneca, *Ep.* 101.4; Plutarch, *Cons. ad Apoll.* 11; Stobaeus, *Ecl.* 3.16.28; 4.41. Of special interest is Seneca, *Ep.* 5, where the Stoic speaks despairingly of 'a mind in a state of anxiety through looking into the future', and of 'projecting our thoughts far ahead of us instead of adapting ourselves to the present'. The result is, 'No one confines his unhappiness to the present'. Seneca adds in this connexion a counter illustration drawn from nature which recalls Mt 6.26–30: 'Wild animals run from the dangers they actually see, and once they have escaped worry no more'. Compare Dio Chrysostom 10.15–16.

Whether unwittingly or not, Matthew does what the tradition did before him in 6.26–30, namely, take up a proverbial notion and use it to make a point contrary to the received sense. Both gnomic statements in 6.34, if taken in themselves, sound pessimistic or stoical (cf. *b. Ber.* 9b). But embedded in their present, evangelical context, they gain a new sense: anxiety for the morrow is foolish because the all-powerful, all-knowing, compassionate Father in heaven is Lord of the future. If sufficient for the day is the evil thereof, God is more than sufficient in the midst of that evil.

The repetition of the phrase, 'Do not be anxious' (cf. 6.25, 31), and the occurrence of the same verb twice in this redactional, concluding verse, leave no doubt as to what is the key subject of 6.25–34 and how important it is for Matthew. The mental vice of anxiety is to be exorcized at all costs. The mind is not to be bicameral, subject sometimes to faith, at other times to anxiety. The truth about God should cast out all fear. For reiteration of the same theme see 10.26–31.

(iv) *Concluding Observations*

(1) 6.19–24 contains three sets of antitheses: earth/heaven (19–21), darkness/light (22–3), mammon/God (24). The focus of the first set is the heart, of the second the eye, of the third service. How are the three antitheses and their foci related? The decision with regard to service (God or mammon) creates either inner light or inner darkness and the resultant ὀφθαλμὸς ἁπλοῦς or ὀφθαλμὸς πονηρός while the state of one's eye (= intent) in turn fixes the heart and determines whether one is treasuring up treasure in heaven or on the earth. In short, the firm decision to serve God fills one with light and assures everlasting treasure while the choice in

favour of mammon creates darkness and leads only to the vain grasping of treasures that will certainly perish.

(2) As 6.25–34 shows us, Matthew thought the task of serving God and not mammon to be no easy achievement. For 6.25–34 functions to give believers assurance; it encourages them to be free from worrying overmuch about earthly cares. But what is so hard about the service for which 6.19–24 beckons? The evangelist must have considered the section an integral part of the sermon on the mount, in which the disciple of Jesus is exhorted, among other things, to give to him who asks, to refrain from turning away one who would borrow, and to let him who wants his coat have it, and his cloak also. Now there is, to state the obvious, nothing easy about all this, and to serve God in such a fashion will naturally lead to insecurity. Will not true discipleship land one in a hard, bad way? To follow the path of 5.38–42 and 6.19–24, the path Jesus himself trod, will cause one to exclaim, But what of my life? (cf. Acts Pet. 12 Apost. 10.17–21). How can I serve my lord if my belly is empty (cf. *Mek*. on Exod 16.4)? These questions were certainly in Matthew's mind, and they led him to place the material in 6.25–34 after 6.19–24. In 6.25–34 Matthew's gemaric and pastoral orientation rises to the surface. Our evangelist is trying to lighten heavy hearts. 6.25–34 reproaches no one. It is an attempt to free believers from anxiety so that, unfettered, they might serve their Lord with alacrity.

(3) Two final observations. (i) The promise that God will take care of his own (cf. 6.26, 30) certainly cannot exclude trial and tribulation. Jesus does not guarantee comfort, prosperity, or health. He does not assert that the righteous will flourish upon the earth, and he holds forth no numbing nepenthe for fortune's slings and arrows. On the contrary, the disciple can expect the buffeting of fortune and difficulty at every turn (5.10–12; 10.16–39; 24.9–13). What then is the point? Jesus promises that the heavenly Father, through divine providence, will give his own what is truly necessary for them if they are to accomplish their God-given tasks. There is a road, and it can be travelled. For the disciple that should be enough. (ii) 6.19–34 was not composed to offer Matthew's readers concrete counsel on what to do with wealth. The section rather calls one to be generous with what one has, to exercise faith in the Father in heaven, to serve God by turning a deaf ear to the smooth words of the harlot mammon. Matthew knew of itinerant missionaries who lived close to poverty (cf. 10.9–10) as well as of well-to-do Christians (see on 4.18–22; 19.21), and he recognized that both of them had their place within the community of Jesus' followers. It was consequently not possible for our writer to do other than set forth general principles regarding earthly needs which each, following a conscience formed by Christian

instruction, could apply to his own particular situation. (Matthew's gospel clearly represents a stage in which the enthusiasm of primitive Christianity is giving way to social organization and practical concerns. This explains why the book's instruction on riches and other matters is prudently nuanced.)[31]

(v) *Bibliography*

D. C. Allison, Jr., 'The Eye is the Lamp of the Body (Matt. 6.22–23 = Luke 11.34–36)', *NTS* 33 (1987), pp. 61–83.

J. Amstutz, ΑΠΛΟΤΗΣ. Eine begriffsgeschichtliche Studie zum jüdisch-christlichen Griechisch, Bonn, 1968.

P. Benoit, 'L'oeuil, la lampe du corps', *RB* 60 (1953), pp. 603–6.

H. D. Betz, 'Kosmogonie und Ethik in der Bergpredigt', *ZTK* 81 (1984), pp. 139–71; translated and reprinted in *Essays*, pp. 89–123.

idem, 'Matthew vi.22f and ancient Greek theories of vision', in Best, *Text*, pp. 43–56; reprinted in *Essays*, pp. 71–87.

W. Brandt, 'Der Spruch von lumen internum', *ZNW* 14 (1913), pp. 97–116, 177–201.

K. Brunner, 'Textkritisches zu Mt 6.28 οὐ ξαίνουσιν statt αὐξάνουσιν vorgeschlagen', *ZKT* 100 (1978), pp. 251–6.

H. J. Cadbury, 'The Single Eye', *HTR* 47 (1956), pp. 69–74.

D. Catchpole, 'The ravens,the lilies and the Q hypothesis', *SNTU* 6–7 (1981–2), pp. 77–87.

Dupont 1, pp. 74–81, 111–13; 3, pp. 272–304.

C. Edlund, *Das Auge der Einfalt*, Copenhagen, 1952.

F. C. Fensham, 'The Good and Evil Eye in the Sermon on the Mount', *Neotestamentica* 1 (1967), pp. 51–8.

R. T. France, 'God and Mammon', *EvQ* 51 (1979), pp. 3–21.

E. Fuchs, 'Die Verkündigung Jesu. Der Spruch von den Raben', in Ristow, pp. 385–8.

Giesen, pp. 166–79.

T. F. Glasson, 'Carding and Spinning: Oxyrhynchus Papyrus No. 655', *JTS* 13 (1962), pp. 331–2.

Goppelt, *Theology* 1, pp. 73–5.

J. G. Griffiths,'Wisdom about Tomorrow', *HTR* 53 (1960), pp. 219–21.

E. P. Groenewald, 'God and Mammon', *Neotestamentica* 1 (1967), pp. 59–66.

F. Hahn, 'Die Worte vom Licht Lk 11,33–6', in Hoffmann, *Orientierung*, pp. 107–38.

P.-E. Jacquemin, 'Les options du chrétien', *AsSeign* 39 (1972), pp. 18–27.

Jeremias, *Parables*, pp. 214–15.

Jülicher 2, pp. 98–115.

P. Katz, 'ΠΩΣ ΑΥΞΑΝΟΥΣΙΝ', *JTS* 5 (1954), pp. 207–9.

---

[31] See further the suggestive article of D. B. Kraybill and D. M. Sweetland, 'Possessions in Luke-Acts: A Sociological Perspective', *PRS* 10 (1983), pp. 215–39; also Davies, *SSM*, pp. 387–401, on 'M and Gemara'.

K. Koch, 'Der Schatz im Himmel', in *Leben angesichts des Todes*, ed. B. Lohse and H. P. Schmidt, Tübingen, 1968, pp. 47–60.

O. Linton, 'Coordinated Sayings and Parables in the Synoptic Gospels', *NTS* 26 (1980), pp. 146–8.

B. A. Mastin, 'Latin Mam(m)ona and the Semitic Languages: A False Trail and a Suggestion', *Bib* 65 (1984), pp. 87–90.

M. Mees, 'Das Sprichwort Mt 6,21; Lk 12,24 und seine ausserkanonischen Parallelen', *Aug* 14 (1974), pp. 67–89.

F. Nötscher, 'Das Reich (Gottes) und seine Gerechtigkeit (Mt 6,33 vgl. Lc 12,31)', *Bib* 31 (1950), pp. 237–41.

M. F. Olsthoorn, *The Jewish Background and the Synoptic Setting of Mt 6,25–33 and Lk 12,22–31*, Jerusalem/Rome, 1975.

W. Pesch,'Zur Exegese von Mt 6,19–21 und Lk 12,33–34', *Bib* 40 (1960), pp. 356–78.

Potwin, pp. 105–10.

J. E. Powell, 'Those "Lilies of the Field" Again', *JTS* 33 (1982), pp. 490–2.

H. Riesenfeld, 'Vom Schätzensammeln und Sorge—ein Thema urchristlicher Paränese. Zu Mt 6.19–34', in *Neotestamentica et Patristica*, ed. W. C. van Unnik, Leiden, 1962, pp. 47–58.

R. L. Roberts, 'An Evil Eye (Matthew 6:23)', *RestQ* 7 (1963), pp. 143–7.

H. P. Rüger, 'Mamonas', *ZNW* 64 (1973), pp. 127–31.

S. Safrai and D. Flusser, 'The Slave of Two Masters', *Immanuel* 6 (1976), pp. 30–33.

Schulz, *Q*, pp. 142–5, 149–57, 459–61, 468–70.

G. Schwarz, 'προσθεῖναι ἐπὶ τὴν ἡλικίαν αὐτοῦ πῆχυν ἕνα', *ZNW* 71 (1980), pp. 244–7.

F. Schwencke, 'Das Auge des Leibes Licht', *ZWT* 55 (1914), pp. 251–60.

E. Sjöberg, 'Das Licht in dir. Zur Deutung von Matth. 6,22ff. Par', *ST* 5 (1951), pp. 89–105.

T. C. Skeat, 'The Lilies of the Field', *ZNW* 37 (1938), pp. 211–14.

Tannehill, pp. 60–7.

Wrege, pp. 109–24.

Zeller, *Mahnsprüche*,pp. 77–94.

XV

THE TREATMENT OF ONE'S NEIGHBOUR
(7.1–12)

(i) *Structure*

For the structure of this passage see pp. 626–7.

(ii) *Sources*

The synoptic parallels to Mt 7.1–12 are these:

Mt 7.1–2	=	Lk 6.37a, 38c	=	Mk 4.24b
7.3–5	=	6.41–2		
7.6				
7.7–11	=	11.9–13		
7.12	=	6.31		

How are they to be evaluated? Given the extensive word-for-word agreement between Mt 7.7–11 and its Lukan twin (see on 7.9), literary dependence one way or the other or the mutual adoption of a common (written) source is almost unavoidable. For which side of the disjunction does one settle? Matthew's use of Luke or Luke's use of Matthew seems, for two reasons, excluded. (1) Characteristically Matthean vocabulary (e.g. ἢ τίς ἐστιν ἐξ ὑμῶν ἄνθρωπος in 7.9, ὁ ἐν τοῖς οὐρανοῖς in 7.11, πάντα οὖν ὅσα ἐάν in 7.12) does not appear in Luke, and the reverse is also true (e.g. Matthew has neither 'Holy Spirit' nor ὑπάρχοντες, both of which occur in Lk 11.13). (2) As will be argued later, the variations between Mt 7.9–10 and Lk 11.11–12 are inscrutable unless one postulates that the two evangelists had slightly different sources before their eyes; that is, redactional contributions do not suffice to explain either Mt 7.9–10 or Lk 11.11–12 on the assumption that one is the source of the other or that both depend upon the exact same source (Q). One is, therefore, led to embrace a modified form of the Q hypothesis. Apparently our two writers drew upon what may be labelled Q^mt and Q^lk, upon two different versions or editions of the same source, Q (cf. p. 121).

Granted the soundness of this conclusion, notable in Matthew is the absence of anything corresponding to Lk 6.37b–8b, which (against Fitzmyer, *Luke* 1, p. 641) is probably Q material (cf. Jeremias, *Lukasevangelium* 1, p. 146): 'Condemn not, and you will not be condemned; forgive, and you will be forgiven; give and it will be given to you; good measure, pressed down, shaken together, running over, will be put into your lap'. Why the omission? The placement of 7.3–5 (on the log and speck on the eye) after 7.1–2 reveals Matthew's concern in this section: do not judge others. Because the material just quoted from Luke (= Q) treats of rewards, its appearance here would detract from the main theme. Matthew prefers to stick to the point.

(iii) *Exegesis*

DO NOT JUDGE (7.1–2)

1–2. Matthew now turns from one social issue, what to do with and about mammon (6.19–34), to another, how to treat one's neighbour. This takes him back to the Q source and the sermon on the plain (cf. Lk 6.37–42). For the theme compare Ps 18.25–6; Rom 2.1 (ἐν ᾧ γὰρ κρίνεις τὸν ἕτερον σεαυτὸν κατακρίνεις); 14.10; 1 Cor 4.5; 5.12; Jas 4.11–12; 5.9; 1 Clem. 13.2 (which would appear to be independent of the synoptics; see Hagner, pp. 135–51); Polycarp, *Ep.* 2.3–5; Justin, *Dial.* 47.5 (agraphon: ἐν οἷς ἂν ὑμᾶς καταλάβω ἐν τούτοις καὶ κρινῶ);[1] and Sextus, *Sent.* 183 (ὁ κρίνων ἄνθρωπον κρίνεται ὑπὸ τοῦ θεοῦ).

Because so much of the sermon on the mount contrasts the Pharisees with the followers of Jesus, and because, in the synoptic tradition, the Pharisees are so often presented as wrongly passing judgement on others (e.g. Mt 9.10–13; 12.1–8; Lk 7.39; 15.1–2; 18.9–14), the command not to judge may in part be intended to implicate the Pharisees, those who, in Matthew's opinion, condemn and judge others (cf. Zahn, p. 302).

μὴ κρίνετε ἵνα μὴ κριθῆτε. In Lk 6.37a this sentence, which reverses the *lex talionis*, begins with καί (redactional?); and for ἵνα (cf. Jas 5.9) Luke has καὶ οὐ.

The imperative μὴ κρίνετε, cannot refer to simple ethical judgements, and believers are not being instructed to refrain from critical thinking (without which they could never choose between true and false religion; cf. 18.15). Jesus himself, after all, delivered himself of numerous polemical utterances, and it would in any case be futile to forbid people to exercise their faculties of discernment (cf. Irenaeus, *Adv. haer.* 4.30.3). One can, however, enjoin mercy, humility, and tolerance, and such is the case with Mt 7.1–2 (cf. 6.14–15; 18.21–2). μὴ κρίνετε implies that the individual, acting upon what Luther called 'self-centred wisdom', is playing the judge (cf. Jn 5.30). He is taking up a rôle he should not be playing because it is reserved for the only capable judge, God. (Cf.

---

[1] Although Justin attributes the saying to Jesus, the Latin translation of the Life of St. Anthony (PL 73.136A) and St. John Climacus (PG 88.812D) attribute it (probably correctly) to the lost Apocryphon of Ezekiel. For discussion see A. Resch, *Agrapha*, TU 30.3–4, Berlin, 1906, pp. 102, 322–4; Jeremias, *Unknown Sayings*, pp. 83–8; and A. Baker, 'Justin's Agraphon in the Dialogue with Trypho', *JBL* 87 (1968), pp. 277–8.

13.36–43, 47–50, where the sorting out of evil from good awaits the great assize). Thus κρίνω is almost synonymous with κατακρίνω = 'condemn' (cf. 12.41–2; 20.18; Rom 2.1, 3). This inference is borne out by the meaning of the verb in the second half of the present clause. 'Do not judge, *lest ye be judged*' means, 'Do not judge, lest ye be condemned [by God at the final judgement]'. Compare Jas 2.13: judgement is without mercy to one who shows no mercy to others. Consider also Mk 9.38–41, where Jesus, opposing his disciples' intolerance, first commands them not to forbid the strange exorcist to use Jesus' name and then declares, 'He who is not against us is for us'. Rabbinic parallels may be found in *b. Roš. Hoš.* 16b; *b. Šabb.* 127b, 151b ('he who is merciful to others, mercy is shown to him by Heaven, while he who is not merciful to others, mercy is not shown to him by Heaven'—a rabbinic 'sentence of holy law'); *t. B. Qam.* 9.30; *y. B. Qam.* 8.10.6c.[2] T. W. Manson wrote: 'The whole business of judging persons is in God's hands, for He alone knows the secrets of men's hearts. This does not mean that we are not to use all the moral insight we possess in order to discover what is right and wrong; but that we are to confine ourselves to that field and refrain from passing judgement on persons. For our judgement is itself a factor in shaping their lives, and a harsh judgement may help a fellow-creature on the road to perdition' (*Sayings*, p. 56).

ἐν ᾧ γὰρ κρίματι κρίνετε κριθήσεσθε. This is a redactional elaboration of 7.1, for which Lk 6.38 (Q; see Schürmann, *Lukasevangelium* 1, p. 363) = Mk 4.24, which Matthew immediately quotes, served as the model. The upshot is parallelism absent from both Mark and Q. Note that the addition of κρίμα increases even further the paronomasia of 7.1–2.

All Christians, not just those in positions of leadership, are the subject of Mt 7.2 and the surrounding verses. Of all may it be said, 'With what sin he hath sinned, in this shall he be judged' (LAB 44.10).

καὶ ἐν ᾧ μέτρῳ μετρεῖτε μετρηθήσεται ὑμῖν.[3] So Mk 4.24, without

---

[2] One is hardly comfortable with the sweeping words of Braun, *Jesus*, p. 97: 'the absolute prohibition of judging that Jesus issues (Matt. 7:1 par.) not only has no Jewish analogy, it contradicts broad Jewish teaching and practice'. What would Braun make of *b. Šabb.* 127b and 151b, or of *ARN* (vers. 2) 19.20b, where the lesson of thinking the best of people despite appearances is taught? See also *m. 'Abot* 2.5: Hillel said, 'Judge not thy fellow until thou art come to his place'. Although not necessarily first century, texts such as these encourage one to infer that when Jesus called people not to judge, he was probably not offering unheard-of counsel but reminding his hearers of a known imperative which they, being human like the rest of us, had difficulty honouring.

[3] αντιμετρηθησεται, which adds clarity but breaks the pattern of assonance in 7.2 (κρι/κρι/κρι; μετρ/μετρ/μετρ), appears in Θ 0233 *f*[13] (28ᶜ) *al* it vgᶜˡ Ath Aug Cyr Hier Lcf.

the καί. So also Lk 6.38 (Q), with τῷ γὰρ αὐτῷ before μετρῷ, with ᾧ after it, and with ἀντι added to the final verb. ἐν means 'according to'. The καί introduces synonymous parallelism: 2a and 2b mean the same thing. The sentence is traditional, the equivalent of bĕmiddâ šeʾādām môdēd bâ môddîn lô (*Mek*. on Exod 13.19, 21; 14.25; 15.3; 5, 8; 17.14; *m. Soṭa* 1.7; *t. Soṭa* 3.1; Tg. Ps.-J. on Gen 38.26; *b. Šabb*. 105b; *b. Sanh*. 100a; *b. Soṭa* 8b; SB 1, pp. 444–6; McNamara, pp. 138–42). For similar statements see Ecclus 16.14; T. Zeb. 5.3; 2 En. 44.5; and Tg. Isa. on 27.8 ('in the measure you were measuring with they will measure you . . .'). The notion of 'measure for measure'—is the picture supposed to be of grain being measured?—was manifestly well-known in ancient Judaism. It was frequently brought into connexion with eschatology, as it is here (cf. Rüger (v), Couroyer (v)). Unlike Lk 6.38, where the emphasis is on God's mercy, Matthew keeps the idea of judgement to the fore.[4]

We need not doubt that Jesus himself used the 'measure for measure' proverb. Although the piece of folk-wisdom might have entered the tradition from without, it has multiple attestation in Mark and Q, and the criterion of coherency is satisfied, for Jesus' eschatological paraenesis took up the law of reciprocity (see e.g. Mt 10.32–3 = Lk 12.8–9).

THE SPLINTER AND THE LOG (7.3–5)

3. As is so typical of the Jesus tradition, the abstract (7.1–2) now melts into the concrete (7.3–5): prosaic utterance becomes vivid parable.

Concerning structure, 7.3 and 7.4 are rhetorical questions which prepare for 7.5, an exhortation addressed to the 'hypocrite'. Concerning content, while the theme of judging others (7.1–2) is continued, the parable in 7.3–5 emphasizes the element of hypocrisy: the fault of the one who will be judged by God for having judged others is self-righteous two-facedness (cf. Lk 18.9–14). For the sense see Rom 2.1 ('Therefore you have no excuse, O man, whoever you are, when you judge another; for in passing judgement upon him you condemn yourself, because you, the judge, are doing the very same things'); Sextus, *Sent*. 90; *b. Qidd*. 70a ('He who accuses another of a fault has it himself)'; *b. B. Meṣ*. 107b; *b. Sanh*. 18a, 19b. For parallels from the Graeco-Roman world see Horace, *Sat*. 1.3.25;[5] Plutarch, *Mor*. 469B,

---

[4] Cf. Neuhäusler (v), p. 109. In Mk 4.24 the context has to do with the reception of Jesus' teaching: 'Take heed what you hear'.

[5] 'When you look over your own sins, your eyes are rheumy and daubed with ointment; why, when you view the failings of your friends, are you as keen of sight as an eagle . . .?'

515D. Recall also the story of David and his anger upon hearing Nathan's parable about the rich man who had taken the poor man's little ewe lamb: the king did not realize that what made him angry in another was his own fault (2 Sam 12.1–15). All too often we search for the faults of others with the lantern of Diogenes while remaining utterly oblivious to our own obvious failings.

Should the saying about the beam and splinter be considered authentic? Jesus was fond of hyperbole and liked parables, and with his special concern for right intention (cf. Vermes, *World*, p. 47), he was much engaged to root out hypocrisy. Furthermore, Gos. Thom. 26 appears to offer us a version of the saying independent of Q (see below). Against these facts, one could refer to the Jewish parallels (to be cited below) and then appeal to the criterion of dissimilarity (cf. Braun, *Qumran* 2, p. 84, n. 6). But as the Jewish parallels have been thought by some to stem from the Christian tradition (see below), and as we in any case know that Jesus took up traditional materials for his own purposes, Mt 7.3–5 may tentatively be traced to Jesus—who was, we should remember, a carpenter at one time (see on 13.55). For the original form of 7.3–5 see on 7.5.

τί δὲ βλέπεις τὸ κάρφος τὸ ἐν τῷ ὀφθαλμῷ τοῦ ἀδελφοῦ σου. So also Luke (although P⁷⁵ 1424 *pc* omit δέ). Use of a common Greek source seems certain. (In Mt 7.3–5 = Lk 6.41–42, fifty out of sixty-four words are shared.) Gos. Thom. 26a appears to go back to a slightly different Greek sentence: τὸ κάρφος . . . σου βλέπεις (so HG, p. 40). κάρφος, which appears in the NT only in Mt 7.3–5 par., means 'splinter' or 'chip' and connotes insignificance. The translation of the KJV, namely, 'mote' (= 'speck of dust'), is probably incorrect; see King, 'Mote' (v). The word is met with only once in the LXX, in Gen 8.11, for *ṭārāp*. In Matthew κάρφος stands for small moral defects while its antithesis, δοκός, stands for sizeable moral defects. Note that both the splinter and the beam are in the eye, which is the 'most conspicuous part of the body' (Bengel, *Gnomon, ad loc.*). On 'brother' in Matthew see on 5.22. For the comedic, striking contrast between the beam and the splinter, which was perhaps proverbial, see *b. 'Arak*. 16b: 'R. Tarfon said, I wonder whether there is any one in this generation who accepts reproof, for if one says to him: Remove the mote (*qêsām*) from between your eyes [or: teeth], he would answer: Remove the beam (*qôrâ*) from between your eyes [or: teeth]' (cf. *b. B. Bat*. 15b).⁶

τὴν δὲ ἐν τῷ σῷ ὀφθαλμῷ δοκὸν οὐ κατανοεῖς; The outcome of someone with a beam in the eye correcting one with a speck in his is

⁶ Schlatter, p. 243; Manson, *Sayings*, p. 58; and Jeremias, *Theology*, p. 19, n. 2, find no difficulty supposing that the rabbinic tradition in *b. 'Arak*. 16b and *b. B. Bat*. 15b might come from the Jesus tradition. This possibility must be conceded, esp. as R. Tarfon is known to have engaged in anti-Christian polemic.

the blind leading the blind. In Luke, δοκόν (= 'beam of wood'; LXX: 10, 4 for *qō(ô)râ*; cf. the rabbinic loan word, *dôqĕyāy'* = δόκια) appears after δέ, a second τήν is then added, and τῷ ἰδίῳ replaces τῷ σῷ. κατανοέω perhaps replaces βλέπω in both Matthew and Luke because an object in one's eye can be noticed but not really seen.

Gos. Thom. 26b readily translates itself back into the following Greek: τὴν δὲ δοκὸν τὴν ἐν τῷ ὀφθαλμῷ σου οὐ βλέπεις. This is so interesting because, while the order of Gos.Thom. agrees with Luke, the σου agrees with Matthew. It would appear, then, that either Gos. Thom. 26b reflects a knowledge of both the First and Third Gospels or it is independent of both. The second alternative is supported by the apparent independence of Gos. Thom. 26a (see above), and if this be accepted, then the agreements between Gos. Thom. 26 and Matthew and/or Luke take us back to a pre-synoptic stage. All this in turn entails that Luke's τῷ ἰδίῳ must be secondary (an inference upheld by the use of σου in the rest of the saying) and that Matthew displaced δοκόν.

4. This verse and the next form a chiasmus:
Or how can you say to your brother:
a   Let me cast out the beam from your eye,
b   and behold,
c   the beam is in your own eye?
d   First cast out
c   the beam from your own eye,
b   and then you will see clearly
a   to cast out the beam from your brother's eye.

ἢ πῶς ἐρεῖς τῷ ἀδελφῷ σου. Luke has the more hypothetical πῶς δύνασαι λέγειν. . . . The 'or' might be Matthean, for ἢ πῶς has no parallel in Mt 12.29, and Luke, according to the text of NA[26], never has the construction. ἐρείς (ἐρῶ: Mt: 30; Mk: 2; Lk: 19) is also probably redactional, Luke's δύνασαι presumably from Q (cf. Jeremias, *Lukasevangelium* p. 147).[7] πῶς ἐρεῖς/ἐρεῖτε translates *'êk tō'mĕrî(û)* in Jer 2.23 and Isa 19.11 LXX.

ἄφες ἐκβάλω τὸ κάρφος ἐκ τοῦ ὀφθαλμοῦ σου.[8] For ἐκ τοῦ Luke has τὸ ἐν τῷ (cf. on 7.5). He also prefaces this clause with the vocative, 'brother'. This adds to the culprit's hypocrisy, for in truth the man is not acting like a brother but more like a parent with child. It cannot be decided whether the third evangelist added 'brother' (cf. Acts 9.17; 21.20; 22.13) or whether Matthew has

---

[7] We reject the suggestion of Black, p. 132, who divines in Matthew (ἐρεῖς) and Luke (δύνασαι λέγειν) different renderings of a Semitic imperfect.

[8] απο (so HG) appears after καρφος in K W Δ Θ 565 700 1010 Maj. εκ has the stronger attestation and is what Matthew wrote twice in 7.5 (cf. Lk 6.42). (Against the impression left by Allen, pp. xxv–xxvi, Matthew does not regularly avoid a compound verb followed by the same preposition; see MHT 4, p. 39.)

dropped it (so Gundry, *Commentary*, p. 121). ἄφες invites permission (BDF § 364; cf. 27.49).

καὶ ἰδοὺ ἡ δοκὸς ἐν τῷ ὀφθαλμῷ σου. Luke has αὐτὸς τὴν ἐν τῷ ὀφθαλμῷ σου δοκὸν οὐ βλέπων; 'And behold' is probably Matthean (see on 1.20) although αὐτός . . . οὐ βλέπων could likewise be Lukan (cf. BDF § 430.1–2).

5. Before setting out to hunt mole hills in faraway places, one should be able to see the mountain before one's face.

ὑποκριτά, ἔκβαλε πρῶτον τὴν δοκὸν ἐκ τοῦ ὀφθαλμοῦ σου, καὶ τότε διαβλέψεις ἐκβαλεῖν τὸ κάρφος ἐκ τοῦ ὀφθαλμοῦ τοῦ ἀδελφοῦ σου.[9] Luke has the infinitive at the end and τὸ ἐν τῷ for ἐκ. With regard to both of these differences, Gos. Thom. 26 concurs with Matthew. But Gos. Thom. 26 (cf. *P. Oxy.* 1.1) goes its own way in not having 'hypocrite' and in not beginning with a command but with ὅταν (contrast *P. Oxy.* 1.1: καὶ τότε). Is this not some indication of independence? (Observe also the absence in Gos. Thom. of anything resembling Mt 7.4 = Lk 6.42a). For 'hypocrite' see on 6.2. Interestingly enough, the word is here applied to believers. According to Jeremias, the Pharisees were the original objects of the warning, for 'hypocrite' is nowhere else in the gospels applied to disciples (*Parables*, p. 167). But the word, which does not appear in Gos. Thom., may not have belonged to the original saying.

Because human beings unhappily possess an inbred proclivity to mix ignorance of themselves with arrogance towards others, the call to recognize one's own faults is a commonplace of moral and religious traditions, including the biblical (cf. Prov 28.13; Jn 9.41; 1 Jn 1.8).[10]

In 7.3 one simply sees (βλέπειν). In 7.5 one sees clearly (διαβλέπειν). In the latter instance one sees in order to help. The stare to find fault becomes the genuinely friendly eye of a brother who is a servant (cf. 18.15). Some commentators, to be sure, fail to discern in Mt 7.3–5 any instruction concerning fraternal correction. For them, the text prohibits judging altogether (cf. 7.1–2): anyone who presumes to admonish or appraise another has a beam in his eye (cf. Jn 8.7; so many, including Bonnard, p. 97; Hill, *Matthew*, p. 147; Guelich, pp. 352–3). In our estimation, this interpretation is indeed plausible with reference to the historical Jesus. He probably will not have been interested in clarifying what preconditions are requisite if one is to make so bold as to estimate

---

[9] To maintain the parallelism between 5a and 5b, δοκον should be placed not where it is in ℵ B C^vid —after σου—but before εκ, as in L W Θ 0233 *f*^1.13 Maj latt (so rightly HG, against NA^26).

[10] Cf. *b. B. Meṣ.* 63b: 'Do not taunt your neighbour with the blemish you yourself have'. *Lam. Rab.* on 3.40: 'Let us first correct ourselves; then let us seek to correct others'. *y. Taʿan.* 2.1.65a: 'Let us pick off the straw from ourselves before we do it to others'.

another's condition and offer advice for correction. Jesus presumably will simply have wished to discourage hypocrisy and self-righteousness. (In line with this, the original saying may be preserved only in 7.3 or 7.3–5a; 7.4–5 or 7.5b could be secondary expansion.) Matters seem otherwise with the redactional level (cf. Schniewind, p. 98; Gundry, *Commentary*, p. 122). The evangelist shows a special concern elsewhere for the proper procedures for dealing with sin seen in others (18.15–20). Moreover, Matthew may have moved ἐκβαλεῖν forward (contrast Luke) in order to shift the emphasis to the act of removal. When to this is added Matthew's characteristic use of the word 'brother' to mean 'Christian brother' (see on 5.22), it is natural to think primarily— though not exclusively (see Luz 1, p. 380)—in terms of intra-ecclesiastical activity.

PEARLS BEFORE SWINE (7.6)

6. Having warned his audience about judging others, Matthew now adds 'gemara' in order to counteract an extreme interpretation of 7.1–5: if there must not be too much severity (vv. 1–5), there must at the same time not be too much laxity (v. 6). Our author is anticipating a problem and searching for a balance, for moral symmetry. The principles advanced in 7.1–5 are not to be abused. They do not eliminate the use of critical faculties when it comes to sacred concerns. One should not always throw the cloak over a brother's faults. One must not be meekly charitable against all reason. Compare 2 Cor 6.14–18.

Although 7.6 has no parallel in Mark or Luke, it should not be considered an editorial creation. (1) Word statistics do not demand Matthean composition.[11] (2) The verse just may have stood in Q^mt, Luke or Q^lk having omitted it as being potentially offensive (cf. Davies, *COJ*, p. 123; Marshall, p. 466). (3) Gos. Thom. 93 appears to preserve a version independent of Matthew:[12] 'Do not give that which is holy to the dogs, lest they cast it on the dung-heap; do not throw the pearls to the swine, lest

[11] μὴ δῶτε appears only once in the First Gospel. The same is true for τὸ ἅγιον with the meaning of 'that which is holy'. κύων: Mt: 1, Mk: 0; Lk: 1. βάλλω: Mt: 34; Mk: 18; Lk: 18. μαργαρίτης: Mt: 3; Mk: 0; Lk: 0. ἔμπροσθεν: Mt: 18; Mk: 2; Lk: 10. χοῖρος: Mt: 4; Mk: 4; Lk: 4. μήποτε: Mt: 8; Mk: 2; Lk: 7. καταπατέω: Mt: 2; Mk: 0; Lk: 2. πούς: Mt: 10; Mk: 6; Lk: 19. στρέφω: Mt: 6; Mk: 0; Lk: 7. ῥήγνυμι: Mt: 2; Mk: 2; Lk: 2.

[12] Cf. Koester, in *TTEC*, p. 182, n. 83. Did. 9.5, by way of contrast, agrees completely with Matthew.

they make it . . . [text breaks]'.[13] (4) A Semitic original is easily constructed (cf. Jeremias (v), though we are hesitant about his hypothesis of a mistranslation).

μὴ δῶτε τὸ ἅγιον τοῖς κυσίν. Note the use of the definite article throughout the rest of the saying. Because dogs in the ancient world were known primarily not as pets[14] but as wild creatures which roamed the streets in packs scavenging for refuse on which to feed, 'dog' became a word of reproach (as in 1 Sam 17.43; 24.14; 2 Sam 9.8; 16.9; Ps 22.20; Prov 26.11; Isa 56.10–11; Diogenes, *Ep.* 44). Compare the English 'cur' and recall that 'Cynic' (= κυνικός, 'dog-like') was used as a term of abuse (as in Diogenes Laertius 6.60). In Deut 23.18, 'dog' = a pagan, male prostitute (*qādēš*), and similar equations are made in other texts (e.g. Mt 15.26–7 = Mk 7.27–8; 1 En. 89.42–9; Ps.-Clem. Hom. 2.19; SB 1, pp. 722–6)— although it would be going too far to assert that 'dog' was a common appellation for the Gentiles (cf. Abrahams 2, pp. 195–6). The question for us is, Are the 'dogs' of Mt 7.6 Gentiles (as in 15.26–7), or do we have here a general term of contempt (cf. Phil 3.2 (dogs = the Judaizing faction); Rev 22.15 (dogs = sinners outside paradise); Ignatius, *Eph.* 7.1 (mad dogs = heretics); *m. Soṭa* 9.15 ('this generation is as the face of a dog' refers to the impiety of Israel))? Surely the latter.[15] 'Do not give that which is holy to dogs' takes up for a novel end a known rule (cf. *m. Tem.* 6.5; *b. Bek.* 15a; *b. Pesaḥ.* 29a; *b. Šebu.* 11b; *b. Tem.* 117a, 130b) in which τὸ ἅγιον means sacrificial meat or leaven (cf. Exod 29.33; Lev 2.3; 22.6, 7, 10–16; Num 18.8–19). In Mt 7.6 this rule, by virtue of its new context, becomes a comprehensive statement about the necessity to keep distinct the realms of clean and unclean (cf. Exod 29.33; CD 12.8–9).[16]

[13] If Gos. Thom. 93 is, as we have affirmed, independent of Matthew, this supports our suggestion that Mt 7.6 might come from Q; for Gos. Thom. 92 recalls Mt 7.7 while Gos. Thom. 94 recalls Mt 7.8. So Matthew and the author of Gos. Thom. have Mt 7.6 in similar contexts. Furthermore, it would seem to follow that, in Q, Mt 7.6 stood beside Mt 7.7–11 = Lk 11.9–13, not beside Mt 7.1–5 = Lk 6.37, 38, 41, 42.

[14] There are, however, indications that dogs were sometimes domesticated; see Tob 6.1 (v.l.); 11.4 (v.l.); Mk 7.27 (?); Philo, *Praem. Poen.* 89; *b. 'Abod. Zar.* 54b; Anacharsis, *Ep.* 8; Ps.-Dionysius, *De div. nom.* 4.25. The Zoroastrians were known to have had great respect for the dog; cf. Herodotus 1.140.

[15] Those who would demur could see in Mt 7.6 a prohibition of mission to the Gentiles (cf. 10.5–6; 15.24); cf. T. W. Manson, *Only to the House of Israel?*, FFBS 9, Philadelphia, 1964, p. 1; idem, *Sayings*, p. 174.

[16] Also, if Mt 7.6 goes back to Jesus—a question we have found no way of answering—his apparent openness to Gentiles (note esp. 8.5–13, also 15.21–8) makes a reference to them unlikely. Our conclusions about Mt 7.6 render uncertain a conjecture many have found appealing, namely, that the Aramaic original had to do not with 'that which is holy' (*qudšāʾ*) but with a 'ring' (*qĕdāšāʾ*; cf. 11QtgJob on 42.11 and the traditional targum on the same verse). Cf. Prov 11.22 and see Perles

Within the context of Matthew (and, we may presume, for the pre-Matthean tradition), 7.6 is to be assigned one of two meanings, and perhaps both are present simultaneously. (1) The saying is an admonition about the necessity to limit the time and energy directed towards the hard-hearted. The gospel of the kingdom—in 13.45–6 the kingdom is a pearl—was to be preached to all; but its heralds were also instructed to shake the dust off their feet when they were not received into a house or town (10.14). They were not to throw away wittingly the words of the gospel. They were not to give that which is holy to dogs or to throw pearls before swine (so Luther). There has to be an economy of truth. (2) Matthew may have had in mind certain esoteric teachings and practices that were not to be made known to outsiders (cf. 1QS 9.17, 22; Philo, *De cherub*. 42, 48; Josephus, *Bell*. 2.141; Ps.-Clem. Rec. 3.1; Gregory Nazianzus, *Orat*. 2.79; Ps.-Dionysius, *De div. nom*. 1.8 *ad fin*).[17] Although God gives good gifts even to evil human beings (cf. 5.45), not everything should be set before everybody. 'Holy things are for the holy'. In this case, the Didache (9.5) would maintain the right spirit of Mt 7.6: those who have not been baptized into the name of the Lord should not receive the Eucharist, for that would be to give that which is holy to dogs (so also Tertullian, Cyril of Jerusalem, Jerome, and many other Fathers).[18] Consider also the rabbinic notion that the words of Torah should not be transmitted to a Goi: *b. Ḥag*. 13a; *b. Ketub*. 111a; SB 1, p. 447 (cf. *b. Šabb*. 127b: 'Let not sacred words enter a place of uncleanness').[19]

(v); Jeremias (v); and Black, pp. 200–2. It is all the more difficult to accept this conjecture because, as Jeremias has observed, there must have been not one but two translation errors: *bʾpy* must have been taken to mean 'before' rather than 'in the nose of'. There is the further difficulty that Gos. Thom. 93, which might go back to an independent translation of the Aramaic, also has 'holy'.

[17] Cf. Davies, *COJ*, pp. 122–4. The theme of hiding sacred mysteries from the uninitiated is nearly ubiquitous in the history of religions. Recall that the short text of Lk 22.15–19 has sometimes been explained as someone's attempt to protect the sacred eucharistic formula from profanation (see Jeremias, *Eucharistic Words*, pp. 157–9).

[18] The range of patristic interpretations is interesting. Elchasai used Mt 7.6 to justify his esoteric, sectarian teachings (so Hippolytus, *Ref*. 9.12). Basilidians referred the verse to non-Gnostics (Epiphanius, *Haer*. 24.5.2), Origen to lapsed Christians (*Princ*. 3.1.17). In Ep. 2 Concerning Virginity 6, true believers are not to minister—i.e. sing psalms or read the Scriptures—where non-Christians (= dogs and swine) are drinking and blaspheming in their feasts. Methodius, *De creatis* 1, pp. 493–4 (Bonwetsch), in a unique interpretation, equated pearls with virtues, swine with pleasures.

[19] Another interpretation has been defended by Guelich, pp. 353–6. Following the lead of G. Bornkamm, 'Bergpredigt', he links 7.6 with the clause in the Lord's Prayer about apostasy: to forfeit what is holy and precious is to succumb to the temptation of apostasy. Lambrecht rightly calls this 'somewhat farfetched' (p. 164).

μηδὲ βάλητε τοὺς μαργαρίτας ὑμῶν ἔμπροσθεν τῶν χοίρων. In tandem with 6a, this is an example of synonymous parallelism. The sense of 6a is the sense of 6b; and 'do not throw' corresponds to 'do not give', 'your pearls' to 'that which is holy', and 'dogs' to 'swine'. For 'pig' occurring with 'dog' as an unclean or despised animal see 1 En. 89.42; 2 Pet 2.22; P. Oxy. V 840.33; b. Šabb. 155b; Horace, Ep. 1.2.26; 2.2.75. Mt 7.6b may have been, like 7.6a, proverbial. Compare Theophylactus Simocatta, Ep. 20: τὰ δῶρα τοῖς χοίροις διένειμε.

Pearls, because of their great value (cf. T. Jud. 13.5; Mt 13.45–6; 1 Tim 2.9; b. B. Bat. 75a), came to be metaphorically used for something of supreme worth, especially of fine wisdom, excellent sayings, or precious teaching: ARN 18; b. Ḥag. 3a; b. Ber. 33b; b. Yeb. 94a; b. Qidd. 39b (cf. Gregory Nazianzus, Orat. 28.2; the Revelation of John the Theologian, end (in ANF 8, p. 586)). Swine, on the other hand, were unclean animals (Lev 11.7; Deut 14.8; Josephus, C. Ap. 2.137), and so they became a symbol of heathen or non-Israelites (ARN 34; SB 1, pp. 449–50) or, as in the present instance, of the unclean or foolish in general (Prov 11.22; 2 Pet 2.22). The 'swine', therefore, together with the 'dogs', are those who have wholly abandoned themselves to vicious courses. They are the hard-hearted and blind so prominent in the gospel tradition (Mt 13.10–13; 15.14; etc.).

μήποτε καταπατήσουσιν αὐτοὺς ἐν τοῖς ποσὶν αὐτῶν καὶ στραφέντες ῥήξωσιν ὑμᾶς. This supplies the reason for the two admonitions just delivered. 'Dogs' and 'swine' desecrate what should be honoured (cf. Prov 23.9; b. Sanh. 90b[20]). καταπατήσουσιν[21] presumably goes with 'swine', ῥήξωσιν with 'dogs'. This makes the arrangement chiastic:

a Do not give dogs what is holy
b Do not throw your pearls before swine
b Lest they (the swine) trample them under foot
a And (lest the dogs) turn to attack you

SEEK AND YOU SHALL FIND (7.7–11)

What is the connexion between 7.7–11 and the preceding verse? Some see none at all and implicitly accuse our evangelist of creating a messy amalgam (cf. McNeile, p. 91; Hill, Matthew, p. 148). According to others, praying and seeking and knocking

[20] 'One who gives terumah (heave-offering) to an ignorant priest is as though he had placed it before a lion: just as a lion may possibly tear his prey and eat it and possibly not, so is an ignorant priest—he may possibly eat it undefiled and possibly defiled'.

[21] καταπατέω occurs with πούς in Dan 7.19 LXX and with τὰ ἅγια in 1 Macc 3.51. Cf. also Ezek 34.18: tirměsŭ běraglêkem.

are all for wisdom, which is necessary if one is to take the speck out of a brother's eye (7.5), or to understand how the principle of 7.6—pearls are not for swine—is to be rightly applied (cf. Schweizer, *Matthew*, p. 172). Still others surmise that 7.7–11 concludes a complex headed by the Lord's Prayer and that the section offers appropriate assurance to those who pray to the Father (cf. Schniewind, p. 99; G. Bornkamm, 'Bergpredigt', p. 430; Guelich, p. 356; cf. Lambrecht, p. 163). Gundry, for his part, avows that 7.7–11 is not primarily concerned with instruction for prayer; rather does the piece serve to introduce the Golden Rule: as God gives good gifts to those who ask him (7.7–11), just so should the disciple do good to others (7.12; *Commentary*, p. 123). Yet one more attempt to fathom what is going on is this: after having been told how to act towards others (7.1–6), the disciples are reminded of how God himself deals with people (7.7–11), and they are to imitate him in his benignity and wisdom (so Alford 1, p. 69). For our own solution, which saves Matthew from the charge of flitting to and fro with no purpose or discernible design, see pp. 625–7.

As to the internal structure of 7.7–11, vv. 7 and 8, which state the thesis and its basis, are parallel to each other, as are vv. 9 and 10, which supply supporting illustrations. V. 11, the conclusion, is an inference drawn from vv. 9–10. Schematically—

7.7   thesis:

> ask→and it will be given you
> seek→and you will find
> knock→and it will be opened to you

7.8   basis:

> everyone who asks→receives
> and he who seeks→finds
> and to him who knocks→it will be opened

7.9   first supporting illustration:
> if a son asks for bread/
>> his father does not give to him a stone

7.10   second supporting illustration:
> if a son asks for fish/
>> his father does not give to him a serpent

7.11   concluding inference, from 7.9–10:
> because God is better than evil men/
> and because God is like a father/
>> how much more . . .

The unity of the section is brought out by the final words of 7.11 (will *give* good things to those who *ask* him), which form a chiastic inclusion with the opening of 7.7 (*ask* and it will be *given*).

7. **αἰτεῖτε καὶ δοθήσεται ὑμῖν, ζητεῖτε καὶ εὑρήσετε, κρούετε καὶ ἀνοιγήσεται ὑμῖν.** So Lk 11.9, with 'And I say to you' prefaced. Compare Gos. Thom. 92 ('Seek and you shall find') and 38 ('There

will be days when you will seek and you will not find me'). The thought belongs to Jewish wisdom, as the following texts show: Prov 8.17 ('I (wisdom) love those who love me, and those who seek me diligently find me'); 1.28 ('They will seek me (wisdom) diligently but will not find me'); Wisd 6.12 (wisdom 'is found by those who seek her'). Compare Eccles 7.23–9. See also Jer 29.13 ('You will seek me and find me; when you seek me with all your heart'; the previous verse, 29.12, concerns prayer); Jn 14.13–14; 15.7; 16.24 (see p. 685); *b. Meg.* 6b, 12b; *Pesiq. R.* 176a; Epictetus, *Diss.* 1.28.20; 4.1.51.

For αἰτέω with δίδωμι in the context of prayer see Philo, *Migr. Abr.* 121 and Jas 1.5. The two passive verbs—δοθήσεται, ἀνοιγήσεται—are obviously theological passives: God gives and God opens doors. αἰτεῖτε and the other two imperatives are in the present tense because asking should be continual. Note that the commands of Mt 7.7 are positive and in this respect contrast with the negative imperatives so heavily concentrated in 6.1–7.6 (where μή is used fourteen times). ζητεῖτε and κρούετε[22] are probably both on a par with 'ask'; that is, they are activities within prayer or identical with prayer—as 7.9–11, where 'ask' alone is used, indicates.[23] For prayer as seeking see 2 Sam 21.1; Ps 24.6; 27.8; 105.4; and Hos 5.15.

According to Marshall, pp. 467–8, there are three ways of understanding 7.7–8. (1) The two verses contain beggars' wisdom: the beggar knows that if he persists he will get what he wants. On this interpretation, the stress is on pertinacity (cf. Lk 18.1–8 and see Jeremias, *Parables*, pp. 159–60, also Gundry, *Commentary*, pp. 123–4). (2) The statement that the one who asks receives, that the one who seeks finds, and that the one who knocks will have the door opened to him, might be drawn from universal experience: people generally get what they want if they are insistent (cf. G. Bertram, *TWNT* 3, pp. 956–7). (3) 7.7–8 may simply be apodictic assertion: Jesus, as the authoritative spokesman of God, is revealing a religious truth which depends not upon worldly experience or wisdom but upon the speaker's authority (so Marshall, p. 468; Schulz, *Q*, pp. 163–4). This last approach is surely the best, at least for the Matthean context. 7.7–11 serves, as we have seen, a function similar to 6.25–34. Both passages support and encourage the disciple who hesitates because of, or who is dismayed at, the great weight of Jesus' heavy imperatives. For the evangelist, then, the point is not persistent effort but the good

[22] κρούω occurs with ἀνοίγω in both Lk 12.36 and Rev 3.20—both times on the lips of Jesus.
[23] *Pace* Zahn, p. 308, and others, knocking does not have to do with seeking entrance into the kingdom of God.

character of the Father as this has been revealed by Jesus. Confirmation of this is to be had in the conclusion: what is emphasized in v. 11 is not human effort but God's gift: 'how much more will your Father who is in heaven . . .'.

Nowhere in Matthew or in the other synoptics is there any explicit reflection on the problem of unanswered prayer (contrast Jas 4.3; for the rabbis see SB 1, pp. 454–5). The confidence that the sincere believer or the united community will be heard and answered seems unbounded (cf. 18.19; 21.22; Jn 14.13; 15.7; 16.23–4; the exception to the rule is Mk 14.32–42). This fact reflects not only the bold and optimistic faith of Jesus but also the enthusiastic beginnings of the church.[24]

8. πᾶς γὰρ ὁ αἰτῶν λαμβάνει καὶ ὁ ζητῶν εὑρίσκει καὶ τῷ κρούοντι ἀνοιγήσεται. So Lk 11.10. Compare Jn 16.24; Jas 4.3; 1 Jn 3.22; Josephus, *Ant.* 8.175. Gos. Thom. 94 has this: 'Whoever seeks shall find (and whoever knocks) it shall be opened to him'. Whereas the impact of v. 7 seems to come from the first half of the clause (ask, seek, knock—all imperatives), here, in v. 8, the accent shifts to the second half (receives, finds, it shall be opened). Verses 7 and 8 are, for this reason, not tautological.

The striking, unqualified 'all' should not be taken absolutely. For in 6.5 and 7 we have met those whose prayers God presumably does not answer. 'All' must refer to 'the sons of the kingdom' (13.38), all those who count as the 'salt of the earth' and the 'light of the world' (5.13–16). See further on v. 11.

In Gos. Thom. 2 this line is found: 'Jesus said: let the one seeking not cease from seeking until he finds, when he finds he will be troubled, and if he is troubled, he will marvel and he will rule over all'. The same sentence appears in *P. Oxy.* 654.1 (fragmentary). Clement of Alexandria cited another version of this saying and attributed it to the Gospel according to the Hebrews: 'The one who marvels shall rule, and having ruled he shall rest' (*Strom.* 2.9.45). Clement also passed on a slightly different and fuller version of the dictum: 'Let the one seeking not rest until he finds. And having found he shall be troubled, and having been troubled he shall rule, and having ruled he shall rest' (*Strom.* 5.14.96). Whether this second variant appeared in the Gospel according to the Hebrews we do not know. It does not seem, in any event, to be an authentic utterance of Jesus but instead an expansion of the traditional material behind Mt 7.7–11. (Cf. Fitzmyer, *Background*, p. 373, who cites J. H. Ropes as affirming authenticity, A. Resch and E. Jacquier as arguing against it.)

9. The reader is now asked a question the answer to which is beyond all doubt: fathers do not, as a rule, mock their sons.

[24] According to Irenaeus, *Adv. haer.* 2.13.10 and 2.30.2, Gnostics quoted Mt 7.7f. to justify their discovery of esoteric truths (cf. Clement of Alexandria, *Strom.* 8.1). One understands why Tertullian, *De praescr.* 8–10, held the verses to be addressed only to Jews and pagans. Christians had, so Tertullian argued, already found.

ἢ τίς ἐστιν ἐξ ὑμῶν ἄνθρωπος ὃν αἰτήσει ὁ υἱὸς αὐτοῦ ἄρτον, μὴ λίθον ἐπιδώσει αὐτῷ;[25] There is a similar sentence in Lk 11.11: 'What father among you (ἐξ ὑμῶν), if his son asks (αἰτήσει ὁ υἱός) for a fish, will instead of a fish give him (αὐτῷ ἐπιδώσει) a serpent'? The Greek words in parentheses indicate the vocabulary shared by Lk 11.11 and Mt 7.9. What is the relationship between the two verses? The problem is complex. Mt 7.10, which in form is very close to Lk 11.12, is, like Lk 11.11, about a son asking for a fish and being given a serpent; while Mt 7.9, which has the same sentence structure as Lk 11.12 (where an egg and a scorpion are the objects), is about a son asking for bread and being given a stone. So although Matthew and Luke have similar sentence forms (Mt 7.9 resembles Lk 11.11, Mt 7.10 resembles Lk 11.12), the content differs, as does the order. Visually:

| Matthew | 7.9 bread/stone | // fish/serpent | 11.11 | Luke[26] |
| | 7.10 fish/serpent | // egg/scorpion | 11.12 | |

Any credible solution to the puzzle formed by these verses must recognize that both Mt 7.10–11 and Lk 11.11–12 are embedded in common Q material. In fact, Mt 7.7–8 is identical to Lk 11.9–10 (twenty-four words are shared and in the same order), and Mt 7.11 is nearly the identical twin of Lk 11.13 (the few minor differences are readily put down to redactional contributions; see below). So there is, it would seem, no getting around the common origin of Mt 7.7–11 = Lk 11.9–13 in Q. Yet as the differences between Mt 7.9–10 and Lk 11.11–12 are sufficiently great to prohibit their derivation from the same Greek source[27]—a fact which goes hard against Griesbach—we have here as near as we can get to proof that Matthew's edition of Q was at points dissimilar from Luke's.

τίς ἐστιν ἐξ ὑμῶν ἄνθρωπος is editorial in 12.11 and probably is here too. Bengel, *Gnomon, ad loc.*, commented: 'A man—one then who is certainly not inhuman'. For ἄνθρωπος as a substitute for the indefinite pronominal adjective (a Semitism) see p. 81. For the use of an interrogative clause where one would expect a relative (another Semitism) see BDF § 469. Perhaps the evangelist added αὐτοῦ after ὁ υἱός because he wished to retain the absolute form, *the* son (so Luke), for Jesus alone. It should be remarked that a

[25] ℵ¹ L W f¹·¹³ Maj lat syʰ Aug Cyp could be original in having (ε)αν αιτηση (cf. 14.7; 18.19; 21.22). But both NA²⁶ and HG reproduce ον αιτησει on the authority of ℵ* B Θ b (a c gˡ h) syᶜ·ᵖ co.

[26] Many mss. of Luke insert 'bread, will give him a stone or also' after 'his son ask for' in 11.11. This is assimilation to Matthew.

[27] Cf. Dodd, *Tradition*, p. 337, n. 1. According to Gundry, *Commentary*, p. 124, Matthew inserted bread because of the Lord's Prayer, in which the heavenly Father gives bread to his own. For other attempts to explain Mt 7.9–10 and Lk 11.11–12 as redactional adaptations of the same source see Marshall, p. 469, who rejects them all and concurs with Dodd in ascribing the variations to the unpredictable workings of oral tradition.

round stone looks like a round loaf of bread; moreover, in 4.3 the devil asks Jesus to turn stones into their 'lookalike', loaves, so the two things were associated in the Q tradition. Recall also that in the feeding narratives (14.13–21; 15.32–9) bread is linked with fish, and ἰχθύς appears in the next verse, 7.10. The verbs in vv. 9–10, the first of which, αἰτήσει, makes a verbal link with the previous verse, are, obviously, gnomic futures. Note the switch from δίδωμι in v. 7 (cf. v. 11) to ἐπιδίδωμι. On the meaning of ἐπί as a prefix see p. 658.

Although v. 11 presupposes that all are engulfed in a morass of evil deeds, the rhetorical question, What father would give his son a stone if he asked him for bread?, anticipates a hearty declamation: None, of course! Here, as throughout the gospels, the possibility that a father might act otherwise than in his son's best interest seems to be no real possibility, so the argument can run without hesitation from the goodness of an earth-bound father to the goodness of the heavenly Father, God (cf. the argument in Isa 49.15). This is precisely what we would expect from Jesus. In his sayings and parables, kings and their servants, priests and Levites, husbandmen and sons may all act perniciously, but never fathers. Does this perhaps not tell us something not only about Jesus' patriarchal world but also his happy experience with Joseph, his own father?

According to some scholars, Mt 7.9 = Lk 11.11 and the following two verses were at one time separate from Mt 7.7–8 = Lk 11.9–10; and even the latter has been held the product of a complex tradition-history (see Crossan, *Aphorisms*, pp. 95–104). Nothing, however, demands any of the proposed reconstructions, and 7.7–8 = Lk 11.9–10, which would not obviously be forceful or memorable of itself, requires a context in order to gain meaning. 'Ask', 'seek', and 'knock' are imperatives whose significance resides not in themselves but in the illustrations that they introduce. Beyond this, if the pieces of Mt 7.7–11 = Lk 11.9–13 did not fit together from the start, how do we account for the coherence of thought and the aesthetically pleasing, balanced structure their meshing makes (see p. 678)? (In accepting the primitive unity of the Q piece, we must depart from Jeremias, *Parables*, pp. 144–5 (following A. T. Cadoux), according to whom 7.9–11 = Lk 11.11–13 was addressed by Jesus to his opponents and was designed to defend God's goodness towards the despised. We must also turn down the proposition that, in the original, 'the theme of "seeking and finding" is not yet formulated as an ecclesiastical admonition for prayer, but reflects the older sapiential theme of seeking after wisdom, revelation, and salvation'; so H. Koester, 'Gnostic Writings as Witnesses for the Development of the Sayings Tradition', in *The Rediscovery of Gnosticism. Vol. I: The School of Valentinus*, ed. B. Layton, Studies in the History of Religion, Leiden, 1980, p. 244. For one thing, there is in the synoptic tradition not one single admonition to seek wisdom; cf. C. E. Carlston, 'Proverbs, Maxims, and the Historical Jesus', *JBL* 99 (1980), p. 92.)

10. A second rhetorical question, much like the first, is now asked. Again the response is not in doubt. Thus the reader inevitably accepts the observations upon which the inference of 7.11 will be drawn.

ἢ καὶ ἰχθὺν αἰτήσει. Lk 11.12a has: ἢ καὶ αἰτήσει ᾠόν. Fish, like bread (7.9), was a staple, and would have been a common food around the Sea of Galilee.

μὴ ὄφιν ἐπιδώσει αὐτῷ; This clause is exactly parallel to 7.9c (contrast Lk 11.11c and 12b); and because in Matthew, unlike Luke, both 7.9 and 10 begin with ἤ, we may infer that Matthew has increased the degree of parallelism between the verses. Lk 11.12b has this: ἐπιδώσει αὐτῷ σκορπίον. In Mt 7.9–10, when a son asks for bread and fish, he is given a stone (a useless item) and a snake (ὄφις).[28] In Luke, however, the son is given a snake and a *scorpion*. Perhaps—although here we can do nothing more than guess—the tradition substituted a harmful thing for a harmless one, increasing the cruelty.

11. This is the conclusion and *telos* of 7.7–11, and it makes plain the object of the entire section: the heavenly Father, with a love surpassing that of human parents, deeply cares for his own and will never turn a deaf ear to their prayers.

εἰ οὖν ὑμεῖς πονηροὶ ὄντες οἴδατε δόματα ἀγαθὰ διδόναι τοῖς τέκνοις ὑμῶν. So Luke, with ὑπάρχοντες (redactional; ὑπάρχω: Mt: 3; Mk: 0; Lk: 15) as the fifth word. 'If you, then, being evil'—a clause which theologians have often taken to support the doctrine of original sin[29]—is not strictly necessary, but it does add force to the argument: notwithstanding that they continually whirl about in the abyss of sin, even human beings can show compassion and give unselfishly. 'Good gift(s)' was a fixed expression used by the rabbis (SB 1, p. 459) and is already found in Ecclus 18.17.

Although usually passed over by the commentators, remark should be made of the ὑμεῖς. With the exception of Mk 10.18 ('Why do you call me good? No one is good but God alone'), the Jesus of the synoptics never includes himself in statements such as Mt 7.11. It would sound strange indeed to hear him say, 'If we, then, being evil . . .'. Perhaps the notion of Jesus' sinlessness has affected the formulation here (cf. 2 Cor 5.21; Heb 4.15; 7.26–8; 1 Pet 1.19; 1 Jn 3.3–5). If so, this was already true in Q, for

---

[28] The *Barbut* (*clarias macamcracanthus*), a type of fish that grows up to five feet long and looks like a snake, might be the ὄφις of our saying; cf. Bailey, p. 137.

[29] The words do at least seem 'plainly [to] assert the actual existence of evil in man and imply the absolute universality of human sin'; so F. R. Tennant, *The Sources of the Doctrine of the Fall and Original Sin*, reprinted, New York, 1968, p. 248. Cf. 19.17; Rom 3; Philo, *Mut. nom.* 1.585. The word, πονηρός, does not imply that 7.11 must at first have been addressed to outsiders. For instructive reflections on Jesus' understanding of sin see R. Bultmann, *Existence and Faith*, New York, 1960, pp. 187–8.

Luke too has the second person plural. Yet maybe we should also consider the possibility that the words of Mt 7.11 = Lk 11.13 faithfully represent Jesus and that in his speech he tended to segregate himself from his hearers. (Compare his use of 'my Father' and 'your Father' and his disuse of 'Our Father'.) Such a suggestion at least has the merit of being consistent with the unanimous failure of the gospels to preserve any signs of Jesus' own consciousness of sin or guilt—a fact doubly peculiar given that the saint so often perceives himself to be 'the chief of sinners' and that it is the truly sinful who are least aware of their sin (cf. 1 Tim 1.15 and note J. A. T. Robinson, *The Human Face of God*, London, 1973, pp. 96–8).

πόσῳ μᾶλλον ὁ πατὴρ ὑμῶν ὁ ἐν τοῖς οὐρανοῖς δώσει ἀγαθὰ τοῖς αἰτοῦσιν αὐτόν. For 'your Father in the heavens' (redactional; see on 6.1), Luke has 'your Father ὁ ἐξ οὐρανοῦ', and for 'good things' (cf. 12.35) he has substituted 'Holy Spirit'. (Q may have run, 'How much more will the Father give from heaven good things . . .' (cf. Jas. 1.17). In this case, the second ὁ in Luke would be a corruption. There is no way to determine whether this is or is not a correct conjecture; but if it is, Matthew must have altered the sense of Q, preferring to connect 'heaven' with 'Father' rather than with the verb.)

The reference to 'your Father who is in heaven' constricts the otherwise seemingly unqualified assertions of 7.7–8: 'Everyone who asks, receives' means 'everyone (who is a child of the Father in heaven and) who asks receives'. With 'how much more' (cf. Ecclus 11.11) compare the rabbinic *'al 'aḥat kammâ wĕkammâ*, as in *b. Ber.* 61b.

The force of 7.11 lies in an inference from the lesser to the greater: if even evil men do the good, how much more God, who is not evil at all (cf. the similar argument in Heb 12.7–11). That this conclusion is the climax of 7.7–11 proves our point with regard to its thrust. Disciples are not so much being called to ask and seek and knock as they are being encouraged to take heart. 7.7–11 embodies, above all, not command but reassurance. The paragraph is intended to build up faith and to make known to disciples their happy privilege. Matthew is trying to reduce anxiety. Compare our remarks on 6.25–34, where, significantly enough, a speech of encouragement is also delivered on the basis of an argument *a minori ad maius* (= *qal wāḥômer*): if God so clothes the grass of the field, how much more. . . .

There is no agreement as to precisely how 'good things' should be understood. Are they the gifts prayed for in the Lord's Prayer (cf. Schweizer, *Matthew*, p. 174)? Or, as Luke has it, principally the Holy Spirit? Should we think of the eschatological benefits of the kingdom (so Guelich, p. 359)? Or is it better to surmise that all needs, temporal and spiritual, are included under the umbrella term, 'good things' (cf. McNeile, p. 92, citing 6.25–34 and Rom

8.32)? In our estimation, the passage's function within the sermon on the mount as a whole holds the key. Like 6.25–34, Mt 7.7–11 serves to offer the disciple assurance in the face of the difficult commands of Mt 5–7. This implies that the 'good things' are precisely all that is required to live the life of faithful discipleship as this is set forth in the great sermon.

Addressing now the issue of the origin of Mt 7.7–11, is the section, for whose unity we have pleaded, dominical or not? It is not difficult to reach a decision. While signs of a post-Easter derivation are absent, a convergence of features takes us straight to Jesus. He was fond of parallelism. He taught confidently that prayer would be heard and answered. He often employed the father/son relationship to illustrate religious truths. Over and above all this, there are possible indications of a Semitic original (cf. Jeremias, *Theology*, p. 25), and the argument of the Q passage is very much like that of 6.25–33, which, as we have argued, is based on dominical material. One should also observe the parallel with the authentic beatitudes. Just as the mourners will laugh, the hungry be filled, and the merciful treated with mercy, so those who pray will receive, those who seek will find, and those who knock will have the door opened to them (cf. Cadoux, p. 210).

John's gospel contains some interesting parallels to Mt 7.7–11. Especially notable is 16.23–24: 'If you ask (αἰτήσητε) anything of the Father, he will give (δώσει) it to you in my name. Hitherto you have asked nothing in my name; ask, and you will receive (αἰτεῖτε καὶ λήμψεσθε), that your joy may be full' (cf. also 14.13–14; 15.7, 16). Because the pairs, αἰτήσητε/δώσει and αἰτεῖτε/λήμψεσθε so strongly recall Mt 7.7–8 = Lk 11.9–10 (where we find αἰτεῖτε with δοθήσεται followed by αἰτῶν with λαμβάνει), the Johannine text just may be an adaptation of the tradition on prayer known from Q. In accordance with this possibility, in John, as in Q, the 'ask and it will be given to you' declaration is brought into conjunction with father/son imagery: 'If you ask anything of the Father he will give it' (so John) is close to 'if his son asks him . . . how much more will your heavenly Father give . . .' (so Q).

THE GOLDEN RULE (7.12)

12. Compare Lk 6.31 (part of the 'love your enemies' complex, as in Q). Although the so-called 'golden rule' sums up in brief the right conduct towards others and therefore appropriately closes 6.19–7.11, a section on social behaviour, 7.12 is not simply the conclusion of 6.19–7.11 (or of 7.1–11). Rather does it bring to a climax the entire central core of the sermon on the mount, 5.17–7.11. (The verse should therefore be printed as a separate paragraph, as in the NEB and HG.) Mention of 'the law and the prophets' takes the reader back to 5.17 and thereby establishes an *inclusio* within which Matthew has treated of the Torah (5.17–48),

given rules for the Christian cult (6.1–18), and offered instruction
and encouragement for life in the world (6.19–7.11). This would
seem to indicate that 'whatever you wish that men would do to
you, do so to them' is—in true rabbinic fashion—a general rule
which is not only the quintessence of the law and the prophets but
also the quintessence of the sermon on the mount and thus the
quintessence of Jesus' teaching in general. In other words, Mt 7.12
gives expression to the *ultimum desideratum*, to the highest
expression of the 'better righteousness'.

This conclusion is certainly consistent with other passages in
Matthew.[30] In 22.34–40 the evangelist has Jesus declare that the
first commandment is to love God and that the second is 'like it'
(= of equal importance; contrast Mark), namely, to love one's
neighbour. (Here too the command to love is that upon which
'depend all the law and the prophets'.) Similarly, at the end of the
list of commandments required for entering into life, Matthew
adds this: 'You shall love your neighbour as yourself' (19.16–30;
contrast Mk 10.17–31). And in 5.43–48 our author chooses to save
for the end, as the last of his six paragraphs on the messianic
Torah, the command to love one's enemies. 5.43–48 is,
accordingly, the climactic paragraph, and it issues in the
exhortation to be perfect as the heavenly Father is perfect. There
can be no doubt, then, concerning the pre-eminence given by the
First Gospel to the demand to love one's neighbour; and as the
golden rule is really just another way of delivering that demand, it
scarcely surprises to find it at the conclusion of Mt 5.17–7.11, the
epitome of Jesus' teaching on discipleship.

The parallels to Mt 7.12 are, as is well known, abundant: e.g., Tob 4.15:
'And what you hate, do not do to anyone' (cf. Gos. Thom. 6 = *P. Oxy.*
654.5); Ecclus 31.15: 'Judge your neighbour's feelings by your own, and in
every matter be thoughtful'; Ep. Arist. 207: 'As you wish that no evil
should befall you, but to be a partaker of all good things, so you should
act on the same principle towards your subjects and offenders . . .'; Philo,
Hypothetica in Eusebius, *Praep. ev.* 8.7.6 (358d): 'Let no man himself do
what he hates to have done to him'; T. Naph 1.6 (Hebrew): 'None should
do to his neighbour what he doth not like for himself'; 2 En. 61.1–2: 'And
now, my children, keep your hearts from every injustice which the Lord
hates. Just as a man asks for his own soul from God, so let him do to every
living soul . . .'; Sextus, *Sent.* 89: 'As you wish your neighbours to treat
you, so treat them' (so also 210b); Did. 1.2: πάντα δὲ ὅσα ἐὰν θελήσῃς μὴ
γίνεσθαί σοι, καὶ σὺ ἄλλῳ μὴ ποίει (cf. Acts 15.20, v. 1.; 15.29, v. 1.);[31] *b.*

[30] In addition to what follows see Barth, in *TIM*, pp. 75–85; Spicq 1, pp. 5–56;
Furnish, *Love*, pp. 74–84; B. Gerhardsson, *The Ethos of the Bible*, Philadelphia,
1981, pp. 48–54; and J. A. Piper, *'Love your enemies'. Jesus' love command in the
synoptic gospels and in the early Christian paraenesis*, SNTSMS 38,
Cambridge,1979, pp. 141–52.

[31] Despite the differences here, one strongly suspects Matthean influence, given

Šabb. 31a: 'A certain heathen came before Shammai and said to him, "Make me a proselyte, on condition that you teach me the whole Torah while I stand on one foot". Thereupon he repulsed him with the builder's cubit which was in his hand. When he went before Hillel, he said to him, "What is hateful to you, do not do to your neighbour: that is the whole Torah, while the rest is commentary thereon; go and learn it"; Tg. Yer. 1 to Lev 19.18: 'What is disagreeable to you, do not do it to him (your neighbour)'; *ARN* 15: ' "Let the honour of thy fellow be as dear to thee as thine own". How so? This teaches that even as one looks out for his own honour, so should he look out for his fellow's honour. And even as no man wishes that his honour be held in ill repute, so should he wish that the honour of his fellow shall not be held in ill repute'; Sent. Syr. Men. 250–1: 'All that is hateful to you, you should not wish to do that to your neighbour'. Greek and Roman parallels include Herodotus 3.142; Isocrates, *Nicocles* 61; and Diogenes Laertius 5.21. For a full list of parallels see Dihle (v). The idea of doing to others as one wishes to be done to is, it should be remembered, almost a universal sentiment. It can be found in Buddhist, Confucian, and Islamic texts (e.g. Confucius, *Analects* 15.23).

The previous paragraph provokes the question, Was Jesus' formulation of the golden rule in any sense creative? In the judgement of many, while first-century Palestinian Judaism was acquainted with a negative version which prudently warned not to harm one's neighbour, Jesus himself advanced a positive version which required an absolute demonstration of love (cf. Schlatter, p. 247; Schürmann, *Lukasevangelium* 1, pp. 349–50; Jeremias, *Theology*, p. 212). There is much room for doubt about this. One cannot, admittedly, cite Ep. Arist. 207 (which contains the positive form) as rebuttal, for it was not composed in Palestine; and the questions hanging over the date and provenance of 2 Enoch as well as the Hebrew fragments of the Testament of Naphtali forbid their citation in this connexion. Ecclus 31.15, on the other hand, comes very close to Jesus' golden rule, and Sirach was not penned in the Diaspora. Further, the differences between the negative and positive formulations are perhaps not as significant as has sometimes been made out (cf. Moore 2, pp. 87–8). The negative formulation does not always presuppose a calculating attitude with its own selfish ends in view:[32] it too can be rooted in a genuine concern for one's fellows.[33] It also bears remarking that the negative and

---

the redactional nature of the first four words in Mt 7.12: πάντα οὖν ὅσα ἐάν.

[32] The popular, common sense notion, Do not harm others lest they harm you, was surely well-known to first-century Jews. Cf. *t. Meg.* 4.16: 'Do, that they will do to you, lend, that they will lend to you, mourn that they will mourn for you, honour in burial, that they will honour you in burial'. This is only enlightened self-interest.

[33] Cf. Guelich, p. 361; Vermes, *World*, pp. 160–1. Although the rule has sometimes been criticized or wrongly exploited for its 'naif egoism' (Bultmann), such egoism is only a reference point which is soon transcended, a place of departure from which the hearer must subsequently move, posthaste. The golden rule cannot be practised without suffering self-denial (cf. Ps.-Clem. Hom 12.32). For this reason it is not bound up with 'utilitarian narcissism' (Breech, p. 55). Mt 7.12 is not just common sense reciprocity, nor does it entail cost/benefit analysis. Our evangelist would have been dumbfounded by Meier's analysis (*Commentary*,

positive versions appear in early Christian literature with little discussion of their differences. Lastly, the command to love one's neighbour *as oneself* (Lev 19.18, 34; cf. Exod 23.4–5) already implies the content of Mt 7.12 = Lk 6.31 (cf. Augustine, *De serm. mont.* 2.22.75), so the claim to find in the synoptic logion profound originality seems ill-conceived and probably stems more from Christian apologetic than from an objective examination of the texts.

If the conclusion just drawn be correct, then, it may be observed, Matthew himself might have known perfectly well that the golden rule was unoriginal with Jesus. That our evangelist could still place it where he does at the culmination of 5.17–7.12 shows us his belief—not always shared by later Christians—that the truth of his Lord's teaching did not necessarily hinge upon its novelty.

πάντα οὖν ὅσα ἐὰν θέλητε ἵνα ποιῶσιν ὑμῖν οἱ ἄνθρωποι, οὕτως καὶ ὑμεῖς ποιεῖτε αὐτοῖς.[34] Compare Epictetus, *Diss.* 2.17.34 (οὕτω καὶ ὑμεῖς ποιεῖτε). Luke has καὶ καθώς (καθώς: Mt: 3; Mk: 8; Lk: 17) for the first four words, the indicative θέλετε for the subjunctive, and ποιεῖτε αὐτοῖς ὁμοίως after ἄνθρωποι. Most of these differences are explicable in terms of Matthean redaction.[35] Note that the unqualified 'men' must include everyone, even enemies (cf. 5.38–48).

The 'therefore' of 7.12a has been understood in several different ways. (1) It can simply be omitted on textual grounds (so Zahn, p. 310). (2) The connexion could be with 7.11 or with 7.7–11: because God treats you well, you must treat others well (cf. Schlatter, p. 246; Gundry, *Commentary*, p. 125). Or, as Chrysostom has it (*Hom. on Mt.* 23.6), if you desire God to hear your prayers (7.7–8), do this, namely, what 7.12 enjoins. (3) 'Therefore' sums up all from 7.1 (so Bengel, *Gnomon, ad loc.*). (4) According to Albright and Mann (p. 84), 7.12 may originally have followed 7.6; the οὖν would then, at least at one time, have connected these two verses (cf. Allen, p. 67). (But there is not a shred of evidence for considering 7.7–11 a secondary insertion.) (5) The conjunction looks back to 7.1–2 (so Plummer, p. 114, tentatively). (6) According to McNeile (p. 93), 'οὖν is not in logical sequence with v. 11, but sums up the Sermon to this point . . .' (cf. Barth, in *TIM*, p. 73; Guelich, pp. 361–2). This must be the correct

pp. 70–1): 7.12 does 'not rise above enlightened self-interest'; it is not 'on a level with the loftier teaching of the double command of love (22:34–40) . . .'. This completely overlooks the significance that 7.12 takes from its context in the Jesus tradition in general and from its context in the sermon on the mount in particular (cf. Luz 1, pp. 389–93).

[34] Because of the seeming lack of connexion with the immediate context the ουν is omitted by ℵ* L 1424 *pc* syᵖ boᵐˢˢ.

[35] πᾶς + οὖν: Mt: 6; Mk: 0; Lk: 1. ἐάν: Mt: 67; Mk: 35; Lk: 29. οὕτως: Mt: 32; Mk: 10; Lk: 21.

solution. 7.12b harks back to 5.17 and, on our structural analysis of the sermon on the mount (see pp. 62–4), thereby fashions an *inclusio*. The verse must accordingly round off 5.17–7.12 and give summary expression to the sermon's most salient or characteristic imperative.

οὗτος γάρ ἐστιν ὁ νόμος καὶ οἱ προφῆται. There is no Lukan parallel. Against Jeremias, *Theology*, p. 212, n. 1, the phrase is almost certainly editorial (see on 5.17). This being so, there is a good chance that Matthew had Hillel's version of the golden rule in mind;[36] or maybe the summary of the law in terms of the golden rule or the command to love was simply familiar to those in the Jewish schools of the first century (cf. Abrahams 1, pp. 18–29). In any event, it cannot be chance that the apostle Paul, a one-time Pharisee, also summed up the meaning of the law in a manner reminiscent of Mt 7.12 and 22.39–40. In Rom 13.8–9 he wrote, 'Owe no one anything, except to love one another; for he who loves his neighbour has fulfilled the law. The commandments . . . are summed up in this sentence, "You shall love your neighbour as yourself" ' (cf. Gal 5.14). These words must reflect either Paul's 'rabbinic' training or, what could be true at the same time, his knowledge of the Jesus tradition. In either case, with regard to the quintessence of the Torah, Paul speaks in unison with Matthew (as well as with the Fourth Evangelist for that matter; see Jn 13.34; 14.21–4).[37]

The idea that the law could be summed up in a general principle is, as we have seen, present in Jewish texts (see further Daube, pp. 63–66; Davies, *SSM*, p. 401, n. 2). In addition to those passages already cited, the following deserve quotation: Philo, *Decal*. 18–19: the Decalogue is the κεφάλαια νόμων (cf. *Spec. leg.* 1.1.1); *Sipra* on Lev 19.18: Thou shalt love thy neighbour as thyself. R. Akiba said: 'That is the greatest principle in the Law'. Ben Azzai said, 'The sentence "This is the book of the generation of man" is even greater than the other'; *b. Ber*. 63a: Bar Kappara expounded, 'What short text is there upon which all the essential principles of the Torah depend? "In all thy ways acknowledge Him and He will direct thy paths" '; *b. Mak*. 23b–24a: the six hundred and thirteen precepts communicated to Moses were reduced to one principle by Habakkuk: But the righteous shall live by faith.

Within the context of the First Gospel, the golden rule is not a principle from which all of the law's commands can be deduced, nor is it the hermeneutical key to interpreting the law or for

---

[36] In the judgement of Neusner 3, pp. 359–60, the attribution of the golden rule to Hillel could be fictitious.

[37] Whether or not the golden rule of Mt 7.12 = Lk 6.31 goes back to Jesus cannot be determined with certainty; see Grundmann, pp. 226–7. The sentiment expressed is, in any event, quite consistent with the spirit of Jesus' teaching.

determining the validity of different commandments (*pace* Barth, in *TIM*, pp. 78–85). Rather is it simply the most basic or important demand of the law, a demand which in no way replaces Torah but instead states its true end.[38] Compare 23.23: there are some commandments which are more weighty than others, but this should not lead to the neglect of lighter matters.

(iv) *Concluding Observations*

(1) If it is indeed correct to see 7.7–11 as the fraternal twin of 6.25–34, and if the two sections really are intended to encourage readers, then it is distortion to think of Matthew as a harsh, unrelenting legalist or an impossibly stern perfectionist. Rather does he have a pastor's heart. He is aware that the sermon on the mount sets forth a well-nigh unattainable ideal and that the disciples who take its imperatives seriously will know themselves to be inadequate for the task. Our evangelist knows all about the storm of anxiety and doubt that will be brought on by Jesus' overwhelming injunctions. This is why, in 6.25–34 and 7.7–11, the sky suddenly clears and the torrential onslaught passes. In these two places our sensitive author, anticipating the reader's perplexity, is moved to make manifest the goodness of the Father in heaven and to write reassuringly about seeking, asking, and knocking. So just as the whole sermon on the mount is set in the context of mercy and compassion (see p. 427, on 4.23–5.2), so within the sermon itself do these two divine qualities become conspicuous and shed their light on all about. In 6.25–34 and 7.7–11 the call to do God's will is interrupted while the good news of God's supportive grace sounds forth.

(2) 'Purity of heart is to will one thing'. So wrote Søren Kierkegaard, and Matthew would have understood. For the evangelist one thing was needful, this being the love enjoined by Jesus Christ. Such love will encourage one to obey Jesus' Torah (cf. 5.21–6, 43–8), to practise right religion in the Christian cult (cf. 6.14–15), and to serve God instead of mammon (cf. 6.22–3). For this cause not only does the first major section of the sermon on the mount (5.17–48) come to its fitting termination in the commandment to love one's enemy, but the entire central core, 5.17–7.12, finds its goal in the golden rule. To love one's neighbour, to do as one would wish to be done unto—that is the law and the prophets.

(3) Because Messiah Jesus himself came to fulfil the law and the

---

[38] So also D. J. Moo, 'Jesus and the Authority of the Mosaic Torah', *JSNT* 20 (1984), pp. 6–11. Cf. Banks, p. 169.

prophets (5.17–20), he must also have perfectly embodied the commandment to love.[39] Matthew, to be sure, never says, in so many words, 'Jesus loved'. Yet take away this tacit idea and the gospel becomes incoherent. As the lover of men and women, Jesus heals the afflicted (4.23–5; 8.2–17; etc.) and proffers encouragement (6.25–34; 7.7–11). He forgives sin (9.1–8) and exhibits mercy (9.10–13, 27–31; 12.1–8; 20.29–23). He shows compassion (9.36; 12.20; 14.14; 15.32) and gives rest to the weary (11.28). And having done all this he does even more: he hands over his life for the sake of others (20.28; 26.28). Jesus is, in fine, the exemplar in love. It follows that the evangelist would not only have concurred with Kierkegaard but also with the author of 1 John, who wrote, 'We love, because he first loved us'.

(v) *Bibliography*

Bailey, *Poet*, pp. 134–41.

H.-W. Bartsch, 'Traditionsgeschichtliches zur "goldenen Regel" und zum Aposteldekret', *ZNW* 75 (1984), pp. 128–32.

N. Brox, 'Suchen und Finden. Zur Nachgeschichte von Mt 7:7b/Lk 11:9b', in Hoffmann, *Orientierung*, pp. 17–36.

R. H. Connolly, 'A Negative Form of the Golden Rule in the Diatessaron?', *JTS* 35 (1934), pp. 351–7.

B. Couroyer, ' "De la mesure dont vous mesurez il vous sera mesuré" ', *RB* 77 (1970), pp. 366–70.

Crossan, *Aphorisms*, pp. 50–4, 95–104, 179–82.

E. Delebecque, 'Sur une hellénisme', *RB* 87 (1980), pp. 590–3.

A. Dihle, *Die goldene Regel*, Göttingen, 1962.

Dupont 1, pp. 50–2, 143–4, 163–7, 172–5.

Friedlander, pp. 226–38.

T. F. Glasson, 'Chiasmus in St. Matthew vii.6', *ExpT* 68 (1957), p. 302.

H. A. Guy, 'The Golden Rule', *ExpT* 70 (1959), p. 184.

W. H. P. Hatch, 'A Syriac Parallel to the Golden Rule', *HTR* 14 (1921), pp. 193–5.

B. Hjerl-Hansen, 'Le rapprochement poisson-serpent dans la prédication de Jésus (Mt 7.20 et Luc 11.11)', *RB* 55 (1948), pp. 195–8.

J. Jeremias, 'Matthäus 7,6a', in *Abraham unser Vater*, ed. O. Betz, M. Hengel, and P. Schmidt, Leiden, 1963, pp. 271–5.

G. B. King, 'The Mote and the Beam', *HTR* 17 (1924), pp. 393–404.

idem, 'The "Negative" Golden Rule', *JR* 8 (1928), pp. 268–79.

K. Koschorke, ' "Suchen und Finden" in der Auseinandersetzung zwischen gnostischem und kirchlichem Christentum', *WD* 14 (1977), pp. 51–65.

---

[39] It is not too much to say that in chapters 8–28 Jesus lives out the words of chapters 5–7. Cf. Thurneysen, p. 18: 'He himself would then be the true content of all his sayings'.

C. H. Kraeling, 'Seek and You will find', in *Early Christian Origins*, ed. A. Wikgren, Chicago, 1961, pp. 24–34.

P. G. Maxwell-Stuart, ' "Do not give what is holy to the dogs" Mt 7:6', *ExpT* 90 (1979), p. 341.

B. M. Metzger, 'The Designation "The Golden Rule" ', *ExpT* 69 (1958), p. 304.

E. Neuhäusler, 'Mit welchem Massstab misst Gott die Menschen?', *BuL* 11 (1970), pp. 104–13.

W. Ott, *Gebet und Heil*, Munich, 1965, pp. 99–112.

F. Perles, 'Zur Erklärung von Mt 7:6', *ZNW* 25 (1926), pp. 163–4.

A. M. Perry,'Pearls before Swine', *ExpT* 46 (1935), p. 381.

R. A. Piper, 'Matthew, 7,7–11 par. Lk 11,9–13: Evidence of Design and Argument in the Collection of Jesus' Sayings', in Delobel, pp. 411–18.

H. P. Rüger, ' "Mit welchem Mass ihr messt, wird euch gemessen werden" ', *ZNW* 60 (1969), pp. 174–82.

Schulz, *Q*, pp. 139–41, 146–9, 161–4.

G. Schwarz, 'Matthäus vii 6a. Emendation und Rückübersetzung', *NovT* 14 (1972), pp. 18–25.

W. A. Spooner, 'Golden Rule', in *Encyclopaedia of Religion and Ethics*, ed. J. Hastings, Edinburgh, 1914, vol. 6, pp. 310–12.

G. Strecker, 'Compliance—Love of One's Enemy—The Golden Rule', *AusBR* 29 (1981), pp. 38–46.

M. Theunissen, "Ο αἰτῶν λαμβάνει', in *Jesus: Ort der Erfahrung Gottes*, ed. B. Casper, Freiburg, 1976, pp. 13–68.

Zeller, *Mahnsprüche*, pp. 113–17, 127–31.

XVI

THREE WARNINGS AND THE CONCLUSION OF MATTHEW'S INAUGURAL SERMON
(7.13–29)

(i) *Structure*

The main issue concerning the structure of 7.13–29 is whether 7.15–23 should be analysed as one unit (cf. Burchard, p. 74; Luz 1, pp. 400–1) or two (7.15–20 + 21–3; so Denaux (v) and Lambrecht, *Sermon*, pp. 183–7). The pertinent considerations are these:

(1) 7.15–20, as the opening sentence makes crystal clear, has to do with false prophets: 'Beware of false prophets' (7.15a). So does 7.21–3, as can be concluded from a comparison of 7.22 ('On that day *many* will say to me, "Lord, Lord, did we not *prophesy in your name*, and cast out demons in your name, and do many *mighty works* in your name?" ') with certain verses in chapter 24. In these last the false *prophets* (24.24), who are *many* (24.5, 11), will come *in Christ's name* (24.5) and do great *signs* and *wonders* (24.24). Those who are condemned in 7.21–3 have all the characteristics of false prophets, a fact which underscores the unity of theme between 7.15–20 and 21–3.

(2) 7.22 (just quoted) seems to borrow the language of Jer 14.14 ('The prophets are prophesying in my name; I did not send them') and 27.15 ('I have not sent them, says the Lord, but they are prophesying falsely in my name'). Again this underlines the theme common to 7.15–20 and 21–3: both have to do with false prophets.

(3) There are six significant verbal links between 7.15–20 and 21–3: ἔρχονται (15)/εἰσελεύσεται (21); ψευδοπροφητῶν (15)/ἐπροφητεύσαμεν (22); ἐπιγνώσεσθε (16, 20)/ἔγνων (23); ποιεῖ/ποιεῖν/ποιοῦν (17, 18, 19)/ποιῶν (21); πᾶν (17, 19)/πᾶς (21); βάλλεται (19)/ἐξεβάλομεν (22).

(4) From first to last, Matthew has built his inaugural sermon out of triads. But if 7.15–23 be more than one unit, then 7.13–27, the concluding section, would not be triadic. Instead of having three parts (7.13–14, 15–23, 24–7), it would have four (7.13–14, 15–20, 21–3, 24–7). Surely this inconcinnity should, if possible, be avoided.

(5) The intimate connexion between 7.15–20 and 21–3 is upheld by three additional correlations. a. The 'wolves in sheep's clothing' (7.15) are just like those who say 'Lord, Lord' but are not truly Jesus' own (7.21–3). b. Those who have prophesied in Christ's name and yet suffer condemnation (7.22–3) certainly deserve the label, 'false prophets' (7.15). c. Just as every tree that does not bear good fruit is cut down and thrown into the fire (7.19), so those who claim to have done great things in Christ's name are rejected by the eschatological judge as evildoers (7.22–3).

As the five points just made reveal, 7.15–20 and 21–3 are tightly knit together and treat of the same subject, false prophets. This moves us to consider 7.15–22 a unit, which in turn impels us to divide 7.13–27 into three sections.

1. The two ways (7.13–14)
   a. Exhortation (13a)
   b. The wide gate and the easy way (13b–c)
   c. The constricted gate and the hard way (14)
2. False prophets (15–23)
   a. Exhortation (15a)
   b. The deeds of the false prophets (15b–20)
   c. Their words on judgement day (21–3)
3. The two builders (24–7)
   a. The wise builder (24–5)
   b. The foolish builder (26–7)

(ii) *Sources*

If we have indeed put forward the correct structural analysis (see further on 7.15), it is an aid to understanding the editor's compositional procedure. The sources of 7.13–29 may be illustrated as follows:

7.13–14 (M,Q^{mt},orQ + heavy redaction)	compare Lk 13.23–4 (Q^{lk} or L)
7.15–20 (Q + heavy redaction)	compare Lk 6.43–4 (Q)
7.21 (Q + heavy redaction)	compare Lk 6.46 (Q)
7.22–3 (Q + heavy redaction)	compare Lk 13.26–7 (Q)
7.24–7 (Q)	compare Lk 6.47–9 (Q)
7.28–9 (editorial)	compare Mk 1.22, 27; Lk 7.1

In Q the sermon on the plain concluded with two units, the first concerned with fruits (7.16–18/Lk 6.43–4, 45), the second with the house upon the rock (7.24–7/Lk 6.47–9). Matthew, however, wished to compose a closing section with two unique features. He wanted first to create yet one last triad. And, secondly, he wanted the opening blessings of the sermon (5.3–12) to be balanced by warnings at the end (cf. the blessings and curses of Deut 28–30). In order, then, to achieve his goals, he (1) moved the two-way saying (7.13–14) forward from its position in Q$^{(mt)}$ (or M), (2) creatively expanded the sayings about fruit (Lk 6.43–4) in order to transform them into a warning about false prophets (7.15–23), and (3) left the parable of the two builders (7.24–7) intact and in place. Thus the rhyme and reason behind Matthew's reordering of Q material in 7.13–27 makes perfect sense. It is moreover our judgement that the procedure envisioned is far easier to fathom than Luke's dissecting the sermon on the mount, which is what the Griesbach hypothesis entails. (For additional failings of the Griesbach hypothesis see on 7.15 (Luke has no parallel to this redactional verse), on 7.16 (Luke seems original over against

Matthew), on 7.17–18 (Matthew's πονηρός is secondary *vis-à-vis* Luke's σαπρός), on 7.20 (Luke is more primitive), on 7.21–2 (Matthew is again less plausibly original than Luke, and Luke omits precisely what is characteristically Matthean), and on 7.24–7 (neither Matthew nor Luke is consistently more primitive).)

(iii) *Exegesis*

THE TWO WAYS (7.13–14)

Although 7.13–14 has a parallel in Lk 13.23–4, one cannot with great confidence posit a common origin in Q. The differences between the two texts are considerable, and while Mt 7.13–14 could be the product of Q and heavy Matthean redaction, other possibilities cannot be excluded. Our paragraph could come from M, Lk 13.23–4 from L, or one might explain matters by recourse to the differences between Q^mt and Q^lk. We leave the problem open.[1]

Deut 11.26 reads: 'Behold, I set before you this day a blessing and a curse'. Compare 30.15: 'See, I have set before you this day life and good, death and evil'. In Jer 21.8 the lines from Deuteronomy are taken up and modified in this fashion: 'I set before you the *way* of life and the *way* of death'. After this, the theme of the two ways is a fixed item of Jewish moral theology. See, for example, T. Asher 1.3–5 ('Two ways hath God given to the sons of men, and two inclinations, and two kinds of action, and two modes (of action), and two issues. Therefore all things are by two ways, one over against the other. For there are two ways of good and evil, and with these two are the inclinations in our breasts discriminating them'); 2 En. 30.15 (God showed Adam 'the two ways, the light and the darkness, and I (God) told him: "this is good and that bad" '; cf. 42.10); *b. Ber.* 28b ('There are two ways before me, one leading to Paradise and the other to Gehinnom, and I dare not know by which I shall be taken . . .'); and *Mek.* on Exod 14.28 (God put before Adam 'two ways, the way of life and the way of death, and he chose for himself the way to death'). See also Ps 1.6; 119.29–32; 139.24; Prov 28.6, 18; Wisd 5.6–7; Ecclus 2.12; 15.11–17; 21.10; 1QS 3.13–4.26; Philo, *Sacr. A C* 2; *Agric.* 103–4; 4 Ezra 7.3–9; *Sipre* on Deut 11.26; *m. 'Abot* 2.9; *ARN* 14, 18, 25; *t. Soṭa* 7.11; *t. Sanh.* 14.4; *b. Ber.* 28b; *b. Ḥag.* 3b; SB 1, pp. 461–3. For early Christianity see Did. 1–6; Barn. 18–20; Herm. m. 6; Ps.-Clem. Hom. 5.7; T. Abr. 11, recension A (under the influence of Matthew); Apost. Const. 1–5. On the theology of the two ways see G. W. E. Nickelsburg, *Resurrection, Immortality, and Eternal Life in Intertestamental Judaism*, Cambridge, Mass., 1972,

---

[1] On the differences between Mt 7.13–14 and Lk 13.24–4 see esp. Jeremias, *TWNT* 6, pp. 920–7. According to Jeremias (and also Manson, *Sayings*, p. 175), Mt 7.13–14 is a moralizing adaptation and expansion of a dominical utterance more faithfully preserved in Luke. Schulz (v), pp. 309–12, and Guelich, p. 385, however, argue for the priority of Matthew. For yet another option see Michaelis (v): Mt 7.13–14 and Lk 13.23–4 quite possibly represent independent developments of two originally distinct dominical words.

pp. 156–65; also M. J. Suggs, 'The Christian Two-Ways Tradition', in *Studies in the New Testament*, ed. D. Aune, Leiden, 1972, pp. 60–74.

Although the motif of the two ways is thoroughly Jewish, it cannot be considered exclusively Jewish. The Tabula of Cebes (1st cent. A.D.) describes the path to true education thus: 'Do you not also see a small door (θύραν) and in front of the door a way (ὁδόν) which is not much frequented; very few (ὀλίγοι πάνυ) pass here; as it were through a trackless waste which seems both rough and rocky? . . . And there seems to be a high hill, and a very narrow (στενή) ascent with a deep precipice on both sides' (15.2–3). Other parallels outside the Jewish and Christian traditions include Hesiod, *Op.* 287–92; Xenophon, *Mem.* 2.21.21–34; Diogenes of Sinope, *Ep.* 30; Libanius, *Or.* 9.

13. Because 7.13b–c and 14, two perfectly balanced lines, are prefaced by a call to enter in at the narrow gate, and because there is no corresponding exhortation about the broad gate, the weight of 7.13–14 comes down not on the wayward but on the heads of would-be disciples, on those who have heard the sermon on the mount and acknowledge its demands. They are being called to flee complacency and to view all save entrance into the kingdom of God as dangerous divertisement. Guided by the words of Jesus, the faithful reader is to put shoulder to the wheel and forsake every obstacle in the way of obtaining the one true good.

εἰσέλθατε διὰ τῆς στενῆς πύλης. In Lk 13.24 this apodictic command—which applies equally to all believers (cf. Chrysostom, *Hom. on Heb.* 7.4)—is introduced by ἀγωνίζεσθε, so the verb which is an imperative in Matthew ('enter in') becomes an infinitive in Luke.[2] For πύλη ('gate') Luke has θύρα ('door'). In the LXX both words translate *petaḥ*, *delet*, *sap*, and *šaʿar*. The 'narrow gate' in Matthew implies difficulty—the difficulty of doing; cf. 7.15–27—and recalls the camel and the eye of a needle saying (19.24; cf. Origen, *C. Cels.* 6.16).

If an authentic saying of Jesus lies behind Mt 7.13–14 and Lk 13.24, it is likely to have been something like this: 'Strive to enter (into life or the kingdom) by the narrow gate (or door)' (cf. Lk 13.24a). This would be a summons to discipleship, to steadfast striving in the cause of Jesus (cf. Perrin, *Rediscovering*, pp. 144–5; Derrett (v), p. 21). How then do we explain Mt 7.13–14? The figure of the gate or door was much less common in Judaism than the figure of the two ways, so it may well be that Jesus' original utterance attracted to itself, for catechetical or other edifying reasons, conventional accretions associated with the theme of the two ways (so Luz 1, pp. 396–7, ascribing the additions to Matthew).

---

[2] According to Jeremias, *Lukasevangelium*, p. 232, the construction in Luke is redactional. According to Hoffmann (v), p. 196, the verb 'to strive' shows Hellenistic influence: 'to strive' to do something is typical of ethical diatribe.

The eschatological orientation of 7.13-14 is manifest (1) from the many similar Jewish texts which are often eschatologically oriented; (2) from the use of 'life' elsewhere in Matthew to refer to the future life of the kingdom; (3) from the word ἀπώλεια, which refers to eternal destruction; (4) from the verb εἰσέρχομαι, which so often in Matthew has an eschatological association (5.20; 7.21; 18.3; 19.23-4; 23.13; cf. Mattill (v), pp. 532-3); and (5) from the parallel with 7.24-7: the building of a house on the sand which then suffers in the eschatological storm is the functional equivalent of entering the wide gate or going down the broad way to destruction, while the building of a house on a firm foundation which then endures the final tempest is the functional equivalent of entering the narrow gate and going down the constricted way to life.

ὅτι πλατεῖα ἡ πύλη καὶ εὐρύχωρος ἡ ὁδὸς ἡ ἀπάγουσα εἰς τὴν ἀπώλειαν.[3] Compare 2 Bar. 85.13: 'There is the sentence of corruption, the way of fire, and the path which bringeth to Gehenna'. The notion that vice is attractive and easy to succumb to is, of course, native to all religion. To sin is natural, to repent unnatural. Compare Diogenes Laertius 4.49 ('The road which leads to Hades is easy to follow') and Tertullian, *Adv. Marc.* 2.13 ('The way of evil is broad and well supplied with travellers; would not all men take its easy course if there were nothing to fear?').

Lk 13.24 has ὅτι after 'narrow door' and after this goes another way. The word statistics do not indicate that the differences can easily be put down to Matthean creativity.[4] Moreover, the two-way theme appears nowhere else in the First Gospel. So 7.13-14 may reproduce largely traditional material (from Q^mt or from M).

Both πλατύς and εὐρύχωρος[5] occur most frequently in the LXX for forms of *rḥb*. For the latter with πύλη see 2 Chr 18.9. The two words (combined also in Isa 33.21 LXX) together connote a lack of striving, of work. Compare Chrysostom, *Hom. on Mt.* 23.7: Jesus 'both declared the carelessness of the generality and instructed His hearers not to regard the felicities of the many but the labours of the few'.

There has been some discussion over just what image should be conjured in the mind's eye by Mt 7.13-14. Should one think of a traveller on a road who is approaching a city gate (cf. Tabula of

[3] η πυλη is missing in ℵ* 1646 *pc* a b c h k Cl Cyp Eus Hipp Lcf Or^pt. See Metzger, p. 19. As the external evidence supports inclusion, 'the gate' was probably dropped in order to create a coherent image (see the commentary).

[4] πλατύς: Mt: 2; Mk: 1; Lk: 3. εὐρύχωρος: only here in the NT. ὁδός: Mt: 22; Mk: 16; Lk: 20. ἀπάγω: Mt: 5; Mk: 3; Lk: 4. ἀπώλεια: Mt: 2 (in 26.8 the word is from Mk 14.4); Mk: 1; Lk: 0.

[5] The word means 'spacious' (so BAGD, s.v.), although the RSV translates it 'easy'.

Cebes 15; so Mattill (v), pp. 543–6)? Or just maybe of a passage on the way (so P. Joüon, according to Jeremias (v), p. 922)? Or, as the gate is mentioned before the way, is it not more natural to envision a gate at the beginning of a road—as in John Bunyan's *Pilgrim's Progress*?[6] In our estimation, none of these questions can be answered affirmatively. If the tradition-history suggested on p. 696 be right, then the theme of the two ways has, along with the image of the gate leading to eternal perdition (cf. 16.18; 3 Macc 5.51; 2 Bar. 59.10; T. Abr. A 11.11; *b. 'Erub.* 19a)[7], been brought into secondary association with the original statement about the gate or entrance leading into eternal life (cf. 4 Ezra 7.6–8; Sib. Or. 2.150; Rev 22.14; T. Abr. A 10.15; Herm. s. 9.12.5; Apoc. Zeph. 3.9; T. Jacob 2.17; *Pesiq. R.* 179b). One cannot, therefore, expect a coherent image to crystallize readily if at all. And in fact, 'gate' and 'way' seem to function synonymously (cf. Bonnard, p. 102). They are, in a sense, set not one before the other but side by side.[8]

According to J. D. M. Derrett (v), all of the standard interpretations of Mt 7.13–14 are less than satisfactory. In his view, the narrow gate and the broad gate are in the same wall, and the key to right comprehension lies in understanding ἀπώλεια as financial 'waste' or 'loss'. Waiting at the broad gate of the city are the tax collectors who fleece all who enter therein. Jesus is instructing his listeners to become like those clever few who seek an inconspicuous wicket or second gate by which they can enter without suffering personal loss. Furthermore, Isa 59.14 has influenced our text: 'Justice [which should be at the gate] is turned back, and righteousness stands afar off; for truth has fallen in the public squares, and uprightness cannot enter'. Derrett even designates 7.13–14 a 'midrash' on Isa 59.14. In all of this we cannot follow him. The connexion with the OT text is tenuous, especially the verbal links ('gate' must be read in). Beyond this, ἀπώλεια is best made out as 'perdition' in view of such two-way passages as 1QS 4.13 and *b. Ber.* 28b (cf. 2 Bar. 85.13). Finally, although Derrett finds Mt 7.13–14 'somewhat jejune' when read in terms of the two-way doctrine, it may be said by way of reply that the originality of the logion lies not in its imagery but in its application. The way to life is no longer the (pre-messianic) Torah but instead the words of Jesus.

καὶ πολλοί εἰσιν οἱ εἰσερχόμενοι δι' αὐτῆς. Compare Lk 13.24b ('Because *many* . . . will seek to enter and will be unable'). The 'many' are not identified—which leaves open the frightening possibility that the reader may end up among them.

From the days of Noah (Gen 6) to the days of Moses (Exod 23.2;

---

[6] Bunyan, it may be observed, connects 7.7 with 7.13–14: the knocking of the former is at the gate of the latter.

[7] The gate of hell is to be distinguished from the gate(s) of death, for which see Job 38.17; Ps 9.13; 107.18; and T. Isaac 4.9.

[8] Buchanan, p. 100, makes the strange suggestion that the narrow way is a mountainside path to a monastery, the broad way a road to Rome.

32) and on to the days of the prophets (1 Kgs 19.10; Ezek 9.8–10; etc.), it is always the multitude, the many, who follow evil. Those that do good are, according to the Scriptures, a minority.

14. This sentence is the negative obverse of 13b–c. 'Broad' becomes 'narrow', 'spacious' becomes 'constricted', 'destruction' becomes 'life', 'many' becomes 'few', and 'those entering' becomes 'those finding'. We find in all this one of the keys to Matthew's outlook. There is a right way and a wrong way. There are those who are perishing and those who are being saved. There are people headed for death and people headed for life. Now such antitheses should not be understood to implicate our evangelist in a simplistic outlook—as though for him everything was black or white. Rather, the stark alternatives that appear so often in the First Gospel drive home the important lesson that one must choose clearly and unambiguously—and if necessary at great personal cost—when the issue is religious truth. There are no options when it comes to God and his demands.

τί στενὴ ἡ πύλη καὶ τεθλιμμένη ἡ ὁδὸς ἡ ἀπάγουσα εἰς τὴν ζωήν.[9] Compare Ps 16.11 ('Thou dost show me the path of life') and 118.19–20. Matthew's τί, which is adverbial, bears the sense of 'how' (cf. *māh*), as in Lk 12.49, and is Semitic (cf. Black, pp. 121–4).

'Life', a word commonly part of two-way passages, means in our text 'eternal life', the life of the kingdom of God. Compare 1QS 4.7; Ps. Sol. 9.5 ('life' opposed to 'destruction'); 14.10; T. Asher 6.3; 4 Ezra 7.48, 82, 129, 137; *b. Ḥag.* 3b; *Mek.* on Exod 14.28. Although in the synoptics '(eternal) life' (= *ḥayyê 'ôlām*) typically refers to the future (as in Mt 18.8–9; 19.16–17), in John it becomes, characteristically, a present reality: 'Truly, truly, I say to you, he who believes has eternal life' (6.47; cf. 3.15–16; 6.51; 11.24–5). Also of interest is the Fourth Gospel's use of 'door' and 'way': Jesus Christ is called both (10.7, 9; 14.6; cf. Ps.-Clem. Hom. 3.52.2: 'I am the gate of life: the one entering through me enters into life').

Because, as 7.24–7 indicates, the sermon on the mount 'in its entirety is to be regarded as "the way to eternal life" . . .',[10] we can understand why the road is so little travelled. To live by the words of Mt 5–7 is, despite 11.25–30, no easy task (cf. our comments on p. 690).[11]

[9] According to Metzger, p. 19, the Semitism, τι, became assimilated to the οτι of 7.13 in ℵ* B* (with δε) N^c 700^c 1010 *pc*. This is uncertain. As Gundry, *Commentary*, p. 128, urges, Matthew's love of parallelism could be invoked in favour of an original οτι.

[10] So Betz, *Essays*, p. 3. Cf. Grundmann, p. 231. Bornhäuser, pp. 205–7, wrongly urges that the narrow gate is the golden rule.

[11] On the use of the image of the two ways in connexion with teaching materials see Bergman (v).

Although we have, so far, translated τεθλιμμένη (a perfect passive participle) as 'constricted', this may well be incorrect. (1) If in 7.13b our author were trying to express the antithesis of 'broad', στενός would have been the natural, obvious choice. (2) While θλίβω appears only once in the First Gospel, the related θλῖψις occurs four times, in 13.21; 24.9, 21, and 29; and only in 13.21 can one doubt that the eschatological tribulation is in view. Further, the use of θλῖψις in conjunction with prophecies of eschatological trial is well attested outside Matthew (Dan 12.1; Hab 3.16; Zeph 1.15; Acts 14.22; Col 1.24; Rev 7.14; Herm. v. 2.2.7). (3) Matthew, like other early Christians, believed that the time between the passion of Jesus and his *parousia* belonged to the 'messianic woes' of Jewish expectation (cf. Allison, pp. 40–50). He would accordingly have had no trouble thinking of the Christian 'way' as a 'way of tribulation'. (4) There are two OT passages in which much of the vocabulary of Mt 7.13–14 appears, and both would have been read by early Christians as eschatological texts. In Isa 26.1–19 we read of 'tribulation' (26.16–17), of entering gates (1–2), and of a straight way (7). And these key words appear in Isa 30.18–26: 'tribulation' (20), 'scanty' (στενός, 20), 'way' (21), 'broad' (23), 'many' (25), 'perish' (25). (5) If the way of the believer is in fact the 'narrow way of tribulation', then its opposite, the 'broad way', is such because it is relatively free of affliction and persecution. This is consistent with Matthew's insistence upon the believer as the one who particularly suffers great difficulties (cf. 5.10–12, 44; 10.16–33; 13.21; 23.34; 24.9–10). And εὐρύχωρος, which basically means 'spacious', can refer to a place of comfort, a place free of molestation (so BAGD, s.v.; cf. Herm. m. 5.1.2), while στενός (and related words) can describe a situation of oppression (as in 2 Cor 4.8; 6.12). For further discussion see Mattill (v), who is followed by Luz 1, pp. 397–8.

καὶ ὀλίγοι εἰσὶν οἱ εὑρίσκοντες αὐτήν. In 7.13 the phrase was, 'those entering through it'. Why the change? Perhaps while 'those entering' are simply carried along unawares to destruction, 'those finding' are people who have actively sought: they have quite intentionally gone against the grain.

Is our line rhetorical, an injunction to decision? Or is 7.14c a dogmatic calculation, that is, a statement of *massa damnata* (cf. 4 Ezra 7.47–51; T. Abr. A 11; 2 Bar. 48.43; *b. Sanh.* 97b; *b. Menaḥ* 29b)? In favour of the second view one could cite 22.14 ('Many are called but *few* are chosen'); but against it one could refer to 8.11 ('*Many* shall come from east and west') and 20.28 ('a ransom for *many*'). If the issue cannot be resolved with certainty, this is so for two reasons. First, Matthew's theology is unsystematic and not perfectly consistent. This is why one verse can speak of the salvation of a few, another of Jesus ransoming many. Secondly, one does well to keep in mind the Semitic habit of making hyperbolic declarations in hortative material. Consider *m. Qidd.* 1.10: 'If a man performs a single commandment, it shall be well with him and he shall have length of days and shall inherit the land;

but if he neglects a single commandment it shall be ill with him and he shall not have length of days and shall not inherit the land'. It would be perverse to take these words literally. They are exhortation. One is to act *as if* the fulfilment of one commandment meant everything (cf. Sanders, *Paul*, pp. 129–47). Similarly, the true meaning of Mt 7.13–14 could be: act *as if* only a very few will enter through the gates of paradise. On this reading, one would do wrong to find in this passage an objective numerical estimate. (Note that in Lk 13.23–4 Jesus does not directly answer the question, Will those who are saved be few? He instead throws the question back at his listeners by commanding them to strive to enter the narrow door.)

ON FALSE PROPHETS (7.15–23)

In order to construct a second warning unit in the closing section of his inaugural sermon, Matthew takes up the Q tradition about good and bad fruit (Lk 6.43–4) and, through expansion, makes it treat of false prophets. His hand is evident throughout.

The major question concerning 7.15–23 is easy enough to ask. Who exactly are the false prophets? An answer, however, is not so easily returned. The options seem to be three. (1) Jewish opponents. According to Lagrange (p. 152), the false prophets should be identified with the Pharisees (so also Hill (v), who thinks this true only for 7.15–20; 7.21–3 concerns another group). According to E. Cothenet (v), we should think of the Zealots. Others have nominated the Essenes (Hjerl-Hanson (v); Daniel, 'Faux prophètes' (v)) or even known figures, including Bar Kokba and Simon Magus (see the critical review by Davies, *SSM*, pp. 199–202). (2) Christian opponents. A gamut of choices falls under this heading. Scholars have discovered polemic against Gnostics or Paulinists (so Weiss, *History* 2, p. 753), against antinomians (see Bacon, p. 348; Barth, in *TIM*, pp. 73–5; Hummel, pp. 64–5), against enthusiasts (so Kingsbury, *Structure*, p. 151; Burnett, pp. 234–47), against rigorous, legalistic Jewish Christians opposed to the Gentile mission (Guelich, pp. 391–3; Gundry, *Commentary*, pp. 132–3), or against individuals who cannot be specified (Aune, pp. 222–4). (3) Strecker (p. 137, n. 4) has defended a third possibility: the evangelist is not lashing out against any particular group but delivering a standard eschatological warning: false prophets will arise in the latter days, so beware!

It is hardly necessary to review in detail the evidence for and against each of the alternatives indicated. The identification with Jewish opponents is uncertain because, as we have argued and will argue, there is a unity of theme between 7.15–20 and 21–3; and as those condemned in 7.21–3 are almost certainly Christians (they say 'Lord, Lord' to Jesus and do wonders in his name), those condemned in 7.15–20 are also, in all probability, professing Christians. As for Strecker's proposal, it suffers because 24.23–8 strongly suggests that, with regard to false prophets, Matthew was concerned with a concrete problem. This leaves us with the option of Christian opponents. Unfortunately, this is all we are left with. Prudence reminds us that we just do not have enough data on which to base a firm decision (although the Gnostic interpretation does seem a bit farfetched; see Davies, *SSM*, pp. 192–208). 'All that can be said is that the norms of Christian behaviour represented by Matthew and his circle are not completely accepted by itinerant prophets whom Matthew thinks should be exposed as charlatans. The false prophets represented a form of antistructure which posed a great threat to the existing structure of the Matthean community' (Aune, p. 224).

15. This verse serves as the heading for 7.16–23; 7.16–20 then tells of the false prophets' deeds, 21–3 of their words.

Schematically:

  I. General warning (15)
    A. 'Beware of false prophets' (15a)
    B. Description: 'who come to you . . .' (15b–c)
  II. The false prophets' deeds (16–20)
    A. General principle: 'By their fruits you will know them' (16a)
    B. Illustrations (16b–19)
      1. Thorns and thistles (16b)
      2. Good trees and bad trees (17–19)
        a. What good trees and bad trees do (17)
        b. What good trees and bad trees do not do (18)
        c. Fruitless trees will suffer the judgement of fire (19)
    C. General principle: 'By their fruits you will know them' (20)
  III. The false prophets' words (21–3)
    A. General principle: 'Not every one who says to me, "Lord, Lord" . . .' (21)
    B. The false prophets speak on judgement day (22)
      1. Claim: we prophesied in your name (22b)
      2. Claim: we cast out demons in your name (22c)
      3. Claim: we did many mighty works in your name (22d)
    C. The response of the judge (Jesus) (23)
      1. 'I never knew you' (23a)
      2. 'Depart from me, you evildoers' (23b)

On the links between 7.15–20 and 21–3, links which justify

thinking of 7.15–23 as all-of-a-piece, see on 7.19 and 21 and pp. 693–4.

προσέχετε ἀπὸ τῶν ψευδοπροφητῶν. The verb is redactional in 16.11 and 12 and has no parallel in 6.1 and 10.17; also, its use with ἀπό (cf. *min*) in warnings seems characteristic of the redactor (Mt: 5; Mk: 0; Lk: 2; cf. Ecclus 6.13; 11.33; 17.14; 18.27). ψευδοπροφήτης occurs also in 24.11 and 24 (Mk: 1; Lk: 1).[12] The false prophets are probably to be thought of as being, at least in part, teachers and preachers; for in 10.41; 13.17; and 23.29, 'righteous (one)' (='one who teaches righteousness') and 'prophet' are in synonymous parallelism (cf. Acts 13.1; Did. 15.1).[13]

Two observations. (1) Because Matthew's church is in the world as a mixed body which will not be refined until the great assize (13.24–30, 36–43), false prophets are only to be expected. And even though the disciple must attempt to distinguish true prophet from false (cf. 7.6), the task is no easy one. It should, therefore, be undertaken in true humility (cf. 7.1–5) and in the knowledge that there will be no perfect community before the consummation. (2) One might conceive of the connexion between 7.15–23 and 13–14 in this fashion: the false prophets prevent others from entering the narrow gate and from following the 'constricted path of tribulation' (cf. 23.13) because they stand before the broad gate, beckoning all to enter in; and, as misleading guides, they also line the broad path (cf. Chrysostom, *Hom. on Mt* 23.7–8).

The warning about false prophets, it is important to note, implies that there were true prophets, and their existence is confirmed by the redactional 10.41 ('whoever receives a prophet because he is a prophet shall receive a prophet's reward') as well as by 23.34 ('I send to you prophets and wise men and scribes, some of whom you will kill and crucify, and some you will scourge in your synagogues and persecute from town to town'; the future tense, which points to the post-Easter period, is redactional). Hence Mt 7.15–23 cannot be taken as polemic against all prophets but only against certain prophets in particular. Who then are the legitimate prophets? We should almost certainly think of Cynic-like itinerants, charismatic teachers (cf. 7.22) who wandered from place to place or through the countryside and who sought to imitate the homeless Messiah by abandoning all worldly security (cf. 10.41; Acts 11.27;

[12] LXX: 10, 9 in Jeremiah. See also 1QH 4.16; Acts 13.6; 2 Pet 2.1; 1 Jn 4.1; Rev 16.13; 19.20; 20.10; 2 Bar. 66.4; Josephus, *Ant.* 8.236, 318; *Bell.* 6.285; Did. 11.5–10; Asc. Isa. 2.12–15; 5.2; SB 1, pp. 464–5.

[13] See further Cothenet (v), pp. 293–9, and D. Hill, 'Christian Prophets as Teachers or Instructors in the Church', in *Prophetic Vocation in the New Testament and Today*, ed. J. Panagopoulos, NovTSup 45, Leiden, 1977, pp. 108–30.

15.32–3; 21.10; Lucian, *Peregrinus* 11–12).[14] They would have treasured such hard sayings as Mt 6.19–21; 8.20, 22; and 19.24. The Didache, which must be as close in time and place to Matthew as any other early Christian document, gives us a fair idea of such radical types whose spiritual descendants begot the later monastic movements; see Did. 10–11.

οἵτινες ἔρχονται πρὸς ὑμᾶς ἐν ἐνδύμασιν προβάτων, ἔσωθεν δέ εἰσιν λύκοι ἅρπαγες. Almost every word of this clause appears more often in Matthew than in Mark or Luke.[15] Does ἔρχομαι carry an eschatological sense (cf. 11.3; 16.27–8; 17.10–12; 24.42–4), or does it allude to the itinerant behaviour of the false prophets (cf. Did. 11.1, 4), or does it simply denote their presence or appearance (cf. 20.28; 21.32)? For 'sheep's clothing' see *Dox. Gr.* 573.21 and recall Aesop's fable of the wolf in sheep's clothing (date uncertain).[16] The expression appears neither in the LXX nor, as far as we have been able to determine, in any extant Jewish text from antiquity. Although a symbolic interpretation is usually— and probably rightly—taken for granted by modern interpreters, as it was by most early Christian writers (cf. Justin, *Dial.* 35; *1 Apol.* 16; Irenaeus, *Adv. haer.* 1, preface; Acts Thomas 79; Ignatius, *Eph.* 5 long recension), Zahn, p. 314, and others have argued that the prophetic garb (cf. 1 Kgs 19.13, 19; 2 Kgs 2.8, 13–14; Heb 11.37; 1 Clem. 17.1: always μηλωτή) is in view (so Böcher (v); Hill (v)). However one decides that issue, the sheep are the congregation, the people of God (cf. Num 27.17; Ps 78.52; 1 En. 89–90; Jn 10.1–30), and among them counterfeit Christians (cf. 7.21–3) have taken up residence. Compare Did. 16.3: 'In the last days the false prophets and corrupters shall be multiplied, and the sheep shall be turned into wolves'. (In *Midr. Rab.* on Est 10.2 Israel is portrayed as a sheep in the midst of wolves (= Gentiles).)

The contrast between inward intention and outward appearance (cf. *b. Yoma* 72b) holds together 7.15–23 and recalls the 'hypocrites' of 6.1–18. For λύκος (cf. the rabbinic *lûqôs*) with ἅρπαξ (cf. L. Proph. Dan. 7) see Gen 49.27 LXX. The wickedness of the wolf moved the writer of T. Benj. 11.1 to write, 'And I [Benjamin] shall no longer be called a ravening wolf' (cf. Gen 49.27); and Tg. Onq. on Gen 49.27 has dropped the designation of Benjamin as a wolf altogether.

---

[14] Lit.: Aune, pp. 211–17; A. E. Harvey, review of G. Theissen, *Movement*, in *JTS* 30 (1970), pp. 279–83; E. Schweizer, *Gemeinde*, pp. 140–8; Theissen, *Movement*, passim.

[15] ὅστις (Mt: 29; Mk: 4–5; Lk: 21), ἔνδυμα (Mt: 7; Mk: 0; Lk: 1), and πρόβατον (Mt: 11; Mk: 2; Lk: 2) in particular are favourites of his.

[16] This fable *may* have been known in first-century Palestine; certainly one can detect the influence of some of Aesop's fables on rabbinic literature; see H. Schwarzbaum, 'Talmudic-Midrashic Affinities of some Aesopic Fables', *Laographia* 22 (1965), pp. 466–83.

Although, against Koester, *Überlieferung*, pp. 183–4, Mt 7.15 is
redactional, the motifs are traditional and the phrases prefabricated. For
the inside/outside contrast see 23.27–8. For the sheep/wolf antithesis see
10.16. For false prophets see 24.23–8. For 'fierce wolves' ravaging the
Christian flock see Acts 20.29. For the prophetic agraphon, 'There will be
false prophets' (in the end time), see Justin, *Dial.* 35.3; Ps.-Clem. Hom.
16.21.4. For the wicked being like or acting like wolves see Homer, *Il.*
4.471; 16.156; Epictetus, *Diss.* 1.3.7; 3.22.35; Ezek 22.27; Jer 5.6; Zeph 3.3;
1 En. 89.10–27; Mt 10.16=Lk 10.3; Jn 10.12; Acts 20.29; Did. 16.13;
2 Clem. 5.2–4. In many of these texts sheep are the victims of wolves (cf.
Philo, *Praem.* 86; 4 Ezra 5.18; Philostratus, *VA* 8.22; Libanius, *Ep.* 194.1).
For the association of wolves with false prophets see Ezek 22.27–8.

Warnings against and prophecies of false prophets were often
delivered in the early church; see Mk 13.21–3; 2 Pet 2.1–22; 1 Jn
4.1–3; Did. 11–12; 16.3–4; Herm. m. 11; Acts Thomas 79
(dependent upon Matthew); Ps.-Clem. Hom. 2.6–12; discussion in
Aune, pp. 222–9. In most of these passages false prophets are a
part of the eschatological scenario. This leads us to surmise that
Matthew saw the false prophets of his own day as the harbingers of
the end-time apostasy—a surmise supported by 24.4–5, 10–12,
23–8 (cf. T. Judah 21.9). The latter times had made their
appearance. See further on 7.23, on ἀνομία.

Did. 16.3–4 almost certainly betrays a knowledge of Mt 7.15–23: 'For
in the last days the *false prophets* and corrupters shall be multiplied, and
the *sheep* shall be turned into *wolves*, and love shall be turned into hate (cf.
Mt 24.12). For as *lawlessness* (ἀνομία) increaseth . . .'. Although our
gospel is not quoted verbatim, the key words, 'false prophets', 'sheep',
'wolves', and 'lawlessness' all appear in Mt 7.15–23. This cannot be
coincidence; and as we have judged Mt 7.15 ('Beware of false prophets
who come to you in sheep's clothing but inwardly are ravenous wolves') to
be redactional, and as we shall judge its association with 7.23 ('Depart
from me, you doers of τὴν ἀνομίαν') to be editorial also, the author of the
Didache or of one of his sources appears to have known the First Gospel.

16. How does one know whether there is a snake beneath the
flowers? How does one discern whether under the exquisite artistic
veneer there lies true coin or false? 7.16ff. addresses the issue and
returns this advice: as faith and works never part company, 'you
will know them by their fruits'.

ἀπὸ τῶν καρπῶν αὐτῶν ἐπιγνώσεσθε αὐτούς. Compare 7.19 and
12.33–5 (this with reference to the Pharisees). Lk 6.44 (ἕκαστον γὰρ
δένδρον ἐκ τοῦ ἰδίου καρποῦ γινώσκεται) must be nearer to Q (cf.
Mt 12.33c).[17] Matthew, unlike the other evangelists, uses

[17] Matthew's hand is evident in at least three particulars: αὐτῶν (which connects
7.16 with the preceding), the plural, 'fruits' (which corresponds to the plural in 7.15;
contrast Luke), and instrumental ἀπό (Mt: 5; Mk: 0; Lk: 0–1).

ἐπιγινώσκω—which here equals the simplex (cf. 14.35; BAGD, s.v. 2a)—only with a person as direct object (contrast Mk 2.8; 5.30; Lk 1.4, 22; 5.22; 7.37; 23.7). The verb may be in the future tense (against Luke) either to emphasize the eschatological dimension—false prophets come at the end of the age—or because 7.16 concerns the time after Jesus (Matthew would in this case be historicizing). (Against Guelich, p. 395, we do not think that the future is employed because the false prophets will only be known or shown up at the judgement. It is far more natural to interpret 7.16–20 as giving guidance to those who are to beware of certain people—even if this does create tension with 7.1–5. Surely Matthew is attempting to give his readers some indication of who in fact the false prophets are.) For fruits as deeds or as the consequences of deeds see on 3.8.

Mt 7.16–20 contains a transposition of the Q source order. 7.16 = Lk 6.44 while 7.18 = Lk 6.43. The Lukan arrangement is original. The First Evangelist has preferred to make the summarizing statement, 'By their fruits you will know them', introduce (7.16) and conclude (7.20) the material gathered in 16b–19 (which includes 7.18 = Lk 6.43).

The principle of 7.16 is known from other texts and must be judged a commonplace. See Ecclus 27.6; Jn 15.2–17; Gal 5.19–23; Jas 3.10–12; Ignatius, *Eph.* 14.2; 2 *En.* 42.14; *b. Ber.* 48a. In Ecclus 27.6; Mt 12.33; Lk 6.43–5; and Jas 3.10–12, 'fruit' is speech, and people are known by their words (cf. Clement of Alexandria, *Paed.* 2.5.45). But in Mt 7.16–20; Jn 15; and Gal 5.19–23 a more comprehensive meaning is manifest: deeds in general. This is probably why Matthew, unlike Luke, has the plural, 'fruits', in 7.16, 17, 18, and 20 (although not in 19, this being a perfect reproduction of 3.8).

μήτι συλλέγουσιν ἀπὸ ἀκανθῶν σταφυλὰς ἢ ἀπὸ τριβόλων σῦκα; Lk 6.44b has: 'For from thorns (ἐξ ἀκανθῶν) they do not gather (οὐ . . . συλλέγουσιν) figs (σῦκα), nor from a bramble bush do they pick grapes (σταφυλήν)'. It is not at all clear how one should set about to explain these two texts. μήτι (cf. Jas 3.11; a negative answer is expected, as in 26.22) could indeed be Matthean (Mt: 4; Mk: 2; Lk: 2), and the use of ἀπό may be explained by its appearance in 7.15 and 20. But how does one account for the ordering of the material?

Matthew: from thorns—grapes Luke: from thorns—figs
      from thistles—figs   from a bramblebush—
                                      grapes

Perhaps we are not dealing with Q but with variants from oral tradition (M and L; cf. Wrege, pp. 136–46; Marshall, p. 273). Or perhaps only one evangelist has reproduced Q, the other M or L.

Or perhaps at this point Q^{mt} and Q^{lk} were not identical (cf. on 7.9). We favour the last option, for Q's sermon on the plain probably had in it something close to Lk 6.43–4.[18] We must, however, admit that a redactional solution cannot be ruled out completely. Matthew could be explained as a reworking of the text in Luke (= Q), to wit: having written of 'thorns', he associated them with 'grapes' because of biblical precedent (Isa 5.2, 4 LXX; cf. *b. Pesaḥ.* 49a); then, having used 'grapes' in the first clause he moved 'figs' to the second; and, finally, our author preferred instead of 'bramblebush' (βάτος) a rough synonym, 'thistle' (τρίβολος; cf. Heb 6.8)—maybe because he thought of βάτος (cf. *sĕneh*) in a favourable light, it having been the bush in which Moses saw the fire of God (Exod 3.2–4; Deut 33.16; Mk 12.26; Lk 20.37; Acts 7.30, 35), or because of the biblical association of ἄκανθαι and τρίβολος (Gen 3.18; Hos 10.8; cf. Heb 6.8).[19]

Jas 3.12 reads: 'Can a fig tree (συκῆ), my brethren, yield olives, or a grapevine figs (σῦκα)? No more can salt water yield fresh'. Granted James' acquaintance with the Jesus tradition, this verse—which agrees with Matthew against Luke in its interrogative form—just might preserve an oral variant of Mt 7.16 = Lk 6.44. Yet this is very far from certain. The thought of good from bad is absent, and there are classical parallels that are even closer to Jas 3.12 (e.g. Epictetus, *Diss.* 2.20.18–19; Plutarch, *Tranq. an.* 13; *Mor.* 472F; Seneca, *Ep.* 87.25).

Gos. Thom. 45 reads: 'Jesus said, They do not harvest grapes from thorns, nor do they gather figs from thistles; f[or] they give no fruit' (καρπός).[20] This is a troublesome text. It agrees on the one hand with Matthew in its order: from thorns—grapes/from thistles—figs. Thus if the literary solution outlined above is on the mark, it would be all but impossible not to infer that the author of Gos. Thom. or his tradition copied Matthew. On the other hand, Gos. Thom. 45 and Lk 6.44 are united against Matthew in three particulars: (1) each has a declarative statement, not a rhetorical question;[21] (2) each has a verb in the second clause as well as the first; and (3) most important of all, the context of each is the same: in Gos. Thom. and Luke the saying about fruit is followed by

[18] So also J. M. Robinson, R. D. Worden, and U. Luz in their essays in *Society of Biblical Literature 1983 Seminar Papers*, ed. K. H. Richards, Chico, 1983, pp. 451–4, 455–71, and 473–9 respectively.

[19] Regardless of one's judgement on the problem of source and redaction, it is difficult to think that Daniel, 'Esséniens' (v), is right to connect 'thorn' with the Hebrew *sĕneh* and find in this an allusion to the Essenes, who had prophets (Josephus, *Bell.* 2.159).

[20] Gos. Thom. 45 does not include the saying about the good and bad tree (Mt 7.17–19 = Lk 6.43). Perhaps Mt 7.15–20 and Lk 6.43–4 are the result of a conflation of two originally distinct sayings, one about trees and fruit (Lk 6.43), another about figs and grapes and thorns and brambles (Lk 6.44); cf. Jeremias, *Lukasevangelium*, p. 148.

[21] For the changing of a statement into a question cf. 6.25–6, 30 par.

the saying about good and evil treasure (cf. also Mt 12.33–4).[22] What is one to conclude?

One might reasonably judge that the author of Gos. Thom. or his tradition knew our two canonical gospels, Matthew and Luke. Yet this would be premature. The highly conjectural literary explanation of Matthew's arrangement (from thorns—grapes, from thistles—figs) is that—highly conjectural. And if one favours instead a solution involving oral tradition or different forms of Q, Gos. Thom. 45 need not depend upon Matthew. The concurrence in order could derive from common, pre-Matthean tradition. Similarly, the agreements with Luke are not as telling as first appears. They can without trouble be explained by common use of Q or a Q-like source—a possibility which gains force because Gos. Thom. 45 does not exhibit any peculiarly Lukan features. We propose, therefore, that while Gos. Thom. 45 *may* betray knowledge of the synoptics, it *need not* do so. Furthermore, given the frequent independence of Gos. Thom. elsewhere, the supposition of its independence here is a sensible verdict.

If Mt 7.16, 18 = Lk 6.43–4 was first uttered by Jesus, its original application cannot be determined. But the principle remains clear. Because like produces like, because evil comes from evil (cf. Jer 13.23–4; *b. Šabb.* 129a), appearances can be telling. The outside will inevitably give away what is inside. False face cannot hide false heart forever. Deeds will ultimately demonstrate nature. Certain actions follow inexorably from certain spiritual causes.

In Matthew the principle of like from like is applied to the problem of distinguishing true prophet from false: the deeds or behaviour of the false prophets will give them away (cf. Did. 11.7–12; Herm. m. 11.7–16; Acts Thomas 79). Yet Matthew is almost certainly doing a bit more than supplying his readers with an objective criterion applicable to their own situation (contrast Deut 13.1–5; 18.20–2; 11QTemple 54.8–18; 61.1–5; 1 Cor 12.4ff.). Rather does 7.15–23 presuppose, in all likelihood, a familiar group whose credentials are already known—if not to us then to Matthew's first audience. This implies that 7.15–23 has the additional function of denouncing that group. The evangelist is scoring points against a known opponent.

The problem of false prophets was never really solved by early Christianity. If in Matthew, the Didache, Hermas, and the Acts of Thomas it is their general behaviour which proves determinative, other documents supply other criteria. According to 1 Cor 12.1–3, the confession, 'Jesus is Lord', is decisive (but see also 12.10; 14.29). Later, in 1 Jn 4.2, the confession becomes more specific: 'every spirit which confesses that Jesus Christ has come in the flesh is of God'. In the last half of the second century, in 3 Cor. 3.34–8 (part of the Acts of Paul),

[22] Interestingly enough, Mt 12.33–7, like Gos. Thom. 45, is preceded by the pericope about blasphemy against the Holy Spirit.

disagreement with the apostle to the Gentiles or with the 'orthodox' tradition becomes the mark of the pseudo-prophet (assuming, that is, that the two itinerants of 3 Cor. 1.2 should be identified as prophets). Ps.-Clem. Hom. 2.6–12 records yet one more method: the true prophet 'always knows all things', speaks the truth, and utters only prophecies that come to pass.

The interpreter should not waste time wondering how anyone could expect to find grapes on thorns or figs on thistles. The expectations of those who gather or harvest are irrelevant, as is the question of whether the appearance of thistles or thorns can be deceiving.[23] Mt 7.16, 18 = Lk 6.43–4 has roughly the same import as does 12.34 = Lk 6.45: the good man out of the good treasure of his heart brings forth good, and the evil man out of his evil treasure produces evil. The subject is the continuity between outward acts and inward states. Bad deeds inhere in bad natures, good deeds in good natures.

For figs with grapes see Ps 105.33; Cant 2.13; Isa 34.4; Jer 5.17; 8.13; Hos 9.10; Joel 2.22. Note also the contrast between the grapevine and the bramble in Judg 9.7–15. The impersonal plural, συλλέγουσιν, which has a passive meaning, is widely regarded as an Aramaism (so BDF § 130.2). Seneca, *Ep.* 37.25, commenting on the maxim, *bonum ex malo non fit*, wrote: 'Good does not spring from evil any more than figs grow from olive trees'. Compare also idem, *De ira* 2.10.6 ('Do you think a sane person would marvel because apples do not hang from the brambles of the woodland? Would he marvel because thorns and briars are not covered with some useful fruit? No one becomes angry with a fault for which nature stands sponsor') and Theognis, *Eleg.* 1.537 ('It is not from the squill that the rose and the hyacinth grow').

17. This positive formulation appears to be a redactional creation modelled on the negative formulation in 7.18, whence most of the vocabulary. The evangelist's love of parallelism is again unmistakable.

οὕτως πᾶν δένδρον ἀγαθὸν καρποὺς καλοὺς ποιεῖ. What one is is what one does: the deeds are the man (cf. 6.22–3). The adverb, οὕτως (redactional), subordinates 7.17–18 to 7.16. The former thus illustrates the latter, which thereby becomes a general principle. ἀγαθός (Mt: 15; Mk: 4; Lk: 4) is presumably Matthean (contrast 12.33). 'To make fruit' (cf. 3.10) is a Semitism meaning to bear or produce fruit (Black, pp. 138–9). The ποιεῖ in this and the next verse is a stylistic correction upon Luke's ἐστὶν . . . ποιοῦν. Given the context, the stress resides not in 17a but in 17b.

---

[23] Cf. Luther: in Mt 7.16 Jesus 'cites an example in plain and simple words that even a child can understand. No one is so naive as to suppose that a thornbush bears figs or grapes' (p. 260).

τὸ δὲ σαπρὸν δένδρον καρποὺς πονηροὺς ποιεῖ. This is the obverse of 17a, with the generic article instead of 'all' and with 'tree' coming after rather than before its adjective. σαπρός (Mt: 5; Mk: 0; Lk: 2) means 'decayed, rotten' (cf. Hos 2.4; Mt 12.33; 13.48), or 'old and worn out' (cf. LSJ, s.v.); here the sense is 'worthless'.[24] Because of the word's association with πονηρούς, 'bad' would be an acceptable translation (so RSV). The bad or evil fruits of a worthless tree are the deeds of the false prophets. The replacement of σαπρός by πονηρός in 17b underlines the ethical content (contrast 12.33; Lk 6.43–4).

18. This is parallel but antithetical to 7.17. Compare 12.33.

οὐ δύναται δένδρον ἀγαθὸν καρποὺς πονηροὺς ποιεῖν, οὐδὲ δένδρον σαπρὸν καρποὺς καλοὺς ποιεῖν. SB 1, p. 467, cites no parallel to 7.18 = Lk 6.43. Perhaps this bespeaks an origin with Jesus, if the criterion of dissimilarity is to be trusted. Lk 6.43 has: 'For there is no (οὐ γάρ ἐστιν; cf. 6.44) good (καλόν) tree bearing bad (σαπρόν) fruit, nor again a bad (σαπρόν) tree bearing good (καλόν) fruit'. For the thought compare Job 14.4 ('Who can bring a clean thing out of an unclean?') and 1 Jn 3.9 ('No one born of God commits sin; for God's nature abides in him'). There is an enigmatic parallel of sorts in Gos. Thom. 43: 'You have become as the Jews, for they love the tree, they hate its fruit, and they love the fruit, they hate the tree'.

Despite the interpretation in Apoc. Pet.[2] 7.75.7–26, Mt 7.18 should probably not be thought of as implying some sort of determinism, as if the world were made up of two sorts of people whose fates are irrevocably fixed. As Chrysostom put it, 'Christ saith not this, that for the wicked there is no way to change, or that the good cannot fall away, but that so long as he is living in wickedness, he will not be able to bear good fruit. For he may indeed change to virtue, being evil; but while continuing in wickedness, he will not bear good fruit' (Hom. on Mt. 23.8; cf. Augustine, De serm. mont. 2.24.79).

19. πᾶν δένδρον μὴ ποιοῦν καρπὸν καλὸν ἐκκόπτεται καὶ εἰς πῦρ βάλλεται. Compare Jn 15.6. In 3.10 (q.v.) these exact words (plus οὖν) are attributed to the Baptist. Why do they appear here too? 7.19 helps bind 7.15–20 to 7.21–3; for while 'tree' and 'fruit' look back to the metaphors of 7.16–18, the prospect of judgement ('cut down and thrown into the fire') points forward to 7.21–3, where

---

[24] Cf. O. Bauernfeind, TWNT 7, p. 97. Manson, Sayings, p. 59: 'This curious use of the Greek word (sapros) may be influenced by the fact that the Aramaic verb "to be evil" (b'ēsh) is etymologically identical with the Hebrew verb bāʾash, "to stink". Also, the wild grapes in Isaiah's parable of the Vineyard (Isa 5.2, 4) have a name in Hebrew, which means literally "stinking things". We may then perhaps think of the "corrupt tree" as a wild tree producing fruit—not rotten—but unsuitable for eating because it is harsh and bitter'.

the setting is the final judgement. Also, the verb, ποιοῦν, binds the two sections together: it occurs in 7.17, 18, 19, and 21. ('Fruit' is here in the singular—contrast 16, 17, 18, 20—because it is so in 3.10.)

20. ἄρα γε ἀπὸ τῶγ καρπῶν αὐτῶν ἐπιγνώσεσθε αὐτούς. Matthew repeats an earlier line, 7.16a. The effect is two-fold. First, the theme of knowledge by fruits is underscored (cf. the repetition for emphasis in 19.30 = 20.16 and 24.42 = 25.13). Secondly, an inclusion is created, marking off 7.16–20 as the first half of 7.15–23.[25]

Although ἄρα (= 'consequently', 'as a result'; cf. Rom 10.17; Heb 4.9) does not introduce sentences in classical usage, it does in the LXX: Gen 26.9 (with γέ) (cf. Lk 11.48; 1 Cor 15.18; Heb 4.9).[26] ἄρα γε appears also in 17.26 (without parallel).

Both 7.19 and 20 are, as already noted, doublets, and it should be remarked that the phenomenon of repetition is relatively frequent in Matthew. See, for example, 3.2 = 4.17; 5.29–30 = 18.8–9; 5.32 = 19.9; 9.13 = 12.7; 10.38 = 16.24; 11.15 = 13.9; and 17.20 = 21.21. Kilpatrick (pp. 84–93) found in this circumstance a liturgical or homiletical interest, and others would have recourse to the overlapping of sources. But in truth many of the lines that are reiterated are simply lines of which the evangelist is particularly fond and which lend themselves to being duplicated for the sake of emphasis: repetition persuades.[27]

21. The subject of false prophets continues, with the accent shifting (1) from their deeds ('fruits') to their words or claims ('many will say') and (2) from recognition by others in the present ('you will know them') to their rejection by Jesus in the future ('I never knew you').

οὐ πᾶς ὁ λέγων μοι· κύριε κύριε, εἰσελεύσεται εἰς τὴν βασιλείαν τῶν οὐρανῶν ἀλλ' ὁ ποιῶν τὸ θέλημα τοῦ πατρός μου τοῦ ἐν τοῖς οὐρανοῖς. The shibboleth, 'Lord, Lord', does not itself save, for it can turn out to hide a false faith. Lk 6.46 has: 'Why do you call me "Lord, Lord", and do not do what I tell you?' This last verse is a *skandalon* for the Griesbach hypothesis. Luke omits precisely what is characteristic of Matthew, as the statistics show.[28] One

---

[25] The *inclusio* does not require that 7.15–20 be thought of as a separate section. Cf. 6.25–34, a unit which has within it an inclusion marked off by μὴ μεριμνᾶτε (in 25) and μὴ μεριμνήσητε (in 31).

[26] According to Thrall, p. 36, the use of the inferential ἄρα in the initial position of a sentence may have been a more common feature of the *koinē* than the extant evidence suggests.

[27] Barth, in *TIM*, p. 59, observes that half of the doublets in Matthew pertain either to the final judgement or to the doing of God's will. For discussion of the doublets that do bear on the synoptic problem see pp. 119–20.

[28] οὐ πᾶς: Mt: 2 (redactional in 19.11); Mk: 0; Lk: 0. Participial forms of λέγω meaning 'saying': Mt: 118; Mk: 36; Lk: 94. εἰσέρχομαι + 'kingdom of heaven': Mt:

may infer either that Matthew used Luke or—and this is far more probable—that Matthew and Luke independently drew upon the same source, Q.[29]

For the common double vocative see Gen 22.11; 46.2; Exod 3.4; 1 Sam 3.10; Mt 23.37; Lk 8.24; 10.41; Acts 9.4; T. Abr. A 14.14; 15.1; Apoc. Abr. 9.1; 2 Bar. 22.2; SB 1, p. 943; 2, p. 258. Sometimes it expresses earnestness. The use of the term, 'Lord', seemingly requires that the false prophets belong to the church, for otherwise the address is reserved in Matthew for disciples or for outsiders seeking to follow or to receive help from Jesus. For 'Lord, Lord' see Est 4.17b LXX; Ps 108.21 LXX; 140.8 LXX; Mt 25.11; b. Mak. 24a; b. Ḥul. 139b. For 'to do the will of the/your Father in heaven' in the rabbis see m. 'Abot 5.20; t. Nazir. 4.7; ARN 41; b. Pesaḥ. 112a. In 7.21, 'the will' refers to God's will as it has been revealed in the sermon on the mount. Note that Matthew's 'the will of my Father' = Luke's 'what I [Jesus] tell you'. This implies the perfect solidarity between Jesus' word and God's will: the one is the other.

'My Father' appears here for the first time in Matthew, 'perhaps precisely because in the next verse Jesus appears as judge, as authorized representative of the Father' (so Schweizer, Matthew, p. 188).

There are three very interesting non-canonical variants of this saying: 2 Clem. 4.5 ('Though ye be gathered with me in my bosom and do not my commandments, I will cast you away and will say to you: Depart from me, I know not whence ye are, ye workers of iniquity'); Gos. Naz. frag. 6 ('If you be in my bosom and do not the will of my Father in heaven, I will cast you out of my bosom'); and Pap. Egerton 2 frag. 2ʳ (τί με καλεῖτε τῷ στόματι ὑμῶν Διδάσκαλον μὴ ἀκούοντες ὃ λέγω). Because, against both Matthew and Luke, 2 Clem. 14.5 and Gos. Naz. frag. 6 agree in the phrase, 'in my bosom' (ἐν τῷ κόλπῳ μου), they appear to preserve tradition independent of the synoptics.[30] At the same time, since the latter has 'the will of my Father who is in heaven', one also suspects, in the case of Gos. Naz. frag. 6, some influence from Matthew. What of Pap. Egerton 2? There has, unfortunately, been no agreement as to whether that fragmentary text—which is to be dated sometime before A.D. 150—draws

---

4; Mk: 0; Lk: 0. ποιέω + θέλημα + πατρός: Mt: 3; Mk: 0; Lk: 0. πατήρ with οὐρανός: Mt: 13; Mk: 1; Lk: 1.

[29] Lk 6.46 is probably closer to Q than is Matthew's version; so Bultmann, History, pp. 116–17; Klostermann, p. 70; Schürmann, Lukasevangelium 1, pp. 379–81; Schulz, Q, p. 427; and Schneider (v); against Bonnard, p. 105; Hahn, Titles, p. 91; and Wrege, p. 147. Also, it is probable that in Q, as in Luke, Lk 6.46 introduced the parable of the two foundations. This means that while the saying was addressed to the disciples in the tradition, Matthew has reinterpreted it and applied it to false prophets.

[30] On 2 Clem. 4.5 see Donfried, pp. 62–8. He argues for independence.

upon our canonical gospels.[31] Our own conclusion is that while *Pap. Egerton 2* does seem to show knowledge of Matthew (see on 8.2), it also probably preserves an independent version of Mt 7.21 = Lk 6.46.[32] Certainly the possibility of a translation variant should be considered. 'Teacher' and 'Lord' could be the equivalents of the honorific *rab* or *mar*, and the ποιῶν/ποιεῖτε of Matthew and Luke might be a correct interpretation of ἀκούω = *šāma*'. ('Hear' = 'obey' in Gen 3.17; Exod 15.26; Mt 18.16; Acts 28.28; and *b. Sanh.* 90a.)

Within its original, pre-Easter context, this saying probably expressed Jesus' 'prophetic self-consciousness',[33] his conviction that his inspired words required whole-hearted obedience (cf. 7.24–7 par.). But in the First Gospel there is much more than this. 'Lord' does not simply mean, as it might have before Easter, either 'revered sir' (cf. 8.2, 6, 8; Mk 7.28; Lk 7.6; Jn 4.11) or 'teacher' (cf. Jn 13.13–14). Instead, the early Christian confession, 'Jesus is Lord' (Rom 10.9; 1 Cor 12.3; Phil 2.11), stands in the background, and the scene called to mind is that of the Son of man sitting on his throne (7.22; 25.31).[34] So in 7.21 Jesus is the judge of the last day who has come before the time to declare openly by what criterion he will separate the sheep from the goats.

What exactly is the fault of those who say, 'Lord, Lord', and do not do what the Father wills? It is not simply inactivity. The false prophets are hardly the victims of what Coleridge diagnosed as Hamlet's fatal flaw, namely, the futile ado of thinking and thinking without ever doing. On the contrary, those rejected by Jesus, the eschatological Lord, have performed apparently great things. They have prophesied, cast out demons, and done many mighty deeds. So what is the problem? Unfortunately, the answer to this question hinges upon the answer to another, namely, Who

[31] Favouring independence are G. Mayeda, *Das Leben-Jesu-Fragment Papyrus Egerton 2 und seine Stellung in der urchristlichen Literaturgeschichte*, Bern, 1946; H. Koester, 'Apocryphal and Canonical Gospels', *HTR* 73 (1980), pp. 119–23; and Crossan, *Other Gospels*, pp. 65–87. Favouring dependence: J. Jeremias, in Hennecke 1, pp. 95–6, and D. F. Wright, 'Apocryphal Gospels', in Wenham, *Tradition*, pp. 210–21.

[32] Such a proposal supports our finding that Mt 7.21 is secondary over against Lk 6.46, for the latter and the saying in *Pap. Egerton 2* are relatively close. For the judgement that *Pap. Egerton 2* shows knowledge of written and oral traditions side by side see P. Vielhauer, *Geschichte der urchristlichen Literatur*, Berlin, 1975, pp. 636–8.

[33] So Bultmann, *History*, p. 151. Cf. Fuller, *Christology*, p. 119, who affirms that Jesus himself upgraded the term *mar* with reference to himself, referring it to 'the authority of his enunciation of God's final, absolute demand'. The authenticity of Mt 7.21 need not (against Hahn, *Titles*, p. 91) be doubted.

[34] According to Betz (v), Jesus is, in 7.21–3, only advocate (cf. 1 Jn 2.1), not judge. This position is only defensible with regard to Betz's hypothetical pre-Matthean setting. In Matthew, Jesus himself is clearly the judge (cf. 16.28; 19.28; 24.30–1; 25.31).

are the false prophets? And because, in our discussion of 7.15, we failed to make any satisfactory identification of the wolves in sheep's clothing, we must for a second time confess our ignorance.[35] All that can be safely asserted is that Matthew, like Paul before him (1 Cor 12–14), did not regard charismatic gifts and extraordinary deeds as definitive pointers to authentic faith.

22. This verse and the next are, it would seem, loosely based upon Q. In Lk 13.26–7 there is this: 'Then you will begin to say, "We ate and drank in your presence, and you taught in our streets." But he will say, "I tell you, I do not know where you come from; depart from me, all you workers of iniquity!" ' Compared with this, Mt 7.22–3 is secondary,[36] a very free redactional construction in the interests of the Matthean context. The evangelist has added several distinctive phrases, changed the subject from unbelieving Jews[37] to false prophets who profess Jesus Christ, and made reference to three prophetic activities. (There are also three activities in Luke—eating, drinking, and teaching.) He has also moved the dialogue from its context in Q. For the parallel in 2 Clem. 4.5 see on 7.21.

πολλοὶ ἐροῦσίν μοι ἐν ἐκείνῃ τῇ ἡμέρᾳ. Compare 24.11: '*Many* false prophets will arise and deceive many'. The similarity between 24.11 and 7.22 upholds a connexion between 7.15–20 and 7.21–3 because it shows the latter no less than the former to treat of false prophets (cf. p. 693).

The eschatological content of 'in that day' (cf. *bayyôm hahû*') is plain; see 24.19, 22, 29, 36, 38; 26.29; also Isa 10.20; Hos 1.5; 2.21 LXX (ἐν ἐκείνῃ τῇ ἡμέρᾳ); Amos 9.11; Zeph 1.15; Zech 12.3–11; 13.1–4; 14.4, 6 (ἐν ἐκείνῃ τῇ ἡμέρᾳ), 8, 9, 13, 20; 1 En. 45.3; Lk 17.31 (ἐν ἐκείνῃ τῇ ἡμέρᾳ); 21.34; 2 Th 1.10; 2 Tim 4.8 (ἐν ἐκείνῃ τῇ ἡμέρᾳ). For the rabbis, who, unlike the OT and Matthew, typically used the expression, 'that day', not of the judgement but of the messianic period or the world to come, see SB 1, p. 468. The setting for 7.22–3 is the last day, the day when the Son of man

---

[35] For the answers others have given see on 7.15. According to Manson, *Sayings*, p. 176, Matthew's text takes aim at antinomianism and indeed has an anti-Pauline orientation. In his view, Mt 7.21 manifestly contradicts the idea contained in Rom 10.9—'If thou shalt confess with thy mouth Jesus as Lord . . . thou shalt be saved'. But see Hill, *Matthew*, p. 152.

[36] Cf. Schulz, *Q*, pp. 424–6; Hoffmann (v), pp. 200–2; Krämer (v); and Gundry, *Commentary*, pp. 131–2. The link between Mt 7.22 and Lk 13.26 was noticed by both Justin Martyr (*Dial.* 76) and Origen (*C. Cels.* 2.49), for they appear to conflate the two verses. Because Mt 7.22–3 is largely redactional, one wonders about the methodology of Boring, who finds (p. 208) that his criteria show 7.22–3 to be the product of an early Christian prophet. Such was also the mistaken conclusion of U. B. Müller, *Prophetie und Predigt im Neuen Testament*, Gütersloh, 1975, p. 176.

[37] According to Hahn, *Titles*, p. 90, these Jews are 'those who followed Jesus in His lifetime but who after His death do not adhere to the church . . .'. If so, Lk 13.26–7 must be a community product.

comes in his glory with the angels and sits on his throne to make judgement (25.31). Then will tares be separated from wheat, the wolves from the sheep. For words or speeches delivered by the condemned at the end see 1 En 63; Mt 25.31–46; Justin, *1 Apol*. 16; *Dial*. 76; *b. ʿAbod. Zar*. 2b–3b. For judgement scenes from ancient Jewish literature see SB 4/2, pp. 1199–1212.

κύριε κύριε, οὐ τῷ σῷ ὀνόματι ἐπροφητεύσαμεν καὶ τῷ σῷ ὀνόματι δαιμόνια ἐξεβάλομεν καὶ τῷ σῷ ὀνόματι δυνάμεις πολλὰς ἐποιήσαμεν; On 'Lord, Lord' see on 7.21. 'Did we not prophesy in your name' borrows the language of Jer 14.14 ('The prophets are prophesying lies in my name; I did not send them . . .') and 27.15 ('I have not sent them, says the Lord, but they are prophesying falsely in my name . . .'; cf. 29.9; Zech 13.5). For the connexion between prophecy and miracles in the Jewish tradition see Josephus, *Ant*. 20.167–72, and *b. Yeb*. 121b.

'In your name' can be taken in several different ways. (1) It could mean, 'in the power of your name' or 'by your authority', as in Jas 5.14 (so SB 1, p. 468, and the vast majority of commentators). This seems the most natural interpretation—until one considers 24.5: 'For many will come in my name, saying, "I am the Christ" . . .'. Here the false prophets (cf. 24.24) who 'come in my name' identify themselves with the Messiah. But what sense does it make to claim the authority of a name if it is in fact one's own? Jesus does not cast out demons in the name of Jesus. (2) One may avoid this dilemma by supposing that the one who 'comes in the name of' Jesus is appealing to Jesus' person and work in order to create the impression that he himself is Jesus returned. This is why the false prophet says, 'I am the Christ' (24.5, 23). The problem with this is that while it makes sense of 24.5, it does not make much sense of 7.21–2, where the false prophet says, 'Lord, Lord', and thus recognizes Jesus as a figure distinct from himself. (3) 'In my name' might simply indicate that the false prophets claim to be Christians. This would be consistent with their being 'wolves in sheep's clothing' and with their saying, 'Lord, Lord'. Yet one would be hard pressed to find any other instances of such a usage of 'in my name' in the NT (but see, perhaps, the later Melch. 9.5.1–11). (4) Perhaps the false prophets use Jesus' name as a charm or magical formula, as in Acts 19.13–17 (cf. Mk 9.38–40). Against this, however, in Acts 19 we have to do with those outside the Christian church, which is not the case here. Furthermore, while the use of a charm for performing exorcisms or healings is well attested, this is not so for prophesying. (5) Those who 'come in my name' could be messianic pretenders who do not necessarily identify themselves with the Christian Messiah. But 7.22, where the false prophets acknowledge Jesus as Lord, would seem to put them in the Christian camp. Their Christian status also follows from the continuity of theme between 7.15–20 and 21–3; for in the former the false prophets have obviously infiltrated the church. (6) Perhaps the most satisfactory solution is this: 'in my/your name' is just not consistently used in the First Gospel. In 7.21–3 'in your name' probably means 'in the power of your name' or 'by your authority' (solution 1) while in 24.5 'in my name' must mean a good deal more: the speaker is trying to make himself out to be Jesus or a messianic figure (solution 2 or 5).

The recognition that miracles and other seemingly supernatural phenomena are not infallible signs of saving faith is common to several NT authors, and it is what makes possible the expectation that the last days will see even evil figures doing great wonders (Mt 24.23–8; 2 Th 2.9–10; Rev 13.13–15; etc.). In Lk 10.20, for instance, Jesus declares, 'Do not rejoice in this, that the spirits are subject to you; but rejoice in that your names are written in heaven'. And in 1 Cor 12–14, the apostle Paul puts tongues and other spectacular manifestations in their place by calling for decency and order in worship and by exalting love above everything else as the more excellent way. Matters are similar in our gospel. The evangelist knows that the gifts of prophecy, exorcism, and other miracles, although far from being bad things in themselves (cf. 10.7–8)[38], are not of utmost import.[39] In particular, they can lead hearts and minds away from the pressing issues of the moment—obedience to the demands of Jesus' inaugural sermon. What Jesus has called for is obedience to his Torah (5.17–48), sincere practice of the Christian cult (6.1–18), and a right attitude towards the things of this world (6.19–7.12). He has beckoned his followers to travel down a very difficult road (7.13–14), a road without the promise of fame and glory, a road which instead holds forth the prospect of persecution (5.10–12), with reward coming only in the future (6.4, 6, 18, 19–21). Hence, and despite 10.8, the spectacular and the showy things that cannot but promote vanity and satisfaction in this world are far from being unambiguous boons. In no way can they be held up as testimony to faith. They do not make possible entrance into the kingdom of heaven. Judgement is not rendered according to spectacular manifestations but according to the demands of

[38] Against Käsemann, *Beginnings*, pp. 83–4, and Hill (v), Mt 7.22 does not indicate that Matthew was opposing Christian enthusiasts; the point is simply that no more than the confession of 'Lord, Lord'—which Matthew certainly did not oppose—are exorcism and prophecy and miracles necessarily signs of true righteousness. Cf. Guelich, p. 401. On the other hand, Matthew, one must concede, had no love for magical practices (Hull, pp. 116–41), and his rejection of such practices may have been related to a dislike of enthusiasts.

[39] Despite Luther, p. 271, there is no indication that the false prophets worked wonders only in the past, when they were still true believers, and that they then suffered a lapsed faith and did miracles no more.

righteousness (5.19–20) and love (7.12; 25.31–46) and the secret matters of the heart (6.1–18).

Mt 7.21–3, we may observe, probably reveals the motive for the later omission of Mk 9.38–9 (= Lk 9.49–50): 'John said to him, "Teacher, we saw a man casting out demons in your name, and we forbade him, because he was not following us". But Jesus said, "Do not forbid him; for no one who does a mighty work in my name will be able soon after to speak evil of me" '. As Mt 7.21 consigns to perdition those who have taken the Messiah's name and done great works, the evangelist could not have Jesus do an about face and announce that 'no one who does a mighty work in my name will be able soon to speak evil of me'.

23. The confession of the false prophets turns out to be nothing but air; and their words are blown away by the curt response of the one they have called 'Lord'.

καὶ τότε ὁμολογήσω αὐτοῖς ὅτι οὐδέποτε ἔγνων ὑμᾶς. This redactional line[40] serves to introduce a phrase taken from Ps 6.9. Lk 13.27, which must be closer to Q (see Jeremias, *Lukasevangelium*, p. 233; Gundry, *Commentary*, p. 132), reads, 'And he will say, "I tell you, I do not know (οἶδα) where you come from" '. Matthew prefers a word stronger than ἐρῶ (so Luke), and he chooses ὁμολογέω[41] because of its solemnity, public character, and legal sense (which connotes irreversibility); its use in the judgement scene of Mt 10.32 may also have been a factor (cf. Rev 3.5). The use of the third person αὐτοῖς ('I will confess to *them*') serves to differentiate the false prophets from Matthew's readers. Matthew is, after all, not concerned with correcting the false prophets but with giving the true sheep a warning. As for the use of the second person just four words later ('I never knew *you*'), this creates a contrast with the threefold σῷ of the false prophets in 7.22. Note also that Matthew has changed the tense: 'I do not know' (perfect with present sense) has become 'I never knew you'. The change was probably made so that 7.23a would cover the protracted period of ministry presupposed by 7.22.

'I never knew you' (cf. 25.12, also in a judgement scene) is not to be taken literally. How could the judge of the earth do right if he knew nothing of those who stood before him? And how could God lack knowledge of any individual? 'I never knew you' is a formula of renunciation and means, 'I never recognized you as one of my own' (cf. Amos 3.2; Jn 10.14; 1 Cor 8.3; 2 Tim 2.12, 19[42]).

---

[40] καὶ τότε: Mt: 7; Mk: 3; Lk: 0. ὁμολογέω: Mt: 4 (redactional in 14.7); Mk: 0; Lk: 2. οὐδέποτε: Mt: 5 (redactional in 21.42 and 26.33; without a parallel in 9.33 and 21.16); Mk: 2; Lk: 2. γινώσκω + accusative personal pronoun: Mt: 3; Mk: 0; Lk: 0.

[41] On this word see esp. O. Michel, *TWNT* 5, pp. 119–220, and D. R. Catchpole, 'The Angelic Son of Man in Luke 12:8', *NovT* 24 (1982), pp. 257–9.

[42] According to Moule, *Birth*, p. 120, n. 2, this 'might be regarded as a (reverse) reminiscence of Matt. vii. 21–3'.

ἀποχωρεῖτε ἀπ' ἐμοῦ οἱ ἐργαζόμενοι τὴν ἀνομίαν.⁴³ Compare
13.41; also Job 21.14; 22.17; Ps 139.19; Justin, *1 Apol.* 16.11; *Dial.*
76.5; 2 Clem. 4.5. Lk 13.27b has: ἀπόστητε ἀπ' ἐμοῦ πάντες ἐργάται
ἀδικίας. Ps 6.9 LXX reads: ἀπόστητε ἀπ' ἐμοῦ πάντες οἱ
ἐργαζόμενοι τὴν ἀνομίαν (alluded to in 1 Macc 3.6). Luke agrees
exactly with the first four words of the LXX, Matthew with the last
four. The situation in Luke is rather easily explained. ἀδικία, a
word found six times in Luke-Acts but not in Matthew or Mark,
replaces ἀνομία, a word which Luke never employs; also, while the
third evangelist has ἐργάτης in four places, he never uses οἱ
ἐργαζόμενοι or ὁ ἐργαζόμενος. The motivations behind the
changes in Matthew, by contrast, are a little less clear. He has
conformed 'workers of unlawlessness' to the LXX, but why the
substitution of ἀποχωρέω (Mt: 1; Mk: 0; Lk: 2; the MT has *sûrû*)
for ἀφίστημι and the dropping of 'all' (the MT has *kol*)? Was
ἀποχωρεῖτε perhaps in Q, Luke having altered it to ἀπόστητε in
accordance with the LXX? Did Matthew dislike ἀφίστημι (Mt: 0;
Mk: 0; Lk: 4)? Is Gundry (*Commentary*, p. 132) correct to urge
that Matthew omitted 'all' because of the desire to avoid repetition
(cf. 7.21)? Although these questions remain unanswered, two
points may be made. (1) In view of the 'pure LXX form running
through the NT quotations from the Psalms, it naturally comes
about that we cannot speak of more than a mode of expression
influenced by the LXX' (Stendahl, *School*, pp. 89–90). (2) Inexact
allusions to Scripture are very common in Jewish literature (note,
e.g. the use of Ps 6.9 in 1 Macc 3.6), especially in the apocalypses
(like Revelation), so the allusion in Mt 7.23 can hardly be
considered anomalous.

There is perhaps some reason to suppose that Ps 6 played a rôle
in early Christian apologetics. In addition to the allusion to Ps 6.9
in the present text, Ps 6.4–5 seems to be alluded to in Jn 12.27.

ἀνομία is often translated 'lawlessness' (so BAGD, s.v.), and the
word has been milked for much by those who think Matthew was
fighting tooth and nail against Christian antinomianism.⁴⁴ There
are problems with this, as a close look at the usage in Matthew
reveals. Neither the Torah nor the Messiah's law is the clear
subject in 13.41; 23.28; or 24.12. In 23.38 and 24.12 the emphasis
seems to fall upon a sinful, inward state, while in 13.41 'doers of
iniquity' is no more than a general descripton of bad deed doers.
Thus, as is the case elsewhere in the NT (e.g. Rom 4.7; 6.19; 2 Cor
6.14; 2 Th 2.3, 7–8; Tit 2.14; 1 Jn 3.4), the strictly legal background

---

⁴³ Θ L *f*¹³ 1424 *al* b vgˢ add παντες (cf. Ps 6.9; Lk 13.27).

⁴⁴ E.g. Barth, in *TIM*, pp. 159–64; Hummel, pp. 64–8; and Cothenet (v).
Contrast Stendahl, *School*, p. xii; Walker, pp. 135–6; Thompson, p. 262, n. 26;
and Stanton, 'Origin and Purpose', pp. 1909–10.

of ἀνομία should not be pressed.[45] Indeed, the word probably has much more to do with eschatology than with law. In Mt 24.12; 2 Th 2.3; and Did. 16.4, ἀνομία characterizes the end period of wickedness, and in Mt 7.23 and 13.41 it belongs to an exclusion formula (cf. 4.10) pronounced at the final judgement (cf. Jub. 23.19; T. Iss. 6.1).

HEARERS AND DOERS OF THE WORD (7.24–7)

The parable of the two builders terminated Q's sermon on the plain. Both Matthew and Luke have let it retain this function in their gospels: the parable concludes both Mt 5–7 and Lk 6.17–49. Interestingly enough, the ending of a discourse with a parable is a Matthean pattern which holds for four of the five major discourses (7.24–7; 13.52; 18.21–35; 25.31–46).

7.24–5 and 26–7 constitute not a double parable (cf. 13.31–3) but a single parable in antithetical parallelism. As usual, the parallelism is much fuller in Matthew than in Luke.

Deut 28.15 reads: 'But if you will not obey the voice of the Lord your God or be careful to do all his commandments and his statutes which I command you this day, then all these curses shall come upon you and overtake you'. Curses follow, including this one: 'You shall build a house, and you shall not dwell in it' (28.30b). Other texts reminiscent of Mt 7.24–7 par. include Prov 10.25 ('When the tempest passes, the wicked is no more, but the righteous is established for ever'); 12.7 ('The wicked are overthrown and are no more, but the house of the righteous will stand'); and 14.11 ('The house of the wicked will be destroyed, but the tent of the upright will flourish'). See also Isa 28.16–17; Ezek 13.8–16; and Boethius, *de Consolatione* 2.4. The closest rabbinic parallels are to be found in *ARN* 24 ('Elisha ben Abuyah says: One in whom there are good works, who has studied much Torah, to what may he be likened? To a person who builds first with stones and afterward with bricks: even when much water comes and collects by their side, it does not dislodge them. But one in whom there are no good works, though he studied Torah, to what may he be likened? To a person who builds first with bricks and afterward with stones: even when a little water gathers, it overturns them immediately') and *m. 'Abot* 3.18 (R. Eleazar b. Azariah used to say: 'He whose wisdom is more abundant than his works, to what is he like? To a tree whose branches are abundant but whose roots are few; and the wind comes and uproots it and overturns it. . . . But he whose works are more abundant than his wisdom, to what is he like? To a tree whose branches are few but whose

---

[45] See Davies, *SSM*, pp. 202–5; A. Sand, 'Die Polemik gegen die "Gesetzlosigkeit" im Evangelium nach Matthäus und bei Paulus', *BZ* 14 (1980), pp. 112–25; and J. E. Davison, '*Anomia* and the Question of an Antinomian Polemic in Matthew', *JBL* 104 (1985), pp. 617–35.

roots are many; so that even if all the winds in the world come and blow against it, it cannot be stirred from its place . . .'; cf. *ARN* 22).

24. πᾶς οὖν ὅστις ἀκούει μου τοὺς λόγους τούτους καὶ ποιεῖ αὐτούς. Compare Philo, *Praem Poen.* 79; Lk 8.21; Jn 12.47–8; Jas 1.25. Lk 6.47a has: 'Everyone coming to me and hearing my words (τῶν λόγων) and doing them (αὐτούς)'. Matthew has added οὖν (Mt: 57; Mk: 5; Lk: 31) and τούτους (Mt: 6 (3 in 7.24–7; 5 with λόγους); Mk: 1; Lk: 5). Luke has perhaps changed 'hears' and 'does' to participles (so Jeremias, *Lukasevangelium*, p. 149) and almost certainly tacked on 47b: 'I shall show you what he is like' (ὑποδείκνυμι: Mt: 1; Mk: 0; Lk: 3; Acts: 2). Luke's 'who comes to me and'—note the connexion with Lk 6.17–18—probably derives from Q (cf. Lk 14.26), Matthew having omitted it because for him 'the coming one' is exclusively a messianic title (cf. 3.11; 11.3; 21.9; 23.39). With πᾶς ὅστις compare the Hebrew *kol 'ăšer*, the Aramaic *kol dî*, and the rabbinic *kōl mî še*. 'Therefore' apparently links 7.24–7 with 7.15–23. Both units concern doing the will of God as opposed to hearing it, and both gain force by calling to mind the great assize. Note the emphatic placement of the personal pronoun ('*my* words' = Jesus' words; cf. 16.18) and the additional emphasis contributed by τούτους (= these words in the sermon on the mount). (On Jesus' lips, 'my words' will have embraced his entire message; cf. Mk 8.38.) ποιεῖ takes up one of the key words of 7.15–23 and continues the point made there: one must *do* what Jesus says. For 'do' + 'word' see Jer 22.4; 11QTemple 54.6. For other statements about the great importance of Jesus' words see Mk 8.38; Lk 11.28; Mk 13.31 = Mt 24.35.

It is perhaps noteworthy that, in 7.24–7, Matthew says nothing at all about studying the words of Jesus. For the evangelist, presumably, it is not studying that is greater but doing. Compare *m. 'Abot* 1.17, which no doubt addresses a tendency in rabbinic Judaism to exalt study at the expense of other action.

ὁμοιωθήσεται ἀνδρὶ φρονίμῳ.[46] Compare the 'to what may he be likened' of *ARN* 24 and *m. 'Abot* 3.18, quoted above. Lk 6.48a has ὅμοιός ἐστιν ἀνθρώπῳ, which reproduces Q (see Jeremias, *Lukasevangelium*, p. 150). ὁμοιόω is Matthean (Mt: 8; Mk: 1; Lk: 3). The future tense adverts to the last judgement; and, as Schweizer observes, just as there are wolves among the sheep (7.15–23) and tares among the wheat (13.24–30) until the end, so do the houses of wise and foolish stand side by side until the Son of man takes his throne in judgement (*Matthew*, pp. 190–91).

Matthew naturally thinks of the builder of a house as male

---

[46] So ℵ B Z Θ *f*(1).13 33 700 892 1241 *al* ff¹ 1 vg syp.hmg sa mae. ομοιωσω αυτον (cf. 11.16; Lk 7.31; 13.18, 20) appears in C L W Maj f h k q syc.h bo Arn Cyp Hil Lcf.

(ἀνήρ). φρόνιμος (redactional: Mt: 7; Mk: 0; Lk: 2) is again paired with μωρός in 25.1–13; compare Ecclus 21.25–6; 1 Cor 4.10; Tit 3.8–9. 'The issue shows plainly enough that one is wise and the other foolish . . . [but] Matthew is apt to paint the lily' (Manson, *Sayings*, p. 61).

ὅστις ᾠκοδόμησεν αὐτοῦ τὴν οἰκίαν ἐπὶ τὴν πέτραν. Compare Apoc. Pet.² 7.70.26–7. The rock is not hearing and doing but the teaching of Jesus as delineated in the great sermon; and to build on that rock, that is, to do the will of the Father in heaven, shows a person to be prudent. Compare Ecclus 22.16–18. It is probably too much to think of an allusion to Peter and his church (cf. 16.18). Lk 6.48b–c reads: 'building (οἰκοδομοῦντι) a house (οἰκίαν), who dug and went down deep and laid a foundation upon rock' (ἐπὶ τὴν πέτραν; cf. 1 Cor 3.10–15). The Third Evangelist has probably added 'who dug and went down deep and laid a foundation',⁴⁷ for the vocabulary seems to be typically Lukan.⁴⁸ In addition, Luke's version detracts from the main issue, which 'is not the amount of labour expended, but the choice of a suitable foundation. The simpler statement of Mt. is to be preferred, as is also Mt.'s dramatic description of the tempest. "Because it had been well builded" (Lk) misses the point. We are to imagine both houses as equally well built. The only difference is that correctly given by Mt.: one was founded on rock and the other on sand' (Manson, *Sayings*, p. 61). For rock as a metaphor of safety see 1 Sam 2.2; Ps 27.5; Mt 16.18.

25. Compare 16.18.⁴⁹ According to Augustine (*De serm. mont.* 2.24.87), the storm that strikes the house built upon the rock stands for the calamities and afflictions of everyday life. Indeed, carried away by allegorical fancy, he equates rain with 'gloomy superstition', rivers with 'carnal lusts', and winds with 'rumours'. But we may well doubt whether 7.25 was intended by Jesus or understood by Matthew to depict the harsh vicissitudes of normal human existence. In the OT the storm often represents God's judgement (Gen 6–7; Isa 28.2; 29.6; 30.30; Ezek 13.10–16; 38.22), and in later Jewish literature the difficulties and trials of the latter days are, despite Gen 9.11, sometimes pictured as terrible tempests (e.g. 1QH 3.14; Sib. Or. 3.689–92; 5.377–80; 2 Bar 53.7–12). In the synoptic tradition itself the story of Noah's flood is taken up in an

---

⁴⁷ According to Jeremias, *Parables*, p. 27, n. 9, Luke has in mind a Hellenistic house with a cellar. This is uncertain. As Gundry, *Commentary*, p. 134, notes, excavation is referred to in *Yal.* 1.766 (Num 23.9).

⁴⁸ σκάπτω: Mt: 0; Mk: 0; Lk: 3. τίθημι: Mt: 5; Mk: 11; Lk: 16. θεμέλιος: Mt: 0; Mk: 0; Lk: 3.

⁴⁹ Ignatius, *Phil.* prologue, long version, conflates Mt 7.25 and 16.18. The result is a consistent image—the church founded upon a rock and weathering the storms of spiritual wickedness.

attempt to portray the eschatological affliction (Mt 24.39 = Lk 17.27). It seems a good guess,then, that Mt 7.24–7 = Lk 6.47–9 should conjure up in the mind the storms of the end times. The troubles facing those who have heard Jesus' words are the eschatological ordeals, from which people are saved by virtue of their obedience to the sermon on the mount (cf. Cadoux, p. 245; Jeremias, *Parables*, pp. 169, 194).

καὶ κατέβη ἡ βροχὴ καὶ ἦλθον οἱ ποταμοὶ καὶ ἔπνευσαν οἱ ἄνεμοι καὶ προσέπεσαν τῇ οἰκίᾳ ἐκείνῃ.[50] The pattern, conjunction + verb + article + element is repeated three times to achieve three perfectly parallel clauses which are then climactically followed by 'and hit upon that house'. Lk 6.48c ('and when a flood arose, the river broke against that house') may or may not be closer to Q. For rains and rivers as symbols of God's judgement see Ps 66.10–12; Isa 30.27–30; Sib. Or. 3.689–91. According to BAGD, s.v., ποταμός, while in Lk 6.48–9 a river rises near the house in question, in Matthew 'the river*s*' are to be understood as mountain or winter torrents which fill the ravines after a heavy rain.

καὶ οὐκ ἔπεσεν. There is a wordplay with προσέπεσαν: 'they fell upon . . . it did not fall'. Luke has this: 'and was not able to shake it', which is redactional (ἰσχύω: Mt: 4; Mk: 4; Lk: 8 (always preceded by οὐκ or μή and usually followed by an infinitive); σαλεύω: Mt: 2; Mk: 1; Lk: 4; Acts: 4).

τεθεμελίωτο γὰρ ἐπὶ τὴν πέτραν. 'On the rock' (cf. Ignatius, *Polyc*. 1.1) is from Q (cf. 7.24 and Lk 6.48b), but it may be repeated here by our evangelist for emphasis. Luke's 'because it had been well built' is redactional and changes the sense: the house stands not because of its good foundation but because it has been well built.

26. Matthew has revised Q so as to make this verse conform to 7.24. The result is perfect parallelism.

The subject switches from the wise man and his house to the foolish man and his dwelling. As we have argued, in the original parable everything turned upon the choice of a foundation. Should one build on Jesus' words or on something else? In Matthew the point is retained: one must direct life according to Jesus' instructions. But 7.24–7 also makes a second point. Just as one must keep to the narrow road (7.13–14) and offer more than lip service (7.21), so too is it expedient to busy the hands once one knows what should be built. It is not enough to hear or read Jesus' words, even if one applauds. Indeed, because Jesus himself commands not study but action, it is hypocrisy to nod in

---

[50] In this verse and 7.27, BDF § 492, on the insufficient authority of six Latin mss. and Cyp Chr Eus, prefers asyndeton: κατεβη η βροχη, ηλθον οι ποταμοι, επνευσαν οι ανεμοι και προσεπεσαν τη οικια εκεινη, και ουκ επεσεν· τεθεμελιωτο γαρ επι την πετραν.

agreement while sitting by the wayside.

The foolish man is introduced as the counterpart of the wise man. As so often in the parables of Jesus, correct behaviour may be observed in one character, incorrect behaviour in another. Compare the two servants of 18.23–34, the two sons of 21.28–31, the two servants of 24.45–51 = Lk 12.35–46, and the two debtors of Lk 7.41–2; also the rich man and beggar in Lk 16.19–31 and the Pharisee and the publican in Lk 18.9–14.

καὶ πᾶς ὁ ἀκούων μου τοὺς λόγους τούτους καὶ μὴ ποιῶν αὐτοὺς ὁμοιωθήσεται ἀνδρὶ μωρῷ. Compare Ezek 33.32 (ἀκούσονταί σου τὰ ῥήματα καὶ οὐ μὴ ποιήσουσιν αὐτά) and *Sipra* on Lev 26.3 ('The one who learns not in order to do, it would have been better for him had he not been born'). In Matthew's mind, only the Jesus of the sermon on the mount guarantees asylum from God's judgement. If one leans on anything else, it will prove to be a weak reed.

Matthew's 'all' and 'these my words' are editorial, both being taken from 7.24 = Lk 6.47. μωρῷ (see on 5.22) is also editorial. In the First Gospel μωρός refers to the folly of not understanding religious truths that should be obvious (23.17, 19) or to the folly of not acting upon what one knows (25.2, 3, 8). Both meanings are appropriate in 7.26. (Unlike Paul, who transforms the word into something ironically positive (1 Cor 1.25; 3.18; 4.10), Matthew maintains a wholly pejorative sense.)

Lk 6.49a–b (ὁ δὲ ἀκούσας καὶ μὴ ποιήσας ὅμοιός ἐστιν ἀνθρώπῳ) is very close to Mt 7.26a when allowance is made for the three editorial insertions noted above.

ὅστις ᾠκοδόμησεν αὐτοῦ τὴν οἰκίαν ἐπὶ τὴν ἄμμον. This differs from 7.24c only in the last word. Rock becomes sand (ἄμμος: Mt: 1, Mk: 0, Lk: 0). The result is this: a sound building technique is replaced by shortsighted senselessness. Who would build a house on sand? Lk 6.49c has: 'building a house on the land without a foundation'. The participle is Lukan as is 'the land without a foundation' (see on 7.24).

27. The fate of those who hear and do not do is next described. They do not weather the storm. Their end is destruction (7.13) and separation from Jesus (7.23). This is the unsoothing note on which the sermon ends. Augustine called it 'fear-inspiring' (*De serm. mont.* 2.25.87).

καὶ κατέβη ἡ βροχὴ καὶ ἦλθον οἱ ποταμοὶ καὶ ἔπνευσαν οἱ ἄνεμοι καὶ προσέκοψαν τῇ οἰκίᾳ ἐκείνῃ. This repeats 7.25 exactly, save that προσέπεσαν gives way to προσέκοψαν (= 'beat against'). Matthew is undoubtedly responsible for the heightening of the parallelism. Lk 6.49 has: 'against which the storm broke'.

καὶ ἔπεσεν. Compare Lk 6.49: καὶ εὐθὺς συνέπεσεν. Luke has created the συν-compound (Jeremias, *Lukasevangelium*, p. 150);

but εὐθύς appears only here in the Third Gospel. Note once again that the parallelism is much greater in Matthew than in Luke: while the former has καὶ οὐκ ἔπεσεν (7.25) and καὶ ἔπεσεν (7.27), the latter has 'and was not able to shake it' (6.48) and 'and immediately it fell' (6.49). For the destruction of the wicked or the house of the wicked in a storm see Job 8.15; Ps 11.6; 83.15; Prov 14.11; Isa 28.15–18; Ahiqar 75 (Lingenberger).

καὶ ἦν ἡ πτῶσις αὐτῆς μεγάλη. The house, symbolizing a person, has collapsed in condemnation, and its ruin is total. Compare Lk 6.49: καὶ ἐγένετο τὸ ῥῆγμα τῆς οἰκίας ἐκείνης μέγα. It is impossible to determine whether Matthew or Luke is here closer to Q. In any event, 'Great was the fall thereof' seems to have been a proverbial expression meaning 'a complete collapse' (cf. Philo, *Mut. nom.* 55; *Migr. Abr.* 80; *Ebr.* 156).

CONCLUSION OF THE INAUGURAL SERMON (7.28–9).

Immediately following the parable of the two builders Luke has this: 'After he had ended all his sayings in the hearing of the people . . .'. The sentence must be judged editorial (Jeremias, *Lukasevangelium*, p. 151). But so must Mt 7.28–9 (see below). This means that if Q contained a concluding line for the sermon on the plain, its wording is forever lost. All one can say is that such a closing sentence, if it did exist, may have combined a remark about Jesus finishing his words with a notice of his going on to Capernaum (cf. Mt 7.28; 8.5; Lk 7.1).

Mt 7.28–9 + 8.1 ('When he came down from the mountain, great crowds followed him') forms, through the repetition of earlier words and phrases, an inclusion with 4.23–5.2. The great wheel of the sermon on the mount has turned full circle.

4.23–5.2	7.28–9
'great crowds followed him' (4.25)	'great crowds followed him' (8.1)
the crowds (5.1)	the crowds (8.1)
the mountain (5.1)	the mountain (8.1)
going up (5.1)	going down (8.1)
teaching (5.2)	teaching (7.29)

Furthermore, 'opening his mouth' (5.2) has as its counterpart 'when Jesus finished these words' (7.28). Thus the beginning and end of the sermon mirror one another. This has the effect of marking off 5.3–7.27 as a distinct literary unit.

The correspondence of introduction and conclusion is also found in two other major Matthean discourses, those in chapters 10 and 13.

9.35–10.5a	11.1
'the twelve disciples' (10.1)	'the twelve disciples'
'cities' (9.35)	'cities'
'teaching . . . and preaching' (9.35)	'teaching and preaching'
'Jesus' with the definite article (9.35)	'Jesus' with the definite article
13.1–3a	13.53
'parables' (13.3)	'parables'
'Jesus' with the definite article (13.1)	'Jesus' with the definite article

28. The crowd—and not just the disciples—has heard Jesus' words (see on 5.1). We are apparently to think of Jesus addressing his disciples in the midst of a crowd that overhears. (7.28 cannot reasonably refer to what the crowd learned later.)

Our evangelist gives no words to the crowd. Whether or not one is to imagine people struck dumb with amazement is uncertain. What cannot be denied, however, is that the silence is artistically and theologically appropriate. In Mt 5–7 only one character opens his mouth. There is no dialogue, there are no questions, and there is no vocal response. Jesus' words are ringed in silence. This focuses all attention on him while it also implicitly impresses upon us his great authority: when he speaks, Jesus is alone and by himself.

καὶ ἐγένετο ὅτε ἐτέλεσεν ὁ Ἰησοῦς τοὺς λόγους τούτους. Compare Num 16.31; Deut 31.1 LXX; 31.24; 32.45; Jer 26.8. Particularly close is 2 Bar 87.1: 'And it came to pass when I had ended all the words of this epistle . . .'. Matthew repeats his closing formula five times, at the end of each major discourse (5–7, 10, 13, 18, 24–5). On the Semitism, καὶ ἐγένετο, see p. 82.

Despite the significant parallels with the conclusions to the other major discourses, 7.28–9 stands out as atypical. This is because it is the only conclusion which does not carry the story forward. 11.1; 13.54; 19.1; and 26.1 all immediately immerse the reader back into the narrative flow. Only after the sermon on the mount is there a pause in which to catch one's breath. This circumstance undoubtedly advertises the uniqueness of 5–7 for the evangelist's work. Matthew's readers are expected to stop and ponder what has been said; they are to realize, however dimly, that the great sermon hides a multitude of profound ramifications and that it is accordingly something to be returned to again and again.

ἐξεπλήσσοντο οἱ ὄχλοι ἐπὶ τῇ διδαχῇ αὐτοῦ. This phrase, borrowed from Mk 1.22, appears again (slightly modified) in the redactional 22.33. Compare also Mk 11.18; Lk 4.32; Acts 13.12. In Mark and Luke, the verb, ἐκπλήσσω, sometimes refers to the reaction that naturally follows an extraordinary event or miracle (Mk 7.37; Lk 2.48; 9.43). This is never so in Matthew's gospel, where the word is reserved exclusively for the response provoked by Jesus' *words* (7.28; 13.54; 19.25; 22.33). The addition by Matthew of ὄχλος (cf. 4.25; 5.1) displaces the impersonal plural of Mk 1.22. The disciples, oddly enough, are not mentioned. We do not hear that they too were amazed.

The passive of ἐκπλήσσω can mean to be 'amazed' or 'overwhelmed' either with wonder, as in 13.54, or with fright, as in 19.25 (cf. BAGD, s.v.). Because both meanings are appropriate to 7.28–9, maybe the distinction just made should here be abandoned. If Jesus' teaching would cause wonder because of its novelty (cf. Mk 1.27; Jn 7.46; and see below),[51] it would also, given that the note of judgement has been rung so loudly at the end of chapter 7, be natural for people to react with fear. (The imperfect tense has the force of indicating continued amazement or wonder, as though the people returned to their homes still pondering what it all meant.)

29. Despite the genuine continuity between the teaching of Jesus and the Jewish Torah, there is something new about the Messiah's speech. His teaching first goes beyond the letter of the law and makes what the evangelist probably understood to be an unprecedented demand for purity of intention and harsh self-denial. Secondly, the teaching is unlike that of the doctors of the law in so far as it depends not upon the OT or Jewish tradition but solely upon the authority of the speaker, who is in this like a true prophet.[52] By what we may call his intuitive awareness of the will of God in its nakedness, Jesus proclaims what all should do. He does not call upon any mediate authority (cf. Abrahams 1, p. 15). The man himself, in daring boldness, is his own authority. He thus rewrites the rules of the serious game he is playing. Contrast *y. Pesaḥ* 6.1.33a: Hillel 'discoursed of the matter all the day, but they did not receive his teaching until he said, Thus I heard from Shemaiah and Abtalion'. Lastly, if it is true, as George Orwell wrote, that 'Orthodoxy, of whatever colour, seems to demand a lifeless, imitative style', then we have in Jesus' fresh and vivid, home-made images sure indication that he spoke for himself and did not follow any party line. This implies novelty of some sort.

If the form and content of Jesus' teaching set him apart in one important particular from the scribal tradition that became

---

[51] One must be cautious here. As Matthew stresses the continuity between Jesus' words and the old Torah, and as he omits Mark's 'new teaching' (Mk 1.27), the element of newness should not be overemphasized. Cf. Davies, *SSM*, pp. 99–106. And yet, given the differences between Jesus' teaching and the tradition (cf. 5.20–6.18) as well as the amazement of the crowds, the people have obviously heard what they have not heard before.

[52] Yet in contrast to the prophets, Jesus does not preface his words with, 'Thus says the Lord'. Jesus instead says, 'But *I* say to you . . .'.

rabbinic Judaism, we should also record the fact that Jesus cannot be lumped in with those imaginative seers who, in composing apocalypses, claimed to be revealing the secrets of heaven. The apocalyptic visionaries, in contrast to the rabbis, appealed less to the OT and tradition than to fantastic experiences of revelation. In 1 Enoch knowledge comes through the seeing of visions and the hearing of angels. The same is true in 4 Ezra. In 2 Enoch there is an ascension into heaven which enables Enoch to learn first-hand about what is above. In 2 Baruch God talks directly to the scribe or gives him visions in the night, in response to prayer and fasting. In the Apocalypse of Abraham the patriarch leaves the earth and follows an angelic guide. And so it goes. The writers of the apocalyptic literature speak not on their own authority but by virtue of purported revelatory experiences. It is otherwise with Jesus. Not only does he fail to cite the OT with regularity or the words of the fathers at all, he also fails—with the apparent exception of Lk 10.18—to relate that he learned religious truths by ascending into heaven or by seeing visions or by hearing angels. He simply addresses the conscience directly and declares, 'I say to you'. Now when we inquire as to how Jesus himself, were he here before us, would explain his apodictic, declarative style, the historical waters suddenly become opaque. We have asked a question we cannot answer. But when we turn from Jesus to Matthew, matters can be penetrated. Jesus speaks as he does because he has direct knowledge of God: the Son knows the Father (11.27). (See also Davies, *SSM*, pp. 431–435.)

ἦν γὰρ διδάσκων αὐτοὺς ὡς ἐξουσίαν ἔχων καὶ οὐχ ὡς οἱ γραμματεῖς αὐτῶν.[53] Matthew has added the possessive pronoun (cf. 4.23; 9.35; 10.17; 11.1; 12.9; 13.54). It serves to distinguish Christian scribes (13.52) from scribes outside the church. Otherwise the evangelist has taken over Mk 1.22b without alteration. 'Their scribes' appears only here in Matthew.

According to H. P. Chajes, *Markus-Studien*, Berlin, 1899, pp. 11–12, someone misunderstood the Hebrew source behind Mk 1.22 = Mt 7.29: *bĕmāšāl* ('in parable') was wrongly rendered as though it were *kĕmōšel* ('as one with authority'). This is highly implausible. The use of parables would not in itself have created astonishment; and in any case Mk 1.22 may well be redactional (so Pesch 1, p. 120). For speculation on the possible relation between Jesus' authority and the rabbinic *rĕšûtā*' see Daube, pp. 205–23. Differentiating between rabbis and scribes (ordinary teachers), he argues that the former had a creative authority the latter did not; so, Daube urges, when the gospels exalt Jesus' authority over the scribes, they are really ascribing to their Lord 'rabbinic authority'. (The problem with this is that Jesus, as we have seen, taught with an authority unlike both of Daube's groups, the rabbis and scribes.)

[53] C* W 33 1241 *pc* lat sy Eus Hil insert και οι Φαρισαιοι after αυτων.

According to 28.18, the Easter event bestowed upon Jesus 'all authority in heaven and on earth'. This would seem to imply that his ἐξουσία was circumscribed before the resurrection. Yet one should not make much of this. Already in the pre-Easter period Jesus can avow, 'all things have been delivered to me by my Father' (11.27). Moreover, the Jesus who speaks in 28.18 with all authority explicitly endorses the pre-Paschal instruction: 'teaching them to observe all that I have commanded you' (28.20). Consequently, the authority of the earthly Jesus is for all practical intents and purposes the same as that of the risen Lord.

One last observation. It is Jesus' teaching, not that of his disciples, which is contrasted with the teaching of the scribes. This is because Jesus and no one else is the source of the Christian *halakah* (cf. van Tilborg, p. 128).

(iv) *Concluding Observations*

(1) The concluding section of Mt 5–7 consists of three protreptic subsections, each of which draws its life from eschatological expectation: 7.13–14 (the two ways), 15–23 (false prophets), 24–7 (the two builders). This is the first instance of a pattern that will be repeated. Thus, the final three units of the missionary discourse in chapter 10 (10.32–3, 34–9, 40–2) have to do with eschatological rewards and punishments; and the same is true of the second triadic group of kingdom parables in chapter 13 (13.44, 45–6, 47–50), this coming right before the closing sentences (13.51–2, 53). The great eschatological discourse, 24.1–25.46, likewise ends with three lengthy parables about the last day (25.1–13, 14–30, 31–46). In fact, of the five major discourses in Matthew, only that in chapter eighteen fails to wind up with a triad treating of the last things. But even here the final unit is a parable about the sad fate of those who fail to forgive their brothers from the heart (18.23–35). So even though the concluding triadic pattern is not inevitable, the eschatological conclusion is. The Matthean discourses, then, consistently reflect the flow of history. The present is always swallowed up by the future, and everything stands under the shadow of the conclusion. All meaning is determined by the issue of things (cf. 2 Bar. 19.4–8).[54]

(2) The prudent man builds his house upon solid rock. Why? In part, we may surmise, because he anticipates the eschatological blessings stored up for the sons of the kingdom (cf. 5.3–12). But he

[54] Q appears to have concluded with an eschatological speech (cf. Lk 17.23–37), and the Didache turns to the last things at its conclusion. So Matthew's habit of concluding with eschatological subjects was probably encouraged by his tradition. Note also that the last speech in all three synoptics is the eschatological discourse.

also does his good and wise work because he knows of the coming eschatological tempest; and, being afraid of it, he acts upon his knowledge. The man accordingly illustrates the maxim, 'The fear of the Lord is the beginning of wisdom' (Prov 1.7; cf. Ecclus 25.10–11). This idea, that the fear of God and his judgement is a proper motive for proper action, runs throughout the eschatological statements of the First Gospel. See 3.7–10; 5.21–6, 29–30; 7.13–14; 10.33; 12.33–7; 16.24–7; 18.7–9, 23–5; 24.43–25.46. The evangelist, in encouraging his readers to seek light instead of darkness, had no qualms about making the threat of judgement a dominant motivating force (cf. Mohrlang, pp. 49, 68–9). For him, the judgement of God was an inescapable reality, and the fear of it only natural.[55]

(3) Chrysostom, in discussing Mt 7.21–3, cites 1 Cor 13.2: 'And if I have prophetic powers, and understand all mysteries and all knowledge, and if I have faith, so as to remove mountains, but have not love, I am nothing' (*Hom. on Mt.* 24.2). The citation is apposite. According to the general testimony of the NT, including Matthew, miracles, *by themselves*, mean nothing. And, at worst, they can feed the selfish ego and lead not to the glorification of God but to the praise of the miracle-worker. The First Gospel, to be sure, is filled with miracles. Jesus is constantly casting out demons and healing people. Yet—and the omission speaks very loudly—our gospel writer fills relatively little space telling the followers of Jesus about the miracles they themselves can do (see only 10.8; 14.28–33; 17.14–21; 18.19; 21.21). And in the sermon on the mount, which is an epitome of teaching on discipleship, there is not one command to perform miracles. Obedience to the messianic Torah, the practice of proper piety, and generous, self-sacrificing conduct in society are what is demanded. One infers, then, that while Matthew took Christian miracles for granted, he did not think them to be of any great moment. The Messiah, admittedly, did miracles aplenty—but only because this was what had been prophesied (cf. 11.2–6). By contrast, miracles are not what is expected of his followers, at least not first of all. The call to righteousness encompasses personal virtue, private devotion, and unselfish social behaviour; and to these things seemingly supernatural powers are incidental. This is why those who do mighty works in Jesus' name will not by that account alone escape condemnation (cf. 7.21–3).

(4) The sermon on the mount ends with a polemical barb which declares the superiority of Jesus' teaching to that of the scribes. This is not the first such stab. In the key passage, 5.17–20, the

---

[55] Matthew seems untroubled by the difficulties that some ancient and modern exegetes have found in ascribing retribution and vengeance to God.

righteousness of Jesus' true followers is contrasted with the righteousness of the scribes and Pharisees. And in the little cult-didache, 6.1–18, proper Christian piety is illustrated by setting up members of the Jewish synagogues as counter examples. In addition, before the sermon, in chapter 3, Matthew takes up the Q material in which the Baptist thunders against the Sadducees and Pharisees who come out to hear him. The polemical bent of our writer's mind becomes even more prominent if Mt 1–2 be read, as it can and often has been read, as being, at least to some degree, a Christian apologetic, an answer to Jewish slanders concerning Jesus' birth and his right to be called a Davidid (see pp. 220–1). The two chapters do in any case associate the scribes and chief priests with the evil king Herod (see 2.4). Hence six of the first seven chapters of Matthew clearly reveal an author engaged in critical dialogue with the Jewish establishment and its leaders. Which is to say: in belonging to the Christian community, Matthew is not so far removed from the synagogue as to pay it no heed. Quite the opposite: he is very much concerned that his readers understand the failings of Judaism and so stay within the Messiah's fold. If, moreover, we are correct in finding the structure of Mt 5–7 to be set up in programmatic antithesis to rabbinic doctrine, specifically to the three pillars of R. Simeon (see p. 134), then are we not confronted by a writer who is worried about more than 'the synagogue across the street' (to borrow Stendahl's phrase)? An affirmative answer commends itself. The scope and grandeur of our gospel and the evident care with which it has been constructed betray the authorial hope that the book be of far-reaching influence and importance. It is but a small step from this inference to the supposition that Matthew hoped his gospel enterprise would prove to be a watershed in Jewish-Christian relations, that it would build up the church by demonstrating the truth of the gospel *vis-à-vis* Judaism as well as supply Christian scribes with powerful weapons with which to confront the rabbinic currents of the day. And it is, again, only a second small step from this to raising questions about Matthew and what is called Jamnia.

(v) *Bibliography*

K. Abou-Chaar, 'The Two Builders: A Study of the Parable in Luke 6.47–9', *NESTTR* 5 (1982), pp. 44–58.

Aune, pp. 222–4.

Barth, in *TIM*, pp. 73–5, 159–64.

J. Bergman, 'Zum Zwei-Wege-Motiv. Religionsgeschichtliche und exegetische Bemerkungen', *SEÅ* 41 (1976), pp. 27–56.

H. D. Betz, 'Eine Episode im Jüngsten Gericht (Mt 7,21–3)', *ZTK* 78

(1981), pp. 1–30; translated into English in *Essays*, pp. 125–57.

O. Böcher, 'Wölfe in Schafspelzen. Zum religionsgeschichtlichen Hintergrund von Matth. 7,15', *TZ* 24 (1968), pp. 405–26.

E. Cothenet, 'Les prophètes chrétiens dans l'Évangile selon saint Matthieu', in Didier, pp. 281–308.

C. Daniel, 'Esséniens, zélotes et sicaires et leur mention par paronymie dans le N.T.', *Numen* 13 (1966), pp. 88–115.

idem, ' "Faux prophètes": surnom des Esséniens dans le sermon sur la montagne', *RevQ* 7 (1969), pp. 45–79.

Davies, *SSM*, pp. 199–205.

A. Denaux, 'Der Spruch von den zwei Wegen im Rahmen des Epilogs der Bergpredigt (Mt 7,13–14 par. Lk 13,23–4). Tradition und Redaktion', in Delobel, pp. 305–35.

J. D. M. Derrett, 'The Merits of the Narrow Gate', *JSNT* 15 (1982), pp. 20–9.

Dupont 1, pp. 44–50, 98–103, 167–72.

D. Hill, 'False Prophets and Charismatics: Structure and Interpretation in Mt. 7:15–23', *Bib* 57 (1976), pp. 327–48.

B. Hjerl-Hansen, 'Did Christ know the Qumran Sect?', *RevQ* 1 (1959), pp. 495–508.

P. Hoffmann, Πάντες ἐργάται ἀδικίας: Redaktion und Tradition in Lk 13,22–30', *ZNW* 58 (1967), pp. 188–214.

Jeremias, *Parables*, p. 194.

idem, *TWNT* 6, pp. 920–7.

Jülicher 2, pp. 259–68.

M. Krämer, 'Hütet euch vor den falschen Propheten: Eine überlieferungsgeschichtliche Untersuchung zu Mt 7,15–23/Lk 6,43–6/Mt 12,33–7', *Bib* 57 (1976), pp. 349–77.

S. Légasse, 'Les faux prophètes. Matthieu 7,15–20', *EF* 18 (1968), pp. 205–18.

Marguerat, pp. 175–211.

A. J. Mattill, Jr., ' "The Way of Tribulation" ', *JBL* 98 (1979), pp. 531–46.

M. Mees, 'Ausserkanonische Parallelstellen zu den Gerichtsworten Mt 7:21–3; Lk 6:46; 13:26–8 und ihre Bedeutung für die Formung der Jesusworte', *VetChr* 10 (1973), pp. 79–102.

W. Michaelis, *TWNT* 5, pp. 42–118.

P. S. Minear, 'False Prophecy and Hypocrisy in the Gospel of Matthew', in Gnilka, *Kirche*, pp. 76–93.

Perrin, *Rediscovering*, pp. 144–5.

G. Schneider, 'Christusbekenntnis und christliches Handeln', in Schnackenburg, *Kirche*, pp. 9–24.

Schulz, *Q*, pp. 309–20, 424–30.

G. Schwarz, 'Matthäus vii 13a. Ein Alarmruf angesichts höchster Gefahr', *NovT* 12 (1970), pp. 229–32.

E. Schweizer, 'Matthäus 7.14–23', in *Gemeinde*, pp. 126–31.

Wrege, pp. 132–55.

Zeller, *Mahnsprüche*, pp. 139–42.